Not Just Another Club

OVER the years, Stan Liversedge has followed the fortunes of
Manchester United with more than a passing interest – as a
sportswriter, he travelled abroad with the team during the
heady days of the Busby era, and he came to know many of
the most famous names who wore the United jersey. He has
written books in collaboration with many top names in
football – Sir Matt Busby among them – and has been the
confidant of more than a few other noted managers, as well as
players.

It goes without saying, then, that this book is written
with genuine authority, and it goes into great detail about
Manchester United's triumphs, tragedies ... and, when
necessary, their blemishes. As someone who, for the best part
of 20 years, worked for Liverpool Football Club, Stan
Liversedge also has a deep understanding of the rivalry
between the Anfield Reds and the Reds of Old Trafford. And
as someone who has known so many famous names in both
camps, he can claim to have more than a passing acquaintance with the greats of the game.

Not Just Another Club

STAN LIVERSEDGE

JANUS PUBLISHING COMPANY
London, England

First published in Great Britain 1996
by Janus Publishing Company
Edinburgh House, 19 Nassau Street
London W1N 7RE

Pictures by courtesy of John Cocks, LP Sports Service
and Peter Beckett.

British Library Cataloguing-in-Publication Data.
A catalogue record for this book is available from the British Library.

ISBN 1 85756 203 8

Cover design Ian Wileman

Photosetting by Keyboard Services, Luton, Beds
Printed and bound in England by
Antony Rowe Ltd
Chippenham
Wiltshire

CONTENTS

'Eric has changed us from possible winners into definite winners ... he suits our style, enjoys the freedom we give him. I've said all along I want him to stay, and together we can work it out.' - ALEX FERGUSON

'Martin Edwards and Alex Ferguson say they're aghast at the severity of his punishment ... I would have thought he got off lightly.' In Sir Matt Busby's day 'Cantona would have been out of the door within five minutes.' - TOMMY DOCHERTY

'No-one would say that what Eric did was right; but everyone in this country went overboard - they wanted to hang him. When Eric comes out for a warm-up, the abuse he gets is unbelievable. Look at what's happening in this country ... Eric is picked out and told he's supposed to set standards. It's a bloody joke.' - PADDY CRERAND

'Abroad, the crowd is too far from the players. Here, the game is warmer. There is even room for love between the crowd and players. The crowd vibrates with the game.' - ERIC CANTONA, in December, 1993.

'When the seagulls are following a trawler, it is because they think the sardines are going to be thrown into the sea.' - ERIC CANTONA, summarily ending a Press conference in March, 1995, after his 14-day prison sentence had been replaced by the imposition of 120 hours' community service.   •

'It may well be that we have put both the League and the FA Cup in jeopardy by the action we have taken, but the reputation of Manchester United is above trophies. What is most important is that the game is bigger than Manchester United, and Manchester United is more important than Eric Cantona.' - United chairman MARTIN EDWARDS, announcing the club's suspension and fine imposed on Cantona after the Selhurst Park incident of January 25, 1995.

'The game needs him; United need him; I bloody need him.' - ALEX FERGUSON, in the summer of 1995.

Chapter 1

DOUBLE TROUBLE!

'It's a shame, but out on the field we can sense people either love or hate United – there's no middle ground. I think that clouds people's judgment of what we've achieved.' – MARK HUGHES, shortly before his transfer from Manchester United to Chelsea.

WHEN the history of Manchester United comes to be rewritten, will United be regarded as unfortunate victims of their own fame – or as mercenary villains? Will Eric Cantona be remembered as the French ace in the pack who inspired United to soaring success – or branded as a hot-head whose absence, through suspension, cost them their chance of European glory and a repeat of the classic League–FA Cup double? Indeed, will the enigmatic Cantona, along with Paul Ince (controversially sold to Inter-Milan) and Roy Keane (who hit the headlines on and off the field) be looked upon as fall-guys, or as big-name players who, by word and deed, sullied United's glittering reputation as the supreme footballing outfit in these islands? And what about manager Alex Ferguson? Will he be revered as Sir Matt Busby was, or remembered as someone who put winning above all else? Only time will tell ... even after the double of '96.

What *IS* certain is that as season 1995–96 got under way, United had become embroiled in one controversy after

1

another, after having seen the championship and the FA Cup slip from their grasp. There followed a summer of simmering discontent for their fans, putting a huge question mark against their prospects for the new campaign, which saw Newcastle United installed as 3–1 title favourites.

Liverpool were quoted at 4–1, Manchester United at 5–1, champions Blackburn Rovers at 7–2; and yet, despite all the doubts, the traumas, the arguments, the magic of Manchester United still cast its spell worldwide ... as I was reminded forcibly when I was in the Red Centre of Australia – Ayers Rock – and *en route* for home via Singapore. In my hotel at Ayers Rock I met Mario, a waiter of Italian extraction (though he was born Down Under), and when he heard that I was from England, he immediately proclaimed his love for Manchester United, the club he had supported from the age of five. In Singapore I digested the comments of *Straits Times* columnist Roger Wright, who offered the view that 'Andy Cole has not really had any chance to latch on to the Cantona connection, with the latter's suspension undoubtedly the big element in United's failure to capture their third successive championship.' United, minus Cantona, had drawn a double blank in the spring of 1995, while their £8.5 million sales of Ince and Hughes sparked off a furore which was swiftly followed by another, as Ukrainian wing-star Andrei Kanchelskis shook the dust of Old Trafford from his feet.

Going back to the *Straits Times* and Roger Wright, he submitted: 'With the mercurial Frenchman around, I think the title would have been safe, despite all Blackburn's efforts. Blackburn did it, in the end ... I cannot hide my feelings of disappointment. The reason? – Blackburn lack glamour. The team seems to lack the flair of United. I would like to conduct a poll of Singaporean British Soccer fans (and there are thousands) and ask them about flair and excitement. I wonder where their sympathies would lie ...' As for Cantona, Wright delivered this verdict: 'He will be back. Reformed, chastened and, hopefully, just as inspirational.' This, of course, after Cantona's future had seemingly been settled with the news that he was signing on for three more years, declaring: 'I'm staying because Manchester United is the biggest club in England, maybe in Europe, maybe in the world.'

From Alex Ferguson, the manager who, finally, had had to go to France to talk Cantona into returning to Old Trafford, had come this warning: 'I think Eric recognises this is the last chance for him in this country. He knows he has to handle it – if he's sent off again, everything will erupt once more. The easiest thing for Eric would have been to run away from this – he has made the hardest decision possible by staying. He has put himself in the firing line, saying "I'm not prepared to let them beat me."' There was another telling quote from Ferguson, on the eve of season 1995–96: 'The game needs him; United need him; I bloody need him.' That certainly sounded like a cry from the heart.

Settling Cantona's future was not Ferguson's only problem. If the Frenchman had declared that he would stay, ultimately, because of his high regard for the manager, Andrei Kanchelskis was proving difficult – indeed, his agent declared that 'Andrei loves the club, the players and the fans; but he cannot work with the manager.' A furious Ferguson rapped back: 'If Andrei says he can't get on with the manager, that's fine. But that's not the issue. He signed a new contract last year for five years – that's the important issue.' And a final parting shot: 'I'll see Andrei at the start of next season.' By then, however, United and Everton were engaged in a dispute over the player.

Meanwhile, United had been accused of greed concerning their commercial activities, and from inside and outside Old Trafford came admissions that others were jealous – indeed, even that in some quarters there was hatred of United. On the eve of the 1995 FA Cup Final Mark Hughes, then United's longest-serving player, summed up: 'It's a shame, but out on the field we sense people either love or hate United – there's no middle ground. I think that fact clouds people's judgment of what we've achieved.' Weeks previously Cantona, having

3

settled for 120 hours' community service in lieu of 14 days in gaol, had uttered some cryptic words of wisdom as he took his leave, almost disdainfully, of the media:

'When the seagulls are following a trawler, it is because they think the sardines are going to be thrown into the sea.' Make of that what you will . . . but his manager left no doubts on one score: 'Eric has changed us from possible winners into definite winners . . . he suits our style, enjoys the freedom we give him.' Some people argued that Cantona had been given too much freedom. One observer of the Old Trafford arena concluded: 'Cantona and Ince were signed because they fitted Ferguson's category of a true United player – they were good enough, and wanted to win. Unfortunately, it has backfired on all of them . . . the loss of the Premiership crown might be regarded as adequate penance.' The same observer wrote, too: 'The club has become the target of a deep and abiding hatred. Chairman Martin Edwards is right when he says players are open to more provocation than they have ever been. What he didn't add, for fear his words might be used against his club, is that United are far and away the most-hated team in the country.'

One Premiership chairman had already spoken of the 'staggering jealousy' of United; a Premier League manager had talked of 'an anti-brigade'; Ferguson had declared there was 'a certain envy' of United. And when it came to settling Cantona's future, he admitted: 'We know it will be difficult for Eric to return to normal football in this country, but we think it is possible ... together, we can work it out.' Contrasting sentiments were expressed by Liverpool's costly defender, Phil Babb, who claimed that if Cantona played in English football again, he would need a machine-gun to keep the opposition's fans off his back.

If Ferguson had his hands full with keeping Cantona and selling Ince and Hughes, he discovered that Kanchelskis presented another problem. Weeks before the end of season 1994–95, the flying winger was said to be seeking a move – first, with his sights on Glasgow Rangers, then with ideas of landing at Liverpool. After Ferguson had rebuked Kanchelskis in no uncertain terms, Everton stepped in – and controversy flared anew as the transfer became an on-off-on-again saga.

Amid all this, United revealed plans to make Old Trafford the most-admired stadium in the land after accusations on TV that they were 'selling their soul' for financial gain. United unveiled a £28 million project to erect Europe's biggest cantilever stand and hoist crowd capacity to 55,300 – the highest in British football. Martin Edwards and United's second Knight of the Realm, Sir Bobby Charlton, were pictured looking admiringly at a model of the development plan which would project Old Trafford not only as a monument to the late Sir Matt Busby, but as a symbol of the success achieved under current manager Alex Ferguson ... who had gambled heavily not only upon the continuing magic of Monsieur Cantona, but upon extracting full value from the £7 million splash on Andy Cole.

As for those televised accusations of greed, the programme also showed clips of Cantona in controversial action, with former United manager Tommy Docherty expressing the view that Busby would not have tolerated the Frenchman's presence at Old Trafford after the infamous Selhurst Park affair. There were also shots of the horrific scenes at the time of the 1958 Munich air disaster, and of United on their 1968 night of European glory, as they won the Champions' Cup at Wembley. There were, too, interviews with fans (some of whom proclaimed eternal devotion to Cantona) and a chat with a former United star, Paddy Crerand, who reminded people that it was Busby who had made Manchester United great. It was, overall, an intriguing miscellany which was presented to the public gaze, as accusations were levelled and refuted, and judgments were pronounced.

But behind the facade of Old Trafford, there remains one indisputable fact: that while Manchester United can claim to stand pre-eminent among all the clubs in the land, in a footballing sense, they have also become the symbol of Big Business in Soccer. From being a bomb-battered shell of a club which could barely afford to pay Busby £13 a week and was in hock to the tune of £15,000 (a small fortune half a century ago), United have become an institution dealing in millions, both on and off the field.

Where Busby conjured up for the fans a footballing empire during the 1950s and 1960s, Old Trafford during the 1990s prospers not only from the massive support flocking through the turnstiles, but from widespread commercial activities ranging from souvenirs and replica strips to executive boxes. In April 1995, a TV programme on Channel 4 accused United of leading Premiership clubs down 'a nasty, mercenary trail'. The programme was entitled 'J'Accuse: Manchester United.' It all seemed a far cry from the days when the club scarcely had two ha'pennies to rub together. But if March 17, 1995 (St. Patrick's Day) was significant for the revelation of United's grandiose plans for a super-stadium, February 6 of the same year passed relatively unnoticed by most people; yet for those who (like myself) had long memories, that day was remembered as the 37th anniversary of what a former newspaper colleague of mine, Frank Taylor, termed The Day A Team Died.

The team in question? Manchester United ... with whom Frank was flying back from a European Cup-tie in Belgrade. That Thursday afternoon in 1958, players, club officials, Pressmen and others perished on a snowswept airstrip at Munich. A handful lingered on, before expiring as they lay in hospital; and a few more lived to tell the tale, harrowing as it was. As United's Elizabethan aircraft slewed to a halt and crashed, all hell was let loose, and one of the finest football teams ever assembled was decimated. So, too, was the Manchester Press corps ... though Frank Taylor survived. He was lucky – and so was I, because I, too, should have been on that plane. Frank recovered, after having been gravely injured (though years later, he still walked with a limp); as for me, I had to cry off the trip at virtually the last minute, because my services were required in the office of my paper, *The People*. So I didn't travel with United, though I did go with them on their first venture back into Europe after Munich, when United met AC Milan in a European tie and we travelled to Italy by train, boat and train again. And during the 1960s, when the side had been rebuilt, I reported on many of United's matches, at home and abroad.

By February 6, 1995, Sir Matt Busby (whom I had known for more than 30 years) had died, and the talk was all about United and a volatile Frenchman called Eric Cantona – who, on the 37th anniversary of Munich, was sunning himself in Guadeloupe, even as the police awaited his presence at South Norwood, in London, to help with the inquiries into the Selhurst Park incident of January 25.

During the Busby years, as I covered United's matches, I became enamoured of the style they displayed, on and off the field: such as when they staged a championship banquet in a plush Manchester hotel and one of the club's directors rose to announce, with due solemnity (this being a Friday evening) that a special papal dispensation had been granted for those guests who wished to partake of meat. Yes, under Busby, the club had genuine style; and this is something which remains true about the club in so many ways today. Yet in recent years, amid the triumphs, there have been incidents which have not reflected well upon the reputation of United – not that it was all sweetness and light in Busby's day. When I discussed the Cantona affair at Selhurst Park with a colleague and suggested that in Busby's day it would have culminated with the Frenchman being slapped on the transfer list, he replied: 'Matt wouldn't have signed him, in the first place.' Well, I don't know about that; Busby allowed George Best a considerable amount of rope when the Irishman was posing all kinds of problems, and he stood by other players at times when criticism became almost strident ... although he did put Denis Law up for sale when the Scottish star virtually demanded more money or a move. Matt won that battle as Law backed down, thus proving that the club was bigger than the individual. And in 1995, there were those disposed to argue that Cantona was proving to be bigger than the club, no matter what the protestations from Ferguson and United. Then again, some folk claimed Best had become a law unto himself, during Busby's time.

The chairman of one club, Burnley's Bob Lord, had some

stinging words to say about United not so long after Munich, when he used the term 'teddy-boys' – and that description hurt Busby. United then were striving to regain their position of power as a footballing force, although some of their younger players came in for criticism. Mark Pearson (they called him Pancho, because of his long, dark sideboards) didn't always endear himself to fans cheering United's opponents, and there came a day when Nobby Stiles needed Alf Ramsey to spring to his defence as the cry went up for him to be axed from England's line-up. Goalkeeper Harry Gregg, signed by Busby for a then world-record fee of £23,000 (don't laugh), not only once blacked a fan's eye, but laid out an England winger in the mud on a cold winter's night – that incident had the home supporters baying for Gregg's blood. Then there was an incident involving a water-pistol and two or three of United's young players which, although little more than a prank, made unwanted headlines.

During the Ferguson era, players such as Cantona, Ince, Keane and Hughes demonstrated that they could more than take care of themselves, and Denis Law put forward the viewpoint that while the Frenchman had been the key player in United's title successes, 'the one flaw people will cite in Eric's make-up is his disciplinary record.' Law himself was once advised by his mother: 'If anyone kicks you, kick them back'. And he admitted: 'As a player not famed for walking away from potential flash-points, I admit I have a genuine sympathy for Cantona. I don't think Eric would be the player he is, if he had a cool, calm attitude. My flare-ups with opponents were never premeditated ... I don't think Eric's are now.' Law revealed: 'I truly wish I'd been blessed with Bobby Charlton's super-cool temperament. I wasn't, though, and if I had just walked away when I sensed injustice had occurred, I really think a vital ingredient of my game would have been missing.'

Well, Denis certainly used to irritate Alan Hardaker (the then League secretary) as he raised an arm in triumph after having scored; and I saw Denis in a bad mood after a European Cup reverse away against Partizan Belgrade, who had been rated as rather easy meat for a team of the calibre of United. Denis admitted he had passed up a good scoring chance, and United knew they should really have done better.

Harry Gregg, who played in that match, once described Matt Busby as a manager who concealed 'the iron fist in a velvet glove', and while this was not an original term, Law certainly felt the impact of that 'iron fist', as did Gregg himself.

Busby lived not only to be 84; he also saw United achieve their long-sought goal as they carried off the title trophy, after more than a quarter of a century of striving. By then, it was Alex Ferguson in charge of team affairs, and so he emulated the old master; and instead of George Best, it was Eric Cantona's name on the lips of the Old Trafford faithful. By the spring of 1995, as United awaited Cantona's return to the fold after his months of suspension, Ferguson and fellow-Scot Kenny Dalglish were engaged in another battle for supremacy in the Premiership, and United's manager was destined this time to finish second-best. Ferguson and Dalglish often appeared to strike sparks off each other, going back to Kenny's days as Liverpool manager, and the rivalry continued as Blackburn Rovers claimed their first championship success since 1914.

Ferguson, indeed, was made to suffer twice over, as Everton won the FA Cup – and he was villified for having sold Ince, Hughes and Kanchelskis, and found himself being called upon to apologise for remarks made about Leeds United fans. United supporters were dismayed to learn that Inter-Milan, far from handing over £7 million or more for Ince, were putting down just £3 million, with the remainder to follow. One fan observed that for £3 million, United wouldn't even have been able to buy Mark Draper (sold by Leicester City to Aston Villa for £3.4 million).

As if to compound a summer of misfortune, the Old Trafford club had to defend itself against charges that it was exploiting the supporters and being greedy, while after a newspaper phone-in verdict that Ferguson should go, United's conduct in the Kanchelskis transfer saga came under critical scrutiny. An ITV Teletext phone poll of more than 5,400 people showed that 75 per cent blamed United for the hold-up of the winger's move to Everton.

Alex Ferguson, of course, has learned how to win titles and trophies, but his critics claim that he could take lessons in how to win friends from the late, great Sir Matt Busby, who seldom, if ever, shouted the odds – even when he was feeling the pressure. Ferguson has lambasted the Football Association on occasion, and made few friends among the fans not only of Leeds, but also of Everton and Blackburn Rovers. One sportswriter claimed he was 'paranoid' about the media and that, 'thanks to the antics of Cantona, Ince and Keane' United had become 'the most disliked team in the country'. The media? After the local evening paper had conducted its phone-in and reported that more than half the 800-odd fans quizzed had said he should go, Ferguson dismissed the verdict like this: 'City fans calling in and making mischief. They'd love to see the back of me ... well, they'll have a long time to wait; a bloody long time.'

Leeds United? An apology was demanded after Ferguson's comments, in his book, about Leeds fans ... 'you can feel the hatred, the animosity.' As for Everton: 'I still can't believe we really lost that Cup Final. I mean, you never like getting beaten by an ordinary team'. And on losing the title to Blackburn Rovers: 'Knowing we were the best team in the country made it no easier.' Ah, yes, Blackburn ... where 'I'm as welcome as the Black Plague. Even when they were nobodies, I wasn't welcome there.' Ferguson did give the Rovers credit for their resilience, team spirit and the quality of striker Alan Shearer – but claimed that 'Blackburn weren't great champions.' Why not? 'People would have expected more from United ... they would have insisted we won it in style.'

The manager whose own team had suffered humiliation in Europe the previous season forecast that in season 1995–96 the Rovers were 'not equipped to make a real challenge – direct football sprinkled with little bits of passing won't work in Europe.' Well, the Rovers did hit trouble in the Champions' Cup – although United's critics could have questioned: 'If

United had been the best team in the country, how come they didn't win the title - and the FA Cup - again in season 1994-95?' As for Ferguson and Kenny Dalglish, they have crossed swords several times, going back to Kenny's days at Liverpool, as well as when he was team boss of the Rovers. Liverpool, like Leeds, Everton and Blackburn, have caused the United manager to bow his head in despair at times, while the rivalry between some of the respective fans has ranged from feelings of jealousy to downright bad temper and shocking manners. Twice, Liverpool have licked United 2-0 to put the Indian sign on their title aspirations - and even when Liverpool defeated Blackburn Rovers 2-1 at Anfield in the final match of season 1994-95, it wasn't sufficient to set up Manchester United as the champions.

Ferguson has referred to 'the bitterness so many feel towards United', and at Upton Park he heard West Ham fans displaying extremely partisan feelings against his team; meanwhile, at Anfield, Liverpool supporters were saluting Dalglish and his Rovers with the chant of 'Champions! Champions!' Ferguson termed Blackburn's £5 million splash on Chris Sutton as 'madness', then spent £6 million, plus a player, on Andy Cole. At one time he had tried and failed to land Peter Beardsley and Paul Gascoigne from Newcastle, and seen Spurs snap up Nick Barmby. Then, having landed Cole, he forecast (as he looked towards the return of Cantona) that Cole would 'get 30 goals for us this year'. Some would claim this was putting Cole under pressure and, indeed, during the early part of season 1995-96, the striker didn't enjoy much luck. He had hit a dozen League goals in 17 games (including five in one match) the previous term ... then came one goal in seven outings by mid-October, 1995.

Like Ferguson, Liverpool manager Roy Evans knows what it is to be under pressure, and Evans declared that 'when we were up there for so long, I heard people saying "Let's get them out - we've had enough." United must feel the same thing. There's always an anti-brigade, but I think it was less for Liverpool than it is for United.' And from Kenny Dalglish, after the title decider in the spring of 1995: 'It's the first time

11

I've known anybody with feelings towards Manchester United hoping that Liverpool would get a result.' Then came the barb: 'Liverpool got the result – but United couldn't help themselves (by only drawing at West Ham). To benefit from a bad result, you have to get your own result.'

United supporters still haven't forgotten (or forgiven) the day in the mid-1980s when their team arrived at Anfield for a match and, as the players stepped down from the coach, someone directed an aerosol spray at their faces. No pun intended, but it left a nasty taste in the mouth, not to mention the eyes, and brought apologies from Dalglish and Liverpool. Ferguson has a memory, too, of taking his team to Anfield – and hearing a Liverpool player call from the dressing-room: 'F*** you!' And more recently Phil Babb was making it very plain that he would like to see Monsieur Eric Cantona cast out of English football – for good.

When Cantona's French lawyer, Jean-Jacques Bertrand, was talking to Martin Edwards about a new deal for the player, Bertrand claimed that 'anything can happen to Eric ... the circumstances are very difficult'. United, indeed, were said to share Bertrand's worry that Cantona had become the focal point of bitter rivalry between United fans and opposition supporters, and there was 'concern in the champions' camp that Cantona is becoming bigger than Manchester United.' Ferguson's flight to France to talk the enigmatic star into returning was regarded by some as a sign that United were ready to bow the knee.

When Alan Shearer received his PFA Player of the Year award in 1995, it was reported that 'hisses and jeers' greeted the screening of the 1994 Player of the Year's face. 'It was an indication that Cantona's infamy stretched across fraternal boundaries, that his brief appearance on the TV monitors around the Grosvenor House Hotel in London should have provoked such an unwelcome response.' The *Daily Mail's* Vic Robbie declared that 'the Cantona issue is like a running sore waiting to be prodded and probed by troublemakers until violence erupts. When he plays again, he will be the target of every foul-mouthed fan in the country, and there will be no shortage of United supporters ready to defend him by whatever method. It is a problem that might have been avoided if Matt Busby had still been alive. I doubt the great man would have allowed the Frenchman to ever wear again the famous red, black, green and yellow or blue of United.' For Messrs. Edwards and Ferguson, according to Robbie, the way out was simple. Having given support to 'a flawed footballer', they should sell him and make a £4 million profit. 'Financially, it makes sense. More importantly, it would defuse what is sure to be an explosive situation every time he plays for United next season.' And Cantona's reappearance on an English field was scheduled for Old Trafford at the start of October – against United's arch-enemies, Liverpool.

According to Ferguson, United are different from any other club in Britain (a claim the Anfield faithful would surely contradict ... Liverpool fans want their team to beat United more than anything else, and they would have relished the knowledge that, after Ferguson had been quoted £3 million for Peter Beardsley, Dalglish snapped him up less than a month later for £1.9 million. They would have relished learning, too, that Newcastle United refused Ferguson permission to talk to Gazza, even though United were prepared to match Spurs when it came down to the fee).

Ferguson concluded that 'you have to think Newcastle don't like us' (this was in the pre-Keegan days), and it has to be confessed that there are indeed plenty of folk who find Manchester United arrogant as a club. Before Ferguson arrived at Old Trafford, there was a certain Tommy Docherty, who, while acknowledging that Fergie was a great manager, also said: 'I don't like Fergie much as a bloke'. The Doc did admit to being 'delighted for the supporters and for the players' on their success, and added: 'I actually enjoy watching them now.' Ferguson's description of The Doc, in answer to other criticism concerning Neil Webb: 'He's a bitter old man.' United's manager also retaliated against former Liverpool skipper Emlyn Hughes, whom he savaged in print, while amid something of a war of words with Kenny Dalglish, the latter was prompted to observe about United: 'It took them 26 years to win it (the title) . . . I hope it doesn't take us that long'. Well, it didn't take Dalglish that long, although the Rovers had waited 81 years when they accomplished their mission in the spring of 1995.

When Leeds United – hammered by their Manchester counterparts in an Old Trafford FA Cup-tie – held Ferguson's team to a draw there in the League, the home fans had to endure taunts from the visiting brigade: 'Where is Eric Cantona?' He, of course, was still serving his suspension after the kung-fu incident at Selhurst Park. At one stage, Vic Robbie was writing, 'Au revoir, Cantona.' Au revoir it wasn't, however, as events unfolded; but whether or not Cantona's 'love affair' with Manchester United would last for three more years remained to be seen. Meanwhile, United continued to be the highest-profile club in the country – as their manager said, back-page or front-page news almost daily. Ferguson, 'a workaholic who prides himself on his football knowledge', maintained that 'success in football is not down to individual honours . . . gaining glory for the club, that's what really matters.' And he declared his conviction that 'managing Manchester United is the biggest challenge in football; it's a job that has grown with the development of the club, and I honestly believe it would prove beyond many managers. I love my job. The fire still burns inside me to bring more success to this club . . .'

Alongside this statement of intent came some words of wisdom from a rival manager, Leeds United's Howard Wilkinson. 'This (management) has always been a precarious profession, but nothing like it is today. The pressure . . . has intensified out of all proportion. We are in an era of instant gratification. To be manager of a football club for more than two years is a considerable achievement. The financial rewards for success are handsome, and there are bound to be casualties. There is no certainty for any of us.' Those were words which would be echoed fervently by many of the men who had been tried in the managerial furnace and adjudged to have failed – including some who had been sacked by Manchester United.

IN 1995, an eight-page contract attracted the top price in a sale of Manchester United memorabilia at Bonhams, in Knightsbridge, London, after a plea by the late Sir Matt Busby's family not to sell his first managerial agreement with Manchester United had failed. When the document went under the hammer at the London auction house, it was sold for £4,200. The contract had been drawn up in 1946, when Busby was on a salary of £13 a week, as United's team boss ... and the anonymous bidder, who described himself as 'a genuine Manchester United fan', thus paid more than six times what Busby had earned in a year. The contract had been entered in the auction by an unidentified vendor who claimed to have received it from someone to whom former United chairman Harold Hardman had given it, more than 30 years previously. Bonhams said they were satisfied the contract was legitimately on offer and, despite the pleas of the Busby family, could not withdraw it from the sale. And so it was knocked down to the mystery buyer ... who put in the bid by telephone. It was reported that Manchester United had deliberately decided not to bid for the contract because of the upset the sale had caused to the Busby family, although the club did put in bids for several items (United bought a scrapbook belonging to Munich victim Tommy Taylor), and the total of 35 lots raised £13,618. The Taylor scrapbook was bought for the club museum at Old Trafford ... the stadium which stands as a lasting monument to the man who made United.

Chapter 2

THE MAN WHO MADE UNITED

'In a game that can so easily break a man, Busby's record is remarkable. He can accept defeat with dignity, is never arrogant in success.' – BILL SHANKLY, then the manager of Liverpool.

IT isn't often that there is what you might call a public turnout for the funeral of a former footballer or manager, but it happened when Bobby Moore, one of England's World Cup heroes, died; and it happened, also, when Sir Matt Busby, the 'elder statesman' of Manchester United, went to his final resting place. The Manchester United faithful lined the streets for his funeral ... there were some too young to remember the great days when Busby was manager at Old Trafford; there were others who, in their mind's eye, relived for a moment or two those past glories as the teams that Busby built achieved so much.

He assembled three great sides during his 25-year span as manager: the first, under Johnny Carey, was assembled against the odds because, in those post-war days, United were impecunious, to say the least – even their Old Trafford ground was unfit for use, because of bomb damage. The second team assembled by Busby saw the birth of the famous Babes ... then, on Thursday, February 6, 1958, the Munich disaster put paid to the cherished hopes that this side would

16

win all the honours going, at home and abroad. Finally came the post-Munich side, the one which first faltered in the quest, then succeeded gloriously on a night of footballing drama at Wembley, as United defeated Benfica, the Eagles of Lisbon, and carried off the European Cup. Along the way, through triumph, tragedy and tears, Matt Busby had remained a constant figure at the helm – even though at one stage he all but threw in the towel.

I first became acquainted with him in 1958, and the last time we talked was in a neighbour's house, enjoying the party hospitality, not many months before he died in January 1994. In the years between, I saw Matt in varying moods ... sombre, as we talked about Munich; smiling, as he savoured celebrating with United; not so pleased, as he reflected upon a European Cup reverse which should have been a victory; determined, as he put bad memories behind him and regained his zest for the job of managing Manchester United. He liked a flutter, he liked a laugh, and he enjoyed a wee dram. He could also let you know when the joke had gone too far. He earned a knighthood, yet he never let you feel he was superior ... he retained what is known as the common touch. I started out by calling him Matt, and that form of address never altered.

He started out as a player who, for a while, appeared to be heading nowhere; indeed, while playing for Manchester City, he confessed in a letter to the girl who was to become his wife that he felt he was 'out of my sphere' in football. But his luck changed, with a switch of position, and so he joined Liverpool (for a fee of £8,000) to become a member of one of the finest half-back lines that club had ever had. By then, he had totalled more than 200 League games for Manchester City, and he clocked up 125 appearances for Liverpool between 1936 and 1940 ... when war came, he managed three matches before going into the Army. The war took six years out of Busby's life, and when he returned to Civvie Street he had learned quite a lot about handling men – after all, he had been a company sergeant-major.

17

Liverpool offered him a coaching job, hinting that he could become manager George Kay's right-hand man. It was from Kay that, as Matt told me, he learned another thing; that 'a team boss must be a fighter, just like his team.' Busby also learned more about handling people ... 'Liverpool kept a player on top wages, even when he wasn't getting a game. And they rewarded his loyal service with a second benefit.' Liverpool were ready to hand Busby a five-year contract, too; and he was wanted by Ayr United, Reading ... and Manchester United, who needed to get back on the rails.

It was on February 19, 1945, that Busby was named as United's manager, although he didn't take charge on a day-to-day basis until October, because he was still waiting to be demobbed. At 35, he was still technically a player on Liverpool's books, and there was talk of Liverpool wanting a transfer fee, should he move as United's player-manager. Busby had spent what he described to me as 'the nine happiest years of my playing life' at Anfield, but the rift caused by his leaving took time to heal – indeed, in a phone call from George Kay, he learned that Liverpool no longer wished him to play in a special exhibition match which was being staged on their ground.

Busby set out to find and groom the best possible young talent, though he did have some decent players to start with ... Johnny Carey, Charlie Mitten, Stan Pearson, Johnny Morris, and Jack Rowley. Carey had crossed the Irish Sea and was very much an unknown when he turned up in Manchester – where his attention was caught by a newspaper placard announcing 'United's Big Capture'. It referred not to him, but to the £5,000 signing of Blackburn centre-forward Ernie Thompson. The last lines of the story related also how 'United have signed a junior from Ireland. His name is J. Carey'. The fans came to admire Carey and call him 'Gentleman Johnny' and, oddly enough, years later he was to manage Blackburn Rovers and steer them to promotion. He was to manage Everton, as well – and find himself being sacked by the then chairman, John Moores, during a taxi ride across London. Later still, Carey became a local government officer in Sale, Cheshire, while as for Stan Pearson, I ran across him when he was running a post-office in the pretty Cheshire village of Prestbury. Like Carey, he was a very unassuming man – and an accomplished footballer in his prime. It would be odd, of course, if all players were cast in the same mould, and Morris and Mitten were two different characters; each man, indeed, crossed swords with Busby before going through the exit door at United. Morris moved to Derby County, Mitten travelled much further afield.

Charlie was well known for his love of greyhound racing, and he was still enjoying 'the dogs' when he had a spell as manager of Newcastle United, while during his days playing for Fulham (after he had left Old Trafford) players used to tell the tale of finding Charlie in the treatment room – applying deep-heat treatment to one of his beloved dogs. It was said that a couple of the Fulham players had to wait their turn until the dog had been dealt with. However, while Charlie was still playing for Manchester United, the day dawned when the lure of Eldorado proved greater than the words of wisdom dispensed by manager Busby. Charlie wasn't the only man to get the 'golden' signs lighting up his eyes – Stoke City's England centre-half, Neil Franklin, was another. The lure of the gold came from Colombia, in the shape of a club named Bogota, and while Busby took the trouble to warn Charlie that he might not find Bogota turning out to be the Mecca he fondly imagined, it made no difference – Charlie was off, despite the further warning that if and when he returned, there would be nothing for him at Manchester United.

Mitten stayed in Colombia and saw out his contract with Bogota, but when (as was inevitable) he came back to England, Busby didn't backtrack; even though, as he told me, 'we could still have done with Charlie's footballing skills'. There was no place in the team for Charlie at Old Trafford, and so he left for Fulham, for what Busby termed 'a good-sized fee'. Years later, Matt was to turn down overtures from abroad for his own services ... and to fend off the Italians when there was talk of Tommy Taylor moving to the land of the lire. Busby, having created another great side, was determined that his finest players would not be prised away by the predatory Italians.

This was the first United side Busby named: Crompton; Walton, Roach; Warner, Whalley, Cockburn; Worrall, Carey, Smith, Rowley, Wrigglesworth. Goalkeeper Jack Crompton gave United sterling service, and when I got to know him I found he was, as ever, a devotee of the man he called 'the boss' through so many years – even after Crompton had moved on.

In those early days, Busby switched players around in the endless search to create a balanced side. Carey and Johnny Aston started out as forwards, ending up as internationals and the finest full-back pairing in England. Centre-half Allenby Chilton, a rock-like figure, kicked off as a wing-half and, like several other United men when they had hung up their boots, he became a manager – although the day came when he lost his job at Grimsby. As Busby was to tell Billy Liddell, when asked about the pitfalls of management: 'I made my bed, and it turned out to be a good one ... but not many managers can say that.'

At £4,000, Jimmy Delaney was a bargain buy, despite warnings that signing him would be a mistake. Some claimed that the Scotland star, who had been out of action for a year because of shoulder trouble, was 'brittle-boned'. Matt got six seasons out of Delaney – and when he did leave, United recouped £3,500 of their original outlay. Like Delaney, Aston, Carey, Chilton and company won international caps; in fact, one Saturday Crompton was the lone player in the side without an international honour to his name. Later, United had almost two teams of internationals; then came the horror of Munich.

In three consecutive seasons United went close to winning the title – second to Liverpool by a point in season 1946–47, runners-up to Arsenal and Portsmouth in seasons 1947–48 and 1948–49. But if 1948 was a disappointment in the League, United compensated in some measure by beating Blackpool 4–2 at Wembley and carrying off the FA Cup. It was a dazzling display of football, too ... after a Cup run which had started with a 6–4 away victory over Aston Villa (who had scored first and went in 5–1 down at half-time). In the semi-final against Derby County, a Pearson hat-trick did the damage, and in the final United twice came from behind to win. Behind the scenes, Busby was grooming the youngsters, too, and United produced a side which won the FA Youth Cup five seasons on the trot. Along the way, the fans flocked in their thousands to see the budding stars ... though the 'old brigade' hadn't quite run out of steam.

After their three consecutive seasons as runners-up during the late 1940s, United finished second again in the spring of 1951, then they were hailed as League champions at the end of the following season. The previous term, Tottenham Hotspur had finished ahead of them; the next time out, it was Spurs who had to concede best to Manchester United. By then, however, the first great team was being broken up, and when United won the championship for the first time in 40 years (their previous success, actually, had been back in 1911), they had a couple of new faces in their side. Winger Johnny Berry (who never played again after Munich) was signed from Birmingham City, after several attempts to land him, and Roger Byrne (who was to become the cool, cultured captain of the Babes) stepped up from reserve-team football to show that he could play in almost any position – when switched from defence to attack, he slammed home seven goals in United's last half-dozen games.

It wasn't one smooth progression after that title triumph, because 12 months later United could do no better than finish in eighth place, and that really was the signal for Busby to launch his newcomers on to the senior scene. The Busby Babes entered the arena ready, willing and able to make their mark; and even today, the names of Edwards, Byrne, Colman, Taylor, Whelan, Charlton, Jones, Blanchflower, Pegg and company spring to mind. There is little doubt that, but for Munich, the Babes would have been the first to capture the European Cup (and no disrespect to Glasgow Celtic, who achieved the feat in 1967 ... nor to the United side which followed, in 1968). The Babes had it all, and as they progressed, they were reinforced by judicious signings such as Harry Gregg and the emergence of Bill Foulkes as a no-nonsense defender. So the honours came to Old Trafford, and the caps were doled out.

In goal at first, there was Ray Wood, then Gregg; at full-back were Byrne and Foulkes, with a lad named Geoff Bent as Byrne's understudy (and he would have walked into any other side). At half-back it was Eddie 'Snake-hips' Colman, Blanchflower or Jones, and Edwards, who could burst through the opposition like a tank and rifle goals. Jones was cast as the stopper type of defender, Blanchflower more the footballer.

Up front, there was the wing menace of Johnny Berry and David Pegg (the later speedy and direct, a maker and scorer of goals), while Liam (Billy) Whelan was a slim, serious-looking, Irishman who provided guile to complement the incisive marksmanship of Dennis Viollet and Tommy Taylor, a spring-heeled leader of the attack. Taylor had cost £29,999 when he was signed from Barnsley, and Busby explained that he hadn't wanted to saddle the lad (who had had to be persuaded to move) with a £30,000 price tag. While Foulkes had carved out a footballing career after a stint down the pit (he was effective at full-back or centre-half), Byrne had dropped back from the left wing to play at No. 3. When it came to Jones and Blanchflower, often it took an injury to decide which of them got into the side.

Edwards, even in United's star-studded outfit, remained a player who was regarded as special, yet he remained also a modest young man – he was still only 21 when Munich claimed him as a victim. Former League referee Peter Rhodes recalls an occasion when he was in charge at an FA Cup-tie on the ground of Hartlepool United, with Manchester United providing the opposition. When the United players went out for a pre-match inspection of the pitch, Edwards looked around in some wonder ... 'I never realised there were League clubs like this,' he told Rhodes. It wasn't so much a putting-down of Hartlepool United as a genuine expression of surprise – and, having visited that Soccer outpost myself more than once during the late 1950s and the 1960s, I could understand what Edwards meant. There wasn't much to the place – if anything, it had a rather ramshackle air about it.

Edwards arrived at United from Dudley, in the Midlands, and Wolves were sorely disappointed when he chose Old Trafford. Jones and Pegg, like Taylor, hailed from Yorkshire, while Colman and Viollet were locals, and Charlton came from the pit village of Ashington. I once visited the two-up, two-down cottage Bobby's mother called home, to talk to her about her famous footballing sons, and she had no false pride.

There were other names on the assembly line of Old Trafford's talent, and they came into prominence more after Munich. Before that day of disaster, however, United had finished as First Division top-dogs in seasons 1955–56 and 1956–57, and in 1957 they were denied the classic 'double' only when Aston Villa beat them in the FA Cup final, after Wood had been so badly hurt that he could no longer keep goal. Still concussed, he made up the numbers as an outfield player, with Blanchflower going in goal.

Munich was one of British football's blackest days, and I saw at first-hand the effect it had on some of those involved. I saw Busby return from Munich still hobbling on sticks; I saw his right-hand man, Jimmy Murphy, battling to keep United functioning until 'the boss' was fit to take charge again. For a long time, Matt hovered between life and death, as did others who survived the air crash. United's manager later told me how he felt he could no longer carry on in football, after such cruel blows to the club, and it was his wife, Jean, who urged him on: 'Those boys who have died would have wanted you to carry on,' she told him. As for Jackie Blanchflower, he told me how the nuns at Munich's Rechts der Isaar hospital had said the last rites over him ... when he had returned home, I used to visit Jackie and his wife, Jean, at their bungalow where they lived with their young daughter, Krista, and we would chat for hours about what had gone before.

They called those who ministered to the crash casualties 'the angels of Munich', and Professor Georg Maurer, who was in charge of the medical-team effort to save lives, advised Busby to get away and drink in the fresh air, to speed his recovery. He did, and eventually returned home in time to see his patched-up team tackle Bolton Wanderers in the FA Cup final – then, as had happened the previous year, United suffered again, with Gregg taking a battering in a goalmouth incident, though he recovered to carry on. Once again, there were no victory celebrations for United.

Apart from the first crop of Busby Babes, there were other youngsters coming through, and the names of Alex Dawson, Ian Greaves, Freddie Goodwin, Colin Webster, Ronnie Cope and Mark Pearson became familiar to Old Trafford fans. Later still, they would hail Nobby Stiles and Sammy McIlroy (the last of the Babes), not to mention a footballing genius from Belfast by the name of George Best. Then there was Johnny Giles, who became Nobby Stiles's brother-in-law and, of course, there were the costly imports Paddy Crerand (£56,000), Denis Law (£115,000), Alex Stepney (£50,000), and 'golden-boy' Albert Quixall (£45,000), plus Stanley Matthews' inside-forward partner from Blackpool, little Ernie Taylor, and Maurice Setters, Noel Cantwell, David Herd and Stan Crowther. United also groomed David Gaskell, who was in goal when they won the FA Cup in 1963.

In so many ways there was an air of excitement, even drama, about those days when United were fighting back after the team had been decimated at Munich, and while there were one or two rough patches along the way, the 1963 Cup triumph provided fresh impetus for club and manager. At Wembley, United made it third-time lucky as they despatched Leicester City by a two-goal margin. There were only two survivors then from the 1958 Cup-final side – Bill Foulkes and Bobby Charlton – with Gaskell getting the vote over Harry Gregg. Cantwell and Tony Dunne (a near-neighbour of mine today) were the full-backs – Dunne, an undemonstrative Irishman in the Carey mould, was an immaculate defender who let his feet do the talking for him, while Cantwell, another intelligent player, had been schooled by West Ham.

24

United's half-back line had class and crunch, with Foulkes flanked by the rugged Setters and the artistic Crerand, while the front line consisted of Giles, Quixall, Herd, Law and Charlton. Giles preferred to play at inside-forward (he became a midfield star for Leeds United, who paid what, at that time, was a high-priced £40,000, though it turned out to be a bargain). With Quixall and Law there, however, Johnny had to settle for a wide berth.

Both Giles and Stiles were to ask Matt Busby for transfers, but while in Nobby's case he was glad to stay (he got his chance when Setters left for Stoke), Johnny decided his future must lie elsewhere. He had been at United since he was a youngster and, as he told me, 'once you've been what you might call the office-boy, somehow you tend to feel you're always regarded as the office-boy. They might not think that, but you do.' So he travelled on, having claimed a Cup-winner's medal. In that final, two goals came from David Herd, a no-frills centre-forward who reckoned his job was to stick the ball in the net, while the mercurial Law was United's other marksman.

If it was skipper Noel Cantwell who went up to collect the Cup, the fans saluted most of all the men who had made it back from Munich ... Charlton, Foulkes and, of course, Busby. It had been a long, hard road that season because, having flirted with the danger of relegation, United finished 19 places down the table and only three points clear. So they were still far from top-dogs, and the cheque book came out again as Busby signed winger John Connelly from Burnley. Then there was a runners-up spot to Liverpool in the League, an FA Cup semi-final – and a return to Europe, which saw United hammered 5-0 by Sporting Lisbon in Portugal after a 4-1 victory flourish by United in the home leg of their Cup-winners Cup-tie. Close to relegation in 1963, close to the championship in 1964 ... and Best arrived on the scene to set the fans tingling with renewed anticipation.

United were on their way back to the top when, at the end of season 1964–65, they won the championship by pipping Don Revie's Leeds on goal average, as both clubs totalled 61 points. The marksmanship of Law proved the difference, as he rifled home 28 goals, and it was sweet revenge for Busby's men, who had seen Leeds demolish their dreams of another Wembley date by winning the FA Cup semi-final duel – after a replay. In 1967, Busby was entitled to smile broadly again, as United were on their way to another Championship and, thereby, qualified for the European Cup.

United rounded off their season in real style, too, finishing undefeated in their last 20 matches and completing their programme by going to Upton Park and handing out a 6–1 hiding to West Ham. It was, the Old Trafford faithful hoped, a sign of things to come in the European Cup, which by then had become the Holy Grail, in much the same way that the Championship became an obsession before Alex Ferguson's men managed to do the trick. The United fans of the 1960s still felt the scars of a Champions' Cup disappointment after the title success of 1965 – United soared to success when they thrashed Benfica 5–1 in their own Stadium of Light in Lisbon, and the sky really did seem to be the limit. Best mesmerised Benfica (including European-Footballer-of-the-Year, Eusebio) as he scored twice, with Charlton, Connelly and Crerand also on the mark. United, indeed, had the ball in Benfica's net three times in the opening 16 minutes.

This was United's team of all-stars, that magical night: Gregg; Brennan, Dunne; Crerand, Foulkes, Stiles; Best, Law, Charlton, Herd, Connelly. And it seemed United were set to finish off the job, as an unrated team from Yugoslavia by the name of Partizan Belgrade barred the way to the Final. I was in Belgrade for the first leg of that game, and Best proved a pre-match problem for Busby – not because he misbehaved, but because his ability to last 90 minutes was in doubt. By the final whistle, everyone wanted to draw a veil over what had gone before ... Best, United now realised, faced a cartilage operation; Law had missed a sitter; and when I went to see Busby in the dressing-room, for once he looked dejected. He asked me to give him a couple of minutes, retreated inside, then reappeared, the usual smile back in place, and answered all my queries. We both knew United should have won, had they played up to anything like their normal standard. And when Partizan went to Old Trafford for the return, we found that the damage had already been done – United simply couldn't pull the chestnuts out of the fire, on home ground. That experience left many people wondering if United were fated never to win the European Cup.

By the end of season 1966–67, United were back in business; once again they were on the trail of that elusive European trophy. They had won the League championship and this time out, they were well and truly on the way to glory. The Champions' Cup trail began with a match against a Maltese club with a familiar Scottish name – Hibernian, who were vanquished, 4–0 on aggregate. Then came a tussle with a Yugoslav club, Sarajevo – which, of course, evoked those unhappy memories of Partizan. But this time there was no mistake; United scored a 2–1 overall success, to take them through to a tie against Polish club Gornik Zabrze, and once again an aggregate 2–1 scoreline was sufficient to pitch United into the semi-finals ... where they were paired with the Spanish greats, Real Madrid.

At Old Trafford, United managed to forge a lead, but by the slimmest of margins – just one goal, struck by George Best. And in the return game the omens looked anything but good as Real lashed in three goals, to make it appear as if they were virtually home and dry, even when the scoreline overall became 3–2. For at that stage, only 15 minutes of playing time remained. Matt Busby confessed to me later that at that moment in time he endured agonies as he visualised his dream being demolished yet again; but when David Sadler put the ball into Real's net, hope suddenly became renewed. It was that most unexpected of marksmen, Bill Foulkes, who became United's hero as he popped up, seemingly from nowhere, to put the finishing touch to a centre from Best ... and that made it 3–3 on the night, and 4–3 on aggregate for United.

You could see that Real's players were distraught; as for their supporters, they were stunned. But there was to be no let-off for Real, as United clung grimly to their task, and so,

27

for the first time, they emerged from a European Cup semi-final knowing that they would be going all the way. Now it was Benfica, the Eagles of Lisbon, whom they would be meeting in the Final – at Wembley – and, of course, memories were stirred of past encounters and dramas since United had blazed the European Cup trail back in 1956, taking on Anderlecht and defying authority.

There had been those who didn't want English clubs competing against the Continentals, but Busby had made a stand and, by 1968, he had seen his club contest three semi-finals, without success, come back after the tragedy of Munich to start out all over again, and savour the moment when another of the survivors from the air crash, Bobby Charlton, led the team out to take on Benfica at Wembley. I was one of the thousands who watched the drama unfold, after a first half in which there had been little to suggest what was to come. I can recall that rare headed goal from Charlton which was cancelled out by one from Jaime Graca; I can recall a magnificent save by Stepney and an astonishing let-off when Eusebio had the chance to clinch things, close to time; I can also recall that sporting moment when Eusebio congratulated Stepney, after United's 'keeper had made a super-save ... and, of course, I can recall the goals that made Manchester United the winners in extra time.

The brilliance of Best produced United's second goal, with extra time no more than two minutes old ... as Benfica's 'keeper dived, despairingly, he could see for himself that the ball was in the net, because he was facing his own goal and had his hands over the line, on the Wembley turf. Meanwhile, the Irishman was wheeling away in triumph. United's third goal came from Brian Kidd, then celebrating his 19th birthday and today Alex Ferguson's right-hand man. Then Charlton struck again, to make it United 4, Benfica 1. The three-goal salvo had come in the space of seven magical minutes and, as Charlton held the gleaming trophy aloft, it was a moment for emotion. Matt Busby admitted to me that he had shed a tear or two, just then. Ironically, he had seen Manchester City depose United as champions in 1968, but it

28

all came good for Busby in the European Cup, and the final accolade was his knighthood. Busby was hailed as 'one of the few managers who can truly face triumph and disaster, and treat those two imposters the same.'

When it was recorded that during the semi-final against Real Madrid, Busby had virtually given up hope of seeing his side claim the Champions' Cup, as United trailed 3–1 during the second leg, it was also recalled that when he walked into the dressing-room at half-time 'the kindly smile had replaced the look of strain and disappointment' as he offered his players encouragement to go out and keep on fighting for a result. I saw that same look of strain and disappointment etched on Matt's face after the defeat by Partizan in Belgrade ... yet, minutes later, he had managed to put the smile back in place as he discussed the débacle.

Busby's managerial career at Old Trafford spanned a quarter of a century, which is a lifetime – and more – for any team boss; indeed, when he had completed a score of years in the hot seat (and at United it became the hottest seat of all), he had remained in office longer than any other manager in the game. By then, indeed, football had seen no fewer than 600 managers arriving and departing during that 20-year period ... in which time Busby had also built three teams, each of them equipped to achieve success.

Jimmy Murphy, whom Matt had hand-picked to be his No. 2, stood as a contrast in some ways with 'the boss'; where Busby was urbane, almost gentle, Jimmy appeared as a man with fire in his belly – fire which he wanted the players to have, too. He was the man called upon to make tough decisions as Busby lay so grievously ill in the Rechts der Isaar hospital, after Munich, and he certainly needed to inject fighting spirit into the patched-up side which consisted of a few old hands and some untried kids. Murphy, like Matt Busby, was offered top jobs elsewhere, but he rejected them, saying: 'Matt respects everybody with whom he has dealings ... My greatest reward was at Wembley in 1958 when the boss came back from Munich, still a sick man. He said, "Thank you, Jimmy. You've done a wonderful job. I'm proud of you."' And Murphy added: 'Our association is founded on mutual respect.'

Bobby Charlton admitted that he had sought Busby's advice often; as did Don Revie, when he was setting out upon the uncharted course of management at Leeds. Revie recalled that Busby answered his every question, when he went to see him at Old Trafford. 'Some men might guard their secrets from others; but not Matt. He demonstrated his wonderful gift for making the man who seeks his advice seem like the most important person in the world.' Bill Shankly, too, was lavish in his praise of Busby – and Shanks, whom I knew well, didn't dispense his favours lightly. He recalled that at a time when Liverpool were going 'flat out for the Championship', they defeated Manchester United at Anfield. Bill said: 'Busby was the first to grab me by the hand and say, "See that you don't let it out of your grasp now, Bill." In a game that can so easily break a man, his record is remarkable. He can accept defeat with dignity, and is never arrogant in success.'

Chapter 3

A NAP HAND OF MANAGERS

'I never interfered with the manager's right to do the job in the way he considered it should be done.' – SIR MATT BUSBY.

MATT Busby reigned as manager of Manchester United from 1945 to 1969 . . . a span of almost a quarter of a century. During the next 17 years or so, United managed to produce a nap hand of managers, some of whom were more or less hand-picked by Busby; but not one of them managed to emulate 'the old man' and steer the Championship trophy back to the Old Trafford sideboard. One fellow-Scot whom Matt and United failed to land was 'the big fellow', Jock Stein; but United had more success when, after their nap hand had failed to deliver, they persuaded another Scot, Alex Ferguson, to travel across the border to Manchester and chance his arm. And the man who had been team boss at Aberdeen finally succeeded in achieving what United and their fans had craved for so many years.

The first to have a go, once Busby had decided it was time to make his exit, was a young, fresh-faced, smiling and good-looking fellow by the name of Wilf McGuinness. He had red blood coursing through his veins, for he had been brought up at Old Trafford and played first-team football for United until dogged by injury. He had been one of the famous Busby Babes, graduating as a wing-half who could make a biting

31

tackle and who, seemingly, was possessed of endless stamina. He became skipper of the England Under-23 side, and graduated to the status of a senior international as he played against Ireland in 1958 and against Mexico in Mexico City. The failure of Wilf McGuinness to nail down the job of managing United on a long-term basis saddened Matt Busby greatly, for he had had high hopes when he spoke in favour of keeping the job 'in the family' with Wilf's appointment. It was in January, 1969, that Busby revealed his wish to step down from the managerial chair, come the end of the season and (as happened when Bill Shankly, then Bob Paisley, then Joe Fagan quit the job at Liverpool) the football world buzzed with speculation as to who could possibly follow such an act.

Busby himself told me that he felt McGuinness should be given his chance, and the first step was for Wilf – then aged 32 – to take charge as the club's chief coach, with the starting date June 1, 1969. McGuinness did achieve some measure of success, too, because he steered United to the semi-finals of both the FA Cup and the League Cup, and he took them to eighth place in the First Division. But such progress was not deemed quite sufficient and, in any event, McGuinness discovered that he had to contend not only with the opposition provided by other clubs, but with problems off the field. In 1970, with the turn of the year approaching, there was a run of poor results which sent United sliding down the table, while in the League Cup they suffered the indignity of being knocked out by Third Division Aston Villa. And as if to compound the problems, rumours became rife that all was not well in United's dressing-room.

Alan Gowling may never have been regarded by United fans as one of the dazzling stars at Old Trafford – such adulation was reserved for the Laws, Charltons and Bests – but he did a very effective job during his time at the club, and he had plenty of brains. He was probably what you might term one of the team's workhorses, like Roger Hunt at Liverpool, but – like Hunt – he had the knack of scoring goals, and he was not lacking in skill or in the ability to see things from 'upstairs' – he could certainly use his head.

I got to know him fairly well, and when we discussed United's team bosses, he reckoned McGuinness was 'on a loser from the start.' It could not be disputed that Wilf had been a team-mate of players who were now having to regard him as 'the boss'; neither could it be disputed that some players had won more medals than Wilf ... and in football, there is a saying that when someone seeks to exert authority, he is likely to be told: 'Show us your medals.' McGuinness had achieved a degree of success at club and international level; he knew the Old Trafford scene as well as anyone; and as a coach he was popular. But when it became a matter of laying down the law, embarking upon a rebuilding job and deciding that some players had become expendable ... 'the writing was on the wall', as Gowling put it.

According to him, some of United's younger players felt they were living in the shadow of big-name stars and there were times when they felt, also, that certain illustrious names were allowed to take liberties. George Best was cited as one of these star names, of course, and Gowling told me he recognised a conflict of personalities between Best and Bobby Charlton during both the McGuinness era, and after Matt Busby had taken charge of team affairs once more – indeed, Gowling claimed it became even more sharply focused then. Gowling considered, however, that in fairness to Best, it should be acknowledged just how much he meant to United – indeed, Gowling reckoned that as well as producing some match-winning performances, the Irish genius believed he sometimes 'carried' the team. In short, he was the ace in United's pack.

So the day dawned when Wilf McGuinness learned he must step down from the top job, and Gowling (who discussed matters with him) felt that, for a time, he was a somewhat bitter man about the way things had gone for him. In Gowling's words, he was 'almost a broken man' and his traumatic experience certainly left its mark; his hair turned white, then he lost it altogether, so that in later years he was to become Soccer's version of the television cop, Kojak.

McGuinness finally left Old Trafford, had a spell managing

York City and in Greece, then wound up on Bury's backroom staff, by which time he had become rather more philosophical about his experiences and could summon up a smile again. Matt Busby, meanwhile, had held sway once more, briefly, after Wilf stepped down, and he told me how saddened he had been by what had happened to his protégé. Matt told me, also, how the dressing-room atmosphere had become affected, with divided loyalties among the players, and as a result of this knowledge, which reached the boardroom, the question of retaining McGuinness as team boss was raised. So, as Wilf resumed coaching the reserves, Busby gave management another go, but by the time he had seen United finish in eighth place he wanted to call it a day again, even though some players remained keen for him to stay as 'the boss'.

Had things gone differently, United's next manager would have been Jock Stein; but while Celtic were not overly happy about United's approach, they did give them permission to talk to their manager ... who, after pondering upon matters, decided to decline the offer, with thanks. So Celtic heaved a sigh of relief, and United had to search elsewhere for the man who would tackle what had become the toughest job in football. Their choice fell upon an Irishman with a genial smile and, seemingly, a streak of steel in his make-up, even if he appeared to be a very quiet man. Frank O'Farrell was the team boss at Leicester City, and he had taken them to promotion. When United chairman Louis Edwards contacted Leicester counterpart Len Shipman, he was given the green light to approach O'Farrell, and Matt Busby met the Irishman to talk things over. In quick time, O'Farrell agreed to become United's new manager, and he was officially installed on July 1, 1971.

It was a strange start to the season, too, because United had to play their first two home matches away from Old Trafford, at Anfield and Stoke, as a result of some supporters having caused problems the previous season during a match against Newcastle United.

O'Farrell (like Ron Atkinson later) seemed destined to

34

bring that elusive Championship trophy to Old Trafford as his team picked up points in real style – by the turn of the year they had a 17-goal marksman in George Best (hat-tricks against West Ham and Southampton), and come the first day of 1972 United (beaten only by Everton and Leeds), topped the table. There was a hiccup or two, as a few players didn't altogether see things the manager's way ... Alan Gowling, having lost his first-team spot and turned down a move to Crystal Palace, agreed to join Huddersfield Town, while Sammy McIlroy was said to have been involved in a row and defied the club. In fact, as Sammy told me, he was ready to blow his top when he thought he had been axed even from United's reserve side ... only to discover that he was being held back so that he could make his mark the following day in the big derby game against Manchester City.

Then, when McIlroy turned up in Belfast, instead of flying with United to Israel, the story came out about the so-called row. In fact, the manager had given Sammy – still only 17 – permission to go home and see his father, who was ill, while the player admitted he needed a break from the game. As it was, a much bigger name was missing when United reached Tel Aviv; because George Best, the centre of rumours about retirement, was said to be in Marbella. So it was left to O'Farrell to issue a statement explaining the McIlroy business – and making it clear he had been upset by Best's absence.

When it came to getting results in the League, United's dreams of a first title trophy since the halcyon days of Busby flickered and faded from view. During one unhappy spell, seven games had been lost in succession. And while United had made two costly signings in Martin Buchan and Ian Storey-Moore, for a total of £320,000, they could do no better than achieve eighth place in the League. Worse was to come, too, because season 1972–73 found United still seeking their first victory after nine matches. It was near the end of September before they won, beating Derby County 3-0 at Old Trafford.

By that time, they were close to the foot of the table and the natives were becoming restless as talk of relegation hung in the air. United held a board meeting and the directors decided to plunge into the transfer market again, this time coming up with Ted MacDougall (£200,000) and Wyn Davies (£65,000). Both players were strikers, and it meant that around £600,000 had been expended upon four recruits in the effort to get the club moving in an upward direction again. Ironically, considering what happened in 1995 when United and Eric Cantona travelled to Selhurst Park, it was a trip there to face Crystal Palace which undid O'Farrell. Palace gave United the full treatment – the final scoreline showed they had rattled home five goals without reply – and only four days after that agonising experience, O'Farrell was being shown through the exit door, despite a suggestion from Busby that he should be given a while longer to see if he could turn things round.

Busby told me that his co-directors were not in a similar frame of mind, however, and when he saw which way the wind blew, 'I didn't rock the boat.' So, three and a half years after Matt had first handed over the reins, United were looking for their third team boss. If O'Farrell had been recognised as one of football's quiet men, the next incumbent at Old Trafford was well and truly one of the game's extroverts. The subject of United's managerial vacancy cropped up when Busby met Tommy Docherty at a match, and it swiftly became apparent that The Doc had more than a passing interest in the job. He was then Scotland's team boss, but on December 22, 1972, he was released to take up the challenge at Old Trafford – as he acknowledged, it was 'the job I've been waiting for all my life.'

His career had taken many twists and turns, and he was noted for his ability to make quick decisions as he wheeled and dealed in the transfer market. For instance, while at Chelsea he was involved in a strange, on-off-on-again transfer saga which finally saw Alex Stepney move to United – and this, only 112 days after The Doc had signed him for Chelsea. Each time the fee, £50,000, was a world record for a 'keeper.

At one stage, it seemed that The Doc intended to play Stepney and Peter Bonetti in alternate games for Chelsea, on the basis that he believed he had the best two goalkeepers in the country on his staff. Alex once assured me that so far as a player was concerned, 'if you're looking for the quiet life, don't sign up with The Doc ... but if you're prepared to flog your guts out, you'll get 100 per cent backing from him.' Stepney, like Sammy McIlroy, made his debut for United in a derby game against Manchester City, and it was Sammy who described Docherty to me as 'a flamboyant character who was a law unto himself. If you got along together – which usually meant doing things the way The Doc demanded – well and good. If you crossed him, watch out!'

Martin Buchan did cross Docherty during a practice match – and, for his pains, was given marching orders. Buchan, a strong-minded character himself, could be caustic, and he had quizzed the manager about his repeated blowing of the whistle as he halted play in order to make points. So The Doc blew the whistle on him. He also blew the whistle in sensational style on several players while he was managing Chelsea, while I had one or two memorable encounters with The Doc, whom I had first met when he was a player with Preston North End. We came into contact again during his Chelsea days, and the cause of our conversation was his decision to send home eight of his players during a week when Chelsea were staying at sunny Blackpool. One of those players was Terry Venables; another was George Graham. It was reported that the eight had broken curfew, although Venables claimed The Doc's cancellation of a night out was not merely as a result of a defeat by Liverpool at Anfield, but the culmination of several disagreements between players and manager. At any rate, the upshot was that Chelsea, minus those eight players, met Burnley and suffered a 6–2 hammering at Turf Moor. Naturally, that defeat made more headline news. By then, former Blackpool captain Harry Johnston was a colleague of mine at *The People*, and he rang in to tell me: 'I've got Tommy Docherty with me ... do you want to talk to him?' Of course, I did! And I managed to get some very quotable quotes from The Doc for Sunday's paper.

I recall a quote, too, after Tony Hateley (father of the

37

Queen's Park Rangers striker) had turned up trumps for Chelsea with a goal which won an FA Cup semi-final, and The Doc triumphantly proclaimed: 'That's what I paid £100,000 for!' I remember being abroad with Liverpool, too, when the news filtered through that Docherty intended to axe Alex Stepney and promote Paddy Roche to the No. 1 spot at United. The Doc reckoned Roche was the man for the future, while Stepney declared that he would back his own record against The Doc's judgment. Roche suffered a nightmare time from which he never seemed to recover (shades of Jim Leighton, as Alex Ferguson axed him for an FA Cup-final replay), so Stepney regained his place and The Doc admitted to having been wrong.

I had another experience with The Doc when I was ghosting a book for Lou Macari, and United's manager was required to vet the material. To cut a long story short, I met Tommy in an hotel in Malta, where I was on holiday and he was attending a function organised by the Malta branch of the United Supporters' Association. The function went on and on, and it was around midnight when I finally made contact with The Doc – who then told me he hadn't even seen the manuscript. So I arranged for him to get a copy on his return to Old Trafford, and there were no more snags. Well, apart from one little matter. Having done a chapter on how Lou saw The Doc, I did another on how The Doc saw Lou Macari (and I have to say Tommy Docherty was as good as gold about this). However, when the serial rights were sold to a national newspaper, a condition was that Docherty's verdict on Macari must be included for extracts, so I told The Doc that he would receive £100 for his co-operation.

He was happy enough about that, but as the weeks went by he began to bombard me with phone calls from Old Trafford, asking when the cash was coming. I explained that we had to wait for payment from the paper. In the end, I became so anxious to get The Doc off my back that I was ready to pay his £100 out of my own pocket – fortunately, at that stage the cheque did arrive and The Doc got his cut. The phone calls stopped.

When it came to wheeling and dealing, Docherty lived up to his reputation. He sold MacDougall, Davies, Willie Morgan, Brian Kidd, Gerry Daly, Jim McCalliog and Steve James; he signed Steve Coppell, Gordon Hill, Stuart Pearson, Jim Holton, Mick Martin, Alex Forsyth, Ron Davies, Tommy Baldwin, Alan Foggon and Paddy Roche. And he gave Denis Law a free transfer – which, in Matt Busby's considered opinion (as he told me later), was a mistake. Busby believed Law was still good enough to get goals. One thing which didn't please Busby was the fact that Law, apparently, learned from the media about the proposal to free him. Matt conceded that this might have arisen from a misunderstanding, but he felt it was unfortunate, any way.

Under The Doc, United suffered relegation, bounced straight back, and savoured the delight of beating Liverpool in the 1977 FA Cup Final to rob them of a unique treble (Liverpool claimed the Championship and the European Cup). United's fast-flowing, ebullient football matched the style of their manager, and the fans who loved to sing 'Que sera, sera...' flocked to Old Trafford in such numbers that during season 1974–75, the average attendance was no less than 48,388 – United regularly got the kind of gates Busby's teams attracted, as does the team assembled by Alex Ferguson today. During the brief sojourn in the Second Division, The Doc's team was never deposed from the top spot from the end of August to the end of the season, and after having roared back to the top flight, they continued to roar as they went to places such as Anfield (in November, 1975) leading the First Division, although in the end they had to settle for finishing sixth as Liverpool (not for the first time) outstripped United at the head of the pack. But Docherty's side had still done enough to earn a place in the UEFA Cup. And if there was a slip in 1976, when underdogs Southampton pipped United for the FA Cup, 12 months later it was Liverpool who fell and Docherty and his players who paraded the trophy around Wembley stadium.

That triumph, however, was to be the last one achieved under Docherty's management, because inside a couple of months he was being shown the exit door – and Matt Busby, who had been instrumental in his arriving at Old Trafford, played a key role in his departure. It revolved around the sensational story of Docherty's affair with the wife of the club's physiotherapist. It seemed to be assumed that The Doc had the assurance of chairman Louis Edwards that his job was safe and that it would all be a seven-day wonder so far as the media was concerned; but, as Busby told me, this couldn't be allowed to happen. Matt related how he returned from holiday to be greeted with the news about the romance and, after a grilling by the media, he thought matters through and concluded that, regrettably, The Doc must go. The way Busby put it to me: 'How could a manager chastise players who misbehaved, when they were aware that he had been involved in something like this? No, it just wasn't on...' So, sadly, Busby indicated that the curtain must come down on The Doc's reign as manager. And it did.

Enter Dave Sexton, a man whose career had been linked with that of Tommy Docherty in more ways than one. When Docherty took over as caretaker manager at Chelsea, he had brought in Sexton as a coach, and Sexton did indeed have a special aptitude for getting the best out of players. Terry Venables termed him 'a student of the game' and reckoned that for Sexton coaching was 'a labour of love'. Later in life, Venables made Sexton a member of his international back-room team. As The Doc progressed to Old Trafford, Sexton became manager at Chelsea, after a playing career with Luton Town, West Ham, Orient, Brighton and Crystal Palace. Then he had returned to Orient as manager and saved them from relegation to the Third Division. That was in 1965, and later that year he joined Fulham as a coach, then moved to Arsenal, where he was named assistant manager in March, 1967. Six months later he was being asked to return to Chelsea as Tommy Docherty's successor, and he did well at Stamford Bridge.

In successive years Chelsea claimed the FA Cup and the European Cup-Winners' Cup, and I was at Old Trafford the night they stunned Leeds United by winning their FA Cup

Final replay, against the odds. The goal that mattered was scored by David Webb, after Leeds had dominated play as they had done at Wembley. By the mid-1970s, however, Chelsea were falling upon difficult times and Sexton departed. He joined Queen's Park Rangers and in two years there achieved a great deal – in fact, they gave Liverpool a real run for their money in the title chase. Sexton, in fact, became a target for several clubs (Arsenal were said to want him as No. 2 to manager Terry Neill) . . . but when he did move on again, it was – to the surprise of some people – away from his southern roots as he travelled north to Manchester United.

Once again, Matt Busby played a major role in securing yet another manager – indeed, what he called 'discreet soundings' had been taken on a previous occasion, while Dave Sexton was managing Chelsea, but the word then was that Sexton felt he should remain loyal to the Stamford Bridge club and his players. When The Doc moved out, it was Busby who suggested United should try again to land Dave Sexton – and this time they got their man. For the first year, he relied upon the team and the style which had brought success for Docherty, acknowledging: 'We played the game the same way'. Like The Doc, he took United to Wembley – an FA Cup semi-final replay success against Liverpool was followed, in season 1978–79, by a Final fling against Arsenal. By then Sexton had recruited several players and United had virtually a new-look side, with former Leeds stars Gordon McQueen and Joe Jordan in their line-up, plus 'keeper Gary Bailey, Mickey Thomas (the replacement for Gordon Hill, who had been sold, to the dismay of some United fans, to Derby County, who were managed by . . . Tommy Docherty), and Jimmy Greenhoff. At Wembley, Arsenal led 2–0 by half-time, and that was the scoreline still, with four minutes to go. Then McQueen struck, and two minutes later McIlroy equalised – only for Graham Rix to provide a cross for Alan Sunderland to beat Bailey. Thus the Cup was won and lost.

Twelve months on, in August, 1980, Sexton was splashing out what, at the time, seemed to be a fortune as he paid £800,000 of United's money for midfield star Ray Wilkins.

41

More than this, United became involved in a battle royal for the Championship, and the issue was decided only in the dying days of the season, when Liverpool triumphed over Aston Villa to snatch the prize, while United conceded victory to Leeds at Elland Road. The following season took a downward turn for Sexton as United faltered, and with the media voicing criticism, the fans also made their feelings felt. At the end of the campaign (a bitter end, as it turned out), United embarked on a run which brought seven successive wins; but the writing was on the wall – Sexton's days were numbered. The hoped-for title challenge had not materialised, and the media gave the manager little respite. The quiet man remained quiet; he suffered in silence; but his fate was decided, and so he went. Manchester United had now seen four managers come and go, and the Holy Grail remained just a mirage.

Some folk claimed that Busby had posed problems for the various managers, but if he did, it was almost certainly because they had had so much to live up to. When I asked Busby outright, he told me that while on occasion he had expressed his views (on the Denis Law transfer, for example), he had never interfered with the manager's right to do the job in the way he felt best. 'I wouldn't have thanked the directors for getting on my back when I was manager,' he told me – adding that even when he felt a manager was making a wrong decision, after having given his opinion, if the manager remained determined to go ahead, he could count on Busby's support. He cited various instances: the time McGuinness dropped both Law and Charlton; the time The Doc promoted Roche at Stepney's expense; the sale of Brian Greenhoff to Leeds; the signing of Wilkins; the transfer of Andy Ritchie, who opted to join Brighton, despite interest from Newcastle United.

Busby wasn't in favour of letting Greenhoff go, but he didn't try to block the deal; and when Sexton revealed that Ritchie could bring United £400,000, it seemed to Busby that the manager was presenting a pretty good case, since Ritchie had been home-produced talent, so the profit was that much greater. Initially Sexton said that in fairness to Ritchie, the player should be put in the picture, and Andy indicated he didn't wish to go, but Brighton proved persuasive in the final analysis. As for Ray Wilkins, there was little Sexton didn't know about him, of course, and after months of delicate negotiation, United were given permission to make an approach. Unfortunately, Chelsea wanted more cash than United had in mind, so that presented another barrier to a deal; yet, though the talk was of £800,000, in the end Sexton was given the go-ahead and Wilkins joined United.

If Alex Ferguson feels United have been a source of envy to some people, Matt Busby believed there were times when the club was held to ransom by clubs in the market as sellers. As chairman Martin Edwards made clear during the mid-1990s, United had always been in the forefront when it came to big-money deals, and they had broken transfer records several times. It was a world-record £23,000 for Harry Gregg; £45,000 for Quixall; £50,000 for Stepney; £115,000 for Law, when he was rescued from what might be termed his Italian misadventure. And the fifth manager to try his luck at Old Trafford – Ron Atkinson – was allowed to spend £2 million on Bryan Robson and Remi Moses, with Robson commanding a cool £1.5 million. Ferguson, who was candid enough to say that Busby had set the standards at Old Trafford, was also willing to concede that, if nothing else, Atkinson would have 'earned his keep' by virtue of having signed Robson, United's Captain Marvel. I doubt if Busby played a part in the arrival of Big Ron; I do know negotiations were conducted at the home of someone who at one time had been a newspaper colleague of mine – John Maddock, later to become the controversial general manager of Manchester City, when the sacking of Peter Reid topped the agenda at Maine Road.

Like The Doc, Atkinson was a larger-than-life character who seemed to have no doubts about his own ability, and he steered United to Cup Finals. In 1983, Jimmy Melia's underdogs from Brighton barred the way at Wembley, but lost out in a replay; and two years later, it was Everton who stood between United and the FA Cup ... in the end,

Atkinson was glad of the scoring ability of match-winner Norman Whiteside ... who also played a major role in blocking the Old Trafford route to stardom for Peter Beardsley (he arrived from Vancouver Whitecaps, and returned without having played even one full League game for United). Later, Peter told me: 'It was just one of those things. Norman Whiteside did so well that he ended up playing in the World Cup for Northern Ireland. I knew the Whitecaps would be happy to have me back, in any event.' So back he went – to become a £150,000 buy by Newcastle and figure in three transfer deals exceeding £1 million each time; £1.9 million from Newcastle to Liverpool, then on to Everton and back to Newcastle. As for Whiteside, he also had a spell with Everton before his career was cut short by injury problems.

Bryan Robson's career was dogged by injury, too, but while Big Ron made way for Alex Ferguson, 'Robbo' lasted long enough to collect a Championship medal – indeed, at the age of 36 he was telling me: 'It's my aim still to be in the team. The lads who finished off the season when we won the Premiership title did a great job – but after 18 months, when I was so frustrated with injuries, I want to be back in the action.' Finally, he became a team boss himself, at Middlesbrough – by which time United had repeated their title-winning act, and added the FA Cup, for good measure. That feat was accomplished under Ferguson (Robson himself steered Boro' into the Premiership), but while Atkinson was United's manager, there was a season when the Championship looked a good bet ... in season 1985–86, United surged through their first 10 matches as winners, every time out; and after battering the opposition, they had conceded only three goals, while scoring 27. It took homespun Luton Town, in match No. 11, to halt the victory roll, as they held United to a draw.

That was merely a hiccup, as United disposed of Queen's Park Rangers and, after a 1-1 draw with Liverpool at Old Trafford, there were victories over Chelsea and Coventry City, so that United went into the fourth month of the campaign with a record which showed they had yet to be beaten. It took a Yorkshire club, Sheffield Wednesday, to do the trick. The date was Saturday, November 9, 1985, when – at Hillsborough – United suffered their first reverse as lanky striker Lee Chapman struck the winner late in the game. Not surprisingly, even before Christmas there were those who predicted that the title race had ended ... yet, as Liverpool have proved time and again, a race is never over until it's been won. At one stage, United had led the chasing pack by 10 points; but that gap was narrowed when Spurs prised a draw out of the game at Old Trafford, and when United were losing away to Leicester City, Liverpool were beating Birmingham City, so that by this time they were no more than two points adrift.

When United beat Aston Villa away and Liverpool lost at Highbury, the gap widened again; but Arsenal were doing United no favours – they went to Old Trafford, and Charlie Nicholas hit the winner there. Chelsea muscled in on the Championship act by moving to within two points of United, and it took a 3–1 win away against Oxford United for Atkinson's team to open up a five-point margin. Mid-January saw the title race becoming ever tighter, with Everton joining Liverpool and Chelsea as challengers to Manchester United, and when United went down by the odd goal in five against Nottingham Forest at Old Trafford (while their three rivals chalked up more points) the leadership changed hands for the first time, as Everton became top dogs. They beat Spurs, United lost at Upton Park, and injuries took their toll at United, as well. They lost their inspirational skipper, Bryan Robson, for three long months, and as United faltered and faded, Liverpool came up on the rails to claim the No. 1 finishing spot. United? To their great sorrow, they could do no better than claim fourth place. The critics sharpened their knives, Atkinson became a major target, and six months later he became United's ex-manager, as they seemed to be on a slippery slope.

Instead of title talk, there were mutterings about relegation; and if Atkinson was deemed to be failing on the football front, he also made headline news as he became involved in a romance. In the end, he departed from Old Trafford as yet another manager who had not been able to deliver the title trophy which, for the United faithful, had become the be-all and the end-all. As for the directors at Old Trafford, they had to turn their attention yet again to finding another team boss who, they so fervently hoped, would at last be able to come up with the Holy Grail. And so it was a case of 'bring on the next one...' with 'the next one' turning out to be a Scot by the name of Alex Ferguson. Long before he arrived physically to be installed in the managerial chair, his name was being canvassed for the hot seat and, of course, judged by his success at Aberdeen, where he had won titles and trophies at home and abroad, he possessed the right credentials ... or did he? The test of time would surely tell.

Chapter 4

THE PASSAGE OF TIME

Enter Alex Ferguson . . . he became the sixth manager to take up the challenge of emulating what Matt Busby had achieved for the club – that of taking the League-title trophy to Old Trafford.

TIME dragged for the fans who followed Manchester United, even though there were occasions when they were able to celebrate success in Cup Finals at Wembley. Time dragged, indeed, for more than quarter of a century, when it came to the quest for that most elusive trophy of them all: the one which proclaimed a club as Champions of the Football League. This, above all, was the one by which you measured success, and from Matt Busby's day to the moment when, under Alex Ferguson, United finally scaled the pinnacle, there were seasons when the Old Trafford faithful (and United's current manager and his players) were driven almost to despair.

The Charity Shield is regarded as a pipe-opener to the campaign for the Championship, and at Wembley in the Charity Shield the champions come up against the holders of the FA Cup. In 1977, for instance, Manchester United and Liverpool tackled each other and, after a scoreless draw, they settled for holding the Shield for six months apiece. Liverpool were to triumph over Arsenal, West Ham and Tottenham Hotspur before they met United once again, this time in

1983 – and United claimed the Charity Shield with a 2-0 victory. Seven years on, and United were sharing the Shield once more, while in 1993 and 1994 they emerged as winners. Even so, for a club of Manchester United's standing, the Charity Shield remained merely a sideshow to the main attraction ... indeed, even the League Cup and the FA Cup, welcome though they were on the Old Trafford sideboard, did not quite make up for that missing Championship trophy.

The record books show that Manchester United were beaten finalists in the Football League Cup (which, of course, has gone under various guises down the years) in 1983, 1991 and 1994, and that they carried off this particular trophy in 1992. In the FA Cup, they finished on the losing end at Wembley in 1976, 1979 and 1995 (under three different managers – Tommy Docherty, Dave Sexton and Alex Ferguson, respectively), while they were winners in 1977 (under Docherty), 1983 and 1985 (the manager was Ron Atkinson on both occasions), and 1990, 1994 and 1996 (when Alex Ferguson was in charge). In season 1982-83, during the Atkinson era, United could just as easily have lost the trophy as won it, while during Docherty's reign at Old Trafford they lost a Final everyone expected them to win, and won a Final which deprived Liverpool of a unique treble.

In 1976, United went to Wembley to meet the under-dogs of Southampton, who had in their side that day a player by the name of Jim McCalliog ... and he had been one of the men that Tommy Docherty had discarded at Old Trafford. It was a perceptive pass from McCalliog that sent striker Bobby Stokes scampering clear of the United defence at Wembley – and as Stokes beat 'keeper Alex Stepney, he was scoring the goal that won the Cup. In season 1982-83, another team of underdogs – this one from Brighton (who were managed by a Scouser called Jimmy Melia) – barred the way to success for United. The teams shared four goals, and the match went into extra time. One of the marksmen for Brighton was Gordon Smith, and he was the man who might well have won the duel – but with the goal seemingly at his mercy, Smith passed up the chance to make a name for himself. And so a replay took place. It turned out to be no contest, as Manchester United struck four times without reply. And that, as they say, is how the cookie crumbles.

It was in season 1982–83, also, that, United went to Wembley for their first ever League Cup-Final appearance, and when their players walked off the pitch it was in the knowledge that their conquerors, Liverpool, had clocked up a hat-trick of successes in the competition – although United had taken them to extra time before going out by the odd goal in three.

Not until 1992 did United get their hands on the League Cup (when Brian McClair's goal enabled them to defeat Nottingham Forest by the only goal of the game), but under Ron Atkinson, United achieved FA Cup success for a second time at the end of season 1984–85. That was a season to be remembered with pleasure, and with sorrow, by football in general and by Manchester United in particular. They knew only too well, having experienced the tragedy of Munich, just what it meant to be closely involved in a Soccer disaster; and the horrific events of the Bradford fire and in the Heysel stadium (when Liverpool met Juventus in the final of the European Cup) overshadowed almost everything else that happened in the game.

In the case of the Heysel disaster, there was swift action by UEFA. While Liverpool voluntarily exiled themselves from European competition, UEFA decided that all English clubs should be banned from taking part, and this meant that Manchester United, having beaten League-champions Everton in the final of the FA Cup, must forfeit their place in the European Cup-Winners' Cup. By the same token, Everton, of course, could not compete in the Champions' Cup. As in 1983, the 1985 Final was a dramatic affair which went to extra time, but on this occasion there was no need for a replay.

United had already overcome opposition from one half of Merseyside, because in their semi-final they had to tangle with Liverpool, and the rivals shared four goals in the first outing, at Goodison Park. The second confrontation took place at Maine Road, and there Mark Hughes and Bryan Robson enabled United to despatch Liverpool by the odd goal in three. This meant that Everton were the team United had to meet at Wembley ... and they, of course, were going for the classic double of League title and FA Cup. United already had one unhappy memory of Everton that season, because the men from Goodison had travelled to Old Trafford and knocked United off the Milk Cup trail by winning 2–1. And while United had reached the quarter-finals of the UEFA Cup that season, they had suffered a shock defeat at the hands of an unsung, almost-unknown team from Hungary by the name of Videoton, who won on penalties.

When it came to the Final of the FA Cup, United defender Kevin Moran carved out a niche in Soccer history for himself, as he became the first footballer ever to be given marching orders in what is recognised as Soccer's showpiece. Moran, always courageous and never intentionally dirty, had a good reputation among fans, as well as players, but he paid the penalty for a somewhat clumsy foul he committed against Peter Reid. In the view of many who saw the incident, few would have argued had Moran simply had his name taken, but the verdict of the referee was final, and it was 'Off you go.' So a dejected Moran trudged off the pitch, and United were left to battle on, a man short. They did themselves justice, however, and they managed to snatch victory from the jaws of defeat as Norman Whiteside scored the only goal.

That FA Cup success was the last one for United until the start of the 1990's ... by which time they were still seeking the Holy Grail – the Championship itself. By season 1985–86 United had been waiting 18 years, and when Ron Atkinson's side clocked up 10 straight wins it appeared that, at long, long, last, the title trophy was there for the taking. Had United managed to overcome Luton Town at Kenilworth Road, they would have equalled Tottenham Hotspur's 1960 record of 11 consecutive victories from the start of the League campaign – but though Mark Hughes struck for United, Brian Stein scored the goal that earned Luton a point and cost United their 100 per cent record.

50

Once Sheffield Wednesday had inflicted a first defeat upon United, the Reds never seemed to be quite the same, all-conquering force of the first three months, and their final placing was fourth, 12 points adrift of champions Liverpool. Instead of another assault the following term, there were three defeats on the trot to plunge United to the foot of the table, and while they had climbed out of the bottom three by October, the following month brought a parting of the ways for the club and manager Atkinson. The axe fell after United had been knocked out of the League Cup with a 4–1 drubbing from Southampton at The Dell. The next day, Atkinson was informed that after more than five years at the helm, he was no longer the manager of Manchester United. Within a matter of hours, Alex Ferguson had been installed as the new Master of Old Trafford.

Ferguson thus became the sixth manager to take up the challenge of emulating what Matt Busby had achieved for the club – that of taking the League-title trophy to Old Trafford ... and, for a while, at any rate, it seemed as if he, too, would be doomed to go the way of his predecessors, despite the success he had achieved during his reign at Aberdeen, who had won not only virtually all the domestic honours, but had beaten Real Madrid in Gothenburg in the Final of the European Cup-Winners' Cup. That was in 1983, and Ferguson was to emulate that success with Manchester United. His first game in charge, however, ended with his team going down 2–0 against one of football's so-called 'unfashionable' clubs, Oxford United. Eventually, United managed to finish in a mid-table position.

Season 1987–88 saw United suffering only two defeats in their first 16 matches, but at the end of the campaign they had to settle for second place behind Liverpool, who had set a new record with 90 points, which meant they were nine points ahead of the Old Trafford club. The following term, and United battled back to beat the odds – not in the title race, but against Liverpool, who in their League game at Old Trafford had stunned the home fans by going into the lead. But United braced themselves and struck back to win the game 3–1, with two of the goals coming inside five minutes. However, once more United had to be satisfied with a mid-table finishing position.

Season 1989–90 saw Ferguson under pressure, as United embarked upon the biggest spending spree in their history ... and crashed, 5–1, against Manchester City as they slid down to the relegation zone. The word 'crisis' began to be bandied about, especially after a 3–0 home defeat by Spurs in the Littlewoods Cup. It was when United met Nottingham Forest in the FA Cup that Ferguson's fortunes took a turn for the better ... and since then, as the record books show, he has scarcely looked back. Two semi-final games against Oldham Athletic, and a 3–3 draw in the Final against Crystal Palace, were followed by a replay winner from Lee Martin which set the Old Trafford club and its manager on the road to even greater glory. Most of all, of course, there was the League Championship – although, even then, there was to be a bitter disappointment before success was achieved.

However, season 1990–91 was notable for the fact that, as he had done once before, Ferguson steered his club – this time not Aberdeen, but Manchester United – to glory in a European tournament. If unrated Videoton had dumped United out of the UEFA Cup in Ron Atkinson's day, another Hungarian side of no-hopers, Pecsi Munkas, found themselves being despatched from the Cup-Winners Cup as United won home and away. Wrexham appeared at Old Trafford, where they lost 3–0, and United also won the return, this time by two clear goals. In the quarter-finals, they defeated Montpellier (for whom Eric Cantona once played) ... although United had to do it the hard way, after a 1–1 home draw. On French soil United won 2–0, to go through and meet Legia Warsaw, who had accounted for Sampdoria in their quarter-final tie.

In the first leg, United fell behind; but they stormed back to score three times, and with the return game at Old Trafford ending in a 1–1 draw Alex Ferguson's men went through to take on Barcelona in the Final in Rotterdam. For the first time in more than two decades, Manchester United had reached the final of a major European competition. Two goals from Mark Hughes (back from his sojourn in Barcelona) more than cancelled out Ronald Koeman's solo late in the game, and so this proved to be consolation for having lost out in the League Cup Final against Sheffield Wednesday, who had scored the only goal. Yet United still had to settle for sixth spot in the First Division table,

Season 1991–92 still had the fans living in hopes ... yet still asking themselves if the Championship would ever be celebrated again – at least, in their time. It seemed, for so long during this bitter-sweet season, that United might at last accomplish their mission, because they stayed the course right to the end and, indeed, appeared to be in the driving seat. Unbeaten in their first 12 matches, United developed an iron-curtain defence as they conceded no more than 14 goals in their first 21 games; yet on New Year's Day Queen's Park Rangers set tongues wagging as they hammered United 4–1 – and this at Old Trafford. Rangers, indeed, had never before achieved victory there. United won four and drew five of their next nine matches, and with six games to go they trailed Leeds United by only a point, while having two games in hand.

But if an FA Cup victory away against Nottingham Forest had proved to be a turning point in the fortunes of club and manager, a home defeat in the League against Forest (coupled with defeats at West Ham and Liverpool) proved to be United's undoing in the title race. On Sunday, April 26, 1992, Leeds United won at Bramall Lane, while Manchester United went down at Anfield – and so, with only one game left for each club, the Championship trophy was destined for Elland Road. Leeds, four points clear, could not be caught. Oddly enough, Nottingham Forest had taken revenge for their Wembley defeat by United in the Rumbelows League Cup Final ... but at least that trophy came to rest on the Old Trafford sideboard, along with the European Super Cup, after a 1–0 victory over Red Star Belgrade on home ground.

So, then, a quarter of a century had passed since Manchester United had last claimed the League title; and down those years, there had been bitter pills to swallow, as well as some consolation prizes scooped up for the club by a succession of managers. Matt Busby had bowed out for the last time towards the end of the 1960's, and he had seen, in turn, men like Wilf McGuinness, Frank O'Farrell, Tommy Docherty, Dave Sexton and Ron Atkinson have a go. Busby was still there, too, when Alex Ferguson came down from Scotland to try his luck. And, at last - at long, long last - Manchester United found that in Ferguson they had the man to get his hands on that glittering Championship trophy. He had arrived during season 1986–87; he had survived some hard times; and, come season 1992–93, he was to emerge as the man who steered United to the first Premier League title.

Chapter 5

GETTING RID OF 'THE STIGMA'

'These players have the opportunity of getting rid of the stigma of not winning the big one for 26 years and giving the supporters what they've really wanted since then.' – ALEX FERGUSON, as United headed for their first title success under his management.

ALEX Ferguson was out on the golf course when he learned that, for the first time in 26 years, Manchester United had become Champions. And they had achieved their objective without even having had to kick a ball ... because on that Sunday afternoon in 1993, struggling Oldham Athletic had done the trick for them. Oldham had gone to Villa Park as no-hopers and sprung such an upset by winning that it ended Aston Villa's bid to grasp the title trophy. It meant that Manchester United, still with two matches to play, could not be overhauled; it meant that Monday night's game at Old Trafford, against Blackburn Rovers, would be one long night of celebration, with the team doing a triumphant lap of honour.

May 2, 1993, was what one observer termed 'the end of the longest wait'. Fans flocked down what was now named Sir Matt Busby Way to celebrate the auspicious occasion; and one young fellow, from Helsinki in Finland, was sufficiently moved that he kissed the brickwork of Old Trafford. Ten years previously, when he was only 12 years old, he had opened an English football magazine and extracted from it a team picture of Manchester United to pin up by his bed. His name then was Ville Leppanen ... later, he changed it to Manu Leppanen, by deed poll. As he explained: 'Manu IS a Finnish name – it was my grandfather's.' By May, 1993, Manu – meaning Manchester United – had become almost his reason for existing.

United manager Alex Ferguson, on the eve of Oldham's Sunday engagement at Villa Park, knew full well that his team held a four-point lead at the top of the table, but he was taking nothing for granted. With Aberdeen, he had claimed three Scottish titles in six years – but he was ready to admit that chasing Manchester United's first Championship since 1967 was a much tougher assignment. He declared that 'it's hard to win a League anywhere ... it was hard at Aberdeen, because we had to beat Rangers and Celtic, and everything is against you up there – resources, support, refereeing decisions which always favoured the Old Firm. But winning in England is even more difficult. United's lack of success over the years has proved nobody has a divine right to win titles down here. It would be an honour, but records don't mean a thing to me. It's this club that matters more.' In uttering that last sentiment, he was echoing the sentiments of the great Sir Matt Busby, who had taken the club to the pinnacle.

Alex Ferguson summed up about his team of triers: 'These players have the opportunity of getting rid of the stigma of not winning the big one for 26 years and giving the supporters what they've really wanted since then.' And that footballing genius of the 1960's, George Best, pointed out that 'every United team has had to live in our shadow ... unfortunately, the shadow we left was too great for many players and managers.' Best, who claimed that United had handed the title to Leeds 'on a plate' the previous year, forecast that the current United side would go on to conquer Europe... 'I think, in 12 months' time, we will see the squad Fergie has built will be a match for any team in Europe. They can go on to lift the European Cup.' Best's timing was out a little bit, in that respect – United were to suffer when they tried conclusions with the Continentals in the Champions' Cup. However, what of Sir Matt Busby, who lived to see his beloved United crowned Champions again? 'My admiration for what Alex has achieved is immense, and I don't want to take any of the shine away. If United win the title (this was just before the Villa débacle) it will be Alex who deserves the recognition.'

Busby made one telling point, also: 'It is a very difficult league to win. You can't just say, because you are Manchester United and the biggest club in Britain, that you should win it. These last few years have been frustrating for many people – I have always felt for the managers when they haven't won.' So just how difficult was it for United to conquer, at last? Well, eight clubs had claimed the title trophy during those 26 'lost' years at Old Trafford: Liverpool 11 times; Everton and Arsenal three times apiece; Leeds United (under Don Revie) twice and again (under Howard Wilkinson); Derby County twice; Manchester City, Nottingham Forest and Aston Villa once apiece. It was recorded that 'the United faithful watched, cursed, pleaded and despaired as successive managers hurled mountains of money at a problem which seemed intractable.'

When comparisons were made between Manchester United, 1960's vintage, and the United side of 1993, it was inevitable that the names of George Best and Ryan Giggs cropped up – even though the one was Irish and the other Welsh. Alex Ferguson, it was said, 'has provided Giggs with the kind of protection which Best was never accorded. In 1967, the world and his sister could tell you more than you needed to know about George, from his taste in ties to the names of the last six ladies in his life. As Manchester's premier tourist attraction, he lived in a state of permanent siege, with buses lined up outside his home so that day-trippers might gasp and gawp. Giggs has suffered no such distractions.'

As for Eric Cantona, his signing was acclaimed as 'the biggest single turning point in United's Championship odyssey'. It was said that the Frenchman was 'the final piece in the Championship jig-saw' – and that 'there were plenty of people who suspected that the signing would be the straw which broke United's challenge.' The writer was not to know how much United were going to miss Cantona when they went – and failed – for a repeat of the Double in the spring of 1995. In 1993 it was 'all power to Fergie's elbow for having the guts to go for him, keeping faith when others muttered their disapproval.'

Striker Mark Hughes admitted that he had had his 'ups and downs with the boss, like quite a few other players. But we've grown to appreciate what he was trying to achieve for United. He shook everybody up when he arrived; he rocked the club, he made us think.' Indeed he did. And from the manager of the French national team, Gerard Houllier, came more praise for United's manager – and for Howard Wilkinson, the man who had taken Cantona into English football in the first place. 'I think Howard did a lot for Eric. The time he spent with Leeds was memorable. But it has been a very good move to Manchester – to collect a second Championship medal in England (he had also won one in France, with Marseille, in 1991) in such a short space of time is truly remarkable. There will be a few managers and coaches wondering if Cantona can do the same job for their clubs.'

United kicked off the season in what amounted to low gear, as Blackburn Rovers and Norwich City set the early pace. United, in fact, had a struggle to translate territorial superiority into goals ... in eight League outings during October and November, they managed only eight goals. So Ferguson was well aware what was needed – after all, he could remember that this same failing had played a serious part in United's faltering finish as they were unable to stave off the challenge from Leeds the previous term. He had tried (and failed) to land David Hirst from Sheffield Wednesday; and then, suddenly, Cantona became available. Ferguson swooped, Cantona made an immediate impact, and United embarked upon an unbeaten run of nine matches, during which they won seven times and rattled in 21 goals. On Boxing Day they went to play Sheffield Wednesday at Hillsborough, were trailing 3–1 ... and ended up sharing the spoils after a sizzling, 3–3 draw. In a barnstorming comeback, Brian McClair struck twice, while it was Cantona whose goal clinched the point. On another trip to Sheffield (for the FA Cup at Bramall Lane) Steve Bruce missed a spot-kick and Manchester United made their exit, beaten by the odd goal in three. They came through their next three League games (one of them at Anfield) with maximum points, however, and kept their nerve after losing by the only goal against struggling Oldham, at Boundary Park.

They still had their critics, as they followed up by only managing to draw three times on the trot, but one of the crunch matches showed that Manchester United had no intention of caving in or even giving up. Norwich City, having despatched Aston Villa and thus boosted their own Championship ambitions, if only briefly, were swept aside at Carrow Road as United beat them 3–1, and a run of five victories in succession ensured that, this time out, there would be no mistake. At Old Trafford in the return against Sheffield Wednesday, Bruce more than made up for his penalty miss in the FA Cup against Sheffield United – first, he headed home a late equaliser and then, with the game deep into injury time (which extended for seven long minutes), he snatched a winner. While Villa were going down 3–0 at Ewood Park, United were winning 2–0 away against Crystal Palace ... no one, then, had the faintest notion about what would happen at Selhurst Park when United met Palace there in January, 1995.

And so Manchester United arrived at the final hurdle; two games left to play, four points clear of Aston Villa, and the Championship at long, long last within their grasp. Oldham's victory at Villa Park was relayed to Alex Ferguson as he played golf that Sunday afternoon – he had reached the final hole when someone walked up to him and imparted the glad tidings. Ferguson termed it 'the most marvellous moment of my career' – not for him any sense of anti-climax – and his Captain Marvel, Bryan Robson, declared: 'It's been a long time, and now no one can throw that 26-year gap in the faces of the young players.' Even as he celebrated the present, however, Ferguson was looking to the future. 'We have the power and the potential to be a major football force for years to come ... the future could not be more exciting.' He didn't know it then, of course, but he would still have a few bitter pills to swallow, before even greater glory.

After the crowning ceremony at Old Trafford, where Blackburn Rovers were duly mastered, the final scene was scheduled for a ground which would become memorable for all the wrong reasons a few seasons later ... Selhurst Park was the venue, with Wimbledon (and not Crystal Palace) as United's hosts. The men from Old Trafford rounded off their season in true Championship style: they finished with seven straight wins, a 10-point lead and a playing record which, remarkably, turned out to be identical to that of the 1967 side. It read: Played 42, Won 24, Drawn 12, Lost 6 ... Goals for 67, Goals against 31 ... Points total 84.

More than 30,000 people turned up for that final outing at Selhurst Park, where gate receipts were a record (£303,000). Ferguson admitted that his players could have been carried away by the carnival atmosphere generated by the fans, 'but we showed a winner's attitude ... the performance was in keeping with the attitude of the whole team.' And as United won 2-1, their supporters enjoyed the spectacle of Bryan Robson striking the winner – that was the first goal he had scored in the Premier League. On this occasion, it was recorded, the tougher Wimbledon tackled, 'the more sophisticated became United's method of dealing with them, not least from Eric Cantona. The Frenchman's flicks and feints assured the ball was gone before the boot came in, and when he eventually tired of the treatment, he exacted retribution with an elbow and knee on John Fashanu in one flowing movement.'

Ryan Giggs had begun the match as a spectator, to give Robson his chance of glory, but when Denis Irwin pulled a muscle, that was the signal for Giggs to join in the action. 'That generated the best from Cantona, who showed some thrilling skills, and it was he who headed a Giggs corner for

Ince to volley home.' As for United's winner: 'Robson timed his run on to Bruce's chip with all his old precision, to spring the offside trap and drive the ball home left-footed.' As they departed for home, masters of all they surveyed, United's players and manager were unaware of what lay ahead, of course.

Manager, players and club would be taking what amounted to a roller-coaster ride over the next couple of seasons, what with the double success of Premiership title and FA Cup, the ups and downs (mostly downs) in Europe and the Cantona controversy, coupled with the unsuccessful bid to retain both the Championship and the FA Cup. And even then, there was more to come, both on and off the field . . . not least, as United achieved another double to rewrite the Soccer history books.

CHAPTER 6

A DREAM COME TRUE

'When I was manager, I was very conscious of the need for the team to do well. Now it's nice to be the club president and leave team affairs to somebody else.' – SIR MATT BUSBY.

SIR Matt Busby left Manchester United a handsome legacy – and a substantial liability. The legacy was the stature of Manchester United, after his long and brilliant stewardship; the liability was that such a legacy made it difficult, if not impossible, for the next man to succeed. And so it proved as, in turn, Wilf McGuinness, Frank O'Farrell, Tommy Docherty, Dave Sexton and Ron Atkinson tried their luck. It took the sixth man, a dour-looking Glaswegian by the name of Alex Ferguson, to restore the somewhat faded fortunes of United ... though he, too, was to admit that at one stage it seemed as if he would become just another one of those who had been tried and found wanting.

Busby and Ferguson had several things in common – for a start, both were Scots. For another thing, they were given votes of confidence by their respective chairmen (in private, not publicly) when the going had become rough. Busby steered United to success in the League, the FA Cup and in Europe; Ferguson emulated those feats as time went by. But not, as he admitted, without a struggle. As the Duke of

Wellington once observed, it was a damned close-run thing. Today, the Old Trafford stadium stands as a magnificent testimony to the job that Busby started – he took over at a time when the place was more or less a bomb-ravaged shell (United played their homes games at Manchester City's Maine Road ground) and the club was virtually broke. What Busby achieved, in retrospect, was little short of a miracle; and he lived to see United and Ferguson prosper even more.

One Sunday morning, after another bad result in the League, Busby went down to Old Trafford and sat brooding a little, pondering on how to improve his team's fortunes. He was taken by surprise when his chairman, a venerable little, white-haired gentleman called Harold Hardman, turned up to tell him, specifically, that he need not worry – he wasn't about to be given the sack. Ferguson, a man who was said to be 'quick to accuse, slow to apologise', also suffered what the Bard called 'the slings and arrows of outrageous fortune'; the knives were out and, according to one report, by 1990, United's manager was 'clinging by his finger-tips' to the job, with 'terrace discontent in the air again.' By then, more than two decades had passed, and United were still in desperate pursuit of their Holy Grail – the Championship.

Ferguson had gone into the transfer market with a vengeance, splashing out £7 million on new players; yet it still appeared as if success in the League would prove elusive. At the end of the season, Liverpool – the bane of United's life – were once again the reigning Champions, while the Old Trafford club languished in 13th place. Liverpool and, to a certain extent also, Leeds United, appear to have dominated Ferguson's thoughts at various times during his term of office at Old Trafford; in the meantime, United's manager confessed that season 1989–90 was 'the watershed' of his career with the club. He was fortunate that the FA Cup came to his rescue – it turned out, as he candidly admitted, to be his 'life-saver'. And even then, success in that glamour competition was not accomplished without some heartache, because when Ferguson axed 'keeper Jim Leighton from the FA Cup

Final replay against Crystal Palace, Leighton felt shattered. Indeed, as he became the object of sympathy from some people, his manager came in for criticism. In one respect, Ferguson couldn't win, since his critics accused him of having ditched Leighton after the drama of the extra-time, 3–3 draw at Wembley; yet many of those critics had been on his back earlier for having kept faith with the 'keeper at a time when his form and confidence had dipped.

The one thing that did vindicate Ferguson, of course, was the result: a 1–0 victory in the replay. And so a tempestuous season came to a more-or-less happy conclusion, after it had seemed at the start that United as a club were passing out of the hands of Martin Edwards and into the control of a gentleman named Michael Knighton (later to become the chairman of another United – this one at Carlisle). Edwards, indeed, told his manager that he had sold the club to Knighton, who made an appearance on the pitch before the opening match against Arsenal to indulge in a ball-juggling act as he wore the club's famous red strip. Not surprisingly, his appearance caused considerable comment. However, when the real thing (meaning the match) got under way, United's fans enjoyed it and they went home well pleased, having seen Arsenal subjected to a 4–1 hiding.

Yet as the season wore on and the derby game against Manchester City arrived, things appeared much less bright – United went home on the wrong end of a 5–1 scoreline, to make this one of Ferguson's worst days in football, and things continued to go badly for a spell – so much so that speculation surfaced about the manager's future. And when United were paired – away – with Nottingham Forest in the FA Cup, the writing seemed to be on the wall, should defeat overtake the Manchester Reds. By that time, the Knighton takeover had fizzled out and Edwards was back in the driving seat, and the day before the Forest match, he summoned the manager to his office. The media had been more or less inviting Edwards to come clean and debate Ferguson's future, but Edwards was not to be lured into that trap;

instead, he told his manager that while he felt United should not go public with the vote of confidence which so often is construed as 'the kiss of death', in private he wished to reassure Ferguson that, win or lose next day, his job remained safe. So Ferguson was vastly encouraged and, against Forest, his team did the talking for him as Mark Robins scored the only goal. United didn't know it then, but they were on their way to Wembley. But while the going was tough, Ferguson needed to keep his nerve.

He was given some assistance by the man who had achieved such greatness at Old Trafford before him. I knew Matt Busby more than 30 years and not only did I respect him – I think I came to understand him, especially after we had worked closely together at one period of time, sharing a wee dram or two in both his home and mine. I had discovered for myself what Harry Gregg termed 'the iron fist in the velvet glove' because, early in my acquaintance with Busby, when I brashly propositioned him about a job for me on the public relations side at United, he wrote back to say that if and when such a job ever did crop up, it would be the directors who decided upon the man to fill it. By and large, though, Busby presented a genial, avuncular visage to everyone he met and, for me, he was the greatest exponent of them all in the art of dealing with the media.

Few managers like these inquisitors. Some managers turn up grudgingly for the after-match Press conference, even when they've won; and even then, sometimes you struggle to make sense of what they're saying. Some managers simply fail to turn up, especially if it's a case of a post-match post-mortem. One of the great things about Busby was his approach to people – he never talked down to them; yet when he became Sir Matt, I did wonder if this signal honour would make a difference. But when I asked him what I should call him now, his eyes twinkled in that familiar fashion as he answered: 'Call me what you've always called me.' And so I still called him simply 'Matt'.

He once confessed to me that during the George Best era (and Best was, for me, the finest footballer ever to grace a

United jersey), he suffered some sleepless nights at times over the Irish wonder-boy. There were occasions, too, when he became exasperated by the errant conduct of Georgie Boy. But he seldom allowed such exasperation to surface in public, and only once after a match did I see him without a smile on his face. He had every right to feel aggrieved, but after he had asked me to give him 'a couple of minutes', he emerged from United's dressing-room with the smile back in place.

That occasion was after United had lost a European Cup semi-final against Partizan Belgrade in Yugoslavia and, as I have said earlier, what made things worse was that in addition to a glaring miss by Denis Law (who admitted, 'I missed a sitter from about a yard'), United had to fly home with the depressing knowledge that they would be losing Best for several weeks. They had gambled on his fitness and lost, just as they had lost the match; now, it was clear, Best *did* need a cartilage operation. So Busby's United, like the team assembled by Alex Ferguson, knew their bad times in Europe, as well as their moments of triumph.

Like Ferguson, also, Busby knew all about media pressure and talk of the sack – which, no doubt, was why United's elder statesman took the time and trouble to dispense bits of sensible advice and encouragement when the pressure was increasing – one of the things to do, as Busby knew from experience, was to give the morning papers a miss. Busby, indeed, to my certain knowledge, was very conscious of the pressures which piled up on Ferguson – after all, apart from his own experiences, he had been a close observer as five other managers had tried to do the business for United before Ferguson arrived from across the Border,

Not many months before he died, Busby told me: 'When I was the manager, I was very conscious of the need for the team to do well; now it's nice to be the club president and leave team affairs to somebody else.' But that didn't mean he ignored how Alex Ferguson felt. Matt also told me, as United were finally homing in on the Championship in 1993: 'I have one ambition left – to see United crowned again.' Typically, though, he added: 'But we shall just have to wait and see...'

Well, he saw his ambition fulfilled, and he was delighted for the club, and for Ferguson. Twenty-six years on, the 'old man' was at Old Trafford again, on a May evening, not only to join in the title celebrations, but to take a bow himself. As for Ferguson, at last he had laid a ghost and restored United to the pinnacle.

Along the way, he had been portrayed so often as an anxious, gum-chewing figure standing outside the dug-out, living every moment of every kick of the ball as his players strove to overcome the opposition. Some folk believed he was too anxious; some didn't enjoy the spectacle of seeing Ferguson's jaws working overtime on that gum, and some smiled to themselves as United failed to deliver a victory for their manager. Alex Ferguson was described to me by a football insider as 'a workaholic', and that description surely fits the man, because he has so often given the appearance of being intense, even obsessed, with his job. Possibly, once United had overcome the final hurdle and snatched the title trophy, he felt able to relax a touch, but certainly he remained a man wanting to be a winner.

A predecessor, Tommy Docherty, hailed Ferguson as 'a great manager', but muted that tribute somewhat by adding that he didn't much like him 'as a bloke'. Someone else, having been in Ferguson's company socially for an evening, came to the conclusion that he was 'a very nice fellow'. I'm sure he does know how to enjoy himself, but never at the expense of the day job. He made this clear not long after moving in at Old Trafford, when he decided United's image of a 'drinking club' must be changed, and it was no secret that several players came to the end of the road because they didn't measure up to the manager's ideas of what they should (or shouldn't) be doing, especially when it came to bending the elbow. 'A hard man, quick off the mark to accuse ... slow to apologise' – that was how one sportswriter, a fellow-Scot to boot, saw Ferguson. He was 'respected for his astute football brain' and earned 'the undying support of his players by being straight and honest with them.' As Mark Hughes, no shrinking violet on the field of play, acknowledged, 'he shook us up.' There may have been some who didn't regard him as the greatest thing since sliced bread but, by and large, he seemed to have got a grip on things and earned the loyalty and respect of the men under his command.

Ferguson was said to be known for 'a volatile temper' – indeed, he admitted this himself – and, like a former manager of Liverpool (Graeme Souness), was reported to have hurled cups around the dressing-room during a half-time harangue when he was managing Aberdeen. So far as I know, it has not been recorded if Ferguson has chucked cups around the United dressing-room, but who would bet on it? If he tells his players what to do, he has also shown he can listen to them, as was illustrated when he signed Eric Cantona from Leeds United. And while he's been described as 'paranoid' about the media, he even listens to the odd journalist. Ferguson heard Steve Bruce and Gary Pallister out as they sang the praises of Cantona and, as top-class defenders, they knew (and Ferguson knew) what they were talking about. I did wonder, though, if United's manager would have gambled around £1 million on the Frenchman had another £1 million signing, Dion Dublin, not broken a leg. As for the journalist, a man I knew well years ago, he tipped off United about Lee Sharpe (more of which elsewhere).

Ferguson has often talked about the quest for success and the problems of achieving it at a club like United, a club he believes to be unique in football. The fact is that because of United's great reputation, built initially by Busby, the greater is the challenge for the manager of the day. Yet Ferguson claimed that he had no hang-ups when he followed Ron Atkinson into football's most demanding job. He has pro-claimed his belief that when it comes to succeeding, it's the Scots who possess the main ingredient ... 'the big thing is determination, the desire to succeed. We can usually respond to any challenge. I can't define the whole thing, but I know what drives us on – it has to be the hunger to be a winner'. This was a verdict a fellow-Scot, George Graham (who claimed half a dozen trophies during his eight-year stint at Arsenal) echoed when he said of Ferguson: 'Like me, he can often be represented as a dour Scot; but the two of us share a relentless ambition to keep on succeeding.'

Think of other Scottish managers who have achieved outstanding success, and the names immediately spring to mind ... Busby, Bill Shankly, Jock Stein (who, it was recorded, acknowledged that rejecting the job at United was 'the biggest mistake' he ever made) ... followed by Ferguson, Graham and Kenny Dalglish, who steered Liverpool to a League-FA Cup double and who matched Ferguson, stride for stride, in successive seasons when the title fight became a slog between United and Blackburn Rovers. Ferguson said that when it came to ambition to succeed, 'so much of it has to do with your background ... your character is formed by the area you come from. Just look at those who worked on the yards on the Clyde.' Well, Ferguson and Dalglish hail from the Glasgow area, while Busby and Shankly were reared in the mining districts.

Ryan Giggs, on the other hand, is Welsh, and Ferguson (perhaps with memories of what happened to George Best) kept young Giggs under wraps for many months. It was a United steward who told Ferguson about the lad playing for Salford Schools, and so Giggs arrived at Old Trafford for trials. Just as Busby knew with Best, so Ferguson knew with Giggs that he had landed someone who had 'something special'. If the credit for Giggs finishing up at United goes to a club steward, I claim credit for being the first sportswriter to bring his name to the attention of a nationwide public, because after I had tipped off *The People* about him, they did a piece on 'the new George Best'. My source was another manager who, of necessity, had to scour the lower reaches of football when he went talent-spotting – he was out and about watching the bigger clubs' reserve sides in the hope of picking up lads who were not quite going to make the top grade. However, while he enthused to me about Giggs, he said sadly: 'I didn't even bother to ask – I could see he had that special ability which would take him to the top. I knew there was no way United would let him slip through the net.' Don't forget that David Platt was one who was allowed to leave Old

69

Trafford – his transfer to Arsenal in 1995 took his overall tally in fees to the £22 million mark.

I have tipped off managers myself . . . I phoned Bob Paisley about Trevor Steven when he was a fledgling at Burnley, and about Marco Gabbiadini when he was a 16-year-old with York City. When Kenny Dalglish managed Liverpool, I rang him to mention Paul Warhurst, then at Oldham; I was sure he could become the replacement for Alan Hansen because, like Hansen, he had everything (well, in my view, he did). Warhurst was comfortable on the ball, could take it and control it from any angle, and possessed a genuine turn of speed. Oldham's one reservation about him, it seemed, was his tendency to have a lapse of concentration at times. But he could play at right-back or centre-back, and I had a notion that he might do well in midfield. Then he went to Sheffield Wednesday, to make his mark also as a striker with England potential. Ultimately, he was signed by Dalglish, for Blackburn Rovers, and after his arrival there I was told that Kenny did go to watch him when he was still playing for Oldham, but that, apparently, he hadn't seen him as a centre-back replacement for the illustrious Hansen. Still, Kenny did sign him, in the end – and Warhurst by then had gone from being a £10,000 player (when Oldham signed him from Manchester City) to one who commanded a fee of £2.75 million (when he landed at Ewood Park).

So now we come to the tale of Manchester United and Lee Sharpe, and I was intrigued to learn how his signing came about, because I was reminded of my days at *The People*, when United were part of my regular Soccer beat and I used to visit the homes of quite a few of the lads who wore the famous red jersey. When they were relaxing at home after training, I would pop in for a chat and, sometimes, I managed to come away with a good story – indeed, one of the players of those days told me: 'The boss (Matt Busby) has warned us about you . . . he says you're dangerous!' I think that was a wind-up, though I could never be sure. However, on one occasion I called at a United player's home, only to discover, as I was invited in, that already ensconced in an armchair was a journalistic rival. His name was Len Noad, and he worked for the *Weekly News*, which came out on a Thursday. I always worried, when I had a story for the Sunday, that the *Weekly News* would beat me to the punch.

When Len saw me, he looked up and grinned. 'Come on then, sit down and take the weight off your feet,' he said, as if he were the host. I hesitated, pondering whether to stay or go, then decided to make the best of a bad job. So we chatted about football in general and nothing in particular, and I left really no wiser than when I had arrived. I certainly didn't pick up a story that afternoon, though I wondered if Len Noad had done so before I got there. Which brings me to Lee Sharpe, because it was thanks to Len that this talented player arrived at Old Trafford.

When Len and his partner, Jimmy Arthur (a Scot) were plying their trade for the *Weekly News*, they knew just about every manager in the business, as well as many players, and I knew that as well as getting stories for their paper, they helped out managers whenever they could. Len eventually retired, as did Jimmy, and the former moved down south, near sunny Torquay. Lee Sharpe at that time was a stripling of 16 and in his first year as a YTS lad at Torquay United, though his home territory was the Birmingham area. Somehow, the Midlands clubs must have missed him – it happens – and there he was, striving to make his mark at a club most folk regard as one of the game's outposts. And there was Len Noad, still keeping his finger on the pulse, as it were. Having been given the tip, Manchester United asked Len to let them know when Sharpe graduated to senior football, and when he did so, the lad went on as substitute and made both goals in a 2–2 draw. He was watched a couple of times, then Alex Ferguson himself travelled to see him in action. As Manchester United fans now know, Sharpe is quick, crosses the ball well, is handy in the air, built to withstand a physical challenge, and knows how to find the net.

Since Torquay were managed by former Spurs star Cyril Knowles, the odds were that he would let his old club know about the youngster who showed such promise, so Ferguson

71

wasted no time. That night, contact was made with Torquay's manager and a deal was set up for Sharpe to become a Manchester United player, the arrangement being that he would sign on his 17th birthday.

Initially, Torquay would pocket a £60,000 fee, with further payments forthcoming according to the youngster's progress. And how he has progressed ... Some years later, when Ferguson snapped up a £7 million player (Andy Cole), he acknowledged that every signing was a gamble, whether you forked out a fortune or merely 'five bob'. Well, he certainly got value for money from Lee Sharpe, and whatever his detractors may say about him, during his time at Old Trafford Ferguson has never been afraid to back his own judgment, whether as a buyer or as a seller. Generally speaking, it has brought results.

In the case of Eric Cantona, he has been accused of allowing the Frenchman to get away with things, in much the same way that Matt Busby was said to have let George Best have too much rope. In view of the fact that Paul McGrath and Norman Whiteside became expendable, while Cantona did not, it's interesting to speculate ... just how would Fergie have handled Best? In an interview when he was talking about events in football, the United manager said: 'We are producing superbly-fit, finely-honed human beings.' Then came the sting in the tail: 'There has been a dramatic improvement in the physical, but not so much the mental side. Emotions run high. When you put players in a situation where in each and every game, the opposition are playing their best game of the season, it's inevitable that their fighting qualities will come to the fore. They have to compete at the highest level because they are winners. Nothing will change that. I am constantly attempting to calm the very nature of the players while, at the same time, attempting to channel their necessary aggression in the right direction. The public should not be deceived by the fact that I operate a policy whereby punitive action against players remains a private matter. Nobody gets away with anything here. At the same time, I reserve the right to retain my loyalty to the players. But they know that if they step out of line, I will sort them out. The fact is, we are where we are because we are winners'.

When it comes to pouring millions of pounds into the transfer market, United's manager is perceived as applying two basic conditions: 'Can he do it for Manchester United – and is he a winner?' On Paul Ince, for example: 'An aggressive player and a winner by nature. He has matured tremendously over the last few seasons. I impress upon him repeatedly the futility of arguing.' This, of course, was before the controversial sale of Ince to Inter-Milan, by which time the player and Ferguson were having something else to say – Ferguson, in fact, was less complimentary about the player's performances during season 1994–95, while Ince was quoted as talking about 'betrayal' in United's decision to part company with him. Even so, Ferguson acknowledged the part Ince had played for the club since his transfer from West Ham ... and suggested, even, that the day might come when the midfield man could return to Old Trafford.

Ferguson, despite those 'ups and downs' referred to by Mark Hughes, said this about the Welsh international: 'He epitomises the kind of winning attitude I look for in a player. He has maintained that spirit ever since I brought him back from Barcelona'. And as for the *enfant terrible*, Eric Cantona ... 'reports that I put my job on the line to keep Eric at Old Trafford are a nonsense. But I do regard him as a very special talent, and his action (at Selhurst Park) has cost him a tremendous amount of money. It could be 10 months before he is fully fit to play for us again. The severity of the punishment we imposed was unprecedented, but we hope Eric will have learned from it. I lost my temper a lot, both as a player and as a manager. But there comes a time when you just cannot afford to do it any more. You have to learn to calm down.' Ferguson put his case for having sold Ince and Hughes (to Chelsea), while welcoming back Cantona, after the player's request to be released from his contract. Ferguson confessed that when it came to the Frenchman, 'the game needs him, United need him, I bloody need him.' In fact, by the time Cantona was scheduled to make his comeback at the start of October 1995, United were on course to challenge boldly for the Championship again, thanks to the youngsters Ferguson had blooded.

Chapter 7

THE FERGUSON FILE

'Nobody is bigger than this club. That has been the case for the last 35 or 40 years, and it's not going to change now.' – ALEX FERGUSON, dismissing a transfer request from Andrei Kanchelskis.

ALEX Ferguson wasted little time in telling his Ukrainian wing ace, Andrei Kanchelskis, where he got off. The Cantona affair was still on the boil in March, 1995, when Fergie decided that for the vital League game against Everton at Goodison Park, Kanchelskis was expendable – although (after United had lost, 1–0) he did restore Andrei to the team for the next match ... a record-breaking, 9–0 triumph over Ipswich Town at Old Trafford, where £7 million striker Andy Cole hit five of the goals. Ironically, Kanchelskis was to be transferred to Everton for £5 million and become the subject of a cash wrangle ... then suffer injury as Everton lost against United at Goodison early in season 1995–96.

However, when Kanchelskis initially asked to go, Ferguson reacted strongly. He revealed that the winger had known since the previous Tuesday that he would be back to face Ipswich on the Saturday, declaring: 'Nobody is bigger than this club. That has been the case for the last 35 or 40 years, and it's not going to change now. Just ask Denis Law – Sir Matt Busby scared Denis half to death.' It wasn't quite like that, as I recall, though Law did back down after having issued what amounted to more or less an ultimatum: 'More money, or I want to go.'

Along with Busby, Leeds United chairman Harry Reynolds and the then Football League secretary, Alan Hardaker, I was in Estoril, Portugal, on football business – Estoril was the venue for a meeting of UEFA – and we had dinner together one evening. It was very late on when Busby learned, via a telephone call initiated by Denis, that the Scot would rather stay at Old Trafford, after all. And so the hatchet was buried – later, in fact, Busby did reward Law ... after the Scot had offered a suitable apology. In the case of Kanchelskis, one word used to describe him at the time he made transfer noises was 'petulant', and Ferguson acknowledged his regret that the wing star had gone public about his wish to leave as he said: 'It is so difficult for me to pick a team now ... there's always going to be a disappointed player.'

Ferguson suffered another disappointment – and the club a blow – not many hours later, because Kanchelskis decided that instead of lining up for United against Wimbledon at Selhurst Park, he would travel to play in what was termed 'a meaningless international friendly' in Slovakia. Was that Andrei's way of cocking a snook at United's manager? Kanchelskis had already booked his place for the next international – Russia versus Scotland in March 1995 – and that was a European-championship qualifier, but he also insisted in putting in an appearance in Slovakia and, of course, he could claim that he didn't wish to jeopardise his chance of selection for the big games. As Ferguson was forced to admit: 'Andrei wanted to go, so there was nothing we could do about it.' But United were still 'disappointed not to have him available for such an important match.'

The player could have taken advantage of a waiver clause in FIFA regulations which forces clubs to release men for a certain number of friendly games in a year, but he opted not to go with United to Selhurst Park, the place remembered for Cantona's kung-fu act several weeks earlier. At the same time

76

that the winger was committing himself to country, not club, further bad tidings came with the news that Paul Ince was being charged with assault in connection with an incident at Selhurst Park.

Like Cantona, Ince was scheduled to appear at Croydon on March 23. However, he had retained his England status as a member of the side which met the Republic of Ireland in the ill-fated Lansdowne Road match, the Football Association having deemed that his status as a member of the community had not been affected by the allegations of assault upon a fan at Selhurst Park. An FA spokesman summed up: 'We will look at the implications of any police moves in the cold light of day, when we have talked with our legal advisers.' Meanwhile, United knew they must soldier on without Kanchelskis against Wimbledon in a match which could propel them back to the top of the table. The absence of Andrei opened the door again for Lee Sharpe, axed the previous Saturday, and when it came to picking and choosing, United's manager issued a reminder that other players had been omitted ... Sharpe, Hughes, Denis Irwin, Steve Bruce, Ryan Giggs, Brian McClair – even Bryan Robson. Bruce had been dropped for a big European game against Barcelona – 'that hurt him deeply, but it was for the good of the club, and he accepted it.'

The other players had accepted their omission, too: 'I had the unenviable task of leaving out Robson on FA Cup-final day, and that after some of his performances had been out of this world.' Ferguson declared that his office door was always open (as was the case in Matt Busby's day) and that his players 'can come in and argue it out with me. And some have.' Sometimes, in the Busby era, a player would go in to see him feeling disgruntled ... and emerge wondering just what all the fuss had been about. There were times when Busby, like Ferguson, was accused of letting players get away with things (for Cantona, read Best), and both managers stood to be shot at, when it came to the way they dealt with star names, on occasion. If Ferguson claimed that 'nobody is bigger than this club', there were those who felt disposed to dispute this, when the name of Monsieur Cantona was mentioned. The media as a whole was critical of United's method of punishing the wayward French star.

After the Football Association hearing, one respected columnist, James Lawton, of the *Daily Express*, was withering in his condemnation of the verdict. Jimmy, whom I have known for many years, wrote that on the day Cantona faced the FA music, 'the tune for the man who has dragged English football into the gutter' was *Pennies from Heaven*. Lawton said Cantona's French lawyer, who had expressed his fears beforehand about the punishment, 'should have rested easy.' The FA was 'very choosy about employing Madame Guillotine. Chop off the head of the odd peasant, send a Swindon Town plummeting the divisions; but upset Manchester United, treat their prodigal son as though he was anything other than a gift to English football, incapable of really behaving like a common thug? Monsieur, you are naive.'

Lawton accused United of having 'squirmed grotesquely on the spike of financial self-interest.' Cantona was 'a hero … he scores beautiful goals, don't you know? He can light up a stadium with one flash of Gallic inspiration. So forget his appalling record. Forget the fact that the Players' Union have agreed with clubs that the striking of a referee demands an automatic life ban. And how far is the attacking of a fan, however provocative, in a spectators' area, in full view of horror-struck women and children, removed from the ultimate crime? So Eric will get a late start to next season. It is not uncommon for him. A nice little goal here, a little suspension there, c'est la vie, mon ami. The Nike contracts may be shaky, but the T-shirts are going a bomb in the souvenir shop. The future will be just fine, and for this assurance we should be grateful to M. Bertrand (Cantona's French lawyer). For he tells us, "Eric is a charming person in private who is under intense pressure because of the bad-boy image that has been pinned on him."' Then Lawton asked: 'But who really did the pinning? What a charmless question.'

Ferguson himself, of course, had known periods of intense pressure since he arrived at United; it had been there for all to see, at times, as he viewed the match action, jaws working rhythmically and concentration writ large upon his face. Ferguson, who claimed that he had never had any 'hang-ups' about the shadow of Busby when he arrived from Aberdeen, where life had been comfortable, knew just how much was expected of him. By the end of season 1986–87 United had climbed to 11th place – a modest-enough improvement since his arrival – and from then on, up to United's Championship success there were see-saw results and placings. But Ferguson was allowed two things in real abundance: the time, and the money, to assemble a squad of players capable of reaching United's goal.

During his first six years, Ferguson invested heavily as 21 players arrived, at a total cost of almost £16 million, while £4.5 million was recouped from the transfer out of 26 players. These were the ins and outs of it: IN – Gary Pallister (£2.3 million); Paul Parker (£1.7 million); Mark Hughes (£1.6 million); Neil Webb and Paul Ince (£1.5 million apiece); Danny Wallace (£1.2 million); Brian McClair (£850,000); Steve Bruce (£800,000); Mike Phelan (£750,000); Denis Irwin (£700,000); Andrei Kanchelskis and Mal Donaghy (£650,000 apiece); Peter Schmeichel (£505,000); Jim Leighton (£450,000); Viv Anderson (£250,000); Lee Sharpe (£180,000); Ralph Milne (£170,000), Neil Whitworth (£80,000); Jules Maiorana (£30,000); Andy Rammell (£25,000); Paul Dalton (£10,000). Some of those recruits (notably Danny Wallace) never really made their mark, while Jim Leighton's experience of being axed from the FA Cup-final replay side left him with bitter memories. Yet he was to play for Scotland again, during 1995, and thus vindicate Ferguson's judgment in having bought him for United in the first place. Neil Webb suffered injuries, while Milne, Whitworth, Rammell, Dalton and Maiorana remained largely anonymous players. Wallace, Phelan and Donaghy virtually dropped out of sight after leaving Old Trafford, although about 10 of the costly recruits turned out, on present-day valuations, to have been extremely good buys.

Kanchelskis brought United a massive, £5 million fee, while the money Ferguson splashed out on players such as Schmeichel, Pallister, Bruce, Irwin, McClair and Sharpe

79

could have been recouped over and over – as, indeed, it was in the case of Ince, while the sale of Hughes at £1.5million, after years of sterling service, almost brought United their money back. By the time Ince left for Inter-Milan, he had been cleared of the assault charge, but his departure, along with that of Hughes and Kanchelskis, brought some hard words from the fans, who were miffed not only about the deals being done, but also about the revelation that Inter, far from shelling out £7million or more on the nose, were putting down only £3million.

I recall a manager telling me, around the time United were in for Ince, how Alex Ferguson had privately expressed some reservations about the problems of negotiation, not least when agents were involved. Ferguson did admit later that in the case of Ince, he had been pleasantly surprised by the way agent Ambrose Mendy had conducted the business – although the deal was not done without a bit of a rumpus, because before he had put pen to paper, Ince was pictured wearing a United jersey. That not only embarrassed United, but it also aroused the ire of former Old Trafford favourite Lou Macari who, at that time, just happened to be the manager of the selling club, West Ham United, and of the Hammers' fans. For a while it seemed the transfer would fall through, but in the end Macari and the Hammers cooled down, Ferguson got the chance to talk transfer business, and the deal was done and dusted.

The return of Hughes to United was another shrewd move by the manager, who believed the player should never have left in the first place. As Terry Venables conceded, Hughes had a rather miserable time while at Barcelona, and his team-mate there, Gary Lineker, reckoned Hughes might well have been too young at the time to make such a big move. Venables had taken both men for season 1986–87, and while Lineker was a hit, Hughes was 'a sad disappointment'. Not that it was all down to the player, as Venables admitted.

He reckoned Hughes found it difficult to settle in a new environment and a new culture – something similar happened when Ian Rush went to Italy – and while Lineker was

26, Hughes was no more than 22. So it might have been better if the Welshman had joined Barcelona a couple of years or so later. Not only did Hughes miss friends and home life, but his form dipped as he found himself being pulled up by referees who didn't exactly take to his robust style of play – one which, remember, had helped to make him such a formidable player in a short time, back home ... and which was to make him just as formidable again, on his return to the English game. There came a day when Sparky received his marching orders, during a UEFA Cup-tie, and Venables felt he had no option but to drop Hughes.

There came a time, also, when the player was farmed out on loan to Bayern Munich ... and while all this was going on, back at Old Trafford Ferguson was keeping track of events. Indeed, he had tried to sign Hughes the year before he finally did land him, but the first time around, Venables rejected the overtures. Then came a day when Hughes – back at Old Trafford – saw the wheel turn full circle as he helped United claim the European Cup-Winners Cup with a 2–1 victory in Rotterdam over ... Barcelona. More than this, Hughes claimed the first United goal and in the second half struck their winner – he produced one of his noted 'spectaculars' as, with both feet off the ground, he directed the ball goalwards in a manner which astonished those unfamiliar with his penchant for doing the unexpected. In a similar way, at Wembley, he rescued United from a semi-final defeat by Oldham Athletic, with mere seconds left on the clock – and United went on to the Final of the FA Cup. No doubt Hughes went into that European Final against Barcelona with the urge to prove a point; he certainly settled the score with those two goals.

If, as report had it, by 1990 Ferguson was 'clinging on by his finger-tips' to his job at United, he got to grips with the challenge in no uncertain manner, to emulate the feats he had achieved as manager at Aberdeen. Along the way, and not for the first time, he trod on a few toes as he spoke his mind – such as when he rapped back at television pundit Jimmy Hill, who had once been a player, then a manager, himself. When Hill managed Coventry City and I interviewed him, he made a point which stuck in my mind: that 'the people who call something a gimmick are those who wish they'd thought of it themselves.' Hill had offered criticism of Cantona after an incident with Norwich City's John Polston and, according to one interested observer, *Independent* feature writer Jim White (a Mancunian, and a United fan to boot), Cantona deserved to be given the red card treatment (he had been booked earlier). Hill's comments were 'modest and appropriate', though he described Cantona's action as 'despicable'. Ferguson, however, took exception and branded Hill 'a prat'.

Ferguson, always driven to succeed, continued to spend United's money after having lashed out close on £16 million of it ... Roy Keane arrived, valued at £3.7 million, and the staggering, £7 million acquisition of Andy Cole was another eye-opener (although Kevin Keegan said time would tell which club had got the better of the bargain). Ferguson had relished pipping Kenny Dalglish for Keane – in fact, Blackburn were unhappy as they claimed that three times Keane had declared his intention of joining them, if and when he left Nottingham Forest. There was even talk of court action by the Rovers but, in the end, they licked their wounds, while Keane became another headliner – though not always for the right reasons – as he made his presence felt with Manchester United. His career had taken off with a vengeance after the one-time, part-time footballer in his native Cork had landed a contract at Forest, following just one trial. Four years later, at the ripe old age of 22, he was an established Republic of Ireland international and playing in the finals of the World Cup in the United States, since when he has become a key player, also, for Manchester United.

He has played various roles (midfield, right-back, at the heart of the defence) and while he didn't set Old Trafford alight early on, he has become a player whom Ferguson talks about in glowing terms, and as a future United captain. Keane survived talk of his being axed from the side at one time, and was candid enough about his style of play: 'I don't go off on mazy dribbles; I pass the ball and run to support people,' he said. He rated himself as a hard worker who played within the team pattern. So Blackburn Rovers missed him, and United got their man – in fact, if the Rovers were miffed about losing out on Keane, they were doubly unhappy when Ferguson nipped in to sign defender David May from Ewood Park for £1 million. May, a first-team regular for the Rovers, jumped at the chance to join United when the time came for him to decide his future, although he, too, had his problems after arriving at Old Trafford, as injury dogged him.

In the big-money power game, Ferguson, Dalglish, Kevin Keegan, Joe Royle, Bruce Rioch and Roy Evans have all become rivals for the finest talent, and each man has had to settle for winning some and losing some. United, for example, failed to land not only Peter Beardsley and Paul Gascoigne, but they also missed out on an up-and-coming talent by the name of Nick Barmby, who was scooped up by Spurs and in 1995 joined Middlesbrough, to become an England international. Yet the United team boss has groomed enough talent of his own at Old Trafford: the Neville brothers, Gary and Philip; Nicky Butt; Paul Scholes; David Beckham; Terry Cooke; and winger Keith Gillespie, who weighed in at £1 million when he joined Newcastle as Andy Cole moved to Old Trafford.

Bryan Robson, who signed Barmby, also rated Keane as a player having 'all the qualities needed to become a truly great midfield player', while Ryan Giggs, so carefully cherished by Ferguson as he made his way towards first-team football, was quickly regarded as 'the great natural talent in the domestic game'. Even at 19, Giggs was coming to the attention of the predatory Italians.

United were swift to snuff out such speculation by coming up with the offer of a five-year contract, as talk centred around a £15 million move. It was said that Ferguson had given Giggs special treatment, that he had been 'keen to protect the youngster from the kind of media attention and commercial exploitation he believes played a major part in the downfall of George Best.' By the mid-1990's Giggs had indeed become a genuine commercial proposition as he was featured prominently in various ways ... after all, it is impossible to keep someone wrapped in cotton wool and away from the world of commerce for ever, especially if they are extremely marketable.

Still, the wraps were taken off United's youngsters only gradually, and even as this was happening, United's manager was well aware of the need to keep pace with the Blackburns, the Liverpools and the Newcastles in that big-money power game. He got Keane and May, but missed out on Alan Shearer, although the Southampton striker had been strongly tipped to land at Old Trafford or, maybe, Spurs. Six months before he arrived at Ewood Park, however, I was being told by someone in the game to 'forget about Shearer going to United – if he does leave The Dell, he's earmarked for Blackburn.' And while Ferguson termed the Rovers' £5 million signing of Chris Sutton 'madness', he might well have had cause to revise this view as Sutton and Shearer combined to pile up a formidable tally of goals during the Rovers' successful tilt at the title in season 1994–95.

Not for the first tine, Ferguson ruffled the feathers of Dalglish, who was prompted to rap back and say that while the Rovers were bringing on youngsters who, in time, would figure in the club's first-team plans, he would continue to sign players who, he felt, would improve his side. An ominous warning of intent to beat off all opposition, whenever possible. And Ron Atkinson, himself no mean spender in the transfer market, had something to say about the Rovers' financial clout.

Atkinson declared that when it came down to the power of money, Blackburn Rovers, backed as they were by Jack Walker's millions, were in a position to stave off all-comers in the chase for big-name players. If other clubs did manage to exert a greater pull, it would be because they were regarded as having greater glamour. And so the millions continued to be poured into the transfer market by the giants of the Premiership, with Newcastle muscling in on the act as they signed Les Ferdinand to counteract Liverpool's £8.5 million acquisition of Stan Collymore, and Everton – having missed out on both these costly strikers – finally claiming as their own the £5 million man, Andrei Kanchelskis. Liverpool had already beaten off opposition from Blackburn for Neil Ruddock, Dalglish had foiled Liverpool in their efforts to land Tim Flowers; and so the transfer merry-go-round went on, despite warnings that expenditure on such a lavish scale could lead to ruin for some clubs, in the final analysis.

One player who had cost United around £1 million, however, was clearly being slotted into a category of his own – the one marked 'priceless'. His name: Eric Cantona. Ferguson had dealt with footballers who, in his considered opinion, could be said to have presented problems one way or another – he made no secret about Paul McGrath and Norman Whiteside having been on what he called 'collision course' with him, though after both men had moved on, you sensed that Ferguson had a real feeling of regret in the case of Whiteside. Ferguson stressed that the club was more important than the individual – more important, for that matter, than he was as the manager, and he came to the conclusion that Gordon Strachan, who had served under him both at Aberdeen and Old Trafford, had 'run out of steam' for United. Strachan could still afford to smile as he helped Leeds pip United for the title. Apart from having demonstrated a ruthless streak when it came to dealing with players, United's manager has not been slow to take decisions affecting men on the backroom staff – though when Archie Knox left, it also left Ferguson unhappy.

Ferguson had taken Knox with him to Old Trafford, where he became the No.2, and when Knox decided to join Glasgow Rangers as right-hand man to Walter Smith, United's manager accepted this as being his prerogative. However, the timing of Knox's departure did not make Alex Ferguson a happy man, while on the backroom side, also, he came to the conclusion that it was time for a change concerning the chief scout, Tony Collins. I knew Tony when he managed homespun Rochdale, and from there he gravitated into scouting with

Bristol City and Leeds United, Then he became Manchester United's chief scout, but as time passed Ferguson felt the need for a change, and he appointed a fellow named Les Kershaw.

In some ways it might have been regarded as a rather surprising choice, because Kershaw was a university lecturer who worked part-time in football, scouting and assessing teams for a London club, although he lived in the Manchester area. By all accounts, he was highly regarded by Terry Venables, however, and initially he took a year's sabbatical from the day job then, ultimately, he made football his full-time occupation as he became Manchester United's chief scout. So Ferguson, who had gone on record as saying that when it comes to the hunger for success, Scots possess that quality in abundance, showed that he wasn't so blinkered that he couldn't recognise talent elsewhere, no matter what the person's nationality ... and, of course, that included a certain Frenchman.

Ferguson on Cantona: 'Eric has changed us from possible winners into definite winners...' And whatever the final verdict on the French star, the verdict on Ferguson's tenure of office at Old Trafford cannot be other than that he has proved a worthy (if more abrasive) successor to Sir Matt Busby. Whether or not (as Kevin Keegan pointed out) United will manage to emulate the feats of a certain other club – Liverpool (22 trophies spread across 17 seasons) – remains to be seen.

CHAPTER 8

THE POWER AND THE GLORY

'When I look at clubs like Manchester United or Blackburn, it is Martin Edwards and Jack Walker who have the power; the glory goes to Alex Ferguson or Kenny Dalglish.' – Former England coach TERRY VENABLES.

CLUB chairmen are not the most-beloved people in football; ask Manchester United supremo Martin Edwards. He has been only too well aware (as he candidly confessed) of his own rating (or lack of it) in the popularity stakes, so far as the Old Trafford fans are concerned. The popular conception of a club chairman is that he's the fellow who issues the 'kiss-of-death' vote of confidence in his manager, often just a matter of weeks, or even days, before wielding the axe. In the case of Matt Busby and Alex Ferguson, they – and their chairmen – proved exceptions to the rule, because each manager survived that dreaded 'vote of confidence'.

So far as I am aware, Aston Villa chairman Doug Ellis didn't give Ron Atkinson (who spent several seasons in the hot seat at Old Trafford) a vote of confidence. Atkinson simply got the chop. He had taken Villa to the Coca-Cola Cup Final the previous season and savoured the sight of his team beating Manchester United at Wembley . . . months later, when things were going much less well for Villa, and at a time when Atkinson was on the verge of moving into the transfer market again, the axe fell. He declared: 'To say I was shocked and stunned is, I can assure you, an understatement.' A few months later he was back in business at Coventry, after the Sky Blues and manager Phil Neal had parted company 'by mutual consent'.

I have known my share of chairmen: John Moores at Everton, Peter Swales at Manchester City, Reg Brealey at Sheffield United, Bill Fox at Blackburn Rovers, Sir John Smith and Noel White at Liverpool, Bob Lord at Burnley, Albert Henshall at Stoke (in the days of Stanley Matthews) and Harry Reynolds at Leeds United. Each man has (or had) his own characteristic. John Moores, for instance, could smile blandly enough, but the smile and the mild appearance concealed a ruthless streak – as was evinced when he fired manager Johnny Carey during a taxi ride across London, while on the way to the annual general meeting of League clubs. Moores also ditched me, after a story I had run about an Everton player. When Carey's successor, Harry Catterick, steered Everton to the League Championship (at that time I was well in with his chairman), Moores asked me: 'How much do you think we should give him, as a bonus?' I was taken aback, but thought quickly and answered: 'I should think £1,000...' Then, with my brain still clicking, I added: 'Tax-free, of course'. That was quite a lot of money, more than 30 years ago.

Peter Swales once told me: 'I can't half pick 'em.' He was referring to the lengthy list of managers who had come and gone during his time at Manchester City, and he admitted: 'The biggest mistake I made was in sacking Tony Book.' But Swales retained Book on the backroom side. Reg Brealey revealed to me that he was ready to sell out at Sheffield United and indicated that if I could find a buyer at around £5 million, I could anticipate a handsome commission. I did my best, but though *The People* ran the story, so far as I know it didn't produce a nibble. (A deal was done, at around £3 million, in the summer of 1995).

Sir John Smith, urbane and possessed of a somewhat autocratic manner, had a habit of terminating telephone conversations rather abruptly. He told me once that for him, Liverpool Football Club was 'almost a religion'. Master-butcher Bob Lord, who ruled at Burnley with a rod of iron, indicated to me that 'I would rather see this club sink into the Third Division than bankrupt it by spending money we haven't got.' Burnley had to sell to survive, by and large.

Bob Lord also told me that when it did come to buying players, 'the manager tells me who he wants – then I tell him whether or not we can afford it.' I once did some articles with Bob Lord for a national Sunday newspaper, and even when he was rapped on the knuckles by the powers-that-be over something he had said, he never complained or tried to blame me. Everton chairman George Watts complained, though, when I was in charge of sport at the *Liverpool Echo*. He rang to say that his club wasn't getting its fair share of publicity – exactly the same complaint the Liverpool direc-tors had made to me at the time I took charge of the *Echo*'s sports department. When Watts told me that 'the *Echo* needs Everton', I retorted: 'Yes, and Everton need the *Echo*.' Whereupon Watts said that had I been standing in front of him, he would have 'clobbered' me. So I went round to see him there and then, and while we had to agree to differ, no blows were struck.

Bill Fox, chairman of Blackburn Rovers and president of the Football League, had been a grammar-schoolmate of mine, and one night at Anfield, when Liverpool had knocked the Rovers out of the FA Cup, he chided me for backing the Anfield Reds. Since I was then the programme editor at Liverpool Football Club, I had to remind him that I had a vested interest in Liverpool's success. If I got into trouble with Bill Fox, Albert Henshall at Stoke got into trouble for calling the then League secretary, Alan Hardaker, 'a dictator' in a story which I ran in *The People*. Albert received a rap over the knuckles, but he didn't hold that against me, and I recall one of my earliest meetings with him ... as I walked into his office, he was seated at his desk, holding his head in his hands. Then he confided: 'I've just had to do a rotten job – tell Frank Taylor he's been sacked'. Albert was almost in tears, and he was genuinely grieving as he talked about having been down to the Victoria Ground to break the bad news to the manager – a man who, like himself, was a very decent human being.

Stoke were in the doldrums and strapped for cash, and they gave the job to Taylor's deputy, Tony Waddington, a one-time young hopeful at Manchester United whose career had been curtailed by injury. He took Stanley Matthews back to Stoke, and signed former United stars such as Harry Gregg, Dennis Viollet, David Herd and Maurice Setters. Matthews inspired such a resurgence of interest that the gate trebled overnight to close on 30,000 – and Stan ended up telling me: 'I hope you don't sleep at night...' At that time he was putting his name to a column in the *Sunday Express*, while still a player, and his testimonial match was coming up. I ran a story in *The People* which concerned the match, and Stan rang to ask me to pull the story out. I told him: 'Sorry – only the editor in London can do that ... I'll give you his number.' That was when Stan said he hoped I would suffer from insomnia, to which I replied: 'Stan, I can assure you, I'll sleep like a babe in arms tonight.' My conscience was crystal-clear.

During Stan's spell at Blackpool, his inside-forward partner was little Ernie Taylor, who signed for Manchester United after Munich. And now that we're back on the subject of Manchester United, it's time to bring in James Gibson, the man who talked Matt Busby into leaving Liverpool and taking on the mammoth task of bringing success to the Old Trafford club. If his decision to move on from Anfield caused feathers to be ruffled there, it wasn't all plain sailing for Busby at Manchester United, and if it was Gibson who landed Busby, it was a small, spare-framed man called Harold Hardman who issued the vote of confidence to United's manager at a time when League results were going awry. The assurance from his chairman – 'You are not to worry ... your job is safe,' Hardman said – was a gesture Matt most certainly appreciated that Sunday morning, as his chairman made a surprise visit to Old Trafford. As Busby told me: 'We just managed to salvage safety in the League ... while winning the FA Cup. It was one of the most harassing periods of my managerial career' – a verdict Alex Ferguson would probably echo when he reflects upon the vote of confidence he received from Martin Edwards.

Their meeting, too, was in private, on the eve of a crucial FA Cup-tie against Nottingham Forest, and the vultures had been hovering, ready to make a meal of things, should United go down and out of the Cup competition. Edwards demonstrated loyalty as he told Ferguson his job wasn't under threat, even if United lost; and, in turn, Ferguson has shown great loyalty to his chairman, and to United ... as did Matt Busby, who (in his own words to me) 'could have become a wealthy man', had he opted to up sticks and go abroad. By the summer of 1995, there was talk that Alex Ferguson was a target for at least one Italian club – just as talk surfaced that Busby had become a magnet for a club from Italy. However, not for him the lure of the lire ...

Busby told me that he felt deeply about United: 'I was in charge of the greatest club in the world, and that was sufficient reward for me.' In fact, he was invited not once, but several times, to take charge of clubs abroad, and he revealed to me that not only did he become the target for an Italian club, but that Athletic Bilbao (whom United had despatched from European competition) had tried to tempt him into going to Spain. In Busby's own words, Bilbao offered him terms 'which few men could have resisted ... I could have become a wealthy man.' Yet Busby stayed on at Old Trafford, where he built three great teams, and he made certain, also, when transfer talk was in the air again, that his star players didn't hit the trail to the land of the lire. One magnet for the Italians was Tommy Taylor, but Busby squashed any suggestion of a deal – his view was that if one man went, the door could well be opened for others to go, and that might lead to an exodus from Old Trafford. Busby remained true to his convictions, and when United achieved success again under Alex Ferguson, their manager of the 1990's was gracious enough to say, in his own hour of triumph, that it was Busby who had set the standards at United – as he declared, also, that Martin Edwards and the board had been 'brilliant' in their attitude towards himself.

Ferguson said that never once had United's directors queried the details of his management, or asked him in what direction he was heading. And it was in what United's manager termed 'my moment of crisis' that Edwards gave him backing before that crucial Cup-tie against Forest. In turn, Ferguson has defended the man who is chairman and chief executive at Old Trafford, while Edwards did go public, as transfer fees shot up, by saying that United would remain in the forefront when it came to breaking records, just as they had done during his father's time as chairman. Later, when a Belgian footballer by the name of Jean-Marc Bosman caused consternation over the transfer system, Edwards had more to say.

When it appeared as if he would be selling out to Michael Knighton, some critics voiced the opinion that he would make a financial killing, and there have been other times when the knives have been out for United's top man, not least because of the kind of cash he earns and because of the club's commercial activities. Alex Ferguson has said, somewhat sadly, that his chairman has been given 'a rough ride' by the public – indeed, Ferguson claimed there was a feeling of resentment towards Martin Edwards from the crowd at Old Trafford. For example, should the chairman appear on the pitch to make a presentation, he could expect that to be the signal for some abuse. One day, Ferguson felt compelled to ask Edwards why he put himself in the firing line, and received this reply: 'I've got to, haven't I?' From United's manager came an acknowledgement that Edwards demonstrates courage in facing up to this unenviable part of the job, and I recall something which Edwards himself said, as United were still on their way towards their goal of claiming the Championship, after a gap of 26 years. At the time, I felt his admission was not only frank – it was astonishing. It concerned his relationship with the rank-and-file supporters who flock to Old Trafford in their thousands and who back

United with such fervent feeling ... the kind of feeling which, seemingly did not extend to United's chairman.

After Martin Edwards had succeeded his father, Louis (he of the smiling, portly figure) and gained accession to the boardroom throne, the man who combined the jobs of chairman and chief executive at a salary estimated at £130,000 a year, overall, confessed that he had never enjoyed any real rapport with United's fans. At that stage of the game, United were going close, but not close enough, to their goal – they were about to lose out to Leeds United in the battle for the title (season 1991–92), and it must have taken some heartsearching for Edwards to make his remarkable admission publicly.

What did he have to say? This: 'I have never regretted being involved with this club – it is my life, and I make no apologies for that. I have to ask myself whether I'm doing the job because I want to be loved by everyone, or for personal love and satisfaction. I can't even say to myself that I'm doing it for the supporters, because I know their opinion of me is not particularly high, and it is very difficult to return something you are not receiving.' Yet Edwards maintained: 'Everything I do is for my love of this club, and there is a wonderful satisfaction to be gained from that fact alone'. Edwards then had been a director for 22 years and chairman for a dozen years, during which time he had indeed taken his share of criticism, as well as having enjoyed seeing United win the FA Cup more than once and achieve success in the European Cup-Winners' Cup.

At that stage, he had allowed his manager the luxury of five years and millions of pounds in the bid to assemble what, manager and chairman so fervently hoped, would turn out to be a championship-winning outfit. And, of course, their hopes were realised thrice over. Yet, before that happy day had dawned, Martin Edwards was making this candid confession: 'If winning the FA Cup on three occasions and the European Cup-Winners' Cup during my time hasn't done the trick, then not even winning the League Championship is going to make me popular here. I have given up all hope on that score – if we had gone on to win the treble this season (1991–92), it probably wouldn't have made the slightest bit of difference'. Maybe; maybe not.

When Edwards was speaking up in defence of his manager, he was at some pains to point out that it had taken Matt Busby seven and a half years to steer the League-title trophy on to the Old Trafford sideboard, though it must be conceded that Busby was starting from scratch, in every sense, whereas Ferguson inherited some decent players and had money to splash in the transfer market. But, at long, long last, there came the day when both Edwards and his manager were able to sit back and relax (temporarily, at least), happy in the knowledge that, once again, albeit after 26 years, the title trophy was Manchester United's property.

On a December day in 1993, as Howard Kendall quit his job at Everton the second time around, and as Liverpool lost 3-1 to Sheffield Wednesday (with Mark Wright and Neil Ruddock each scoring an own goal, and Ian Rush banished to the substitutes' bench), Alex Ferguson was expressing his delight because, it must have seemed for him, Christmas had come early. He had just signed a new deal at Old Trafford which, it was suggested, would earn him well over £1 million during the coming four years, and this was his due reward for having taken the Premiership trophy to Old Trafford. That gloomy first Saturday in December, 1993, Merseyside fans found their cup of woe overflowing as they endured the misery of seeing Manchester United on their way to Liverpool's once-proud and unchallenged claim to be the supreme Soccer club in the land, while Everton then were being rated the poor relations, reportedly £4 million in the red. Indeed, Howard Kendall had just seen his side shunted out of the Coca-Cola Cup by none other than ... Manchester United, and, it was said, he had decided to quit after Everton had blocked a £1.5 million move for United striker Dion Dublin. As for Liverpool, they were acutely aware that, despite the millions they had lashed out, United had forged a dozen points clear at the top and were considered certainties to retain the title trophy. By then, in fact, the bookies (seldom wrong) were offering odds as to which club would finish second to United.

All in all, then, a time for Martin Edwards and Alex Ferguson to feel that all was right with the world and that the sweat, effort and expense really had proved to be worthwhile. There was also, perhaps, good cause for Ferguson (the manager who had spoken up for his chairman) and Edwards (the chairman who had consistently backed his manager) to reflect upon the experiences and the views of another household name in the game: Terry Venables. The former England coach had had what might well be termed a rather stormy relationship with chairman Alan Sugar at Tottenham Hotspur, as Venables came towards the end of his managerial stint there.

Once upon a time, that innovative football coach, Malcolm Allison, had brought in a psychologist in an effort to put the players of Crystal Palace in a positive frame of mind, and one of the things the psychologist had told them was this: 'You cannot have the power *and* the glory, in this game.' Reflecting upon that statement years later, Venables admitted that he had come to realise just how true it was, when he considered clubs such as Manchester United and Blackburn Rovers during the 1990's. It was Martin Edwards and Jack Walker who wielded the power, Alex Ferguson and Kenny Dalglish who could bask in the glory. Venables acknowledged that being the chairman of a football club, the man at the top, 'is a different business.' During his days at Queen's Park Rangers he had Jim Gregory as his chairman, and he said of Gregory: 'He had the power, while the manager had the glory – or the sack.' More than a few managers would echo that sentiment although, in Venables' case, when he did move out from Loftus Road, it was of his own volition, because he had been tempted by the bait of managing Spanish glamour-club Barcelona.

As for Alex Ferguson, when talk of retirement in 1997 was in the air (United then were bidding for a repeat of the double, in season 1994–95), Martin Edwards declared: 'We have no plans to groom a successor. Alex is 53, and when his contract ends in two years' time, a lot will depend on when he thinks he has had enough.' Then Edwards made another important point.

'But if he is still feeling great, still in good health and wants to stay in the job, I don't see why he shouldn't continue. We are very happy with him, and we hope that situation will continue for a good many years.' This prompted Ferguson to reply: 'The only change I would contemplate over the next few years would be to bring someone in to work alongside me; but, take it from me, I will continue to be the man in charge.' He spelled out his continued, driving ambition as he declared: 'The important thing is to keep on winning something every season.' Twenty-four hours after having made that statement, Ferguson was expanding upon it in a manner which must have made some people ponder ... possibly, for instance, his right-hand man at Old Trafford, Brian Kidd, who might have been asking himself a few questions about the manager's mention of bringing in 'someone to work alongside me.'

The next news was that Ferguson was reported to have nominated Kidd as his eventual successor. It was said that United's manager, 'reacting to a series of stories suggesting he has considered retiring in 1997, preferred the version which sees him carrying on for a good few years yet, then seeing his assistant take over.' Ferguson was then quoted: 'Whatever happens in the next few years at this club, Brian Kidd will have a big say in the running of it. He has done a fantastic job, and that will always be recognised. If Brian wanted the job when I step down, he would get it.'

Ferguson hadn't quite finished with the quotes, even then. Four days before he was scheduled to visit Buckingham Palace to collect his CBE (by coincidence, it was around the time Eric Cantona and Paul Ince were due in court), United's manager was insisting, according to an interviewer, that he remained fit, full of vigour and ambition, and that 'he scoffs at speculation that he will abdicate the hot seat in favour of Brian Kidd within a couple of years.'

One thing Ferguson did acknowledge: that 'managers are

under pressure as never before ... if they have three bad games, they're out.' He conceded there was 'that little extra pressure in being manager of Manchester United, because we are the biggest name in the game. We are either on the front page or the back page of every national newspaper every day. Sometimes it's good, sometimes it's bad. We're high-profile ... but there are times when it can be very difficult to handle. Every game is like a Cup final for us – that's not a cliché, it's a fact. We are Manchester United, everybody wants to beat us.'

At a time when unrated, Second Division York City were inflicting a 3–0 defeat upon United in the first leg of a Coca-Cola Cup-tie, at Old Trafford, United's chairman was reacting, too – to the news that Belgian footballer Jean-Marc Bosman had successfully challenged the legality of the system under which a club could demand a transfer fee for a player whose contract had expired. The news broke in Luxembourg, and it was revealed that the interim verdict of Advocate-General Carl Otto Lenz would go before the full European Court of Justice, whose binding decision was expected some months hence. Martin Edwards, chairman of the club rated as the wealthiest in the land, declared: 'I think this will mean a paradise for agents and players. Money is no longer going to be circulated in the game ... it will go in wages and transfer fees, and that means there won't be the same money flowing at the lower end of the game. If the transfer system is abolished, players will be looking for higher wages because no fees will be involved. It will affect the smaller, selling clubs ... it won't affect the larger clubs and, in some ways, it will be an advantage to us. It means players will have the freedom to go to whichever club they want. Ambitious players are going to lean towards successful and wealthier teams, the clubs that will give them what they want in terms of wages.'

Edwards admitted: 'We might lose an expensively-recruited player for nothing – but, likewise, we can bring a new man in for nothing, as well. In the long run, the bigger players are always going to want to play for the bigger clubs.' Hard on the heels of Edwards' assessment came the news that 'investors in the Stock Exchange seemed unmoved by the ramifications of the Bosman case ... United's shares were up 8p at 206p in the wake of bullish predictions of a bumper financial report by the company which will be announced early next month.' And Edwards acknowledged: 'I don't see why this radical move should affect our valuation on the Stock Market. I think it's fairly neutral, from our point of view.' He added: 'In the past there has been a restriction in the transfer market – if we felt a club was asking too high a price, we tended to duck out of the auction. Now players will decide where they want to go themselves.

'I'm sure the lower clubs in the Premier League will be concerned with this far more than United, Liverpool or Arsenal. I know where the big players want to be. This move will drive down transfer fees. If a footballer has only one year to go on his contract, you're not going to throw big money at that situation when you know later you will get him for nothing.'

Chapter 9

THIS 'STAGGERING JEALOUSY'

'This jealousy towards Manchester United is quite staggering.'
– former Leeds United chairman LESLIE SILVER.

WHAT have Alex Ferguson, Paddy Crerand, former Leeds United chairman Leslie Silver, and Liverpool manager Roy Evans got in common? They have all made a point of referring to the jealousy and envy of others when it comes to Manchester United. Ferguson, for example, declared there was 'a certain envy' of United; Silver talked about 'the staggering jealousy' towards United; Evans spoke of the 'anti-brigade', and Crerand rapped: 'I suppose it would make a lot of people happy if United won nothing. There is a great deal of jealousy about United because of who they are and what they stand for. It's always hard when you're Manchester United. You need to be special to be a part of this club.' Well, Crerand was once a part of United, as a player, and these days he still identifies closely with the club.

Of course, it's impossible to expect Paddy, whom I first got to know during the 1960's, to be impartial when it comes to United. He revered the late Sir Matt Busby, and has remained a constant supporter and defender of the club which Busby built up to greatness. Paddy – also a defender of Eric Cantona, as United sought to keep the French star at Old Trafford; admitted to having been given the red-card treatment himself 'six or seven times', and he could 'lose the heid', as they say north of the Border, when he judged he was being treated unfairly by opponents. But he always tried to play football in the United manner.

On the eve of the FA Cup semi-final between United and Crystal Palace (who had been United's opponents in the League at Selhurst Park the previous January, when Cantona was dismissed), Crerand declared his footballing philosophy this way: 'I want to be thrilled by watching adventure in my football'; and he offered the view that 'Eric has found his natural home here.' Another of United's former stars made a telling point, too – that 'it's harder to play for Manchester United than for any other club in the country.' That verdict came from Mark Hughes who, at the time, was United's longest-serving player, and who in the summer of 1995 joined Chelsea. It was the absence of Cantona and the fact that £7 million-man Andy Cole was Cup-tied which brought a reprieve for Hughes – not always an angel himself during the heat of the action – and he had been a favourite of the fans for his ability to produce a spectacular rescue act. He had more to say about the reaction of other people to United, also, on the eve of the 1995 FA Cup Final.

Hughes, recalling United's final League match of season 1994–95, when they drew against West Ham at Upton Park and thus missed out on a third successive Championship, reflected: 'We walked off to jeers and abuse. I hoped the genuine football fans would acknowledge how close we'd come to achieving a really remarkable feat. That kind of reaction is becoming widespread. It does make it harder for us to win things; but it also makes us more determined. We have to keep at arm's length the people trying to knock us down or undermine us.' Hughes also acknowledged: 'It's a shame, but out on the field we sense people either love or hate United. There's no middle ground. I think that clouds people's judgment of what we've achieved. I wish people would step back and look at how we've tried to play the game. I think they might react differently when they see us in action.

100

We feel that wherever we go, people want to see us for the wrong reasons. We know we have brought some of this on ourselves, but people are now just looking for excuses to have a go at us.'

Hughes claimed: 'That has become the easy approach for a lot of our critics. I think everybody here deserves great credit that, after such a difficult season, we have taken our defence of the League title to the final day and that we're back at Wembley to defend the FA Cup. But the crowd reaction at West Ham was very disappointing. We had lost the title that day, but nobody could doubt the effort we'd put in, or the way we'd played.' Nobody could deny that United had kept right on going, in the face not only of opposing teams and fans, but of almost day-by-day controversy. Hughes conceded: 'The lads in our dressing-room will hold up their hands and admit they've done wrong. Everything we do, on or off the field, is analysed.'

He protested that 'we're only human ... we all have our failings.' And he stressed: 'But the disciplinary rules are laid down for everyone – if you're sent off, you're banned. You take your punishment.' He claimed, however: 'When it's a United player, though, a national debate is started. Our misbehaviour seems to generate a campaign to get United players punished more severely. That's because we're in the public eye so much.' Critics of United, no doubt, would argue that it was up to the players of such an illustrious club to make doubly sure they didn't transgress, and let their often-sublime football do the talking for them.

Most people would admit that it was Eric Cantona who inspired United to their first Championship for 26 years, and that he was the key man again when they achieved the double 12 months later. Coming up to the FA Cup semi-final in 1995, Crerand admitted there was 'a strong possibility' that United would miss out on the title and on their bid to reach Wembley; he didn't deny, either, that what had happened at Selhurst Park on January 25 had probably cost the club its chance of retaining the Championship trophy. According to Alex Ferguson (and it is difficult to disagree with him),

101

United threw away the Championship in season 1991–92, when they finished second to Leeds United ... inspired by (guess who?) ... Monsieur Cantona. Leeds totalled 82 points, Manchester United 78.

If there was one good thing about it, however, perhaps it was that Leeds as Champions made a change from Liverpool – who had been the nation's premier club during Ferguson's first half-dozen seasons at Old Trafford. Season 1985–86 had ended with Liverpool claiming not only the title, but the FA Cup, under the astute management of Kenny Dalglish, and later he and Ferguson were to cross swords on more than one occasion, as Kenny progressed from Anfield into limbo, thence to Blackburn Rovers and yet another Championship. Season 1986–87 saw Everton taking over at the top from Liverpool, while United finished in mid-table; and 12 months later, Liverpool were back as Champions, with United the runners-up.

One year on, and the United faithful were cheered somewhat as Arsenal snatched the title trophy in a dramatic cliffhanger at Anfield, but at the end of season 1989–90, Liverpool were laughing again as they made good their vow to climb back to the top ... while Manchester United languished in 13th place. Then it was Arsenal back on top, Liverpool second and United sixth; and after that came Leeds, with United pipped at the post. Not surprisingly, then, Alex Ferguson has often appeared to be preoccupied by the doings of Liverpool and, to a lesser degree, Leeds. Both clubs have caused him to hold his head in despair and, it has to be admitted, also, that the rivalry between Manchester United, Liverpool and Leeds United has caused feelings not just of jealousy, but sometimes downright bad temper. Ferguson, indeed, has spoken of 'the bitterness so many people feel towards Manchester United' ... and this anti-United feeling has surfaced time and again, even when Sir Matt Busby passed away.

Busby died on Thursday, January 20, 1994, aged 84. He had lived to see his beloved club regain the Championship crown, after all the years of striving. The following Saturday, when United met Everton at Old Trafford, the stage was set for a tribute to Busby and a game of football which would do credit to the great man's memory. Close on 45,000 saw Ryan Giggs score the only goal, and Alex Ferguson was moved to say: 'I think today you saw a precious talent...'

That same day, as happened at Old Trafford, clubs around the country observed a minute's silence in tribute to Busby, the man who had made Manchester United not merely great throughout the land, but world-famous. Twenty-four hours later, when Blackburn Rovers met Leeds United at Ewood Park, the pre-match tribute to Busby was scheduled – but as home supporters stood with bowed heads and in silence, the occasion was marred by the chant of 'There's only one Don Revie!' from some people masquerading as Leeds United supporters. The Leeds players were disgusted by this moronic act – former Manchester United player Gordon Strachan, for instance, could be seen shaking his head in despair – and Revie himself (who in his time had sought Busby's sage advice) would have been desperately upset, had he been alive to witness the mindless manner in which some of those so-called Leeds fans behaved.

The then Leeds chairman Leslie Silver felt it imperative to call a board meeting, and an official apology was issued to United and the Busby family. It was said that any fans who were identified as having been among the offenders would be banned for life from Leeds United, and Silver himself declared that 'this jealousy towards Manchester United is quite staggering... I can only stress the relationships we have with our friends at Old Trafford ... at board, management and playing levels we have nothing but healthy respect for each other' – a view which would certainly be echoed by those in charge of affairs at Anfield, as well as Manchester United. As Liverpool manager Roy Evans said: 'When we were up there for so long, I heard people saying, "Let's get them out – we've had enough." Manchester United must feel the same thing now. There's always an anti-brigade, but I think it was less for Liverpool than it is for Manchester United.' It cannot be denied that relations between the fans of Leeds United and those of Manchester United have not always been of the best, and the same applies to the fans of Liverpool and Manchester United. More than anything, the Anfield faithful want their team to beat the Reds from Old Trafford, such is the off-the-field rivalry.

For their part, the Manchester United diehards consider that their favourites are superior to all others – indeed, more than one critic of United has claimed that there is an air of arrogance about the club itself. When it comes to Liverpool and Leeds United, there is little or no love lost between the supporters of these two clubs and those who so fervently follow the fortunes of Manchester United. The transfer of Eric Cantona to Old Trafford was regarded more as a defection by those who had idolised him at Elland Road, and during the 1990's the supporters of both Uniteds have taken every opportunity to bait each other, while – as a Manchester United fan reminded me 10 years after the event – the aerosol-spray episode at Anfield was still vivid in the memories of some of the Old Trafford faithful. And while Alex Ferguson's comments about 'a certain envy of United' were not directed at either Liverpool or Leeds, he hasn't forgotten the occasion when he heard a Liverpool player call from the dressing-room: 'F*** you '

Not that United's team boss has been averse to saying his piece, either – sometimes in controversial style, sometimes scathingly; and after Leeds United had been hailed as Champions (thanks in part to a Sheffield United own goal at Bramall Lane), leaving Manchester United to finish as second-best, Ferguson talked about those people who had said this had been a two-horse race in an inferior league. Clearly stung, he made the point forcibly that folk hadn't said this when Liverpool were cock of the walk and clocking up a title-winning margin of a dozen points. According to Ferguson, Manchester United *are* different from any other club in Britain ... according to the faithful at Anfield and Elland Road, this would surely be a matter for debate. I'm not sure about the Leeds brigade, but I do know the Liverpool fans want their team to beat United above all – the more so since the title went to Old Trafford.

Ferguson acknowledged that when Kenny Dalglish managed the Anfield club, he made two inspired signings in John Barnes and Peter Beardsley. Would you believe that, had events turned out differently, it would have been Barnes and Beardsley of United? Ferguson was a mite miffed, indeed, when he failed to land Barnes from Watford, Beardsley (and Paul Gascoigne) from Newcastle ... and an up-and-coming star by the name of Nick Barmby. Like Liverpool and Arsenal, when Barnes was still at Watford, United were informed by Watford's then manager, Graham Taylor, that the player was available. At that stage, there was talk of Barnes going abroad, but Dalglish nipped that in the bud when he swooped to land Barnes for Liverpool at £900,000. It was Dalglish, also, who persuaded Sweden's World Cup captain, Glenn Hysen, to opt for Anfield, after he had been a target for Manchester United – although Ferguson reckoned that in the long run United did the better deal by signing Gary Pallister.

Even so, Pallister ended up costing United far more than they had bargained for because, initially, when they had tried to talk Middlesbrough into doing a deal for £400,000, they were told it would take another £100,000 to clinch matters. When Pallister did make the trip to Old Trafford, ultimately, the fee was a cool £2.3 million. As for Beardsley, he had already been briefly at Old Trafford, during another managerial era – though he had never made even one full League appearance while he was there from Vancouver Whitecaps. As he told me later, when he was a Liverpool star: 'Nothing really went wrong ... Norman Whiteside got his chance, and he took it so well that he went on to play for Northern Ireland in the World Cup. It was just one of those things, and I wasn't too unhappy, because I knew the Whitecaps would be glad to have me back'. Arthur Cox brought Beardsley back into the Newcastle fold, at £150,000 – then Dalglish splashed what was then a record fee of £1.9 million to take the player to Liverpool. Yet Beardsley could well have become a Manchester

105

United man the second time around, because Alex Ferguson made a play for him.

At that time, Newcastle's manager was Willie McFaul and, according to Ferguson, Manchester United were quoted no less than £3 million ... less than a month before Beardsley fetched up at Anfield. When I talked to Peter about his transfer, he told me: 'At the end of the day, Liverpool were the only club actually to put down their money for me.' When Ferguson revealed his abortive attempt to land Beardsley, he claimed that Newcastle had also refused him permission to talk to Paul Gascoigne, even though Manchester United were prepared to match Tottenham Hotspur when it came to the fee. Ferguson was critical of Newcastle – 'You have to think Newcastle don't like us – either it's just one of those things, or some people are jealous.'

When Liverpool wound up as Champions at the end of season 1987–88 (and went to Wembley for the FA Cup, although they lost that one to Wimbledon), Ferguson admitted not only did he not like it, but that he had pondered upon whether or not the time had come to break up his own team and start buying. Perhaps at the back of his mind was the knowledge that a previous manager at Old Trafford (Busby) had felt the need to assemble not one great side, but three great sides: the one skippered by Johnny Carey during the 1940's, the one captained by Roger Byrne which was decimated at Munich, and the one which contained Best, Law, Crerand and Charlton, and which carried off the European Cup in 1968.

If Ferguson had a preoccupation with Liverpool, it was not surprising, what with the continued run of success the club had enjoyed under Shankly, Paisley, Fagan and Dalglish. United's manager was very conscious of the demands not only from within the Old Trafford boardroom, but from the thousands of fans who had suffered as Liverpool lorded it over all for a span of some 20 years. Like Ron Atkinson in his day as United's manager, Ferguson got a kick out of seeing his side get a result at Anfield, although after one 3-1 victory there he was needled when Liverpool coach Ronnie Moran (who, like Ferguson, can be an abrasive character) claimed the better side had lost.

Ferguson's view was that United had taken Liverpool apart, and he was to concede that the Moran comment might even have been lurking at the back of his mind when his team suffered a knock-out blow in the Cup – there and then, he decided he was not prepared to put up with Liverpool's domination of English football any more, and he resolved to change everything and assemble an Old Trafford outfit which could go on to claim the Championship. Ferguson concluded that his main rivals were Dalglish and Arsenal's then manager, George Graham. United's team boss also had what he called 'a gut feeling' that if he didn't have a stab at it, he wouldn't be regarded as having made the grade in English football. No doubt he knew that there were those who reckoned winning trophies in Scotland, even with Rangers and Celtic as rivals, didn't compare with what people rated 'the hardest league in the world' – meaning the top division in English football.

There seemed to be an affinity between Ferguson and Graham which, the United manager would probably have admitted, didn't exactly exist between himself and Dalglish – indeed, on one noteworthy occasion after a match at Anfield, when Ferguson was expounding his views, Dalglish appeared on the scene, carrying daughter Lauren in his arms. As he walked past the assembled media, he was reported to have informed them that they might as well talk to his daughter – they would get just as much sense out of her. Former Liverpool and England captain Emlyn Hughes became a target for scathing comment from United's manager, after Hughes had criticised him. Ferguson had rested winger Andrei Kanchelskis and Hughes, claimed Ferguson, reckoned he had 'bottled it'. Ferguson declared that Hughes had constantly criticised during 18 months in which United's manager had 'gone through purgatory', striving to get things right at Old Trafford, and Hughes was accused of having resorted to 'gutter journalism'. Ferguson also rounded on other football folk – players and managers-turned-critics –

who, he said, 'stand on their heads for the sake of being controversial, and don't care who they hurt in the process.'

Ferguson has often looked like a man under stress – when Leeds United pipped their Manchester counterparts for the Championship, it was like a dagger blow to the Old Trafford boss and his team, and the same thing applied at the end of season 1994–95, when a repeat of the double eluded Manchester United.

In the season when Leeds took the title, and again when Blackburn Rovers lost 2–1 at Anfield and still walked away with the prize, Liverpool defeated Manchester United by a 2–0 margin on both occasions, and that caused much rejoicing among the Anfield faithful. The words of a former Anfield idol, Bill Shankly, might well have echoed in Ferguson's brain to haunt him ... 'Football isn't a matter of life and death; it's more important than that.' According to United's manager, had you been able to witness the looks on the faces of his deflated players after their defeat by Liverpool, you would have come to the conclusion that they appreciated this was 'much more than just another game of football.'

When United finished first in the spring of 1994, thus denying Blackburn Rovers the Championship prize, Kenny Dalglish reflected on an incident in a shock defeat for the Rovers at Southampton and termed it a turning point – but for that, he believed the Rovers might still have gone on to take the title. There was another blast from Dalglish after he had seen his side deprived of a last-gasp equaliser at Old Trafford during season 1994–95, as the two clubs went neck-and-neck for the title trophy. As it happened, that didn't affect the ultimate result, though at the time Dalglish branded referee Paul Durkin's decision to disallow a goal as 'a disgrace'. Having viewed the incident on television, Dalglish declared: 'I can't see any reason for the goal being chalked off.'

Before the contest, he had called for a strong display from the referee; after the final whistle, when asked if he thought Durkin had been influenced by the capacity Old Trafford crowd, Dalglish said: 'That's the sixty-four-thousand-dollar question. You'd better ask the referee. The television replays prove it was a goal.' Ferguson rapped back: 'Kenny wanted a perfect referee today. He wanted a strong referee, and I believe he got his wish. I've watched the incident on television, and if that goal had stood, we would have been complaining. Shearer gave Keane a shove – that's absolutely clear.'

A neutral observer, sportswriter Tony Lanigan, summed up that 'Dalglish was right; the goal should have stood.' But, tongue in cheek, Lanigan added: 'He can't have everything his way. Glory with Celtic, more than 100 caps for Scotland, countless medals with Liverpool, three Championships as the Anfield manager, and then given 30-odd million to spend as boss of Blackburn Rovers. And Alan Hansen likes him. He was due a bad throw of the dice, and he got it at Old Trafford when Sherwood's brave header was disallowed and Blackburn were denied the point that could have made all the difference in the destination of the title.' Lanigan wasn't to know, of course, that the Rovers were destined still to triumph ... though only just.

Dalglish, for his part, was to have another go – this time at critics of the Rovers – and it was reported that he 'mocked Champions Manchester United as old hostilities flared again with Blackburn's title rivals.' Dalglish was quoted thus: 'It took them twenty-six years to win it – I hope it doesn't take us that long.' On the eve of the Manchester derby game at Maine Road and his own team's clash with Sheffield Wednesday, the war of words opened up as Paul Ince added fuel to the flames by declaring: 'The pressure can be intense – but we know we can handle it... We'll have to wait and see if Blackburn can.' The previous season, Gary Pallister had said his piece, along with Alex Ferguson, before a confrontation with the Rovers at Ewood Park (which Blackburn won, 2–0).

Dalglish clearly hadn't forgotten that little matter, as he countered: 'I read the same script last year. Our lads haven't got any pressure on them. Most of the pressure in football is felt at the other end of the table.' Dalglish again: 'Nothing Ince says will affect us. The players don't need anything like this to fire them up. They've got their pride and passion, a drive to win, and they don't need any extra incentive. We're the only club to have pushed United over the last two years, and though there was disappointment here last season, there was also tremendous satisfaction at having come from nowhere to go so close.' It was then coming up to the middle of February, 1995, and (wouldn't you have guessed it?) that man Cantona joined in the arguments as he defended United's £7 million acquisition of Andy Cole.

On the eve of the now-notorious match against Crystal Palace at Selhurst Park, and just after his header had applied the *coup de grace* to Blackburn Rovers at Old Trafford, Cantona raised a few eyebrows as he delivered this verdict: 'If you look at the prices of transfers in England today, getting Cole for £7 million is like getting him free. When you see defenders costing over £3 million – and I will not mention names – and you see Cole, I think we have done a very good deal.' As a matter of interest, it was a defender who had cost some £3.5 million – Liverpool's Phil Babb – who was to have an astonishing go at Cantona shortly after he had been given his marching orders at Selhurst Park – even if the words had been ghost-written.

Meanwhile Cantona, still talking about Cole, claimed: 'I prefer to talk about quality, rather than money, but if he costs that much, he must be one of the best players in England. We are a big club, there are many great persons here, and he is just another one. I'm not talking just about the players; I mean the manager, chairman and the people who run the bars. It's not about Mark Hughes, Andy Cole or Eric Cantona; it is about working together. That is the way we win.' Then the Frenchman reflected on what he saw as a shift in the balance of power in the title race.

After United's victory over the Rovers (which meant that the Old Trafford club had done the double over Dalglish's team), Cantona said, and rightly so: 'It was an important result, especially for the points, but also for the psychology. Now they know where we are and what we can do. From now, game after game will have more pressure ... we know how to

110

handle the pressure, because we have won two Champion-ships. They don't know, because they have never done.' According to Cantona, the title race had become 'like a 100-metres race, where you have to be strong, you have to be a man. Before, it was for children.' He declared: 'We have the experience, but we cannot rely on that; we must be patient and remember we must fight for the right to make our experience count. We need everyone fit in the last three months, coming back at the right time.' What Cantona couldn't know, at that moment in time, was that while he would be fit enough, he would be conspicuous by his absence from United's side because of suspension and, therefore, he would not be able to take part in the final lap of the Championship race. As Paddy Crerand later conceded, when the finishing line was in sight, United's failure to stay the course in the title race could probably be pinned on the Frenchman's absence through those final, testing weeks.

Moreover, as the fate of Manchester United unfolded, the words spoken months previously by chairman Martin Edwards sprang ominously to mind ... while some people had derided the club's suspension of Cantona as little more than a mild form of punishment, Edwards had gone on record as saying that this could kill off the club's bid for honours. And it did.

CHAPTER 10

TRIAL BY TELEVISION

'We went 26 years without winning the title, and we were still the most famous club in the country – by miles. Do Manchester United need any more prestige? – There is an aura about United because of the way we play the game.' – Former United star PADDY CRERAND.

ONCE upon a time, Matt Busby had a shop – to be precise, the Red Devils' Souvenir Shop, which stood on the forecourt at Old Trafford. It was managed for a time by Matt's son, Sandy (once a young hopeful with United), and – as its name implied – it dealt in souvenirs associated with the club Busby had built. In the words of Paddy Crerand, 'he was the man who put it all together' – including the Red Devils' Souvenir Shop. Once upon a time, in fact, Busby's connection with the shop made headlines which, as he admitted to me, surprised him. By 1995, United were still making news (as usual) – this time, because they were being accused on television of being greedy and exploiting their supporters. Where the original Red Devils' Souvenir Shop had dealt initially in hundreds, then thousands, by 1995 United's marketing and merchandising branch was dealing in millions. From little acorns do big oaks grow...

Busby explained to me just how he came to acquire the Souvenir Shop: 'I was surprised that the news about my

112

connection made headlines, because I had been firmly under the impression that people generally knew I owned the shop.' To remove any doubts, he told me how it all developed. 'A year before I retired as manager, I had an idea about taking over the shop, which was doing only fair business. When I did retire, I told the board I would be prepared to pay for the stock and take the shop over. It was as simple as that. In a way, I became one of the pioneers of the souvenir-shop industry.'

He was not to know that, in the year after his death, the club he loved would be put on trial by TV because of its commercial enterprises. When it came to the Red Devils' Souvenir Shop, Busby made one thing crystal-clear: 'There was no secrecy about my move; neither did I feel I should have to advertise it to the world. Furthermore, my business venture could just as easily have blown up in my face, rather than turn out to be a success. So I took the gamble, off my own bat. When the subject was raised at the club's annual general meeting, reference was made to the fact that the shop didn't figure in the club's account's.' The explanation: it couldn't, because the shop was owned privately, by Matt Busby; and his family had an interest in it. 'I immediately made this clear to the shareholders, and my answer was accepted happily enough.'

By 1995, United's shareholders were being mentioned again, this time in a Channel 4 television programme, 'J'Accuse: Manchester United'. The narrator was Hunter Davies, and the programme featured former United manager Tommy Docherty, plus an assortment of other people with football connections, supporters and journalists, including Mihir Bose and Jim White – the latter, a feature writer on the *Independent*, was also a self-confessed Manchester United fan. The programme levelled the charge against United that the club had become greedy for money to the extent that it was in the business of exploiting fans. Screened in April, 1995 (as United were going for a repeat of the double), it pulled no punches as Davies declared that when it came to United's report for the past year, 'in half a sentence it almost dismissed what, in recent years, was United's most brilliant achievement' – League title, FA Cup and Charity Shield – while over the next two dozen pages it detailed United's success in the world of business. Davies asserted: 'Money has taken over.' He claimed the club was in danger of severing its ties with its cultural and geographical roots. Davies talked about profits of £11.5 million and an annual turnover of almost £44 million, and he went on the attack.

Like this: 'In the mass pursuit of money, they are in the process of selling their soul. United are more famous, worldwide, than the Rovers' Return. I worry about the way the club is capitalising on this brilliance.' He added: 'Yes, there is money to be made at Old Trafford.' Indeed, there is, as a report issued after the title trophy had been won and lost, demonstrated in no uncertain manner. It said: 'United may have lost their title to Blackburn Rovers, but they still finished top of the Premiership Cash League'. The report revealed that United had earned close on £3 million from the £41 million share-out to the top clubs from the lucrative TV deal with BSkyB and the BBC. Champions Blackburn Rovers may have picked up a merit bonus of £897,600 for having claimed their first title trophy in 81 years ... but when it came to pulling power, their overall pay-out of £2.716 million was eclipsed by their rivals from Old Trafford who, having finished second-best in League and FA Cup, still banked £1.22 million in facility fees alone during season 1994–95, and figured in no fewer than 32 televised League games – seven more than the Rovers.

Second-placed they may have been; yet United scooped up no less than £856,800 in merit money, in addition to the £860,000 share-out which every single one of the Premiership clubs received. So United's final cheque added up to a massive £2.938 million. Little wonder there was such a frantic struggle by the also-rans to survive in such a money-spinning branch of football. The facility fees totalled £10.34 million for the season, and the Rovers collected £958,000 of this – in fact, this was the second-highest amount, because United's £1.22

million was the jackpot figure. The share-out of the overall sum of £10.32 million merit money was governed by a club's final position in the Premiership – Wimbledon, for instance, took £247,000 for having featured only five times on TV, yet their total rake-off was £1.67 million, thanks to a finishing place of ninth. Indeed, this put them ahead of Arsenal, who drew £1.66 million. So there could be no mistaking the immense pulling power of Manchester United, who had the crowds flocking to Old Trafford and the TV cameras homing in ... though not always in homage.

Hunter Davies, born in Renfrew, brought up in Carlisle, and a self-confessed Tottenham Hotspur supporter since he moved to London in 1958, has acquired a considerable reputation as an author and broadcaster. He has written more than 30 books (ranging from a biography of Wordsworth to one of The Beatles); perhaps his greatest claim to fame came with publication of *The Glory Game* – naturally, it was about football and, more specifically, it dealt with the doings of Spurs. It became what might be termed a football classic. Davies also admitted to having followed the fortunes of Manchester United, although to a lesser degree than Spurs, but during the television programme he was caustically critical of the Old Trafford club as he talked about 'the curious double standards of United', and what he called an 'obsession' with making money.

Davies claimed: 'Last year they got £26 million from merchandising, advertising, sponsorship, TV and catering, but only £18 millions from gate receipts and match pro-grammes.' He said United had 42 players and 31 coaching and ground staff – 73 people 'to get the lads out on the pitch', as he put it – while 123 people were employed in the merchandising and administrative departments. According to Davies, 'United no longer have players; they have assets.' He cited Paul Ince, Ryan Giggs, Lee Sharpe – 'even Denis Irwin is an asset' – and said that Eric Cantona was the club's greatest asset. Then he asked: 'But what happens when your assets start misbehaving?' Davies declared: 'Cantona is no longer simply someone who wins games – he also makes profits.' Cantona was pictured in clips showing him in controversial action, and on a Nike commercial he looked inscrutable – even arrogant, some might have said – as he intoned, in English: 'I have been punished for striking a goalkeeper, for spitting at supporters, for throwing my shirt at a referee, and for calling my manager a bag of shit.' Those last few words came out more as 'a bag of sheet', while at one stage during the commercial Cantona rolled his eyes in an upwards direction, then closed them, as if to suggest that the whole scene had become just too much to bear.

Tommy Docherty entered the arena and, in his usual, pungent style, observed: 'Sir Matt Busby – God rest his soul – would turn in his grave if he saw some of the things happening now. If Sir Matt was in charge of Cantona, he would have been out of the door within five minutes – no hesitation.' Well, United persuaded Cantona to stay, rather than showing him the exit door ... meanwhile, the TV show rolled on, as Davies declared that on match day 'the United experience is as frenetic as going to see a *Take That* concert at Wembley. The club exploits this ready market of 44,000 weekly ... now the shopping bag (bearing United's name) has replaced the scarf as the ultimate accessory.' Davies also recorded that 'United have changed their strip six times in the last four years' and asked: 'Could it be something to do with the fact that there is a huge market among fans for replica strips?'

Tommy Docherty chimed in, as he talked about the family with two or three children – naturally, the kids wanted track-suit tops or shirts, yet the gear bought only a few months previously had been replaced by yet another strip, and The Doc said: 'You know what kids are like ... they want up-to-date ones.' As he accused United of 'exploiting that type of thing', he made reference to a one-time notorious high-wayman, declaring that 'When Dick Turpin took your money off you, at least he wore a mask.' A few months after the TV programme, a newspaper report claimed: 'United have angered their fans by introducing yet another new kit – the Premiership runners-up are facing more criticism from supporters and consumer groups with their second shirt-unveiling in six months. Having produced a third-strip, blue-and-white Umbro shirt in January, United will launch another £40 top in August.' One story accused United of having sought to keep the change 'under wraps after announcing ticket-price rises, but they are scrapping the black away kit launched two years ago in favour of a grey one.' The report declared United had been 'condemned by the newly-formed Manchester United Independent Supporters' Association for "insensitive profiteering" only weeks after raising admission to Old Trafford next season.'

The association's secretary, Andy Walsh, was quoted: 'Why aren't the vast profits from these replica-shirt deals used to subsidise match tickets? United announced half-year profits of £11.5 million, yet they still feel it necessary to sting fans' pockets by encouraging them to buy another shirt. They are exploiting their position as the leading club in the country by cashing in on the fashion market. My season ticket has shot up from £266 to £304, yet there will be fewer Premier League games next season.'

While Nigel Griffiths, Shadow Consumer Affairs Minister, urged the Office of Fair Trading to commission a report on the football-strip industry – 'We are in danger of seeing Premiership Soccer becoming the preserve of giant corporations and rich people ... this is taking gross advantage of the loyalty of fans, with many parents pressurised by their children to buy the latest kit' – Umbro marketing chief Tim Gardiner was counter-attacking, as he said: 'The three United shirts each have a two-year lifespan. Children wear them day in, day out, and get full value for money.' And a United official, Ken Ramsden, was quoted: 'We are not ashamed to change. Our pricing is fair, not cynical. We are spending £28 million on stadium improvements, and have to find the money from somewhere.'

Now, back to the April television programme and Hunter Davies, who spoke of the 'non-footballing things United have put their name to.' He said: 'You can take out United insurance, have a Mother's Day meal in the banqueting suite, have your wedding at the ground.' And Davies asked: 'What next – an Old Trafford funeral service, perhaps, with a member of the first-team squad in attendance?' Davies referred to a Manchester United credit card which, he claimed, was 'acceptable at leading stores everywhere ... but, sadly, not at Old Trafford's ticket office.' And this prompted him to ask: 'So how do you get a ticket?' He then explained that 'most tickets are pre-sold' and mentioned that when it came to the executive boxes from which you could view a match at Old Trafford in luxurious style, there were '100 companies on the waiting list.'

Davies informed his audience: 'To apply for a ticket you have to enter a lottery, which means you have to join the club. And that costs £10 a year.' Davies said there were more than 100,000 members, which meant that United raked in £1 million – 'but if you don't get a ticket, you don't get your £10 back.' Davies summed up: 'Not a happy picture for the average United fan. There are often only 10,000 tickets going spare for any given match.' Davies further declared: 'United and the other big clubs have sold out their birthright – our birthright – through greed and short-sightedness. As United's support gets bigger and bigger, their hard-core support gets pushed further and further aside.' He added: 'United have all the money to market themselves as our national team.'

On the eve of the 1995–96 season, it was reported that 'all Manchester United home matches are already sold out for the new Premiership season', although there was a reminder that 'major ground improvements at Old Trafford have reduced the capacity to 30,000 ... it will eventually rise to 55,300 when the new tier is completed, making it one of the best stadia in Europe.' Meanwhile, back to the television programme, which showed a clip of a coach-load of supporters arriving for a game at Old Trafford. It gave an insight into the way United have become what might be considered a national institution, because these particular supporters had had to set out at six o'clock that morning. They were members of the North Devon Supporters' Club, and for them the chance to watch United in action for 90 minutes meant a round trip of some 600 miles. As Davies pointed out, they could have gone to a game much closer to home (Plymouth, Exeter, Torquay, for instance), but they clearly wanted more. And as the secretary of the North Devon Supporters' Club was quick to confirm: 'If it were possible to get the tickets, I could run two or three coaches.' Hunter Davies declared that Manchester United were 'interested in taking, not giving', of being 'concerned more about its national pulling power than serving its own people.'

The scene shifted from Old Trafford to the less-salubrious atmosphere of a London club's ground – Leyton Orient's – and in an interview with the Orient stadium director, John Goldsmith (whose job including trying to market Orient memorabilia), the admission came that this was indeed a difficult task – not least, because shops no more than a mile or two from Orient's ground were displaying Manchester United's wares. So, if you wanted Orient kit, the London club's own shop was the place to get it. Inevitably, Goldsmith confirmed: 'We can't compete.' And United manager Alex Ferguson said that he must be 'ever mindful' that United are 'a massive machine' involving many people. 'We are talking about a public limited company.' As Ferguson spoke about 'the passion of the people' being greater than anywhere else, he was talking not only about the many thousands who support Manchester United with such astonishing fervour; he was talking, also, about a vast, money-making machine, an enterprise which thinks and deals in millions. Davies declared that 'the rich get richer, the poor get poorer ... football used to be about glory, romance and loyalty, not about exploitation and multi-national corporations.' He asserted: 'That's exactly what Manchester United is now.'

He reminded people that the club had become Manchester United plc in 1991, when it was floated on the Stock Market and 'major institutions have taken the opportunity to buy into the club.' For example, the BBC staff pensions fund had a three per cent slice of the cake, while another organisation had around seven per cent. When it came to shareholdings, Davies said that United chairman Martin Edwards held 'a

119

whopping, twenty-eight point four per cent', making his stake worth in the region of £21 million. Referring to the average United fans who had followed the team for a long time, Davies claimed: 'They hate the tacky merchandise, have to struggle to get tickets.' As for what he termed 'the over-priced programme', it was 'little more than a mail-order catalogue.'

When he moved on to discuss the Cantona incident at Selhurst Park in January 1995, Davies pointed out that share prices fell by 5p, knocking something like £3 million off the club's value. Cantona? He was 'no longer simply someone who wins games – he is someone who makes profits. So calls for him to be sacked from English football were always going to fall on deaf ears in the boardroom.' Davies further claimed that immediate apologies from the club 'were not quite forthcoming', while the programme included a clip of Cantona's kung-fu act at Selhurst Park as he lunged, two-footed, at a fan. Tommy Docherty, talking about the penalty imposed upon Cantona by his club and by the Football Association (a ban until after September 30, 1995, as well as fines) disagreed with the viewpoint that this punishment was too heavy.

He said: 'When the Football Association added 10 games, Martin Edwards and Alex Ferguson say they're aghast at the severity of the added punishment . . . I would have thought he got off very lightly indeed.' And while the Frenchman appeared somewhat haughty on the TV programme as it translated his own words, Hunter Davies talked about the 'arrogance' of Manchester United and said the club 'get more from peripheral activities than through the turnstiles.' He declared: 'Football is not just a commodity; it's an emotion. United's business should be Match of the Day, not Supermarket Sweep. When pure greed takes over a football team, the idea of fair play goes out of the window.' Davies reminded people what had happened to United during season 1994–95 when they had tried conclusions with the Continentals in the Champion's Cup – United, he said, were 'rubbish in Europe' – and he asserted: 'What worries me is where they are leading us. They are encouraging a cartel of other rich clubs on a nasty, mercenary trail which, eventually, could betray their own legend and the spirit of football. I have nothing against the team itself; what I do worry about is the way the club is capitalising on its brilliance.'

Needless to say, the arguments and accusations made by Davies, Docherty and others on the programme evoked a strong reaction, as United refuted the charge that fans were being ripped off. Back came the answer that 'all our commercial work is for the good of the club' as a gentleman called Danny McGregor, who was concerned with United's commercial dealings, went on the offensive. He rapped back: 'We're not ripping off anybody ... thanks to commercial enterprise, we have the best stadium in the country, and we're able to go ahead and spend £28 million on a new stand – to make more room for the fans.'

When the subject of replica-strip changes was aired, of course, United could counter – with perfect truth – that not one of the club's supporters was forced to buy even a single item; it was purely a matter of choice. If the strips sold well, then that, surely, was evidence of the demand. And, as McGregor reminded people: 'If it wasn't for the fact that we have got our commercial house in such good order, we would not have the likes of Andy Cole running out of the tunnel at Old Trafford.' McGregor and United received backing from another person with close links to the game: Johnny Flacks, chairman of the Greater Manchester and Lancashire branch of the Football Supporters' Association. Flacks, who seemingly had refused to take part in the TV programme, was quoted as having said that it became 'blatantly obvious that it was designed to put the boot into the club over its commercial activities', and he declared: 'The FSA has no objection to clubs making money on the commercial side, provided it is ploughed back into the club to improve facilities and bring in the best players.' Well, nobody could have accused United of being penny-pinching in the transfer market, or of making their supporters put up with outmoded facilities at Old Trafford. Indeed, United could

121

seriously claim that when it came to crowd comfort and capacity, the sky was virtually the limit – or it would be, once the new cantilever stand was completed.

On the eve of the 1995 FA Cup semi-final between United and Crystal Palace, it was Tommy Docherty who offered some words of comfort to Alex Ferguson, as he said it wouldn't be the end of the world, should United fail to reach Wembley (not that The Doc could see this happening). But: 'they're in Europe, regardless (having qualified for the UEFA Cup); they could still win the title (they didn't); and (it came down to money again) with such fanatical support, they're already overwhelming winners of the "Commercial Cup"'. Winners of the 'Commercial Cup' or not, it was reported that United chairman Martin Edwards was 'livid at one more TV documentary portraying the club as a monument to rapacity' … and, of course, while United for their part preserved a dignified silence on the subject, they could well have presented their own, justifying version of the story.

As it was, and not for the first time, a committed Red sprang to the club's defence with some forthright views – indeed, Paddy Crerand, a £56,000 signing by Matt Busby and a hero of the 1968 European Cup triumph, was less an apologist and more a defender of the faith as he rapped back in blistering style at United's critics. He defended Eric Cantona; he defended the club. On Cantona: 'No-one would say that what Eric did that night (at Selhurst Park) was right; but everyone in this country went overboard; they wanted to hang him. When United play away and Eric comes out for a warm-up, the abuse he gets is unbelievable – and he's only kicking in.' Crerand spoke about 'what's happening in this country' and said, scathingly: 'Eric is picked out and told he's supposed to set standards. It's a bloody joke.'

Crerand also demanded to know what was wrong with Manchester United getting support from all around the country, and he gave this answer: 'We went 26 years without winning the title, and we were still the most famous club in the country – by miles. We might not get into the Champions' League next season (United didn't), and it's said we will miss

122

the prestige. Do Manchester United need any more prestige? There is an aura about United because of the way we play the game.' Critics might claim there was a touch of arrogance about that last sentence, but few could deny the argument that when United are on song, they are a delight to watch.

Chapter 11

BLACK EYE FOR A FAN

'Matt Busby gave me the biggest verbal roasting of my life.' –
Former United goalkeeper HARRY GREGG.

IT may come as a surprise to those who have declared
themselves in favour of, or against, Eric Cantona, to learn
that the volatile Frenchman was not the first Manchester
United player to have a go at a football fan. It happened
during Matt Busby's days at Old Trafford, when one of his
star players took a swing at a football follower and gave the
fan a 'shiner'. The same player was also regarded as a villain
when he laid out an England international cold in the cloying
mud of Ewood Park, one dark winter's night – and hailed as a
hero on two other memorable occasions. The man in
question: Harry Gregg.

He and I go back a long way – more than 35 years – and I
am godfather to his son. During his career at Doncaster
Rovers and Manchester United, Harry landed in trouble
more than once – as he said: 'I've been praised and insulted,
cheered and jeered. There are grounds where I'm not
welcome (shades of Alex Ferguson referring to visits to
Blackburn), and grounds where I love to play.' The old
football saying is that 'you have to be daft to be a goalkeeper';
and some folk reckoned that if he wasn't daft, Harry Gregg
was the maddest of them all. I knew differently ... even if I did

have one or two up-and-downers with him myself. He could be cussed, he could be fiery; he could be a joker, such as when he kidded team-mates that during a quiet spell in a game he lit up a cigarette and took a few puffs. He was a hero at Munich, a hero in what became known as the Battle of Belfast. And when his first wife was terminally ill, he lavished as much care upon her as any man could have done. Cross him at your peril; make a friend of him, and you had made a friend for life.

Greggy had two careers at United: as a world-record-priced 'keeper, and as a goalkeeping coach. His playing career at Old Trafford spanned more or less a decade, though he was never awarded a testimonial, and he had to wait until the summer of 1995 – 37 years after the horror of Munich – to receive belated recognition of his services to Soccer with the award of an MBE. That, in the eyes of some, was less than his due after his bravery at Munich, when he crawled back into the wreckage of the aircraft to rescue a baby girl. Years later, I played a part in ensuring that he and that girl – now grown up and celebrating her coming of age – were reunited as they appeared together on television.

Like Eric Cantona, Harry Gregg was regarded as less than a hero, on occasion. After the Selhurst Park affair Gordon Taylor, chief executive of the Professional Footballers' Association, talked of a 'lynch-mob mentality', while Graham Kelly, chief executive of the Football Association, expressed that body's concerns about racial abuse and taunts from spectators. Harry Gregg was once a candidate for a near-lynching, and once he felt the cutting edge of a knife thrown from the crowd – when he looked down to see what had struck him, he discovered his leg was bleeding. His team-mate in those days, Charlie Williams (then a centre-half, later one of television's *The Comedians*), once stopped a heavy salt cellar – with his head. And from first-hand experience during more than 30 years of reporting on football matches, I can verify that there were times when I wondered if I would get home in one piece. For instance, one day at Ewood Park where Blackburn Rovers were playing Newcastle United (then going flat-out for the

First Division), the atmosphere became distinctly unhealthy as the Rovers took the lead and there were immediate chants of 'Geordie aggro! Geordie aggro!' Fortunately, Newcastle equalised, and the threat of a riot was snuffed out. I know Harry Gregg will remember Ewood Park, too – I was there the night he flattened England winger Bryan Douglas, a Rovers idol, and the home fans were baying for Greggy's blood. There was also the time when Harry tangled with a fan who had a Rovers connection, and there was talk of prosecution. In fact, the Blackburn Rovers connection began on January 24, 1953, for Harry Gregg.

He was then with Doncaster Rovers and making his debut, and with his side 3–1 up against Blackburn, the outlook seemed rosy enough – until centre-forward Tommy Briggs (a beefy individual who once scored seven goals in one match) challenged the Doncaster 'keeper for the ball, at the same time that a full-back came charging across, as well. In the resultant collision Gregg's right arm was shattered, with two bones near the elbow being smashed, so off he went. Then came that winter's night when Greggy was playing for Manchester United at Ewood Park, and as he and Douglas went up for the ball, Gregg cleared with one fist and caught Douggie with the other. The Rovers star went down as if poleaxed – out cold. The next thing, Gregg was down on his knees, and Rovers trainer Jack Weddle was racing to the rescue.

The way Harry told it to me afterwards was like this: 'Right through the game, a Rovers player had been impeding me every time the ball came across into the goalmouth. I'd become frustrated and fed-up with this treatment, so I decided that the next time it happened, I'd do something about it.' It was only when he saw Douglas lying face down in the mud that Harry realised something: 'I'd caught the wrong man.' And later he apologised publicly to Douggie. But in the meantime, Jack Weddle had arrived on the scene and was giving Gregg a hard time verbally, while tending to the fallen idol. Gregg's Irish temper surfaced, and he reacted, telling Weddle that if he didn't 'shut it' he would get the same sort of treatment. No blows were struck, however, and afterwards Matt Busby smoothed ruffled feathers behind the scenes, while Greggy told me: 'When I saw Douggie lying in the mud, I was afraid he'd choke to death, so I began to turn him over – that was when Jack Weddle arrived, and we had a barney.' The match ended with United winning, to add insult to injury.

Harry Gregg almost 'chinned' me on one occasion – that was when I called at his home one afternoon, and when he came to the front door I could tell he wasn't in a happy mood. Neither was I, as it happened, and before I knew what was what, I was telling him: 'You bloody footballers are all the same – you make me sick!' Then I saw one of those ham-sized fists begin to bunch, and I added swiftly: 'Hey – I'm not big enough for you to hit!' Which brings me to the story of the fan who was given a 'shiner' by Harry Gregg – it happened when United played Luton Town away, and as the players were walking off the pitch at the end, Harry found his path blocked by a stranger.

He told me how he did his best to avoid the fan, but could make no headway; then he realised matters were becoming 'rather difficult' – in fact, he reckoned the fan was about to hit him ... so Harry got his blow in first. Naturally, the incident made headlines and there was talk of court action, while Harry felt impelled to apologise to just about everyone. He was advised to keep his mouth shut when it came to dealing with the media, but when United arrived back in Manchester, I had the job of trying to get Harry to say his piece. He wasn't feeling talkative, however, as he hurried along the railway platform towards the exit, and he warned a photographer that if he didn't desist from trying to get some shots, he would 'smash the camera'.

Matt Busby hadn't been at the match but he hauled Harry in on the Monday morning and made it crystal-clear that he was far from amused. He gave the 'keeper what Harry described to me as 'the biggest verbal roasting of my life ... and I'd had my ups and downs with Peter Doherty at Doncaster.' As it turned out, the whole thing ended on a happier note, because when United met Blackburn Rovers at the start of the season, who should be there but the man from the match at Luton – he hailed from Blackburn, and before the game, got hold of Harry for a friendly chat. He also saw his team win. Harry had already learned, during a heart-to-heart with the fan at Luton, after the incident there, that he intended to forgive and forget, so that was that.

When it came to the Battle of Belfast, Northern Ireland were playing Italy in a World Cup qualifier at Windsor Park – but when the Hungarian referee, Istvan Zolt, was stranded, fogbound in London, the powers-that-be decided the match would still go ahead . . . as a friendly. This didn't go down well with the 50,000 folk who had paid good money to see a World Cup tussle, and the Irish referee – Tommy Mitchell – who had been appointed in Istvan Zolt's place, must have wondered what he had done to deserve such treatment. He sent one Italian player off, the fans got hold of another and subjected him to a mauling, players went in with bone-crunching tackles which could have maimed opponents and, when they were not doing this, they were raising their fists to each other. The game ended in an atmosphere of chaos, with the home fans seeking Italian blood and Irish team-captain Danny Blanchflower telling each of his players to escort an Italian player to safety. Harry Gregg was credited with having felled four people who had ideas about wreaking havoc on Italian players.

Italian newspapers laid into the fans as they wrote about 'a scene of savagery and unbelievable cowardice . . . collective hysteria, unchained fury.' Members of Parliament got up to speak about the matter, Italian football chiefs declared that if Italy had to return to Belfast for the real thing, the World Cup qualifier must be played 'behind closed doors and barricaded gates'. Italian team-manager Alberto Foni insisted: 'The tie must go to London or Glasgow' . . . but when it did go on, it was still played in Belfast. This time, there was no pitch invasion, and Northern Ireland went through to the World Cup finals in Sweden, where Harry Gregg was voted the world's No.1 goalkeeper.

As it happened, he was followed at Old Trafford by another 'keeper who cost a world-record fee: Alex Stepney. Gregg had cost £23,000, Stepney cost £50,000 – and he, too, made headline news as he was accused of having clouted an opponent who played for the South American club, Estudiantes. It was a World-Club championship duel, with the first leg in Buenos Aires, where Nobby Stiles received marching orders and missiles were hurled at United's players.

Stiles was sent off after having made a gesture of dissent, while team-mates such as George Best, Bobby Charlton and Francis Burns suffered from the attentions of Estudiantes players. So, for the Old Trafford return, Stiles was an absentee – and during the match, Best was shown the red card. David Sadler, meanwhile, had two front teeth loosened and had his lip cut. And after all the shirt-tugging and other minor misdeeds of mayhem, the match was over ... which was when Stepney was accused of having swung a punch at an opponent. The television cameras captured what was called 'an embarrassing incident' as the United 'keeper ran off the field at the final whistle.

Stepney explained to me later what had happened. Like this: 'As I left the field, I was boiling inwardly.' That, he said, was at the way United had failed to take their chances, and at the way some of his team-mates had been treated by opponents. 'When I saw one of their players coming towards me, I didn't make any particular effort to get out of his way – I caught him with my arm, carried on towards the tunnel, still with my mind in a tangle of emotions.' Alex admitted that when he realised he could be in trouble, he was shaken; but, as with the Gregg incident at Luton, it became a case of 'Let's forget it'.

So even in Matt Busby's day there were alarms and excursions involving United players: Nobby Stiles, for instance, was one who came in for criticism because of his style of play, and had Alf Ramsey taken heed of Nobby's critics, he would have axed him from England's World Cup team. As it was, Nobby collected a winner's medal, just as he did in the European Cup in 1968 – and along the way, he certainly triumphed over adversity, because after having been knocked down by a bus when he was a youngster, it was feared he might lose his sight. But he went on to play for the club he idolised ... he used to stand on the railway bridge at Old Trafford and watch his heroes such as Carey and Chilton arriving for training. But he never sought their autographs: 'I was too shy,' he said.

Although he defied medical opinion, his eyesight was not of the best, and there came a time when he was advised to wear contact lenses. At one stage, however, he had problems playing under floodlights (he found he was mistiming tackles and interceptions), and it took him 18 months or so to adjust to the point where he got it right. At least one of his team-mates had noticed Nobby was having problems with his eyesight quite early on, and on one memorable occasion, at a reception for the England and Scotland teams, Nobby slipped out of the room midway through the meal, then went back to what he fondly imagined to be his seat ... only to discover that he wasn't back with his team-mates, but that he had walked into a wedding reception.

At one stage Nobby (who had made his debut for United in October, 1960, at the age of 18) felt that he wasn't really making progress as he would have wished, and that a transfer might be the solution. But with the departure of Maurice Setters to Stoke City, Nobby found that the way was paved for him to nail down a regular first-team place, and so he made the big breakthrough. The undertaker's son from Collyhurst had arrived. For a player who became Nobby's brother-in-law – Johnny Giles – the scenario became somewhat different as he decided to try his luck with Leeds United, and while some thought Don Revie had gone 'over the top' in paying £40,000 for Giles, Johnny went on to become a star at Elland Road.

Stiles and Giles both came to the fore with Manchester United after the Munich disaster, and another famous name – Michael Parkinson – had something to say about the effects of the air crash ... not just on the Old Trafford club, but on teams the post-Munich United came up against. Parkinson declared that some of United's opponents 'felt compromised by the public's overwhelming desire that nothing but good should happen to what was left of the Busby Babes' ... but in the 1958 FA Cup Final 'Bolton and Lofthouse put paid to that dream by winning 2–0, with Lofthouse settling matters by shoulder-charging Gregg into the net.'

Parkinson was referring to the Final between United and Bolton Wanderers – which, in one respect, was virtually a carbon copy of the 1957 Final, when Aston Villa's Peter McParland tangled with United 'keeper Ray Wood, who suffered concussion and was taken out of the stadium at half-time to be tested on whether or not he would be fit to resume in goal. He wasn't, so he played outfield, with Jackie Blanchflower going between the posts. In 1958 it was Bolton's Nat Lofthouse who bundled Harry Gregg and the ball over the line for a goal – something which, today, would have resulted in the striker being penalised for having treated a goalkeeper in such cavalier fashion. Gregg was laid out for the count – *a la* Bryan Douglas at Ewood Park – and the incident was recalled when Lofthouse became the subject of a 'This Is Your Life' programme on TV.

Parkinson, who interviewed Lofthouse when the former player was nearing his 70th birthday, wrote that 'nothing distracted him from his job, which was to fill the net with footballs and, if necessary, goalkeepers.' Harry Gregg was flown over from his home near Coleraine for the TV show, and confirmed then what, years earlier, he had told me ... if he'd had the chance, that afternoon at Wembley, he would have wreaked vengeance on the Bolton centre-forward. When Parkinson referred to Munich, that struck a chord, as well, because while I missed that trip with United (my boss was ill, so I was required to stay behind in the office), I saw how Munich affected various survivors, among them Harry Gregg – he suffered blinding headaches for a spell and, in desperation, he used to bind a tie as tightly as he could around his forehead in an attempt to subjugate the pain.

Parkinson admitted that when Gregg was laid out cold at Wembley in 1958, 'there was much debate' about the legality of the Lofthouse challenge; 'it certainly wasn't pretty but, by

131

God, it was effective.' So effective that when United trainer Jack Crompton arrived to douse Gregg with cold water and try to restore him to his senses, Harry was too groggy even to realise just who had caught him, or that a goal had been awarded.

Lofthouse, who rated Tom Finney and George Best 'the two most complete players I ever saw', reckoned 'we were all tough' in his day; and one former Manchester United hero, Jimmy Delaney, would have echoed that sentiment after he had come up against Harry Gregg. This time it was a benefit match and Delaney was the idol of Derry City, having steered the Irish League club to Cup glory. Delaney was once a bargain buy by Matt Busby, and he became a hero in the first great team Busby assembled at Old Trafford ... but he didn't feel much like a hero during that benefit match when he and Greggy collided. As Harry went up to catch the ball, his knees caught Delaney in the face. Both players were carried off, and it was late that night before Delaney recovered consciousness.

He required something like a score of stitches to his face, while as for Gregg, his knees were causing him considerable pain – so much so that the following day he visited hospital. His mission was twofold: to see how Delaney was faring, and to have his painful knee X-rayed. The collision between the players had sent a fair number of Delaney's teeth flying, and – with two still unaccounted for – there appeared to be a school of thought that the missing molars might well be embedded in Gregg's knee(s).

During Gregg's decade at Old Trafford, he played along-side some of the best ... Charlton, Law, Stiles and Best, who as a new boy showed the United 'keeper that he was no mug. During a practice session Best beat Harry, who decided it was 'beginner's luck' and gave the youngster a chance to score another goal – only this time, Gregg was deliberately allowing Best to get a glimpse of an opening. Best didn't fall for it – he still beat the 'keeper – and, said Harry, 'that was when I realised the kid was something special.' So was Denis Law, who became the acknowledged 'King' at Old Trafford, although one man didn't exactly sing his praises after Busby had spent £115,000 of United's money to bring Denis back from Italy.

The man in question was the then League secretary, Alan Hardaker, a somewhat abrasive character who, in true Yorkshire manner, could call a spade a bloody shovel. While I was in Estoril with Busby, Hardaker and Leeds chairman Harry Reynolds, the talk centred on Law, and Hardaker suggested the £115,000 fee had been over the odds. He was always irked when he saw Denis, having scored a goal, raise his arm in salute ... Alan reckoned a player should just stick the ball away, then go back to doing his job. On this occasion in Estoril, as we sat having dinner, Alan incurred Busby's displeasure with his comments about the value or otherwise of Law. I won't say that Matt bridled, but he reacted sharply, making it clear that he felt Denis had been worth every penny of the fee. 'He's scored goals for us, helped us to improve Old Trafford and fill it with fans.' And thus ended the debate.

CHAPTER 12

ERIC THE RED

'On the pitch I do what I have to do. I score goals, I make goals and teams win.' – ERIC CANTONA.

THE fans of Leeds United turned Eric Cantona into what one sportswriter called 'a cult hero'. Cantona, however, lived to see the day when they were giving him what is coloquially referred to as 'some stick' ... because, although he was playing football at Elland Road, he was wearing the colours of Manchester United. And it was reported that Leeds fans 'regard him as an arrogant deserter who dumped them for United three months ago.' On the eve of the Premier League clash between the two Uniteds, Leeds Supporters' Club chairman Ray Fell forecast that Eric would be in for 'a hot reception', adding: 'When he first went to Manchester United, he was still idolised by Leeds fans; but attitudes have hardened. The feeling now is that he deserted the camp because he was chasing a transfer. The rivalry between Leeds and Manchester United made it harder to stomach. Eric seems to think Leeds fans still love him, but the whole thing is now looked upon by our people as a dark episode.'

The darkest episode of Cantona's controversial career came on a winter's night at Selhurst Park, the home of Crystal Palace, when he was shown the red card (yet again) and, after some turbulent action involving a Palace fan, he was banned by Manchester United for the remainder of the season and fined two weeks' wages, estimated at £20,000. Cantona then became the subject of the great debate, dependent upon whether you thought he had become a victim or a man who deserved to be given the order of the boot from English football.

The catalogue of Cantona's previous offences (and red cards) added up to a considerable list, as did the number of clubs for which he had played, both in his native France and in this country. He had been introduced to English football by Sheffield Wednesday, whose manager at the time, Trevor Francis, knew Continental quality when he saw it; after all, he had included in his own, distinguished playing career a spell in Italy and, like Cantona, he had donned an international jersey. However, the relationship between Cantona and Wednesday was fated to be brief, to put it mildly. No more than a few days after having been put through his paces indoors (because the weather was too bad for football on real grass), Cantona's stay was coming to its conclusion. When Wednesday wanted him to remain a while longer and demonstrate what he could do on the real thing, he upped and left.

Enter Leeds United, whom he helped to the Championship ... which, ironically, meant pipping Manchester United at the post. Leeds went to Sheffield United's Bramall Lane ground and scored a victory which set them up to clinch the title, while a 2–0 defeat for Manchester United, at the hands of arch-rivals Liverpool, doomed them to disappointment. So for the fans of Leeds, Cantona was then the hero – but not for much longer. He went with Leeds to Wembley for the Charity Shield pipe-opener to the season, and contributed a hat-trick of goals as Leeds came out on the right side of a 4–3 scoreline against Liverpool, who had won the FA Cup. The ecstatic Leeds supporters hailed the Frenchman as their hero.

Then came his move to Manchester United, for around £1 million ... and the mood changed, as the good vibes began to disappear, so far as the Elland Road brigade were concerned.

Stories started to circulate that the relationship between Cantona and Leeds manager Howard Wilkinson had deteriorated, not least because the down-to-earth Wilkinson was bent on demonstrating just who was the boss. While he was with Leeds United, Cantona had become such a major figure on the Elland Road scene that he had begun to cast a shadow, it was claimed, which suggested that he was larger even than the club for which he played.

Cantona was to be quoted: 'Those who accept being in my shadow are the most intelligent people because they know that I make them win. And certainly there are those who don't accept it. Howard Wilkinson didn't and when that happens, we separate...' Cantona was also quoted as saying: 'In life I do what I want and, as much as possible, I will continue to do what I want. But on the pitch I do what I have to do. I score goals, I make goals and teams win.' Come December 1992 and the Frenchman and Leeds United were on the verge of parting company. There was a transfer request: 'When I decide something, I do it quickly,' said Cantona, and he added: 'Your first thought is often your best one.' It didn't turn out that way at Selhurst Park, though, on January 25, 1995 ... but Cantona wasn't to know that at the end of 1992.

Howard Wilkinson is a manager not given to using flowery phrases, and when you're in his company, it quickly becomes evident that he thinks before he does open his mouth. At an after-match Press conference, when the questions start coming, he will pause and deliberate, then give a sensible answer, as befits someone who has played the game professionally, invested more than £25 million on players as a manager, and progressed in an upwardly-mobile direction through the ranks. Wilkinson, known as 'Wilko' to the media men, was a schoolteacher who worked as a Football Association staff coach in Yorkshire. He has coached a variety of England-international squads and seen his name linked with the top England job. As a manager, he steered one club to the Northern Premier League title, and another to the Championship of the Football League. He also became chairman of the

136

League Managers' Association, so he has had a significant voice in the affairs of football. In short, also, he talks a lot of common sense. When it came to Cantona, Wilkinson revealed that the player 'wanted to go ... he did ask for a transfer, and it was in everyone's best interests that he went. He was not prepared to abide by the rules and conditions which operate for everybody else here.'

This, it was suggested, could be taken to mean that Leeds United's manager either couldn't, or wouldn't, guarantee Monsieur Cantona a first-team place – and that Cantona, in turn, wasn't prepared to settle for a second-best option which could mean him being a substitute. Cantona told the world: 'People who saw my matches can judge for themselves. They must have been saying to themselves, "This bloke's a genius – we don't understand. Perhaps there's some other problem."' He added: 'I understand how the Leeds supporters feel, and I know that no words of mine will placate them. All I can say is that the love I have for them remains intact.' He also maintained that he still respected the manager of Leeds United.

Cantona declared that he believed Howard Wilkinson to be 'a good bloke ... I left Leeds on very good terms with him, and I want them to stay that way.' Indeed, not long after he had become a Leeds United player, the Frenchman was proclaiming that was the happiest time of his chequered career, and the fans were certainly enamoured of him as they drooled and chanted, 'Ooh, aah, Cantona...' As Cantona observed after his move to Old Trafford: 'Leeds were my first English experience, and I have to thank Howard Wilkinson for my understanding of the game in this country.' One thing in which the manager of Leeds United exercised patience was the little matter of explaining things when it came to crossing the language barrier. And Cantona appreciated that. At the same time, he forecast that he was going to have 'a nice adventure with Manchester United, just like I had at Leeds.'

He also declared his intention of never playing in France again: 'my ambition is to help Manchester United become English champions.' He was wrong, and he was right. Not only did he play for France again, and on his native soil; he also helped Manchester United become the champions in two successive seasons, which meant he had set a unique record of having won three Championship medals in successive seasons with two different clubs. And he captained his country ... although he wasn't to know that he would forfeit this honour, as well as a place in Manchester United's side – or that United and the police would become involved in a war of words over him.

One thing which, apparently, struck the Frenchman, was that the quality of football in this country was diminished because of the number of matches the clubs are expected to play, and Manchester United chairman Martin Edwards placed some emphasis upon this point, too, as his club went to Wembley for the FA Cup Final in 1994. He pointed out that this would be United's 63rd game of the season – a formidable number of matches, to be sure, although other clubs (such as Liverpool and Leeds United) had become accustomed to playing even more games during the course of a campaign when they were winning trophies at home and abroad.

Martin Edwards admitted that things could have gone terribly wrong, and that at one stage of the season he could see three domestic trophies slipping away from Manchester United's grasp. 'What has pleased me more than anything is that we have claimed the Championship in a year when we also reached two Cup Finals,' he said. 'We've been locked in a colossal number of games ... the next trip to Wembley will be our 63rd match of the season, and to win the League with that sort of commitment as well is fantastic. We've gone for everything. I always felt that if we hadn't won the League, it wouldn't be because we weren't the best side, but because we simply over-stretched ourselves. There was a big danger of that in the Wembley semi-final with Oldham.' Then, everything looked to be lost, with less than a minute to go – but Mark Hughes produced one of his spectacular scoring efforts to salvage a replay ... which United won.

Edwards confessed: 'Everything flashed before me when

we went into the second period of extra time. We had lost to Villa in an earlier Cup Final (the Coca-Cola Cup) and I thought we were struggling again. I really couldn't see a goal coming ... I could see everything crumbling. I thought, "That's two out of three going down." The effect of going out of the FA Cup might have had the wrong impact on the players. Mark Hughes's goal revived the season for us.' Indeed it did, because United cruised through the replay against deflated Oldham and went on achieve the double.

Eric Cantona made a pertinent point when he reminded people that 'you have to be ceaselessly at a peak, physically, to win. When you're tired, you don't win.' And when you've just been granted a reprieve, it has two effects – for Manchester United, that Hughes goal against Oldham was a real reviver, while for their opponents it was a flattener. Cantona, having discussed matters with United skipper Bryan Robson, reckoned that 'people shouldn't play such a direct game when they're on the pitch every three days for two months – it's not physically possible. At times like that you need instinctive players capable of construction and keeping the ball.' True enough. The pressure of having to play so often meant that players didn't know how to vary their game – they 'don't know how to play another kind of football ... or don't want to play another kind.' Thus the Cantona philosophy.

Cantona's interest in painting, poetry and philosophy has been well documented, and when it comes to Soccer he has summed up his outlook in this manner: 'I score goals, I make goals and teams win. Wherever I go, teams win ... yes, even if I don't stay very long.' The man who claimed that boredom was his worst enemy and that he never looked back, became the most charismatic – and controversial – figure in English football, let alone at Manchester United, since the halcyon (and sometimes turbulent) days of George Best. Cantona, indeed, became the most emotive subject at a time when the game itself was going through a sticky patch, with a rash of allegations about 'bungs', bribery, drugs and refereeing decisions. As a matter of fact, within a fortnight or so of Cantona having been sent off at Selhurst Park, the letters

139

about him were dropping thick and fast through the letter-box of the Football Association at Lancaster Gate in London – chief executive Graham Kelly revealed that there had been more than 1,000 epistles.

There was even a phone-in on the radio about the Cantona affair, and one irate caller demanded to know why, on the night itself, the police hadn't arrested the Frenchman and carted him off to 'the nick'.

It was suggested that if a spectator had vaulted over the fencing, raced on to the ground and assaulted a player, he would have been hauled away in summary fashion and finished up in the police van. That thought had occurred to me, and I quizzed a senior police official on the subject. He simply shrugged and told me: 'There was no need to arrest anyone . . . they knew where they could get hold of Cantona when they wanted to talk to him.' As events turned out, when the police indicated that they were ready to interview the Frenchman, they were kept waiting because he had flown to foreign climes for a break in order to escape the media attention to which he was being subjected back in Manchester.

It was reported that, privately, some members of the police had expressed surprise and disappointment that Cantona hadn't been arrested, along with the Crystal Palace fan who had been involved, that night at Selhurst Park, and that their colleagues had come up with an answer to that one – the answer being that if there had been an arrest, in full view of the crowd, there could have followed even more ugly scenes . . . possibly, even, a riot. In view of what happened at Stamford Bridge when Millwall defeated Chelsea in an FA Cup replay which required a penalty shoot-out, it does seem understandable that the police at Selhurst Park had no wish to inflame an already-volatile situation. As the Cantona debate raged on and the police awaited his return from the island of Guadeloupe, I happened upon the story of another player who had been on the pitch at Selhurst Park that infamous night in January – John Salako, the winger who at that time was a Palace player.

During his career he had been struck down by a series of injuries which, it seemed, threatened to destroy the promise of a lengthy international career in an England shirt. However, at the age of 26 (which made him two years younger than Cantona) Salako had made an astonishing comeback after two knee injuries which had left doctors in the United States (whence he had travelled, to undergo revolutionary treatment) debating just how to tell the player that his footballing days were numbered.

Fortunately for Salako, the doctors had managed to effect a cure, and by the time he was lining up against Manchester United at Selhurst Park, he was also looking to resurrect his international career – indeed, by the summer of 1995 he had become a £2 million target for Newcastle United (a move he opted to reject, as he decided later to join Coventry City).

So what did John Salako have to say about the Cantona affair? This ... 'It wasn't until I got back to the dressing-room that I sat down and thought, "Did he really do that?"' And the Palace player added: 'My mind went back a week to Everton, where we lost badly and there were kids shouting such foul abuse, really getting personal, that I thought I'd like to have said something, or retaliated. You think to yourself, "Who are these people who can talk to you like that?" But a professional must always walk away and say, "Leave it, because you're better than that"'. Salako's philosophy: 'You must rise above it all. The behaviour of players is vital on and off the field, because we are ambassadors for our clubs – and for the game. It can be hard ... people can pester you ... but if it's a test, then we have to pass it. Some of them are just waiting for us, as pros, to let ourselves down, and there are plenty of opportunities for them to report on us.'

Salako had more to say, when it came to the subject of racial taunts. 'Ninety per cent of it I can take, because there's no real intent behind it. But there are times when I think they would really do harm if they could get to you. I'm trying to concentrate on the field, but people will use whatever tactics they can to put you off. Some of it's quite frightening.' At the same time, the player acknowledged: 'Footballers have let

141

themselves down badly, so we should carry some of the can. In any walk of life you get people who can't quite handle it.

'We are happy to thrust sixteen- or seventeen-year-old players into the limelight, and there's no counselling if they need help to cope. I was in an FA Cup-final team at 21, getting £250 a week. At big clubs, some kids are on £2,000 a week, playing in front of 40,000 crowds, and they're expected to deal with everything. It's hard to enjoy the game, these days. Winning is so important, because winners get everything and losers get nothing.'

Well, on the subject of kids, Alex Ferguson kept the wraps on a teenager named Ryan Giggs as he also kept him away from the prying eyes of the media. Giggs became a public figure soon enough, as it was – and as for Cantona, he was also in the spotlight, at a club which has the highest profile in the country. Under Ferguson, Manchester United have begun to emulate the feats of the old master, Matt Busby, and it was United's first great manager who once said something which remains valid to this day. 'I won't deny it is pleasant to succeed. But winning at all costs is not the true test of achievement. There is nothing wrong in trying to win, so long as you don't set the prize above the game. There is no dishonour in defeat, so long as you play to the limit of your strength and skill. What matters above all is that the game is played in the right spirit.' It seems to me that this is a message which the Football Association should order to be carved in tablets of stone, if necessary, and in sufficient numbers for a tablet to be hung behind the dressing-room door of every football club in the country.

Chapter 13

'A NIGHT OF UNALLOYED DISGRACE'

'I thought, "Oh, my God... he's going to do something stupid."
I've never been so scared in my life.' – WOMAN FOOTBALL
FAN who witnessed at close quarters Eric Cantona's
kung-fu act at Selhurst Park.

IT started out as just another football match, on the night of
January 25, 1995; it ended up with one of the central
characters, a volatile French international by the name of Eric
Cantona, launching a two-footed, kung-fu-style assault on a
belligerent fan, then being hauled up before the Football
Association on a charge of having brought the game into
disrepute ... this, a matter of days after Cantona had
attended a London police station and been charged with
common assault.

Twenty-four hours before he was due to face the Football
Association's three-man commission of inquiry, Cantona's
French lawyer, Monsieur Jean-Jacques Bertrand, was express-
ing his fears that the player – already suspended by his club,
Manchester United, until the end of the season, as well as
having been fined two weeks' pay – would find himself being
banned from the game worldwide and thus becoming a
Soccer outcast. Bertrand said: 'He faces an extension of his

ban to all federations ... he could be banned from playing soccer for the rest of his life.'

Bertrand and United's lawyer, director Maurice Watkins, were deputed to represent Cantona at the hearing, with manager Alex Ferguson reported to be available for 'moral support' and United chairman Martin Edwards appealing beforehand that the Football Association should consider United's suspensions and fine punishment enough for the errant Frenchman.

So what WAS all the fuss about, and what DID happen during that match which became one of the most-debated for many a year? One writer summed up after the event: 'Eric Cantona's boots and fists hung over Selhurst Park like a nasty smell, as Manchester United had to prepare to retain their Premiership title without the man who has become their heartbeat. The loss of two points which denied them the opportunity to replace Blackburn Rovers at the helm of English football was minimal punishment for a night of unalloyed disgrace.' In fact, the loss of two points could be said to have killed off United's title aspirations, no matter that on the final day of the season they could only draw, as the Rovers lost. In retrospect, perhaps the major damage had been done at Selhurst Park.

It has to be said that Crystal Palace, themselves in dire need of points as they fought to ensure Premiership survival, displayed a readiness to 'get stuck in' and battle like tigers in the bid to contain their illustrious opponents. Yet it seemed as if their efforts would be in vain as defender David May (who had been snapped up from Blackburn Rovers) scored only his second goal for United to put them in the lead. Palace, however, were not quite finished, and with little more than 10 minutes' play remaining, they managed to scramble an equaliser. By then, of course, it was a matter of United's 10 men striving to hold out – although there were still times when they had threatened to stretch their slender lead (such as when £7 million-man Andy Cole, who hadn't then hit the target in 11 appearances, snatched at a shot and drove the ball wide, and when Roy Keane sent in a cross which was met

144

by Lee Sharpe ... whose goalbound effort struck the cross-bar).

United were unhinged when John Salako broke through towards the penalty box – yet even then, there were opportunities for Alex Ferguson's side to hack the ball away, as Palace players tried to direct it goalwards. In the end, with 'keeper Peter Schmeichel and May coming to grief, it was Palace skipper Gareth Southgate who drove home a left-footer through a ruck of players.

So United were denied the chance to occupy the top spot for the first time since late November, and when the post-match inquest was held, Alan Smith – then the manager of Crystal Palace – claimed that the Cantona incident 'unsettled us more than it unsettled them.' Certainly United's 10 men battled hard after the dismissal of Cantona – which was followed by the explosive affair, early in the second period of the match. Mere minutes after the restart, Schmeichel launched the ball half-way into the Palace half of the field and, as Cantona and Palace defender Richard Shaw reacted, the Frenchman was seen to aim a kick at his opponent. The immediate reaction of referee Alan Wilkie was to show Cantona the red card.

The millions watching the match via television then saw the Frenchman apparently walking away – and the next moment, it seemed, all hell was let loose as Cantona launched himself towards a fan who was on the other side of the barrier. Cantona, indeed, might well have done himself a severe injury, because he fell backwards, and after being seen to raise his fists towards the fan, he was finally escorted away and out of sight. Television, however, captured not only the moment of fury which erupted as the player launched his two-footed assault, but also the expressions on the faces of people in the immediate vicinity of the incident ... faces which showed not only fear, but absolute bewilderment, after what the spectators had just witnessed. Two sisters (one aged 10, the other 12) were close to the action. The 10-year-old, Stephanie West, from Dorking, in Surrey, was quoted afterwards: 'I didn't want to watch. I put my hands up to my mouth. I was very frightened.' And afterwards? 'I was just confused ... I couldn't think properly about it all. That night when I was in bed I thought about it all, and it made me cry.' Her father related how both girls had collapsed in tears on their return home, with Stephanie especially distraught and, seemingly, a victim of 'delayed shock.' The father said: 'They had never seen such hatred ... there was a torrent of abuse pouring off the terraces. It was that which upset them more than anything. They kept asking me on the way home, "Why do people have such hatred? Why do they get so angry?" It was very shocking to them.'

The elder sister, Louisa, told how 'the crowd kept shouting all kinds of things which are unprintable – every sentence contained about three swear-words as Cantona came towards us. Cantona stopped, like he was trying to make sure what was being said – this one fan was waving his finger at Cantona, telling him to get off the pitch and shouting at him – then he lunged at him, and it all started. I can understand him (Cantona) being angry and upset, but I don't think he had the right to hit him, even though the man was shouting very nasty things. It was really scary. We have seen violence on TV and things like that, but we have never seen it so close.' The girls' father declared himself to be 'desperately disappointed with Cantona ... the children dearly love Manchester United, and we are sorry at the way the club's name has been dragged into this.'

Another fan, Kathy Churchman, from East Grinstead, was also quoted. There was 'that look' in Cantona's eyes ... 'you see it in films, but not at football matches. He suddenly stopped and looked towards us. I thought, "Oh, my God, he's going to do something stupid". I've never been so scared in my life. Cantona jumped over the fence and landed a karate kick. It missed my face by an inch and left stud marks on my coat and my leg. Cantona threw a punch, and that just missed me, too. I had mud splattered down the side of my face. I would never want to see him play in this country again. There was not a sign of sorrow over what he had done. He arrived at that match a hero, he left it a hooligan.'

146

Not everyone condemned totally. A Nottingham business-man (described as 'a neutral and no apologist for Cantona') called the office of a national newspaper to declare that 'the bile aimed at Kanchelskis (because he was Russian), McClair (Scots), Parker (black and seated on the bench) and the Frenchman (foreign and a genius) was beyond belief...' As for those in the game – former United players and the players' own top man, Gordon Taylor (chief executive of the Professional Footballers' Association) – they had their say. Taylor, while admitting 'there is no excuse for Cantona's conduct', warned of the danger of 'a lynch-mob mentality.'

Taylor argued: 'He (Cantona) has a Gallic temperament and he appears to have been highly intimidated by the circumstances here. Eric could have been escorted to the dressing-room in a better way. It seems everyone wants to come down on Eric like a ton of bricks and forget his positive contribution to the game. While action has to be taken, too many people have been quick to say he should never play again. That's a knee-jerk, emotive reaction.'

Knee-jerk, emotive or not, former United players were swift in their condemnation of the Frenchman, although he did have some who were prepared to defend him. Alex Stepney (once involved in an on-field rumpus himself, and a hero of United's 1968 European Cup triumph), declared that 'Cantona must go from the club.' He argued that 'George Best was provoked all the time, but over the years he handled it very well. No player is bigger than the club, I don't care who he is. Somebody has to make a stand, and I think the FA will do so by banning him for life.' The Football Association decided to add to the punishment imposed by Manchester United, but decreed that Cantona could return to English football at the beginning of October, 1995. Which he did.

Former United captain Bill Foulkes, a survivor of the Munich disaster, summed up: 'Going into the crowd is behaving like a hooligan – that's nothing to do with sport.' And ex-United manager Tommy Docherty declared: 'What he (Cantona) did was outrageous. It should never have been seen on a football ground and should never be seen again.

147

His disciplinary record is appalling.' George Best, however, claimed it was 'stupid' to talk about banning Cantona for life – 'that would be ridiculous. He got involved in something he shouldn't have done, but I wouldn't belittle him.' As for referee Alan Wilkie, who showed Cantona the red card: 'I've been in this game 17 years, and I have never known something like this to happen. I am sure the FA will act swiftly, but it is not for me to speculate on what action they might take.'

A United supporter, Mark Tierney, was quoted, too: 'It's the worst that's happened to this club since Matt Busby died.' And a United shareholder, Joan Moore, made the point that 'Eric is a role model for United fans. The kids copy what they see him do on the pitch, and they might now copy what they've watched him do on television.' And so the Cantona debate rumbled on, while the Football Association (and the police) waited to talk to him. Meanwhile, it was recorded that 'the loss of Cantona to English football would blow a huge hole in what has become a multi-million-pound industry.'

Manchester United Football Club, it was said, 'is in the super-league of product marketing, and Cantona has played a key part in generating its wealth, attracting sponsors to the club and customers to its shops. It has a superstore at Old Trafford, one in the centre of Manchester, and branches in Plymouth, Dublin and Belfast. It is also planning to open branches in Tokyo and Sydney. Last year the club reported a 6.6 per cent increase in profits before tax and transfer fees to £8.2 million. Its share price was hit by Wednesday's incident, however, with more than £3 million knocked off the club's value.' Then the report switched to the American sportswear giant, Nike, 'which is thought to pay Cantona between £150,000 and £200,000 a year to wear its boots. The company refused to quantify its return in terms of sales, but it is known to be immense.'

Nike's initial reaction, it was reported, was that it had no intention of dropping Cantona, 'but after the FA announced the disrepute charge, a slightly different line emerged. A spokesman said, "We will be speaking to Eric and examining

148

the situation. There will be no rash decisions."' Later still, after Cantona had appeared in court and been sentenced to two weeks in gaol (he then used his right of recourse to appeal and, subsequently, undertook 120 hours' community service in lieu of going to prison), Nike's public-relations manager, Simon Taylor, said there were no plans to review the deal, which was due to expire after the 1996 European Championships.

Taylor said that Cantona, who was wearing Nike boots when he attacked the fan, had already been severely punished. 'Hopefully, the case is closed when the final decision is made. We would never condone violence in any sport ... Eric realised what he did was very wrong. Let's hope he can carry on playing the sport we all love to see him play.' And while Cantona's Nike boots were in the news, it was reported that another sportswear manufacturer, Umbro, was paying United big money – said to be £10 million to £12 million – over a period of six years 'for the right to cash in with massive sales of replica kit', while the consumer electronics giant, Sharp, 'has paid United £4 million since 1982 to have its name emblazoned across the players' shirts.'

Such talk, of course, related to very high finance, while on a more personal note there was the story about Cantona's new book, about to be launched. Mention was made of 40,000 copies about to go on sale, with a spokesperson talking of the Frenchman doing a signing session for buyers who wanted their copy to be autographed by the player. There was a suggestion that the book launch had been delayed; but, delayed or not, there would be plenty of time for Cantona to pen his autograph on the inside cover of the book, should his fans queue to buy it, because after the Football Association hearing, the verdict was that Cantona could not resume his soccer career until after September 30, 1995, and that he must pay another fine (this again was one of £10,000).

The Association's chief executive, Graham Kelly, indicated that if people thought Cantona had got off lightly, this certainly was not the case – altogether, he would be out of football for eight months and, of course, at that stage he still

149

had to make his appearance in court (as did Matthew Simmons, the fan with whom he had tangled at Selhurst Park). It was recorded that both Cantona and the fan (who was charged with two offences of threatening behaviour) faced the possibility of prison, as well as a fine – a maximum of six months in gaol and a £5,000 fine, if convicted.

What was termed 'the long shadow of the absent Cantona' stretched not only over Old Trafford; it had its effect elsewhere. Four clubs – Barcelona, Valencia, Inter-Milan and Sao Paulo, of Brazil – were said to have expressed interest in signing him, should United finally decide to let the Frenchman go, although the verdict of FIFA, following upon the Football Association's decision, meant that Cantona was barred from playing football worldwide, until after September 30. Well, apart from one far-flung outpost, that is. As the newspaper headline proclaimed, Mongolia was 'the only Cantona bolt-hole.'

The paper reported: 'Eric Cantona has had his Football Association ban extended worldwide by FIFA. A FIFA statement said, "The player is banned from all football activities throughout the world up to and including September 30, 1995."' There was one loophole, however. The report added: 'In theory, Cantona could ply his trade in Mongolia for the duration of his ban. The Asian country is currently in dispute with FIFA, and a spokesman said, "The only place where we currently have doubts about our jurisdiction is Mongolia. I understand talks are ongoing to clarify that situation."'

On a more mundane (and far more credible) note, it was also reported that Monsieur Cantona was now expected to give youngsters at Old Trafford the considerable benefit of his expertise when it came to the art of coaching, during the months that he must endure his enforced absence from the field of play. That kind of thing – coaching – was something which another household name in football – Sir Stanley Matthews – had spent many years doing, at home and abroad. By the time the Cantona affair had blown up, Sir Stan had reached the venerable age of 80 and was about to be fêted yet

150

again. He said the Cantona incident at Selhurst Park had 'sickened me' and went on record like this: 'For a professional to lose his temper like that is inexcusable. A lot of ex-players are for him ... they are wrong. He was a very naughty boy and deserves to be punished. I have never seen anything like it, and I don't think football will again.'

Matthews recalled: 'Before the war, if you got sent off, you were booed by your own fans. And if you were sent off, you never played for England again.' In a playing career spanning 33 years, Matthews was never booked – he played his first League game for Stoke City in 1932, when he was 17, his last in 1965, by which time he had reached the age of 50. He reflected: 'Once on the field, I never heard anything ... I just got my head down and got on with the game. That's what professionals have to do. Provocation is no mitigation.'

However, a slightly different tack was taken in a story which emanated from the United States, where it was reported that, like Eric Cantona, a sports star had landed himself in trouble after having charged into the crowd to punch a heckling spectator. Basketball ace Vernon Maxwell was fined about £13,000 and banned for 10 games for his sins, and the Houston Rockets player decided that he would not appeal against his punishment ... instead, he would sue the fan who had so provoked him. Furthermore, a team-mate of Maxwell's observed: 'I bet you, deep down, every NBA player is living this incident through Maxwell. There are a lot of hecklers who come to games and conduct themselves in a way where they deserve to be punched.'

No doubt there would be a considerable number of soccer players in this country, never mind Eric Cantona, who would echo that comment with genuine feeling. The Football Association's Graham Kelly, in fact, was at pains to stress: 'We're concerned with the increasing level of abuse that footballers have to suffer. We don't think it's acceptable, and we don't think it's part of the game. We have already had talks with the Commission for Racial Equality, and we hope to speak to leading politicians about a further initiative in this respect.' Kelly reminded people that Cantona 'faces a court case, has been dealt with by Manchester United, has lost money, lost the captaincy of the French team and suffered double the fine he could have suffered in court. I don't think you could say he has not suffered for his actions of January 25. He has said there will be no repetition of this incident.'

Kelly declared that the Frenchman 'recognises the gravity of the situation'; and, while recognising, also, that footballers like Cantona are paid vast sums of money each week and that they know beforehand that they are liable to be subjected to taunts from the terraces (taunts they are expected to ignore), the Football Association did stress that it had taken into account the provocation Cantona had had to endure at Selhurst Park. Cantona himself, having agreed with Manchester United that he would not appeal against the punishment imposed by the Football Association, could make no comment at that time because of his impending court case.

United's solicitor, Maurice Watkins (who was also a member of United's board), did have something to say, however. Like this: 'I've spent quite a bit of time over the past few weeks with Eric. We have talked about the situation, and I believe he will do his best. I think that is also the confidence Mr Ferguson has in him. I hope he will spend his time quietly in training and, hopefully, at peace; then, when he returns, we hope he will settle down quickly in the team and delight the fans as he has already done over the last few years.' There were a great many expressions of hope in that dissertation and, as one observer summed up: 'Amen to that.'

CHAPTER 14

THE CANTONA DOSSIER

'It is significant that for all the problems Cantona has had since leaving us, he was never in bother during his time at Leeds. I don't mean that as any reflection on Manchester United, but it's great credit to Howard Wilkinson.' – Leeds United's then chairman LESLIE SILVER.

THEY were listed as 'The Sins of the Season' and 'Ten Years of Trouble'. And the name of French footballer Eric Cantona figured prominently. Those 'Sins of the Season?' – November 1994 ... Bruce Grobbelaar accused of having taken a bribe to make sure Liverpool lost a match. He was charged with having brought the game into disrepute, while an Arsenal and England forward, Paul Merson, was admitting to having had problems relating to cocaine, alcohol and gambling. He was ordered to spend six weeks in a rehabilitation clinic. Then came December, and the Premier League launched an inquiry into allegations of transfer kickbacks. It was claimed that George Graham, then Arsenal's manager, had received £285,000 as part of a £1.57 million transfer deal that took Danish international John Jensen to Highbury in 1992. Arsenal were later to sack Graham, who repaid a large sum of money, plus interest, to the Highbury club.

Come January 1995, and Eric Cantona was seen by millions to launch a two-footed attack on a fan after having been sent off at Selhurst Park – he was suspended by Manchester United until the season's end, fined an estimated £20,000, and faced a disciplinary commission the following month ... by which time more soccer trouble had erupted, as referee Rodger Gifford was attacked by a Blackburn Rovers supporter after the Ewood Park match against Leeds United, while Chelsea's Dennis Wise was convicted of assaulting a taxi-driver (he was cleared, on appeal).

After a pitch invasion by Chelsea fans who had seen their side lose an FA Cup-tie (in a penalty shoot-out) against Millwall, mounted police threw a cordon across the Stamford Bridge pitch ... and Eric Cantona, on holiday in the Caribbean, was hitting the headlines again, this time as he was alleged to have attacked ITN reporter Terry Lloyd. That same month (February 1995), there was mayhem at Lansdowne Road, Dublin, where England met the Republic of Ireland in what was supposed to be a friendly match – but, inside half an hour, as the Irish team went a goal up, England fans rioted and the match was abandoned.

The 'Ten Years of Trouble' went back to March 1985, when Millwall fans wrecked Luton Town's Kenilworth Road ground during an FA Cup-tie which ended with 31 policemen being hurt, and in May of that year came the horrific, Heysel-stadium disaster. In May, 1988, fans invaded the Stamford Bridge pitch after Chelsea's play-off defeat by Middlesbrough, while a year later Birmingham fans spilled on to the pitch and attacked their own players after Crystal Palace had taken the lead. That was a mere month after the Hillsborough disaster had accounted for the lives of 96 Liverpool supporters. In May 1990, Leeds fans went on the rampage in Bournemouth before and after the win which sealed the Second Division Championship for Howard Wilkinson's side (there were 73 arrests) and in March, 1993, when Manchester City and Tottenham Hotspur met in the FA Cup on a Sunday afternoon, mounted police restored order as City fans invaded the Maine Road pitch (Spurs won the tie).

In October 1993, Dutch police arrested 197 England supporters when violence flared in Amsterdam before the

154

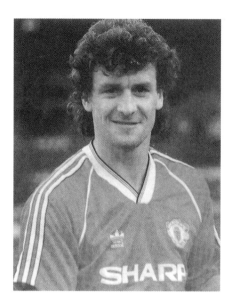

Mark Hughes . . .
'It's a shame, but
out on the field we
can sense people
either love or hate
United'.

Steve Bruce, who
became the first
Englishman to skipper a
double-winning side . . .
he left for Birmingham
City with the thanks of
Manchester United
ringing in his ears.

Comeback day for Eric Cantona . . . and in the background, one of his critics . . . Liverpool defender Phil Babb.

It's all over, and Ryan Giggs salutes the home fans after United have drawn 2–2 with Liverpool on Cantona's comeback day.

United's
£7 million man,
Andy Cole, who
answered his
critics after a
five-star display
against Ipswich
Town. But
Cole's place
was in jeopardy
during the run-
in to the finale
of season
1995–96.

Ryan Giggs takes on Phil Babb – the man who said of Eric Cantona: 'If it were
up to me, I'd ban him from English football for good'.

The best goalkeeper in Europe . . . but even Peter Schmeichel couldn't stop this brilliant effort from Liverpool's Robbie Fowler.

Bargain-buy, Lee Sharpe in action against Steve McManaman.

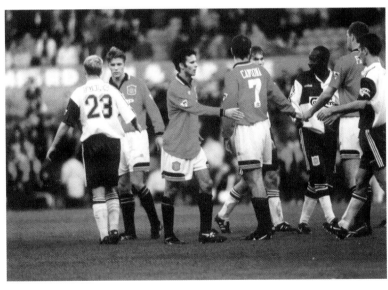

Handshakes all round, and Eric Cantona comes through his eagerly-awaited return to English football after having helped United earn a point against arch-rivals Liverpool.

Airborne duel between Gary Pallister and Ian Rush . . . the United man cost a club-record fee at the time of £2.3 million.

At last . . . players who brought United their glittering triumph in 1968.

Manchester United's 'elder statesman' . . . Sir Matt Busby, pictured with daughter Sheena shortly before his 84th birthday.

Bob Lord – chairman of Burnley, and the man who referred to United players as 'teddy boys' . . . a description which hurt Matt Busby.

Manager-turned commentator . . . Tommy Docherty, former team boss at Old Trafford, who featured in a TV programme which was heavily critical of United's commercial activities.

Kenny Dalglish . . . he and Alex Ferguson crossed swords on more than one occasion.

Action-man Harry Gregg, who was a Munich hero and who became involved in controversy surrounding games at Kenilworth Road and Ewood Park. Another record-priced 'keeper signed by United', Alex Stepney, also found himself the centre of controversy after a world-club-championship match against Estudiantes.

United's playing squad for season 1962–63 – the season they flirted with relegation, and won the FA Cup.

Munich survivors . . . and some newcomers. This was the United squad after the Munich air disaster had decimated Matt Busby's all-star team.

Derby-game day, and it's Matt Busby the player (left) leading out Liverpool as they meet Everton.

The cup that cheers . . . United skipper Noel Cantwell with the trophy, after victory over Leicester City in the 1963 final.

Sharing the spoils – and the players of Manchester United and Liverpool get together with the Charity Shield after having drawn at Wembley in 1990.

Keane

One of the aces in Matt Busby's pack . . .
George Best in action. By the mid-1990s
United had another charismatic hero in
Eric Cantona, and Best was saying: 'I
would pay to see him play'.

Ince

Kanchelskis

Men who tried to bring the title trophy to Old Trafford, but had to settle for something less, clockwise from left: Frank O'Farrell, Tommy Docherty, Dave Sexton, Ron Atkinson (pictured walking out at Wembley with skipper Bryan Robson and Liverpool manager Joe Fagan) and Wilf McGuinness.

One of the finest players ever to grace a United jersey – Duncan Edwards, who became one of the victims of Munich.

It was heartache for 'keeper Jim Leighton when he was axed by Alex Ferguson for the 1990 FA Cup-final replay against Crystal Palace, but Leighton vindicated Ferguson's judgment in having signed him for United, as he moved on and regained his Scotland place in 1995.

Making a point – Bill Shankly, who said of Matt Busby: 'In a game that can so easily break a man, Busby's record is remarkable. He can accept defeat with dignity, is never arrogant in success'.

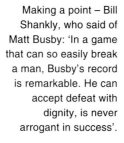

Action Man . . . and match winner. Eric Cantona left an indelible mark on the 1996 FA Cup-final by scoring the goal that took the trophy to Old Trafford.

Alex Ferguson relaxing at a social occasion.

UNITED'S LEAGUE RECORD DURING THE BUSBY ERA

Season	P.	W.	D.	L.	F.	A.	Pts.	Position
1946-47	42	22	12	8	95	54	56	Second
1947-48	42	19	14	9	81	48	52	Second
1948-49	42	21	11	10	77	44	53	Second
1949-50	42	18	14	10	69	44	50	Fourth
1950-51	42	24	8	10	74	40	56	Second
1951-52	42	23	11	8	95	52	57	Champions
1952-53	42	18	10	14	69	72	46	Eighth
1953-54	42	18	12	12	73	58	48	Fourth
1954-55	42	20	7	15	84	74	47	Fifth
1955-56	42	25	10	7	83	51	60	Champions
1956-57	42	28	8	6	103	54	64	Champions
1957-58	42	16	11	15	85	75	43	Ninth
1958-59	42	24	7	11	103	66	55	Second
1959-60	42	19	7	16	102	80	45	Seventh
1960-61	42	18	9	15	88	76	45	Seventh
1961-62	42	15	9	18	72	75	39	Fifteenth
1962-63	42	12	10	20	67	81	34	Nineteenth
1963-64	42	23	7	12	90	62	53	Second
1964-65	42	26	9	7	89	39	61	Champions
1965-66	42	18	15	9	84	59	51	Fourth
1966-67	42	24	12	6	84	45	60	Champions
1967-68	42	24	8	10	89	55	56	Second
1968-69	42	15	12	15	57	53	42	Eleventh
1969-70	42	14	17	11	66	61	45	Eighth

Former top League referee Peter Rhodes . . . he reported Eric Cantona to the Football Association after an incident at Bramall Lane; but no action was taken.

The standard Matt Busby set . . . and the figures speak for themselves.

World Cup match against Holland (431 fans were deported) and by May 1994, it was being recorded that Millwall hooligans had twice invaded the pitch as their side crashed out of the First Division play-offs, with Derby County 'keeper Martin Taylor being kicked to the ground as he sought safety. The chairman of a northern Premier League club also felt the impact of supporter hostility on home ground...

It happened at Manchester City's Maine Road at the height of the takeover battle between Francis Lee and Peter Swales, with chairman Swales being pelted by fans and having egg splashed over his new, blue jacket. Lee, of course, had done nothing to encourage such wayward behaviour by so-called City supporters, while Swales admitted that he could understand the fans' frustration – although the action of this mindless minority was too much for him to stomach. Whatever his faults and mistakes during a lengthy spell as City's chairman, Swales had never been less than a committed supporter, and he had allowed a string of managers to spend millions in the quest to achieve parity with rivals United. He was a City fan to the day he died.

If Swales generated so much feeling among the Maine Road faithful, Eric Cantona generated more passionate argument than probably any other player in the history of the English game – even though he was French. Alex Ferguson admitted that Cantona was 'different in his nature ... his temperament, cultural background, almost everything, in fact. Little wonder he's not on the same wavelength as the rest of us.' Leeds United's chairman, at the time, Leslie Silver, contrasted his manager's approach to the Cantona situation when the French star played for the Elland Road club. 'It is significant that for all the problems Cantona has had since leaving us, he was never in bother during his time at Leeds. I think that shows the quality of management here. I don't mean that as any reflection on Manchester United, but it's great credit to Howard Wilkinson.'

As it happened, when Cantona returned to Elland Road wearing the colours of Manchester United, the Leeds fans gave him a hot reception and he retaliated by spitting – an

155

offence which brought him a £1,000 fine. Cantona's catalogue of misdemeanours stretched from 1987 to 1995, during which period of time he had played for more than half a dozen clubs. Wherever he had played, something had happened during each of those eight years ... starting back in 1987, when he was playing for Auxerre and was fined heavily after having given his own goalkeeper, Bruno Martini, a black eye.

The following year Cantona was in trouble at international level – he was told he would be banned from the French team for a year after he had sworn at coach Henri Michel. Cantona was reported as having labelled Michel 'one of the most incompetent managers in world football'. Come 1989, and Cantona was being suspended indefinitely by Marseille after having kicked the ball into the crowd and thrown his jersey at the referee – these actions had been in protest when he found he was being substituted. He was then loaned to Bordeaux and to Montpellier ... where, in 1990, he was banned for 10 days after having hurled his boots into the face of a teammate. Cantona confessed: 'I had a dressing-room fight with Jean-Claude Lemoult. I threw my boots in his face.'

In 1991 Cantona was suspended for three matches after having thrown a ball at the referee, and when he appeared at a disciplinary hearing, he yelled the word 'idiot!' ... then was promptly informed that the ban would be doubled. By that time, he was wearing the colours of Nimes. The following year Cantona was trying his luck with Sheffield Wednesday, but because of bad weather his first week's training was limited to work on artificial turf, and when he was invited to stay a second week, with a view to seeing how he performed on grass, he moved on ... to Leeds United, who forked out £900,000 for him. With Leeds he savoured the delight of collecting a Championship medal, then – having hit a hat-trick in the Charity Shield match against Liverpool – he was off to Old Trafford for a £1 million fee. By 1993 he was in trouble for having spat at a Leeds fan on his return to Elland Road, and more problems were posed for Manchester United and their wayward French star as, in the November,

United tried conclusions with Turkish club Galatasaray in the European Cup. United got their comeuppance ... so did Cantona. At the end of the match in Istanbul he was given marching orders by referee Kurt Rothlisberger – whom, it was alleged, he had labelled a cheat. Cantona was also involved in a fracas with the Turkish police, and the upshot of it all was that he was suspended for four European matches – a ban which was liable to cost his club dearly.

The year 1994 was notable (if that is the appropriate word) for Cantona being banned for five matches after having suffered the indignity of being sent off twice in four days – the first time at Swindon (where he was seen to stamp on an opponent, John Moncur), and the second time at Arsenal's Highbury ground (where he went for an early bath after having committed two bookable offences). In May of that year Cantona was accused of having stamped on the then Coventry City player, Phil Babb, during the match at Old Trafford, though no action was taken (Babb himself had something to say later), then in July, when Cantona attended the World Cup Finals in the United States, he was put in handcuffs after having swung a punch at a tournament official. The Frenchman had been ejected from the Press box at the semi-final between Brazil and Sweden in Pasadena, and he was later released by the security guards.

When United entered a pre-season tournament in Scotland, Cantona was sent off after having fouled Glasgow Rangers' Steve Presley, and the sequel was another ban, for three games. The downside continued when an advert was banned from British television because of bad language ... the upside came when Cantona was named PFA Player of the Year and (as he scored twice in the FA Cup final) a double as he collected not only a winner's medal, but his third consecutive League-championship medal. For good measure, he was named captain of his country. As 1995 dawned, however, the Cantona penchant for getting into trouble revealed itself again, this time during an FA Cup-tie against Sheffield United at Bramall Lane, where home player Charlie Hartfield was shown the red card. Cantona, who had kicked Hartfield, escaped punishment, while the Sheffield player copped it for having retaliated. That incident happened early in January, in a match which was televised, and before the end of the month another televised game provoked a furore throughout the nation. This was the notorious kung-fu incident at Selhurst Park on the night of January 25.

By the time Cantona was sunning himself in the Caribbean, his club were playing Manchester City at Maine Road, and ill-feeling became apparent between the rival fans – indeed, some United supporters to whom I spoke, admitted that for a time the atmosphere was intimidating. A week or so later, Leeds United were due to meet their Manchester counter-parts in an FA Cup-tie at Old Trafford ... and, not surpris-ingly, there was much speculation about what might happen. Leeds manager Howard Wilkinson counselled his club's supporters to be on their best behaviour, while Manchester United declared their readiness to place Cantona in what was termed 'protective custody' as he was instructed to steer clear of Old Trafford while the two Uniteds were engaged in their Cup confrontation.

It was reported that 'the "Keep Cantona Cool" policy is backed by both chairman Martin Edwards and manager Alex Ferguson', and the latter offered this explanation: 'I think it will be wise to keep Eric away from Old Trafford at the weekend'. That could be construed as a masterly statement of diplomacy since, as Ferguson admitted, 'there may be some people present who would see his presence as inflammatory.' It was also recorded that from the Leeds supporters' point of view, 'Cantona's defection from Yorkshire to Lancashire remains the transfer that provokes the most heated debate among Leeds supporters. They will jump at the chance to revel in the player's current crisis as he sits out the rest of the season, suspended by his club and awaiting FA action over his assault on a fan at Crystal Palace.

'The Old Trafford hierarchy are also well aware that it will not be solely Leeds followers who attempt to incite the errant Frenchman to react in the wake of his explosive behaviour at Selhurst Park last month and his attack on an ITN reporter in

Guadeloupe at the weekend.' It was suggested that Cantona might take legal action against ITN for what was termed defamation and violation of his privacy while on holiday in the Caribbean. United chairman Martin Edwards declared that Cantona was 'in a very unfortunate situation.'

'I feel very sorry for him ... he will be followed around wherever he goes. The pressure on him is getting worse. People are looking for a reaction from him, whatever he does.' Of course, a large number of people would argue that after the Selhurst Park affair, the Frenchman had brought retribution upon himself; and a former United footballer, Eamon Dunphy, now an observer of, and writer about the modern soccer scene, looked back at what had happened in his own country, at Lansdowne Road, in Dublin, and delivered this verdict: 'The atmosphere in the major English football grounds is not one of healthy rivalry, sporting fraternity and enjoyment of the occasion. It is hate. Sheer hate.' He was not alone in thinking this.

159

Chapter 15

CARIBBEAN CAPERS

'It may not be the sacred duty *of the media to discover what happened next, but it would be a pretty bloody stupid organisation that didn't. And what happened next was intriguing...' – Daily Mail* columnist IAN WOOLDRIDGE.

ERIC Cantona generated an explosion of thousands of words and almost acres of newspaper space, after his televised antics at Selhurst Park. There were few moments when you could smile about things, though one report did contribute a moment of light relief. It began: 'Positively the last word on Cantona.' It went on: 'It seems that, having lashed out, he is being treated for a lower-leg injury.' Then the explanation: 'This, you will no doubt he sorry to hear, is not Cantona, the hurdler, but Cantona, a four-year-old gelding who runs on the flat. Ooh, aah, Cantona, to give the horse his full name, sustained a hoof ailment during his holiday on a Yorkshire stud farm. He was named by a consortium of Leeds businessmen who revered the two-legged version during his time at Leeds United.'

The report went on: 'According to *Timeform*, racing's bible of form analysis, the gelding is "one to treat with caution at present." But Tony Sweetman, whose wife, Eve, now owns the horse, claims he is an absolute gent. "Mind you", he adds, "he is a very haughty, disdainful creature and always seems to be looking down his nose" '

Two journalists had something to say about Monsieur Eric Cantona (the Manchester United footballer) being allowed to slope off on holiday at a time when the police back home were studying his case and considering when to summon him for interview. The *Daily Mail*'s Vic Robbie wrote that 'Manchester United were applauded for banning Cantona for the rest of the season, even if some of us believed they were too lenient. They were seen to be upholding the discipline of a great club. A follow-up statement by United director Maurice Watkins, a lawyer, seemed perfectly understandable. No official or player, including Cantona and Paul Ince, who was alleged to have struck a spectator, would discuss the Selhurst Park incident until any legal action by the police or disciplinary action by the FA had been taken.'

Then Robbie pounced. 'Yet less than 48 hours later, there was Ince in a Sunday newspaper (the *News of the World*), with whom he has a contract, protesting his innocence. Even as Watkins was making his statement, the club were giving Ince the go-ahead, and on Sunday said there would be no disciplinary action against the player. Perhaps someone at Old Trafford could tell Mr Watkins what is happening at his club, and then tell us.' At a later date, when Ince appeared in court, he was cleared of assault. As for Cantona, there was a great to-do about the wisdom or otherwise of his club allowing him to take a holiday abroad, knowing he would be called on at some stage by the police, though Alex Ferguson sprang to the defence of both club and player when he talked about the media having camped out by Cantona's home, and about wishing to ensure that the Frenchman got away from the pressures and attentions of the media for a spell. The police made it known they were not happy when, having decided to summon Cantona to South Norwood, they found he was sunning himself abroad, while United became involved in a war of words, claiming the police had been aware Cantona was away.

Enter the noted columnist Ian Wooldridge, who is never

short of a pithy comment or two, and he referred to 'the bizarre sequence of events that have led to Cantona sunbathing on a Caribbean beach at the height of the English soccer season.' He claimed that 'they evidently strike Alex Ferguson as being some private matter,' adding: 'I think we will be the judge of that.' Referring to the Selhurst Park affair which was witnessed by millions of television viewers and was 're-screened later in every news bulletin', Wooldridge said: 'There are bound to be a few viewers sufficiently unlethargic to say, "Good heavens, how interesting". Inevitably, the more alert among them will want to know the consequences. Was Cantona charged with GBH? Did the spectator die of his injuries?' Wooldridge declared: 'It may not be the sacred *duty* of the media to discover what happened next, but it would be a pretty bloody stupid organisation that didn't. And what happened next was intriguing. Instead of staying around to help the police with their necessary inquiries, Mr Cantona and his family, apparently with Mr Ferguson's approval, fled to the island of Guadeloupe "to escape media attention."'

Wooldridge pointed out that Alex Ferguson 'must be aware that Manchester United do attract some attention and that even when he isn't hacking away at disgusting spectators, Cantona, with his aesthetic appreciation of fine art, poetry and philosophy, is a figure of some interest.' There was more in the same vein as Wooldridge referred to 'the player's futile attempt to disappear'. And, of course, with their reputation for putting the boot in, the tabloids could have been counted upon to chase after Cantona like ferrets diving down a hole. So it seemed a trifle naive to hope that Cantona would achieve peace and solitude simply by taking a plane to Guadeloupe – an island which was only a few hours' flying time from these shores.

When the news broke of Cantona's confrontation with the ITN reporter on Guadeloupe, it coincided with the victory United had scored over Manchester City at Maine Road – a victory which had taken United back to the top of the table. 'If a picture paints a thousand words, the expressions of the Manchester United hierarchy said it all,' wrote one observer –

162

and he wasn't referring to expressions of triumph. 'Just minutes earlier manager Ferguson and chairman Edwards had been all smiles ... a thumping, 3–0 victory ... but when news began to filter through of a thumping of a startlingly different kind on the sun-kissed beach of Guadeloupe, the United chiefs were clearly stunned. Cantona had survived as a United star only after hours of soul-searching by Ferguson and Edwards following his kung-fu attack on a supporter at Crystal Palace ... so shaken were Ferguson and Edwards by the incident in Guadeloupe that neither could trust themselves to comment sensibly.'

The *Mail on Sunday* carried a story from the Caribbean isle, where Cantona had been found and was quoted as saying he intended not only to return to England, but to carry on playing for United. According to the paper, Cantona had been holidaying with his family at a rented, beachfront villa; he had signed autographs, posed for photographs with souvenir hunters, and acknowledged greetings from other holiday-makers on the French-owned strip of territory. And, 'as the warm ocean waters lapped the beach, Cantona talked to the *Mail on Sunday* ... He denied he was trying to a avoid detectives who had ordered him to report to South Norwood for questioning. He said, "There is no disrespect. It is a misunderstanding. I promised my wife and son a vacation. They are my main priority." He confirmed that he wants to return and play for Manchester United next season. "Yes, I will stay with United next season, I promise."' The paper reported that one of the few non-French guests at the resort had said Cantona looked 'angry and glum at first, but as the days went by he perked up no end. He's got a lot of support here.'

When it came to Cantona's failure to show up at South Norwood, United hit back at claims that their star had been out of order, with Ferguson declaring bluntly: 'The police knew Eric was going on holiday, and they never said he couldn't leave the country. At no time was an appointment made for the police to see Eric. There seems to be a lack of communication on their side of things. The suggestion that he has tried to dodge the police is stupid. He'll be back next week and ready to see the police then. We had to get Eric away – television crews and media people were camped outside his house, and more were arriving by the day. It would have been impossible for him and his family to remain at home.' Apparently, United received word from the police that Cantona's presence at South Norwood was required 48 hours later – by which time he was already abroad.

Gordon Taylor, chief executive of the Professional Footballers' Association, who had pledged to speak for Cantona at the FA disciplinary hearing, reflected that the news from Guadeloupe would add to 'the campaign to drive him out of the country ... you wonder if he can survive, with the rival fans waiting for his return, and you wonder if he'll even tolerate his suspension. If the FA impose extra punishment, they'll ask FIFA to implement it. If that happens, Eric will be running out of countries where he can play.' Well, the FA did, and so did FIFA ... and Cantona did 'tolerate' his overall suspension as, despite one request to be released from his contract, he was persuaded by his manager to bite the bullet and stay at Old Trafford.

United's chairman, admitting the club suspension might jeopardise Cup and League ambitions, declared: 'The reputation of Manchester United is above trophies. What is most important is that the game is bigger than Manchester United, and Manchester United is more important than Eric Cantona. He's accepted the punishment. It is severe, and it says everything. We had a duty to the game.' There were those in the media, however, who begged to differ with United on the claim that Cantona's punishment had been 'severe'.

One report claimed United had 'effectively given Cantona a slap on the wrist ... the club ignored demands to sack the hot-tempered Frenchman.' The *Daily Mail*'s Neil Harman wrote: 'With one eye on their responsibility and the other fixed firmly on their profit and loss account, United couldn't bring themselves to do the right thing and show Cantona the door.' This was written before events in Guadeloupe. Harman declared that suspension of the volatile Frenchman to the end of the season 'is limp-wristed tolerance of a star from whom they can derive even more cash in Cantona shirts, Cantona wrist watches and Cantona mugs, through the families who follow them. Cantona means big bucks. If United retain the title and enter the UEFA Champions' League again, they obviously feel they are in better shape to win the Champions' Cup and its attendant fortune with the errant Frenchman, rather than without him.' United, as events unfolded, didn't retain the Championship crown. Harman was moved to ask: 'Is a club like United – called the biggest club in the world – so desperate that they are willing to accept a player like Cantona pulling on a red jersey again?'

Harman quoted the Football Association's Director of Public Affairs, David Davies (a former TV reporter) as having described the Selhurst Park incident as 'beyond belief', and delivered this verdict: 'That Cantona is still considered worthy of employment by United is equally unbelievable.' But FA supremo Sir Bert Millichip had a different viewpoint when he spoke about the Guadeloupe affair. 'I had great sympathy for him (Cantona) that people were chasing him all over the world. They have followed him around to take pictures of him.' Millichip rightly pointed out that the Guadeloupe business was totally unrelated to football, and said he had sympathy for people 'looking for a bit of peace.' And a gentleman from Cheshunt, felt impelled to write to a newspaper in defence of Cantona . . . 'it's time something was done about unwarranted intrusions by the media.'

As the debate still raged about the actions of the volatile Frenchman, Cantona finally returned from the sun-kissed island, to be pictured on television as he walked – unsmiling, as usual – and pushing a trolley through the airport after having arrived back on his native soil. One thing was for sure: love him or loathe him, deify or disparage him, proclaim his guilt or defend him to the death, it had to be conceded that the Continental and Caribbean capers attributed to Monsieur Cantona (and his misdeeds while with Manchester United) constituted a formidable list of talking points.

CHAPTER 16

'BAN HIM FOR GOOD!'

'If it were up to me, I'd ban him from English football for good.' – Liverpool's £3.5 million defender, PHIL BABB, after the Eric Cantona kung-fu incident at Selhurst Park.

I am no *Sun* worshipper; neither do I survey the *Mirror* each morning to see if my face is my fortune. At the same time, as an experienced journalist, I can admire the excellence with which these tabloid dailies are put together, technically speaking – not to mention the gusto with which they pursue their quarry whenever they scent a good story. When Graeme Souness was under siege as the manager of Liverpool, he offered this serious and intelligent opinion: 'I don't believe it is possible to organise a university course that could educate managers in how to handle the media properly in these times. We are caught in a tabloid war.' He could say that again – and again.

The *Sun* became a newspaper reviled and despised by many Liverpudlians after its treatment of the Hillsborough disaster, and there have been many lurid headlines in the various tabloids which have not endeared them to those whose jobs are concerned with professional football (the tabloids, indeed, might well have felt disposed to spell soccer in a more meaningful manner ... Socker). Souness, like

166

Manchester United manager Alex Ferguson, has fallen foul of the media on occasion – and, like Ferguson and Kenny Dalglish, discovered that one team in particular tended to give him grief. The team in question: Wimbledon.

In the spring of 1988, the Dons shocked Liverpool and their fans by going to Wembley as the underdogs and walking away with the FA Cup. In fact, Wimbledon scored other notable victories over Liverpool to the point where, for a considerable spell, they became regarded as their bogey-team. To the credit of both Souness and Dalglish, neither man slated Wimbledon – on the contrary, each gave the Dons due praise for having managed to keep up with the Joneses of the Premiership (and that is not intended to be a reference to the formidable Vinny).

Manchester United have good cause to remember and reflect upon Wimbledon, too, because they were involved in an exceptionally-contentious confrontation with the Dons. Yet Alex Ferguson, like Souness and Dalglish, has admitted that in many ways he could not help but admire the tremendous team spirit engendered by the London outfit. No 'southern softies', they ... As Ferguson said, Wimbledon have long enjoyed 'knocking the big clubs for six', and it was a match at Wimbledon which left Manchester United with such unhappy memories, not least because an incident in the tunnel made headline news.

The referee on that occasion was the experienced Brian Hill (who, in the 1988 FA Cup final, ruled out a Peter Beardsley goal and then conceded that, with hindsight, he might well have applied the advantage rule instead of having blown for a Wimbledon foul on the Liverpool player). When Manchester United and Wimbledon tangled, a few minutes from the end of the match, Brian Hill blew his whistle and summoned a senior police officer – it was learned later that the referee had requested a police escort should be available at the final whistle to ensure that he was able to leave the field in safety. Another referee, Keith Cooper, was to acknowledge that he took similar precautions after having encountered problems with fans elsewhere. In this instance, Brian Hill made his exit without any apparent problem, while United's players (having lost 2–1 and seen former team-mate Terry Gibson score both goals) went over to salute the fans who had travelled from Manchester.

It was when the players were walking up the tunnel on their way to the dressing-room that trouble erupted, as United's Viv Anderson and Wimbledon's John Fashanu came up against each other, and the next thing that happened, according to United's manager, was that 'all hell was let loose', with various players becoming involved. Meanwhile, Anderson lay unconscious. Naturally, there was a Football Association commission to determine who, if anyone, was to blame for the fracas, and the commission in its wisdom decided that Fashanu should be suspended for three matches and fined £2,000, while Anderson did not escape scot-free . . . he was fined £750, and suspended for one game.

It was recorded that the commission was satisfied that Fashanu had struck Anderson, but that the United player had directed comments at the Wimbledon striker which were 'insulting and improper'. Like Vinny Jones, Fashanu is regarded as someone who, in his time, has done considerable work for charity, but while Alex Ferguson was perfectly willing to give Fash full credit for this, it didn't prevent United's manager from claiming that when Fashanu later put his name to a newspaper article striving to justify himself, he was 'totally out of order'. Which brings me to two more newspaper articles (one of which appeared under Fashanu's name) containing references to Manchester United star Eric Cantona. I picked up a tabloid one morning to read that Fashanu was urging the Frenchman, in effect, to 'clean up your act', and that piece appeared several months before the notorious Selhurst Park affair. I must admit that my immediate reaction was to wonder if football's powers-that-be would take stock and come down hard on Fash for the comments he had made.

In fact, I spoke to someone who has close connections with the Professional Footballers' Association, and when we discussed the Fashanu article, I was told: 'When I read what

Fash had said, I thought it was a bit heavy...' The Football Association obviously thought so, as well, because a fine of £6,000 was imposed on the former Wimbledon player, and some months later, his comments were recalled as the Selhurst Park incident blew up.

It was pointed out that when it came to considering the likely punishment for Eric Cantona, Fashanu had been made to pay up for having spoken up. And as the arguments about Cantona raged, occupying acres of newspaper space, the Frenchman became more and more the subject of debate – so much so that his name even figured in the newspaper leader columns. Through the course of the past half-century, a handful of Frenchmen have been accorded such treatment in the British Press ... there was the aged and ailing Marshal Pétain, a hero of the First World War; there was the shifty-eyed Pierre Laval, considered by many to have been a traitor to his native land during World War Two; there was the unsmiling, arrogant-looking General Charles de Gaulle; there was president Francois Mitterrand; there was Jacques Delors; and there was Monsieur Cantona, the enigmatic footballer.

The *Daily Mail* leader column said of him: 'Hugely gifted, a joy to watch, a hero to his fans. Cantona is all of these. He is also a disgrace to football and civilised behaviour. Cantona may not care tuppence about letting down the youngsters who idolise him. Indeed, is anyone in football really bothered about setting an example? Yobbery is commonplace and often excused. The game is awash with stories of bungs and bribes (John Fashanu, along with Bruce Grobbelaar and Hans Segers, was to find himself caught up in bribery allegations). Rich clubs like Manchester United cynically exploit their supporters with unnecessary – but highly profitable – changes of strip ... If our national game is to salvage its reputation, Cantona must be banned. Not for a season, but for life. Anything less would be a craven surrender to the power of money.'

Tough talk, indeed; and one of Cantona's fellow-professionals, Liverpool's record-priced defender, Phil Babb, also went into print as he contributed his thoughts in a full-page article in the *Irish Times* under the heading *PHIL BABB'S NOTEBOOK*. The article was acknowledged to have been ghost-written; nevertheless, it was a remarkable piece – not least because of the use in an Irish family newspaper of the notorious F-word.

The article appeared on Saturday, January 28, 1995 (three days after the kung-fu affair at Selhurst Park, and hard on the heels of the Merseyside derby game), and one intriguing aspect was that before he got to Monsieur Cantona, Babb reflected upon a magazine interview which two of his team-mates, Robbie Fowler and Steve McManaman, had given. What they were quoted as having said was picked up by some of the tabloids and, according to the *Phil Babb's Notebook*, 'by football standards, it was quite risqué'. Babb was quoted: 'Shanks (Bill Shankly) is turning in his grave, apparently. Nobody knows what Roy Evans (Liverpool's manager) is thinking about it all. He seems in good form. He's always like that, though. Maybe some knuckles will get rapped. Maybe there'll be a fine or two. Nobody seems too concerned. The lads at the centre of it all are saying they've been stitched up. I'm getting a bit of flak because I know the guys from the magazine.

'I'm asking Steve and Robbie if they said what the magazine says they said. Well, yes, they did, but ... If you don't want them to print it, don't say it, I tell them. You know what journalists are like, you know a magazine like *Loaded* isn't interested in the 'two cats and two kids' stuff. So here I am on derby day giving out advice on how to handle the media ... Anyway, I tell the guys that if they don't want it printed, they shouldn't say it. Then we're off doing a couple of light sprints, and before they can come back and ask me if I've got any qualifications for giving media lessons, we're off on the bus to the hotel.'

So there was Phil Babb, dispensing words of wisdom about the media ... and then, right at the end of the broadsheet page came another 10 paragraphs which, to say the least, were bound to cause some comment, since they concerned

Eric Cantona, and what had happened at Selhurst Park a few days previously ... and at Old Trafford in the final League match of season 1993–94, when Babb was playing for Coventry City against Manchester United.

On the United-Crystal Palace game at Selhurst Park, Babb was quoted: 'I thought Cantona was so far out of order. He's had a suspect temperament that everyone has known about, but he's overstepped the mark in a big way this time. The FA have given him 14 days to come up with a reply, and I'm looking forward to hearing it.' Then followed some tongue-in-cheek comments. The article continued: 'When you look at the incident, it's so amazing that it's easy to forget this guy has just been sent off for lashing out at a player on the pitch. So there's two incidents. He's frustrated, he's got a bit of abuse, like we all get, and he's lashed out at a spectator, jumped right over the mark.' Then came the punchline: 'If it were up to me, I'd ban him from English football for good. I mean, you go out to a park game on a Sunday and you see a local league match and, if some of the lads have a fight, they're looking at getting big bans.

'Guys at that level who keep getting into trouble, get banned for five years sometimes. You can't have another law for professionals. Nobody is watching those guys in their amateur leagues, they aren't role models. They're just run-of-the-mill lads playing for fun, but the suspensions they get for fighting each other are unreal. For hitting a spectator, it's hard to imagine what punishment they'd be given. Then you have a guy who has captained his country. In terms of world soccer he's a megastar, and he's just gone and completely flipped his lid. No matter who you are, you can't be allowed to get away with that.' Babb then switched to the United-Coventry City match at Old Trafford.

'I met Eric in the way most defenders meet Eric, in the last game of the season last year. He'd already done his suspensions and had the Moncur incident at Swindon, and this was the last game of the season and United had already won the League.' Babb reckoned 'there wasn't anything building up between us in the game' – then claimed that as he was closing

Cantona down, the Frenchman 'lifted his studs as I stretched for the ball.'

Babb also made the claim that 'I could have had my career ended' and he demanded to know: 'How can a manager defend that?' He said that Alex Ferguson 'comes out and says he doesn't know what all the fuss is about. They're saying that if the ref. didn't see anything and no player has complained, then forget about it.' And in one pungent and extraordinary sentence (extraordinary to me, at any rate), Babb declared: 'To be honest, I heard that and I just thought, "Fuck off."' He also argued: 'There is no justification for sticking by him (Cantona) ... I can't see Cantona playing in this country again. What sort of stick can he expect from supporters around the country if he plays again? He's going to need a machine-gun to keep them off his back in the future.' Well, Cantona did make a comeback, in October 1995, when the opposition on parade at Old Trafford was ... Liverpool, whose team included Phil Babb.

Babb's article offered the view that while it had been shaping up for a good title race, 'now, maybe, Manchester United's season is in ruins' – a prediction which turned out to be bang on the mark, as United failed to retain either the title trophy or the FA Cup. Babb further commented in the *Irish Times*: 'You can't have one guy who is bigger than football because of his talent. It doesn't look like I'll be seeing him (Cantona) again for quite a while. His skill will be missed, but that's the price football has to pay.' The final line on the page read: 'In an interview with Tom Humphries.' And I must admit that I wondered if Phil Babb had vetted every word which had appeared under his name on that particular page of the paper.

I also wondered about the reactions not only of Monsieur Cantona, but of Manchester United, Liverpool and the Professional Footballers' Association, once Babb's reported comments had been digested – they might well not be familiar with the *Irish Times*, but *The People* newspaper picked up the story and ran it boldly across the back page under a by-line which read: 'Exclusive, by Frank Johnstone.'

172

I reflected upon a conversation I had had with a member of the Manchester United staff after Cantona had arrived at Old Trafford. The Frenchman apparently did have an interpreter, but my contact told me: 'I think Eric understands English better than he lets on.' So it was logical to assume that he would have understood *The People* story, had he seen that particular issue of the paper ... on which I had once worked, along with Frank Johnstone, whom I have known for more than 30 years.

I decided to check with Frank about the story, so I rang him at his home in Ireland. He was quite open about what had happened and how *The People* had learned about the Phil Babb story – Frank himself had spotted the article in the *Irish Times* and informed *The People* about the contents, as they concerned Eric Cantona. Hence the story which led the back page of the English tabloid on the Sunday morning. And *The People* story kicked off: 'Liverpool star Phil Babb wants Eric Cantona banned from English football for life. And in a blistering attack on Manchester United, he claims boss Alex Ferguson has let him get away with murder. Babb's comments will infuriate United fans, especially as they come from one of their arch-enemies. The Republic of Ireland international, a £3.7 million signing from Coventry last September, is the first Premier League "pro" to publicly attack Cantona, who sensationally assaulted a Crystal Palace fan on Wednesday.

' "If it were up to me, I'd ban him from English football for good," said Babb. "It would be a shame to lose him from the game, but football can survive without him." ' *The People* story went on to say that Babb claimed Cantona could have caused him to miss the 1994 World Cup Finals ... 'I could have had my career ended.' According to Babb, 'the *Daily Mirror* got the stills from the TV coverage and they caught it perfectly. He's got six studs slap-bang on my knee, and the ball is two feet away.'

When I talked to Frank Johnstone, he told me he had not spoken to Babb and that the player was claiming – with perfect truth – that he had never spoken to *The People*. So far

173

as I am aware, that story died a death without any action having been taken over it . . . except in the case of one person. Because, although I suspected (indeed, I was virtually certain) that neither Liverpool nor Manchester United would wish to fan the flames of controversy any further, with Cantona being so obviously deep in trouble over the Selhurst Park incident, I also felt that some comment was called for from someone who held a position of authority in football. So I contacted Gordon Taylor, the chief executive of the Professional Footballers' Association.

Gordon, whom I have known for years, is highly respected in the game – at one time, a few years ago, he might well have become a leading light on the Football League side – and I felt sure that he would listen to my questions . . . the first of which was: 'Has your association had any reaction from anyone about the comments attributed to Phil Babb?' Gordon answered: 'Yes, the matter was referred to me . . .' By Manchester United, by Eric Cantona, by Liverpool? 'By a supporter . . .' As yet, there had been no reaction from United or from Liverpool, while as for Cantona, 'at the moment, Eric has enough problems without adding fuel to the flames.'

What else did Gordon Taylor say? This: 'Everyone is entitled to his opinion, and everyone knows his (Cantona's) temperament has let him down. Since everyone is entitled to his opinion, Phil Babb is entitled to his. John Fashanu made some points about Cantona – that is the nature of the game, and that is free speech.' In fact, as I have said, Fashanu's comments in a newspaper had cost him a £6,000 fine – a substantial amount to pay for 'free speech.' – as I am sure Gordon would have conceded.

Gordon did add, when we were talking, a comment that 'the whole game condemns what Cantona did, and it would be naive to think that all professionals would lock arms and be totally in support of him.' As for anticipating Manchester United's likely reaction, the chief executive of the PFA told me: 'I imagine United would prefer to let things go' . . . and I wasn't disposed to argue with that assumption. Thus the carefully-constructed comments of the chief executive of the

PFA, and I, for one, could understand his desire not to spark off further controversy.

So far as I am aware, the comments attributed to Phil Babb were never called into question by the Football Association – though he did suffer suspension himself, after having been sent off in a game against Nottingham Forest, for having brought down Steve Stone. Babb thus became the first Liverpool player to have been given marching orders during season 1994–95, although it was recorded that there had been 'much debate' as to whether or not the decision of referee Gary Willard to dismiss Babb had been justified. Whether or not Liverpool hauled Babb up and took action over his newspaper comments about Cantona is another matter ... I certainly never saw anything to suggest that this had happened. However, football clubs do tend to try to keep their business to themselves.

Going back to that final League match of season 1993–94 at Old Trafford – the game which prompted Babb to go public in the *Irish Times* – I checked with a former Liverpool stalwart of the 1970's, Phil Neal, who later became the manager of Bolton Wanderers and then Coventry City. Phil told me immediately: 'Oh, yes – I remember it well enough; in fact, I can see the incident now.' Neal and I were then talking some nine months after the match in question, so what happened had clearly stuck in his mind.

He said: 'Manchester United had won the title ... it was the big presentation day. Had it been mid-season, more might have been made of the incident. Phil went in to nick the ball and Cantona went in very late, with his studs up. Fortunately, Phil Babb wasn't hurt.' Well, Babb was certainly forthright in the views he expressed about the Frenchman, although I cannot imagine that the powers-that-be at both Anfield and Old Trafford would be too happy at the manner in which the Liverpool defender had gone public. And while Babb might ponder upon the likely reaction of rival fans, should Cantona reappear on an English football field, I wondered, also, how the supporters of Manchester United would react to Phil Babb, the next time he went out to play for his club at Old

Trafford. In the event, the match ended honours even, at 2–2 (Cantona made one goal, and scored the equaliser from a penalty) – and there were no reports of trouble.

Chapter 17

THE GEORGE AND ERIC SHOW

'I would pay to go and watch Eric Cantona play.' – Former
United star GEORGE BEST.

HOW, you might wonder, would Sir Matt Busby have
handled Eric Cantona? When Denis Law issued what virtually was an ultimatum – 'More money, or I want to go' –
Busby told the world that the club was bigger than the
individual, and promptly put Law on the transfer list. It
was Denis who did the backing down, in the end ... he
actually signed a private letter of apology to the club while,
in turn, Busby did reward him later as he informed Law
(also privately) that he would be getting a new contract
which carried with it an increase in pay. Thus was honour
satisfied.

When it came to George Best, Matt handled his wayward
Irish star with kid gloves at times, while at others he 'played
hell' with him, as he told me. Matt, indeed, confessed to me
that more than once George gave him sleepless nights ... just
as, no doubt, Eric Cantona has given Alex Ferguson one or
two moments of insomnia. If Cantona is worth the kind of
money clubs pay today (reputedly more than £10,000 a
WEEK), what would Best command in these affluent times
for footballers who reach the top? And if Cantona now,
having joined United for around £1 million, were to bring

them more than five times that sum, what would Best, in his pomp today, have brought his old club? It's a fair bet that people would be talking in terms of more than £15 million ... after all, that's the kind of money which was bandied about when the talk was of Ryan Giggs becoming a target for the Italians.

Giggs and Cantona are playing in a different age to that of Best, and United chairman Martin Edwards has spoken of the abuse players face (the Football Association's Graham Kelly also echoed this) when they play on the grounds of opponents. Edwards declared: 'It is becoming increasingly difficult for players not to respond. Football has become very provocative.' He could say that again; and his comments were confirmed by the *Daily Mail*'s chief football writer, Neil Harman, who summed up: 'What he (Edwards) didn't add, for fear his words might be used against his club, is that United are far and away the most-hated team in the country.' Then Harman asked: 'Why?'

His answer: 'There are many plausible explanations ... the size of the club, the extent of others' jealousy, the fact that referees seem besotted by them, the indulgence of the manager towards players who should be publicly slapped down and the arrogance with which they often go about their business.' There was a comment, too, by one of the Labour Party's former big guns, Roy Hattersley – a noted Sheffield Wednesday supporter – that when Cantona joined United he was moving to 'a club noted for its phenomenal success, its astronomical salaries and the collective arrogance of its players. Cantona fitted in exactly.'

And so to the manager who, it was claimed, had battled in the boardroom to persuade his directors that the volatile French ace in the pack should not be jettisoned and put up for sale ... Ferguson said Cantona was 'the best player I have ever worked with', a man who, perhaps, bottled up his emotions 'to the point where they are liable to burst out disastrously in matches ... Everyone knows there is that side to his nature' – but 'his worst offences are certainly not premeditated. It is a total loss of control, like that horrible

178

explosion at Selhurst Park. You never see a trace of that Cantona on the training ground. I know he had a record of warring at his French clubs, but here I sometimes think he is too quiet and unemotional. He can go out on the field and do something diabolical, something that nobody in his right mind could condone. It nearly always happens when he has decided he has been wronged and the referee is doing nothing about it. Then he resolves to exact his own justice, which is madness.'

Yet, having also admitted that Cantona's reaction was 'usually so blatant that it is instantly self-destructive', United's manager indicated that he was prepared to assume the responsibility for rehabilitating the Frenchman. 'I intend to keep working on him and with him . . . I have to impress upon him that there will be players and teams (and what about the fans of opposing clubs?) who will set out to wind him up. He simply has to be prepared for it, and accept it. That's what I will be working on with him during his period of suspension. I still believe he could have an important role at Manchester United.'

Ferguson was candid enough to admit, also, that 'in the early days, I had my card marked and was told I was taking a risk'. He added: 'But you gamble on every player. You may as well gamble on one who lifts people out of their seats (something Everton manager Joe Royle was to say about Andrei Kanchelskis, the winger he signed from United). Sometimes he just boils over, but that kind of temperament makes him a great player. Eric's main problem is he is so honest, and sees injustice as the biggest crime of all.'

Possibly Cantona saw the two-week gaol sentence which was originally imposed upon him as yet another example of injustice – certainly United chairman Martin Edwards led the chorus of complaint against it, while Cantona's agent, Jean-Jacques Amorfini, declared: 'His lawyers advised him to plead guilty, and that's the result. They're all out to get him . . . I can tell you, he won't stay in that country a lot longer.' Well, it was touch and go for a while, as Cantona retreated to France and Alex Ferguson followed, to talk him into returning to these shores. According to Martin Edwards, the Frenchman had been punished three times for one offence. Be that as it may, Cantona – like George Best before him – could seldom, if ever, escape from the glare of publicity, good or bad during his career at what everyone associated with Manchester United (not least, their ardent fans) believed to be the biggest club in the country, if not the whole wide world.

Considering the former United idol (Best) and the Frenchman who became a 1990's cult hero, it seems that there are certain parallels – and, of course, some differences. Once upon a time, Best acquired a house in the Cheshire countryside, and people travelled from miles around, simply to stand and stare, hoping that they would catch a glimpse of their idol in what had become a goldfish bowl. In the case of Monsieur Cantona, he acquired a dwelling not too far from Old Trafford – something which, according to one observer, was quite a clever move on the player's part because, by choosing such a locality (in contrast to some of his team-mates who resided in Cheshire's stockbroker belt), Cantona had given folk the chance to feel that he was just like one of them. Which, of course, he wasn't, and isn't. How could he be, when someone like George Best was saying of him: 'I would pay to go and watch Eric Cantona play'?

One journalist declared that Cantona could be capable of being 'a genius and an idiot' in the space of 45 minutes; another phrased it rather differently . . . 'We need that kind of genius; we need him back very quickly.' Yes, in spite of the fact that as Cantona was being charged with misconduct and having brought the game into disrepute, the Football Association's chief executive, Graham Kelly, was going on television and saying, for all to hear: 'What happened last night (at Selhurst Park) was a stain on our game.'

The Cantona philosophy was reflected by various quotations from the great man himself . . . 'I don't give a damn' (this was before the events at Selhurst Park) and 'I don't have to justify myself to journalists or TV.' One compliment from a manager, he claimed, was worth more than the offerings of any old journalist. And one journalist admitted that 'people can't understand what makes him tick.' Cantona was 'a one-off ... I don't think anyone in this country has experienced someone like him.' They were saying the same sort of thing about George, the genius at Manchester United during the 1960's, as they reported that Eric Cantona had made his professional bow for Auxerre at the age of 17, and that his transfer to Marseille came about for a French record fee of £2 million.

The Channel Islands, of course, lie between England and France, and it was a professional footballer from those parts, the Blackburn Rovers and England international, Graeme le Saux, who elevated Eric Cantona unhesitatingly, as he declared the Frenchman to be 'the best player in his position in the League ... he can change games in an instant.' Cantona certainly changed things in a match against the Rovers at Old Trafford when he headed United into the lead with a wonder goal ... and he certainly changed things when he got his marching orders at Selhurst Park, then made his two-footed lunge at a spectator. Le Saux declared, with absolute truth, that 'in the history books we will all look back, and he will be one of the greats.' Footballing greats, Le Saux meant.

Cantona, described by a journalist as 'a larger-than-life cult figure', was quoted as saying that, given the choice, he would change nothing ... 'Whatever people say or do won't make me change.' And after the Football Association had decided to extend his suspension, he remained an enigma, giving no hint as to what he might be feeling, even though he was said to have felt remorse and expressed his apologies for his action. If anything could be read from his expression, it appeared to amount almost to a look of haughty disdain.

As Matt Busby told me, George Best caused him problems time and again, and he would haul the Irishman up after yet another troublesome affair. When you talked to Best after a match, his demeanour was modest, his speech was low-key, and it seemed as if butter wouldn't melt in his mouth. In short, you couldn't help but like him. And Matt told me how,

181

when he had a face-to-face with Best, George would promise: 'It won't happen again, boss.' And it didn't ... for a while. Best on Eric Cantona, with the hindsight of his own experiences: 'The word genius is often abused. But when you look at Cantona, you see someone who doesn't have to work at it. Someone like Kevin Keegan had to work hard at his game, week in, week out. I couldn't explain how or why I did things ... Eric can't explain how or why he does it.'

Cantona, talking about managers: 'I have the most admiration for the manager who wins ... the one who manages to win without restricting players and shouting.' And on Maradona: 'For me, he is an inspiration. He has got it all. For me, he is the greatest.' Cantona was to join with Maradona in the summer of 1995, as the star from South America sought to band his fellow-professionals together.

Back to George Best: 'I hate comparisons with myself. I have had a lot of run-ins with the Press, and my mad moments on the field, as well ... similar to Eric. The pressure is something he has to live with. It's a very difficult side of being in the public eye. I still have it, 25 years after I finished playing.' The media attention on the day Eric made his Old Trafford comeback was something which might well have been reserved for royalty. When it was suggested to Best that, privately, Alex Ferguson must have asked himself if he had 'indulged' Cantona too much, the Irishman recalled: 'Busby took a lot of stick because they said he didn't know how to handle me. But he did it privately.'

Cantona on scoring goals: 'A good goal is important, it is beautiful.' And 'what pleases me most is when a team plays to win ... even in defeat, Johan Cruyff is great.' It was 'better to lose 7–3 than to go for a no-score draw and lose 1-0.' And when he was voted the Players' Player of the Year: 'I owe my success to Manchester United.' Cantona confessed that 'everyone makes silly mistakes ... I have done something silly, and the critics were against me. I am proud when they talk about me, whether it's good or bad.' The Frenchman was speaking before the events of Selhurst Park, and while Manchester United said he regretted his actions there and that he would continue his career with them, there was an air of uncertainty, even as he prepared for his comeback, that life would ever go on in the way it had done before all the trouble erupted. It was reported that 'no one has yet managed to penetrate the mystery of Cantona ... only one person knows, for sure.'

That kind of thing was being said about the Irish genius, George Best, during Busby's days as manager at Old Trafford – as a matter of interest, Matt once told me he believed George should have become the first millionaire footballer in these islands ... as to whether or not he did, neither I nor Busby had any idea. Best had arrived at United as an unknown kid from Belfast who had cost not a penny in the transfer market; on the other hand, Cantona was a £1 million investment by United, as befitted his status as an established international. Best still had to make his mark, but it didn't take him long to do just that – as I have related elsewhere, Harry Gregg discovered this when he put young George to the test during a training session. It turned out to be the other way round, with Best putting the 'keeper to the test! And, like Harry Gregg, Matt Busby swiftly realised Best was 'something special' – though when we discussed the controversial Irishman, Matt shook his head more than once as he smiled somewhat ruefully while reflecting upon past events.

It was United's scout in Northern Ireland, Bob Bishop, who first spotted the talent of Best, and in quick time he steered the youngster in the direction of Old Trafford. George left Belfast when he left school, arriving at United in 1963, and by the time he had reached the venerable age of 17 he was not only a first-teamer, but an international (he was just 17 years and 328 days old when he donned the green jersey for the first time), and while he never made it to the Finals of the World Cup, he gave millions untold pleasure as he demonstrated his God-given skills. Busby told me how George 'raised the roof' with his marvellous ability – and, as he shook his head yet again, Matt also told me: 'He raised my blood pressure, too, at times.' Like Cantona, Best was inspirational; in United's European Cup-winning season he was joint top

183

League marksman, with 28 goals ... and he was voted European Footballer of the Year. Proof, indeed, (if any were needed), of the esteem in which he was held as a player who excited and entertained.

He toured 'down under' with United in 1967, when it was recorded that he had once been 'a shy, retiring young Irish boy who spent most of his evenings listening to records in his digs after training in the day with Manchester United.' The report continued: 'Now he has become the darling of the gossip columnists.' Maybe Eric Cantona didn't quite become the 'darling' of the gossip columnists, but he certainly generated as much publicity as did Best during his time at Old Trafford. Cantona has fallen foul of referees several times since he joined United and, in fairness, he has taken his share of whacks from opposing players – as did Best. There was one notable occasion when the man in the middle made it clear to a tough-tackling defender that he must desist from giving Best such rugged treatment – only to hear the aggrieved defender protest: 'What else do you expect me to do? He's making me look a right idiot!'

Like Cantona, Best made monkeys of defenders, and he scored some fantastic goals. He showed courage, too – such as the time he went to hospital after a car crash, then walked out to catch the team coach for a match at Newcastle. Best donned his United jersey at St James's Park, then went out and scored as his side drew, 2-2; what's more, he produced a scintillating performance ... just as he did on tour in New Zealand when United rattled in the goals and Best, dazzling, delighted the 20,000 crowd as he struck a hat-trick. At one stage, one of the New Zealand officials sat holding his head in his hands, muttering to himself, 'Oh, no ... he's got it again...' He was referring to the fact that, once more, Best had claimed possession of the ball.

Perhaps Best's most impressive display came against Benfica – not in the 1968 European Cup Final, but in Lisbon's Stadium of Light. Matt Busby certainly rated it so as he told me: 'George turned on his own, distinctive brand of magic.' There was one move where Best collected the ball, checked as

184

he pulled it back, then dummied before slotting the ball past the 'keeper. It was recorded that 'every time he got the ball, he inspired United'. They defeated Benfica 5–1, and afterwards it was reported that there was an incident concerning Best.

'A man came at him with a knife – to hack off a lock of hair as a souvenir.' And during the 90 minutes of match action, Best had the girl fans among his audience screaming 'El Beatle! El Beatle!' On his return to Manchester, his Beatle-cut hairstyle was topped by a sombrero, as the cameras flashed and photographed him yet again.

Not every trick came off for George Best, of course – and, come to that, not every trick was witnessed by an adoring public. By the same token, while Alex Ferguson has said that Cantona poses no problems in training, there were times when Best gave training a miss ... and he also missed trains. However, it was during a training session that George had even Matt Busby drooling over his skills, as he toe-ended the ball against an opponent's shin, collected the rebound and drilled the ball past the goalkeeper. 'A deliberate piece of artistry' was how Busby summed it up to me.

Off the park, like Cantona, Best could make money almost as easily as he seemed to earn his wages at Old Trafford, and in Ken Stanley (who, for a spell, was also the official agent for the England team) he had someone who, I am convinced, really took the time and trouble to look after his interests. But Ken told me of one occasion when, after he had worked long and hard on the player's behalf, George failed to put in the scheduled appearance. And Ken Stanley admitted to me: 'Nothing George did would surprise me...' According to former United team-mate Alan Gowling, there was 'a conflict of personalities' between Best and Bobby Charlton. 'Bobby was the epitome of the professional, George much more the instinctive footballer who could turn on the flash of genius. Bobby believed that players needed to be totally dedicated; George had a different viewpoint and, in his own fashion, he proved it.' Not unlike Monsieur Cantona, one might say – a player who has never been accused of giving less than 100 per cent, in training or in match action. And neither was George Best – even if he didn't turn up in time to catch the train when United were *en route* to London for a game against Chelsea.

This was something which, according to Gowling, 'Bobby could neither understand nor stomach' ... yet, again in Gowling's own words, the talent of Best made him 'the best all-round footballer I have ever seen.' Another observer wrote: 'The sight of Best's frail-looking figure conjuring the ball away from a rival defender with magic dexterity is enough to send any soccer fan away from the ground bubbling with excitement. Not even the brilliance of Law or Charlton can push the young Irishman into the background when United are playing.'

Cantona, of course, is no frail-looking figure – he stands more than six feet tall and, where Best was willowy, the Frenchman appears to be as strong as an oak tree. But, like Best, Cantona can send the fans home bubbling with excitement – or, of course, arguing the toss about him. If Alex Ferguson was (and is) faced with problems as to the best method of handling Cantona, he can reflect that this was no more than Matt Busby experienced when it came to maintaining a grip on young George Best ... who, in the World Cup year of 1966, was such a shining light for Manchester United. That year, as most people will instantly recall, was a great year for English football, because we won the World Cup – and, as a fairly recent advert proclaimed, it was a great year, also, because it was in 1966 that Eric Cantona was born.

Football clubs prefer to wash any dirty linen in private, and Busby used the privacy of his office for those face-to-face confrontations with an erring Best. It was there that Matt would 'play hell with him', at times, and adjure the wayward Irishman not to stray again. In response, George would assure Busby that 'it won't happen again' ... just as, so we were informed, Monsieur Cantona had pledged not to transgress again, after having expressed remorse over the Selhurst Park affair. According to Busby, Best was 'a jumble of contradictions' – a phrase which some might apply to

186

Cantona. Busby's theory was (though he couldn't be certain) that 'fame possibly came too soon for George to handle.'

Once, as George was recovering in hospital after a cartilage operation, he was visited by team-mate Harry Gregg, who (with Busby's blessing) advised his fellow-countryman to reflect upon the way things had gone, and to get his life back on the rails. Harry told me that George admitted he would dearly love to do that thing ... but, as Harry had to acknowledge, it wasn't as easy as that. Like Eric Cantona in a later era, Best was the constant focus of media attention and lived his life in a goldfish bowl.

Busby once advised his Irish star to find a nice girl and settle down to married life. Matt awoke one morning to read in the papers that George had indeed got himself a girl and that, apparently, there was serious talk of a wedding. It seemed that George had met the young lady during a club trip to Scandinavia, and when Matt taxed him about it, he was informed: 'You're always on at me about settling down and getting married ... that's what I'm going to do!' To which Busby replied that he didn't expect George to talk about getting wed to a lass he'd known for only a couple of weeks or so. Not long afterwards, that particular romance was dying a death.

Busby told me that 'as a footballer, George was the one who gave me the most enjoyment', and I would go along with that verdict 100 per cent. He was the finest all-round footballer I have ever seen – he had that special talent which, to quote Busby, 'put him in a class apart', and those who were privileged to see Best in full, flowing action were often entranced and will surely never forget his skills. The fans of today, no doubt – and they probably never even saw Best in full flight – would claim that Eric Cantona, too, is 'in a class apart' ... when he concentrates on playing sublime and skilful football.

Sammy McIlroy was truly the last of the players to come off the Old Trafford assembly line which produced the famous Busby Babes and, like Best, he arrived as a young innocent from Belfast. However, he was so unhappy during his early days here that he took every possible chance to leg it for home – and he would have stayed there, too, had his Dad not told him to get himself back to Manchester United, where his future lay. Sammy was labelled 'the new George Best' and, like George, he was spotted by Bob Bishop.

While Best became closely acquainted with the big-city, bright lights of Manchester, McIlroy found that 'life in the big city was all too much for me'; and, perhaps (at first, anyway), George Best, too, had the feeling that it was 'all too much' for him to handle ... the contrast between Belfast – which has a small-town atmosphere – then the adulation of the multitude of fans. Sammy admitted to me that he often felt alone in Manchester, and this is understandable, given the fact that he was young, on his own for long hours, and homesick. He made his United debut in front of 63,000 fans, in a derby game against Manchester City, and he was playing in the same side as Best, who had been his idol back home. It was Best who provided the pass for McIlroy to score, Best who later treated his fellow-countryman to the bottle of champagne which George had promised, should Sammy hit the target in that match. Sammy can also recall an occasion when Best's memory was not quite as good...

It happened when McIlroy was picked to play for Northern Ireland (the match was at Hull), and he and Best arranged to meet at the railway station and travel together. 'George told me not to worry about getting the tickets for the train...' Naturally, Sammy was keyed up for this, his debut game at international level, and he arrived early at the station. He waited and waited and, as time passed, he got into a bit of a panic – because there was no sign of George. Eventually, he dashed to the booking office and bought his ticket. On arrival at Hull, he was buttonholed by team-boss Terry Neill, who demanded to know where Best was.

Hesitantly, the international new boy began to explain what the arrangement had been; and, of course, like Neill, he was wondering where George Best had got to. This time, however, it wasn't a case of the missing genius ... it transpired, when Best finally did make his appearance, that he had completely forgotten about the arrangement to travel with Sammy by train. Instead, he had travelled by car – and, naturally, he was profuse in his apologies to McIlroy.

When I talked to Sammy about Best, he told me: 'I always liked him. George was one on his own ... an enigma in so many ways ... yet I couldn't help but like him, apart from admiring his footballing ability.' I have yet to meet the man who expressed dislike of George Best; even those for whom he posed problems would smile as they shook their heads and find a good word to say on his behalf. However, I can recall the words of a former Northern Ireland captain, the illustrious Danny Blanchflower, brother of Manchester United's Jackie. Danny wrote a column in the *Sunday Express*, and one day he was moved to compose a few thoughts about Best.

Like this: 'Already he has won recognition as one of the most brilliant young players in the world. It's hard to believe that one boy can be blessed with so much talent, and that fate will not take some sort of quick revenge on him.' Fate did indeed play its part in the life of George Best ... just as fate has played its part in the life of Eric Cantona. When the French enigma had been banned from football for months in 1995, a writer from Dublin offered the view that Eric could make a living outside football. 'I am not being facetious in suggesting that Eric should think seriously about going into film-making – he is obviously adept at martial arts and is extremely marketable. He has the natural arrogance and machismo of a Schwarzenegger.' A verdict with which Cantona himself might well agree.

CHAPTER 18

THE REFEREE'S REPORT

'I reported Don Revie under Rule 25 of the Football Association's own code, and it was under this rule that sent in a report on Eric Cantona. The incident was clear enough, and Rule 25 says you MUST report any instance of misconduct; but the Football Association took no action.' – Former Football League referee PETER RHODES.

ERIC Cantona and Manchester United probably don't know this – not a lot of people do – but the Frenchman would have been hauled up before the Football Association on yet another misconduct charge, had a certain former top-class League referee had his way. What is more, this one-time referee himself once gave a football fan 'a belting' which felled the fan and left him lying unconscious. The Cantona business had nothing to do with the now-infamous affair at Selhurst Park in January, 1995; this incident had happened 16 days earlier, at Sheffield United's ground. What the ex-referee saw there prompted him to put Cantona 'on report' to the Football Association.

Somewhat to my surprise, when I spoke to the former referee, Peter Rhodes, he expressed a certain sympathy with Cantona – not about the Bramall Lane incident or the Selhurst Park business, but because of the constant media attention the Frenchman had had to endure in the weeks that followed. What surprised me was that the sympathy came from a no-nonsense Yorkshireman with a record of having been one of the strictest referees in the business ... ask Malcolm Allison, Denis Law, Ian St John, Billy Bingham, or Jack Charlton. Rhodes it was who, after having handled a match at Manchester City's Maine Road ground, reported Allison – as a result, Allison was fined and banned from the touchline for a spell.

In the case of Ian St John, Rhodes braved the wrath of the Anfield faithful as he gave the fiery Scot the red-card treatment after Ian had indulged in an act of retaliation (his tormentor also joined him for an early bath). Law and Bingham were given the red-card treatment, too, after having committed offences in games refereed by Rhodes – in Bingham's case, the match between Everton and Brazilian champions Bangu was being played in Manhattan, New York. It was a tournament involving the champion clubs of England and Scotland, and those from countries in Europe and South America. Rhodes told me: 'An opponent fouled Billy, who had beaten his man all ends up. Billy retaliated by planting a perfect uppercut into his opponent's solar- plexus ... so Billy just had to go.'

When it came to Don Revie, then managing Leeds United, Rhodes sent in a critical report to the Football Association after Revie had 'torn into referee Ray Tinkler, who had been handling the game between Leeds and West Brom. An Albion player broke through and the linesman signalled that he was onside, so Tinkler allowed play to run on. West Brom scored a goal – which, Leeds claimed, cost them the title – and afterwards Revie gave the referee some stick, in public. What he should have done was to voice his complaint privately, to the Football Association.' So Revie was hauled up before the Football Association ... and years later, Rhodes took issue with Jack Charlton – he acknowledges that he isn't Big Jack's No. 1 fan, and says: 'I suppose he would say the same about me.' Rhodes recalled being at a function where Jack was billed to speak, and 'he got stuck into me almost as soon as he'd been introduced. He told his audience it had been suggested to him that Peter Rhodes had been the most influential referee in England since the war – adding, "If you believe that, you'll believe anything." So far as I was concerned, Jack was in deadly earnest when he said his piece, and I imagine that at the back of his mind was the time I had put Revie in front of the Football Association commission.'

Which brings us to Denis Law, whom Rhodes first refereed when the Scot was an unknown teenager playing in Huddersfield Town's third team at Beck Lane, Heckmondwike, Yorkshire, and later, when Law had become a record-priced, £115,000 signing by Manchester United. Rhodes told me: 'When I first came across Denis, he had a squint and probably weighed around four stone, wet through. The squint was cured by a simple operation, and he grew to become one of the best strikers in the game. But when he was still making his way with Huddersfield, I refereed their game against Sheffield United, and I've still got an old newspaper cutting which relates how, at one stage, I went across to young Law and told him: 'You and I each have 15 years to go in this game – and this is how I want the game played.'

Rhodes was a tough nut, all right – as a trainee pilot in the RAF, he survived an horrific plane crash which left him hanging, upside-down, half in and half out of the aircraft . . . and, seemingly, with a broken back which would put paid to his ever walking again. He recalled: 'For around 30 to 40 minutes I was unconscious, suspended there, and when I did come to, I realised two things – that a farmer who had seen the plane crash had arrived, and that I was saturated in aviation fuel which was dripping on to me. I could tell I'd broken my back, and it turned out I'd also fractured my skull, while my face was a terrible mess. They got me to hospital, and I was encased in plaster from head to toe – I faced the prospect of being paralysed. But after about a year in hospital, things looked brighter and, gradually, I made a complete recovery.' As he spoke, Rhodes was so matter-of-fact about the whole thing . . . he's not a man for histrionics, as players found when, having recovered enough to walk, he showed he could also run fast enough to keep up with play in

League matches. Indeed, he lined a European Cup final between AC Milan and Benfica, and was on the League list for two decades.

There were times when he was a thorn in the side of authority, too – another blunt-talking Yorkshireman, the then League secretary, Alan Hardaker, had more than one set-to with Rhodes, who was acting in his capacity as chairman of the Association of Football League Referees and Linesmen. Eventually, Rhodes quit the League list to go refereeing in America – which was how he came to be handling the Everton-Bangu game in New York. Home or abroad, Rhodes refereed with authority – 'I meant what I said, and players knew it' – as Denis Law discovered anew after he had returned from Italy. Law himself revealed in later years that his mother had once advised him: 'If anyone kicks you, kick them back' – on the basis that if he didn't, then people would carry on kicking him. Denis admitted, too, that he was sent off three times – once for giving 'a mouthful' to a referee ... whose name happened to be Peter Rhodes.

He told me how it happened: 'Denis had fouled Alan Ball – it was little more than an ankle-tap – and I awarded a free-kick. As I walked alongside Law, I received a very rude reply. Paddy Crerand must have heard this, and he obviously realised what was liable to happen next, because he came across to Denis and told him, "You don't swear at this referee" ... whereupon Denis rapped back, "Why not? – He's a real c..."' At the disciplinary hearing, which took place in a Sheffield hotel, Paddy and Denis said the word used was "coot", and journalists outside the room where the hearing was being held, were amazed to hear laughter ... I had asked both players just what kind of a bird a coot was.'

Rhodes exerted his authority on the pitch, not least with players regarded as tough-nuts. Jack Charlton? 'He was hard, but fair – he wasn't a crippler'. Denis Law? 'He might disregard an opponent who got in the way while he executed a bicycle kick, but he was never a player who would deliberately put his boot up an opponent's backside – and I

193

can think of one former international who would have had no compunction about doing that.'

Rhodes, whose League career ran for 20 years up to 1968, told me: 'It was only during my last five years that I really needed to crack down. These days, you get infinitely more dissent – and players now earn so much money that if they're sent off, there is little or no financial hardship. Some of them treat referees with contempt. For me, the biggest farce was the action of Manchester United – having fined Cantona two weeks' pay (estimated at £20,000) and suspended him, they embarked upon negotiations with him, apparently for an improved contract. I feel great sorrow that United have fallen from their previous high standards of conduct – five players sent off during season 1994–95 gives the impression that they're determined to win and don't give a damn. I feel United have let themselves – and the memory of Matt Busby – down. They may well point out that after more than 25 years in the wilderness, they won the championship, and that is what their fans wanted, but anyone could be forgiven for thinking United have developed a win-at-all-costs attitude.'

Referring to earlier days, Rhodes reckoned that, generally speaking, United were not noted for 'dishing it out', although at various times, some of their players showed they could look after themselves in no uncertain manner. He recalled the late, great Duncan Edwards – 'from my point of view, he could be one of the hardest players to handle . . . he was such a big lad, and when he went into a tackle or embarked on one of those surging runs, opponents needed to look out. It wasn't that Duncan was a dirty player – just that he didn't know his own strength.' Edwards, capped at 18, had claimed 18 international honours when he died, a victim of Munich, at the age of 21. Had he lived, he might well have outstripped Bobby Charlton when it came to collecting international caps. Charlton, like Harry Gregg and Bill Foulkes, survived Munich, and the post-Munich side included signings such as the craggy Maurice Setters and Stan Crowther, while Nobby Stiles later broke through to first-team football.

It was the transfer of Setters to Stoke City that paved the

way for Nobby to make the big breakthrough – not that he didn't have his critics. There were those who claimed Alf Ramsey and Matt Busby should give Nobby the cold-shoulder treatment, but neither manager gave way, and Stiles wound up with a World Cup-winner's medal. Peter Rhodes told me: 'Players like Allenby, Chilton, Gregg, Crerand ... they played the game like the man's game it is, but they weren't necessarily dirty. Crowther and Setters were very hard men, too, but while you had to referee them, they knew how far to go. And while Stiles came in for some stick, at times, he was a little terrier and a very good tackler ... though, again, not cast in the same mould as a couple of other characters I could name. They would "do" an opponent without a second thought – I have to say that neither played for Manchester United.

'Years ago, it was the custom for referees to get a club's games home and away, each season, and for several years on the trot I refereed matches between Manchester United and Sunderland. For some reason I could never explain, those games always seemed to begin in an unpleasant sort of atmosphere, though I can't say I ever experienced trouble. Matt Busby never encouraged the rough stuff in his teams, and Denis Law was the only one I recall having taken to task. Years later, I was in London and happened to bump into Denis – in Harrods, of all places – and when we chatted, I mentioned the game he played in the third team for Huddersfield, in the Yorkshire League. He admitted he didn't remember me then, and while he obviously hadn't forgotten the sending-off incident, he took one point which I made. In fact, he seemed a bit embarrassed when, having been told that he didn't recall my having refereed him in those early days, I reminded him of the old footballing maxim that "the best referees are the ones you don't notice!"'

Like Eric Cantona, Rhodes had a run-in with a football fan. 'It happened as I was coming off the pitch at the end of a game and I realised a gang of louts were heading for me. One of them – he would be about 18 – came at me and, as he did, I didn't wait for him to strike first ... I caught him slap-bang on the side of his jaw and laid him out. His eyeballs began to roll upwards, his legs began to buckle, then he went down and out for the count. Naturally, the League got on to me about what had happened, so I explained just how it was, and said I had treated the man exactly as I would have treated a burglar whom I'd found in my home at midnight. I made no apology for my action, and the whole thing was allowed to die a death.'

By 1995 Football Association spokesman Mike Parry was saying: 'We must not have the situation where referees fear for their safety at Premier League grounds – it's absolutely critical that we avoid any repetition of this at any stadium.' By 'this', he meant what had happened at Ewood Park, where a home fan had raced on to the pitch and had a go at referee Rodger Gifford after Blackburn Rovers' game against Leeds United had ended 1–1, and on a highly-controversial note. Around that time, also, Everton chairman Peter Johnson was defending his manager, Joe Royle, after a defeat at Newcastle where referee David Elleray had dismissed two Everton men and booked five more. It was Elleray who, on October 1, 1995, had the job of taking the Manchester United-Liverpool match ... the game in which, after months on the sidelines, Eric Cantona made his long-awaited comeback.

Going back to the Newcastle game, Everton's manager had condemned Elleray's performance as 'the most insensitive display of refereeing I have seen in 30 years', while Johnson claimed: 'Referees are becoming the new stars – that cannot be right. I'm sorry to have to say this, but we now have a major referee problem, and I don't think I'm alone in believing this. Standards are slipping.' Elleray's reaction: 'It seems scapegoats are always needed in football, and referees are the easiest targets. Everybody else takes their turn at being a winner or loser, but we can never win.'

As it happened, the man in charge of Everton's FA Cup duel with Newcastle United in March 1995, had something to say, too, about the life of the referee in modern-day football. Sympathising with Rodger Gifford, Keith Cooper recalled: 'Fans attacked me four years ago, and now I ask for a police escort from every match I referee. It is an indication of how

196

much the game has changed in the 12 years or so I've been on the list. I have even had to endure telephone calls to my home which have threatened me and my family.' Cooper said that after a controversial game at West Brom, 'the linesmen and I were making our way off the field when we were attacked by several spectators, and were fortunate not to be badly hurt. That left a lasting impression ... ever since, I always make a point of asking for two officers to come on to the pitch at half-time and full-time to accompany the linesmen and myself.' Shades of Brian Hill when he officiated at the Wimbledon-Manchester United match.

Cooper spoke of having had 'hate mail' after he had sent off two players in a match between Leicester City and Coventry City, while 'the lines to my home were hot with calls telling me what they'd do to me or my family. In times of adversity a referee has to try to smile ... our greatest problem is that if a referee makes even one mistake, it gets magnified, especially if it has a direct bearing on the outcome of a match. It's getting to the stage where you are not allowed to make an error of judgment. A referee has to be a certain type of person – if it's too hot for him, he has to decide whether he wants to stay in the kitchen. It's certainly getting hotter.' And the heat was on when Sheffield United met Manchester United in the third round of the FA Cup on January 9, 1995, and the referee issued marching orders to home player Charlie Hartfield. After the critics (and there were a few) had had their say, it was Peter Rhodes who took action – by reporting Eric Cantona to the Football Association. So let us see what the fuss was all about ... and, first, let me say that I have no particular love for *The People* newspaper, even though that paper employed me for around 30 years.

Alex Ferguson reckoned that during his first six months as manager of Manchester United, *The People* linked him with more than 100 players. That figures ... but whatever you may think about the tabloid Sunday paper, it certainly went upmarket when it recruited Brian Glanville, one of the major names in sporting journalism. Come to that, the former deputy leader of the Labour Party, Roy Hattersley, also commands genuine respect as a knowledgeable commentator on football, as well as politics. Glanville has travelled the world on soccer safari; Hattersley is known as a dedicated follower of Sheffield Wednesday – I have seen him at Hillsborough on a fairly regular basis – and each of these writers had an opinion to expound on what happened when Manchester United and The Blades met at Bramall Lane. Their views centred around Monsieur Eric Cantona, with Glanville proclaiming that if Manchester United retained the Frenchman for season 1995–96, 'that would surely be a dereliction of duty, as it would be on the FA's part if they allowed it.' (They did.)

Glanville acknowledged that Alex Ferguson's dilemma was 'an agonising one ... Keep Cantona, turn a blind eye to his blackness, and win titles. Cast him out, and go back to the days of being the nearly team which choked and froze on the last lap.' Glanville declared that 'Cantona's disciplinary record in France was atrocious' and that 'with United, he has been involved time and again in violent incidents; and if on one or two occasions he may have been unjustly treated, these were more than balanced by such events as those at Norwich, when he back-heeled John Polston in the face, and when he took a sly kick at Sheffield United's Charlie Hartfield, whose retaliation got him sent off. In those circumstances, Cantona escaped unscathed.' As for Roy Hattersley, he wrote of some incidents involving Cantona being 'remarkable because they were so unsavoury', declared that 'many of the fouls – which were obvious on the TV replays – were committed behind the referee's back. Hartfield was sent off for striking Cantona a glancing (but nevertheless unforgivable) blow.

'The slow-motion replay revealed that he was responding to a surreptitious Cantona kick. Retaliation is always unpalatable, but in the past couple of years too many football fracas have been started by Cantona' – a player described by the *Daily Mail*'s chief soccer writer, Neil Harman, as 'the unexploded hand-grenade Leeds were more than happy to hand on to someone else'. Harman also wrote: 'He showed no remorse for the outburst (when United met Galatasaray)

198

in 1993 which provoked a frenzied attack on him and his fellow-United players in the tunnel. Domestically, he was sent off at Swindon for plunging his studs into the chest of John Moncur, then dismissed four days later at Arsenal when two tackles, with varying degrees of intent, were punished.'

Writers such as Glanville, Hattersley and Harman have shown the other side of the Cantona coin, for they have liberally praised his talents as an outstanding footballer, while condemning his penchant for turning footbrawler. Peter Rhodes, too, acknowledged that in Cantona, Manchester United secured a player who, like Johnny Carey and George Best in Busby's day, was capable of producing some compelling moves; but while Carey in particular turned in one impeccable performance after another, he also demonstrated that he was possessed of an equable temperament – which was why the Old Trafford faithful called him 'Gentleman Johnny'.

It was while the football world was still agog with the misdemeanours of Cantona after the Selhurst Park affair that Rhodes revealed to me his action in reporting the wayward Frenchman to the Football Association over another incident which occurred during the Bramall Lane Cup-tie – but Rhodes was not referring to the Cantona-Hartfield affair. This eagle-eyed former referee had spotted yet another bit of bother, and he told me: 'The referee was Robbie Hart, from Darlington, and it was while he was dealing with Hartfield – and had his back to Cantona – that the second incident happened.

'I saw one of Hartfield's team-mates begin to remonstrate with Cantona ... who then bunched a fist and took a swing at this player. He missed him by no more than a whisker,' Well, Rhodes may have quit refereeing years ago, but he is still in a position to blow the whistle on offenders, should he see something which, in his view, brings the game into disrepute. Rhodes retains various offices in the game at local level and, therefore, he is entitled to report to the Football Association any act of misconduct which he witnesses being committed by a player. He exercised that right after having viewed the

Bramall Lane Cup-tie on BBC television, and he was adamant and crystal-clear about what he saw. He invoked Rule 25 of the Football Association's own charter – as he told me: 'I reported Don Revie under this rule, and he was hauled up before an FA Commission. And it was under the same rule that I sent my report on Cantona to the Football Association. The rule is quite clear – in fact, it is specific. It does not say that anyone who sees something which amounts to misconduct may or should report the matter to the FA ... it states that you MUST report it.'

So what happened, then, after Rhodes had sent in his report? 'I heard nothing from the Football Association, so after about 10 days I rang Lancaster Gate to inquire what was happening. The FA's spokesperson, a lady, told me my letter had not been received, and suggested I send a copy of it. Which I did. I was more than a little surprised to get a reply stating that since there had been no complaint from Sheffield United, no action was proposed concerning my report on Cantona. In my view, by not taking action on my complaint, the Football Association was not sticking by its own rule. The incident was clear enough to me – I saw just what happened while I was watching television. The way is open for someone to go to the highest courts in the land and seek a "judicidial review" against the FA. This would compel the Football Association to stick strictly to its own rules and regulations, thus avoiding a charge that it is selective.' Rhodes's argument recalled the complaint by Liverpool's Phil Babb, after he had alleged that Cantona had 'lifted his studs and aimed them at my knee' during a game when Babb was playing for Coventry City at the tail-end of season 1993–94.

Rhodes also referred to a high-profile incident in another high-profile match, making a pertinent point as he talked about the Rugby Union international between England and Wales at Cardiff the day before Manchester United met Leeds United in an FA Cup-tie at Old Trafford in February 1995. He recalled: 'Wales had a player – John Davies – sent off ... he was the first to be shown the red card in the Five Nations Championship; and in something like three hours, he had been made aware of his fate. He was banned for 60 days. There was an appeal against the penalty, but it was dismissed. I would like to know why, if Rugby Union could dispense disciplinary justice so swiftly, it took the Football Association until almost the end of February to deliver its verdict on the Cantona affair relating to his dismissal and his subsequent actions at Selhurst Park on January 25.' Considering that Graham Kelly, the chief executive of the Football Association, had not hesitated to go on record and brand Cantona's kung-fu action at Selhurst Park as 'a stain on our game', other people might have been inclined to wonder, as well.

201

CHAPTER 19

THE LOST TITLE FIGHT

'Manchester United have won the title for the past two seasons, but they have no God-given right to win it again.' – Blackburn Rovers striker ALAN SHEARER.

BY the end of February 1995, Manchester United remained on course for the FA Cup-Premiership double, after having done a demolition job on Leeds United in the fifth round of the Cup contest and having hauled themselves to within two points of Blackburn Rovers in the title race. The bookies, seldom wrong, made United 9–2 to stage a repeat of their double act of the previous season. In the Cup quarter-final, United faced Queen's Park Rangers – over whom they had done the double in the League; and in the meantime, they had chalked up another double, this time over their most persistent title rivals, Blackburn Rovers. They had also beaten challengers Newcastle United at Old Trafford and drawn at St James's Park.

Magpies manager Kevin Keegan, having seen his side give Liverpool a 3–0 hiding at St James's Park (a hat-trick for Andy Cole), had predicted that no one could stop Manchester United from claiming the title: 'the rest will have to catch the ferry,' he declared, when it came to competing in Europe. His forecast proved to be bang on the mark, as United not only collected their first Championship in more than a quarter of a century, but went on to do the double. And by March 1995, they were aiming for a repeat performance.

Faded challengers Nottingham Forest had been the only team to win at Old Trafford, while Newcastle trailed in third place. As for Blackburn, United had 'stuffed' them 4–2 at Ewood Park in the October, while local rivals Manchester City were dismissed with a five-goal mauling, then subjected to a 3–0 defeat in the February return. In between times, on January 25, 1995, at Selhurst Park, United had failed to put one across Blackburn Rovers as they were held to a draw by Crystal Palace, with Eric Cantona making headlines on the front and back pages. In that match, the fact that former Blackburn defender David May had hit the target for United was recorded merely as a by-line.

As football argued whether or not Cantona should have been shown the exit door, there was debate, also, as to whether or not United could continue to make their challenge for the double – and their inspirational Frenchman had played a seemingly significant part just before his suspension, as he headed the goal that sank Blackburn at Old Trafford. It was a match which ended in fierce argument, though, because the Rovers had had what they considered to be a good goal ruled out. When they 'equalised' in the dying moments, it was claimed that Alan Shearer had committed a foul by pushing, as he went up to nod the ball towards marksman Tim Sherwood, but Rovers manager Kenny Dalglish was adamant that he could see nothing wrong, and that the referee's decision could have cost Blackburn the title (as it turned out, it didn't).

Not surprisingly, Alex Ferguson saw things in a different light. He said that before the game Dalglish had expressed the hope that the game would have a strong referee – and, Ferguson claimed, this was exactly what Kenny had got. It mattered not, though, what either manager felt; what counted was the referee's decision. And the Rovers' goal was ruled out. By the time Leeds tried their Cup luck at Old Trafford in February, the title countdown was looming ... Leeds walked out, knowing they had not been beaten in 1995, and returned to the dressing-room a chastened side. And Manchester United turned their attention, once again, to Premiership business.

There were just over a dozen League games to go, starting with a mid-week match against Norwich City at Carrow Road, then another away date, against Everton at Goodison Park. After that, it was relegation-haunted Ipswich Town at Old Trafford, a tough one away against Wimbledon, Tottenham Hotspur at Old Trafford, Liverpool at Anfield, then Arsenal at home, plus Leeds and Southampton, to make it three on the trot (unless an FA Cup semi-final intervened) at Old Trafford. The last five League games were against Leicester City at Filbert Street (a top-versus-bottom affair), Chelsea at Old Trafford, Coventry City (now managed by former United team-boss Ron Atkinson) at Highfield Road, Sheffield Wednesday at home, and a wrap-up match away against a West Ham side which could well be fighting for Premiership survival ... as, indeed, was the case with Coventry City.

At Carrow Road, United triumphed 2–0, though they came unstuck at Goodison Park, where £4 million striker Duncan Ferguson hit Everton's lone-goal winner. At Old Trafford against Ipswich, the Suffolk side were Cole-axed, as £7 million man Andy Cole claimed five of the nine goals United scored – without reply. Even so, Blackburn Rovers won at Villa Park, so they retained the leadership ... although the goal difference had been overturned with that stunning, 9–0 massacre of Ipswich. As for Cole, he had claimed more League goals in one game than any other player had done in Manchester United's history, and he revealed the motivation which had inspired him: 'Ever since I've been here, people have been saying I'm not worth the money. I've been slaughtered. Well ... I've proved them all wrong. People have kept saying I have to prove this, and prove that. The other United players, the manager and the supporters have been brilliant. They are the main people I have to please. That's the main challenge for me – and I know things can get even better.' Well, United had clocked up their most emphatic League victory since they defeated Wolves 10–1 back in

October, 1892, and the display against Ipswich had Alex Ferguson purring with satisfaction. And so United travelled on, to Selhurst Park, where they tackled ... Wimbledon.

That encounter revived unhappy memories of what had happened in the match against Crystal Palace a few weeks earlier, when Eric Cantona had cut loose; and against Wimbledon, it looked odds-on another draw ... until, with the final minutes looming, Steve Bruce stabbed the ball home as he nutmegged 'keeper Hans Segers. Once again, this was a match which ended in controversy, although this time out it was Wimbledon manager Joe Kinnear who was escorted from the touchline, while his chairman, Sam Hammam, also became involved in the argument. As for Alex Ferguson, he candidly admitted that United had been fortunate to claim three points which propelled his team back to the top – though only for 24 hours, since Blackburn beat Arsenal the following night. The United manager said of Bruce's winner: 'I believe the 'keeper dropped the ball, and Bruce had every right to go for it. Whether or not he fouled the 'keeper in doing it we will only know when we watch the video. It's a lucky victory.'

Wimbledon's manager said he was not complaining about the goal, but about the dismissal of left-back Alan Kimble for a second bookable offence – a dismissal which had come about mere minutes before Bruce struck. Kinnear claimed: 'Kimble must be the only man in the world to be sent off for not standing 10 yards away from a corner.' There was a touch of irony, too, about the fact that Kinnear had not wanted the game to go on, while Ferguson was in favour of getting it out of the way. The pitch had required three inspections, after a heavy downpour (it was to be used again the next night, for a Coca-Cola Cup semi-final between Liverpool and Crystal Palace); and Kinnear, it was said, would have been content to give the pitch a rest, considering the semi-final scheduled for the next night. As it turned out, it was United who had to play the waiting game – their sixth-round FA Cup-tie against Queen's Park Rangers gave Blackburn the chance to pick up points in the League against Ron Atkinson's Coventry City.

It was Dion Dublin, a £1 million signing by Alex Ferguson and a £2 million buy by Coventry, who gave the Sky Blues the lead, Alan Shearer (striking his 32nd goal of the season) who dragged the Rovers level, so that the match ended 1–1, with Blackburn now four points ahead of United, who had a game in hand. Kenny Dalglish, striving to give his players an injection of self-confidence, said: 'People seem to have more respect for my players than maybe they have for themselves. A bit more self-belief wouldn't do them any harm.' It was a viewpoint echoed by Graeme le Saux, who declared: 'If we don't win, I want to know we've been beaten by a better side, not by our own shortcomings. It would be sad if a lack of self-belief cost us the title.' Alex Ferguson, meanwhile, was predicting that the title race would go 'right to the wire', with the last five games being important ... 'if we're still in contention by then, I would fancy our chances.'

He pointed out that while Blackburn were 'very competitive', United had six of their last 10 games at Old Trafford, while the Rovers must play six matches away, against their four at home. 'That might give us a slight advantage.' Alan Shearer chipped in to say his equaliser at Coventry 'could be the one that wins us the title.' And the Rovers were happy when United, at home to Tottenham Hotspur, failed to find the net, despite constant pressure. A Hughes header hit a post, the woodwork also denied Cole and 'keeper Ian Walker palmed a Giggs drive round a post then clawed away a powerful, goalbound header from Ince. And that was all in the first 45 minutes. In the second half, Klinsmann went close for Spurs, Barmby and Anderton passed up scoring chances, and Rosenthal cleared off the line, while a fierce drive from Cole struck 'keeper Walker on the chest. The 0–0 result meant that Blackburn remained three points ahead, with United having a single-goal advantage when it came to goal difference. Nine games to go for each club ... and Ferguson admitting: 'We never do things easily – we have our supporters hanging on to the last gasp, and it will be the same this season.'

United's manager praised 'keeper Peter Schmeichel, who

had kept 11 clean sheets: 'Since he came back from injury, his form has been sensational. He is the best goalkeeper in Europe.' A tribute to make the giant Dane glow with satisfaction ... even if Ferguson was still pondering on the problem of winger Andrei Kanchelskis, who had been at odds with the club in recent weeks. And by the time Blackburn had beaten Chelsea, the United manager faced another poser, because that result hoisted the Rovers six points clear ... Shearer chalked up his 100th League goal, and United had to tackle Liverpool at Anfield 24 hours after the Rovers-Chelsea game. Liverpool, indeed, could still have a say in the destination of the title trophy, because apart from meeting United, they had a final home game against the side managed by Kenny Dalglish.

All in all, United seemed to have the easier task as the clubs came to the final countdown – Arsenal, Leeds, Chelsea, Sheffield Wednesday and Southampton at home, Liverpool, Leicester, Coventry and West Ham away. Blackburn faced Everton, Queen's Park Rangers, Leeds United, West Ham and Liverpool away, and Crystal Palace, Manchester City and Newcastle United at Ewood. And from Alan Shearer came this assessment: 'Of course, I am proud of the 100 goals (77 of them for the Rovers in 89 games), but I couldn't have done it without the rest of the lads. There are no stars in our dressing-room. United have won the title for the past two seasons, but they have no God-given right to win it again, and we don't feel under any pressure. We are enjoying ourselves. I'm sure there will still be a lot of ups and downs to come, and we know we get nothing for being on top now. It's what happens at the end of the season that counts, and we are confident.'

With eight games to go, the Rovers had 76 points, so they needed 14 to hit the 90-point target which is generally regarded as being a title-winning total. Three home wins would put them on 85 points, leaving them to average a point from each of their five away games. United could hope to collect 15 points from their home matches, to take them on to 88, leaving them to pick up two (maybe three) points from four away outings.

At Anfield, however, Alex Ferguson must have wondered if this was to be a repeat of the season when Leeds had pipped United for the prize – because, once again, Liverpool scored twice without reply – well, once through Redknapp, and (with five minutes to go) when Bruce put the ball into his own net. So United were six points adrift of Blackburn, though two home games in succession could be crucial, since Blackburn had to play at Loftus Road, and at Goodison Park. Bruce endured an unhappy afternoon all round at Anfield, being booked, as well as scoring an own goal. This took him over the 40-point mark for the season and meant he would miss the League game against Leeds and the FA Cup semi-final.

As Liverpool clinched victory, the contrast between the home bench and that of the visitors was stark, and said it all. Liverpool's backroom team were on their feet and giving their feelings full-throated voice... while alongside sat a glum-looking Ferguson and a thoughtful-looking Brian Kidd. Ferguson admitted later: 'I don't think we deserved anything ... we've won big games to keep us in contention all season, but in the past week we've drawn with Spurs and now lost at Liverpool. We needed to win this one.' And as the games against Arsenal and Leeds loomed, Ferguson knew he would lose both Bruce and Lee Sharpe through suspension, while Roy Keane, Ince and Hughes were all walking a disciplinary tightrope – each was just one caution away from an automatic ban which would condemn them to miss the Cup semi-final.

Ferguson conceded: 'I can't protect them when we're chasing the Championship. They will just have to get on with it.' And apart from the disciplinary aspect, United had David May still recovering from a hernia operation and Paul Parker 'nowhere near ready', after an ankle operation. Yet when Arsenal arrived at Old Trafford, United's manager got his pep-talk absolutely right, as he questioned his players' attitude. Ruthlessly, he told them he wanted to know if they still retained their hunger for success: 'I had to ask the question of them ... you can get used to success, and forget how you achieve it.'

Ferguson got just the response he wanted, as Arsenal were swept aside with a three-goal salvo which cut Blackburn's lead to three points. But after two more games – one at Goodison, the other at Old Trafford – the title pendulum swung back Blackburn's way ... by then, the Rovers were five points clear, with a game in hand. It left Ferguson admitting: 'I think that Blackburn can only throw the League away now. We're hoping for a Devon Loch situation (in which the seemingly-certain winner of the Grand National faltered and fell). We've got to win our last six games – but we won't give in.'

Against Everton at Goodison, Blackburn rattled in two goals – then had to hang on grimly, to grind out a fortunate victory. After the 2–1 result, Kenny Dalglish admitted: 'We were fortunate to get three points. We had good fortune around the goalmouths, and I hope our luck stays that way until the end of the season.' Twenty-four hours later, United found it impossible to break down the stubborn resistance of Leeds United at Old Trafford, so the game ended scoreless. United could also reflect that while Leeds were playing a part once more in thwarting their bid for the title, Blackburn had won at Goodison ... where Joe Royle's team had beaten the men from Old Trafford. Now United must hope Blackburn lost at Loftus Road, at Leeds and at Anfield in the final match.

As United had failed to get goals in three of their last four games, Ferguson must have pondered, also, on the wisdom of having dismissed Blackburn's £5 million splash on Chris Sutton as 'madness' – between them, Sutton and Shearer had shared 46 goals in Premiership games, with Sutton having contributed 15. And during the Old Trafford match against Leeds, the home fans had had to endure the taunt of: 'Where is Eric Cantona?' Where, indeed? As United chairman Martin Edwards had admitted weeks earlier, suspending Cantona could well have jeopardised his club's chances in both League and Cup. Now Cantona's absence was clearly appearing costly, to say the least.

The draw against Leeds was not Ferguson's only worry. Kanchelskis returned from international duty with Russia and had to miss the crucial League match – which led to

United's manager declaring: 'We're really angry, because Andrei allowed himself to be given eight pain-killing injections to play for Russia. That is a policy we would never pursue. We don't go down that road with injections like this.' Kanchelskis, who had been troubled all season by a stomach-muscle injury, finally required a hernia operation – and there was more controversy when, on the eve of the FA Cup final against Everton, his agent declared that the player and his manager didn't get on. The agent claimed Kanchelskis was asking to leave United almost daily, with Ferguson responding bluntly by saying that the player was expected to honour his contract.

Meanwhile, at Loftus Road, Blackburn beat Queen's Park Rangers with a goal from Sutton ... who warned United: 'We're not going to blow it; Alex Ferguson might as well keep quiet.' The Rovers were eight points clear, and the bookies had stopped taking bets on the destination of the title trophy, even though six matches remained. Sutton declared: 'We are so serious, so desperate, so focused ... we've read what Alex Ferguson has said about us, but we're treating it all as kidology. Each time we win, it's another notch towards the title.'

Yet United chipped away at Blackburn's lead as they won 4–0 at Leicester and the Rovers dropped two points at Leeds, where Brian Deane scored a last-gasp equaliser for the home side. Ferguson then seemed in upbeat mood: 'It could be the biggest triumph in our history if we take the title – and if Blackburn keep throwing points away, the situation could change.' Twenty-four hours later, however, he was talking in a different vein, after Chelsea had held United to a 0–0 draw at Old Trafford. He was driven to admit that if God were a United fan, 'He's got to act now. It's left us looking for miracles.' A few hours on, and a headline boldly proclaimed that Fergie's prayer had been answered!

Astonishingly, at Ewood Park, Kenny Dalglish and his players had been left feeling stunned by Manchester City's smash-and-grab victory in a game of five goals, so the title race had been thrown open again ... and it remained a close-run thing right to the final day, as the Rovers lost 2–0 against West Ham at Upton Park, while United went to Highfield Road and beat Coventry City 3–2 ... leaving Blackburn to face Newcastle United at Ewood. There was a wry spark of humour in Ferguson's pre-match comment, as he announced his intention of giving Ewood Park a miss: 'I'm as welcome in Blackburn as the Black Plague. Even when they were nobodies I wasn't welcome there. I don't think I'll watch it on television, either ... why torture yourself?' Why, indeed? Ferguson certainly didn't want to watch Alan Shearer despatching the Magpies as he struck the only goal of the game!

Then Manchester United took up their option to win one of their matches in hand as former Blackburn Rover David May drilled home the winner against Sheffield Wednesday at Old Trafford. United stole closer still to Blackburn as they beat Southampton 2–1, with the help of a disputed penalty. So the title contestants came to the final day of reckoning ... Blackburn couldn't be caught, should they win at Anfield; but if they drew or lost, and United won at West Ham, the title trophy would remain at Old Trafford ... as it would do, should goal difference emerge as the deciding factor.

Ferguson scoffed at any suggestion that Liverpool would give the Rovers any assistance: 'It would be an insult to suggest Liverpool will not do all they can to beat Blackburn,' he declared, adding: 'Liverpool have won 18 Championships and four European Cups, and know all about what it's like to earn honours. It's beyond thinking for anyone to suggest they'd not try, just because of Kenny's associations with the club.' A verdict echoed by Liverpool manager Roy Evans: 'I want to finish the season with a win for our fans.'

So it was Blackburn on 89 points, United on 87 – and everything to play for, as the teams walked out at Anfield and at Upton Park. When it came to goals, the Rovers had scored 79, conceded 37, while United had scored 76, but conceded only 27. After United's final home game, against Southampton, Eric Cantona had joined in the team's farewell lap of honour, with the fans' applause reaching thunderous proportions ... how they wished the Frenchman could have been

211

available over past weeks ... and especially now, for the showdown with West Ham!

From Anfield, the news was flashed to Upton Park: Blackburn had gone ahead through Shearer – and then it was 1–1, with John Barnes having equalised. United themselves had gone a goal down, but been spurred to even greater effort after Brian McClair had equalised. As the second half wore on, United had every outfield player in the Hammers' half of the field, and the ball repeatedly pinged around the penalty area ... but still a winner would not come. The atmosphere? That was electric – and, perhaps, remarkable, in that West Ham fans were clearly not on United's side as they fought to retain the Championship crown, while at Anfield the Liverpool faithful were cheering for the Rovers, while wanting their own favourites to sign off with a victory.

Once again, it all demonstrated that Manchester United could look no further than their own diehards for support. As Kenny Dalglish admitted when it was all over: 'It's the first time I've known anybody with any feelings towards Manchester United hoping that Liverpool would get a result. Liverpool got the result (an injury-time winner from Jamie Redknapp, who had been signed by Dalglish), but United couldn't help themselves. To benefit from a bad result, you have to get your own result first.' Blackburn had so nearly blown it ... only seven points from the possible 18 on the final lap told its own story. Once it was all over, the Kop saluted the Rovers with the chant of 'Champions! Champions!' Down in London, Ferguson swallowed his bitter disappointment to say: 'All credit to Blackburn. Anyone who gets 89 points deserves the championship.'

Yet United's manager didn't forget to salute his own players – he's never one to sell them short – as he reflected: 'Most leagues are won in the mid-80's. They've gone well beyond that, which is because of us. It's taken a very good team to take our Championship, and we could not have done more to stop them than we did today. Over the last four years, we've contested four Championships and lost only 22 games out of 168. That is magnificent, and our players can be proud of themselves.' So, as Dalglish joined Brian Clough and Herbert Chapman as one of only three managers to have steered two different clubs to the Championship, Alex Ferguson faced the task of lifting his players for one final flourish – the FA Cup final against Everton. 'Right now, they're very disappointed, but I'm sure they'll lift themselves for the final.' Ferguson could reflect that in almost any other season, United's tally of 88 points would have been sufficient to stave off the challenge from any other club for the title trophy. They hadn't lost this title fight by a knock-out, either, or even on points ... but by just one solitary point.

CHAPTER 20

THE BITTER END

'It's been a nice week for us – that's for sure. Sometimes you don't get what you deserve. – ALEX FERGUSON, after having seen United lose the FA Cup and the League-title trophy in the space of eight days.'

BEWARE the ides of March . . . Thus the warning words from one Will Shakespeare. In the Roman calendar, the Ides refers to the 13th day of the month, except for March, May, July and October, when the Ides fell on the 15th. As it happened, the sixth round of the FA Cup for Manchester United was scheduled for Sunday, March 12, 1995 – and the 40,000 and more fans who regularly flocked to Old Trafford were in no mood to give thought to possible disaster, as their favourites made it to the quarter-finals of the Cup and gave notice to Blackburn Rovers that they intended to take the title fight to the final round.

Newcastle United had snuffed out the FA Cup hopes of the team managed by Kenny Dalglish, while his old sparring partner at Anfield, Ian Rush, had had the audacity to hit a hat-trick in a Coca-Cola Cup-tie at Ewood Park and thus despatch the Rovers from that competition. So two avenues into Europe had been blocked – which left only the League. Blackburn's Graeme le Saux declared that Cantona's ban was United's loss . . . 'we must make sure it becomes our gain. We still feel a bit humble about where we are. The Rovers try to go on with a quiet sense of purpose, while United get all the attention. We're just not as grand. They're seen as superstars, and get put under more pressure because of it.'

Le Saux added a rider: 'Sometimes people crack in the limelight ... we've seen that.' Yet the Rovers man reckoned: 'It's not over yet; they're strong enough to cope, and this setback could even end up knitting them closer together.' – a viewpoint echoed by former United manager Tommy Docherty, as he still tipped his old club to retain the title, and declared that the players at Old Trafford would 'roll up their sleeves' and demonstrate that there could be life after Cantona. When Le Saux was asked if the Rovers would view it as a hollow triumph, should they claim the Championship, he had a short, sharp answer: 'Are you kidding? If anyone tries that one, I'll just give my medal a rub, hold it up and look at how well it shines in the light!'

United's ground had become almost an impregnable fortress: just two defeats in more than 60 games through two and a half years. Chelsea had dared to go to Old Trafford and win during season 1993–94, Nottingham Forest had managed it during season 1994–95. As for the FA Cup, rank outsiders Wrexham had had the temerity to visit United's ground and give the home fans a scare or two. Wrexham had acquired a reputation as giant killers – ask Arsenal! – and a matter of days after the banishment of Cantona, they tried conclusions with United in the fourth round. There was no Cantona, no Cole (Cup-tied), no Hughes (injured) and no Bruce (suspended) ... and with only 10 minutes gone, Wrexham snatched the lead.

Minutes later, however, Denis Irwin put them in their place as he equalised, and when Ryan Giggs flicked home goal No.2, the writing was on the wall. Each time United breached the Wrexham defence, there came a chorus of 'Ooh, aah, Cantona!' from the home fans, and even some of the Welsh club's 6,000-strong travelling support ended up joining in. Eventually, United ran out worthy winners by a three-goal margin (McClair, Irwin (penalty) and an own goal from

Wrexham skipper Tony Humes). Then it was into round five for United, and the Old Trafford confrontation with Leeds United.

On the morning of the Cup-tie, *The People* newspaper forecast that United and Cantona were 'bracing' themselves for a swingeing, £250,000 fine from the Football Association after its disciplinary hearing, due in five days' time. Meanwhile, the managers of both Uniteds were talking calmly about the match of the day. Leeds team boss Howard Wilkinson had already asked his club's supporters to act in a sporting and responsible manner at Old Trafford – and there were 6,500 ready to make the trek across the Pennines. Wilkinson also expressed his understanding of United's problems concerning Cantona and made it clear he harboured no ill-will to anyone, while at the same time giving praise to his managerial counterpart at Old Trafford. For his part, Alex Ferguson stressed that players, officials and directors of both clubs had the friendliest of relations, as he looked forward to a tie playing in sporting style.

United had just written off the prospect of a £2 million payday from the sale of Mark Hughes, after Cantona had been banned – they had now offered Hughes (a target for Everton) a new deal. Chairman Martin Edwards called it 'a financial sacrifice' ... 'This could have cost us around £2 million, but things have changed suddenly. It's a footballing decision, rather than a financial one'. Hughes, back after injury, provided United with a boost; as for Leeds, they had to rejig because of the absence of Carlton Palmer and Brian Deane. Former Liverpool captain Alan Hansen, now a TV pundit, expressed his fears for Leeds, considering their line-up ... and within minutes of the kick-off, he was being proved right.

Two goals inside the first five minutes set the tone, and the home fans began to taunt the Leeds support. Manchester City had lost their Cup-tie at Newcastle hours earlier, and the Old Trafford brigade began to chant: 'Are you Manchester City in disguise?' Every time a Manchester United player got the ball, he was cheered; every time a Leeds man gained possession, he was roundly booed. Steve Bruce scored his

216

first goal since August, Hughes capped an emotional return by getting his name on the scoresheet, McClair was another marksman; and while Leeds briefly raised the hopes of their fans, it was a case of too little, too late.

When substitute Tony Yeboah scored, to make the margin 2–1, Leeds fans were in with a shout for the first time, and they began to display banners bearing the names of Barcelona, Galatasaray and Gothenburg (in reference to Manchester United's failure to achieve anything in the European Cup). But when Hughes planted a header past John Lukic, to get his name on the scoresheet, the writing was on the wall. Alex Ferguson said: 'This is a club where players become legends, and "Sparky" has been a hero for 10 years. It's amazing that when the big games come round, he scores.' Ultimately, Hughes was to move on, to Chelsea, however.

That Cup triumph left United's fans cock-a-hoop and relishing the prospect of a home quarter-final tie against Queen's Park Rangers, whom United had already beaten twice during the season. United had now been installed at 9–2 for the double, and were Cup favourites at 9–4. On Saturday, March 11, the Klinsmann-inspired Spurs went to Anfield and stole a last-gasp, stunning victory, while Crystal Palace and Wolves drew, 1–1. Twenty-four hours later, it was United and Rangers at Old Trafford, and after 90 minutes Ray Wilkins (once an £800,000 signing by United) and his men had been eclipsed by Alex Ferguson's double-chasers. Goals from Lee Sharpe and Denis Irwin (a superb, swerving free-kick bent round the defensive wall) put United into the semi-finals for the second successive season ... and they were paired with Crystal Palace (winners of the replay with Wolves) at Villa Park. Everton, having come out on top against Newcastle at Goodison Park, had to meet Tottenham at Elland Road.

United had Bruce missing through suspension, while Kanchelskis failed a late fitness test, so they went into their semi-final knowing Wembley was the big goal, since they had virtually blown their chance of retaining the title – though their manager remained defiant, as he said: 'You never know what happens ... it's not over yet.' It didn't bother him if his

217

team had to play extra time to reach Wembley: 'It will be worth any effort if reaching Wembley makes up for disappointment in the League.'

Crystal Palace were struggling for Premiership survival – but in Cup competitions, they had rattled in 25 goals while conceding only eight in 13 ties. And their latest signing, Ray Houghton, from Liverpool, reminded everyone how Palace, underdogs against Liverpool in the 1990 semi-final, had battled through to win 4–3, after extra time. Houghton had then been on the receiving end; now he declared: 'We know we're the underdogs – but it was exactly the same five years ago. There are a lot of similarities between the 1990 Palace team and this one. Earlier that season we had beaten them 9–0, and everybody expected Liverpool to win again, handsomely. It shows, on the day, anyone can win in a one-off semi-final.' Indeed, it did, because while everyone was talking about the 'dream final' between Manchester United and Spurs, Everton simply took no notice as they hammered Tottenham, to reach Wembley. Four goals went into the Spurs net, with Daniel Amokachi, Everton's £3 million signing, a two-goal hero.

Against Palace, United were shocked as they fell behind to a goal from Iain Dowie, but a Denis Irwin free-kick (aided by a slight deflection) beat 'keeper Nigel Martyn, with 20 minutes to go, and while that was the end of scoring during normal time, there were more goals in the extra period ... Chris Armstrong for Palace, Gary Pallister for United. However, no one could break the deadlock, so a replay it had to be ... with United cruising through. Once again, though, it was at some cost, because the United headlines were for all the wrong reasons, as tempers flared and Roy Keane was shown the red card after he had been fouled by and stamped on Palace skipper Gareth Southgate, then tangled with Darren Patterson.

It started with Keane winning the ball with a high-looking tackle, then being floored by Southgate. As Keane rose, he was seen – and the clip was viewed by millions watching on TV – to stamp his boot on the prostrate Palace skipper.

During a melée, Keane's international team-mate, Ray Houghton, was pictured rushing in, eyes blazing, while Patterson and Armstrong also became involved, though it was Patterson who came into closest contact with Keane.

Referee David Elleray, no stranger to controversy, had no hesitation in sending off both Keane and Patterson, and the backlash rebounded upon United, as their 'crime sheet' for the season was listed in detail ... Keane, five bookings, one sending-off; Ince, four bookings, one sending-off; Hughes, three bookings, one sending-off; Cantona, one booking, one sending-off; Parker, one sending-off. Before the match, the respective managers had gone on to the pitch to plead with the fans for good behaviour. It was a match in which United skipper Bruce was just back, after his two-game suspension. And Alex Ferguson commented afterwards: 'It's incredible, on this, of all nights. Roy deserved to be sent off ... we'll handle it as we always do, in our own way. We don't need to broadcast to the world what we're doing.' Pressed about Keane's dismissal and its effect on the game's image, Ferguson rapped: 'I've said it's silly. You can't excuse it. He could have cost us the League now, missing three games.'

Inside the next 24 hours there was talk that Keane could even miss the remainder of the season, including the FA Cup final, and as the arguments raged, the critics had a field-day. Ferguson did attempt to defend Keane in one respect, as he revealed: 'Roy suffered a bad tackle in the first half and needed seven stitches in an ankle (that injury would keep him out of two games, any way). We weren't going to play him in the second half, but he insisted on carrying on. We were just getting Brian McClair ready when he got sent off. You should never listen to players...' The question arose as to whether United would listen to the critics, as they tore into the club, while Graham Kelly, the Football Association's chief executive, had his say.

He declared: 'The two players were sent off on a night when the need for self-control was paramount. It is vital that the FA take a stand. It is no good condemning misbehaviour unless we are prepared to act. We are. The two players concerned disregarded the pleas for good behaviour made publicly by, among others, their own managers. I do not believe there can be any credible argument against the action we are taking. In our view, there is a case to answer before a commission.' So Keane and Patterson were charged with having brought the game into disrepute.

Yet, while one headline proclaimed it was 'Time for United to read the Riot Act', club chairman Martin Edwards still questioned the furore surrounding Keane, as he asked: 'Do they want us to put him in gaol?' Edwards declared that the policy already laid down by the FA provided for a three-match suspension for violent conduct, and argued: 'To talk about things beyond that sounds crazy. What about all the other players who have been sent off for similar offences? Will their cases be reconsidered? Everyone has gone overboard about this (shades of what Paddy Crerand had said about Cantona, and what Mark Hughes had said about the fuss made when it was United players who misbehaved).

'Keane was reacting to a tackle. It was a nasty tackle; he retaliated, and he shouldn't have. It's right that he was sent off, that he should be banned. He will also be fined by the club. What do people want us to do – sentence him to two weeks in gaol?' Edwards and United were said to be 'fuming' at what they saw as 'the FA responding to outside pressure', and it was further said that United's reputation 'has taken a noticeable dent this season, with the Cantona affair and now Keane's disgrace leading some to question the club's image in the game.' The critic was not wrong there.

Edwards, however, countered this charge by claiming: 'Our disciplinary record over the years is pretty good. Players who are booked or sent off are fined; but why should we tell the world what internal punishments we give? It's our business. We don't condemn our players in public. That policy goes back to Matt Busby's day.' Even so, the tide of criticism swelled, with one observer writing: 'United argue that the whole world is sniping at them, but they are offering their critics a generously wide target. Someone at Old Trafford needs to get a grip, and be seen to get a grip. The man responsible for the players is Ferguson, who has brought the more notorious individuals to the club but prefers to keep private the penalties imposed on them for their frightening lack of discipline.

'That would be fine and dandy if the punishments were seen to be having a deterrent effect. Just to fine a player who earns in excess of £8,000 a week does no good whatsoever, if he simply goes out and offends again. It has come to the stage where – if they need reminding of the great honour it is to play for United – the message needs to be reinforced. If they fall short of those standards, there should be no place for them at Old Trafford. Cantona and Keane have fallen a long way short, and whatever Ferguson may think, the prevailing mood in the game is that we don't want these sort of people in it.'

The voice of the supporter was added to the debate when Tony Kershaw, chairman of the National Federation of Supporters Clubs, declared that Cantona should quit English football. 'He will be baited by fans and goaded by rival players ... referees will have a nightmare, especially if he is closely involved in a challenge for the ball, for some players do cheat. The reaction he will get is unacceptable, as far as I'm concerned. It is too big a price for the game to pay, and I don't think he should play in this country again.' Kershaw did claim it was wrong to suggest Cantona was partly to blame for the incident when a Crystal Palace supporter lost his life: 'His name may have been chanted, but I think it was a case of hooligans looking for any excuse for a fight. I enjoy watching Cantona play, and I understand why United want him to stay. But the club couldn't handle George Best, and I don't think they can handle Cantona ... It's not as if he's been sent off just once; he's constantly been involved in trouble.'

Another observer pointed out that Keane had had his moments of trouble while at Nottingham Forest, but United were accused of having 'turned a blind eye to his past record, and the sense of the player being an accident waiting to happen has merely grown since he arrived.' It was further recorded that 'the behaviour of certain individuals is eating away at the soul of Manchester United...' And there was yet another accusation levelled at the Old Trafford club, this time about its commercial activities.

'What is just as alarming is that the directors may be too busy congratulating themselves on the profits from their merchandising and marketing prowess that they don't have the wit to see it.' It was pointed out that while Sir Bobby Charlton had said the directors had made their manager aware of the responsibility and behaviour required of players who pulled on a United jersey, 'clearly, the message got lost in the translation.' This, then, was the atmosphere in which United set about facing up to their final half-dozen League games, while bracing themselves, also, for the Wembley confrontation with Everton ... a confrontation in which they would be without Cantona, the Cup-tied Cole, and Kanchelskis, who was booked for a hernia operation.

Chairman Edwards might well have reflected upon the fears he had expressed some weeks previously – that by fining and suspending the errant Frenchman, United could have put both League title and FA Cup in jeopardy. As United moved into the fateful, final weeks of the campaign, those fears must have returned to haunt him.

As for Keane, some 48 hours after his dismissal at Villa Park, he was making a fulsome, all-round apology for his action on the pitch. A cynic might have wondered if the apology came at the instigation of United, although no doubt it would be vehemently denied that it was designed to act as some kind of damage-limitation exercise, with the threat of a Cup-final ban hanging over the player. Keane spoke of 'two seconds of madness' as he admitted: 'I over-reacted ... other players rushing in made it 10 times worse. It's the first time I've been sent off, and I have never gone out to hurt anybody. I've often been "done" myself, but I've never gone out to "do" another player. I didn't really put any weight on my boot, but I shouldn't have done it at all. Immediately, I thought, "Bloody hell, what a stupid thing to do with the season having so many other problems". It was two seconds of madness, and I had no doubt I was to be sent off.'

Keane admitted: 'I have let everyone down – the fans, the club, myself and my family. I know what I did was wrong. It came at a bad time after the death of the fan at the week-end, and the atmosphere was hostile. I sincerely offer my apologies.' Whether or not this would be sufficient for Keane to escape a further ban remained to be seen, when the FA came to consider his offence. Meanwhile, manager Ferguson was saying: 'Not every player has the temperament of a Bobby Charlton (a point made by Denis Law). I'm just hoping we can finish the season with a smile on our faces (United didn't). We have lots of good young players available.' Right there and then, United needed all the good young players they could lay their hands on, considering how their senior stars were in the wars, one way and another.

Ferguson had already made it clear that Keane could expect to be punished by the club . . . 'Roy regrets what he did, and he could regret it even more. Apart from anything the FA might do, we will be without him with injury and then suspension just before the Cup Final, and who knows whether he will get his place back? I don't intend to nail him to the cross publicly, because that is not my style, but he knows the score, and we will handle it our way.' It was reported that United would fight any attempt to try to make an example of Keane beyond the normal, three-match punishment for a violent-play dismissal. 'United officials will contest any additional suspension and could put the FA's disciplinary procedure to the ultimate test. United are also upset that Southgate, whose tackle sparked the Villa Park flare-up, escaped without even a caution.' In the event, Keane served a three-match ban and was able to line up in United's Wembley side. But the quest for the FA Cup turned out to be a lost cause, as Everton won with a goal from Paul Rideout, to give manager Joe Royle a stunning reward for his few months in charge at Goodison Park. Anders Limpar broke from midfield, slipped an astute pass to Matt Jackson, whose cross was rammed against the bar by Graham Stuart – but Rideout nodded home the rebound, as 'keeper Schmeichel was left stranded and the hamstrung Bruce could only stand and stare.

Bruce had tweaked a hamstring not long before, and he left the scene of the action at half-time, making way for Ryan Giggs, who did his utmost to inject the necessary firepower into United's desperate attacking forays. During the second period, as United laid siege to Everton's goal, 'keeper Neville Southall clawed one goalbound effort to safety, tipped another over (with some help from the crossbar) and pulled off an astounding, double-barrelled save from substitute Paul Scholes. Even Schmeichel joined in the United attacks as they drove forward during the dying minutes ... but the goal that could have saved United's season never arrived. Alex Ferguson paid Southall a handsome compliment – 'He had a marvellous game ... I think he has won them the Cup' – while also offering the view that 'I think we deserved better.' Yet, more than anyone, he knew what Manchester United had really missed – the inspiration of Cantona, who had sat behind him during the 90 minutes of action. Ferguson and the Frenchman, chewing gum in tandem, could only watch anxiously as those words of chairman Martin Edwards proved to be prophetic – United's grip on the title trophy had been prised loose by Blackburn Rovers, with Everton having wrested the FA Cup from them and, to make matters worse, Liverpool having claimed the Coca-Cola Cup. It had been a season of Northern supremacy, but for Manchester United, it was one in which they had finished up with nothing to show for their efforts. They had gone marching on, right to the end – but what a bitter ending it had turned out to be.

ON Sunday, October 1, 1995, Eric Cantona made his long-awaited comeback in English football – at Old Trafford, against Manchester United's arch-rivals, Liverpool. The match ended in a 2–2 draw, with Cantona having made United's opening goal and scored their equaliser after Robbie Fowler had struck twice for the opposition. In mid-week, Cantona played against York City in the Coca-Cola Cup return, but even he couldn't ensure that United edged through ... after their 3–0 reverse at Old Trafford, their 3–1 victory at Bootham Crescent was too little, too late. The following Saturday, Cantona was in action again, this time for the reserves against Leeds United. It was a game aimed at improving his match fitness, but after only 18 minutes he had to bow out, through injury. However, his brief appearance had demonstrated beyond doubt the charismatic hold he had on United fans ... no fewer than 21,502 people turned up to watch the game and, with Premiership matches not on the fixture list because of forthcoming international matches, the gate at United's reserve game turned out to be the highest in the country, on the day. The top gate for an Endsleigh League First Division match was 15,335 at Portman Road, where Ipswich Town met Wolves.

Chapter 21

MOMENT OF TRUTH

'Eric is desperate to play... it has been a long time for him. We all hope our fellow-pros will give him a break and not try any silly antics.' – Former United captain STEVE BRUCE.

THIRTY-ODD miles down the East Lancashire Road, 30,000 voices rose on the night air as the chant went up: 'United! United!' This, however, was not the chorus of the Old Trafford faithful, but the partisan support of Liverpool – hailing the news that arch-rivals Manchester United were trailing in their UEFA Cup-tie against Rotor Volgograd. Liverpool themselves were playing Russian opposition and, while the Anfield Reds progressed, United went out... just as they were to go out of the Coca-Cola Cup, despatched by the so-called no-hopers of York City. Which made it a traumatic start for Manchester United, in season 1995–96; though if there was one consolation, it was that they were challenging strongly for the leadership of the Premiership – and Eric Cantona was back, after his enforced, eight-month exile.

The close season had brought United their share of problems, with the controversial transfers of Paul Ince and Mark Hughes, and the on-off-on-again saga of Andrei Kanchelskis, who finally joined Everton amid an atmosphere of acrimony, as United agreed to sell, pulled the plug, then at last allowed the player to go, while relations between the clubs became strained to the point where Everton chairman Peter Johnson was seething as he declared: 'The full story will come out eventually, but for now I can say that United's behaviour has been nothing less than disgraceful. We have signed the deal that was first put to them 18 days ago. They have not considered the player or the public's perception of football in all this.'

The argument had centred around the demand from Kanchelskis's Russian club, Donetsk, for a £1.14 million cut of the £5 million Everton had agreed to pay United – and as the transfer saga dragged on, it meant he had to miss the first two rounds of the European Cup-winners Cup, in which Everton were involved. On the day the deal did go through, United chairman Martin Edwards confirmed: 'No amount is payable by United to Kanchelskis in respect of his transfer.' Everton, it was reported, had agreed to foot the bill regarding the player's cut – said to be £1.2 million. And to add injury to what Everton perceived to be insult, when United played at Goodison Park, Kanchelskis was carried off after having collided with Lee Sharpe.

While all this was going on, Eric Cantona had taken himself off to France, after a rumpus over his inclusion in a work-out against Rochdale. And the fans around the country still argued the rights and wrongs of his readmission to English football, come October 1. From Lymington, in Hampshire, came this riposte: 'Alex Ferguson should stop making excuses for Cantona. The Frenchman should take a course on sportsmanship and how to play by the rules. Until he does, he will never be accepted in this country' (a claim which would be stridently refuted by the United supporters). And another epistle: 'Why waste all this time, effort and money to retain the services of the fiery French footballer? It could be put into a team of up-and-coming youngsters who are being held back due to lack of funds and sponsors. Such a scheme could produce some professionals who might just learn more about loyalty.' (Had the writer, from Leyland in Lancashire, not heard of Scholes, Butt, Beckham, the Neville brothers and Terry Cooke?)

Going back to Cantona's involvement in the closed-doors game against Rochdale, the Football Association wanted an explanation on this one, considering the Frenchman's ban was from 'all football activities' until after September 30. Mike Parry, the FA's spokesman, said: 'When we saw pictures of Eric playing, we looked at the details of the suspension.'

The conclusion? 'Any match against another club could be interpreted as being in breach of the ban. We have written to United asking for their observations.' In a fax to the Football Association, United argued that the Rochdale game could not be viewed as anything more than a trial – there were no fans, and there had been 18 substitutions. The matter ended with United agreeing not to include Cantona in any more practice matches against outside opposition.

Cantona, however, had been sufficiently irked to depart for France; so Ferguson followed him there, to try to talk him into a change of heart, after the Frenchman had sought his release from United. Ferguson succeeded; Cantona declared: 'If we had not such a special relationship, I would have left United a long time ago.' Ferguson said: 'He had set his heart on playing against Liverpool when his ban ends, and I think he saw that prospect disappearing when the FA inquired about the match against Rochdale.' Ferguson revealed that Cantona had felt so frustrated that he had phoned Inter-Milan to see if they were still interested in him.

While Cantona waited in the wings, United lost their first League match, at Villa Park, then embarked upon a run which shot them up the table. Fergie's fledglings did him proud – until they encountered Rotor Volgograd and York City. Even then, after the first leg of the UEFA Cup-tie, on foreign soil, United had cause to be happy with a 0–0 result, plus a 3–0 League win over Bolton Wanderers. When York City arrived at Old Trafford, United's team was even younger than the one which had seen off Bolton, though Ferguson tempered enthusiasm with words of caution.

He declared: 'They won't let me down. I don't want to dampen their enthusiasm, because they are really enjoying themselves. A year ago, this would have been a really big night for them ... if they just see this as an ordinary game, they'll have a hard night.' And they did – because after 90 minutes, cock-a-hoop York had won 3–0. Worse was to come, because Rotor Volgograd tried their luck at Old Trafford and forged a 2–0 lead, and while United fought back to draw 2–2 and preserve their unbeaten home record in Europe, they went out of the UEFA Cup on the away-goals ruling.

So the scene was set for the moment of truth: the return of Cantona, in the home game against Liverpool. The Frenchman lived up to expectations, too, as he made an early goal and struck from the penalty spot to salvage a point after Robbie Fowler had scored twice for Liverpool. Cantona joined the fray after two of his team-mates had spoken up for him – Peter Schmeichel declaring that 'he has gone through an eight-month nightmare ... nobody has done him any favours.' Schmeichel offered the view, also, that 'he has changed ... I'm sure you'll see a different and better Eric. I rate Eric as one of the five most gifted players there have ever been in the world. To have him back will be a huge bonus; his reappearance will add to the young players' confidence.' Ryan Giggs chipped in, too: 'He brings so much out of the rest of the team.'

From their then skipper Steve Bruce (who departed in a shock move to Birmingham City towards the end of May), came a plea for others to give Cantona a break, as he reflected upon his own experiences and some comments made by his manager. Answering criticism of United's summer sales when he penned his first programme notes of the season, Ferguson had reminded the players still at Old Trafford that he remained totally committed to the club – and wasn't interested in anyone who felt unable to match that commitment. Bruce, the first Englishman to captain a double-winning side, was an appreciative audience for his manager's remarks as he said: 'I don't believe the demands of playing for United have changed that much since I came here in 1987.'

Bruce could remember vividly his own debut game – a victory at Portsmouth which still left Ferguson critical of the manner in which it had been achieved. By 1995, Bruce was reflecting on the departures of Paul McGrath and Norman Whiteside and saying: 'We were in a transitional period ... the team was evolving. But there were those who would love to play for United, and those who think they know what it's like, who will never grasp what it takes to be a Red.' On the previous campaign, when United 'seemed to be fighting on all fronts, what with injuries and suspensions', it was 'all stacked against us, but we fought through and got ourselves into a position where we should have won the title. How we didn't beat West Ham on the final day is still incredible ... Blackburn will never really appreciate how close they came to losing it.' Like Mark Hughes, Bruce reckoned it was 'sad that people either love or hate us ... we've given great entertainment in recent years. We've stepped off the rails a bit at times, but there is the minutest focus on us all the time, and people are just waiting to condemn us.'

Well, Eric Cantona had been condemned by plenty of people when he threatened to defect from Old Trafford – an ITV poll of more than 1,200 gave the verdict that 57 per cent said 'Yes', when asked: 'Do you think Cantona was betraying the club with his transfer request?' On the eve of the Frenchman's comeback, Bruce issued a plea for tolerance and understanding as he said: 'We all hope our fellow-pros will give him a break and not try any silly antics. Let's just enjoy Eric and his football ... he is a special talent, and it will be a shame if he can't show that.' Ferguson added his piece when he pointed out: 'It's possible there will be defenders who will try to take him over the edge, but we have referees to handle that. You want fairness and the same treatment as everyone else. You don't ask that Eric should be treated any differently.' Ferguson's plea was answered by former Liverpool captain Ian Rush, who maintained he and his teammates would not be found guilty of trying to lure Cantona back into trouble. And they didn't.

But there was trouble of a different kind for Cantona – he was to suffer an injury which kept him out of the game against Manchester City, and he came up against a player who admitted to having sought to 'wind him up' in the Coca-Cola Cup return at York, where United's 3–1 victory was too little, too late. York midfielder Nigel Pepper confessed: 'I had a couple of dips at Eric, and he didn't react one bit. I had some goes at him and caught him once – there was no intent on my part, but I still got him. Eric didn't even say a word to me – he just turned around and had a go at the referee. I can applaud him now for not reacting... He's such a good player, people will always get tight and try to hit him. In any game the knocks are going to come his way.' Pepper himself started a suspension shortly afterwards, for having accumulated cautions.

If Cantona didn't fall foul of the referee at York, team-mate Roy Keane did, in the League game against Blackburn Rovers at Ewood Park. United won 2–1; Keane was sent off by referee David Elleray, who had handled Cantona's comeback game against Liverpool, and was no stranger to controversy. Elleray showed Keane the red card for 'diving' in the penalty area – a verdict Keane disputed as he insisted: 'I'm not a diver. I didn't agree with the referee's decision. There are so many different opinions, and I have mine – disagreeing with the interpretation that I dived.' A former referee, Brian Hill (once the man in the middle at another United match – against Wimbledon – which caused a furore after the final whistle) reckoned that while Keane 'wouldn't say boo to a goose when he was at Nottingham Forest, he has changed his spots since moving to United, and made life difficult for referees.'

Alex Ferguson, however, described Keane as 'one of the best we've ever had at Old Trafford', while Forest coach Liam O'Kane – admitting that Keane had 'a short fuse' – declared: 'I've never seen anyone who did the simple things so well. He'll end up as one of the greats.' So once more a United player had folk arguing about him ... and there was more to be said about the mercurial Cantona, by people within the game.

Gordon Taylor, chief executive of the Professional Foot-ballers' Association, admitted that he had considered 'extremely seriously' whether or not to warn his members to refrain from provoking the Frenchman. 'I reached the decision that there was no reason why a special case should be made for an individual player. We all know Cantona's main problem lies in his temperament, and there is always the possibility of opposing players looking to rile him. Cantona is undoubtedly a special player in terms of his outstanding talent, but there has to be a limit to how many times you can make a special case for him. If the message has not got through to him now, then perhaps it never will.'

Sir Bobby Charlton claimed: 'From a skill point of view, I would not swap him for any other player in the world ... we have to hope he has learned a lot from his experience. He loves to play, and I don't believe he will want to be put out of the game again. But who knows? He's an absolute pleasure to watch when he's performing to the peak of his ability. I am not on tenterhooks about his return, but I am prepared for anything.' A verdict echoed by Cantona's fellow-countryman, David Ginola, who had arrived on the English Soccer scene to star for Newcastle United. Ginola's view: 'Eric is 29, and it's too late for him to change. I would hope he has learned his lesson, but we will have to wait and see.' And United chairman Martin Edwards confessed: 'We have stood by him, and we can only hope he appreciates that. He has a new contract, a new start with us. It is up to him now – we are all holding our breath.' Especially when Cantona was due to return to London for his first major test on the ground of a Premier League club.

United's date with Chelsea towards the end of October, 1995, would bring the Frenchman – injury permitting – up against not only the Chelsea team and their fans, but in contact once more with the referee who had sent him off at Selhurst Park the previous January. Alan Wilkie played the reunion down somewhat, as he said: 'If it is offered, I will be only too glad to shake Eric's hand. I'm looking forward to the game...

'I have refereed Eric in three matches, including his first-ever game in England, and I've never had to speak to him before that Palace game.' Wilkie also said: 'The main reason everyone loves refereeing United is because there's such a Cup-tie atmosphere...' And he was speaking on the eve of Cantona's appearance in the Coca-Cola Cup return at York, where the result prompted noted columnist John Junor (a Cantona fan) to pen a pithy piece as he termed Alex Ferguson 'one of the great managers of all time' and the Frenchman 'a peerless player'. Yet there was a sting in the tail as Junor wrote: 'Wasn't it a joy to see them (United) knocked out by tiny, humble York City, a team 56 places below them in the League, a team which had cost just £91,000 in transfer fees compared with the £17.5 million Alex Ferguson has spent on his side?' And Junor reminded folk: 'Isn't it upsets like this which make Soccer still the most exciting spectator game in the world?'

It was another Cup upset (the UEFA Cup) which damaged United's financial calculations, as well as their reputation. The club's share value slumped by £11 million as shares fell by 18p to 193p. The City analysts blamed the drop directly on United's failure to overcome Rotor Volgograd and it was suggested that success in the European tournament, coupled with exclusive Sky television coverage, should have been worth up to £6 million to United. And yet ... while 'times are changing in football, United look sure to stay the fattest cats in the Premiership. Helped by transfers out, Britain's most profitable club raised profits 86 per cent. to £20 million in the year to July. Not bad, without winning a major trophy! But then, United are no ordinary club. Their phenomenal success in merchandising – from tea mugs to duvets and videos – generated £23 million sales, up 65 per cent.' Thus ran a report in October, 1995 – though it added: 'Sensibly, chairman Martin Edwards concedes growth of this kind is unlikely to be sustained and will now try to improve margins rather than rely on raising turnover... An early exit from Europe means no repeat of last year's £4.5 million windfall from the Champions' League.'

But all was not lost – far from it. 'A new kit-sponsorship deal with Umbro could be worth up to £25 million over five

233

years. There is the prospect of more cash from Sky TV, and ground improvements will lift capacity to 55,000 next year. Filling it seems a formality.' More than this, of course; by the start of 1996, United's manager hoped his all-star team would be heading not only for another championship, but for success in the FA Cup. They might be two down, but there still remained two to go...

Two months to go to the turn of the year, and it was Newcastle United first (eight wins, one defeat, with the explosive shooting of Les Ferdinand and the subtle promptings of David Ginola); Manchester United second (with Cole having managed only one goal in seven games and young Scholes pressing his claims for a place). Would the Magpies blow up, as they had done the previous term – or would they justify their rating as the bookies' title favourites? And could Cole get anywhere close to that 30-goal target Alex Ferguson had set for him as he savoured the prospect of Cantona's comeback? – The pressure was increasing all round; indeed, it all indicated that the championship race would be close and go right to the wire once more.

As Manchester United prepared to take on Chelsea at Stamford Bridge, former Old Trafford star Mark Hughes (now with the opposition) warned Cantona that he would be in for a noisy reception. More than this: 'The hostility from crowds to United players is worse than anything I've ever experienced, even when I was playing for Barcelona in highly-charged Spanish games, or for Bayern Munich in Germany.' Hughes declared: 'The venom from opposition fans reached a higher level than ever in the wake of the incident at Crystal Palace last season. The backlash to Eric made it worse for the rest of us. A lot of people wanted United to fall flat on their faces.

'That feeling has probably carried on now ... Eric will have to live with that. The one big difference I've noticed from being a Chelsea player is that there isn't anything like the hostility shown towards me now in away games that I felt when I was playing for United.' Chelsea team-mates had warned Hughes that their match at West Ham would

234

engender 'a little extra feeling and that the atmosphere in the ground would be particularly charged. It was nothing like my visit to Upton Park with United in the last game of last season' (when the championship was wrested from United). On Cantona: 'A lot of people gain a great deal of pleasure from watching him play – even if they don't admit to it. Undoubtedly, some are attracted to him because they don't know what's going to happen next. Will there be an explosion?

'It's talent like Eric's we need to nurture and protect. At the moment, people are trying to destroy his kind of ability. Hopefully, he won't be sparked into doing anything silly again in the future. He did let the side down ... it wasn't just that we would have had Eric in the team for the last three one a half months of the season ... the whole club would have been spared the sideshow that events surrounding that night at Selhurst Park created. That made it impossible just to go out and play. I think Eric is aware of these facts now.'

Hughes and his Chelsea team-mates were made to suffer, as United (with Cantona staying out of trouble, while still displaying deft touches of skill) won 4–1, though Hughes did have the consolation of getting his name on the scoresheet. Meanwhile, at St James's Park, Newcastle hammered in half a dozen goals against Wimbledon. For the Manchester club, there was good news and bad news; while they beat Bryan Robson's Middlesbrough at Old Trafford, Roy Keane was sent off for the second time during the season and the third time during 1995. His offence: swinging a punch at Boro' striker Jan-Aage Fjortoft, after the players had become involved in some shirt-pulling. Alex Ferguson remained tight-lipped about Keane's dismissal, saying only that this was the penalty when a player raised his fist.

The red card meant a four-match suspension for the Irishman – who then underwent surgery for a hernia problem and thus missed his country's vital play-off match against Holland (which the Republic lost) for a place in the 1996 European championships. Keane was also missing when United took on Liverpool at Anfield, although they welcomed the return of Peter Schmeichel and Ryan Giggs.

However, this turned out to be an unhappy occasion, as Liverpool won 2–0 and United played in a manner which left their manager giving his players a rap. Ferguson was doubly dismayed, because Newcastle's 1–0 victory over Everton 24 hours previously had opened up a seven-point gap at the top of the table, so defeat at Anfield meant that both Merseyside clubs had contributed towards United's misery.

Ferguson's verdict on his team: 'I don't think the players showed the passion required for this type of football. When we play Liverpool I, and everyone connected with the club, expect the players to fight. In the first half, the players didn't fight; in the second half, they showed a little bit of passion and made a game of it . . . but we don't want to mask a really poor performance. Particularly in the first half, it was the most lifeless United performance for years, especially coming at this place. This was a bad performance that we're not accepting at all. A few players in the Liverpool defence had an easy time, because we never got near them. For some of our players, coming to Anfield with United was a new experience – but the rest have played here, and there's no excuse. Liverpool dominated the midfield – they showed the passing to keep possession, and we never really made a tackle on them'.

United's manager may have repeated himself several times during that peroration, but there was no mistaking his message – knowing, also, as he did, that his team faced tough fixtures immediately afterwards, against Leeds United and table-topping Newcastle. This 'public rebuke hurled at his players' by an 'incensed' manager demonstrated just how unhappy the display had made him. And with Andy Cole – substituted for a second time – still only with three goals to his name, there was speculation that his place was in jeopardy.

It was no consolation to United's manager that another striker who had been off-key (Liverpool's Stan Collymore) had been denied a hat-trick only by virtue of fine saves from Schmeichel and the woodwork. United's 'keeper made five superb saves against British football's costliest player, and when Schmeichel was beaten, he saw the ball strike the angle

236

of post and bar. The 'keeper also made his own contribution to his manager's condemnation of the team's display when he said the time had come for United to 'waken up', or their chance of claiming the championship would disappear. And as Ferguson looked to 1996, he fervently hoped for a change in fortune – not only for his own United, but for Newcastle United. He was not to know, at that stage, that the Magpies' lead would be whittled away as the weeks of 1996 went by, nor that his team would be contesting the final of the FA Cup with Liverpool ... nor that Cantona, far from exploding, would keep his cool and produce such consistent scoring form that he would be voted the sportswriters' Footballer of the Year. The *Daily Mail*'s Neil Harman, one of Cantona's fiercest critics immediately after the Selhurst Park affair, was prompted to write, at the end of November, 1995: 'He's not quite angelic, but such a sense of serenity has descended on Cantona that United can be carried to the Premiership title on the cultured spread of his wings.'

The end of 1995 did bring one cloud on United's horizon, as it was reported that they faced 'the cold shoulder from other clubs over their youth-recruitment tactics.' The story referred to the signing of two starlets ... 'rival clubs are threatening to boycott fixtures against the Old Trafford youth teams.' United were scheduled to appear before an FA disciplinary inquiry after Arsenal and Oldham Athletic had complained that Matthew Wicks, son of former defender Steve Wicks, and David Brown had left these clubs, respectively, to join Manchester United. Manchester City manager Alan Ball, commenting on United's so-called 'aggressive' approach towards recruitment of young talent nurtured by other clubs, claimed: 'They've been doing it for years ... they take all our best youngsters. We have written to them to say we will pull out of all fixtures at youth level, unless they stop.'

City were reported to have been furious when 14-year-old Steve Flitcroft, brother of their former England Under-21 player, Garry, left the Maine Road school of excellence to join United. Oldham chairman Ian Stott, an FA councillor, declared: 'I can understand clubs wanting to make a protest by refusing to play against United. We have complained because we are making a stand. We feel there ought to be firm guidelines to prevent this sort of thing happening.' Oldham's complaint that Brown had been 'poached' was revealed at the same time as the news broke about Wicks, who had joined Arsenal as an 11-year-old and, after having signed associated-schoolboy forms for them, agreed professional terms with United. He was currently captain of the England Under-18 side.

United were charged under an FA rule concerning the inducement of young players to switch clubs, and when it came to Wicks, Arsenal were said to be seeking £1.5 million compensation – though they would drop their claim, if he rejoined them. Alex Ferguson said: 'The boy is unhappy. He has not been settled at the club in the last few weeks, and he's felt homesick.' But he maintained: 'He's not going to Arsenal until certain agreements are made.' The upshot was that United were found guilty of having poached Wicks and Brown. In the case of the former, there was a compromise solution as Wicks agreed to return to Arsenal, so United had only to pay the costs of the hearing. United maintained that they had not breached regulations and that a fine would have been harsh. An FA spokesman confirmed, however, that United had escaped a minimum, £50,000 fine only because the player had gone back to Highbury. 'United were found guilty,' he said, adding: 'There was certainly the prospect of a very large fine, because it is an issue the FA feels very strongly about.' In the case of David Brown, United were fined £20,000, and a commission ruled that they must pay Oldham £75,000 for the youngster, with possible further sums, depending upon his progress at Old Trafford. In total, Oldham could collect half a million or more.

United director Maurice Watkins maintained: 'It's all about interpretation of the regulation ... it's a technical matter. We are a hostage to fortune, because young players want to play for us. They and their parents see that we develop talent and give first-team opportunities to young players. It is the players who come to us after turning down other offers. If somebody wants to play for us and not another club, I can't see how you can make them play against their wishes. We believe the rules support our actions, and we are acting within them.' Ian Stott called for a new code of conduct, in the wake of the David Brown case. 'It is important that cases like this are brought and won, if the ever-increasingly costly investment in youth development is to be maintained,' he declared.

Maurice Watkins spoke up, also, when it was reported that United might join Europe's biggest clubs in a breakaway super-league, unless UEFA agreed to scrap its restriction on foreign players for the three major European tournaments. Like other clubs, United felt they had been penalised because they had not been able to field their strongest side when playing in Europe. Watkins claimed: 'It seems clear from the outcome of the Bosman case that there should be no restriction on clubs fielding European Union players. Already the Premier League has embraced the ruling. It is our view that UEFA should exist to run competitions within the law.' That, however, was for the future ... of more immediate concern for United was their assault on the championship and the FA Cup, as 1996 was ushered in. Kevin Keegan was in upbeat mood after a Newcastle victory over Arsenal ... 'If we keep playing like that, we will win something,' he declared. The win came shortly after Andy Cole had struck to help Manchester United beat the Magpies 2–0 at Old Trafford.

During the early days of 1996, French-international defender William Prunier rejected the chance to stay at Old Trafford, after having been offered only a short-term deal, and as Alex Ferguson sought to reinforce his side after injuries to Gary Pallister and Steve Bruce, he reflected that if Newcastle had beaten his team, 'it could have been a gap of 13 points.'

At the same time, Ferguson was admitting that he had erred in playing Peter Schmeichel against Spurs at Tottenham, after the 'keeper had injured himself during the warm-up. Schmeichel played for 45 minutes, Spurs took control of the game, and beat United 4–1. United had enjoyed success against another London club, Queen's Park Rangers, with Andy Cole having hit his third goal in successive games. When it came to the FA Cup, Sunderland gave United a scare at Old Trafford – Ferguson admitted: 'We're lucky to be in the competition.' A late goal from Cantona – shades of things to come! – robbed the First Division side of victory as they shared a four-goal thriller ... and in the League, the points gap between the United of Manchester and the United of Newcastle had been narrowed to seven points. As Roy Keane observed: 'Bloody hell – there's a lot of difference between that number and 13. They're catchable now.'

And Cantona? Sir Bobby Charlton was musing on his rehabilitation as the anniversary of the Selhurst Park incident came round. Like this: 'What he did at the time was really wrong; but he's paid the penalty and he's behaved.' And Neil Harman was asking: 'Has English football ever experienced such a transformation, from the devil incarnate to docile do-gooder?' The headlines had just hailed Cantona as a peace-maker at Upton Park. And after United had managed to overcome Sunderland in the Roker Park replay, Cantona was being hailed again for his reactions at Reading's Elms Park ground in the fourth-round FA Cup-tie. A coin thrown on the pitch hit a linesman, though it was thought the target was Cantona. Referee Jeff. Winter said: 'If this was supposed to be a test for Eric, he passed with flying colours.' And United won 3–0.

Next stop, Selhurst Park ... where he produced what was termed 'an authoritative performance' in a 4–2 victory, took the captain's armband when Bruce went off injured, and scored twice. 'Eric had done it again ... back at the scene of his most shameful moment, the Frenchman had returned in triumph to keep United's title hopes alive.'

There came the day of the FA Cup derby game against Manchester City ... and two more items of news to ponder. City manager Alan Ball branded the penalty verdict that turned this duel United's way 'a shocker.' City had taken an early lead, then referee Alan Wilkie awarded a controversial spot-kick which Cantona despatched, to pave the way for

United's 2–1 win. Meanwhile, United fans learned that they could now attend Old Trafford for weddings, as well as match of the day, and United lost a battle with Lazio for the signature of South African defender Mark Fish. On the commercial front, United revealed they had agreed a six-year sponsorship deal with Umbro to confirm their ranking as British football's wealthiest club . . . and this, just two months after having announced record profits of £20 million. The Umbro contract had still had two years to run, and a spokesman said: 'Everyone can take it as read that the deal reflects the size and stature of United as a world footballing power.' It was believed the club would pick up £10 million each year. As for players, United had set aside no less than £8 million for transfer deals, if need be. And it was reported that in the past year the club's merchandising wing had more than doubled its turnover to £5.25 million – the bulk of this created by shirt sales . . . more of which later.

Ryan Giggs was said to have signed 'the most lucrative sponsorship deal in British football' for an individual player – his agreement with Reebok 'could earn the United star £6 million over the next six years.' Even the likes of Cantona – match-winner and peacemaker in the explosive game against West Ham – and Paul Gascoigne 'cannot match the money available to the 22-year-old winger.' It was said the deal required a sustained spell of success by club and player to exploit its full potential, but it was worth 'a minimum £300,000 a year to Giggs until 2002, assuring him of at least £1.8 million.' Bonuses linked to sales and success could increase the player's earnings. As for Andy Cole, his last-minute header may have ensured victory in the Roker Park Cup replay . . . but his admission that 'it's not been the best of seasons for me' was merely a foretaste of what was to come. By the time United had reached Wembley and were coming to the crunch in the title race, Cole was sitting on the bench and sweating on a place in the first-team line-up.

Chapter 22

DOUBLE DELIGHT!

'I love the team ... hate the club.' – Manchester United supporter.

ALEX Ferguson fell foul of players at Leeds United, and most especially of Newcastle United manager Kevin Keegan ... Manchester United fell foul of their fans – yet again – and twice in swift succession. It was the spring of 1996, and the championship race was coming to the boil, as Ferguson's team also prepared to meet their arch-rivals, Liverpool, in the FA Cup at Wembley. The row had been sparked off by remarks Ferguson had made, in the wake of an Old Trafford victory over Leeds United. The aftermath came when, having also beaten Leeds, Newcastle were about to depart from Elland Road. Keegan, interviewed on television, appeared almost incandescent with rage as he gave his Old Trafford counterpart a tongue-lashing.

It had started in mid-April, when Ferguson was critical of the Leeds players – and remember, there had been an occasion in the past when he had felt compelled to apologise to the Elland Road club. Now he was terming the Leeds' players' efforts in recent matches as 'pathetic' and saying: 'On that performance (against Manchester United) they should be a top-six team. They're not. They're struggling, so they've been cheating on their manager.' One report suggested that

Ferguson had 'a vested interest in winding up the resolve of the Elland Road playing staff' – their next match would be against Newcastle. 'But Ferguson is also dismayed at the way sections of the Leeds crowd have turned on Howard Wilkinson', a manager he so admired.

Ferguson declared that Wilkinson's players 'owe it to him to produce some good performances in their last three games, and that will help the fans realise they have a first-class manager'. Leeds captain Gary McAllister rapped back: 'It's nice to see Ferguson is so concerned about Leeds – but we can keep our own house in order. Our concern is getting points and putting in good performances in our remaining games ... frankly, I'd have thought Fergie's only concern would be for his team to do the same'. Leeds defender John Pemberton, describing Ferguson's 'cheating' accusation as 'garbage', declared: 'It's Ferguson's way of trying to wind us up for the Newcastle game.'

Like Manchester United, Newcastle defeated Leeds 1–0 – then came the Keegan explosion. 'You don't say the sort of thing he (Ferguson) has done recently. He went down in my estimation, after what he said. You've got to send him a tape of this game (Newcastle and Leeds), haven't you? I've kept quiet until now ... we're still fighting for the title, and he has got to go to Middlesbrough and get something – and I will love it if we beat them.' Keegan's voice rang with barely-contained fury and – naturally – the media made the most of the rumpus. They even called upon the stress experts and the psychiatrists to forecast the result of the Keegan outburst ... would it backfire, or would it wind up his own team to go out and do the business against Nottingham Forest? One expert said: 'I have never seen a manager as angry or emotional as Keegan appeared to be. But it will have gone down well with Newcastle supporters and players, and should help to motivate them.' Ironically, Newcastle's match-winner at Leeds had been former Manchester United player Keith Gillespie, while back at Old Trafford Andy Cole, who had moved in the opposite direction in the £7 million deal, was finding himself in and out of the side.

The championship battle had see-sawed, as United chased Keegan's team during the second half of the season, and one match in particular put the spotlight not only on a poor performance by Ferguson's side, but upon United's commercial activities. Shortly before United met Leeds, they had to play at Southampton; and what happened there was totally unexpected.

The Saints were fighting for Premiership survival, and they won, 3–1. It was reported: 'The Saints provided divine intervention on behalf of Newcastle and guaranteed a fight to the finish for the title. They thought it was all over ... but it isn't now!' Ferguson rounded on his defence after this debacle – a first defeat in 19 games – as he said: 'We cannot be proud of our defending; we were absolutely terrible'. What sparked off more discussion was the fact that at half-time United switched their strip – from grey to blue-and-white stripes. Not that it made any difference to the result. Ferguson later offered an explanation that the grey strip made it difficult for his players to distinguish their team-mates against the backdrop of the fans – and, in any event, 'the players prefer the blue, and so do I.' Of course, the feelings of the kit manufacturers had to be considered, but in the final analysis, they owned up to being at fault. The result at The Dell meant that Ferguson's team had 73 points, with three games to go; Keegan's team had 67 points, with five games to go.

Back to the change of strip, and Manchester United were accused of 'a rip-off' as they announced that they would be ditching that 'unlucky' grey. 'It means England's biggest and wealthiest club will be launching three strips next season, leading to claims that thousands of fans who flock to buy replica shirts are being cheated. Fans wanting to wear the club's latest colours will thus have to pay out three times'. Tony Kershaw, secretary of the National Federation of Football Supporters' Clubs, declared: 'You can only sum it up as a rip-off. Changing all three kits in the course of one season is totally unfair to fans of all age groups, not just children.' When it was revealed that a white away strip would replace the grey, United chairman Martin Edwards, looking po-faced as he faced the TV cameras, announced that the white shirts (to be worn for only one season) would be discounted by a tenner. Clearly, the club hoped this would placate fans who had spent £30 to £40 a time on the grey kit.

It was then reported that Umbro would be footing the bill for the £10 discount, and their managing director, Alan Hadfield, said: 'We chose the grey – it has been as popular as any Manchester United change kit is. If we put a strip on the market that players are struggling to see each other in, then we are to blame'. The firm said the particular shade had been the problem – other teams (including England) had worn grey without any complaints. As the arguments about the strip changes flourished among the fans, I was interested to hear the observations of one dyed-in-the-wool United supporter. He, too, had been talking to fans he knew and he told me that one of then had expressed this succinct opinion: 'I love the team … hate the club'.

Labour leader Tony Blair had attacked football clubs who constantly changed team strips, and as long ago as a year before the debacle at The Dell one observer of the game had suggested that Manchester United would soon be changing their shirts at half-time, as he singled out the club and criticised its commercial activities. By the last day of April, 1996, the fans were being informed of another fact – that thousands of season tickets in the new stand at Old Trafford were set to triple in price to £1,169 a year. 'It will make then the most costly in the land,' said a report. One section would be designated an 'executive area' for season 1996–97, with higher-quality catering and car-parking facilities. 'These 2,300 prime seats are being advertised at £995 each plus VAT, although in the old cantilever stand the same spots were available for £340.'

United assistant secretary Ken Ramsden explained: 'We also have executive areas in the south stand where the tickets will be the same price. We have taken a commercial route, but feel it has proved in the best interests of everyone with a successful team playing in the best surroundings'. The report said that fans relocated when the old stand was demolished were advised that they would be able to claim back their old seats – 'but have only just learned the cost.' And Chris Robinson, chairman of the Independent Manchester United Supporters' Association, said: 'It does appear that money is more important than loyalty.'

Still, the team was going well, and the defeat by Southampton (after 15 wins in 16 games) proved to be merely a blip, as United defeated first Leeds, then Nottingham Forest – whose manager, Frank Clark, had made it clear that his players would not be yielding one inch either to Manchester United or to Newcastle United, whom they would be meeting during the last week of the campaign. The fact that Clark had once played for Newcastle was irrelevant – he was concerned only with ensuring that Forest gave of their best. Their best wasn't good enough at Old Trafford, where they were turned over in a 5–0 rout, so it was left to Newcastle to see if they could emulate Manchester United when they visited the City Ground.

Meanwhile, Eric Cantona could look forward to receiving his Footballer-of-the-Year award shortly before the FA Cup final ... and the sportswriters were looking forward to hearing what he had to say, in his acceptance speech. Apart from one or two columnists who had expressed their reservations, Cantona's award was declared to be no more than his due, considering the way he had behaved and the contribution he had made to United's cause – not least when it came to sticking away single goals which had won matches as the title race headed for its conclusion. There was the winner he struck against Newcastle at St James's Park which left manager Ferguson saying: 'Eric has scored a lot of important goals – his record is fantastic – and we certainly don't win many games when he's not in the team.' That victory had taken Manchester United to within a point of Newcastle, and before long it would be Newcastle who were chasing their Old Trafford rivals.

Once again, cash came into the championship equation as

it was reported that Manchester United's status as new title favourites had sent their shares soaring by 13p on the Stock Exchange. 'Cantona's goal increased the value of Manchester United plc by £7.9 million as the shares hit their highest point for the year at 280p each. Investors are clearly attracted by the prospect of seeing United win the Premier League and compete in the lucrative European Champions' Cup next season ... last September, after they were knocked out of the UEFA Cup, the share price slumped to 197p.

While Manchester United's fortunes had risen both on the field and off it, Newcastle had headed for the final showdown with heart-breaking results at Anfield and Ewood Park. Liverpool had clinched a last-gasp, 4–3 victory; Blackburn Rovers had staged a similar rescue act ... with a Geordie, young Graham Fenton, the player who struck twice to win the encounter. And he had been brought up as a Newcastle supporter. Back at Old Trafford, Alex Ferguson was not pinning his hopes solely upon Monsieur Cantona ... he was agonising over what to do about Andy Cole. And revealing the identity of 'the young footballer Manchester United will not sell at any price'. Coming towards the end of February, 1996, Ferguson had cited 21-year-old Paul Scholes as being irreplaceable in his plans for the future; by the beginning of March, United's manager was predicting, also, that Cole would 'take off' again as a marksman, after having reached double figures for the season during a 6–0 blitzing of Bolton by United.

Ferguson pointed out that Cole could not be rated merely in terms of goals scored – 'he's an all-rounder now ... you can't count his involvement in goals for others. He puts defenders under pressure, makes them really tentative.' As for young Scholes (13 goals in 17 starts), 'I see him as the long-term replacement for Eric Cantona. We would never consider selling Scholes – he is too valuable to the club. Scholes can fill Eric's boots; he has great vision and can open up defences with his passing skills. He can slot into the creative role that Cantona has made his own for us. Paul also has that priceless eye for a goal.' It was Cantona who had scored one

247

goal and made the other in United's FA Cup quarter-final win over Southampton, Cantona whose 'classic piece of piracy' took United to the top of the table with a 1–1 result away against Queen's Park Rangers, Cantona whose goal (his 14th of the season) secured a 1–0 victory over Arsenal at Old Trafford, and Cantona whose goal against Spurs put United three points clear of Newcastle. As for Scholes and Cole, the former was a two-goal man in the six-goal romp against Bolton, the latter was on the mark as United despatched Chelsea in their FA Cup semi-final. And yet again, the cash equation cane into it as the financial columns recorded that United 'score on transfers.'

The story, on the eve of the semi-final, recorded that the recent upsurge in United's share price 'is set to continue if Britain's most valuable football club wins the FA Cup semi-final or the Premiership. For United, which has increased its market value 65 per cent. to £158 million since August, success on the pitch works straight through to its share price. It jumped sharply after the club agreed a £60 million, five-year sponsorship deal with Umbro. The club is expected to report half-year profits of £11.9 million, up from £7.3 million. Much of the boost has come from the £5 million sale of Andrei Kanchelskis. The sale has created a surprise, £4.2 million surplus on the club's transfer account, more than making up for loss of gate receipts caused by the closure of the north stand for rebuilding, according to latest forecasts by house-broker Merrill Lynch. With the north stand re-opened, crowd capacity will rise from 44,000 to 55,300. Ticket revenue is expected to rise by £3 million a season on 75 per cent capacity.'

As Alex Ferguson set his players a title target of 81 points, he could bask in the glow of knowing that his fledglings had come good, too – the Neville brothers had been called into the England squad, ready to become the first brothers to play for England since the hey-day of the Charltons; and Nicky Butt and David Beckham had more than played their parts in the side's surge to the top and to Wembley. Yet there remained the question mark over Andy Cole, who had been

248

substituted in the win over Arsenal after he had passed up three clear-cut chances – though Ferguson did say his costly striker 'is cursed by incredibly bad luck in front of goal.' Cole had never been dropped since his arrival at Old Trafford, but he was replaced again late on, during the game against Spurs, and he had had what were described as 'two heart-to-heart discussions with Ferguson' in the 48 hours preceding the match. His goal tally then was 10, in 34 games. Scholes had scored a dozen in half as many appearances. Cole's former club had briefly regained the top spot as they 'answered the doubts over their staying power' with a 3–0 win over West Ham (Faustino Asprilla had celebrated his first home goal for the Magpies).

One man who appeared to have no doubts – about Manchester United's crop of young talent – was England coach Terry Venables. He watched United knock Chelsea off the Wembley trail, then said: 'The maturity United's young-sters showed was outstanding, and a significant factor in why they were able to beat Chelsea without Bruce, Pallister and Irwin. I have already brought Gary Neville into the England defence and called up Phil for the match against Bulgaria ... there's no doubt in my mind that Beckham and Butt will join them in the England squad. The four of them can be vital parts of the England team looking forward to the next World Cup.' Even so, Alex Ferguson was being tipped to use some of that £8 million available for new faces ... 'United will send a high-powered delegation to Amsterdam to watch the man acclaimed as one of the fastest wingers in Europe, George Donis'; and: 'Alex Ferguson will make his first major signing for more than a year, with the capture of brilliant Dutch midfielder Edgar Davids'. Donis was playing in a European Cup semi-final for Panathinaikos, Davids was starring for Ajax.

Of more immediate concern to Ferguson was his team's showing in the League derby game against Manchester City at the start of April, and once more Cantona delivered the goods. 'He is performing like a player possessed ... having provided all the Premiership goals which earned United three wins and a draw in March, the Frenchman proceeded to demonstrate his particular relish for the frenetic air of a Manchester derby'. United won, 3–2, at Maine Road, and Cantona struck his eighth goal in six Manchester meetings to start the ball rolling. United needed those goals, because Newcastle's Peter Beardsley also struck – twice in four minutes – to put his team's title challenge back on track against Queen's Park Rangers. One tribute to Cantona came from an opposing goalkeeper, Southampton's Dave Beasant. 'You can see a change in Eric; he doesn't seem to get involved. When he took a kick from our players, he just accepted it – rather than react, he has got up and got on with the game.'

Another day, another crunch game – against Coventry City, managed by former United boss Ron Atkinson and battling to stay in the Premiership. It was Cantona who provided a close-range finish to ensure a 1–0 victory as he hit his seventh goal in eight games between March 3 and April 8. Newcastle, Southampton (the FA Cup), Queen's Park Rangers, Arsenal, Spurs, Chelsea (he set up a goal for Cole, hit a post and cleared off his own line in this FA Cup duel), Manchester City and Coventry ... they had all felt the impact of Cantona's striking power and skills. United's win over Coventry was followed by Newcastle's setback at Blackburn, to leave the Magpies six points adrift. And then came the news that Cantona was the Footballer of the Year.

Newcastle's Les Ferdinand had claimed the Player-of-the-Year award from his fellow-professionals, but Ferguson declared: 'There can be no question that Eric is the outstanding player of the season. He is the best footballer in the country and has been over the past few months. It's a long season, and sometimes, when the PFA draw up their short list for their award before Christmas and then announce their player of the year in March, you can get an unfair situation. Eric's form over the last three months has been sensational.' The Frenchman had scored 17 goals in 33 appearances since his return to action in the October. His reaction? – 'I am proud and privileged to have been voted Footballer of the Year. It is a tremendous honour for me and my country ... it

is also a great tribute to the players at Manchester United.'
And Neil Harman wrote of Cantona: 'He changed, so why
couldn't we? The coronation of Cantona justifies both his
astonishing metamorphis and that of those who were his
chief accusers. England's football writers have not only
chosen the best footballer in this country, but should toast in
vintage on May 9 their own ability to repent.' Not that every
sportswriter totally agreed . . . Harman's *Daily Mail* colleague,
Jeff. Powell, posed a few questions, while the *Daily Express*
columnist, James Lawton, while agreeing that Cantona 'is
unquestionably Footballer of the Year', also declared: 'But he
is not, suddenly, a combination of Superman and Mother
Teresa'. Lawton said Cantona had behaved in a professional
manner for six months . . . 'someone like Peter Beardsley has
been doing it for the best part of 20 years.'

Lawton also suggested that 'in the rush to acknowledge
Cantona's reformation – and the sustained brilliance of his
play this season – we shouldn't forget the burden of debt he
had to repay.' Another writer, the *Mail on Sunday*'s Joe
Melling, recorded that Cantona's emergence as the 49th
player to win the coveted award since 1948 was 'a transformation that seemed barely possible and owes much to the
management skills of Alex Ferguson. In the first instance, he
responded to Cantona's moment of madness (at Selhurst
Park) by suspending the Frenchman to the end of the season
. . . then he was forced to make an urgent flight to France for a
rendezvous with Cantona in Paris . . . it seemed the Frenchman was on the threshold of abandoning England for Italy.'
Ferguson told Melling: 'I was not going to kick him out; I was
determined to see it through.' And Melling declared: 'Now
Cantona the outcast is embraced among the game's most
distinguished performers. The vote (by the football writers)
proves he has won over many who, a short while ago, were
scathing in their condemnation.'

But if Cantona was able to smile with quiet satisfaction,
Ferguson was still wrestling with the problem presented by
Cole. He had 10 days 'to reflect on whether he can put his
absolute trust in Cole to deliver United the championship he

was specifically purchased for. Only two matches remain of what has become an increasingly torrid period for the 24-year-old. Ferguson has shown a remarkable tolerance towards Cole...' But as United faced up to Nottingham Forest – the last team to win at Old Trafford, 16 months – previously Ferguson made his decision. He axed Cole and replaced him with Scholes, who had not figured in a starting line-up since December 9. It was Scholes who set United off on their five-goal spree by scoring the first and settling any nerves his team-mates right have had. Ferguson said the dropping of Cole was 'no great deal... it wasn't an easy decision, but it was the correct one.' And so United opened up a six-point lead, then Newcastle went to Leeds and won – and Kevin Keegan verbally lambasted his Old Trafford counterpart. Come Thursday night, would the title trophy be going to Manchester, or would the race be going right to the wire? – It all depended upon Newcastle's performance at Nottingham Forest's City Ground.

On May 2, 1996, four events occurred at widely different places in England. In a Manchester hospital, Peter Swales died suddenly. For many years he had been chairman of Manchester City, but despite all his efforts to see that City outshone Manchester United, he was doomed to disappointment and, in the end, he was ousted by Francis Lee, a former City player. Swales had also been chairman of the England international committee which appointed the national team managers, but his reign as the top man there ended with the departure of Graham Taylor. On the day Swales died, Glenn Hoddle was named the new team coach of England. On that same day, also, Matthew Simmons – the fan who had been involved in the Cantona kung-fu affair at Selhurst Park – was gaoled for a week after an astonishing physical attack on the prosecuting lawyer. Simmons had been found guilty of using threatening words and behaviour during the Crystal Palace–Manchester United match more than a year previously. The magistrates had refused to accept his claim that he did not provoke Cantona into the attack upon him. Simmons was fined £500, ordered to pay £200 costs and banned from football grounds for a year. In the event, he walked free after just one night in gaol.

The fourth event occurred on the evening of May 2, and at Nottingham Forest's City Ground Ian Woan struck a goal, with quarter of an hour to go, which labelled Newcastle United's experience there a 'heart-breaker'. That goal equalised a stunning strike from Peter Beardsley which had given Newcastle the lead they so desperately sought ... but the 1–1 result left them two points behind Manchester United, so the final day of reckoning would come on the Sunday, at Middlesbrough and at St James's Park, One sentence summed it all up ... 'United will win the title if they avoid defeat at Middlesbrough after Newcastle were caught by Woan's sucker punch at Forest...' So the stage was set for a dramatic, last-day battle between four teams. As the story said, 'it may not be quite all over, and publicly Kevin Keegan's men still cling to the belief that they can win their first championship in 69 years; but in their hearts, they feel the dream has disappeared.' It was further recorded: 'Surely, only a miracle can prevent the title going to Old Trafford for the third time in four years. A miracle it would be if Bryan Robson – for so long the spiritual leader of United – inflicted the defeat on Alex Ferguson's side Newcastle are now praying for.'

The miracle didn't happen, for Newcastle ... as they trailed 1–0 to Spurs, their rivals were scoring, and scoring again at the Riverside stadium. David May broke the deadlock against Middlesbrough, Andy Cole – and what joy it gave him! – knocked in a second goal, and Ryan Giggs rounded off a 3–0 victory which was accomplished in the style of true champions. Newcastle did manage an equaliser, but it didn't really matter. Manchester United were crowned champions for the third time in four years ... and, remarkably, even before the kick-off at Middlesbrough the bookies were making Alex Ferguson's team the 13–8 favourites to win the title the following season! Newcastle? – They were quoted at 100–30, with Liverpool sandwiched in between at 3–1.

Ferguson and Liverpool manager Roy Evans dined with

each other shortly before the FA Cup final, which Ferguson believed could turn out to be 'the most thrilling since the Matthews final, when Blackpool came from behind to beat Bolton in 1953.' Evans wasn't quite so optimistic, though he did concede that 'the ingredients are there.' Ferguson recalled that when he was handed the United job close on a decade earlier, his brief was to get the upper hand on Liverpool – and that remained the situation as the two managers approached Wembley. Ferguson: 'I told West Ham manager Harry Redknapp in January that the battle for the championship would be between us and Liverpool. He looked at me as though I had flipped. Newcastle were about 10 points clear at the time ... but from day one this season it was Liverpool who concerned me most'. Liverpool did make a few slips, but Ferguson claimed: 'It happened for us in the Premiership ... however, I didn't get it too wrong, because the showdown is at Wembley.' Indeed, it was.

Evans recalled that when Ferguson arrived at United, 'Liverpool were the best', but he acknowledged: 'The boot is on the other foot now. United are the best, and we have to strive to become better than them.' Evans revealed that some Liverpool fans had told him they would be satisfied if United were beaten twice in the season, but 'that's rubbish ... I would have been more than happy to have lost both our League games against United if we had gone on to be champions.' Liverpool in fact, had taken four points out of six from United. And now? – 'Both of us are going to Wembley to win...'

It didn't turn out to be the classic Ferguson had forecast, but the result went right for United – and Eric Cantona (who else?) emerged as the match–winner. The Footballer of the Year, whose demeanour had been modest when accepting his award, was lauded again by the sportswriters as the man who had saved the final from being virtually a non-event. 'Cantona carved out a piece of history as United lifted the FA Cup to clinch English football's first Double Double ... Eric the Magnificent's 85th-minute winner lit up a disappointing final and capped a superb season for the Frenchman. It was his

19th goal in a season that has seen United clinch their third title in four years and Alex Ferguson lift his eighth major trophy as Old Trafford boss. Cantona's goal completes a rehabilitation that started against Liverpool in October last year ... yesterday he paid tribute to the United fans who stood by him during his suspension.'

Cantona: 'For eight months I was banned, but during every game they remembered me, even if it was just for 15 seconds. I will never forget that. I respect them, love them, try to give them the pleasure they need to receive.' It was recorded that as Cantona – captain for the day – walked up the steps to the Royal box, a rival supporter appeared to spit at him. 'Cantona completely ignored it and just seemed to smile. Ferguson also appeared to be punched as he mounted the steps, and angrily pointed out his assailant to police and stewards.' As the Frenchman confirmed that he would be staying with United 'certainly for the next two years', Ferguson declared his pride in the entire squad and said of Cantona's goal: 'It was a perfect time to score – not a lot of time to recover. Although Eric had a quiet game, the manner of his goal was marvellous, with his composure and accuracy. It needed something like that to break the deadlock.' The goal had come from a David Beckham corner which 'keeper David James punched clear. The ball was deflected off Ian Rush to Cantona, on the edge of the box, and the Frenchman unleashed a powerful drive which evaded Liverpool defenders and hit the back of the net. Thus was the FA Cup final won and lost, thus was the historic double achieved.

Peter Rhodes, the former referee who had been critical of both Cantona and United some months previously, now delivered this verdict on the Frenchman: 'I give him full marks ... the court scene involving the man (Matthew Simmons) who reacted in the way that he did, after having been handed his punishment, showed what kind of provocation Cantona had been facing at the time of the Selhurst Park incident. United got him at a bargain fee, and it has to be admitted that he now looks the bargain of all time. As for United, the emphasis now seems to me to be more on skill

255

than possibly it was in the fairly recent past. I think the emphasis has changed for the better. Some of their young-sters are very skilled indeed, and all credit to Alex Ferguson for having pinned his faith in them.'

When it came to the way United operate in finding and grooming young talent, Rhodes could cite the case of a player on his own doorstep. 'United sent Brian Kidd to York to watch City's youth-team 'keeper on a Saturday morning ... they liked what they saw and paid £100,000 cash down, with a lot more to come if he makes the grade. Fergie is a very effective manager, a very shrewd operator; and he was deservedly named Manager of the Year.' However, Manches-ter United being Manchester United, they and their manager were back in the headlines just days after the Wembley triumph – and this time the news concerned a possible new contract for Ferguson, whose term still had a year to run. At 54, he was said to be looking for a deal which would take him to the age of 60 – and a rise in pay. Chairman Martin Edwards: 'Alex has done a great job ... we hope he remains with us for a long time. At the end of the day, he has an idea of his valuation, we have our own idea; and then it's a matter for negotiation.' But United's chairman also said: 'In the Green-bury Report (on directors' pay) there is a strong recommen-dation to all plc's against contracts that last longer than three years. That applies to managing directors, managers and chairmen. We have to be mindful of that.' Ferguson's answer was that he hoped the main aspects of the contract would be sorted out before he went on holiday at the week-end ... 'I can then leave the whole matter in the hands of my advisers to clarify while I'm away. I would like the whole matter sorted out as soon as possible.'

Forty-eight hours later, it was clearly make-up-your-mind time, both for United and for their manager. He was saying, pointedly: 'My future should be decided by this evening – one way or the other.' He was said to be 'clearly furious that the club's record-breaking season has not convinced the plc board that he is the man to take them into the next Millennium.' Ferguson, looking grim-faced, was pictured as he was about to embark upon talks with chairman Martin Edwards, and the next news was that 'he was locked in a crisis meeting with his chairman this afternoon.' Edwards had gone into the meeting still saying that 'we hope very much that Alex is still our manager in six years' time – but whether it takes one contract or a couple of contracts is another matter.'

It was reported that after all the success he had brought to the club, 'the proud Scot believes it is demeaning to have to fight for the contract he wants' and that 'Ferguson also feels angry that he has to argue for an increase in his £250,000-a-year salary with a chairman whose salary last year was £290,000, on top of which he drew a further £720,000 in dividends from his shares in the club'. It was further recorded: 'Edwards will be only too aware that there will be a massive backlash from United supporters if he fails to reach agreement with the manager who has made Manchester United the most successful club in British Soccer over the past five years.' The way one United fan – who had backed them for the double – put it to me: 'After what he's done for the club, they should make him a Freeman of the city, never mind give him a six-year contract.'

Several hours later, Ferguson was pictured, smiling, and it was revealed that he and United had reached agreement on a deal which would keep him at Old Trafford until the year 2000. He had become 'the highest-paid manager in British football after agreeing a four-year contract worth £2.6 million...' Ferguson's verdict: 'It's been a long, long day, and I'm glad it's all over. At times the delay has been frustrating, but it was never in my mind to walk out. You have to see it through, argue your case. That's what I have done.' And, having rested his case, he went off on holiday.

As for Monsieur Eric Cantona, he was having what might be termed the last word (or two). Whether or not they turned out to be famous last words remained to be seen ... he declared: 'Manchester United are good enough to win the European Cup – I will definitely be ready for the challenge.'

CALIFO
AND WEST

THE ROUGH GUIDE

ROUGH GUIDE CREDITS

Series Editor: Mark Ellingham
Editorial: Martin Dunford, John Fisher, Jack Holland, Jonathan Buckley,
               Greg Ward, Richard Trillo, Jules Brown
Production: Susanne Hillen, Kate Berens, Gail Jammy
Typesetting: Greg Ward and Andy Hilliard

Acknowledgements

Deborah: the Californians, Brett Bennett and Rick Olson for their help and friendship researching the guide; and the English, Ron Bosley, Pauline Burton, and Antoinette (aka "Toni the Truth") Ring for their usual support.

Jamie: for invaluable assistance above and beyond the call of duty, my grateful appreciation goes out to Tom Stilz in Washington, Kathy Taylor and Susan Bladholm in Oregon, Jeanine Breshears in Portland, Jackie French in Bend, John Poimiroo in Yosemite, Capt. John Stone on Whidbey Island and Helen Chang in San Francisco. For encouragement and support I'm also indebted to Mom, Dad and Bobbie, Brando and Judah, the townspeople of Pendleton, Oregon and most of all to Catherine Robson.

Mick: Fred Sater, Rosemarie Wosewick, Laurie de Selms, Sandy Bartosh, Inez Savage, Meg Neff, Marcella Streets & Joe Sheehan, and Rachel Huntingford.

Wendy: BJ Stokey at the Port of Seattle, Lynne Pierce, Larry Whiteman, E. Trindle, André Havard and Bridget Ferguson.

Continuing thanks to **Martin Dunford**, who edited the first edition of this book, Catherine Mulvenna for proof-reading, and, on this new edition, the authors would also like to thank Mr Greg Ward for being himself . . .

Reprinted twice in 1993 by Rough Guides Ltd, 1 Mercer Street, London WC2H 9QJ.
Distributed by Penguin Books, 27 Wrights Lane, London W8 5TZ.
Previously published by Harrap Columbus.

Typeset in Linotron Univers and Century Old Style to an original design by Andrew Oliver.
Printed by Cox & Wyman, Reading.
Incidental illustrations in Part One and Part Four by Ed Briant.
Basics illustration by Cathie Felstead; Contexts illustration by Sally Davies.

672p.
Includes index.

British Library Cataloguing in Publication Data

A catalogue record for this book is available from the British Library.
ISBN 1-85828-057-5 (previously published by Harrap Columbus under ISBN 0-7471-0272-4)

CALIFORNIA
AND WEST COAST USA

WRITTEN AND RESEARCHED BY

DEBORAH BOSLEY, WENDY FERGUSON,
JAMIE JENSEN AND MICK SINCLAIR

With additional accounts by
Lucy Ackroyd, Susan Compo,
Donald Hutera and Emilie Strauss

Edited by
GREG WARD

THE ROUGH GUIDES

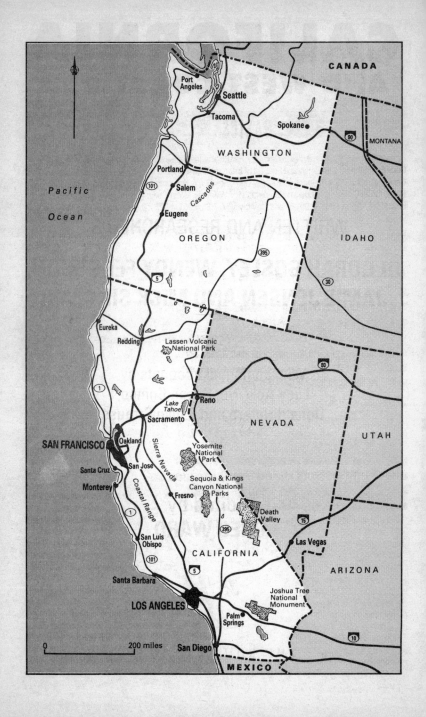

CONTENTS

Introduction vi

INTRODUCTION

You'd have to have grown up in a cave not to have some impression of **California and West Coast USA**. No region of the world, perhaps, has been as publicised, and idealised, as California, and none lives up to the hype to quite the same degree. Whatever else it may be, the West Coast really is a terrestial paradise of sun, sand, surf and sea, and it has a whole lot more besides: high mountain ranges, fast-paced glitzy cities, deep primeval forests, and hot dry deserts. The area as a whole – California, Washington *and* Oregon – really has the lot.

Having zoomed from the Stone Age to Silicon Valley in little more than a couple of centuries, the West Coast doesn't dwell on the past. In some ways this part of America represents the ultimate "now" society, with all that entails – life is lived very much in the fast lane, and conspicuous consumption is emphasised to the exclusion of almost everything else. But this is only one side of the coin; the deeper sense of age here often gets skimmed over. Provided you get out of the cities, it is readily apparent in the landscape: dense groves of ancient trees, primitive rock carvings left by the aboriginal Native American culture, and the eerie ghost towns of the Gold Rush pioneers. California especially is a land of superlatives, full of the oldest, the tallest, the largest, the most spectacular, all of which goes far beyond local bravura.

It's important to bear in mind, too, that the supposed "superficiality" of the West Coast – an image promoted as much by Americans on the *East* coast as by foreigners – is largely a myth, even if the area's endeavours to gain cultural credibility can sometimes seem crude and brash. Politically, it's probably the USA's most schizophrenic region, home state of some of its most reactionary figures – Ronald Reagan and Richard Nixon to name just two – yet also the source of some of the country's most progressive political movements. Some of the fiercest protests of the Sixties emanated from here, and in many ways this is still the heart of liberal America. Consider the level of environmental awareness (outside the cities at least) which puts the smoky East to shame; and the fact that the West Coast has set *the* standard for the rest of US (and the world) regarding gay pride and social permissiveness. Economically, too, the region is crucial, whether it's in the traditionally dominant film industry, the recently ascendant music business, even in the increasingly important financial markets – in which Los Angeles (the unquestionable capital of the West Coast) has come to set the pace.

Where To Go
The three West Coast states – California, Washington and Oregon – together cover as much land as Western Europe: keep in mind that distances can be huge, and that you won't, unless you're here for an extended period, be able to see everything on one trip.

In an area so varied it's hard to pick out specific highlights. You may well start off in **Los Angeles**, far and away the biggest and most stimulating city: a maddening collection of freeways and beaches, seedy suburbs and high-gloss neighbourhoods and extreme lifestyles that you should see at least once, even if you make a quick exit for more relaxed locales. From Los Angeles you have a number of choices. You can head south to **San Diego** – a smaller, up-and-coming city, with broad, welcoming beaches and a handy position close to the Mexican border; or you could push inland to the Californian **desert** areas, notably **Death Valley** – as its name suggests, a barren inhospitable landscape of volcanic craters and wind-swept sand dunes that in summer (when you can fry an egg on your car bonnet) becomes the hottest place on earth. Most people, though, make the steady journey up the **Central Coast**: a gorgeous run, by car especially, following the shoreline north through some of the state's most dramatic scenery, and taking in some of its liveliest small towns, notably Santa Barbara and Santa Cruz.

The Central Coast makes the transition from Southern to Northern California – a break that's more than just geographical. **San Francisco**, at the top end, is California's second city, and about as different from LA as it's possible to get: the coast's oldest, most European-looking city, set compactly over a series of steep hills, its wooden houses tumbling down to water on both sides. San Francisco also gives access to some of the state's most extraordinary scenery, not least in the national parks to the east, especially **Yosemite**, where powerful waterfalls cascade into a sheer glacial valley that's been immortalised by Ansel Adams and countless others in search of the definitive landscape photograph.

North of San Francisco the physical look changes once again. The climate is wetter up here, the valleys that much greener, providing a gentle introduction to the backcountry beauty of **Oregon** – a more provincial state than California in almost every way, with rugged hiking routes for the asking, particularly along the coast. Even its largest city, **Portland**, has a refreshing small-town cosiness. **Washington**, too, is a long way from the beach culture of Southern California, like Oregon divided into two distinct entities by the Cascade mountains. The west is wet and fertile, with thick, lush forests and the mountains of the **Olympic Peninsula**; to the east – beyond the charred wasteland left by **Mount St Helens** – the arid desert is home to a handful of one-horse towns and some hardy farmers. The focus for the Northwest region as a whole, the tough port of **Seattle**, set on the deep natural bay of the **Puget Sound**, provides plenty to detain you on the way north into Canada.

Climate

California's climate comes close to its sub-tropical ideal. In **Southern California** in particular you can count on endless days of sunshine from May to October, and warm dry nights – though **LA**'s notorious smog is at its worst when the temperatures are highest, in August and September. Right along the **coast** mornings can be hazily overcast, especially in May and June, though you can still get a suntan – or sunburn – even under greyish skies. In winter temperatures drop somewhat, but more importantly it can rain for weeks on end, causing massive mudslides that wipe out roads and hillside homes. Inland, the deserts are warm in winter and unbearably hot (120°F is not unusual) in summer; desert nights can be freezing in winter, when, strangely but beautifully, it can even snow. For serious **snow**, head to the mountains, where hiking trails at the higher elevations are blocked from November to June almost every year; skiers can take advantage of well-groomed slopes all over the three states.

The coast of Northern California is wetter and cooler than the south, its summers tempered by sea-breezes and fog, and its winters mild but wet. **San Francisco**, because of its exposed position at the tip of a peninsula, can be chilly all year, with summer fogs tending to roll in to ruin what may have started off as a pleasant sunny day. Head a mile inland, and you're back in the sun. **Oregon** and **Washington** are both mixtures, dismally grey and wet on the west side of the Cascade mountains between October and June, though with gentle blue-skied summers, giving a moderate tan without frazzling. Winters, while soggy, are rarely really cold. East of the mountains, the drizzle stops and the temperatures become more extreme – pleasant in spring, less so in summer, and with colder winters.

DAYTIME TEMPERATURES (MAX & MIN F)	Jan		April		July		Oct	
San Diego	65	46	68	54	76	63	73	58
Los Angeles	65	47	71	53	83	63	77	57
Fresno	55	36	75	47	99	63	80	48
San Francisco	55	42	64	47	72	54	71	51
Death Valley	65	37	91	61	116	87	91	51
Seattle	44	35	57	42	71	53	59	46
Portland	44	33	60	42	77	55	62	46

PART ONE

THE
BASICS

THE BASICS

GETTING THERE

Flight routes and prices to the West Coast from Britain vary wildly. Several major airlines have frequent non-stop flights to the major cities of Los Angeles, San Francisco, Seattle; others have so-called direct services (a flight is called "direct" so long as it keeps the same flight number throughout its journey), which may land once or twice on the way. You could also, if you wanted to see a little more of the country, fly somewhere else entirely in the US and travel on from there on an internal flight, perhaps using a discounted air pass or VUSA fare (see p.17) – though this will be more expensive than flying to the West Coast direct. Inclusive holidays and fly-drive deals are another way of saving money – see below for details.

FROM LONDON

Wherever and however you go, the most expensive time to travel is **high season**, roughly between June and August and a week on either side of Christmas. May and September are slightly less pricey, while any other time of year is considered **low season** and cheaper still. At any time of year, midweek flights cost less than weekend ones.

When **booking a flight** it's important to shop around for the best price: either by scanning the travel ads in the Sunday papers, London's *Time Out* or one of that city's many giveaway maga-

zines, or by phoning the airlines direct or contacting one of the agents mentioned overleaf. The details we've given are the latest available, but by the time you read them they're likely to have undergone at least subtle changes.

Most of the **non-stop flights from London** to the West Coast are to Los Angeles, the hub of the region's air travel. Fewer travel non-stop to San Francisco and Seattle, and you can't fly non-stop at all to San Diego or Portland – although connections on to all these cities via Los Angeles and other US cities are plentiful.

Non-stop flights take ten or eleven hours to reach Los Angeles, San Francisco or Seattle from London. Most leave around midday, which means you land during the afternoon, local time; the return journey is an hour or so shorter, flying through the night and arriving in London from Los Angeles or San Francisco in time for breakfast, and from Seattle in time for lunch.

More airlines have **one-stop direct flights** to the West Coast. Travelling this way obviously adds time – at least four hours – to the journey, and if you dislike hanging around airport lounges you should check the details carefully before booking.

As for **ticket types**, **standby** deals (open-dated tickets which you pay for and decide later when you want to fly) are rare and usually offer little or no savings over the much more common **Apex** returns. With these, seats must be booked at least 21 days in advance, and you must stay a minimum of seven nights. There's no great difference in **fares** from London to any particular West Coast city (although LA can cost £10–30 less than the others): they range from around £500 for a midweek flight in low season to over £600 for a weekend flight in high season. It's always worth phoning the airlines to check on whatever current reductions they may be offering: increased competition on transatlantic routes has recently prompted the major carriers to make attractive short-term offers, coming down as low as £300 return to anywhere on the West Coast. Such reductions carry a hefty number of restrictions: tickets must be booked thirty days in advance and paid for within 48 hours, you must fly midweek, and you usually can't change your plans after booking. Recently **"Instant Saver"** tickets have been introduced by several of the main airlines;

these tickets can be booked one day in advance and are completely inflexible. If this arrangement suits you, there are considerable savings to be made.

You can get a precise picture of the options by contacting an **agent** (we've listed some opposite), who may also – especially if you're under 26 or a student – be able to knock up to £150 off regular Apex fares, bringing prices down to around £350 return: your best bet when there are no special airline deals. Some also offer *"open jaw"* tickets, which enable you to fly into the US through one city and out from another one, making your own arrangements for internal travel. With one of these, you might, for example, combine New York and Los Angeles for around £325, or Seattle and Los Angeles from £400. You can also pick up cut-price seats on **charter flights** through a number of **specialist operators** – excellent value, especially if you're travelling from elsewhere in Britain, although they tend to be limited to the summer. Their brochures are available in most high-street travel agents, and you can also contact them direct at the addresses given below. If you're really on a tight budget you may be able to travel as a **courier**. Most of the major courier firms offer opportunities to travel cheaply and deliver a package of some kind (see the Yellow Pages or addresses

opposite) and prices can be as low as £200 return. Normally, though, you're required to sacrifice your baggage allowance (only hand-baggage is allowed) and fit in with some tight restrictions on when to travel.

Finally, you could also take a flight to **New York or another East Coast city** and travel on from there – handy if you want to see a little more of the country before the West Coast. Again, agents are the best source of cheap deals, especially to New York – to which you can pick up seats for under £300 if you shop around.

FROM ELSEWHERE IN BRITAIN

There are no scheduled non-stop flights to the West Coast from anywhere in Britain other than London; but there are still plenty of other options to consider.

From **Glasgow**, *Northwest* have six flights a week via New York or Boston to Los Angeles and other West Coast cities; *American Airlines* have a similar service from **Manchester** via Chicago, and *British Airways* will throw in a free shuttle from Manchester to connect up with their transatlantic services. And, even cheaper, the charter flights run by some of the companies mentioned above often leave from UK regional airports, especially Stansted and Manchester.

FLIGHTS FROM LONDON

The following carriers operate **non-stop flights** from London to the West Coast
(all from Heathrow unless stated otherwise).

Air New Zealand, from Gatwick three times a week to Los Angeles.

American Airlines, daily to Los Angeles.

British Airways, daily to Los Angeles and San Francisco; five a week to Seattle in high season, two in low season; daily to Los Angeles from Gatwick.

TWA, daily to Los Angeles and San Francisco.

United Airlines, daily to San Francisco.

Virgin Atlantic, daily to Los Angeles.

The following carriers operate **one-stop direct flights** from London to the West Coast
(all from Gatwick unless stated otherwise).

British Airways, five a week from Heathrow in high season via Los Angeles to San Diego; two a week in low season via Chicago to Seattle.

Continental, daily via Denver, Miami, Houston or Newark to Los Angeles, San Francisco and San Diego.

Delta, daily via Cincinatti or Atlanta to Los Angeles, San Francisco and San Diego.

Northwest, four a week via Minneapolis to Los Angeles, San Francisco and Seattle.

TWA, daily from Heathrow via Los Angeles or New York to San Diego and San Francisco; daily from Heathrow via New York to Seattle and Portland.

AIRLINES AND AGENTS

AIRLINE ADDRESSES IN BRITAIN

Air New Zealand, Elsenore House, Fulham Palace Road, London W6 (☎081/741 2299).

American Airlines, 15 Berkeley Street, London W1 (☎071/572 5555).

British Airways, 156 Regent Street, London W1 (☎081/897 4000).

Continental, Beulah Court, Albert Road, Horley, Surrey RH6 7HZ (☎0293/776464).

Delta, Victoria Plaza, Victoria Station, London SW1 (☎0800/414767).

TWA, 200 Piccadilly, London W1 (071☎439/0707).

Northwest, 8 Berkeley Street, London W1 (☎0345/747800).

United, 193 Piccadilly, London W1 (☎071/990 9900).

USAir, Piccadilly House, Regent Street, London SW1 (☎0800/777333).

Virgin Atlantic, Sussex House, High Street, Crawley RH10 1DQ (☎0293/562000).

LOW-COST FLIGHT AGENTS IN BRITAIN

Campus Travel, 52 Grosvenor Gardens, London SW1 (☎071/730 8111) and many other branches around the country.

Council Travel, 28a Poland Street, London W1 (☎071/437 7767).

Travel Cuts, 295a Regent Street, London W1 (☎071/637 3161).

STA Travel, 74 Old Brompton Road, SW7; 117 Euston Road, NW1 2SX: telephone enquiries (☎071/937 9971); 25 Queens Road, Bristol BS8 1QE (☎0272/294399); 38 Sidney Street, Cambridge CB2 3HX (☎0223/66966); 88 Vicar Lane, Leeds LS1 7JH; 75 Deansgate, Manchester M3 21BW (☎061/834 0668); 36 George Street, Oxford OX1 2QJ.

MAJOR COURIER FIRMS

CTS Ltd ☎081/844 2626
DHL ☎081/890 9393
IML ☎081/847 5621

Nomad ☎081/570 9277
Polo Express ☎081/759 5838
TNT Skypack ☎071/240 2240

ADDRESSES IN IRELAND

Aer Lingus, 41 Upper O'Connell St, Dublin 1 (☎01-377777 or☎01-370191).

Delta, 24 Merrion Square, Dublin 2 (☎1-800/768075).

USIT, Aston Quay, O'Connell Bridge, Dublin 2 (☎01/778117); 13b College St, Belfast BT1 6ET (☎0232/324073).

FROM EIRE

If you're under 26 or a student, the best fares **from Eire** are through *USIT* (see above). They currently offer a standard rate for all the West Coast destinations served by *Delta* and *Aer Lingus* (LA, San Francisco, San Diego, Seattle) for IR£582. Flights from Shannon may be marginally cheaper.

Student-only fares to New York, Boston or Chicago go for around IR£369 return. If you don't qualify for student or youth reductions, the full Apex fare, with all its attendant restrictions to the East Coast is in the region of IR£400. Naturally prices vary seasonally; *Aer Lingus* also have occasional special offers. The cheapest deals of the lot come if you're prepared to travel via London, on *Northwest* – the single fare to the US East Coast is £IR204.

FROM EUROPE

Although the national airlines of all European countries have non-stop flights to the West Coast, their prices are usually far in excess of anything you'll find in the UK, and you'll nearly always save money by booking a flight from London. The exceptions are the cut-price charter flights periodically offered in the major cities; ask at your nearest travel agent for details. The cheapest deals of all from continental Europe, so long as you don't mind where you land in the US, are with *Icelandair*, who fly from Luxemburg to Baltimore, Chicago, Detroit, New York and Orlando.

FROM AUSTRALIA AND NEW ZEALAND

From Australia and New Zealand, there are no cheap alternatives to Apex fares. A return from Sydney to Los Angeles is around Aus$1400 with *Air New Zealand, Continental, United* or *Qantas*. The same airlines, except *Qantas*, also fly from Auckland to Los Angeles for a return fare of around NZ$1800. If you do fly from down under, consider breaking your journey in Honolulu, Hawaii, where most flights stop anyway; you can usually stay over for as long as you like at no extra charge.

INCLUSIVE HOLIDAYS

Packages – fly-drive, flight/accommodation deals and guided tours (or a combination of all three) – can be a good way of skirting potential problems once you're on the West Coast, and most work out cheaper than arranging the same trip yourself. The drawbacks are the loss of flexibility and the fact that flight/accommodation schemes often use hotels in the mid-range to expensive bracket – cheaper accommodation is almost always readily available. There are a great many packages to choose from and your high street travel agent will have plenty of brochures.

FLY-DRIVE

Fly-drive deals, which give cut-rate (and sometimes free) car hire when buying a transatlantic ticket, are always cheaper than hiring on the spot and give great value if you're intending to do a lot of driving. On the other hand, you'll certainly have to pay more for the flight than you would if you booked it through an agent. The airlines, *Northwest* and *TWA*, and tour operators *American Airplan* and *Jetsave* (addresses on previous page), offer reasonable deals, and the competition between them means it's always worth phoning to check on current special offers. Normally, however, there's little to choose between them: prices begin at £55 per week for a small family saloon, working up to £130 per week for an estate, usually including 750 to 1000 free miles. Be sure to watch out for the hidden extras, though, like "drop-off" charges, which can be as much as a week's rental. Remember, too, that while you can drive in the US with a UK licence, there may be problems with hired vehicles if you're under 25. For complete car-hire and driving details, see "Getting around" below.

FLIGHT AND ACCOMMODATION DEALS

There's really no end of **flight and accommodation packages** to all the major cities on the West Coast, and although you can always do things cheaper independently, you won't be able to do the *same* things cheaper – in fact the equivalent room booked by itself will probably be a lot more expensive. *STA Travel* (address on p.5) offer "City Packages" using hostel accommodation in Los Angeles or Seattle, which work out at $10 to $15 per night plus the airfare. And there are any number of tour operators offering other, more costly deals. *Virgin Holidays* are about the cheapest: with them seven nights in LA or San Francisco plus a return flight will set you back between £600 and £700 a head, including car hire. See also "Sleeping", p.20, for details of pre-booked accommodation schemes.

TOURING AND ADVENTURE PACKAGES

A simple way to take in a large chunk of the West Coast without worrying too much about the practical details is using a specialist **touring and adventure package**, which includes transport, accommodation, food and a guide. Some of the most adventurous carry small groups around on minibuses and use a combination of budget hotel and camping accommodation (camping equipment, except sleeping bag, provided). Most also have a food kitty of around £20 a week, with many meals being prepared (and eaten) communally, although there's plenty of time to leave the group and ferret about on your own.

There are a number of UK-based operators, of which *Trek America* are fairly typical, running two-week trips around the high spots of California and Oregon for £300–320 excluding flights. Other operators include *Contiki, Top Deck* (brochures from youth/student orientated travel agents) and the more unorthodox San Francisco-based *Green Tortoise* (see "Getting around"), whose two-to-three day trips to Yosemite or week-long tours of Northern California cost $50 to $150.

If your main interest is **backcountry hiking**, the San Francisco-based *Sierra Club* offer a range of tours all including food and guide, taking you into otherwise barely accessible parts of the High Sierra wilderness. The tours are summer-only, cost around $300 for two weeks and are heavily subscribed, making it essential to book at least three months in advance. You'll also need to join the club ($38).

TOUR OPERATORS

AmeriCan Adventures, 45 High Street, Tunbridge Wells TN1 1XL (☎0892/511894).

American Pioneers, PO Box 229, Westlea, Swindon SN5 7HJ (☎0793/881882).

Contiki Travel, Wells House, 15 Elmsfield Road, Bromley BR1 1LS (☎081/290 6422).

Explore Worldwide, 1 Frederick Street, Aldershot GU11 1LQ (☎0252/319448).

Green Tortoise, PO Box 24459, San Francisco, CA 94124 (☎415/ 821-0803).

Greyhound, Sussex House, London Road, East Grinstead, West Sussex RH19 (☎0342/317317).

Sierra Club, c/o Outings Dept, 730 Polk Street, San Francisco, CA 94110 (☎415/776-2211).

Top Deck, 131 Earls Court Road, London, SW5 (☎071/244 8641).

Trek America, Trek House, The Bullring, Deddington, Oxford OX15 0TT (☎0869/38773).

Virgin Holidays, Sussex House, High Street, Crawley, West Sussex RH10 1BZ (☎0293/775511).

VISAS AND RED TAPE

To enter the US for less than ninety days you'll need a full UK passport (not a British Visitor's Passport) and a visa waiver form, which you'll be handed to fill in either by your travel agent, the airline when you check in, or on the plane. You must present it to immigration on arrival. Citizens of Eire, Australia and New Zealand must have a non-immigrant visitor's visa before arriving.

To obtain a visa, fill in the application form available at most travel agents and send it with a full passport to the nearest US Embassy or Consulate. Visas are not issued to convicted criminals and anybody who owns up to being a communist, fascist, or drug dealer. You'll need to give precise dates of your trip, and declare that you're not intending to live or work in the US (if you are intending to do either of these things, see p.38).

IMMIGRATION

During the flight, you'll be handed an **immigration form** (and a customs declaration: see below), which must be filled out and, after landing, given up at immigration control. On the form you must give details of where you are staying (if you don't know write "touring") and the date you intend to **leave** the US. Part of the form will be attached to your passport, where it must stay until you leave, when an immigration or airline official will detach it.

Besides the form, the officer will be interested in how you intend to support yourself during your stay. If you're intending to stay for more than a couple of weeks, you may be asked to show a return ticket and ample means of support: about $250 per week is considered sufficient, so it's wise to have a stash of travellers' cheques and credit cards to flash (bring all you can muster even if you don't intend to use them). If you're **staying with friends**, you'll need to provide their address and phone number, which may be checked if the officer sees fit to do so. If you've written "touring" on the immigration form, you'll be asked where you intend to spend your first night. Saying "a hotel" or "a hostel", and giving a broad indication that you know how to find one, should suffice.

There are, of course, ways to bend the rules slightly. One of the more popular methods is to borrow enough money to get into the country, afterwards returning it using an international money order. Overall it will certainly help if you appear reasonably respectable. It's unfortunately still true that entry will be eased if you're white, look middle class, and are polite, well-spoken and sober. And even if you are thinking of working in the US, don't, whatever you do, say so.

CUSTOMS

Customs officers will relieve you of your customs declaration and ask if you have any fresh foods. If you say "yes" you'll have to hand them over and probably won't get them back, certainly not in the case of meat or fruit; say "no" and they might decide to check your baggage anyway. You'll also be asked if you've visited a farm in the last month: if you have, you could well lose your shoes. The **duty-free allowance** if you're over seventeen is two hundred cigarettes and one hundred cigars, and, if you're over 21, a litre of spirits.

As well as foods and anything agricultural, it's also prohibited to carry into the country any articles from Vietnam, North Korea, Kampuchea or Cuba, obscene publications, and, oddly enough, lottery tickets, chocolate liqueurs or Pre-Columbian architecture. Anyone caught carrying drugs into the country will not only face prosecution but be entered in the records as an Undesirable and probably denied entry for all time.

EXTENSIONS AND LEAVING

The date stamped on the form in your passport is the **latest** you're legally entitled to stay. Leaving a few days after may not matter, especially if you're heading home, but more than a week or so can result in a protracted – and generally unpleasant – interrogation from officials which may cause you to miss your flight. Overstaying can also cause you to be turned away the next time you try to enter the US.

The simplest way to stay on is to **cross** either the Mexican or Canadian border, preferably before your time is up, and come back (allowing a decent interval – at least a day) ready to answer any tricky questions. You may be searched, so make sure you don't have a library card or anything else that might indicate you have an unofficial, semi-permanent US address; your diary may also be examined. All being well, you'll routinely have a new leaving date stamped in your passport.

Alternatively, you can do things the official way and get an **extension** before your time is up. This can be done by going to the nearest **US Immigration and Naturalization Service (INS)** office (their address will be under the "Federal Government Offices" listings at the front of the phone book). They will automatically assume that you're working illegally and it's up to you to convince them otherwise. Do this by providing evidence of ample private finances and, if possible, bring along an upstanding American citizen to vouch for your worthiness. Obviously you'll also have to explain why you didn't plan for the extra time initially – saying your money lasted longer than you expected, or that a close relative is coming over, are well-worked excuses.

HEALTH AND INSURANCE

If you're coming from Europe, you don't require any innoculations to enter the US. But **insurance**, while not compulsory, is essential. The US has no national health system, and you can lose an arm and a leg (so to speak) having even minor medical treatment. Insurance policies can be bought at any high-street travel agent or insurance broker. In Britain, the cheapest are generally *Endsleigh*, who charge around £35 for a fortnight to cover life, limb and luggage. Their forms are available from most youth/student travel offices (though their policies are open to all), or direct from 97–107 Southampton Row, London WC1 (☎071/436 4451) and many regional offices. On all policies, read the small print to ensure the cover includes a sensible amount for medical expenses – at least $100,000 – and that they'll fly you home in the event of serious injury. If you have anything **stolen** (including money), register the loss imme-diately at the nearest police station (addresses in the *Guide*, or under "Police" in the Emergency list-ings at the front of the phone book). They'll issue you with a reference number to pass on to your insurance company – an accepted alternative to the full statement insurers usually require.

If you need to see a **doctor**, lists can be found in the Yellow Pages under "Clinics" or "Physicians and Surgeons". British Consulates (addresses in the "Listings" sections of the *Guide*) can also provide selected names. A basic consultancy fee is from $50 to $75, payable in advance; medicines aren't cheap either – keep receipts for all you spend and claim it back on your insurance policy when you return.

Many **minor ailments** can be remedied using some of the fabulous array of potions and lotions available in a **drugstore** (found on almost every corner), but bear in mind that many pills available over the counter in Britain need a prescription in the US. Brand names can be confusing; if in doubt ask at the nearest **pharmacy** (there's one in every drugstore). More seriously, if you're involved in an **accident**, medical services will rush to your aid and charge you later. For an accident that doesn't need an ambulance, we've listed casualty depart-ments in the *Guide*; ditto for dental treatment.

One of the most serious health problems affecting the West Coast is **AIDS**. The compara-tively high number of HIV-positive cases has led to a more informed and open attitude towards the virus than is the case in Britain. It hardly needs to be said, however, that casual sex with-out a condom is wildly irresponsible.

COSTS, MONEY AND BANKS

At the time of writing, the exchange rate was £1 to $1.65, making the US a fairly cheap country to visit. Many items: petrol, booze, cameras and cigarettes, for example, cost less than in Britain. That said, you will still need to watch your wallet carefully if you're on any kind of budget.

COSTS

Your biggest expense is likely to be **accommo-dation**: the cheapest city hotel costs upwards of £13 a night, many more from £20 to £30, while those in rural areas cost a few pounds less. You can sometimes cut costs by using hostels (£3–6), or camping (free–£7), but you should remember that money for accommodation is something immigration officers will take into account when you enter the country.

Food is no problem at all. For just £5 or £6 a day you'll be able to afford a fairly basic life-support diet, spending £10 to £12 means you'll be dining pretty well. Beyond this, everything hinges on how much sightseeing, drinking, clubbing and socialising you're intending to do. If you plan to do much of any of these – especially in a major city – expect to get through upwards of £35 a day.

MONEY AND BANKS

US currency comes in green, equally sized bills worth $1, $5, $10, $20, $50 and $100 and rarely seen larger denominations. The dollar is made up of 100 cents in coins of **1 cent** (known as a penny), **5 cents** (a nickel), **10 cents** (a dime), and **25 cents** (a quarter). Very occasionally you might come across **JFK half-dollars** (50¢), **Susan B. Anthony dollar coins**, or a **two-dollar bill**. Change (quarters are the most useful) is necessary for buses, cigarette and soft drink dispensers, and telephones, so always carry plenty.

TRAVELLERS' CHEQUES AND CREDIT CARDS

The bulk of your money should be carried as **US dollar travellers' cheques** (US *travelers' checks*); travellers' cheques in other currencies may as well be from the moon. Dollar cheques can be changed in banks, but are as good as cash virtually everywhere – so plenty of $10 and $20 cheques are useful.

Travellers' cheques can be bought in Britain over the counter at any bank and many building societies whether you have an account or not: there's usually a charge of one or two percent of the amount ordered. The most widely recognised cheques are *American Express*, available from Lloyds, the Royal Bank of Scotland and the TSB; *Visa* travellers' cheques from the Co-op, Yorkshire and Barclays banks; and *Thomas Cook* travellers' cheques, sold by their major agents and the Midland Bank.

When changing travellers' cheques in a bank (less often, if ever, elsewhere) you'll be asked for **identification**; a driving licence or passport will suffice. Don't worry about using travellers' cheques anywhere that displays a sign saying *no*

checks – this refers to personal or social security (US "welfare") cheques. For **emergency phone numbers** to call if your cheques (and/or credit cards) should be stolen, see "Police and Thieves".

PLASTIC MONEY AND CASH MACHINES

Plastic money is readily acceptable: *Visa, Access* (known in the US as *Mastercard*) and *American Express* will do nicely in most shops, restaurants and for many other services, but remember that fluctuating exchange rates may result in spending more than you expect when the item shows up on your statement. When hiring a car or checking into a hotel you may well be asked to show a credit card to establish your credit worthiness – even if you intend to settle the bill in cash.

Provided you know your PIN (personal identification number), most major credit cards, and some bank and building society cash cards (such as *Abbey National*'s *Abbeylink*) can be used to draw up to $500 a day from the **cash machines** (US "Automatic Telling Machines" or "ATMs"; *Cirrus, Honor* and *Plus* are the biggest networks). It's essential, though, that you check the latest details with your credit card company before departing – otherwise the machine may simply gobble up your plastic friend. *American Express* card holders can use the travellers' cheque and cash dispensers found at airports and in larger cities.

BANKS

Banking hours are generally 10am to 3pm Monday to Thursday and 10am to 5pm on Friday. Most major banks – *Bank of America, Citibank, Security Pacific, Wells Fargo* – will change dollar travellers' cheques for their face value (although a few are known to charge for this – ask first to be sure). These banks can also **change foreign travellers' cheques and currency** – usually a frustratingly tedious task. You'll probably – depending on the amount and number of cheques – end up paying a lower commission at an exchange bureau: *Thomas Cook* is the most widely found name; and some banks operate airport exchange offices. Rarely, if ever, do hotels change money.

EMERGENCIES

If you're flat broke and at a loss for what to do, don't give up hope: there are several alternatives still available.

The easiest way to get money is to have someone in the UK send you some through **Western Union**. All they need do is hand over the loot to any UK Western Union agent (call Freefone 100 and ask for *Western Union* to find the address of the nearest one), which you then collect (less a ten percent commission) from any Western Union office in the US (for the nearest one: ☎1-800/326 6000). The transfer is instantaneous.

Alternatively, arrange for someone to transfer cash from any branch of **Thomas Cook** in Britain via telex to one of their branches on the West Coast. The main addresses are given in the *Guide*, and they're all in local phone books. The actual transfer of funds is, again, instantaneous; the cost is £25.

If there's time, get someone to buy an **international money order** and post it to you. The cost of this is minimal, but you have to rely on airmail and should allow seven days for arrival. It can be cashed at any post office, and is a quicker way to acquire funds than being sent an **ordinary cheque**, which takes two to three weeks to clear. Other possibilities include **selling blood** (see the Yellow Pages for agencies and hospitals, you can get $12 for a pint) or **working illegally** (see p.38). You might also throw yourself on the mercy of the **British consulate** in Los Angeles, San Francisco or Seattle (addresses in the *Guide*), who will – in worst cases only – repatriate you (on arrival in the UK, you'll have to surrender your passport until you've repaid the airfare) but will never, under any circumstances, lend you money.

The numbers to ring if you lose your travellers' cheques are:

American Express ☎1-800/221-7282
Thomas Cook ☎1-800/223-2131
Visa ☎1-800/627-6811

COMMUNICATIONS: TELEPHONES AND POST

Because of the strong emphasis placed on business efficiency, and the fact that Americans in general demand excellent service, all forms of communication in the US *have* to be good – something that's especially true on the commercially important and comparatively far-flung West Coast.

TELEPHONES

West Coast **telephones** are run by *Pacific Telephone (Bell System)* commonly abbreviated to *PacBell* – and linked to the nationwide *AT&T* network. The **dialling tone** is a continuous lowish hum; the **ringing tone** is long nasal squawk with short gaps; the **engaged (US "busy") tone** a series of rapid blips; **number unobtainable** (rare) is a single high-pitched squeak. Dial-phones are scarce: the vast majority are the push-button kind, emitting a different audio tone for each button pressed. Some numbers, particularly those of consumer services, employ letters as part of their "number", for example ☎1-800/822-TAXI to call a cab company in Los Angeles. The letters are on the buttons. For help, call the **operator** (☎0).

Public telephones invariably work and are everywhere – on street corners, in railway and bus stations, hotel lobbies, bars, restaurants – and they take 25¢, 10¢ and 5¢ coins. The cost of a **local call** from a public phone (ie within the same area code) varies according to the actual distance being called (some area codes cover vast territories). Minimums are 20¢, plus a further amount depending on how long you talk. Many government agencies, car hire firms, hotels and other services have a **toll-free number**, for which you don't have to pay anything: at a public phone simply insert a dime, which you'll get back when you hang up. These numbers always have

WEST COAST AREA CODES

619	San Diego and Eastern California	408	Northern Central Coast
714	Orange County	415	San Francisco
213	Los Angeles	510	The Bay Area
310	West Los Angeles and the South Bay	916	Sacramento and the Gold Country, and inland Northern California
818	Los Angeles Valley regions		
805	Southern Central Coast and southern San Joaquin Valley	707	Northern California Coast
		206	Western Washington
209	Central and northern San Joaquin Valley, and western Sierras	509	Eastern Washington
		503	Oregon

INTERNATIONAL CODES

From the US, dial ☎011 followed by:

UK 44
Eire 353

Australia 61
New Zealand 64

To place a phone call **to** the US from Britain, simply dial ☎01-01 followed by the relevant number.

USEFUL NUMBERS

Emergencies ☎911. Ask to be connected with the required emergency service: fire, police or ambulance.

Local directory information ☎411
Long distance directory information ☎1
(Area Code)/555-1212

Toll-free directory enquiries ☎1-800/555-1212.
Operator ☎0

the prefix 800. Numbers with the prefix 900 are pay-per-call phone sex and sports lines, varying from $1 to $20 a call.

Non-local calls ("zone calls"), to more distant numbers within the same area code, cost much more, and sometimes require you to dial 1 before the seven-digit number. Pricier still are **long-distance calls** (ie to a different area code), for which you'll need plenty of change – stuff it into the machine when the recorded voice tells you to. If you still owe money at the end of the call, the phone will ring immediately and you'll be asked for the outstanding amount (if you don't cough up, the person you've been calling will get the bill). Non-local calls and long-distance calls are far cheaper if made between 6pm and 8am, and calls from **private phones** are always much cheaper than those from public phones. Detailed rates are listed at the front of the **telephone directory** (the "White Pages", a copious source of information on many matters).

Phone calls from a hotel room are usually more expensive than from a public phone (and there are usually public phones in any hotel lobby). On the other hand, many hotels offer free local calls from rooms – check when you arrive.

The West Coast has roughly fifteen **area codes** – three-figure numbers which must precede the seven-figure number if you're calling from a region with a different code. In the *Guide*, we've only included the area codes where it's not clear from the list above which you should use.

International calls can be dialled direct from private or public phones, though obviously you'll need to load the (public) phone with money first. You can get assistance from the **international operator** (☎1-800/874-4000), who may also interrupt every three minutes asking for more money, and again call you back for any money still owed immediately after you hang up. One alternative is to **reverse charges (US "call collect")** by dialling ☎1-800/44-55-667, which will connect you for free with a British operator. The **cheapest rates** for international calls to Europe are between 11pm and 7am on weekdays, and all day at weekends, when a direct-dialled three-minute call will cost roughly $6.

LETTERS AND POSTE RESTANTE

Post offices are usually open Mon–Fri 9am–5pm, and Sat 9am–noon. They're the best places to buy **stamps** and send mail that you want to arrive quickly – though stamps are also available from vending machines on the walls outside, and there are blue **mail boxes** on many street corners. **Airmail** between the West Coast and Europe generally takes about a week to arrive. Obviously postcards are the cheapest thing you can send home (40¢). Aerogrammes are slightly dearer (45¢), while letters up to half an ounce in weight (a single thin sheet) will set you back 50¢, and the cost mounts steadily with every sheet you add.

Sending ordinary **mail within the US** is normally swift and reliable, costing 29¢ for a letter weighing up to an ounce. Addresses are written much the same way as in Britain, although the last line of the address is made up of an abbreviation denoting the state (in California, "CA") and a five-figure number. This is the **zip code**, denoting the local post office, and without it letters are liable to get lost or at least delayed. If you don't know the zip code, phone books carry a list for their service area; or ask at any post office.

In the US, **poste restante** is known as "**General Delivery**". Letters can be sent c/o General Delivery to any post office in the country but *must* include the post office's zip code, and

will only be held for thirty days before being returned to sender – so make sure there's a return address on the envelope. If you're receiving mail at someone else's address, it should include "c/o" and the regular occupants' name; otherwise it too is likely to be returned.

Rules on sending **parcels** are very rigid: packages must be in special containers bought from post offices, and sealed according to their instructions. Parcels are sent by land unless airmail is specified and, not surprisingly, costs increase the further the destination and the heavier the parcel. To send anything out of the country, you'll need a **customs declaration form**, available from a post office.

To send a **telegram** (sometimes called "a wire") don't go to a post office but to a *Western Union Office* (listed in the Yellow Pages). If you have a credit card, you can phone and dictate your message. **International telegrams** are slightly cheaper than the cheapest international phone call: one sent in the morning from the West Coast should arrive at a British address the next day. For domestic telegrams ask for a **mailgram**, which will be delivered to any address in the country the following morning.

INFORMATION, MAPS AND THE MEDIA

Before you leave, it's worth contacting the *United States Travel and Tourism Administration* (USTTA) for their range of free maps, leaflets and so on – though they're unable to help with very much else. Their UK office is at 22 Sackville Street, London W1 (Mon–Fri 10am–4pm; ☎071/439 7433); and they also have offices in Australia at Suite 6106, MLC Centre, King & Castlereagh Streets, Sydney, NSW 2000 (☎2/223-4055, 2/223-4099 or 2/223-4666), and in West Germany at Bethmannstrasse 56, 6000 Frankfurt-Main (☎29-5211, 29-5212 or 29-5213). Anywhere else you'll have to rely on the American embassy or consulate for information.

More specific information can be obtained from the West Coast's three **State Tourist Offices**, though you need to be very specific about your interests, and write well in advance. Addresses are:

California Office of Tourism, Suite 1600, 801 K Street, Sacramento, California 95814 (☎916/322-2881).

Washington Tourism Development, 101 General Administration Building, AX-13, Olympia, Washington 98504 (☎206/753-5600).

Oregon Tourism Division, 595 Cottage Street NE, Salem, Oregon 97310 (☎503/378-3451).

ON-THE-SPOT INFORMATION

Once on the West Coast, you'll find most large towns have at least a **Visitors and Conventions Bureau** (typically Mon–Fri 9am–5pm, Sat 9am–1pm), with detailed information on their area. In addition there are **Chambers of Commerce** almost everywhere – designed to promote local business interests but also holding local maps and information and with a positive attitude towards helping travellers. Most communities will also have a number of local **free newspapers** (see below) carrying news of events and entertainment.

MAPS

Each of the state tourism offices issues free **maps** of their region – usually fine for general driving and route planning. To get hold of one, either write to the office directly or call at any visitors bureaux. Most Oregon visitors bureaux will also be able to give you the immensely informative *Oregon Passenger Services* map, which details all the long-distance public transport services around the state. Of the commercially available maps, the best are the three *Rand McNally* state maps, each costing £1.99. If you're travelling further afield in the US, the *Rand McNally Road Atlas* (£9.95) is a worthwhile investment, covering the whole country plus Mexico and Canada. If you need something more detailed for **hiking** purposes, for example, camping shops generally have a good selection, and park ranger stations in national parks, state parks, and wilderness areas all sell good quality local hiking maps for $1 or $2.

Most good UK bookshops carry a fair selection of maps of the West Coast (though rarely much on hiking). If you can't find what you want, try a specialist map stockist like *Stanfords*, 12–14 Long Acre, London WC2 (☎071/836 1321), who also run a mail-order service. Bear in mind, too, that if you're an *AA* or *RAC* member, you can get free maps (and help) from the *American Automobile Association (AAA)* (☎1-800/336-4357), based at 8111 Gatehouse Road, Falls Church, VA 22047, but with offices in every city.

NEWSPAPERS

Due mainly to its vast size, the US had no national **newspapers** at all (aside from the gloriously tacky sex-and-scandal weekly, the *National Enquirer*, 75¢) until the arrival of the colour *USA*

Today a few years back. This didn't do much to change reading habits, though: take one look at its shallow stories, dredged up from around the country, and you'll see why Americans prefer their newspapers grainy, inky and local. The only newspaper that's read all over the West Coast is the *Los Angeles Times*, which gives probably the best coverage of West Coast, national and world events in the country. Otherwise, newspapers tend to excel at reporting their own area but generally rely on agencies for their foreign – and even some national – reports.

One good thing US newspapers share is their low cost: 25–35¢, with Sunday editions (enormous affairs, though taken up largely by ads) selling for $1–1.25. You buy newspapers from vending machines on street corners. Other US papers, like the widely read and influential *New York Times*, cost slightly more and are sold through specialist outlets in the big cities (addresses in the *Guide*).

Every community of any size has at least a few **free newspapers**, found in street distribution bins or just lying around in piles. It's a good idea to pick up a full assortment: some simply cover local goings-on, others provide specialist coverage of interests ranging from long-distance cycling to getting ahead in business – and the classified and personal ads can provide hours of entertainment. Many of them are also excellent sources for bar, restaurant and nightlife information, and we've mentioned the most useful titles in the *Guide*.

TELEVISION

TV in the US comes in quantity. Often there'll be thirty-odd channels to choose from, most of them filled with sycophantic chat-shows and banal sitcoms (frighteningly, you soon realise that British TV imports only the "best" of the genre), frequently interrupted by commercials. On the other hand, if you have no qualms about exploiting people's greed, American **quiz shows** can be addictive – and those involving word puzzles are surprisingly good for improving your American-English. As for **news coverage**, local news is, as ever, comprehensive: a couple of hours each night, usually from 5pm until 6pm and 10pm until 11pm, normally followed by an hour of **national and international news**. Unsurprisingly this is much less thorough, and world events which don't directly affect the US barely get a look in. The **major networks** (ABC, CBS and NBC), each with an affiliated local station, have long dominated US broadcasting, although Rupert Murdoch's Fox network is fast making incursions, and each city has a number of independent stations.

You won't find commercials – or any sort of news – on the non-commercial **PBS** channels, where programmes are paid for by viewer subscriptions, individuals or special interest groups – a policy which gives rise to anything from entire evenings of British comedy to hours of high-class costume drama. Similarly with the **public access** channels, which give airtime to anybody (New Age astrologists, right-wing fanatics) organised enough to put a half-hour programme together.

There's also **cable TV**, widely found in motels and hotels – although sometimes you need to pay a couple of dollars to watch it. Most cable stations are no better than their network rivals, but there are a few more specialised channels that are worth a look. The **ARTS** channel broadcasts enjoyable, if always po-faced, arts features, imported TV plays, author interviews and the like. **CNN** (Cable News Network) is an around-the-clock news channel. **HBO** (Home Box Office) shows recent mainstream movies. The **Weather Channel** has detailed local and national weather updates, along with informative features. And there is, of course, **MTV** (Music Television), which threatened to turn the music industry on its head in the early Eighties but now has a diet of non-stop rock videos (on hourly rotation) that's for the most part wearyingly mainstream.

Other cable channels – each major city has at least a dozen – are even more narrowcast: at the end of the dial you'll frequently find Japanese soap operas and earnest half-hour interviews with people claiming to have come back from the dead. Soccer fans should scan the Spanish-language channels, which often show matches from Europe.

Entire **TV listings** can be found in local newspapers or the weekly (also Murdoch-owned) *TV Guide* (60¢), available just about everywhere.

RADIO

Radio stations are even more abundant than TV channels, and the majority, again, stick to a bland, commercial format. Except for news and chat, stations on the AM band are best avoided in favour of the FM waveband, in particular the nationally funded **public** and **college stations**, both found on the left of the dial (88-92 FM). These invariably provide diverse and listenable fare, be it bizarre underground rock or obscure literary programming, and they're also good sources for local nightlife news. If you're not tuned in to one of these you may as well adopt the American habit of regularly swapping frequencies, skipping between the re-run Eagles tracks until you find a crazed phone-in.

GETTING AROUND

Although distances can be great, getting around the West Coast is seldom much of a problem. Certainly, things are always easier if you have a car, but between the major cities there are good bus links and – although much less frequent – a train service. The only regions where things are more difficult are the isolated rural areas, though even here, by adroit forward-planning, you'll be able to get to the main points of interest without too much trouble on local buses and charter services, details of which are in the relevant sections of the *Guide*.

BY BUS

Bus is by far the cheapest way to travel. The main long distance service is *Greyhound* (see box overleaf), who link all major cities and many smaller towns. In isolated areas buses are fairly scarce, sometimes only appearing once or twice a week, and here you'll need to plot your route with care. But between the big cities, buses run around the clock to a fairly full timetable, stopping only for meal breaks (almost always fast-food dives) and driver change-overs. *Greyhound* buses are more comfortable than you might expect, too, and it's feasible – and not too uncomfortable – to save on a night's accommodation by travelling overnight and sleeping on the bus. Any sizeable community will have a *Greyhound* station; in smaller places the local post office or petrol station doubles as the stop and ticket office. If you're miles from anywhere, simply flag down the bus from the side of the road – they almost always stop.

Fares – for example $46 from Los Angeles to San Francisco one-way – are expensive but not staggeringly so, and can sometimes be reduced by travelling on weekdays (except Friday), when cheaper fares may be offered. If you're intending to travel all over the West Coast – or the rest of the US – by bus, you'll save a packet by buying a *Greyhound* **Ameripass** in advance. These must be bought before you leave the UK: from *London Student Travel*, 52 Grosvenor Gardens, London SW1W 0AG (☎071/730 3402); through any branch of *Thomas Cook;* or from *Greyhound*'s UK office at Sussex House, London Road, East Grinstead, West Sussex RH19 1LD (☎0342/317317). The passes give unlimited travel within a set time limit: four days (£45), seven days (£75), fifteen days (£120), or thirty days (£150). Extensions can be bought in the US for the dollar equivalent of £10 a day. The first time you use your pass, present it to the ticket clerk saying where you want to go. The pass will be dated (which becomes the commencement date of the ticket) and your destination is written on a page which the driver will tear out and keep as you board the bus. Repeat this procedure for every subsequent journey.

A few years ago, *Greyhound* absorbed its major rival, *Trailways*, and incorporated all their routes into its own schedules. You may still, however, occasionally spot a *Trailways* depot that hasn't been closed down or a bus that hasn't been renamed. During 1990, many *Greyhound* drivers went on strike protesting against "unfair management practices", only to be sacked by the company, who then recruited new staff. This caused many fraught scenes as buses arrived at picketed *Greyhound* stations, totally disrupted timetables, and led to the dismissed drivers vowing to set up a rival bus company. As it stands, *Greyhound* services are running fairly normally, though there's every indication that many of their routes may be sold off to local companies in the near future.

Greyhound produces a condensed **timetable** of major country-wide routes, but this isn't particularly useful and you'd do better to plan your route with the fuller regional timetables available free from *Greyhound* stations in the US. You can also phone the local terminal for information (we've included the main *Greyhound* phone numbers in the *Guide*; others will be in the phone book).

An **alternative**, in every sense, is *Green Tortoise*, whose buses, furnished with foam cushions, bunks, fridges and rock music, ply the major West Coast cities, running between Los Angeles and San Francisco once-weekly for $30 one-way, and between San Francisco and Seattle or Portland twice-weekly for $49 one-way. Reservations are recommended and can be made through local agents: in Los Angeles ☎310/392-1990; in San Francisco ☎415/821-0803; in Seattle ☎206/324-RIDE; and in Portland ☎503/937-3603. Outside California, call toll-free on ☎1-800/227-4766. *Green Tortoise* also run well-priced tours of the West Coast; see p.6 for details.

Bear in mind that fair-sized distances can be covered for very little money (if also very slowly) using **local buses**, which connect neighbouring districts. It's possible, for example, to travel from San Diego to Los Angeles for $3, but it'll take all day and at least three changes of bus to do it.

BY TRAIN

Travelling on the *Amtrak* **rail** network is a far less viable way of getting about. The system isn't at all comprehensive on the West Coast, and is much more expensive than taking a *Greyhound* – Los Angeles to Seattle, for example, costs $159 one-way. That said, it certainly has its fans: all the major cities are connected and the carriages clean, comfortable and tidy, and rarely crowded.

You can cut **fares** greatly by using one of the three **rail-passes** valid in the region, each of which gives free travel for 45 days. The **National Rail Pass** ($299) can be used on all US trains; the **Western Region Rail Pass** ($239) covers everywhere west of Chicago and New Orleans; and the **Far Western Rail Pass** ($159) is good for all the West Coast routes, valid as far east as Salt Lake City and Flagstaff (for the Grand Canyon).

These passes can be bought from *Amtrak* stations in Los Angeles, San Francisco and Seattle on production of your passport, or from *Amtrak*'s UK agent: **Destination Marketing Limited**, at 2 Cinnamon Row, Plantation Wharf, York Place, London SW11 3TW (☎071/978 5222).

AMTRAK AGENTS IN BRITAIN

Albany Travel, 190 Deansgate, Manchester M3 3WD (☎061/8330202).

American Express Holidays, Portland House, Stag Place, Victoria Street, London SW1 (☎071/834 5555).

Amtrak/Destination Marketing, 16 Bedford Square, London WC1 (☎071/323 0898).

Compass, 9 Grosvenor Gardens, London SW1 (☎071/828 4111).

Thistle Air Ltd, 22 Bank Street, Kilmarnock, Ayrshire (☎0563/31121).

For Amtrak info in the US, phone ☎1-800/USA-RAIL

BY PLANE

Taking a **plane** is obviously the quickest way of getting about the West Coast, and much less expensive than you might expect; indeed flying can be cheaper than travelling by train, and often only a little more costly than taking the bus. Planning ahead and buying your tickets in the UK before you leave can save as much as thirty percent on internal flights – something known as a **Visit USA** ticket, available from any travel agent and handy if you just want to make a couple of hops to cover long distances quickly. Once on the West Coast, you can take advantage of special offers, such as *Southwest Airlines* $49 fare between any two California cities.

If you're planning a lot of flying across the West Coast – and/or the rest of the country – you'll be better off with an **air pass**: these are available in the UK only from all the main American airlines (and by *British Airways* in conjunction with *USAir*) usually with the proviso that you cross the Atlantic with them. All the air pass deals are broadly similar, involving the purchase of at least three **coupons** (for around £180; £45–55 for each additional coupon), each valid for a flight of any duration in the US. The best deal really depends on which airline has the strongest connections in the region you intend to visit: study the possibilities carefully before committing yourself. Also worth considering is *Delta*'s pass for an unlimited number of standby flights over thirty days; available for the sterling equivalent of $449 ($749 for sixty days).

CAR HIRE AND DRIVING

UK nationals are allowed to **drive** in the US on a full UK driving licence, but under-25s may encounter problems if trying to **hire a car** and will probably get lumbered with a higher than normal insurance premium; those under 21 will find it impossible. Car hire companies will also

expect you to have a credit card; if you don't have one they may let you leave a hefty **deposit** (at least $200) but don't count on it.

Often the cheapest way to **hire a car** is either to take a fly-drive deal (see p.6) or book **in advance** with a major agent like *Alamo, Avis, Budget, Hertz, Holiday Autos* or *Thrifty* – all of which have offices in Britain. *Holiday Autos* (☎071/491 9000) tend to be the cheapest, charging around £70 a week for a four-door saloon, with sub-compacts going for as low as £58 a week with **free unlimited mileage** – an important consideration if you're planning to do a lot of miles.

Alternatively, **once there** a number of local and indigenous US companies (*Rent-a-Heap, Rent-a-Wreck, Dollar* and many others) hire out new – and not so new – vehicles. They are certainly cheaper than the big chains if you just want to spin around a city for a day, but free mileage is not included, so they work out far more costly for long-distance travel. Most firms have offices at airports, and addresses and phone numbers are comprehensively documented in the Yellow Pages. You can, with most firms, leave the car in a different city to the one in which you hired it, though this will incur a **drop-off charge** that's sometimes as much as a week's rental.

CAR-HIRE FIRMS

TOLL-FREE NUMBERS IN THE US

Alamo ☎1-800/327-9633

Avis ☎1-800/331-1212

Budget ☎1-800/525-0700

Dollar ☎1-800/421-6868

Hertz ☎1-800/654-3131

National ☎1-800/328-4567

Thrifty ☎1-800/376-2277

Value ☎1-800/ 327-2501

When you hire a car, read the small print carefully for details on **Collision Damage Waiver (CDW)**, a form of insurance which often isn't included in the initial hire charge but which you should think about taking out. At $10–12 a day, this can add substantially to the total cost, but without it you're liable for every scratch to the car – even if it wasn't your fault.

DRIVEAWAYS

A variation on hiring is a **driveaway**, whereby you drive a car from one place to another on behalf of the owner. The same rules as for hiring apply, but you should look the car over before taking it as you'll be lumbered with any repair costs, and a large fuel bill if the vehicle's a big drinker.

The most common routes are between West Coast and New York, although there's a fair chance you'll find something that needs shifting up the coast, from Los Angeles to San Francisco or Seattle. You don't have to drive flat out, although four hundred miles a day is considered reasonable. Look under "Driveaways" in the Yellow Pages and phone around for the latest offers.

HIRING AN RV

Besides cars, **campervans** (US "Recreational Vehicles" or **"RVs"**) can be hired for around £170 a week, although outlets are surprisingly rare (Americans tend to own rather than rent them). Two, in LA and San Francisco respectively, are *El Monte Rents* (☎818/443-6158), 12061 E. Valley Blvd, CA 91732, and *Western RV Rentals* (☎415/532-7404), 4901 Coliseum Way, Oakland CA 94601. Again, though, it's easier and cheaper to book in advance from Britain.

Most travel agents who specialise in the US (see "Touring and Adventure Packages", p.6) can arrange RV rental, and usually do it cheaper if you book a flight through them as well. A price of around £300 for a five-berth van for two weeks is fairly typical.

DRIVING

Once you have a vehicle, you'll find **petrol** (US "gasoline") is fairly cheap at around $1.25 a gallon for **unleaded** petrol, which most cars use. In California and Washington most petrol stations are self-serve; in Oregon, all stations have attendants who'll pump the petrol for you. Most hire cars have **automatic transmission**, power-

assisted brakes, and power-assisted steering. If you're unfamiliar with these features, take a steady chug around the block to get used to them.

American **miles** are the same as British miles but sometimes **distances** are given in **hours** – the length of time it should take to drive between any two places. There are obviously other differences between driving in the US and in Britain, not least the fact that rules and regulations aren't always nationally fixed, though in the three West Coast states they're fairly uniform. One rule which is national, of course, is **driving on the right**. This can be remarkably easy to forget – some people draw a cross or tie a ribbon on their right hand to remind them.

ROADS

There are several **types of road**. The best for covering long distances quickly are the wide, straight and fast **Interstate Highways**, usually at least six-lane motorways and always prefixed by "I" (eg I-5) – marked on maps by a red, white and blue shield bearing the number. Even-numbered Interstates usually run east–west and those with odd numbers north–south.

Driving on these roads is easier than it first appears, but you need to adapt quickly to the American habit of **changing lanes**: US drivers do this frequently, and overtake on both sides. In California and Washington (but not Oregon) it's also permitted to stay in the fast lane while being overtaken on the inside. Big overhead signs warn you if the road's about to split towards two different destinations (this happens quite often), or an exit's coming up. Sometimes a lane *must* exit, and if you lose concentration you're liable to leave the Interstate accidently – no great calamity as it's easy enough to get back on again. **Missing an exit** is more annoying – U-turns are strictly illegal, and you have to continue on to the next exit.

A grade down, and broadly similar to British dual carriageways and main roads, are the **State Highways** (eg Hwy-1) and the **US Highways** (eg US-395). Some major roads in cities are technically state highways but are better known by their local name. Hwy-2 in Los Angeles, for instance, is better known as Santa Monica Boulevard. In rural areas, you'll also find much smaller **County Roads**; their number is preceded by a letter denoting their county. In built-up areas **streets** are arranged on a grid system and labelled at each junction.

AMERICAN DRIVING/CAR TERMS

Antennae	Aerial	*Parking Brake*	Hand brake
Denver Boot	Wheel clamp	*Speed zone*	Area where speed limit decreases
Divided Highway	Dual carriageway		
Fender	Bumper/Car wing	*Stickshift*	Gear stick/manual transmission
Freeway	Limited access multi-lane motorway, often raised above street level	*Trailer*	Caravan
		Trunk	Boot
		Turn-out	Lay-by
Gas(oline)	Petrol	*RV*	Recreational vehicle, often a massive mobile home with multiple bedrooms, kitchen and bathroom
Gridlock	Traffic jammed in every direction		
Hood	Bonnet		
No standing	No parking or stopping	*Windshield*	Windscreen

RULES OF THE ROAD

Although the law says that drivers must keep up with the flow of traffic, which is often hurtling along at 70mph, the official **speed limit** on the West Coast is 55mph (65mph on some stretches of I-5), with lower signposted limits – usually around 30–35mph – in built-up areas. There are no **spot fines** but if given a ticket for **speeding**, your case will come to court and the size of the fine will be at the discretion of the judge; $75 is a rough minimum. If **the police** do flag you down, don't get out of the car and don't reach into the glove compartment as the cops may think you have a gun. Simply sit still with your hands on the wheel; when questioned, be polite and don't attempt to make jokes.

As for other possible violations, US law requires that any **alcohol** be carried unopened in the boot of the car, and it can't be stressed enough that **driving while intoxicated (DWI)** is a very serious offence. If a police officer smells alcohol on your breath, he/she is entitled to administer a breath, saliva or urine test. If you fail, they'll lock you up with other inebriates in the *drunk tank* of the nearest jail until you sober up. Your case will later be heard by a judge, who can fine you $200 or in extreme (or repeat) cases, imprison you for thirty days. Less serious offences include making a **U-turn** on an Interstate or anywhere where a single unbroken line runs along the middle of the road; **parking on a highway**; front-seat passengers riding without fastened **seatbelts**; and even, in California, **running out of fuel**. At **junctions**, one rule is crucially different from the UK: you can turn right on a red light if there is no traffic approaching from the left; otherwise red and amber mean stop.

Once at your destination, you'll find in cities at least that **parking meters** are commonplace. Charges for an hour range from 25¢–$1. **Carparks** (US *parking lots*), charge up to $10 a day. If you park in the wrong place (such as within ten feet of a fire hydrant) your car is likely to be towed away or **wheel-clamped**; a sticker on the windscreen tells you where to pay the $30 fine.

If you **break down** in a hired car, there'll be an emergency number pinned to the dashboard. Otherwise you should sit tight and wait for a Highway Patrol, who cruise by regularly. Raising your car bonnet is recognised as a call for assistance, although women travelling alone should, obviously, be wary of doing this (see "Women's West Coast", p.33).

HITCHING

Where it's legal, **hitching** may be the cheapest way to get around but it is also the most unpredictable, even potentially dangerous, especially for women travelling alone. Small country roads are your best bet: in rural areas it's quite common for the locals to get around by thumb. One place *not* to hitch is Los Angeles: if you do, the chances are you'll be lucky if you live to regret it. Anywhere else, observe the general common sense rules on hitching: make sure you sit next to a door that's unlocked, keep your luggage within reach, refuse the ride if you feel unsure of the driver, and demand to be let out if you become suspicious of his/her intentions.

Hitching is illegal in Oregon, in parts of Washington, and on the outskirts of many cities, and is always prohibited if done by standing on the road (as opposed to beside it) or by a freeway entrance sign – rules which are enforced. On Interstates, thumb from the entrance ramps only.

Another, slightly less risky, technique is to strike up a conversation with likely-looking drivers in roadside diners or gas stations. Safer still is to scrutinise the "**ride boards**" on university campuses, although drivers found this way will usually expect a contribution towards fuel costs.

CYCLING

In general, **cycling** is a cheap and healthy method of getting around all the big **cities**, some of which have cycle lanes and local buses equipped to carry bikes – strapped to the outside. In **country areas**, certainly, there's much scenic, and largely level, land, especially around Sacramento and the Wine Country.

Bikes can be **hired** for $8–15 a day, $45 a week, from outlets usually found close to beaches, university campuses, or simply in areas which are good for cycling; the local visitors centre will have details. Apart from the coastal fog, which tends to clear by midday, you'll encounter few **weather** problems (except perhaps sunburn) but remember that the further north you go, the lower the temperatures become. Expect rain in Washington and Oregon.

For **long-distance cycling** you'll need a good quality, multi-speed all-terrain bike, maps, a helmet (not a legal necessity but a very good idea), and a route avoiding Interstates (on which cycling is illegal). It's also wise to cycle north to south, as the wind blows this way in the summer, and can make all the difference between a pleasant trip and acute leg-ache. Of **problems** you'll encounter, the main one is traffic – mobile homes driven by buffoons who can't judge their width, and, in Northern California, Washington and Oregon, enormous logging trucks whose slipstream will pull you toward the middle of the road. Be particularly careful if you're planning to cycle along Hwy-1 on California's central coast: besides heavy traffic, it has tight curves, dangerous precipices, and is prone to fog.

If you're camping as well as cycling, look out for the **hiker/biker campsites**, which are free of cars and campervans and are common in California and Oregon, less so in Washington. For more information in advance of your arrival, write to the *American Youth Hostels Association* (address under "Sleeping", p.22); *Bikecentennial*, PO Box 8308, Missoula, MT 59807 (☎406/ 721-1776); or the *Sierra Club* (address on p.32). Also worth getting are two free and very informative leaflets: the *Oregon Bicycling Guide* and *Oregon Coast Bike Route*, issued by the *Department of Parks and Recreation*, 525 Trade Street SE, Salem, Oregon 97310; and the *Washington Bike Map and Freeway Guide* from the *Public Affairs Office, Washington State Department of Transport*, Transportation Building KF-01, Olympia, Washington 98504.

SLEEPING

Your major expense on the West Coast is going to be accommodation. You can obviously trim costs greatly by camping or sleeping in a dormitory-style hostel, which can cost from nothing to around $10. But in major cities campsites tend to be on the outskirts and hostels in short supply, making it more likely that you'll need to use hotels and motels. These cost anything upwards of $20, and many hotels will set up a third single bed for $10–15 on top of the regular price, reducing costs considerably for three people sharing. By contrast, the lone traveller will have a hard time of it: "singles" are usually double rooms at an only slightly reduced rate.

Wherever you stay, you'll be expected to **pay in advance**, at least for the first night and perhaps for further nights too, particularly if it's high season and the hotel's expecting to be busy. Payment can be in cash or in dollar travellers' cheques, though it's more common to give your credit card number and sign for everything when you leave. **Reservations** are held until 5pm or 6pm unless you've notified the hotel you'll be arriving late. Most of the larger chains have an advance booking form in their brochures and will make reservations at another of their premises for you.

Since cheap accommodation is always taken up quickly, **book ahead** if possible in the cities, using the suggestions in the "Finding a place to stay" sections of the *Guide*, or checking the options and addresses listed below.

HOTELS AND MOTELS

Hotels and **motels** are essentially the same thing – motels tend to be located beside the main roads away from city centres – and the cheaper ones are pretty basic affairs. In general, though, there's a uniform standard of comfort everywhere – double rooms with bathroom, TV and phone – and you won't necessarily get a vastly better room by paying, say, $50 instead of $30. Over $50, the room and its fittings simply get bigger and more luxurious, and there'll probably be a swimming pool which guests can use for free. Paying over $100 brings you into the decadent realms of the en suite jacuzzi.

Very few hotels or motels bother to compete with the ubiquitous diners and offer **breakfast**, although there's a trend towards providing free coffee (from paper cups) and sticky buns on a self-service basis from reception (US *the lobby*).

In most places you'll be able to find cheap one-off hotels and motels simply by keeping your eyes open – they're usually advertised by enormous roadside signs. Alternatively, there are a number of budget-priced **chains** whose rooms cost around $20 to $35. Cheapest of these are *Motel 6*, widely found in all three states, and, in California only, *EZ-8*. Higher on the budgetary scale, *Best Western*, *Howard Johnson's* (California only), *TraveLodge*, and *Quality Inns* all do reasonably priced rooms for $35 to $50. Pricier still are *Nendel's* (Washington and Oregon only) *Ramada*, and *Vagabond* (California only) – though if you can afford to pay this much ($50–100) there's normally somewhere nicer to stay.

Many of the higher-rung chains offer **pre-paid discount vouchers**, which in theory save you money if you're prepared to pay in advance – British travellers must purchase them in the UK. These usually cost £30 to £60 a night for a minimum of two people sharing, and it's hard to think of a good reason to buy them. True, you may save a nominal amount on the fixed rates, but better-value accommodation is not exactly difficult to find in the US, and you may well regret the lack of flexibility such schemes will give your travels.

When it's worth blowing a hunk of cash on somewhere really atmospheric we've said as much in the *Guide*. Bear in mind the most upscale establishments have all manner of services which may appear to be free but for which you will be expected to **tip** in a style commensurate with the hotel's status – ie *big*.

BED AND BREAKFAST

Forget English seaside resorts and greasy bacon and eggs: **bed and breakfast** on the West Coast is often a luxury – even the mattresses have to conform to a standard of comfort far higher than those in hotels. Typically, the bed and breakfast inns, as they're usually known, are restored buildings in the smaller cities and more rural areas – although the big cities also have a few. Even the larger establishments tend to have no more than ten rooms, without TV and phone but often with plentiful flowers, stuffed cushions and an almost over-contrived homely atmosphere; others may just be a couple of furnished rooms in someone's home, or an entire apartment where you won't even see your host.

While always including a huge and wholesome breakfast (five courses is not unheard of), prices vary greatly: anything from $30 to $200 depending on location and season. Most fall between $45 and $75 per night for a double, a little more for a whole apartment. Bear in mind, too, that they are often booked well in advance.

For a list of inns in each state, send a SAE to:

For California: **Bed and Breakfast International** 151 Ardmore Road, Kensington, CA 94707.

For Washington: **The Washington Bed and Breakfast Guild**, 2442 NW Market Street, Seattle, Washington 98107.

For Oregon: **Oregon Bed and Breakfast Directory**, 230 Red Spur Drive, Grants Pass, Oregon 97527.

For bed and breakfast rooms and apartments in the main Californian cities and along the Central Coast: **Colby International**, 139 Round Hey, Liverpool L28 1RG (☎051/220 5848).

YS AND YOUTH HOSTELS

Aside from the odd private hostel in the larger cities, there are two kinds of cheap hostel-type accommodation in the US: YMCA/YWCA hostels (known as "*Y's*") offering mixed-sex accommodation or in a few cases women-only accommodation, and straight official *AYH* youth hostels.

Prices in the less plentiful **YMCA hostels** range from around $8 for a dormitory bed to $18 to $30 for a single or double room. Facilities can include a gymnasium and swimming pool, and sometimes a cheap cafeteria.

More common are the regular *AYH* **youth hostels**. There are about sixty on the West Coast, most in popular hiking areas, though a few in the bigger cities and tourist centres. At $6 to $10 (a few dollars more for non-members) per night per person they are clearly the cheapest option under a roof. The *International Youth Hostel Handbook (Volume II)* has a full list, and is available from the British *Youth Hostel Association* headquarters/shop, at 14 Southampton Street, London WC2 (☎071/836 8542), where you can also buy a year's *IYHF* **membership** for £8.30 (£4.40 if you're under 21). The informative *American Youth Hostel (AYH) Handbook* ($5) is only available from hostels in the US or direct from the *AYH* national office: PO Box 37613, Washington, DC 20013-7613 (☎202/783-6161).

Particularly if you're travelling in high season, it's advisable to **book ahead** by writing to the relevant hostel and enclosing a deposit, or by sending an *IYHF Advance Booking Voucher*, which costs £4 – a sum then knocked off the bill at the hostel – available from any international youth hostel office or specialist travel agent (though first check that the hostel you're after

accepts them – a few don't). Beds reserved in this way will be held until 9pm. Some hostels will allow you to use a **sleeping bag**, though officially they should (and many do) insist on a **sheet sleeping bag**. You can buy these for around £10 from the London *YHA* shop, or they can be hired at the hostel. The maximum stay at each hostel is technically three days, though this is again a rule which is often ignored if there's space. Few hostels provide meals but most have **cooking** facilities, and there's almost always a curfew some time between 10pm and midnight; alcohol and smoking are banned.

CAMPING

In the US, **camping** is done at a **campground**; a camp*site* is the spot where one pitches one's tent or hooks up one's *RV* to the electrical supply. We've used "campsite" in the British sense throughout the *Guide*, but you'll obviously find the same word used in the American sense everywhere you travel. Campsites range from the primitive (a flat piece of ground that may or may not have a water tap) to others which are more like open-air hotels, with shops, restaurants and washing facilities. Naturally enough, prices vary accordingly, ranging from nothing for the most basic plots, up to $12 a night for something comparatively luxurious. There are plenty of campsites but often plenty of people intending to use them: take special care over plotting your route if you're camping during public holidays or the high season, when many sites will be either full or very crowded. By contrast, some of the more basic campsites in isolated areas will often be completely empty whatever time of year you're there, and if there's any charge at all you'll need to pay by leaving the money in the bin provided.

YOUTH HOSTEL INFORMATION

Local youth hostel information can be found at the following *AYH* council offices:

California

San Diego Council, 1031 India Street, San Diego, CA 92101 (☎619/239-2644).

Los Angeles Council, 1502 Palos Verdes Drive, Harbor City, CA 90710 (☎310/831-8846).

Central CA Council, PO Box 28148, San Jose, CA 951159 (☎408/298-0670).

Golden Gate Council, 80 Beach Street, Suite 396, San Francisco, CA 94109 (☎415/771-4646).

Washington

Washington State Council, 419 Queen Anne Avenue, Suite 108, Seattle, WA 98109 (☎206/281-7306).

Oregon

Oregon Council, 650 W. 12th Street, Room 9, Eugene, OR 97402 (☎503/683-3685).

Two private companies oversee a multitude of campsites all over the West Coast, although these are almost exclusively for *RVs*. For their brochures and lists contact *California Travel Parks Association*, PO Box, 5648, Auburn, CA95604 (☎916/885-1624); and *Kampgrounds of America (KOA)*, PO Box 30558, Billings, Montana 59114 (☎406/248-7444). More tent-friendly sites can be found in the West Coast's **state parks** (see p.32). In California these can be can be booked ahead (for a $3.75 fee) through a computerised system called MISTIX, part of the *Ticketron* ticket agency, who have offices in most towns or can be phoned on ☎1-800/446-7275. A full brochure and list of state park campsites is available from the *Department of Parks and Recreation*, PO Box 942896, Sacramento, CA 94296 (general info ☎916/445-6477). In Washington and Oregon the rule tends to be first-come-first-served, although a few sites operate a high-season reservation system. Write for information and listings to *Washington State Parks and Recreation Commission*, 7150 Cleanwater Lane, KY-11, Olympia, Washington 98504 (☎206/753-2027); or *Oregon State Parks*, 525 Trade Street SE, Salem, Oregon N7310 (☎503/378-6305).

Fully half the land on the West Coast is in the public domain, and, if you're backpacking, you can **camp rough** pretty much anywhere you want in the gaping **wilderness areas** and **deserts**. You must always, however, get a **Wilderness Permit** first (either free or $1) from the nearest park rangers' office. You should also take the proper precautions: carry sufficient food and drink to cover emergencies, inform the park ranger of your travel plans, and watch out for bears and rattlesnakes, and the effect *your* presence can have on *their* environment. See "Backcountry Camping, Hiking and Wildlife" on p.31. For more information on these undeveloped regions – which are often protected within either "national parks" or "national forests", again see p.32 – contact, in California, the *Western Regional Information Office*, National Park Service, Fort Mason, Bldg 201, San Francisco, CA 94123 (☎415/556-0560); or the *US Forest Service*, 630 Sansome Street, San Francisco, CA 94111 (☎415/556-0122). In Washington and Oregon contact the *Pacific North West Regional Office*, National Park Service, 20001 Sixth Avenue, Seattle, Washington 98121 (☎206/442-0170).

FOOD AND DRINK

It's not too much of an exaggeration to say that on the West Coast you can eat whatever you want, whenever you want. Whether it's for basic daily sustenance or for a special social occasion, Americans dine out much more than British people. On every main street, a mass of restaurants, fast-food places and coffeeshops try to outdo one another with their bargains and special offers.

Things are further improved by the fact that California is one of the most agriculturally rich – and health-conscious – parts of the country. Junk food is as common as anywhere else in the US, but the state also produces its own range of highly nutritious goodies: apples, dates, grapes, kiwi fruits, melons, oranges and peaches are everywhere, joined by abundant fish and seafood from the ocean and high-quality meat and dairy goods. You'll rarely find anything that's not fresh, be it a bagel or a spinach-in-Mornay-sauce croissant (California's mix'n'match food concoctions can be as anarchic as its architecture), and even fast-food won't necessarily be rubbish. Washington and Oregon, too, are healthy places, between them producing the lion's share of the nation's apples, alongside plentiful apricots, berries and pears, and although there are more of the traditional American ribs, steak and burger menus this far north, again it's seafood that predominates, at least west of the Cascades. There's also excellent beef in the cattle country to the east of the mountains.

BREAKFAST

For the price, on average $3 to $5, breakfast is the best-value and most filling meal of the day. Go to a **diner**, or, slightly smarter, a **café** or **coffeeshop**, all of which serve breakfast until at least 11am, with some diners serving them all day. There are often special deals at earlier times too, say 6–8am, when the price may be even cheaper.

The breakfasts themselves are pretty much what you'd find all over the country. **Eggs** are the staple ingredient, in a variety of styles: "sunny side up" (fried on one side, leaving a runny yolk), "over" (flipped over in the pan to stiffen the yolk), or "over easy" (flipped for a few seconds giving a just a hint of solidity to the yolk). **Omelettes** are popular, usually made with three eggs and with more exotic fillings (avocado, for instance) than you would ever come across at home. There is usually also some form of **meat** available: ham or bacon, streaky and fried to a crisp; or sausages, skinless and spicier than the British version, sometimes shaped as disc-like "sausage patties".

All breakfasts come with **toast**: rye, white or wholewheat bread generally – though around San Francisco you may be offered the white, dense and tangy **sourdough bread**. Alternatives are an **English muffin** (actually a crispy crumpet), or, in trendier places, an **American muffin** – a fruitcake made with bran and sugar. If you wish, you can add **waffles** or **pancakes** to the combination, consumed swamped in butter with lashings of maple syrup. A concession to California's love of light food is the option of **fruit**; typically apple, banana, orange, pineapple or strawberry, wonderfully styled and served on their own or with pancakes, though costing as much as a full-blown fry-up.

Wherever you eat, it'll be washed down by as much **coffee** as you can stomach: refills are nearly always free and waiters will keep supplying mugfuls until you ask them to stop. Rarely other than fresh, coffee is either "regular" or "decaff" (de-caffeinated); it will come with a small jug of **"cream"** (usually **"half-and-half"**, half-milk, half-cream): **American milk** is normally homogenised, spreading the cream right through it. If you're buying coffee **"to go"** (takeaway), you'll be asked in advance how you want it. If you

want black coffee say so; if you want just milk (as opposed to "half-and-half"), simply ask for "milk" – though you may then be asked if you want "2%" (semi-skimmed) or "1%" (skimmed).

Tea is less commonly drunk than coffee, but isn't hard to find. Be warned, though, that anything called "English tea" will be a poor-quality brew made with weak tea-bags or an inferior Earl Grey. Better to try the wide range of **herbal teas** available: apple and cinnamon, blackcurrant, emperors (a very spicy herb) and ginseng, peppermint and camomile, and a huge selection of others. A cup will cost from 30¢ to $1, and be served straight or with lemon rather than milk.

LUNCH AND SNACKS

Most West Coast workers take their lunch-break between 11.30am and 2.30pm, and during these hours you should look for the low-cost **set menus** on offer – generally excellent value. Chinese restaurants, for example, frequently have help-yourself rice and noodles or dim sum feasts for $4 to $6, and many Japanese restaurants give you a chance to eat sushi much more cheaply ($7–10) than usual. Most Mexican restaurants are exceptionally well-priced all the time, and you can get a good-sized lunch in one for $4 to $5. In Northern California, Washington and Oregon, watch out for any seafood restaurant that sells **fish and chips**: the fish is breaded and then fried – a vast improvement on English batter – and the chips are actually chipped potatoes rather than the American french fry matchsticks you'll normally find. A plateful will be about $4. Look, too, for **clam chowder**, a thick, creamy shellfish soup served almost everywhere for $2 or $3.

As you'd expect, there's also **pizza**, available from both familiar chains like *Pizza Hut* and *Pizzaland*, and unfamiliar ones like *Shakey's*. All are dependable and offer broadly the same range; count on paying around $6 for a basic two-person pizza. If it's a warm day and you can't face hot food, look for a deli (see below) that has a **salad bar**, where you can help yourself for $2. Consider also the West Coast's favourite healthy fast-food: **frozen yoghurt**, which is sold in most places by the tub for $1.50, or through chains like *Heidi's*.

For **quick snacks**, you'll find many **delis** do ready-cooked meals for $2 to $3, as well as a range of **sandwiches "to go"**, which can be meals in themselves, filled with a custom-built combination of meat, cheese, seafood, pasta and salad. **Bagels**, also, are everywhere: thick, chewy rolls with a hole in the middle, filled with anything you fancy. **Street stands** sell hot dogs, burgers, tacos, or a slice of pizza for around $1, and most shopping malls have ethnic fast-food stalls, often pricier than their equivalent outside, but usually edible and filling. Be a little wary of the grottier **Mexican fast-food** stands if you're buying meat, although they're generally filling and very cheap. There are chains, too, like *El Pollo Loco* and *Taco Bell*, which sell swift tacos and burritos for around $3. And of course the inevitable **burger chains** are as ubiquitous here as anywhere in the US: *Wendy's*, *Burger King* and *McDonalds* are the familiar names, though there are others yet to cross the Atlantic, including *Jack-in-the-Box* – a drive-through takeaway where you place your order by talking to a plastic clown (and with a recently updated menu including croissants and shrimp salads).

Finally, just about any of these places will serve **soft drinks** (*sodas*). *Coke* and *Pepsi* are the market leaders, hotly pursued by *7-Up*, *Dr Pepper* and several others. Each brand is available in caffeine-free and sugar-free varieties (there's even, in reaction to this, a brand, *Jolt*, which promises "all the sugar and twice the caffeine"). You can buy sodas from street-vending machines and in supermarkets for about 50¢ a can, or from a fast-food outlet in three sizes for between 50¢ and $1: small (large), regular (bigger) and large (massive), each with ice added by the shovelful.

GLOSSARY OF AMERICAN FOOD TERMS

A la mode	With ice cream	Hash browns	Fried grated potato
Au jus	Meat served with a gravy made from its own juices	Hero	Sandwich made with French bread
BLT	Bacon, lettuce and tomato toasted sandwich	Home fries	Thick-cut fried potatoes
		Jello	Jelly
Broiled	Grilled	Jelly	Jam
Brownie	A fudgy, filling chocolate cake	Maitre d'	Head waiter
		Muffin	Small cake made with bran and/or blueberry
Brunch	A midday meal taken at weekends, with drinks	Pecan pie	Pastry shell filled with pecan nuts and syrupy goo
Caesars Salad	Cos lettuce in egg dressing with anchovy paste, olives and lemon served with garlic croutons and parmesan cheese	Popsicle	Ice lolly
		Potato chips	Crisps
		Pretzels	Savoury circles of glazed pastry
Check	Bill	Seltzer	Fizzy/soda water
Chips	Potato crisps	Sherbet	Sorbet
Clam chowder	A thick soup made with clams and other seafood. Very tasty and, with bread, almost a meal in itself	Shrimp	Prawns
		Soda	Generic term for any soft drink
		Maryland soft-shell crab	A kind of crab whose shell is soft and edible
Club sandwich	Large, overstuffed sandwich	Squash	Marrow
Doggy bag	Not a bag but a stylish wrapping-up of your leftovers for reheating later at home	Tab	Bill
		Teriyaki	Chicken or beef, marinated in soy sauce and grilled
		Waffles	Like pancakes but thicker and crispier; egg batter cooked in an iron and served with maple syrup, honey or butter
Egg-plant	Aubergine		
English muffin	Toasted bread roll, similar to a crumpet		
Fillet	The same meaning as in England but pronounced "fillay"	Waldorf salad	Celery, chopped apple and walnuts served on lettuce leaves with a mayonnaise dressing
Frank	Frankfurter (hot dog)		
(French) fries	Chips		
Half-and-half	Half cream, half milk	Zucchini	Courgettes

FREE FOOD AND BRUNCH

Some **bars** in the US are used as much by diners as drinkers, who turn up in droves to fill up on the free **hors d'oeuvres** laid out by a lot of city bars between 5pm and 7pm Monday to Friday – an attempt to nab the commuting classes before they head off to the suburbs. For the price of a drink you can stuff yourself silly on chilli, seafood or pasta, though bear in mind it will help to look like an office worker; look like a tramp and you won't get in.

Brunch is another deal worth looking out for: a cross between breakfast and lunch that's indulged in at weekends (though Sunday is more usual) between 11am and 2pm. For a set-price ($8 and up) you get a light meal and a variety of complimentary cocktails or champagne. Perfect for serious daytime boozing.

RESTAURANTS

Even if it often seems swamped by the more fashionable regional and ethnic cuisines, traditional **American cooking** is found all over the West Coast. Portions are big and you start with **salad**, eaten before the main course arrives. There's a choice of salad dressing and you'll need to state your preference: *Italian* (like European *French*, a moist, straightforward combination of oil, vinegar and mayonnaise), *French* (*not* like European *French*; much creamier with more lemon), *Thousand Island* (thin and best eaten with seafood), *Ranch* (thick, cheesy and spicy) or *Blue Cheese* (thick, creamy, with bits of blue cheese); if none of these appeal to you, ask for "dry". Some restaurants have a salad bar from which you help yourself while waiting for the main course.

Main dishes are dominated by enormous **steaks**, **burgers**, piles of **ribs** or half a **chicken** (roast **turkey**, incidentally, is only eaten hot on Thanksgiving Day, otherwise it's served cold in sandwiches). Vegetables include french fries or a baked potato, the latter commonly topped with sour cream and chives. Order a burger as you would a steak, asking for it rare, medium-rare, medium or well-done. Often the burgers will taste like steaks: thick and juicy.

There's also a good choice of **fish and seafood**, especially in Washington and Oregon, where enormous hunks of ocean fish are consumed as eagerly as meat. West of the Cascades particularly, fish is a speciality, not least salmon – either served straight or stuffed, or sometimes in unlikely mixes with pasta.

Shellfish is popular here too, including Washington's highly rated **dungeness crab** – smoother and creamier than the average crab – **clams**, and, most strikingly, Puget Sound **geoduck** (pronounced "gooeyduck"): huge molluscs of intensely phallic appearance.

Cheapest of the American food chains is the California-wide *Sizzler*, although you'll rarely need spend more than $10 for a solid blowout anywhere.

By contrast, it's **California Cuisine**, geared towards health and aesthetics, that's raved about by foodies on the West Coast – and rightly so. Basically a development of French *nouvelle cuisine*, utilising the wide mix of fresh, locally available ingredients, California Cuisine is based on physiological efficiency – eating only what you need to and what your body can process. Vegetables are harvested before maturity and steamed to preserve a high concentration of vitamins, a strong flavour – and to look better on the plate. Seafood comes from oyster farms and the catches of small-time fishermen, and what little meat there is tends to be from animals reared on organic farms. The result is small but beautifully presented portions, and high, high prices: not unusually $50 a head for a full dinner with wine; the minimum you'll need for a sample is $15, which will buy an entrée. To whet your appetite, starters include mussels in jalapeno and sesame vinaigrette, snails in puff pastry with mushroom puree, and, among main courses, roasted goat's cheese salad with walnuts, swordfish with herb butter and tuna with cactus ratatouille.

Restaurants serving California Cuisine build their reputation by word of mouth; if you can, ask a local enthusiast for recommendations, or simply follow our suggestions in the *Guide*, especially in Berkeley, the recognised birthplace of California Cuisine. Not to be totally left out, Washington and Oregon have come up with **Northwest Cuisine**, which is similar to California Cuisine but has more emphasis on fish, and, again, is only found in expensive restaurants.

Of other American regional cooking, it's **Cajun** that's currently in vogue. Also known as "creole", it originated in Louisiana as a way of saving money by cooking-up leftovers. It's centred on black beans, rice and seafood, and is always highly spiced. There are a few relatively inexpensive places to find it (charging around $8), but its current cachet has pushed prices up tremendously, and in most places it's not really a budget option.

GLOSSARY OF ETHNIC FOOD TERMS

MEXICAN

Arroz	Rice, usually pepared in tomato sauce	*Mariscos*	Seafood
Burritos	Folded tortillas stuffed with refried beans or beef, and grated cheese	*Menudo*	Soup made from a cow's stomach, said to be a cure for hangovers
Chiles Rellenos	Green chillies stuffed with cheese and fried in egg batter	*Nachos*	Tortilla chips topped with melted cheese
Enchiladas	Soft tortillas filled with meat and cheese or chilli and baked	*Salsa*	Chillies, tomato and onion and cilantro, served in varying degrees of spiciness
Fajitas	Like tacos but a soft flour tortilla stuffed with shrimp, chicken or beef	*Tacos*	Folded, fried tortillas, stuffed with chicken, beef or (occasionally) cow's brains
Frijoles	Refried beans, ie mashed fried beans	*Tamales*	Corn meal dough with meat and chilli, wrapped in a corn husk and baked
Guacamole	A thick sauce made from avocado, garlic, onion, and chilli, used as a topping	*Tortillas*	Maize dough pancakes used in most dishes
Margarita	*The* cocktail to drink in a Mexican restaurant made with tequila, triple sec, lime juice and limes, and blended with ice to make slush. Served with or without salt	*Tostada*	Fried, flat tortillas, smothered with meat and vegetables
		Quesadilla	Folded soft tortilla containing melted cheese

ITALIAN

Cacciatore	"Hunter's style" – cooked with tomatoes, mushrooms, herbs and wine	**Pasta**	
		Cannelloni	Large pasta tubes, stuffed with minced meat and tomato and baked
Calzone	Pizza folded in half so the topping is inside	*Cappelleti*	"Little hats" stuffed with chicken, cheese and egg
Alla Carbonara	Sauce made with bacon and egg	*Cappelli d'angeli*	"Angel's hair", very fine pasta strands
Alla Veneziana	Cooked with onions and white wine	*Fettucini*	Flat ribbons of pasta
Alfredo	Tossed with cream, butter and cheese	*Fusilli*	Pasta spiral
		Gnocchi	Pasta and tomato dumplings
Al forno	Cooked in the oven	*Linguine*	Flat pasta noodles, like tagliatelle
Posillipo	Tomato cooked with garlic, Neapolitan style	*Manicotti*	Squares stuffed with cheese; ravioli are the same only with meat
Puttanesca	Literally "whore style", cooked with tomato, garlic, olives, capers and anchovies	*Tortellini*	Rings of pasta stuffed with either spiced meat or cheese
Zabaglione	Dessert of whipped egg yolks, sugar and marsala	*Vermicelli*	Very thin spaghetti
		Ziti	Small tubes of pasta, often baked with tomato sauce

JAPANESE

California Roll	Mild tasting sushi with a slice of quocado	*Sake*	Strong rice wine, drunk hot
		Sashimi	Thinly sliced raw fish eaten with soy sauce or *Wasabi*
Gyoza	Meat and vegetable dumplings		
Karagei	Fried chicken	*Sushi*	Raw fish wrapped up in rice in seaweed (see next page)
Larmen	Noodles in spicy broth		
Negimayaki	Sliced beef with scallions	*Tempura*	Seafood and vegetables deep-fried in batter
Okonomi	Literally "as you like it", usually used with regard to sushi when choosing the topping	*Tonkatsu*	Deep-fried pork with rice
		Wasabi	Hot green horseradish sauce

JAPANESE (CONTINUED)

Sushi/sashimi

Anago	Sea eel	*Nigiri*	Rice topped with fish
Ebi	Shrimp	*Tai*	Red snapper
Ikura	Salmon roe	*Tekka(maki)*	Tuna with rice rolled in
Kappa(muki)	Cucumber with rice and		seaweed (*nori*)
	seaweed	*Toro*	Extra meaty part of the tuna
Maguro	Tuna	*Chirashi*	Mixed fish on rice

CHINESE

Cantonese	**Szechan/Hunan**		**Dim Sum (Cantonese)**	
Chow	*Ch'ao*	Stir-fried	*Bao, bau*	Bun
Doufu	*Tofu*	Bean curd	*Cha Shew Bao*	Steamed bun filled with sweet
Fun, fon	*Fan*	Rice		cubes of roast pork
Gai, gee	*Chi*	Chicken	*Chow fun*	Fried rice noodles
Har, ha	*Hsia Jen*	Shrimp (prawns)	*Chow mai fu*	Rice vermicelli
Hew	*Shao*	Roasted	*Har Kow*	Shrimp dumplings
Jyuyuk	*Jou*	Pork	*Jook*	Congee, or rice gruel
Ngow yuk	*Niu Jou*	Beef	*Kow, gow*	Dumplings
Opp	*Ya*	Duck	*Lo Mein*	Mixed noodles
Ow	*Cha*	Deep-fried	*Mai fun*	Thin noodles
Yu	*Yu*	Fish	*Tang mein*	Soup noodles
			Wontons	Thin-skinned dumpling filled with
				fish or meat

Although technically ethnic, **Mexican** food is so common that it often seems like (and, historically, often is) an indigenous cuisine, especially in Southern California. What's more, day or night, it's the cheapest type of food to eat: even a full dinner with a few drinks will rarely be over $10 anywhere except in the most upmarket establishment. West Coast Mexican food is different from what you'll find in Mexico, making more use of fresh vegetables and fruit, but the essentials are the same. Lots of rice and kidney beans, often served refried (ie boiled, mashed and fried), with variations on the **tortilla**, a thin maize dough pancake that comes in several ways. You can eat it as an accompaniment to your main dish; wrapped around the food and eaten by hand (a **burrito**); folded, fried and filled (a **taco**); rolled, filled and baked (an **enchilada**); or fried flat and topped with a stack of food (a **tostada**). One of the few options for vegetarians in this meat-orientated cuisine is the **chile relleno**, a green pepper stuffed with cheese, dipped in egg batter and fried.

Other ethnic cuisines are plentiful too. **Chinese** food is everywhere, and can often be as cheap as Mexican. **Japanese** is more expensive and fashionable – sushi is worshipped by some Californians – although it costs less than it does in Britain. **Italian** food is popular, but can be expensive once you leave the simple pastas and explore the exotic pizza toppings or the specialist Italian regional cooking that's fast catching on in the major cities. **French** food, too, is widely available, though always pricey, the cuisine of social climbers and power-lunchers and rarely found outside the larger cities. **Thai**, **Korean**, and **Indonesian** food is similarly city-based, though usually cheaper; **Indian** restaurants, on the other hand, are thin on the ground just about everywhere and often very expensive – although as Indian cuisine catches on the situation is gradually changing for the better, with a sprinkling of moderately priced Southern Indian food outlets. There's also a surprisingly impressive number of **Basque** restaurants in many West Coast farming regions, reflecting the background of many of the local settlers.

Whatever you eat and wherever you eat, **service** will always be enthusiastic and excellent, mainly due to the American system of **tipping**, on which the staff depend for the bulk (and sometimes all) of their earnings. You should always top up the bill by fifteen or twenty percent; not to tip at all is severely frowned upon. Many (not all), restaurants accept **payment** in the form of credit/charge cards: if you use one, a space will be left to fill in the appropriate tip. Travellers' cheques are also widely accepted with ID (see p.10).

DRINKING

American **bars** and **cocktail lounges** are pretty true to their popular image: long dimly lit counters with a few punters perched on stools before a bar-tender-cum-guru, and tables and booths for those who don't want to join in the drunken bar-side debates. In freeway-dominated Los Angeles, though, the traditional neighbourhood bar is as rare as the traditional neighbourhood; there are exceptions, but LA bars tend to be either extremely pretentious or extremely seedy, neither good for long bouts of social drinking. On the other hand, San Francisco is the consummate boozing town, still with a strong contingent of old-fashioned, get-drunk bars that are fun to spend an evening in even if you don't plan to get legless. In Washington, you'll also find **taverns**, similar to bars but selling just beer and wine.

To **buy and consume alcohol** on the West Coast you need to be 21, and could well be asked for ID even if you look much older. **Licensing laws and drinking hours** are, however, among the most liberal in the country (though laws on drinking and driving are not; see p.19). Alcohol can be bought and drunk any time between 6am and 2am, seven days a week; and, as well as bars, nightclubs and restaurants are nearly always fully licensed. You can buy beer, wine or spirits more cheaply and easily in supermarkets, many delis, and, of course, liquor stores (closed on Sundays and public holidays in Washington).

For the most part, American **beer** is as unremarkable as its European reputation suggests: fizzy and tasteless and not very strong, consumed to quench the thirst rather than to get drunk. Brands such as *Budweiser*, *Miller* and *Schlitz* are found everywhere, as is *Michelob*, the only nationally sold variety likely to find fans among British beer drinkers. Happily there are alternatives. The full-bodied, San Francisco-brewed *Anchor Steam* beer is available across much of the region, and the many "microbreweries" of Washington and Oregon turn out handcrafted lagers, ales and stouts which are on a par with anything you can buy in Britain. The best and most widely found is *Henry Weinhard's*, although most areas have their own speciality: try *ESB* or *Red Hook Ale* in Seattle, *Grants* in Yakima, *Deschutes Black Butte Porter* in Bend, Oregon, or

the product of any of Portland's dozen fine breweries. Northern California's *Red Tail Ale* is also worth keeping an eye out for. Otherwise do what most locals do and stick to **imported** beers, especially the Mexican brands *Bohemia*, *Corona*, *Dos Equis*, *Superior* and *Tecate* (though for the really unadventurous, British brands are easily found in the big cities). Expect to fork out $1 for a glass (just over a British half-pint) of draught beer, slightly more for a bottle or an imported beer. Don't forget that in all but the more pretentious bars, several people can save money by buying a (quart or half-gallon) **"pitcher"** of beer for $3 to $5. If bar prices are a problem, you can stock up with **six-packs** from a supermarket ($2–5 for domestic, $4–8 for imported brews).

If you're partial to the Californian **wines** available in Europe, like *Gallo* and *Paul Masson*, you may be surprised to learn that they are held in low regard on the West Coast, and produced in plants resembling oil refineries. Most people prefer to drink the produce of the West Coast's innumerable smaller wineries – invariably good, with the best of the lot coming from the Napa and Sonoma Valleys, made from French-strain grapes and predominantly dry. Wines are categorised by grape-type rather than place of origin: *Cabernet Sauvignon* is probably the most popular, a light and easily drunk red. Also widespread are the heavier reds – *Burgundy*, *Merlot* and *Pinot Noir*. Among the whites, *Chardonnay* is very dry and flavourful, and generally preferred to *Sauvignon Blanc* or *Fumé Blanc*, though these have their devotees. The most unusual is the strongly flavoured *Zinfandel*, which comes as white, red or rosé. In the Northwest, too, mainly east of the mountains in Washington and in Oregon's Willamette Valley, there are many quality wineries, a lot of which experiment with fruits and berries, producing tasty concoctions made from raspberry, loganberry, blackberry and rhubarb.

You can learn a lot about West Coast wine by taking a **winery tour**, mostly including free tastings (although some charge $4–5 for a full glass or two), a number of which we've mentioned in the *Guide*. Or, before leaving home, write to the Wine Institute, 165 Post Street, San Francisco, CA 94108, for their informative booklet and winery directory. The best lesson of all, of course, is simply to buy the stuff. It's fairly inexpensive: a decent glass of wine in a bar or restaurant costs under $2, a bottle $5 to $8. Buying from a supermarket is cheaper still – just $3 to $6 a bottle.

COCKTAILS

Bacardi	White rum, lime and grenadine – not the brand name drink	Manhattan	Vermouth, whisky, lemon juice and soda
Bellini	Champagne with peach juice	Margarita	Tequila, triple sec and lime (or strawberry) juice
Black Russian	Vodka with coffee liqueur, brown cacao and Coke	Mimosa	Champagne and orange juice
Bloody Mary	Vodka, tomato juice, tabasco, Worcester sauce, salt and pepper	Mint Julep	Bourbon, mint and sugar
		Negroni	Vodka or gin, campari and triple sec
Brandy Alexander	Brandy, brown cacao and cream	Pina Colada	Dark rum, light rum, coconut, cream and pineapple juice
Champagne cocktail	Brandy, sugar and champagne	Screwdriver	Vodka and orange juice
Daiquiri	Dark rum, light rum and lime, often with fruit such as banana or strawberry	Silk Stocking	Gin, tequila, white cacao, cream and sugar
		Tequila Sunrise	Tequila, orange juice and grenadine
Harvey Wallbanger	Vodka, galliano, orange juice	Tom Collins	Gin, lemon juice, soda and sugar
Highball	Any spirit plus a soda, water or ginger ale	Vodka Collins	Vodka, lemon juice, soda and sugar
Kir Royale	Champagne with cassis		
Long Island Iced Tea	Gin, vodka, white rum, tequila, lemon juice and Coke	Whisky Sour	Bourbon, lemon juice and sugar
Mai-Tai	Dark rum, light rum, cherry brandy, orange and lemon juice	White Russian	Vodka, white cacao and cream

As for **spirits** ("hard liquor"), this is where the US really excels: the range, even in a run-of-the-mill bar is enough to put the best-stocked British pub to shame. Whatever you order you'll get it in a glass full of ice ("on the rocks"); to avoid this demand it "straight up". You need to be careful when ordering whisky. Unless you ask for Scotch or Irish you'll be served the heavier-tasting *bourbon*, the more common brands of which are *Jim Beam, Old Grandad, Wild Turkey* (*Jack Daniels* is not technically a bourbon as it's made in Tennessee, not Kentucky). There are startling arrays of different gins and vodkas (*Stolychnaya* or "stoly" is the most popular), and always a good selection of rums from white to dark to every shade in between, including the explosive *Bacardi 151* – 75 percent pure alcohol. Remember that in America, a Martini is a cocktail made with gin and a dash of white vermouth; if you want the British kind use the generic term, pronouced "vermooth". Spirits generally cost $1 "a shot" – a slightly larger measure than the UK "single".

Cocktails are extremely popular, especially during **happy hours** (usually any time between 5pm and 7pm) when drinks are half-price and there's often a buffet thrown in. Varieties are innumerable, sometimes specific to a single bar or cocktail lounge, though there are a few standards listed above, any of which will cost between $2 and $5.

POLICE AND THIEVES

No one could pretend that the West Coast is trouble-free, although away from the major urban centres (and throughout Washington and Oregon), crime is a lower-key issue than you might think. Even the lawless reputation of Los Angeles is far in excess of the truth, and most of the city, by day at least, is fairly safe; at night, though, a few areas are completely off-limits. Members of the notorious LA gangs are a rare sight outside their own territories (which are usually well away from where you're likely to be), and they tend to kill each other rather than tourists. By being careful, planning ahead, and

taking care of your possessions, you should, generally speaking, have few real problems. If you do, the police are usually helpful and obliging to foreign visitors although they'll be less sympathetic if they think you brought the trouble on yourself.

One way you might accidently break the law is by **jaywalking**. If you cross the road on a red light or anywhere except an intersection, and are spotted by a cop, you're likely to get a stiff talking-to – and possibly a ticket, leading to a $20 fine.

STREET CRIME

The biggest problem for most travellers is the threat of **mugging**. It's impossible to give hard and fast rules about what to do if you're confronted by a mugger. Whether to run, scream, or fight depends on the situation – but most locals would just hand over their money.

Of course, the best thing is simply to avoid being mugged, and there are a few basic rules worth remembering: *don't* flash money around; don't peer at your map (or this book) at every street corner, thereby announcing you're a lost stranger; even if you're terrified or drunk (or both), *don't* appear so; *avoid* dark streets, especially ones you can't see the end of; and in the early hours stick to the roadside edge of the pavement so it's easier to run into the road to attract attention.

If the worst happens and your assailant is toting a gun or (more likely) a knife, try to stay calm: remember that he (for this is generally a male pursuit) is probably scared too. Keep still, don't make any sudden movements – and hand over your money. When he's gone you'll be shocked, but try to find a cab to take you to the nearest police station. Here, report the theft and get a reference number on the report to claim insurance (see "Health and Insurance", p.9) and travellers' cheque refunds. If you're in a big city,

ring the local *Travelers Aid* (their numbers are listed the *Guide*) for sympathy and practical advice. For advice specifically for women in case of mugging or attack, see p.33.

STOLEN PASSPORTS AND TRAVELLERS CHEQUES

Needless to say, having bags snatched which contain travel documents can be a big headache, none more so than **losing your passport**. You can't get home without it, and it can be an extremely tough process to get a new one. The only British Consulate on the West Coast which (very grudgingly) issues passports under normal circumstances – the others do but only in emergencies – is in Los Angeles at 3701 Wilshire Boulevard (☎213/385-7581). If you're in LA at the time, things will be reasonably straightforward. If you're not you'll need to ring them giving an address where they can send you an application form, and enclosing any ID you still have plus a $30 reissuing fee. Better than parting with your ID (especially if all you have left is a driving licence) is to send a *notarized* (ie specially stamped) photocopy of it. Most banks have a notary who can do this for you at little or no charge. The passport issuing process can take six weeks: to speed things up, the Consulate can telex record departments in Britain – but they won't do this until you've sent them a $10 telex fee.

Another common problem is **lost travellers' cheques**. You should keep a record of the numbers of your cheques separately from the actual cheques, and if you lose them, ring the issuing company on its toll-free number (see box on p.11). They'll ask you for the cheque numbers, the place you bought them, when and how you lost them, and whether it's been reported to the police. All being well, you should get the missing cheques reissued within a couple of days – and perhaps an emergency advance to tide you over.

BACKCOUNTRY CAMPING, HIKING AND WILDLIFE

The West Coast has some fabulous backcountry and wilderness areas, coated by dense forests and capped by great mountains. Unfortunately, while still immensely rewarding, it isn't all as wild as it once was, thanks to the thousands who

tramp through each year. If you're intending to do the same, you can help preserve the special qualities of the environment by observing a few simple rules. For practical information on travelling through the deserts, see Chapter Three.

The US's protected backcountry areas fall into a number of potentially confusing categories. **State parks** are state-run parks, often around sites of geological or historical importance (not necessarily even in a rural area). **National parks** are federally controlled and preserved areas of great natural beauty. Around national parks, you'll often find areas of **national forest** also federally administered but with much less protection. More roads run through national forests and often there is some limited logging and other land-based industry.

CAMPING

When **camping rough**, check that fires are permitted before you start one; if they are, use a stove in preference to local materials – in some places firewood is scarce, although you may be allowed to use deadwood. In wilderness areas, try to camp on previously used sites. Where there are no toilets, **bury human waste** at least four inches into the ground and a hundred feet from the nearest water supply and campsite. **Burn rubbish**, and what you can't burn, carry away. A growing problem is water-borne *Giardia*, a bacteria causing an intestinal disease, symptoms of which are chronic diarrhoea, abdominal cramps, fatigue and loss of weight, that requires treatment. To avoid catching it, **never drink** from rivers and streams, however clear and inviting they may look (you never know what unspeakable acts people – or animals – further upstream have performed in them). Before you drink it, **water** that isn't from taps should be boiled for at least five minutes, or cleansed with an iodine-based purifier (such as *Potable Aqua*) or a *Giardia*-rated filter, available from camping or sports shops.

HIKING

When completing the form for your **wilderness permit** (see "Sleeping", p.20), be sure to ask a park ranger for weather conditions and general information about the hike you're undertaking. Hiking **in the foothills** should present few problems but you should check your clothes frequently for **ticks** – pesky blood-sucking insects which are known to carry diseases. If you have been bitten, get advice from a park ranger. Another annoyance around water are **mosquitos**. Beware, too, of **Poison Oak**, a shrub that grows all over the West Coast, usually among oak trees, with leaves in groups of three with prominent veins and shiny surfaces. If you come into contact with this, wash your skin (with soap and cold water) and clothes as soon as possible – and don't scratch; the only way to ease the itching is to smother yourself in calamine lotion or to take regular dips in the sea. **In the mountains** late snows are common, giving rise to the possibility of avalanches and meltwaters, which make otherwise simple stream crossings hazardous. For hiking trips of lengthy duration (2–3 days or more) it goes without saying that you should be properly prepared with all necessary equipment, supplies, maps and common sense. For the best hiking guides and information (and organised tours, see p.7), contact the **Sierra Club**, 730 Polk Street, San Francisco, CA 94109 (☎415/776-2211).

WILDLIFE

You're likely to meet many kinds of wildlife on your travels through the wilderness, but only bears, rattlesnakes and black widow spiders are likely to present problems. With due care, many potential difficulties can be avoided.

Some campsites are equipped with **bear lockers**, which you are obliged to use to store food when not preparing or eating it. When camping in other areas where bears are present, store food in airtight containers inside sacks and suspend them from a tree branch (one strong enough to support the food but not a bear), preferably about twenty feet high and at least ten feet from where you're sleeping. Bears are enthusiastic eaters who think nothing of wrenching off a car door or wrecking the boot to get to whatever food they can smell inside.

Never feed a bear: it'll make the bear dependent on humans for food and cause them to be increasingly troublesome to visitors. Remember that bears within state and national parks are protected, but if they spend too much time around people the park rangers are, depressingly, left with no option but to shoot them.

If a bear visits your camp, scare it away by banging pots and pans. If it doesn't go, you should. Leave backpacks open and lying on the ground so a bear can examine the contents without tearing them apart. Be wary of **bear cubs**: they may look cute and cuddly but the mother will be close by and won't welcome the attention you're paying to her infant. Finally, if you get rather too close to a bear for comfort, keep calm, lie slowly down on the ground and stay there without moving. The bear will get bored and move away.

Rattlesnakes (only the female actually rattles), which live in the drier foothills and desert areas, seldom attack unless provoked: do not tease or try to handle them. Rattlesnake bites are rarely fatal but you might suffer severe tissue damage. If you are bitten, contact a ranger or doctor immediately. It's a wise precaution to carry a **snakebite kit**, available for a couple of dollars from most sports and camping stores. **Black widow spiders** are quite common in the backcountry of eastern Washington and Oregon, and, again, their bites should be reported straight away.

For more on the hazards of snakes and spiders, see p.204; and for more on West Coast wildlife generally, see *Contexts*.

WOMEN'S WEST COAST

Women on the West Coast have made great advances over the last couple of decades, and although the women's movement has lost some impetus in recent years its achievements persist: women's bars, bookstores and support centres are testimony to continuing, and widespread, female commitment on the West Coast. Women really do have positive, and demanding, roles; and the New Age movement is going some way towards reassessing ideologies on femininity, though it prefers esotericism to the political arena. A shame, because in the midst of Republican ruination of abortion rights, the women's movement needs all the solidarity it can muster.

Practically speaking, though a woman **travelling alone** is certainly not the attention-grabbing spectacle on the West Coast that she can be elsewhere in the world (or even the US), you're likely to come across some sort of harassment. By and large this will be fairly similar to what you'd get at home, though it may be less subtle (as with other things here). In a land obsessed with all things physical, it's no surprise that women here, in particular, are under incredible pressure to *look* perfect and mens' attitudes towards you may reflect this.

More serious than the odd offensive comment, **rape** statistics in the US are high, and it goes without saying that you should *never* **hitch** alone – this is widely interpreted as an invitation for trouble, and there's no shortage of weirdos to give it. Similarly if you have a car, be careful who you pick up: just because you're in the driving seat doesn't mean you're safe. If you can, avoid travelling at night by public transport – deserted bus stations, while not necessarily threatening, will do little to make you feel secure, and where possible you should team up with another woman.

West Coast **cities**, especially San Francisco can feel surprisingly safe. But as with anywhere, particular care has to be taken at night. **Mugging** is nowhere near the problem it is in New York, but you can't relax totally – though a modicum of common sense can often avert disasters. Walking through unlit, empty streets is never a good idea, and if there's no bus service (and you can afford it), take cabs – if not, an escort. Ignoring creeps who bother you is no guarantee that they'll go away – either move yourself or be assertive to the point of verbal aggression: in most cases this does the trick. It's true that women who *look* confident tend not to encounter trouble – those who stand around looking lost and a bit scared are prime targets. Provided you listen to advice and stick to the better parts of a town, going into **bars** and **clubs** alone should pose no problems: there's generally a pretty healthy attitude towards women who choose to do so and your privacy will be respected – only extremely unevolved specimens will assume you're available. If in doubt, gay and lesbian bars are usually a trouble-free alternative.

Small towns in rural areas are not blessed with the same liberal attitudes toward lone women travellers that you'll find in the cities. Here, in most cases, aggravation will come in the form of an annoying little man who approaches you in a bar with a well-worn cliché or two. On the whole, he'll be harmless, but use your judgement and if you're not sure, tell him in no uncertain terms to leave you alone. If your **vehicle breaks down** in a country area, walk to the nearest house or town for help; *don't* wait by the vehicle in the middle of nowhere hoping for somebody to stop – they will, but it may not be the kind of help you're looking for. Should disaster strike, all major towns have some kind of rape counselling service available; if not, the local sheriff's office will make adequate arrangements for you to get help, counselling, and, if necessary, get you home.

Specific **women's contacts** are listed in the city sections of the *Guide*, but for good back-up material get hold of *Places of Interest to Women* (Ferrari Publications, PO Box 35575, Phoenix, Arizona; $7), a yearly guide for women travelling in the US, Canada, the Caribbean and Mexico.

GAY AND LESBIAN WEST COAST

The gay scene on the West Coast is huge, albeit heavily concentrated in the major cities. San Francisco, where anything between a quarter and a third of the voting population is reckoned to be gay or lesbian, is the premier gay city of the world; Los Angeles comes a close second, and up and down the coast gay men and women enjoy the kind of visibility and influence those in other places can only dream about. Gay politicians, and even police officers, are more than a novelty here and representation at every level is for real. Resources, places, facilities and organisations are endless.

In Los Angeles, the gay population has been growing steadily since the earliest days of the movie industry – a job which gave considerably greater freedom of lifestyle than most others at the time. Later, during World War II, the military purged suspected homosexuals at their point of embarkation. For those expecting to serve in the Pacific war zone, this meant they got off in San Francisco – where, unable to face the stigma of a return home, many remained, their ranks later swelled by gays who lost their government jobs during McCarthy's swipes of the 1950s.

In both cities, the activism of the 1960s highlighted gay issues, but they only became fully mainstream topics in the 1970s, when, particularly in San Francisco, gays organised themselves into the largest and most influential minority group in the city. Politicians realised that the gay vote was the difference between winning and losing and quickly got on the case. In 1977 San Francisco got its first city official on the Board of Supervisors, the openly gay Harvey Milk. Milk's hero status was assured forever when, in 1978, he was assassinated by another councillor, the conservative Dan White.

Since the heady Seventies, however, and in the face of the AIDS crisis, the energies of gay men and women have been directed to the protection of existing rights and helping victims of the disease. California has lost many to AIDS, but the state, perhaps more than anywhere else, has responded quickly and with compassion and intelligence: public health programmes have had hitherto unheard of sums of money pumped into them, and attitudes across the board are broad-minded and supportive.

Ghettoisation, then, is no longer a problem for West Coast gays, although there are sizeable, predominantly gay areas in almost all the major cities – San Diego's **Hillcrest**, Los Angeles' **West Hollywood**, San Francisco's **Castro** district, Seattle's **Capitol Hill** – and even Portland has an impressive number of gay bars and clubs and a strong lesbian scene. However, although tolerance is high everywhere, the liberal attitudes of the major cities are not always reflected in the West Coast's more isolated areas.

For a complete rundown on local **resources**, **bars** and **clubs**, see the relevant city chapter of the *Guide*. Of national and statewide **publications** to look out for, by far the best is *Bob Damron's Address Book* (PO Box 11270, San Francisco CA 94101; $12) a pocket-sized yearbook full of listings of hotels, bars, clubs and resources, available in both state and national editions from almost any decent bookshop. Also useful is *Gay Yellow Pages* (Ferrari Publications, PO Box 292, Village Station, New York, NY 100114; $8.95). There's also *The Advocate* (Liberation

Publications, 6922 Hollywood Blvd, Los Angeles CA; $2.50), a bi-monthly national gay news magazine, with features, general info and classified ads (not to be confused with *Advocate Men*, which is a soft-porn magazine). Specifically lesbian publications are harder to find: the most useful is

Gaia's Guide (132 W. 24th St New York, NY 10011; $6.95), a yearly international directory with a lot of US info. In Oregon, the monthly magazine, *Lavender Network*, covers local gay and lesbian activities, and is sold in most liberal bookstores.

SPORT

Americans are sport-mad, and nowhere in the country do the various forms of athletic activity and competition have a higher profile than on the West Coast, particularly in California. All the big cities have at least one team in each of the major professional sports – baseball, football, and basketball – sometimes as well as supporting sides in the more unusual spectator sports of indoor soccer, volleyball, ice hockey, wrestling, even roller derby.

Less expensive, but just as exciting as the professional games, are the **intercollegiate sports** – college and university teams, competing against one another in the Pacific-10 Conference, usually with an enthusiasm fuelled by passionate

local rivalries: in Los Angeles, USC and UCLA have an intense and high-powered sporting enmity, with fans on each side as vociferous as any European soccer crowd. In the San Francisco Bay Area, the rivalry between UC Berkeley and Stanford is akin to that of Oxford and Cambridge; and in Washington and Oregon intra-state feuds between the state colleges and universities fill up the sporting year.

BASEBALL

Baseball, much like cricket in its relaxed, summertime pace and seemingly byzantine rules, is often called "America's pastime". Games are played – 162 each season – all over the US close

THE RULES OF BASEBALL

The basic set-up looks like the English game of rounders, with four **bases** set at the corners of a 90-foot square **diamond**; at the bottom corner the base is called **home plate** and serves much the same purpose as do the stumps in cricket. Play begins when the **pitcher**, standing on a low **pitcher's mound** in the middle of the diamond, throws a ball at upwards of 100mph, making it curve and bend as it travels towards the **catcher**, who crouches behind home plate; seven other defensive players take up **positions**, one at each base and the others spread out around the field of play.

A **batter** from the opposing team stands beside home plate and tries to hit the ball with a tapered, cylindrical wooden bat. If the batter swings and misses, or if the pitched ball crosses the plate above the batter's knees and below his chest, it counts as a **strike**; if he doesn't swing and the ball passes outside of this **strike zone**, it counts as a **ball**. If the batter gets **three strikes** against him he is **out; four balls** and he gets a free **walk**, and takes his place as a **runner** on first base.

If he succeeds in hitting the pitched ball into **fair territory**, the wedge between the first and third bases, the batter runs towards first base; if the opposing players catch the ball before it hits the ground, the batter is **out**. Otherwise they field the ball and attempt to relay it to first base before the batter gets there; if they do he is **out**, if they don't the batter is **safe** – and stays there, being moved along by subsequent batters until he makes a complete circuit of the bases and scores a **run**. The most exciting moment in baseball is the **home run**, when a batter hits the ball over the outfield fences, a boundary 400 feet away from home plate; he and any runners on base when he hits the ball each score a run. If there are runners on all three bases it's called a **grand slam**, and earns four runs.

The nine players per side bat in rotation; each side gets **three outs** per **inning**, and there are **nine innings** per **game**. Games normally last two to three hours, usually during the day, though increasingly games are taking place at night. There are no tied games; the teams play **extra innings** until one side pulls ahead and wins.

on every day from April to September, with the league championships and the World Series, the final best-of-seven playoff, lasting through October. Watching a game, even if you don't understand what's going on, can be at the least a pleasant day out, drinking beer and eating hot dogs in the sun: tickets are cheap and the crowds usually friendly and sociable.

TEAMS AND TICKETS

In 1991, some of the best **teams** in the Major Leagues were from California. The **Oakland A's**, many times champions of the American League, and the **Los Angeles Dodgers**, finished at the top of their divisions; other clubs, including the **San Francisco Giants**, didn't fare so well. **Tickets** for games cost $5 to $12 per seat, and are generally available on the day of the game. Along with other Major League clubs in San Diego, Anaheim (where the California Angels play) and Seattle, there are also numerous **minor league** clubs, known as **farm teams** because they supply the top clubs with talent – in small towns across the three states. Details are included in relevant chapters of the *Guide*.

AMERICAN FOOTBALL

Increasingly popular in England thanks to coverage by Channel Four, **football** in America attracts the most obsessive and devoted fans of any sport, perhaps because there are fewer games played – only sixteen in a season, which lasts throughout the autumn. With many quick skirmishes and military-like movements up and down the field, it's ideal for television, and nowhere is this more apparent than during the **televised games** which are a feature of many bars on Monday nights – though most games are played on Sundays.

The game lasts for four fifteen-minute quarters, with a fifteen-minute break at halftime. But since time is only counted when play is in progress, matches can take up to three hours to complete, mainly due to interruptions for TV advertising. Commentators will discuss the game throughout to help your comprehension, though they use such a barrage of statistics to illustrate their remarks that you may feel hopelessly confused. Not that it matters – the spectacle of American football is fun to experience, even if you haven't a clue what's going on. Players tend to be huge, averaging about six feet five inches and weighing upwards of seventeen stone; they look even bigger when they're suited up for battle in shoulder pads and helmets. The best players become nationally known celebrities, raking in millions of dollars worth of fees for product endorsements on top of astronomical salaries.

TEAMS AND TICKETS

The main West Coast **teams** are the San Francisco **49ers**, and the Los Angeles **Rams** and the Los Angeles **Raiders**, all of whom are always near the top of the National Football League (NFL) – the professional league. Other teams are the San Diego **Chargers**, and the Seattle **Seahawks**. There are no second division equivalents, though the **college teams**, particularly USC and UCLA, serve as a training ground for future NFL stars. **Tickets** for professional games cost between $15 and $35; college games $5 to $10. Details are in the *Guide*.

THE RULES OF AMERICAN FOOTBALL

The **rules of the game** are fairly simple: the **field** is 100 yards long by 40 yards wide, plus two **endzones** at each end; there are two teams of eleven men. The game begins with a **kickoff**, after which the team in possession of the ball tries to move downfield to score a **touchdown**, while the opposing team tries to stop them. The attacking team has four chances to move the ball forward ten yards and gain a **first down**; otherwise they forfeit possession to the opposition. After the kickoff the **quarterback**, the leader of the attack, either passes the ball to a **running back**, or throws the ball through the air downfield to a **receiver**. Play ends when the man with the ball is tackled to the ground, or if the pass attempt falls incomplete.

A **touchdown**, worth six points, is made when a player crosses into the defending team's endzone carrying the ball; a **field goal**, worth three points, is scored when the **placekicker** – always the smallest man on the team and usually the lone foreigner – kicks the ball, as in rugby, through the **goalposts** that stand in the endzone. If the attacking team has failed to move the ball within scoring range, and seems unlikely to gain the required ten yards for another first down, they can elect to **punt** the ball, kicking it to the other team. A change of possession can also occur if the opposition players manage to **intercept** an attempted pass.

BASKETBALL

Basketball is one of the few professional sports that is also actually played by many Americans, since all you need is a ball and a hoop. It's a particularly popular sport in low-income inner-city areas, where school playgrounds are packed with young hopefuls.

The professional game is played by athletes of phenomenal agility, seven-foot-tall giants who float through the air over a wall of equally tall defenders, seeming to change direction in mid-flight before slam-dunking the ball (smashing it through the hoop which such force that the back-board sometimes shatters) to score two points. Games last for an exhausting 48 minutes of play-ing time, around two hours total. The most excit-ing clubs are the **Los Angeles Lakers**, who play their games in front of a crowd of celebrities (actor Jack Nicholson, for example, has a season-long front court seat) and the "Rip City" **Portland Trailblazers,** who lost to the Lakers in the 1991 Western Divsion championship. Other profes-sional teams include the Seattle **Supersonics**, the Golden State **Warriors** (who play in Oakland), the Sacramento **Kings** and the slowly improving Los Angeles **Clippers**. **UCLA** long dominated the college game, winning national championships throughout the 1960s, though now they struggle to keep up with the other university sides. **Tickets** cost $10 to $30 for professional games, $4 to $10 for college level; details in the *Guide*.

PARTICIPANT SPORTS

Surfing is probably the best-known West Coast pastime, forever identified with California by the songs of the Beach Boys and Frankie Avalon. The California coast up to San Francisco is dotted with excellent surfing beaches. Some of the finest places to catch a wave, with or without a board, are at **Tourmaline Beach** near San Diego, at **Huntington Beach** and **Malibu** in Los Angeles, along the coast north of **Santa Barbara** and at **Santa Cruz** – where there's also an excellent surfing museum.

Cycling is an increasingly popular sport, with the West Coast home to some highly competitive, world-class road races, particularly around the Wine Country north of San Francisco. One innova-tion developed here, and since adopted by bicycle messengers around the globe, was the heavy-duty, all-terrain **mountain bike**, designed to tackle the slopes of Mount Tamalpais in Marin County. There, and elsewhere in California, you can rent bikes for $10 to $15 a day; see "Getting Around", p.20, for more on general cycling.

Skiing is the biggest mass-market participant sport, with downhill resorts all over the West Coast – where, believe it or not, it snows heavily (almost) every winter. In fact, the Sierra Nevada mountains of California offer some of the best skiing in the US, particularly around Lake Tahoe, where the 1960 Winter Olympics were held. Washington and Oregon, too, have a number of resorts. You can hire equipment for about $30 a weekend, plus another $20 to $30 a day for lift tickets.

A cheaper option is **cross-country skiing**, or ski-touring. There are a number of backcountry ski lodges in the Sierra Nevada and in the Cascades of Washington and Oregon, offering a range of rustic accommodation, equipment rental and lessons, from as little as $10 a day for skis, boots and poles, up to about $100 for an all-inclusive weekend tour.

All these, and other, sporting outlets and facil-ities, are detailed in the relevant chapters of the *Guide*.

FESTIVALS AND HOLIDAYS

Someone, somewhere is always celebrating something on the West Coast, although apart from national holidays, there are few festivi-ties shared throughout the region. Instead there is a disparate multitude of local annual events: art and craft shows, county fairs, ethnic celebrations, music festivals, rodeos, sandcastle building competitions, and many others of every hue and shade. To find out more, write to the relevant State Office of Tourism (addresses, p.13) for a full list, or simply phone the visitors center in a particu-lar region ahead of your arrival and ask them what's coming up. For the main festivities in Los Angeles see Chapter Two, p.168.

The one event which is found all along the West Coast itself is the seasonal **whale watch-ing**. During November and December, Grey Whales migrate from the Arctic to their breeding grounds off the coast of Baja California, making their return journey during February and March. Along the coast in these months you'll often find open-air whale-themed events, generally with a display or talk about the whales, and with food, drink and even music supplied, as people peer out to the ocean hoping for (and usually getting) a glimpse of the great creatures.

NATIONAL FESTIVALS

The biggest of the US's **national festivals and holidays** is **Independence Day** (4 July) when the entire country grinds to a standstill as Americans get drunk, salute the flag and partake of firework displays, marches, beauty pageants and more, all in commemoration of the signing of the Declaration of Independence in 1776. Less all-American is **Halloween** (31 October), which is not a public holiday despite being one of the most popular yearly flings. Traditionally it has kids running around the streets banging on doors demanding "trick or treat" and being given pieces of candy; these days such activity is confined to rural areas, and Halloween has grown into a

massive gay celebration in Hollywood and San Francisco's Castro district, marked by mass cross-dressing and general licentiousness. More sedate is **Thanksgiving Day** (last Thursday in November), the third big event of the year and essentially a domestic affair with relatives returning to the familial nest to stuff themselves with roast turkey, and (supposedly) fondly recall the landing of the Pilgrim Fathers and the start of the European colonisation of North America.

PUBLIC HOLIDAYS

On both Independence Day and Thanksgiving Day, shops, banks and offices will be closed for the full day, as they will on most of the **other public holidays**: New Year's Day; Martin Luther King's Birthday (15 January); President's Day (third Monday in February); Memorial Day (last Monday in May); Labor Day (first Monday in September); Columbus Day (second Monday in October); Veteran's Day (11 November); and Christmas Day. Good Friday is a half-day holiday, and Easter Monday is a full day holiday.

STAYING ON

There are a whole range of visas, depending on your skills and length of stay, but unless you've got relatives (parents or children over 21) or a prospective employer to sponsor you, your chances at best are slim. Finding long-term accommodation is a lot simpler, although by no means cheap.

FINDING WORK

Illegal work, once quite easy to find, has become a major headache in recent years, since the Government introduced fines of up to $10,000 for employers if caught employing a foreigner without a **social security number** (which effectively proves you're part of the legal workforce). Understandably, most are now reluctant to hire travellers.

Even in the traditionally more casual establishments like restaurants and bars, things have really tightened up, and if you do find work it's likely to be of the less visible, poorly paid kind — washer-up instead of waiter. Temporary **agency work** without the proper papers is a long shot too; opt for unskilled work like cleaning and

While it may be a great place to live, it's becoming increasingly difficult to work on the West Coast. For an extended legal stay, you should apply for a special working visa at any American Embassy *before* you set off for the States. (For other ways of extending your stay, see "Visas and Red Tape", p.7).

construction and your chances are better. **Agricultural work** is always available on Californian farms during harvest, but often entails working miles away from major centres and is wearying "stoop" (continually bending over) labour; the apple-picking season in Washington and Oregon is another good bet. The best way to find farm work is to check with the nearest university, which will have noticeboards detailing what's available. There are usually no problems with papers in this kind of work – simply because you won't be asked for them – and if you can stick it out the pay is often good and comes with some basic kind of board and accommodation. Finally, **housecleaning** and **babysitting** are feasible, if not very well-paid options. Check the notices in supermarkets, drugstores, local papers and, again, universities. As with anything, it's **who** you know that counts; the more contacts you've got, the better chance you have of finding somebody to put some work your way. Don't be afraid to ask around: the West Coast responds to an enterprising spirit.

There is, of course, the option of making up a social security number or borrowing somebody else's, but this means borrowing their identity, too: it's too tricky to bother with, as well as being highly illegal. In an effort to get around the recent stringency, more and more people are opting into **marriages of convenience**, usually on the basis of some kind of payment to the person willing to marry you. While such marriages are common, they're no guarantee of a **Green Card** (the cherished document that declares you legally entitled to work and reside in the US). Indeed the authorities treat all marriages involving foreigners with suspicion, and will interview you rigorously; should they suspect that your marriage is not legitimate, you qualify for immediate deportation.

Students have a slightly better chance of prolonging their stay on the West Coast if they can get on to an *Exchange Visitor Programme*, for which participants are given a *J-1 visa* that enti-

tles them to accept paid summer employment and apply for a social security number. However, you should note that most of these visas are issued for jobs in American summer camps, which aren't everybody's idea of a good time. If you're interested contact: *BUNAC* (232 Vauxhall Bridge Road, London SW1; ☎071/630 0344), or *Camp America* (37 Queens's Gate, London SW7; ☎071/589 3223).

FINDING A PLACE TO STAY

West Coast **apartment hunting** is not the nightmare it is in, say, New York: accommodation is plentiful and not always expensive, although the absence of housing associations and co-ops means that there is very little really cheap accommodation anywhere except in very isolated country areas. Accommodation is almost always rented unfurnished so you'll have to buy furniture; expect to pay around $600 a month for a studio or one-bedroom apartment, $900 per month for two to three bedrooms in Los Angeles or San Francisco, half this in Seattle. Most landlords will expect one month's rent as a deposit, plus one month in advance. Utilities, such as gas and electricity, are all charged monthly, and work out slightly cheaper than those in Britain.

There is no statewide organisation for accommodation so you'll have to check out the options in each place. By far the best way to find somewhere is to ask around – often short-term lets come up via word of mouth. Otherwise rooms for rent are often advertised in the windows of houses and local papers have "Apartments For Rent" sections. In **Los Angeles**, the best source is the *LA Weekly*, although you should also scan the *LA Times* classifieds. In **San Francisco** check out the *Chronicle* and the free *Bay Area Guardian*, *East Bay Express* – and, for women, *Bay Area Women's News*. In **Seattle**, the place to look is the *Seattle Weekly*. **Housing agencies** do exist, but unfortunately require two weeks' rent as a finding-fee.

DIRECTORY

ADDRESSES Though initially confusing, American addresses are masterpieces of logical thinking. Generally speaking, roads in built-up areas are laid out to a grid system, creating "blocks" of buildings: addresses of buildings refer to the block, which will be numbered in sequence, from a central point, usually downtown; for example, 620 S. Cedar will be six blocks south of downtown. In small towns, and parts of larger cities, "streets" and "avenues" often run north–south and east–west respectively; streets are usually named (sometimes alphabetically), avenues generally numbered.

CHILDREN Travelling with kids is problem-free on the West Coast. Hotels and restaurants are well-used to them, most state and national parks organise children's activities, much of the coastline has nature trails – and of course Disneyland and Universal Studios in Los Angeles are the ultimate in kids' entertainment. It's a good idea, though, to limit your trip to a comparatively small area, avoiding long, boring journeys on the Interstates.

CIGARETTES AND SMOKING Cigarettes are sold in virtually any food shop, drugstore or bar, and also from vending machines on the outside walls of these establishments. A packet of twenty costs around $1.50 – much cheaper than in Britain – though most smokers buy cigarettes by the carton for around $10. You should be aware that smoking is a much-frowned-upon activity in the US, even though no government

measures have been taken against tobacco advertising. It's possible to spend a month in the States without ever smelling tobacco; most cinemas are non-smoking, restaurants are usually divided into non-smoking and smoking sections, and smoking is universally forbidden on public transport and in elevators.

CONTRACEPTION Condoms are available in all pharmacies. If you're on the pill, it is obviously best to bring a supply with you. If you run out, you can get more with a prescription from any doctor.

DATES In their numerical form, dates are written differently in the US than in Europe: 4.11.92 is not 4 November but 11 April.

DEPARTURE TAX All airport, customs and security taxes are included in the price of your ticket.

DISABLED VISITORS Well-catered for. Most public buildings have been modified for disabled access, curb cuts are standard, and the more recent buses have lowering platforms for wheelchairs, and, usually, understanding drivers.

DRUGS Possession of under an ounce of the widely consumed marijuana is a non-criminal offence on the West Coast, and the worst you'll get is a $200 fine. Being caught with more than an ounce, however, means facing a criminal charge for dealing, and a possible prison sentence. Other drugs are, of course, completely illegal and it's a much more serious offence if you're caught with any. Of the most widespread, crack and PCP ("angel dust") are confined to ghetto areas and the only contact you'll have with them will be if an addict tries to rob or kill you (statistically improbable). Ordinary cocaine, by contrast, is still the drug of the rich, though the sharp decrease in its street price means it's much more prevalent than before. The fad for designer drugs such as Ecstasy, with which the West Coast became associated for a while, has largely faded.

ELECTRICITY 110V AC. All plugs are two-pronged and rather insubstantial. Some travel plug adapters don't fit American sockets.

FLOORS In the US, what would be the ground floor in Britain is the *first* floor, the first floor the *second* floor and so on.

PART TWO

CALIFORNIA

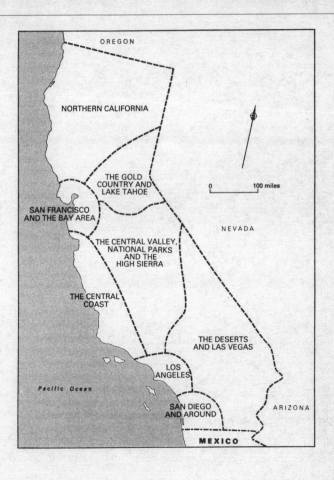

OREGON

NORTHERN CALIFORNIA

THE GOLD
COUNTRY AND
LAKE TAHOE

SAN FRANCISCO
AND THE BAY AREA

THE CENTRAL VALLEY,
NATIONAL PARKS
AND THE
HIGH SIERRA

THE CENTRAL
COAST

NEVADA

0   100 miles

THE DESERTS
AND LAS VEGAS

LOS
ANGELES

Pacific Ocean

SAN DIEGO
AND AROUND

ARIZONA

MEXICO

CHAPTER ONE

SAN DIEGO AND AROUND

F ree from smog, jungle-like entwinements of freeways, and shocking
extremes of wealth and poverty, **San Diego** and much of its surrounding
county represent the acceptable face of Southern California. Pipped by
Los Angeles in the race to become *the* Southern Californian city, San
Diego was for a long time thought of as an insignificant spot between Los
Angeles and Mexico, but it is now exacting revenge on its overgrown rival 125
miles to the north. Built on a gracefully curving bay, San Diego is not only

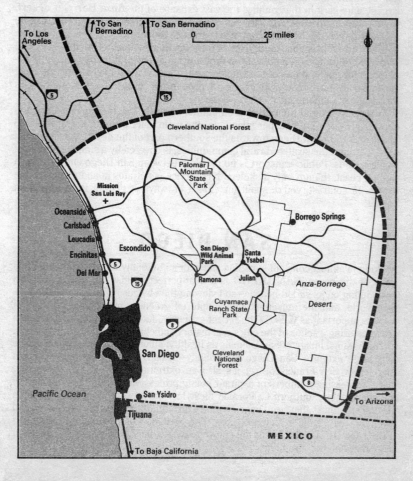

To Los Angeles

To San Bernadino

To San Bernadino

0   25 miles

Cleveland National Forest

Palomar Mountain State Park

Mission San Luis Rey

Oceanside

Carlsbad

Leucadia

Encinitas

Del Mar

Escondido

San Diego Wild Animal Park

Santa Ysabel

Borrego Springs

Ramona   Julian

Anza-Borrego Desert

Cuyamaca Ranch State Park

San Diego

Cleveland National Forest

Pacific Ocean

San Ysidro

Tijuana

To Arizona

MEXICO

To Baja California

scenically inviting, it also has a range of museums that is among the nation's most impressive, an evocative and nowadays well-tended history, several major tourist attractions, and much to discover away from the usual visitors' points of call. The second biggest city in California, it is also easy to explore and get to know fairly quickly – even cyclists have a good time.

Not surprisingly, the city is very much the social and commercial hub of San Diego County, and there are big changes as you travel out from the metropolis. The **North County** divides into two quite different sections: the small and often enticing beach communities strung along the coast from the northern edge of San Diego itself to the rugged chaparral of the Camp Pendleton marine base; and, inland, the vineyards and avocado groves of a large agricultural area which reaches east towards much wilder and more mountainous land. Most settlements away from the coast are tiny and insular, and some have barely changed since the Gold Rush: a number of deep forests and several state parks are ideal for exploration by hiking and taking obscure back roads. San Diego County also holds the largest state park in the country: the vast expanse of the **Anza-Borrego desert**, which, with its multifarious varieties of vegetation and geological quirks, can be as rewarding as the better-known desert areas to the north.

In the other direction, south from San Diego, there's little between the city and Mexico. **Tijuana**, just 25 miles from downtown San Diego is an obvious jumping-off point for explorations of the whole country, and while it may not be the most appealing destination in Mexico, it's a good place to spend a few hours – as thousands of Californians do each weekend.

Transport around the region is straightforward. By car, I-5, skirting along the coast, and I-15, a little deeper inland, are the main links with the north, while I-8 heads east from San Diego towards the southern part of the desert. The area east of I-15, around the scattered rural communities, is covered by a simple network of smaller roads. Public transport is no problem between San Diego and the North County coast, though only a skeletal bus service penetrates inland and on to the desert. In contrast, you're spoilt for choice on ways of getting to the Mexican border.

SAN DIEGO

Basking in almost constant sunshine and with its humidity tempered by the proximity of the ocean, **SAN DIEGO** is a near-perfect holiday resort. Anyone can enjoy idling on its varied beaches and viewing the obvious sights: San Diego Zoo, Sea World, and the museums and sculptured greenery of Balboa Park. But at least as important as these is the recent expensive facelift given to the downtown area, restoring a sense of the city's real history and character.

The national image of San Diegans as healthy, affluent and conservative is true to a large extent – San Diego is certainly cleaner, and cleaner-cut, than Los Angeles or San Francisco. Yet it's also an extremely amiable and easy-going place. Increasing numbers of aspirant young professionals – the embodiment of the comfortable Southern Californian lifestyle – have swept away the reputation for dull smugness that San Diego acquired through the Sixties and Seventies and given the city quite a different face. The presence of two college campuses (SDSU and UCSD) also keeps the cobwebs away – and helps sustain the image of a city that's on the up-and-up.

The telephone **Area Code** for San Diego and the surrounding area is ☎619.

The first European to land on Californian soil, the Portuguese adventurer Juan Rodríguez Cabrillo (in the employ of the Spanish), put ashore at Point Loma, a spot about ten miles from the centre of present-day San Diego, in 1542. White settlement didn't begin until two centuries later, however, with the building of a mission – the first in California – and a garrison, on a site overlooking San Diego Bay. Conflict between *Californios* and the fresh waves of settlers from the Midwest led to the raising of the Stars and Stripes over San Diego in 1847, an event closely followed by the transference of the Mexican provinces to the US. But San Diego missed out on the new mail route to the west and was plagued by a series of droughts through the 1860s, causing many bankruptcies. The arrival of the trans-continental Santa Fe railroad, soon followed by the building of the *Hotel del Coronado*, resulted in an economic boom through the 1880s. A few decades later came the first of two international expositions in Balboa Park, which were to establish San Diego (and the park itself) nationwide.

In terms of major trade and significance the city has long played second fiddle to Los Angeles, although it has benefited to a large extent from a military presence. During World War II, the US Navy took advantage of the numerous sheltered bays and made San Diego their Pacific Command Center – a function it retains to the present day. The military dominates the local economy, along increasingly with tourism, not least in the hundreds of families who arrive in the city each week to watch their offspring participate in the Marine Academy's graduation ceremony.

Arrival and information

Drivers will find it easy to reach the city centre from any of three Interstates: I-5 is the main link from Los Angeles and passes through the northern parts of the central city; from the east, I-8 runs through Hotel Circle before concluding in Ocean Beach; I-15, the main route from inland San Diego County, cuts through the city's eastern suburbs.

All forms of **public transport** leave you in the heart of downtown San Diego: **trains** use the Santa Fe Depot, close to the western end of Broadway, while the **Greyhound** terminal (☎239-9171) is even more central at Broadway and First Avenue. Lindbergh Field **airport** is only two miles from downtown, so low-flying jets are a feature of the city. There are two terminals, East and West, connected by bus #2 ($1.25) with downtown, the service starting around 6am and finishing just after midnight. Obviously, given the distance, cabs into town aren't vastly expensive, and quite a few hotels – even some of the budget ones – offer their guests a free airport limo service. All the main **car hire** firms have desks at the airport.

Information

A good first stop in the city is the **International Visitor Information Center**, downtown at F Street and First Avenue (daily 8.30am–5pm; ☎236-1212), which has maps and all kinds of information on San Diego and around, including accommodation. Another useful source is the *AYH* office at 1031 India Street (Mon–Sat 9.30am–4.30pm; ☎239-2644 or ☎234-3330), whose telephone gives local hostel information outside business hours. A couple of free weekly publications, the *San Diego Reader* and *Metropolitan*, which can be found in many shops, bars and clubs, should be scanned for their eating and entertainment info; there's also the tourist-aimed *In San Diego Today*.

Getting around

By day, **getting around** San Diego without a car is easy, whether using buses, the tram-like Trolley, or a hired bike. Travelling is harder at night, with all but the major public transport routes closing down around 9pm. The transit system won't break anyone's budget but a number of cut-rate tickets and passes can reduce costs over a few days or weeks.

Buses

Seven transit companies operate **buses** in the San Diego area in an integrated system, although in the city by far the most common is *San Diego Transit* (information: ☎233-3004). Buses have a flat-rate fare of $1.25 (or $1.50 on the small number of express routes), transfers are free (with a one-hour time limit), and fares should be paid when boarding with exact money (dollar bills are accepted). In general, the bus service is reliable and swift, with even comparatively far-flung spots connected to downtown – known on route maps and timetables as "Center City" and very much the hub of the network – at least twice an hour.

USEFUL SAN DIEGO BUS ROUTES

The following buses connect **Downtown San Diego** with the surrounding area:

Balboa Park #7, #16, #25.	**Hillcrest** #3, #11, #25.	**Mission Beach** #34.
Coronado #19, #901, #903.	**Imperial Beach** #901.	**Ocean Beach** #35.
East San Diego #1, #15.	**La Jolla** #34.	**Pacific Beach** #30, #34.

Bus Information

If you intend to travel on San Diego's local buses, call into **The Transit Store**, 449 Broadway (Mon–Sat 8.30am–5.30pm, Sun noon–5pm; ☎234-1060), for detailed timetables, the free *Regional Transit Guide*, the Day Tripper Transit Pass, monthly passes, and 10-Ride tickets (see below), and to have any queries answered.

The Trolley

Complementing bus travel around the city is the **San Diego Trolley** (often called the "Tijuana Trolley"), a tram-like vehicle which runs on tracks through the streets, covering the sixteen miles from the Santa Fe Depot (departures from C Street) to the Mexican border crossing at San Ysidro. For stops in San Diego, fares are 50¢–$1, to the border $2. Tickets should be bought from the machines at Trolley stops, and occasionally an inspector may appear and demand proof of payment. Apart from being a cheap way to reach Mexico, the Trolley is a link to the southern San Diego communities of National City, Chula Vista and Palm City, and, from the "transfer station" at Imperial and 12th Avenue, its Euclid Avenue line makes much of southeastern San Diego easily accessible. Services depart

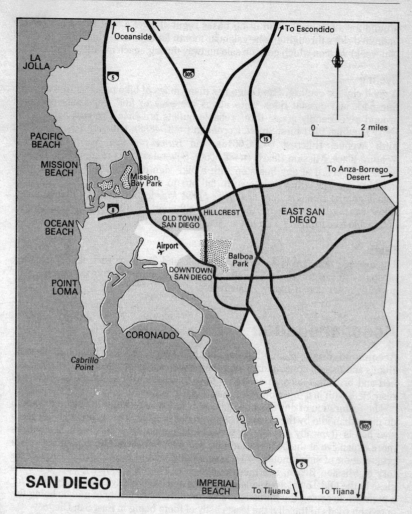

every fifteen minutes throughout the day; the last service back from San Ysidro leaves at 1am, so an evening of south-of-the-border revelry and a return to San Diego the same night is quite possible.

Cut-rate tickets and passes

If you're going to be around for a while and intend to use public transport a lot, buy the **Day Tripper Transit Pass**, which lasts one or four days ($4–12) and is valid on any San Diego Transit bus, as well as the San Diego Trolley and the San Diego Bay ferry (which sails between Broadway Pier in downtown and Coronado, $1.50 each way; see p.64 for more details). For longer stays with less bus-riding, a better deal might be the **10-Ride Ticket** costing $9 ($11.50 for express routes). If you're around for a few weeks and using buses regularly, get a **Monthly Pass**, giving unlimited rides throughout one calendar month for $45, or the half-price (in effect two-week) version which goes on sale midway through each month.

Cycling

A good city for **cycling,** San Diego has many miles of bike paths as well as some fine park and coastal rides. Hire shops are easy to find, especially prevalent around bike-friendly areas: three reliable outlets are *Bike Coronado*, at the Old Ferry Landing, 2101 First Street, Coronado (☎437-4888), *Hillcrest Bike Shop*, 3934 Fifth Avenue, Hillcrest (☎296-0618), and *Hamel's Action Sport Center*, 704 Ventura Place, Mission Beach (☎488-5050). Several city bus routes allow bikes to be carried; board at any bus stop with a bike sign underneath it and tack your machine securely (they're known to fall off) to the back of the bus. For more details get the *How To Take Your Bike For A Ride* leaflet from the Transit Store. Bikes can also be taken on the Trolley, although for this you need a permit, obtainable free from the *AYH* office (see "Information").

Taxis

The average **taxi** fare is $3 for the first mile and $1.70 for each mile thereafter, obviously cheap for several people sharing but otherwise too expensive to be anything other than a luxury or last resort.

Accommodation

Accommodation is plentiful throughout San Diego, at prices to suit all pockets. Hotels and motels are abundant, and there's also a decent selection of hostels and bed and breakfast accommodation – only travellers with tents are likely to feel restricted, with just one campsite being a viable option.

The restoration of downtown – the best base if you're without a car and want to do more than idle by the ocean – has given rise to a batch of surprisingly inexpensive hotels (typically $25–35 for a double) in renovated buildings. Sleeping is more expensive at the beaches (around $40–50 in winter, $50–60 in summer) in a proliferation of small motels – for accommodation ideas in the beach-bum territory of Mission Beach, see the box opposite. There's another group of motels close to the Old Town, a reasonable place to be if you're driving or just staying for a night while seeing the immediate area, and there are plenty of motels lining the approach roads to the city, the least costly of them being in East San Diego.

Especially if you're arriving in summer, it's wise to book in advance – where this is essential, we've said as much below – though the Visitor Information Center (see "Information") has a large stock of accommodation leaflets (many of which carry discount vouchers) and will phone a hotel, motel or hostel on your behalf for free. Specifically **gay** accommodation possibilities are listed on p.74.

Downtown

Armed Services YMCA, 500 W Broadway (☎232-1133). Well-equipped budget option between the *Greyhound* and train stations, and popular with military personnel as much as travellers. Dormitory accommodation for *IYHA* members for $9, and single and double rooms for $20 and $35 respectively.

Beechwood Motel, 465 Fourth St (☎696-9694). Small and cosy, and within an easy walk of everything in downtown. Singles $19, doubles $30.

Churchill's Castle, 827 C St (☎1-800/621-5640). Bizarre attempt to recreate a European castle, complete with turrets and moat. Singles $42, doubles $46.

Corinthian Suites, 1840 Fourth Ave (☎236-1600). Nicely furnished rooms which include cooking facilities. Singles $35, doubles $40.

Downtown Inn, 600 G St (☎238-4100). Pleasant modern hotel, with cooking facilities and fridges in each room. Singles from $24, doubles from $29.

Horton Grand, 311 Island Ave (☎1-800/544-1886). Classy, modernised hundred-year-old hostelry whose staff dress in Victorian-era costumes. Singles $114, doubles $124.

Hotel St James, 830 Sixth St (☎234-0155). Gracious old building tastefully refurbished, though the comfortable rooms are slighty poky. Singles and doubles around $80.

Jim's San Diego, 1425 C St (☎235-0234). Small, shared rooms aimed at backpackers. $15 a night, $90 a week.

The Maryland Hotel, 630 F St (☎239-9243). Amenable restored hotel, if somewhat lacking in frills, in a good downtown location. Singles from $17; doubles from $25.

Marriot Suites, 701 A St (☎1-800/962-1367). Swish high-rise overlooking the yacht harbour – quiet periods can bring big reductions on the regular rates. Singles $135, doubles $150.

Pickwick Hotel, 132 W Broadway (☎234-0141). Though large and characterless, this shares a building with the *Greyhound* station, so it's an inexpensive place to flop down after a long bus journey. Singles $29, doubles $35.

YWCA, 1012 C St (☎239-0355). An atmospheric Twenties structure with women-only accommodation, in small dorms ($8.25 plus key deposit) or tidy private rooms: single $13, double $26.

7 & 1 Mototel, 1919 Pacific Hwy (☎1-800/624-9338). Location is the strong feature: a quiet section of downtown close to the waterfront embarcadero; all rooms have fridges and coffee-makers. Singles from $42, doubles from $45.

The Old Town

EZ-8, 4747 Pacific Hwy (☎295-2512). Unexceptional, but with the area's lowest rates. Singles $32, doubles $37.

Old Town Inn, 4440 Pacific Hwy (☎1-800/225-9610). Serviceable base within a few strides of the Old Town's liveliest areas. Singles from $35, doubles from $60.

Old Town Travelodge, 2380 Moore St (☎1-800/292-9928). Spacious, if ordinary, chain motel in a good location. Singles from $40–50, doubles from $45–55 according to season.

Old Town Padre Trail Inn, 4200 Taylor St (☎297-3291). Unpretentious family-run motel. Singles from $35, doubles from $40.

Ocean Beach and Point Loma

Ebb Tide Motel, 5082 W Point Loma Blvd (☎224-9339). Modestly sized motel that's handy for the beach. Singles from $40, doubles from $50.

MISSION BEACH ACCOMMODATION

Apartments rented by the week make up the bulk of the accommodation in Mission Beach – a great place to be if your primary concerns are sea, sun and surf. Typically sleeping four to six people, they cost from $250–300 a week, and can be a good deal for several people sharing, although it's essential to book at least six months ahead. A number of agents offer deals; try *Beach & Bayside Vacations*, 3958 Bayside Walk (☎800/553-2284) or *Sandcastle Beach Rentals*, PO Box 90661 (☎488-1395).

Loma Lodge, 3202 Rosecrans St (☎222-0511). Among the cheapest in the district, with a beckoning pool and complimentary breakfast; good for exploring the peninsula though not close to the beach. Singles from $30, doubles from $37.

Ocean Villa Motel, 5142 W Point Loma Blvd (☎224-3481). Usefully placed for the sands, with ocean-view rooms. Singles from $30, doubles from $35.

Point Loma AYH Hostel, 3790 Udal St (☎223-4778). Ideal for the beach but awkward for getting about the rest of San Diego – the hostel's six miles from downtown with bus #35 – but a well-run and friendly hostel, with shared rooms; members $10, others $13.

Coronado

El Cordova, 1351 Orange Ave (☎1-800/367-6467). Lovely rooms and gardens for which reservations should be made at least six months ahead. Singles from $72, doubles from $77, two-bedroom suites from $122.

El Rancho, 370 Orange Ave (☎435-3101). Tiny motel whose rooms are equipped with micro-wave ovens, fridges and relaxing decor. Singles and doubles $50–70, according to season.

Hotel Del Coronado, 1500 Orange Ave (☎522-8000). The place that put Coronado on the map and which is still the area's major tourist sight (see "Coronado and Imperial Beach") – it's been pampering wealthy guests for over a century. Singles and doubles from $145.

Mission Bay, Mission Beach and Pacific Beach

Bahia Resort Hotel, 998 W Mission Bay Drive (☎1-800/288-0770). Sprawling pleasure complex curling around the waters of Mission Bay; a watersports fans' delight. Singles and doubles from $95.

The Beach Cottages, 4255 Ocean Blvd (☎483-7440). Beside the beach but away from the crush – a relaxing place to spend a few days of quiet tanning. Singles and doubles from $60–90 according to season.

Beach Haven Inn, 4740 Mission Blvd (☎1-800/367-6467). Not the cheapest around but a fine place to unwind. Singles and doubles $60–80 according to season.

Santa Clara Motel, 839 Santa Clara Place (☎488-1193). No-frills rooms within an easy walk of the hectic Mission Beach sands. Singles from $45, doubles from $50.

Sleepy Time Motel, 4545 Mission Bay Drive (☎483-4222). Unspectacular but well-priced on the main approach road to Mission Beach. Singles from $30, doubles from $34.

Surf & Sand Motel, 4666 Mission Blvd (☎483-7420). Homely accommodation close to the beach. Singles and doubles from $50.

La Jolla

La Jolla Cove Motel, 1155 Coast Blvd (☎1-800/248-2683). Easily the cheapest billet from which to discover La Jolla. Singles and doubles $55–65 according to season.

La Valencia Hotel, 1132 Prospect St (☎1-800/451-0772). Within the radiant pink walls Hollywood celebs enjoyed themselves during the Twenties; today the place is less glamour-ous but no less plush. Singles and doubles from $135.

Prospect Park Inn, 1110 Prospect St (☎1-800/345-8577). Well-priced for the area, with views over the ocean and complimentary breakfast and afternoon tea. Singles from $75, doubles from $85.

East San Diego

Aztec Budget Inn, 6050 El Cajon Blvd (☎1-800/225-9610). Standard motel, adequate for a night or two. Singles from $31, doubles from $39.

Campus Hitching Post, 6235 El Cajon Blvd (☎583-1456). Only possession of a pool sets it apart from its neighbourhood rivals. Singles from $28, doubles from $30.

Morgan's Motel, 5115 El Cajon Blvd (☎287-7800). Small motel with good-sized rooms and good rates. Singles from $30, doubles from $35.

Camping

Of the city's half-dozen **campsites**, only two accept tents. The best-placed of these is *Campland on the Bay*, 2211 Pacific Beach Drive (☎1-800/BAY FUN), linked to downtown by bus #30; the alternative, *San Diego Metro KOA*, 111 N Second Avenue (☎1-800/762-CAMP), is fifteen miles south in Chula Vista – from downtown, take bus #29 or the Trolley to 24th Street.

Bed and breakfast

Bed and breakfast accommodation is in ever increasing supply in San Diego, nowhere more so than in the Hillcrest district where several elegant Victorian homes are throwing open their doors to guests. The pick of them are the *Britt House*, 406 Maple Street (☎234-2926), around $100; the *Keating House*, 2331 Second Avenue (☎239-8585), from $70; and *Hill House*, 2504 A Street (☎239-4738), between $55 and $75. For details of bed and breakfast in other areas, contact the Visitor Information Center (see p.47), or send $3.95 for the *Bed & Breakfast Directory for San Diego*, PO Box 3292, San Diego 92103 (☎297-3130).

The City

You never feel under pressure in San Diego to do anything other than enjoy yourself. Though the work-hard play-hard ethic is as prevalent here as anywhere else in Southern California, the accent is very strongly on the second, more pleasurable, part of the equation. Indeed, the city, with its easily managed central area, scenic bay, lively beaches, plentiful parks and commendable museums, is hard not to like from the moment you arrive – even New York streetpeople are known to migrate to San Diego for the winter.

The city divides into several fairly easily defined sections. You'll probably spend at least some of your time in **downtown**, where anonymous high-rise bank buildings stand shoulder-to-shoulder with more personable structures from San Diego's earlier boom days, bestowing the district with a daytime mood more welcoming than is usual in American city centres. Besides being the nucleus of the public transport network, downtown contains a fair chunk of the city's nightlife, and has much inexpensive accommodation. A few miles northeast, the well-maintained parkland of massive **Balboa Park** not only contains San Diego's major museums and the highly rated San Diego Zoo, but is perfectly suited for strolls and picnics beside the walkways which cut around the many acres of carefully nurtured plant-life. A similar distance northwest of downtown is where the city really got started: the first white settlement growing up beneath the hill that was site of the original San Diego mission, an area now preserved as **Old Town San Diego**. The sense of history here is often powerfully evoked and quite believable, despite the inevitable grouping of Mexican-themed shops and eateries, which strain credibility – though not to the extent that you should be put off visiting. A couple of other districts close to downtown don't have any points of interest as such, but can be worth a call for different reasons. You might find yourself staying in **East San Diego**, whose cheap accommodation and large college campus liven up what is an otherwise featureless sprawl; while **Hillcrest's** eclectic mix of trendy yuppies, solvent bohemians, and would-be artists make it one of the city's best areas for ethnic eating and intellectually slanted nightlife.

More appealing for pure relaxation are the beach communities – all within easy reach of downtown and good for a half-day trip out (or longer, if bronzing beside the briny is your main reason for being in San Diego). There's **Ocean Beach**, extremely lively on its sands but the exclusive and wealthy community that's developed a little way inland is tempering its reputation for all-out partying. The rugged **Point Loma** peninsula, on which Ocean Beach stands, forms the western wall of San Diego Bay, with trees along its spine and a craggy shoreline often marked by explorable tidepools – though no fun at all for sunbathing. Across the bay directly south of downtown, **Coronado** is a plush and well-manicured settlement, reflecting the wholesome nature of the large naval base to which it's home. Traditionally, Coronado's visitors have been wealthy health-seekers, here for its seabreezes, palm trees and famous (and expensive) hotel. Just beyond, and much less upscale, **Imperial Beach**'s chief draw is simply the quiet of a seldom-crowded stretch of sand, and, if you're into such things, the horse-riding trails nearby. These days much of Ocean Beach's former youthful vitality has moved to **Mission Beach**, eight miles northwest of downtown, and the adjoining, and slightly more salubrious, **Pacific Beach** – linked by a beachside walkway which, on any weekend, is where you'll find San Diego at its most exuberant. The city is at its most chic, however, a few miles further north up the coast, in visually stunning **La Jolla**, whose coastline of almost too-perfect caves and coves is matched on land by short, litter-free streets lined by small coffeeshops and art galleries, and a tantalisingly designed modern art museum.

Downtown San Diego

Always vibrant and active, **DOWNTOWN** contains the real pulse of San Diego and is much the best place to begin seeing the city. Improvement and renovation initiatives begun in the late 1970s have restored many of the city's older buildings, resulting in several blocks of stylishly renovated Twenties architecture, while the sleek bank buildings of more recent times symbolise the city's growing economic importance on the Pacific Rim. Though downtown is largely safe by day, be warned that at night it can be an unwelcoming place, and you should confine your after-dark visits to the restaurants and clubs of the comparatively well-lit and well-policed Gaslamp District.

Along Broadway

One of the most memorable first impressions of San Diego is that received by travellers arriving at the **Santa Fe Railroad Depot**. The station's tall Moorish archways, built to welcome visitors to the 1915 Panama-California Exposition in Balboa Park, still evoke a sense of grandeur. They also mark the western end of **Broadway**, the main strip slicing through the middle of downtown.

The most hectic portion of Broadway is the block between Fourth and Fifth Avenues, where the pedestrian traffic is a broad mix: shoppers, sailors, yuppies, street bums and others, some lingering around the fountains on the square outside Horton **Plaza** (Mon–Fri 10am–9pm, Sat 10am–8pm, Sun 11am–6pm) – San Diego's major upmarket shopping place and a posing platform for the city's spoilt young brats. Though in essence a typical American shopping mall, Horton Plaza differs in that it has no roof, making the most of the region's sunny climate: a deliberate attempt to resemble a Mediterranean plaza, albeit one with pseudo Art

ID Should be carried at all times. Two pieces should diffuse any suspicion, one of which should have a photo: driving licence, passport and credit card(s) are your best bets.

LAUNDERETTES All but the most basic hotels do laundry but it'll be a lot cheaper (about $1.50) for a wash and tumble dry in a launderette (US *laundromat*) – found all over the place. Take plenty of quarters.

MEASUREMENTS AND SIZES The US has yet to go metric, so measurements are in inches, feet, yards and miles; weight in ounces, pounds and tons. Liquid measurements differ too: American pints and gallons are about four-fifths of British ones. Clothing sizes are easier, always two figures less what they would be at home. For example, a British women's size 12 is a US size 10. To work out shoe sizes, simply add 1½ to your British size.

PUBLIC TOILETS Don't exist as such in cities. Bars, restaurants and fast-food outlets are your best bets, although technically you should be a customer.

TAX Be warned that sales tax is added to virtually everything you buy in a shop but isn't part of the marked price. In California the current rate is 8.25%; in Washington 6.25% (in Seattle 7.9%); Oregon has no sales tax at all. Hotel tax is around 5–8% of your bill.

TEMPERATURES Always given in Fahrenheit.

TICKETS For music, theatre, sports, and camping reservations, use *Ticketron*, whose offices are everywhere and listed in the phone book, and through whom you can buy tickets over the phone using your credit card number.

TIME The West Coast runs on Pacific Standard Time (PST), eight hours behind GMT in winter and three hours behind the East Coast. British Summer Time runs almost concurrent with US Daylight Saving Time – implemented from the last Sunday in April to the last Sunday in October – causing a seven-hour time difference for two weeks of the year.

TIPPING You really shouldn't leave a bar or restaurant without leaving a tip of at least fifteen percent (unless the service is utterly disgusting): it causes a lot of embarrassment and nasty looks, and a short paypacket for the waiter/waitress at the end of the week. The same applies to hotel porters, toilet attendants, etc.

WORLD SERVICE You can keep in touch with British and world events by listening to the World Service of the BBC, broadcast to the Western US for eight hours daily. Programmes are on the short wave band but frequencies and timings vary. For the latest details write for the free *Programme Guide* to BBC External Services Publicity, Bush House, PO Box 76, Strand, London WC2.

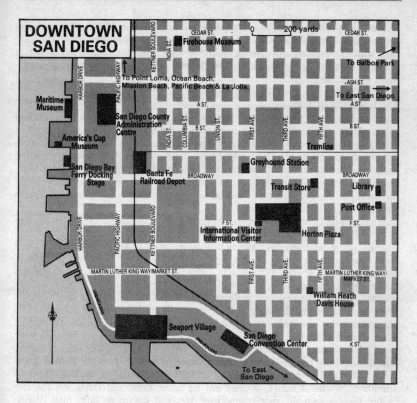

DOWNTOWN SAN DIEGO

Deco features and the odd dollop of Victoriana. Completed in 1985 for a cool $140 million, Horton Plaza became the centrepiece of the new-look downtown, and gave the signal for prices to soar in the nearby condo developments. The top level, with its open-air eating places, is the one to make for. Although the food may be more expensive here than in the streets, it's fun to sit over a coffee or snack and watch the parade go by – a technique especially rewarding on Saturday when the suburban mall rats are showing off their latest t-shirts and $100 wraparound shades. Few of the stores are worth much more than a browse, but don't miss the 21-foot-tall **Jessop Clock,** on level one, made for the California State Fair of 1907.

Further along Broadway things begin to get tatty and dull, but walk a couple of blocks or so for the secondhand bookshops (such as *Wahrenbrock's Book House,* 726 Broadway) and the **library,** 820 E Street (Mon–Thur 10am–9pm, Fri & Sat 9.30am–5.30pm), which has book sales on Friday and Saturday and an extensive reference section where you can pore over Californian magazines and newspapers. Tucked away on an upper floor of the library, the **Wangenheim Room** (telephone for an appointment to be shown around; ☎236-6278) holds the obsessive collection of local turn-of-the-century big-wig, Julius Wangenheim, including Babylonian clay tablets, palm leaf books from India, silk scrolls from China and many more trans-global curios documenting the history of the printed word – worth a stop for its oddity value.

Much less odd, but a useful time-passer, the **Firehouse Museum,** six blocks north of Broadway at 1572 Columbia Street (Sat & Sun 10am–4pm; free), dutifully maintains fire-fighting appliances, helmets, axes, and has photographs vividly recalling some of San Diego's most horrific fires – and the men, horses and equipment who tackled them.

The Gaslamp District

South of Broadway, the **Gaslamp District** occupies a sixteen-block area running south to K Street, bordered by Fourth and Seventh avenues. This was the heart of San Diego when it was still a frontier town, and was, according to local opinion, full of "whorehouses, opium dens and guys getting rolled". The area remained at the core of local carnality for years: street prostitution, though illegal from 1916, flourished here until the 1970s, when the revitalisation operation cleaned things up – and the city's flesh-for-sale moved to the erotic-dancer bars near the Sports Arena, a couple of miles northwest.

What you find now are smart streets lined with classy cafés, expensive antique stores, art galleries – and gaslamps, albeit a modern kind powered by electricity. There's also a relatively high police profile designed to keep the area clean and safe. A tad artificial it may be, but the Gaslamp District is intriguing to explore, not least for the scores of mainly late nineteenth-century buildings in various stages of renovation. They're best discovered – and the area's general history gleaned – during the two-hour **walking tour** (Sat 10am & 1pm; $2) which begins from the small cobbled square at the corner of Fourth and Island avenues. The square is within the grounds of the **William Heath Davis House** (Wed–Sun 10am–4pm; $2.50), included in the walking tour, though also visitable on your own. It was William Davis who founded "New Town" San Diego in 1850, believing that a waterfront location (the fledgling city had previously been located a few miles inland and to the north – the site of Old Town San Diego, see below) would stimulate growth. It didn't, at least not for some time, and Davis left the city before long, eventually dying penniless. He, and the more influential Alonzo Horton, are remembered in the house through photos, while the fittings and furnishings re-create something of the mood of their times.

Even without the walking tour, there's a lot to be enjoyed around this area simply by keeping your eyes open. One of the finest interiors in the whole city is in *Johnny's 801,* a seafood restaurant at 801 Fourth Avenue, restored in the style of the tavern which opened here in 1907. Diners stuff themselves with crabs' legs beneath an epic stained glass dome and above a tiled floor once described as "the handsomest floor in the state" – even if you're not hungry, drop inside for a look. Also worth a peek is the **Horton Grand**, a hotel opposite the William Davis House. This has been painstakingly rebuilt in Victorian style with original artefacts from what was one of the raunchiest hotels in the country; the management claim that it was the site of the "Canary Cottage", one of the West's more notorious brothels. If you fancy staying here, see "Accommodation".

The Embarcadero, Seaport Village and around

Over the last couple of years, the once-shabby streets south of the Gaslamp District have been transformed by the arrival of elegant, expensive condos – providing a fitting setting for the San Diego Convention Center, a $165-million boost to civic pride which opened in 1989, and is booked solidly with high-powered meetings into the twenty-first century. For non-convention-going visitors, the most interesting facet of the building is the sail-like roof imitating the yachts tethered in the marina of the *Marriot Suites* hotel, just beyond, which also indicate the beginning of the **Embarcadero**, a pathway which continues for a mile or so along the bayside curling around to the western end of downtown.

Favoured by San Diegan strollers, joggers and kite-flyers, most out-of-towners get no further along the embarcadero than **Seaport Village,** a twee but mildly enjoyable collection of souvenir shops and restaurants, often with free clown and puppet shows laid on for kids. Make a point of strolling the full length of the embarcadero however, as it makes a enjoyable route to the nautically flavoured museums on Harbor Drive, which is also the departure point for the ferry to Coronado (see "Coronado and Imperial Beach").

The first of the museums is the **America's Cup Museum**, on the B Street Pier (daily 10am–6pm; $3), celebrating the trophy first competed for in 1851, after the owners of a New York shipyard developed a super-fast schooner, *America*, and challenged British yachtsmen to a race around the Isle of Wight. The history of the cup is loaded with controversy, intrigue and no small measure of xenophobia, but sadly these facets are barely acknowledged in the museum, which is primarily a collection of models and drawings of vessels which have contested the 27-inch-high cup (the cup itself is occasionally displayed). It was a local bastion of conservatism, the San Diego Yacht Club, that regained the trophy for the US from Australia in 1987, an excuse for much patriotic hullabaloo (the twelve-metre sloop that did the deed, the *Stars & Stripes*, stands outside the museum), and is masterminding the defence of the trophy in the next contest, which will be held off San Diego in May 1992.

A few yards north of the B Street Pier, there's further sailing fare to be found in the **Maritime Museum** (daily 9am–6pm; $5), comprising three vintage sailing craft: the most interesting being the *Star of India*, built in 1863 and now the world's oldest still-afloat merchant ship. Alongside, the *Berkeley*, which served for sixty years as a ferry on San Francisco Bay, and the *Medea*, a small steam-powered yacht, are of very minor appeal.

Landlubbers nonplussed by the bayside museums should explore the **San Diego County Administration Center** (Mon–Fri 8.30am–5pm), one of the most distinctive public buildings in California: a rich burst of Spanish colonial with a beaux-arts arrangement of gold and azure tiles. It's one of the unsung beauties of San Diego and from Harbor Drive you can walk right through the foyer to the main entrance, on the way viewing the *Guardian of Water* statue (on the Harbor Drive side) and the three interior murals.

Balboa Park and San Diego Zoo

The thousand sumptuous acres of green **BALBOA PARK** contains one of the largest groupings of museums in the US. Yet its real charm is simply itself: its trees, gardens, traffic-free promenades – and a thumping concentration of Spanish colonial-style buildings.

Balboa Park was a wasteland inhabited by cacti, rattlesnakes and lizards until 1898, when a local woman, Kate Sessions, began cultivating nurseries and planting trees there in lieu of rent. The first buildings were erected for the 1915 Panama-California Exposition, held to celebrate the opening of the canal. The memories of its success lingered well into the Depression, and in 1935 another building programme was undertaken for the California-Pacific Exposition.

THE BALBOA PARK MUSEUMS: PRACTICAL INFORMATION

Ideally, you should **come** to Balboa Park on the first Tuesday of the month when admission to almost all the museums is free. On the other hand, don't come on a Monday, when the bigger collections are closed. None of the museums is absolutely essential viewing but at least three – the Museum of Man, the Timkin Gallery, and the Museum of Art – could collectively keep you engrossed for a few hours. The cheapest way to see them is to buy the $9 **Balboa Park Passport**, which allows admission to any four of the park's museums. To buy the passport, and to pick up general information, call at the **information center** (9.30am–4pm; ☎239-0512) inside the House of Hospitality, clearly signposted from the park entrances.

The park, within easy reach of downtown with **buses** #7, #16 or #25, is large but fairly easy to **get around** on foot – if you tire, the free Balboa Park tram runs frequently between the main musuem groupings and the car parks.

Along El Prado: the major museums

Opposite the House of Hospitality, strains of the music lessons held in the Casa del Prado often permeate through to the adjacent **Timkin Art Gallery** (Tues–Sat 10am–4.30pm, Sun 1.30pm–4.30pm; free), filled with high quality art that makes the stiflingly formal atmosphere and the evangelical zeal of the attendants worth enduring. Inside are fine works from the early Renaissance to the nineteenth century, including impressive pieces by Rembrandt and El Greco, and a stirring collection of Russian icons.

By contrast, the **San Diego Museum of Art** (Tues–Sun 10am–4.30pm; $5, students $2) has few individually striking items: many of the major names are represented, but not by their most acclaimed work. There's a solid stock of European paintings from the Renaissance and succeeding styles through to the "Europe in Transition" canvases from the nineteenth century (matched by a fairly uninspiring selection from the same century in the US), and finally some welcome bright rooms of moderns. The biggest surprises, perhaps, are amid the exquisitely crafted pieces within the Asian section, mainly from China and Japan but with smaller representations from India and Korea. Outside, don't miss the **Sculpture Court and Garden**, which you can walk into for free at any time, with a number of formidable works, most notably those by Henry Moore and Alexander Calder.

The contents of the **Museum of Man** (Tues–Sun 10am–4.30pm; $3, students $1), which straddles El Prado, veer from the banal to the excellent – and into the truly bizarre. The demonstrations of tortilla-making and Mexican loom-weaving are painfully forced, while the large number of replicas – particularly the huge "Mayan" stones which dominate the ground level – would have more impact simply as photos. But there's much to be seen and be fascinated by, not least the Native American displays; the temporary shows, too, can be absorbing.

The structure between the House of Hospitality and the Space Theater (see below) replicates the *Electric Building* – built for the 1915 Expo to display the latest gadgetry – and it houses four small museums. Of these, just two will occupy you for more than a few minutes: the **Museum of Photographic Arts** (Tues–Sun 10am–5pm, Thurs until 9pm; $2.50, students $1), mounting challenging temporary shows, and the **Museum of San Diego History** (Wed–Sat 10am–

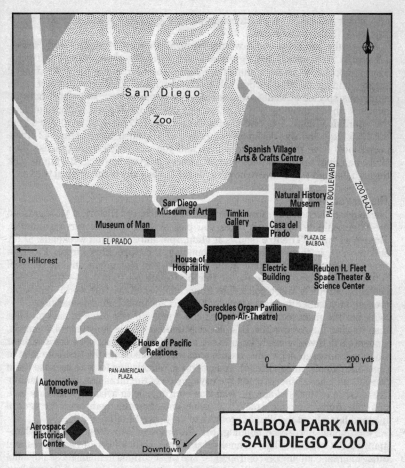

BALBOA PARK AND
SAN DIEGO ZOO

4.30pm; $2), virtually next door, cleverly charting the booms and busts that have
turned San Diego from uninviting scrubland into the fifth biggest city in the US
within 150 years. Of the building's other collections, the **Hall of Champions**
(Mon–Sat 10am–4.30pm, Sun noon–5pm; $2, students $1) is dull unless you're
knowledgeable on American sports, and San Diegan athletic achievers especially;
and only the craftsmanship put into creating scaled-down versions of large
chunks of the US and the tracks crossing them, make the **San Diego Railroad
Museum** (Fri 1–5pm, Sat & Sun 11am–5pm ; $1) viewable.

The **Reuben H. Fleet Space Theater and Science Center** (daily 9.45am–
9.30pm; theater $4–6; science center $1), close to the Park Boulevard end of El
Prado, is one of the most recent and most hyped features of Balboa Park, with a
"gee whiz" attitude out of step with everything around it. The Science Center has
a lame batch of kid-oriented exhibits, although impressive sensations can be
induced by the Space Theater's dome-shaped tilting screen and 152 loudspeak-

ers, which will take you on stomach-churning trips into volcanoes, over water-falls, even through outer space.

Across the plaza, the more worthy **Natural History Museum** (daily 10am–4.30pm; $4, students $1), has a great collection of fossils, a comprehensive if some-what unappetising array of stuffed creatures, an entertaining hands-on mineral section, and an affecting section called "On The Edge", dealing with a few of the numerous species of wildlife whose existence is threatened, and which pulls no punches when explaining why. A short walk behind the Natural History building, the **Spanish Village Arts and Crafts Center** (daily 11am–4pm; free) dates from the 1935 Expo and was designed in the style of a Spanish village. Some 42 crafts-people now have their workshops here and you can watch them practise their skills: painting, sculpture, photography, pottery or glass working. It's fun to walk through, though you'd have to be pretty loaded to buy any of the original works.

The rest of the park

The major collection away from El Prado is the Aerospace Historical Museum, and the fifteen-minute walk to it takes you past several spots of varying interest. There's a **Puppet Theatre** (shows at 11am, 1pm and 2.30pm on weekends; $1.50, children $1), in the Pacific Palisades building; the **Spreckles Organ Pavilion** (free Sunday concerts) is home to the world's largest pipe organ; and the series of cottages comprising the **House of Pacific Relations** (Sun 1.30–4.40pm; free), contains extremely kitsch collections from countries all over the world – enjoy the proffered tea, coffee and cakes but don't expect any multi-cultural education.

All but the most technically minded could find a better place to pass an hour than touring the **Aerospace Historical Museum** (Tues–Sun 10am–4.30pm; $4, students $1): if you're really keen to see a replica of *The Spirit of St Louis* (aviator Charles Lindbergh began the journey that was to make him the first solo pilot to cross the Atlantic in San Diego), you can do so quickly and for free because it's in the entrance hall. Otherwise, on the paying side of the turnstiles, there's a numb-ing mass of portraits of anyone who was ever anyone in aviation, and fairly tedi-ous collections of model planes, real planes and other things through the ages of manned flight from the Wright brothers to the Space Shuttle.

Next to the Aerospace building, the **Automotive Museum** (daily 10.30am–4pm; $3.50) continues the technological theme, with a host of cars, bikes and other internal-combustion contraptions. The most curious item for those not auto-fixated, however, is the *Lincoln Continental* which carried President Reagan to a would-be assassin's bullet in 1981.

San Diego Zoo

The **San Diego Zoo** (daily March–Oct 9am–5pm, rest of the year 9am–4pm), immediately north of the main museums, is one of the city's biggest and best-known attractions. As zoos go, it's undoubtedly one of the world's best, with a very wide selection of animals – among them very rare Chinese pheasants, Mhorr gazelles, and a freak-of-nature two-headed corn snake – and some pioneer-ing techniques of keeping them in captivity: animals are restrained in "psycholcg-ical cages", with moats or ridges rather than bars. It's also enormous, and you can easily spend a full day here; indeed it's too expensive to consider visiting for just a couple of hours. Take a bus tour early on to get a general idea of the layout, or the vertiginous *Skyfari* which whisks you through the air over the heads of the humans as well as the animals. But bear in mind many of the creatures get sleepy in the heat of midday and retire behind bushes to take a nap. There's a Children's Zoo as well, with a variety of walk-through bird cages, and an animal nursery.

Basic **admission** is $10.75; the bus tour costs $3; the *Skyfari* $1.50; and the Children's Zoo is 50¢ for everyone older than three years. Should you intend giving the place your all, buy the the *Deluxe Tour* ticket ($15) which covers admission to both zoos, the bus tour, and a ride on the *Skyfari*.

Centro de la Cultural Raza

Visiting all the museums in Balboa Park or spending hours threading through the crowds at the zoo, could well leave you too jaded even to notice the unassuming round building on the edge of the park beside Park Boulevard. This, the **Centro de la Cultural Raza** (Wed–Sun noon–5pm; free), mounts strong temporary exhibits on Native American and Hispanic life in an atmosphere altogether less stuffy than the showpiece museums of the park – make the time for it.

Old Town San Diego

In 1769, Spanish settlers chose what's now Presidio Hill as the site of the first of California's missions. As the soldiers began to leave the mission and the presidio, they settled at the foot of the hill. This was the birthplace of San Diego, later to be dominated by Mexican officials and afterwards the early arrivals from the eastern US, and the area is now preserved as **OLD TOWN SAN DIEGO** (locally referred to as "the Old Town") a state historical park that holds a number of original adobe dwellings, together with the inevitable souvenir shops.

Practical information

To **get to the Old Town,** use bus #4 or #5 from downtown; by car, take I-5 and exit on Old Town Avenue, following the signs. Alternatively, from I-8 turn off onto Taylor Street and head left on Juan Street. Most things in the park which aren't historical – the shops and restaurants – open around 10am and close at 10pm, but the **best time** to be around is during the afternoon, when you can learn something of the general history of the area and enter the more interesting of the adobes (including several which are otherwise kept locked) with the excellent **free walking tour**, which leaves at 2pm from outside the Machado y Silvas Adobe by the plaza. Details on this, and other aspects of the park, can be found at the **visitor center**, inside the park on San Diego Avenue (daily 10am–6pm).

The park and around

Many of the old structures are thoughtfully preserved and contain many of their original furnishings, giving a good indication of early San Diegan life. Of the places not covered on the walking tour, one of the more significant is the **Casa de Estudillo** on Mason Street (summer daily 10am–6pm, rest of the year daily 10am–5pm; $2), built by the commander of the presidio, José Mariá de Estudillo, in 1827. Next door, the **Casa de Bandini** was the home of the politican and writer Juan Bandini and the social centre of San Diego during the mid-nineteenth century. Following the switch of ownership of California, the house became the *Cosmopolitan Hotel*, considered among the finest in the state, and some of the elegant features of that period can still be seen in the dining room. You can wander through the rest of the building freely, and reward yourself with a lavish Mexican lunch in the courtyard restaurant; see "Eating".

Many of the other buildings in and around the park need little more than a passing glance, though one justifying a longer look is the **Whaley House**, just beyond the park gates on San Diego Avenue (Wed–Sun 10am–4.30pm; $3). The first brick house in California – once the home of Thomas Whaley, an early San Diego luminary – displays furniture and photos from his time, and a reconstruction of the courtroom which the building contained from 1869. A few strides south of the Whaley House, a slightly spooky **cemetery**, once the site of public executions, holds tombs whose inscriptions read like a Who's Who of late nineteenth-century San Diego.

Modest though it is, the cemetery makes a better stop than the **San Diego Union Building**, where the city's newspaper began in 1868; the Old West memorabilia inside the **Seeley Stables** (times as Casa de Estudillo; admission with the same ticket); or the **Heritage Park**, just north on Juan Street, where several Victorian buildings have been gathered from around the country – to be inhabited at weekends by period-attired history fanatics.

It's more productive to walk along Conde Street and peer into the atmospheric, sculpture-filled interior of the **Old Adobe Chapel**, dating from the 1850s and used as a place of worship until 1917. The lack of markers to the chapel means that visitors often unknowingly pass it by. On the other hand, many deliberately choose to avoid one of the park's more curious places: the **Mormon Battalion Visitors Center** (daily 9am–9pm; free), which commemorates the two-thousand-mile march of the Mormon Battalion after the assassination of the religion's founder, Joseph Smith, in Carthage, Illinois, in 1844. The Battalion occupy a crucial and heroic place in Mormon history; after passing close to San Diego, where a few of their number settled, they continued to what became Salt Lake City. There they established a community too remote to suffer further persecution – and now too big and powerful to be threatened by non-believers. Provided you're not spiritually over-susceptible (Mormons are always eager to recruit) and can tolerate the sentimental accounts, it adds up to an absorbing hour.

Bazaar del Mundo

A re-creation of a Mexican street market, **Bazaar del Mundo** fills a corner of the park. Though ringed by gift shops, it's enjoyable enough on a Sunday afternoon, when there's free music and folk-dancing in its tree-shaded courtyard. It's also a fair place to **eat**: stands serve fresh tortillas, *La Panaderia* sells Mexican pastries for a dollar, and a couple of restaurants are worth a longer meal break – see "Eating" for fuller details on Old Town dining.

Presidio Hill: the Serra Museum – and the San Diego Mission

The Spanish-style building which now sits atop Presidio Hill is only a rough approximation of the original mission – moved in 1774 – but contains the intriguing **Junípero Serra Museum** (Tues–Sat 10am–4.30pm, Sun noon–4.30pm; $2): a gathering of Spanish furniture, diaries and historical documents pertaining to the man who led the Spanish colonisation of California, and an acerbic commentary on the struggles of a few devoted historians to preserve anything of San Diego's Spanish past against the wishes of dollar-crazed developers.

Outside the museum, pause awhile by the Serra Cross, a modern marker on the site of the original mission. To find the actual mission, you'll need to travel six miles north to 10818 San Diego Mission Road, where the **Mission Basilica San Diego de Alcalá** (daily 9am–5pm; $1), was relocated to be near a water source and fertile soils – and to be further from the likelihood of attack by rebellious Indians. The present building (take bus #43 from downtown) is still a working parish church (mass daily at 7am and 5pm), and is one of the least visited of all the California missions, a peaceful complex that gives welcome respite from the nearby freeways – a mood perhaps enhanced by the decay which seriously affects parts of the building, despite a thorough renovation programme begun in the 1930s. Walk through the dark and echoey church to the garden, where two small crosses mark the graves of Indian neophytes – making this California's oldest cemetery – and to the chapel's fourteenth-century stalls and altar, imported from Spain. A small **museum** holds a collection of Native American craft objects and historical articles from the mission, including the crucifix held by Junípero Serra at his death in 1834. Despite accusations that the missionary campaign was one of kidnapping, forced baptisms, and treatment of Indians as virtual slaves, Serra was beatified during 1988 in a ceremony at the Vatican, the Pope declaring him a "shining example of Christian virtue and the missionary spirit".

Ocean Beach and Point Loma

Once ruled by a drug-running chapter of Hells Angels, **OCEAN BEACH**, accessible on bus #35 from downtown, is now one of the more sought-after addresses in San Diego. Vacant plots with a sea view regularly change hands for half a million dollars, and the single-storey adobe dwellings, lived in by several generations of Portugese fishing families, that characterised the area as recently as a decade ago, have virtually disappeared – the few that remain look like dinky-sized outhouses beside the opulent newer structures. The new money is less in evidence along Voltaire Street, which closes in on the sea rife with the trappings of beach culture: rows of cheap snack bars, surf and skate rental shops, and t-shirt stalls. The beach itself can still be enjoyable for those with the right inclination – especially at weekends, when you really shouldn't bother coming unless you're in the mood to party.

Further south from the pier – and the best of the beaches – rise the dramatic **Sunset Cliffs**. While a great vantage point for watching the sun go down, the cliffs are notoriously unstable and more than a few people have tumbled over the edge after an afternoon of excess on the beach. Beyond here, you're into the hilly and very green peninsula of **POINT LOMA** – much of it owned by the navy, which has been beneficial in keeping some of the more attractive parts of the coastline unspoilt and accessible to the public. You can get here direct from downtown by taking bus #2 and transferring to #6 at Rosecrans and 30th Avenue, but there's little to see until you get to the southern extremity, and the **Cabrillo National Monument** (July to Labor Day daily 9am–dusk, rest of the year daily 9am–5.15pm; $3 for cars, $1 for pedestrians and cyclists). It was here that Cabrillo and crew became the first whites to land in California, though that's as far as the historical interest goes, for they quickly reboarded their vessel and sailed away. The startling views from this high spot, however, across San Diego Bay to the downtown skyline and right along the coast to Mexico, easily repay the journey here, and there's ample opportunity for discovering the marine life in the numerous tidepools around the shoreline, reachable by way of a clearly marked **nature walk**, beginning close to the monument.

Also nearby, a **visitor center** informs on what creatures can be spotted and when the tides are most willing to reveal them (obviously the pools are flooded at high tide). If your timing is wrong, climb the hill to the **old San Diego lighthouse**, the interior of which can be toured. As it happens, the structure led an unfulfilled life: soon after it was built it was realised that the beacon would be obscured by fog, and another lighthouse was erected at a lower elevation.

Facing the Pacific, a mile or two from the monument, a platform makes it easy to view the November to March **whale migration**, when scores of grey whales pass by on their journey between the Arctic Ocean and their breeding grounds off Baja California.

Coronado and Imperial Beach

Across San Diego Bay from downtown, the bulbous blob of **CORONADO** is a well-scrubbed resort community with a major naval station occupying its western end. It's of very limited interest, save for an historic hotel and the engagingly long and thin streak of sands – a natural breakwater for the bay – that runs south. The simplest way to get here is on the **San Diego Bay ferry** ($1.50 each-way) which leaves Broadway Pier daily on the hour between 10am and 10pm, returning on the half-hour. Alternatively use bus #910 (or #19, though this only goes as far as the naval station) from downtown.

By road, you cross the **Coronado Bridge** (drivers without passengers have to pay a $1.50 toll), its struts decorated with enormous murals depicting daily Hispanic life, best seen from the community park beneath the bridge in the district of Barrio Logan.

The town of Coronado grew up around the **Hotel del Coronado**, a whirl of turrets and towers erected as a health resort in 1888. Using Chinese labourers who worked in round-the-clock shifts, the aim was to lure the ailing rich from all parts of the US – a plan in which it succeeds to this day, although the hotel and its elaborate architecture has lost much of its charm thanks to the high-rises which have gone up close by. If you're passing, the place is certainly worth dropping into for its glamour-soaked history. Through the lobby and courtyard a small **museum** records the hotel's past. It was at the "del", as it's locally known, in 1920 that Edward VIII (then Prince of Wales) first met Mrs Simpson (then a Coronado housewife) – a contact which eventually led to their marriage and his abdication from the British throne, and remembered here by an unintentionally hilarious cardboard head stuffed on top of a dinner suit. More thrilling is the tablecloth signed by Marilyn Monroe and the rest of the cast who filmed *Some Like It Hot* here – outside, past the tennis courts occasionally graced by world champions but more commonly by moneyed geriatrics, are the sands and palms on and around which much of the movie's action took place.

Silver Strand and Imperial Beach

From the hotel, Silver Strand Boulevard continues from Coronado over a narrow strip of glistening sands. There are plenty of good spots to stretch out and relax – though no food and drink facilities at all – foremost among them being **Silver**

Strand State Park. At the end of Silver Strand Boulevard, down-at-heel **IMPERIAL BEACH** is a contrast to smart Coronado, but does have a pleasant and fairly isolated beach. There's little other excitement beyond the helicopters periodically buzzing in and out of the naval air station. If the peace appeals, nearby **Border Field State Park** – a flat area noted for its horse trails – might be another reason to come, and is only five miles from the Mexican border (to reach it, take the Trolley from PALM CITY, a few blocks inland along Palm Avenue).

If you do come this far and don't have a car, you can get back to San Diego by taking buses #32 or #33 from the neighbouring PALM CITY (also on the Trolley route), which return through dreary CHULA VISTA and NATIONAL CITY.

East San Diego and Hillcrest

Scruffy **EAST SAN DIEGO** is largely suburban sprawl, only really of interest for the cheap motels and restaurants close to the SDSU campus. That said, you might want to venture into its western fringes as far as 1925 K Street, the site of **Villa Montezuma** (Wed–Sun 1pm–4.30pm; $3). Ignored by the majority of visitors to San Diego, possibly due to its location, the villa's a florid show of Victoriana, with a rich variety of domes and all manner of loopy eccentricities. Local kids know the villa simply as the "haunted house" – a nickname which doesn't seem unreasonable when you catch sight of the place. It was built for Jesse Shepard – English-born but noted in the US as composer, pianist, author and all-round aesthete – and paid for by a group of culturally aspirant San Diegans in the 1880s, and the glorious stock of furniture remains, as do many ornaments and oddments and the dramatic stained glass windows. It's a house which well reflects Shepard's introspective nature and interest in spiritualism, both of which must have been entirely out of step with brash San Diego through the boom years. **To get to the villa** without a car, you can either make the long walk (about 45 minutes) from downtown, take buses #3, #5 or #16, each stopping within about five blocks, or use the Trolley, transferring to the Euclid Avenue line and getting off near 20th Street.

North of downtown and on the northwest edge of Balboa Park, **HILLCREST** is an increasingly lively and artsy area, thanks to the wealthy liberals who've moved into the district in recent years. It's also the centre of the city's **gay community**. Go there (it's easily reachable from downtown) either for something to eat – there's a selection of interesting cafés and restaurants (detailed under "Eating") – or simply to stroll around the fine gathering of Victorian homes.

Mission Bay and Sea World

Heading northwest from downtown towards the coast, you pass through the unre-deemed area surrounding the Sports Arena – popular with military personnel for its topless bars and with unfussy tourists for its plain but cheap hotels – before reaching MISSION BAY, whose mudflats quickly become a landscaped expanse of lagoons and grassy flatlands usually crowded with watersports fanatics. Mission Bay is also the setting for San Diego's most popular tourist attraction, **Sea World** (daily 9am–dusk; $24.95). It's a good place to bring kids, though the high price dictates that you allow a whole day if you do come. Highly organised and cleverly run, Sea World has a large number of exhibits and timetabled events (get the day's schedule as you enter), ranging from "performances" by killer whales and dolphins, designed to demonstrate the creatures' intelligence and skills, to the eerie sight of the heads of hundreds of moray eels protruding from the hollow rocks of the Fobidden Reef display. Of the rest, two features in particular draw the crowds: the Shark House, where all manner of sharks circle menacingly, although none of them is as violent or as demonstrative as the infamous Great White, an eat-anything monster that Sea World hope one day to raise and keep in captivity; and the Penguin Exhibit – a mock Antarctica, where hundreds of the birds noisily jump around on ice and dive into the water, where they're visible through glass.

Mission Beach and Pacific Beach

Anyone of a nervous disposition, and without a physique suitable to be seen in bathing apparel, might well find **MISSION BEACH**, just west of Mission Bay, too hot to handle. On the other hand, the raver-packed sands, scantily clad torsos, and surfboard-clutching hunks might be precisely what you've come to the West Coast for. If so, your only headache will be finding accommodation (see "Sleeping") and negotiating the bumper-to-bumper traffic that fills Mission Boulevard – the one and only through-road – during the summer, when hiring a bike is the fastest way to get about (see "Cycling").

First impressions may suggest otherwise, but the city authorities have made major endeavours to limit the anarchic hedonism long associated with this classic example of Southern California beachlife, including approving the opening of the squeaky-clean Belmont Park, by Ocean Front Walk, a collection of swimwear shops, a pricey fitness centre, and stalls selling candyfloss, toffeeapples, and other traditional seaside fare – it's encouraged more families to use the area but so far made little impact on the beach's freewheeling character.

Cross from the social inferno of Mission Beach into **PACIFIC BEACH**, immediately north, and things become much more sedate. Here, expensive oceanside homes with tidy lawns set a refined tone, although there's still plenty to enjoy – a more than serviceable beach around Crystal Pier, and Garnet Avenue running inland from the pier, lined by funky eating places and nightspots. Adept surfers are no strangers to Pacific Beach either, a mile north of the pier, Tourmaline City Surf Park is reserved exclusively for their use and is regularly pounded by promising waves.

La Jolla and around

"A nice place ... for old people and their parents", wrote Raymond Chandler of **LA JOLLA** in the 1950s, though this didn't stop him moving here (his former house is at 6005 Camino de la Costa) and setting much of his final novel *Playback* in the town, re-naming it "Esmeralda". Since Philip Marlowe concluded his last case, La Jolla has been infused by new money and fresh vitality, and its opulence is now less stuffy and more welcoming. The main section, around Prospect Street and Girard Avenue, has spotless sidewalks flanked by tidy grassy verges, and there are numerous chic art galleries side-by-side with equally chic cafés.

This means it's expensive, too, but it's worth coming at least to savour the town's unique (if clearly contrived) elegance and the **La Jolla Museum of Contemporary Art,** 700 Prospect Street (Tues–Sun 10am–5pm, Wed open until 9pm; $3, students $1, free Wed 5–9pm), which has a huge – and regularly changing – stock of paintings and sculptures from 1955 onwards. Minimal, Pop and California schools are in evidence, bolstered by a strong range of temporary shows, not to mention fabulous views of the Pacific surf crashing against the rocks immediately below the building's huge windows.

The museum was once the home of Ellen Scripps, whose seemingly endless reserves of wealth were injected into La Jolla through the first half of the century. It was she who commissioned architect Irving Gill (who raised several distinctive public buildings in La Jolla) to design her house, and even today the Scripps name is almost everywhere, not least in the small, neat, and exquisitely tasteful, **Ellen Scripps Park**, just outside the museum on the seaward side. Where the park meets the coast is the start of **La Jolla Cove**, much of it an ecological reserve, with an underwater park whose clear waters makes it perfect for snorkelling. You can climb down to explore the caves just below the street level, or continue around the curving shore towards the pier and the **Scripps Aquarium and Oceanographic Museum** (daily 9am–5pm; free), whose tanks of colourful Pacific fish, and displays of other marine life, provide a less costly alternative to Sea World.

Around La Jolla

Beyond the Scripps Aquarium, La Jolla Shores Drive winds uphill to join North Torrey Pines Road, the main route northward. From the bluff that the road ascends, there's a great view over the ocean, and, if you're lucky, of daredevil hang-gliders launching themselves into the void. For a less heart-stopping sight pull up at **Torrey Pines State Preserve** (daily 9am–sunset; free), to admire one of the country's rarest species of pine tree – this being one of just two surviving stands of the Torrey Pine. Whatever their rarity, however, the pines are not especially distinctive, although these, thanks to salty conditions and stiff ocean breezes, do manage to contort their ten-foot-frames into a variety of tortured, twisted shapes. The half-mile **Guy Fleming trail** offers a chance to view them at close quarters and, at the head of the trail, a small **museum** and **interpretive center** will tell you more than you thought there was to know about Torrey pines.

Beyond the preserve, there's a steady descent into Del Mar, a town described under "Around San Diego".

Inland from La Jolla

Despite the scenic potential of the setting, a hillside rising above La Jolla, the **University of California at San Diego (UCSD)** campus is a bland affair, only meriting a call if you fancy trekking around to locate the various specially commissioned works, scattered around the 1200-acre grounds, which constitute the **Stuart Collection of Sculpture**. The first acquisition, in 1983, has yet to be bettered: Niki de Saint Phalle's *Sun God*, a large colourful bird whose outstretched wings welcome visitors to the car park opposite Peterson Hall. To find the rest, get a leaflet from the office in the Visual Arts Building.

Without the benefit of a car, you can reach the campus with bus #34 from downtown, which ends its route a mile or two away at a spick-and-span shopping mall called *University Towne Square*. Come here for the commendable shows of indigenous arts and crafts from around the globe staged at the **Mengei International Museum of World Art** (Tues–Sat 11am–5pm; suggested donation $2), worth seeking out among the upmarket stores.

Eating

Wherever you are in San Diego, you'll have few problems finding somewhere to eat that offers good food and good value. Everything from crusty coffeeshops to stylish ethnic eateries are in copious supply, and many of them offer attractive special reductions, advertised outside and in the publications listed under "Information".

Downtown

Alfonso's, 135 Broadway. Impressive range of mid-priced Mexican favourites, to eat in or takeaway.

Anthony's Fish Grotto, 1360 Harbor Drive. Cut-price off-shoot of a local seafood institution, justly famed for its freshly caught main courses.

Athens Market Taverna, 109 W F St. Popular Greek eaterie with fine food at affordable prices – and belly dancers gyrating between the tables at weekends.

Café Lulu, 419 F St. Taking orders until 4am, this is downtown's latest-opening food spot, offering delicate quiches and lasagne, plus a large selection of coffees to help you stay awake.

California Café, Top Floor, Horton Plaza. A good place to sample California cuisine without busting your budget; the daily specials are the best bet.

Chuey's Numero Uno, 1894 Main St. Mexican food institution that's been handing out massive portions for decades.

Croce's Restaurant & Jazz Bar, 802 Fifth Ave. Pricey but excellent range of pastas and salads; the Sunday jazz brunch is the talk of the town. See "Nightlife".

Dick's Last Resort, 345 Fourth Ave. Regular American fare served by the bucket in a deliberately brash setting, with flea-market furniture and loud-mouthed waiters. Fun if you're in a convivial mood.

Filippi's Pizza Grotto, 1747 India St. Thick and chewy pizzas in an entertaining small room at the back of an Italian grocery.

Galaxy Grill, 522 Horton Plaza. A Fifties-style diner that's the prime location in this upscale shopping mall to munch a burger and watch the well-groomed crowds glide by.

La Gran Tapa, 611 B St. Classy Spanish restaurant with tempting *tapas*, though the regular menu can be pricey.

Grand Central Café, 500 Broadway. Shares a building with the YMCA (see "Accommodation") and provides wholesome, inexpensive dishes throughout the day (closed Sunday).

Johnny M's 801, 801 Fourth Ave. Quantity takes precedence over quality, though the piles of seafood are still very edible inside what's one of the downtown's most impressive historic interiors – see "Downtown".

Old Columbia Bar & Grill, 1157 Columbia St. Solid American lunches to be consumed while gazing at the workings of the in-house brewery, which produces several ales worth sampling. See "Nightlife".

Olé Madrid Café, 425 F St. Enjoyable mid-priced Spanish restaurant, with an informal ambience aided by flamenco singers.

Pacifically Fish, 624 E St. Fresh fish and a good choice of chowders and seafood cocktails, all at fair prices.

The Pepper's Café, 905 Fourth Ave. Traditional breakfasts and lunches, given a California styling in every way except cost.

Super Taco Loco, 1153 Sixth Ave. Tremendous stock of takeaway taco, with every imaginable filling.

Veva's Mexican Café, 739 E St. Very cheap Mexican fare, featuring regional specialities.

Hillcrest

The French Side of the West, 2202 Fourth St. A fixed price ($18.50) buys a slap-up French dinner with a choice of main courses – worth the extravagance.

The Gathering, 4015 Goldfinch St. Stylish, but unpretentious café with a carefully chosen menu of well-prepared food – and the home-baked muffins are a delight.

The Good Egg, 7947 Balboa Ave. Until 9am, as much coffee as you can drink for 5¢, provided you buy a breakfast: the gigantic pancakes created from various mouthwatering ingredients are a wise choice.

Ichibin, 1449 University Ave. Few better places exist to enjoy quality Japanese cuisine: the combination platters are extremely wel -priced.

Kung Food, 2949 Fifth Ave. Succulent vegetarian cuisine, in a non-smoking environment.

Quel Fromage, 523 University Ave. Coffee bar with a range of brews, plus the ritual serving of tea and scones in the afternoon; a few lightweight hot meals are also on offer, and browsable newspapers and magazines are plentiful.

San Diego Chicken Pie Shop, 3801 Fifth Ave. Known for fifty years for its chicken pie dinners, also serves a few other American classics in informal surrounds.

Stefano's, 3671 Fifth Ave. Finely prepared meals, a relaxing atmosphere and decent prices, makes this the top place in the area for Italian food.

Thai Chada, 142 University Ave. Exquisite gourmet Thai dishes at modest cost, with heaps of care lavished on both food and service.

Old Town

Aztec Dining Room, 2811 San Diego Ave. Reliable Mexican outlet just north of the tourist-infested haunts of the Old Town, and very popular with locals.

The Brigatine, 2444 San Diego Ave. Sumptuous seafood in inventive styles in this award-winning, but not too expensive (especially during the 4–7pm happy hour), eaterie.

Café Coyote, Old Town Esplanade, 2461 San Diego Ave. In a tacky tourist-shopping mall but with a good southwestern-influenced menu; usually patronised by cruising late-teens.

Casa de Bandini, 2660 Calhoun St. Lovely place to relax and linger over a Mexican lunch, and soak up the sounds of the *mariachi* band from the patio of one of the Old Town's landmark buildings.

Casa de Pico, Bazaar del Mundo. Impressive selection of quality Mexican food but the incessant crowds tend to be off-putting.

Hamburguesa, Bazaar del Mundo. The liveliest restaurant in this always-crowded section of the Old Town. A mind-boggling variety of burgers, and more predictable Mexican offerings.

Irish Rose, 2707 Congress St. Small selection of very edible, very affordable salads and sandwiches, and a stock of gourmet coffees and teas.

Kelly's Pub, 2222 San Diego Ave. Besides the chance to guzzle imported European beers, there's a reasonable selection of modestly priced sandwiches. See "Nightlife".

Old Town Mexican Café y Cantina, 2498 San Diego Ave. Lively and informal Mexican diner; only at breakfast are you unlikely to have to queue for a table.

Ocean Beach and Point Loma

Broken Yok, 3350 Sports Arena Blvd. Omelettes of many sizes and fillings, accompanied by a formidable variety of muffins. Also in Pacific Beach, see below.

The Old Ocean Beach Café, 4967 Newport Ave. Casual beachside diner favoured by locals.

Souplantation, 3960 W Point Loma Blvd. Great selections of natural foods, imaginative pastas and an astounding choice of homemade soups.

Qwiig's Bar & Grill, 5083 Santa Monica Ave. Crisp salads and ultra-fresh seafood are the trademarks here – or simply devour a bucket of oysters while gazing over the ocean.

The Venetian, 3663 Voltaire St. Excellently priced pizzas and pasta dishes, a fine reward for a hard day's tanning on the beach.

Coronado

Kensington Coffee Company, 1106 First St. Aromatic coffees, imported teas, and food limited to pastries but good for a tasty snack.

McP's Irish Pub, 1107 Orange Ave. Earthy bar that proffers a neat line in lunchtime sandwiches and stews. See "Nightlife".

Mexican Village Restaurant, 120 Orange Ave. Long-standing Mexican diner of ballroom dimensions, patronised as much for its margaritas and music as for its food.

Miguel's Cocina, 1359 Orange Ave. Brilliant fish tacos and a full range of other Mexican delights.

Stretch's, 943 Orange Ave. For the health-conscious eater, extremely good-for-you meals using only the freshest, natural ingredients.

Mission Beach and Pacific Beach

Broken Yok, 1851 Garnet Ave. The city's egg specialists creating yet more omelettes; see "Ocean Beach and Point Loma" for further comments.

China Wok, 3825 Mission Blvd. Eat-in or takeaway Chinese food that can be just the job for a substantial snack.

The Eggery, 4130 Mission Blvd. A coffeeshop with imagination, serving breakfasts until 2pm and many other worthwhile dishes throughout the day.

Giulio's, 809 Thomas Ave. Dependable Italian food at more-than-fair prices.

Luigi's Italian Restaurant, 3210 Mission Blvd. Enormous pizzas and a rowdy beachside atmosphere, bolstered by competing TV sets.

The Red Onion, 3125 Ocean Front Walk. Beside the beachside boardwalk, with a riotous atmosphere as huge helpings of Mexican food are washed down with killer margaritas. See "Nightlife".

Saska's, 3768 Mission Blvd. Laidback dining place where substantial breakfasts are served all day and (nearly) all night, alongside the usual selection of lunch and dinner items.

La Jolla

Ashoka, 8008 Girard Ave. Slightly pretentious Indian restaurant, but the $7 lunch buffet is unmatched.

Café Budapest, 5656 La Jolla Blvd. A welcome find if cravings for goulash soup or stuffed red cabbage suddenly strike.

Clay's Texas Pit Bar-B-Q, 5752 La Jolla Blvd. Stuffing yourself with fried chicken and corned beef hash may seem rather uncouth in La Jolla, but this low-cost diner is a carnivore's dream.

Pasha's, 110 Torrey Pines Rd. Gourmet Afghan restaurant that doesn't hike up its prices: delicious meat and vegetarian dishes.

Star of India, 1025 Prospect St. Mostly northern Indian cuisine, but with a good stock of vegetarian dishes.

Sammy's, 402 Pearl St. Delicious, woodfired pizza with fillings ranging from goat cheese to Peking duck.

Sushi on the Rock, 1277 Prospect St. Tempting array of sushi combination platters served to a soundtrack of rock and reggae.

East San Diego

A-Dông, 3874 Fairmount Ave. The cut-rate lunch specials of this Vietnamese restaurant make a special trip worthwhile – the dinners are pretty good, too.

California Club Sushi Bar, 5522 El Cajon Blvd. Outstanding sushi spot, which also serves some Chinese specialities and run-of-the-mill American dishes.

Dookie's, 4125 El Cajon Blvd. Gloomy but good-value American eaterie, with large portions, small costs, and a pianist soothing tired dinner-eaters.

Nightlife

San Diego's arch conservatism is apparent even in the city's **nightlife**: money is lavished on snob-appeal pursuits such as classical music and opera, but the crowds flock to a large batch of much-of-a-muchness beachside discos and boozy live music venues – or pass the evening in a coffee bar. It may be narrow in scope, but there is at least plenty going on. For full listings, pick up the free *San Diego Reader*, or buy (35¢) the Friday edition of the *San Diego Union*.

Bars

The Daily Planet, 1200 Garnet Ave, Pacific Beach (☎272-6066). Sizeable sports bar with a 3–6pm happy hour, and cut-price drinks offered through the evening.

Foggy Notion's, 3655 Sports Arena Blvd. Watch the newspaper ads for the bizarre theme nights, chiefly an excuse to guzzle reduced-rate drinks.

Old Columbia Bar & Grill, 1157 Columbia St, Downtown. Where discerning beer hunters enjoy ales and lagers brewed on the premises. See "Eating".

Pacific Beach Brewhouse, 4475 Mission Blvd, Pacific Beach. Enticing array of home-brewed beers and a crowd eager to try them.

Red Onion, 3125 Ocean Front Walk. Beachside Mexican restaurant whose bar is the social hotspot of Mission Beach. See "Eating".

Coffee bars

Java, 837 G Street, Downtown. The antidote to surfer-dominated beach clubs, where the intellectually inclined browse current affair magazines and imbibe from a fine stock of coffees and teas.

Quel Fromage, 523 University Ave, Hillcrest. Linger over a coffee while reading overseas newspapers or viewing the small-scale art exhibitions. See "Eating".

Upstart Crow, Seaport Village, Downtown. Coffee bar fused with a bookstore which makes for a lively cross-section of customers – and a surfeit of reading material.

Live music venues

B St California Grill & Jazz Bar, 425 W.B St, Downtown (☎236-1707). Upmarket jazz haunt for slinky sophisticates.

Blind Melons, 710 Garnet Ave, Pacific Beach (☎483-7844). Earthy, live blues croaked out seven nights a week.

MAJOR VENUES

Any big name in contemporary music visiting San Diego is likely to appear at one of the following **major venues**:

The Bacchanal, 8022 Claremont Mesa Blvd (☎560-8000).

Copley Symphony Hall, 750 B St, Downtown (☎699-4205).

San Diego Convention Center, 111 W Harbor Drive, Downtown (☎570-1222).

San Diego Sports Arena, 3500 Sports Arena Blvd (☎224-4176).

Tickets

Assuming they're available, **half-price tickets** for theatre and classical music events for that evening can be bought at *Times Arts Tix*, between Horton Plaza and Broadway (Mon 10am–4pm, Tues–Sat 10am–7pm; ☎238-3810).

Otherwise, tickets for all major shows are available from the venue or through *Ticketmaster*. ☎278-TIXS.

Bodie's, 253 F St, Downtown (☎236-0898). Rowdy bar with rock, blues and R&B combos nightly.

The Casbah, 2812 Kettner Blvd, Downtown (☎294-9033). Varying roster of blues, rock and indie bands.

Casey's Pub, 714 Garnet Ave, Pacific Beach (☎274-5523). The nightly band can be anything from young hopefuls to fading Californian rock legends making their last stand.

Club Mick's, 4190 Mission Blvd, Pacific Beach (☎581-3938). Old style rock'n'roll most nights, reggae on Tuesday.

Croce's Top Hat, 805 Fifth Ave, Downtown. Classy jazz in the back of a pricey restaurant; has a jazz brunch on Sunday. See "Eating".

Ingrid's Cantina, 805 Fifth Ave, Downtown. Adjoining Croce's (see above), with R&B bands every night.

Island Saloon, 104 Orange Ave, Coronado (☎435-3456). Rocks to local R&B groups on Fridays and Saturdays.

José Murphy's, 4302 Mission Blvd, Pacific Beach (☎270-3220). Rock, blues, and the odd bit of soul, are the norm at this popular beachside venue.

Kelly's Pub, 2222 San Diego Ave, Old Town (☎543-9767). Unexceptional rock bands but a reasonable hangout if you're staying close to the Old Town. See "Eating".

McP's Pub, 1107 Orange Ave, Coronado (☎435-05280). Rock and blues fare, with folk music early in the week. See "Eating".

Patrick's II, 428 Fifth St (☎233-0377). No-frills bar with matching R&B bands nightly.

Spirit, 1130 Buenos Ave, Mission Bay (☎276-3993). Glam, metal, thrash and indie bands all get a look-in at this long-running alternative venue open every night.

Texas Teahouse, 4970 Voltaire St, Ocean Beach (☎222-6895). Live music most nights, usually in an R&B mould.

Winston's, 1921 Bacon St, Ocean Beach (☎222-6822). Rock bands most nights, reggae on Thursday.

Clubs and discos

Club Emerald City, 945 Garnet Ave, Pacific Beach (☎483-9920). Lively disco with drink specials at weekends.

Confetti, 5373 Mission Beach Rd, Pacific Beach (☎291-1184). Average music but this spacious disco is famed for its cut-rate drinks and free food offers.

Diego's, 860 Garnet Ave, Pacific Beach (☎272-1241). Beach-crowd disco with best-bikini contests among the fun, and vintage rock'n'roll flings on Friday and Saturday.

The Hop 3105 Ocean Front Walk, Mission Beach. Filled on Friday and Saturday for its Fifties-themed rave-ups.

Sub Zero, 7375 El Cajon Blvd, East San Diego (no phone). Alternative club, much patronised by students, with industrial and underground rock sounds.

Winter's, 5880 El Cajon Blvd, East San Diego (☎582-1814). Occasional live bands but better-known for its psychedelic, house, and alternative disco nights.

Theatre

There's a thriving **theatre** scene in San Diego, with several mid-sized venues putting on quality shows and many smaller fringe venues. Tickets range from $20–25 for a major production, to $10–15 for a night on the fringe. The *San Diego Reader* carries a full listing. The main venues are the *Old Globe Theater*, part of the *Simon Edison Complex for the Performing Arts* in Balboa Park (☎234-5623), the two *Gaslamp Theaters*, 444 and 547 Fourth Avenue (☎234-9538), the *Civic Theater*, 202 C Street (☎236-6510), and the *La Jolla Playhouse*, at the Mandell Weiss Center on the UCSD campus (☎534-39600).

Comedy

Three clubs regularly host **comedy** acts bound for the more glamourous venues of LA or New York. The cheapest shows, around $7, are in midweek; expect to pay from $8 to $10 on Friday or Saturday. The venues are *Comedy Isle*, at the *Bahia Resort Hotel*, 998 W Mission Bay Drive, Mission Bay (☎488-6872); the *Comedy Store*, 916 Pearl Street, La Jolla (☎454-9176); and *The Improv*, 832 Garnet Avenue, Pacific Beach (☎483-4521).

Cinemas

Despite possessing a large number of **cinemas**, going to the movies in San Diego offers few alternatives to the latest Hollywood blockbusters. Scan the newspapers for full listings – admission is usually $5 to $8, a few dollars less for most matinee shows. For more adventurous fare – foreign-language films, monochrome classics or cult favourites – find out what's on at the *Ken*, 4061 Adams Avenue (☎283-5909), and look for Monday-evening screenings at the San Diego Public Library, 820 E Street (☎236-5489).

Classical music and Opera

From October to May, the well-respected *San Diego Symphony Orchestra* appear at the Copley Symphony Hall, 750 B Street (☎699-4205), tickets are $10–35. During the summer, the orchestra plays outdoors at the Summer Pops series in Marina Park South by the Embarcadero. The *San Diego Opera*, frequently boasting top international guest performers during its January to May season, is based at the Civic Theater, 202 C Street (☎232-6510); cheapest seats are $11, but $6 standing-tickets are usually on sale half an hour before curtain-up.

Gay San Diego

Mostly centred on the Hillcrest area, San Diego's **gay and lesbian** population makes its presence felt through a number of publications and resource centres, and a network of gay bars and clubs. Also, several hotels and bed and breakfast inns are noted for their friendliness towards gay and lesbian travellers – though none is exclusively gay.

Publications and resource centres

The primary source of gay and lesbian news and views is the free *San Diego Gay Times*, appearing weekly and distributed through gay bars and clubs, many of the city's coffee bars, and through most gay-run businesses. Look out, too, for the *San Diego Lesbian Press*, published six times a year. You can learn more by calling at the **Lesbian and Gay Men's Center**, Suite 2, 3780 Fifth Avenue (Mon–Fri 6–10pm; ☎692-GAYS); and, although its services are aimed at all women, the **Women's Center**, 2467 E Street (☎233-8984), is a useful source of lesbian info.

Bars and clubs

Club West Coast, 2028 Hancock St. Disco spread across three floors: expect loud sounds and blinding lights.

The Flame, 3780 Park Blvd. Relaxed lesbian club, open from early evening to early morning.

Number One Fifth Avenue, 3845 Fifth Ave. Where smartly dressed gay men sip cocktails on the patio.

Peacock Alley, 1271 University Ave. Gay male video disco, though women are usually welcome.

Shadows, 4046 30th St. Enjoyable, neighbourhood-style bar patronised by gay men and lesbians, and sporting a booming jukebox.

Gay Accommodation

Balboa Park Inn, 4302 Park Blvd (☎298-0283). Sizeable bed and breakfast inn, in Hillcrest within walking distance of Balboa Park and its museums. Singles and doubles $65–100.

Clarkes Flamingo Lodge, 1765 Union St (☎1-800/822-0133. Friendly hotel decorated in high-camp tropical style. Singles and doubles from $33.

Hill House, 2504 A Street (☎239-4738). Affordable near-luxury in a bed and breakfast inn filled by fireplaces and rocking chairs. Singles and doubles $55–80.

Siesta Motor Inn, 1449 Ninth Ave (☎239-9113). Fairly ordinary motel but well-placed for Hillcrest and Balboa Park. Singles $33, doubles $38.

Listings

Airlines *American* 9665 Chesapeake Drive, Suite 225 (☎232-4050); *Delta* 409 Camino del Rio, Suite 100 (☎298-4344); *Northwest* 1026 Third Ave (☎1-800/225-2525); *TWA* 1200 Third Ave (☎295-7009); *United* 2375 Airline Rd (☎234-7171); *US Air*, Suite 208, 7851 Mission Center St (☎1-800/428-4322).

American Express 1640 Camino del Rio, Mission Valley (☎297-8101).

Amtrak Reservations ☎239-9021; information ☎1-800/872-7245.

Arts and entertainment hotline For a recorded run-through of events, phone ☎234-ARTS.

Beach and surf conditions ☎225-9492.

Car Hire *Avis* 3875 N Harbor Drive (☎1-800/331-1212); *Budget* 2535 Pacific Highway (☎297-2900); *Hertz* 3871 N Harbor Drive (☎1-800/654-3131); *Thrifty* 2100 Kettner Blvd (☎1-800/367-2277).

Chemists 24-hour pharmacy at Sharp Cabrillo Hospital, 3457 Kenyon St, between downtown and Ocean Beach (☎221-3400 or ☎221-3711).

Flea Market The huge *Kobey's Swap Meet* takes place at the Sports Arena, 3500 Sports Arena Blvd; Thurs–Sun 7am–3pm.

Hospitals For non-urgent treatment, the cheapest place is the Beach Area Community Health Center, 3705 Mission Boulevard in Mission Beach; ☎488-0644.

Library The main public library branch is at 820 E St (Mon–Thur 10am–9pm, Fri & Sat 9.30am–5.30pm).

Left Luggage At the *Greyhound* terminal, and Santa Fe Depot.

Post Office For poste restante use the main office at 2535 Midway Drive, between downtown and Mission Beach (Mon–Fri 8.30am–5pm, Sat 8.30am–4.40pm; zip code 92138; ☎293-5410). For anything else, the downtown post office is usually more convenient: 815 E St (Mon–Fri 8.30am–5pm, Sat 8.30am–noon).

Rape Crisis Centre/Hotline 2467 E Street (☎233-3088).

Sport Football: the *San Diego Chargers* play in the Jack Murphy Stadium in Mission Valley (☎280-2121). Baseball: the *San Diego Padres* play in the same stadium as the Chargers, tickets from the stadium office or *Ticketron* (☎283-4494).

Surf Report ☎225-9492.

Thomas Cook Suite 170, La Jolla Gateway, 9191 Towne Center Drive (☎453-0270).

Ticketron For the nearest of San Diego's many branches call ☎565-9947, or simply look in the phone book.

Traveler's Aid At the airport, daily 9am–10pm (☎231-7361); downtown, Suite 201, 1122 Fourth Avenue, Mon–Fri 8.30am–5pm (☎232-7991).
Victims of Crime Helpline ☎236-0101.
Weather ☎289-1212.
Western Union ☎236-9338.
What's On A recorded run-down of what's on and what's open: ☎239-9696.

AROUND SAN DIEGO

San Diego County lies largely north of the city, and it veers from small, sleepy suburban communities to completely open – and rugged – country. Passing through at least some of it is unavoidable, though how much time you actually spend in the region depends on whether you want to allow several days to camp out and follow forest and desert hikes, or simply to dash along the coast as fast as possible to Los Angeles.

The towns of the **North County Coast** stretch forty miles north from San Diego in a pretty much unbroken line as far as the Camp Pendleton marine base, which divides the county from the outskirts of Los Angeles. There's often little to distinguish one community from another, all chiefly populated by a strange mix of slick San Diego commuters and beach bums, and the main attraction is the coast itself: miles of fine sandy beaches and great opportunities for swimming and surfing. Otherwise there's little to take up your time on the way to LA. **Inland**, the North County is quite different, with no sizeable towns and given over to farming as far as the terrain allows, the outlook one of thick forests, deep valleys and mile-high mountain ranges. Besides a few reminders of the ancient indigenous cultures, remnants from the mission-era, and a few tiny settlements – some of which can comfortably consume an hour or two of your time – it's best to make for the area's state parks and enjoy some leisurely countryside walks.

Nature comes in more extreme forms in the **Anza-Borrego desert**, which fills much of the eastern part of the county with severe vistas pacified by several oases and stacks of unusual vegetation. The desert also has an interesting history, having been part of the great natural barrier between the eastern US and the promised land in the early days of the West's settlement – the ghosts of pioneer travellers are rife.

Finally there's Mexico, or more accurately the Mexican border city of **Tijuana**. To be honest this isn't up to much, giving the merest hint of how Mexico really is and a much stronger taste of the US's comparative affluence – most visitors are shoppers and it's hard to avoid the commercial trappings. However, it is at least a different country, and is extremely easy to reach from San Diego. Visit if only to say you've been there.

The North County Coast

The tall bluff that marks the northern edge of the city of San Diego and holds Torrey Pines State Preserve (described under "North from La Jolla"), forms the southern boundary of **DEL MAR**, a smart and pleasant little town whose **race-course** is famous throughout the West for its meetings between late June and early September. If you're around between late June and early July, the **Southern California State Exposition** is held at the Del Mar Fairgrounds, with barbecues and livestock, and a fair amount of contemporary arts and music events. The same venue also stages the **Jumping Frog Jamboree** during the last week of April, a peculiar – and cruel – event to which you can either bring your own frog or hire one for the day. There's little else to delay you in Del Mar, however, although the railway station is just a pebble's throw from an inviting beach.

Cheaper and more enjoyable, **SOLANA BEACH** – the next town north – makes a better place for an overnight stop than Del Mar. A throng of motels line the coast road, there's some decent nightlife (the *Belly Up Tavern*, 143 S Cedros Avenue, is one of the major mid-sized music venues in the area), and during the day striking views over the ocean from the Solana Beach County Park. If you're driving, take a quick detour inland along Hwy-8, passing the rolling Fairbanks Ranch (built by the film star, Douglas Jnr) to **RANCHO SANTA FE**: a small but extremely rich community shaded by trees and given its distinctive Spanish architectural flavour through the 1920s and 1930s.

On the coast north of Solana Beach, the strangely tagged **CARDIFF-BY-THE-SEA** was named according to the wishes of its founder's English wife – which also explains the presence of Manchester and Birmingham avenues. Names aside, the city has little to enjoy other than proximity to **San Elijo Beach State Park**, with its landscaped **campsite** overlooking the sands, which makes a good base for exploring two rather more appealing communities a short way along the shore. The first, **ENCINITAS**, is a major flower-growing centre, its abundant blooms at their best during the spring, when soft waves of colour from the flowers cast a calm and collected air over the whole place. It's no surprise that an Indian guru chose the city as the HQ of the *Self Realization Fellowship*, whose **Meditation Gardens,** 216 K Street (Tues–Sun 9am–5pm; free) are open to all. There's further flower power nearby at the **Quail Botanical Gardens**, 230 Quail Gardens Drive (summer daily 8am–6pm, winter daily 8am–5pm; free). From a financial as well as a geographical viewpoint, Encinitas makes a sensible base for further exploration: *Budget Motels of America*, 133 Encinitas Boulevard (☎1-800/624-1257) has doubles from $40.

Neighbouring Encinitas to the north, **LEUCADIA**'s rustic buildings evoke something of an old California hippy mood, though the town is fairly staid, save for the surfer-filled cafés and bars close to **Moonlight Beach**.

Carlsbad

Surfers also constitute the major element of **Carlsbad State Beach** (with a busy cliff-top campsite), marking the edge of **CARLSBAD**, one of the few coastal communties with a past worth shouting about. During the early 1880s, water from a local spring – proffered by a pioneer settler to thirsty passengers passing through on the Santa Fe Railroad – was deemed to have the same invigorating qualities as the waters of Karlsbad, a European spa-town in what was then Bohemia (now part of Czechoslovakia). Carlsbad thus acquired its name and a money-spinning reputation as a health resort.

A good way to catch up on Carlsbad's full history is to take the two-hour guided **walking tour** run by *Muffin Tours* (☎729-4484), which costs $4 and begins at 9.30am each Tuesday from the **Convention and Visitors Bureau**, inside the former rail depot at Elm Avenue and State Street (☎434-6093). Even if you miss the walking tour, drop into the Hanseatic-style **Hanse Gift Shop** (Mon–Sat 10am–5pm, Sun 1pm–4.30pm), where you can ask to be shown into the small **museum** around the original – now dry – well. A selection from the city's past is gleefully maintained here by local history fanatics, including two 400-year-old bronze busts of King Karl and his queen from Karlsbad, sitting incongruously among the postcards.

Other than the campsite mentioned above, accommodation in Carlsbad tends to be pricey. There are couple of well-priced places to **eat,** however: *Pollos Maria*, 3055 Harding Street, has fast but tasty Mexican food; and, out from the centre but easily spotted by its "Danish windmill", is a branch of *Pea Soup Andersen's*, 850 Palomar Airport Road.

Oceanside, Mission San Luis Rey and around

The most northerly town on the San Diego county coast, **OCEANSIDE** is dominated by the huge Camp Pendleton marine base and has little to redeem itself. But the town is a major transport centre, for the county and *Greyhound* bus services, and is the easiest place (without a car) from which to reach **Mission San Luis Rey** (Mon–Sat 10am–4pm, Sun noon–4pm; $2), four miles distant on Mission Avenue (Hwy-76) with local bus #313: the largest of the Californian missions, founded in 1789 by Padre Laséun, and once housing three thousand Indians. Franciscan monks keep the impressively restored mission's spiritual function alive while the **museum** and serene candle-lit **chapel** evoke earlier times. Even if you don't go inside, look around the foundations of the guards barracks immediately outside the main building, and, across the road, the remains of the mission's ornate sunken gardens.

The strong sense of history at the mission is fast being diluted by new property developments all around – commercial spillover from Oceanside that is creeping into the community of SAN LUIS REY itself. To escape, push on another two miles beyond San Luis Rey to **Rancho Guajome**, a twenty-room adobe building erected in the mid-eighteenth century as home for the newly married Cave Cortes and Ysidora Bandini, who turned the place into a major social gathering-place. Among the many celebrities entertained at the ranch were Ulysses S Wright and Helen Hunt Jackson, who, according to legend, based the central character of *Ramona*, her gushingly sentimental tale of Indian life during the mission era, on Ysidora's maid. After Cortes' death in 1874, Ysidora fought to maintain the upkeep of the place but over the years it fell into a dilapidation that was halted only when the building was bought by the county authorities. There are **free guided tours** of the house each weekend at 2pm, but at any other time just walk in to the courtyard – whose still fountains and ragged greenery make a spooky suggestion of glamorous times past.

Highway 76 continues inland to Mission Asistencia San Antonio de Pala, and to the Palomar Observatory, both described below. Along the coast beyond Oceanside, the **military** have kept their territory in its raw state, creating a vivid impression of how stark the land was before industrialisation took hold. When manoeuvres aren't in progress, it's possible to pitch a tent in the lower parts of the camp area, close to the uncluttered **beach**. The northern part of the camp, around the San Onofre Nuclear Plant, is popular with surfers because the plant's by-products apparently keep the water warm – though you might prefer to stay clear.

The North County Inland

About forty miles north of San Diego on I-15, accessible on buses #20, #810 or #820 from downtown San Diego, the dormitory city of **ESCONDIDO** is known to almost any American aged over 55 for one thing: the **Lawrence Welk Museum,** 8860 Lawrence Welk Drive (daily 10.30am–5pm; free), some eight miles further along I-15. Welk is the world's leading creator of "champagne music" – a gooey, anodyne noise that makes Liberace sound like the Sex Pistols. The man himself lives nearby and can sometimes be spotted, mobbed by drooling admirers. The museum, stocked with souvenirs from Welk's fairly tedious life, is only worth the journey if you're seriously into hagiography. Otherwise, Escondido has little to detain you, though the **Convention and Visitors Bureau,** 720 N Broadway (Mon–Fri 8.30am–5pm, Sat 9am–4pm; ☎1-800/848-3336), is useful if only to gather ideas on where to head next.

North from Escondido

S6 leads out from Escondido **Mission Asistencia San Antonio de Pala** (Tues–Sun 10am–3pm; $1), close to the junction with Hwy-76 from Oceanside. Built as an outpost of Mission San Luis Rey, this lay in ruins until the Cupeno Indians were ousted from their tribal home (to make room for the building of Warner Hot Springs) and moved to this area, where the mission was revived to serve as their church. The buildings here now are rarely used and all reconstructions of the originals, but they're not without atmosphere, supplemented by the breeze whispering through the gaping windows and the eerie silence hanging over the cemetery. If you want to stay overnight, there's a small basic **campsite** opposite the mission.

Continuing east, Hwy-76 runs into **Cleveland National Forest** and a good sprinkling of **campsites** (both state- and federal-run). The enormous forest stretches south from here almost to the Mexican border, although less-than-hardcore backpackers tend to prefer the **Palomar Mountain State Park** (info: ☎789-0191), on S7, for its cooler, higher altitude (some parts rise above 5000 feet) and enjoyable, and fairly unarduous, hiking trails. Capable of seeing a billion light-years into the cosmos, the 200-inch telescope of the **Palomar Observatory** on S6 (daily 9am–4pm; free) is something of a legend in astronomy circles. As a visitor, it's not possible to view the distant galaxies directly, but look in on the observatory's impressive collection of deep-space photographs taken using the powerful telescope.

East from Escondido

A few miles east from Escondido on Hwy-78 (bus #307), the **San Diego Wild Animal Park** (summer daily 9am–5pm, winter daily 9am–4pm; $14.50) is the major tourist target in the area: a 2000-acre enclosure that's about as enjoyable as any safari park, a place to spend the day rather than a brief stop-off. It's obviously a place for kids, and attractions include a sizeable aviary, noisy with the massed squawks of tropical birds, a mock-African Bush, a Kilimanjaro hiking trail, not to mention elephant-rides and various films and exhibitions. Admission also includes a fifty-minute ride on the Wgasa Bush Line Monorail, which skirts through the outer reaches of the park, where the animals – among them lions, tigers, cheetahs, deer, monkeys – roam in relative freedom.

THE NORTHEAST RURAL BUS SYSTEM

The only **bus service** through the sparsely populated northeastern section of the county is the reliable but infrequent *North East Rural Bus System* (☎765-0145; calls answered Mon–Fri 7–11am and 1–5pm) which links San Diego with Ramona and Santa Ysabel daily except Sunday, and continues on into the Anza-Borrego desert (though sometimes only once a fortnight).

The best departure point in San Diego is Grossmont Center near El Cajon, roughly ten miles east of downtown (get there with city bus #15). It's strongly advisable to phone at least a day in advance to check schedules – and you must phone ahead if you want to be picked up from Cuyacama State Park. The buses can be boarded either at marked stops, or, where there are none, by simply flagging the vehicle down. A consolation for the scarcity of buses are the low **fares**: just $2.25 from San Diego to Julian, for example.

In contrast to the crowded coast, the population – and the landscapes – become increasingly sparse as you press further east along Hwy-78, into a region that's a near-impossible nut to crack without personal transport (for details of the *North East Rural Bus Service* service, see the box above). If you're coming this way by car directly from San Diego, use S67 and join Hwy-78 at RAMONA, eighteen miles from Escondido, and continue east for sixteen miles to **SANTA YSABEL**, a tiny crossroads community enlivened only by *Dudley's Bakery*, famous far and wide for its homebaked breads and pastries at giveaway prices – it's hard to miss at the junction of Hwy-78 and Hwy-79 – and the tiny **Santa Ysabel Mission**, a 1924 replacement of a 1818 original, that sits in moody isolation beside Hwy-78 as you approach the town.

A different atmosphere prevails in **JULIAN**, seven miles from Santa Ysabel on Hwy-78, and surrounded by trees – a sure sign that you're entering the foothills of the mountains which divide the coastal side of the county from the desert. Hard as it may be to believe today, the discovery of gold here in 1869 turned Julian into the second-biggest town in the San Diego area. Since then, the local population has stayed constant at around 1500, and has earned more from harvesting apples than from precious metal: the cider and apple pies made and produced here bring thousands of weekend visitors.

With its little buildings and carefully nurtured downhome charms, you'll like Julian as soon as you arrive, but a short stroll reveals little of consequence beyond the shops and restaurants (the *Julian Café* has the best atmosphere, but for better food try *Kendal's Café* on B Street) grouped along Main Street. Nonetheless, Julian makes a fine overnight stop on the way to or from the Anza-Borrego desert, and the **Chamber of Commerce**, on Main Street (Mon, Tues & Fri; ☎765-1857), has plenty of info on the town's dozens of **bed and breakfast inns**. Among these, the *Julian Hotel*, at the junction of Main and B streets, is the oldest still-functioning hotel in the state, whose week-night rates ($50–85) are fairly typical; expect to pay $10 or $20 more at weekends.

If you find yourself with a few spare hours to while away in Julian, one good place to spend the time would be in the midst of the absorbing clutter of the **Pioneer Museum**, on Hwy-78 just off Main Street (Tues–Sun 10am–4pm; $1). At the overpriced **Eagle Gold Mine Museum**, off C Street (daily 9am–4pm; $6), you can get an inkling of the below-ground perils faced by the town's early settlers.

Cuyamaca Rancho State Park

Without the time or the inclination to venture into the Anza-Borrego desert, head nine miles south from Julian along Hwy-79 and spend at least a few hours among the oaks, willows, pines and firs that fill the **Cuyamaca Rancho State Park**. Even if you stay for days, you won't see everything: from lush meadows to stark mountain peaks, the park spans 25,000 acres, and is crisscrossed by a hundred miles of hiking trails

The most rewarding of the trails is the **Cuyamaca Peak Trail,** a steep, three-and-a-half-mile climb to a 6500-foot summit giving views east to the desert and west to the Pacific Ocean. Start the trail, and pick up information and maps, from **park headquarters** (☎765-0755), beside Hwy-79 in the heart of the park. At the same place, check the latest on the park's **campsites**, strung along Hwy-79, they're the only accommodation on offer. For some historicial back-up to the scenery, drop into the excellent **Indian Museum** (daily 8.30am–4.30pm; free), showing the formidable resistance of the local Indians to Spanish attempts to cut down the area's forests. The same tribe, in fact, also strongly resisted the arrival of the settlers from the eastern US, and was one of the last to be forced on to reservations.

The Anza-Borrego Desert

The largest state park in the country, the **ANZA-BORREGO DESERT** consumes 600,000 acres and offers a diverse variety of plant and animal life as well as a legend-strewn history spanning Indian tribes, the first white trailfinders and Gold Rush times. Some of Anza-Borrego can be covered by car, although four-wheel-drive vehicles are necessary for the more obscure – and most interesting – routes, and there are over five hundred miles of hiking trails where vehicles are not permitted at all. If you do come, bear in mind that all the usual preparations and precautions for desert travel should be taken (see p.203).

The best **time to come** is between October and March, when the daytime temperatures are around the mid-eighties (nights are much cooler). Obviously summer months are fiercely hot, often above 100°F, and the place is then best left to the lizards, although most campsites stay open all year. The desert **blooming season**, between March and May, is popular, when scarlet octillo, orange poppies, white lilies and purple verbena, and other peacock-like wildflowers are a memorable – and fragrant – sight.

The park

The western section is the first part of the park you'll see coming from Julian, and contains some of the more interesting historical debris. Scissors Crossing, the junction of Hwy-78 and S2, was once part of the **Butterfield Stage Route,** the first regular line of communication between the eastern states and the newly settled West, which began service from 1857. **Blair Valley**, on S2 towards the southeast corner of the park, holds a campsite and some shops, and **Box Canyon** is a passage carved through the rock by the Mormon Battalion of 1847 (see p.62). Some miles further on, the **Vallecito Stage Station** is an old adobe stage rest stop which gives a good indication of the comforts – or lack of them – of early desert travel. To the south lies the least-visited portion of Anza-Borrego, good for isolated exploration and undisturbed views around Imperial Valley, where there's a vivid and spectacular clash as grey rock rises from the edges of the red desert floor.

S22 leads east from Borrego Springs (see below) past a memorial marker to Peg Leg Smith, an infamous local spinner of yarns from the Gold Rush days who is further celebrated by a festival of tall stories – the **Peg Leg Liars Contest** – which takes place at this spot on the first Saturday in April; anybody can get up before the judges and fib their hearts out, the most outrageous tales earning a modest prize. Roughly four miles further on, a track leads to **Font's Point** and a view over the **Borrego Badlands** – a long sweeping plain devoid of vegetation whose strange, stark charms are oddly inspiring. **Ocotillo Wells State Vehicular Recreation Area**, ten miles to the east, is the only place in Anza-Borrego where dune buggies and dirt bikes are permitted. Owners drive like demons around and around in a maelstrom of tossed-up sand and engine noise. If you're tempted to join them, information is available from Recreation Headquarters (daily 8am–5pm; ☎767-5391) – otherwise stay well clear.

Anza-Borrego Practicalities

The one sizeable settlement in the park is the resort community of **BORREGO SPRINGS** at the end of S3. It's worth avoiding except as a place to gather supplies (which in any case are more expensive here than outside the desert) and to use the **Visitor Information Center** at 200 Palm Canyon (June–Sept weekends and holidays 10am–3pm, rest of the year daily 9am–5pm; ☎767-5311), a mile or so west of the town centre, which has the lowdown on everything about the desert, and full details on accommodation. Nearby, a footpath leads from the large *Borrego Palm Canyon* campsite into **Borrego Palm Canyon**, where there's a dense concentration of desert palms – the only palms native to California.

The campsite is among the biggest of the many in the park, along with *Tamarisk Grove*. Both organise **guided hikes** and regular discussion and activity evenings led by a park ranger, which can be very informative on local history and wildlife. Places can be reserved through MISTIX (essential for holidays and weekends, and in the March–May blooming season). Other campsites fill on a first-come-first-served basis; those in the backcountry always have space and you can camp anywhere without a permit, although it's advisable to let a park ranger know your plans. The more primitive sites are free, others charge according to their facilities – around $4 to $6 a night per person in most places.

If you're not feeling adventurous enough to camp, the **hotels** in Borrego Springs tend to be pretty expensive. Only *Oases* at 366 W Palm Drive (☎767-5409) is at all affordable, with rooms from $42.

Tijuana

TIJUANA has the odd distinction of being both the least interesting place in Mexico and one of the most visited cities in the world. Twenty million people a year cross the border here, most of them Californians on day-long shopping expeditions seeking somewhere cheaper and more colourful to spend money than their local mall. And they find it: blankets, pottery, cigarettes, tequila, dentistry or car repair – everything is lower-priced in Tijuana than in the US (though more expensive than in the rest of Mexico), and all of it is hawked with enthusiasm.

What's most dramatic about Tijuana for first-time arrivals is the abrupt realisation of the vast economic gulf separating the two countries. Crossing the frontier area takes you past beggars crouched in corners and dirty children scuffling for change thrown by tourists. It's both a depressing and revealing experience. For regular visitors, however, it's a shock that soon fades; it's also unrepresentative of Tijuana itself which is, in fact, one of the wealthiest Mexican cities, thanks to its duty-free status and the large number of Southern Californian manufacturing companies who are relocating south of the border to exploit the cheaper work force here.

Whatever its faults, Tijuana is, at least, quite unique, and you could hardly find a more intriguing day-trip out from San Diego. However, it's not typically Mexico, and if you want a proper taste of the country you'd do well to hurry on through. Things are also much safer these days than was the case a decade or so ago when Tijuana lived up to a rough border town image. Then prostitution was rife and the streets extremely creepy after dark; these days the red-light area is limited to the easily avoided blocks around the junction of Avenida Artícula and Mutualismo. Provided you take the usual amount of care there's little danger in most parts of town.

The main streets and shopping areas are a mile or so from the border in **downtown**, where the major thoroughfare is Avenida Revolución, lined with street vendors and people trying to hassle you into the shopping emporiums. Stroll up and down for a while to get the mood and then retire to one of the plentiful bars and watch the throng in the company of a sizeable margarita (in the bigger bars expect to pay $1.50 for a large one, $1 for a tequila, and about 50c for a beer). At night, the action mostly consists of inebriated North American youths dancing themselves silly in flashy discos – not hard to find around the main streets.

As a break from rampant commercialism, visit the **Centro Cultural Fonapas** (daily 11am–9pm) – rising like a huge golf ball from ramshackle city skyline, on the corner of Paseo de los Héroes and Mina. It has strong accounts of regional Mexican cultures, through multi-media shows and temporary exhibitions, but there's a steep $5 admission fee for the English language show at 2pm. If you understand Spanish, you can get the same for just 1000 pesos at 6pm.

Practical details and travel onwards

Getting to Tijuana from San Diego could hardly be easier. The San Diego Trolley ends its route close to the elevated concrete walkway which leads over the border, as does bus #932 from the Santa Fe Depot in downtown San Diego. If you arrive by *Greyhound*, you'll have to cross the border on foot and reboard for the ride into Tijuana proper – hardly worthwhile since the Tijuana bus station is some miles from the centre.

Crossing into Mexico, **border formalities** are minimal: you simply negotiate a turnstile and you're there. Customs and immigration checks are only carried out 25km inside the country, so you only need to be carrying a Mexican Tourist Card (available free from any Mexican consulate in the US – see the phone book for the one nearest you; and also, somewhat unofficially, at the border) if you're continuing on from Tijuana. Returning to the US, however, the formalities are as stringent as anywhere (see *Basics*, p.8). Even if you've just travelled down for the day, you will need to satisfy the usual entry requirements. Dollars are accepted as readily as pesos everywhere in Tijuana, but although you can **change money** at any of the banks along Avenida Revolución, it's only worth doing so if you're travelling further into Mexico. Only Bánamex will change travellers' cheques.

If you do want to sample Tijuana's discos into the small hours and stay overnight, the **accommodation** options are fairly good. You'll spend much less here for a **hotel** room than you would north of the border, and many decent lodgings can be found close to the central streets. The ones to try first are *Hotel del Mar*, Calle 1a 1948 (☎685-7302), $7.50 for a double, the similarly priced *Hotel San Jorge*, Avenida Constitución 506 (☎685-8540), and *Hotel Paris*, Calle 5a 1939 (☎685-3023), usually $12 for a double. For comparative opulence, splash out for the *Hotel Nelson*, Avenida Revolución 502 (☎854303), which charges $22 for a double. If none of these appeal or have space, there are plenty more in the same area; just take your pick.

As for **travelling further into Mexico**, on the whole the northwest of the country has little to tempt visitors, and many people head straight for Mexico City and the regions beyond. A closer option, though, is the peninsula of Baja California, which has miles of unspoilt coast and a few moderately sized cities. Wherever you go, the invaluable *Real Guide to Mexico* ($11.95) is available in most San Diego bookshops.

travel details

Trains
From San Diego to Del Mar (10 daily; 30min); Oceanside (10; 45min) San Clemente (1; 1hr 8min) San Juan Capistrano (10; 2hr 15min); Anaheim (9; 3hr); Downtown Los Angeles (10; 2hr 45min).

Buses
From San Diego to Oceanside (18 daily; 1hr); Anaheim (12; 2hr 15min); Long Beach (7; 2hr 15min); Downtown Los Angeles (22; 2hr).

From Grossmont Center (San Diego) to Ramona (4 a week; 1hr 10min); Santa Ysabel (4; 1hr 35min); Julian (2; 1hr 30min), Borrego Springs (2; 2hr 50min); Cuyacama (5 a month; 2hr 10min); Scissors Crossing (3; 2hr 35min); Butterfield Ranch (3 a month; 2hr 50min).

International buses
From San Diego to Tijuana (14 daily; 50min).

CHAPTER TWO

LOS ANGELES

The rambling metropolis of **LOS ANGELES** sprawls across the floor of a great desert basin in a colourful melange of fast-food joints, shopping malls, palm trees and swimming pools, bounded by snow-capped mountains and the Pacific Ocean, and held together by an intricate network of high-speed freeways rising above a thousand square miles of architectural anarchy. It's an extremely visual, often voyeuristic, city, and famously hard to make sense of – understandable, in F. Scott Fitzgerald's phrase, "only dimly, and in flashes".

For all that, Los Angeles can surprise you with a powerful sense of familiarity. The entertainment industry has played a major role in popularising images of the city ever since the first film-makers arrived in the 1910s, attracted by a climate which allowed them to film outdoors year-round, plenty of cheap open land on which to build elaborate stage sets, and a varied enough collection of nearby landscapes to form the backdrop to just about anywhere in the world. Since then, the money and glamour of Hollywood has acted as a magnet to countless thousands of aspiring actors, writers, designers and, more recently, would-be rock stars. The myth of overnight success is very much part of the LA mind-set, not to mention the prospect of the next big earthquake. This is a place of extremes, where tomorrow can bring acclaim or disaster, lending a unique, on-the-edge, almost unhinged personality to the city . . . LA, certainly, is like nowhere else on earth.

It's also a very young city. As recently as a hundred years ago, Los Angeles was a balanced bi-cultural community of white American immigrants and wealthy Mexican ranchers, with a population of under 50,000. It was only on completion of the transcontinental railways in the 1880s that the city really began to grow, since when the population has doubled every ten years. From the late nineteenth century onwards, hundreds of thousands descended upon the basin, lured by the widely advertised virtues of life in America's sub-tropical paradise. Ranches were subdivided into innumerable suburban lots and scores of new towns, and land speculators marketed an image of Los Angeles which survives to this day, its most pervasive symbol the family sized suburban house (with a swimming pool and two-car garage) set amidst the orange groves between the mountains and the sea in a glorious land of sunshine. The real boom years came after World War II when many of the veterans who'd passed through on their way to the South Pacific came back and stayed, buying government-subsidised houses and finding well-paid work in the mushrooming aeronautics industry – which still accounts for one in four jobs in Southern California.

Once heralded as the world's most up-to-date city, and spurned by its detractors as "nineteen suburbs in search of a city", LA now seems to have come of age. The many museums that have gone up in the past decade reflect its emergence as an energetic international centre of visual art, and the forest of skyscrapers that has sprung up downtown is proof of its key position as the high-finance gateway between America and the Far East. Yet LA still doesn't *feel* like a city in the European sense. It really *is* difficult to get around without a car. What's more, no Angeleno seems to notice the contradiction inherent in mud-wrestling venues and porno cinemas next door to quality bookshops and trendy restaurants. Or, indeed, in an infrastructure that contains both a 50,000-strong homeless population and some of the highest standards of living in the world. It's precisely this flood of endless possibilities and opposites, however, that makes LA so exciting and strangely addictive, and everywhere else you go afterwards somehow tame and almost predictable. As David Puttnam summed it up: "leaving Los Angeles is like giving up heroin".

Arriving and information

Arriving in LA is potentially one of the most nervewracking experiences you're ever likely to have. However you get to the city, and especially if you're not driving, you're faced with a sprawling urban monster that can be a source of bewilderment even for people who've lived in it for years. Provided you don't panic, however, and follow our guidelines, the city is far from the savage beast it first appears.

By plane

All European and many domestic **flights** use **LAX** (officially titled Los Angeles International Airport but always known by its abbreviation), sixteen miles southwest of downtown LA. Once through customs, if you're not hiring a car (if you are, see "Driving and car hire" below), take the free **"C" shuttle bus** (not "A" or "B", which serve the car parks), running 24 hours a day from each terminal, to the LAX Transit Centre at Vicksburg Avenue and 96th Street, where numerous local **buses** (the RTD and others) leave for different parts of LA. See "Getting around the city" below for more bus details.

The main alternative to regular buses are minibus services such as **Airport Shuttle** (☎971-8265) and **SuperShuttle** (☎1-800/325-3948) – which run to downtown, Hollywood, West LA and Santa Monica (the *SuperShuttle* also goes to Long Beach and Disneyland) and deliver you to your door. If you're heading for the Santa Monica area, or the South Bay, another possibility is the **Coast Shuttle** (☎310/417-3988). Fares vary depending on your destination, but are generally around $15, with a journey time of between 30 and 45 minutes. The buses run around the clock from outside the baggage reclaim areas (tickets are sold from kiosks in the baggage reclaim area, or pay when you board) and you should never have to wait more than fifteen or twenty minutes for one. **Taxis** from the airport are always expensive: reckon on around $25 to downtown, $30 to Hollywood and $70 to Disneyland. Unlicensed taxi operators may approach you and offer flat fares to your destination; if tempted, bargain fiercely.

The vast majority of flights into LA use LAX, but if you're arriving from elsewhere in the US, or Mexico, you may land at one of the **other airports** in the LA area – at Burbank, Long Beach, Ontario or Newport Beach. These are similarly well-served by car-hire firms, and we've listed the main bus routes from them on p.91. If you're going somewhere that we haven't listed, phone the RTD (☎626-4455) on arrival and tell them where you are and where you want to go.

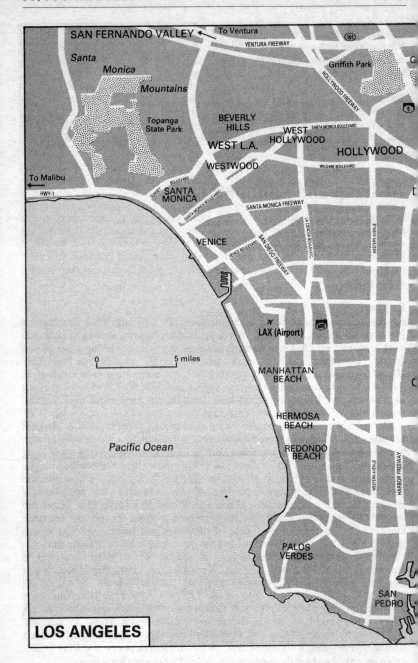

SAN FERNANDO VALLEY — To Ventura

VENTURA FREEWAY

Santa

Monica

Mountains

Griffith Park

G

HOLLYWOOD FREEWAY

5

Topanga
State Park

BEVERLY
HILLS

WEST
HOLLYWOOD

SANTA MONICA BOULEVARD

WEST L.A.

HOLLYWOOD

WESTWOOD

WILSHIRE BOULEVARD

To Malibu

HWY-1

BOULEVARD

SUNSET

SANTA
MONICA

SANTA MONICA BOULEVARD

SANTA MONICA FREEWAY

LA CIENEGA BOULEVARD

WESTERN AVENUE

VENICE

VENICE BOULEVARD

SAN DIEGO FREEWAY

✈ LAX (Airport)

405

MANHATTAN
BEACH

HERMOSA
BEACH

0   5 miles

REDONDO
BEACH

WESTERN AVENUE

HARBOR FREEWAY

Pacific Ocean

PALOS
VERDES

SAN
PEDRO

LOS ANGELES

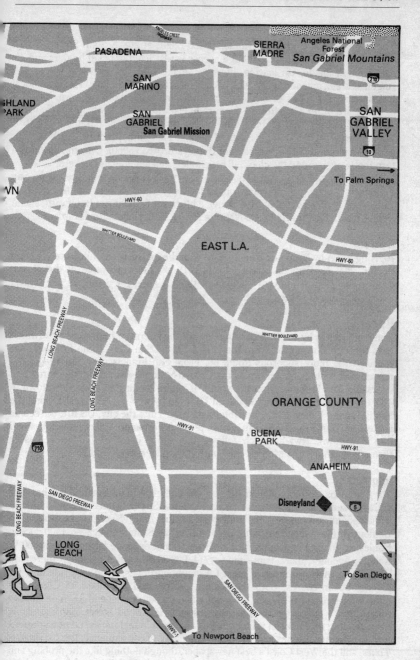

By bus

The main **Greyhound** bus terminal (☎620-1200), at 208 E Sixth Street, is in a seedy section of downtown – though access is restricted to ticket holders and it's safe enough inside. On leaving, however, make sure you turn left, across Los Angeles Street, and not right – which leads into deepest Skid Row. The major local bus stops are three blocks on, along Broadway, in the heart of downtown.

There are **other Greyhound terminals** elsewhere in LA, which handle fewer services: in Hollywood at 1409 Vine Street (☎466-6381); in Pasadena at 645 E Walnut Street (☎792-5116); in Santa Monica at 1433 Fifth Street (☎310/394-5433); and in Anaheim at 1711 S Manchester Boulevard (☎635-5060). Only the downtown terminal is open round-the-clock; all have toilets and left luggage lockers.

Green Tortoise also run services to LA (☎329-1990) once a week from San Francisco, stopping in downtown outside *Gorky's Café*, 536 E Eighth Street, in Hollywood at *McDonalds* on Vine Street, a block south of Sunset Boulevard, and in Venice just behind the *Interclub Network Hostel*, 2221 Lincoln Boulevard.

By train

Arriving in LA by **train** you'll be greeted with the expansive architecture of Union Station, 800 N Alameda Street (☎624-0171), on the north side of downtown. Trains also stop at outlying stations in the LA area; for a full list see "travel details" at the end of the chapter.

By car

The main routes by **car** into Los Angeles are the interstate highways, all of which pass through downtown. From the east, I-10, the San Bernardino Freeway, has replaced the more sonorous Route 66. From San Francisco or San Diego, the most direct route is I-5, known as the Golden State Freeway, from the north, and the Santa Ana Freeway from the south. If you're looking to avoid downtown, I-405, the San Diego Freeway, splits off I-5 to go by way of LAX, West LA and the San Fernando Valley. Of the non-interstate routes into the city, US-101, the scenic route from San Francisco, cuts across the San Fernando Valley and Hollywood into downtown; Hwy-1, which follows the entire coast of California, passes through Malibu, Santa Monica, the South Bay and Orange County.

Information

For free maps, accommodation suggestions and general information, LA has four **visitors centres**: downtown at 695 S Figueroa Street (Mon–Fri 8am–5pm, Sat 8.30am–5pm; ☎689-8822); in Hollywood at the *Janes House*, 6541 Hollywood Boulevard (Mon–Fri 9am–5pm; ☎461-4213); in Santa Monica at 1400 Ocean Boulevard (daily 10am–4pm; ☎310/393-7593); and opposite Disneyland at 800 W Katella Avenue (daily 9am–5pm; ☎714/999-8999). Less usefully, there are **Chambers of Commerce** in most LA neighbourhoods, good as a rule only for picking up brochures. Both the visitors centres and Chambers of Commerce often offer free **maps** of their area, but you'd do better to spend $1.75 on *Gousha Publications*'s fully indexed "Los Angeles and Hollywood Street Map", available from vending machines in visitor centres and most hotel lobbies. Of **newspapers and magazines**, LA has just one daily newspaper of consequence: the *Los Angeles Times,* still the West Coast's best newspaper, though nothing like the probing and incisive journal it once was. Of the free papers, much the fullest and most useful is

LA MEDIA

TV STATIONS

2 KNXT CBS
4 KNBC NBC
6 KCET PBS
7 KABC ABC

9 KHJTV Independent
11 KTTV Fox
13 KCOP Independent

RADIO STATIONS

KABC 790 AM News and current affair chat shows.

KFWB 980 AM The best news source, also talk-shows.

KLON 88.1 FM Knowledgeably presented jazz and blues.

KCRW 89.8 FM Santa Monica college radio; great drama, music and much more.

KXLU 89.9 FM Classical and salsa, interspersed with rapid rock shows.

KSAK 90.1 FM Album rock.

KPFK 90.7 FM Varied, but mostly modern, specialist music shows.

KFAC 92.3 FM Classical music.

KNX 93.1 FM Soft rock album tracks.

KZLA 93.9 FM Country music.

TTWV 94.7 FM Known as "The Wave", the major New Age station.

KLOS 95.5 FM Album rock.

KFSG 96.3 FM Christian.

KLSX 97.1 FM Classic rock tracks.

LA Weekly, with over a hundred pages of news, features and listings. A poor second is the less feature-packed *LA Reader*, although it is worth picking up, its reviews and comments much more down-to-earth than the *Weekly*'s.

Getting around the city

The only certainty when it comes to **getting around** LA is that wherever and however you're going, you should allow plenty of time to get there. Obviously, this is partly due to the sheer size of the city but the confusing entwinements of freeways and the tailbacks common during rush hours can make car trips lengthy undertakings – and the fact that most local buses stop on every corner hardly makes bus travel a speedy alternative.

Driving and car hire

The best way to get around LA – though by no means the only way – is to **drive**. Despite the traffic being bumper-to-bumper much of the day, the **freeways** are the only way to cover long distances quickly. The system, however, can be confusing, especially since each stretch can have two or three names (often derived from their eventual destination, however far away) as well as a number. Four major freeways fan out from downtown: the Hollywood Freeway (a section of US-101), heads northwest through Hollywood into the San Fernando Valley; the Santa Monica Freeway (I-10) crosses West LA to Santa Monica; the Harbor Freeway (I-110) runs south to San Pedro; and the Santa Ana Freeway (I-5) passes Disneyland and continues through Orange County. For **shorter journeys**, especially between downtown and the coast, the wide avenues and boulevards are a better option, not least because you get to see more of the city.

All the major **car hire** firms have branches all over the city (simply look in the phone book for the nearest office or call one of the numbers below), and most have their main office close to LAX, linked to each terminal by a free shuttle bus. Cheapest are *Thrifty* (☎1-800/367-2277), who charge $29 a day, $129 a week; among the others are *Avis* (☎1-800/331-1212), *Budget* (☎1-800/527-0700) *Hertz* (☎1-800/654-3131) and *National* (☎310/670-4950), who all do reliable vehicles for upwards of $30 a day, $150 a week. A number of other companies specialise in everything from old bangers to Batmobiles. *Rent-a-Wreck*, 12333 W Pico Boulevard (☎310/478-0676), hire out mid-Sixties Mustang convertibles; *Dream Boats*, 8536 Wilshire Boulevard (☎310/659-3277), specialise in pink Cadillacs and '57 T-birds. Expect to pay $50 per day.

Parking is only a problem in downtown and Westwood, where passing motorists are known to park just because they see a space. Anywhere else there is usually plenty of room, either at the meters on the street or in shopping mall car parks, which are normally free but usually with a two-hour limit (for more on West Coast driving and the perils of parking, see *Basics*).

Public transport

Until the underground Metrorail train system becomes fully operational in the mid-1990s (so far only the **Blue Line** section between downtown and Long Beach is running; departures are every fifteen minutes throughout the day and the one-way fare is $1.10), **public transport** in LA is mainly limited to **buses**, most of which are run by the *Southern California Rapid Transit District* – abbreviated to **RTD**. Although initially bewildering, the gist of the RTD network is quite simple: the main routes run east–west (ie between downtown and the coast) and north–south (ie between downtown and the South Bay). Establishing the best transfer-point if you need to change buses can be difficult, but with a bit of planning you should have few real problems – though you should always allow plenty of time.

Ten free area brochure/maps are available from RTD offices, and diagrams and timetables for individual routes can be picked up on the bus (you could also try

---

RTD ROUTES

#1–99 – local routes to and from downtown.

#100–299 – local routes in other areas.

#300–399 – limited-stop routes (usually rush hours only).

#400–499 – express routes to and from downtown.

#500–599 – express routes in other areas.

#600–699 – special service routes (for sports events and the like).

The MAIN RTD OFFICES are:

419 S Main St (Mon–Fri 8am–4.30pm). 515 S Flower St, on level B of Arco Plaza (Mon–Fri 7.30am–3.30pm).

6249 Hollywood Blvd (Mon–Fri 10am–6pm).

For **route and transfer information**, phone ☎626-4455 (6am–11.30pm); be prepared to wait your turn, and be ready to give precise details of where you are and where you want to go. Other **local transport services** include: *Orange County (OCTD)* ☎714/636-7433; *Long Beach (LBTD)* ☎310/591-2301; *Culver City* ☎837-5211; *Santa Monica* ☎310/451-5445.

asking for the free **Bus System Map**, which covers the entire network, although these have not been printed for some time due to the route disruption caused by the Metrorail construction). Buses on the major arteries between downtown and the coast run roughly every fifteen minutes between 5am and 2am; other routes, and the **all-night services** along the major thoroughfares, are less frequent, usually half-hourly or hourly. The standard **single fare** is $1.10; **transfers**, which can be used in one direction within the time marked on the ticket (usually three hours), cost 25¢ more; **express buses** (a limited commuter service), and any others using a freeway, are 35¢ extra. Stuff the correct money (coins or notes) into the slot when getting on. If you're staying a while, you can save some money with a **Monthly Pass**, which costs $42 (slightly more to include express buses) and also gives reductions at selected shops and travel agents. There's also the **Downtown DASH**, buses with a flat fare of 25¢ that ply two routes through the centre of downtown roughly every ten minutes between 6.30am and 6pm on weekdays, every fifteen minutes between 10am and 5pm on Saturday, but not at all on Sunday.

A number of other **local public transport services** supplement the RTD network ; also, **Greyhound** run buses between most of the major districts of LA.

You won't necessarily need to use **taxis** much, but if you do want one they can be found at most transport terminals and major hotels (they don't cruise the streets). Otherwise phone: among the more reliable companies are *Independent Cab Co.* (☎1-800/521-8294); *LA Taxi* (☎627-7000); and *United Independent Taxi*

MAJOR LA BUS ROUTES

From LAX to:
Downtown #42, #439 (weekdays only) #607 (rush hours only).
Long Beach (via Redondo Beach) #232 .
West Hollywood #220 (for Hollywood change to #1 along Hollywood Boulevard or #4 along Santa Monica Boulevard.

To and from downtown:
Along Hollywood Blvd #1.
Along Sunset Blvd #2 .
Along Santa Monica Blvd #4 .
Along Melrose Ave #10 .
Along Wilshire Blvd #20, #21, #22 .

From downtown to:
Santa Monica #22.
Venice #33, #333, #436 (express).
Forest Lawn Cemetery #90, #91.
Exposition Park #40, #42, #81.
Huntingdon Library #79.
Burbank Studios #96.
San Pedro #446 (express), transfer to #146 for Catalina terminal, #147 for Ports O'Call Village.
Manhattan Beach/Hermosa Beach/ Redondo Beach #439 (express).
Redondo Beach/Palos Verdes #443.
Long Beach #60, #368, #456 (express).
Disneyland #460 (express).

Greyhound within LA
From downtown to:

Hollywood (15 daily; 25min).
North Hollywood (12; 40min).
Santa Monica (9; 35min).
Long Beach (12; 35min).
Anaheim (14; 45min).
Huntington Beach (1; 1hr 40min).
Newport Beach (2; 1hr 55min).

Laguna Beach (2; 2hr 20min).
Dana Point (2; 2hr 30min).
San Juan Capistrano (2; 1hr 30min).
San Clemente (8; 2hr 10min).
Glendale (4; 55min).
San Fernando (6; 1hr 20min).
San Bernardino (7; 1hr 50min).

(☎653-5050 or 1-800/822-TAXI). The basic fare is $1.90, plus $1.40 for each mile: not cheap, but good value for several people sharing over a fairly short distance. The driver won't know every street in LA but will know the major ones; ask for the nearest junction and give directions from there.

It's even possible to take a **boat** from LA: a number of daily **ferries** run to Avalon, the main (indeed only) town on the island of **Catalina**, just off the coast, from San Pedro, Long Beach or Newport Beach. Details on p.149.

Cycling

Cycling in LA may sound perverse, but in some areas it can be one of the better ways of getting around. There are beach bike paths between Santa Monica and Redondo Beach, and from Long Beach to Newport Beach, and many equally enjoyable inland pedals, notably around Griffith Park, the grand mansions of Pasadena and along the LA River. Contact *AAA* (☎741-3111), *Caltrans* (☎620-3550) or the *LA Department of Transportation* (☎485-3051) for maps and information.

The best place to **hire a bike** for the beaches is on Washington Street around Venice Pier, where there are many outlets, including *Spokes'n'Stuff* (☎310/650-1067 or ☎310/306-3332); during summer there are also bike-hire stands on the beach. For Griffith Park, use *Woody's Bicycle World*, 3157 Los Feliz Boulevard (☎661-6665). Prices range from $8 a day for a clunker to $15 a day and up for a ten-speed. For similar cost, the beachside stores also rent out **rollerskates**, although connoisseurs get equipped at the specialist *Roller Skates of America*, at 64 Windward Avenue (☎310/399-4481), off the Boardwalk in Venice.

Walking

Some people are surprised to find pavements in LA, let alone pedestrians, but **walking** is the best way to see much of downtown and a number of other districts, such as the central section of Hollywood. You can structure your strolling by taking a **guided walking tour**, the best of which are organised by the *Los Angeles Conservancy* (☎623-CITY), whose treks cover art deco landmarks and just about anything upright. Among many alternatives, they run downtown tours every Saturday, leaving the *Biltmore Hotel* on Olive Street at 10am (reservations essential; $5). You can also take guided **hikes** through the wilds of the Santa Monica Mountains and Hollywood Hills free of charge every weekend with a variety of organisations, including the *Sierra Club* (☎387-4287), the *State Parks Department* (☎818/706-1310) and the *Santa Monica Mountains Conservancy* (☎620-2021). In addition there are many marked hiking trails for self-guided exploration, some of the most inviting being in Griffith Park.

Guided coach tours

If you're feeling really lazy you could always see something of the city from the window of a **guided coach tour**. These vary greatly in cost and quality. The **mainstream tours** carrying large bus-loads of tourists around the major sights are only worth considering if you're very pushed for time, since none of them covers anything which you couldn't see for yourself at less cost. Often better value are **specialist tours** tailored to suit particular interests, and usually carrying smaller groups of people. There are also, as you'd expect in LA, the **studio tours** of film and TV production areas, covered on day trips by most of the mainstream operators, though again you'll save money by turning up independently.

MAINSTREAM TOURS

By far the most popular of the mainstream tours is the half-day "stars' homes" jaunt. Usually including the Farmer's Market, Sunset Strip, Rodeo Drive, the Hollywood Bowl, Chinese Theater, as well as, of course, the "stars' homes", this is much less tempting than it sounds – frequently no more than a view of the gate at the end of the driveway of some TV or celluloid celeb. Among other programmes are tours around the Westside at night, to the beach areas, the Queen Mary and Spruce Goose, day-long excursions to Disneyland, even shopping trips to the Mexican border city of Tijuana.

Costs range from $25–40 per person; a number of companies run tours and their leaflets are strewn over hotel lobbies and visitor centres. You can make reservations (and be picked up from) most hotels. Otherwise simply drop into or phone one of the following booking offices:

Casablanca Tours, at the *Hollywood Roosevelt*, 6362 Hollywood Blvd (☎461-0156).

Gray Line Tours and *Starline Tours,* at the Janes House, 6541 Hollywood Boulevard (☎856-5900).

Hollywood Fantasy Tours, 1721 N Highland Ave (☎1-800/782-7287).

Oskar J's Tours, 13455 Ventura Blvd (☎818/785-4039).

SPECIALIST TOURS

To give a general idea of the broad scope of specialist tours, we've listed some of the better ones below, each costing around $30 per person. For more suggestions, pick up the free *LA Visitors Guide* from hotels and visitors centres, which has a full listing. Early reservations, a week or so ahead, are essential.

The California Native, 6701 W 87th Place (☎310/642-1140). A one-day trip to the mountain and desert regions on the fringes of LA, taking in Old West historical sites and the infamous San Andreas fault, cause of the city's earthquakes.

Grave Line Tours, PO Box 931694, Hollywood (☎310/392-5501). Two and a half hours in the back of a 1969 Cadillac hearse pausing at the scene of nigh-on every eventful death, scandal, perverted sex act and drugs orgy that ever tainted Hollywood and the surrounding area. Leaves daily at noon from the corner of Hollywood Boulevard and Orchid Avenue.

Hollywood on Location, 8644 Wilshire Blvd (☎310/659-9165). Not strictly a guided tour, they provide the inside info on the TV shows and movies being shot on location around the city over a 24-hour period, and directions on how to get to them. It can make for an enjoyable fling but is hardly practical if you're without a car, and there's no guarantee that you'll see anything memorable – many sets are closed or inaccessible.

STUDIO TOURS

For some small insight into how a film or TV show is made, or just to admire the special effects, there are guided tours costing $6–20 at *Burbank Studios*, *NBC Televison Studios*, *Universal Studios*, all in the San Fernando Valley; see p.165. If you want to be **part of the audience** in a TV show, the street just outside the Chinese Theater is the major solicitation spot: TV company reps regularly appear handing out free tickets, and they'll bus you to the studio and back. All you have to do, once there, is laugh and clap on cue.

Accommodation

Finding a **place to stay** in LA is easy; finding somewhere that's cheap and well-located is difficult, though not impossible. If you're driving, of course, you needn't worry about staying in a less than ideal location – a freeway is never far away. Otherwise you'll need to be a sight more choosy about the district you plump for – getting across town can be a time-consuming business.

As always, **motels** and cheap **hotels** start at around $30 for a double, but – along with many of the major mid-range chains – many are situated in unappealing or out-of-the-way areas, and awkward to reach by public transport. Often you'll find you gain by paying a little more for a decent location in any of a number of other, non-chain mid-range hotels. Failing that, there is also a batch of **bed and breakfast inns** – though these are expensive and are frequently fully booked. For those on a budget, **hostels** are dotted all over the city, many in good locations, though at some stays are limited to a few nights; there are also a number of college and **university dorms** and **fraternity houses** that let out space during summer, although they're not necessarily any cheaper than the lowest-priced hotels. **Camping** is possible: there are a few campsites on the edge of the metropolitan area (although you can camp rough if you're hiking in the San Gabriel mountains), but getting to them is only viable if you're travelling by car.

LA is so big that if you want to see it all without constantly having to cross huge expanses, it makes sense to divide your stay between several **districts**. Prices – and options – vary by area. Downtown and its immediate vicinity has probably the best assortment of cheap hotels and plenty more in the mid-range bracket; Hollywood has a few cheap and many mid-range hotels; while more salubrious West LA, Santa Monica, Venice and Malibu are predominantly mid-to-upper range territory. All of these districts are good bases for seeing LA by car or public transport (and all have at least a hostel or some cheaper-scale accommodation), but if you've arrived on a late flight, or are leaving on an early one, it might be handy to stay near the airport. Hotels near LAX are blandly similar and in the $60–100 price range but all have complimentary limo service to and from the airport terminals. Alternatively, and much cheaper, there is a hostel and a campsite nearby.

Among options further out, the South Bay and Harbor Area carries a good selection of low to mid-range hotels (and a hostel) strung mostly along the Pacific Coast Highway, and is well-connected with other parts of town. It's only worth staying in Orange County, thirty miles southeast of downtown, if you're aiming for Disneyland or are travelling along the coast: hotels under $70 a night are a rarity, although there is a hostel and a few coastal campsites in easy reach.

Since there are no booking agencies, and visitors centres do not make accommodation reservations (though they will offer information and advice), you can only make a **booking** through a travel agent or by phoning directly; do so as early as possible (six months ahead is not uncommon, but a month is often enough), especially if arriving between May and September. Almost without exception, hotels are cheaper if booked by the week than the night. Unless stated otherwise, the hotel **prices** listed below are for double rooms per night in summer. Campsite prices, as elsewhere in the US, vary according to whether you arrive on foot or by vehicle. The prices we give are for arriving by car and pitching a tent; charges for campervans will be slightly more.

Specific **gay** accommodation options are listed on p.191.

Downtown and around

Hotels and motels

Brandon Hotel, 735 S Hartford Ave (☎483-0361). Between Seventh and Eighth Street – a dodgy neighbourhood but the hotel is safe and clean. $25–36.

City Center Motel, 1135 W Seventh St (☎628-7141). Small and informal. $38–40.

Figueroa Hotel, 939 S Figueroa St (☎1-800/421-9092). Well-placed mid-range hotel on the northern side of downtown, with a jacuzzi-equipped pool and 24-hour coffee shop. $72–84.

Holiday Inn Convention Center, 1020 S Figueroa St (☎1-800/465-4329). Big and impersonal, usually filled with convention delegates, but within easy reach of all of downtown. $95.

Holiday Inn Downtown, 750 Garland Ave (☎1-800/465-4329). On the western fringe of downtown beside the Harbor Freeway. $80–96.

Howard Johnson's LA Central, 1640 Marengo St (☎1-800/654-2000). Between downtown and East LA, with a daytime shuttle bus to the heart of downtown. $67.

Jerry's Motel, 285 S Lucas Ave (☎481-0921). Small and good value. $37–40.

Kent Inn, 920 S Figueroa St (☎626-8701). Tidy, no-frills lodgings, with a small swimming pool and self-service launderette. $50–55.

Mitchell Hotel, 1072 W Sixth St (☎481-2477). Slightly seedy but basically safe. $28.

Nutel Hotel, 1906 W Third St (☎483-6681). A few blocks from MacArthur Park and a mile from the heart of downtown. $36–44.

Orchid Hotel, 819 S Flower St (☎624-5855). Near the Financial district but a simple walk to anywhere in downtown. $35.

Park Plaza, 607 S Park View St (☎384-5281). Facing MacArthur Park, this has a sumptuous lobby and marble floor, though the rooms are ordinary. $40–45.

Royal Host Olympic Hotel, 901 W Olympic Blvd (☎626-6255). At the southwest corner of downtown, price includes a meal voucher for the adjoining restaurant. $45.

Expense account hotels

Biltmore Hotel, 506 S Grand Ave (☎1-800/421-8000). Classical architecture combined with modern luxury to make your head swim. $190.

The Westin Bonaventure, 404 S Figueroa St (☎1-800/228-3000). With gleaming futuristic towers and a built-in shopping mall, this is as close as you can get to the 21st century without leaving the present. Price includes use of the gymnasium. $185.

Bed and Breakfast

The Eastlake Inn, 1442 Kellam Ave (☎250-1620). Meticulously restored Victorian house in the preserved quarter of Angelino Heights. $65–99.

Terrace Manor 1353 Alvarado Terrace (☎381-1478). Built in 1902 and one of the better preserved in a noted terrace of Victorian houses. $60–90.

Hollywood

Hostels

Hollywood AYH Hostel, 1553 N Hudson Ave (☎467-4161). Situated in central Hollywood close to Hollywood Blvd, room rates are $29 for singles and $39 for doubles, with cheaper beds – $9 for members, $11 for others – in dorms. Maximum stay for non-members of two nights; no advance booking.

Hotels and motels

Academy Hotel, 1621 N McCadden Place (☎465-1918). Just off Hollywood Blvd. Small and pleasant. $40.

Best Western Hollywood, 6141 Franklin Ave (☎464-5181). Part of the nationwide chain; in the heart of Hollywood. $59–69.

Dunes Sunset Motel, 5625 Sunset Blvd (☎1-800/452-3863). On the eastern side of Hollywood, also good for reaching downtown. $45–59.

Hastings Hotel, 6162 Hollywood Blvd (☎464-4136). Somewhat downbeat and seedy, but if you can find a clean room, take it. It'll be the cheapest on the boulevard. $35.

Holiday Inn Hollywood, 1755 N Highland Ave (☎1-800/465-4329). Expensive and massive, but perfectly placed. $89–132.

Hotel Hollywood, 5825 Sunset Blvd (☎1-800/445-0021). The best at the price in central Hollywood. $75.

Howard's Weekly Apartments, 1738 N Whitely Ave (☎466-6943). Just off Hollywood Blvd, this imposes a minimum stay of three nights; $95–145 for a double, cheaper if booked several months in advance.

Saharan Motor Hotel, 7212 Sunset Blvd (☎874-6700). Unexciting but functional, and comparatively cheap for its useful location. $45–50.

St. Moritz Hotel, 5849 Sunset Blvd (☎467-2174). Rather poky, but the cheapest in central Hollywood. $25.

Expense account hotels

Hollywood Roosevelt, 7000 Hollywood Blvd (☎1-800/423-8262). The first hotel built for the movie greats, lately revamped and reeking with atmosphere – though the rooms are plain. $125.

West LA

Campus accommodation

Mira Hershey Hall, 801 Hilgard Ave (☎310/825-3691). Part of the UCLA campus, with two-bedded rooms available during the summer vacation (mid-June to mid-Sept) for $32. Must be booked at least a month in advance. Fraternities and sororities also have space which they rent out; details from the *Pan-Hellenic Sorority Council* (☎310/206-1285) or the *Inter Fraternity Council* (☎310/825-8409).

Hotels and motels

Bevonshire Lodge Motel, 7575 Beverly Blvd (☎936-6154). Well-situated for both West LA and Hollywood. $44.

Deseret Motel, 10572 Santa Monica Blvd (☎310/474-2035). Faded and ordinary, but the cheapest option this close to the centre of Beverly Hills. $36–50.

Hotel Del Flores, 409 N Crescent Drive (☎310/274-5114). Three blocks from Rodeo Drive. Minimum stay of two nights. $37–40.

Le Reve Hotel, 8822 Cynthia St (☎1-800/424-4443). A few blocks north of Santa Monica Blvd. Elegant suites in the style of a French provincial inn; $75 and up.

Wilshire Orange Hotel, 6060 W Eighth St (☎931-9533). Close to Hancock Park and the LA County Museum of Art; reservations require a $45 deposit. $35–55.

Expense account hotels

Beverly Hills Hotel, 9641 Sunset Blvd (☎1-800/792-76327). For power breakfasts and selling screenplays. $190.

Chateau Marmont, 8221 Sunset Blvd (☎626-1010). One-time haunt of John and Yoko; earlier saw the likes of Boris Karloff, Greta Garbo, Errol Flynn, Jean Harlow *et al*. $125 and up.

Le Parc, 733 N West Knoll (☎1-800/424-4443). Each room a suite with cooking facilities – popular with British rock stars. $145 and up.

Santa Monica, Venice and Malibu

Hostels

Interclub Network Hostel, 2221 Lincoln Blvd, Venice (☎310/305-0250). Six-bed dorms and a free shuttle bus to and from LAX. Closed 11am-4pm, with a 1am curfew. Five-day maximum stay. $12 per person on production of a passport or backpack.

Jim's at the Beach, 17 Brooks Ave, Venice (☎310/399-4018). Beachside dormitory accommodation on production of a passport. $15 per night; $90 per week.

Marina Hostel, 2915 Yale Ave, Marina del Rey (☎310/301-3983). On the edge of yachty Marina del Rey but only a mile from Venice Beach. No curfew, open 24 hours. $12 per person.

Santa Monica International Hostel, 1436 Second St, Santa Monica (☎310/392-0325). Newly built *AYH* hostel just a few strides from the Santa Monica sands. Members $9, others $13.

Share-Tel International Hostel, 20 Brooks Ave, Venice (☎310/392-0325). Small apartments for several people sharing. $13 per night or $90 for a week.

Venice Beach Cotel, 25 Windward Ave, Venice (☎310/399-7649). Very beachy atmosphere: dorm beds for $12–15 and private, ocean-view rooms for $28–45.

Hotels and motels

Breakers Motel, 1501 Ocean Ave (☎1-800/634-7333). A block from Santa Monica Pier. Large airy rooms. $75.

El Tovar by the Sea, 603 Ocean Ave (☎310/451-1820). Every room has a sea-view. $75.

Hotel Carmel, 201 Broadway (☎310/451-2469). The best bet in Santa Monica, two blocks from the beach. $35 a night, $210 a week.

Hotel Santa Monica, 3102 Pico Blvd (☎1-800/231-7679). In the heart of Santa Monica itself, a mile from the beach. $50–65.

Malibu Riviera Motel, 28920 Pacific Coast Hwy (☎213/457-9503). $55 rooms just outside town, ideal if you're planning a drive up the coast.

Santa Monica Travelodge, 1525 Ocean Ave (☎1-800/255-3050). One of the nationwide chain. $58–80.

Star Dust Motor Hotel, 3202 Wilshire Blvd (☎310/828-4581). A mile from the beach. Doubles for $50, and outside "cottages", holding up to four people. $60 nightly, $350 weekly.

Venice Beach Hotel, 25 Windward Ave (☎310/399-7649). With some of the cheapest rooms in Venice, and a relaxed atmosphere. $45.

Expense account hotels

Santa Monica Beach Hotel, 1700 Ocean Ave (☎310/458-6700). Santa Monica's first new hotel for twenty years and worth the wait: a deluxe affair overlooking the ocean and the Santa Monica pier, often in demand as a film-set. From $185.

Campsites

Leo Carrillo State Beach Park (☎818/706-1310). Located in Malibu partly on the beach, 25 miles northwest of Santa Monica on Pacific Coast Highway, and served twice an hour in summer by RTD bus #434. $12.

Near LAX

Hostels

Bill Baker International Youth Hostel (AYH), 8015 S Sepulveda Blvd (☎776-0922). Summer only. Connected by RTD bus #42 with the LAX transit terminal. Open 7.30am–9pm, with an 11.30pm curfew. Members $7, others $10.

Hotels and motels

Capri Motel, 8620 Airport Blvd (☎645-7700). A mile northeast of LAX, with a swimming pool. $40–60.

The Cockatoo Inn, 4334 Imperial Highway (☎1-800/262-5286). This country-style inn may be in a faceless suburb, but it's just a stone's throw from LAX and serves a complimentary breakfast. $45–50.

Geneva Budget Motel, 321 W Manchester Blvd (☎677-9171). The cheapest in the area. No limo service but a cab from LAX should be under ten dollars. $40.

LAX Hotel, 1804 E Sycamore Ave (☎1-800/421-5781). Just south of LAX; convenient for the South Bay. $58–67.

Trade Winds Hotel, 4200 W Century Blvd (☎1-800/852-0012). In boring Inglewood, but every room is a suite, and there's a complimentary champagne hour. $60.

Campsites

Dockweiler Beach County Park (☎310/305-9545). On Vista del Mar, almost at the western end of the LAX runways. $10.

The South Bay and Harbor Area

Hostels

Los Angeles International Hostel (AYH), 3601 S Gaffey St, building #613 (☎310/831-8109), *RTD* bus #232 passes close by, and the *SuperShuttle* from LAX will bring you here for $13. Ideal for seeing San Pedro, Palos Verdes and the whole Harbor area, and overlooking the ocean. Open 7–9.30am and 4pm–midnight. Members $9.25, others $12.25; private rooms $22.

Hotels and motels

At Ocean Motel, 50 Atlantic Ave (☎310/435-8369). Serviceable base from which to explore Long Beach and vicinity. $45.

City Center Motel, 255 Atlantic Ave (☎310/435-2483). Unexceptional but pefectly adequate for a couple of nights. $46.

Palos Verdes Inn, 1700 S Pacific Coast Highway (☎1-800/421-9241). Affordable luxury on the edge of Redondo Beach, and at the foot of the Palos Verdes hills. $85–93.

Seahorse Motel, 233 N Sepulveda Blvd (☎1-800/854-3380). In Manhattan Beach, a few blocks from the sands. $58.

Sea Sprite Ocean Front Apartment Motel, 1016 Strand (☎310/376-6933). Small and next to the beach. $42–55.

TraveLodge Hermosa Beach, 901 Aviation Blvd (☎1-800/553-1145). A branch of the uninspiring, but functional, chain. $59–64.

Quality Inn Torrance, 4111 Pacific Coast Highway (☎1-800/228-5151). A mile inland from Redondo Beach. $52.

Hotel Queen Mary, Pier J, Long Beach (☎1-800/421-3732). The rooms are cramped converted cabins inside the former ocean liner. $80 and up.

Around Disneyland

Hostels

Fullerton Hacienda Hostel (AYH), 1700 N Harbor Blvd (☎714/738-3721). New and comfortable, on the site of a former dairy farm. Open 4pm–9.30am. *OCTD* bus 43A stops outside. Members $8.50, others $11.50.

Hotels and motels

Anaheim Angel Inn, 1800 E Kattela Ave (☎1-800/358-4400). Fairly plain but well-priced and placed. $36–59.

Motel 6, 921 S Beach Blvd (☎714/827-9450). Closer to Knotts Berry Farm than Disneyland but the cheapest around. $35–45.

Park Place Inn, 1544 S Harbor Blvd (☎714/776-4800). The newest of two dozen hotels ringing Disneyland all owned by the Stovall family and giving good value. Others in the chain, all costing around $60, include *Apollo Inn*, 1741 S West St (☎714/772-9750), *Cosmic Age Lodge*, 1717 S Harbor Blvd (☎714/635-6550), and *Space Age Lodge*, 1176 W Katella Ave (☎714/827-9450).

Expense account hotels

The Disneyland Hotel, 1150 W Cerritos Ave (☎714/778-6600). The price does not include admission to the park, although the Disneyland monorail does stop right outside. $150 and up.

The Orange County Coast

Hostels

Huntington Beach Colonial Hostel (AYH), 421 Eighth St, Huntington Beach (☎714/536-3315). Four blocks from the beach and mostly double rooms. Sleeping bags are allowed. It's closed between 9.30am and 4.30pm, and operates an 11pm curfew, although you can hire a key for $1 (plus a $10 deposit). Members $7.50, others $9; ten-day stays for $65 when there's space.

Hotels and motels

Hotel Laguna, 425 S Coast Highway (☎714/494-1151). In the centre of Laguna Beach. If you have the cash, this is the place to spend it. Atmospheric and comfortable, and nearly every room has a sea-view. $85–110.

Sail-Inn Motel, 2627 Newport Blvd (☎714/675-1841). Basic accommodation but the least costly in the Newport area. Close to Balboa Peninsula. $75–80.

Seacliff Motel, 1661 S Coast Highway (☎714/494-9717). A mile south of Laguna Beach but right on the ocean. $80–90.

Sea Lark Motel, 2274 Newport Blvd (☎1-800/858-8956). Three miles inland from Newport Beach, but certainly the cheapest in the vicinity. $35.

Campsites

Bolsa Chica Campground (☎714/848-1658). Facing the ocean in Huntington Beach. $12.

Doheny State Beach Campground (☎714/496-6171). At Dana Point, this is often packed with families, especially at weekends. $12.

San Clemente State Beach Campground (☎714/492-7146). Two miles south of San Clemente. $12.

The San Gabriel and San Fernando Valleys

Hotels and motels

Belair-Bed & Breakfast, 941 N Frederic Ave (☎818/848-9227). By far the best value in Burbank. $35.

Econo Lodge, 1203 E Colorado Blvd, Pasadena (☎818/449-3170). Friendly budget chain motel, usefully placed for exploring Pasadena. $40—45.

Safari Inn, 1911 W Olive Ave (☎1-800/845-5544). Pricey, but handy for visiting the studios. $56 and up.

Expense account hotels

The Huntington Hotel, 1401 S Knoll, Pasadena (☎818/568-3900). Utterly luxurious refurbishing of a landmark 1906 hotel discreetly tucked away in residential Pasadena. From $145.

Campsites

Chilao Flat, on Hwy-2 twenty miles northeast of Pasadena (☎818/574-1613). The only campsite in the San Gabriel Mountains which you can drive to, though there are plenty of others accessible on foot. For more details contact the Angeles National Forest Ranger Station at 701 N Santa Anita Ave, Arcadia (☎818/574-1613).

LA'S MUSEUMS

Aerospace Building p.113.
Avalon Museum p.150.
Burbank Studios p.165.
Cabrillo Marine Museum p.147.
California Afro-American Museum p.113.
Children's Museum p.106.
Fisher Gallery p.112.
Forest Lawn Museum p.164.
George C. Page Discovery Center p.130.
Gene Autry Western Heritage Museum p.126.
Grier-Musser Museum p.112.
Hall of Economics and Finance p.113.
Hall of Health p.113.
Hollywood Wax Museum p.123.
Huntington Library and Art Collections p.163.
J. Paul Getty Museum p.142.
La Brea Tar Pits p.130
LA County Museum of Art p.129.
LA County Museum of Natural History p.113.

Laguna Beach Museum of Art p.158.
Long Beach Museum of Art p.148.
Maritime Museum (San Pedro) p.148.
Max Factor Museum p.122.
Movieland Wax Museum p.153.
Municipal Art Gallery p.120.
Museum of Contemporary Art (MOCA) p.106.
Museum of Flying p.140.
Museum of Neon Art (MONA) p.109.
Museum of Science and Industry p.113.
Newport Harbor Art Museum p.157.
Norton Simon Museum p.161.
Pacific Asia Museum p.160.
Richard Nixon Library and Birthplace p.155.
Skirball Museum p.112.
Southwest Museum p.118.
St Elmo's Village p.130.
Universal Studios p.165.
Wells Fargo Museum p.107.
Will Rogers Museum p.142.

THE CITY

Spilling over a vast flat basin and often lacking well-defined divisions, **LA** is not a city in the usual sense. Instead, it's a massive conglomeration of inter-connected districts, not all of which have that much in common. Travelling from one side of LA to the other will take you through virtually every social extreme imaginable, from mind-boggling beachside luxury to the severest inner-city poverty anywhere in the US – a chaos that's the result of the last century's rapid growth within a confined area. With the basin bordered by desert to the east, mountains (north) and ocean (west), the millions of new arrivals who have poured in during the last hundred years have had to fill the spaces between what were once geographically quite isolated and small communities, creating a metropolis on the most mammoth scale.

If LA has a heart, however, it's **downtown**, in the centre of the basin with towering office blocks punctuating what's for the most part a very low and level skyline. With everything from avant-garde art to the abject dereliction of Skid Row, downtown offers a taste of almost everything you'll find elsewhere around the city, compressed (unusually for LA) into an area of small, easily walkable blocks. It's a good place to get your initial bearings, and, usefully, the hub of the transport network. **Around Downtown**, a serviceable label for a hotch-potch of areas with little in common except being adjacent to or fanning out from downtown, demonstrates still more of LA's diversity: from the elaborate Victorian relics of the turn-of-the-century suburbs, and the later art deco buildings which characterised the city in the Twenties, to the centre of LA's enormous Hispanic population, home to some rare sights of enjoyable street-life, and the sprawl of dull and desperate neighbourhoods that make up South Central LA.

Away from downtown, you'll probably spend most of your time in the broad corridor that runs twenty-five miles west to the coast. Here are LA's best-known and most interesting districts, the first of which, **Hollywood**, has streets caked with movie legend – even if the genuine glamour is long gone. Tourists flock here, and it's also where some of LA's most freaky street people choose to parade themselves. Adjoining **West LA**, on the other hand, is home to the city's newest money, shown off in the incredibly expensive shops of Beverly Hills and the posey eateries and nightspots of the Sunset Strip, and on its western edge merging into **Santa Monica and Venice** – the quintessential coastal LA of palm trees, white sands, and laid-back living. The coastline itself is perhaps the major draw, stretching north from here twenty miles to the northern edge of LA and **Malibu**, noted for its celebrity residences and their keenly guarded privacy.

South along the coast from Venice, the three **South Bay beach cities** are quieter, lived in by middle-class, middle-brow commuters, and a long way in spirit from the more bustling and fad-conscious portions of the city. The beaches are the sole focus of attention here, and are good enough to warrant a short visit, the bluffs and coves leading on to the **Harbor Area** – though, again, despite recent facelifts and some mildly enjoyable resort-areas, there's nothing that will detain you for more than half a day.

Orange County, directly east of the Harbor Area, is mainly lifeless suburban sprawl, and the only reason most people come here is to visit **Disneyland**, the city's biggest single tourist attraction and the granddaddy of all theme parks. If you're not keen on seeing "the happiest place on Earth" – as Disneyland calls

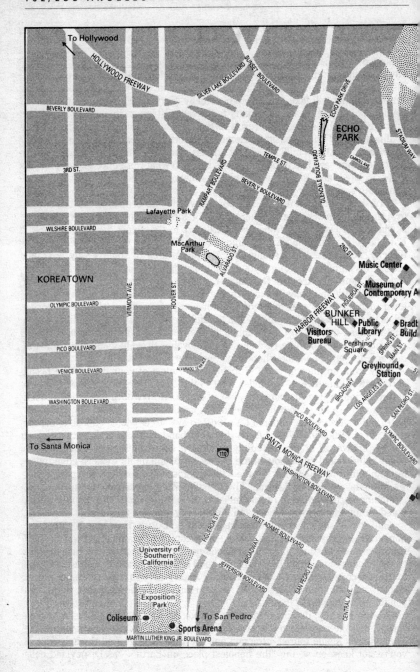

To Hollywood

HOLLYWOOD FREEWAY

SILVER LAKE BOULEVARD

SUNSET BOULEVARD

ECHO PARK DRIVE

BEVERLY BOULEVARD

ECHO PARK

STADIUM WAY

TEMPLE ST.

CARROLL AVE.

3RD ST.

RAMPART BOULEVARD

BEVERLY BOULEVARD

GLENDALE BOULEVARD

Lafayette Park

WILSHIRE BOULEVARD

MacArthur Park

ALVARADO ST.

2ND ST.

Music Center

KOREATOWN

VERMONT AVE.

HOOVER ST.

Museum of Contemporary Art

OLYMPIC BOULEVARD

FIGUEROA ST.

HARBOR FREEWAY

BUNKER HILL

Public Library

Bradbury Building

PICO BOULEVARD

Visitors Bureau

Pershing Square

SPRING ST.

MAIN ST.

VENICE BOULEVARD

ALVARADO TERRACE

Greyhound Station

SAN PEDRO ST.

WASHINGTON BOULEVARD

BROADWAY

LOS ANGELES ST.

To Santa Monica

110

PICO BOULEVARD

OLYMPIC BOULEVARD

SANTA MONICA FREEWAY

WASHINGTON BOULEVARD

FIGUEROA ST.

WEST ADAMS BOULEVARD

University of Southern California

BROADWAY

JEFFERSON BOULEVARD

SAN PEDRO ST.

CENTRAL AVE.

Exposition Park

To San Pedro

Coliseum

Sports Arena

MARTIN LUTHER KING JR. BOULEVARD

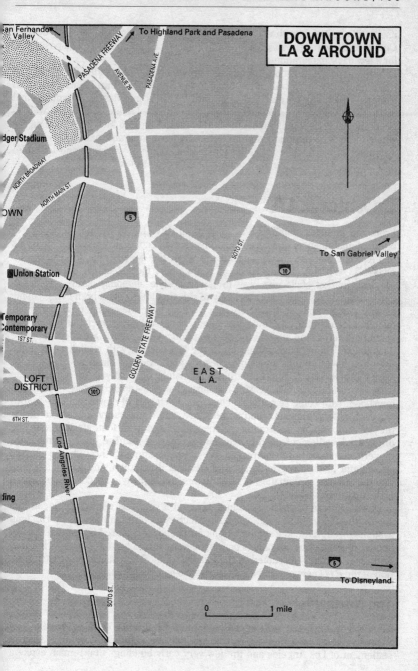

San Fernando Valley

To Highland Park and Pasadena

PASADENA FREEWAY

AVENUE 26

PASADENA AVE

DOWNTOWN
LA & AROUND

dger Stadium

NORTH BROADWAY

NORTH MAIN ST

OWN

5

SOTO ST

To San Gabriel Valley

Union Station

10

emporary
Contemporary

1ST ST

GOLDEN STATE FREEWAY

EAST
L.A.

LOFT
DISTRICT

101

6TH ST

Los Angeles River

ding

5

To Disneyland

SOTO ST

0   1 mile

itself – it's best to hug the coast and continue south, along the **Orange County Coast**, whose string of surprisingly individualistic communities is well-positioned for a few days' exploration on the way to San Diego.

In the opposite direction, LA has also grown on the other side of the hills that make up the northern wall of the basin to the **San Gabriel and San Fernando Valleys**, which stretch east and west until LA fades into desert, mountains and ocean. The valleys are distanced from mainstream LA life socially as well as geographically, their inhabitants the butt of most Angeleno hick jokes, and on the whole there is no reason to venture here. The few honourable exceptions include a number of worthwhile art collections and a couple of working (and tourable) film studios, as well as the most famous of LA's cemeteries.

Downtown LA

From the homeless families on the steps of City Hall to the phallic towers of multinational finance, nowhere else do the social, economic and ethnic divisions of LA clash quite as loudly and clearly as in the square mile that makes up **DOWNTOWN LA**. In the space of a few short blocks, adobe buildings and Mexican market stalls give way to Japanese-style shopping plazas and avant-garde art galleries, and you're as likely to rub shoulders with a high-flying yuppie as with a down-and-out drunk. Though it's long been the commercial and enter-tainment focus of the city, and always the seat of local government, as businesses spread out across the basin in the post-war boom years, so the area became more dilapidated. Things have picked up in the last decade, with revitalisation initia-tives that have brought museums, theatres and a rash of plush new condos for young professionals. But these have ultimately only served to intensify the extremes, and downtown remains the most changed – and changing – LA neigh-bourhood, with some remarkable contrasts. Each part of downtown has its own share of history, museums and architecture, and it makes most sense to divide the area into simple geographic segments and see it on foot, starting with the original LA settlement on the **Northside**, crossing into the brasher and more modern corporate-tower-dominated **Westside**, continuing through the chaotic streets and historic movie theatres of **Central downtown**, and finally stepping into the strange combination of street bums and high-style art collections which make up the **Eastside**.

Downtown can easily be seen in a day, and if your feet get tired you can hop aboard the *DASH* **buses** (25¢ flat-fare) which run every ten minutes on two loop systems through the key sections (look for the silver-coloured bus stops). Forget about bringing a car: not only is parking expensive and hard to come by, but traf-fic is also constantly disrupted by the building of the Metrorail; in any case it's the hub of the *RTD* network and easily accessible by public transport.

The Northside

To see downtown LA, start at the beginning. **El Pueblo de Los Angeles**, off Alameda Street, was the site of the original late eighteenth-century Mexican settlement of Los Angeles and the few very early buildings that remain evoke a strong sense of LA's Spanish and Mexican origins. The **plaza church** is the city's oldest and now serves as a sanctuary for Central American refugees who have come to the US illegally (the right of immigration officers to enter the church to evict them is an ongoing controversy). There's also the city's first **Firehouse**, with a small but intriguing roomful of firefighting gear, and the handsome mission-style **Pico House**, now closed to the public but LA's most luxurious hotel when it opened in 1870. **Olvera Street**, which runs north from the plaza, is a less successful restoration, contrived in part as a pseudo-Mexican village market and saved only by its lighthearted grouping of food and craft stalls.

Olvera Street was the creation of one Christine Stirling, who along with other powerful citizens and help from the city government tore down the slum she found here in 1926 and built much of what you see today, incorporating some of the salvageable historic structures. For the next twenty years she organised fiestas and worked to popularise the city's Mexican heritage while living in the early nineteenth-century **Avila Adobe** at 10 Olvera Street – touted as the oldest structure in Los Angeles, although almost entirely rebuilt out of reinforced concrete following the 1971 earthquake. Inside the house are two **museums** (Tues–Sun 10am–3pm; free) – one an idealised view of pueblo-era domestic life; the other, across the landscaped courtyard, telling the cleaned-up, official, version of how the LA authorities connived to get a secure supply of water for the city (for the real story, see p.166).

Across the street, a **Visitors Center** in the Sepulveda House offers the usual information, and shows an informative free film (Mon–Sat 11am & 2pm) on the history of Los Angeles. For a more detailed look at the Pueblo area, there are also free **guided walking tours** (☎628-1274) leaving on the hour between 10am and 1pm, Tuesday to Saturday, from the building next to the Firehouse.

Union Station, across Alameda from Olvera Street, echoes LA's roots in a rather different way – a magnificent example of monumental mission-style municipal architecture, finished in 1939. The running-down of the country's rail network means it's not the evocative point of arrival and departure it was conceived as, but the building itself is in fine condition, with a spacious vaulted lobby, heavy wooden benches, intact deco signs, and flanking courtyards planted in informal combinations of fig trees and jacarandas. Once it thronged with passengers; now it sees just a few trains each day, although its projected future use as a terminal on the Metrorail should go some way towards bringing back the crowds.

Union Station may be a fine expression of monumental urban architecture but its construction wasn't welcomed by everyone, having been built on the site of LA's original Chinatown. Many of the displaced families moved to an area just west and north of Olvera Street, and by 1938 what's now **CHINATOWN** was established, along North Broadway and North Spring Streets. It's not the bustling affair you'll find in a number of other US cities, however, and there's little point in turning up here except to eat in one of the restaurants (see p.179).

Across the channel of the Santa Ana Freeway from Olvera Street, the **Civic Center** is a collection of plodding bureaucratic office buildings around a lifeless plaza. The exception to this, the art deco **City Hall**, known to the world through LA cop badges seen in TV shows ever since *Dragnet*, was as late as 1960 the city's tallest structure, and there's a 360-degree view of sprawling Los Angeles from the observation deck at the top of its 28-storey tower.

Northeast of City Hall, at 310 N Main Street, the **Children's Museum** (summer Tues–Fri 11.30am–5pm, weekends 10am–5pm, rest of the year Wed & Thurs 2.30pm–5pm, weekends 10am–5pm; children $3, adults $3.50 but free on Wed and Thurs afternoon), is largely uninspired but a good place to dump the kids. More edifying, on the south side of the Civic Center plaza, are the free tours of the **Los Angeles Times** building (11am and 3pm weekdays), which show how the West Coast's biggest and some say best newspaper is put together. The *Times* of fifty years ago was the right-wing mouthpiece of its power-hungry owner, Harry Chandler. Though the paper gained a liberal reputation through the Seventies and became well respected for its coverage of events in Central America, its editorial stance has again shifted, reflecting the conservative swing of the US in the Eighties.

The Westside

Up until a century ago the area south of the Civic Center, **BUNKER HILL**, was LA's most elegant neighbourhood, its elaborate mansions and houses connected by funicular railway to the growing business district down below. As with all of downtown, though, the population moved before long to stylish new suburbs and many of the old homes were converted to rooming houses, later providing the backdrop for many low-budget detective movies.

The funicular, too, which ran above Third Street between Hill and Olive, was torn down in 1969 to make way for the massive office towers which now form the heart of the growing **FINANCIAL DISTRICT**. As you'd imagine, this isn't the city's most fascinating neighbourhood. Most of the fifty-storey towers have a concourse of shops and restaurants at their base, high-style shopping malls designed to provide some synthetic sort of street-life for the brokers and traders, jaded from the day-to-day routine of setting up mega-buck deals.

The Museum of Contemporary Art

The largest and most ambitious development in the district is the **California Plaza** on Grand Avenue, a billion-dollar complex of offices and luxury condominiums being built around the **Museum of Contemporary Art (MOCA)** (Tues–Sun 11am–6pm, Thurs & Fri until 8pm, closed Mon; $4, students $2, free Thurs 5–8pm), which opened at the end of 1986 in an effort to raise the cultural stature of the area (and of LA) and was funded by a one percent tax on the value of all new downtown construction. Designed by showman architect Arata Isozaki as a "small village in the valley of the skyscrapers", it justifies a visit for the building alone, whose playful exterior adds a welcome touch of colour to the often dour downtown skyscrapers.

The barrel-vaulted entrance gate on Grand Avenue opens on to an outdoor sculpture plaza, off which are the ticket booth, the museum store and the entrance to the administration wing, covered in diamond-shaped green aluminum panels with bright pink joints. A stairway leads down from the upper plaza to a smaller courtyard, between the museum café and, last, the main entrance to the galleries.

The brainchild of the high-rollers of the LA art world, MOCA was put together as a gesture of goodwill – and, cynics say, to raise the value of the works they loan for display. Much of the gallery is used for temporary exhibitions, but the bulk of the permanent collection is from the Abstract Expressionist period, work by Frank Kline, Mark Rothko and the impressive multi-media memorials of Antoni Tapies and Jean Fautrier. There's also Pop Art, espoused by Robert Rauschenberg's urban junk and Claes Oldenburg's papier-mâché representations of hamburgers and gaudy fast foods.

That said, there are no singularly great pieces among the established names, and you can usually find much more compelling ideas expressed amid the paintings and sculpture of the rising stars in the stock bequeathed by collector Barry Lowen. These are hard to categorise but are something of a greatest hits collection of work by artists you're likely to come across in the trendier city galleries – Jennifer Bartlett, David Salle, Anselm Kiefer, Eric Fischl, Ellsworth Kelly, to name a few – and side-by-side they show off the diversity and accomplishment of contemporary American art.

The theatre on the lower floor hosts some bizarre multi-media shows and performance works, as well as the more standard lectures and seminars (☎621-2766 for details). A ticket to MOCA also gets you into The Temporary Contemporary, the museum's open exhibition space on the Eastside of downtown, described on p.109.

Around MOCA

If MOCA's highbrow tone gets too demanding, there's relief in the shallow but amusing **Wells Fargo Museum** (Mon–Fri 9am–4pm; free) at the base of the shiny red towers of the *Wells Fargo Center*. It tells the history of *Wells Fargo & Co*, the bank of Gold Rush California, with among other things a two-pound nugget of gold, some mining equipment and a simulated chance to experience the stagecoach journey from St Louis to San Francisco in 1859.

A block away, the unmistakeable shining glass tubes of the **Westin Bonaventure Hotel** defined the skyline of a futuristic Los Angeles in the movie *Bladerunner*. Its lobby doubles as a shopping mall and office complex – an M.C. Escher computer-generated drawing of spiralling ramps and balconies that is disorientating enough to make it necessary to consult a colour-coded map every twenty yards to remind you where you are. But brace yourself and step inside for a ride in the glass lifts that run up and down the outside of the building, giving views over much of downtown and beyond.

The *Bonaventure*'s lifts also give a bird's-eye view of the fire-damaged shell of one of LA's finest buildings, the Los Angeles **Public Library** across the street, which has been closed since an arson attack a few years back. The concrete walls and piers of the lower floors, enlivened by Lee Laurie's figurative sculptures symbolising the Virtues of Philosophy and the Arts (currently obscured by the renovation work) form a pedestal for the squat central tower, which is topped by a brilliantly coloured pyramid roof. The library, built in 1926, was the last work of architect Bertram Goodhue, and its straightforward pared-down manner set the tone for many LA buildings, most obviously the City Hall.

In exchange for planning permission, the developers of the **Library Tower** office block across Fifth Street – the tallest building west of Chicago – have agreed to pay some fifty million dollars toward the restoration of the library. Huge steps around the base of the tower curve up to Bunker Hill between a series of terraces with outdoor cafés and boutiques – not wildly thrilling but as good a way to ascend the hill as any.

Central Downtown

Though it's hard to picture now, **Broadway** once formed the core of Los Angeles' most fashionable shopping and entertainment district. Today many of its movie palaces and department stores are the clothing and jewellery stores of a bustling Hispanic community, a cash-rich hustle and bustle where pesos change hands as much as dollars, all to a soundtrack of salsa music blaring from ghetto-blasters nailed to the wall. The most vivid taste of the area is to be had amid the pickled pigs' feet, sheeps' brains and other delicacies inside the **Grand Central Market**, on Broadway between Third and Fourth. It's a real scrum but the best place (at least for carnivores) to enter the spirit of things.

The **Bradbury Building** across the street makes for a break from the mayhem of the market, its magnificent sunlit atrium surrounded by wrought-iron balconies, and open-cage lifts alternating up and down on opposite sides of the narrow court, with elaborate open staircases at either end. The building is an art director's dream, and most of the income for this 1893 office building does indeed come from film-shoots.

Aside from the street-life, the best thing about Broadway is the great movie palaces of the **THEATER DISTRICT** – monuments to escapism whose "enchanted realms" still function today. For the price of a ticket (around $5) you can view the glorious interiors for yourself. Two are especially noteworthy: next to the Grand Central Market, the opulent 1918 **Million Dollar Theater**, its whimsical terracotta facade mixing buffalo heads with bald eagles in Hollywood Spanish Baroque, was built by theatre magnate Sid Grauman, who went on to build the Egyptian and Chinese theatres in Hollywood. The **Los Angeles Theater**, at 615 S Broadway, is even more extravagant, built in ninety days for the world premiere of Charlie Chaplin's *City Lights* in 1931, and crowning what had become the largest concentration of movie palaces in the world. The plush lobby behind the triumphal arch facade is lined by marble columns supporting an intricate mosaic ceiling, while the 1800-seat auditorium is enveloped by trompe l'oeil murals and lighting effects.

With the advent of TV, the rise of the motor car and LA's drift to the suburbs, the movie palaces lost their customers and fell into decline. **Pershing Square**'s underground car park was an attempt to bring the punters back – a task in which it failed, and many of the movie houses are these days showing exploitation and Spanish-language films to sadly depleted numbers. Pershing Square itself also hasn't fared well, turned from what was downtown's only public park and political focal-point into a miserable target for litter and down-and-outs.

The buildings around the square have – albeit after years of neglect – emerged rather better. The most prominent of these, the **Biltmore Hotel**, stands over the west side of the square, its three brick towers rising from a Renaissance Revival arcade along Olive Street. The grand old lobby that was the original main entrance has an intricately painted Spanish beamed ceiling which you can admire over a pricey glass of wine. A block south, the art deco **Oviatt Building** is another sumptuous survivor. The ground floor housed LA's most elegant haberdashery, where dapper types like Clark Gable and John Barrymore would shop, and has since been converted into the exquisite and expensive *Rex II* restaurant. If you can't afford this, the lifts, which open on to the street level exterior lobby, are at least worth studying, with hand-carved oak panelling, designed and executed by Parisian craftsman Réné Lalique.

The Eastside

A block east of Broadway, downtown takes a downturn in LA's **SKID ROW**: a shabby, downtrodden area around Los Angeles Street between the *Greyhound* station and City Hall that has a slightly threatening air – though by day at least it's fairly safe. It's been a seedy neighbourhood for some time now, and it has the arty associations to match. The Doors posed for the cover of their album, *Morrison Hotel*, here, and Charles Bukowski is just the latest of the booze'n' broads school of writers to use the bars and poolhalls as a source of material. Otherwise there's nothing of interest; indeed, over the last ten years the northern boundaries of Skid Row have been pushed back by the sanitised shopping precincts of **LITTLE TOKYO** – the clearest evidence of the Japanese money which accounts for most of the new construction in LA these days. For a quick taste of this, the place to make for is the **Japanese American Cultural and Community Center**, 244 S San Pedro Street, for its **Doizaki Gallery** (Tues–Sun noon–5pm; free), showing traditional and contemporary Japanese art and calligraphy. The centre also includes the **Japan America Theater**, where Kabuki theatre groups regularly perform.

From the cultural center, a zig-zagging pathway takes you through the Shoji screens, sushi bars, shops and Zen rock gardens of **Village Plaza**, and out of Little Tokyo to the **Temporary Contemporary** at 152 N Central Avenue (hours and prices same as MOCA, p.106) – an exhibition space in a converted police garage that shows works by contemporary artists other LA museums won't touch. Initially developed, as its name suggests, as the temporary home of the Museum of Contemporary Art, the success of the gallery was such that it was kept on as an alternative exhibition space to the more refined main building. A spaceframe awning and steam-shrouded bamboo garden marks the entrance, otherwise hidden away behind a multi-storey car park and derelict buildings.

Many of the warehouses and industrial premises east of Alameda Street have been converted into a **LOFT DISTRICT** of artists' studios, small galleries, and best of all, the world's only **Museum of Neon Art (MONA)**, at 704 Traction Avenue (Tues–Sat 11am–6pm; $2.50), which preserves and displays works of neon, electric and kinetic art, and has some great old flashing signs and a changing exhibit of engaging contemporary pieces. Among the many **galleries**, mostly open between 11am and 5pm every day except Mondays, one of the most interesting is the artist-operated **Los Angeles Contemporary Exhibitions (LACE)**, 1804 Industrial Street – three expansive floors of painting, sculpture and video installations at the cutting edge of the LA art scene, plus a performance space and well-stocked bookshop. More commercially orientated but still good for a look are *LA Artcore* and *Double Rocking "G"* both at 652 S Mateo Street, and *Cirrus*, 542 S Alameda Street, which has an outstanding range of prints and monographs.

Around Downtown

The LA sprawl begins as soon as you leave downtown, the diverse environs of which tend to be forgotten quarters, scythed by freeways, and with large distances separating their few points of interest. Added together, however, there's quite a bit worth seeing, in areas either on the perimeters of downtown or simply beginning here and continuing for many miles to the south or east. The districts immediately west of downtown, around **Angelino Heights** and **Echo Park**, are where the upper crust of LA society luxuriously relocated itself at the turn of the century in groupings of wooden Victorian houses, mostly in impressive states of preservation – vivid indicators of the prosperity of their time, just as the nondescript drabness surrounding them now evidences the blight which later befell the area. Much the same applies to the streets around **MacArthur Park**, although they still contain some of the impressive commercial architecture which set the stylistic tone for the city in the Twenties.

The other areas which surround downtown are too widely separated for it to make sense to try to see them consecutively; each is ten to thirty minutes by car or bus away from the next. Directly south of downtown, the long succession of unimaginative low-rent housing developments is interrupted only by the contrast of the **USC Campus**, populated by bright-eyed well-off students, and the neighbouring **Exposition Park**, with acres of gardens and several museums – a couple of which merit going out of your way to see. Beyond here, the deprivation resumes, leading into LA's most depressed area – the vast urban nightmare of **South Central LA**. A chilling counterpoint to the commercial vibrancy of downtown, this forms the main route between downtown and the Harbor Area, and, while it's not a place to linger, it does give a picture of the grim reality behind LA's glamourous myths. An immensely more appealing place to visit is the Hispanic-dominated **East LA**, the largest Mexican city outside Mexico, and a buzzing district of markets, shops and street-corner music that gives a tangible insight into the other, relatively unacknowledged, side of LA. North of downtown is rather less hectic, and holds amid the preserved homes of the **Highland Park District**, the **Southwest Museum**, which has a fine and extremely comprehensive collection of Native American artefacts.

Angelino Heights and Echo Park

Long before there was a Malibu or a Beverly Hills, some of the most desirable addresses in Los Angeles were in **ANGELINO HEIGHTS**, LA's first suburb, laid out in the flush of a property boom at the end of the 1880s on a hilltop a little way west of downtown. Though the boom soon went bust, the elaborate houses that were built here, especially along **Carroll Avenue**, have survived and have recently been restored as reminders of the optimism and energy of the city's early years. There's a dozen or so in all, and most repay a look for their catalogue of late-Victorian details – wraparound verandahs, turrets and pediments, set oddly against the downtown skyline; one, with a weird Great Pyramid roof, was even used as the set for the haunted house in Michael Jackson's *Thriller* video. All the homes are private, and not generally open to visitors, though the Angelino Heights Community Organisation (☎413-8756) sometimes offers tours.

At the foot of the hill, to the west of Angelino Heights, **Echo Park** is a tiny park of palm trees set around a lake. In the large, white, arcaded building on the northern edge, the evangelist **Aimee Semple McPherson** used to preach fire and brimstone sermons to five thousand people, with thousands more listening in on the radio – the first in a long line of network evangelists. "Sister Aimee" died in mysterious circumstances in 1944, but the building is still used for services by her Four Square Gospel ministry, who dunk converts in the huge water tank during mass baptisms.

MacArthur Park and around

Wilshire Boulevard leaves downtown between Sixth and Seventh Streets as the main surface route across twenty-five miles of Los Angeles to the Santa Monica beaches. It was named by and for entrepreneur Gaylord Wilshire, who made a fortune selling an electrical device that claimed to restore greying hair to its original colour. Wilshire used the proceeds from this and other ventures to buy up a large plot of land west of Westlake Park, later renamed **MacArthur Park**, through the centre of which he ran the wide thoroughfare. When the property market collapsed in 1888, Gaylord discovered politics, ran for Congress (and lost), and later moved to England, where he became friends with George Bernard Shaw and the Fabian Socialists.

The park has since fallen into disrepair, but its patches of green and its large lake provide the nearest relief to the sidewalks of downtown. Half a mile west, the **Bullocks Wilshire** department store is a seminal building of art deco Los Angeles, the most complete and unaltered example of late 1920s architecture in the city. Built in 1929 in what was then a beanfield in the suburbs, *Bullocks* was the first department store outside downtown, and the first to embrace the automobile, with its main entrance (though the foyer is lavish enough) at the back of the building adjacent to the car park. Transportation was the spirit of the time, and throughout the building there are mural and mosaic images of planes and ocean liners that glow with activity in a studied celebration of the (then) modern world. Odd, really, that the actual merchandise on sale now is fairly dowdy: *Bullocks* is still very much a retail business, but there's nothing about the store which urges anyone to consume.

The **Ambassador Hotel**, just past Vermont Avenue at 3400 Wilshire, is another landmark building, though also rough around the edges these days and perhaps scheduled for demolition. The *Ambassador* had its best days from the early Twenties to the late Forties when its *Cocoanut Grove* club was a favourite nightspot, and the hotel was the winter home of transient Hollywood celebrities. The large ballroom and nightclub (though closed, it still stands in much-altered form in the front garden of the hotel) hosted some of the early Academy Award ceremonies, and was featured in both the first two versions of *A Star is Born* – though it's the kitchen which was the scene of the hotel's most notorious event. On 5 June 1968 **Bobby Kennedy** was fatally shot here while trying to avoid the press by sneaking out the back way after winning the California Presidential Primary.

From the *Ambassador* you can either continue west up the so-called "Miracle Mile" (p.129) or, two blocks south of Wilshire, between Vermont and Western, look in on **KOREATOWN**, the largest concentration of Korean people outside Korea and five times bigger – and infinitely more genuine and lively – than Chinatown and Little Tokyo combined. If you want to eat Korean food there's no better place – see p.179 for details.

Bonnie Brae Street and the West Adams District

The area to the south of MacArthur Park, on the southwestern edge of downtown, was another integral part of LA's residential expansion in the late nineteenth century and a number of early Victorian houses have survived unscathed, grouped together around small parks between Wilshire Boulevard and the USC Campus. **Bonnie Brae Street**, two blocks east of MacArthur Park, holds the best examples, one of which, at 403 S Bonnie Brae Avenue, has been turned into the **Grier-Musser Museum** (Wed–Sat 11am–4pm; $3), whose Victoriana-stuffed innards should satisfy the most avid fan of the period.

On the south side of the Santa Monica Freeway, along Hoover Boulevard, the **West Adams District** is another former rich district that has become something of a slum. It does, however, have a kind of attraction in the **Paul Ziffren Sports Resource Center**, 2141 West Adams Street (Mon–Fri 10am–5pm; free; phone to be shown around; ☎730-9696), which has films and photographs of great moments in sporting history.

The USC Campus and Exposition Park

The **USC CAMPUS**, a few minutes south of downtown on buses #40 or #42, is an enclave of wealth in what is one of the city's poorer neighbourhoods. Students here are thought of as more likely to have rich parents than brains (USC is a fee-paying university and one of the most expensive in the country) and the stereo-type can often seem borne out by their easy-going, sun-tanned, beach-bumming nature – and the fact that the university is more famous for its sporting prowess than academic achievement. There have been attempts to integrate the campus population more closely with the local community, but for the moment at least USC is something of an elitist island, right down to its own fast-food outlet.

Though sizeable, the campus is reasonably easy to get around. If you do want to visit, however, you might find it easier to take the free hour-long **walking tour** (Mon–Fri 10am–2pm by appointment; ☎743-2183). Without a guide, a good place to start is in the **Doheny Library** (during academic year Mon–Fri 8am–5pm, Sat 9am–5pm; free), where you can pick up a campus map and pass an hour investi-gating the large stock of overseas newspapers and magazines on the second floor. Another place for general information is the **Students Union** building just across from the library. Of things to see, USC's art collection is housed in the **Fisher Gallery** on Exposition Boulevard (during academic year, Tues–Sat noon–5pm; free). This stages several major international exhibitions each year, and has a broad permanent stock. Elsewhere in the building, smaller shows of students' creative efforts are displayed in the *Helen Lindhurst Architecture Gallery* (Mon–Fri noon–6pm, Sat noon–5pm; free) and *Helen Lindhurst Fine Arts Gallery* (Mon–Fri 9am–5pm; free).

The campus is also home to the **George Lucas Film School**, named after the producer who studied here with Steven Spielberg, which is a decidedly main-stream rival to the UCLA film school in Westwood. A short walk from the film school, the **Arnold Schoenburg Institute** (Mon–Fri 10am–4pm; free) is a study centre devoted to the pioneering composer. Schoenburg, born in Austria in 1871, came to the US to escape the Nazis, and spent the fourteen years before his death in 1951 in LA. His wide influence on modern musical thought – largely through his experiments with atonal structures – is even more remarkable when you consider he had no formal training. In the reception area is a mock-up of his studio, while the small auditorium displays personal mementoes from his life. During term-time, students often provide free lunchtime concerts of the great man's music.

Just off the campus proper, on the other side of Figueroa Street, the Hebrew Union College's **Skirball Museum** (Tues–Fri 11am–4pm, Sun 10am–5pm; free) devotes several rooms to describing some of the history, beliefs and rituals of the Jewish religion. Inasmuch as it concentrates on more mystical elements of the faith it's fairly absorbing, although anything dealing with the more controversial political ramifications is conspicuously absent.

Exposition Park

Across Exposition Boulevard from the campus, **EXPOSITION PARK** is, given the grim nature of the surrounding area, one of the most appreciated parks in LA, incorporating some lush landscaped gardens, a major sports stadium and a number of decent museums.

It's large by any standards, but the park retains a sense of community – a feeling bolstered by its function as favourite lunch-place for gangs of picnicking schoolkids. After lunch, their number-one spot tends to be the **California Museum of Science and Industry**, set among a cluster of museums off Figueroa Street (daily 10am–5pm; free), for its working models and thousands of pressable buttons – although its displays are uncritical, and marred by a bizarrely sited *McDonalds* propositioning museum-goers as they cross from one half of the museum into the next. Just outside, the **Hall of Health** (daily 10am–5pm; free), has a replica "classic" American diner carrying displays on what not to eat if you want to stay healthy.

If you are tempted to the park simply for the fun of playing games, make for the neighbouring **Hall of Economics and Finance** (daily 10am–5pm; free), where with the aid of a few machines you can wreck the American economy and destroy the stock market – though all the simulations are, again, irritatingly lightweight. Next door, the **Aerospace Building** (daily 10am–5pm; free), marked by the DC10 parked outside, is even blander: a few models and displays pertaining to space and the predicting of the weather. Better instead to head for the **California Afro-American Museum** (daily 10am–5pm; free), which has temporary exhibitions on the history, art and culture of black people in the Americas. Not surprisingly the range can be very diverse, but what's shown is often very stimulating – despite which it's one of the least visited museums in Exposition Park.

The **Los Angeles County Museum of Natural History** (April–Sept Tues–Sun 10am–5pm, weekends 9am–6pm, rest of the year Tues–Sun 10am–5pm, closed Mon; $3, students $1.50, free on the first Tuesday of the month) may also have greater appeal. Apart from fielding the biggest collection, it's also the nicest building in the park – an explosion of Spanish Revival with echoey domes, travertine columns and a marble floor. Foremost among the exhibits is a tremendous stock of dinosaur bones and fossils, and some individually imposing skeletons (usually casts) including the crested "Duck-billed" Dinosaur, the skull of a Tyrannosaurus Rex, and the astonishing frame of a Diatryma – a huge bird incapable of flight. But there's a lot beyond strictly natural history in the museum, and several hours are not too long to allow for a comprehensive look-around. In the fascinating Pre-Columbian Hall, which records central American culture prior to the Spanish invasion, you'll find Mayan pyramid murals and the complete contents of a Mexican tomb (albeit a reconstruction). The Californian history sections usefully document the early (white) settlement of the region during the Gold Rush times and after, with some amazing photos of Los Angeles in the Twenties. Topping the whole place off is the gem collection: several breathtaking roomfuls of crystals, their qualities enhanced by special lighting. Among the treasures, look out for the caseful of sparklers thought to have been part of the Russian Tsar's Crown Jewels.

On a sunny day, keep some spare time for walking through Exposition Park's **Rose Garden** (daily 9am–5pm; free). The best months for doing this are April and May, when the flowers are at their most fragrant, although that's also when the bulk of the 45,000 annual visitors come by to admire the 16,000 rose bushes and the downright prettiness of their setting.

South Central LA

Lacking the scenic splendour of the coast, the glamour of West LA and the history of downtown, **SOUTH CENTRAL LA** is hardly a place that ranks on the tourist circuit. But even if wealthy white LA would like to pretend it doesn't exist, it's an integral part of the city, if only in terms of size: a big, roughly circular chunk reaching from the southern edge of downtown to the northern fringe of the Harbor Area. The population is mostly black with a few pockets of Hispanic and Asian, joined here and there by bottom-of-the-heap, working-class whites. Oddly enough, it doesn't look so terribly rundown at first sight, mostly made up of detached bungalows enjoying their own patch of palm-shaded lawn. But the picture is deceptive, and doesn't conceal for long the fact that just about all the people here are very poor, get an abysmal deal in schooling and work, and have little chance of climbing the social ladder and escaping to the more affluent parts of the city.

South Central LA is also the heartland of the notorious **LA gangs**. There are reputedly over sixty of these, with around 70,000 members between them, the largest being the Crips and the Bloods. The gangs have existed for forty years, and it's only recently, with the massive amounts of money that can be made through controlling the local drug trade, that violence has escalated and automatic weaponry (not least Uzi machine guns) has become affordable to gang members. It can be a bloody – and lethal – business, and although most fatalities (there are about five hundred a year) are a direct result of drug-trade rivalry, there's lately been an increase in "drive-by shootings" – where a vehicle pulls up, gang shouts are heard from inside, and a gang-member steps out, spraying pedestrians with bullets. The vast majority of these killings take place in established gangland areas, and it was indicative of LA's entrenched racial and social divisions that it wasn't until the death of a single white professional woman during a shoot-out in West LA in 1987, that a gang-related death caused widespread publicity and led to major anti-gang initiatives on the part of the police. The resulting clamp-downs have seen a thousand arrests made on a single night but on the whole have made little real headway in tackling the problem – and seem unlikely to do so until the outlook for people in LA's poorer sections improves.

Despite the violence, you're unlikely to see much evidence of the gangs beyond the occasional blue or red scarf (the colours of the Crips and Bloods) tied around a street sign to denote "territory"; and you stand even less chance of witnessing inter-gang warfare. As for personal danger, passing through South Central LA by car is quite safe, but be wary, especially after dark, of delays at traffic lights. If walking (only do this in daylight) the major threat is if you look white and rich (and like a scared tourist); obviously you shouldn't ask for hostility and resentment, and a possible mugging, by waving wads of dollars, expensive cameras, jewellery or watches around.

What will strike you much more than the gangs is the sheer monotony of the place: every block for twenty-odd miles looks much like the last, enlivened periodically by fast-food outlets, dingy supermarkets and uninviting factory sites. You can glimpse much of this by driving past on the Harbor Freeway (Hwy-110), which links downtown to the Harbor Area, or by way of one of the more minor roads such as Central Avenue. Failing that, a longer journey is to take local bus #53 (as opposed to the express buses which take the freeway), which uses Central Avenue between downtown and DOMINGUEZ HILLS, just north of Long Beach.

Watts

WATTS, on the southernmost fringe of downtown, is barely part of South Central LA, but it almost earned a place in LA folk history to match Hollywood following the six-day **Watts Riot** of August 1965. The arrest of a 21-year-old unemployed black, Marquette Frye, on suspicion of drunken driving, gave rise to charges of police brutality and led to bricks, bottles and slabs of concrete being hurled by the local community at police and passing motorists during the night. The situation had calmed by the next morning, but the following evening both young and old black people were on the streets, giving vent to an anger generated by years of what they felt to be less than even-handed treatment by the police and other white-dominated institutions. Weapons were looted from stores and many buildings set alight (though few residential buildings, black-owned businesses, or community services like libraries and schools, were touched); street barricades were erected, and the events took a more serious turn. By the fifth day the insurgents were approaching downtown, which – along with the fear spreading through white LA – led to the call-out of the National Guard: 13,000 troops arrived, set up machine-gun placements and road blocks, and imposed an 8pm–dawn curfew, which caused the rebellion to subside.

In the aftermath of the uprising, which left 36 dead, one German reporter said of Watts, "it looks like Germany during the last months of World War II" – and much of it still does – Watts is by far the ugliest part of South Central LA. There was, for a short time after the riots, a more positive attitude to the area, and promises of investment were forthcoming. These, however, haven't amounted to much in the long-term; indeed any forward strides made through the Seventies have been wiped out by wider economic decline. The only time since the riots that anyone has shown an interest was in 1975 when members of the revolutionary Symbionese Liberation Army (SLA), who had kidnapped publishing heiress Patti Hearst, fought a lengthy – and televised – gun battle with police until the house they were trapped in burned to the ground. The site of the battle, at 1466 E 54th Street, is now a vacant lot, though the surrounding houses are still riddled with bullet holes.

The one good reason to come here is to see the **Watts Towers** (sometimes called the **Rodia Towers**), at 1765 E 107th Street. More than a bit of mystery surrounds these structures and their maker Simon Rodia. Made from iron, stainless steel, old bedsteads and cement, and decorated with fragments of bottles and around 70,000 crushed sea-shells, they're striking pieces of street art. Rodia had no artistic background or training at all, but laboured over the towers' construction from 1921 to 1954, refusing all offers of help and unable to explain either their meaning or why he was building them at all. Once finished, Rodia left the area, refused to talk about the towers at all, and faded into complete obscurity. As part of a restoration programme, the towers have been under cover for some time, but their upper portions are easy to see.

If you're seriously interested in black history, take a look at the **Dunbar Hotel**, 4225 S Central Avenue. Built in 1928, it was the first hotel in the US built by and for black people, who otherwise found it impossible to find accommodation in LA. It's currently being converted into a history and cultural centre for the community.

Compton, Inglewood and Gardena

Between Watts and the Harbor Area, only a few districts are of passing interest. Acquiring worldwide fame through being the home of many of LA's rappers – NWA for example sang venomously of its ills on their album *Straight Outta Compton* – **COMPTON** is not a place where strangers should attempt to sniff out the local music scene. History buffs secure in their cars, however, might fancy a stop at the **Dominguez Ranch Adobe**, 18127 S Alameda Street (Tues & Wed 1–4pm, second & third Sun of each month 1–4pm; free), now restored and chronicling the social ascent of its founder, Juan Jose Dominguez – one of the soldiers who left Mexico with Padre Serra's expedition to found the Californian missions and whose long military service was acknowledged in 1782 by the granting of these 75,000 acres of land. As the importance of the area grew, so did the power of Dominguez's descendants, who became powerful in local politics.

On the other side of the Harbor Freeway, west of Watts, **INGLEWOOD** is unenticing in itself but is home to the **Hollywood Park Racecourse,** a landscaped racetrack with lagoons and tropical vegetation, and even a state-of-the-art computer-operated screen to give punters a view of the otherwise obscured back straight. Next door are the white pillars which ring **The Forum**, the 17,000-seat stadium which is the headquarters of both the *LA Lakers* (basketball) and the *LA Kings* (hockey); see p.199 for more on LA sport.

One of the safer segments of South Central LA, **GARDENA**, a few miles south, is best known for its large Japanese population and, more importantly, a city ordinance which permits gambling – rare in California. Along Vermont and Western Avenues, half a dozen or so clubs devoted to poker are combined with restaurants and cocktail lounges, which charge a half-hourly rental on seats (from $1 to $24). Food and drink is served round the clock, though the bars are separate from the tables. Slightly tacky perhaps, but if you're desperate for a flutter…

East LA

You can't visit LA without being made aware of the Hispanic input to the city's demography and character, whether it be through the thousands of Mexican restaurants, the innumerable Spanish street names – or, most obviously, through the large numbers of Spanish-speaking people on the streets. None of this is surprising given LA's proximity to Mexico, but equally apparent are the clear distinctions between the latino community and white LA. As a rule it's the former who do the menial jobs for the latter, and, although a great number live in the US lawfully, they're also the people who suffer most from the repeated drives against illegal immigration.

There are strongly Hispanic neighbourhoods all over LA, but the key one is **EAST LA**: a sizeable fist of the city which begins two miles east of downtown, across the concrete-clad dribble of the Los Angeles river. The Mexicans who lived here long before the white settlers arrived were joined by millions more from the late nineteenth century onwards, coming to work chiefly in agriculture. As the white inhabitants gradually moved west towards the coast, the Mexicans stayed, creating a vast Spanish-speaking community that's more like a Mexican barrio than part of a North American city.

In East LA (commonly abbreviated to "ELA" or "East Los") the activity tends to be outdoors, in cluttered markets and busy shops. White visitors are comparatively thin on the ground but you are unlikely to meet any hostility on the streets during the day, although this is less the case at night – or any time of day in the rough and very male-dominated bars.

Besides soaking up the streetlife there are few specific things to see, although many impressive community-sponsored murals decorate the main thoroughfares. The best plan is just to turn up on a Saturday afternoon (the liveliest part of the week) and stroll along **Brooklyn Avenue**, which begins at the northeast edge of Boyle Heights and features some wild pet shops, with free-roaming parrots and cases of boa constrictors, and a number of **botanicas shops**, which cater to practitioners of *Santeria* – a religion that is equal parts voodoo and Catholicism. Browse amid the shark's teeth, dried devil fish and plastic statuettes of Catholic saints and buy magical herbs, ointments or candles after consulting the shopkeeper and explaining (in Spanish) what ails you. Only slightly less exotic fare can be found in **El Mercado de Los Angeles**, 3425 E First Street, an indoor market not unlike Olvera Street but much more authentic. Afterwards go to the junction of Soto Street and Brooklyn, where at 5pm each afternoon *Norteños* combos (upright bass, accordian, guitar and banjo sexto) freely showcase their talents, hoping to be booked for weddings; failing that, listen to the mariachi bands that strike up at 6.30pm outside the *Olympic Donut Shop*, at First Street and Boyle Avenue, four blocks south of Brooklyn Avenue.

The Highland Park District

North of downtown the Pasadena Freeway curves its way along a dry riverbed towards the foothill community whose name it bears. The freeway, LA's first, was completed in 1940 as the Arroyo Seco Parkway. Highway engineers have since learned their lessons, but be aware that this antiquated roadway has "stop" signs on the on-ramps and exit curves so sharp that the speed limit is 5mph.

Beside the freeway, two miles from downtown, the **HIGHLAND PARK DISTRICT** has a number of exuberantly detailed Victorian houses brought together from around the city to form **Heritage Square** (weekends noon–4pm), a fenced-off ten-acre park. Just beyond the next freeway exit, at 200 E Avenue 43, the **Lummis House** (Wed–Sun 1–4pm) is the well-preserved home of Charles F. Lummis, a publicist who was at the heart of LA's nineteenth-century boom. Unlike many of the real-estate speculators and journalists who publicised various aspects of the Southern Californian good life, Lummis did some genuinely good deeds: he was an early champion of civil rights for Native Americans, and worked to save and preserve many of the missions, which were then in ruin. His house was a cultural centre of turn-of-the-century Los Angeles, where the literati of the day would meet to discuss poetry and the art and architecture of the Southwest. Lummis built this house for himself in an ad-hoc mixture of mission and medieval styles, naming it *El Alisal* for the many large sycamore trees (*Alisal* in Spanish) that shade the gardens. He constructed the thick walls out of rounded granite boulders taken from the nearby riverbed, and the beams over the living room of old telephone poles. The front doors are similarly built to last, made of thick wood reinforced with iron and weighing a literal ton, while the plaster and tile interior is rustically kitted out with hand-cut timber ceilings and home-made furniture.

The Southwest Museum

The foundation of the **Southwest Museum** (Tues–Fri 11am–5pm, Sun 1pm–5pm; $4.50), which rises castle-like below Mount Washington, was Charles F. Lummis's most enduring achievement. Half a mile north of the Lummis House (take bus #83 along Figueroa Street from downtown), the museum is the oldest in Los Angeles, founded in 1907. Its name however is a bit deceptive – the recently renovated museum displays Native American artefacts from all over North America, with exhibits of Pre-Columbian pottery, coastal Chumash rock art and a full-size Plains Indian Cheyenne tepee. The museum also hosts travelling exhibitions, and its educational programme of lectures, films and theatrical events have made it an international centre for indigenous American cultures. The Braun Research Library has an unmatched collection of recordings and photographs of Native Americans from the Bering Straits to Mexico, and the museum shop features Navajo rugs, kachina dolls and turquoise jewellery, as well as an extensive selection of books and specialist publications. Although people in LA scarcely know about the museum, it's well worth an afternoon.

Hollywood

The violet hush of twilight was descending over Los Angeles as my hostess, Violet Hush, and I left its suburbs headed towards Hollywood. In the distance a glow of huge piles of burning motion-picture scripts lit up the sky. The crisp tang of frying writers and directors whetted my appetite. How good it was to be alive, I thought, inhaling deep lungfuls of carbon monoxide.

S.J. Perelman

If there's a single place-name that epitomises the glamour, money and overnight success that LA supposedly offers, it's **HOLLYWOOD**. Ever since American movies, and their stars, became the international symbols of the good life, Hollywood has been a magnet to millions of tourists on once-in-a-lifetime pilgrimages and an equally massive assortment of hopefuls drawn here by the thought of riches and glory. Even if the real prospects of success were one in a million, enough people were taken in by the dream to make Hollywood what it is today – a weird combination of insatiable optimism and total despair. It may be a cliché, but Hollywood *does* blur the edges of fact and fiction, simply because so much *seems* possible here – and yet so little, for most people, actually is.

The truth is that Hollywood was more a centre of corruption and scandal than the city of dreams the studio-made legend suggested. Successful Hollywoodites actually spent little time here – they left as soon as they could afford to for the privacy of the hills or coast. Many of the big film companies, too, long ago relocated well away from here, leaving Hollywood in isolation, with prostitution, drug

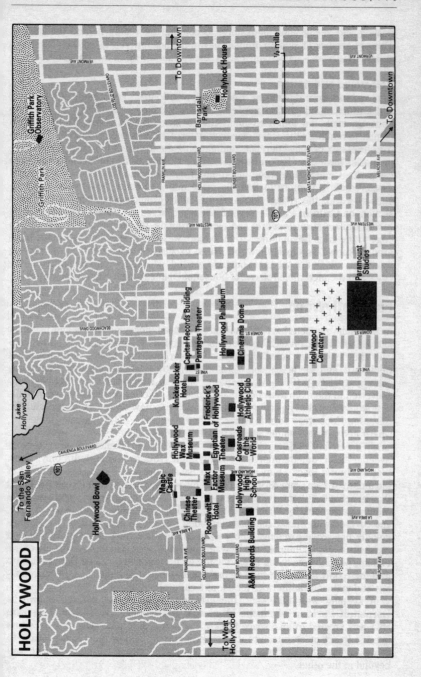

dealing and seedy adult bookstores becoming the reality behind the fantasy. Things have brightened up dramatically in the last few years, but the district can still be dangerous – if not to the extent that you should think twice about coming.

Hollywood orientation

Approaching from downtown, **East Hollywood** is the first taste of the district, and a more mundane first impression than this largely soulless tract of cheap housing would be tough to find. Things pick up in **Central Hollywood**, a compact area that's the real movie history territory, swarmed around by an eccentric street-mix of social derelicts and gawping dumb-struck tourists. Whether the memories have been hammed-up into tacky shrines, or forgotten and turned into car parks, Central Hollywood has them in quantity, and you'd have to be avidly uninterested in filmlore to find the place dull. Protecting Hollywood from the outside world, the rising slopes of the Santa Monica Mountains constitute a section of **Griffith Park** – several thousand acres of nature offering rugged hiking trails and busy sports and picnic grounds, that forms a scenic northern edge to the area. Beyond the park, the more westerly of the slopes form the high-ground known as the **Hollywood Hills**: exclusive homes perched on snaking driveways which are the most tangible reminders of the wealth generated in the city – and the incredible roll-call of household names which have sprung from it.

East Hollywood

In the main characterised by dilapidated houses, decaying hotels and used car lots, **EAST HOLLYWOOD** is the drabbest section of Hollywood – though historically the district has some significance. **Silverlake**, four blocks north of Sunset Boulevard, and the area's sole splash of brightness – and centre of a large gay community (see p.190) – was home to some of Hollywood's first studios, now converted in the main to trendy restaurants and galleries. Walt Disney opened his first studio at 2719 Hyperion Avenue in 1926 (it's now a grocery store); and the Keystone Kops were born in Mack Sennett's studio at 1712 Glendale Boulevard, where just a single sound studio remains. Time is better spent, however, on a small green hill close to the junction of Hollywood Boulevard and Vermont Avenue, at the quietly impressive **Hollyhock House** (guided tours only, Tues, Wed & Thur at 10am, 11am, noon & 1pm, Sat and the first, second and third Sun of the month at 1pm, 2pm & 3pm; $1.50). This was the first of architect Frank Lloyd Wright's contributions to LA, though it was largely designed, with minimal acknowledgement, by Wright's student, Rudolph Schindler. Completed in 1921, and covered with Mayan motifs and imbued with an art deco fervour, it's an intriguingly obsessive dwelling, whose original furniture (now replaced by detailed reconstructions) continued the Mayan conceptual flow. The bizarre quality of the building was obviously too much for the oil heiress owner, Aline Barnsdall, who lived here only for a short time before donating both the house and the surrounding land to the city authorities for use as a cultural centre.

In keeping with this wish, the grounds of the house became known as **Barnsdall Park**, in which the **Municipal Art Gallery** (Tues–Sun 12.30–5pm; 50¢) was erected to give space to new Southern Californian artists. If you've no interest in art or architecture, the park is one of the few quiet spots locally to enjoy a view: the Hollywood Hills in one direction and all of downtown and beyond in the other.

A HISTORY OF HOLLYWOOD

Given its racy character, it's odd to think that Hollywood started life as a temperance colony, intended to provide a sober God-fearing alternative to raunchy downtown LA, eight miles away by rough country road. Purchased and named by a pair of devout Methodists in 1887, the district remained autonomous until 1911, when they were forced, in return for a regular water supply, to affiliate their own city to LA as a suburb. The film industry, meanwhile, gathering momentum on the East Coast, needed somewhere with guaranteed sunshine and a diverse assortment of natural backdrops to enable pictures to be made quickly, and somewhere to dodge patent laws which had restricted film-making in the east. Southern California, with its climate, scenery and isolation, was the perfect spot. A few offices affiliated to eastern film companies were opened downtown from 1906, but independent hopefuls soon discovered the cheaper rents on offer in Hollywood. The first studio opened here in 1911, and within three years the place was packed with film-makers – many of them, like Cecil B. de Mille who shared his barn-converted office space with a horse, destined to be the big names of the future.

The ramshackle industry expanded fast, bringing instant profits and instant fame, and the hopefuls who arrived eager for a slice of both soon swamped the original inhabitants, outraging them with their hedonistic lifestyles. Yet movie-making was far from being a financially secure business, and it wasn't until D.W. Griffith's *The Birth of a Nation* was released in 1915, that the power of film was demonstrated. The right-wing account of the American Civil War caused riots outside cinemas and months of critical debate in the newspapers – and for the first time drew the middle-classes to the screens to see what all the fuss was about. It was also the movie which established the narrative style and production techniques that became standard.

The modern industry took shape from the 1920s on, when film production grew more specialised and many small companies either went bust or were incorporated into one of the handful of bigger studios which came to dominate film-making. Hollywood didn't care what it made as long as it sold; one successful swashbuckler or western spawned dozens more until the market was swamped and a new genre hurriedly dreamt up. During World War II Hollywood became a propaganda weapon, offering devasted Europe an escape into a rose-tinted view of American life, a falsehood that defined the industry's course for the next few decades. Despite the continued existence of a more creative side – such as the hard-bitten *film noir* style from the mid-Forties – it's been big names, big bucks and conservatism that have kept Hollywood alive. There was a brief flourish during the Sixties, and the early Seventies saw a host of innovative movies funded by the big studios but the last ten years have been less inspiring, seeing a return to safe, often epic escapism. With its profits gnawed into by television and rock music, the industry today rarely even thinks about taking risks.

Central Hollywood

The myths, magic, fable and fantasy splattered throughout the few short blocks of **CENTRAL HOLLYWOOD** would put a medieval fairytale to shame. With the densest concentration of faded glamour and film mythology in the world, the rich sense of nostalgia pervades everything here, and makes the area deeply appealing in a way no measure of tourists or souvenir postcard stands can diminish. Although you're much more likely to find a porno theatre than spot a real star (no bona-fide somebody would be seen dead here these days), the decline which blighted the area from the early Sixties is fast receding, as prolonged efforts by local authorities have gone some way to reclaiming the area and making it safe. Nevertheless the place still gets hairy after dark, with on-leave marines strutting along the sidewalks and Hispanic adolescents cruising Hollywood Boulevard in flashy customised autos. Soak up the history during the day, and return at night to sample the more heady – though seldom dangerous – street-life.

Along Hollywood Boulevard

Following Hollywood Boulevard west, the junction of **Hollywood and Vine** is a juxtaposition of street names that still tingles the spines of dedicated Hollywoodphiles, some of whom can be spotted standing in respectful silence before crossing the road. During the golden years the rumour spread that any budding star had only to parade around this junction to be seen and sized-up by the film directors (the major studios were then in close proximity), who nursed coffees behind the windows of neighbouring restaurants. In typical Hollywood style the whole tale was blown wildly out of proportion, and while many real stars did pass by, it was only briefly on their way to and from work, and the crossing did nothing but earn a fabulous reputation. The only thing marking the legend today, apart from disappointed tourists, is a small plaque on the wall of the *New York Pizza Express*.

A block on along Hollywood Boulevard from Vine Street, 1714 Ivar Avenue is home to the bulky **Knickerbocker Hotel**, now an old people's home but the place where the widow of legendary escapologist, Harry Houdini, conducted a rooftop seance in an attempt to assist her late spouse in his greatest escape of all. During the Thirties and Forties, the hotel had a reputation for letting to some of Hollywood's more unstable characters and a number of lesser-name suicides plunged from its high windows. At 1825 Ivar Street is the flea-bag rooming house where author and screen-writer **Nathanael West** lived during the late Thirties, after coming west to revive his sagging financial situation. Gazing over the street's parade of extras, hustlers and make-believe cowboys, he penned the classic satirical portrait of Hollywood, *The Day of the Locust*.

Back on Hollywood Boulevard, at number 6608, **Frederick's of Hollywood** with its purple and pink facade, is Hollywood's idea of a landmark. Opened in 1947, it has been (under-) clothing Hollywood's sex-goddesses ever since, and many more mortal bodies all over the world through its mail-order outlet. Inside, the **lingerie museum** (free) displays some of the company's best corsets, bras and panties, donated by a host of happy big-name wearers, ranging from Lana Turner to Belinda Carlisle.

A little further on, the **Egyptian Theater** (number 6708) was financed by impresario Sid Grauman, who with this building modestly sought to re-create the Temple of Thebes, and had the usherettes dress as Cleopatra. The very first Hollywood premier (*Robin Hood*, an epic swashbuckler starring Douglas Fairbanks Snr), took place here in 1922. It's now divided into several smaller cinemas and has lost much of its appeal, despite the minor Egyptian motifs that adorn the concrete pillars.

Lovers of high camp should instead turn left for the **Max Factor Museum** at 1666 Highland Avenue (Mon–Sat noon–4pm; free), the shrine (no less) to the man who made-up a thousand faces. Emigrating from Russia, where he had a wigs and cosmetics shop, in 1904, Max Factor made for Hollywood armed with a specially thinned grease-paint in cream form which he insisted would be the perfect on-camera make-up. It was, and through the great years of the movies he amassed a fortune. The atmosphere of the museum is as hagiographical as you'd expect. In celebration of the early days, a photo of Tsar Nicolas III sits incongrously between Henry B. Walthall and Ben Turpin, the moviemen who gave the first screen tests to the Factor product, and there's a photo gallery of stars smothered in Factor produce. The strangest object here is the "beauty calibrator" – a gruesome implement used for measuring the cranium and assessing a person's cosmetic needs.

Less fun, at least during the daytime, is the **Hollywood Wax Museum** (daily 10am–midnight, until 2am on Fri & Sat; $7): a naff selection of dummies of the obvious people. Besides Spock's ears, Marilyn's backside and Dolly's breasts, is a replica of da Vinci's painting *The Last Supper* – very peculiar, as are many of the people who stumble in during the small hours . . .

Much of the pavement along this stretch of Hollywood Boulevard is marked by the brass name-plates that make up the **Walk of Fame** (officially beginning at Hollywood and Vine). The laying of the plates began in 1960, instigated by the local Chamber of Commerce who thought enshrining the big-names would somehow restore the boulevard's glamour and boost tourism. Selected stars have to part with several thousand dollars for the privilege of being included; you may as well walk straight on over them.

Nothing as vulgar as money can taint the appeal of the foot and hand prints embedded in the concrete concourse of the **Chinese Theater** at 6925 Hollywood Boulevard. Opened in 1927, this was intended as a lavish setting for premieres of swanky new productions. Through the halcyon decades, this was *the* spot for movie first-nights, and the public crowded behind the rope barriers in their thousands to watch the aristocrats of film arriving for the screenings. The foot-and-hand-prints-in-concrete idea came about when actress Norma Talmadge accidentally (though some say it was a deliberate publicity stunt) trod in wet cement while visiting the construction site with the owner Sid Grauman. The first formally to leave their marks were Mary Pickford and Douglas Fairbanks Snr, who ceremoniously dipped their digits when arriving for the opening of *King of Kings*, and the practice has continued into the present – R2D2, the robot from *Star Wars*, just one of the latter-day big cheeses. It's certainly fun to work out the actual dimensions of the film stars, and to discover if your hands are smaller than Julie Andrews's or your feet are bigger than Rock Hudson's (or both), despite the tourists who swarm around the place. As for the building, it's an odd western version of a classical Chinese Temple, replete with dodgy Chinese motifs and upturned dragon tail flanks. Try to take a peek at the art deco splendour of the lobby even if you're not going in for a movie.

If the schmaltz makes you nauseous, there's more straight-faced Hollywood history directly opposite at the **Roosevelt Hotel**. Also opened in 1927, this was movieland's first luxury hotel and it fast became the meeting place of top actors and screenwriters, its *Cinegrill* restaurant feeding and watering the likes of W.C. Fields, Ernest Hemingway, and F. Scott Fitzgerald, not to mention hangers-on like Ronald Reagan. In 1929 the first Oscars were presented here, beginning the long tradition of Hollywood rewarding itself in the absence of honours from elsewhere.

As Hollywood's pizzazz faded so did the *Roosevelt*, but after a fabulous refit job through the mid-Eighties, luxury is again the operative word. Peek inside for a view of the splashing fountains and elegantly weighty wrought-iron chandeliers of its marble-floored lobby, and for the intelligently compiled pictorial **history of Hollywood** on the second floor. As you might expect, the place is thick with legend: on the staircase from the lobby to the mezzanine, Bill "Bojangles" Robinson taught Shirley Temple to dance; and the ghost of Montgomery Clift (who stayed here while filming *From Here To Eternity*) apparently haunts the place, announcing his presence by blowing a bugle.

Along Sunset Boulevard

Further veins of Hollywood nostalgia can be tapped directly south of the central section of Hollywood Boulevard, on and around the less touristy **Sunset Boulevard**, which runs parallel. You might start your explorations at the corner of **Sunset Boulevard** and **Gower Street**. During the industry's formative years, when unemployed movie extras hopeful of a few days' work with one of the small local B-movie studios would hang around here, the junction earned the nicknames "Gower gulch" and "poverty row".

Now an office block, the delectable Spanish Revival-style building at 6525 Sunset Boulevard was known from the Twenties until the Fifties as the **Hollywood Athletic Club**. Another of Hollywood's legendary watering holes during the golden years, it hosted among others Charlie Chaplin, Clark Gable and even Tarzan himself beside the Olympic-sized pool; in the apartment levels above, John Barrymore and John Wayne held drinking parties. Until a few years ago, a few pieces of general memorabilia were displayed in the lobby, though now the practice has stopped. Look in to see if it's been revived.

The grouping of shops at the **Crossroads of the World**, at 6672 Sunset Boulevard, isn't much to look at now, but when finished in 1936 it was one of LA's major tourist attractions. The central plaza is supposed to resemble a ship, surrounded by shops designed with the motifs of Tudor, French, Italian and Spanish architecture – the idea being that the shops are the ports into which the shopper would sail. It may sound tacky, but time has been kind, and considering the more recent and far brasher and vulgar architecture found in LA, this has a definite, if muted, charm.

The Hollywood Memorial Cemetery

Despite the beliefs of some of their loopiest fans, even the biggest Hollywood stars have been mortal. Consequently the many LA cemeteries which hold their tombs get at least as many visitors as the city's museums. One of the least heralded and least dramatically landscaped of them, though with more than its fair share of big names, is the **Hollywood Memorial Cemetery**, close to the junction of Santa Monica Boulevard and Gower Street and suitably overlooked by the famous water tower of the neighbouring *Paramount Studios* (whose even more famous gates are just around the corner on Santa Monica Boulevard).

In the southeastern corner of the cemetery, the cathedral mausoleum sets the tone for the place, a solemn collection of tombs that includes, at number 1205, the resting-place of **Rudolph Valentino**. Ten thousand people packed the cemetery when the celebrated screen lover died aged just 31 in 1926, and to this day on each anniversary of his passing (23 August), at least one "Lady in Black" will likely be found mourning – a tradition which started as a publicity stunt in 1931 (the first weeping damsel claimed to be a former paramour of Valentino's but was exposed as a hired actress) and has continued ever since. While here, spare a thought for the more contemporary screen star, Peter Finch, who died in 1977. His crypt is opposite Valentino's and tourists often lean their rears unknowingly against it while photographing Rudolph's marker.

Fittingly, outside the mausoleum, the most pompous grave in the cemetery belongs to **Douglas Fairbanks Snr**, who with his wife Mary Pickford did much to introduce social snobbery among the movie-making people. Even in death Fairbanks keeps a snooty distance from the pack, his achingly ostentatious memorial, complete with sculptured pond, only reachable by a shrubbery-lined path from the mausoleum. On the way out of the cemetery, one of the more overlooked graves is that of **Virginia Rappe** – a small-time actress doomed to be remembered as "the girl in the Fatty Arbuckle scandal". In 1921, star comedian Fatty Arbuckle was charged with the rape and manslaughter of Rappe following a "drunken orgy" in a San Francisco hotel. Rappe was pronounced dead from a ruptured bladder and Arbuckle faced three trials before being acquitted. Despite the verdict, popular opinion doubted his innocence, and his career was finished.

Griffith Park

The combination of gentle greenery and rugged mountain slopes making up vast **GRIFFITH PARK**, between Hollywood and the San Fernando Valley (daily 5am–10.30pm, mountain roads close at dusk; free), is a welcome escape from the mind-numbing hubbub almost everywhere else in the city. The largest municipal park in the country, it's also one of the few places where LA's multitude of racial and social groups at least go through the motions of mixing fairly happily together. Above the landscaped flat sections, where the crowds assemble to picnic, play sports or visit the fixed attractions, the hillsides are rough and wild, marked only by foot and bridle paths, leading into desolate but appealingly unspoilt terrain that gives great views over the LA basin and out to the ocean. Bear in mind, though, that while the park is safe by day, its reputation for after-dark violence is well founded.

Practical points . . . and hiking tips

There are four **main entrances** to Griffith Park. Western Canyon Road, north of Los Feliz Boulevard, leads to the Ferndell. Vermont Avenue, also north of Los Feliz Boulevard, leads to the Greek Theatre and the bird sanctuary. Crystal Springs Drive, off Riverside Drive, takes you to the Ranger Station; and the Los Feliz exit of the Golden State Freeway (I-5) leads to the Zoo and Travel Town. Bus #97 runs along Los Feliz Boulevard beside the park from downtown but there is no public transport inside the park, and you'd do better to cycle. The closest place to **hire a bike** is *Woody's Bicycle World*, 3157 Los Feliz Boulevard (☎661-6665).

The steeper parts of Griffith Park, which blend into the foothills of the Santa Monica Mountains, are the focus of a variety of **hikes**. Free maps are available at the **Ranger Station**, at 4730 Crystal Springs Road (☎655-5188) – also the starting point for **guided hikes** and atmospheric **evening hikes**, held whenever there's a full moon. The rangers also have maps for drivers that detail the best vantage-points for views over the whole of Los Angeles, not least from the highest place in the park – the summit of Mount Hollywood.

Around the park

Western Canyon Road enters the park through **the Ferndell** – as the name suggests, a lush glade of ferns, from which numerous trails run deeper into the park – continuing up to the **Observatory** (Sun–Fri 1–10pm, Sat 11.30am–10pm; free): familiar from its use as a backdrop in *Rebel Without a Cause*, and with moderately interesting science displays and a Laserium and Planetarium (shows every hour; $4). More enticingly, on clear nights when something is afoot in the cosmos, there are brilliant views through the powerful **telescope** (daily 7–10pm; free) mounted on the roof.

Descending from the observatory by way of Vermont Canyon Road (effectively the continuation of Western Canyon Road) brings you down to the small **bird sanctuary**, set within a modest-sized wooded canyon. A park ranger leads an informative 45-minute walking tour at 1pm on Sunday, pointing out the various species which have been encouraged to nest here. Across the road is the **Greek Theater**, an open-air amphitheatre which seats nearly five thousand beneath its Greek-style columns – though if you're not going in for a show (the Greek is a venue for big-name rock, jazz and country music concerts during summer) you'll see just the bland exterior.

The **northern end** of the park, over the hills in the San Fernando Valley, is best reached directly by car from the Golden State Freeway, although you can take the park roads from close to the Greek Theater (or explore the labyrinth of hiking trails) which climb over the park's hilly core. At the end of the journey, don't bother with the cramped **LA Zoo** (summer daily 10am–6pm, rest of the year daily 10am–5pm; $5) or the old locos of the **Travel Town Transportation Museum** (May to Oct Mon–Fri 10am–5pm Sat & Sun 10am–6pm; slightly reduced hours rest of the year; free) – a far better reason to be in this section of the park is the **Gene Autry Western Heritage Museum** (Tues–Sun 10am–5pm; $5), bearing the name of the "singing cowboy" who cut over six hundred discs from 1929, starred in blockbusting Hollywood Westerns during the Thirties and Forties, and became even more of a household name through his eponymously titled TV show in the Fifties.

Autry fans hoping for a shrine to the man who pined the immortal *That Silver Haired Daddy of Mine*, are in for a shock, however: the **collection** – from buckskin jackets and branding irons to the emotive sculptures of turn-of-the-century Western artist Frederic Remington and the truth about the shoot-out at the OK Corral – is a serious and very credible attempt to explore the mindset and concerns of those who participated in the US's colonisation of the West. It also puts into context the later role of the movie industry in spoonfeeding a totally false impression of the region's past to millions of people all over the world.

Engaging in a different way are the narrow underground passages of the **old zoo**, a mile south, reached by way of a small tunnel behind some high fences near the merry-go-round in the **Crystal Springs area**. These eerie surrounds once contained bears and tigers, and it's easy to believe there may still be some lurking here as you creep about in the near-silence. The rest of the Crystal Springs area is a favourite picnic spot, and a place to watch amateur baseball games on the adjacent diamond or drop into one of the numerous other shows – motorbike contests and the like – which happen nearby.

Also close by, opposite the entrance to the park on the corner of Riverside Drive and Los Feliz Boulevard, is the **William Mulholland Memorial**

Fountain, whose watery cascades are a reminder of the man credited with building the aqueduct in 1902 which gave the city its first reliable supply of water – a feat that's part of a long saga laced with scandal and corruption.

The Hollywood Hills

Apart from the chance to appreciate how flat the LA basin is, the views from the **Hollywood Hills** feature perhaps the oddest, yet most opulent, selection of properties to be found anywhere. Around these canyons and slopes, which run from Hollywood itself into Benedict Canyon above Beverly Hills, mansions are so commonplace that only the half-dozen fully blown castles (at least, Hollywood-style castles) really stand out.

Mulholland Drive, which runs along the crest, provides a glimpse of some of the notorious abodes – Rudolph Valentino's extravagant **Falcon Lair**, Errol Flynn's **Mulholland House**, the former home of actress Sharon Tate, where the last of the Manson family killings took place, and any number of run-of-the-mill million-dollar residences belonging to an assortment of luminaries, visionaries, former politicians and movie moguls – some of whom have helped forge LA's reputation for ostentatious and utterly decadent living.

Unfortunately, though, there's no real way to explore in depth without your own transport and a knowledgeable friend to help pinpoint the sights, spread widely across every hillside. You could use one of the guided tours (p.92), but for the most part you can't get close to the most elaborate dwellings anyway, and none are open to the public.

The Hollywood Sign

One thing you can see from more or less anywhere in Hollywood, is the **Hollywood Sign**, erected to spell "Hollywoodland" in 1923 as a promotional device to sell property at the foot of the hills. The "land" part was removed in 1949, leaving the rest as a world-renowned symbol of the entertainment industry here. It's also (unjustifiably) become one of the world's most famous suicide spots, ever since would-be movie star Peg Entwhistle terminated her career and life here in 1932, aged 24. It was no mean feat – the sign being as hard to reach then as it is now: from the end of Beachwood Drive she picked a path slowly upward through the thick bush and climbed the fifty-foot high "H", eventually leaping from it to her death. Stories that this act led to a line of failed starlets desperate to make their final exit from Tinseltown's best known marker, however, are untrue – though many troubled souls may have died of exhaustion while trying to get to it. There's no public road (Beachwood Drive comes nearest, but ends at a closed gate) and you'll incur minor cuts and bruises while scrambling to get anywhere near. In any case, the bother really isn't worthwhile.

Lake Hollywood

Hemmed in among the hills between Griffith Park and the Hollywood Freeway, **Lake Hollywood** feels like a piece of open country in the heart of the city. The clear, calm waters, actually a reservoir intended to lubricate the whole of LA in times of drought, make a delightful spot, surrounded by clumps of pines in which squirrels, lizards and a few scurrying skunks and coyotes easily outnumber the people. The point is, there's no social kudos associated with being seen trotting around the footpaths which encircle the lake – which may explain why so few Angelenos deem it worthy of their presence. Their loss, nature's gain.

The only way to reach the lake is by car. The **lake access road** is only open 7am–noon & 2–7pm on weekdays, and 7am–7.30pm on weekends: to get to it, turn right onto Dix Street (a block north of Franklin Avenue), left into Holly Drive and climb to Deep Dell Place; from there it's a sharp right into Weidlake Drive and left past a "no through road" sign.

The Hollywood Bowl

Where Highland Avenue hits the Hollywood Freeway, a twenty-minute walk from Hollywood Boulevard, the **Hollywood Bowl** is an open-air auditorium with more fame than it deserves. The first musical note was struck here in 1921, and the Beatles played here in the mid-Sixties, but the Bowl's principal function is as home to the Los Angeles Philharmonic, who give evening concerts from July to September. These are far less highbrow than might be imagined. It's long been the done thing to consume a picnic in the grounds before making the climb to one's seat, and nowadays the consumption tends to continue throughout the show, often rendering the music barely audible above the crunching of popcorn and fried chicken, and the clink of empty wine bottles rolling down the steps. It's obviously not a choice spot for lovers of fine music, but can be fun nonetheless.

More, but not much more, about the Bowl's history can be gleaned from the video show inside the small **Hollywood Bowl Museum**, close to the entrance (July to Sept daily 9.30am–4.30pm, until 9.30pm on concert days, rest of the year Tues–Sat 9.30am–4.30pm; free), where there's also a routine collection of musical instruments from around the world.

West LA

LA's so-called "Westside" begins immediately beyond Hollywood in **WEST LA**, which contains some of the city's most expensive neighbourhoods. Bordered by the foothills of the Santa Monica Mountains to the north and the Santa Monica freeway to the south, West LA is fashionable LA, at the sharp end of all that's new and happening in the city, and perhaps closer than anywhere else to embodying the stylish images that the city projects to the outside world. Actually, once you're there, the reality is often less dazzling: away from the showcase streets are the usual long, residential blocks, only marginally less drab than normal with their better tended lawns, swisher supermarkets, cleaner gas stations – and a higher class of fast food stand.

The single best reason to come is the engrossing collection of the **LA County Museum of Art**, on the eastern perimeter of West LA in the still firmly Jewish **Fairfax district**. It's not until you cross west of Fairfax Avenue that West LA truly reveals itself in **West Hollywood** – a major centre for art and design, clogged by posey eateries and boutiques and, less chic, the clubs at the core of the city's music scene. **Beverly Hills**, a little way west, is less gregarious but more affluent: you may find you need an expense account to buy a sandwich but nonetheless it's a matchless place to indulge in upscale window shopping on the way to the more roundly appealing **Westwood Village**. The main business in this low-rise, Spanish Revival near-pedestrianised area has always been movies (seeing them rather than making them). The original deco palaces still remain, a short way from the **UCLA Campus** – the second of LA's university sites and home to a number of galleries and museums.

Although several sections are best seen on foot, overall West LA is a large area and can be a problem to get around without a car. With a bit of advance planning, though, you won't need more than a couple of bus rides (and often only one) to cross from one part to the next.

The Fairfax District and the LA County Museum of Art

The West LA section of Fairfax Avenue, between Santa Monica and Wilshire Boulevards, is the backbone of LA's Jewish community. Apart from countless kosher butcher's shops and delicatessens there's little specifically to see, but by local standards it's a refreshingly vibrant neighbourhood, and easily seen on foot. The graceful facade of the **Pan-Pacific Auditorium**, off Fairfax on Beverly Boulevard, still standing despite the fires that have destroyed the rest of the building is probably the area's most tangible landmark, built as an exhibition space in 1938, and a startling sheer example of the machine-age ethos, more like a sleek sports car than an exhibition hall.

Fairfax continues down to the lacklustre wooden structures of **Farmer's Market**, at the junction with Third Street (June to Sept Mon–Sat 9am–8pm, rest of the year Mon–Sat 9am–6.30pm; Sun 10am–5pm): overrated as a place to eat and drink although the stalls are groaning under fresh fruit and veg. Further on, the *May Company* department store on Wilshire Boulevard was built in 1934 to announce the western entrance to the premier property development of the time, the **Miracle Mile**, as it was named, which stretched along Wilshire from here to the edge of downtown and the *Bullocks Wilshire* department store (p.111), and is still lined with art deco-era monuments. Look out particularly for the **Wilshire Tower** at number 5514, a Zigzag Moderne tower stepping up from a streamlined two-storey pedestal, and, just east of La Brea Avenue, the 1929 black and gold **Security Pacific Bank**. However, many of the businesses have relocated to Century City or downtown, and most of the office blocks are empty now.

The LA County Museum of Art and the La Brea Tar Pits

Oddly enough, the **LA County Museum of Art** or LACMA (Tues–Fri 10am–5pm, weekends until 6pm; $4, students $1.50) is one of the least impressive of the buildings along the Miracle Mile. It was plopped down in 1965 in a fit of municipal mindedness that has never really taken root. The buildings aside, though, some of the collections of applied art here are among the best in the world, and despite the loss of Armand Hammer's fine stock of paintings to his own museum in Westwood, it justifies a lengthy visit.

The LACMA is an enormous museum, and you'd be best off picking the periods you're interested in and sticking to them – there's no way you could see the lot in one go. Pick up a map of the complex from the information desk in the new Anderson building, since the various collections are continually shifted around from one wing to another. The pick among many excellent collections of South East Asian sculpture and Middle East decorative arts is the **Fearing Collection**, consisting of funereal masks and sculpted guardian figures from the ancient civilisations of Pre-Columbian Mexico. There's also a broad selection of works by

contemporary local artists, particularly Richard Diebenkorn. Where the museum really excels, however, is in its specialisations, notably the prints and drawings in the **Robert Gore Rifkind Center for German Expressionist Studies**, which includes a library of magazines and tracts from Weimar Germany, and the **Pavilion for Japanese Art**. This is a recent addition to the museum, built in a way that's supposed to resemble the effects of traditional *shoji* screens, filtering varying levels and qualities of light through to the interior. Displays include painted screens and scrolls, ceramics, and lacquerware, rivalling the collection of the late Emperor Hirohito as the most extensive in the world.

The roof combs of the pavilion make a playful reference to the tusks of a model mastodon slowly sinking into the adjacent **La Brea Tar Pits** (Tues–Sun 10am–5pm; $5, students $1.50, free on the second Tues of each month), a large pool of smelly tar ("*la brea*" is Spanish for tar) surrounded by full-size models of mastodons and sabre-tooth tigers. In prehistoric times, such creatures tried to drink from the thin layer of water covering the tar in the pits, only to become stuck fast. Millions of bones belonging to the animals (and one set of human bones) have been found here and reconstructed in the adjacent **George C. Page Discovery Center** (hours and admission as for the County Art Museum). Tar still seeps from the ground, and, during 1988, a by-product, methane gas, caught fire underground and spread flames through the Fairfax streets.

St Elmo's Village

Not far from the art works on display in the County Museum, **St Elmo's Village** at 4836 St Elmo Drive, a mile south of Wilshire (☎931-3409), is a popular version of community art-in-action. An arts project now over twenty years old, the colourful murals and sculptures here grew out of efforts to foster a constructive and supportive environment for local youth. It's now also the site of the **Festival of the Art of Survival**, a yearly celebration of slightly hippy-flavoured folk and popular art and music held each Memorial Day; drop by if you can.

West Hollywood

Between Fairfax Avenue and Beverly Hills, **WEST HOLLYWOOD** is the newest of LA's constituent cities. Owing to a number of legal technicalities, it was for many years a separate administrative entity from the rest of Los Angeles, notorious for its after-hours vice clubs and general debauchery. Things changed in 1983, however, when the autonomous city of West Hollywood was established, partly to clean up the place and partly to represent the interests of the predominantly gay community. There are still sleazy rent-boy areas around La Brea Avenue in the east, but much of the rest has smartened up considerably, from the new sculpture garden down the centre of **Santa Monica Boulevard**, the main drag of West Hollywood, to the flashy danceclubs and designer clothes appearing over the rest of the neighbourhood.

Melrose Avenue, LA's trendiest shopping street, runs parallel to Santa Monica Boulevard three blocks south, a streetscape which at times seems to have been lifted out of a low-budget 1950s sci-fi feature: neon and art deco abound among a fluorescent rash of designer and second-hand boutiques, exotic antique shops, avant-garde galleries and high-fashion eateries. Record shops, too, are everywhere, all good for checking what's going on locally. The west end of

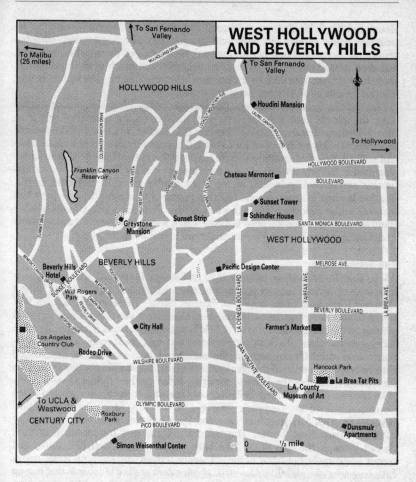

WEST HOLLYWOOD
AND BEVERLY HILLS

To San Fernando
Valley

To Malibu
(25 miles)

MULHOLLAND DRIVE

HOLLYWOOD HILLS

To San Fernando
Valley

◆Houdini Mansion

COLDWATER CANYON DRIVE

LAUREL CANYON BOULEVARD

To Hollywood

Franklin Canyon
Reservoir

LOMA VISTA

HOLLYWOOD BOULEVARD

BOULEVARD

Chateau Marmont■

◆ Sunset Tower

■ Schindler House

SANTA MONICA BOULEVARD

Greystone
Mansion

Sunset Strip

WEST HOLLYWOOD

BEVERLY HILLS

Pacific Design Center

MELROSE AVE.

Beverly Hills
Hotel

FAIRFAX AVE.

LA BREA AVE.

Will Rogers
Park

BEVERLY BOULEVARD

LA CIENEGA BOULEVARD

◆ City Hall

Farmer's Market ■

Los Angeles
Country Club

Rodeo Drive

WILSHIRE BOULEVARD

SAN VICENTE BOULEVARD

Hancock Park

■ La Brea Tar Pits

L.A. County
Museum of Art

To UCLA &
Westwood

CENTURY CITY

OLYMPIC BOULEVARD

Roxbury
Park

PICO BOULEVARD

0   ½ mile

◆Dunsmuir
Apartments

Simon Weisenthal Center

Melrose is more upmarket, with furniture shops and art galleries spread out around the hulking, bright blue glass mass of the **Pacific Design Center**, a wholesale furniture marketplace on Melrose at San Vicente Boulevard known locally as the "Blue Whale" for the way it fits alongside its low-rise neighbours.

The stylistic extremes of Melrose Avenue are reflected in the area's domestic architecture as well. Three blocks east of La Cienega, the 1922 **Schindler House**, at 833 N King's Road (tours Wed, Sat & Sun 1–4pm, and by appointment ☎651-1510; donations), was the blueprint of California modernist architecture for years after, with sliding glass doors, exposed roof rafters, and open-plan rooms facing on to outdoor terraces – banal in replication but compelling in the original. The house was actually first conceived as two houses, one for the architect R.M. Schindler and his wife, one for a second couple, sharing a central kitchen and planned in an S-shape with each wing curling around a private garden. Coming from his native Austria via Frank Lloyd Wright's studio to work on the Hollyhock

House (p.120), Schindler was so pleased with the mild California climate that he built this house without any bedrooms, romantically planning to sleep outdoors year-round in covered porches on the roof; he misjudged the weather, however, and soon moved inside. To save money Schindler did much of the construction work himself, allowing him to try out new ways of building. The house is now used as the offices of *Arts and Architecture* magazine.

Four blocks west, **La Cienega Boulevard** divides West Hollywood roughly down the middle, separating the next-wave trendies on the Hollywood side from the establishment *couturiers* on the Beverly Hills border. La Cienega ("the swamp" in Spanish) holds a mixture of LA's best and most expensive French restaurants and art galleries, and continues south, passing the glitzy **Beverly Center** shopping mall at Beverly Boulevard – a seemingly inpenetrable fortress of brown plaster that was thrown up in 1982 on top of the fun but faded **Beverlyland** funfair. Another landmark structure, and one that managed to survive the wrecker's ball by some adroit repositioning, is the **Tail o' the Pup**, the world-famous hot-dog stand shaped like a (mostly bun) hot dog, which was recently moved a block away from La Cienega to 329 San Vicente Boulevard to make way for a hotel.

The Sunset Strip

Above west Hollywood, on either side of La Cienega Boulevard, the roughly two-mile long conglomeration of restaurants, plush hotels and nightclubs on Sunset Boulevard has long been known as **Sunset Strip**. These establishments first began to appear during the early Twenties, along what was then a dusty dirt road serving as the main route between the Hollywood movie studios and the West LA "homes of the stars". F. Scott Fitzgerald and friends spent many leisurely afternoons over drinks here, around the swimming pool of the long-demolished *Garden of Allah* hotel, and the nearby *Ciro's* nightclub was *the* place to be seen in the swinging days of the Forties, surviving today as the original *Comedy Store*. With the rise of TV the Strip declined, only reviving in the Sixties when a scene developed around the landmark *Whiskey-a-Go-Go* club, which featured seminal psychedelic rock bands such as Love and Buffalo Springfield during the heyday of West Coast flower-power. The striptease clubs and headshops that lined Sunset through the mid-1970s have been replaced by hi-tech hi-fi stores and trendy restaurants, but many of the old names remain, and the Strip is still one of LA's best areas for nightlife. Also striking after dark are the billboards that line up above the street: fantastic commercial murals often animated with eye-catching gimmicks.

Greta Garbo was only one of many stars and starlets to appreciate the quirky character of the huge Norman castle that is the **Chateau Marmont Hotel**, towering over the east end of the Sunset Strip at no. 8221. Built in 1927 as luxury apartments, this stodgy block of white concrete has long been a Hollywood favourite. Howard Hughes used to rent the entire penthouse so he could keep an eye on the bathing beauties around the pool below, and the hotel made the headlines a few years ago when comedian John Belushi died of a heroin overdose in the hotel bungalow that he used as his LA home. Across the street, the corner of Sunset and Crescent Heights Boulevard was the site of the **Garden of Allah** hotel, once an infamous watering hole for celebs, now remembered only by a small plastic scale-model in a glass case behind the concrete bank building that replaced it.

Beverly Hills and Century City

Beverly Hills, Century City, everything's so nice and pretty,
all the people look the same, but you know they're so damn lame.

Circle Jerks

Probably the most famous small city in the world, **BEVERLY HILLS** has over the years sucked in more than its fair share of wealthy residents. Here, though, the money is discreet rather than vulgar, revealed more by the immaculate shops and squeaky clean streets than ostentatious displays. It's not a particularly welcoming place, especially if your clothes don't match the quietly elegant attire of the residents – the pets in Beverly Hills are better dressed and groomed than some of the people elsewhere in LA. There's time enough, though, to stroll the designer-crammed stores of Rodeo Drive and, if you're driving, take a spin by the mansions up in the canyons before the police (and Beverly Hills has more police per capita than anywhere else in the US) ask for your ID.

Beverly Hills divides into two distinct halves, separated by the old railway line down Santa Monica Boulevard. **Below the tracks** are the flatlands of modest houses on rectangular blocks, set around the "Golden Triangle" business district that fills the wedge between Santa Monica and Wilshire Boulevards. **Rodeo Drive** cuts through the triangle in a two-block-long concentrated showcase of the most expensive names in international fashion. It's an intimidatingly stylish area, each boutique trying to outshine the rest: none as yet charges for admission, though some require an invitation (for a couple of the most interesting, see p.194).

Above the tracks is the upmarket part of residential Beverly Hills, its gently curving drives converging on the pink plaster **Beverly Hills Hotel**, on Sunset Boulevard and Rodeo Drive. The wildly overgrown but luxurious hotel was built in 1913 to attract wealthy settlers to what was then a town of just five hundred people, and it still has the social caché that makes its *Polo Lounge* a prime spot for movie execs to be seen power-lunching. You can call in for a taste of life in the fast-lane, but you'll need $5 to buy a beer.

In the verdant canyons and foothills above Sunset lie many palatial estates, often hidden away behind landscaped security gates. **Benedict Canyon Drive** climbs from the hotel up past a good number, beginning with the first and most famous: the lavish **PickFair** mansion, built for Mary Pickford and Douglas Fairbanks in 1919 and setting the tone for the exclusive community that has grown up around it. From the gate at 1143 Summit Drive you can just glimpse the house, now owned by Jerry Buss, the high-profile owner of the LA Lakers basketball team. Further up Benedict Canyon, Harold Lloyd's **Green Acres**, where he lived for forty years, with its secret passageways and large private screening room, survives intact, though the grounds, which contained a waterfall and a nine-hole golf course, have since been broken up into smaller lots. Above here, Cielo Drive turns off to the west, twisting up the canyon into the Hollywood Hills (see p.127).

The grounds of the biggest house in Beverly Hills, Greystone Mansion, are now maintained as a public park by the city, who use it to disguise a massive underground reservoir. Though the fifty-thousand-square-foot manor house is rarely open, you can visit the 16-acre **Greystone Park** at 905 Loma Vista, from 10am–5pm daily. You might recognise it as the "Whispering Glades" mortuary from the movie *The Loved One*, much of which was filmed here. Up the hill are the fabulously expensive tract homes of **Trousdale Estates**, a late-Fifties exercise in ostentatious banality, with two sub-repro Greek columns per stucco shed – and, as a bonus, a panoramic view.

Century City

The only tall buildings punctuating West LA's flat skyline are the gleaming spires of **CENTURY CITY**, just west of Beverly Hills, erected during the Sixties on the backlot of the *20th Century Fox* film studios. The plate-glass office towers aren't at all inviting, rising sharply and inhospitably skywards from sidewalks which have never been used – a perhaps typically Sixties disaster, planned at a time when sweeping gestures toward sweeping vistas were the order of the day. The massive **ABC Entertainment Center** complex, on Avenue of the Stars, might conceivably bring you here – its *Schubert Theater* is one of LA's leading live theatres, specialising in touring productions of the latest Andrew Lloyd Webber hit (see p.189).

Along the south edge of Century City, **Pico Boulevard** is quintessential LA: mile after mile of single-storey shopfronts, auto parts stores and delis, with a mini-mall on every other corner. To the west, look through the front gates of the still-working **20th Century Fox** film and TV studios to catch a glimpse of the intact New York City street set used for the production of *Hello Dolly!*

Less frivolously, just east of Century City, below Beverly Hills, an inauspicious white building houses the **Simon Wiesenthal Center for Holocaust Studies** at 9760 West Pico (Mon–Thurs 10am–4pm; free), US headquarters of the organisation devoted to tracking down ex-Nazis, and with an extensive library and a small but unforgettable museum documenting concentration camp atrocities.

Westwood Village and the UCLA campus

Just west of Beverly Hills, on the north side of Wilshire Boulevard, **WESTWOOD VILLAGE** is one of LA's more user-friendly neighbourhoods, a grouping of low-slung redbrick buildings that went up here in the late 1920s, along with the nearby campus of the nascent University of California at Los Angeles (UCLA). It's an area that's easily negotiated on foot, and one very much shaped by the proximity of the university campus, which is really the lifeblood of the area.

Broxton Avenue, the main strip of Westwood Village, was for many years the weekend cruising strip for Westside teenagers, and although the street is now closed to cars it is still packed on Friday and Saturday nights with hordes of kids making the circuit of record stores and video parlours. It's also a big moviegoing district, with thirty or so cinemas within a quarter-mile radius. None of the more than ten thousand seats in Westwood's theatres is reserved, and people-watching while queuing up for the latest blockbuster is often half the fun.

Much of the Spanish Revival design of the original layout has survived the intervening years of more unimaginative construction, though the ordinary businesses of the old days have been replaced by fancy boutiques and designer novelty shops. The tower at the end of the street belongs to the 1931 **Fox Westwood Village** which, together with the neon-signed *Bruin* across the street, is sometimes used by movie studios for "sneak" previews of films to gauge audience reaction. Check the Calendar section of the *LA Times* for showings.

The UCLA Campus

The **UCLA campus** is the dominant feature in Westwood, a grouping of Italianate buildings spread generously over well-landscaped grounds. It's worth a wander if you've time to kill, particularly for a couple of worthy exhibition spaces. The student union building, at the north end of Westwood Boulevard, half a mile north of the village, has a bowling alley, a good bookstore and a "rideboard" offering shared-expense car-rides; and there's a decent coffee house, in Kerckhoff Hall just behind.

Stop at one of the information kiosks located at various spots around campus to pick up a **map**. Of things to see, the spacious rotunda of the **Powell Library**, on one side of the central quadrangle, was where Aldous Huxley put in long hours at the card catalogues in the late 1930s, researching his novel *After Many a Summer*, based on the life and legend of William Randolph Hearst. In Haines Hall, there is a well-respected **Museum of Cultural History** (Wed–Sun, noon–5pm; free), which has often intriguing exhibitions of contemporary anthropological studies; and, at the northern end of campus, the **Wight Art Gallery** holds a variety of visiting exhibitions (Tues–Fri 11am–5pm, weekends 1–5pm; free).

Nearby, UCLA's **film school** has a reputation for producing offbeat filmmakers rather than espousing traditional Hollywood production values; it also has one of the most extensive collections of old films and TV programmes in the world, examples of which are shown every day, often for free, in the large auditorium in **Melnitz Hall**. Check the bulletin board in the lobby for the current schedule.

Once you've exhausted all this, you could do worse than visit the Franklin D. Murphy **Sculpture Garden**, which contains work by Rodin, Maillol, Moore and other modern artists under the June blooms of the jacaranda trees – an ideal spot for a snack.

South of the Village

South of the village, **Westwood Boulevard** has more cinemas, a few interesting shops and a number of specialist bookstores below Wilshire Boulevard. This section of Wilshire exploded in the 1970s with oil-rich high-rise developments, leading to a change of scale that would seem bizarre anywhere outside of LA. Modest detached houses sit next to twenty-storey condominium towers in which penthouse apartments with private heliports sell for upwards of $12 million.

Inside one of the towers, on the corner with Westwood Boulevard, the **Armand Hammer Museum of Art and Culture Center** (Wed–Mon noon–7pm; $4.50) is one of the city's best – and most debated – art stashes, amassed over seven decades by the flamboyant and ultra-wealthy boss of the Occidental Petroleum Corporation. Art critic Robert Hughes called the paintings here "a mishmash of second or third-rate works by famous names", but while the Rembrandts and Rubens are less than stunning, the nineteenth-century pieces more than make amends, with Van Gogh's intense and radiant *Hospital at Saint Remy* being the jewel among them. In a separate gallery, the museum's costliest acquisition is also the most disappointing: the *Codex Hammer* – which Hammer bought for $2 million and renamed after himself – comprising of pages from the notebooks of the sixteenth-century visionary artist-engineer Leonardo da Vinci. Now suspended between plexiglass panels above an English translation of their contents, the pages are filled by vague ramblings on hydraulics.

Outside the musuem, at the end of the driveway behind the tiny *Avco* cinema, you'll find Hammer's speckled marble tomb, sharing the tiny cemetery of **Westwood Memorial Park** with the likes of movie stars Peter Lorre and Natalie Wood, wildman jazz drummer Buddy Rich, and the lipstick-covered plaque that marks the resting place of **Marilyn Monroe**. Since her death in 1962, Monroe's ex-husband, Joe DiMaggio, has sent a bouquet of red roses twice-weekly to be placed in the basket alongside.

Santa Monica, Venice and Malibu

Set along an unbroken, twenty-mile strand of clean, white-sand beaches, and home to a diverse assortment of LA's finest stores, restaurants and art galleries, the small, self-contained communities that line the **Santa Monica Bay** feature some of the best of what Los Angeles has to offer, with none of the smog or searing heat that can make the rest of the metropolis unbearable. The entire area is well served by public transport, near (but not too near) the airport, and there's a wide selection of cheap accommodation, making the area a good base for seeing the rest of LA.

Santa Monica, set on palm-tree-shaded bluffs above the blue Pacific, is the oldest, biggest and best-known of the resort areas. Once a wild beachfront playground, and the memorable location for many scenes from the underworld stories of Raymond Chandler, it's now a self-consciously healthy and liberal community, which has enticed a large expatriate British community of writers and rock-stars, ranging from Rod Stewart to Johnny Rotten.

Directly south, **Venice's** once-expansive network of canals and the beachfront boardwalk brings together a lively mixture of street performers, roller skaters and casual voyeurs – and is one of the few places in LA where people actually walk for fun.

North from Santa Monica along the Pacific Coast Highway, **Pacific Palisades** is a gathering of hugely expensive suburban houses clinging to the lower foothills of the nearby mountains. Aside from some pioneering post-war architecture, however, there's nothing to consume your time, except perhaps pushing a few miles inland to **Will Rogers State Park**, home and museum of one of the legends of the American West, and with some rewarding hiking paths leading into the neighbouring canyons.

A few miles further along the coastal road, the **J. Paul Getty Museum** is rightly acknowledged as one of the world's finest collections of classical art, and reason enough alone for visiting the area. Close by, **Topanga Canyon** has more hiking, its reputation as haven of back-to-nature hippiedom gone, but still with a surprisingly wild set of trails leading into the the deep, wooded canyons and sculptured rock outcrops of the Santa Monica Mountains.

Malibu, at the top of the bay, twenty miles from Santa Monica and the northernmost edge of LA, is a whole other world. Its beach colony houses are owned by those who are famous enough to need privacy and rich enough to afford it. For all that, you don't have to be a millionaire to enjoy its fine surfing beaches, or the birds, seals – and, in migrating season, whales – for which this part of the coast is noted.

Santa Monica

As little as a century ago, most of the land between **SANTA MONICA** and what was then Los Angeles was covered by beanfields and citrus groves, interrupted by the occasional outposts of Hollywood and Beverly Hills. Like so much of the state, the land was owned by the Southern Pacific Railroad, who tried – and failed – to make Santa Monica into the port of Los Angeles, losing out to other interests who dredged the harbour at Wilmington, near Long Beach. The linking of the beachfront with the rest of Los Angeles by the suburban streetcar system meant the town instead grew into one of LA's premier resorts – a giant funfair city that was the inspiration for Raymond Chandler's anything-goes "Bay City", described in *Farewell My Lovely*. Today Chandler wouldn't recognise the place: changes in the gaming laws and the advent of the private swimming pool have led to the removal of the offshore gambling ships and many of the bathing clubs, and Santa Monica is among the city's more elegant seaside towns – a transformation currently being hurried along by an influx of fashionable residents.

Santa Monica lies across 26th Street from West LA, and splits into three distinct portions. The town itself, holding a fair slab of Santa Monica's history and its day-to-day business, sits on the coastal bluffs; below there's the pier and beach; while Main Street, running south from close to the pier towards Venice, is Santa Monica's more residential quarter, with designer-eateries and fancy shops.

The town

Santa Monica reaches nearly three miles inland, but most things of interest are situated within a few blocks of the beach. The **Visitor Information Office** (daily 10am–4pm; ☎310/393-7593) in a kiosk just south of Santa Monica Boulevard, along Ocean Boulevard in Palisades Park (the cypress-tree-lined strip which runs along the top of the bluffs), makes a good first stop. Its handy free map shows the whole of the town and the routes of the Santa Monica *Big Blue Bus* transit system, a useful Westside complement to the *RTD* network.

Two blocks east of Ocean Boulevard, between Wilshire and Broadway, the **Santa Monica Promenade** is the closest the town comes to having a high street, a pedestrianised stretch popular with buskers and itinerant evangelists, and lined by a variety of low-rent shops. Browse through the many secondhand and fine art book shops, check out the latest Spanish-language movies, or, of a Wednesday, sample the offerings at the weekly **farmer's market**, which sets up along Arizona Street on either side of the mall. The mall is anchored at its southern end by the expensive **Santa Monica Place**, a white stucco shopping precinct styled by noted LA architect Frank Gehry. The atrium fountain was recently replaced by a twenty-foot-tall sandcastle, but otherwise *Santa Monica Place* has the usual assortment of chain stores, plus a food hall where you can sample fast-food from around the world.

Santa Monica has many pockets of artistic endeavour, with a number of fine **art galleries** selling works by emerging local and international artists. There's a concentration around the *Ruth Bachofner Gallery* at 926 Colorado Avenue, just east of Lincoln Boulevard, while some of the biggest names in the art world are handled by the *James Corcoran Gallery* at Fifth Street and Santa Monica Boulevard. For a change of pace from the unflinchingly contemporary, explore the **Angel's Attic** at 516 Colorado Street (Thurs–Sun 12.30–4.30pm;

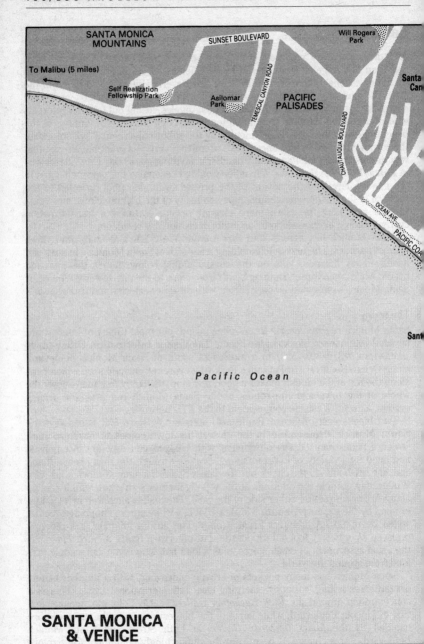

SANTA MONICA
MOUNTAINS

SUNSET BOULEVARD

Will Rogers
Park

To Malibu (5 miles)

Self Realization
Fellowship Park

Asilomar
Park

PACIFIC
PALISADES

Santa
Can

TEMESCAL CANYON ROAD

CHAUTAUQUA BOULEVARD

OCEAN AVE.

PACIFIC COA

San

Pacific Ocean

**SANTA MONICA
& VENICE**

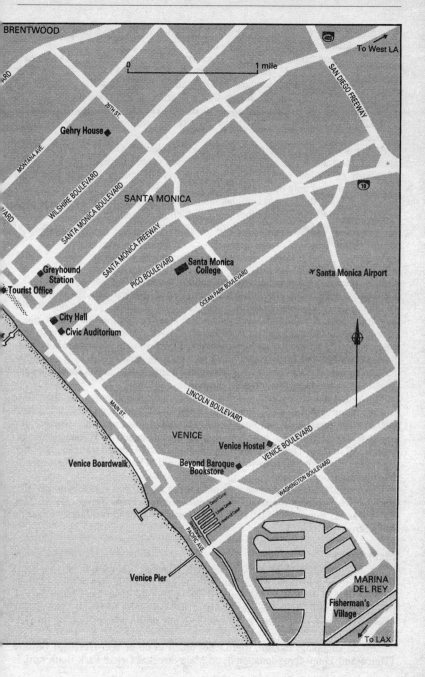

BRENTWOOD

0   1 mile

26TH ST

MONTANA AVE.

Gehry House ◆

WILSHIRE BOULEVARD

SANTA MONICA BOULEVARD

SANTA MONICA

SANTA MONICA FREEWAY

PICO BOULEVARD

Santa Monica College ◆

OCEAN PARK BOULEVARD

SAN DIEGO FREEWAY

To West LA

405

10

⊀ Santa Monica Airport

Greyhound Station ■
Tourist Office

City Hall ■
Civic Auditorium ◆

MAIN ST.

LINCOLN BOULEVARD

VENICE

Venice Hostel ◆

Venice Boardwalk

Beyond Baroque Bookstore ◆

VENICE BOULEVARD

WASHINGTON BOULEVARD

PACIFIC AVE.

Venice Pier

MARINA DEL REY

Fisherman's Village

To LAX

$3 – proceeds go to autistic children), a collection of Victorian toys, dollhouses and miniatures in a Queen Anne-style house.

Further inland, Santa Monica has a few worthwhile places, though it's less easy to stumble upon them. On the northern border, **San Vicente Boulevard**'s grassy tree-lined strip is a joggers' freeway, and races through the plush houses of **Brentwood**, including the house where Marilyn Monroe was found dead in 1962, at 12305 5th Helena Drive. South of San Vicente, reflecting the upward mobility of the area, are the flashy novelty and clothing shops of **Montana Avenue**.

At the southeast corner of Santa Monica Boulevard, Ocean Park Boulevard spears off to another place you'd be unlikely ever to stumble upon by chance, the **Museum of Flying** (daily 10am–5pm; free), at the Santa Monica Municipal Airport (now used only by private planes). The major employer in the early years of Santa Monica, the Donald Douglas Aircraft Company, had its main factory here – birthplace of the DC-3 and other planes which pioneered commercial aviation – and the old premises display Sopwith Camels and Spitfires among a number of vintage aircraft.

The pier and beach

Despite the many features on top of the bluffs, the real focal point of Santa Monica life is down below, on the 'beach and around **Santa Monica pier**, the only reminder that the city was ever anything but a quiet coastal suburb. Jutting out into the bay at the foot of Colorado Avenue, the pier is in the tradition of seaside piers, recently expanded after half of it was washed away by winter storms, with new rides, a giant helter-skelter and a well-restored 1922 wooden **carousel** (daily 9am–6pm; 50¢ a ride) – which featured, along with Paul Newman, in the 1973 movie *The Sting*. The pier also has shooting galleries and bumper cars, and is sometimes the site of free concerts and assorted celebrations.

The grand beach houses just north of the pier were known as the "Gold Coast", because of the many Hollywood personalities who lived in them. The largest, now the **Sand and Sea** beach club, was built as the servants' quarters of a massive 120-room house, now demolished, that belonged to William Randolph Hearst. MGM boss Louis B. Mayer owned the adjacent Mediterranean-style villa, where the Kennedy brothers were later rumoured to have had their liaisons with Marilyn Monroe.

If you're not intending to stretch out on the sands, you can follow the **bike path**, which begins at the pier, twenty miles south to Palos Verdes. Or, on foot, wander south along the beach to Pico Boulevard and head two blocks inland to Main Street.

Main Street

Santa Monica underwent a major change following completion of the Santa Monica Freeway in 1965, which brought the beachfront homes within a fifteen-minute drive of downtown and isolated the bulk of the town from **Main Street**, five minutes' walk from the pier – where the collection of novelty shops, kite stores and classy restaurants has grown into one of the prime shopping districts on the Westside.

Beyond shopping, though, there's not much to do or see. **Heritage Square** (Thurs–Sun 11am–4pm; donations), on Main Street at Ocean Park Boulevard, is the city's effort to preserve some of its architectural past in the face of the onslaught of new money: an assortment of houses moved here to escape demolition and displayed alongside informative exhibitions on the history of the Santa Monica area. Not all of Santa Monica has been so lucky, however. Ocean Park Boulevard was one of the main routes to the coast via the old streetcars of the *Pacific Electric*, and the entire beachfront between here and the Venice border, overshadowed by massive grey condominiums, used to be the site of the largest and wildest of the amusement piers, the fantastic **Pacific Ocean Park**. "P-O-P", as it was known, had a huge rollercoaster, a giant funhouse and a boisterous midway arcade, described by architectural historian Reyner Banham as a "fantasy in stucco and every known style of architecture and human ecology". Sadly, not a trace remains.

Venice

Immediately south of Santa Monica, **VENICE** was laid out in the marshlands of Ballona Creek in 1905 by developer Abbot Kinney as a romantic replica of the northern Italian city, a twenty-mile network of canals, lined by sham palazzos and waterfront homes, that was intended to attract artsy folk from Los Angeles to sample its sub-European Bohemian air. It never really caught on, and the coming of the automobile finished it off altogether. Many of the canals were filled in, and the area, now annexed by the city of Los Angeles, fell into disrepair, with most of the homesites being taken over by oil wells – an era that features in Orson Welles' film *A Touch of Evil*, in which derelict Venice stars as a seedy border town.

Kinney was, however, ahead of his time. A fair bit of the original plan survives, and the pseudo-European atmosphere has since proved just right for pulling in the artistic community he was aiming at, making Venice one of the coast's trendier spots. Chic cafés and restaurants abound near the beach, and there is a strong alternative arts scene, centred around the **Beyond Baroque Literary Arts Center and Bookshop** in the old City Hall at 681 Venice Boulevard (Mon–Fri 10am–5pm; ☎310/822-3006), which holds regular readings and workshops of poetry, prose and drama.

Windward Avenue is the main artery of the town, running from the beach into what was the Grand Circle of the canal system, now paved over and ringed by a number of galleries and the Venice post office, inside which a mural depicts the early layout. The original Romanesque **arcade**, around the intersection with Pacific Avenue, leads to the beach and is alive with health food shops, used-record stores, and roller-skate rental stands. The whitewashed walls of the original hotels, and of the Venice Pavilion on the beach, are here and there covered by colourful and portentous giant **murals**: one of Venice in the snow, another, just north, the *Fall of Icarus*. The few remaining **canals** are just a few blocks south, below Venice Boulevard and east of Pacific, where the original quaint little bridges survive, and you can sit and watch the ducks paddle around in the stagnant waters.

It's **Venice Beach** that draws most people to the town. Nowhere else does LA parade itself quite so openly and as sensuously as it does along the **Venice Boardwalk**, a wide pathway also known as Ocean Front Walk. Year-round at weekends and every day in summer it is packed with people and people-watchers, jugglers, fire-eaters, Hare Krishnas and roller-skating guitar players. You can buy anything you might need to look like a local without ever leaving the beach: cheap sunglasses, t-shirts, Walkmans and tennis shoes. South of Windward is **Muscle Beach**, a now legendary outdoor weightlifting centre where serious-looking hunks of muscle drive some serious iron, and high-flying gymnasts swing on the adjacent rings and bars. Spend ten minutes watching and you'll find Narcissus is alive and well, and working on his biceps.

Incidentally, be warned that **Venice Beach at night** is a dangerous place, taken over by street gangs, drug dealers and assorted psychos. Even walking on the beach after dark is illegal, and anywhere in the immediate vicinity you should take great care.

Pacific Palisades and Will Rogers State Park

The town of **PACIFIC PALISADES**, which rises on the bluffs two miles north of Santa Monica pier, is slowly but very surely falling away into the bay, most notice-ably on the point above Chautauqua Boulevard and Pacific Coast Highway, other-wise known as "PCH". With each winter's rains, a little bit more of the bluffs gets washed away in mudslides, blocking traffic on PCH, and gradually shrinking the backyards of the clifftop homes. There are few places of interest among the suburban ranch houses, although some of the most influential buildings of post-war LA were constructed here – **Charles Eames' house**, for example, at 203 Chautauqua Street, fashioned out of prefabricated industrial parts in 1947.

In complete contrast, and a better place to spend a few hours, a mile east along Sunset Boulevard from the top of Chautauqua is the **Will Rogers State Historic Park** (daily 8am–dusk; free, parking $4), a steep climb from the RTD bus (#2) stop. This was the home and ranch of the Depression-era cowboy philosopher and journalist Will Rogers, one of America's most popular figures of the time, renowned for his downhome, commonsense thinking, and the saying that he "never met a man he didn't like". The overgrown ranch-style house serves as an informal **museum** (daily 10am–5pm; free), filled to overflowing with cowboy gear and Indian art; and the 200-acre park has miles of foot and bridle paths, one of which leads up to the top of Topanga Canyon.

The J. Paul Getty Museum

From Pacific Palisades, PCH follows the curve of the bay towards Malibu. Three miles or so on, a huge French chateau towers above the shore, an imposing house that inadvertently marks the otherwise easily missed entrance to the **J. Paul Getty Museum** at 17985 Pacific Coast Highway (Tues–Sun 10am–5pm; free; ☎310/458-2003), housed in a replica Pompeiian Villa that holds the Getty collection of Greek and Roman antiquities. If driving, you must make parking reservations by phoning well in advance; otherwise take RTD bus #434 from Santa Monica, and ask the bus driver for a free pass.

The Getty Museum opened in 1974, displaying the art collection of the colossally wealthy oil magnate, John Paul Getty, who began collecting art in the 1930s, at first showing it in his house. Two years after the museum opened Getty died, leaving $1.3 billion to continue the work he had started: an unprecedented sum for any museum, which has made this one notorious in the art world for having more money than it knows what to do with. Under American tax laws, the Getty Trust must spend five percent of its endowment, or $100 million, every year, which means in effect that the museum is able to outbid anyone in the world to get what it wants, thereby inflating international art prices beyond the reach of most institutions and encouraging shady behaviour among the museum's suppliers. A sizeable part of the collection was speedily acquired by a curator who bought over-priced works by the crateload on behalf of private individuals, who then bequeathed the art to the museum and claimed the cost as a (often gigantic) tax write-off*.

Even so, you'd be mad to miss the place while you're in LA. The fake Roman Villa, a copy of the *Villa dei Papiri* in Pompeii, is gorgeously sited high above the ocean, and – sour grapes aside – the quality of the **exhibits** helps the Getty Museum rank among the world's finest museums. The collection is not surprisingly determined by the enthusiasms of Getty himself. There's a formidable array of his major interest, Greek and Roman statuary, including the only remaining work (an athlete) of Lysippos, sculptor to Alexander the Great; and a feast of ornate furniture and decorative arts, with clocks, chandeliers, tapestries and gilt-edged commodes, designed for the French nobility from the reign of Louis XIV, filling several overwhelmingly opulent rooms. Getty was much less interested in painting – although he did scoop up a very fine stash from the Renaissance and Baroque periods, including works by Rembrandt, Rubens, de la Tour and more – but a large collection has been amassed since his death, featuring all the major names from the thirteenth century to the present: drawings by Raphael and Bernini, paintings of the Dutch Golden Age, a handful of French Impressionists, to name just a few. By contrast, there's also an extensive and highly absorbing collection of photographs by Man Ray, Lazlo Moholy-Nagy and notable others.

When the proposed new branch of the museum, designed by architect Richard Meier for a site above Brentwood in the Santa Monica Mountains, opens in 1995, only the antiquities will be left on display at the existing museum.

Topanga Canyon

A mile beyond the Getty Museum, a turning leads up into **Topanga Canyon**, a fermenting ground for West Coast rock music in the Sixties, when Neil Young, the Byrds and other artists moved here, holding all-night jam sessions in the sycamore groves along Topanga Creek. The canyon still has the wildness which attracted them, especially in winter and early spring, when mudslides threaten houses and waterfalls cascade down the cliffs, and the hillsides are covered in golden poppies and wildflowers. A hundred and fifty thousand acres of these mountains and the seashore have been protected as the **Santa Monica Mountains National Recreation Area**, but as yet very few people take the chance to walk the trails in search of the fine views and fresh air, catching sight of the many deer, coyotes and the odd mountain lion that still live here. The *Santa Monica Mountains Conservancy* (☎620-2021) offers free guided hikes

---

* One recent scandal concerned the so-called *Malibu Venus*. This ancient Greek statue was unveiled here in 1988, amid allegations that it was pilfered from the ruins of Agrigento and demands from the Italian government for its repatriation.

throughout the mountains most weekends, and there are self-guided trails through the canyon's **Topanga State Park**, off Old Topanga Canyon Road at the crest of the mountains, with spectacular views out over the Pacific.

Beyond Topanga Canyon, the beaches and ocean-views are blocked off by mile after mile of private homes all the way to Malibu. There are a few signposted beach-access points but most of the rock-stars and others who can afford to live here treat the sands and seas as their own. Although any bit of land below the high-tide line is legally in the public domain, you're sure to feel like a trespasser.

Malibu

Everyone has heard of **MALIBU**; the very name conjures up images of beautiful people sunbathing on a palm-fringed beach and lazily consuming cocktails. And for once the image is not so very far from the truth – even though you might not think so on arrival. As you enter the small town, the succession of ramshackle surf shops, fast-food stands and real estate agents scattered along both sides of PCH around the graceful **Malibu Pier** doesn't spell money in itself; but the secluded communities just inland are as wealthy as any in the entire US.

The south-facing beach next to the pier, **Surfrider Beach**, was the surfing capital of the world in the 1950s and early 1960s, popularised by the many *Beach Blanket Bingo* movies filmed here, starring the likes of Annette Funicello and Frankie Avalon. It's still a big surfing spot: the surf is best in late summer, when storms off Mexico cause the waves to reach upwards of eight feet. Just beyond is **Malibu Lagoon State Park**, a nature reserve and bird refuge; birdwatching walks around the lagoon are offered some weekends, and there's a small **museum** (Tues–Sat 10am–4pm; free), detailing the history of the area.

Most Malibu residents live in the houses and small ranches that hide away in the narrow canyons on the edges of the town, together forming a well-off, insular community with a long-established dread of outsiders. Up until the Twenties all of Malibu was owned by one **May K. Rindge**, who hired armed guards and dynamited roads to keep travellers from crossing her land on their way to and from Santa Monica. Rindge fought for years to prevent the state from building the Pacific Coast Highway across her property, but lost her legal battle in the State Supreme Court, and her money in the Depression. Her son took over the ranch and quickly sold much of the land, establishing the **Malibu Colony** at the mouth of Malibu Canyon as a haven for movie stars. There's very little to see here except the garage doors of the rich and famous; if you must, you can enter on foot or cycle a mile or so along PCH, on the other side of the hill. You'd do better, though, just visiting the **Trancas Market**, near the gated entrance to the colony – good both for star-spotting and stocking up on food and drink before a day on the sands.

Much of **Malibu Creek State Park**, at the crest of Malibu Canyon Road along Mulholland Drive, used to belong to *20th Century Fox* studios, who filmed many Tarzan pictures here and more recently used the chaparral-covered hillsides to simulate South Korea for the television show *M.A.S.H.* The four-thousand-acre park includes a large lake, some waterfalls, and nearly fifteen miles of hiking trails. Nearby **Paramount Ranch**, another old studio backlot, has an intact Western Town movie set, where you can play gunfighter, near Mulholland Drive on Cornell Road.

The beaches

Five miles along the coast from Malibu Pier is the largest of the Los Angeles County beaches, **Zuma Beach**, whose huge carpark is popular with San Fernando Valley high school kids, who drive over Kanan-Dume road to escape the sweltering inland summer heat. Adjacent **Point Dume State Beach**, below the bluffs, is a lot more relaxed, especially up and over the rocks at its southern tip, where **Pirate's Cove** is used by nudists. The rocks here are also a good place to look out for seals and migrating grey whales in winter, as the point juts out into the Pacific at the northern lip of Santa Monica Bay.

Another five miles along PCH, where Mulholland Drive reaches the ocean, is **Leo Carrillo State Beach Park**, the northern border of LA County and the end of the RTD bus (#434) route. The mile-long sandy beach is divided by Sequit Point, a small bluff that has underwater caves and a tunnel you can pass through at low tide. Leo Carrillo is also the nearest and most accessible **campsite** for the rest of LA (see p.97). Five miles further on, at **Point Mugu State Park**, there are some very good walks through mountain canyons, and campsites right on the beach. Point Mugu is also the site of the US Navy's Pacific Missile Test Center, which takes up most of the five miles of coast south of VENTURA, at the southern edge of the Central Coast.

The South Bay and Harbor Area

South of Venice and Marina del Ray, the coast is dominated by the runways of LAX and the oil refineries of EL SEGUNDO. Beyond here begins the eight-mile coastal strip of the South Bay beach towns: **Manhattan Beach**, **Hermosa Beach** and **Redondo Beach**. These are poorer (though not poor), quieter, more suburban and smaller than the Westside beach communities. Along their shared beach-side bike path the joggers and roller-skaters are more likely to be locals than posers from other parts of LA, and all three can make a refreshing break if you like your beaches without pretentious packaging. Each has a beckoning strip of white sand, and Manhattan and Hermosa especially are well-equipped for surfing and beachsports. They're also well connected to the rest of the city: within easy reach of LAX and connected by regular buses (#439 and #443) to downtown LA.

Visible all along this part of the coast, the large vegetated peninsula of **Palos Verdes** looks more tempting than it really is, much of it an upmarket residential area, although the comparatively rough-hewn little city of **San Pedro** is a worthwhile destination around the far side (not least for the local youth hostel, the area's cheapest accommodation by a long way; see p.98) sited on the LA harbour, the busiest cargo port in the world and still growing. On the other side of the harbour, **Long Beach**, connected to downtown by express bus #456, is best-known as the resting place of the Spruce Goose and Queen Mary – two enormously popular tourist sights which rather mar the low-key appeal of the place itself.

Perhaps the most enticing, and certainly the strangest place in the area is **Catalina Island**, only twenty miles offshore and easily reached by ferry. It's almost completely conserved wildland, with many unique forms of plant and animal life and just one small, offbeat centre of population – Avalon.

Manhattan Beach, Hermosa Beach and Redondo Beach

Accessible along the bike path from Venice, or by car along Pacific Coast Highway, **MANHATTAN BEACH** is a likeable place with a healthy well-to-do air, home mainly to white-collar workers whose middle-class stucco homes tumble towards the beach, uncluttered by high-rise hotels. There's not much to see or do away from the beach, but then that's the main reason for coming. Surfing is a major local pastime, there's a two-week international surf festival each August, and the city is a major centre for beach volleyball, evidenced by the profusion of nets across the sands. For a break from sport, sun and sand, the bars and cafés along Manhattan Beach Boulevard are places to be seen (details p.170). If you can, call at the **Historical Center**, in the post office building at 425 15th Street (Tues–Thurs 9am–1pm; free), for its entertaining collection of photos and oddments from the city's early times. If these whet your appetite, you can buy (for $1) a map describing a history-flavoured **walking tour**.

HERMOSA BEACH, across Longfellow Boulevard, is more down-at-heel than Manhattan Beach, its houses less showy, with a younger, more effervescent mood. The centre, near the foot of the pier around Hermosa and Pier Avenues, is an unlikely setting for one of the South Bay's best-known nightspots, *The Lighthouse* (see p.185). Once more there's little of note except the beach, though you should take a look in the **Either/Or** bookshop at 124 Pier Avenue, once a haunt of writer Thomas Pynchon, which has a voluminous fiction selection and wide variety of New Age tomes, as well as stacks of free publications littering its floor.

Despite some long family oriented strips of sand, and fine views of Palos Verdes' stunning greenery, **REDONDO BEACH**, south of Hermosa, is less inviting. Scores of condos and tall hotels line the beach, and the food and drink spots around the yacht-lined King's Harbor are off-limits to impecunious visitors.

The bike path turns inland here to finish in the featureless blue-collar suburb of TORRANCE: an unfortunate end to an otherwise scenically dramatic ride. If you've pedalled this far and still have some energy, a better route is straight ahead around the Palos Verdes peninsula.

Palos Verdes

A great green hump marking LA's southwest corner, **PALOS VERDES** isn't of special interest, but the bluffs and coves along the protected coastline can be enjoyable to explore. Malaga Beach, by Torrance County Beach just south of Redondo, is a popular scuba-diving spot; Abalone Cove, reached from the car park on Berkentine Road, off Palos Verdes Drive, has some lively rockpools; and, a couple of miles east at the end of a path off Peppertree Drive, Smugglers Cove is a renowned **nudist beach**.

While you're in the area, don't miss **Wayfarer's Chapel**, at 5755 Palos Verdes Drive (daily 9am–5pm; free). Designed by Frank Lloyd Wright's son, Lloyd, it's a tribute to the eighteenth-century Swedish scientist/mystic Emanuel Swedenborg. The ultimate aim is for the redwood grove around the chapel to grow and entangle itself around the glass-framed structure – a fusing of human handiwork with the forces of nature of which Swedenborg would have been proud.

A few miles further on, just before the end of Palos Verdes Drive, **Point Fermin Park** is a small tip of land prodding into the ocean. In the park is a curious little wooden lighthouse dating from 1874 (no admittance), and a whale-watching station where you can read up on the winter migrations. There's also the less seasonally dependent thrill of hang-gliders swooping down off the cliffs.

From the park, it's an easy stroll along Bluff Place and down the 29th Street stairway to Cabrillo Beach and the excellent **Cabrillo Marine Museum**, at 3720 Stephen White Drive (Tues–Fri noon–5pm, weekends 10am–5pm, closed Mon; free). A diverse collection of marine life has been imaginatively and instructively assembled: everything from predator snails and the sarcastic fringehead (a rare fish whose strange name makes sense once you see it) to larger displays on otters, seals and whales.

San Pedro and around

About three miles further on along Bluff Place, the scruffy harbour city of **SAN PEDRO** is in stark contrast to the affluence of the rest of Palos Verdes. It was a small fishing community until the late nineteenth century, when the building of the LA harbour nearby brought a huge influx of labour, much of it drawn from the migrants who arrived on the ships, chiefly from Portugal, Greece and Yugoslavia. Many of these, and their descendants, never left San Pedro. They lent a striking racial mix to the town, manifest around the narrow sloping central streets in one of LA's densest groupings of ethnic groceries.

Some of this history is revealed in the **Maritime Museum** (Sun–Tues 10am–5pm; free), on the harbour's edge at the foot of Sixth Steet, while the **Bloody Thursday Monument**, on the corner of Sixth Street and Beacon Street close to the City Hall, is another reminder of the city's gritty past. It marks the 1934 strike by local waterfront workers, commemorating the two who were killed when police and private guards opened fire. A fifteen-minute walk along the shore from the museum is the overrated **Ports O'Call Village** – a dismal batch of wooden and corrugated iron huts supposedly capturing the flavour of exotic sea-ports around the world. Give it a miss.

Between San Pedro and Long Beach (connected by *LBTD* bus #142, or RTD #146) soar two tall road bridges, giving aerial views of oil wells and docks, and the vast Naval Supplies Center (through which the buses sometimes pass to pick up civilian workers). Just inland, the community of **WILMINGTON** is home to the palatial Greek-style **Banning House** at 401 E Main Street (guided tours Tues–Sun at 12.30pm, 1.30pm, 2.30pm & 3.30pm; free). A mid-nineteenth-century entrepreneur, Phineas Banning made his fortune when the value of the land he purchased here increased astronomically as the harbour was developed. Through his promoting of the rail link between the harbour and central LA, he also became known as "the father of Los Angeles transportation" – no mean accolade at a time when the local transport system was one of the best in the world.

Long Beach

Not so long ago you would have given **LONG BEACH** a miss. Once the stamping ground of off-duty naval personnel, its porn shops and sleazy bars caused God-fearing local parents to put the place off-limits to their young, and for tourists the attractions were just the wrong side of seedy. The last ten years, however, have seen a billion-dollar cash injection into the town that has led – in the downtown area at least – to a spate of new office buildings, a convention centre, new hotels, a swanky shopping mall and a clean-up campaign that has restored some of the best turn-of-the-century buildings on the coast. Inland from downtown, however, the story is different – grim, uninviting, housing developments on the perimeter of the impoverished district of South Central LA (see p.114).

Downtown Long Beach is clearly the place to spend most of your time, with, especially along Pine Avenue, the best of Long Beach's rescued architecture and numerous thrift stores, antique/junk emporiums and bookshops. Nearby, on Third Street, is the succinctly named **"The Mural"**, whose depiction of the Long Beach population appears to be contemporary but was in fact painted in the Thirties under Roosevelt's New Deal, unwittingly predicting the racial mixture which Long Beach attained much later. From the mural, the pedestrianised Promenade leads towards the sea, passing the concrete open-air auditorium – often the site of free art and music events – and crosses the busy Ocean Beach Boulevard into **Shoreline Village**, a belt of eateries and entertainments arranged along the waterfront. It's a bit contrived but okay for a quick look, especially at weekends when much of young Long Beach assembles here to parade itself.

Ocean Boulevard leads away from Shoreline Village down to **Breakers Hotel**: twelve storeys of Spanish Revival pinkness topped by a green copper roof. A mile further on, 2300 Ocean Boulevard was once owned by Fatty Arbuckle and now houses the **Long Beach Museum of Art** (Wed–Sun noon–5pm, Thurs until 9pm; suggested donation $2), neatly fringed by a sculpture garden. Inside is a small but quality collection of contemporary Southern Californian art, and some very avant-garde screenings from the **video annexe** – phone ☎310/439-2119 to check what's showing. Another mile in this direction, the **Belmont Shores** area was built by old and is maintained by new money. Along its main thoroughfare, Second Street, a collection of designer shops and yuppie-frequented cafés, sustains the affluent style of the surrounding avenues, where many of the wealthy Long Beachites of the Twenties had their homes.

A short way north, **Rancho Los Alamitos** (Wed–Sun 1–5pm; free), is one of Long Beach's two restored ranches, with free hour-long guided tours that bestow a good sense of one side of Californian life during the early part of the century. While around the Rancho, you may as well drop by the very green grounds of the **CSULB campus** (*LBTD* bus #12 runs here from downtown Long Beach), and view the extravagant plant-life of the **Japanese Garden** (Tues–Thurs 9am–4pm, Sun 1–4pm; free), or the art and local history exhibitions inside the **University Art Museum**, on the fifth floor of the university library at 1250 Bellflower Boulevard (Tues–Sat 11am–5pm, closed during university holidays; free). Follow Pacific Coast Highway to Long Beach Boulevard and turn right, and you reach the second of the old farmsteads, **Rancho Los Cerritos** (Wed–Sun 1–5pm; free) – another fine place to absorb something of the way local life used to be, before the discovery of oil and the building of the harbour.

The Spruce Goose and Queen Mary

Long Beach's two most famous attractions are not indigenous at all. Both the Spruce Goose and Queen Mary (daily 10am–6pm; $17.50 for both) were acquired by the local authorities with the aim of bolstering tourism – something at which they have resoundingly succeeded. They lie across the bay, opposite Shoreline Village, but are easily accessible either by a lengthy walk, a short ride on *LBTD* bus #181, or by way of the pricey ($2 each way) "Water Taxi", which leaves every half an hour between 11.30am and 6pm from Shoreline Village.

The **Spruce Goose** at least has some direct connection with Long Beach. It was over the harbour that the enormous flying boat – the largest wooden plane ever constructed – skimmed in 1947, on its first and only flight. Built by the Howard Hughes Corporation for the government war effort, it was intended to transport men and machinery – up to 750 troops could fit into its cargo hold – to the beach-heads of Europe. But by the time it was finished the war had ended and doubts were expressed as to Hughes' motives, a common charge being that he was satis-fying his own eccentricities at the taxpayers' expense (the nickname "Spruce Goose" was first applied in scorn by a Congressman, and Hughes hated it).

Uniqueness makes the thing worth seeing, if you can afford it, even if in the age of jumbo jets its size isn't as impressive as might have been once. You can climb on to the plane for a brief peek into the cockpit and cargo hold, but at least as interesting as the plane are the short film-shows about the enigmatic Hughes himself, and a small gathering of personal memorabilia.

The **Queen Mary**, next door to the plane and now kitted out as a luxury hotel, is as tangible a testament to the hypocrisy of the British class system as you'll find. The suggestion is that all who sailed on the vessel – the flagship of the *Cunard Line* from the Thirties until the Sixties – enjoyed the extravagantly furnished lounges and the luxurious cabins, all carefully restored and kept spark-ling. But a glance at the spartan third-class cabins reveals something of the real story – and the tough conditions experienced by the impoverished who left Europe on the ship hoping to start a new life in the US. The red British telephone kiosks around the decks and the hammy theatrical displays in the engine room and wheelhouse – closer to *Star Trek* than anything nautical – don't help.

Catalina Island

Though it's overlooked by many foreign visitors, **CATALINA ISLAND** is favoured by Californians in the know, a mix of uncluttered beaches and wild hills twenty miles off the coast. Since 1811, when the indigenous Gabrileño Indian population were forced to resettle on the mainland, the island has been in private ownership, and has over the years grown to be something of a resort – a process hastened by businessman William Wrigley Jnr (part of the Chicago-based chew-ing gum dynasty), who financed the construction of the Avalon Casino, a building which is still the major landmark. Since then, to their credit the islanders – there are two thousand of them – have resisted the grosser aspects of tourism. The hotels are unobtrusive among the whimsical architecture and cars are a rarity; to get about, local people either walk (the "city" of Avalon covers just one square mile), ride bikes or drive electrically powered mokes.

FERRIES TO CATALINA

From Long Beach to Avalon (2–4 daily; 1hr 50min); Two Harbors (2 weekly; 2hr).

From Newport Beach to Avalon (1 daily; 2hr 30min).

From San Pedro to Avalon (5–7 daily; 1hr 30min); Two Harbors (1–2 daily; 1hr 30min).

Getting to Catalina ... and staying there

Depending on season, a return trip to Avalon from San Pedro or Long Beach costs between $20 and $28 on **ferries** which run several times daily, operated by *Catalina Cruises* (☎1-800/888-5939) and *Catalina Express* (☎519-1212). From Newport Beach (see p.156) to Avalon, the *Catalina Passenger Service* (☎714/673-5245) runs a daily round-trip, costing around $20. If you get seasick or feel extravagant there are also air connections.

If you want to stay for longer than a day, be warned that hotel **accommodation** in Avalon is pricey – often upwards of $80 – and most beds are occupied throughout the summer and at weekends. The tourist information offices mentioned below, will help you find a bed: the cheapest **hotel** is usually the *Atwater* (☎1-800/4-AVALON), around $50; the only budget option is the **campsite** (☎310/510-0303) on the town's western fringe. This too is fully booked most summer weekends but on weekdays and out of season there's usually space. In Catalina's interior, the only places to stay are the basic campsites at Black Jack and Little Harbor; again, reservations have to be made in advance (☎310/510-0303).

Avalon

Avalon can be fully explored in an hour. For maps and details, call into either the **Information Center** (☎1-800/428-2566) opposite the entrance to the pier, or the **Chamber of Commerce** (☎310/510-1520), actually on the pier. They also offer **tours** of the island, ranging from whistle-stop town tours and short voyages in glass-bottomed boats to a fuller three-hour affair (starting at 9am and costing $19.50) – the only way to see the interior of Catalina without hiking. Mokes, for which you need a full driving licence, and bikes (both of which are banned from the rough roads outside Avalon) can be hired from the stand opposite the *Busy Bee* restaurant on Bay Shore Drive.

The best way to see Avalon is on foot, beginning at the **Avalon Casino** ($2, includes museum), a sumptuous 1920s structure, with mermaid murals, gold leaf ceiling motifs and an Art Deco ballroom. The collections at the adjoining **museum** (Easter to October Mon–Sat 1–4pm & 8–10pm, Sun and holidays 1–4pm) include Native American artefacts from Catalina's past.

On the slopes behind the Casino, the **Zane Grey Pueblo Hotel** is the former home of the Western author, who visited Catalina with a film crew to shoot *The Vanishing American* and liked the place so much he never left. Grey built this pueblo-style house, complete with beamed-ceiling and a thick wooden front door. It's now a hotel, with rooms named after his books, and makes a handy place to rest after climbing the hill, both to admire the views over Avalon and the bay, and to examine the few items kept from Grey's time.

The interior

If possible, venture into the **interior** of Catalina. You can take a tour (see above) if time is short; if it isn't, get the free permit from the information centre in Avalon that allows you to hike and camp. The carefully conserved wilderness holds a wide variety of flora and fauna, some of it unique. Keep an eye out for the Catalina Shrew, so rare it's only been sighted twice, and the Catalina Mouse, bigger and healthier than its mainland counterpart thanks to abundant food and lack of natural enemies. There are also buffalo – descended from a herd of fourteen left behind by a Hollywood film crew – and deer, mountain goats, lizards and rattlesnakes.

Anaheim: Disneyland and around

Life in Anaheim, California, was a commercial for itself, endlessly replayed.
Nothing changed; it just spread farther and farther in the form of neon ooze. What
there was always more of had been congealed into permanence long ago, as if the
automatic factory that cranked out these objects had jammed into the on position.

Philip K. Dick, *A Scanner Darkly*

In the early 1950s, illustrator/film-maker Walt Disney conceived a theme park
where his cartoon caracters – Mickey Mouse, Donald Duck, Goofy and the rest,
already indelibly imprinted on the American mind – would come to life, and his
already fabulously successful company would rake in even more money from
them.

Disneyland opened in 1955, in anticipation of the acres of orange groves thirty
miles southeast of downtown – **ANAHEIM** and inland **Orange County** – becoming the nexus of population growth in Southern California. The theory proved
correct, and the area around Anaheim – staunchly conservative suburbs made up
of mile after mile of unvarying residential plots – is still one of the US's fastest
growing areas, though much of this could be put down to the presence of
Disneyland itself, without which the local economy would be much the poorer.

Certainly the park, and the scores of hotels and restaurants that have opened
up in its wake utterly dominate the Anaheim area, and the boom doesn't look like
slowing. If you're not coming to see Disneyland, you may as well give the place a
miss: it hasn't an ounce of interest in itself. But if you do come, or are staying in
one of Anaheim's many hotels, the creakier rides at **Knotts Berry Farm** go
some way to restoring wholesome notions of what amusement parks used to be
like; the **Movieland Wax Museum** is mildly entertaining; and, on an entirely
different note, the **Crystal Cathedral** is an architecturally imposing – and
unflinching – reminder of the potency of the evangelical movement. If you're a
sports fan, note also that both the *LA Rams* (football) and the *California Angels*
(baseball), play at Anaheim Stadium; see p.199 for the facts.

Disneyland

It's hard to think of anything that comes closer to demonstrating the wishful
thinking of the modern US than **DISNEYLAND** (summer daily 9am–midnight,
rest of the year daily 10am–6pm, until midnight on Sat & Sun; $27.50), its simu-
lated realities in many ways reflecting the problem-free world average America
dreams of. The most famous, most carefully constructed, most award-winning
theme park anywhere – and to some extent the blueprint for imitations worldwide
ever since – Disneyland is a phenomenon, the ultimate escapist fantasy. Even
though LA opinion is divided as to whether Disneyland should be avoided or
revelled in, it's worth experiencing once. Kids enjoy it, no question; and in any
case, it might be said that if you don't want to visit a place where real life is
distorted in the pursuit of "happiness", perhaps you shouldn't be in the US at all.

The admission price is high enough to prevent you coming for a quick look
around, and you'll need to stay all day to get your money's worth; entry includes
all the rides, although during peak periods you might have to queue for hours to
get on them. Remember, too, that the emphasis is on family fun. While it's been
known for people to cruise around Disneyland on LSD, the authorities take a dim

view of anything remotely anti-social, and eject those they consider guilty – in other words, stay sober, look normal, and smile a lot.

Bear in mind that Disneyland is not LA's only large-scale amusement park; the whirlwind rides at Magic Mountain for example (see p.166) are consistently better.

Practicalities

Disneyland is at 1313 Harbor Boulevard, Anaheim, about 45 minutes by **car** from downtown using the Santa Ana Freeway. By **train** from downtown, six services a day make the half-hour journey to Fullerton, from where *OCTD* bus #40 or #41 will drop you off at Disneyland. By **bus**, use RTD #460 from downtown, which takes about 90 minutes, or the quicker *Greyhound* service, which runs thirteen times a day, and takes 45 minutes to Anaheim, leaving an easy walk to the park. From Long Beach, RTD bus #149 connects both Knotts Berry Farm and Disneyland, taking just over an hour.

As for **accommodation**, try to visit Disneyland just for the day and spend the night somewhere else. It's not a very appealing area, and anyway most of the hotels and motels close to Disneyland cost well in excess of $70 per night. Cheaper options are a little further out; for details see p.99.

A massive central kitchen produces all the **food** that's consumed in the park (you're not permitted to bring your own), unloading popcorn, hot-dogs, hamburgers and other all-American produce from the many stands by the ton. For anything healthier or more substantial, you'll need to leave the park and travel a fair way. Our "Eating" listings on p.174 suggest some options.

The park

The only way to enjoy Disneyland is to jump into it with both feet; don't think twice about anything and go on every ride you can. From the front gates, **Main Street** leads through a scaled-down, camped-up replica of a turn-of-the-century Midwestern town, filled with small souvenir shops, food stands and penny arcades, to Sleeping Beauty's Castle, a pseudo-Rhineland Valley palace at the heart of the park. **Adventureland**, nearby, contains two of the best rides in the park: the *Pirates of the Caribbean*, a boat trip through underground caverns, singing along with drunken pirates; and the *Haunted Mansion*, a riotous "doom buggy" tour in the company of the house spooks. While here, make a point of taking the *Jungle Cruise* through the audio-animatronic jungles of the Congo, with a live narration that's the only part of Disneyland taking the mickey out of Mickey Mouse.

Less fun is **Frontierland**, the smallest and most all-American of the various themelands, taking its cues from the Wild West and the tales of Mark Twain, who grew up in the same town – Hannibal, Missouri – as Walt Disney.

Fantasyland, across the drawbridge from Main Street, shows off the cleverest but also the most nauseatingly sentimental aspects of the Disney imagination: *Mr. Toad's Wild Ride* through Victorian England, *Peter Pan* flying over London, and *It's a Small World* – a tour of the world's continents in which animated dolls sing the same cloying song over and over again.

There's only one spot in the park where you can actually see the outside world: by looking over the boundary walls when riding the *Skyway* cars that travel via a dangling cable from Fantasyland into **Tomorrowland.** This is Disney's vision of the future, where the *Space Mountain* roller-coaster zips through the pitch-blackness of outer space, Michael Jackson dances in 3-D in the movie *Captain E-O*, and R2D2 pilots a runaway space cruiser through the *Star Wars* galaxy of Luke Skywalker and Darth Vader.

In addition to these fixed attractions, there are over-the-top **firework displays** every summer night at 9pm, and all manner of parades and special events celebrating important occasions – such as Mickey Mouse's birthday.

Around Disneyland

It's hard to escape the clutches of Disneyland even when you leave: everything in the surrounding area seems designed to service the needs of its visitors. There are a few places within easy reach which offer a chance to forget, at least temporarily, its existence, but if Disneyland has given you a taste for distortions of reality, there's the Richard Nixon Library and Birthplace to enjoy in Yorba Linda.

Knott's Berry Farm

Those who find the actuality of Disneyland considerably less enjoyable than the hype might prefer the more traditional **Knott's Berry Farm** (summer daily 10am–midnight, Sat 10am–1am, rest of the year daily 10am–6pm, Sat 10am–10pm, Sun until 7pm; $21.95). This relaxed, rough-at-the-edges park was born during the Depression when people began queuing up for the fried chicken dinners prepared by Mrs Knott, a local farmer's wife. To amuse the children while they waited for their food, Mr Knott reconstructed a Wild West ghost town and added amusements until the park had grown into the sprawling carnival of roller-coasters and thrilling rides that stands today. Something of a dampener on the fun, however, is the knowledge that the place is no longer owned by the Knotts but by the Robert Welch family – founders of the John Birch Society and still active in extreme right-wing politics. Knott's Berry Farm is four miles northwest of Disneyland, but also on the RTD #460 route from downtown, off the Santa Ana Freeway at Beach Boulevard in BUENA PARK.

Across the street, the **Movieland Wax Museum** (summer daily 9am–9.30pm, winter 10am–9pm; $11.95), is a Madame Tussaud's for the Hollywood set, displaying a collection of wax dummies posed in scenes from favourite films and TV shows. The Marx Brothers, Captain Kirk and the crew from the Starship Enterprise, and Arnold Schwarzenegger may not be essential viewing, but they're good for a laugh.

The Crystal Cathedral

The impressive **Crystal Cathedral** (daily 9am–4pm; free), on the other side of Disneyland in GARDEN GROVE, just off the Santa Ana Freeway on Chapman Avenue, is a rather less frivolous attraction. Designed in tubular space-frames and walls of plate glass by architect Philip Johnson, it forms part of the vision of the Reverend Robert Schuller. A hard-sell evangelist, not content with the the world's first drive-in church (next door to the cathedral), he commissioned this dramatic prop to boost the ratings of his televised Sunday sermons, shows which reach their climax with the special Christmas production, using live animals in biblical roles and people disguised as angels suspended on ropes. Schuller raised $1.5 million for the construction of the building during one Sunday service alone – a statistic worth pondering as you stroll around the echoey interior.

RICHARD M. NIXON: A LIFE IN POLITICS

Qualified as a lawyer, fresh from wartime (non-combat) service in the US Navy, Richard Milhouse Nixon **entered politics** as a Republican Congressman in 1946, without so much as a civilian suit to his name. A journalist of the time observed that Nixon employed "the half-truth, the misleading quotation, the loose-joined logic" to cast doubts on his rival – traits he was to perfect in the years to come.

Shortly after arriving in Washington, the fresh-faced Nixon joined the **House UnAmerican Activities Committee**, a group of reds-under-the-bed scare mongers led by the fanatical Joseph McCarthy (whose greatest achievement, perhaps, was to make Nixon look like a moderate). Through the now-notorious anti-communist "witchtrials", McCarthy and Nixon wrecked the lives and careers of many loyal Americans who had idealistically flirted with communism in their youth.

Nixon's meteoric rise culminated in becoming Eisenhower's Vice President in 1953, aged just 39. Seven years later, Nixon was defeated in his own bid for the nation's top job by the even younger John F. Kennedy, a loss which led him into the **"wilderness years"**. Staying out of the public spotlight, he took a highly lucrative post with a Los Angeles law firm and wrote *Six Crises*, a book whose deep introspection came as a surprise – and convinced many of the author's paranoia.

Seeking a power base for the next presidential campaign, Nixon contested the governorship of California in 1961. His humiliating defeat prompted a short-lived "retirement" and did nothing to suggest that seven years later he would beat Ronald Reagan to the Republication nomination and be **elected president** in 1969.

Nixon had attained his dream, but the country he inherited was more divided than at any time since the Civil War. The **Vietnam conflict** was at its height, and his large-scale illegal bombing of Cambodia earned him worldwide opprobrium. He was however able to bask in the glory of a slight thaw in the Cold War: a change of direction by Mao Tse-tung improved relations with China, and the first strategic arms limitation talks (SALT) treaties were agreed with the USSR.

Recession and unemployment didn't prevent Nixon's decisive re-election in 1972, but his second term was ended prematurely by the cataclysmic **Watergate Affair**. In January 1973, seven men were tried for breaking into and bugging the headquarters of the Democratic Party in the Watergate building in Washington, an act which was discovered to have been financed with money allocated to the Campaign to Re-elect the President (CREEP). From their testimonies, a trail of deceit lead deep into the corridors of the White House – and eventually to the president himself.

Nixon may not have sanctioned the actual bugging operation, but there was ample evidence to suggest that he participated in the cover-up. Ironically, Nixon's insistence on taping all White House conversations in order to ease the writing of his future memoirs was to be the major stumbling block to his surviving the crisis. Facing the threat of impeachment, Nixon **resigned** in 1974.

The full pardon granted to Nixon by his successor, Gerald Ford (appointed to the vice-presidency during Watergate – some allege, on the condition of such a pardon being given) did little to arrest a widespread public disillusionment with the country's political machine. The rose-tinted faith, long held by many Americans, in the unflinching goodness of the President *per se* seemed irredeemably shattered.

Remarkably, however, the years since Richard Nixon's ignoble demise have seen him quietly seek to establish elder-statesman credentials, opining on world and national affairs through books and newspaper columns. Watergate is increasingly touted as a mistake, ruthlessly exploited by his enemies. These days, Nixon has a growing number of admirers, and there's even an only half-joking campaign to have him contest the presidency in 1992.

Yorba Linda: the Richard Nixon Library and Birthplace

Mickey Mouse may be its most famous resident, but conservative Orange County's favourite son is Richard Milhouse Nixon, born in 1913 in what's now the freeway-caged **YORBA LINDA**, about eight miles northeast of Disneyland. Here, the **Richard Nixon Library and Birthplace**, 18001 Yorba Linda Boulevard (Mon–Sat 10am–5pm, Sun 11am–5pm; $4.95), is a shrine to the one-time US president who forged a career from lies and secrecy, and finally resigned from the world's most powerful job in total disgrace. Besides offering a chance to dwell on a fascinating rise to – and fall from – power, the popularity of the unrelentingly hagiographical library (really a museum) evinces one of the strangest features of the contemporary US: the rehabilitation of Richard Nixon.

Oversized gifts from world leaders, amusing campaign memorabilia, and a laugh-a-line collection of obsequious letters written by and to Nixon (including one he despatched to the boss of *McDonalds* proclaiming the fast-food chain's hamburgers to be "one of the finest food buys in America") form the core of the exhibition, but it's in the constantly running archive radio and TV recordings that the distinctive Nixon persona really shines through.

Although famously humiliated in 1960's live TV debates with John F. Kennedy (refusing to wear make-up, Nixon perspired freely under the TV lights and was seen as the embodiment of sleaze), Nixon had earlier used the medium to save his political life. In 1952, the discovery of undeclared income precipitated the "fund crisis", which cast doubts over Nixon's honesty. Incredibly, with the **"Checkers speech"**, Nixon convinced 58 million watching Americans of his integrity with a broadcast to rival the the worst soap opera. Exuding mock sincerity, Nixon cast himself as an ordinary American struggling to raise a family, buy a house, and provide for the future – and climaxed his performance with the statement that, regardless of the damage it may do to his career, he would not be returning the cocker spaniel dog (Checkers) given to him as a gift and now a family pet.

Throughout the museum, Nixon's face leers down in Big Brother fashion from almost every wall, but only inside the **Presidential Auditorium** (at the end of the corridor packed with notes attesting to the president's innocent role in the Watergate Affair) do you get the chance to ask him a question. In a career packed with controversy and shady dealing, many possible questions spring to mind, but the choice is limited to those already programmed into a computer. Ten or so minutes after making your selection, Nixon's gaunt features will fill the overlarge screen and provide the stock reply – as endearingly and believably as ever.

The Orange County Coast

As Disneyland grew, so did the rest of Orange County. Besides providing tourist services, the region become a major centre for light industry and home to many of the millions who poured into Southern California during the Sixties and Seventies – its population density is even greater than that of neighbouring, more metropolitan, Los Angeles County. But it was expansion without style, and those who could afford to soon left the anonymous inland sprawl for the more characterful coast. As a result, the **ORANGE COUNTY COAST**, a string of towns stretching from the edge of the Harbor Area to the borders of San Diego County 35 miles south, is suburbia with a shoreline: swanky beachside houses line the sands and the general ambience is easy-going, conservative and affluent.

As the names of the main towns here suggest – **Huntington Beach, Newport Beach** and **Laguna Beach** – there's no real reason beyond sea and sand to visit. But they do provide something of a counterpart to LA's more cosmopolitan side, and form appealing stopovers on a leisurely journey south. You might even spy a bit of countryside: unlike most of the city's other districts, the communities here don't stand shoulder-to-shoulder but are a few miles apart, in many instances divided by an ugly power station but sometimes by a piece of undeveloped coast. The one place genuinely meriting a stop is just inland at **San Juan Capistrano**, site of the best kept of all the Californian missions – the only slab of proper history to be found in these parts. Further on, there's little before you reach adjoining San Diego County, but the campsite at **San Clemente** provides the only cheap accommodation along the southern part of the coast.

If you're in a rush to get from LA to San Diego, you can skip the coast by passing through Orange County on the inland San Diego Freeway. The coastal cities, though, are linked by the more adventurous Pacific Coast Highway (PCH), part of Hwy-1, which you can pick up from Long Beach (or from the end of Beach Boulevard, coming from Anaheim). *OCTD* bus #1 rumbles along PCH roughly hourly throughout the day. *Greyhound* connections aren't so good: San Clemente gets eight buses a day, but Huntington Beach and Laguna Beach just two, and most *Greyhound* buses bound for San Diego use the freeway. *Amtrak* is a good way to get from downtown LA (or Disneyland) to San Juan Capistrano, but the only other coastal stop is at San Clemente. One point to remember is that you can travel all the way along the coast from LA to San Diego using local buses for about $3 – though you should allow a full day or more for the journey.

Huntington Beach

HUNTINGTON BEACH, is the first place of any interest on the Orange County coast, wildest of the beach communities and one that you don't need a fortune to enjoy. It's a compact little place composed of engagingly ramshackle single-storey cafés and beach stores grouped around the foot of a long pier. The beach is the sole focus: it was here that Californian surfing began – imported from Hawaii in 1907 to encourage curious day-trippers to visit on the *Pacific Electric Railway*. During the day massed ranks of mixed-ability surfers attempt to coax a ride from even the smallest wave; at night, everyone lays aside their boards and joins in the barbecues, cooked on the beach's own fire-rings. Once you've exhausted the beach and the local shops, there's not much else, although Huntington Beach is a good place to be based for a while, with Orange County's cheapest beds in the **youth hostel** at 421 Eighth Street, three blocks from the pier (see p.99 for details).

Newport Beach and Corona Del Mar

Ten miles south from Huntington, **NEWPORT BEACH** could hardly provide a greater contrast. With ten yacht clubs and ten thousand yachts, this is upmarket even by Orange County standards, a chic image-conscious town that people visit to acquire a tan they can show off on the long stretches of sand or in the bars alongside. You'll need a pocketful of credit cards and a viewable physique to join them, but the sheer exclusivity of the place may be an attraction in itself.

Newport Beach is spread around a natural bay that cuts several miles inland, but *the* place to hang out is on the thin **Balboa Peninsula**, along which runs the three-mile-long beach. The most youthful and boisterous section is about halfway along, around Newport Pier at the end of 20th Street. North of here, beachfront homes restrict access; to the south the wide sands are occupied by a sporty crowd and, further along, around the second of Newport's two piers, the **Balboa Pier,** by seasiding families. Balboa Pier is the most touristy part of Newport, but it does hold a marina from which you can to escape to Catalina Island (p.149), or spend $6 on a 45-minute boat-ride around Newport's own, much smaller, islands.

On the peninsula there's little in the way of conventional sights, but you might cast an eye over the exterior (no public access) of the constructivist-style **Lovell House**, on 13th Street, designed by Rudolph Schindler and finished in 1926. Described by one contemporary critic as "epoch making", it is raised on five concrete legs, with the living quarters jutting out towards the edge of the sidewalk, and formed the basis of the architect's international reputation.

Away from the peninsula, Newport Beach is hard to get around and hardly worth the effort unless you're driving. However, bus #1 stops on the northern edge of the peninsula, at 32nd and Balboa Streets, and continues south through the other major part of Newport: a monumental feat of landscaping called **Newport Center**, filled by high-rise offices, unimaginably pricey shops, and the much-hyped **Newport Harbor Art Museum** at 850 San Clemente Drive (Tues–Sun 11am–5pm, Fri also 6–9pm; donation requested), which occasionally stages brilliant exhibitions of Southern Californian art.

Just a few miles along PCH from flashy Newport, **CORONA DEL MAR** is a much less ostentatious place, worth a short stop for its unpretentious beach and the **Sherman Foundation Center**, devoted to the horticulture of the American Southwest and raising many vivid blooms in its **botanical gardens**. Between here and Laguna Beach lies an invitingly unspoiled three-mile-long hunk of coastline, protected as **Crystal Coves State Park**. It's perfect to explore on foot, far from the crowds. Bus #1 stops alongside.

Laguna Beach

Nestling among the crags around a small sandy beach, **LAGUNA BEACH** grew up late in the nineteenth century as a community of artists, drawn by the beauty of the location. You need a few million dollars to live here nowadays, but there's a relaxed and tolerant feel among the inhabitants, who span everything from rich industrialists to the remnants of the Sixties era when Laguna became a hippy haven – even Timothy Leary was known to hang out at the *Taco Bell* on PCH. The scenery is still the great attraction, and despite the massive growth in population Laguna remains relatively untarnished, with a still flourishing minor arts scene manifest in the high number of craftshops and galleries crammed into the narrow streets.

PCH passes right through the centre of Laguna, a few steps from the small main **beach**. From the north side of the beach, an elevated wooden walkway twists around the coastline above a conserved **ecological area**, enabling you to peer down on the ocean and, when the tide's out, scamper over the rocks to observe the tide-pool activity. From the end of the walkway, make your way through the legions of posh beachside homes (which often make beach access difficult) and head down the hill back to the centre. You'll pass the **Laguna Beach Museum of Art** (summer Tues–Sun 11.30am–9pm, winter Tues–Sun 11.30am–4.30pm; free), which has changing exhibitions from its stock of Southern Californian art from the 1900s to the present-day. Bus #1 continues a couple of miles south to less-touristed **SOUTH LAGUNA**, where the wonderfully secluded Victoria and Aliso beaches are among several below the bluffs.

Laguna's festivals

Laguna hosts a number of large summer **art festivals** over a six-week period during July and August. The best-known (and most bizarre) of them is the **Pageant of the Masters**, a kind of great paintings charade in which the participants pose in front of a painted backdrop to portray a famous work of art. It might sound ridiculous, but it's actually quite an impressive display and takes a great deal of preparation – something reflected in the prices: $10 for the cheapest tickets for shows which sell out months in advance (though you may be able to pick up cancellations on the night). The idea for the pageant was hatched during the Depression as a way to raise money for local artists, and the action takes place at the Irving Bowl, close to where Broadway meets Laguna Canyon Road, a walkable distance from the Laguna Beach bus station. The pageant is combined with the **Festival of the Arts** held at the same venue during daylight hours.

The excitement of both festivals waned during the Sixties and a group of hippies created the alternative **Sawdust Festival**, in which local artists and craftspeople set up makeshift studios to demonstrate their skills – now just as established but a lot cheaper and easier to get into than the other two. It takes place at 935 Laguna Canyon Road (take bus #57) and admission is $3.

Dana Point

From Laguna it's often possible to see **Dana Point**, a fat promontory jutting into the ocean about four miles south. It was named after sailor/author Richard Henry Dana Jnr, whose *Two Years Before The Mast* – a novel of life on the high seas in the early days of California – described how cattle hides were flung over these cliffs to trading ships waiting below. He ended his voyaging career here in 1830, and there's a statue of him and a replica of his vessel, *The Pilgrim*, at the edge of the harbour – part of what's now a town spread over the entire headland. Both are fairly unremarkable, however, as indeed is the place as a whole, although you'll need to pass by on your way to San Juan Capistrano. The **Orange County Marine Institute** (Mon–Sat 10am–3.30pm; free) has informative displays on tide-pool and sea-life; **Doheny State Beach** is overwhelmed by a huge campsite (see p.99).

San Juan Capistrano and San Clemente

Three miles inland from Dana Point, accessible on bus #91 along Del Obispo, off PCH, the town of **SAN JUAN CAPISTRANO** was built in a period-style derived from the nearby **Mission San Juan Capistrano** on Camino Capistrano (summer daily 8.30am–7pm, Oct to mid-May daily 8.30am–5pm; $3), which is where the bus stops (it's a five-minute signposted walk from the *Amtrak* station). The seventh in California's chain of missions, this was founded by Junipero Serra in 1776; and within three years was so well populated that it outgrew the original chapel. Soon after, the **Stone Church** was erected, the ruins of which are the first thing you see as you walk in. The enormous structure had seven domes and a bell-tower but was destroyed by an earthquake in 1883. For an idea of how it might have looked, visit the full-sized reconstruction – now a working church – just northwest of the mission, finished in 1985.

The rest of the mission is in an excellent state of repair, due largely to a restoration programme which began in 1895. The **chapel** has most atmosphere: small and narrow, decorated by Indian drawings and Spanish artefacts from the mission's founding, and set off by a sixteenth-century altar from Barcelona. In a side-room is the chapel of St. Pereguin: during the Seventies, a woman suffering from cancer prayed for six months to the saint asking to be cured, and afterwards her doctor declared that the cancer had indeed disappeared. Now the tiny room is kept warm by the heat from the dozens of candles lit by hopeful cancer sufferers who arrive here from all over the US and Mexico.

The other restored buildings reflect the mission's practical role during the Indian period: the kitchen, the smelter, the workshops used for dyeing, weaving and candle-making. There's also a rather predictable **museum**, which gives a broad historical outline of the Spanish progress through California and displays odds and ends from the mission's past.

The mission is also noted for its **swallows**, popularly thought to return here from their winter migration on 19 March. They sometimes do arrive on this day – along with large numbers of tourists – but the birds are much more likely to show up as soon as the weather is warm enough and there are enough insects on the ground to provide a decent homecoming banquet.

San Clemente

Back on PCH, bus #1 ends its journey at the K-mart Plaza shopping centre, and you need to take bus #91 to continue the couple of miles south into the town of **SAN CLEMENTE**. This is a pretty little place, its streets contoured around the hills lending an almost Mediterranean air. It's predominantly, however, a retirement town, and although there's a decent campsite (see p.99 for details) the chances are that under-fifties won't be entertained for long. Best to push on south to San Diego with *Greyhound* (at 306 S Camino Real) or *North County Transit District* bus #305.

The San Gabriel and San Fernando Valleys

The northern limit of LA is defined by two long, wide valleys lying over the hills from the central basin, starting close to one another a few miles north of downtown and spanning outwards in opposite directions – east to the deserts around Palm Springs, west to Ventura on the Central Coast. It's true to say you wouldn't miss an awful by not visiting the valleys at all, but they do give a picture of what life is like in some of LA's more downbeat suburbs, and there is a certain amount to see.

Spreading east, the **San Gabriel Valley** was settled by farmers and cattle ranchers who set up small towns on the lands of the eighteenth-century Mission San Gabriel. The foothill communities grew into prime resort towns, luring many here around the turn of the century; the largest of them, **Pasadena** now holds many elegant period houses, and the brilliant but underpublicised Norton Simon

Museum. Above Pasadena, the slopes of the San Gabriel Mountains are littered with explorable remains from the resort days, and make great spots for hiking and rough camping, although you'll nearly always need a car to get to the trailheads. The areas around Pasadena are generally less absorbing, although, to the south, WASP-ish **San Marino** is dominated by the **Huntington Library**, a stash of art and literature ringed by botanical gardens that itself makes the journey into the valley worthwhile.

The **San Fernando Valley**, spreading west, is *the* valley to most Angelenos: a sprawl of tract homes, mini-malls, fast-food drive-ins and auto parts stores. It has more of a middle-American feel than anywhere else in LA, inhabited – at least, in the popular LA imagination – by macho men and bimbo-esque "Valley Girls", who even have their own dialect ("Valley Talk" – see "Glossary"). There are a few isolated sights, notably **Forest Lawn Cemetery** – an over-the-top statement in graveyard architecture that's hard to imagine anywhere except in LA – but otherwise, beyond a couple of minor historical sites, it's the **movies** which bring people out here. Rising land values in the 1930s pushed many studios out of Hollywood and over the hills to **Burbank**, an anodyne community now overpowered by several major film and TV companies, whose behind-the-scenes tours are the only chance in LA to see the basics of film-making. Don't be tempted, incidently, to go to North Hollywood, an unattractive district named by its architects in an attempt to cash in on associations with the "real" Hollywood.

Pasadena

Marking the entrance to the San Gabriel Valley, **PASADENA** is as much the home of the grand dames of Los Angeles society as it is to the "little old lady from Pasadena" of the Beach Boys song. In the 1880s, wealthy East Coast tourists who came to California looking for the good life found it in this foothill resort ten miles north of Los Angeles, where luxury hotels were built and railways cut into the nearby San Gabriel mountains to lead up to taverns and astronomical observatories on the mile-high crest. Many of the early, well-to-do visitors stayed on, building the rustically sprawling houses which remain, but as LA grew so Pasadena suffered, mainly from the smog which the mountains collect. The downtown area is currently undergoing a major renovation, with modern shopping centres being slipped in behind Edward Hopperish 1920s facades, but the historic parts of town have not been forgotten. Maps and booklets detailing self-guided tours of Pasadena architecture and history are available from the **Pasadena Convention and Visitors Bureau** at 171 S Los Robles Avenue (Mon–Fri 9am–5pm, Sat 10am–4pm; ☎818/795-9311). If you're around at the right time, watch out also for the New Year's Day **Tournament of Roses**, which began in 1890 to celebrate and publicise the mild Southern California winters, and now attracts over a million visitors every year to watch its marching bands and elaborate flower-covered floats.

A block north of Colorado Boulevard, a replica Chinese Imperial Palace houses the **Pacific Asia Museum** at 46 N Los Robles Avenue (Wed–Sun noon–5pm; $2), which has a wide range of objects from Japan, China and Thailand – though if you have even the slightest interest in the art of South East Asia, your time would be better spent at the collection of the Norton Simon Museum, quarter of a mile away on the other side of downtown.

The Norton Simon Museum

You may not have heard of the **Norton Simon Museum**, but its collections, housed in a modern building at 411 W Colorado Boulevard (Thurs–Sun noon–6pm; $5, students $2.50), are in many ways broader in range and more consistently excellent than either the County or Getty museums. Established and still overseen by the eponymous industrialist, who made his millions selling ketchup and soft drinks, the museum (perhaps because of its unfashionable location) sidesteps the hype of the LA art world to concentrate on the quality of its presentation. You could easily spend a whole afternoon – or two – wandering through the spacious galleries.

The core of the museum's collection is Western European painting from the Renaissance to the modern period. The museum has a massive collection, much of it rotated, but most of the more major pieces are on view constantly. There are Dutch paintings of the seventeenth century – notably Rembrandt's vivacious *Titus, Portrait of a Boy* and Frans Hals' quietly aggressive *Portrait of a Man*; Italian Renaissance work from Pietro Longhi and Guido Reni; and, most striking of all, seventeenth-century Spanish religious narratives by Francisco de Zurburán, not least a striking *Saint Francis in Prayer*. Among more modern works, there is a good sprinkling of French Impressionists and Post-Impressionists: Monet's *Mouth of the Seine at Honfleur*, Manet's *Ragpicker* and a Degas capturing the extended yawn of a washerwoman in *The Ironer*, and works by Cezanne, Gauguin, Van Gogh. Perhaps the most extraordinary painting in the entire collection is Picasso's *Woman with Book*, finished in 1932 and a far cry from his earlier Mondrian-like *La Pointe de la Cité*, also here.

As a counterpoint to the Western art, the museum has a fine collection of **Asian sculpture**, including a very sexy 2000-year-old *Yakski* figure – a divinity associated with fertility and fecundity, taken from the railings of a Buddhist *stupa* – and many highly polished Buddhist and Hindu figures, a mix of the contemplative and the erotic, some inlaid with precious stones.

On the way out, don't forget to drop into the musuem **bookshop**; apart from having lower prices than any other art bookstore in LA and being superbly stocked, you get a free print just by handing over your ticket stub.

The Gamble House

Behind the museum, Orange Grove Avenue leads into a hillside neighbourhood containing some of Pasadena's finest houses. The **Pasadena Historical Society**, on Walnut and Orange Grove (Thurs–Sun 1–4pm; $4), has displays on the history of Pasadena and is decorated with its original 1905 furnishings and paintings. The building later became the Finnish Consulate, and much of the folk art on display here comes from Pasadena's "twin town" of Jarvenpää in Finland.

But it's the **Gamble House**, 4 Westmoreland Place (Thurs–Sun noon–3pm; $4, students $2), which brings people out here. Built in 1908, and one of the masterpieces of (and greatest influence on) Southern Californian vernacular architecture, it's a style you'll see replicated all over the state, at once relaxed and refined, freely combining elements from Swiss chalets and Japanese temples in a romantic, sprawling shingled house. Broad eaves shelter outdoor sleeping porches, which in turn shade terraces on the ground floor, leading out to the spacious lawn. The interior was crafted with the same attention to detail, and all of the carpets, cabinetry and lighting fixtures were designed specifically for the house and are in excellent condition.

The area around the Gamble House is filled with at least eight other less lavish **houses** by the two brothers (the firm of "Greene & Greene") who designed it, including Charles Greene's own house at 368 Arroyo Terrace, which leads down into the Arroyo Seco via Holly Street. A quarter of a mile north of the Gamble House is a small, concrete block house by Frank Lloyd Wright, *La Miniatura*, which you can glimpse through the gate opposite 585 Rosemont Avenue. All of these houses are private.

Into the foothills

Below the Gamble House, the western edge of Pasadena is defined by the Arroyo Seco canyon. Arroyo Boulevard winds along here, under the slim and soaring **Colorado Boulevard Bridge**, a spot favoured by stunt flyers in the barnstorming 1920s. It continues up through Brookside Park to pass the 104,000-seat **Rose Bowl** (Mon–Fri 8am–4pm; free): site of the 1984 Olympic soccer competition and one potential host of the 1994 World Cup – as well as a lively **flea-market** on the second Sunday of each month. On the other side of the Foothill Freeway, **Descanso Gardens** (daily 9am–4.30pm, $3), in the La Canada district, concentrates all the plants you might see in the mountains into 155 acres of landscaped park. The gardens are especially brilliant during the spring, when all the wildflowers are in bloom.

From La Canada, the **Angeles Crest Highway** (Hwy-2) heads up into the mountains above Pasadena. This area was once dotted with resort hotels and wilderness camps, and today you can hike up any number of nearby canyons and come across the ruins of old lodges that either burned down or were washed away towards the end of the hiking era in the 1930s, when automobiles became popular. One of the most interesting of these trails, a five mile round trip, follows the route of the Mount Lowe Railway, once one of LA's biggest tourist attractions, from the top of Lake Avenue up to the old railway and the foundations of **"White City"** – formerly a mountaintop resort of two hotels, a zoo and an observatory. A brass plaque embedded in concrete is the only evidence of the resort, and even this is slowly becoming overgrown with pine trees and incense cedars. The Crest Highway passes through the **Angeles National Forest**, where you can hike and camp most of the year and ski in winter to Mount Wilson, high enough to be the major siting-spot for TV broadcast antennae, and with a small **museum** (daily 10am–4pm; free) beside the 100-inch telescope of the defunct 1904 Mount Wilson Observatory. From here, if it's clear, there are sweeping views out over the entire Los Angeles area.

East of Pasadena: Arcadia and Sierra Madre

Foothill Boulevard, parallel to the Foothill Freeway (I-210), is better known as part of the one and only **Route 66**, formerly the main route across the US "from Chicago to LA, more than 3000 miles all the way". The freeway stole Route 66's traffic, and following Foothill Boulevard out of Pasadena nowadays leads to the adjacent town of **ARCADIA**, whose **State and County Arboretum** on Baldwin Avenue (daily 9am–5pm; $3, free the third Tues of each month) has forests of trees arranged according to their native continent. The site was once the 127-acre ranch home of "Lucky" Baldwin, who made his millions in the silver mines of the Comstock in the 1870s. He settled here in 1875, and built a fanciful white palace along a palm-treed lagoon, later used in the TV show *Fantasy Island*, on the site of the 1839 Rancho Santa Anita. He also bred horses, and raced them on a neighbouring track which has since grown into the **Santa Anita Racetrack** (Oct to April Wed–Sun 1–6pm; $3–$6.50), still the most beautiful and glamorous racetrack in California.

The district of **SIERRA MADRE**, on the northern edge of town, lies directly beneath Mount Wilson and is worth a visit if you're a hiker. A seven-mile round trip trail up to the mountain's summit has recently been restored and is now one of the best hikes in the range. The trailhead is 150 yards up the private Mount Wilson Road.

South of Pasadena: the Huntington Library

South of Pasadena, SAN MARINO is a dull, uppercrust little suburb with few redeeming features beyond the **Huntington Library, Art Collections and Botanical Gardens**, off Huntington Drive at 1151 Oxford Road (Tues–Sun 1–4.30pm; advance reservations are required on Sun; free, parking $2). Part of this is made up of the collections of Henry Edwards Huntington, the nephew of the childless multi-millionaire Collis P. Huntington, who owned and operated the Southern Pacific Railroad – which in the nineteenth century had a virtual monopoly on transportation in California. Henry was groomed to take over the company from his uncle, but was dethroned by the board of directors and took his sizeable inheritance to Los Angeles, where he bought up the existing streetcar routes and combined them as the *Pacific Electric Railway Company*. It was a shrewd investment: the company's "Redcars" quickly became the largest network in the world, and Huntington the largest landowner in the state, buying up farmlands and extending the streetcar system at an enormous profit. He retired in 1910, moving to the manor house he had built in then-genteel San Marino, devoting himself full-time to buying rare books and manuscripts and – in an ironic twist of fate – marrying his uncle's widow Arabella and acquiring her collection of English portraits.

A covered pavilion has a bookshop and information desk, where you can pick up a self-guided walking tour of each of the three main sections. The **Library**, right off the main entrance, is a good first stop, its two-storey exhibition hall containing numerous manuscripts and rare books, such as a Gutenberg Bible, a folio edition of Shakespeare's plays and – the highlight – the **Ellesmere Chaucer**, a c.1410 illuminated manuscript of *The Canterbury Tales*. The displays around the walls of the room trace the history of printing and of the English language from medieval manuscripts to a King James Bible, through Milton's *Paradise Lost*, Blake's *Songs of Innocence and Experience*, to first editions of Swift, Coleridge, Dickens, Woolf and Joyce.

To decorate the **main house**, a grand mansion done out in Louis XIV carpets and later French tapestries, the Huntingtons travelled to England and came home laden with the finest art money could buy. Most of it still hangs on the walls. Unless you're a real fan of eighteenth-century English portraiture, head straight through to the back extension, added when the gallery opened in 1934, which displays, as well as works by Turner, van Dyck and Constable, the stars of the whole collection: Gainsborough's *Blue Boy* and Reynolds' *Mrs Siddons as the Tragic Muse*.

There are also paintings by Edward Hopper and Mary Cassatt, and a range of Wild West drawings and sculpture, in the newish **Scott Gallery for American Art**. For all the art and literature, though, it's the grounds that make the Huntington really special, and the acres of beautiful themed **gardens** surrounding the buildings include a Zen Rock Garden – complete with authentically constructed Buddhist Temple and Tea House. There's also a Desert Garden, which has the world's largest collection of desert plants, including twelve acres of cacti in an artful setting – a distillation of the natural landscape of Los Angeles. While strolling through these botanical splendours, you might also call in on the Huntingtons themselves, buried in a Neo-Palladian mausoleum at the northwest corner of the estate, beyond the rows of an orange grove.

Glendale and Forest Lawn Cemetery

GLENDALE, eight miles north of downtown and the gateway to the San Fernando Valley, was once a fashionable suburb of LA. Now it's a nondescript dormitory community hovering between the Valley and LA proper, and the only reason to come here is to visit the Glendale branch of **FOREST LAWN CEMETERY** at 1712 S Glendale Avenue (daily 9am–5pm; free) – immortalised with biting satire by Evelyn Waugh in *The Loved One*, and at the vanguard of the American way of death for decades. Founded in 1917 by a Doctor Hubert Eaton, this fast became *the* place to be seen dead, its pompous landscaping and over-sized artworks attracting celebrities by the dozen to buy their own little piece of heaven.

It's best to climb the hill and see the cemetery in reverse from the **Forest Lawn Museum**, whose surprising exhibits include, among a hotch-potch of old artefacts from around the world – coins from ancient Rome, Viking oddments, medieval armour – and one of the mysterious sculpted figures from Easter Island, which was discovered being used as ballast in a fishing boat in the days when the statues could still be removed from the island. How it ended up here is another mystery, but it is the only one on view in the US.

Next door to the museum, the grandiose **Resurrection and Crucifixion Hall** houses the largest piece of religious art in the world, *The Crucifixion* by Jan Styka. Unfortunately you're only allowed to see it during the ceremonial unveiling every hour on the hour (and you'll be charged $1 for an eyeful). Besides this, Eaton owned a copy of da Vinci's *Last Supper*, and, realising that he only needed one piece to complete his set of "the three greatest moments in the life of Christ", he commissioned American artist Robert Clark to produce *The Resurrection* – an effort which is also only viewable when unveiled, though this happens on the half-hour. If you can't be bothered to stick around for the showings (with both, in any case, the size is the only aspect that's particularly impressive), you can get a good idea of what you're missing from the scaled-down replicas just inside the entrance.

From the museum, walk down through the terrace gardens – loaded with sculptures modelled on the greats of classical European art – to the **Freedom Mausoleum**, where you'll find a handful of the cemetery's better-known graves. Just outside the mausoleum's doors, Errol Flynn lies in an unspectacular plot (unmarked until 1979), rumoured to have been buried with six bottles of whisky at his side, while a few strides away is the grave of Walt Disney. There are no great attractions inside the mausoleum itself unless you're on a real Hollywood pilgrimage. If you are, you'll find Clara Bow, Nat King Cole, Jeanette MacDonald and Alan Ladd handily placed close to each other on the first floor. Downstairs are Chico Marx, and his brother Gummo – originally an active member of the comedy team, who later spurned the limelight to become the Marx Brother's agent and business manager. To the left, heading back down the hill, the **Great Mausoleum** is chiefly noted for the tombs of Clark Gable (next to Carole Lombard, who died in a plane crash just three years after marrying him), and Jean Harlow, in a marble-lined room which cost over $25,000, paid for by fiancé William Powell.

A number of **other Forest Lawn cemeteries** continue the style of the Glendale site, to a much less spectacular degree. There's a Hollywood Hills branch in Burbank (6300 Forest Hills Drive, close to Griffith Park) which has a strong roll call of ex-stars – Buster Keaton, Stan Laurel, Liberace, Charles Laughton and Marvin Gaye – but little else to warrant a visit. The others, even less interesting, are at Covina Hills, Cypress and Long Beach.

Burbank and the studios

While Hollywood carries the name that's synonymous with the movie industry, many of the studios, if they were there at all, moved out of Tinseltown long ago, and much of the nitty-gritty business of actually making films goes on over the hills in otherwise boring **BURBANK**.

Near the junction of the Ventura and the Hollywood freeways are a number of **film and television studios**, including *Disney NBC*, at 3000 W Alameda Street (daily 9am–4pm; $7), offer a ninety-minute tour of the largest production facility in the US, and a chance to be in the audience for the taping of a programme (☎818/840-3537 for free tickets).

The **Burbank Studios** (Mon–Fri at 10am, 10.30am, 2pm & 2.30pm; $20; ☎818/954-1744), which combines the old *Warner Brothers* and *Columbia* studios on Barham Boulevard just south of the freeway, is perhaps more interesting, laying on an instructive, fairly technical behind-the-scenes look (called the "VIP tour") at how a movie is made, touring the backlot stage-sets and including an actual filming whenever possible. Try to reserve a place a month in advance if possible – tours are limited to thirty people a day.

The largest of the old backlots belongs to **Universal Studios**, whose tours (summer daily 8am–10.30pm, rest of the year Mon–Fri 10am–8pm Sat & Sun 9.30am–8pm; $24.95), are more tourist-aimed affairs, four hours long and more like a trip around an amusement park than a film studio. The first half consists of a narrated tram-ride through a make-believe set where you can experience the fading magic of the parting of the Red Sea and a collapsing bridge; the second takes place inside the Entertainment Center, where otherwise unemployed actors and stuntmen engage in convincing Wild West shootouts and the so-called Miami Vice Action Spectacular stunt show. The *Universal Amphitheater*, which hosts pop concerts in summer, is part of the complex too, as is a brand-new twenty-screen movie theatre complex, with a lobby reminiscent of 1920s movie palaces; there's also the *Victoria Station* restaurant, which has the old departures board from London's Victoria Station hanging above the bar.

Los Encinos State Historic Park and northwards

West of Universal Studios the Ventura Freeway passes below the increasingly expensive hillside homes of SHERMAN OAKS and ENCINO, close to which the **Los Encinos State Historic Park** on Balboa Boulevard (Wed–Sun 10am–5pm, tours 1–4pm; $1) is all that remains to be seen of the original Indian settlement and later Mexican *hacienda* here. The high-ceilinged rooms of the 1849 adobe house open out on to covered porches, shaded by oak trees (in Spanish "encinos") and kept cool by the two-foot-thick walls.

West of Encino, Topanga Canyon Boulevard crosses the Ventura Freeway, leading south towards Malibu (p.144) or north to **Stony Point**, a bizarre outcrop of sandstone that has been used for many budget Western shootouts. The area certainly has a desolate spookiness about it, and it comes as little surprise to learn that during the late Sixties, the Charlie Manson "family" lived for a time at the **Spahn Ranch**, just west at 12000 Santa Susana Pass. In recent years however, it has become a popular venue for LA's contingent of lycra-clad rock climbers.

The Mission San Fernando

At the north end of the Valley the San Diego, Golden State and Foothill freeways join together at I-5, the quickest route north to San Francisco. Under the interchange, the **Mission San Fernando** at 15151 San Fernando Mission Boulevard (daily 9am–4.30pm; $2) was completely rebuilt following the 1971 earthquake, with nicely landscaped courtyards and gardens. Eighty-odd years ago, the then-dilapidated mission featured in several films made by Hollywood pioneer D.W. Griffith, not least *Our Silent Paths*, his tale of the Gold Rush.

Magic Mountain

A short way past the cascading spillway of the LA Aqueduct (see below), Hwy-14 splits off east across the Mojave desert, while I-5 continues north past Valencia and **Magic Mountain** (summer daily 10am–midnight, rest of the year weekends only; $18, plus $3 parking), a three-hundred-acre complex that has some of the fastest and wildest rollercoasters and rides in the world – all a hundred times more thrilling than anything at Disneyland.

THE LA AQUEDUCT

Just beyond the Mission San Fernando, I-5 runs past two of LA's main reservoirs, the water stored in which has been brought hundreds of miles through the **LA Aqueduct** from the Owens Valley and Mono Lake on the eastern slopes of the Sierra Nevada mountains. The water tumbles down a great concrete spillway above the freeway, at the southern end of which is an impressive engineering feat.

However, with all due respect to the expertise involved, the legality of the arrangements by which the City of Los Angeles gained control of such a distant supply of water is still disputed. Agents of the city, masquerading as rich cattle-barons interested in establishing ranches in the Owens Valley, bought up most of the land along the Owens River, before selling it on, at personal profit, to the City of Los Angeles. These sharp practices provided the inspiration for Roman Polanski's 1974 movie *Chinatown*.

THE FACTS

Consumption, of all kinds, is taken very seriously in LA. Bargain hunting is a major preoccupation, but there's also tremendous importance attached to squandering – and being seen to squander – loads of bucks on something simply because it's in vogue. The fact that social **drinking** is far less popular than it is up the coast in San Francisco further highlights this obsession with doing things in a prescribed way: spontaneous revelry seems anathema to LA, and many bars and pubs are full of people posing while waiting to meet friends, before heading off to pose again somewhere more exotic. Lately, **coffee bars** have become the places to be seen – not least because they won't leave a hardened socialite too drunk to drive home. Even **eating** isn't spared the vagaries of fashion. While it is unbelievably easy to dine well and cheaply, there are scores of restaurants who'll whack up their prices on the back of a good review, and get away with it because they know the place will be packed with first-timers who'll impress their cohorts by claiming that they've been eating there for years.

Nightlife, too, is conditioned by the style of the moment, but the sheer verve of the club scene, and the fact that LA is centre of the American rock industry – new bands haven't broken through until they've won over an LA crowd – means there's seldom an evening without something exciting going on. Other musical tastes, country, jazz and blues, for example, are widely catered to, though are not what the city does best, probably because they're just not fashionable enough. Opera and classical music are scantily represented – though there are some bold theatre groups and, naturally, the very latest films.

You might, of course, be too exhausted with daytime pursuits to have much strength left for the evening. The city's **shops** are great sappers of energy, and touring the more outrageous ones can be a great insight into LA life – revealing who's got the money and what they're capable of wasting it on.

As always, it's easiest to **get around** by car, especially if you're staying out late. The RTD runs 24-hour services on the main routes through most of the busiest night-time areas – between downtown, Hollywood, West LA and the coast. If you're going anywhere else, you should check the bus schedules carefully since there's often no public transport after 9pm. The best sources of **what's on information** are the free *LA Weekly* and *LA Reader*, and the "Calendar" section of the Sunday *Los Angeles Times*. Additionally, the college radio stations (see p.89) carry details, previews and sometimes free tickets for forthcoming events.

Drinking: bars, pubs and coffee bars

That LA's **bars and pubs** are rarely the scruffy boozing places found elsewhere in the US is due at least in part to the easy availability of alcohol for home consumption, through any number of liquor stores and supermarket outlets. Many are worth going to to people-watch as much as to drink, although there are plenty of genuinely seedy and dimly lit dives – probably not dangerous, but best avoided if you're unsure.

You can get a drink, at least a beer or a glass of wine, in most restaurants, and for serious, uninterrupted drinking there are bars and cocktail lounges on every other corner – just look for the neon signs. For places with a bit more character,

LA'S FESTIVALS

January

1 Tournament of Roses in Pasadena. A parade of floral floats and marching bands along a five-mile stretch of Colorado Boulevard.

February

Early The Japanese New Year is celebrated around Little Tokyo with traditional arts.

First full moon after 21 Chinese New Year. Three days of dragon-float street parades and cultural programmes, based in Chinatown.

March

17 St Patrick's Day. A parade through downtown and related events all over the city, with some bars serving green beer.

End The Academy Awards are presented at the Shrine Auditorium, with much moviebiz spectacle.

April

Early The Blessing of the Animals. A long-established Mexican-originated ceremony held to thank animals for the services they provide to mankind. Many locals arrive in Olvera Street bearing their pets, have them blessed, then watch the attendant parade.

May

5 Cinco de Mayo. A day-long party to commemorate the Mexican victory at the battle of Puebla (and not Mexican Independence Day as some Californians think). Besides a spirited parade in Olvera Street, there are celebrations with Mexican food, drink and music in most LA parks.

July

Middle Watts Jazz Festival. Two days of free music with the Watts towers as a backdrop.

August

First two weeks Culmination of the South Bay's International Surf Festival, where globally famed surfers compete.

September

4 LA's birthday. A civic ceremony and assorted street entertainment around El Pueblo de Los Angeles to mark the founding of the original pueblo in 1781.

Last two weeks Los Angeles County Fair in Pomona, in the San Gabriel Valley. The biggest County Fair in the country, with livestock shows, eating contests and fairground rides.

October

Second weekend LA Street Scene. Free rock music, fringe theatre and comedy on the streets of downtown. Usually running at the same time is the West Hollywood Street Festival, a display of handmade arts and crafts and a general slap-on-the-back for LA's newest constituent city.

November

End Hollywood Christmas Parade. The first and best of the many Yuletide events, with a cavalcade of mind-boggling floats.

however, the recommendations below are useful either for an entire evening's socialising or a quick splash on the way to somewhere else. As you'd expect, they reflect their locality: a clash of beatniky artists and financial whizz-kids in downtown, the legacy of the movies and the subsequent arrival of leather-clad rock fans in Hollywood, the cleaner-cut trendiness of West LA, a batch of jukebox and dartboard-furnished bars in Santa Monica evidencing the British contingent in the area, and the less fashionable, more hedonistic beachside bars of the South Bay. Most are open from 6am until 2am, though you're liable to be drinking alone if you arrive for an early liquid breakfast; busiest hours are between 9pm and midnight. A number of bars and restaurants also have **happy hours**, when drinks are usually half-price and there'll be some sort of free food. These can be ideal for either getting drunk cheaply, or just stuffing yourself for the cost of a beer. If you want something of the bar atmosphere without the alcohol, present yourself at one of the fast-growing band of **coffee bars** – more gregarious than you might expect, and varied in style and clientele.

Downtown

Al's Bar, 305 S Hewitt St. At the heart of the Loft District art scene; drink cans of cheap beer in small, smoke-filled rooms, with a pool table and occasional live acts.

Casey's Bar, 613 S Grand Ave. White floors, dark wood-panelled walls and nightly piano music, a regular drop-in spot for office-workers on their way home.

Yee Me Loo, 690 N Spring St. A Chinatown bar that looks like a set from *Farewell My Lovely*.

Hollywood

Boardners, 1652 N Cherokee Ave. A likeably unkempt neighbourhood bar – a rarity in the heart of Hollywood but very welcome.

Cat and Fiddle, 6530 Sunset Blvd. Unpretentious, boisterous but comfortable pub with English beers on draught and occasional live jazz (see "Live Music", p.183).

Gorky's, 1716 Cahuenga Blvd. A new branch of the famous downtown eaterie, worth a call for its big bar and great beers.

Musso and Frank's, 6667 Hollywood Blvd. If you haven't had a drink in this 1940s landmark bar, you haven't been to Hollywood. It also serves food (see p.177).

The Power House, 1714 N Highland Ave. Enjoyable heavy-rockers watering hole just off Hollywood Boulevard; few people get here much before midnight.

Small's KO, 5574 Melrose Ave. The newest and hippest bar, but with the atmosphere of a morgue; charges an admission fee if anyone famous is inside.

West LA

Barney's Beanery, 8447 Santa Monica Blvd. Well-worn pool-hall bar, stocking over two hundred beers. It also serves food (see below).

The Ginger Man, 369 N Bedford Drive. Looks like a New York media-persons' bar but has the atmosphere of a neighbourhood pub; it also has a small café.

Molly Malone's Irish Pub, 575 S Fairfax Ave. Self-consciously authentic Irish bar, from the music to the shamrocks in the foaming Guinness (see also "Live Music").

The Polo Lounge, 9641 Sunset Blvd, in the *Beverly Hills Hotel*. It's worth the price of a drink (at least $5) to watch Hollywood in action – mainly fat-cat producers making deals on the phone or showing off an endless stream of expensive young escorts.

Tom Bergin's, 840 S Fairfax Ave. Great place for Irish Coffee.

Yesterday's, 1056 Westwood Blvd. Drink fruit daiquiris on the balcony upstairs, overlooking Westwood Village.

Santa Monica, Venica and Malibu

Crown and Anchor Pub, on the Santa Monica Pier. English-style pub without much atmosphere but with imported British brews.

McGinty's Irish Bar, 2615 Wilshire Blvd. Friendly, often raucous small pub with dartboards and, frequently, live music.

Rebecca's, 2005 Pacific Ave. The hottest bar in ever-so-trendy Venice, with an interior composed of crocodiles and octopi dangling from the rough wooden ceiling.

S.S. Friendship, 112 West Channel Rd, Pacific Palisades. Welcoming beachfront bar with a mix of gay and straight but mainly local people, from 11am until 2am daily.

Ye Olde King's Head, 116 Santa Monica Blvd. Jukebox, dartboards and signed photos of all your favourite rock dinosaurs.

Ye Old Mucky Duck, 1810 Ocean Ave. Another English-style pub.

The South Bay and Harbor Area

Brennan's, 3600 Highland Ave, Manhattan Beach. Live-wire bar with rock bands providing the background music.

Hennessey's Tavern, 313 Manhattan Beach Blvd. Sedate compared to some in the area, but often with live bands.

Shellback Tavern, 116 Manhattan Beach Blvd. Relaxed, beachy atmosphere.

Coffee Bars

Highland Grounds, 742 N Highland Ave. The poshest and most pose-worthy of LA's coffee bars.

Java Coffee House, 7286 Beverly Blvd. Good selection of coffees and a refined pseudo-bohemian atmosphere.

Oynx Sequel, 1802 N Vermont Ave. Tea and cakes alongside the coffees, and much reading and philosphical chat.

The Pik-Me-Up, Sixth St at La Brea. Draw on a dishwater cappucino and then draw on the broken furniture in this amusing would-be beatnik's hangout. Occasional poetry readings, too.

HAPPY HOURS AND BRUNCH

Many bars and some restaurants have **happy hours**, usually from 5pm until 7pm, when drinks are cheap and there'll be a selection of help-yourself snacks: taco dips, crisps or popcorn. A few offer piles of free food that you can attack once you've bought a drink – and thereby save the cost of dinner later on. We've listed some of the best of them here; otherwise just look out for signs on bar windows and their ads in the newspapers.

Sunday brunch, a light meal costing around $10 accompanied by complimentary drinks, is not the big deal in LA that it is in, for example, New York: most Angelenos don't get up early enough (brunch is usually 11am–2pm) and the booze, while free, isn't exactly free-flowing even when you do catch the eye of the person serving you. If you are interested, though, look out for a branch of *Arriba*, a Mexican fast-food chain who do a decent brunch; or again check the newspaper ads.

Happy hour venues

Barragan Cafe, 1538 W Sunset Blvd. More for half-priced drinking than free food, but this Mexican restaurant reputedly produces the most alcoholic margarita in LA.

Cat and Fiddle, 6530 Sunset Blvd. No food but drinks at half-price, enabling you to prepare for an evening of looking cool in this trendy hangout (see p.186).

Lawry's California Center, 568 San Fernando Rd. Even the cut-price drinks aren't particularly cheap but the setting is unbeatable – outside tables on a lushly vegetated patio.

Traditions, on the USC campus. Packed with students tucking into the gratis chicken wings and meatloaf, and getting very drunk at the same time.

Eating: budget food and restaurants

LA **eating** covers every extreme: whatever you want to eat and however much you want to spend, you're spoilt for choice. You should, however, try to take at least a few meals in the more exotic eateries, if only to watch the city's many self-appointed food snobs going through their paces. If, on the other hand, you simply want to load up quickly and cheaply, the options are almost endless, and include free food available for the price of a drink at **happy hours**. In general, restaurants are open from noon until around midnight, sometimes closing between lunch and dinner, although many fast food outlets stay open around the clock – you'll find a list of the best of these on p.175.

Budget food is as plentiful as in any other US city, ranging from reasonably wholesome sit-down fare in street corner coffee shops and cafés – which, due to price and convenience, may well be where you'll do the bulk of your eating – to the burgers of the big franchises. Almost as common, and just as cheap, is **Mexican food**. Oddly perhaps, this is the closest thing to an indigenous LA cuisine – most notably in the *burrito*, a filled tortilla that's rarely seen in Mexico – and available everywhere, both from street vendors and comfortable restaurants.

Given the city's appetite for ethnic cooking, regular **American** restaurants are not as common as you might expect, and not especially cheap either. Even more costly are chic restaurants offering the delicate morsels of **California cuisine** and, increasingly prevalent, **Cajun** cooking – both mainly centred on West LA. A better value option is, as ever, **pizza**, both ordinary and, more expensively, extravagant designer-pizzas specific to LA, covered with weird and wonderful toppings. **Italian** cuisine proper comes in many regional varieties, and in sometimes riotous restaurants, but bear in mind it can get pricey beyond the basic pasta dishes.

Chinese cooking can be found all over the city, but is at its most affordable and atmospheric in Chinatown. **Japanese** food, and more specifically sushi, is not as popular as it once was but is still widely available. The comparatively few **Thai** and **Korean** restaurants are also worth seeking out; the latter especially has yet to be discovered by the LA foodies and offers very good value.

You'll find other ethnic cuisines go in and out of fashion too. **Indian**, for example, is on the rise at present and a growing number of restaurants are opening up, slowly exposing the city to the varied styles – and charging plenty for doing so. In contrast, **Middle Eastern** and **Ethiopian** restaurants retain a low enough profile to be well-priced and satisfying. **Vegetarian** and **wholefood** outlets, while abundant, often seem geared more to complementing a lifestyle than satisfying a hunger: ecologically sound but costly. On a similar note, LA has some of the best chefs in the world if money is no object: we've included a handful of **expense account** restaurants for blow-outs and gourmet celebrations. There are also a few gay-run restaurants which, besides the food, offer a good way to discover more about the city's gay and lesbian networks (see p.190).

Budget food: coffee shops, delis, diners and drive-ins

Budget food is everywhere in LA, at its best in the many small and stylish **coffee-shops**, **delis** and **diners** which serve wholesome soups, omelettes, sandwiches and so on that can be healthy, cheap and quick; indeed it's easy to exist entirely this way and never have to spend much more than $5 for a full meal.

There are of course the internationally franchised fast-food places on every street – *McDonald's*, *Burger King* et al and locally based chains of **hamburger stands**, most open 24 hours a day. *Fatburger*, originally at San Vicente and La Cienega on the border of Beverly Hills, and *Tommy's*, which started near downtown at 2575 Beverly Blvd, both have branches everywhere.

Sadly, but surely, the best of the 1950s **drive-ins**, like *Tiny Naylors* in Hollywood, last seen in Wim Wender's LA saga *The State of Things*, have been torn down to make room for mini-malls, although *In-n-Out Burgers* drive-ins are all over the San Gabriel and San Fernando Valleys.

Downtown

Clifton's Cafeteria, 648 S Broadway (☎485-1726). A cafeteria complete with redwood trees and a waterfall; the food is cheap and good too.

Downtown LA, 418 E First St (☎680-0445). Artsy and innovative small café that's popular with designers and politicos.

Gorky's Café, 536 E Eighth St (☎627-4060). Round-the-clock diner that's a hangout for many painters, sculptors and general arty types. Excellent omelettes, soups and sandwiches at cheap prices.

John's Burgers, 101 S Main St (☎617-7556). Great range of highly fattening sandwiches and meat and rice dishes – all dirt cheap.

Langer's Deli, 704 S Alvarado St (☎483-8050). "When in doubt, eat hot pastrami" says the sign, though you still have to choose from over twenty ways of having it, and a huge deli selection.

Lindsey's, 112 W Ninth St (☎624-6684). Lively and comfortable café that's a cut above the usual coffee shop standard, serving large and fresh-looking salads, thick burgers and delicious pastries.

The Pantry, 877 S Figueroa St (☎972-9279). There's always a queue for the hearty portions of downhome American cooking, 24 hours a day.

Phil's Coffee Shop, 100 Spring St (☎628-3632). Simple, cheap diner close to City Hall.

Phillipes Famous French Dip Sandwiches, 1001 N Alameda St (☎628-3781). Spit-and-sawdust café, a block north of Union Station. Long communal tables and a decor that's not changed since 1908.

Trio's Grill, 200 S Broadway (☎629-4610). Mostly fried and stodgy food, to be consumed in the company of larger-than-life downtown characters.

Vickman's Restaurant and Bakery, 1228 E Eighth St (☎622-3852). Open 3am–3pm for workers in the adjacent produce market. Great homemade pies.

Hollywood

Hampton's, 1342 N Highland Ave (☎469-1090). Choose from over fifty toppings for your gourmet hamburgers, plus an excellent salad bar.

Mel'n'Rose's, 7315 Melrose Ave (☎930-0256). Runny omelettes and $3 burger specials in a garish Fifties-style setting.

Millie's Inc, 3524 Sunset Blvd (☎661-55392). 1940s-style diner with counter-top jukebox and hearty breakfasts. Fresh biscuits and gravy, and spicy fried potatoes.

Village Coffee Shop, 2695 Beachwood Drive (☎467-5398). A classic laid-back coffee shop in the hills below the Hollywood sign.

Yukon Mining Co., 7328 Santa Monica Blvd (☎851-8833). Excellent coffee shop that bears not a hint of schizophrenia as it caters both to the local gay community and the old-timers from the neighbouring senior citizens home. Open 24 hours.

West LA

The Apple Pan, 10801 W Pico Blvd (☎475-3585). The best hamburgers in the world, finished off with a slice of freshly baked apple pie.

The Authentic Café, 7605 Beverly Blvd (☎939-4626). Keep an eye out for this easy-to-miss but hard-to-forget Santa Fe-style desert eatery. Mexican food, mixed in with spicy Chinese and the obligatory designer pizzas. Bring your own beer.

Barney's Beanery, 8447 Santa Monica Blvd (☎654-2287). Infinite variety of hot dogs, hamburgers and bowls of chili, and over two hundred bottled beers, amid dimly lit pool tables.

Caffe Latte, 6254 Wilshire Blvd (☎936-5213). The many blends of tea and coffee are reason enough to visit, though this small eaterie also produces well-priced pasta dishes.

Canter's Delicatessen, 419 N Fairfax Ave (☎651-2030). Huge sandwiches for $7, with excellent kosher soups. Open 24 hours.

Cassell's Hamburgers, 3266 W Sixth St (☎480-8668). No-frills, lunchtime-only take-away hamburger stand that some swear by.

Duke's, 8909 Sunset Blvd (☎310/652-9411). Many a rockstar's favourite café when housed in the *Tropicana* mote. Still brings in a motley crew of night owls. Weekends open until 4am.

Ed Debevic's, 134 N La Cienega Blvd (☎310/695-1952). Fifties-style diner with singing waitresses and pricey beer.

Hard Rock Cafe, in the *Beverly Center*, Beverly Blvd at San Vicente Blvd (☎310/276-7605). Long waits and loud music but the food's not half-bad . . . and the locals no longer have to fly all the way to London to buy their t-shirts.

Johnny Rockets, 7507 Melrose Ave (☎651-3361). Chrome and glass, Fifties-derived hamburger joint, open until 2am on weekends.

John O'Groats, 10628 W Pico Blvd (☎310/204-0692). Excellent cheap breakfasts and lunches. Not a place to come to if you're in a hurry.

Johnny's Coffeeshop, 6101 Wilshire Blvd (☎938-3521). Genuine old-style coffee shop, for sturdy portions scoffed from the counter top or snug booths.

Kate Mantillini, 9109 Wilshire Blvd (☎310/278-3699). Worth stopping for a $5 cappucino just to get a look at the flashy interior. Open 24 hours.

The Melting Pot, 8490 Melrose Ave (☎652-8030). Fresh soups and sandwiches.

Nate'n'Al's, 414 N Beverly Drive (☎310/274-0101). The best-known deli in Beverly Hills, popular with movie people.

Le Petit Four, 8654 Sunset Blvd (☎310/659-0484). Gourmet lunch spot with great pastries.

Ships, corner of La Cienega and Olympic Blvd (☎310/652-0401). The best food of any coffee shop in LA; try the *Ship Shape* hamburger, on sourdough bread, with a chocolate shake. Open 24 hours.

Tail o' the Pup, 329 N San Vicente Blvd (☎310/652-4517). Worth a visit for the roadside pop architecture alone though the dogs and burgers are plenty good too.

Santa Monica, Venice and Malibu

Bicycle Shop Café, 12217 Wilshire Blvd, Santa Monica (☎310/826-7831). Pseudo-bistro that's as good a place to drink as to eat, serving light meals and salads.

Café Beignet, 234 Pico Blvd, Santa Monica (☎310/396-6967). Clean-cut coffee shop in a bowling alley. Excellent fried chicken and seafood, plus the eponymous tasty pastries.

Café Montana, 1610 Montana Ave (☎310/829-3990). Good breakfasts and excellent salads and grilled fish in this art gallery-cum-café on the newest strip of upmarket Santa Monica.

Café 50s, 838 Lincoln Blvd, Venice (☎310/399-1955). No doubts about this place: Ritchie Valens on the jukebox, burgers on the tables . . .

Deli Malibu, 3894 Cross Creek Rd, Malibu (☎310/456-2444). For upmarket Malibu, the deli delights such as finely prepared pastrami and chopped liver are well priced – but don't expect to escape for less than $15 each.

Gilliland's, 2424 Main St, Santa Monica (☎310/392-3901). Highly eclectic menu of good and hearty foods, from tangy samosas to a thick Irish stew.

Pioneer Boulangerie, 2102 Main St, Santa Monica (☎310/399-7771). Open-air cafeteria and bakery by the beach, serving soups, salads and deli foods.

Rae's Diner, 2901 Pico Blvd, Santa Monica (☎310/828-7937). Classic 1950s diner behind a turquoise blue facade, open 6am–10pm. Don't miss the fresh biscuits and gravy breakfasts.

Reel Inn, 18661 Pacific Coast Highway, Malibu (☎310/456-8221). Low-key seafood diner beside the beach, with appealing prices and a good atmosphere.

The Rose Café, 220 Rose Ave, Venice (☎310/399-0711). Wide variety of pasta dishes and salads in this sunny Venice hangout.

The Sidewalk Café, Venice Boardwalk (☎310/399-5547). Breakfast on the beach, and watch the daily parade of beach people pass by. Live music most evenings.

Zucky's, 431 Wilshire Blvd at Fifth St, Santa Monica (☎310/393-0551). New York Jewish-style deli and coffee shop: lively if garish and open 24 hours.

The South Bay and Harbor Area

Café 50s, 140 Pier Ave, Hermosa Beach (☎374-1955). Juicy hamburgers and bulbous sandwiches in a Fifties Americana setting. Slightly pricey but fun.

Egg Co. Café, 350 N Sepulveda, Manhattan Beach (☎374-9177). Eggs and other fried goodies served for breakfast and lunch.

Gwene's Pantry, 443 E Broadway, Long Beach (☎437-7037). Very tasty, if slightly expensive, British-flavoured fare such as steak and kidney pie and cornish pasties.

Joe Just's, 301 Pine St, Long Beach (☎436-9821). A purveyor of fine deli sandwiches for sixty years; good place for a bite while exploring Long Beach.

Legends, 5236 E Second St, Long Beach (☎433-5753). Big portions of ribs, burgers and sandwiches in a sports-themed setting.

The Local Yolk, 3414 Manhattan Ave, Manhattan Beach (☎546-4407). As the name suggests, everything done with eggs, plus muffins and pancakes.

Queen's Restaurant, 101 Los Alamitos Ave, Long Beach (☎432-5000). Buffet food laid out on groaning tables beneath historic photos of Long Beach and live sports on TV.

Russell's, 5656 E Second St, Long Beach (☎434-0226). Worth a trip to sample the great burgers and fresh pies.

Tony's Famous French Dip Sandwiches, 701 Long Beach Blvd, Long Beach (☎435-6238). The title tells all, but alongside the French dips is a beckoning array of soups and salads.

Disneyland and around

Angelo's, 511 S State College Blvd, Anaheim (☎714/533-1401). Straight out of *Happy Days*, a drive-in complete with roller-skating car-hops, neon signs, vintage autos and, incidentally, good burgers. Open until 2am on weekends.

Belisle, 12001 Harbor Blvd, Garden Grove (☎714/750-6560). Open 24 hours for filling sandwiches, meat pies and a variety of things baked.

Knott's Berry Farm, 8039 Beach Blvd, Buena Park (☎714/827-1776). People flocked here for the delicious fried chicken dinners long before Disneyland was around, and they still do.

Orange County Coast

Bennie the bum's Diner, 238 Laguna Ave, Laguna Beach (☎714/497-4786). A Fifties-style diner with art deco flourishes, fine coffee and foamy milkshakes. Open 24 hours a day, which makes it ripe for observing Laguna's Bohemian/yuppie social mix.

The Place Across The Street From The Hotel Laguna, 440 S Coast Highway, Laguna Beach (☎714/497-2625). Pastas, salads and sandwiches with home-baked bread.

This is just a checklist of places to satisfy hunger at all hours. For full restaurant reviews, see the appropriate sections.

Downtown
Gorky's Café, 536 E Eighth St (☎627-4060).
The Pantry, 887 S Figueroa St (☎972-9279).
Pacific Dining Car, 1310 W Sixth St (☎483-6000).

Hollywood
Yukon Mining Co., 7328 Santa Monica Blvd (☎851-8833).

West LA
Canter's Delicatessen, 419 N Fairfax Ave (☎651-2030).

Kate Mantillini, 9109 Wilshire Blvd (☎310/278-3699).
Ships, corner of La Cienega and Olympic Blvd (☎310/652-0401).

Santa Monica, Venice and Malibu
Zucky's, 431 Wilshire Blvd (☎310/393-0551).

Disneyland and around
Belisle, 12001 Harbor Blvd (☎714/750-6560).

Orange County Coast
Bennie the bum's diner, 238 Laguna Ave (☎714/497-4786).

Renaissance Bakery, 234 Forest Ave, Laguna Beach (☎714/494-9240). Delicate pastries which are enjoyable to munch on the outside benches.

Ruby's, Balboa Pier, Newport Beach (☎714/675-RUBY). The first of the retro-streamline 1940s diners that have popped up all over LA and one of the best.

The San Gabriel and San Fernando Valleys

Beadle's Cafeteria, 850 E Colorado Blvd, Pasadena (☎818/796-3618). Stodgy, meat-and-two-veg cafeteria that's been around for years.

Dora's Oak Knell Sandwich Shop, 724 E Greene St, Pasadena (☎818/795-3881). One-table wooden shack serving generous portions. LA's closest thing to a transport cafe.

Dr. Hogly-Wogly's Tyler Texas Bar-B-Q, 8136 Sepulveda Blvd, Van Nuys (☎818/780-6701). Queue up for the chicken, sausages, ribs and beans, some of the best in LA.

Goldstein's Bagel Bakery, 86 W Colorado Blvd, Pasadena (☎818/796-1904). When money's tight, feast on day-old 15¢ bagels; otherwise enjoy fresh pastries, coffees and teas.

Pasadena Creamery, 50 W Colorado Blvd, Pasadena (☎818/796-1904). Delicious gelato ice cream and frozen yoghurt in a range of flavours and toppings.

Pie'n'Burger, 913 E California Blvd, Pasadena (☎818/795-1123). Classic coffee shop, with good burgers and excellent fresh pies.

Rose City Diner, 45 S Fair Oaks Ave, Pasadena (☎818/793-8282). A Fifties-style diner serving great omelettes – and more – all day and most of the night.

Mexican

LA's **Mexican** restaurants are the city's best – and most plentiful – eating standby, serving tasty, healthy and filling food for as little as $5 a head, including the requisite ice-cold bottle of *Bohemia* or *Corona* beer. They're at their finest and most authentic in East LA, on the borders of downtown, the centre of LA's huge Hispanic community, although there's a good selection of more sanitised examples all over the city. Aside from restaurants, there are less enticing but even cheaper (though without the beer) Mexican fast-food outlets like *Taco Bell*, *Pollo Pollo*, *Pollo Rico* and *El Pollo Loco* (the best of the bunch) just about everywhere.

Downtown and around

El Cholo, 1121 S Western Ave (☎734-2773). One of LA's first Mexican restaurants and still one of the best, despite the drunken frat-rats from USC.

El Tepayac, 812 N Evergreen Ave, East LA (☎267-8668). Huge burritos and very hot salsa that sometimes cause huge queues.

King Taco Warehouse, 4504 E Third St, East LA (☎264-4067). More like a mini-mall than a restaurant, with every kind of taco imaginable.

Luminarias, 3500 Ramona Blvd, Monterey Park (☎268-4177). Slightly sanitised but making up for it with some unusual views: two freeways and a women's prison. (Also live salsa music; see p.186).

Hollywood

Burrito King, 2109 W Sunset Blvd at Alvarado St (☎413-9444). Excellent carnitas burritos and tasty tostadas from this small stand across the car park from a car wash; open until 2am.

El Conchinito, 3508 W Sunset Blvd (☎668-7037). Halfway between a Mexican and Jamaican restaurant, serving exotic-looking combinations of grilled meats and delicate sauces, and fresh fruit licuados.

El Coyote, 7312 Beverly Blvd (☎939-2255). Stodgy Mexican food, and lots of it. Cheap, strong margaritas are the house speciality.

LA Olé, Wilshire Blvd at Western Ave (☎383-6394). If you like unremarkable Mexican food washed down by shots of *Jose Cuervo*, this is the place to come: it's great for loud and boisterous parties.

Lucy's El Adobe, 5536 Melrose Ave (☎462-9421). Above-average Mexican food.

Yuca's Hut, 2056 N Hillhurst Ave (☎662-1214). Tasty burritos al fresco.

West LA

Casa Carnitas, 4067 Beverly Blvd (☎667-9953). Tasty Mexican food from the Yucatan Peninsula: the dishes are unmistakeably inspired by Cuban and Caribbean cooking; lots of seafood, too.

La Salsa, 11075 W Pico Blvd at Sepulveda (☎310/479-0919); and in Westwood Village at 10959 Kinross Ave (☎310/208-7666). A pilgrimage spot for Spike Jones fans (he immortalised the road junction in his hit, *Pico and Sepulveda*), and for lovers of soft tacos and dangerously hot salsa.

Santa Monica, Venice and Malibu

Freddy's Cantina, 11520 W Pico Blvd (☎310/479-6149). Excellent and authentic enchiladas at William Burroughs' favourite (and relatively unknown) LA eatery.

Marix Tex-Mex Playa, 118 Entrada Drive. Pacific Palisades (☎310/459-8596). Flavourful fajitas and massive margaritas in this rowdy but stylish beachfront cantina.

Sabroso, 1029 W Washington Blvd (☎310/399-3832). Chic Mexican food, with all of the flavour but none of the rice-and-beans stodginess: duck tacos and smooth *mole* sauces, on a cactus-filled patio.

The South Bay and Harbor Area

The Mardi Gras, 401 Shoreline Village Drive, Long Beach (☎310/432-2900). Worth coming to for the raucous, festive atmosphere on weekends, as much as for the heaps of food.

Pancho's, 3615 Highland Ave, Manhattan Beach (☎310/545-6670). Big portions, comparatively cheap for the area.

La Playita, 16 Fourteenth St, Hermosa Beach (☎310/374-9542). The Mexican breakfasts are a good start to a day on the beach, as are the dinners to finish the evening off.

The San Gabriel and San Fernando Valleys

Don Cuco's, 3911 Riverside Drive, Burbank (☎818/842-1123). Good local eatery, close to Burbank studios, that does a great Sunday brunch.

Merida, 20 E Colorado Blvd, Pasadena (☎818/792-7371). Unusual Mexican restaurant, featuring dishes from the Yucatan Peninsula; try the spicy pork wrapped up and steamed in banana leaves.

American, California Cuisine and Cajun

Down-to-earth **American** cuisine, with its steaks, ribs, baked potatoes and mountainous salads, has a deceptively low profile in faddish LA, although it's available almost everywhere and usually won't cost more than $10 for a comparative blowout. Much more prominent – and more expensive, at upwards of $15 – is **California Cuisine**, based on fresh local ingredients, more likely grilled than fried, and stylishly presented. The current rage is for spicy, fish-based **Cajun** cooking, still available in authentic form and fairly cheaply, at around $8 for a stomach-full – though you'll pay twice as much at somewhere trendy.

Downtown and around

Mr. Jim's Pit Bar-B-Que, 3809 S Vermont Ave near Exposition Park (☎737-9727). Also at 5403 S Vermont (☎778-6070) and 10303 Avalon Blvd in Watts (☎757-0221). Slabs of LA's best ribs smothered in your choice of barbecue sauce, and served with baked beans and a sweet potato tart.

Pacific Dining Car, 1310 W Sixth St (☎483-6000). Styled to look like an English supper club inside an old railroad carriage, and open 24 hours a day for steaks. Breakfast is the best value.

Hollywood

Columbia Bar and Grill, 1448 Gower St (☎461-8800). Standard American food in a spacious restaurant, owned and run by "Trapper John", Wayne Rogers from TV's *M.A.S.H.*

Musso and Frank's Grill, 6667 Hollywood Blvd (☎467-7788). Since it opened in 1919 anyone who's anyone in Hollywood has been seen munching away in the dark-panelled dining room, though at $15 for a bacon and eggs breakfast you definitely pay for the atmosphere.

West LA

Angel City, 7505 Melrose Ave (☎655-0955). The biggest and least crowded of the Melrose bijou eateries, serving excellent versions of the now-standard grilled fish and fresh pasta dishes, plus murderously good desserts.

Border Grill, 7407½ Melrose Ave (☎658-7495). Quality Cajun cooking, with a host of daily specials enlivening the already tempting menu.

Citrus, 6703 Melrose Ave (☎857-0034). The trendiest and best of the newer upmarket restaurants, serving California cuisine in an outdoor setting indoors. Reservations are essential; lunch for two will be around $50.

City, 1280 S La Brea (☎938-2155). Be sure to leave space for the irresistible desserts in this glutton's paradise – pricey though.

Green's Soul Food, 5766 Rodeo Rd (☎295-9111). Ribs, cornbread, chitterlin's and black-eyed peas – Southern cooking at its best, and with a great jukebox.

The Gumbo Pot, 6333 W Third St in the Farmer's Market (☎933-0358). Delicious and dead-cheap Cajun cooking; try the *gumbo yaya* of chicken, shrimp and sausage, and the fruit-and-potato salad.

Stratton's Grill, 1037 Broxton Ave, Westwood Village (☎310/208-8488). Honest-to-goodness American food: steaks grilled slowly over a mesquite fire, excellent chilis and creamy soups, in a former bank building.

Italian

After years of having nothing more exotic than the established takeaway pizza chains – *Piece o' Pizza* and *Shakey's* are among the more widespread names – LA has woken up to the delights of regional Italian cuisine, and there is a growing number of specialist restaurants, especially around the Westside, serving up more refined and varied **Italian** food. Another recent phenomenon is the **designer-pizza**, invented at Hollywood's *Spago* restaurant (where it costs $10 just for a slice) and made to a traditional formula but topped with duck and shitake mushrooms and other exotic ingredients. The problem with all this is that it doesn't come cheap: even a pasta dish in the average Italian restaurant can cost upwards of $8, and the least elaborate designer-pizza will set you back around $15.

Downtown

La Bella Cucina, 949 S Figueroa St (☎623-0014). Fabulous pizzas and homemade pastas, with the accent on northern and rural Italian cuisine.
California Pizza Kitchen, 330 S Hope St (☎626-2616). Inventive pizzas, very chewy and very nourishing; not cheap but worth the extravagance. Also in West LA.

Hollywood

Palermo, 1858 N Vermont Ave (☎663-1178). As old as Hollywood, and with as many devoted fans, who flock here for the stodgy pizzas and gallons of cheapish red wine.
Sarno's, 1712 N Vermont Ave (☎662-3403). A crowded hangout with live opera and a wild atmosphere. The food's pretty good too, but expensive.

West LA

California Pizza Kitchen, 12 N, La Cienega Blvd (☎310/854-6555). Slightly pricey but super-stylish designer-pizza joint, always packed and serving good salads and calzone. Another branch in downtown.
Mario's, 1001 Broxton Ave, Westwood (☎310/208-7077). Far and away the best pizza in West LA; try the house special pesto in place of tomato sauce for a real treat. Also serving a wide range of pasta dishes.
Pizzeria Santo Pietro, 1000 Gayley Ave (☎310/208-5688). Good pizzas and a pleasant, youthful atmosphere in the heart of Westwood Village.

Santa Monica, Venice and Malibu

Boston Wildflour Pizza, 2616 Lincoln Blvd (☎310/392-8551); 2807 Main St (☎399-9990). Excellent spinach salads plus wholewheat pizzas.
La Scala Presto, 11740 San Vincente Blvd (☎310/826-6100). Fresh pizzas and pasta.

The South Bay and Harbor Area

Mangiano, 128 Manhattan Beach Blvd (☎310/318-3434). Fairly pricey but worth it for the specialist northern Italian seafood.

The San Gabriel and San Fernando Valleys

Scarantino, 1524 E Colorado Blvd, Glendale (☎818/247-9773). Good, low-priced Italian food.

La Scala Presto, 3821 Riverside Drive, Burbank (☎818/846-6800). Stylish and tasty antipasti, pizza and fresh pasta.

Chinese, Japanese, Thai and Korean

There are high-style sushi bars and dim sum grazeries, popular with Far East businessmen and fast-lane yuppies alike, around the fashionable sections of LA in which you can easily eat your way through $20. Cheaper and much less pretentious outlets tend not surprisingly to be downtown, in Little Tokyo and Chinatown, where you can get a fair-sized meal for under $10. Sushi's late-Seventies popularity is being overtaken by Thai and Korean food, although the latter has as yet to spread beyond the confines of Koreatown. Expect to pay $10 to $15 for a Thai or Korean meal.

Downtown and around

Chinese Friends, Mandarin Plaza, 964 N Broadway (☎626-1837). Chinese food at American coffee shop prices, and noodles with everything.

Curry House, 123 Astronaut Ellison Shoji Onizuka (☎620-0855). Serving LA's latest craze: Japanese curry and spaghetti dishes – worth investigating.

Dong Il Jang, 3455 W Eighth St (☎383-5757). A cosy Korean restaurant where the meat is grilled under your table.

Far East Cafe, 347 E First St, Little Tokyo (☎628-1530). A Chinese restaurant straight out of the darkest *film noir*. Cheap food and private wooden booths, popular with cops and robbers from the nearby jail.

Grandview Gardens, 944 N Hill St (☎624-6084). Where discerning dim-sum-eaters show up for lunch.

Mandarin Deli, 727 N Broadway (☎623-6054). Very edible and very cheap noodles, dumplings, and other hearty staples.

Miriwa, 750 N Broadway (☎687-3088). Cavernous and often crowded dim sum restaurant serving cheap and excellent food that's well worth the wait.

Mon Kee, 679 N Spring St (☎629-6717). For years this has been the best Chinese restaurant in LA, specialising in fresh seafood dishes: shrimp, deep-fried cod and a mouthwatering ginger crab.

Shibucho, 333 S Alameda St (☎626-1184). Excellent sushi bar in the heart of Little Tokyo; if possible, go with someone who knows what to order, as no one seems to speak English.

VIP Palace, 3014 Olympic Blvd (☎388-9292). Korean restaurant, especially strong on spicy barbecued beef.

Hollywood

Katsu, 1972 N Hillhurst Ave (☎665-1891). Sushi bar for the cyberpunk brigades; the only colour is in the artfully presented bits of fish on your plate.

West LA

Chung King, 11538 W Pico Blvd (☎310/477-4917). The best neighbourhood Chinese restaurant in LA, serving spicy – and lately fashionable – szechuan food: don't miss out on the *bum-bum* chicken.

Mandarette, 8386 Beverly Blvd (☎310/655-6115). One of the first of the yuppie dim sum eateries.

Ping Tong Café, 7015 Melrose Ave (☎931-2580). Among the least expensive of the city's many Thai restaurants, boasting a large range of vegetarian dishes.

Santa Monica, Venice and Malibu

Chin Chin, 11740 San Vicente Blvd (☎310/826-2525). Flashy but not overpriced dim sum café, open till midnight.

Flower of Siam, 2553 Lincoln Blvd (☎310/827-9986). Thai food guaranteed to set your taste buds on fire.

Todai, 201 Arizona Ave (☎310/451-2076). All-you-can-eat sushi is a long-accepted concept in LA; indulge to your heart's content for under $8 at lunchtime or $15 in the evening.

The San Gabriel and San Fernando Valleys

Casa de Oriente, 2000 W Main St, Alhambra (☎818/282-8833). Dim sum at its best: pork baos, potstickers and dumplings, and delicious sweets.

Gen Mai-Sushi, 4454 Van Nuys Blvd (☎818/986-7060). Japanese-style vegetarian restaurant with brown rice, sushi and seasonal macrobiotic dishes.

Indian, Middle Eastern, Ethiopian

Indian restaurants are thin on the ground in LA, but Indian food is enjoying an upsurge in popularity, and the number is growing – with menus often embracing uniquely Californian dishes. **Middle Eastern** eateries are similarly few, and those that do exist tend to be fairly basic, as do the city's even fewer **Ethiopian** food outlets. Most of the Indian and Middle Eastern restaurants are in Hollywood or West LA, and fall into a fairly mid-range price bracket – between $8 and $12 for a full meal, less for a vegetarian Indian dish.

Hollywood

Addis Ababa, 6263 Leland Way, a block south of Sunset Blvd (☎463-9788). Unpretentious Ethiopian food, served with fresh *injera* bread.

India Inn, 1638 N Cahuenga Blvd (☎461-3774). One of the few good, low-cost Indian restaurants in LA.

Paru's, 5140 Sunset Blvd (☎661-7680). Southern Indian food, all vegetarian and lightly spiced. Serves brunch on weekends.

Shamshiry, 5229 Hollywood Blvd (☎469-8434). The best of the Iranian restaurants that have been established in West LA since the fall of the Shah, offering kebabs, pilafs and exotic sauces.

West LA

Ashoka Cuisine, 1043 S Fairfax Ave (☎993-0027). Despite the taped sitar music, the tandoori dishes are worth indulging in, as are the delicious desserts.

East India Grill, 345 N La Brea Ave (☎936-8844). Southern Indian cuisine given the California treatment: included among the pleasures on offer are spinach curry and curried pasta.

Raja, 8875 W Pico Blvd (☎310/550-9176). Sample the excellent value $6.75 lunch buffet if you can – in the evening you'll spend a lot more.

Walia, 5881 W Pico Blvd (☎310/933-1215). This small Ethiopian restaurant looks like an African hut. You'll eat well for under $10.

Santa Monica, Venice and Malibu

Red Sea, 1551 Ocean Blvd (☎310/394-5198). Delectable Ethiopian food in a cosy and pleasingly priced restaurant.

Vegetarian and wholefood

It's small wonder that mind- and body-fixated LA has a wide variety of **wholefood** and **vegetarian** restaurants, and even less of a shock that the bulk of them are found on the consciousness-raised Westside. Some vegetarian eateries can be very cheap ($3–4) but watch out for the ones that flaunt themselves as a New Age experience and include music – these can be three times as dear.

Downtown

The Kingsley Gardens, 4070 W Third St (☎389-5527). A range of international meat-free dishes, plus a macrobiotic menu and a mouthwatering range of sugar-free desserts.

Hollywood

Inaka, 131 S La Brea Ave (☎936-9353). Vegetarian and macrobiotic food with a strong Japanese theme. Live music on weekends.

West LA

The Golden Temple, 7910 W Third St near Fairfax Ave (☎655-1891). The food is healthful, if dull, and the candlelight and the music of this Sikh-run vegetarian restaurant will soothe stressed-out nerves.

The Good Earth, 1002 Westwood Blvd (☎310/208-8215). The best of a chain of health-food restaurants: good food and friendly service at reasonable prices; also excellent breads and cakes.

Nowhere Café, 8009 Beverly Blvd (☎655-8895). Slightly costly but extremely good-for-you wholefood meals.

Source, 8301 Sunset Blvd (☎656-6388). Started as a hippy hangout during the 1960s, and still serving the healthiest mostly veggie food on Sunset Strip.

Santa Monica, Venice and Malibu

The Comeback Inn, 1633 W Washington Blvd (☎310/396-7255 or ☎310/396-6469). Carefully prepared vegan food, set off by live music in the evenings and on weekend afternoons.

The Fig Tree, 429 Ocean Front Walk, Venice (☎310/392-4937). Tasty veggie fare and grilled fresh fish on a sunny patio just off the Boardwalk.

Govinda's, 9624 Venice Blvd (☎310/836-1269). A range of meat-free dishes, from vegetarian Indian dishes to cauliflower quiche, complemented by a well-stocked juice bar.

Inn of the Seventh Ray, 128 Old Topanga Rd, just off Topanga Canyon (☎310/455-1311). The ultimate New Age restaurant, serving vegetarian and other wholefoods. Excellent desserts, too.

Oasis Café, 1439 Old Santa Monica Mall (☎310/393-0940). Deli-style specialities and a continually evolving menu that's often very cheap.

Shambala Café, 607 Colorado Ave (☎310/395-2160). The menu includes chicken but is otherwise meat-free. Some interesting seaweed dishes.

The South Bay and Harbor Area

Good Stuff, Strand and 13th St (☎310/374-2334). Tidily presented veggie fare, though not too cheap.

The Spot, 110 Second St, Hermosa Beach (☎310/376-2355). A staggering array of vegetarian dishes, based on Mexican and other international cuisines.

Expense account restaurants

If you've finally sold the screenplay that's been rumbling around the desk drawer or are being treated to a meal by some top-cat producer – or you just want to impress someone – LA sports any number of **top-notch restaurants** which serve superb food in consciously cultured surroundings. Prices are uniformly high: at most places a light lunch will set you back at least $25, and a full dinner can cost anything up to three times that, not always including wine.

Chinois on Main, 2709 Main St (☎310/392-9025). The man who created designer-pizza at *Spago* afterwards turned his sights across the Pacific to China and opened what's now LA's most popular restaurant, serving sizzling dishes like fresh fish in garlic and ginger, all designed to go with the green-and-black decor.

L'Orangerie, 903 N La Cienega Blvd (☎310/652-9770). "Very pretty, very romantic, very French and very expensive" is how *Gault-Millau* describes it; if you haven't got the $150 it takes to sit down, enjoy the view from the bar.

Patout's, 2260 Westwood Blvd (☎310/475-7100). Exquisite and authentic Cajun cooking, from gumbos to trout and crab in lemon, to beef with crawdad sauce, all served with impeccable style.

Il Rex, 517 S Olive St (☎627-2300). Possibly the most expensive but definitely the most elegant and beautiful restaurant in LA, housed in the Réné Lalique-crafted one-time haberdashery. The pasta dishes are excellent.

Nightlife: clubs and discos

LA's **clubs** are the wildest in the country. Ranging from absurdly faddish hangouts to industrial noise cellars, even the more image-conscious joints are often more like singles bars, with plenty of dressing-up, eyeing-up and picking-up (and sometimes not much else) going on, and everybody claiming to be either a rock star or in the movies. If you don't fall for the make-believe, the city's nightlife jungle can be great fun to explore, if only to eavesdrop on the vapid *Less Than Zero* dialogue. Nowadays many of the more interesting and unusual clubs are actually homeless, run by a couple of DJs specialising in a musical/fashion theme and operating wherever and whatever night of the week they can in a borrowed space. As a result, the trendier side of the clubscene is hard to pin down, and you should always check the *LA Weekly* or the *LA Reader* before setting out – or ask likely looking clubbers in record or clothes stores for suggestions. If all you want to do is dance, there are also plenty of mainstream **discos** – a far simpler proposition, and much like discos anywhere else in the world.

Not surprisingly, Friday and Saturday are the busiest nights, but during the week things are often cheaper, and though less crowded, rarely any less enjoyable. Everywhere, between 11pm and midnight is the best time to turn up, things usually hitting their peak from midnight to 2am. There's nearly always a cover charge, usually from $5 to $10, and a minumum age of 21 (it's normal for ID to be checked), and you should obviously dress with some sensitivity to the club's style – there's no point in turning up at a Motown fling dressed from head to foot in leather. That said, prohibitive dress codes are a rarity, and although there may be a bigger welcome if you look completely outrageous, you won't be excluded from anywhere purely on account of your clothes.

Downtown

God Save The Queen, 912 S San Pedro St (☎856-8980). Various indie, goth and glam sounds for a well-dressed-down crowd. Saturday only; $10.

Mayan, 1038 S Hill St (☎746-4287). Convince the doorman that you deserve to be allowed in and your reward is a place among the cool and most fashionable of LA, eager to shake a leg in gorgeous surrounds. Friday and Saturday; $15.

Stock Exchange, 605 S Spring St (☎627-4467). Take the Art Deco interior of the old Pacific Stock Exchange, insert a million-dollar sound and light system and charge $5 a drink, and you've got LA's flashiest club. Wed–Sat; $15.

Variety Arts Center, 940 S Figueroa St (☎623-9100). If it's still standing despite its long-threatened demolition, this fading 1930s palace offers one of the best nights out in LA, with a large auditorium, a spacious dancehall and a rooftop bar. Cover varies. See also "Live Music" below.

Hollywood

Arena, 6655 Santa Monica Blvd (☎962-4485). Work up a sweat to funk, hip-hop and house sounds on a massive dance floor inside a former ice factory. Friday; cover varies. See "Gay and Lesbian LA".

Club Hollywood, 6904 Hollywood Blvd, opposite the Chinese Theater (☎465-3145). Café, bar, games room and dancing; $5–10.

Club Lingerie, 6507 Sunset Blvd (☎466-8557). Long-enduring, stylish modern dance club with intimate bar and music varying from rockabilly to jazz to post-industrial thrash; $5–10. See also "Live Music".

Continental Club, 1743 Cahuenga Blvd (☎461-9017). Looks like an old bus depot, and has an inside *Crush Bar* playing Motown hits; $5.

Florentine Gardens, 5951 Hollywood Blvd (☎464-0706). Stuck between the Salvation Army and a porno theatre, but very popular with the faddish youth of LA; $5–10.

Probe, 836 N Highland Ave (☎461-8301). Ultra-trendy but friendly club that hosts top DJs playing whatever's hot; $8.

1970, 5060 Sunset Blvd (☎669-1000). Seventies music (and dress) from the Sex Pistols to Sister Sledge. Sunday only; $5.

West LA

Cocoanut Teaszer, 8117 Sunset Blvd (☎654-4773). Poseurs, rockers and voyeurs mix uneventfully on the two dance floors. No cover before 9pm, otherwise $5.

Crayons, 10800 W Pico Blvd (☎310/475-0970), in the Westside Pavilion. Fluorescent dinosaurs decorate this bar/café/nightclub. Jazz some nights, no cover, and bands at the weekends – when it's $5.

English Acid, Wed at 7969 Santa Monica Blvd (☎960-9444). Noises from the first British invasion, circa mid-Sixties, and from subsequent ones; $5.

Twenty/20, 2020 Avenue of the Stars (☎937-2020). Hi-tech setting for hi-tech dance sounds, enjoyed by street-credible would-be socialites; $10–15.

Live Music

LA has a near-overwhelming choice if you're looking for **live music**. Ever since the nihilistic punk bands of a decade or so ago – Circle Jerks, X, Black Flag – drew the city away from its cocaine-sozzled laid-back West Coast image, LA's **rock music** scene has been second to none in the States, to the extent that it has replaced the film industry as the quick route to riches and fame. There's a proto-rock star at every corner, and the guitar case is in some districts (notably Hollywood) an almost *de rigueur* accessory. The punk phenomenon has, of course, long since been overtaken, and nowadays the trend is for various heavy metal hybrids, varying from 100mph thrash-metal and its wild, teenage devotees to, more recently, glam-metal, which mates classic heavy rock poses with more acceptably mainstream music. Guns 'n Roses are one name that's had international success; most of the other current bands have yet to spread their name further than the confines of the city. Conversely, one musical genre of sigificance which you won't hear much about in most clubs is **rap***.

In addition to local talent there are always plenty of British and European names in town, from major artists to independents. There's an enormous choice of **venues**, and inevitably it's a constantly changing scene, but the clubs we've listed are established enough to still be around when you read this. Most open at 8pm or 9pm; headline bands are usually onstage between 11pm and 1am. Admission ranges from $8 up to $15 and you should phone ahead to check set times and whether the gig is likely to sell out (if it is you can have tickets held at the door up to showtime). As with discos, you'll need to be 21 and will almost certainly be asked for ID. As ever, *LA Weekly* is the best source of **listings**.

Rock music is very much the lifeblood of the live scene, but there are plenty of less fashion-conscious alternatives around the city. **Country music** is fairly prevalent, at least away from trendy Hollywood, and the Valleys are hotbeds of hillbilly and swing. There's **jazz**, too, played in a few genuinely authentic downbeat dives, though more commonly found being used to improve the atmosphere of a restaurant. There's never any obligation to eat in these places, however, and entry will often be free, although in most cases it does help to be fairly tidily dressed.

The lively Latin dance music of **Salsa**, immensely popular among LA's Hispanic population, was promoted heavily by record companies in the city during the mid-Seventies but failed to cross over into mainstream acceptance. It's still found, mostly in the bars of East LA, though it's worth saying that (aside from the places we've listed) these are very male-orientated gathering places and visitors may well feel out of place – though they're rarely dangerous.

Finally there's a small but steadily growing live **reggae** scene, occasionally featuring biggish names but more often sticking to the increasingly numerous local bands – for up-to-the-minute news of reggae shows, phone the **reggae hotline**; ☎310/281-6770.

The big performance venues

Tickets for these shows will cost between $15 and $30, and should be bought in advance from a branch of *Ticketmaster* (outlets all over, check details in phone book) or over the phone by credit card.

Greek Theater, in Griffith Park (☎460-6488). An outdoor, summer only venue with a broad range of big name musical acts.

Hollywood Palladium, 6215 Sunset Blvd (☎466-4311). Once a big band dancehall, with an authentic Forties interior.

---

* Despite the global influence (and notoriety) of South Central LA rap acts such as NWA, they hardly get a look-in locally. Don't, by the way, go hunting down the local rappers in their home territory – see "South Central LA" for why you should stay clear.

LA Sports Arena, 3939 S Figueroa St (☎480-3232). Cavernous with no atmosphere at all, perfect for mega metal bands.

Pantages Theater, 6233 Hollywood Blvd (☎462-3104). An atmospheric art deco theatre, in the heart of historic Hollywood.

Universal Amphitheater, Universal Studios, Burbank (☎818/980-9421). A huge but acoustically excellent auditorium with regular rock shows.

Rock venues

Café Largo, 432 N Fairfax Ave (☎852-1073). Intimate cabaret venue which often features LA's more unusual live bands. Free–$10.

The Central, 8852 Sunset Blvd (☎310/652-5937). Less painfully trendy than many clubs. Tuesday jam nights have cheap drinks. Cover $3–6.

Club Lingerie, 6507 Sunset Blvd (☎466-8557). Wide-ranging venue that's always at the forefront of what's new; $3–8. See also "Nightlife: clubs and discos".

Doug Weston's Troubadour, 9081 Santa Monica Blvd (☎310/276-6168). The best-known club for the heaviest riffs and shaggiest manes; $4–6.50.

Gaslight, 1608 N Cosmos St (☎466-8126). In the 1960s, this compact bar hosted hippyfavourites such as Iron Butterfly and the Seeds; nowadays it sees a good selection of new bands from LA and beyond – usually four nightly. Free–$4.

Gazzari's, 9039 Sunset Blvd (☎310/273-6606). A temple of hard rock, with name-bands on Fri and Sat, hopefuls on Sun; $6–10.

Helen's Anti-club, 4658 Melrose Ave (☎667-9762). Once great, but few worthwhile bands play here now; $3–6.

King King, 467 S La Brea Ave (☎934-5418). Poky scene of bluesy rock fare. Cover varies, rarely over $3.

Lhasa Club, 1110 N Hudson Ave (☎461-7284). Not just bands but poetry, video and art too. No booze; $2–5.

The Lighthouse, 30 Pier Ave, Hermosa Beach (☎310/372-6911). A broad booking policy which spans rock, jazz, reggae and more; cover varies.

Music Machine, 12220 W Pico Blvd (☎310/820-5150). The wildest club west of Hollywood for aspiring rock acts and more established blues and reggae; $4–8.

Raji's, 6160 Hollywood Blvd (☎469-4552). Back-room of an Indian restaurant that makes a good airing place for up-and-coming local bands; free–$5.

The Roxy, 9009 Sunset Blvd (☎310/276-2222). The showcase of the music industry's new signings, intimate and with a great sound system. Also has "pay-to-play" nights for unknown bands; $8–15.

Shamrock, 4600 Hollywood Blv (☎666-5240). Unappealing exterior hides the joys of various scruffy rock, punk and psychobilly combos; usually free.

Whisky-a-Go-Go, 8901 Sunset Blvd (☎310/652-4202). Recently done-up after many years as LA's most famous rock and roll club, nowadays mainly hard rock; $5–10.

8121, 8121 Sunset Blvd (☎654-4887). In the cellar of the Cocoanut Teaszer (see "Nightlife: clubs and discos") with five acoustic – or quiet electric – bands nightly; free.

Country and folk venues

The Foothill Club, 1922 Cherry Ave, Signal Hill (☎494-5196). A glorious dancehall from the days when hillbilly was cool, complete with mural showing life-on-the-range. Seven nights a week, doors open at 5pm; no cover.

The Forge, 617 S Brand Blvd, Glendale (☎818/246-1717). A few big names but mainly country cult figures. Free country and swing dancing lessons, Wed–Sun; $5, includes two drinks.

Longhorn Saloon, 21211 Sherman Way, Canoga Park (☎818/340-4788). Live country and blues-ish bands every night except Mon. Frequent star-studded jam sessions; $3.

McCabe's, 3103 W Pico Blvd, Santa Monica (☎310/828-4403). The back room of LA's premier acoustic guitar shop; long the scene of some excellent and unusual shows; $5–10.

Molly Malone's Irish Pub, 575 S Fairfax Ave (☎935-1577). Traditional Irish music and American folk; no cover. See also p.169.

The Palomino, 6907 Lankershim Blvd, North Hollywood (☎818/764-4010). Long the best place to catch visiting Country and Western singers, also good for rhythm and blues and the odd goth gig; $5–10.

The Silver Bullet, 3321 South St, Long Beach (☎310/634-6960). A riotous Country and Western talent competition every Tuesday; $3. The regular Top 40 bands are worth avoiding.

Jazz

The Baked Potato, 3738 Cahuenga Blvd, N Hollywood (☎818/980-1615). A small but near-legendary contemporary jazz spot, where many reputations have been forged; $8.

Birdland West, 105 W Broadway, Long Beach (☎310/436-9341). Very stylish venue with good names. Cover varies.

Blue Note Café, 11941 Ventura Blvd, Studio City (☎818/760-3348). Cramped room where burgers and beers are wolfed down to the accompaniment of loud, spirited jazz; cover varies.

Bon Appetit, 1061 Broxton Ave, Westwood (☎310/208-3830). Rock-jazz fusion in a consciously European setting; cover varies.

Cat and Fiddle Pub, 6530 Sunset Blvd (☎468-3800). This pseudo-English pub (see p.169) has jazz on Sunday from 6pm, usually mainstream quintets; no cover.

Coffee Emporium, 4325 Glencoe Blvd, Marina del Rey (☎823-4446). A 1950s coffee house that leaps into the present with "New Age" jazz on Fri and Sat; $5.

Comeback Inn, 1633 Washington Blvd (☎310/396-7255). Cosy bar with varied jazz sounds nightly at 9.15pm; $7.

Nucleus Nuance, 7267 Melrose Ave (☎939-8666). A busy room whose bluesy-flavoured jazz is as much for dancing as listening to; $5.

Sausalito South, 3280 Sepulveda Blvd, Manhattan Beach (☎310/546-4507). Everything from fusion to salsa; no cover.

System M, 213A Pine St, Long Beach (☎310/435-2525). Coffee house-cum-exhibition space which often has jazz of the more experimental kind; cover varies.

Vine St. Bar and Grill, 1610 N Vine St (☎463-4375). An elegant and tiny jazz club, where leading players sometimes stop by for some unannounced gigs; $10.

Salsa

Casa Rivera, 9001 E Telegraph Rd, Pico Rivera, East LA (☎949-8381). Salsa most nights and *jarocho* music from Veracruz, a sort of festive mariachi, once a week; cover $3 on Wed, Fri & Sat; no cover rest of the week.

Luminarias, 3500 Ramona Blvd, Monterey Park, East LA (☎268-4177). A hilltop restaurant (see p.176) with live salsa reckoned to be as good as its Mexican food; no cover.

Miami Spice, 13515 Washington Blvd, Venice (☎310/306-7978). Cuban restaurant with scintillating salsa sounds on Thurs and Sun; no cover.

Quiet Cannon, 901 Via San Clemente, Montebello, East LA. Three bars and dance floors, and salsa every Wed; no cover, but dress smart.

Reggae

Golden Sails Hotel, 6285 E Pacific Coast Highway (☎310/498-0091). Has some of the best reggae bands from LA and beyond on Fri and Sat; $5.

Jamaica West, 2205 Lincoln Blvd (☎310/587-2926). Live bands Fri and Sat; cover varies.

Kingston 12, 814 Broadway, Santa Monica (☎310/451-4423). The only seven-nights-a-week venue for reggae music. Small and comfortable; $10.

Classical music and opera

Considering its size and stature in the other arts, LA has very few outlets for **classical music**. The *Los Angeles Philharmonic*, the only major name in the city, perform regularly during the year, and the *Los Angeles Chamber Orchestra*, based at 315 W Ninth St (☎622-7001), appear sporadically at different venues; there are also **free concerts** performed by students of the Schoenburg Institute on the USC Campus at lunchtime during term. But otherwise attractions are thin, and you may have to rely on what is at least a fairly regular influx of internationally known performers throughout the year. Watch the press, especially the *LA Times*, for details, and expect to pay from $8 to $30 for most concerts, much more for really big-names. If you want to listen to **opera** you should really go to San Francisco, although the *Los Angeles Light Opera* stage productions between May and October, as do *Opera Pacific* (☎714/553-0699), who perform both grand opera and operettas. Prices can be anything from $15 to $80.

Classical venues

The Ambassador Auditorium, 300 W Green St, Pasadena (☎622-7001). Superb acoustics and many international stars between September and May.

The Dorothy Chandler Pavilion, in the *Music Center* 1365 N Grand Ave, Downtown (☎972-7211 or 480-3232). From October until May home to the LA Philharmonic Orchestra, who perform at 8pm on weeknights and at 2.30pm on Sunday.

The Hollywood Bowl, 2301 N Highland Ave, Hollywood (☎850-2000). The LA Philharmonic give open-air concerts here each Tues–Sat evening from July to September (see p.128 for more on the Bowl).

Orange County Performing Arts Center, 600 Town Center Drive, Costa Mesa (☎714/556-ARTS or 480-3232). Home of the Pacific Symphony Orchestra and Opera Pacific.

The Pacific Amphitheater, 100 Fair Drive, Costa Mesa (☎310/410-1062). A big open-air venue, Orange County's answer to the Hollywood Bowl.

The Shrine Auditorium, 3228 Royal St (☎748-5116), box office at 655 S Hill St (☎749-5123). A bizarre building that hosts regular performances by choral and gospel groups.

Royce Hall, on the UCLA campus (☎310/825-9261). Classical concerts often involving big names throughout the college year.

Wilshire Ebell Theater, 4401 W Eighth St (☎939-1128). A Renaissance-style building with sporadic concerts.

Dance

The last fifteen years or so have seen an increase in **dance** activity in LA, with two major ballet companies – the *Los Angeles Ballet* and the *Joffrey Ballet* – relocating on the West Coast after making their name in New York, accompanied by the growth of a number of small modern ensembles. There are also steady visits by companies from around the world, and although the city as yet lacks a specialist dance venue, there's always something going on somewhere, whether it be classical ballet or modern variants.

The big event of the year is the **Dance Kaleidoscope**, which features the cream of LA dance, held over two weeks at the John Anson Ford Theater and organised by the *Los Angeles Area Dance Alliance (LAADA)* (☎465-1100) – a co-operative supported by all of LA's smaller dance companies that provides a central source of information and a bi-monthly newsletter called *Dance Flash*. This, and the usual listings magazines and newspapers will have all the latest details. Expect to pay from $5 to $15 for a small local production, and anything up to $50 for a major show.

Dance venues

Ambassador Auditorium, 300 W Green St, Pasadena (☎304-6161). Some of the bigger international shows play here.

Japan America Theatre, 244 S San Pedro St (☎680-3700). Dance and performance works drawn from Japan and the Far East.

John Anson Ford Theater, 2850 Cahuenga Blvd (☎972-7200). Besides the summer Dance Kaleidoscope, this open-air venue also has one-off productions by local groups.

Dorothy Chandler Pavilion, part of the *Music Center*, 1365 N Grand Ave (☎972-7211 or 480-3232). A venue of the *Joffrey Ballet* and other major names.

Santa Monica College Studio Stage, 1900 Pico Blvd, Santa Monica (☎310/4452-9214). Often stages daring new pieces by modern LA choreographers.

Shrine Auditorium, 3228 Royal St (☎748-5116). Usually hosts at least one quality international ballet company during the spring.

UCLA Center for the Performing Arts, 10920 Wilshire Blvd (☎310/825-9261). Runs an Art of Dance series between September and June which usually has an experimental emphasis.

Comedy

An awful lot of gags are cracked every night all over LA, from the mouths of famous, soon-to-be famous and utterly-without-hope comics, both stand-up and improvisational, at a range of **comedy clubs** across the city. Most of the clubs are in Hollywood or West LA: they usually have a bar, charge a cover of $5–12, and put on two shows each evening, generally starting at 8pm and 10.30pm – the later one being the more popular. The better-known venues are open every night but are often solidly booked on Friday and weekends; other venues have comedy only on certain nights.

Comedy venues

The Comedy Club, 49 S Pine Ave, Long Beach (☎310/437-5326). A mixed range of hopeful stand-up comics.

Comedy & Magic Club, 1018 Hermosa Beach (☎310/372-1193). Strange couplings of naff magic acts and good-quality comedians.

The Comedy Store, 8433 W Sunset Blvd (☎656-6225). LA's comedy showcase and popular enough to be spread over three rooms – which means you're usually okay turning up on spec at weekends. Always a good line-up too.

Funny You Should Ask, at the *Melrose Theater*, 733 N Seward Ave (☎465-0070). Mainly improvisational, with a house team creating some fine routines from audience suggestions.

Groundling Theater, 7307 Melrose Ave (☎934-9700). Another pioneering improvisational venue where only the gifted survive.

The Ice House, 24 N Mentor Ave, Pasadena (☎818/577-1894). The comedy mainstay of the valley, very established and fairly safe.

Igby's Cabaret, 11637 Tennessee Place, (☎310/477-3553). Fairly new and boasting some surprise big-name turns alongside entertaining hopefuls.

The Improvisation, 8162 Melrose Ave (☎651-2583). Known for hosting some of the best acts working in the area. Book ahead.

LA Comedy Cabaret Club, 17271 Ventura Blvd, Encino (☎818/501-3737). Stand-up comics of mixed worth.

LA Connection, 13442 Ventura Blvd, Sherman Oaks (☎818/784-1868). An improvisation showcase for highly rated obnoxiousness specialists. Seldom less than memorable.

The Laugh Factory, 8001 Sunset Blvd (☎656-8860). Stand-ups of varying standards and reputations, with the odd big-name.

Upfront Comedy Showcase, 1452 Third Street Promenade, Santa Monica (☎310/319-3477). Nightly improvisational comedy based on audience suggestions.

Theatre

LA has a very active **theatre** scene. While the bigger venues host a predictable array of clapped-out old musicals and classics starring a crowd-pulling line-up of big film-names, there are over a hundred "equity waiver" theatres with less than a hundred seats, enabling non-equity-card-holders to perform, and a vast – and incestuous – network of fringe writers, actors and directors. Tickets are less expensive than you might expect: a big show will set you back upwards of $15 (matinees are cheaper), smaller shows around $6 to $10, and you should always book ahead.

We've listed the pick of both the major and fringe theatres, but a quick way through the maze is to phone *Theatrix* (☎466-1767) which handles reservations and provides details on what's playing at several of the smaller venues; or see the *LA Times*' weekend "Calendar" section.

Fringe theatres

Gene Dynarski Theater, 5600 Sunset Blvd (☎466-1767). Small-time character actor Dynarski built this likeable little theatre himself to rent out to small companies.

Groundling Theater, 7303 Melrose Ave (☎934-9700). One of the more consistently interesting venues on the fringe.

Odyssey Theater, 12111 Ohio Ave (☎310/826-1626). This place mounts engaging productions of everything from Sondheim to Sam Shepard and beyond. Also has smaller spaces for one-person shows.

Powerhouse Theater, 3116 Second St, Santa Monica (☎310/392-6529). Adventurous and risk-taking experimental shows.

Richmond Shepard Theater, 6476 Santa Monica Blvd (☎465-5567). A multi-theatre complex with poetry as well as plays.

Major theatres

Coronet Theater, 368 N La Cienega Boulevard (☎310/276-7461). Home of the LA Public Theater, whose productions include the odd famous name, and whose lively bar is patronised by excessively theatrical types.

Mark Taper Forum, 135 N Grand Avenue, downtown (☎972-7690). Theatre in the three-quarter round, frequently innovative new plays.

Schubert Theater, ABC Entertainment Center, Century City (☎310/553-9000). The only good thing about Century City is that you can come here to ogle the razzamatazz musicals.

Westwood Playhouse, 10886 Le Conte Avenue, Westwood (☎310/208-5454). One of the smaller of the major thatres, often with one-person shows.

Film

LA being the centre of the world **film** industry, it's no shock to find that many major feature films are released here months (sometimes years) before they play anywhere else in the world, and a huge number of cinemas show both the new releases and the long-serving faves – though there are comparatively few places screening independent and foreign movies. Depending on where you go and what you see, a ticket will be around $6.

For **mainstream cinema**, the numerous movie theatres around Westwood have the biggest screens and best sound systems in LA, and show the widest batch of first-run features. The newest rival to Westwood is the eighteen-screen *Cineplex Odeon*, at Universal Studios (☎818/508-0588), a plush complex which includes a pair of pseudo-Parisian cafés. Another, more enterprisingly programmed, is the *Beverly Cineplex*, in the Beverly Center, which has fourteen tiny auditoriums featuring a mix of first-run blockbusters and (slightly) more artsy fare.

For **cheap and free films**, the places to hit are the *Bing Theater* at the County Art Museum, 5905 Wilshire Blvd (☎857-6010), which has afternoon screenings of many neglected Hollywood classics and charges just $1; the USC and UCLA campuses also often have interesting free screenings aimed at film students, announced on campus notice boards. Otherwise, the best places to find **arthouse and cult films** are the *New Beverly Cinema*, 7165 Beverly Blvd (☎938-4038), especially strong on imaginative double bills and the *Nuart Theater*, 11272 Santa Monica Blvd (☎310/478-6379), which also runs rarely seen classics and documentaries. Short seasons of **foreign-language films** are often showing at the city's eight *Laemmle Theaters*, at Figueroa at Third St, downtown (☎617-0268); 11523 Santa Monica Blvd, West LA (☎310/477-5811); 8556 Wilshire Blvd, Beverly Hills (☎310/652-1330); 9036 Wilshire Blvd (☎310/274-6869); in Santa Monica at 1332 Second St (☎310/394 9741); in Pasadena at 2588 E Colorado Blvd (☎818/793-6149) and 2670 E Colorado Blvd (☎818/796-9704); and in Encino at 17200 Ventura Blvd (☎818/981-9811).

If you're looking for a golden-years-of-film **atmosphere**, you'll need either to take in an action triple bill in one of the historic downtown movie palaces (described on p.108), where the delirious furnishings may captivate your attention longer than the all-action triple-bills; or visit one of the Hollywood landmarks. *The Chinese Theater*, 6925 Hollywood Blvd (☎468-8111) with its large screen and six-track stereo sound, art deco interior, shows limp MOR films; as does the *Egyptian Theater*, 6708 Hollywood Blvd (☎467-6167). If these don't appeal, you could always indulge in the near-wraparound screen of the *Cinerama Dome*, 6360 Sunset Blvd (☎466-3401).

Gay and Lesbian LA

Although nowhere near as big as that of San Francisco, the **gay scene** in LA is far from invisible, and gay people are out and prominent in workplaces and environments right across the city. Of a number of specific areas where gays tend to locate, best-known is the autonomous city of West Hollywood, which has a gay-led council and has become synonymous with the (affluent, white) gay lifestyle, not just in LA but all over California. The section of West Hollywood on Santa Monica Boulevard between Doheny Boulevard and Crescent Heights has many restaurants, shops and bars that are primarily aimed at gay men. The other overtly gay community is Silverlake, at its most evident in the gay-orientated bars and restaurants along Hyperion Boulevard. (For more on the Gay and Lesbian West Coast, see "Basics".)

Gay resources

AIDS Project Los Angeles, 7362 Santa Monica Blvd (☎876-8951). Sponsors fundraisers throughout the year and an annual walkathon.

Gay and Lesbian Community Services Center, 1213 H Highland Ave (☎464-7400). Counselling, health testing and information. They also publish a useful bi-monthly magazine called *The Center News*.

Bookshops

A Different Light, 4014 Santa Monica Blvd (☎668-0629). The city's best known gay and lesbian bookshop, with monthly art shows, readings, women's music events and comfortable chairs for lounging.

Publications

Act Up, PO Box 26601, CA 90026 (☎664-2052). Bi-monthy newsletter challenging the official response to AIDS.

The Advocate, 6922 Hollywood Blvd (☎871-1225). A national gay men's magazine, the California edition has statewide listings and classified ads.

Compass, PO Box 1586, Hollywood (☎874-4838). General gay news magazine, free in gay bars, restaurants, hotels, etc.

Dispatch, 8380 Santa Monica Blvd (☎877-1045). A free bi-weekly listing arts and events.

Edge, 6900 Meirose Ave (☎934-5922). Fortnightly magazine with general features on the LA gay scene.

Frontiers, c/o Media Concepts, 7985 Santa Monica Blvd (☎877-1045). Fortnightly magazine with gay-orientated political articles and general arts information for Southern California.

Gay Community Yellow Pages, 2305 Canyon Drive (☎469-4454). Gay businesses, publications, services and gathering places listed yearly.

The Leather Journal, 7985 Santa Monica Blvd (☎877-1045). Magazine with a leather and S&M slant.

The News, PO Box 60869. Monthly review with general arts features of interest to the gay and lesbian communities.

Reactions, 12319 Ventura Blvd (☎818/877-1000). A free bi-monthly with features and political news.

Gay hotels

Gay couples will find themselves readily accepted at just about any LA **hotel**, but there are a few that cater especially for gay travellers and can also be useful sources of information on the LA gay scene generally.

Coral Sands Hotel, 1730 N Western Ave (☎1-800/367-7263). Exclusively geared towards gay men. The rooms face the inner courtyard pool. $80 and up.

The Selby Hotel, 1740 N Hudson Ave (☎469-5320). Also aimed solely at gay men. Shared bathrooms. $36.

Studio Hotel, 1611 Vista del Mar (☎460-6000). Gay men and women only. Art deco in design, built on old movie lot. $160 per week.

Gay and Lesbian restaurants

Again, gays won't find themselves made unwelcome anywhere in LA, but there are a few eateries that cater specifically to gay men and lesbians.

Casita de Campo, 1920 Hyperion Ave (☎662-4255). Great Mexican food and a comfortable atmosphere.

Gloria's Cafe, 3603 W Sunset Blvd (☎664-5732). Popular local hangout that's a great spot for dinner, especially Cajun.

French Market Place, 7985 Santa Monica Blvd (☎654-0898). A themed eaterie that's at least as much fun as Disneyland.

The Rose Tattoo, 665 N Robertson St (☎310/854-4455). Elegant dining for both women and men.

Gay and Lesbian nightlife: bars and clubs

Mainly for men

Arena, 6655 Santa Monica Blvd (☎962-4485). Large dance floor throbbing to funk and hi-energy grooves – and sometimes live bands – on Wed, Sat and Sun; $8–10.

Le Bar, 2375 Glendale Blvd, Silverlake (☎660-7595). Quiet and welcoming, with a pool table.

Circus, 6655 Santa Monica Blvd (☎462-1291). A long-running disco with the latest dance music and three bars. Men only on Tues; gay men and women on Fri.

Catch One, 4067 W Pico Blvd (☎734-8849). Sweaty dance barn packed, mostly with gay men, every weekend; $5.

Corral Club, 3747 Cahuenga Blvd (☎818/796-6900). Male dancers and videos; no alcohol, the slogan is "hard men soft drinks".

Detour, 1087 Manzanita, Silverlake (☎664-1189). A friendly and quite cheap denim and leather bar.

Rage, 8911 Santa Monica Blvd (☎758-7243). Very flash gay men's club playing the latest hi-n-r-g hits. Drinks are cheap, the cover varies.

Revolver, 8851 Santa Monica Blvd (☎550-8851). Club in which you can watch yourself dancing with yourself on giant video screens hanging above the dance floor. The definitive West Hollywood gay bar.

Score, 107 W Fourth St (☎625-7382). A comfortable disco and bar; cover $2, includes one free drink.

Mainly for women

Code Blue, 11150 Olympic Blvd (☎310/281-9903). Home to "the beautiful people" – the glamorous side of the women's movement.

Les Beans, 10836 Venice Blvd (☎310/836-6710). Feminist art gallery, coffee house, and vegetarian restaurant.

The Oxwood Inn, 13713 Oxnard St, Van Nuys (☎818/997-9666). After sixteen years in the same San Fernando Valley location, this Country and Western women's bar has become a mainstay. It's open Friday and Saturday nights, has no cover charge and features a pool table.

Peanut's, 7969 Santa Monica Blvd (☎654-0280). Eclectic, mixed crowd and a variety of bizarre sideshows, plus a massive dance floor. Men also welcome most nights, call for details; cover $6, $9 weekends.

Seven Hail Marys, call for location (☎310/672-0512). "A Club for Women with Alternative Rituals" the spiel goes; actually a Friday night haunt that plays 1950s, 1960s and 1980s music. It also has a TV lounge equipped with biker magazines.

Women's LA

It's hardly surprising that a city as big as LA should have such an organised **women's** network, with many resource centres, bookshops, publications and clubs. Women travellers are unlikely to encounter any problems which aren't applicable to all the West Coast (for more on which see "Basics", p.33), but the resources here are much more developed.

Any of the following are good sources of general and detailed information on the local women's movement, though there's an inevitable crossover with the city's sizeable lesbian community – for bars catering only to women, see "Gay and Lesbian LA", above.

Resource centres

Connexxus Women's Center, 9054 Santa Monica Blvd (☎310/859-3960). Primarily lesbian in orientation, a drop-in centre offering group counselling and discussions.

Gay and Lesbian Community Services Center, 1213 N Highland Ave (☎464-7400). Health and human services and public education.

International Gay/Lesbian Archives, Natalie Barney/Edward Carpenter Library, 1654 Hudson Ave (☎463-5450). Archives containing feminist books and periodicals. Mon–Fri noon–5pm.

NOW LA, 1242 S La Cienega Blvd (☎310/652-5572). The local branch of the National Organization for Women provides a referral service, and is also able to answer phone inquiries.

The Women's Building, 1643 Eighteenth St, Santa Monica (no phone). Features everything from exhibits, performances and films to writing groups and various theme-related workshops.

Women's bookshops

Bookworks, 3517 Centinela Ave (☎310/398-1932). New and used books, feminist cards, badges, and posters. Closed Mon.

Bread and Roses, 13812 Ventura Blvd, Sherman Oaks (☎818-986 5376). In the heart of the San Fernando Valley, this store caters to women of all social, racial, ethnic and sociological backgrounds.

Page One, 966 N Lake Ave, Pasadena (☎818/798-8694). Books by and for women, and non-sexist children's books.

Sisterhood Bookstore, 1351 Westwood Blvd (☎310/477-7300). This Westside landmark, just south of Westwood Village, has books, music, cards, jewellery and a comprehensive selection of literature pertaining to the women's movement both nationally and internationally.

The Uprising, 3125 E Seventh St, Long Beach (☎310/438-8922). A combination bookstore, theatre, and gallery specialising in the arts.

Publications

LA Woman. Los Angeles' largest women's magazine, profiling local personalities and providing a calendar of events, available from mainstream newsstands.

Lesbian News. A weekly women's movement publication, also on sale at newsstands.

Women's Yellow Pages. P.O. Box 66093, Los Angeles 90066 (☎310/398-5761). A yearly published listing of over 1400 women-owned businesses and services. Call or write for a free copy.

The Shops

You can buy virtually anything, anywhere, anytime in LA. The level of disposable income in the wealthy parts of the city is astronomical, and much of it gets blown on designer frocks, trendy novelties and all manner of trivial purchases – enough to give the careful, budget-conscious shopper a heart attack. It's all very much part of LA life, though, and whether you want to pop out for a new light bulb or pair of socks, lay waste to a wad or simply be a voyeur in the orgy of acquisition, there are, besides the run-of-the-mill retailers you'll find anywhere, big **department stores**, expansive **malls** and the thoroughly exclusive **Rodeo Drive** – each perfect for doing all of these things. The city also has a good assortment of **specialist shops**, sporting extensive selections of books, records, clothes and just sheer oddities – not to mention the fantastic finds you can make at the city's **thrift stores** and **garage sales**. There's an equally diverse assortment of **food shops**, from corner delis and supermarkets to fancy cake shops and gourmet markets.

General and expense account shopping

Each neighbourhood will have a collection of **ordinary shops** and mini-malls, much the best sources of cheap toiletries and staples at places like *K-mart* and *Pic'n'Save*, the latter specialising in dirt cheap discontinued goods. A step up from these in price and quality, though still good for general shopping, are the city's **department stores**. A couple, *Bullocks Wilshire*, at 3050 Wilshire Boulevard, and the *May Company*, 6067 Wilshire, merit a call for their Twenties architecture rather than their uninspiring merchandise. More upmarket are *Neiman Marcus*, 9700 Wilshire Boulevard, who sell everything from $5 Swiss truffles to his'n'her leopard-skins, and *Nordstrom*, 10830 Pico Boulevard (in the Westside Pavilion) – a clothes, shoes jewellery and cosmetics store that provides regular customers with a personal "shopper" (ie an employee who does all the legwork around the shop and comes back with a choice of goods). Rather more useful for basic purchases is *Robinson's*, 9900 Wilshire Boulevard, where you could spend hours picking through the enormous selections of clothing and household items.

Department stores in LA, however, come second to the massive **malls**, often resembling self-contained city suburbs as much as shopping precincts, around which Angelenos do the bulk of their serious buying. Swishest of all the malls is the seven-acre *Beverly Center*, bordered by Beverly Boulevard and La Cienega Boulevard, and San Vicente Boulevard and Third Street, where you'll find designer-stores, fourteen cinemas, and if you're interested, ample opportunities for star-gazing. Broadly similar, if slightly lower on the social scale, are *The Westside Pavilion*, 10800 Pico Boulevard, and *Century Square*, 10250 Santa Monica Boulevard. If you actually want to buy something, use the more mainstream and affordable *Glendale Galleria*, Central Avenue and Wilson Street in Glendale, or the vast *South Coast Plaza*, 3333 Bristol Avenue, Costa Mesa, just off the Santa Ana Freeway.

Rodeo Drive

The black hole for expense accounts is **Rodeo Drive** in Beverly Hills, a solid line of exclusive stores to which you might be drawn by sheer curiosity. One store worth looking into is *Fred Hayman*, at 273 N – one of the first stores on Rodeo Drive and housing the autographed photos of a number of Hollywood celebs alongside its mostly Italian designer-menswear. Another is *Polo Ralph Lauren*, 444 N which caters to well-heeled WASPS who fancy themselves as canine-fixated English gentry. Besides thousand-dollar suits and monogrammed Wellingtons, there are exquisitely carved walking sticks and mounted game heads, and a huge assortment of wooden dogs, bronze dogs and paintings of dogs.

Clothes

The only place to find really cheap **clothes** bargains is in a thrift store (see below), although if you have the money LA gives a great choice: either in the department stores and malls listed above or the smaller specialist shops with lines, particularly in classic American and designer-wear, that are hard to beat. A few places worth trying are:

American Rag, 150 S La Brea Ave. The best place for classic Amercian styles from the Thirties to the present day.

Atomic Age, 8308 W Third St. Men and women's clothes and accessories from the Twenties to the Sixties.

The Back Room, 8525 W Pico Blvd. A cut-price stockist of women's designer clothes, often at half the price you'll find elsewhere.

Ragtime Cowboy, 5332 Lankershim Blvd, N Hollywood. Secondhand American classics.

Third Faze, 1157 N La Brea Ave. A discount store that's constantly updating its stock: look for "$10 sales" when anything, trousers, shirts, skirts, sweaters, and silk ties, costs just that.

Thrift stores and garage sales

With their hordes of secondhand clothing and furniture, **thrift stores**, broadly similar to British *Oxfam* shops, often come close to being unofficial museums of social history, fun just to browse around even if you don't intend to buy anything. They're all over LA, but the best tend to be in the Valleys and hinterlands of Orange County; indeed, the city of Orange contains two of the finest, the *Goodwill Thrift Store,* 1828 E Collins Avenue and the *Salvation Army Thrift Store*, 686 N Tustin Avenue. **Garage sales**, held on private lawns by house-owners having a clearout, can also be sources of unusual household paraphernalia. They are advertised in the classified sections of newspapers and by ad-hoc roadside signs.

Finally, consider a trip to the **Garment district**, in the southeast corner of downtown, where a number of outlets sell marked-down designer wear.

Food and drink

Since eating out is so common, you may never have to shop for **food** at all. But if you're preparing a picnic, or want to indulge in a spot of home cooking, there are plenty of places to stock up. **Delis**, many open round the clock, are found on more or less every corner in LA; **supermarkets** are almost as common, some open 24 hours, or at least until 10pm – *Lucky's, Alpha-Beta, Pavilion, Ralph's* and *Trader Joe's* are the names to look out for. There are also **ethnic groceries and markets** and – although much more expensive – the **gourmet markets and shops**, not to mention a bizarre collection of one-off outlets for all kinds of food oddities, mainly clustered in fashionable West LA. To buy **drink** you need go no further than the nearest supermarket (*Trader Joe's* is the cheapest and best) or a branch of *Liquor Barn*, open between 6am and 2am; addresses in the phone book.

Specialist shops

Viktor Benes Continental Pastries, 8718 W Third St. The place for freshly baked bread, coffeecakes and Danish pastries.

The Buttery, 2906 Main St, Santa Monica. The best soft, chewy cookies in the city, and also selling croissants and bread.

The Cheese Store, 419 Beverly Drive, Beverly Hills. Over 400 types of cheese from all over the world, including every kind produced in the US.

Famous Amos, 7181 W Sunset Blvd. Although the dark, crisp, chocolate or nut-spattered cookies made here are now available all over LA, this is the original, and even has tables for those who can't wait.

Mrs Field's Cookies, 443 N Beverly Dr, Beverly Hills. Chewy, sweet cookies, made to a "secret recipe" that has plenty of devoted fans. Also at 907 Westwood Blvd, Westwood.

West Hollywood Upper Crust, 640 N Robertson Blvd. A combined bakery and coffee-house where you can find all manner of croissant fillings and a huge variety of pastries and cakes.

Ethnic groceries and markets

Bay Cities Importing, 1517 Lincoln Blvd, Santa Monica. Like a gigantic deli, with piles of fresh pasta, spices, meats, sauces and many French and Middle Eastern imports.

Bezjian's Grocery, 4725 Santa Monica Blvd. Indian and Middle Eastern fare.

Enbun, Japanese Village Plaza. Artfully arranged Japanese foods including the freshest fish, cut to order for sashimi.

Gianfranco, 11363 Santa Monica Blvd. All Italian: pastas, cheeses, stuffed shells and meatballs.

El Mercado, 3425 E First St, East LA. Three floors of authentic Mexican food: chilis, chay-otes and mouthwatering desserts.

Gourmet markets

Ashford Market, 1627 Montana Ave, Santa Monica. Three gourmet shops linked together, offering pastas, breads, pastries, and many exotic fruits and vegetables.

Chalet Gourmet, 7880 W Sunset Blvd. Quality meats, fish, dairy and baked foods.

Charmer's Market, 175 Marine St, Santa Monica. Exotic fresh fruit and vegetables.

Irvine Ranch Market, ground floor of Beverly Center, 142 San Vicente Blvd. Fabulously stocked with the freshest meats and fish, also with row after row of herbs, fruits and spices.

Books

There sometimes seem to be as many bookshops in LA as there are people. Of the ubiquitous **discount chains**, which have spread across the US in the last few years, *Crown* offer the latest hardbacks and blockbusters plus many more (and magazines) at knock-down prices, as do *Doubleday, B. Dalton* and *Waldenbooks*.

One of the few small **general bookshops** to survive is, in fact, LA's oldest: *Fowler Brothers*, at 717 W Seventh Street, open since 1888, with a broad range of new books sold by knowledgeable staff.

More encouragingly perhaps, the city is exceptionally well served by a wide-range of **specialist bookshops** and many **secondhand bookshops**, worthy of several hours' browsing along the miles of dusty shelves.

Given the large number of **authors** who live in LA, **signing sessions** are also fairly common – check posters in bookstores or newspapers for details if you're interested.

Specialist bookshops

Bodhi Tree, 8585 Melrose Ave. New Age and occult books.

A Change of Hobbit, 1853 Lincoln Blvd, Santa Monica. Packed with fantastic fiction, and staffed by experts.

Dangerous Visions, 13606 Ventura Blvd, in Sherman Oaks. Sci-fi and fantasy with a special leaning towards children's titles.

Hennessey and Ingalls, 10814 W Pico Blvd. An impressive range of art and architecture books which may otherwise be hard to find; also rare posters and catalogues.

Larry Edmunds Book Shop, 6658 Hollywood Blvd. Stacks of books on every aspect of film and theatre, and movie stills and posters.

Midnight Special, 1350 Santa Monica Blvd. A general bookshop but with excellently filled shelves of politics and social sciences.

Scene of the Crime, 13636 Ventura Blvd, in Sherman Oaks. New and used collection spanning everything criminal from hard-boiled private dicks to whodunnits, housed in a small room done up in the manner of the study of a country mansion.

Secondhand books

Acres of Books, 240 Long Beach Blvd, Long Beach. Worth a trip to the South Bay just to wallow in LA's largest secondhand collection.

Book City, 6627 Hollywood Blvd. Tightly packed from floor to ceiling with eclectic titles.

Marlow's Bookshop, 6609 Hollywood Blvd. New and secondhand books. Specialises in rare magazines.

Records

If anything, **record shops** are more plentiful than bookshops in LA. What's more, with the current exchange rate, it can be cheaper to buy British albums here than at home – imports are $12 to $15, while most US albums cost around $9. That price, remarkably, goes for CDs too, so in fact these days only the secondhand specialists bother to stock significant numbers of actual records.

Aron's Records, 1150 N Highland Ave. Secondhand discs – all styles, all prices, huge stock.

House of Records, 2314 Pico Blvd. Singles from 1949 to the present.

Moby Disc, 14410 Ventura Blvd, Sherman Oaks. Secondhand and deletion stockist.

Mr Records, 2924 Wilshire Blvd. Rare items, especially obscure Beatles' waxings.

Music and Memories, 10850 Ventura Blvd, Studio City. Almost entirely devoted to Frank Sinatra, though they also stock singers who sound like Frank too.

Poo-Bah Records, 1101 E Walnut Ave, Pasadena. American and imported New Wave.

The Record Connection, 8505 Santa Monica Blvd. Deleted Sixties stuff and classical rarities.

Rhino Records, 1720 Westwood Blvd. The city's biggest selection of international independent releases.

Tower Records, 8801 Sunset Blvd and 1028 Westwood Blvd. The first "supermarket" record store – with vast stocks of everything.

Vinyl Fetish, 7305 Melrose Ave. Besides the punk and post-punk merchandise, a good place to discover what's new on the LA music scene.

Oddities

The following stores sell things which – often deliberately – don't fit into any recognisable category. If none take your fancy, simply saunter down to the "7000" block of Melrose Avenue, where many shops proffer deco and deco-style antiques, ornaments and junk.

Bead Werk, 10895 Pico Blvd. Rare and unusual beads from all over the globe.

Heaven, 10250 Santa Monica Blvd, West LA. Completely silly stock of one-off t-shirts, cheap monster disguises, and many vulgar varieties of bubblegum.

The Last Wound-Up, 7374 Melrose Ave. Only stocks things which can be wound up.

Soap Plant/Wacko 7400 Melrose Ave. Hideous ornaments, bizarre greetings cards and horrible household items – all utterly useless.

Twigs, 1401 Montan Ave, Santa Monica. Everything, even furniture, made from twigs.

Listings

Airlines Most major airlines have offices at several locations around LA; these are just the main addresses: *American*, 6310 W Vincente Blvd (☎1-800/424-7225); *British Airways*, 380 World Way West (☎1-800/247-9297); *Continental*, 7700 World Way West (☎1-800/435-0040); *Delta*, 529 W Sixth St (☎386-5510); *Eastern*, 518 W Sixth St (☎772-5880); *Northwest Airlines*, 504 W Sixth St (domestic: ☎1-800/225-2525; international ☎1-800/447-4747); *Pan Am*, 533 W Sixth St (☎1-800/221-1111); *TWA*, 508 W Eighth St (domestic: ☎484-2244; international: ☎484-9311).

Airports *LAX* ☎310/646-5252; *John Wayne, Orange County* ☎714/834-2400; *Long Beach* ☎421-8293; *Hollywood/Burbank* ☎840-8847; *Ontario* ☎714/785-8838.

American Express Downtown at 901 W Seventh St (☎627-4800); in Beverly Hills at 327 N Beverly Dr (☎234-8277).

Amtrak General enquiries ☎1-800/USA-RAIL; Union Station information and reservations ☎624-0171.

Automobile Club of Southern California, 2601 S Figueroa St (☎741-3111). For maps and other motoring information.

Babysitting Some hotels can arrange this, or try the *Baby Sitters Guild*, 6362 Hollywood Blvd (☎469-8246).

Banks All banks have branches all over the city, though if you're in downtown, Hollywood or West LA, you'll find the following handily placed: *Bank of America*, 525 S Flower St (☎389-3702), 6300 Sunset Blvd (☎464-0511); *Security Pacific*, 100 S Broadway (☎626-2441), 6777 Hollywood Blvd (☎468-2018); *Union Bank*, 900 S Main St (☎236-6875), 94444 Wilshire Blvd (☎228-7035); *Wells Fargo*, 333 S Grand Ave (☎253-3000), 6320 W Sunset Blvd (☎255-0333).

Beach info Weather conditions ☎310/457-9701; surfing info ☎379-8471.

Bike hire See p.92.

Coastguard ☎310/590-2225.

Chemists 24-hour pharmacies at *Thrifty's Drugs*, 333 S Vermont, Downtown (☎735-7305), and *Kaiser Permanente* in the LA Medical Center, 4867 Sunset Blvd, Hollywood (☎667-8301). Consult the phone book for chemists in other areas.

Consulates *UK* 3701 Wilshire Blvd (☎385-0252); *Eire* 4021 Royal Oaks Place, Encino (☎818/981-6464); *Australia* 611 N Larchmont Blvd (☎469-4300); *New Zealand* 10960 Wilshire Blvd (☎310/477-8241).

Directory Enquiries Local ☎411; Long distance 1/Area Code/555-1212.

Doctors *SOS Doctor* on call 24 hours a day: ☎222-1111.

Dental Treatment The cheapest place is the *USC School of Dentistry* (☎743-2800), on the USC Campus, costing $20–200. Turn up and be prepared to wait all day.

Earthquakes Small earthquakes happen all the time in LA, usually doing no more than rattling supermarket shelves and making dogs howl nervously, but once in a while they're are powerful enough to cause serious damage and fatalities. The worst in recent times was on 9 February 1971, which measured 6.1 on the Richter scale and brought down freeway overpasses and a number of buildings and resulted in 65 deaths. Since then the authorities have instigated a programme of making existing buildings "quake-safe" and placing restrictions on new ones – a strategy which seems, in the light of a 5.8 richter scale earthquake on 1 October 1987 that killed only one person, to be paying off. If a sizeable earthquake strikes, try to be under something sturdy, such as a doorframe, and away from windows or anything made of glass. Afterwards, don't use telephones or electricity unless you have to, as this may overload the systems. It's no comfort, for visitors or residents, to know that the widely feared "Big One", a quake above 7.5 on the Richter Scale, is due to hit some time in the next thirty years.

Emergencies ☎911. For less urgent needs: ambulance ☎483-6721; fire ☎384-3131 or ☎262-2111; paramedics ☎262-2111; police ☎625-3311.

Flea markets/Swap meets In Pasadena at the Rose Bowl, second Sunday of each month. In Orange County at the Costa Mesa Fairgrounds, each Saturday.

Hospitals with casualty departments Cedars-Sinai Medical Center, 8700 Beverly Blvd (☎310/855-6517); Good Samaritan Hospital, 616 Witmer St (☎397-2121); UCLA Medical Center, corner of Tiverton and Le Conte St in Westwood Village (☎310/825-2111).

International Newspapers Both the USC and UCLA campuses have libraries holding recent overseas newspapers for browsing. Day-old English and European papers are on sale at *Universal News Agency*, 1655 N Las Palmas (daily 7am–midnight), and *World Book and News*, 1652 N Cahuenga Blvd (24 hours).

Launderettes All over the city, but useful ones in popular areas include *Launderland*, 747 S Union St, Downtow and *Melrose Laundromat*, 4671 Melrose Ave. See the phone book for a complete list.

Left Luggage At *Greyhound* stations and LAX for $1 a day ($2 for larger lockers). There's no left luggage at Union Station.

Lifts There are ride boards on both USC and UCLA campuses.

Lost Property For something lost on the RTD call ☎937-8920.

Mexican Tourist Office, Suite 224, 10100 Santa Monica Blvd (☎310/203-8151). Call in for general information and to pick up a Tourist Card – necessary if you're heading over the border. Open Mon–Fri 9am–5pm.

Money exchange Outside of banking hours daily at LAX until 11.30pm. On Saturday also at *Deak-International*, main office at 677 S Figueroa St from 10am–4pm.

Park info City Parks: ☎485-5555; County Parks ☎738-2961; National Parks Service ☎818/888-3770.

Post offices The city's main post office is downtown at 901 S Broadway (☎617-4413), open Mon–Fri 8.30–6pm, Sat 7am–1.30pm. For Poste Restante here, use zip code 90014. Others include 1615 N Wilcox, Hollywood (☎464-2194), open Mon–Fri 8.30am–5pm, Sat 8.30am-noon, zip code 90038.

Rape hotline ☎262-0944.

Road Conditions For a recorded message ☎626-7231; if you want to speak to someone, ☎620-3550, Mon–Fri 8am–5pm.

Sierra Club The LA branch of this mountain hiking and camping club is at 3550 W Sixth St (☎387-4287), open Mon–Fri 10am–6pm.

Smog Like many other things in the city, LA's smog is more hype than reality. However, the city's basin has always been hazy, and, now exacerbated by motor vehicles, the air quality *is* often very poor and, especially in the Valleys in late summer, can sometimes be quite dangerous. An air-quality index is published daily, and if the air is really bad, warnings are issued on TV, radio and in the press.

Sport Baseball: the *LA Dodgers* (☎224-1400) play at Dodger Stadium near downtown, seats $4–10; *California Angels* (☎714/937-6761), at Anaheim Stadium in Orange County, seats $4–10. Basketball: the *LA Lakers* (☎637-1300) are at the Forum, in Inglewood, seats (often impossible to get) $10–20. Football: the *LA Rams* (☎714/937-6761) also play at Anaheim

Stadium, seats $15–30; *LA Raiders* (☎747-7111) in the LA Coliseum, near downtown, seats $15–30. Hockey: *LA Kings* are also based at the Forum (☎310/419-3182), seats $10–25.

Thomas Cook No central branches but offices at: Business Travel Center, 360 N Sepulveda Blvd, El Segundo (☎640-3010); 455 E Ocean Blvd, Long Beach (☎310/437-0764); and 238A S Lake Ave, Pasadena (☎818/792-7168).

Ticketron The major LA office is 6060 W Manchester Ave (☎310/216-6666); they, or the phone book, will have details of the others.

Time ☎853-1212.

Traveler's Aid ☎310/646-2270 Mon–Fri 9am–4pm. At other times a recorded message on ☎686-0950.

Victims of Crime Resource Center ☎1-800/842-8467.

Weather ☎554-1212.

travel details

Buses
From Los Angeles to Las Vegas (13 daily; 6hr 15min); San Francisco (9; 11hr); San Diego (7; 3hr).

Trains
From Los Angeles 6–8 daily to Fullerton (for Disneyland)/Anaheim/San Juan Capistrano (35 min/44min/1hr 15min); San Clemente (1; 1hr 30min). Additionally there is 1 train and 4 connecting buses daily to Glendale/Van Nuys/Oxnard/Ventura (15min/30min/1hr 30min/1hr 57min); To Pasadena (1 daily; 24min); San Bernadino (2; 1hr 32min); San Francisco (1; 11hr 5min); Las Vegas (1; 6hr 55min); Salt Lake City (1; 16hr); Kansas (1; 16hr 35min); Albuquerque (1; 16hr 50min); Denver (1; 28hr 20min); Omaha (1; 38hr 40min); Chicago (1; 4hr 45min).

CHAPTER THREE

THE DESERTS AND LAS VEGAS

T he **deserts** of Southern California represent only a fraction of the half a million square miles of North American Desert that stretch away eastwards into another four states, and cross the border into Mexico in the south. Contrary to the monotonous landscape you might expect, California's deserts are a varied and ever-changing kaleidoscope, dotted with occasional harsh little settlements. The one thing you can rely on is that it will be uniformly hot and inhospitable – and dry (though desert rainfall is highly irregular, and a whole year's average of three or four inches may fall in a single storm). Most of the 25 million acres that make up the desert are protected in state parks, but it's not all entirely unspoiled. Three million acres are used by the US Government as military bases for training and weapons testing, and when underground nuclear explosions aren't shaking up the desert's fragile ecosystem, the region's many fans flock here to do their damage. City-dwellers work out their urban frustration by tearing around on dune buggies, motorbikes and four-wheel-drive vehicles; acid-freaks and bikers come here to relate to the mysticism of the place and have wild parties, and there are of course the hordes of hikers, rock-climbers and environmentalists, miners, scientists and ranchers, each claiming the land for their sole use. The Bureau of Land Management nervously referees between the warring parties and tries to set aside areas for each group.

In spite of all this, most of the desert remains a wilderness, and with a little foresight can be the undisputed highlight of a trip to California. Occupying a quarter of the state, California's desert divides into two distinct regions: the **Colorado** or **Low Desert** in the south, stretching down to the Mexican border and east into Arizona, and the **Mojave** or **High Desert**, which covers the south-central part of the state. The Low Desert is the most easily reached from the coast and LA, with the extravagantly wealthy **Palm Springs** serving as an access-point. The hiking trails around **Joshua Tree** are the big attraction for serious desert-people, bridging the divide between Low and High Desert in a vast silent area of craggy trees. In contrast, **Imperial Valley** to the south – agricultural land, though you could pass through without realising anyone lived there – and the **Salton Sea** beyond, is undiluted Low Desert. The heat is searing, and unless you're headed for states beyond there's no point making this part of your itinerary. Interstate 10 crosses the Low Desert from east to west and carries a considerable flow of traffic – not unusually, packs of bikers that head out at weekends for a long ride and some high jinks in the popular gambling resorts like **Lake Havasu City** that dot the stunning **Colorado River** region on the California/ Arizona border.

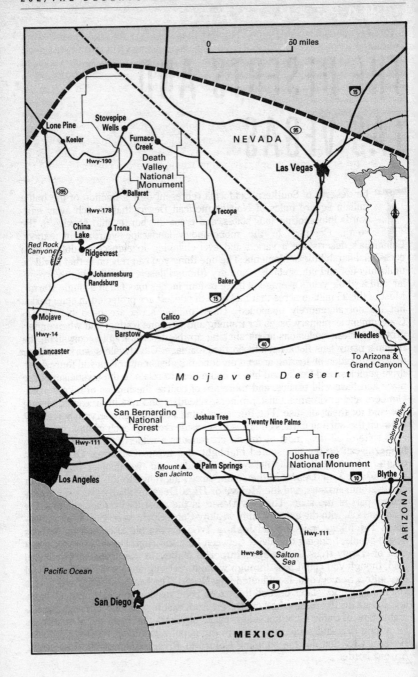

Barstow on I-15 is often a first stop for those heading into the High Desert. From here it's possible (and popular) to make the long and tiring trip to the neon oasis of **Las Vegas**, just across the border in Nevada, for some legalised gambling. Afterwards you can loop back by way of (the only) public transport to **Death Valley**, which utterly dominates the High Desert – so hot, and so remote, that it's almost a region unto itself.

With the exception of Palm Springs, **motels** are low in price, and you can budget for under $40 per night. **Public transport** however, is more of a problem: Los Angeles connects easily with the major points – Palm Springs, Barstow, Las Vegas – but on arrival you're stuck without a car. Also, your car will need to be in very good working order – don't rely on the Thunderbird you picked up in LA for $250 to get you through the worst of the desert. Three major highways cross the desert from east to west. I-15 cuts directly through the middle of the Mojave on its way from Los Angeles to Las Vegas, joined at Barstow, the Mojave's largest town, by I-40, which then heads east to the California border at Needles, and beyond to the **Grand Canyon**. I-10 takes you from LA through the Palm Springs and Joshua Tree area of the Colorado Desert to the town of Blythe, on the border with Arizona. Some fast, empty, secondary roads can get you safely to all but the most remote areas of the desert; but be wary of using the lower-grade roads in between, which are likely to be unmaintained and tricky.

Desert survival

Only the well prepared can enjoy the desert with any sense of security. Hazards abound, but are easily circumvented by a little forward-thinking and common sense. Hikers are the most vulnerable, especially those who venture beyond the designated areas of the state parks, but drivers too should not be blasé and take considerable precautions whatever their destination. Above all *think*. Tell somebody where you are going, and write down all the pertinent information, including your expected time of return. Carry an extra two days' food and water and never go anywhere without a map.

Climate and water

First and most obviously you're up against a pretty formidable **climate**. This varies from region to region, but the basic safety procedures remain the same: not only are you doing battle with incredible heat, but at high elevations at night you should be prepared for below-freezing temperatures too. Between May and September, when the temperatures in Death Valley can get up to 136°F, you really shouldn't come at all (although of course people do); outside of those months the temperature hovers around the mid-nineties. At any time of year, you'll stay cooler during the day if you wear full-length sleeves and trousers: shorts and a vest will expose you to way too much sun – something you won't be aware of until it's too late; also, a wide-brimmed hat and a pair of *good* sunglasses will spare you the blinding headaches that can result from the desert light. You may also have to contend with **flash floods**, which can appear from nowhere: an innocent-looking dark cloud can turn a dry wash into a raging river. Never camp in a dry wash and don't attempt to cross flooded areas until the water has receded.

You can never drink enough **liquid** in the desert: the body loses up to a gallon every day and even when you're not thirsty you should keep drinking. Before setting off on any expedition, whether on foot or in a car, *two* gallons of water per person should be prepared. Waiting for thirst, dizziness, nausea or other signs of dehydration before doing anything can be dangerous. If you notice any of these symptoms, or feel weak and have stopped sweating, it's time to get to the doctor. Watch your alcohol intake too: if you must booze during the day, compensate heavily with pints of water between each drink.

Roads: on wheels and on foot

To survive the rigours of the desert you have to be cool in more ways than one. Don't let adventure get the better of you and go charging off into the wilderness without heeding the warnings. There are, of course, butch types who'll tell you otherwise and insist on hiking through Death Valley in the summer, but the desert is rarely conquered by a pioneering spirit alone and every year people die here. **Roads and highways** across much of the desert are not maintained, and in an area where it's often a challenge to make it across existing dirt roads, trailblazing your own path through the desert is insanity. Of course you'll be tempted, so hire a dune buggy or four-wheel-drive and tear about one of the off-road driving areas that are specifically designated for such lunacy.

Among **other things you should take along**, an emergency pack with flares, a first aid and snakebite kit, matches and a compass is mandatory, and a shovel, tyre pump and extra petrol are always a good idea. A few white towels to drape over the dashboard, steering wheel and back ledge will save you a lot of discomfort when you get back in your car after leaving it parked for a few hours. If the car's engine does overheat, don't turn it off; instead turn the front end towards the wind and pour some water on the front of the radiator, turn the air-conditioning off and heating up full blast to cool the engine quickly. In an emergency, never panic and leave the car: you'll be harder to find wandering around alone. Only the roads through the national parks during summer are completely deserted; in all other areas, a fair volume of traffic will ensure your rescue.

When **hiking**, try and cover most of your ground early morning: the midday heat is too debilitating, and you shouldn't even think about it when the mercury goes over 90°F. Almost all parks will require you to register with them – this is very wise, especially for those who are hiking alone. If you get lost, find some shade and wait. So long as you've registered, the rangers will eventually come and fetch you.

Wildlife

Most people's biggest fear of the desert – quite rightly – is of encountering **poisonous creatures**. While **black widow spiders** and **scorpions** are non-aggressive, they are extremely venomous and easily disturbed. At first the bite is like a sharp pin-prick, but within hours the pain becomes severe, usually accompanied by swelling and acute nausea. In the event of a bite, apply a cold compress and constrict the area with a tourniquet to prevent the spread of venom; work antiseptic into the puncture, drink lots of water, bring your temperature down by resting in a shady area – and always seek medical help immediately. **Tarantulas** are not at all dangerous. A leg span of up to seven inches should help you to avoid them, but if you're unlucky and get bitten don't panic; cleansing with antiseptic is usually sufficient treatment once you've got over the initial pain.

Of all the **snakes** in the California desert, only the rattlesnake is poisonous. Again these are easy to avoid if you know where to look. When it's hot be careful of shaded areas under bushes, around wood debris, old mining shafts and piles of rocks. When it's cooler, snakes favour sunning themselves out in the open, but won't be expecting you and if disturbed will attack. Of course you might not be able to tell a rattler from any other kind of snake; in fact many rattlers don't rattle at all; if in doubt, best assume it is one. If the worst happens you'll soon know. Within ten minutes you'll experience swelling, discolouration and intense pain. You should of course be carrying a snakebite kit. But if you haven't got one and medical attention doesn't seem possible for several hours you'll have to "cut & suck" yourself. As with spider bites you need to restrict the venom with a band; sterilise the edge of a razor blade with a match and cut through the bite-marks lengthwise (in the same direction as your bones and veins) no more than a quarter of an inch deep and half an inch long. Draw the lymph (there should be hardly any blood) out with your mouth and spit after each suction. Gruesome, but, literally, a life-saver.

Nasty critters aren't the only things to avoid. Most **cacti** present few problems, but you should keep an eye out for the eight-foot *cholla*, or *jumping cholla* as they're called for the way they seem to jump off and attach themselves to you if you brush past. Don't use your hands to get them off, you'll just spear all your fingers; instead use a stick or comb to flick it off and remove the remaining spines with tweezers. The large pancake-pads of *prickly pear* cactus are also worth avoiding: as well as the larger spines they have thousands of tiny, hair-like stickers that are almost impossible to remove. You should expect a good day of painful irritation before they begin to wear away. For more on the delights of desert flora and fauna, see *Contexts*.

LOW DESERT: PALM SPRINGS AND JOSHUA TREE

Despite the Low Desert's hundreds of miles of beauty and empty highways, most visitors have no intention of getting away from it all. They're heading for where it's at – the irrefutable capital of the desert, **Palm Springs**. These few square miles are overrun with famous, star-struck, ageing and aspiring strains of humanity whose community and lifestyle can both attract and repel. It is said, not completely in jest, that the average age and average temperature of Palm Springs are about the same – a steady 88. This is a town that sprays its olive trees to ensure that olives won't grow olives (they're too "messy"), and fines homeowners who don't maintain their property to what local officials deem to be a suitable standard. Despite its shortcomings, you'll find it hard to avoid: it's the first stopping-point east from LA on I-10, and centre of a resort area – the **Coachella Valley** – that stretches out for miles around, along Hwy-111. The valley's farming communities have the distinction of being part of the most productive irrigated agricultural centre in the world, growing dates, oranges, lemons and grapefruits in vast quantities, though sadly they're being steadily eaten up by the condos and complexes that comprise the ever-growing Palm Springs industry. Really, even though the great outdoors might seem less appealing from the side of a pool, you should make an effort to push beyond the area's comforts to get any idea of what a desert is *really* like.

Fortunately you don't have to travel impossible distances to see the desert at its natural best. **Joshua Tree National Monument**, one of the most startling of California's state parks, lies one hour's drive east of Palm Springs, three and a half from LA. It's connected by bus from both, and though a day trip in a fast car would do, you might find it better to give Joshua Tree a weekend to get to grips with its sublime landscape, taking in the sunsets and the howl of coyotes at twilight. For all but the extra-bold, this is usually enough. The desert east of the monument, to the Colorado River and Nevada, and south to the Mexican border, is arid and uncomfortable; you needn't make the effort unless you're racing to places beyond.

Palm Springs

The delightful informality of the area makes it possible for you to observe the likes of Frank Sinatra at a nearby table in a popular restaurant, or Red Skelton strolling down the street, or former President Ford swinging a golf club on the fairway.
                                                                    California Office of Tourism

With its manicured golf courses, condominium complexes and some seven hundred millionaires in residence, **PALM SPRINGS** does not conform to any typical image of the desert. Biggest of the Coachella Valley resort towns, it sits in the lushest agricultural area of the Colorado Desert, with the massive bulk of Mount San Jacinto glowering over its low-level buildings, casting an instantaneous and welcome shadow over the town in the late afternoon. Since Hollywood stars were spotted having a bit of mineral rejuvenation out here in the 1930s, it has taken on a celebrity status all its own, a symbol of good LA living, away from the amorphous city itself. Only two hours' drive from the city, its clean, dry air and sunshine have made it irresistible as a place to bring down stress levels in a jacuzzi, and tone and tan with the rich and famous. High-school kids arrive in their thousands for the drunken revelry of **Spring Break** (the two weeks at the end of March and beginning of April – a period you'd be wise to avoid). Things got so bad a few years back that police had to close off the major roads to avoid near-riots amongst the over-excited teenagers. There are also those who come here not to get drunk, but to dry out: the *Betty Ford Center*, smack in the middle of town, draws a star-studded patient list to its booze- and drug-free environment, attempting to undo a lifetime's behavioural disorders in a $20,000 two-week stay.

Purpose-built for luxury and leisure, Palm Springs isn't so much a place as a state of mind. This is handy, as you'll need to adapt fast to its high prices, uniformly boring architecture (apart from the *fabulous* homes of the stars) and, for those not into pro-celebrity golf or expensive restaurants, an appalling lack of things to see or do. Nonetheless this is the desert, and the town's siting is superb, surrounded by beautiful Indian Canyons with the snowcapped mountains behind. Sunbathers abound. Meteorologists have noted changes in the humidity of the desert climate around Palm Springs, which they attribute to the moisture absorbed from the hundreds of swimming pools – the consummate condo accoutrement for the millionaires, and the only place you're likely to want to be during the day. When scarce water supplies aren't being used to fill the pools or nourish the nearby orchards, each of Palm Springs' vast network of golf courses receives around one million gallons daily to maintain its rolling green pastures.

Palm Springs wasn't always like this. Before the wealthy settlers moved in it was the domain of the **Cahuilla Indian Tribe**, who lived and hunted around the San Jacinto Mountains, to escape the heat of the desert floor. They still own much of the town, and via an odd checkerboard system of land allotment, every other square mile of Palm Springs is theirs and forms part of the **Agua Caliente Indian Reservation** – a Spanish name which means "hot water", referring to the ancient mineral springs on which the city rests. The land was allocated to the tribe back in the 1890s, but exact zoning was never settled until the 1940s, by which time the development of hotels and leisure complexes was well under way. The Indians, finding their land already built upon, were left with no option but to charge rent, a system which has made them the richest Indians in America. Today it is estimated that there are one hundred members of the Cahuilla with individual land-holdings worth $2 million or more.

Getting there and getting around

Palm Springs lies 120 miles east of Los Angeles along the Hwy-111 turnoff from I-10. Arriving by **car**, you drive into town on E Palm Canyon Drive, the main thoroughfare through Palm Springs. Coming by **bus**, you'll arrive at the *Greyhound* terminus at 3111 N Indian Ave (☎325-2053), linked with LA ten times daily – a three-hour journey, and, at $23 for a one-way ticket, the cheapest way to get here. *Desert Stage Lines* (☎367-3581) operate from the same terminal and connect Palm Springs to Twentynine Palms and Joshua Tree. **Trains** link LA with Indio, 25 miles away from downtown Palm Springs and connected by regular bus. You can also **fly** here but this can be expensive – should you find a bargain, you'll land at the *Palm Springs Municipal Airport*, 3400 E Tahquitz-McCallum Way (☎323-8161), from where you take #2 bus downtown.

Travel to the resorts around Palm Springs – **Cathedral City, Rancho Mirage, Palm Desert, Indio, La Quinta** – is possible with the *Sun Bus* (☎343-3451), which operates daily from 6am to 6pm and charges 75¢ to get around town, plus 25¢ for each additional zone beyond. It's unlikely that you'll need to use the bus to get around Palm Springs itself: downtown is no more than several blocks long and wide, and provided you don't mind the sun, walking is easy. To get the absolute best out of Palm Springs and the surrounding towns, though, you should think about *car hire*. *Foxy Wheels*, 222 Amado Road (☎619/320-8299), have cars for as little as $28 per day, but for good deals on weekly rates, try one of the larger companies like *Avis Rent A Car*, 455 E Tahquitz Way (☎619/325-1331) and *Hertz Rent A Car*, 244 N Indian Avenue (☎619/778-5120).

Accommodation

Palm Springs was designed with the rich in mind, and big luxury **hotels** far outnumber the affordable variety. One way of getting round this is to visit in summer when temperatures rise and the prices drop. Many of the bigger hotels slash their prices by up to seventy percent, and even the smaller concerns give twenty to thirty percent off. The north end of town, along Hwy-111, holds the cheaper places, most perfectly acceptable and all with pools. Bed and breakfast inns are a rare commodity and unless you have a specific recommendation, you shouldn't exhaust yourself trying to find one. If you're travelling in a group, it may work out cheaper to **rent an apartment**: many of the homes in Palm Springs are used only for a brief spell and let out for the rest of the year. Again summer is the best and cheapest time to look, but there is generally a good supply throughout the year. Palm Springs' daily paper, the *Desert Sun*, has rental information in its classified pages, and many rental agencies operate around town – the **Visitor Information Agency**, 2781 N Palm Canyon Drive (☎619/778-8418) will be able to point you to the more affordable ones, as well as supplying an exhaustive selection of maps, including one that details the homes of the famous (see "Downtown Palm Springs" for the celebrity tour). **Camping** is neither the done thing, nor really a viable option: campsites do exist but they're strictly campervan territory. Tent-carriers will have a better time exploring Joshua Tree.

Listed below are some of the more reasonable options, with **summer rates** quoted; add approximately $10 to $20 to get the winter rate. Their low prices mean they fill up quickly and you must book in advance in the popular October to April period.

Hotels and motels

Best Western Tropics Hotel, 411 E Palm Canyon Drive (☎619/327-1391). Comfortable mid-range hotel with pool, restaurant and bar. Rooms range $55–120 per night.

Desert Ho, 120 West Vereda Sur (☎619/325-5159). Small hotel with nine large rooms set around a beautiful pool and gardens, facing Mt San Jacinto – a mile or two north of downtown, but if you've got a car it's good value for money with rooms from only $48 per night.

Casa Cody, 175 South Cahuilla Rd (☎619/320-9346). Probably the only one of Palm Spring's few bed and breakfast inns that's affordable. Attractive Southwestern-style collection of hotel rooms and apartments set in shady garden. Rooms from $45, apartments from $120 per night.

The Regent Hotel, 960 North Palm Canyon Drive (☎619/325-7374). Centrally located motel, walking distance from shops and restaurants. Ask for the rooms with private patios. Rooms from $40.

Travelodge, 333 E Palm Canyon Drive (☎619/323-2775). Good quality motel chain that regularly has weekend offers to look out for. Mid-week prices start at $60.

Budget Inn Motel & Spa, Corner of I-10 and Indian Ave, North Palm Springs (☎251-1425). Doubles from $45 per night.

Case de Camero, 1480 N Indian Ave (☎320-1678). Doubles from $45.

Casa de Camino, 1447 N Palm Canyon Drive (☎325-9018). Doubles from $35.

Desert Hotel, 285 N Indian Ave (☎325-3013). Probably the only place in town without a pool, but cheapest of the lot with doubles from $25.

Motel 6, 595 E Palm Canyon Drive (☎327-2004). Most central of the cheapies, this one is a ten-minute walk from downtown with a good pool and doubles from $32.

Palm Canyon Inn 1450 S Palm Canyon Drive (☎320-7767). Small, stylish motel, five minutes from downtown with good-sized rooms and pleasant pool & jacuzzi area. Rooms range $35–70.

Super 8 Lodge, 1900 N Palm Canyon Drive (☎322-3757). Good mountain views and doubles from $55.

Downtown Palm Springs

Downtown Palm Springs stretches for about half a mile along Palm Canyon Drive, a wide, bright and modern strip full of expensive boutiques and restaurants. By day, people wear visors and swoon in air-conditioned shopping malls; by night, the youth take over and cruise the main drag in their four-wheel-drives with their stereos blaring.

Should your budget not run to the conventional extravagance of a luxury stay in Palm Springs, there are a handful of things to do that won't break the bank. The **Palm Springs Desert Museum**, 101 Museum Drive (Tues–Fri 10am–4pm, Fri & Sat 10am–5pm; $3.50), is a part-art, part-natural history collection, funded by the locals in pursuit of some kind of prestige and cultural heritage. Whatever the motives, it's a fine museum, luxuriously housed and with strong collections of Native American and Southwestern art – so large, that despite the enormous exhibition space, only a small part can be shown at any given time. The only permanent display is the late actor William Holden's collection of Asian and African art. The natural science exhibits are surprisingly interesting and focus on the variety of animal and plant life in the desert, proving that it's not all sandstorms and rattlesnakes.

Rich people love to buy art, and the concentration of wealth in Palm Springs has fostered a disproportionate number of **art galleries**, along and around Palm Canyon Drive. The *B. Lewin Galleries*, 210 S Palm Canyon Drive, is most impressive, with the world's largest collection of Mexican paintings, including works by Diego Rivera, Gustavo Montoya, Rufino Tamayo and Carlos Merida. The *Nelson Rockefeller Collection*, 777 E Tahquitz Way (☎619/320-9554) has an equally highbrow collection and by appointment you can rub shoulders with connoisseurs looking for premium investments. For something a bit more lighthearted you should try the *T.R.H. Gallery*, 1090 N Palm Canyon Drive, an original comic-strip art gallery with world-famous cartoonists and Disney animation exhibitions. Good fun also is **Ruddy's General Store Museum**, 221 South Palm Canyon Drive (winter Thur–Sun 10am–4pm, summer Sat & Sun noon–6pm; 50¢), a lovingly recreated general store from the 1930s, in authentic detail with all the original showcases, fixtures, signs and products from humbler desert days.

Downtown's most anarchic piece of landscape gardening can be seen at **Moorten's Botanical Gardens**, 1701 S Palm Canyon Drive (daily 9am–4pm; $2), a bizarre cornucopia of every desert plant and cacti, lumped together in no particular order but interesting for those who won't be venturing beyond town to see them in their natural habitat. A mile from downtown, the now condo-crowded **Desert Hot Springs** was the site chosen for its isolation by Cabot Yerxa, the drop-out son of a high-tone East Coast family, who preferred a life of hardship in the desert to his Ivy-League life back home. **Cabot's Old Indian Pueblo**, 6716 E Desert View Avenue (Wed–Mon 9.30am–4.30pm; $1.50) was his life's labour: a four-storey house made from bits and pieces he found in the desert that took over twenty years to complete. Five minutes away, **Kingdom of the Dolls**, 66071 Pierson Boulevard (Tues–Sun noon–5pm; $2.50), took almost as long to put together, tracing a million years of human history in doll figurines – great for killing a bit of time, but if you've got other plans, don't change them.

Knowing that they're in the thick of a mega-star refugee camp, few can resist the opportunity to see the homes and country clubs of the international elite on a **celebrity tour**. As tacky as they are, these tours have some appeal, and allow you to spy voyeuristically on places like Bob Hope's, and the star-studded area of Palm Springs known as **Little Tuscany** – Palm Spring's prettiest quarter, where the famous keep their weekend homes. The best part of the tour is not the houses, but the fascinating trivia about the lives of those who live in them. The Gabor sisters come in for a lot of stick (between them they've been married eighteen times), particularly Zsa Zsa, famous for her ability to strip her ex-husbands of all their assets (they say she's launching a new perfume to rival Liz Taylor's

Passion – it's called *Citation*, just slap it on). Several companies offer tours, the best of them being *Palm Springs Celebrity Tours*, 174 Palm Canyon Drive (☎325-2682), who conduct hour-long tours for $10 and slightly longer affairs taking in the country clubs and the Sinatra estate (where Frank used to bring Ava Gardner at the height of their romance) for $14. Of course if you've got a car, you can do it yourself with a map of the stars' homes from the Visitor Information Agency, but you'll miss the sharp anecdotal commentary that makes it such fun.

One reason people come here is to enjoy the Californian obsession with all things physical and get fit. The **mineral spring** which the Cahuilla discovered on the desert floor over a hundred years ago has grown into an elaborate and sophisticated spa and hotel complex. For $10 you can enjoy the "basic spa experience" at *Spa Hotel and Mineral Springs*, 100 N Indian Avenue (daily 8am–7pm; ☎325-1461). Just as therapeutic is a swim in the **olympic-sized pool** in the *Palm Springs Leisure Center*, Sunrise Way at Ramon Road (daily 11am–5pm; $3; ☎323-8278), a good alternative to the often crowded, and invariably small, hotel pools.

Around Palm Springs

Most visitors to Palm Springs never leave the poolside, but a hardcore of desert enthusiasts still visit for the **hiking** and **riding** opportunities in the **Indian Canyons**, on part of the Agua Caliente Reservation that lies to the east of downtown. Centuries ago, ancestors of the Cahuilla tribe settled in the canyons and developed extensive communities, made possible by the good water supply and animal stock. Crops of melons, squash, beans and corn were grown, animals hunted and plants and seeds gathered for food and medicines. Evidence of this remains and despite the near extinction of some breeds, mountain sheep and wild ponies still roam the remoter areas. To reach the best of them, follow S Palm Canyon Drive about three miles southeast to the clearly signposted entrance. Of the three canyons here, **Palm Canyon** and **Andreas Canyon** are very beautiful and have the easiest hiking trails. About fifteen miles long, they're surprisingly lush oases of waterfalls, rocky gorges and palm trees, easily toured by car, although you should get out and walk for at least a few miles. A tiny trading post sells hiking maps, refreshments, even racoon hats, though to indulge in real wild west fantasy you should see things on **horseback**. The *Smoke Tree Stables*, 2500 Toledo Avenue (☎327-1372), offer one-, two- and four-hour riding tours of the Canyons, from $18 per hour – well worth it, especially if you go early morning (tours start from 7am) to escape the truly uncomfortable midday heat.

To the west of Palm Springs, **Tahquitz Canyon** is similarly spectacular with high waterfalls and clear-water pools for swimming, but the hiking trails are not as easily negotiated, and should not be attempted lightly. To discourage amateurs, entrance is restricted to those with special permits, available from the *Agua Caliente Tribal Office*, 960 E Tahquitz Way (☎327-6412).

Sections of the canyons and surrounding land are set aside for the specific lunacy of **trailblazing** in jeeps and four-wheel-drives. If you're a good, experienced driver with nerves of steel (or know one), you should hire your own from *Dune Off-Road Rentals*, 59755 Hwy-111 (☎619/325-0376) about four miles north of town, for around $50 for half a day. If you can't face the driving and want to learn something about the area as you tear about, then the **guided jeep adventure** is probably more your mark: *Desert Adventures*, 68-733 Perez Road (☎619/324-3378) offer excellent half-day tours of the Santa Rosa mountains for around $25 per hour, or $70 for half a day. The tour takes you across the desert floor and over two thousand feet up through Big Horn Sheep preserves, spectacular cliffs and steep-walled canyons. It's a bit expensive, but brilliant fun for the fearless.

Bland by comparison, the **Morongo Reservation**, off I-10 near BANNING west of Palm Springs, does however have the excellent if tiny **Malki Museum** (daily 10am–4pm) – a hotchpotch of Native American family heirlooms squashed into display cases, the aim of which is to give people an understanding of Native American culture and its importance in the Southwest before the big bucks came to town. Rooting through, you'll find the history of local tribes traced from centuries ago to their survival into the modern age.

When the desert heat becomes too much to bear, you can travel through five climatic zones from the arid desert floor to snow-covered alpine hiking trails on top of Mount San Jacinto on the **Palm Springs Aerial Tramway**, Tramway Drive, just off Hwy-111 north of Palm Springs (daily 8am–9pm; $13 ☎325-1391). Every half an hour large cable cars grind and sway over eight thousand feet to the Mountain Station near the summit. Literally breathtaking, it's well worth the nerve-wracking ascent for both the view, some 75 miles all the way to the Salton Sea, and the welcome change from the blistering heat to temperatures that drop as much as 50°F. There's a **bar** and **restaurant** (where, for a $4 food voucher you can eat as much as you want) at the Mountain Station. Concrete-paved trails (hardly the hiker's dream) stretch for a couple of miles around. Should sub-alpine ecology not interest you, there's always the option of a snowball fight.

Despite an inhospitable climate, animal life flourishes in the desert, something you can see in safety at Palm Desert, twelve miles southwest of Palm Springs along Hwy-111. The **Living Desert**, 47900 Portola Avenue (Oct–May daily 9am–5pm; $3.50), is home to coyotes, foxes, Big Horn sheep, snakes, gazelles and eagles, on view around a series of trails that cover the 1200-acre park. There's also a **botanical garden**, but this is only worth a look in spring when the desert is in bloom; at other times it's just a load of undistinguishable cacti.

After sundown

Palm Springs has a pretty disappointing selection of reasonable **restaurants**, and it doesn't have the **nightlife** you'd imagine either. It's not unknown for people to choose to get drunk in their hotel room – or to go into LA for the night. Much closer at hand, however, is Cathedral City, ten miles down the road.

Eating

The desert heat is stifling enough to suppress the healthiest of appetites, and most people go all day on nothing and suddenly find themselves ravenous at dusk. Sadly but unsurprisingly, few of the **restaurants** in Palm Springs merit their high prices, and supermarket shopping is a better bet for the budget-conscious. *Von's* in the Palm Springs shopping mall, is open from early morning until around 11pm for supermarket goods, but for good natural and wholefoods try *Oasis Natural Foods,* 188 S Indian Avenue.

Frying Fish, 123 N Palm Canyon Drive. Something a bit more exotic; sushi for around $10 per enormous platter.

Louise's Pantry, 124 S Palm Canyon Drive. Fifties-looking diner, where none of the waitresses is under sixty and the servings are huge. Especially good for breakfast.

Nates, 100 S Indian Avenue. Good, large portions of deli-food.

Sizzler's, 725 S Palm Canyon Drive. Reliable if unexciting steak and salad chain-eatery. Fill up on a three-course meal for around $9.

Swifty's Fifties Diner, 411 E Palm Canyon. Open 24hrs and good for sandwiches, burgers and breakfasts.

Le Vallauris, 385 West Tahquitz Way (☎619/325-5059 – reservations only). Palm Spring's best restaurant does not exactly hide its light under a bushel, describing itself as "*the* restaurant where the Stars entertain their friends"; and you are indeed likely to run into one or two once-renowned artistes. If star-gazing is not your style, the Californian/French cuisine is excellent, and the service impeccable. The price, however, is around $50 per head.

Wheel-Inn Eat, ten miles west on I-10 at the CABAZON exit (marked by two fifty-foot concrete dinosaurs). Humble, 24-hour desert truck-stop with a burly clientele and cheap enormous portions of food – so unpretentious you'd think they'd never heard of Palm Springs.

Palm Springs Bars and Clubs

If you're determined to spend your evening in Palm Springs, and you're not a member of one of the exclusive country clubs, you'd better be disco-crazy or you'll have to content yourself with dinner and an early night.

Cecil's, 1775 E Palm Canyon Drive (☎320-4202). Slightly more bearable than *Zelda's*, its music and customers rather easier to digest.

Pernina's, 340 N Palm Canyon Drive. Conceivably this club would be a great place to take a quiet drink and listen to the pianist were it not for the post-retirement gaggle that fill it up.

The Saloon, 225 S Indian Avenue. The best of a sorry bunch, with a bit more of a down-to-earth, beer & pretzels approach to drinking.

Zelda's, 169 N Indian Avenue (☎325-2375). Pick-up joint for a crowd that should really be in bed, Sun–Thurs only.

Cathedral City

Unlike Palm Springs, **CATHEDRAL CITY** ("Cat City"), about ten miles east of town along Hwy-111, has many cheap eating options (albeit of the chain variety), some fairly groovy **bars,** and a thriving **gay scene**. It's ten minutes by car or twenty on the #20 bus from Palm Springs. *El Gallito Café*, 68820 Grove Street, just off Hwy-111, is a busy Mexican cantina that has the best food for miles and often queues to match – get there around 6pm to avoid the crowds. *The Carriage Trade Restaurant*, 68–599 Hwy-111, does a hearty set menu for around $11; and for good steaks and burgers, go to *The Desert Broiler*, 35–955 Date Palm Drive.

The majority of Cat City's **bars** are gay, and unlike their sobered counterparts in California's cities, most still go for it with 1970s-style abandon – definitely the best laugh you'll have in the desert, gay or not. *Daddy Warbucks*, 68–981 E Palm Canyon Drive, is a wild scene with "whipped cream fighting" on Sunday and talent contests on Wednesday. At "jig with a pig" evenings at the *C.C. Construction Co.*, 68–449 Perez Road, you can shimmy with a gay cop and mix with a good-natured drag-queen crowd.

Listings

Area Code ☎619.

Bike Rental *Burnett's Cycles*, 429 S Sunrise Way (☎325-7844). Bicycles for around $25 per day. Frankly, it's cheaper to hire a car (see "Getting there and getting around", above).

Bookstore *Bookland,* 102 N Palm Canyon Drive (☎325-1020). Travel guides, paperback fiction, maps etc.

Chemist *Thrifty Drug and Discount Store,* 366 S Palm Canyon Drive.

Clinic *Palm Springs Health Department,* 3255 Tahquitz-McCallum Way (☎328-8533). General health care as well as VD and Family Planning clinics, charged on a sliding scale according to income.

Dry Cleaning *American Cleaners and Laundry,* 364 S Indian Ave.

Hairdressers *A Cut Above,* 333 N Palm Canyon Drive (☎325-1007).

Laundry *Ramon Coin-Op,* 222 E Ramon Road at Indian Ave (5am–9pm).

Post Office 333 E Amado Rd (Mon–Fri 8.30am–5pm; ☎325-9631).

Taxi *Desert Cab* ☎324-8233.

Travel Agency *Las Palmas Travel,* 403 N Palm Canyon Drive.

What's On Call the *Palm Springs Recreation Department* (☎323-8279) for a recording of arts and entertainments around town.

Joshua Tree National Monument

In a unique transitional area where the high Mojave meets the lower Colorado desert, 850 square miles of freaky-looking trees, their branches ragged and gnarled, flourish in an otherwise sparsely vegetated landscape, making **Joshua Tree National Monument** the most unusual, and fascinating, of California's national parks. With neither the sweeping sand dunes of Death Valley nor the ubiquitous wealth of Palm Springs, it conforms to no other image of the California desert. In recognition of its uniqueness, and the need for its preservation, the state park system took the area under its jurisdiction in the 1930s and has vigilantly maintained its beauty ever since. If you're staying in Palm Springs, there's no excuse not to visit; if you've further to come, make the effort.

The grotesque trees, which can reach up to forty feet in height, have to contend with extreme aridity and rocky soil, and with the exception of springtime, when creamy white blossom grows in clusters on the tips of the branches, the strain of their struggle to survive is evident. Complementary to the trees are great rockpiles, heaps of boulders pushed up from the earth by the movements of the San Andreas fault, which runs directly below. Often as high as a hundred feet, their edges are rounded and smooth from thousands of years of flash floods and winds.

In all it's a mystical, even unearthly, landscape, best appreciated at sunrise or sunset when the whole desert floor is bathed in red light; at noon it can feel like an alien and threatening furnace, with temperatures often reaching 115°F in summer, though dropping to a more bearable 70°F in winter. If you're visiting between May and October you must stick to the higher elevations to enjoy Joshua Tree with any semblance of comfort. In the low desert part of the monument, the Joshua trees thin out and the temperature rises as you descend below sea level. Over eighty percent of the monument is designated wilderness – get out of the car at least once or twice and note the silence.

History

"Joshua Tree" may be a familiar name nowadays, thanks to U2, but previously it was almost unknown. Unlike the vast bulk of the state, no man, save Indians, prospectors and cowboys has had the chance to spoil it. Despite receiving less than four inches of annual rainfall, the area is surprisingly lush, and although craggy trees and rockpiles are what define Joshua Tree today, it was grass that attracted the first significant pioneers. Early cattlemen heard rumours of good pastures from the forty-niners who hurried through on their way to the Sierra Nevada gold fields. The natural corrals made good sites for cattle rustlers to brand their illegitimate herds before moving them out to the coast for sale. Ambushes and gunfights were common. Seeking refuge in the mountains, rustlers, by chance, discovered small traces of gold and sparked vigorous mining operations that continued until the 1940s. To the Mormons who travelled through here in the 1850s, the area signified something entirely different; they saw the craggy branches of the trees as the arms of Joshua leading them to the promised land – hence the name.

Joshua Tree Practicalities

About an hour's drive northeast from Palm Springs, Joshua Tree National Monument is best approached from Hwy-62, which branches off I-10 just outside Palm Springs and takes you past the small town of Joshua Tree to the northern entrance and **Park Headquarters** at **TWENTYNINE PALMS**. In the absence of hotel accommodation in the monument itself, you may be glad of the good **motels** and scattering of restaurants here. Alternatively, if you're coming from the south, there is an entrance and visitors centre at **COTTONWOOD**, seven miles north of I-10 on the Cottonwood Spring Road exit.

From either point you have a choice of routes through the monument; it's worth stopping at one of the visitor centres to collect maps. Passes into the monument cost $5 and are valid for seven days. Casual observers will find a day trip by car plenty, though it's a nice idea to camp over for a couple of nights, and serious rock-climbers and experienced hikers may want to take advantage of the excellent if strenuous trails throughout the monument.

Twentynine Palms

The appealing desert settlement of Twentynine Palms is neither a gloating leisure spot nor a totally useless hellhole, but a small, serviceable kind of place that enjoys good weather and low-key living. Just two minutes' drive from the monument, and an all-important water source for local people, it's a fairly busy town by desert standards , stretching for about a mile along Hwy-62 with a fair selection of places to eat, drink and bed-down. The climate has been considered perfect for convalescents ever since physicians sent World War I poison gas victims here for treatment of their respiratory illnesses, and development of health spas and real estate offices has been considerable. If you're without a car, the town will also be your point of arrival, via *Desert Stage Lines* (☎367-3581), based in Palm Springs.

Unquestionably, the best place in town to stay is the *Twenty-Nine Palms Inn*, 73950 Inn Avenue (☎619/367-3505), located on the only privately owned oasis in the High Desert. Twelve adobe cabins are set around attractively arid grounds and gardens, and a central pool area contains a restaurant and bar. Owned by the same large family since 1928, this is not your average American accommodation. As the owner puts it, "We don't get the safe travellers". Healers and psychics gather around an energy spot in the grounds to get centred, cleanse their chakras and generally do the business. Prices range from $40 per person, per night for the most basic cabin, to around $70 for the more luxurious versions.

Among the cheaper options nearby are the *29 Palms Motel*, 71487 Twentynine Palms Highway (☎619/367-2833), and the *Sunset Motel*, 73842 Twentynine Palms Highway (☎619/367-3848). Both have perfectly acceptable pools and rooms from around $28 per night, but nowhere near as much fun as the Inn.

Camping

Joshua Tree has nine **campsites**, all concentrated in the northwest except for one at Cottonwood by the southern entrance. All have wooden tables, places for fires and pit toilets, but only two (*Black Rock* and *Cottonwood*) have water supplies. *Black Rock* and *Indian Cove* can only be reached from within the monument if you have a four-wheel-drive vehicle; otherwise you have to retrace your steps to the entrances on Hwy-62. Camping is free, on a first-come-first-served basis, and no reservations are allowed, unless you are travelling as part of an educational or study group, in which case you should make a reservation by calling ☎619/367-7511, and expect to pay a nominal fee (around $10).

Hiking trails and highlights

The best way to enjoy the monument is to be selective in your explorations. As with any desert area, you'll find the heat punishing and an ambitious schedule impossible. The rangers and staff at the visitors centres will be able to recommend the most enjoyable routes, depending on what you want to see, whether you want to hike and how experienced you are. Slide shows, free maps and brochure will prepare you for the journey ahead. Never venture anywhere without a map. Many of the roads are unmarked, hard to negotiate and restricted to four-wheel-drive use. If a road is marked as such, don't think about taking a normal car – you'll soon come to a grinding halt, and it could be quite a few panic-stricken hours before anybody finds you.

If you're hiking **stick to the trails**: Joshua Tree is full of abandoned gold mines and while the rangers are fencing them as quickly as possible, there are hundreds they don't even know about. Watch for loose gravel around openings, undercut edges, never trust ladders or timber, and bear in mind that the rangers rarely check mines for casualties. Some of the shafts contain water and poisonous fumes, and even if you survive a fall are popular hangouts for snakes, scorpions and spiders. Even on the easier trails allow around an hour per mile: there's very little shade and you'll tire quickly. If the dryness and heat of desert hiking make you shy from most of the trails, start with one of the easiest: **Fortynine Palms Oasis**, accessible via a 1½-mile trail from Canyon Road, six miles from the visitor centre at Twentynine Palms. To the west of the oasis, quartz boulders tower around the Indian Cove camping area, and a trail from the eastern branch of the campground road leads to **Rattlesnake Canyon** – its streams and waterfalls (depending on rainfall) breaking an otherwise eerie silence amongst the monoliths.

Moving south through the monument, follow the trails through **Hidden Valley**, where cattle rustlers used to hide out, to the rain-fed **Barker Dam**, to the east: Joshua Tree's crucial water supply, built around the turn of the century by cattlemen (and rustlers) to stop the poor beasts from expiring halfway across the monument. Among the more negotiable trails around here is the one to **Lost Horse Mine**, 450 feet up – in its day a pretty profitable mine, making an average of $20,000 a week at its height. The hike will take you through abandoned mining sites, building foundations and equipment still intact.

If you're **driving**, you can reach **Key's View** from here. This 5185-foot-high spot was named after Bill Keys, an eccentric trigger-happy miner who raised his family in this inhospitable landscape until he was locked away in the 1920s for shooting one of his neighbours over a right-of-way argument. He was revered for being a tough desert rat and indefatigable miner, who dug on long after less hardy men had abandoned the arid wasteland. The best views in the whole monument can be had from up here, on a good day as far as the Salton Sea and beyond to Mexico – a brilliant desert panorama of badlands and mountains. To the east of Key's View, Geology Tour Road leads down through the best of Joshua Tree's **rock formations**.

There's **tougher stuff** on the eastern side of the monument around **Pinto Basin**, a notorious danger-zone when the flash floods strike. To cover it on foot, it's essential that you **register** at one of the visitor centres first and check the trail conditions with the rangers. You'll need to be well-armed with maps and water supplies, and on the whole it's unwise even to attempt it unless you're a very experienced hiker or are travelling as part of a group. If you do reach here, you'll find no Joshua trees and few other signs of life: the sun bakes these low elevations to a near wasteland where only *cholla cactus* can survive.

Around Joshua Tree

Directly **north** of Joshua Tree, the only real settlement is the huge *Marine Corps Training Center*, the largest military base in the world and home to war games and other nefarious military activities. More comfortingly, there are several sights northwest, in **Yucca Valley**. The **Hi-Desert Nature Museum**, 57117 Twentynine Palms Highway (Wed–Sun 1–5pm; free), holds a largely poor collection of paintings and tacky souvenirs, but some commendable catches of snakes and scorpions; the **Desert Christ Park**, 57090 Twentynine Palms Highway (sunrise–sundown; free), has a number of massive fifteen-foot concrete figures depicting tales from the Bible – a fittingly bizarre conclusion to the region.

The Imperial Valley and Salton Sea

The chances of you making it **south** beyond Joshua Tree and Palm Springs are slim. This patch of the Colorado desert is the least friendly of all the Californian desert regions, and unlike Death Valley, where there are at least some tourist facilities, has little to encourage exploration. In any case, intense heat makes journeys in the winter uncomfortable and in the summer near impossible.

Sandwiched between Hwy-111 and Hwy-86, which branch off I-15 soon after Palm Springs and the Coachella Valley, the area from the **Salton Sea** down to the furnace-like migrant-worker towns of the agricultural **Imperial Valley** lies in the two-thousand-square-mile Salton Basin: aside from a small spot in Death Valley, the largest area of dry land below sea level in the Western Hemisphere – and probably one of its least appealing. Hwy-86, for what it's worth, is California's most notorious two-lane highway, with a staggering record of deaths and accidents. There's not a lot to come here for unless you're heading for the Mexican border, and even then there are better routes you could take. Years ago, there was a (failed) attempt to make the Salton Sea into a resort, and the campervan parks and retirement homes around around its rim remain, though they're sadly shorn of very much life. There's a wildlife sanctuary in the southern portion of the Salton Sea, but otherwise it's a rather blighted and hostile part of the state. You'd do better to plough straight through this part of California and head into the Colorado River area in Arizona (see p.220).

HIGH DESERT

Desolate, lifeless and silent, the **Mojave Desert**, mythic badland of the west, has no equals when it comes to hardship. Called the High Desert because it averages a height of around two thousand feet above sea level, the Mojave is very dry and for the most part deadly flat, dotted here and there by the prickly bulbs of a Joshua tree and an occasional abandoned miner's shed. For most, it's the barrier between LA and Las Vegas, an obstacle to get over before they reach the city; and, short on attractions as it is, you may want to follow their example. But you should linger a little longer just to see – and smell – what a desert is really like: a vast, impersonal, extreme environment, sharp with its own peculiar fragrance, and in spring alive with acres of fiery orange poppies – the state flower of California – and other brightly coloured wildflowers.

You will at least have relatively little company. If LA is the home of the sports car, the Mojave is the land of the dust-covered flat-bed truck, driven by the few who manage not to perish out here. The only other sign of life is the miserable military sub-culture marooned on huge weapons-testing sites. There is a hard-core group of desert fans: backdrop for the legion of "road movies" spawned by the underground film culture in the late 1960s and early 1970s, the Mojave is a favourite with bikers and hippies drawn by the barren panorama of sand dunes and mountain ranges. But otherwise visitors are very thin on the ground, and for most of the year you can rely on being almost entirely alone.

I-15 cuts through the heart of the Mojave, dividing it into two distinct regions. To the north **Death Valley**, the hottest place on earth, is a distillation of the classic desert landscape: an arid, other-worldly terrain of brilliantly coloured, bizarrely eroded rocks, mountains and sand dunes, 150 miles from the nearest town. To the south, **Barstow** is the lacklustre capital of the Mojave, redeemed only by its location halfway between LA and Las Vegas on I-15, which makes it both a potential stopover between the two points and a good base for the surrounding attractions, explorable by dune-buggy, on horseback, or even on foot.

The area between Barstow and Las Vegas is known as the **"Devil's Playground"** for its eerie isolation, though apart from some spectacular sand dunes you might as well push on through – Death Valley is that much more dramatic, and the amenities are rather random, catering for the odd geologist or desert specialist that manages to make it out here. South and east of here, close to the Nevada and Arizona borders, the desert is at its most demanding, utterly empty, inhospitable, and potentially miserable, and the only reason you might find yourself here is if you're driving through on the way to **Arizona** or the **Grand Canyon**.

Most people prefer to do their Mojave sightseeing from the comfort of an air-conditioned car, and in any case public transport is woefully inadequate. There are two routes up to Death Valley, which is where just about everybody is heading. If you're driving from LA, Hwy-14 and later on either US-395 or Hwy-178 take you right there. By public transport, *Greyhound* buses from LA connect Barstow and Baker on their way to Las Vegas, from where you can pick up the only public transport connection into Death Valley. *Amtrak* also passes through Barstow on its way to Las Vegas, and can make a great change from the monotony of desert driving.

Barstow

Just a few hours from LA along the dusty, seemingly endless I-15, **BARSTOW** looms up out of the desert, providing a welcome opportunity to get out of the car. Though capital of the Mojave, it's a small town, consisting of just one main road lined with a selection of motels and restaurants that at least make an overnight stop possible. There, however, its appeal ends. A relentless sun manages to keep people in their air-conditioned homes for a good part of the day, and during the hottest part of the year Barstow can seem more like a ghost town.

Arriving, accommodation and eating

At the junction of Barstow Road and I-15, the **California Desert Information Center** (daily 9am–6pm; ☎619/256-8617) has a good selection of maps of the surrounding area, lodging and restaurant guides and various flyers on local attractions. If you're arriving by bus, you'll be dropped at the *Greyhound* terminus on First Street, a few blocks from Main Street (☎256-8757), from which eight buses daily run between LA and Las Vegas. Also on First Street is the *Amtrak* Station (☎872-7245), stopping-point of one train daily from LA to Vegas.

Main Street is the best place to look for a **motel**. All are of a similar standard and price, generally only distinguished by the condition of the neon sign outside. Cruise up and down until you find the best deal, but among those you might try are: *Imperial 400*, 1281 E Main Street (☎256-6836), doubles from $29; or closest to the bus station and cheapest, *The Torches Motel*, 201 W Main Street (☎256-3308), which has doubles from $25. You can **camp** seven miles from Barstow in **Calico**, a re-created ghost town (see below) with shaded canyons where you can pitch tent or hook-up campers for $4 per night including showers. **Food** in Barstow is far from exotic but is plentiful and cheap. Restaurants sit snugly between the many hotels on Main Street and are usually of the rib and steak variety, although you can get good Mexican food at *Rosita's*, 540 W Main Street, or a reasonable Chinese meal at the *Golden Dragon*, 1231 E Main Street. Evening entertainment comes in the form of a few grubby bars frequented by bike gangs, the least threatening of which is the *Katz*, 1st and Main Street, open from 6am to 2am.

The town and around

Most people who stop in Barstow are not here to enjoy the desert, but to visit the hideously contrived **Calico Ghost Town** (daily 9am–5pm; $5) seven miles north along I-15. In the late nineteenth century Calico produced millions of dollars worth of silver and borax and supported a population of almost four thousand. Set in the colour-streaked Calico Hills, it's an attractive location, but subject to the extreme heat of the Mojave, it was quickly deserted when the silver ran out. It's since been rather cynically – and insensitively – restored, with tacky souvenir shops and hot-dog stands, and a main thoroughfare lined with saloons, an old school house, a vaudeville playhouse and shops kitted-out in period-styles. However, miles of mining shafts and tunnels are open to crawl around in until claustrophobia forces you up for air.

Calico is only brightened by its festivals, held throughout the year. The best of these is the end of March Spring Festival, which features the **World Tobacco Spitting Championships**. Huge beast-like men gather to chew the wad and direct streams of saliva and tobacco juice at an iron post, cheered on by rowdy crowds who take their sport seriously and their drink in large quantities. As the men (women are most definitely not allowed to compete) battle for the titles of best distance and most accurate spitter, the celebrations are jollied along by gallons of beer and some good bluegrass bands.

A few miles north of Calico along I-15 to the Minneola exit, the **Calico Early Man Site** (Wed–Sun 8.30am–4pm), more popularly known as the "Calico Dig", has become one of the most important archaeological sites in North America since it was discovered in 1968, its findings of old tools and primitive shelter (around 200,000 years old) having dated mankind's existence far earlier than was previously thought. Pick up details of a self-guided tour from the small caravan which serves as an information office. It's of fairly specialist interest, but the fact that the primitive civilisation that lived here made these tools when the climate was more akin to Britain's temperate drizzle is something to ponder on.

Of equal prehistoric importance, but far more vivid, the **Rainbow Basin**, twenty minutes north of town along Fort Irwin Road, is a rock formation which after thirty million years of wind erosion has been exposed as a myriad of almost electric colours. The fossilised remains of animals and insects are clearly visible, but most visitors will probably be content to weave the car through the tricky four-mile loop road around the canyon and marvel at the prettiness of it all.

Heading east on the other main highway out of Barstow, I-40, just past DAGGET, the Department of Energy's **Solar One Power Plant**, marked by a hundred-acre field of mirrors, is a surreal example of how California is putting its deserts to use. It's no longer open to the public, but is worth a look from the road anyway. Anyone who has seen the film *Bagdad Café* will remember the light reflections the mirrors give off for miles around.

Finally, if you're sick of being cooped up in a hot car, consider trekking around on **horseback**, particuarly at sunrise or sunset when the temperatures are more manageable and the colours rich in the extreme. The *Pan McCue Ranch* (☎254-2184), in **YERMO**, eight miles east of Barstow along I-15, has daily riding tours across high desert terrain and through canyons. Long tours are available, but an hour or two – costing around $25 – is probably enough. If the plodding horses of Pan McCue aren't quick or scary enough for you, you could always try finding an all-terrain-vehicle to go **dune-buggying** in. After wrecking much of the desert's fragile ecosystem, dune-buggying and biking have been confined by law to the dunes south of Barstow – though, ridiculously, the town has no facilities for hiring the vehicles. Try asking around in the town, or travel out to the dunes themselves and get friendly with one of the riders there.

Baker and the Eastern Mojave

Unless you're completely at a loss for something to do, you'll miss little by skipping the **Eastern Mojave**. There's nothing much to see, few tourist facilities and the emptiness is unmatched by anywhere else in the state. With a car, Hwy-127 north from **BAKER**, the main supply source in the region, is a possible route into Death Valley. Otherwise, if you're heading for Las Vegas and looking for likely lunch-spots, the spectacular sand dunes around **Kelso**, aka the "Devil's Playground", are worth a stop, though even this requires a significant diversion, taking the Kelbaker Road exit thirty miles southeast off I-15 at Baker. The five-mile stretch of dunes reaches up as high as seven hundred feet, making for an unbeatable photo-opportunity if nothing else.

The Colorado River Area

Whilst you'd be well advised to steer clear of the Eastern Mojave, the eastern portion of the **Colorado Desert** is not so bleak. In recent years small resorts have sprung up along the **Colorado River.** The strength of the river, over a thousand miles long, has by this southern stage of its course been sapped by a succession of dams (though even in the Grand Canyon there are white-water rapids), until here it proceeds towards the Gulf of California in a stately flow, marking the western boundary of the state as it goes. The stretch between Needles, the small border town on I-40. and Blythe, also on the state line a hundred miles south where I-10 meets Hwy-95, and especially **Lake Havasu City**, the mini-city in between the two, is the area to concern yourself with. Small waterfront settlements dot its course, some more interesting than others, but most dependent on the desire (or means) for watersports. In times of economic boom these small towns flourish, crammed with weekend boating parties, windsurfers, skiers etc, but in the last few years the average weekender has had to tighten his belt and some of the towns are struggling. To get round this the bigger towns have taken advantage of Arizona gambling laws, turned themselves into mini-Vegases and are enjoying considerable popularity with packs of bikers that make a weekend of driving across the desert, spending all their money on gambling and drink and then riding back again. Not all that bad an idea.

Lake Havasu City

The Colorado River's busiest resort, **LAKE HAVASU CITY** – which you'll have heard of, if not by name, as home to the displaced British landmark, **London Bridge** – is a strange mix of modern American mediocrity and mock-traditional British-bullshit. For all that, it's not intolerable. At night, when the bridge is lit up it can even induce some serious nostalgia for the homesick traveller. By day, the bridge makes an incongruous sight, but without question looks a hell of a lot better in the middle of the desert with the Chemehuevi mountains behind it than it ever did between South London and the City. The resort's developer, millionaire Robert P. McCulloch, bought the bridge (thinking it was Tower Bridge – or so the story goes) for 2.4 million dollars in the late 1960's, and painstakingly shipped it across the Atlantic Ocean and much of the continental US chunk by chunk before reassembling it over a channel dug to divert water from Lake Havasu, creating an island on the other side of the bridge known as Pittsburgh Point. Despite a glorious climate and development aimed squarely at the visitor, Lake Havasu doesn't really pull it off as a holiday destination, but as a stopover for a day or two it's pretty damned good.

Use Lake Havasu mainly as a place to rest, but if you have to get out and explore you should head for the **Colorado River Indian Reservation**, (daily 8am–sundown; $3) clearly signposted from Hwy-95, about twenty miles south of town. The attraction here is the reservation's collection of prehistoric giant rock figures or *intaglios*, originally made by "carving" the desert floor to shape, shedding the darker top layer of rock to reveal the lighter layers of sand beneath. The figures are so huge (up to 160 feet high) that it's hard to tell what you're looking at, but gaze long enough and you can discern a four-legged animal, and a human and spiral design – whether for artistic or religious purposes it's unclear.

The **Parker Dam** near the small village of Parker, just before the entrance to the reservation is worth a drive across only in passing to admire the modern engineering that halts the flow of the mightly Colorado River on its path to the Gulf of California.

Practicalities

To its credit, Lake Havasu City is adequately endowed with affordable accommodation, a surfeit of inexpensive restaurants and even a *Greyhound* bus that stops daily on its way to Las Vegas; the buses leave from *McDonalds*, 100 Swanson Avenue, a block from London Bridge. Fortunately for those without cars, anything you'll need is within walking distance of the bridge.

Motels are abundant. Those closest to the centre include the *Aztec Motel*, 2078 Swanson Avenue (☎602/453-7172), where spacious one-bedroom suites cost $35 per night, the *Windsor Inn Motel*, 451 London Bridge Road (☎602/855-4135), with rooms from $28, and *Pioneer Hotel of Lake Havasu*, 271 S Lake Havasu Avenue (☎1-800/528-5169) which for a little more ($40–60) offers its own casino.

Lake Havasu's **restaurants** can't boast exotic cuisine, but almost all are good value for money and offer large, wholesome portions. You'll make your own discoveries easily, but to get you started you might try: *Shrugrue's* in the Island Fashion Mall at the end of London Bridge, that offers fresh fish, salads, pasta and traditional American fare; *Max & Ma's*, 90 Swanson Avenue, is a diner-style place that serves great breakfasts, sandwiches and steaks; *New Peking Chinese Restaurant* at 2010 McCulloch Blvd, specialises in excellent Mandarin and Szechuan cooking which you should be able to scoff for under $12 per head.

Las Vegas

When the bronzed visage of Engelbert Humperdinck – or whichever showbiz grizzly is gracing *Caesar's Palace* at the time – leers out from a Nevada billboard, you know you're approaching **LAS VEGAS**: a flat, sprawling, hot city that's almost entirely devoted to serving people's greed. The first hours in Las Vegas are like entering another world: one where the religion is luck, the language is money, and time is measured by revolutions of a roulette wheel. Once acclimatised the whole spectacle is voyeuristically enjoyable (assuming your aim isn't to stake your savings in pursuit of a fortune). But don't stay too long – after more than two days the ceaseless pursuit of dollars can sap your faith in humanity.

The Spanish name of the city means "the meadows" and is derived from the fact that the high water-table here is the only place in the otherwise barren region capable of supporting vegetation. The first non-native discovery of these lush acres was made in 1829, after which they became a stopover on the Spanish trading route to Los Angeles. A few decades later, the Mormons bought Las Vegas from the Paiute Indians for $18 and established a short-lived mining township, but in 1905, when money was needed to build a rail link between Los Angeles and Salt Lake City, Las Vegas land was auctioned off in lots. Twenty-five years on, those who bought a slice of the city saw their investment pay off handsomely when the federal government began the building of the Boulder (now "Hoover") Dam, forty miles away (see p.227), bringing thousands of workers – and their wages – into the area.

Ironically, Nevada was the first state to outlaw gambling, though it was legalised in 1931, ostensibly to raise taxes for building schools. Even then, things remained fairly small-scale until 1940 when the first combined casino and hotel opened on what's now the Strip, and its instant success spawned many more. One such establishment, the *Flamingo*, which opened in 1946 financed by mobster Bugsy Segal, cemented Las Vegas's links with organised crime and instigated the system of attracting people to the gaming tables with the bribe of bargain-priced beds, food, drink and entertainment.

The policy Segal pioneered still holds today – Las Vegas is one of the cheapest places to sleep and eat in the US. It has also gone all-out to sweep away its sleazy image and become the scene of good clean fun. Yet, despite the full-frontal glamour, the enduring image isn't high-spending playboys (who are seldom seen away from their complimentary hotel suites and secluded tables on the Strip), but of ordinary working people standing for hours at a stretch feeding quarters from buckets into slot machines.

The city: basic orientation

Las Vegas divides into two distinct districts: **downtown** and **the Strip**, separated by three miles of the wide, ruler-straight, Las Vegas Boulevard, lined by petrol stations, fast-food drive-ins, and wedding chapels – getting married being simpler in Nevada (few formalities and no blood tests) than any other state (see also Reno). The Strip has the larger and more glamorous casino-hotels, but its blocks are big and during the day give little protection from the scorching sun. Night is the best time to come, when the Strip's at its brightest and gaudiest, and people set about the tables with a vengeance. If you're just passing through Las Vegas, one wild night on the Strip can be a lot of fun; if you spend any longer than 24 hours here you'll soon be desperate for some semblance of normality, in which case you should head downtown to the more compact and less star-struck few blocks of casinos grouped around so-called "Glitter Gulch", the neon-illuminated junction of Main and Fremont Streets. Frankly, the **rest of Las Vegas** needn't concern you at all, either given over to ordinary residential districts or the business community – mining is the biggest industry after the the gigantic tourist trade here.

Arriving, getting around, and information

By **train** you'll arrive in downtown Las Vegas: the station's platform leads directly into the *Union Plaza Hotel*, 1 Main Street. The **Greyhound** terminal (☎382-2640) is at 200 Main Street in downtown, and arriving buses also stop on the Strip, outside the *Stardust Hotel*, 3000 N Las Vegas Boulevard. **Flights** land at McCarran Airport, a mile from the Strip and four from downtown. Many hotels have free buses to collect their guests, otherwise there are frequent minibuses to the Strip ($3) and downtown($4.50).

Local buses are run by the *Las Vegas Transit System* (☎384–3540), and the most useful route is #6 between the Strip and downtown, which runs 24 hours a day. The standard single fare on all buses is $1; pay with correct money as you board. Given the comparatively small area and lack of places to go beyond the two main districts, you're unlikely to need a **taxi**. But if feeling flush after a winning session, it's handy to know they have a basic fare of $1.70 and charge $1.40 for each mile; taking a cab between downtown and the Strip costs around

$8. Traffic, on Friday and Saturday nights especially, so clogs the Strip that it's quicker to use the I-15 freeway to get around.

For **information**, pick up the free *What's On in Las Vegas, Today in Las Vegas* and *LVT*, which lie around hotel receptions and other public areas. They each carry details of accommodation, buffets, the latest shows, and general bumph and discount vouchers. There's also a **Convention and Visitors Bureau** at 3150 Paradise Road (Mon–Fri 8am–5pm; ☎733-2323), next to the vast Convention Center, near the Strip.

Moving on from Las Vegas

If you're relying on public transport, Las Vegas is a major connection point for **Death Valley** and the **Grand Canyon**. While there are no scheduled services, *LTR Stage Lines* (☎702/384-1230) run a charter bus to Death Valley, but you have to call to check on price and the random frequency of the service, which operates from September to May only; in summer, you'll have to hitch.

Buses to the Grand Canyon run year-round courtesy of the *Nava-Hopi* line (☎774-5003), who have one bus a day into the Canyon, $25 one-way. That journey takes virtually the entire day, in searing desert heat, so you might consider **flying**, which offers the added bonus of aerial views of Lake Mead and the Canyon itself. *America West* (☎1-800/247-5692), *Scenic Airlines* (☎1-800/634-6801) and *Air Nevada* (☎1-800/634-6377) all operate several flights daily, with a bottom-rate single fare of around $50.

Las Vegas accommodation

Despite the fact that Las Vegas has some 85,000 motel and hotel rooms (most of them hitched to casinos so you can eat, sleep and gamble and never have to breathe fresh air), it's best to book **accommodation** ahead if you're on a tight budget, or arriving on Friday or Saturday – upwards of 250,000 people descend upon the city every weekend. Many West Coast newspapers have ads outlining the latest Vegas accommodation bargains, so check these before setting off – virtually all hotels and motels offer a variety of discounts and food vouchers, which can help to stretch those holiday dollars. Be sure to get the rate confirmed for the duration of your stay – that $25-a-night room you found on Tuesday may cost $100 on Friday.

With rooms so cheap there's very little point in **camping**, which is surprisingly pricey. The only place where tents are welcome is at the *KOA Campground*, 4315 Boulder Hwy (☎451-5527), five miles from downtown (to which it's linked by a free shuttle bus), costing $15 for two people and another $4 for each additional adult. Several hotels have adjoining campervan parks, costing around $8 per night: in downtown at the *California Hotel*, 12 Ogden Street (☎385-1222); and, on the Strip, at *Circus Circus*, 2880 S Las Vegas Boulevard (☎1-800/634-3450), or the *Hacienda*, 3950 Las Vegas Boulevard (☎739-8214).

There's also **emergency accommodation**, genuinely laid on for those who have squandered their last dime on a potential jackpot. The *Transient Service Center*, 200 W Bonanza Road (☎384-4477), is run by the Salvation Army and provides a free bed and two daily meals: you must be there before 4.30pm and can't go out after that time. The *Rescue Mission*, 405 W Wilson Avenue (☎382-1776), is similar and only accepts guests between between 9am and 4pm.

Hostels and motels

AYH Youth Hostel, 1236 S Las Vegas Blvd (☎382-8119). Halfway between downtown and the Strip, charging members $9, non-members $12, with a $5 key deposit.

Las Vegas Independent Hostel, 1208 S Las Vegas Blvd (☎385-9955). Cheap and cheerful hostel with bare-bones accommodation; $10 a night.

Motel 6, 195 E Tropicana Ave (☎798-0728). The largest branch of this nationwide chain; just off the south end of the Strip. Doubles from $25.

Inexpensive hotels

Circus Circus, 2880 S Las Vegas Blvd (☎734-0410 or ☎1-800/634-3450). Hugely popular, family orientated Strip hotel, with circus acts performing live above the casino floor. Doubles from $28.

El Cortez Hotel, Fremont St at Sixth St (☎385-5200 or ☎1-800/634-6703). Older and smaller than most, this recently modernised downtown hotel is one of the better bargains around. Doubles from $20.

Imperial Palace, 3535 S Las Vegas Blvd (☎731-3311 or ☎1-800/634-6441). Huge and characterless Strip hotel, but with a great antique car collection and supposedly the best odds. Doubles from $30.

Nevada Hotel, 235 S Main St (☎385-7311). Basic but pleasant doubles from $25.

Moderate to expensive hotels

Caesar's Palace, 3570 S Las Vegas Blvd (☎731-7110 or ☎1-800/634-6001). Still the showcase of the Strip hotels. Doubles start at $100 a night, and keep going to well over $1000.

California Hotel, First St and Ogden Ave (☎385-1222). One of the most popular mid-range hotels in downtown Vegas, with doubles from $40.

Excalibur, 3850 S Las Vegas Blvd (☎597-7777 or ☎1-800/937-7777). Arthurian legend built much larger than life, with drawbridges, turrets and nightly jousting matches; staff have to call guests *M'Lord* and *M'Lady*. When it opened in 1990 it was the largest hotel in the world. Doubles from $50.

Riviera, 2901 S Las Vegas Blvd (☎734-5110 or ☎1-800/634-6753). Among the older and larger Strip hotels, with one of the less intimidating casinos. Doubles from $60 a night.

Tropicana, 3801 S Las Vegas Blvd (☎739-2222 or ☎1-800/634-4000). The best and least posey of the Strip hotels, at least as far as non-gambling activities go, with swim-up gaming tables around the world's largest indoor-outdoor swimming pool. Doubles from $50 a night.

Seeing Las Vegas: Downtown, the Strip and around

If, like most arrivals, you're in Las Vegas solely to gamble, there's not much to say beyond the fact that all the casinos are free, open 24 hours a day, and feature a healthy variety of ways to lose money: wheels of fortune, video poker, card games with lightning-fast dealers, loads of craps, the bingo-like Keno, and much more besides. It comes with entertainment, cheap drinks (free to gamblers) and food. Once the casinos are exhausted (or rather once *you're* exhausted) there's very little else.

Downtown

In **DOWNTOWN** the action centres around Fremont Street. Regular punters may have their own favourites, but the casinos here are much the same; all have a friendlier feel than their flashy counterparts on the Strip and the odds are considered more favourable by those in the know. Several of the casinos also hold free gambling lessons, though these should be treated with scepticism – it's unlikely they'll want you to win.

All the **casinos** are close together and it's a simple business to trot between them. The *Union Plaza*, facing the junction of Main and Fremont Streets, has the most businesslike mood but is still good for a stroll around, while the least pretentious downtown joint is *El Cortez*, at the other end of the line of casinos along Fremont. Of the others, squashed in between, *Binion's Horseshoe* is worth a look, mainly because it's the venue of the *World Series of Poker* each May, and sees some spirited wagering of all kinds year-round. Almost opposite, the *Four Queens* has one of downtown's rare non-gambling ways to pass the time: **Ripley's Believe It or Not** (Sun–Thurs 9am–midnight, Fri & Sat 9am–1am; $4.95), part of a chain of museums that seems to have spread all over the West. Robert Ripley made many worldwide hunting and gathering trips during the 1920s, returning to California with unusual anecdotes and bizarre curios by the thousand, later describing many of them in an immensely popular newspaper cartoon series called "Believe It or Not". The exhibits here include many painfully compelling specimens from his enormous stock – a half-human statue, a Grandfather clock made out of pins, and a Chinese mange cure, to list just three of a good hour's worth.

The Strip

In contrast to downtown's close-knit affability, **THE STRIP** (the 3000 blocks of Las Vegas Boulevard) gives full reign to the mythical Las Vegas gloss: the big shows, the big casinos, the big spenders. You'll find all three at **Caesar's Palace**, and, once you're delivered inside the building by moving walkway past a full-sized replica of Caravaggio's *David*, it's also not uncommon to see male employees dressed as Roman centurions and waitresses made-up and attired to suggest lineage to Cleopatra. It's all more high-tack than Roman-style decadence, of course, and you should endure the spectacle for as long as you can before making the short trip to the nearby **Circus Circus**, which attempts to outdo *Caesar's* with its live circus acts: a trapeze artist here, a fire-eater there, usually performing above dense crowds – this being the most family orientated spot on the Strip. **Excalibur**, with its vast drawbridge, crenellated towers, and relentless pseudo-medieval "pageantry" is also worth experiencing. The other Strip casinos are best seen from the outside and at night, when the millions of neon bulbs earn their keep.

For what they're worth, there are a few things tucked away which don't require any form of betting. Best of the bunch is the **Old-Tyme Gambling Museum** (daily 9am–1pm; $1) in the *Stardust Hotel*, 3000 N Las Vegas Boulevard: a well-arranged collection detailing the intimate relationship between gambling and the American West (it was how the early pioneers passed the time, and what got quite a few of them killed), with great displays on the legendary figures of card-playing such as "Wild" Bill Hickock and "Poker" Annie – one of the few women to excel in what was a strongly male-dominated pursuit – and a mesmerising stock of one-armed bandits. Less worthwhile is the **American Museum of Historical Documents** (Mon–Wed 10am–6pm, Thurs & Fri 10am–9pm, Sun noon–5pm; free), inside the 34-acre *Fashion Show Mall* on the north side of the Strip. It's more of a shop than a museum but you can walk in and cast an eye over the many original documents pertaining to everything from space travel to pop music – odd bits of paraphernalia like autographs from the Beatles, signed lunar astronaut photos and a facsimile of the Declaration of Independence. Only in moments of desperation should you head for the **Antique Auto Collection** (daily 9.30am–11.30pm; $3.75), inside the *Imperial Palace*, 3535 S Las Vegas Boulevard, an unalluring batch of cars which belonged to equally unalluring people – Adolf Hitler and Bugsy Segal just two examples. Similarly worth avoiding are the awful dinosaurs of the so-called **Museum of Natural History** (Fri & Sat 9am–9pm, Sun–Thurs 9am–6pm; $5), 3700 N Las Vegas Boulevard.

Off the Strip

If the slick high-rise casinos become too much, make your way two miles east to the comparative serenity of the **Liberace Museum** at 1775 E Tropicana Avenue (Mon–Sat 10am–5pm, Sun 1–5pm; $3.50). Popularly remembered as a smarmy toad who knocked out torpid toe-tappers, the earlier days of Liberace (he died in 1987) make for interesting study. He began his career playing piano in the rough bars of his native Milwaukee; only a decade later, in the 1950s, he was being mobbed by screaming adolescents and ruthlessly hounded by the scandal-hungry American press. All this is remembered by a yellowing collection of cuttings and family photos. The trappings of later wealth – electric candelabra, bejewelled quails eggs with inlaid-pianos, glittering cars and more – are here too, but overall the museum isn't the gathering of over-the-top kitsch you might expect. The music, on the other hand, piped into the scented toilets, hasn't improved with age.

Not far away, off Maryland Parkway, the campus of the University of Nevada feels refreshingly free of gambling and the showbusiness tack of the city, and boasts a much better natural history collection in the **University Museum of Natural History** (Mon–Fri 9am–5pm, Sat 10am–5pm; free), which has excellent features on desert ecology and wildlife, including cases of snakes and other indigenous inhabitants.

Eating

Eating is never difficult or expensive in Las Vegas. Nearly all the casinos offer round-the-clock **buffets** which everyone can use. **Breakfast**, normally served from 7am until 11am, is the least expensive meal of the day, with the cheapest, most basic versions to be had from 99¢, and scantier variations – a small fried egg and a thin pancake – sometimes free with a voucher. A **buffet lunch** costs around $4 or $5, and is served until about 5pm, when it mutates into **dinner** and the price rises by a couple of dollars – although the food will often be exactly the same. There's rarely any restriction on how much you can take from the buffet – the array can include prime rib, chops, meatballs, chicken, spaghetti, rice, potatoes, and a few vegetables, with slices of pie and/or ice-cream to follow – and waiters and waitresses will provide endless (non-alcoholic) drinks. In general, the food on offer is in line with the poshness of the hotel; not surprisingly, the higher the set charge, the better the food and choice will be. The top spot for a full splurge is *Caesar's Palace*, particularly their $6.95 lunch. The cheapest is usually in *Fitzgeralds* on Fremont Street in downtown, with the *Fremont* not far behind, while you'll find the best value food at the *Golden Nugget* and at *Circus Circus*.

Drinks – beer, wine, spirits and cocktails – are freely available in all the casinos to anyone gambling, and very cheap for anyone else. If you're sick of the casinos, there are hundreds of regular **restaurants** – good enough value if you're prepared to spend a bit more. The tourist magazines all carry extensive lists; the ones listed below are only a few suggestions.

Battista's Hole in the Wall, 4041 Audrie St (☎732-1424). Serves pricey but stylish Italian food in a lively setting, enhanced by strolling accordion players and all-you-can-drink complimentary house wine.

Café Santa Fe, 1213 Las Vegas Blvd (☎384-4444). Great omelettes and fresh salads, and other meat-based all-American fare.

Casa Tequila, 1815 E Charleston Blvd (☎384-0651), Mexican place offering an 11am–3pm Mexican lunch for $3, including a margarita.

Chapalas, 3335 E Tropicana Ave (☎451-8141). Daily happy hours, 3–6pm, with enormous helpings of Mexican food and cheap drinks.

Marie Callender's , 600 E Sahara Ave (☎734-6572). Known throughout the West Coast for its home-baked pies and serves great homemade soups.

Oh No Tokyo, 4455 W Flamingo Rd (☎876-4455). Assorted sushi for $6, lunch or dinner, and a wide variety of other Japanese food.

That's entertainment

Besides gambling, or just watching, the other main forms of Las Vegas **entertainment** include credibility-straining "spectaculars" featuring golden-throated warblers and bad comedians, topped off with leggy dancing girls and thumping music. Show seats are $10 on average, but expect to pay (a lot) more if the likes of Frank Sinatra or Dean Martin are topping the bill. Tickets are available from the venues, or can be booked by phone. Full details of what's coming up are in the tourist magazines.

Near Las Vegas: Lake Mead and the Hoover Dam

Almost as many people as go to Las Vegas visit **LAKE MEAD**, an artificial expanse of water about thirty miles southeast of the city. It's undeniably worth seeing – the blue waters a vivid counterpoint to the surrounding desert – but it can get excruciatingly crowded all year round. If you want to sail, scuba-dive, water-ski or fish, there are plenty of places to do so along the lake's 500-odd miles of shoreline; get the details and make bookings through any travel agent before arriving, and bear in mind that accommodation is limited to campervan-dominated campsites. Otherwise, the best plan is to come from Las Vegas for a day, taking a look at the lake and, more interestingly, the massive dam which created it.

Without your own transport, the only way to get to Lake Mead and the dam is on a guided tour. Most travel companies in Las Vegas run these daily; the *Gray Line* (☎384-1234) price of $22,50 for a five-hour tour is fairly typical. If you're driving, there's a choice of two routes: Lake Mead Boulevard runs from north Las Vegas to North Shore Road, which skirts the northern section of the lake; or, driving directly to the dam, use Hwy-93 from central Las Vegas, through the mining town of HENDERSON, and BOULDER CITY, where there's a useful **Visitors Center** (daily 8.30am–4.30pm; ☎293-4041). Besides practical information on the area, this has exhibitions on regional geology and plant life.

Fifteen miles further on from Boulder City, the **Hoover Dam** was known as the Boulder Dam until it was renamed by President Roosevelt at the opening ceremony in 1935, in honour of the previous president, who had been the prime mover in its construction. Designed to block the Colorado river and provide low-cost electricity for the cities of the southwest, it's one of the tallest dams ever built (760ft).

Hwy-93 from Boulder snakes through the rocky ridges of the Black Mountains before crossing the dam, and there are plenty of places to stop and admire the sheer bulk of the structure, composed of sufficient concrete to build a two-lane highway from the West Coast to New York. It's also worth taking one of the informative half-hour **guided tours** (daily in summer 8am–6.45pm, rest of the year 9am–4.15pm; $1), on which you can descend by lift to view the dam's insides.

The Western Mojave

The western expanse of the Mojave Desert spreads out on the north side of the San Gabriel Mountains, fifty miles from Los Angeles via Hwy-14, a barren plain that drivers have to cross to reach the alpine peaks of the eastern Sierra Nevada mountains or **Death Valley**, at the Mojave's northern edge. The few towns that have grown up in this stretch of desert over the past couple of decades are populated in the main by two sorts of people: retired couples who value the dry, clean air; and aerospace workers, employed in one of the many military bases or aircraft factories. **Lancaster**, near Edwards Air Force Base, is the largest town and one of the few places to pick up supplies; **Mojave**, thirty miles north, is a main desert crossroads and the last place to fill up your tank after dark for the next hundred miles. Hwy-14 joins up with US-395 another forty miles north, just west of the huge naval air base at China Lake and the faceless town of **Ridgecrest**, worth a look for its museum of Native American petroglyphs.

Lancaster and the Antelope Valley

From the north end of LA's San Fernando Valley, Hwy-14 cuts off from I-5 and heads east around the foothills of the San Gabriel mountains, passing by **Placerita Canyon**, site of an early gold discovery that's been preserved as a nature reserve (daily 9am–5pm; free). Ten miles further on stands the massive sandstone outcrop of the **Vasquez Rocks**, once a hiding place for frontier bandits and bank-robbers, and later used by Hollywood movie studios as the backdrop for low-budget Westerns. Beyond here Hwy-138 cuts off east, heading up to the ski resorts and lakes along the crest of the San Gabriel Mountains, while Hwy-14 continues across the sparsely settled flatlands of the Mojave Desert.

The biggest town for miles is **LANCASTER**, a sprawling community of pensioners and caravan parks whose economy is wholly based on designing, building and testing aeroplanes, from B-1 bombers for the military to the record-setting *Voyager*, which flew non-stop around the globe in 1987. It's a dull place, but may be worth an overnight stop if you want to get an early start out of LA or to see the desert before the sun heats everything to an unbearable degree. The **Chamber of Commerce** at 44943 W 10th Street (☎805/948-4518), just off J Street, the main drag, has information on places of interest in the desert, and on accommodation – on offer for $30 a night at **motels** like the *Tropic* (☎805/948-4912) at 43145 Sierra Highway, on the east side of town; and the *All-Star Inn* (☎805/948-0435) at 43540 W 17th Street, just off Hwy-14.

Unlikely as it seems at first glance, there are some things to see in the surrounding area, known as the **Antelope Valley**. In the spring, the **California Poppy Reserve** is in full bloom, fifteen miles west of Hwy-14 on Lancaster Road.

Depending upon the amount and timing of the winter rains, the poppy display peaks between March and May, when the reserve is covered in bright orange blossom; the **visitor center** (daily 9am–5pm in season; ☎724-1180) has interpretive displays of desert flora and fauna. The building itself is proof that passive-solar, underground architecture works: built into the side of a hill, it keeps cool naturally and is powered entirely by an adjacent windmill.

Saddleback Butte, seventeen miles east of Lancaster via Avenue J, is a 3650-foot peak whose slopes are home to one of the best collections of Joshua trees. It's also a likely spot to catch a glimpse of the Desert Tortoise, for whom the park provides a refuge from the motorcyclists and dune buggy enthusiasts who tear around the region; there is water and **camping** available for $3 a night.

The desert and dry lake beds north of Lancaster make up **Edwards Air Force Base**, the US military testing ground for experimental, high-speed and high-altitude aircraft. **Tours** (Mon–Fri 10am & 1pm; free) of the facility include a short film (a jingoistic cross between *The Right Stuff* and *Top Gun*) and a look at hangars full of unique aeroplanes, including the missile-like *X-15*. The base is also one of the landing spots for the Space Shuttle, and thousands of people make the journey out here to welcome the astronauts home.

MOJAVE, strung out along the highway thirty miles north of Lancaster, is a major junction on the interstate railway network, though it's used solely by goods trains; Hwy-58 follows the railway tracks east to Barstow and west to Bakersfield. The town itself – mostly a mile-long highway strip of petrol stations, $25-a-night motels and franchised fast-food restaurants, open around the clock – is the last place to fill up on food and petrol before continuing north into the Owens Valley (see p.310) or Death Valley.

Ridgecrest and Randsburg

Beyond Mojave the desert is virtually uninhabited, and the only things that mark the landscape are the bald ridges of the foothills of the Sierra Nevada mountains that rise to the west, though you might see the odd ghostly sign of the prospectors who once roamed the region in search of gold and less precious minerals. Twenty-five miles north of Mojave, Hwy-14 passes through **Red Rock Canyon**, where brilliantly coloured rock formations have been eroded into a miniature version of Utah's Bryce Canyon; the highway passes right through the centre of the most impressive section, though if you walk just a hundred yards from the road you're more likely to see an eagle or coyote than another visitor. There's water, and a fairly primitive free **campsite**.

North of Red Rock Canyon, Hwy-14 merges into US-395. Five miles west of the junction via Hwy-178 sits the sprawling desert community of **RIDGECREST**. Dominated by the military, in this case the huge China Lake Naval Weapons Center, jet fighters scream past overhead taking target practice on land that's chock-full of Indian **petroglyphs**. Though access to the sites is strictly controlled, you can get some idea of the native culture of the Mojave Desert by visiting the **Maturango Museum**, on China Lake Boulevard at 100 E Las Flores Street (Tues–Sun 10am–5pm; $1). The museum has exhibits on both the natural and cultural history of the region, including examples of the rock-cut figures.

Fifteen miles south of Ridgecrest on US-395, the last working gold mine in California, the Yellow Aster Mine, breathes a little life into the near-ghost town of **RANDSBURG**. The **Desert Museum**, 161 Butte Avenue (weekends 10am–5pm;

free), has displays on the glory days of the 1890s, when upwards of three thousand people lived in the town, mining gold, silver and tungsten out of the arid, rocky hills. If you're keen on mining lore, stop in for a beer at the *White House Saloon* across the street, which also has bed and breakfast packages for $30 a night.

Approaching Death Valley

From the west there are two routes toward Death Valley National Monument, of equal length and running along either side of the China Lake Naval Weapons Base. Five miles west of Ridgecrest, US-395 runs north along the west side of China Lake up to the dry bed of what used to be Owens Lake; the water that would naturally flow in the lake has been diverted to Los Angeles, and is carried south by the aqueduct which parallels US-395. Just south of here, Hwy-190 cuts off due east past the tumbledown wooden ruins of DARWIN, a ghost of a mining town that was built by prospectors searching for seams of silver, inspired by tales of an Indian who repaired an explorer's rifle by fashioning a gunsight out of solid silver. Nearby, and more interesting, are the **Darwin Falls**, three miles south of Hwy-190 along a dirt road and four miles west of the junction with Hwy-178; follow the creek up a small canyon to the beautiful spring-fed waterfall.

The less-travelled route loops sixty miles around the eastern side of Naval Weapons Range, and allows the quickest access into the more mountainous backcountry of Death Valley*. Wildrose Road, the continuation of Hwy-178 beyond Ridgecrest, curves through the chemical plants of TRONA past the gold-mining town of BALLARAT – whose eroded adobe ruins still stand in the foothills three miles east of the highway – before joining Hwy-190 for the final fifteen miles east to the entrance to Death Valley. What makes this route worthwhile is the option of following the steep Mahogany Flat Road, which cuts off Wildrose Road thirteen miles south of Hwy-190, up and over the Panamint Mountains to **Telescope Peak** (see p.234), the highest and coolest part of the monument. The road is well-maintained, but although there is excellent **camping**, the nearest food, drinking water or petrol are 25 miles away, at Stovepipe Wells Village.

Death Valley National Monument

As its name suggests, **Death Valley** is an inhuman environment: barren and monotonous, burning hot and almost entirely without shade, much less water. At first sight it seems impossible that the landscape could support any kind of life; yet it's home to great variety of living creatures, from snakes and giant eagles to tiny fishes and Bighorn sheep. But it's the rocks that you come to see: deeply shadowed, eroded crevices at the foot of sharply silhouetted hills, whose exotic mineral content turns million-year-old mudflats into rainbows of sunlit phosphorescence.

Throughout the summer, the air temperature in Death Valley averages 120°F, and the ground can reach near boiling point; it's best to stay away at this time unless you're a real glutton for sweaty, potentially fatal punishment. Better to come during the spring, especially March and early April, when the wildflowers

---

* On a more sinister note, this part of the desert was where Charlie Manson and his "Family" planned their reign of terror while holed up in an old mining camp in Goler Wash, just outside the southeast corner of the monument.

are in bloom and daytime temperatures average a manageable 65°F, dropping to the mid-forties at night. Any time between October and May it's generally mild and dry, with occasional rainfall on the surrounding mountains causing flash floods through otherwise bone-dry gulleys and washes.

The central north–south valley for which the monument is named is just one part of the monument, surrounded by many more, equally inhospitable desert valleys. High above stand the less-visited but far cooler mountain peaks – from where you can see at once both the highest (Mount Whitney) and the lowest (near Badwater) points in the continental US. It's the central valley which contains the monument's two main outposts for provisions and accommodation: **Stovepipe Wells** and **Furnace Creek**, where the **visitor center** (daily 8am–9pm in winter, 8am–5pm in summer; ☎786-2331) and a small **museum** of Death Valley history is located. There is a $5 entrance fee, payable at the park entrance, where you'll be given a map of the region.

Geology and history

The sculpted rock layers exposed in Death Valley, tinted by oxidised traces of various mineral deposits, comprise a nearly complete record of the earth's past, from 500-million-year-old mountains to the relatively young fossils of marine animals left on the valley floors by Ice Age lakes, which covered most of the low-lying areas of the park. There is also dramatic evidence of volcanic activity, as at the massive Ubehebe Crater on the north side of the monument.

Human beings have lived in and around Death Valley for thousands of years, beginning about ten thousand years ago when the valley was still filled by a massive lake; the climate was then quite mild and wild game was plentiful. Later, wandering tribes of Desert Shoshone Indians wintered near perennial freshwater springs in the warm valley, spending the long, hot summers at cooler, higher elevations in the surrounding mountains; there is still a small, inhabited Shoshone village near the *Furnace Creek Inn*.

The first white people passed through in 1849, looking for a short cut to the Gold Rush towns on the other side of the Sierra Nevada; they ran out of food and water but managed to survive and give Death Valley its name. For the next 75 years the only people willing to brave the hardships of the desert were miners. They searched for and found deposits of gold, silver and copper, though the most successful mining endeavours were centred on borates, a harsh alkaline used in detergent soaps. In the late nineteenth century borate miners developed twenty-mule-team wagons to haul the powders across the deserts to the railroad line at Mojave. In the 1920s the first tourist facilities were developed, and in 1927 the mining camp at Furnace Creek was converted into the *Furnace Creek Inn*. Six years later the two million acres of Death Valley and around were purchased by the US government, to be preserved as a national monument.

Getting there and information

Death Valley is a long way from anywhere; the only scheduled public transport is from **Las Vegas**, 140 miles to the southeast, from where the *LTR Stage Lines* (☎702/384-1230) leave roughly every other day September to May, not at all in summer. Otherwise, you'll have to drive. Las Vegas is the nearest city to Death Valley; hire a car and take US-95 past Nellis Air Force Base and the US nuclear weapons test range, through Beatty, Nevada, where you'll find a number of cheap

motels, (see below for details). Coming from Barstow, Hwy-178 enters from the southeast past **Tecopa Hot Springs**, a free, public, natural hot springs that is a popular winter retreat for pensioners and others who appreciate a long hot soak. Perhaps the prettiest drive heads east from Lone Pine (see p.311) past the dry bed of Owens Lake and Panamint Springs – where there's a petrol station and a $40-a-night motel, twenty miles from the park entrance.

Besides the main visitor centre at Furnace Creek, the centre of Death Valley, there are **ranger stations** close to the park boundaries where you can pick up a free map and up-to-date information on tours and activities. The main ones are on the west side of the park at *Wildrose Campground* on Hwy-178; at *Emigrant Campground* near Stovepipe Wells on Hwy-190; and on the northern edge of the park at Scotty's Castle.

Accommodation, camping and eating

Reservations for overnight accommodation in any of the monument's **three hotels** should be made as early as possible, particularly during the peak times of Thanksgiving, Christmas and Easter holidays. The cheapest option is the *Stovepipe Wells Village* (☎786-2387), on Hwy-190 about twenty miles northeast of Furnace Creek, which has double rooms from $45; prices drop to $38 a night during the June to August period. Otherwise there are two costly alternatives: the plush rooms of the *Furnace Creek Inn* will set you back between $175 and $250 a night for a double; across the road and about half a mile north is the more reasonable *Furnace Creek Ranch*, at $65 to $90 for a double. Both hotels are located on natural oases but have very limited facilities in summer; both are operated by the same company – the **Fred Harvey Consortium** – who run almost everything in the monument. For reservations phone (☎619/786-2345 or ☎1-800/622-0838) or write to PO Box 1, Death Valley, CA 92328. You'll save yourself a packet by staying **outside Death Valley** altogether, travelling the 35 miles past Furnace Creek along Hwy-95 to **BEATTY**, Nevada: the *El Portal Motel* (☎702/553-2912) on the west side of town or the *Stagecoach Motel* (☎702/553-2419) on the east side both have double rooms for $35 a night, less in summer.

Camping is the best and cheapest way to enjoy Death Valley. All of the campsites in the monument are operated by the National Park Service; most cost $5 a night, though sites without a water supply are free; sites cannot be reserved and stays are limited to thirty days to cut down on people moving in for the winter. The biggest and most easily accessible sites are at **Furnace Creek** (where there's room enough for over a thousand tents and caravans), and at **Stovepipe Wells** – though the smaller site at **Mesquite Spring**, near Scotty's Castle on the north side of the monument, is much more pleasant. The only place you can be assured of finding some shade is in the canyons on the forested slopes of Telescope Peak, on the western edge of the monument, where there are three sites, **Wildrose**, **Thorndike** and **Mahogany Flat**, just off the mostly paved Wildrose Road. They're free, but be sure to purify the water before drinking.

There's not a great variety of **places to eat** in Death Valley – you're limited to the hotel dining rooms and coffee shops at the three main resorts. The best of the bunch are at the *Furnace Creek Ranch*, where the *Panamint Pizza* parlour and adjacent *Senor Coyote's Mexican Restaurant* do good value meals until 10pm. To quench a thirst after a day in the sun, do as the few locals do and head to the *Corkscrew Saloon*, also at *Furnace Creek Ranch* and open until 1am.

In the Valley

You can get an unforgettable feel for Death Valley just by passing through, and you could quite easily see almost everything in a day. If you've got neither much time nor your own (reliable) transport, regular scheduled three-hour **coach tours** ($21) are offered during the winter months by the *Furnace Creek Inn*, on which you can view the main and most impressive sights in air-conditioned comfort. If you do have the time, though, aim to spend at least a night here, if possible camped out somewhere far from the main centres of activity. Even if you've got your own car, the best way to experience the huge and empty spaces, and the unique landforms, of Death Valley is to leave the roads and crowds behind and wander off – taking care to remember the way back. Sunrise and sunset are the best times to experience the colour that's bleached out by the midday sun, and they're also the most likely times for seeing the wildlife, mostly lizards, snakes and small rodents, that hide out through the heat of the day.

Many of the most unusual sights are located south of Furnace Creek. A good first stop, seven miles along Hwy-178/Badwater Road, is the **Artist's Palette**, an evocatively eroded hillside covered in an intensely coloured mosaic of reds, golds, blacks and greens. Another sixteen miles south, **Badwater** is an unpalatable but non-poisonous thirty-foot-wide pool of water, loaded with chloride and sulphates, that's also the only home of the endangered, soft-bodied Death Valley snail. From the pool a four-mile hike across the hot, flat valley floor, drops down to the **lowest point in the Western Hemisphere**, at 282 feet below sea level.

Zabriskie Point, overlooking Badwater and the Artists's Palette off Hwy-190, four miles south of Furnace Creek, was the inspiration for Antonioni's eponymous 1960s film. More rewarding, but less accessible, is **Dante's View**, 25 miles south of Furnace Creek and ten miles off Hwy-190 on a very steep (and very hot) road. The view from both points is best during the early morning, when the pink and gold Panamint Mountains across the valley are highlighted by the rising sun.

Near Stovepipe Wells on the western side of the monument spread the most extensive of Death Valley's **sand dunes**, some fifteen rippled and contoured square miles of ever-changing dunes, just north of Hwy-190 to the east of the campsite and ranger station. West of the campsite, at the end of a ten-mile dirt road, stand the sheer black walls of **Marble Canyon**, on which ancient Indians scratched mysterious petroglyph figures.

Outside the Valley

Some of the best places in the monument are well outside the actual valley of Death Valley, notably **Telescope Peak**, on the western side of the monument, and **Ubehebe Crater** to the north, an old volcanic crater whose ashen walls have mellowed to an earthy orange tinge. Neither of these see many (if any) tourists: they're well out of the way. **Scotty's Castle**, in contrast, is the most popular single stop in the monument, and hordes of overheated tourists brave impending sunstroke waiting in long queues for the chance to wander through the surreal attraction of this unfinished but still luxurious mansion.

Scotty's Castle

On the north edge of the monument, 45 miles from the visitor centre, **Scotty's Castle** (tours daily 9am–5pm; $5) is an extravagant Spanish Revival castle built during the 1920s as the desert retreat of wealthy Chicago insurance broker Albert Johnson, but known and named after the cowboy, prospector and publicity hound, "Death Valley" Scotty, who managed the construction, and claimed the house was his own, financed by his hidden gold mine. The million-dollar house features intricately carved wooden ceilings, waterfalls in the living room and, most entertaining of all, a remote-controlled player piano; plans for swimming pools and elaborate gardens were shelved when Johnson lost a fortune in the Wall Street Crash of 1929. In winter, the most popular time to visit, you may have to wait as long as three hours for a place on one of the hour-long **tours** of the opulently furnished house, left pretty much as it was when Johnson died in 1948. Scotty himself lived here until 1954, and is buried just behind the house.

Ubehebe Crater and Racetrack Valley

Five miles west of Scotty's Castle – though it might as well be five hundred miles for all the people who venture a look – gapes the half-mile wide **Ubehebe Crater**, the rust-tinged result of a massive volcanic explosion; a half-mile south sits its thousand-year-old younger brother, **Little Hebe**. Beyond the craters the road continues west for another twenty dusty miles to **Racetrack Valley**, a 2½-mile long mudflat across which giant boulders seem slowly to be racing, leaving faint trails in their wake. Scientists believe that the boulders are pushed along the sometimes icy surface by very high winds; sit and watch (but don't hold your breath) from the rock outcrop at the northern end, known as the **Grandstand**.

Skidoo Ghost Town and Telescope Peak

To escape the heat and dust of the desert floor, head up Emigrant Canyon Road, off Hwy-190 in the west, into the Panamint Mountains. Ten miles up the canyon, a dirt track turns off to the east toward **Skidoo Ghost Town**, where only a few ruins – and a number of roaming wild mules – remain from what in 1915 was a gold-mining camp of seven hundred people.

The main road leads another, very steep, fifteen miles, over Emigrant Pass and Wildrose ranger station, past massive, beehive-shaped stone kilns used in the 1880s to make charcoal for use in the smelters of local silver mines. At its end in the juniper and pine forests of Mahogany Flat, there's a free **campsite** (purify water before drinking) and the trailhead for the strenuous twelve-mile round-trip hike up **Telescope Peak**: at 11,000 feet the highest – and coolest – point in the monument. The trail climbs nearly three thousand feet from the trailhead, skirting a pair of 10,000-foot peaks before reaching the summit and its grand panorama of Death Valley, and across to Mount Whitney and the eastern face of the Sierra Nevada mountains – 75 miles to the west.

travel details

Trains
From LA to Indio, 25 miles from Palm Springs (3 weekly; 3hr); Barstow (2 daily; 4hr); Las Vegas (1; 7hr).

Buses
From Palm Springs Desert Stage Lines to Joshua Tree (4 daily; 1hr 30min).

From LA Greyhound to Palm Springs (10 daily; 3hr); Barstow (13; 4hr); Las Vegas (13; 6hr 15min).

From Las Vegas LTR Lines to Death Valley (summer charter service, usually at least 3 weekly; 2h 30min); Grand Canyon Nava-Hopi Bus Lines (1 daily; 5hr).

CHAPTER FOUR

THE CENTRAL COAST

After the hustle of LA and San Francisco, the four hundred miles of coastline in between – the **Central Coast** – can seem like the land that time forgot: sparsely populated outside the few medium-sized towns, and lined by clean, sandy beaches that are often little disturbed by modern life. Indeed, first-time visitors, and those who rarely set foot out of the cities, may be surprised to find just how much of the region survives in its natural state. The mountain ranges that separate the shore from the farmlands of the inland valleys are for the most part pristine wilderness, sometimes covered in thick forests of tall and slender redwood trees, while, in winter especially, fast-flowing rivers and streams course down valleys to the sea. All along the shore, sea otters and seals play in the waves, and endangered grey whales pass close by on their annual migration from Alaska to Mexico.

Big Sur, where the brooding Santa Lucia mountains rise steeply out of the thundering Pacific surf, is the heart of the region, and the best place to experience this untouched environment at its most dramatic. Nature aside, though, the Central Coast also marks the gradual transition from Southern to Northern California. The two largest towns here, **Santa Barbara** and **Santa Cruz**, are poles apart: Santa Barbara, a hundred miles north of Los Angeles, is a conservative, wealthy resort; Santa Cruz, 75 miles south of San Francisco, is a throwback to the 1960s, where long hair and tie-dye are still the style of the day. What they have in common is miles of broad clean **beaches**, with often chilly but always clean water and excellent surf, and a branch of the University of California energising the local nightlife. In between, the small town of **San Luis Obispo** provides a langorous contrast to them both, and is a feasible base for the Central Coast's biggest tourist attraction, **Hearst Castle**, the opulent hilltop palace of publishing magnate William Randolph "Citizen Kane" Hearst, open daily for guided tours.

The Central Coast is also one of the most historic parts of the state, and contains the bulk and the best of the late eighteenth-century Spanish colonial **missions** – the first European settlements on the West Coast, set up to convert the natives to Christianity while co-opting their labour at the same time. Almost all of the towns that exist today grew up around the adobe walls and red-tiled roofs of these Catholic colonies, strung out along the Pacific, each deliberately sited a long day's walk from the next and typically composed of a church and a cloistered monastery, enclosed within thick walls to prevent attacks by Indian tribes. **Monterey**, a hundred miles south of San Francisco, was the capital of California under Spain and later Mexico, and today retains more of its early nineteenth-century architecture than any other city in the state; it's also a good base for one of the most beautiful of the missions, which stands three miles south in the uppercrust seaside resort of **Carmel**.

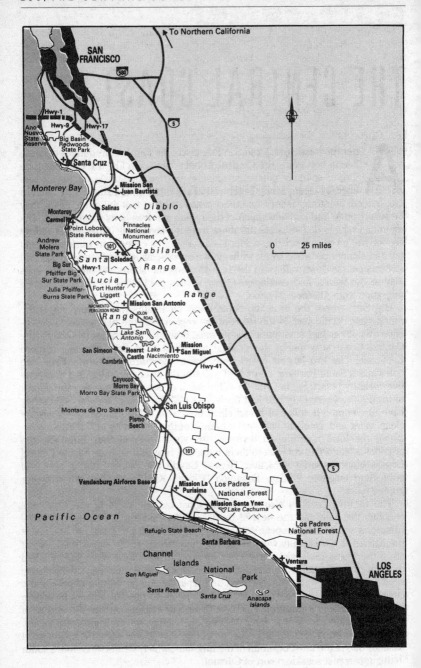

Getting around is easy by California standards: some of the best views in the state can be had from *Amtrak*'s Coast Starlight train, which runs bang along the coast up to San Luis Obispo before cutting inland north to San Francisco. *Greyhound* buses stop at most of the towns, particularly those along the main highway, US-101 – though a better route, if you've got a car, is the smaller Hwy-1, which follows the coast all the way but takes twice as long. **Places to stay** don't always come cheap but are easy to find, at least outside of summer weekends when otherwise quiet towns and beaches are packed solid with holidaying families. Opportunities for **camping** are plentiful, too, in a string of state parks, beaches and forests.

The Channel Islands National Park

Stretching north from Catalina Island off the coast of Los Angeles, a chain of little-known desert islands have been protected in their natural state as the **CHANNEL ISLANDS NATIONAL PARK,** offering excellent hiking and close-up views of sea lions, as well as fishing and skin-diving through the many shipwrecks in the crystal-clear Pacific waters. Only the smallest and nearest, **Anacapa Island**, is easily accessible, via the *Island Packers* (☎642-1393) **ferry** which leaves daily at 9am from 1867 Spinnaker Drive in Ventura Harbor, three miles west of US-101, and returns at 5pm. The fifteen-mile trip, takes two hours each way (costing $30), and there's a free, very basic **campsite** half a mile's walk from the landing cove. Be sure to bring plenty of **food** and especially **water**, as none is available on the boat or on the island.

The **other islands** are more difficult to visit, and require prior arrangements; the largest two, Santa Cruz and Santa Rosa, remain privately owned, with no public transport except for occasional trips from Santa Barbara, organised by the *Nature Conservancy* (☎962-9111). The most distant island, San Miguel – fifty miles offshore – is the burial place of sixteenth-century Spanish explorer Juan Cabrillo, and for many years was used by the military as a bombing and missile range.

Even if you can't spare the full day it takes to visit the islands, it's worth stopping by the **Visitors Center** (daily 8am–5pm, ☎644-8262), next to the ferry landing in Ventura Harbor, which has well-presented displays on the geology and the native plant and animal life of the islands, including seals, sea lions, pelican rookeries and giant kelp forests. It also has up-to-date information on arranging trips to all of the Channel Islands.

Ventura and Ojai

The valleys of suburban Los Angeles meet the Pacific coast at **VENTURA**, a long-standing farming and fishing community that's slowly being submerged beneath an overlay of fast-food restaurants and mini-malls. The only real reason to stop is to catch a ferry out to the offshore Channel Islands, from the harbour fifteen miles southwest of the town, but if you've got a few minutes to spare, be sure to look in on the seemingly time-warped town centre, just north of the intersection of US-101 and Hwy-1, around the restored church of **Mission San Buenaventura** at 225 Main Street (daily 10am–5pm; 50¢), founded in 1782. A block from the mission, on

Main Street, there are two small but reasonably engaging museums: the **Albinger Archaeological Museum**, at 113 E Main Street (Tues–Sun 10am–4pm; free), has exhibits explaining 3500 years of local history, from ancient Native American cultures to the mission era; across the street the **Ventura County Historical Museum** (Tues–Sun 10am–5pm; donations) takes up where it leaves off, with exhibits on local pioneer families and their farming equipment.

Nestled in the hills above Ventura, the small town of **OJAI** (pronounced "O-hi") is a wealthy resort community that's a centre for the exclusive health spas and tennis clubs that dot the surrounding countryside. It's also headquarters of the Krishnamurti Society, which spreads the word of the theosophist who lived and lectured here during the 1920s. For details, contact the Ojai **Chamber of Commerce**, (☎646-3000); otherwise, about the only place in town worth stopping at is *Bart's Books*, an outdoor bookshop at Canada and Matilija, with an excellent selection of secondhand books.

There are two natural **hot springs** off scenic Hwy-33, six miles north of Ojai, near the $5-a-night **campsite** at Wheeler Gorge in the **Los Padres National Forest**. Within the forest, the Sespe Condor Reserve is the protected home of the world's largest bird, the nearly extinct **California Condor**. Although it has a wingspan of over eight feet, it's very rarely spotted by even the most devoted watchers; in fact, the last-known pairs were captured in 1987 and taken to the San Diego Zoo, where they have since doubled their number to over fifty. The first of these are due to be re-released into the wild early in 1992, so with a bit of luck you may catch a glimpse of one.

Santa Barbara

The eight-lane freeway that races past the oil wells and offshore drilling platforms along the coast beyond Ventura slows to a more leisurely pace a hundred miles north of Los Angeles at **SANTA BARBARA**, a monied seaside resort that for years has been known as the "home of the newly wed and the nearly dead" – a not entirely inaccurate demographic summary of the place. The completion of the US-101 freeway in 1991, and the replacement of much of the downtown district with a vast modern shopping mall, are sure signs that this once quaint and quiet refuge is slowly but surely turning into yet another identikit Southern California town.

Home to Ronald Reagan, and weekend escape for much of the old money of Los Angeles, it's a conservative town, but undeniably beautifully sited. Rising on gently sloping hills above the Pacific, the insistent red-tiled roofs and white stucco walls of the low-rise buildings form a quickly familiar background to some of California's finest examples of Spanish Revival architecture, while the golden beaches are wide and clean, lined by palm trees along a gently curving bay. Locals look tanned and healthy, playing volleyball, surfing or cycling along the shore.

Arrival, information and getting around

Getting to Santa Barbara is easy. Hourly *Greyhound* **buses** (☎965-3971) from LA and San Francisco stop downtown at 34 W Cabrillo Street; **trains** (☎687-6848) stop once a day in each direction at the old Southern Pacific station at 209 State Street, a block west of US-101. For more **information** on Santa Barbara, or for

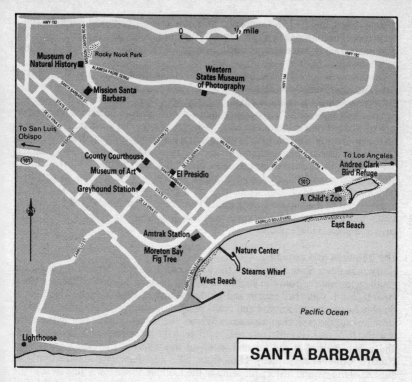

SANTA BARBARA

help with finding a place to stay, contact the **Visitor Information Office** on East Beach at 1 Santa Barbara Street (☎966-9222). **Getting around** Santa Barbara is simple and painless: a free shuttle bus loops around the downtown area on weekdays, while the *Santa Barbara Metropolitan Transit District* (☎683-3702) covers the outlying areas for a flat fare of 50¢.

The town centre

The homogenised feel of Santa Barbara is no accident. Following a devastating earthquake in 1925, the city authorities decided to rebuild virtually the entire town in the image of an apocryphal mission-era past – even the massive, modern El Paseo shopping mall is covered in pseudo-whitewashed adobe plaster – with numerous arcades linking shops, cafés and restaurants. It's reasonably successful, if inevitably rather twee, the square-mile of the town centre squeezing between the south-facing beaches and the foothills of the Santa Ynez mountains. **State Street** is the main drag, home to a friendly assortment of diners, bookshops, coffee bars and nightclubs catering to the needs of the locals rather than visitors.

The town's few remaining, genuine mission-era structures are preserved as the **Presidio de Santa Barbara** (Mon–Fri 10.30am–4.30pm, Sat & Sun noon–4pm; donations), the centre of which, the two-hundred-year-old barracks of the old fortress, **El Cuartel**, stand two blocks off State Street on Perdido Street. The second-oldest building in California, this now houses historical exhibits and a scale model of the small Spanish colony. The more recent past is recounted in the Historical Society **museum**, a block away at 136 E de la Guerra Street, (Tues–Sun noon–5pm; free).

On the corner of State and Anapamu streets, the **Santa Barbara Museum of Art** (Tues–Sat 9am–5pm, Thurs until 9pm, Sun noon–5pm; free) is of more interest, a refreshingly accessible small museum with some fine classical Greek and Egyptian statuary and a fairly comprehensive collection of American painting, as well as some French Impressionists. Just east of here, on Anapamu, the **Santa Barbara County Courthouse** is the one first-rate piece of Spanish Revival architecture in Santa Barbara, an idiosyncratic variation on the mission theme that has been widely praised as one of the finest public buildings in the US. Take a break in the sunken gardens, explore the quirky staircases, or climb the seventy-foot-high **clocktower** (daily 9am–5pm; free) for a view out over the town. Two blocks up State Street the landmark **Arlington Theater** is an intact and still-functioning 1930s movie palace and performance venue, whose *trompe l'oeil* interior simulates a Mexican village plaza.

The beaches and around

Half a mile down State Street from the town centre, Cabrillo Street runs along the south-facing shore, from the yacht and fishing harbour beyond palm-lined **West Beach** to the volleyball courts and golden strand of **East Beach**, which every Sunday hosts an outdoor arts and crafts market. At the foot of State Street take a stroll among the pelicans on **Stearns Wharf**, the oldest wooden pier in the state, built in 1872 and recently restored, with seafood restaurants, ice cream stands and a fish market at the far end. Also on the wharf is the **Sea Center and Nature Conservancy** (daily 11am–5pm; $1), an educational centre that's an annexe of the natural history museum in the foothills above town. Just west of the pier there's an open-air, fifty-metre swimming pool ($2), where world-class athletes keep in shape, and you can hire a **windsurfer** from *Sundance Windsurfing* at 29 State Street (☎966-2474), for $10 an hour – lessons are $35 for two hours, including board rental – or a **bicycle** from *Beach Rentals* at 8 W Cabrillo Street (☎963-2524) for $15 a day. They'll also give you a map of Santa Barbara's extensive system of bike paths; the longest and most satisfying leads west along the bluffs all the way to Isla Vista and UCSB (see p.243), and passes a mile or so above the never-crowded, creekside **Arroyo Burro Beach** (locally known as "Hendry's"), four miles west of the wharf at the end of Las Positas Road. Alternatively head along the beachfront bike path two miles east to the Santa Barbara **zoo** (daily 10am–5pm; $4), and cycle around the **Andree Clark Bird Refuge** (free) just beyond, an enclosed saltwater marsh where you can see a variety of seabirds, including egrets, herons and cormorants.

The foothills: the Mission and the museums

One sight that's worth leaving the beach for is in the hills above the town: **Mission Santa Barbara**, (daily 9am–5pm; $1), the so-called "Queen of the Missions", whose colourful twin-towered front is the most beautiful and impressive of all the California missions, sitting majestically in well-landscaped gardens overlooking the city and the ocean. The present structure was finished and dedicated in 1820, built of local sandstone to replace a series of three adobe churches which had been destroyed by earthquakes; a small **museum** displays historical artefacts from the mission archives. Get there by bus #22, or walk or ride the half-mile, from State Street up Mission Street and Mission Canyon. Just beyond the mission at 2559 Puesta del Sol Road, the **Natural History Museum** (Mon–Sat 9am–5pm, Sun 10am–5pm; $3), has intriguing and informative displays on the plants and animals of the ecosystems of Southern California, and an entrance constructed out of the skeleton of a Blue Whale. Across the road, **Rocky Nook Park** is a great place to picnic or wander among the trees; and, half a mile east of the mission, the excellent **Western States Museum of Photography**, at 1321 Alameda Padre Serra (daily 10am–4pm; free), displays over a thousand antique cameras – and, more interestingly, mounts changing exhibitions of works by some of the world's best contemporary photographers.

Accommodation

Holding some of the West Coast's most deluxe resorts – it's the sort of place movie stars go to get married, or to spend their honeymoon – Santa Barbara is among the priciest places to stay, with rooms averaging over $110 a night. While there's no hostel, and few places under $75, with a bit of advance planning it shouldn't take too big a bite out of your budget. The least expensive – and most of the more moderate – places are booked solid throughout the summer, but if you get stuck, two bureaux, *Accommodations Santa Barbara* (☎687-9191) and *On The Town* (☎687-7474), will try to find you a room for no charge; the *Bed-and-Breakfast Guild* (☎1-800/776-9176) can set up room for you at one of the many local inns. Also, while there's no camping in Santa Barbara proper, there are lots of places along the coast to the north and in the Santa Ynez Valley in the mountains above (see below for details).

East Beach Lodge, 1029 Orilla del Mar (☎965-0546). Standard motel just off the sands of East Beach. Doubles $40 mid-week, from $60 at the weekend.

Hotel State Street, 121 State St (☎966-6586). Near the wharf and beach in a characterful old Mission-style building, with free morning tea and coffee. Doubles $30–55.

Miramar Hotel Resort, 1555 S Jameson Lane (☎969-2203). Slightly faded, once elegant beach resort with a private strand and sea view rooms starting around $65.

Motel 6, 443 Corona del Mar (☎564-1392). Inexpensive but extremely popular beachfront lodging in no-frills chain motel. There's another one north of the town centre at 3505 State St (☎687-5400). Doubles $32.

San Ysidro Ranch, 900 San Ysidro Lane (☎969-5046). Gorgeous, ultra-posh resort (Jackie and JFK spent their honeymoon here), in the hills south of town. Private cottages in lovely gardens start at $150 a night.

Tropicana Motel, 223 Castillo St (☎966-2219). Above-average motel with nice pool, a short walk from State St or the beach. Doubles from $55, more in summer.

Eating

Because of its status as a prime resort area, Santa Barbara has a number of very good and very expensive restaurants, but it also has numerous more affordable options that offer a range of good food. Since it's right on the Pacific, there's not surprisingly a lot of seafood (and sushi) places along the north end of State Street; Mexican places are also numerous and of a very high standard.

Charlotte Cafe, 742 State St (☎966-1221). Pleasant downtown cafe open all day. Also excellent takeaway salads and sandwiches, for an inexpensive al fresco lunch.

Joe's Cafe, 536 State St, (☎966-4638). Long-established bar and grill. A great place to stop off for a burger and a beer, more or less halfway between the beach and the downtown museums.

Paradise Cafe, 702 Anacapa St (☎962-4416). Stylish, slightly upmarket 1940s era indoor/outdoor grill, with good steaks and ultra-fresh seafood.

Pescado's, 422 N Milpas St (☎965-3805). Excellent grilled fish and Mexican seafood specialities, plus an evening Happy Hour.

RG's Giant Hamburgers, 922 State St (☎963-1654). Voted biggest and best burgers in Santa Barbara many years running. Good salads too, and breakfast daily from 7am.

Zia's, 421 N Milpas St (☎962-5391). Upscale but not expensive Santa Fe-style New Mexican restaurant, with subtle variations on the tacos-and-burritos theme: fried chiles stuffed with pine nuts and melted cheese, Hopi blue-corn tortillas, and the like.

Drinking and nightlife

There are quite a few cafés, bars and clubs along the entire length of State Street, especially in the downtown strip. You'll find good jazz at *Joseppi's* (see below), while the *Society for Jazz and World Music* (☎962-3575), puts on a variety of interesting new music all over town.

For the most up-to-date nightlife listings, check out a copy of the free weekly *Santa Barbara Independent*, available at area bookshops, record stores and 7–11 convenience stores.

Carnaval, 634 State St (☎962-9991). Hot spot, playing an array of dance music and hosting biggish name indie bands.

Espresso Roma, 728 State St (☎962-7241). Serves up an excellent espresso and is lively from early morning until late every night.

Joseppi's, 434 State St (☎962-5516). The town's best jazz.

Sojourner Coffee House, 134 E Canon Perdido (☎965-7922). Coffee, beer, wine, and a range of vegetarian food, in a friendly, hippyish setting, with live music some nights.

Zelo's, 630 State St (☎966-5792). One of Santa Barbara's most fashionable bars, which evolves into a dance club as the night wears on.

Santa Barbara listings

Airport Santa Barbara Airport, eight miles from the town centre, near UCSB at 515 Marxmiller Drive in Goleta (☎967-5608), has a limited and very expensive scheduled service to other Californian cities. Carriers include *American Eagle* (☎564-1441 or ☎1-800/433-7300) and *United* (☎964-6863 or ☎1-800/241-6522).

Area Code ☎805.

Bookshops *Earthling Books*, on the corner of State and Victoria streets has an excellent general selection of books. If you're looking for maps and hiking guides, try *Pacific Travellers Supply*, at 529 State St.

Camping and hiking For information on the vicinity of Santa Barbara (and the many good trails easily accessible from downtown), or to find out how to reach the area's many natural **hot springs**, contact the *US Forest Service* office in Goleta, near UCSB at 6144 Calle Real (☎683-6711).

Car Hire The cheapest is *Ugly Duckling Rent-a-car*, 311 W Montecito St (☎962-6670), which rents late-model cars for as little as $20 a day plus 10¢ a mile. The chain offices are *Budget*, 414 Chapala St (☎963-6651) and *Hertz*, 319 W Carrillo St (☎963-3336).

Hospital 315 Camino del Remedio (☎964-4819).

Post Office 836 Anacapa St, just east of State St, (☎963-0593). Open Mon–Fri 8.30am–5pm, Sat until 10am; zip code 93102.

On from Santa Barbara

A few miles along the coast from Santa Barbara, the twenty-five-year-old campus of the University of California at Santa Barbara – UCSB for short – is better-known for its volleyball teams than academics. The characterless town of ISLA VISTA borders the campus on the west, and staircases lead down the bluffs to a sandy **beach** that has some good tidepools, and, at the west end, a popular surfing area at Coal Oil Point; the estuary nearby has been preserved as a botanic study centre and nature refuge.

All along this part of the coast the **beaches** face almost due south, so the surf is very lively, and in winter the sun both rises and sets over the Pacific. About twenty miles out from Santa Barbara, **El Capitan State Beach** is a popular surfing beach, with many campsites, while **Refugio State Beach**, another three miles along, is one of the prettiest beaches in California, with stands of palm trees dotting the sands at the mouth of a small creek. Inland on Refugio Road, up the canyon high in the hills, stands Rancho El Cielo, the one-time Western White House of retired President **Ronald Reagan**. If the first two campsites are full, there are more spaces at **Gaviota State Beach**, ten miles west; it's not as pretty, but there's a fishing pier and a large wooden railway viaduct that bridges the mouth of the canyon. All state beach campsites cost $10 a night, $2 if you're on foot, and parking is $4; reservations are handled through MISTIX.

Just beyond Gaviota the highways split, US-101 heading inland and the more spectacular Hwy-1 branching off nearer the coast. Half a mile off the highway, but a world away from the speeding traffic, is the small **Las Cruces hot spring**, a pool of 95°F mineral water set in a shady, peaceful ravine. Take the turnoff for Hwy-1, but stay on the east side of the freeway and follow a small road to the dirt car park at the end. Walk along the trail up along the creek until you smell the sulphur.

The Santa Ynez Valley

An alternative to the coastal route out of Santa Barbara is to take Hwy-154 up and over the very steep **San Marcos Pass** through the **Santa Ynez Valley**, a pleasant route through a prime wine-growing region that's popular with leather-clad bikers and masochistic cyclists.

Three miles out of Santa Barbara, the **Chumash Painted Cave**, on Painted Caves Road, has walls painted with pre-conquest Chumash Native American art. On the other side of the San Marcos Pass the *Cold Springs Tavern*, under the massive concrete arch bridge at 5995 Stagecoach Road, is a good place to stop for a beer.

Two miles beyond the San Marcos Pass, Paradise Road follows the Santa Ynez River up to **Red Rocks**, an excellent swimming area amidst the stoney outcrops. **Lake Cachuma**, six miles further along Hwy-154, is a popular recreation area with a large **campsite** charging $8 a night; it's not actually a lake but a massive reservoir that holds the overstretched water supply for Santa Barbara.

Beyond the lake, Hwy-246 cuts off to SOLVANG, while Hwy-154 continues on through the vineyards around **LOS OLIVOS**, where wineries like the *Ballard Canyon Winery*, at 1825 Ballard Canyon Road, offer free tours and tastings (daily 11am–4pm).

Solvang and around

It is difficult to imagine anyone falling for the sham windmills and plastic storks that fill the town of **SOLVANG**, but people come by the coachload to see the community, which was established in 1911 by a group of Danes looking for a place to found a Danish folk school. Nowadays the town, three miles off US-101 on Hwy-246, lives off tourism, and locals dress up in traditional Danish costume to entertain visitors. Shops sell things imported from Denmark, but about the only things that make the town worth a stop are the fresh coffee and pastries.

There's marginally more interest in the **Mission Santa Ines** (daily 10am–5pm; $1) on the eastern edge of town, founded by Spanish friars a hundred years before the Danes arrived. The mission is unremarkable in itself, but has curious plaques thanking the Franciscan fathers for improving the lives of the native Chumash tribes, and a gift shop with an obsessive assortment of crucifices and devotional items. If this doesn't grab you either, you'd really do better to give it all a miss and stop by **Nojoqui Falls County Park**, six miles from Solvang off US-101, where a gentle ten-minute walk brings you to a 75-foot waterfall. The route to the park is, in any case, gorgeous, winding along Alisal Road under thick garlands of Spanish moss that dangle from a canopy of oak trees.

Lompoc

Hwy-1 splits off US-101 near Gaviota on a marvellous route through the inland valleys of the Santa Ynez mountains. **LOMPOC**, the only town for miles, calls itself the "flower-growing capital of the world", and claims to produce as much as three-quarters of the flower seeds sold on earth, the products of which during summer form a thick carpet of colour over the gently rolling landscape of the surrounding countryside. For information on the flowers contact the **Lompoc Valley Chamber of Commerce** (☎736-4567).

Lompoc is also the home of Vandenburg Air Force Base, where various new missiles and guidance systems get put through their paces over the Pacific Ocean. Their vapour trails are visible for miles, particularly at sunset, though the only way to see any of it up close is by the *Amtrak* Coast Starlight train, which runs along the coast north from Santa Barbara. The route was writer Jack Kerouac's favourite rail journey, and he worked for a while as a brakeman on the train.

The **beaches** along this section of coast are secluded and undeveloped, and nearly inaccessible much of the year, either because of bad weather or impending missile launches. **Jalama Beach**, at the end of a twisting fourteen-mile road off Hwy-1, spreads beneath coastal bluffs where you can camp overnight for $6; **Ocean Beach**, a broad strand at the mouth of the Santa Ynez River, ten miles west of Lompoc, has large sand dunes that are the nesting grounds of many seabirds.

La Purisima Mission

Four miles east of Lompoc, **La Purisima Mission State Park** (daily 9am–5pm; $1), is the most complete and authentic reconstruction of any of the 21 Spanish missions in California, and one of the best places to go to get an idea of what life might have been like in these early colonial settlements. *La Mision la Purisima Concepcion de Maria Santisima*, as it's called, was founded in 1787 on a site three miles north of here and by 1804 had converted around fifteen hundred Chumash tribespeople, though five hundred of these died in a smallpox epidemic over the next two years. In 1812 an earthquake destroyed all the buildings, and the fathers decided to move to the present site. The complex did not last long, however, after the missions were secularised in 1834, and over the next hundred years they were all but abandonded, pillaged by treasure-hunters and used as stables.

The buildings that stand here today were rebuilt on the ruins of the mission as part of a Depression-era project for the unemployed. From 1933 to 1940 over two hundred men lived and worked on the site, studying the remaining ruins and rebuilding the church and outbuildings using period tools and methods. Workers cavorted in puddles of mud to mix in the straw to make the adobe bricks, roof timbers were shaped with handtools, and even the colours of the paints were made from native plants.

The centre of the mission is a narrow church furnished as it would have been in the 1820s; nearby, at the entrance, small but engaging displays of documents and artefacts from the mission era and photographs of the reconstruction are housed in the old wagon house that serves as **museum** and gift shop. On week-ends throughout the summer there are "living history days", when the volunteers dress up as padres and Indians, and hold a traditional Mass, along with craft demonstrations – fun if you like that kind of thing.

Pismo Beach and Avila Beach

Most of the land along the Santa Maria River, 75 miles north of Santa Barbara, is given over to farming, and both Hwy-1 and US-101 pass through a number of small agriculture-based towns and villages. Some seem hardly to have changed since the 1930s, when thousands of Okies, as they were known, fled to the region from the Dustbowl of the Midwest – an era portrayed in John Steinbeck's novel, *The Grapes of Wrath*. They were notoriously poor: just off US-101, the little town of **NIPOMO** was the site of **Dorothea Lange**'s very famous 1936 photograph of a migrant mother who had just been forced to sell the tyres off her truck. Twenty-five miles north of Lompoc, Hwy-1 passes through the centre of **GUADALUPE**, a small farming village where Spanish far outnumbers English on the signs and advertisements and the dusty streets are lined by ramshackle saloons, cafés and vegetable stands. At the mouth of the river, five miles west of the highway at the end of Main Street, large **sand dunes** surround wetlands that are an essential habitat for endangered sea birds.

Pismo Beach

The dunes stretch up the coast for ten miles north, reaching as far as two miles inland and ending just south of the loud and characterless holiday town of **PISMO BEACH**, where the two highways merge. The central portion of the dunes, three miles south of the town, is open to off-road vehicle enthusiasts, who excite themselves flying up and over the sandpiles of the **Pismo Dunes Vehicle Recreation Area** in dune buggies and four-wheel-drives, motoring along the beach to reach them. Inland from the grey beach, the northern quarter of the dunes is protected as a **nature reserve**, and is a good place to hike around and play Lawrence of Arabia.

North from the nature reserve, between the town and the dune buggy area, a number of beachfront **campsites** line Hwy-1. The **Pismo Beach State Park**

(☎469-2684) has hot showers and beach camping for $5 a night, and is a good place to see the black and orange Monarch butterflies that spend the winter in the eucalyptus trees here and leave before the summer crowds arrive. The once-plentiful **Pismo clams** that gave the town its name, however (from the local Indian word *pismu*, or "blobs of tar" that the shells resemble), have been so depleted that any you might dig up here these days are probably under the four-and-a-half inch legal-minimum size.

Throughout the summer there's an hourly *SLOCAT* **bus** service (☎541-BUSS), costing 50¢ a ride, between Pismo and Avila Beach and the town of San Luis Obispo; *Greyhound* **buses** (☎543-2121) also stop on Price Street in downtown Pismo Beach five times a day in each direction.

Avila Beach

The coastline north of Pismo Beach is more rugged and interesting, with caves and tidepools below ever-eroding bluffs, and sea lions in the many coves. **Avila Hot Springs**, three miles north off US-101 on Avila Beach Drive, is a natural hot spring with a snack bar and grocery store between arcade games and a swimming pool; there's also **camping** for $12 a night.

The three-mile-long strand in front of the summer resort town of **AVILA BEACH** is the last outpost of Southern California beach life, with a high concentration of tumbledown dive-bars and cafés, and one good budget motel, the *Surfside Resort*, 256 Front Street (☎595-2300). Teenagers on the loose from their families cruise the boardwalk, while anyone old enough takes refuge in **bars** like *The Gang Plank Cafe* or *Miss Barbara's*, at 480 Front Street. The party atmosphere continues all summer long, and no one seems to mind the presence of nearby oil refineries and the **Diablo Canyon Nuclear Plant**, which straddles an earthquake fault six miles up the coast. (For what it's worth, three long bursts of a loud siren indicate catastrophe.) The scenic route north from here to San Luis Obispo, **See Canyon Drive**, cuts off north a mile from US-101, climbing gradually up the narrow, overgrown canyon between sharply profiled volcanic cones, with great views out over the Pacific.

San Luis Obispo

SAN LUIS OBISPO, ten miles northeast of Avila Beach and almost exactly halfway between LA and San Francisco, is a main stopoff for both *Amtrak* trains and *Greyhound* buses, and, although a few miles inland, makes the best base for exploring the nearby coast. It's still primarily an agricultural town, and a market centre for the farmers and ranchers of the surrounding countryside, something which contributes to its Middle American feeling – though the eight thousand students at the adjacent Cal Poly campus help keep things reasonably active. The town also has some of the Central Coast's best architecture, from turreted Victorian residences south of the town centre to some fine commercial buildings, not to mention any number of good places to eat, a couple of pubs, and – outside summer holiday weekends – places to stay for the asking. Though it's generally a quiet backwater, San Luis made the news a couple of years ago by enacting a controversial ban on smoking in all public places – bars, cafés, shops and offices – which is still in effect.

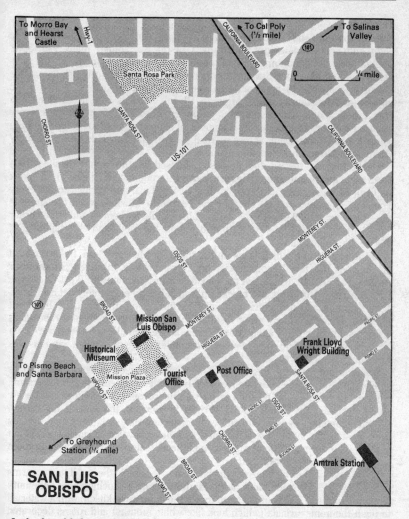

SAN LUIS OBISPO

Arrival and information

The *Greyhound* terminal is at 150 South Street (☎543-2121), half a mile down Higuera Street from the centre of town near US-101, and there are hourly bus connections with both LA and San Francisco. *Amtrak* trains (☎541-5028) stop once a day in each direction at the end of Santa Rosa Street, half a mile south of the business district. The **Chamber of Commerce** office at 1039 Chorro Street (☎543-1323) has a free walking-tour map highlighting much of the town's best architecture, and can help with finding a place to stay. To find out **what's on** and where, check out the free weekly *New Times* newspaper or tune to the excellent, non-commercial community radio stations, both of which have telephone events hotlines: KCPR 91.3 FM (☎544-4640) or the KOTR 94.3 FM (☎927-5021).

The town

San Luis is eminently walkable, with a compact core centred around the late eighteenth-century **Mission San Luis Obispo de Tolosa** (daily 9am–5pm; free), a fairly dark and unremarkable church that was the prototype for the now-ubiquitous red tiled roof, developed as a replacement for the original, flammable thatch in response to arson attacks by Native American tribes. Between the mission and the tourist office, **Mission Plaza**'s terraces step down along San Luis creek, along which footpaths meander, crisscrossed by bridges every hundred feet and overlooked by a number of shops and outdoor eateries on the south bank. Downstream, across a small park, is the San Luis Obispo County **Historical Museum** (Wed–Sun 10am–6pm; free), a low-key collection of local artefacts tending toward the domestic, housed in the richly detailed 1904 Carnegie Library building. **Higuera Street** (pronounced Hi-gear-a), a block south of Mission Plaza, is the main drag of San Luis, and springs to life every Thursday afternoon and evening for the **Farmer's Market**, when the street is closed to cars and filled with vegetable stalls, mobile barbeques and streetcorner musicians. All of San Luis comes out to sample the foods and entertainment of this weekly county fair.

Monterey Street, which leads up the hill from Mission Plaza, holds some of the best of the town's commercial buildings, notably the 1884 **Sinsheimer Building** at no. 849, which has the only cast-iron facade on the West Coast, the **J.P. Andrews Building**, two blocks up, which has an elaborately detailed frontage of granite and terracotta, and, a block further on, the art deco **Fremont Theatre**. There are many other distinguished **buildings** south of the business district, some of which – along Marsh Street above Santa Rosa Street – were built for railway workers and their families, a reminder of the days when San Luis was a bustling railway town.

Standing out from the many turn-of-the-century houses, built for middle-class families in a variety of exuberant late Victorian styles, with turrets and towers and other exotic touches, is a doctor's surgery on the corner of Santa Rosa and Pacific Street designed by **Frank Lloyd Wright** in 1955, at the end of his career. Wright's confident experimentation with forms and materials is as bold here as ever, most visibly in the abstracted images of the local volcanic landscape, cut-out of plywood to form a frieze of windows and the clerestory above the waiting room – complete with signature hearth.

If you have neither the time nor the inclination to sample the small-town charms of San Luis, at least stop to look at the **Madonna Inn**, a shocking pink behemoth along the highway just south of town that is the ultimate in kitsch, with a waterfall to flush the gents' urinals (which look like whale mouths) and rooms decorated according to themes, ranging from fairy-tale princesses to Stone Age cavemen. A very different sort of place is the **Shakespeare Press Museum** on the Cal Poly campus (Mon–Fri by appointment; ☎756-1108) – nothing to do with Shakespeare at all, but a great collection of old printing presses and lead typefaces, collected mainly from the frontier newspapers of California's Gold Rush towns.

San Luis Obispo accommodation

Monterey Street was the site of the world's first **motel** – the *Mo-tel Inn* – long gone now but with a spirit that lives on in the other motels that line the street up to its junction with US-101. Rates and availability fluctuate greatly depending on the time of year, but are generally quite inexpensive; there's also a bed-and-breakfast reservation service, *Megan's Friends* (☎544-4406), who can help you find a room in a local home or a nearby inn. There's no hostel, and the best camping nearby is south of town beyond Pismo Beach, or north off Hwy-1 in Morro Bay.

Adobe Inn, 1473 Monterey St (☎549-0321). Newly redecorated, English-owned motel with nice rooms from $55 a night, including breakfast.

La Cuesta Motor Inn, 2074 Monterey St (☎543-2777 or ☎1-800/543-2777). Equally popular with businesspeople and holiday travellers, with spacious modern rooms and a good sized swimming pool and spa. Doubles from $65.

Lamplighter, 1604 Monterey St (☎543-3709 or ☎1-800/843-6882). Older but comfortable motel, popular with families. Doubles from $50 a night.

Madonna Inn, 100 Madonna Way (☎543-3000). Local landmark (see description above) offering range of theme-decorated rooms from $80 a night.

Eating and drinking

Higuera Street is the place to head to **eat**, especially during the Thursday afternoon Farmer's Market, when cars are banned and local eateries set up barbecues and food stands amidst the jostling, good-natured crowds. There are also a couple of popular bars and cafés on and just off Higuera, around the Mission Plaza area.

Brubeck's, 726 Higuera St (☎541-8688). Upmarket bar and grill serving salads and grilled fresh fish, with live jazz most nights.

Chinatown Cafe, 861 Palm St (☎543-1818). Since the 1930s this family run place has been putting out the central coast's best Chinese food at low prices.

The Graduate, 990 Industrial Way (☎541-0969). A mile east of the centre, but worth a trip for the cheap beer and huge piles of food (all-you-can-eat specials before 9pm). Dancing nightly until 2am, popular with Cal Poly students.

Hudson's Grill, 1005 Monterey St (☎541-5999). Lively collegiate beer and burger bar that's open until midnight.

Linnaea's Cafe, 1110 Garden St, off Higuera (☎541-5888). Fairly new and very successful small cafe, serving up good espresso and a variety of tasty breakfasts and lunchtime sandwiches. After dark, the menu turns to top-notch pastries, pies and cakes, and yet more coffee; there's usually live music as well.

Spike's, 570 Higuera St (☎544-7157). With one of the best beer selections on the California Coast – you can join their "Drink your way around the world" club and get a free beer for every dozen you sample – nobody minds if the burgers aren't that special.

Tortilla Flats, 1051 Nipomo St at Higuera (☎544-7575). Raucous, neon-lit Mexican restaurant, better known for copious margaritas than great food, but with free Happy Hour nachos and dancing from 9pm.

Morro Bay and the coast north to Cambria

North of San Luis Obispo the highways diverge again, US-101 – and the trains and buses – speeding up through the Salinas Valley (see p.254), while Hwy-1 takes the scenic route along the coast. **Morro Rock**, twelve miles on, was (local lore claims) named by the sixteenth-century explorer Vizcaino, who thought it looked like the Moorish domes of southern Spain. Nowadays it's off-limits to the public in order to protect the nesting areas of the endangered peregrine falcons; in any case it's most impressive from a distance, dominating the fine harbour at **MORRO BAY**, where the local fishing industry unloads its catch to sell in the many fish markets along the waterfront. The adjacent town is accessible from San Luis Obispo via *SLOCAT* **bus** #7, though apart from the many seafood restaurants the only places worth

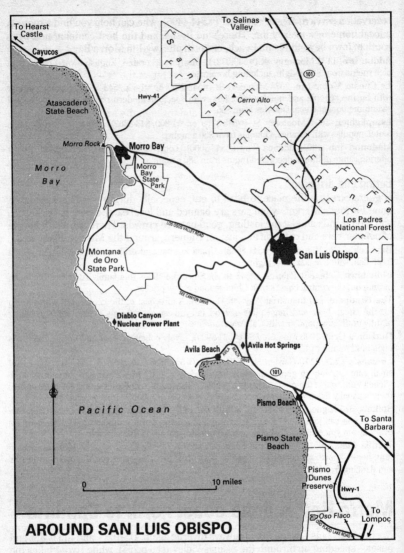

AROUND SAN LUIS OBISPO

coming here for are spread out around the bay, miles from public transport. One of the best views of the rock and surrounding coastline can be had from the top of **Cerro Alto**, eight miles east of Morro Bay off Hwy-41, a 2620-foot volcanic cone with good hiking and **camping** for $5 a night.

Closer in, on a point above the bay a mile south of town at the end of Main Street but providing a good view of Morro Rock, there's a small **Museum of Natural History** (daily 10am–5pm; $1); the **campsite** across the street, in Morro Bay State Park (reservable through MISTIX), costs $10 a night and has hot showers. Across the bay, the thin sandy peninsula that protects the harbour is hard to reach except by boat, or via a two-mile hike from Los Osos Valley Road – it's entirely undeveloped and about the only place where you stand a chance of finding any of the once-abundant Pismo Clams.

Montana de Oro State Park, four miles south at the end of Los Osos Valley Road, is much more primitive than the Morro Bay park, and has some excellent tidepools. The windswept promontory stands solidly against the crashing sea, offering excellent hiking along the shore and through the sagebrush and eucalyptus trees of the upland hillsides, which in the spring are covered in golden poppies.

The next town north along Hwy-1, **CAYUCOS**, was originally a small port built by Englishman James Cass in the 1870s, though it's now a sleepy place ranged along sandy beaches. Surprisingly, it has some of the area's best **nightlife** in the *Cayucos Tavern*, in the heart of the two-block-long ramshackle centre, with live bands at weekends, and late-night poker games for gamblers.

The small town of **CAMBRIA**, ten miles north, is a good place to stay if you're visiting Hearst Castle, another ten miles further on. Hidden away in a wooded valley half a mile off Hwy-1, Cambria was an established town serving the local ranchers and fishermen long before Hearst Castle became the region's prime tourist attraction and to some extent these days trades on its past, with a synthetic Olde English quarter along the highway. Skip this and head directly to the older and much nicer section half a mile east on Main Street, where the shops, restaurants and art galleries cater as much for locals as visitors.

There's not a lot to see or do in Cambria, but for **food and drink** the town excels. One of the best breakfasts this side of anywhere can be had at *Barbara's Cafe*, 2094 Main Street, while *Camozzi's Saloon*, 2262 Main Street, is a rumbustious cowboy bar with occasional live bands. For a **place to stay**, try the *Bluebird Motel* (☎927-4634) at 1880 Main Street, with rooms from $35. The *Cambria Pines Lodge* (☎927-4200) on Burton Drive on the hill above the town, caters to large groups and conferences, but has very large, family size rooms from $65 for a double, and sometimes live music in its rustic, comfortable main bar. There are also many bed-and-breakfasts in town, starting at $60 a night for a double; for details, contact the **Chamber of Commerce**, 767 Main Street (daily 10am–4pm; ☎927-3624).

Hearst Castle and San Simeon

Forty-five miles northwest of San Luis Obispo, **HEARST CASTLE** sits on a hilltop overlooking rolling ranchlands and the Pacific Ocean. Far and away the biggest single attraction for miles, and second only to Disneyland in the state, the former holiday home of publishing magnate **William Randolph Hearst** brings in over a million visitors a year, and is one of the most opulent and extravagant houses in the world. Its interior combines walls, floors and ceilings stolen from European churches and castles with Gothic fireplaces and Moorish tiles, and is filled to over-flowing with Greek vases and medieval tapestries. It's actually more of a complex of buildings than a "castle". Four guesthouses surround the hundred-room main *Casa Grande* – the whole thing surrounded originally by a free-roaming zoo of lions, tigers, bears and zebras – in which Hearst held court over the most famous politicians and movie stars of the 1920s and 1930s. Winston Churchill, Charlie Chaplin, George Bernard Shaw and Charles Lindbergh were just a few who accepted Hearst's invitation to come and stay for as long as they liked.

Hearst Castle, which Hearst himself referred to as "the ranch" (the official name is now "Hearst-San Simeon State Historic Park"), manifests all the subtlety and lightness of touch one would expect from the man whose domination of the national media inspired Orson Welles' classic film *Citizen Kane*. Construction began after his mother's death in 1919, on the southern edge of the 250,000-acre ranch he inherited. The work, managed by architect Julia Morgan, was never actually completed: rooms would often be torn out as soon as they were finished in order to accommodate some bits and pieces of old buildings Hearst had just acquired, and much of the rough reinforced concrete of the structure is still exposed. The main facade, a twin-towered copy of a Mudejar cathedral, stands at the top of steps which curve up from an expansive swimming pool filled with pure spring water and lined by a Greek colonnade and repro statues. Inside the house, ketchup and mustard bottles complete the place-settings of fine crystal and china on the long dark oak table of the baronial dining hall, festooned with banners from Siena's *Palio*.

Hearst Castle Practicalities

You have to take one of the guided **tours** (daily 8am–3pm, until 5pm in summer; $10 each) if you want to see the house and grounds. Tour One, an introductory spin around a guesthouse and the main rooms of the *Casa Grande* which includes a short film, is best for the first visit. If you're coming back a second time, or are simply fascinated (and rich) enough to stay for a whole day, there are three other

---

W.R. HEARST – *CITIZEN KANE*

It would be quite easy to portray William Randolph Hearst (or "W.R") as a power-mad monster, but in retrospect he seems more like a very rich, over-indulged little boy. Born in 1863 as the only son of a multi-millionaire mining engineer, he was avidly devoted to his mother, Phoebe Apperson Hearst, one of California's most sincere and generous philanthropists, a founder of the University of California and the *Traveler's Aid* society.

Hearst learned his trade in New York City working for the inventor of inflammatory "Yellow Journalism", Joseph Pulitzer, who had four rules for how to sell newspapers: one – emphasise the sensational; two – elaborate on the facts; three – manufacture the news; four – use games and contests. When he published his own newspaper, Hearst took this advice to heart, his *Morning Journal* fanning the flames of American imperialism to ignite the Spanish-American War of 1898. As he told his correspondents in Cuba: "You provide the pictures, and I'll provide the war". Hearst eventually controlled an empire that at its peak during the 1930s sold twenty-five percent of the newspapers in the entire country, including two other New York papers, the *Washington Times*, and the *Detroit News* – as well as *Cosmopolitan* and *Good Housekeeping* magazines. In California Hearst's power was even more pronounced, with his San Francisco and Los Angeles papers controlling over sixty percent of the total market.

Somewhat surprisingly, considering his war-mongering and extreme nationalism, Hearst was fairly middle-of-the-road politically, a lifelong Democrat who served two terms in the House of Representatives but failed in bids to be elected Mayor of New York and President of the US. Besides his many newspapers, Hearst owned eleven radio stations and two movie studios, in which he made his mistress Marion Davies a star. He was forced to sell off most of his holdings by the end of the Depression, but continued to exert power and influence until his death in 1951 aged 88.

tours offered: Tour Two takes in the upper floors of the main house, including Hearst's library and bedroom suite, which occupies an entire floor; Tour Three concentrates on one of the guesthouses; Tour Four emphasises the grounds and gardens (summer only). Each tour includes a look at the swimming pool. For more information, or to arrange for a wheelchair – there are lots of stairs – phone (☎927-2020).

All tours take about two hours, including the half-hour bus ride each way up and down the hill, and leave from the car park and visitors center on Hwy-1, where you buy tickets. Reservations, always a good idea and necessary in summer, when tours sell out hours in advance, can be made through MISTIX (☎1-800/444-7275). While waiting for your tour bus, find out more about Hearst and his castle from the excellent but poorly signposted **museum** (daily 9am–5pm, free) in the rear half of the visitors centre, beyond the point where you board the buses.

The only way to get to Hearst Castle without your own transport is on an organised **coach trip**. Three companies offer these: from San Luis Obispo *San Simeon Stages* (☎772-3562; $32 per person) leave daily at 7am, returning early afternoon; from Monterey, *Steinbeck Country Tours* (☎408/625-5107; $45) and *Gray Line Tours* (☎408/373-4989; $40) leave at 8am for the hundred-mile trip along the scenic Big Sur coast, returning at 6pm. Prices include transport and a guaranteed ticket on the introductory tour.

San Simeon . . . and north

The boarded-up pier of **SAN SIMEON**, an all-but-abandoned harbour town along the coast just north of Hearst Castle, is where all of Hearst's treasures were unloaded, as were the many tons of concrete and steel that went into the building of the house. Before the Hearsts bought up the land, San Simeon was a whaling and shipping port, of which all that remains is a one-room schoolhouse and the 1852 *Sebastian's Store*, a combination post office, café, and souvenir shop. The beach south of the pier is protected by San Simeon Point, which hooks out into the Pacific, making it safe for swimming. Along the highway three miles south there's a concentrated blot of **motels**, petrol stations and fast-food restaurants – handy if you arrive in the middle of the night; and there's **camping** available along the beach for $10 a night, again reservable through MISTIX.

North of Hearst Castle the coastline is mostly rolling grasslands and cattle ranches, still owned and run by the Hearst family, with few buildings on the distant hills. An exception to the isolation is the *Piedras Blancas Motel* (☎927-4202), seven miles north, which has double rooms off-peak for $45. Beyond here the highway seems to drop off in mid-air, marking the southern edge of Big Sur, probably the most dramatic stretch of coastline in America.

The Salinas Valley and Steinbeck Country

If you're in a hurry, US-101 through the **Salinas Valley** takes four hours to cover the 220 miles between San Luis Obispo and San Francisco, compared to the full day (at least) it takes to drive the more scenic coast along Hwy-1 through Big Sur. In any case, as both *Greyhound* and *Amtrak* take the inland route, you may not have the choice; of the two, *Greyhound* is for once the better option, as its local buses stop at all the small, rural towns. The four-lane freeway closely follows the path of *El Camino Real*, the trail that linked the 21 Spanish **missions** – each a day's travel from its neighbour – through the miles of farmland along the Salinas River that are some of the most fertile in the nation.

This region is also popularly known as **Steinbeck Country** for having nurtured the Nobel Prize-winning imagination of writer **John Steinbeck**, whose naturalistic stories and novels, including the epic *East of Eden*, were set in and around the valley. To get a good impression of the character of the place while driving through, tune in to the non-stop Hank Williams songs on AM1010.

The Salinas Valley

North of San Luis Obispo over the steep Cuesta Pass, US-101 drops down into the **Salinas Valley**, and, before long, **ATASCADERO**: a small town laid out to a curiously grand plan in 1914 that centres on its Palladian **City Hall**, a huge redbrick edifice whose domed rotunda now houses a small **museum** (Mon–Sat 1–4pm; free) describing the area's history.

PASO ROBLES, eight miles north, is a thriving little town surrounded by horse ranches, nut farms and a number of small, family operated **wineries** that are among the finest in the state. Take a free and friendly tour (daily 10am–5pm) of the *Estrella River* winery, six miles east of town on Hwy-46. Another ten miles east, at the junction of Hwy-41 near Cholame, pay your respects at the small monument on the site where **James Dean** met his maker in a silver Porsche Speedster in 1955.

It's worth taking a break from your journey to have a look at the most intact and authentic of California's Spanish missions, **Mission San Miguel Arcangel** (daily 9.30am–4.30pm; donations), just off US-101, two blocks south of the *Greyhound* station in the small town of **SAN MIGUEL**. Built in 1816, it's the only mission in the chain not to have suffered the revisionist tendencies of a restoration. It was actually used for a while as a saloon and a dancehall, though the chapel has been left pretty much unscathed, with colourful painted decoration and a marvellous sunburst reredos. The other buildings are interesting in their rough imprecision, with irregularly arched openings and unplastered walls forming a courtyard around a cactus garden.

There's a second mission, accessible only by car, twenty miles west of US-101 along the Jolon Road (G-18), which splits off the highway twelve miles north of San Miguel. The **Mission San Antonio de Padua** (daily 9.30am–5pm; donations) is a rarely visited restoration of the 1771 settlement that gives a very good idea of what life might have been like for the missionaries and their converts. This mission was among the most prosperous of the entire chain, and around the extensive grounds, in a wide valley of oak trees and tall grasses, a number of scattered exhibits describe the work that went on in the long-abandoned vineyard, tannery and gristmill.

There's a monastic peace to Mission San Antonio these days, and the brown-robed Franciscan friars who live here are rarely disturbed, despite being in the middle of the Hunter Liggett Army Base; indeed the only sign of the military is at the gates of the base, five miles east of the mission, where you'll have to show your passport or some form of identification. The large house across the valley from the mission used to belong to William Randolph Hearst, who sold it and most of the land between here and Hearst Castle to the government in 1940. The **Nacimiento-Fergusson Road** leads from the mission on a harrowing but picturesque journey over the mountains, past three $4-a-night **campsites**, to Big Sur (see p.257).

Nearby **JOLON** has a market and petrol station, and the washed-out ruins of an 1840s stagecoach stop at the Old Dutton Hotel. The San Antonio Reservoir, five miles southeast, has swimming, **camping** and showers along the west shore, as does the Nacimiento Reservoir further south.

The Jolon Road loops back to US-101 at **KING CITY**: "the most metropolitan cow town in the West", as it likes to be known. On the town's western edge, just off US-101, San Lorenzo Park is the site of the **Agricultural and Rural Life Museum** (daily 9am–5pm; free), to where Monterey County has moved old barns, farmhouses and a one-room schoolhouse. The park also has an $8-a-night **campsite** with hot showers, along the Salinas River. Backpacking permits for the **Ventana Wilderness** in the Santa Lucia Mountains, which divide the Salinas Valley from the Big Sur coast, are handled by the **US Forest Service Office** at 406 S Mildred Avenue (☎968-1578).

Soledad and the Pinnacles National Monument

SOLEDAD, a quiet farming community twenty-five miles further north, has a definite Mexican flavour, its *panaderias* selling cakes and fresh tortillas and making it a good place to stop for a bite to eat, or to stock up on food and drink before heading up into the hills and the bizarre **Pinnacles National Monument**, twelve miles east on Hwy-146 – where grotesque volcanic spires stand out in brilliant red and gold colours against the blue sky. Best visited in the spring, when the air is still cool and wildflowers cover the hillsides, a two-mile trail leads from the **campsite** at the end of Hwy-146, the only road, to the multi-coloured, 600-foot face of the **Balconies** outcrop – good for **rock-climbing** – and a nearby series of talus **caves**, formed by huge boulders that have become wedged between the walls of the narrow canyons. The pitch-black caves were popular with bandits who would hide out here after robbing stagecoaches. There's a visitors centre on the eastern side of the monument but the hundred-mile detour to reach it is hardly worth the bother, since most of what there is to see is on the west side.

Mission Soledad (daily except Tuesday 10am–4pm; donations), just west of US-101 on the south side of town, lay neglected for over a hundred years until there was little left but a pile of mud. The mission was never a great success, perhaps because of its full name, which translates as the "most sorrowful mystery of the solitude", suffering through a history of epidemics, floods and crop failures. Parts have been dutifully restored, though the **ruins** adjacent to the rebuilt church are the most evocative section.

More pleasurable are the **Paraiso Hot Springs** (☎678-2882; $10), five miles further west, high above Soledad in the foothills of the Santa Lucia Mountains: a palm-treed oasis looking out across the Salinas Valley to the Gabilan Mountains and the Pinnacles National Monument. The natural hot springs here were popular with the local Indians for their healing properties, and have been operated as a commercial venture since 1895; you can **camp** here overnight for an additional $4 per person.

While you pamper yourself in the steamy water, it's worth remembering that most Californians know Soledad for one thing only: as site of the **Soledad State Penitentiary** – a grim building looming alongside US-101 two miles north of town where Black militant "Soledad Brother" George Jackson was imprisoned for many years.

Salinas

The second-largest city between LA and San Francisco, and the seat of Monterey County, **SALINAS**, twenty miles north, is a sprawling agricultural town of 85,000 people. It's best known as the birthplace of Nobel Prize-winning writer **John Steinbeck**, and for the **California Rodeo**, the biggest in the state, held here during the third week in July. These attractions aside, you may well find yourself here anyway: Salinas is a main stop for *Greyhound* buses and the Coast Starlight train, and makes an excellent and inexpensive base for exploring the perhaps more obvious attractions of the **Monterey Peninsula**, twenty miles away over the Santa Lucia mountains, with the *MST* bus #21 making the 45-minute trip every hour (see p.263).

Salinas practicalities
Greyhound buses (☎424-1626) between LA and San Francisco stop hourly in the centre of town at 200 Salinas Street, and *Amtrak* trains (☎422-7458) once a day in each direction, two blocks away at 40 Railroad Avenue. For a **place to stay** try the *Traveller's Hotel* at 16 E Gabilan Street (☎758-1198), two blocks from the Greyhound station, which has slightly seedy double rooms for $18 a night; otherwise choose from the many $30-a-night **motels** along Main Street on either side of US-101. For help with finding a place to stay, and for a free **map** and guide to the places which Steinbeck wrote about, contact the **Chamber of Commerce** at 119 E Alisal Street (Mon–Fri 9am–5pm; ☎424-7611). There are quite a few good **Mexican restaurants** around the city, the best and most central being *Rosita's Armory Café*, 231 Salinas Street, open daily from 9am until 3am for fine food and stiff margaritas.

The town ... and Steinbeck Country
Salinas and the agricultural valley to the south are often bracketed together as Steinbeck Country. The writer **John Steinbeck** was born and raised in Salinas, though there's not a lot left to remind you of his presence: he left the town in his mid-twenties to live in Monterey and later in New York City. His childhood home at 132 Central Avenue has sadly been turned into an English-style tearoom, but the **Steinbeck Room** of the public library two blocks away at 110 W San Luis Street (daily 10am–6pm; free) displays a variety of manuscripts and memorabilia.

Steinbeck's **stories** are as valuable and interesting for their historical content as for their narratives. *The Grapes of Wrath*, his best-known work, was made into a film starring Henry Fonda while still at the top of the bestseller lists, having captured the popular imagination for its portrayal of the miseries of the Joad family on their migration to California from the Dust Bowl. *Cannery Row* followed in 1945, a nostalgic portrait of the Monterey fisheries, which ironically went into steep decline the year the book was published. Steinbeck spent the next four years writing *East of Eden*, an allegorical retelling of the biblical story of Cain and Abel against the landscape of the Salinas Valley, in which he expresses many of the values which underlie the rest of his work. Much of Steinbeck's writing is concerned with the dignity of labour, and with the inequalities of an economic system that "allows children to go hungry in the midst of rotting plenty". Although he was circumspect about his own political stance, when *The Grapes of Wrath* became a bestseller in 1939 there was a violent backlash against Steinbeck in Salinas for what were seen as his Communist sympathies.

To this day the town is a hotbed of labour disputes, with the gap between the wealthy owners and agribusiness empires that run the giant farms and the low-paid manual labourers who pick the produce still unbridged. In the 1960s and early 1970s the United Farm Workers union, under the leadership of Cesar Chavez and Dolores Huerta, had great success in organising and demanding better pay and conditions for the almost exclusively Latino workforce, most notably masterminding a very effective boycott of the valley's main product, lettuce. But in the 1990s, workers are once again under siege, with wages less than half of what they were a decade ago amidst increasing worries about the dangers of exposure to pesticides and agricultural chemicals.

Knowing this, Salinas is definitely not the sort of place where you'd expect to find a large public sculpture by a major avant-garde artist, but **Claes Oldenburg's** *Hat in Three Stages of Landing* is just that: a triad of giant yellow steel cowboy hats floating above the grass between the Salinas Community Art Gallery and the Rodeo Grounds, at 940 N Main Street. On the outskirts of town, at the end of West Laurel Drive half a mile west of US-101, the **Boronda Adobe** (daily 9.30am–5pm; free) lies in the middle of rich farmland, virtually unaltered since its construction in 1848, alongside other historic structures that have been brought to the site as part of an expanding regional history centre.

Between Salinas and the Monterey Peninsula, twenty miles distant via Hwy-68, are a couple of other places of divergent interest. **SPRECKELS**, five miles south-west, is a small factory town with an arts-and-crafts feel, built in 1898 for employees of the Spreckels sugar factory, at the time the largest in the world: the small torchlike wooden objects on the gable ends of the many workers' cottages are supposed to represent sugar beets. Parts of the movie *East of Eden* were filmed here, including the famous scene when James Dean – playing Cal – hurls blocks of ice down a chute to get his father's attention.

Along Hwy-68 halfway to Monterey is **Laguna Seca Raceway** (☎373-1811), where race driver and part-time actor Paul Newman keeps in practice on the two-mile road course; races are held throughout the summer, and there's **camping** for $5 a night, year-round.

Big Sur

The California coastline is at its most spectacular along the ninety miles of rocky cliffs and crashing sea known as **BIG SUR**. This is not the lazy beachfront of Southern California, but a sublime landscape at the edge of a continent, where redwood groves line river canyons and the Santa Lucia mountains rise straight out of the blue Pacific. Named by the Spanish *El Pais Grande del Sur*, the "big country to the south" (of their colony at Monterey), it's still a wild and undeveloped region, except for occasional outposts along the narrow **Hwy-1**, which follows a tortuous, exhilarating route carved out of bedrock cliffs five hundred feet above the Pacific Ocean, passing by mile after mile of rocky coves and steep, narrow canyons.

Before the highway was completed in 1937, the few inhabitants of Big Sur had to be almost entirely self-sufficient, farming, raising cattle and trapping sea otters for their furs. The only connections with the rest of the world were by infrequent steamship to Monterey, or by a nearly impassable trail over the mountains to the Salinas Valley. Perhaps surprisingly, even fewer people live in the area today than did a hundred years ago, and most of the land is still owned by a very few families, many of whom are descendants of Big Sur's original pioneers. Locals have banded together to fight US government plans to allow offshore oil-drilling, and to protect the land from obtrusive development. If you'd like to know more about Big Sur's history and the contentious present, an excellent free **guide** to the area, *El Sur Grande*, is available at ranger stations and the post office in the village of Big Sur.

The coast is also the protected habitat of the sea otter, and grey whales pass by close to the shore on their annual winter migration. Visit in April or May to see the vibrant wildflowers and lilac-coloured ceanothus bushes, though the sun shines longest, without the morning coastal fog, in early autumn through until November. Hardly anyone braves the turbulent winters, when violent storms drop most of the eighty inches of rain that fall each year, often taking sections of the highway with it into the sea. Summer weekends, however, see the roads and campsites packed to overflowing – though even in peak season, if you're willing to walk a mile or two, it's still easy to get away from it all.

The best way to see Big Sur is slowly, leaving the car behind to wander through the many parks and wilderness preserves, where a ten-minute walk can put miles between you and any sign of the rest of the world. Hitching is quite good all along the narrow Hwy-1, which is also a perennial favourite with cyclists, and the only **public transport** is by *MST* bus from Monterey, twice a day in each direction (see "travel details" at the end of the chapter).

Much the most interesting stretch of Big Sur is the northern end, ranged along the wide and clear Big Sur River, twenty-five miles south of Monterey and focusing on **Pfeiffer Big Sur State Park**, where you can swim among giant boulders, hike up redwood canyons to a waterfall or sunbathe on a fine sandy beach. The nearby village of Big Sur is the only settlement of any size, with a number of grocery stores, petrol stations and a few places to eat and drink.

We've gathered all our **accommodation** and **eating** recommendations for the Big Sur area into the comprehensive listings starting on p.261.

The southern extent of Big Sur

The southern coastline of Big Sur is the region at its most gentle – not unlike Portugal's Algarve, with sandy beaches hidden away below eroding yellow-ochre cliffs. The landscape grows more extreme the further north you go. Twenty miles north of Hearst Castle, a steep trail leads down along Salmon Creek to a coastal waterfall, while the chaparral-covered hills above were booming during the 1880s with the gold mines of the **Los Burros Mining District**.

Another ten miles north, the cliffs get steeper and the road more perilous around the vista point at **Willow Creek**, where you can watch the surfers and the sea otters playing in the waves. **Jade Cove**, a mile north, takes its name from the translucent California jade stones that are sometimes found here, mainly by scuba divers offshore. The rocky cove is a ten-minute walk from the highway, along a trail marked by a wooden stile in the cattle fence.

Just beyond the Plaskett Creek **campsite**, half a mile north, **Sand Dollar Beach** is a good place to enjoy the surf or watch for **hang-gliders**, who launch themselves from sites in the mountains off the one-lane Plaskett Ridge Road. This steep road is good fun on a mountain bike, and passes by a number of free primitive campsites along the ridge, ending at the paved Nacimiento-Fergusson Road. Check at the **Pacific Valley ranger station** (☎927-4211) for up-to-date information on backcountry camping, since some areas may be closed in summer during the peak of the fire season. They also handle the twenty-five permits a day allowed to people wanting to hang-glide, ten of which are given out on a first-come first-served basis on the day. **Pacific Valley Center**, just north of the ranger station, has a petrol station, a grocery store and a good coffee shop, open from 8am until dark.

The Nacimiento-Fergusson Road twists up the canyon over the mountains to the Salinas Valley past the well-preserved Mission San Antonio de Padua (see p.254), though the views are better coming the other way. Two miles north, Limekiln Creek is named after the hundred-year-old limekilns that survive in good condition along the creek behind the privately owned **campsite**. In the 1880s local limestone was burned in these kilns to extract lime powder for use as cement, then carried on a complex aerial tramway to be loaded on to ships at Rocklands Landing. The ships that carried the lime to Monterey brought in most of the supplies to this isolated area.

ESALEN, ten miles further north, is named after the local Native Americans, the first tribe in California to be made culturally extinct. Before they were wiped out, they frequented the healing waters of the natural **hot spring** here, at the top of a cliff two hundred feet above the raging Pacific surf – now owned and operated by the *Esalen Institute* (☎667-2335) and open weekday nights from midnight to 5am for a $5 charge. Since the 1960s, when all sorts of people came to Big Sur to smoke pot and get back to nature, Esalen has been at the forefront of the "New Age" human potential movement. Today's devotees tend to arrive in BMWs on Friday nights for the expensive, reservation-only massage treatments, yoga workshops and seminars on Eastern religion and philosophy.

Julia Pfeiffer Burns State Park (daily dawn–dusk), three miles north of Esalen along McWay Creek, has some of the best day hikes in the Big Sur area: a twenty-minute walk from the parking area leads under the highway along the edge of the cliff to an overlook of a waterfall that crashes into a cove below Saddle Rock. A less-travelled path leads down from Hwy-1 two miles north of the waterfall (at milepost 37.85) through a two-hundred-foot-long tunnel to the wave-washed remains of a small wharf at Partington Cove, one of the few places in Big Sur where you can reach the sea.

Nepenthe and Pfeiffer Beach

Further north, or at the south end of the *MST* #21 bus route from Monterey, stands **Nepenthe**, a complex of restaurants and shops named after the mythical drug which induces forgetfulness of grief. On the hilltop site, where starcrossed lovers Orson Welles and Rita Hayworth once shared a cabin, the excellent restaurant here has been run since the 1960s by the family of master-knitter and painter, Kaffe Fassett, who grew up in Big Sur – though *Cafe Amphora*, on a rooftop terrace just down the hill, is more affordable and has equally impressive views. Downstairs there's an outdoor sculpture gallery and a decent bookstore, including works by, among others, Henry Miller, who lived in the area on and off until the 1960s. The **Henry Miller Memorial Library** (daily, hours vary; ☎667-2574) across Hwy-1 displays an informal collection of first-edition books and mementoes of the writer's life, collected – along with countless stray cats – in the house of Miller's old friend Emil White.

Big Sur's best beach is two miles north, where a barely marked road leads west from Hwy-1 a mile down Sycamore Canyon to **Pfeiffer Beach**, a sometimes windy, white sand beach dominated by a charismatic hump of rock whose colour varies from brown to red to orange in the changing light. Park where you can at the end of the road, and walk through an archway of cypress trees along the lagoon to the sandy beach, which closes at dusk.

Big Sur River and village

Two miles north of Pfeiffer Beach, and 65 miles north of Hearst Castle, Hwy-1 drops down behind a coastal ridge into the valley of the Big Sur River, where the village of **BIG SUR** and its range of cafés, grocery stores, motels and petrol stations along a half-mile stretch of Hwy-1 is probably the most feasible base for seeing Big Sur. For details of eating and accommodation options, see the listings below.

Just south of the village, **Pfeiffer Big Sur State Park** is one of the most beautiful and enjoyable parks in California, with miles of hiking trails and excellent swimming along the Big Sur River – which in late spring and summer has deep swimming holes among the large boulders in the bottom of the narrow steep-walled gorge. The water is clean and clear, nude sunbathing is tolerated (except on national holidays, when the park tends to be overrun with swarms of screaming children) and since it's sheltered a mile or so inland the weather is warmer and sunnier than elsewhere along the coast. This is also the centre for information on all the other parks in the area, and the main **campsite** in the entire Big Sur area.

The most popular hiking trail in the park leads to the sixty-foot **Pfeiffer Falls**, half a mile up a narrow canyon shaded by Redwood trees from a trailhead opposite the entrance. The thoroughly functional bridges over the river have an understated grace, as does the nearby amphitheatre – built by the Civilian Conservation Corps during the Depression – where rangers give campfire talks and slide shows about the Big Sur area.

Just south of the park entrance, across the road from the Big Sur **post office**, the US Forest Service **ranger station** (☎667-2423) handles the camping permits that are required for the Ventana Wilderness in the mountains above. A popular hike leads steeply up from the Pine Ridge trailhead behind the station six miles into the mountains to **Sykes Hot Springs**, just downstream from the free **campsite** at Sykes Camp along the Big Sur River, continuing fifteen miles over the Santa Lucia mountains to the **Tassajara Zen Buddhist Center**, where the monks may reward your efforts with an invitation to bathe in the natural hot springs.

Big Sur accommodation

In keeping with Big Sur's backwoodsy qualitites, most of the available accommodation is in rustic (but rarely inexpensive) mountain lodges, and the very few rooms on offer are full most nights throughout the summer, especially on weekends. Mid-range accommodation is limited to a few cabins and motels, usually adjoining a privately operated campground or right along the highway, and not really ideal for getting the total Big Sur experience. Almost everything is lined up in what's known as Big Sur village, along a six-mile stretch of Hwy-1 around the Big Sur River, 25 miles south of Carmel.

All the listings below are ordered from south to north.

Lodges and cabins

Big Sur Lodge, in Pfeiffer Burns State Park (☎667-2171). Good-sized modern cabins arranged around a large swimming pool; popular with families, and costing $70–110 a night.

Deetjen's Big Sur Inn, on Hwy-1 near Julia Pfeiffer State Park (☎667-2377). The southernmost, oldest and perhaps nicest of the Big Sur lodges, with twenty very different rooms handcrafted from thick redwood planks, all with fireplaces and costing from $55–110 a night.

Fernwood, off Hwy-1 in the heart of the Big Sur village, (☎667-2422). Family orientated resort right on the Big Sur river, offering camping spots ($9–15) and accommodation in rustic cabins ($55–75 a night for two people). See under "Camping" below for further, similar establishments.

River Inn Resort, at the north end of the Big Sur village (☎667-2700 or ☎1-800/548-3610). Woodsy lodge with a handful of very nice (and very pricey) rooms overlooking the river, and more basic motel-style rooms across Hwy-1; rates vary from $45 to $130 a night.

Camping

Much the most exciting option for campers are the **public campsites** all along the Big Sur coast, and a few less developed ones in the mountains above, where you can also see deer, bobcats and mountain lions. Sites along the coast are popular year-round, and all are available for up to $10 a night ($2 if you're on foot or bicycle) on a first-come, first-camped basis, so get there early in the day to ensure a space. Reservations are, however, only taken at Pfeiffer Big Sur State Park, through MISTIX.

There are also four commercially operated **campsites** around the village of Big Sur: *Ventana* (☎667-2331); *Fernwood* (☎667-2422); *Riverside* (☎667-2414); and *Big Sur* (☎667-2322). All cost about $20 a night, offer deluxe facilities, and accept reservations; they also let cabins for $60 a night.

Plaskett Creek. Thirty miles north of Hearst Castle, across the highway from the ocean.

Kirk Creek. Five miles north and more exposed, but right on the ocean. The *Nacimiento* and *Ponderosa* campsites are up in the hills about ten miles inland on the Nacimiento Fergusson Road.

Julia Pfeiffer-Burns State Park. Fifteen miles north, with free but very basic walk-in sites for backpackers just south of the main gate.

Pfeiffer Big Sur State Park. Just south of the village of Big Sur, this is the main campsite in the area, with hot showers, a well-stocked store and a launderette.

Andrew Molera State Park. Backpackers only, free and bang on the ocean at the mouth of the Big Sur River.

Botcher's Gap. Eight miles inland from Hwy-1 on Palo Colorado Road, eighteen miles north of the village of Big Sur. A good base for exploring the Ventana Wilderness.

Big Sur eating and drinking

Most of the places to eat and drink in Big Sur are attached to the inns and resorts listed above. Many of these are fairly basic burger-and-beer bars right along the highway, but there are a few special ones worth searching out, some for their good food and others for their views of the Pacific. Because of its isolation, prices anywhere in Big Sur are around twenty-five percent higher than you'd pay in town.

Cafe Amphora, at Nepenthe, (☎667-2660). Subtly prepared wholefood concoctions served up on a sunny, outdoor terrace. Big Sur's best views and a dozen healthy and flavoursome variations on Eggs Benedict, plus a range of coffees and ice-cold bottles of Red Tail Ale. Up the hill, the more steak-and-seafood orientated *Nepenthe* (☎667-2345) has a raging fireplace and a somewhat James Bondish, apres-ski atmosphere.

Deetjen's Big Sur Inn, on Hwy-1 near Julia Pfeiffer State Park (☎667-2377). Excellent, unhurried breakfasts ($5) and a variety of top-quality fish and vegetarian dinners ($12–25) in homely, redwood-panelled room.

Fernwood Burgers, Hwy-1 in Big Sur village (☎667-2422). For burgers or fish-and-chips, this budget diner is the place. There's a small grocery store/deli in the same building if you want to pick up supplies for a picnic.

Glen Oaks Restaurant, Hwy-1 in Big Sur Village (☎667-2623). Gourmet California cuisine, mostly fresh fish and pasta dishes, in a cozy, flower-filled cottage.

River Inn Resort, at the north end of the Big Sur village (☎667-2700 or ☎1-800/548-3610). Tasty range of sautéed and grilled seafood starters and hearty main dishes, served in a spacious, redwood-log dining room. In summer there's a lovely riverside garden, and a sunny terrace where you can linger over lunch or an evening drink; in winter, the fireplace attracts locals and visitors in about equal numbers.

North to Monterey

Andrew Molera State Park (daily dawn–dusk), three miles north of Big Sur Village and reached by a short, easy walk along the rocky beach, is the largest park in Big Sur, though it's rarely visited. It occupies the site of what was the El Sur Ranch, one of the earliest and most successful Big Sur cattle ranches, run by Englishman Juan Bautista Roger Cooper, whose cabin is preserved here. You can hire **horses** from the stables (☎625-8664), and take a guided tour.

From the north end of the park the Old Coast Road takes off inland from Hwy-1 up over the steep hills, affording panoramic views out over miles of coastline. The part-paved, roughly ten-mile road winds over wide-open ranch lands and through deep, slender canyons until it rejoins the main highway at **Bixby Creek Bridge**, fifteen miles south of Carmel. When constructed in 1932 this was the longest single-span concrete bridge in the world, and is the most impressive (and photogenic) engineering feat of the Coast Road project.

A mile and a half north, beyond the **Point Sur Lighthouse**, a paved road turns off up **Palo Colorado Canyon**, past a number of houses and the remains of an old lumber mill obscured behind the redwood trees, finishing up eventually at Botcher's Gap campground on the edge of the Ventana Wilderness. On the coast at the foot of the road, the derelict buildings at **Notley's Landing** were once part of a bustling port community. The northernmost stop on the wild Big Sur coast is at **Garrapata State Park** (daily dawn–dusk), three miles south of Point Lobos and the Monterey Peninsula. A mile-long trail leads from Hwy-1 out to the tip of **Soberanes Point** – a good place to watch for sea otters and grey whales.

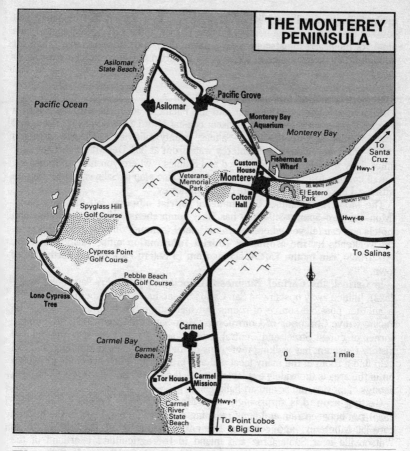

The Monterey Peninsula

Waves which lap quietly about the jetties of Monterey grow louder and larger in the distance . . . and from all around, even in quiet weather, the low, distant, thrilling roar of the Pacific hangs over the coast and the adjacent country like smoke from a battle.

Robert Louis Stevenson, *The Old Pacific Capital.*

The dramatic headlands of the **Monterey Peninsula** mark the northern edge of the spectacular Big Sur coast, a rocky promontory where gnarled cypress trees amplify the collision between the cliffs and the thundering sea. The towns here thrive on the tourist trade, though each has a character very much its own. **Monterey**, largest of the three and a lively harbour town, was the capital of California under the Spanish and Mexicans, and retains many old adobe houses and places of genuine historic appeal alongside some overstated tourist traps. **Carmel-by-the-sea**, on the other hand, three miles to the south, is a contrivedly quaint village of million-dollar holiday homes, best known for the many golf courses that line the coast nearby. **Pacific Grove**, at the very tip of the peninsula amid its most arresting scenery, is smaller than both its neighbours, and far enough off the beaten track to preserve its Victorian seaside character reasonably intact.

Arrival, information and getting around

The Monterey Peninsula juts out into the Pacific to form the Monterey Bay, a hundred miles south of San Francisco; coastal Hwy-1 cuts across its neck, and Hwy-68 links up with US-101 at Salinas, twenty miles east. *Greyhound* **buses** (☎373-4735) stop along the Monterey waterfront at 351 Del Monte Avenue four times daily from both San Francisco and Salinas – where you have to transfer if you're coming from the south. *Amtrak* **trains** also stop in Salinas, connecting up with local buses for the 45-minute trip to Monterey.

The Monterey Chamber of Commerce **tourist office** at 380 Alvarado Street (Mon–Fri 9am–5pm; ☎649-3200) has fairly comprehensive listings of hotels and motels and can tell you where the youth hostel (summer only) is set up this year. On weekends try the **Monterey Tourist Information** office (daily 9am–6pm; ☎372-7568), run by the *YMCA*, across from El Estero Park on the north side of town.

In Carmel, the **Carmel Business Association** (Mon–Fri 9am–5pm; ☎624-2522), hidden away upstairs on San Carlos Street, half a block south of 7th Street, is another possible source of rooms but has little other information, while the Pacific Grove **Chamber of Commerce** (Mon–Sat 9am–5pm; ☎373-3304), on the corner of Forest Street and Central Avenue, across the street from the natural history museum, has walking tour maps of the town's historic buildings and can help find a room in the many local bed and breakfasts. The best guide to **what's on** in the area is the widely available freebie, the *Monterey Peninsula Review*, with listings of movies, music and art galleries.

Getting around is surprisingly easy: *Monterey-Salinas Transit* buses (☎899-2555) run between 7am and 6pm, radiating out from Transit Plaza in the historic core of Monterey, and covering the entire region from Big Sur north to Watsonville near Santa Cruz and inland to the agricultural heartland of the Salinas Valley. The region is divided into four zones: the peninsula, Salinas, Big Sur, and the north coast; fares are 75¢ per zone, and an all-day, single zone pass costs $2. The most useful routes are bus #4 and #5, which link Monterey with Carmel; #21, which runs between Monterey and Salinas; and #1, which runs along Lighthouse Avenue out to Pacific Grove; there's also a free shuttle bus from downtown to the Monterey Bay Aquarium on Cannery Row. The only way to get to Big Sur on public transport is on bus #22, which leaves twice a day, in summer only.

Another option is to **hire a bike**: near Pacific House and the Wharf, the *Doubletree Inn* (☎649-4511) rents out cruisers for $15 a day, and *Bay Bikes*, 640 Wave Street in Cannery Row (☎646-9090) have good quality mountain bikes for $25 a day; they're also in Carmel (☎625-BIKE) on Lincoln between Fifth and Sixth. For more leisurely riding, *Moped Adventures* (☎373-2696) at 1250 Del Monte north of the Wharf have a range of bikes including tandems, plus mopeds at $50 for a three-hour session.

Monterey Peninsula accommodation

What Santa Barbara is to southern California, the Monterey Peninsula is to the north, making it among the most exclusive and expensive resort areas in California, with **hotel** and **B&B** room rates averaging $120 a night. This may tempt you to stay elsewhere – in Santa Cruz, or in agricultural Salinas – and come here on day trips; the other budget option is to avail yourself of one of the many **motels** along Fremont Street, two miles north of the centre of Monterey and reachable on *MST* bus #9# or #10. The only **camping** within walking distance is in Veteran's Memorial Park, site of Steinbeck's fictional Tortilla Flat, at the top of Jefferson Street in the hills above town; it's only $2 a night if on foot, or $10 per car.

Hostel and motels

AYH Monterey Youth Hostel (373-4166). Dorm beds cost around $10, but you'll have to phone first to track down the hostel's current location; it seems to move each year.

Carmel River Inn, Rio Road at Hwy-1, Carmel (☎624-1575). Clean and pleasant, no-frills motel that was the model for Brian Moore's novel *The Great Victorian Collection*. Right on the banks of the Carmel River, near the beach and Carmel Mission, with the cheapest rooms in town; doubles from $45.

Motel 6, 2124 Fremont St, Monterey (☎646-8585). Basic, no-frills motel, but you'll have to reserve a room months in advance to avail yourself of their $40-a-night doubles. Others nearby include the *Driftwood Motel*, 2362 N Fremont St (☎372-5059), and the *Lone Oak Motel*, 2221 Fremont St (☎372-4924).

Pacific Grove Motel, Lighthouse Ave at Grove Acre (☎372-3218). Basic, small motel in marvellous setting, 100 yards from the sea. Doubles $35 in winter, from $50 in summer.

Hotels and B&Bs

Asilomar Conference Center, 800 Asilomar Blvd, Pacific Grove (☎372-8016). Rustic, hand-crafted cabins, and more modern lodge accommodation in splendid beachfront location. Doubles from $50 a night, including a full breakfast.

Green Gables Inn, 104 Fifth St, Pacific Grove (☎375-2095). One of the prettiest houses in a town of fine homes, on the waterfront just a few blocks from the Monterey Bay Aquarium; plush doubles cost $90–160 a night.

Monterey Sheraton, 350 Calle Principal, Monterey (☎649-4234). Luxurious modern hotel right at the heart of historic Monterey, with views out over the bay and peninsula. Doubles cost from $140 in peak season, though in winter and spring they offer a good value "Aquarium Special" for $110, including two tickets to the Monterey Bay Aquarium.

Pacific Grove Inn, 581 Pine Ave at Forest, Pacific Grove (☎375-2825). Thoughtfully modernised 1904 mansion with spacious rooms, five blocks from the shore. Doubles from $60.

Seven Gables Inn, 555 Ocean View Blvd, Pacific Grove (☎372-4341). Great views out over the beautiful coast from this immaculately restored, antique-filled Victorian mansion. Doubles from $90, including full breakfast and afternoon tea and scones.

Monterey

The town of **MONTEREY** rests in a quiet niche along the bay formed by the forested Monterey Peninsula, proudly proclaiming itself the most historic city in California, a boast which for once may be true. Its compact town centre collects some of the best vernacular **buildings** of California's Spanish and Mexican

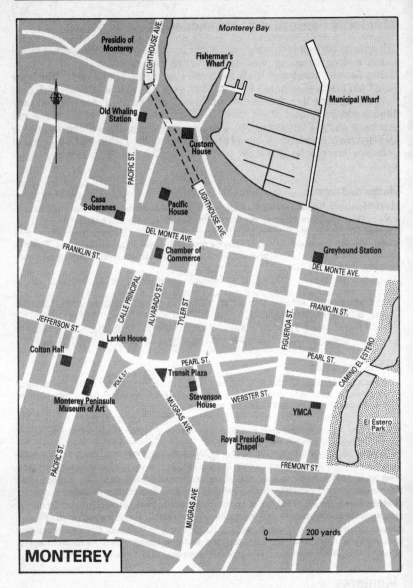

Monterey Bay

Presidio of
Monterey

Fisherman's
Wharf

Municipal Wharf

LIGHTHOUSE AVE.

Old Whaling
Station

Custom
House

PACIFIC ST.

Casa
Soberanes

Pacific
House

LIGHTHOUSE AVE.

DEL MONTE AVE.

FRANKLIN ST.

Chamber of
Commerce

Greyhound Station

DEL MONTE AVE.

CALLE PRINCIPAL

ALVARADO ST.

TYLER ST.

FIGUEROA ST.

FRANKLIN ST.

JEFFERSON ST.

Larkin House

PEARL ST.

CAMINO EL ESTERO

Colton Hall

POLK ST.

Transit Plaza

PEARL ST.

Monterey Peninsula
Museum of Art

MUGRAS AVE.

Stevenson
House

WEBSTER ST.

YMCA

El Estero
Park

PACIFIC ST.

Royal Presidio
Chapel

FREMONT ST.

MUGRAS AVE.

0   200 yards

MONTEREY

colonial past, most of which stand unassumingly within a few blocks of the tourist-thronged waterfront. Many have survived in pristine condition, and can be
found, now preserved as the **Monterey State Historic Park**, scattered throughout the quarter-mile square of the modern city. A loosely organised, roughly mile-
and-a-half-long **Path of History** connects the 35 sites, which tend to be open

daily from 10am–5pm, and park rangers lead guided walking tours on weekends (11am and 2pm; $3.50; ☎649-7118) leaving from the Customs House, near the waterfront at the foot of Alvarado Street, the main street of Monterey. The single best stop, one not to be missed if you've got an afternoon to spare, is the **Monterey Bay Aquarium**, a mile west of town, at the end of the Steinbeck-memorialising Cannery Row.

Some history

Monterey was named by the Spanish merchant and explorer Vizcaino, who landed in 1602 to find an abundant supply of fresh water and wild game after a seven-month voyage from Mexico. Despite Vizcaino's enthusiasm for the site, the area was not colonised until 1770, although it played a pre-eminent role in the development of California thereafter. Under the Spanish the *Presidio de Monterey* was the military headquarters for the whole of Alta California, and thereafter Monterey continued to be the leading administrative and commercial centre of a territory that extended east to the Rocky Mountains and north to Canada, but had a population, excluding native Americans, totalling less than seven thousand.

American interest in Monterey was at first purely commercial, until 1842 when an American naval commodore received a false report that the US and Mexico were at war, and that the English were poised to take California. Commodore Catesby Jones anchored at Monterey and demanded the peaceful surrender of the port. Two days later the American flag was raised, though the armed but cordial US occupation lasted only until Jones examined the official documents closely, and realised he'd got it all wrong. When the Mexican-American War began in earnest in 1846 the United States took possession of Monterey without resistance. The discovery of gold in the Sierra Nevada foothills soon focused attention upon San Francisco, and Monterey became something of a backwater, hardly affected by the waves of immigration which followed.

Old Monterey

The best place to get a feel for life in old Monterey is at the **Larkin House**, on Jefferson Street a block south of Alvarado, home of the first and only American Consul to California and successful entrepreneur, Thomas Larkin. New England-born Larkin, the wealthy owner of a general store and redwood lumber business, was one of the most important and influential figures in early California. He was actively involved in efforts to attract American settlers to California, and lobbied the Californians to turn towards the United States and away from the erratic government of Mexico. Through his designs for his own house, and the Customs House near Fisherman's Wharf, Larkin is credited with developing the now-common Monterey style of architecture, combining local adobe walls and the balconies of a Southern plantation home with a puritan Yankee's taste in orna-ment. The house, the first two-storey adobe in California, is filled with many millions of dollars' worth of antiques, and **tours** (hourly 10am–4pm, except Tues; $1) are obligatory. The gorgeous surrounding gardens are open all day.

Larkin, as unhappy with the American military government as he had been with the Mexicans, helped to organise the Constitutional Convention which convened in Monterey in 1849 to draft the terms by which California could be admitted to the US as the 31st state – which happened in 1850. The meetings were held in the grand, white stone building across the street from his house, the then newly completed **Colton Hall**, now an engaging **museum** (daily 10am–5pm; free) furnished as it was during the convention, with quill pens on the tables and an early map of the West Coast, used to draw up the boundaries of the nascent state.

The oldest building in Monterey, the **Royal Presidio Chapel** (daily 8am–6pm; free), stands at the top of Figueroa Street, half a mile east. This small and much-restored Spanish colonial church was built in 1795 as part of a mission founded here by Junipero Serra in 1770, the rest of which was soon removed to a better site along the Carmel River.

Robert Louis Stevenson, the decline of Monterey ... and the waterfont

The Gold Rush of 1849 bypassed Monterey for San Francisco, leaving the community little more than a somnolent Mexican fishing village – which was pretty much how the town looked when a twenty-nine-year-old, feverishly-ill Scotsman arrived by stagecoach, flat broke and desperately in love with a married woman. **Robert Louis Stevenson** came to Monterey in the autumn of 1879 looking for Fanny Osbourne, whom he had met while travelling in France two years before. He stayed here for three months, writing some articles for the local newspaper and telling stories in exchange for his meals at Jules Simoneau's restaurant behind what is now the **Stevenson House** (daily 10am–4pm, closed Wed), halfway between the Larkin House and the Royal Presidio Chapel at 530 Houston Street. The old rooming house is now filled with memorabilia of the writer and the time, much of it collected by Stevenson on his travels around the South Sea Islands.

Stevenson witnessed Monterey – no longer politically important but not yet a tourist attraction – in transition, something he wrote about in his essay *The Old and New Pacific Capitals*. He foresaw that the lifestyle that had endured since the Mexican era was no match for the "Yankee craft" of the "millionaire vulgarians of the Big Bonanza", like Charles Crocker whose lavish *Hotel Del Monte*, which opened a year later (the site is now the Naval Postgraduate School, east of downtown), turned the sleepy town into a seaside resort of international renown almost overnight. The touristy nature of Monterey has evolved over the years to the point where catering to visitors is now the town's main livelihood. A good deal of the trade is concentrated along the waterfront, around the tacky **Fisherman's Wharf**, where the catch-of-the-day is more likely to be overweight families from San Jose than the formerly abundant sardines. Most of the commercial fishermen moved out long ago, leaving the old wharves and canneries as relics of a once-prosperous industry, and the source of scraps of fish which the tourists buy to throw at the fat sea lions floating in the dirty water under the piers.

A block from the wharf, at the foot of Pacific Street, the whale bone pavement in front of the **Old Whaling Station** is one of Monterey's more unusual sights; a block east, the **Customs House** is the oldest governmental building on the West Coast, portions of which were built by Spain in 1814, Mexico in 1827, and the US in 1846. The balconied building has been restored and now displays 150-year-old crates of confiscated coffee and liquor in a small museum inside. More interestingly, across the pedestrianised plaza the **Pacific House** has been a courthouse, a rooming house and a dancehall in the years since its construction in 1847. It is now the best of the local **museums** (daily 10am–5pm, free), with displays on Monterey history and a collection of Native American artefacts.

Cannery Row and the Monterey Bay Aquarium

A waterfront **bike path** runs from the wharf along the disused railway two miles out to Pacific Grove, following the one-time Ocean View Avenue, renamed **Cannery Row** after John Steinbeck's evocative portrait of the rough-and-ready men and women who worked in and around the thirty-odd fish canneries here. During World War II Monterey was the sardine capital of the Western world, catching and canning some 200,000 tons of the silvery fish each year. However, overfishing meant that by 1945 the fish were more or less all gone, and the canneries were abandoned, falling into disrepair until the 1970s, when they were rebuilt and redecorated and converted into shopping malls and flashy restaurants. Many have adopted names from Steinbeck's tales, and now pack in the tourists as profitably as they once packed sardines. It's all rather phoney, and the only time to come here is the early evening, to take advantage of the cheap food and drinks on offer during the many Happy Hours.

Ride, walk or take the free *MST* shuttle from Fisherman's Wharf to the end of Cannery Row to visit its one (very) worthwhile feature: the engaging **Monterey Bay Aquarium** (10am–6pm daily; $9, students $6). Built upon the foundations of an old sardine cannery, and housed in buildings that blend a sense of adventure and discovery with pleasant promenades along Monterey Bay, the acclaimed aquarium and study centre exhibits over five thousand marine creatures in innovative replicas of their natural habitats. Sharks and octopi roam around behind two-foot-thick sheets of transparent acrylic, there's a 300,000 gallon Kelp Forest tank and a touch pool where you can pet your favourite bat rays. Try, also, to catch the sea otters at feeding time, usually 11am, 2pm, and 4.30pm: endlessly playful critters that were hunted nearly to extinction for their furs – said, with some two million hairs per square inch, to be the softest in the world.

Pacific Grove

PACIFIC GROVE stands curiously apart from the rest of the peninsula, less known but more impressively sited than its two famous neighbours. The town began as a campsite and Methodist retreat in 1875, a summertime tent city for revivalist Christians in which strong drink, naked flesh and reading the Sunday papers were firmly prohibited. The Methodists have long since gone, but otherwise the town is little changed. Its quiet streets, lined by pine trees and grand old Victorian wooden houses, are visited each year by hundreds of thousands of golden Monarch butterflies, who come here from all over the western US and Canada to escape the winter chill. The insects form orange and black blankets on the same trees, near the lighthouse at the very tip of the peninsula, and are the town's main tourist attraction, protected by local law.

Downtown Pacific Grove is centred upon the intersection of Forest and Lighthouse avenues, two miles northwest of central Monterey on *MST* bus #1. The **Bookworks** bookshop and café (daily 9am–10pm), two blocks north at 667 Lighthouse Avenue, is the place to pick up more detailed guides to the local area, or just stop for a cup of coffee and a pastry. A block down Forest Street, on the corner of Central Avenue, the **Pacific Grove Museum of Natural History** (daily except Monday, 10am–5pm; free) has an interesting collection of local wildlife, including lots of butterflies, over four hundred stuffed birds, a relief model of the undersea topography and exhibits on the ways of life of the aboriginal

Costanoan and Salinan Indians. Across the park, the **Chautauqua Hall** was for a time in the 1880s the focus of town life, as the West Coast headquarters of the instructional and populist Chautauqua Movement, a left-leaning, travelling university which reached thousands of Americans long before there was any accessible form of higher education. Nowadays the plain white building is used as a dance-hall, with a three-piece band playing favourites from the Thirties and Forties every Saturday night, and square dancing on Thursday.

About the only reminder of the fundamentalist camp-meetings are the intricately detailed, tiny wooden **cottages**, along 16th and 17th Streets, which date from the revival days: in some cases wooden boards were simply nailed over the frames of canvas tents to make them habitable year-round. Down Central Avenue at 12th Street, at the top of a small wooded park overlooking the ocean, stands the deep red Gothic wooden church of **Saint Mary's By-The-Sea**, Pacific Grove's first substantial church, built in 1887, with a simple interior of redwood beams polished to a shimmering glow, and an authentic signed Tiffany stained-glass window, nearest the altar on the left.

Ocean View Boulevard, which runs between the church and the ocean, circles along the coast around the town, passing the headland of **Lovers Point** – originally called Lovers of Jesus Point – where preachers used to hold sunrise services. Surrounded in early summer by the colourful red and purple blankets of blooming iceplant, it's one of the peninsula's best **beaches**, where you can lounge around and swim from the cosy, protected strand, or hire a glass-bottomed boat and explore the sheltered cove. Ocean View Boulevard runs another mile along the coast out to the tip of the penisula, where the **Point Pinos Lighthouse** (weekends and holidays 1–4pm; free), is at around 150 years the oldest operating lighthouse on the California coast.

Around the point, the name of the coastal road changes to Sunset Drive – which will make obvious sense if you're here at that time of day – and leads on to **Asilomar State Beach** – a wilder stretch with more dramatic surf, too dangerous for swimming, though the rocky shore provides homes for all sorts of tidepool life. The **Butterfly Trees**, where the Monarchs congregate, are on Ridge Road, a quarter of a mile inland along Lighthouse Avenue. Hwy-68 from the end of Sunset Drive takes the inland route over the hills, joining Hwy-1 just north of Carmel, while the **Seventeen Mile Drive** ($6), a privately owned, scenic toll road, loops from Pacific Grove along the coast south to Carmel and back again, passing by the golf courses and country clubs of Pebble Beach. Halfway along stands the trussed-up figure of the **Lone Cypress**, subject of many a postcard, and there are enough beautiful vistas of the rugged coastline to make it almost worth braving the hordes who pack the road on holiday weekends.

Carmel

Set on gently rising headlands above a sculpted, rocky shore, **CARMEL**'s reputation as a rich resort belies its origins. There was nothing much here until the San Francisco earthquake and fire of 1906 led a number of artists and writers from the city to take refuge in the area, forming a Bohemian colony on the wild and uninhabited slopes that soon became notorious throughout the state. Figurehead of the group was the poet George Stirling, and part-time members included Jack London, Mary Austin and the young Sinclair Lewis. But it was a short-lived alliance, and by the 1920s the group had broken up and an influx of wealthy San

Franciscans had put Carmel well on its way to becoming the ghetto of exclusivity it is now.

Certainly, there is little about the town today to welcome travellers of modest means and low credit-rating, and Carmel instead often seems the very epitome of parochial snobbishness. Local laws, enacted to preserve the rustic character of the town, prohibit parking meters, street addresses and postal deliveries (all mail is picked up in person from the post office); planning permission is required to cut down any tree, so they sprout everywhere, even in the middle of streets; and franchise stores or restaurants are banned outright within the city limits. For these aspects alone Carmel is probably worth a look at least, and the chance to catch a rare glimpse of ex-mayor Clint Eastwood may make the sterile shopping mall atmosphere worth bearing for an hour or so, but without a doubt the town's best feature is the largely untouched nearby coastline, among the most beautiful in California.

Carmel's centre, fifteen minutes south of Monterey on *MST* bus #4 or #5, doesn't have much to recommend it – largely designer-shopping territory, in which Armani and Ralph Lauren rub shoulders with mock-Tudor tearooms and a number of **art galleries**, filled with boring watercolour renderings of golf scenes and local seascapes. The galleries are concentrated along Dolores Street between Fifth and Sixth Street, and it's worth at least looking in on the *Weston Galley* on Sixth Street, which hosts regular shows of the best contemporary photographers and has a permanent exhibit of works by Fox Talbot, Ansel Adams and Edward Weston – who lived in Carmel for most of his life. To get the lowdown on the rest, check out the free, widely available *Carmel Gallery Guide*.

Fortunately, the contrivedness of the town centre doesn't extend to the coastline, which is gorgeous and relatively unspoilt. **Carmel Beach**, down the hill at the end of Ocean Avenue, is a tranquil cove of emerald blue water bordered by soft white sand and cypress-covered cliffs, though the tides here are deceptively strong and dangerous – be careful if you chance a swim. A mile south from Carmel Beach along Carmel Bay, **Tor House** was, when built in 1919, the only building on a then treeless headland. The poet Robinson Jeffers (whose very long, starkly tragic narrative poems were far more popular in his time than they are today) built the small cottage and adjacent tower by hand, out of granite boulders he carried up from the cove below. Hourly guided **tours** (Fri & Sat 10am–4pm; $5, students $3.50; ☎624-1813) of the house and gardens, including a rather obsequious account of the writer's life and work, are given year-round, and advance reservations are essential.

Another quarter of a mile along Scenic Road, around the tip of Carmel Point, **Carmel River State Beach** is a mile long and less visited than the city beach, and includes a bird sanctuary on a freshwater lagoon that offers safe and sometimes warm swimming. Again, if you brave the waves, beware of the strong tides and currents, especially at the south end of the beach, where the sand falls away at a very steep angle causing big and potentially hazardous surf.

Carmel Mission

Half a mile or so up the Carmel River from the beach, also reachable by following Junipero Avenue from the centre of town, **Carmel Mission** (daily 10.30am–4.30pm; donations) – *La Misión San Carlos Borromeo del Rio Carmelo* – was founded in 1770 by Junipero Serra as the second of the California missions and the headquarters of the chain. Father Serra never got to see the finished church – he died before its completion and is buried under the floor in front of the altar. The sandstone church was finally completed by Father Lasuén in 1797, and has since been well restored. The facade is unexpectedly exotic and whimsical; flourishes on the central pediment resemble cattle horns, and the interior walls curve gently into the vaulted ceiling to interesting effect. Some three thousand local Indians are buried in the adjacent **cemetery**, and three small **museums** in the mission compound recount the history of the missionary effort alongside ornate silver candleholders, decorated vestments and relics of the life of Father Serra.

Point Lobos State Reserve

Two miles south of the mission along Hwy-1, accessible on *MST* bus #22, the **Point Lobos State Reserve** (daily 9am–dusk; $5 parking fee is valid at all Big Sur parks as well) gives some of the best undisturbed views of the ocean and a chance to see everybody's favourite furry creature, the sea otter, in its natural habitat. The park, named for the *lobos del mar*, the noisy, barking sea lions that group on the rocks off the tip of the reserve, protects some of the few remaining Monterey Cypress trees on its knife-edged headland, despite being buffeted by relentless winds. Craggy granite pinnacles, landforms which inspired Robert Louis Stevenson's *Treasure Island*, reach out of jagged blue coves below, close to which sea lions and otters play in the crashing surf.

A number of hiking trail loop around the reserve, giving good views down into deep coves where sea otters are likely to be seen surfing in the waves. The sea here is one of the richest underwater habitats in California, and California gray whales are often seen offshore, migrating south in January and returning with young calves in April and early May. Because the point juts so far out into the ocean, you have a good chance of seeing them from surprisingly close, often as little as a hundred yards away.

Except for a small car park, the reserve is closed to cars, so queues sometimes form along the highway to wait for a parking space. A worthwhile guide and map is available for 50¢ at the entrance.

Monterey Peninsula Eating

There are many excellent places to eat all over the three city Peninsula area, though because it's a holiday resort, be prepared to spend a bit more than you'd have to elsewhere. By and large the offerings are standard American fare, with steaks and seafood starring on most restaurant menus, with pricey Mexican places playing off the Hispanic heritage. For a full list of the hundreds of eating options in the Peninsula area, check out a copy of the free, weekly and widely available *Entertainment and Dining Review*. If you're on anything like a tight budget, the best cheap eats are on the north side of Monterey along Fremont Street, and in the shopping malls along Hwy-1 south of Carmel.

Inexpensive

Belleci's Deli, 470 Alvarado St, Monterey (☎373-4240). Wide variety of hot or cold sandwiches, burgers and Italian food at rock-bottom prices.

Chutney's Gourmet Cafe, 230 Crossroads Blvd, Crossroads Mall, Hwy-1, Carmel (☎624-4785). Eccentric menu featuring range of soups, salads, sandwiches and burgers in lively, unpretentious café setting.

Mediterranean Market, Ocean Ave and Mission St, Carmel (☎624-2022). Perfect for packing a picnic basket for a day on the sands, full of fine cheeses, deli meats, bread and wine.

Mom's Home Cookin', 1287 Fremont St, Monterey (☎394-9191). Great BBQ ribs and chicken, plus cornbread, collared greens and all the fixin's. Out in the motel district north of Hwy-1.

Old Monterey Cafe, 489 Alvarado St, Monterey (☎646-1021). More than you can eat breakfasts, with great omelettes and buckwheat pancakes, plus tasty sandwiches; daily 7am–2.30pm except Tuesday.

Toot's Lagoon, on Dolores below Seventh St, Carmel (☎625-1915). Good-sized portions on a wide-ranging menu – pizzas, salads, steaks, burgers, fresh fish and famous BBQ ribs – popular with families and birthday celebrants.

Tuck Box Tearoom, Dolores St between Ocean and 7th, Carmel (☎624-6365). Breakfast, lunch and afternoon tea in half-timbered mock-Tudor Olde Englande setting. Pricey and kitsch but fun.

Moderate to expensive

Cafe Fina, middle of Fisherman's Wharf, Monterey (☎372-5200). Pasta dishes, wood-oven pizzas, and of course, grilled fresh fish in the Wharf's most style-conscious setting.

Fishwife Restaurant, 1996 Sunset Drive at Asilomar, Pacific Grove (☎375-7107). Long-standing local favourite, serving great food at reasonable prices – King Prawns sautéed in red peppers and lime juice with rice and steamed vegetables for $10 – in homely, unpretentious surroundings.

La Boheme, Dolores St between Ocean and 7th, Carmel (☎624-7500). Fine dining the Carmel way – in a scaled-down replica of a French country hotel courtyard, complete with whitewashed walls and hanging laundry. Multi-course, *prix-fixe* meals for $17.50 plus wine and service.

Pepper's Mexicali Cafe, 170 Forest Ave, Pacific Grove (☎373-6892). Gourmet Mexican seafood Californified into healthy, high-style dishes that won't put too big a whole in your wallet.

Triples, 220 Oliver St, Monterey (☎372-4744). Light and healthy "California Cuisine", fresh fish and great salads, on a sunny outdoor patio or inside historic Duarte's Store. Behind the Pacific House in the Monterey State Historic Park.

Drinking and nightlife

A number of clubs on the Monterey Peninsula feature a fairly sedate range of live and canned music, though things do pick up a bit in September, when it hosts the world-class Monterey Jazz Festival at the County Fairgrounds east of town; phone ☎373-3366 for more information. Besides the places listed below, most restaurants have a bar or cocktail lounge, generally filled with middle-aged golfers.

The Club of Monterey, Alvarado and Del Monte St (☎646-9244). Fairly young and upscale crowd at this DJ-dance club; darts and pool tables downstairs. Cover $1–8, with occasional live acts.

The Firehouse, 414 Calle Principal, Monterey (☎649-3016). Characterful cocktail lounge in historic brick fire station, with free live music weekend nights.

Monterey Bay Club, in the Sheraton Monterey (☎649-4234). Evening jazz, from Dixieland to modern, most nights.

Monterey Brewing Company, 700 Cannery Row, Monterey (☎375-3634). Good, micro-brewed lagers and ales, bar food, and nightly live rock or blues bands.

Portofino Cafe, 620 Lighthouse Ave, Pacific Grove (☎373-7379). Casual café with acoustic folk and jazz musicians on weekend nights, cover under $5.

Monterey Peninsula listings

Area Code ☎408.
Car Hire *Rent-a-Wreck*, 95 Central Avenue, Pacific Grove (☎373-3356) have old bangers and a range of newer cars from $20 a day. All the national chains have outlets as well.
Hearst Castle Tours *Steinbeck Country Tours* (☎625-5107) and *Gray Line* (☎373-4989) both offer all-day trips through Big Sur to Hearst Castle, costing $45 per person including a guaranteed ticket for the $10 introductory tour of the mansion. *Steinbeck Tours* also do an enjoyable 4-hour Peninsula circuit, if you don't have your own transport or can't face trying to park.
Post Office 565 Hartnell St in downtown Monterey (☎372-5803). Open Mon–Fri 8.30am–5pm, zip code 93940.
Ticketron For camping and Hearst Castle reservations, 711 Cannery Row (☎649-4289); open daily 10am–5pm.
Whale Watching *Randy's Fishing Trips* (☎372-7440) run half- and full-day trips from December to April to watch the migrating gray whales.

North from Monterey

The landscape around the **Monterey Bay**, between the peninsula and the beach town of Santa Cruz, 45 miles north, is almost entirely given over to agriculture. **CASTROVILLE**, ten miles north along Hwy-1, is surrounded by farmland which grows more than 85 percent of the nation's artichokes (try them deep-fried in one of the local cafés), while the wide **Pajaro Valley**, five miles further north, is covered with apple orchards, blossoming white in the spring. The marshlands that ring the bay at the mouths of the Salinas and Pajaro rivers are habitats for many of California's endangered species of coastal wildlife and migratory birds. At **Elkhorn Slough Estuarine Sanctuary**, near the lively fishing port of MOSS LANDING – a good place to stop for seafood – you may spot a falcon or an eagle among the many pelicans that call it home. The **beaches** along the bay are often windy and not very exciting, though they're lined by sand dunes into which you can disappear for hours on end.

Sunset State Beach, fifteen miles south of Santa Cruz, has $10-a-night **campsites** along a seven-mile strand; four miles inland, east of Hwy-1, the earthquake-devastated town of **WATSONVILLE** was more or less the epicentre of the October 1989 Loma Prieta tremor that rattled San Francisco, and its once-quaint downtown of ornate Victorian houses and 1930s brick structures was virtually flattened. Though it hasn't been rebuilt, it's still the main transfer-point between the Monterey and Santa Cruz bus systems, so you may well pass through.

San Juan Bautista

Inland, on US-101 between Salinas and the San Francisco Bay Area, **SAN JUAN BAUTISTA**, seventeen miles north of Salinas, is about the only place worth making for: an old Mexican town that's hardly changed since it was bypassed by the railway in 1876. The early nineteenth-century **Mission San Juan Bautista** (daily 10am–4pm; donations), largest of the Californian mission churches, stands on the north side of the town's central plaza, its original bells still ringing out from the belltower; the arcaded monastery wing which stretches out to the left of the church contains relics and historical exhibits. If it all looks a bit familiar, you may have seen it before – Alfred Hitchcock's *Vertigo* was filmed here.

Most of the town that grew up around the mission has been preserved as a **state park** (daily 9am–5pm; free), with sporadic exhibits interpreting the restored buildings. On the west side of the plaza, the two-storey, balconied adobe **Plaza Hotel** was a popular stopping-place on the stagecoach route between San Francisco and Los Angeles; next door, the 1840 **Castro House**, administrative headquarters of Mexican California, later belonged to the Breen family – survivors of the ill-fated Donner Party (see p.455) – who made a small fortune in the Gold Rush.

Across from the mission, the large **Plaza Hall** was built to serve as the seat of the emergent county government, but when the county seat was awarded instead to HOLLISTER (a small farming community eight miles east, and scene of a motorcycle gang's rampage that inspired the movie *The Wild One*), the building was turned into a dancehall and saloon. The adjacent stables display a range of old stagecoaches and wagons, and explain how to decipher an array of cattle brands, from "lazy H" to "rockin double B". The commercial centre of San Juan Bautista, a block south of the plaza, lines Third Street in a row of evocatively decaying facades. If you're hungry, the best of the half-dozen **places to eat** is the *Mission Café*, on the corner of Mariposa Street.

Santa Cruz

Santa Cruz is part of the post-orgy world, the world left behind after the great social and sexual convulsions. The refugees from the orgy – the orgy of sex, political violence, the Vietnam War, the Woodstock crusade – are all there, jogging along in their tribalism.

Jean Baudrillard, America

Seventy-five miles south of San Francisco, **SANTA CRUZ** is a hard place to pin down. In many ways it's the ideal Californian coastal town, a heady mix of intellect and pure pleasure that's perfect for a few days' stopover on your way north or south. And there are any number of things to occupy you, from surfing or sunning yourself along the many miles of beaches, hiking around the surrounding mountaintop forests, to riding the Big Dipper – the largest and wildest wooden roller coaster on the West Coast. But there's another side to Santa Cruz: the town has grown unwieldily over the last couple of decades, and in spite of a reputation for sixties liberalism, its suburbs have a redneck feel more akin to the Central Valley than the laid-back languid coast; and there's a long-term town-versus-gown split between the locals and the students from UCSC. Only rarely do you get the impression of a resort totally at ease with itself, and the underlying conflicts are one of the many reasons why the town has been so slow to rebuild following the destruction wrecked by the 1989 'quake.

This tension adds spice to a visit to Santa Cruz. The town's reputation as a holdout from the 1960s is an enduring one – which is only fitting since this is where it all began. Ken Kesey and his Merry Pranksters turned the local youth on to the wonders of LSD years before it defined a generation, a mission recorded by Tom Wolfe in *The Electric Koolaid Acid Test*, and the area is still considered among the most politically and socially progressive in California. It's also surprisingly untouristed. No hotels spoil the miles of wave-beaten coastline – in fact, most of the surrounding land is used for growing fruit and vegetables, and roadside stands are

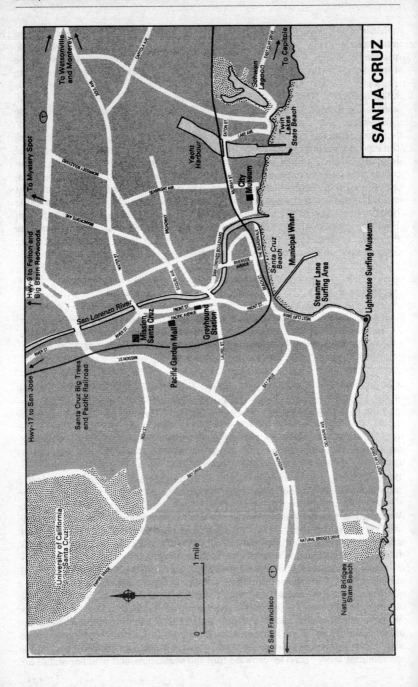

SANTA CRUZ

To Watsonville and Monterey

To Capitola

To Mystery Spot

Schwan Lagoon

HWY 108

CAPITOLA AVE

Yacht Harbour

EATON ST

LAKE AVE

Twin Lakes State Beach

EAST CLIFF DRIVE

MONTEREY BOULEVARD

SEABRIGHT AVE

City Museum

MURRAY ST

BAY ST

BRANCIFORTE AVE

BROADWAY

Hwy 9 to Felton and Big Basin Redwoods

WATER ST

SOQUEL AVE

SAN LORENZO BOULEVARD

RIVERSIDE AVENUE

Santa Cruz Beach

Municipal Wharf

THE BROADWALK

BEACH ST

To San Jose

San Lorenzo River

RIVER ST

FRONT ST

Mission Santa Cruz

FRONT ST

Steamer Lane Surfing Area

Pacific Garden Mall

PACIFIC AVENUE

Greyhound Station

RIVER ST

WEST CLIFF DRIVE

MISSION ST

LAUREL ST

Lighthouse Surfing Museum

Hwy 17 to San Jose

Santa Cruz Big Trees and Pacific Railroad

HIGH ST

BAY DRIVE

MISSION ST

BAY DRIVE

DELAWARE AVE

1 mile

NATURAL BRIDGES DRIVE

University of California, Santa Cruz

EMPIRE GRADE

To San Francisco

WEST CLIFF DRIVE

Natural Bridges State Beach

0

SANTA CRUZ

more likely to be selling apples or sprouts than postcards and souvenirs. Places to stay are for once cheap and easy to find, and the town sports a range of bookshops and coffee houses, as well as some lively bars and nightclubs where the music varies from hardcore surf-punks to long-time local Neil Young and friends.

Arrival, information and getting around

Greyhound buses from San Francisco stop four times a day at 425 Front Street (☎423-1800), in the centre of town; *Peerless Stages* from Oakland and San Jose in the San Francisco Bay Area stop here another six times a day, as do *Green Tortoise* buses. It's more difficult to get to Santa Cruz from the south: only one *Greyhound* bus a day runs from Monterey, though local *MST* and *SCMTD* buses link up with *Greyhound* in Monterey and Salinas via Watsonville. By **car**, Santa Cruz is on Hwy-1, 75 miles south of San Francisco, 45 miles north of Monterey; Hwy-17 runs over the mountains, 33 miles from US-101.

For information contact the **Santa Cruz Visitors Bureau** at 710 Front Street (Mon–Fri 9am–5pm; ☎425-1234), who can help with finding a place to stay and sell a map of Santa Cruz's historic districts for $1. To find out **what's on** in the area, check out the many free newspapers, like the weekly *Good Times* and monthly *Santa Cruz Magazine*, both available at **Bookshop Santa Cruz** (☎423-0900), relocated since the earthquake in temporary, tentlike quarters at the corner of Cedar and Chestnut.

Santa Cruz has an excellent **public transport** system, centred on the Metro Center at 920 Pacific Avenue, and operated by the *Santa Cruz Metropolitan Transit District* or *SCMTD* (daily 7am–6pm; ☎425-8600), who publish *Headways*, a free bilingual guide to getting around the area. The basic fare is $1 an all-day pass is $2, and a five-day pass costs $10. Some of the most useful routes are: #1, which runs up the hill to UCSC; #71 to Watsonville; #67 along the eastern beaches; #3 to the western beaches. Route #35, which runs up into the mountains to Big Basin Redwoods State Park, is equipped with bike racks.

Though there are buses to most of the beaches, you might find it easier to get around by **bicycle**: *Clark's Cyclery*, 927 Pacific Avenue (☎458-9551), rents bikes from $15 a day, as does the *Fun Spot*, 35 Front Street (☎429-6448) while the nearby *Go-Skate* also rent out roller skates and surfboards. If you feel particularly daring, you can even get ocean-going **kayaks** from *The Kayak Shack* (☎662-8433) on the wharf.

The town

After the overcharged tourism of the Monterey Peninsula across the bay, Santa Cruz – a quiet, easy-going community of 45,000 residents plus some ten thousand students – comes as a welcome surprise, spread out at the foot of thickly wooded mountains along a clean, sandy shore. There's not a lot to see in the town, almost all of which is within a ten-minute walk of the beach, apart from the many blocks of Victorian wooden houses – but the feel of the place is a treat.

The sluggish San Lorenzo river wraps around the town centre, two blocks east of the **Pacific Garden Mall**, a landscaped, prettified and pedestrianised stretch of Pacific Avenue that, before the earthquake made most of the buildings uninhabitable, used to be Santa Cruz's main street, lined with bookshops, record stores and cafés, and populated by fossilised fallout from the 1960s, who beg for spare change while street musicians drone out old Bob Marley songs.

One place that survived the tremor is the ornate **Octagon Building**, at the north end of the Mall on the corner of Cooper Street. The brick and stone structure was completed in 1882 as the Santa Cruz Hall of Records, and it now houses a **museum** of local history (Mon–Sat noon–5pm; free), with exhibits that dwell on the Victorian era. Three blocks away, on High Street, fragments dating from the region's earlier Spanish colonial days are shown off in the restored army barracks, next to a scaled-down copy of **Mission Santa Cruz** (daily 9am–5pm; donations). The original adobe church was destroyed by an earthquake in the middle of the nineteenth century; the replica that stands on its site today is dwarfed by a large Gothic Revival church next door.

Between the town centre and the beach, **Beach Hill** rises at the foot of Pacific Avenue, its slopes containing some of Santa Cruz's finest turn-of-the-century homes, like the striking Queen Anne style house at 417 Cliff Street and the slightly odd structure around the corner at 912 3rd Street, constructed out of the remains of a shipwreck.

The Boardwalk and around

Standing out at the foot of the low-rise town, the **Santa Cruz Boardwalk** (summer daily 11am–7pm, weekends until 10pm, winter weekends only; free admission, rides 60¢–$1.50 each, unlimited rides $10.95) stretches half a mile along the sands, the last surviving beachfront amusement park on the West Coast. First opened in 1907 as a gambling casino, the elegant *Cocoanut Grove* at the west end has recently been restored, and the 1940s Swing bands that play in the grand ballroom on weekend evenings offer a change of pace from the raucous string of Dodgem cars, shooting galleries, Log Flume rides and Ferris Wheels that line up beside the wide beach, filled in with every sort of arcade game and test of skill. Though packed solid on summer weekends with Silicon Valley teenagers on the prowl, most of the time it's a friendly funfair where barefoot hippies mix with mushroom farmers and their families. The star attraction is the **Big Dipper**, a wild and wooden roller coaster that's listed on the National Register of Historic Places and often doubles for Coney Island in the movies.

Half a mile west of the Boardwalk, the hundred-year-old wooden **Municipal Pier** juts out into the bay, crammed with fish and chip shops and seafood restaurants, at the end of which people fish for crabs – you don't need a licence to fish, and can hire tackle from one of the many bait shops. Just east of the Boardwalk, across the San Lorenzo River, the small **Santa Cruz City Museum** (Tues–Sat 10am–5pm, Sun noon–5pm; $1), marked by a concrete whale, has concise displays describing local animals and sea creatures, and a brief description of the local Native American culture.

The beaches

The **beach** closest to town, along the Boardwalk, is wide and sandy and has lots of volleyball courts and water that, in August and September at least, is plenty warm enough for swimming. However, not surprisingly it can get very rowdy, especially during the annual Clam Chowder Festival (every February) and the Brussel Sprouts Festival, held each October. For a bit more peace and quiet, or to catch the largest waves, simply follow the coastline east or west of town to one of the smaller beaches hidden away at the foot of the cliffs: most are undeveloped and easily accessible.

From the City Museum, **East Cliff Drive** (and *SCMTD* buses #67 and #68) winds along the top of the bluffs, past many coves and estuaries. The nearest of the two coastal lagoons that border the volleyball courts of **Twin Lakes State Beach**, half a mile east, was dredged and converted into a marina in the 1960s; the other, **Schwan Lagoon**, is still intact, its marshy wetlands serving as a refuge for sea birds and migrating waterfowl. Beyond Twin Lakes there's another long strand of beach, with good tidepools at Corcoran Lagoon, a half mile on.

East Cliff Drive continues past popular surfing spots off rocky **Pleasure Point**, to the small beachfront resort of **CAPITOLA**. The small town, three miles east of central Santa Cruz, began as a fishing village, living off the many giant tuna that populated the Monterey Bay, but soon became popular as a holiday spot, with its own railway line. The large wooden trestle of the now-disused railway still dominates the town, rising over the soft sands of **Hooper Beach**, west of the small fishing pier.

Capitola is especially attractive in late summer, when the hundreds of begonias – the town's main produce – are in bloom. Any time of year, stop by *Mr Toot's*, upstairs from 221 Esplanade, a café and bakery with great views out over the bay and live music most nights. **New Brighton State Beach**, a mile east of Capitola, is the nearest **campsite** to Santa Cruz (see "Camping" below for details).

The beaches west of the Santa Cruz Boardwalk, along **West Cliff Drive**, see some of the biggest waves in California, not least at **Steamer Lane**, off the tip of Lighthouse Point beyond the Municipal Pier. The ghosts of surfers past are animated at the **Surfing Museum** (daily noon–4pm; free), housed in the old lighthouse on the point, which holds surfboards ranging from the twelve-foot redwood planks of the early pioneers to modern, hi-tech, multi-finned cutters. A clifftop bicycle path, and the half-hourly *SCMTD* bus #3 along Mission Street, runs two miles out from here to **Natural Bridges State Park**, where waves have cut holes through the coastal cliffs, forming delicate arches in the remaining stone; three of the four bridges for which the park was named have since collapsed, leaving large stacks of stone sticking out of the surf. The park is also famous – like Pacific Grove further south – for its annual gathering of Monarch Butterflies, thousands of whom return each winter.

Above Santa Cruz: UCSC and the mountains

The **University of California, Santa Cruz**, on the hills above the town and served by *SCMTD* bus #1, was designed and built during the mid-1960s and is fairly unique: students don't take exams or get grades, and the academic programme stresses individual exploration of topics rather than rote learning.

Architecturally, too, it's deliberately different, its park-like campus divided up into small, autonomous colleges, where deer stroll among the redwood trees overlooking Monterey Bay – a decentralised plan, drawn up under then-Governor Ronald Reagan, that cynics claim was intended as much to diffuse protests as to provide a peaceful backdrop for study. You can judge for yourself by taking one of the guided tours that start from the **visitors center** (☎429-2495) at the foot of campus, and be sure to keep an eye out for signs of the major expansion that's in the works, which will enable UCSC to absorb the overflow from overcrowded UC campuses elsewhere. If you don't manage to get yourself invited to spend the night by a friendly student, there are dormitory rooms available for rent in summer.

On the south side of the San Lorenzo River, three miles up Branciforte Drive from the centre of town, there's a point within the woods where normal laws of gravity no longer apply: trees grow at odd angles, balls roll uphill and bright yellow stickers appear on the bumpers of cars that pass too close to the **Mystery Spot** (daily 9.30am–4.30pm; $3). Many explanations are offered – including its being an extra-terrrestrial signalling device that's wreaking havoc with local physics – but most of the disorientation is caused by the not-quite-square corners and perspective tricks used in the various exhibits, spread out around the cool forest.

High up in the mountains that separate Santa Cruz from Silicon Valley and the San Francisco Bay Area, *SCMTD* bus #35 runs down to the village of **FELTON**, five miles north of Santa Cruz on Hwy-9, where the hundred-year-old **Big Trees and Roaring Camp Narrow Gauge Railroad** (daily noon–4pm, weekends only in winter, departing every 90 minutes; $10; ☎335-4484) steams through the massive trees that cover the slopes of the Henry Cowell Redwoods State Park along the San Lorenzo River gorge. The **covered bridge** a mile east of town is also worth a look, if you've got a car; it spans the river between heavily wooded slopes.

Buses continue further up the mountains to the **Big Basin Redwoods State Park**, an hour's ride from Santa Cruz, where acres of three hundred-foot-tall redwood trees cover some 25 square miles of untouched wilderness, with excellent hiking and camping. A popular "Skyline-to-the-Sea" backpacking **trail** steps down through cool, moist canyons, ten miles to the coast at **Waddell Creek Beach** – fifteen miles north of Santa Cruz and a favourite spot for watching world-class windsurfers negotiate the waves – from where *SCMTD* bus #40 will take you back to town.

Santa Cruz accommodation

Compared to most California beach resorts, places to stay in Santa Cruz are inexpensive and easy to come by, especially during the week or outside of summer. One of the saddest losses caused by the 1989 earthquake, from a visitor's point of view, was the characterful old *St George Hotel*, whose fate was yet to be decided at time of writing. The following is a range of options; most offer good-value weekly rates as well. Camping in and around Santa Cruz is abundant and varied, from beaches to forests and points in between.

Camping

New Brighton State Beach, Capitola (☎688-3241). Three miles south of Santa Cruz on the edge of the beachfront village of Capitola, set on bluffs above a lengthy strand. Has hot showers, plots cost $14 a night.

Henry Cowell Redwoods State Park, Hwy-9 (☎335-4598). In the hills above town and UC Santa Cruz, in a redwood grove along the San Lorenzo River. Bus # 35 serves the park, and plots cost $10 a night.

Big Basin State Park, Hwy-236 (☎338-6132). High up in the hills; plots with showers for $10, and numerous backcountry pitches ($1) for hikers and mountain bikers. An excellent overnight trek, from the redwoods to the Pacific, is described above.

Hostels and motels

Santa Cruz Hostel, 511 Broadway, (☎423-8181 or ☎423-8304). The cheapest bed in town, basically a bunk set up in a high school gym; $10 a night for AYH members, plus $2 for non-members. The location sometimes varies from year to year, so phone to check.

Pigeon Point Lighthouse Hostel, Pescadero (☎415/879-0633). Located some 25 miles north of town, near Ano Nuevo State Reserve, but well worth the effort for a chance to bunk down in the old lighthouse keepers quarters. Dorm beds $9 per person, plus $2 for non AYH members; private rooms $23 a night for two, and there's an excellent hot tub ($5 per hour) hanging out over the thundering surf.

The Best Inn, 320 Ocean St (☎458-9220). Across the river from the centre of town, with clean, no-frills double rooms from $25. Very popular in summer.

Capri Motel, 337 Riverside Ave (☎426-4611). One of a dozen $30-a-night, $130-a-week motels near the beach and the Boardwalk. Others include *Aladdin's*, 50 Front St (☎426-3575); the *Mardi Gras*, 338 Riverside Ave (☎426-3707); and the more salubrious *Lanai Motor Lodge*, 550 Second St(☎426-3626), on Beach Hill.

Hotels and B&Bs

Capitola Venetian Hotel, 1500 Wharf Road, Capitola (☎476-6471). Quirky, aging beachfront hotel just across the bridge from Capitola's lively esplanade. All rooms have kitchens, some are two-bedroom suites; doubles cost from $50 per night in midweek, $80 weekends, or $250 per week.

Cliff Crest Inn, 407 Cliff St (☎427-2609). Nicely furnished 1887 Queen Anne-style Victorian home set in lovely gardens at the top of Beach Hill. Rates from $80 for a double room, includes a full breakfast and afternoon sherry.

Sea and Sand Inn, 201 West Cliff Drive (☎427-3400). Small and well-placed hotel overlooking the bay, beaches and Steamer Lane surfers; doubles from $75.

Eating

Eateries in Santa Cruz run to two extremes: health-conscious, tofu-fired vegetarian fare and all-American burger-and-beer bars. In between there are bakeries and sandwich shops, and good seafood from a number of restaurants on the wharf.

Inexpensive

The Bagelry, 320-A Cedar St (☎429-8049). Spacious but usually packed bakery selling coffees and cakes and an infinite range of filled bagels, open early until late.

Dharma's, 4250 Capitola (☎462-1717). A little way south of central Santa Cruz. Cheap and healthy fast food; used to be called *McDharma's* before being sued for breach of trademark.

El Paisano, 605 Beach St at Riverside (☎426-2382). Very good and inexpensive Mexican place with great tamales a speciality. Two blocks from the Boardwalk and beach.

Positively Front Street, 44 Front St (☎426-1944). Hyperactive burger bar with good range of beers, just off the Boardwalk at the foot of the wharf.

Zoccoli's Deli, 1101-C Cedar St at Center (☎423-1711). Great old Italian delicatessen, displaced by the earthquake but still serving up great cheap food, including a minestrone that's a meal in itself.

Moderate to expensive

Edgewater Bar and Restaurant, 215 Espanade, Capitola (☎475-7215). One of many good restaurants lined up along the beach, this one offers steaks and seafood and sunset cocktails. Others nearby include *Margaritaville* (☎476-2263).

Emi Restaurant, 1003 Cedar St (☎423-7502). Housed in the old Santa Cruz Hotel, with top-rate Korean food; before or after, head to the upstairs cocktail and jazz lounge.

Miramar, 45 Municipal Wharf (☎423-4441). Long-established, family owned seafood restaurant, with gorgeous views – especially at sunset – of the Pacific and seafront homes. Recently revamped menu and reasonable prices.

Shadowbrook, 1750 Wharf Road, Capitola (☎475-1511). Very romantic steak and seafood place, stepping down along the banks of a creek.

Drinking and nightlife

Santa Cruz has a range of espresso bars and coffee houses to rival any big city, and it also has the Central Coast's best nightlife, with a number of unpretentious and unthreatening bars and nightclubs where the music varies from heavy-duty surf-thrash to lilting reggae to the rowdy rock of local resident Neil Young.

The Catalyst, 1011 Pacific Ave (☎423-1336). The best bet for catching big name touring artists and up-and-coming locals, this medium-sized club has something happening nearly every night. Usually 21 and over only, cover varies.

Front Street Pub, 516 Front St (☎429-8838). Premises-brewed lagers and ales – try the Amber Ale or their fairly stout Porter – and live music or comedians most nights.

Kuumbwa Jazz Center, 320 Cedar St (☎427-2227). The Santa Cruz showcase for trad and modern jazz, friendly and intimate with cover ranging $1–15.

Mr Toot's Coffee House, 221A Esplanade (upstairs), Capitola (☎475-3679). Bustling tea-and-coffee café overlooking the beach and wharf, with live music most nights; open 8am until midnight (at least) every day.

Santa Cruz Coffee Roasting Co, 121 Walnut Ave (☎423-7250). Just the place to start the day off right, with an excellent range of coffees, by the bean or by the cup.

Listings

Area code ☎408.

Gay Lesbian and Gay Community Center (☎429-2060).

Hospital Santa Cruz Dominican Hospital, 1555 Soquel Drive (☎476-0220); bus #71.

Police 809 Center St (☎429-3714).

Post office 850 Front St (☎426-5200). Open Mon–Fri 8.30am–5pm. General Delivery zip code 95060.

The coast north to San Francisco

The **Ano Nuevo State Reserve**, twenty miles north of Santa Cruz, was named by the explorer Vizcaino, who sailed past on New Years Day 1603. It's a beautiful spot to visit at any time of year, and in winter you shouldn't miss the chance to see one of nature's most bizarre spectacles – the mating rituals of the Northern Elephant Seal. These massive, ungainly creatures, fifteen feet long and weighing up to three tons, gather on the rocks and sand dunes to fight for a mate. The male's distinctive, pendulous nostrils aid him in his noisy honking, which is how he attracts the females; their blubbery forms are capable of diving deeper than any other mammal, to depths of over 4500 feet. Obligatory three-hour **tours** (☎415/879-0227; $5) are organised during the breeding season; throughout the year you're likely to see at least a few, dozing in the sands. See *Contexts* for more on the Elephant Seal's mating habits, and on other coastal creatures as well.

Just north of Ano Nuevo, Gazos Creek Road heads inland three miles to **Butano State Park**, which has ten square miles of redwood trees, views out over the Pacific and a $6-a-night **campsite**. Another two miles north along Hwy-1, and fifty miles south of the Golden Gate Bridge, the beginning of the San Francisco Peninsula is marked by the **Pigeon Point Lighthouse**, where you can spend the night (see p.281) in the old lighthouse keeper's quarters and soak your bones in a hot tub, cantilevered out over the rocks. Pigeon Point took its name from the clipper ship, *Carrier Pigeon*, that broke up on the rocks off the point, one of many shipwrecks that led to the construction of the lighthouse in the late nineteenth century.

The cargo of one of these wrecked ships inspired residents of the nearby fishing village of **PESCADERO**, a mile inland on Pescadero Road, literally to "paint the town", using the hundreds of pots of white paint that were washed up on the shore. The two streets of the small village are still lined by white, wooden buildings, and the descendants of the Portuguese whalers who founded the town keep up another, more enticing tradition, celebrating the **Festival of the Holy Ghost** every year, six weeks after Easter, with a lively and highly ritualised parade. Pescadero is also well known as one of the better places to **eat** on the entire coast, with an excellent restaurant, *Duarte's*, serving fish dinners and fresh fruit pies, and *Dinelli's Café* with Greek food and tasty fried artichoke hearts.

travel details

Trains

From LA *Amtrak* leaves once a day at 9.55am for Santa Barbara (2hr); San Luis Obispo (5hr); Salinas (7hr 30min); San Jose (9hr) and Oakland (11hr), from where a shuttle bus connects to San Francisco.

From San Francisco one train a day leaves Oakland at 8.40am on the same route.

Long-distance buses

From LA *Greyhound* express buses stop at Santa Barbara (15 daily; 2hr); San Luis Obispo (10; 5 hr 30min); Salinas (9; 8hr); and San Francisco (9; 11hr).

From San Francisco *Greyhound* runs to Salinas (9 daily; 2 hr 30min); San Luis Obispo (8; 6hr); Santa Barbara (8; 9hr); and LA (8; 11hr). There are also direct services between San Francisco and Santa Cruz (4 daily; 2hr 30min); and Monterey (4; 3hr 30min).

From LA to San Francisco *Green Tortoise* has a scheduled service once weekly in each direction up and down the coast.

From Oakland and San Jose *Peerless Stages* to Santa Cruz (7 daily; 2 hr).

CHAPTER FIVE

THE CENTRAL VALLEY, NATIONAL PARKS AND THE HIGH SIERRA

The vast **interior** of California – stretching three hundred miles from the Mojave Desert in the south right up to the Gold Country and northern California – is split down the middle by the massive Sierra Nevada mountains. To the west spreads the wide floor of the agricultural Central Valley (also known as the San Joaquin Valley), while on the eastern side, the mountains drop off sharply from the central ridge of the High Sierra into the desert plain of the Owens Valley. It's a region of unparalleled beauty, yet the ninety percent of Californians who live on the coast are barely aware of the area, and mention of it can often provoke laughter at its popular hicksville image.

The **Central Valley** is radically different from anywhere else in the state. During the 1940s, the land was made super-fertile by a massive programme of aqueduct building, using water flowing from the mountains to irrigate the area. The valley, as flat as a pancake, is now almost totally comprised of farmland, periodically enlivened by scattered cities that offer a taste of ordinary Californian life away from the glitz of LA and San Francisco.

From the valley, a gentle ascent through rolling, grassy foothills takes you into dense forests of huge pine and fir trees, interspersed with placid meadows and tranquil lakes and cut by deep rocky canyons. The most impressive sections are protected within three **national parks**: **Sequoia** and **Kings Canyon** – whose prehistorically huge trees form the centrepiece of a rich natural landscape – and **Yosemite**, where towering walls of silvery granite, artfully shaped by Ice Age glaciers, are invigorated by a number of cascading waterfalls. No roads penetrate the hundred miles of wilderness in between, but the entire region is crisscrossed by hiking trails leading up into the pristine alpine backcountry of the **High Sierra**, which contains the glistening summits of some of the highest mountains in the country. When you see them from the eastern side, their Spanish name, *Sierra Nevada*, makes sense: loosely translated it means "snow capped sawblade", which perfectly describes the sharply serrated ridges that stand high above the deserted **Owens Valley**, whose few isolated towns serve as supply-points for hikers and skiers bound for the mountains.

Drivers who aren't particularly interested in exploring the wilds can simply barrel through on I-5, an arrow-straight interstate freeway through the western edge of the Central Valley that's the quickest route between LA and San Francisco. If you're more curious than that, twice-daily **trains** and frequent *Greyhound* **buses**

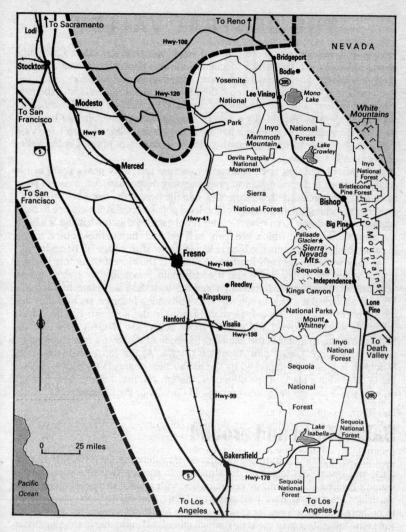

run through the the valley, stopping at the larger cities and towns along Hwy-99 – two of which, Fresno and Merced, have bus connections to Yosemite. Otherwise getting to the mountains can be a problem without a car, though hitching a ride with other wilderness-bound travellers is a fairly safe bet; with a bit of advance planning, you might be able to join one of the many camping trips organised by the *Sierra Club*, the California-based environmentalist group (see p.6). Despite its sparse population, the Owens Valley is easy both to reach and to get around, with a daily *Greyhound* service along US-395 between LA and Reno, Nevada, and the *Trailhead Shuttle Service* ferrying hikers, bikers and skiers to the main High Sierra trailheads.

THE CENTRAL VALLEY

The Central Valley grows more fruit and vegetables than any other agricultural region of its size – a fact which touches the lives, in one way or another, of its every inhabitant. The area is much more conservative and mid-Western in feel than the rest of California, but even if the nightlife begins and ends with the local ice-cream parlour, after the big cities of the coast it can all be refreshingly small-scale and enjoyable. Admittedly nowhere has the energy to detain you long and, between the settlements, the drab hundred-mile vistas of almond groves and vineyards can be sheer torture; as can the weather – summers in the Central Valley are frequently scorching.

Bakersfield, the first town you come to across the rocky peaks north of Los Angeles, is hardly the valley's most prepossessing destination, but in recent years its **country music** scene has burgeoned into the best in the state. It also offers a museum recording the beginnings of the local population, and the chance to mess around on the nearby Kern river. Greater rewards lie further on: **Visalia** is a likeable community, near which are two well-restored turn-of-the-century towns, **Hanford** and **Reedley**, and the bizarre would-be Swedish village of **Kingsburg**.

In many ways the region's lynchpin, **Fresno**, is the closest thing to a bustling urban centre the valley has – and it's just about impossible to avoid. Though economically thriving, it's frequently voted the least desirable place to live in the US, and on arrival it's easy to see why – its redeeming features, such as they are, take a bit of time to discover. Beyond Fresno, in the northern reaches of the valley, lie sedate **Merced** and slightly more boisterous **Modesto** – where the highlight of the calendar is the annual celebration of the town's role as the inspiration for George Lucas' film *American Graffiti*. At the top end of the valley **Stockton** is scenically improved by the delta which connects the city to the sea but is otherwise a place of few pleasures, though you may have to pass through on your way from San Francisco to the Gold Country or the national parks.

Bakersfield and around

Looming unappealingly from behind a forest of oil derricks, **BAKERSFIELD** has a flat and featureless look that does nothing to suggest that this is one of the nation's liveliest country music communities, with a batch of venues where local musicians are ready to blow your socks off. Other than music, there's little reason to be here: the town owes its existence to the fertile soil around the Kern River (once the longest river in the state), which stimulated agriculture, and the discovery of local oil and gas deposits. The **Kern County Museum & Pioneer Village,** 3801 Chester Avenue (Mon–Fri 8am–5pm, Sat & Sun 10am–5pm; $2), documents Bakersfield's development with an impressive collection of over fifty (mostly) restored buildings, many of them dating from the late-nineteenth or early twentieth century. The cumulative effect is to emphasise how boring the place is today – with the exception of its music.

Practicalities

Bakersfield is an important public transport hub: you have to come here from LA by *Amtrak* bus to catch the train through the valley to San Francisco and Northern

California, and travelling by *Greyhound* (1820 18th Street; ☎327-7371) you may well need to change routes here – although overnight stops are rarely necessary. The **Visitor Information Center**, 2101 Oak Street (Mon–Fri 8am–5pm; ☎805/861-2367), and the **Chamber of Commerce**, 1033 Truxton Street (Mon–Thurs 8.30am–5pm, Fri 8.30am–4pm; ☎805/327-4421), can supply factual information.

Stay in tune with Bakersfield's country-music persona by **eating** at *Zingo's*, 2625 Pierce Road, a 24-hour truckstop whose frilly-aproned waitresses deliver plates of diner staples. Cheapest **overnight stays** are at *EZ-8*, 2604 Pierce Road (☎322-1907), and the *Roadrunner Motel*, 2619 Pierce Road (☎805/323-3727), both $30-35.

COUNTRY MUSIC IN BAKERSFIELD

The main – and quite possibly only – reason to dally for more than a few hours in Bakersfield is to hear **country music**; on any weekend the town's numerous honky-tonks reverberate to the sounds of the best country musicians in the US, many of them resident in the town.

The **roots** of Bakersfield's country music scene are with the Mid-Western farmers who arrived in the Central Valley during the Depression, bringing their hillbilly instruments and campfire songs with them. This rustic entertainment quickly broadened into a variety of more contemporary styles developed in the bars and clubs that began to appear in the town, where future legends such as Merle Haggard and Buck Owens (who now, incidently, owns the local country-music radio station, KUZZ 107.9 FM) cut their teeth. A failed attempt to turn Bakersfield into "Nashville West" during the Sixties, and bring the major country-music record labels here from their traditional base, has left the town eager to promote the distinctive "Bakersfield Sound": a far less slick and commercial affair than its Tennessee counterpart.

If you don't get to hear any live music, you can gain an inkling of the Bakersfield Sound from the 1988 hit, *Streets of Bakersfield*, a duet by Buck Owens and Dwight Yoakam – and visit the Country Music museum due to open in 1993, charting the rise and rise of Bakersfield's music, in the grounds of the Pioneer Village.

Venues

To find out **what's on**, read the Friday edition of the *Bakersfield Californian*, check the flyers at the tourist offices mentioned below, or phone one of the venues we've listed. Fridays and Saturdays are the liveliest nights, although there's often something to enjoy during the week, if only the free **country-dancing lessons** offered at many of the town's bars. There's never a cover charge, and live sets usually entail one band playing for four or five hours from around 8pm and taking a fifteen-minute break every hour. Stetson hats and flowery blouses are the sartorial order of the day, and audiences span generations, ranging in age from twenty-one to ninety-one.

Most **venues** are hotel lounges or restaurant backrooms, though one not to be missed is *Trouts*, 805 N Chester Ave (☎805/399-6700), a country-music bar that's been in business nearly forty years. Close by, you might also investigate *Cassidy's*, 4500 Pierce Road (☎805/631-9303); *Junction Lounge*, 2620 Pierce Road (☎805/327-9651); or the *Sutter Street Bar & Grill*, at the *Ramada Inn*, 3535 Rosedale Highway (☎805/327-0681). Another group of worthwhile venues are a half-hour drive across town: *Brandy's Tavern*, 2700 S Union Ave (☎805/831-9853); *Little Bit Country*, 3317 State Road (☎805/393-8044); and *Porter's House*, 10701 Hwy-78 (☎805/366-6000). If it's a Sunday, make for *Ethel's*, on Alfred Harrel Highway, on the way to Krenville State Park, a beer'n'burger shack (usually closed during September) which stages enjoyable afternoon jam sessions featuring local musicians.

Around Bakersfield: The Kern River and Lake Isabella

After a night spent in the smoky honky-tonks, you might like to clear your head by taking a drive out of Bakersfield to **Lake Isabella**, 45 miles northeast on Hwy-178. Both the lake, and the Kern River which feeds it, offer a range of watery activities: fishing, boating, and rafting trips (many companies run trips, including *Sierra South*, 11300 Kernville Road; ☎619/376-3745), ranging from novice-standard jaunts to more adventurous two- and three-day trips on the foaming portions of the river, where previous experience and a medical test are necessary before casting off. At **KERNVILLE**, on the northern shore of the lake, you can get on-the-spot facts from the **Cannel Meadow District Ranger Office** (summer daily 8am–4.30pm, winter Mon–Fri 8am–4.30pm; ☎619/376-3781). From Kernville, the twisting and narrow **Western Divide Highway** (closed in winter and during bad weather) crosses the neighbouring Greenhorn Mountains and the Sequoia National Forest towards US-395, which runs through the Owens Valley (see p.310), eventually ending up on the edge of Death Valley (see Chapter Three).

Visalia and Tulare County

As you leave Bakersfield heading north on Hwy-99, the oil wells fade into full-blown agricultural territory. You can turn east onto Hwy-190 at Tipton for PORTERVILLE and the Sequoia National Forest (the forest headquarters at 900 W Grand Avenue – ☎209/784-1500 – has information on trails across the mountains and the national parks). Otherwise there's nowhere meriting a stop until you reach Tulare County, some seventy miles north of Bakersfield, where several small communities repay quick visits.

Visalia

The first and largest of the towns north of Bakersfield is **VISALIA**, just west of Hwy-99 on Hwy-198. Due to a large oak forest which offered both shade and home-building material, Visalia was the first place in the Central Valley to be settled. Although the forest is gone, there are still large numbers of oaks and eucalpytus planted around the city and local people put an extraordinary amount of care into the upkeep of parks and gardens. In short, it's a pretty place, with a calm and restful air – if you're seeking anything more active you'll be disappointed.

Visalia's features are best seen on foot: self-guided walking tours of its older parts can be obtained free from the **Convention and Visitors Bureau**, 720 W Mineral King Avenue (Mon–Fri 8.30am–5pm; ☎209/734-5876; 24hr info ☎209/732-2711); or you could visit the **Tulare County Mooney Grove Park and Museum** (Museum: Wed, Thurs, Fri & Mon 10am–6pm, Sat & Sun noon–6pm; closed Tues; $1.50), about two miles from the city centre at the end of South Mooney Boulevard. The museum has a hotchpotch of local historical curios, and in the park you'll find the *End of the Trail* statue, originally made for the 1915 Panama Pacific Exhibition in San Francisco, which portrays the defeat of the Indians at the hands of advancing white settlers. Intentionally gloomy, the statue became well known throughout the West, and still inspires a host of copies and numerous snap-happy tourists.

Practicalities

Visalia has a wide choice of places to **eat**: the *Gum Bo Chinese Buffet*, 101 W Main Street, has a cheap lunch buffet; *Pita Mania*, 225 W Main, provides Greek snacks; and *BJ's Kountry Kitchen,* 2363 Mooney Boulevard (closes at 2pm), and *Kay's Kafé*, 215 N Giddings Avenue, have inexpensive American-style breakfasts and lunches. $30–35-a-night **motels** are plentiful along Mineral King Avenue: *El Rancho*, no. 4506 (☎209/734-9271), and *Motel Ashri*, no. 4801 (☎209/627-2885), are as good as any.

Moving On

In Visalia, you're well-placed for both the Sequoia National Park (46 miles away on Hwy-198, see p.297) and the northern end of the Sequoia National Forest – seventeen miles from Visalia on Hwy-245, which branches off Hwy-198. On the way to the Sequoia National Park, **Lake Kaweah** provides an opportunity to waterski and catch fish, and is the best **camping** option in the area: either at *Horse Creek* (☎805/597-2301) beside Hwy-198, or, more expensively, at the **Kaweah Park Resort** (☎805/561-4424), a little further east near THREE RIVERS.

West from Visalia: Hanford

Twenty-four miles west of Visalia on Hwy-198, **HANFORD** was named after James Hanford, a paymaster on the Southern Pacific Railroad who became popular with his employees when he took to paying them in gold. The town formed part of a spur on the railroad and became a major stopover on the route between Los Angeles and San Francisco, which it remains – although rail travellers are far fewer today than they once were.

The leftovers from the railway's boom era are what capture one's attention. In the centre of town the now spotless and spruced-up buildings around Courthouse Square were the core of local life at the turn of the century. The honey-coloured **Courthouse** (Mon–Sat 10am–6pm, Sun 10am–5pm; closed Aug; free) retains many of its Neoclassical features – not least a magnificent staircase – and has, more recently, been occupied by shops and galleries. As you'd expect, the old Hanford jail, rather pretentiously modelled on the Paris Bastille, is only a ball-and-chain's throw away, now doing time as a restaurant (*La Bastille*), although you can wander through to see the old cells – now and again used for secluded dining. Opposite the restaurant, the grandiose Ionic columns of the Civic Auditorium make it easy to locate the adjoining **Veterans' Building**, in which many of the objects and memorabilia from Hanford's glory years are stashed.

Much less ostentatiously, rows of two-storey porched dwellings, a few blocks east of the square, mark the district which was home to most of the eight hundred or so Chinese families who came to Hanford to work on the railroad. At the centre of the community was the **Taoist Temple** on China Alley (groups of 6–20 only and by appointment; $1 per person; more details from the Visitor Agency, see below). Built in 1893, the temple served a social as well as a spiritual function, providing free lodging to work-seeking Chinese travellers, and was used as a Chinese school during the early Twenties. Everything inside is original, from the teak burl figurines to the marble chairs, and it's a shame that entry is so restricted. You can, however, take a look at another institution of Hanford's

Chinese community: the **Imperial Dynasty Restaurant**, two doors along from the temple, still run by the family who opened it fifty years ago. The interior is simple and modest, but the fame of the cooking has spread far and wide and prices have risen as a result.

For more information on Hanford, use the **Visitor Agency** at 213 W Seventh Street (Mon–Fri 8am–5pm; ☎209/582-0483).

North from Visalia: Kingsburg and Reedley

Over half the inhabitants of **KINGSBURG**, twenty miles north of Visalia on Hwy-99, are of Swedish descent, but it's only in the last twenty-five years that they've sought to exploit their roots, converting the town's buildings to Swedish-style architecture and plastering their windows and walls with tributes to the Swedish royal family and the Dana Horse (an object traditionally carved by woodcutters from the Dalarna district of Sweden). Save for such peculiarities, it hardly warrants a call, except perhaps on the third Saturday in May when it stages – predictably – a Swedish festival.

Compared to Kingsburg, **REEDLEY**, five miles east, is a metropolis, though beyond its main thoroughfare – G Street – it's just as quiet. The pinnacles of local entertainment are watching the patient weavers at the **Mennonite Quilting Centre**, 1010 G Street (usually Mon–Fri 8.30am–5pm; free), and exploring the strange **Burgess Hotel** at 1726 11th Street. This one-time doss-house has been revamped with each room decorated in a style of a different country, city or historical period. Usefully, it's not very expensive – you can bed down in the less exotic "San Francisco" or "bi-centennial" rooms for $28. Or just step in off the street and reel with astonishment at the attempt to recreate Morocco in the lobby.

Fresno

Almost classic in its ugliness, **FRESNO** is very much the hub of business in the Central Valley. Caught between being a farming-flavoured town and a fully-blown commercial city, Fresno seems to have missed out on the restoration programmes that have improved similar communities elsewhere in California, while its solution to traffic congestion has been to insert a freeway plumb through its centre. It's significant, too, that the symbol of bland consumerist America – the indoor shopping mall – was first seen here. For all that, Fresno does have its good points (not least a daily bus service to Yosemite) and, since the town can't easily be avoided, it's handy to know about them.

Downtown Fresno is the business heart, with not much to view except the hopefully named **Metropolitan Museum of Art, Science & History**, 1555 Van Ness Avenue (Wed–Sun 11am–5pm; $2), which covers a bit of (almost) everything, mainly with temporary exhibitions. A short walk away, the **Fresno Art Center**, 2233 N First Street (Tues–Sun 10am–5pm; $2), has a similarly worthy but slightly desperate selection of paintings, sculpture and lithographs. There's more compelling stuff in the **Meux Home Museum** (guided tours Fri–Sun noon–3.30pm; free) at the corner of Tulare and R Street, just behind the *Amtrak* station. Built for what in the late nineteenth century was the staggering sum of twelve thousand dollars, this was the home of a doctor who arrived from the

Deep South, bringing with him the novelty of a two-storey house and a plethora of trendy Victorian features. What isn't original is a convincing reconstruction, and the turrets, arches, and even an octagonal master-bedroom, help make the place stylish and absorbing – and quite out of synch with the Fresno which has sprawled up around it.

Given its reputation for almond-growers and cattle-rustlers, Fresno's so-called **Needle** (or **"Tower"**) **District**, three miles north of Downtown along Van Ness Avenue, comes as a pleasant surprise. Proximity to the City College campus made the area something of a hippy hangout during the Sixties; today it has a well-scrubbed liberal bent plus several blocks of antique shops and bookstores, ethnic eateries and coffee bars to fill a few hours of idle browsing.

Over the railway tracks at the end of Olive Avenue, the tree-filled **Roeding Park** is the home of the Fresno **zoo** (daily 10am–5pm; $3), a couple of amusement parks and a lake, and is where Fresnoites come to convince themselves that the city is a nice place to live. Ensconced here on a sunny day, you could almost start believing them.

Around Fresno

Seven miles southwest of the city, close to Hwy-99, Kearney Boulevard is a long, straight and exotically planted thoroughfare that was once the private driveway of Martin Kearney, an English-born turn-of-the-century agricultural pioneer and raisin mogul who had the road built to reach his abode, the **Kearney Mansion** (Fri–Sun 1–4pm; $3) – maintained in the opulent French Renaissance style to which Kearney seemed addicted. He had even grander plans to grace Fresno with a French chateau, the mind-boggling plans for which are displayed here. Regarded locally as something of a mystery man, Kearney apparently led a pacey social life on both sides of the Atlantic, which may explain why he perished following a heart attack during an ocean crossing.

Also close to Hwy-99, about five miles further north, are the remarkable **Forestiere Underground Gardens** at 5021 W Shaw Boulevard (mid-June to early September Wed–Sun 10am–4pm, rest of the year weekends and holidays only; $4). These 65 underground rooms, including a two-storey house and a chapel, all with furnishings and full facilities, were hewn out of solid earth by an Italian farmer, seeking to make the most of his allotment of land – an eminently sensible idea, given Fresno's proneness to baking summer temperatures.

Practicalities

Details on everything in and around the city (and transport to and from the national parks) can be checked at the **Convention and Visitors Bureau**, 690 M Street (Mon–Fri 8am–5pm; ☎209/233-0356). The **bus** and **train** terminals are both in downtown Fresno: *Greyhound* at 1033 Broadway (☎209/268-9461) and *Amtrak* at the junction of Tulare and Q Street (☎209/252-8253).

If you need to **spend a night in Fresno** – almost a necessity if you're travelling the length of the valley or are heading for Yosemite – you'll find the usual glut of cheap motels on the city fringes. More central are the *Vagabond Motor Hotel*, 1807 Broadway (☎209/268-0916), $30 to $40 for a double, and *Motel Orleans*, 888 Broadway (☎1-800/485-7550), $30 a double.

The indoor **farmers market** (Mon–Sat 9am–9pm), at the corner of Divisadero and Tulare Street, and the **outdoor produce market**, on the corner of Merced and N Street (Tues, Thurs, Sat 7am–3pm) are good spots to pick up fresh, cheap **food**. Otherwise, there are a lunch buffets for around $5 at *Diners Smorgasbord* in the *Fulton Mall* on Fresno Street, and the *Sante Fe Hotel* (11.30am–1.30pm), next door to the *Amtrak* station. If they don't appeal, the *Baker Street Café* on the ground floor of the *Hilton Hotel*, 1055 Van Ness Avenue, knocks out some good-priced lunches.

Moving On

Travelling onwards, Fresno has the most direct road link from the valley to Yosemite National Park (p.303), with Hwy-41. Hwy-180 runs south to Kings Canyon National Park (p.300). To get to Yosemite by bus, contact *McCoy's Charter Service* (☎209/268-2237) who run five services a week; the three-hour journey costs $14.

Continuing north: Merced and Modesto

The best thing about sluggishly paced **MERCED**, fifty miles north of Fresno, is its courthouse, a gem of a building in the main square that's maintained as the **County Courthouse Museum** (Wed–Sun 1–4pm; free). The striking Italian Renaissance-style structure, with columns, elaborately sculptured window frames and a cupola topped by a statue of the Goddess Of Justice (minus her customary blindfold), was raised in 1875, dominating Merced then as it still does now. Impressively restored in period style, the courtroom retained a legal function until 1951, while the equally sumptuous offices were vacated in the 1970s, leaving the place to serve as storage space for local memorabilia – most exotic among which is a Taoist shrine, found by chance in the back room of a Chinese restaurant.

Merced has convenient **bus links to Yosemite** (twice daily for $15 with *Yosemite Via Bus*; ☎209/722-0366; or once daily for $13 with *California Yosemite Tours*; ☎209/383-1563 or ☎383-1570), but there's little reason to hang around the town itself. The **Convention and Visitors Bureau** at 1880 N Street (Mon–Fri 8.30am–5pm; ☎384-3333) can provide any information you may need.

Six miles out of Merced, close to the dormitory community of ATWOOD, the **Castle Air Museum** (daily 10am–4pm; free), adjoins an airforce base. It displays thirty-odd military aircraft – mostly bulky bombers with a few fighters thrown in – and has a slightly less militaristic collection of aviation paraphernalia too.

Modesto

Forty miles further along Hwy-99, **MODESTO** was the childhood home of film director George Lucas, and the city became the inspiration (though not the location) for his film, *American Graffiti*, the classic portrayal of growing up in small-town America during the late 1950s. Unbeknown to the general cinema-going public, the movie contains a number of references to local people, particularly the teachers who rubbed Lucas up the wrong way in his formative years.

Modesto has a less than action-packed nightlife, but the fine art of **cruising** still continues along McHenry Avenue, which has replaced the favoured strip of Lucas's time, the four-block-strip on Tenth Street between G and K Streets – close to which (at 1404 G Street) the *A&W Root Beer Drive-In* has roller-skating waitresses in celebration of the celluloid connection. Better still is **"graffiti**

night" – a special commemoration of the movie which takes place on the first Saturday after graduation (the second or third week in June) each year. Throughout the appointed day, authentic autos of the fabled era are dusted off and driven through the city, while in the evening Modesto teenagers of all ages take to their vehicles and participate in a bumper-to-bumper cruise along McHenry Avenue. The event is so popular that regular traffic through the city becomes severely disrupted, and the police have to limit the number of circuits. To find out exactly when graffiti night is due to take place, contact the **Visitors and Conventions Bureau**, 1114 J Street (Mon–Fri 8am–5pm; ☎209/577-5757).

It may seem hard to believe, but Modesto does have a history stretching back beyond duck-tail haircuts and bobby-sox, having grown through the usual Central Valley mix of farming and the railway. Its (comparatively) distant past is encapsulated by the shabbily grand **Modesto Arch** – erected in 1912 over Ninth and I Street to attract attention to the city's expanding economy – and, more imposingly, the Victorian **McHenry Mansion** at 906 15th Street (Tues–Thurs & Sun 1–4pm; free), which is jam-packed with fixtures, fittings and the personal features of a family whose fate was linked with Modesto's for years. Robert McHenry was a successful wheat-rancher who did much to bring about a general uplift in the agricultural well-being of the area. It's surprising to think the luxurious dwelling was still being rented out as cheapish apartments as recently as the early 1970s.

A few minutes' walk from the mansion, the **McHenry Museum**, 1402 I Street (Tues–Sun noon–4pm; free), originally financed by the McHenry family, sports mock-ups of a doctor's office, blacksmith's shop, dentist's surgery and gathering of cattle brands, revealing something of bygone days, although lacking the period atmosphere of the mansion. Adjoining the museum is the **Central California Art League Gallery** (Tues–Sat 11am–4pm; free), with a show of regional painting and sculpture that should consume no more than a few minutes.

Stockton and around

Perched at the far northern limit of the Central Valley, the immediately striking thing about **STOCKTON** is the sight of ocean-going freighters so far inland. The San Joaquin and Sacramento rivers converge here, creating a vast delta with thousands of inlets and bays, and a man-made deep-water channel enables vessels to carry the produce of the valley's farms past San Francisco and directly out to sea. But the geography which aided commerce also saddled Stockton with the image of being a grim place to live and a tough city to work in. During the Gold Rush it was a supply stop on the route to the gold mines, and it became a gigantic flophouse for broken and dispirited ex-miners who gave up dreaming of a fortune and returned here to toil on the waterfront. Though valiant efforts have been made to shed this reputation and beautify the less attractive quarters, it's still primarily a sleeves-rolled-up city of hard work.

The downtown area has a scattering of buildings evoking the early decades of the century – thanks to which Stockton is often in demand as a film set. John Huston's downbeat boxing picture, *Fat City*, for example, was shot here. The walkway along the side of the channel offers views of pleasure craft and takes you through the moderately interesting **Waterside Warehouse**, a mix of shops and pricey snack-stops inside a converted storehouse. In a similar vein, though marginally more appealing, the blocks bordered by Harding Way and Park Street, and El Dorado and California streets, a short way out of the centre, have been preserved as the **Magnolia Historical District**, with sixteen intriguing specimens of domestic architecture spanning seven decades from the 1860s. To find them all, pick up the free leaflet from the **Convention and Visitors Bureau** at 46 W Fremont Street in downtown Stockton (Mon–Fri 8.00am–5pm; ☎1-800/888-8016).

Roughly a mile from the Magnolia district, in Pershing Park alongside Victory Avenue, Stockton gathers totems of its past in the varied and large stock of the **Haggin Museum**, 1201 N Pershing Avenue (Tues–Sun 1.30–5pm; free). Not surprisingly, much is given over to agriculture, including the city's finest moment: the invention by local farmers of a caterpillar tread to enable tractors to travel over muddy ground, adapted by the British for use on tanks and standard-use since for the military everywhere. In tremendous contrast, the museum also contains a batch of nineteenth-century French paintings, including works by Renoir and Gauguin, and Bouguereau's monumental *Nymphs Bathing*.

Practicalities

Stockton's *Greyhound* station is at 121 S Center Street (☎209/465-5781); *Amtrak* at 735 S San Joaquin Street (☎209/946-0527). Even travelling by public transport doesn't mean you have to stay overnight in Stockton – connections both onwards to San Francisco and south down the valley are plentiful – but it can be worth stopping to **eat**: ethnic restaurants being in good supply. For Mexican food there's *Arroyo's*, 324 S Center Street (closed Mon and evenings), *Chili's Bar & Grill*, 5756 Pacific Avenue, or *Porfi's*, 2302 Pacific Avenue; for Chinese try *On Lock Sam*, 333 S Sutter Street, or *Dave Wong's*, 5602 N Pershing Avenue. Of regular American food, steaks and seafood are on offer at the *Catfish Café*, 1560 W March Lane.

There's a **campsite** eight miles south of Stockton – Dos Reis Park (☎209/953-8800), just off I-5, – but staying in the city means spending $60 to $80 in one of the plentiful mid-range chain **hotels**. The pick of these are the *Stockton Vagabond Inn*, 33 N Center Street (☎1-800/522-1555), and *La Quinta*, 2710 W March Lane (☎1-800/531-5900).

Around Stockton: Micke Grove Park and Lodi

If Stockton begins to pall, or it's too nice a day to spend in a city, venture five miles north along Hwy-99 for the pastoral relief – at least outside weekends and holidays – of the **Micke Grove Park** (daily 8am–dusk), an oak grove which holds a Rose Garden, a Japanese Garden and a zoo. It also features the **San Joaquin Historical Museum** (Wed–Sun 1–5pm; free), recording the evolution of the local agricultural industry and, more revealingly, the social history which accompanied it. Don't miss the Stockton clamshell dredge bucket, a tool used in the reclamation of the delta and restored and displayed as if a major work of art.

Beyond the park, on the way north to Sacramento, the state capital (see p.430), sits **LODI**, a small country town immortalised in song by Creedence Clearwater Revival ("oh lord, stuck in Lodi again"), though these days best known for its mass-market **wineries**, several of which have daily tours and tastings. You can get a full list from the Lodi **Chamber of Commerce**, 215 W Oak Street (☎209/334-4773), or the Visitors Bureau in Stockton.

THE NATIONAL PARKS

The reason most coastal Californians grit their teeth and head through the Central Valley is to reach the **national parks** which cover the foothills and upper reaches of the Sierra Nevada Mountains. The southernmost of these, **Sequoia** and **Kings Canyon**, are home to forests of ancient giant sequoia trees and an array of other animal, vegetable and mineral spectacles, and there is ample opportunity for some intrepid hiking. But the biggest draw, and one of the few not-to-be-missed places in California, is the mile-deep and mile-wide valley of **Yosemite**, bounded by the greatest walls of sculpted stone on earth. The world's best rock-climbers spend years here mastering the near-vertical granite faces, while millions of shutter-bug tourists overload the fairly limited facilities each summer to admire the waterfalls that tumble down to the valley floor.

Mercifully, the hordes are easily avoided, either by arriving outside of peak holiday times or, better still, by simply packing a tent and heading into the three thousand square miles of untouched backcountry either protected within the parks proper or the surrounding **national forests**.

Sequoia and Kings Canyon

Separate parks but jointly run, **SEQUOIA AND KINGS CANYON** contain an immense variety of geology, flora and fauna. **Sequoia National Park**, as you might expect from its name, contains the thickest concentration – and the biggest individual specimens – of giant sequoia trees to be found anywhere. These ancient trees tend to outshine (and certainly outgrow) the other features of the park, which is made up of an assortment of meadows, peaks, canyons and caves. With a few exceptions, **Kings Canyon National Park** doesn't have the big trees but compensates with a gaping canyon gored out of the rock by the Kings River, which cascades in torrents down from the High Sierra during the snowmelt period. The few established sights (like the drive-through Auto Log) of both parks are near the main roads and concentrate the crowds, leaving the vast majority of the landscape untrammelled and unspoilt but well within reach for willing hikers.

Sequoia and Kings Canyon practicalities

Unfortunately there's no **public transport** of any kind to either of the parks, and the only way to get there (other than hitchhiking) if you're not driving is the day-long **guided tour** from the Visalia *KOA* campsite (☎1-800/322-2336) – although even this requires a minumum of six people and is costly at $20 per person. **By car**, on the other hand, things are pretty simple: the closest large town to the parks is Visalia, just under fifty miles distant on Hwy-198, or there's a slightly longer drive using Hwy-180 from Fresno.

A **fee** of $5 per car, or $2 per person for those on foot, will be collected at the entrance stations; in return you'll be allowed in and given a copy of the free newspaper, *Sequoia Bark*, which has details and timetables for the numerous **guided hikes** and other interpretive activities, as well as general information on the parks.

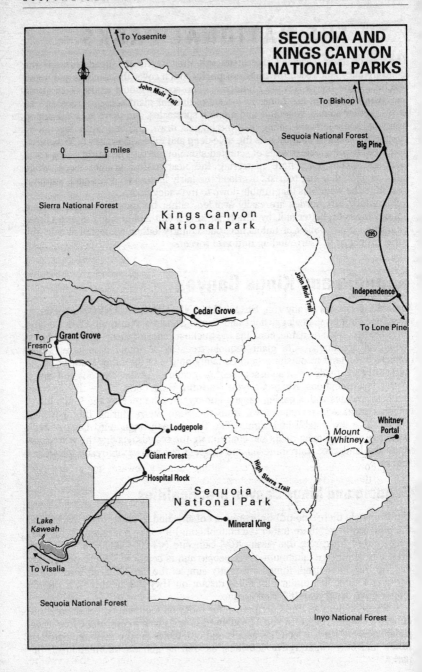

Accommodation

Other than camping, the cheapest places to stay are the motels lining the approach roads, a few miles from the park entrances. Most of these are broadly similar, though two which stand out are the *Snowline Lodge*, on Hwy-180 (☎209/336-2300), around $50, and the similarly priced *Badger Creek Ranch Resort*, a one-time drug rehabilitation centre, whose comfortable cabins fill a large area beside Hwy-245 (☎209/337-2340).

Inside the parks, all facilities, including **accommodation**, are managed by *Guest Services Inc* (☎209/561-3314). Sleeping under a roof is restricted to the cabins at Giant Forest Village, Grant Grove and Cedar Grove, and motel rooms at Stony Creek, about five miles from Grant Grove and just outside the park boundary. Most of the rooms are simple but adequate and some have stoves for cooking. Space is at a premium during the high season (May to October), although you can usually pick up cancellations on the day. Summer prices range from $28 for the most basic cabin, to $97 for a deluxe version with bathroom and comfy beds. Winter makes the cheaper cabins too cold to sleep in, when you'll need to spend around $35 for one of the mid-range type. There are also a few very basic cabins at **Bearpaw Meadow Camp** (☎209/561-3341), eleven miles east of Giant Forest on the High Sierra Trail; cost is $22.

Except during public holidays, there is always plenty of **camping space** in the parks, at a cost of $4–8 (recorded information: ☎209/565-3351). **In Sequoia**, the busiest campsite is *Lodgepole* (☎209/565-3338; bookable through MISTIX); Mineral King has two campsites, *Atwell Mill* and *Cold Springs*, both basic but with piped water and plenty of peace and quiet; and near the park entrance on Hwy-198 are the campervan-dominated *Potiswa*, and the less crowded *Buckeye Flat*. **In Kings Canyon**, there are the *Sunset*, *Azalea* and *Crystal Springs* campsites, all close to Grant Grove, and *Canyon View*, *Moraine*, *Sheep Creek* and *Sentinel*, dotted around Cedar Grove. For **backcountry** camping get a free permit from a visitors centre or ranger station.

Eating

There are **food** markets and cafeterias at Giant Forest Village, Lodgepole and at Cedar Grove Village, though prices will be higher than outside the park. The only fully-fledged **restaurant** in either park is *Giant Forest Lodge Dining Room* at Giant Forest Village, which can offer fitting culinary rewards for a hard day's hiking, though you'll easily lay waste to $20.

USEFUL PHONE NUMBERS

Park headquarters ☎209/565-3341.
Recorded camping info ☎209/565-3456.
Recorded weather and road info ☎209/565-3306.

Sequoia National Park

The two main centres in **SEQUOIA NATIONAL PARK** are Giant Forest and Lodgepole – the accommodation bases and starting-points for most of the hiking trails. To the south there's also the more isolated Mineral King area. While trees are seldom scarce – where the giant sequoias can't grow there are thick swathes of pine and fir – the scenery varies throughout the park: sometimes subtly, sometimes abruptly. Everywhere paths lead through deep forests and around meadows; longer treks rise above the treeline to reveal the barren peaks and gorgeous sights of the High Sierras.

The **history of the park** is laced with political intrigue. In the 1880s the Giant Forest area was bought by the *Co-Operative Land Purchase and Colonisation Association*, a group of individuals known as the Kaweah Colony that had the idea of forming a workers' colony here. They began what became the four-year task of building a road from the Central Valley up to Giant Forest, intending to start commercial logging of the huge trees there. Due to legal technicalities, however, their rights to the area were disputed, and in 1890 a bill (probably instigated by a combination of agricultural and railway interests) was passed by the Senate which effected the preservation of all sequoia groves. The colony lost everything, and received no compensation for the road, which remained in use for thirty years – although decades later the ex-leader of the colony acknowledged that the eventual outcome was of far greater benefit to society as a whole than his own scheme would have been.

Giant Forest and around

Entering the park on **Hwy-180 from Visalia**, you pass **Hospital Rock**, easily spotted by the side of the road and decorated with rock drawings from a Native American settlement first established here in 1350. The rock got its name from a trapper who accidently shot himself in the leg and was treated here by the local tribe – who are further remembered by a small exhibition telling something of their evolution and culture.

From Hospital Rock, the road soon becomes the Generals' Highway and climbs swiftly into the densely forested section of the park, the aptly labelled **GIANT FOREST**. Giant Forest Village, near the junction with Crescent Meadow Road, offers food and accommodation (see above), and makes a good base for exploring the features of the area.

Six miles along a marked trail from the village (or a short car ride along Crescent Meadow Road and then a fifteen-minute walk), is the dramatic **Moro Rock**, a granite monolith streaking wildly upward from the green hillside. Views from its remarkably level top can stretch 150 miles across the Central Valley and, in the other direction, to the towering Sierras. A masonry staircase makes climbing the rock comparatively easy although the altitude can be a strain. Reputedly the rock also makes a good platform for feeling vibrations of distant earthquakes.

Continuing along Crescent Meadow Road you pass the **Auto Log,** chiselled flat enough to enable motorists to drive on to it (hence its name), and pass under the **Tunnel Log**: a tree which fell across the road in 1937 and had a vehicle-sized hole cut through it. Further on, **Crescent Meadow** is, like other grassy fields in the area, more accurately a marsh, and too wet for the sequoias which form an impressive boundary around. The trail around its perimeter leads to **Log Meadow**, to which a farmer, Hale Tharp, searching for a summer grazing ground for his sheep, was led by local Indians in 1856. He became not only the first white man to see the giant sequoias but also the first person actually to live in one – a hollowed-out specimen which is still here, remembered as **Tharp's Log**. From here hardy backpackers can pick up the John Muir Trail and hike the 74 miles to

Mount Whitney (the tallest mountain in the continental US, see p.311). Several less demanding trails cover the couple of miles back to Giant Forest Village.

Just north of Giant Forest on the Generals' Highway (and reachable on foot by various connecting trails) is the biggest sequoia of them all. The three-thousand-year-old **General Sherman Tree** is 275 feet high, with a base diameter of 36 feet (and was, for a time, renamed the Karl Marx Tree by the Kaweah Colony). While it's certainly a thrill to be face-to-bark with what is widely held to be the largest living thing on the planet, its extraordinary dimensions rather pale besides those of the almost equally monstrous sequoias around – and the other tremendous batch that can be seen on the **Congress Trail**, which starts from the General Sherman tree.

When you've had your fill of the magnificent trees, consider also a trip to one of the park's caves. Nine miles from Giant Forest along a minor road, the **Crystal Cave** (guided tours mid-June to early Sept 10am–3pm on the hour and half-hour, rest of the year Fri–Mon 10am–3pm on the hour; $3) has a mildly diverting batch of stalagmites and stalactites.

Lodgepole and around

Whatever your plans, you should stop at Lodgepole Village – four miles along the Generals' Highway from Giant Forest Village – for the geological displays, film-shows and general information on offer at the **Visitors Center** (daily 8am–5pm; ☎209/563-3341 ext 631). Lodgepole is at one end of the Tokopah Valley, a glacially formed canyon (not unlike the much larger Yosemite Valley) that's a piece of cake to explore on the **Tokopah Valley Trail** – which leads from Lodgepole through the valley to the base of Tokopah Falls, beneath the 1600-foot **Watchtower** cliff.

The top of the Watchtower, and the great view of the valley from it, are accessible by way of the **Lakes Trail**, a popular trek, nearly seven miles in length, taking in a fatiguing rise in altitude of 2300 feet. Many walkers turn around at the first of the three lakes on the route, Heather Lake, although if you want to camp along the trail, pressing on for another mile brings you to Emerald Lake, where's there's a **campsite**. The path ends at Pear Lake, a mile further on, which also has a camping area. For the really adventurous (and experienced), both the latter lakes make good start-points for self-guided trekking into the mountains.

The sharpest ascent of all the Lodgepole hikes is on the **Alta Peak & Alta Meadows Trail**, which rises four thousand feet over seven miles. If you don't fancy this in its entirety, the trail splits after slightly more than three miles: from here there's a choice between the easy, level walk to Alta Meadow and its fine views of the surrounding peaks (and the chance to pursue another trail for four miles to the desolate Moose Lake); or the daunting near-vertical (a two thousand-feet rise) hike to Alta Peak – which has even more stunning panoramas.

Mineral King

Lying in the southern section of the park, **MINERAL KING** can only be reached in summer by the century-old twisting Mineral King Road, which branches from Hwy-198 near THREE RIVERS. Eager prospectors built the thoroughfare hoping the area would yield silver. It didn't, the mines were abandoned and the region – the only part of the high country accessible by car – was left to a couple of (very basic) campsites and near-complete tranquillity. Once here you can celebrate the failure of the Disney Corporation's plans to decimate the area by building a ski-resort – they were defeated when the area was added to the national park – by hiking up over steep Sawtooth Pass and into the alpine bowls of the glaciated basins beyond. Pick up practical information at the **ranger station** by the side of the road (summer daily 7am–5pm, rest of the year weekends only 7am–5pm; ☎209/561-3341 ext 812).

Kings Canyon National Park

KINGS CANYON NATIONAL PARK is a wilder, less visited park than Sequoia, with just one real road, skirting the colossal canyon and ending close to Cedar Grove, the only place inside the park with accommodation and eating facilities (see above) and starting-point for most of the marked hikes.

Away from Cedar Grove, you're on your own. The vast untamed park has a maze-like collection of canyons and a sprinkling of isolated lakes – the perfect environment for careful self-guided exploration. To get here, **from Fresno** Hwy-180 runs into the park through the Sequoia National Forest at the Big Stump entrance near Grant Grove; **from Sequoia National Park** simply follow the Generals' Highway, which ends at Grant Grove.

Grant Grove, the Big Stump Area and Hume Lake

Confusingly, **GRANT GROVE** is an enclave of Kings Canyon National Park within the Sequoia National Forest but unless you're planning a major backcountry hike across the parks' boundaries you'll have to pass through here before reaching Kings Canyon proper. In Grant Grove there's a useful **Visitors Center** (daily 8am–5pm; ☎209/335-2315) and the General Grant and Robert E Lee giant sequoias, as well as the massive stump of another which was cut down to be taken to the 1875 World's Fair in Philadelphia – an attempt to convince cynical easterners that such enormous trees really existed.

National forests are federally administered but enjoy much less protection than national parks, and are often exploited for logging and mining. Sequoia National Forest is no exception. A mile from Grant Grove, the **BIG STUMP AREA** is named after the big stumps which litter the place – remnants from the first logging of sequoias carried out during the 1880s. A mile-long nature trail leads through this scene of devastation. It's hardly an enjoyable experience, even if you can spot the ageing remains of flumes used to transport logs to the valley.

Hume Lake and around

About five miles north of Grant Grove, on a minor road between the Kings Canyon Highway and Quail Flat, **HUME LAKE** was built as an artificial lake to provide water for logging flumes, it now forms the heart of an under-populated area that's a good place to **spend a night**. Beside the lake, the comparatively large *Princess* campsite charges $6 a night although there are seven other free, less developed **campsites** in the vicinity, all handily placed for the local hiking trails. If you want to walk through the area and into either park, stop off before Hume Lake at CLINGAN'S JUNCTION and the **Hume Lake Ranger District Office** (June–Aug daily 8am–4.30pm, rest of the year Mon–Fri 8am–4.30pm; ☎209/338-2251), who can offer full details on the local campsites and trails.

Kings Canyon Highway

Kings Canyon Highway, Hwy-180, runs from Grant Grove through the Sequoia National Forest and Hume Lake and descends sharply into the steep-sided Kings Canyon, at the foot of which the various forks of the Kings River often gush furiously. Some measurements claim this is the deepest canyon in the US; whatever the facts, its wall sections of granite and gleaming blue marble and the yellow pockmarks of yucca plants are visually outstanding. It's extremely perilous to wade into the river though: people have been swept away even when paddling close to the bank in a seemingly placid section.

Near the foot of the canyon, the road passes **Boyden Cave** (summer daily 10am–5pm on the hour; $4), whose curious interior has a number of bizarre formations grown out of the forty-thousand-year-old rock, their impact intensified by the stillness and coolness inside. The cave stays at a constant 55°F, causing the numerous snakes and small animals who fall in through the hole in the roof to enter instant hibernation.

Cedar Grove

Once properly into the national park, the canyon sheds its V-shape and gains a floor, where **CEDAR GROVE VILLAGE** is named for the incense cedars which grow in proliferation around it. With a smattering of log cabins, a food store and snack-bar, several campsites and, across the river, a **ranger station** (Mon–Thurs 7am–3pm, Fri & Sat 7am–5pm; ☎209/565-3341), this is as close to a built-up area as the park gets.

The main things to see around here, apart from the obvious appeal of the scenery, are the flowers: Leopard lilies, shooting stars, violets, Indian paintbrush, lupines and others, and a variety of birdlife. The longer hikes through the creeks, many seven or eight miles long, are fairly stiff challenges and you should carry drinking water. An easy alternative, however, is to pootle around the edge of **Zumwalt Meadow**, a beckoning green carpet four miles from Cedar Grove Village and a short walk from the road, beneath the forbidding grey walls of Grand Sentinel and North Dome. The meadow boasts a collection of big-leaf maple, cattails and creek dogwood, and there's often a good chance of an eyeful of animal life.

Just a mile further, Kings Canyon Road comes to an end at **Copper Creek**. Thirty years ago it was sensibly decided not to allow vehicles to penetrate further. Instead the multitude of canyons and peaks which constitute the Kings River Sierra are networked by **hiking paths**, all accessible from here and almost all best enjoyed armed with a tent and some provisions.

The Sierra National Forest

Consuming the entire gaping tract of land between Kings Canyon and Yosemite, the **SIERRA NATIONAL FOREST** boasts some of the Californian interior's most beautiful mountain scenery, though it's less well known – and less visited – than either of its national park neighbours. A federally run area which lacks the environmental protection given to the parks, many of the rivers here have been dammed and much of the forest developed into resort areas that are better for fishing and boating than hiking. That said, there are far fewer people and any number of remote corners to explore, not least the rugged, unspoilt terrain of the vast **John Muir Wilderness**, which contains some of the starkest peaks and lushest alpine meadows of the High Sierra. If you want to discover complete solitude and hike and camp in isolation, this is the place to do it – the sheer challenge of the environment can make the national parks look like holiday camps. But don't try any lone exploration without thorough planning aided by accurate maps, and don't expect buses to pick you up when you're tired. Public transport is virtually nonexistent.

For practical information in advance call in at the **forest information office**, Room 3017 of the Federal Building, 1130 O Street, in Fresno (Mon–Fri 8.30am–4pm; ☎209/487-5155). Once there you can rely on a number of district ranger offices scattered around the forest, all listed below. The forest splits into two main regions: the **Pineridge** district, accessible by way of Hwy-168; and in the north – the only place you can get to by public transport – **Bass Lake** and the Mariposa district, just off Hwy-41 between Fresno and Yosemite.

The Pineridge district and the John Muir Wilderness

The best place for adventurous hiking is the **PINERIDGE** district, forty miles east from Fresno using Hwy-168, where around KAISER PASS you'll find the most isolated alpine landscapes. The campsites around here are all free, although there are also rooms – and evening entertainment – at the *Vermillion Valley Resort* close to EDISON LAKE. Usefully, the resort runs buses to the trailheads which lead into the adjoining **John Muir Wilderness**; if you want to do some serious hiking, or even just spend the night camped out under the stars, you'll need to get a free wilderness permit from the **ranger station** (daily 7.30am–5pm, ☎209/841-3311) along Hwy-168, a mile south of Shaver Lake. If you're planning to come in late spring or early autumn, bear in mind that the area is prone to bad weather even at these times, and that the road and trails may be closed.

Deep in the forest to the southeast, reachable by a mountain road from Shaver Lake (five miles east of Pineridge), DINKLEY CREEK, on the Kings River, is an unsurpassed spot for **white water river rafting**, at its most exciting during the meltwater period from early to mid-summer, when the river is at its swiftest. In addition there are **sequoia groves** around McKINLEY GROVE, with free camping close by; and tracks from the Wishon and Courtwright reservoirs lead into the Woodchuck and Red River Basin portions of the John Muir Wilderness. For more detailed information, consult the **Kings River Ranger District Office** (Mon–Fri 8am–4.30pm; ☎209/855-8321) at the southern edge of the district, close to Pine Flats Reservoir on Trimmer Springs Road.

Bass Lake and the Mariposa district

Without a car, the closest you can get to the wilderness is OAKHURST, centre of the Mariposa district and just seven miles north of the pine-fringed **BASS LAKE** – much the biggest tourist attraction in the area and a stamping-ground of Hell's Angels in the Sixties. The leather and licentiousness, memorably described in Hunter S. Thompson's book *Hell's Angels*, are however long gone, and nowadays Bass Lake is (although crowded in summer) simply a good base for hiking and camping – especially if you don't manage to get to the national parks.

For general information, use the **Bass Lake Visitor Station** on road 222 (daily 8am–4.30pm; ☎209/683-3214); the **Mariposa Ranger District Office** in

Oakhurst (daily 8am–4.30pm; ☎209/683-4665) has local hiking and camping details. As an alternative to the fully equipped **campsites** around the lake, solidly booked during the summer (make a reservation as early as possible through MISTIX), you could use either *Ducey's Bass Lake Lodge* on road 342 on the northern side of the lake (☎209/642-3131), where four-berth rooms cost as little as $30; or the similarly priced *Miller's Landing* on road 222, which skirts the lake's southern flank (☎209/642-3633). Again, booking ahead is essential.

Yosemite National Park

> *No temple made with hands can compare with the Yosemite. Every rock in its walls seems to glow with life. Some lean back in majestic repose; others, absolutely sheer or nearly so for thousands of feet, advance beyond their companions in thoughtful attitudes, giving welcome to storms and calms alike, seemingly aware, yet heedless, of everything going on about them.*
>
> John Muir, *The Yosemite*

More gushing adjectives have been thrown at **YOSEMITE NATIONAL PARK** than at any other part of California. But however excessive the hyperbole sometimes seems, once you enter the park and turn the corner which reveals Yosemite Valley – only a small part of the park but the one at which most of the verbiage is aimed – you realise it's actually an understatement. For many, **Yosemite Valley** is, very simply, the single most dramatic piece of geology to be found anywhere in the world. Just seven miles long and one mile across at its widest point, it's walled by near-vertical, mile-high cliffs whose sides are streaked by cascading waterfalls and whose tops, a variety of domes and pinnacles, form a jagged silhouette against the sky. At ground level, too, the sights can be staggeringly impressive. Grassy meadows are framed by oak, cedar and fir trees, with a variety of wild flowers and wildlife – deer, coyotes, even black bears, are not uncommon.

Sadly, though perhaps understandably, tourists are even more common, and if you're looking for a little peace it's advisable to avoid the Valley on weekends and holidays. That said, the whole park is diverse and massive enough to endure the crowds: you can visit at any time of year, even in winter when the waterfalls turn to ice and the trails are blocked by snow, and out of high summer even the valley itself resists getting crammed. Further-flung reaches of the park, especially around the crisp alpine Tuolumne Meadows, and the completely wild backcountry accessible beyond them, are much less busy all year round – nature in just about the most peaceful and elemental setting you could imagine. Everywhere you go it is, of course, essential to be careful not to cause ecological damage or upset the wildlife population.

Some history

Yosemite Valley was created over thousands of years by glaciers gouging through and enlarging the canyon of the Merced River; the ice scraped away much of the softer portions of granite but only scarred the harder sections, which became the present cliffs. As the glaciers melted a lake was formed which filled the valley, eventually silting up to create the present valley floor.

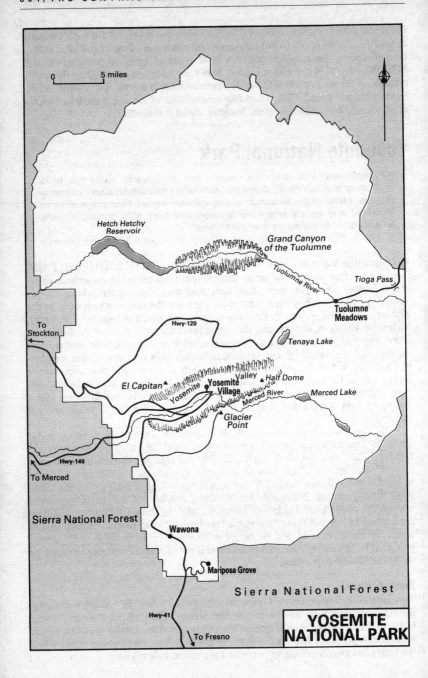

0   5 miles

Hetch Hetchy
Reservoir

Grand Canyon
of the Tuolumne

Tuolumne River

Tioga Pass

To
Stockton

Hwy-120

Tuolumne
Meadows

Tenaya Lake

El Capitan ▲

Yosemite   Valley   ▲ Half Dome
Yosemite
Village

Merced Lake

Merced River

▲ Glacier
Point

Hwy-140

To Merced

Sierra National Forest

Wawona

● Mariposa Grove

Sierra National Forest

Hwy-41

To Fresno

**YOSEMITE
NATIONAL PARK**

Native American tribes occupied the area quite peaceably until the mid-nineteenth century, when the increasingly threatening presence of white Gold Rush settlers in the Central Valley led to the tribes here launching raiding parties to the nearest encampments. In 1851 Major James Savage led a force, the Mariposa Battalion, in pursuit of the Indians, trailing them into the foothills and beyond, and becoming the first white men to set foot in Yosemite Valley. It wasn't long before the two groups clashed properly, and the Indians were moved out to white settlements to make way for farmers, foresters and, soon after, tourists (the first group of sightseers arriving in 1855). Moves were quickly afoot to conserve the natural beauty of the area: in 1864 Yosemite became the first State Park in the country and a few decades later the army were called in to prevent farmers' sheep stripping vegetation from the hillsides.

John Muir, a Scottish immigrant who travelled the entire area on foot, reputedly carrying no more than a notebook, a tin cup and a supply of tea, spearheaded the conservation movement which led to the founding of the *Sierra Club*, with the express aim of keeping Yosemite in particular relatively unspoilt. In 1913, the construction of a dam in the Hetch Hetchy Valley just north of Yosemite to provide water for San Francisco was a setback in the battle to keep Yosemite free of development (many think the struggle to prevent it led to John Muir's death the following year). But the publicity actually aided the formation of the present National Park Service in 1916, which promised – and has since provided – greater protection.

Practicalities

Getting to Yosemite by car is straightforward. Three roads enter the park from the west: Hwy-41 from Fresno, Hwy-140 from Merced and Hwy-120 from Stockton and the San Francisco Bay Area. The only road into the eastern side of the park is Hwy-120, the Tioga Pass Road, which branches off US-395 close to Lee Vining – though this is closed during winter. If you do drive, be aware that **petrol** can be hard to come by, especially after 6pm, so fill up before heading into the mountains.

Public transport into the park is less easy, but possible, all services running to Yosemite Village. From the Central Valley, *McCoy's Charter Service* (☎209/268-2237) leaves each weekday from Fresno (from the *Greyhound* station, *Amtrak* station and airport), for a one-way fare of $15; *Yosemite Via Bus* (☎209/722-0366) runs twice-daily from Merced *Greyhound* station for a round-trip fare of $35; and *California Yosemite Tours* (☎209/383-1563 or 383-1570) connects with the morning train from San Francisco to Merced and returns in time for the evening train back, costing $18 one way. From the east, *Yosemite Transit* (☎209/372-1240) run from Lee Vining twice a day from July to Labor Day for $25 one way. See "travel details" at the end of the chapter for more information.

Generally speaking, anything called a **sightseeing tour** which begins outside the park will involve you in an unsatisfying race through the valley. Packages you might want to consider, however, are *Green Tortoise*'s (☎1-800/227-4766) two-and three-day transport and accommodation deals (including camping at Tuolumne Meadows) from San Francisco, costing upwards of $79 per person, excluding food.

Orientation and information

Roughly in the centre of the park's 1200 square miles, **Yosemite Valley** is where the three roads from the Central Valley end up, and is home to the park's most dramatic scenery. At the southern edge of the park are **Wawona** and the **Mariposa Grove**, which Hwy-41 passes on its way to the valley, 27 miles further on. **Tuolumne Meadows** is in the high country, sixty-odd miles northeast of the valley, close to the Tioga Pass entrance (Hwy-120) on the eastern side of the park.

Everything commercial in Yosemite is run by the *Yosemite Park and Curry Company,* a division of multinational entertainment conglomerate MCA. As a result prices are uniformly higher than outside the park, but not unaffordable. For **general information** phone ☎209/372-0265, or (for a recording) ☎209/372-0264; and for **weather and road conditions** ☎209/372-4605. Or drop in at one of the park's two visitors centres (see below).

Accommodation and camping

Once in the park, **accommodation** can be a problem; it's best to book in advance and bear in mind that anything other than camping can be surprisingly expensive. The valley is where most people make for, and it holds most of the fixed accommodation. For hotel reservations phone ☎209/252-4848. Camping information is on ☎209/372-4845 , but camping reservations should be made through *Ticketron* (in the US toll-free ☎1-800/452-1111; from the UK ☎312/902-1919).

Of **hotels** in the valley, *Yosemite Lodge* has some cabins for under $30 out of season, $40 in summer; rooms are much dearer, starting around $70 – though substantial reductions can be obtained if you stand by for cancellations (hang around the reception area after 4pm). *Curry Village,* a mile from Yosemite Village, has similarly priced rooms but also offers fixed tents and cabins for upwards of $25. If money's no object, you can take a double room at the *Ahwahnee Hotel* for $180. Outside the valley, there's only the *Wawona Hotel,* in Wawona itself, with rooms at around $55, or the canvas tent cabins at Tuolumne Meadows, available only in summer for $35.

Even **camping in the valley**, costing $2 to $10, requires a reservation between April and November; otherwise you'll need to show up at the Curry Village Reservations Office very early in the morning and hope for cancellations. There are a number of campsites: *Sunnyside Walk-In,* just west of *Yosemite Lodge,* is popular with rock-climbers and has the most bohemian reputation; *Lower Pines, Upper Pines* and *North Pines,* at the east end of the valley, are used mainly by campervans. Calmer and quieter are *Backpacker's Camp,* behind *North Pines,* and *Lower River* and *Upper River,* a mile east of Yosemite Village. Camping anywhere else in the valley is strictly forbidden.

The main place for **camping outside the valley** is at Tuolumne Meadows, which is mainly occupied by campervans but has plenty of more hiker-friendly sites. The *Yosemite Creek* site, halfway between the valley and Tuolumne along Hwy-120, is ideal for escaping the crowds, and rarely fills even in summer. There are also many **primitive campsites in the backcountry** specifically for hikers and marked on hiking maps, but bear in mind that even these may be full at peak times. To use them, or to camp elsewhere in the backcountry, you must (as far in advance, and with as flexible an intinerary, as possible) get a **wilderness permit**, available by post from the Wilderness Office, Box 577, Yosemite National Park CA 95389, or from the nearest visitors centre no more than 24 hours in advance.

Getting around

Throughout the summer, free **shuttle buses** operate around the valley floor, running in one direction only around a loop which passes through, or close to, all the main points of interest, trailheads and accommodation areas. In high season they run between 7.30am and 10pm, slightly reduced hours at other times. There is no similar transport anywhere else in the park, though there are summer buses to specific outlying points of interest – Tuolumne Meadows for example. **Cars** spoil everybody's fun on the valley floor; if you're driving in just for the day, leave your vehicle in the day-use car park at Curry Village.

In any case, cycling is the best way to get around: a number of good **bicycle paths** cross the valley floor but **bike hire** is limited to the outlets at *Yosemite Lodge* and *Curry Village* which charge $4.25 per hour or $14.75 per day. Failing that there are always **guided tours** (☎209/372-1240), which range from the rather dull two-hour valley floor spin, costing $12.50, to the all-day Grand Tour for $34.50 which includes Mariposa Grove and Glacier Point. These are bookable from accommodation reception areas, as are a variety of guided **horseback trips**, most of which loop around the base of Half Dome. A number of **guided hikes** are offered as well; details can be found in the free *Yosemite Guide*, handed out at park entrances or from the visitors centres at Yosemite Village and Tuolumne Meadows. The *Mountain Shop* in Curry Village (☎372-1244) rents out backpacks, sleeping bags and other outdoor essentials.

Serious climbing

Many **rock-climbers** base themselves at the *Sunnyside Walk-In* campsite, near *Yosemite Lodge;* for the seriously interested this is a good place to pick up climbing tips, and to find out why the regulars have bestowed somewhat psychedelic names to certain routes: "Separate Reality" and "Ecstasy" being just two. A more organised introduction to the climber's craft is offered by the *Yosemite School of Mountaineering*, who run a beginners' class at Tuolumne Meadows daily in summer that costs $30 (details from any of the visitor centres or by phoning ☎209/372-1244). The school is also the source of the "Go Climb a Rock" t-shirts that are Yosemite's best-selling souvenir.

Food, drink and entertainment

Shopping for just about anything is cheaper outside the park, but if necessary the essentials – food, drink, film – can be found in the stores around Yosemite Village, Curry Village, Wawona and Tuolumne Meadows. For cooked meals, there's a tacky cafeteria and a good but fairly pricey *Mountain Room Broiler* at *Yosemite Lodge,* plus a range of diners and snack bars in Yosemite Village, the best of which is *Degnan's Deli*, where massive sandwiches cost around $4. One of the most beautiful restaurants in the US, the baronial *Ahwahnee Dining Room*, has the best (and most expensive) food in Yosemite – especially during the winter when they bring in top chefs for weekend gourmandising (☎372-1489 for reservations).

Yosemite Village is the centre of the park's **evening entertainment**, in the form of talks, photographic shows and even theatrical productions. The *Yosemite Guide* has the full programme, and lots of other useful information. *Yosemite Lodge* also has the valley's liveliest **bar**.

Yosemite Valley

Even the most evocative photography can only hint at the pleasure to be found in simply gazing at **Yosemite Valley**. From massive hunks of granite to the subtle colourings of wild flowers, the variations in the valley can be both enormous and discreet. Aside from just looking, there are many easy walks around the lush fields to waterfalls and lakes, and much tougher treks up the enormous cliffs. Whichever way you decide to see it, the Valley's concentration of natural grandeur is quite memorable. If there is a drawback, it's that this part of Yosemite is the busiest, and you're rarely far from other visitors or the park's commercial trappings; a couple of days exploring the Valley leave you more than ready to press on to the park's less populated regions.

Yosemite Village

Very much the heart of things in the Valley is **YOSEMITE VILLAGE**, around which are the main shops and post office, and the useful **Visitors Center** (June daily 9am–6pm, March, April & May daily 9am–5pm; ☎209/372-4461 ext 333), which has information, maps and geological displays and is a source of the free hiking permits necessary for overnight trips to the backcountry.

Beside the visitors centre, the small but interesting **Indian Cultural Museum** (Fri–Tues 10am–noon & 1.30–4pm; free), is divided between a roomful of artefacts from the local Native Americans and, outside, a reconstructed group of their buildings. There's something of the more recent past to be found in the nearby **cemetery**, which holds the unkempt graves of some of the early white settlers who attempted to farm the valley, and often perished in its isolation. By contrast, and worth a quick look even if you don't intend to stay there, is the **Ahwahnee Hotel**, a short signposted walk from Yosemite Village. Built in 1927 from local rock, it was intended to blend into its surrounds and attract the richer type of tourist. It still does both fairly effortlessly, and has a viewable collection of paintings of Yosemite around the lobby and dining room.

Around the valley floor

There's little, however, to divert attention from Yosemite's beckoning natural features for long. It's true that you'll never be alone on the valley floor, but most of the crowds can be left behind by taking any path which contains a slope.

The easiest place to reach, just a few minutes' walk from *Yosemite Lodge*, at the western end of the valley, is **Lower Yosemite Falls** (shuttle bus stop 7). Frankly these are disappointing, barely worth even the minimal effort required to get there. Much more exciting is the 3½-mile walk from the *Sunnyside* campsite, behind *Yosemite Lodge*, which leads to the base of **Upper Yosemite Falls**. This almost continuous ascent is very sapping on the leg muscles, but you get fine views over the valley on the way up, and, at the end, a chance to appreciate the power (and volume) of the water as it crashes almost 1500 feet in a single cascade. The top of the falls can be reached by way of another trail, about six miles long, which branches off at a signposted point on the way up. The falls are at their most dramatic during the meltwater period of May and June; by August they're often reduced to a trickle.

An easy trail leads from Lower Yosemite Falls around the edge of the valley floor to **Mirror Lake**, a mile from shuttle bus stop 17. This compellingly calm lake – its meditative stillness due to the fact that it's slowly silting up – lies beneath the great bulk of Half Dome, the rising cliff reflected on its surface, and is best seen in the early morning, before too many tourists arrive.

Besides the two Yosemite Falls, three other waterfalls can be easily reached from the valley. One of the more sensual is **Bridalveil Falls**, a slender ribbon at the valley's western end, and a shortish walk from the village. More rugged are **Vernal and Nevada Falls**, to which a trail begins at the *Happy Isles Nature Centre*, on the southeastern side of the valley (shuttle bus stop 16). The route is steep and can be wet and slippery – it's not referred to as the "mist trail" for nothing – but otherwise is not especially tough, and the visual rewards of reaching either or both falls are tremendous. The Nevada falls are a mile or so further on from Vernal, from where much longer trails continue up the back of Half Dome and on to Tuolumne Meadows; if you're really keen (and well prepared) the **John Muir Trail** heads from the top of the falls over two hundred miles south to the summit of Mount Whitney.

The big cliffs: El Capitan and Half Dome

Of the two major peaks which you can see from the valley, **El Capitan**, rising some 3500 feet above the floor, is the biggest piece of exposed granite in the world, twice the size of the Rock of Gibraltar. A sense of its dimensions can be gleaned by the fact that rock-climbers (Yosemite Valley draws mountaineers from all over the world to test their abilities on the demanding granite faces) fast become invisible to the naked eye from ground level. The best time for attempting an assault is early summer or autumn; during the height of summer the rock face can reach 100°F. Much the same applies to **Half Dome**, the sheerest cliff in North America, only seven percent off the vertical. You can hike to its top by way of a steel staircase hooked on to its curving back from the far end of Little Yosemite Valley, six miles from the top of Nevada Falls; if you plan a one-day assault, you'll need to start at the crack of dawn.

Views of the Valley: Glacier Point

The most spectacular views of Yosemite Valley are from **GLACIER POINT**, the top of a 3200-foot almost sheer cliff, 32 miles by road from the valley. It's possible to get there on foot using the very steep four-mile track which begins at the western end of the valley, beside Hwy-41, though the lazy person's method is to use the bus (details above) to go up and to take the trail down. The valley floor lies directly beneath the viewing point, and there are tremendous views across to Half Dome (easy from here to see how it got its name) and to the distant snow-capped summits of the High Sierra. The road is often closed between September and May, sometimes longer, due to the likelihood of snowfalls at this altitude.

Outside the Valley

However crowded the valley might be, the rest of the park sees very few tourists. Even places you can get to by car, like **Wawona** and **Mariposa Grove** on the park's southern edge, remain peaceful most of the time, and if you're willing to hike a few miles and camp out overnight, the 99 pcrcent of Yosemite that's untouched by road contains acres of pristine scenery, especially around **Tuolumne Meadows**, on the eastern border of the park.

Wawona and the Mariposa Grove

If you're driving to Yosemite from Fresno, you'll probably pass through **WAWONA**, 27 miles west of the valley on Hwy-41, whose landmark is the *Wawona Hotel*, fronted by its unmistakable wooden verandah. Close by, the **Pioneer Yosemite History Center** is a collection of buildings culled from the early times of white habitation. These are good for a scoot around, and, once you're away from the main road, the area makes a quiet spot for a picnic.

The **Mariposa Grove**, three miles east of Hwy-41 on a small road which cuts off just past the park's southern entrance, is the biggest and best of Yosemite's groves of giant sequoia trees. To get to the towering growths, walk the 2½-mile loop trail from the car park at the end of the road, which is also served by a free tram from the entrance. The most renowned of the grouping, well-marked along the route, is the **Grizzly Giant**, thought to be 2700 years old. It's also worth dropping into the **Mariposa Grove Museum** (free), which has modest displays and photos of the mighty trees. For more on the life of the sequoia, see *Contexts*.

Tuolumne Meadows

On the eastern edge of the park, the alpine **TUOLUMNE MEADOWS** have an atmosphere quite different from the valley; here, at 8500 feet, you almost seem to be level with the tops of the surrounding snow-covered mountains and the air always has a fresh, crisp bite. That said, there can still be good-sized blasts of carbon monoxide at peak times in the vicinity of the campsite – the only accommodation base in the area and within easy reach of the park's eastern entrance at Tioga Pass (Hwy-120). But it's a better starting-point than the Valley for backcountry hiking into the High Sierras, where seven hundred-odd miles of trails, both long and short, crisscross their way along the Sierra Nevada ridge. Also, because the growing season is short so high up, early summer in Tuolumne reveals a plethora of colourful wild blossoms.

Between July and mid-August, a bus links Tuolumne and Yosemite Valley. At other times (except winter when the road is closed) it should be fairly easy to hitch a lift from the valley. Alternatively, it's possible to hike between the two centres using part of the **John Muir Trail**, a distance of roughly 25 miles from the Happy Isles trailhead. The Pacific Crest Trail, stretching from Mexico right up to Canada, also passes through Tuolumne, and there are innumerable other paths into the canyons and valleys in the area. One of the best hikes leads north and west through the Grand Canyon of the Tuolumne River; get the full details from the **Visitors Center** (daily in summer 8am–7.30pm; ☎209/372-0263) at the Tuolumne campsite.

THE HIGH SIERRA
AND OWENS VALLEY

Unlike the forested western slope of the Sierra Nevada Mountains, which has been eroded over time and rolls gradually into the rich farmland of the Central Valley, the towering eastern peaks of the **High Sierra** drop abruptly down to the largely desert – and deserted – landscape of the **Owens Valley** far below. Very nearly the entire range is preserved as wilderness, and hikers and mountaineers can get higher much more quickly here than almost anywhere else in California: well-maintained roads lead to trailheads at over ten thousand feet, providing quick access to the stark terrain of spires, glaciers and clear mountain lakes. **Mount Whitney**, at almost 14,500 feet the highest point in the continental US, marks the southernmost point of the chain, which continues north for an uninter-rupted 150 miles to the backcountry of Yosemite National Park.

Running along the opposite wall of the five-mile-wide Owens Valley are the **White Mountains**, nearly as high but drier and more inhospitable than the High Sierra, and home to the gnarled **Bristlecone Pines**, the oldest living things on earth. In between, US-395 runs the length of the sparsely populated valley – which has few signs of settlement at all beyond the sporadic roadside towns and the larger **Bishop**. Finally, at the far northern tip of the valley, there are the placid blue waters of **Mono Lake**, set in a bizarre desert basin of volcanoes and steaming geysers and the subject of an ongoing battle between environmentalists and the City of Los Angeles, which is draining the water of the lake – and in fact the whole of eastern California – to dangerously low levels.

US-395 is the lifeline and pretty much only access to the area, travelled daily by *Greyhound* and with plenty of cheap motels along its length and campsites in the nearby foothills. From the valley, there is a shuttle bus service to the main High Sierra slopes and trails run by *Backpackers Shuttle Service*, whose minivans carry passengers from *Greyhound* stations or other points in the Owens Valley to trail-heads in the Eastern Sierra between Mount Whitney and Yosemite; arrange-ments should be made well in advance ($10 per person, $20 minimum per trip; ☎619/873-4453). With a bit of advance planning, you could sign up with one of the many locally based outfits who organise rock-climbing, ski-touring and cycling expeditions to get you to the great outdoors (see p.318).

Mount Whitney

Rising out of the northern reaches of the Mojave Desert, the Sierra Nevada Mountains announce themselves with a bang two hundred miles north of Los Angeles at **Mount Whitney**, the highest point on a silver-grey knifelike ridge of pinnacles that forms a nearly sheer wall of granite, eleven thousand feet above the valley below. Mount Whitney lies on the eastern border of Sequoia National Park, and its sharply pointed peaks dominate the small roadside town of **LONE PINE** at its feet. The view of the High Sierra summits from the town is fantastic, and was captured by photographer Ansel Adams in an oft-reproduced shot of the full moon suspended above the stark cliffs.

Lone Pine and around

The town of Lone Pine itself is not all that impressive, consisting mainly of motels and petrol stations strung out along US-395. But it makes a good base for exploring the area, particularly if you're not prepared to camp out. *Greyhound* buses from Los Angeles stop on the north side of town at 107 N Main Street once a day at 11pm. If you're looking for a **motel**, try *Trails Motel* (☎619/876-5555), five blocks south on US-395 at 633 S Main Street, or the *Frontier Best Western* (☎1-800/231-4731), 1008 S Main Street – both with doubles from $38. There are a couple of decent restaurants along the highway, like the *Sportsman Café* at 206 S

Main Street and the *High Sierra Inn* across the road, both open from 6am until 10pm daily; for hamburgers or a milkshake stop at the *Frosty Freeze*, 701 S Main Street. In summer, the **swimming pool** at the high school opposite is open daily ($1) if you feel the need to cool off; after a week in the mountains, you can get **cleaned up** at *Kirk's Sierra Barber Shop*, 104 N Main Street, which has hot showers for $2. For more information on local services, contact the Lone Pine **Chamber of Commerce** at 126 S Main Street (daily 9am–5pm except Sun; ☎619/876-4444).

For information on hiking or camping, stop by the **Interagency Visitor Center** (daily 8am–4.45pm; ☎619/876-4252), a mile south of town on US-395 at the junction of Hwy-136, which leads east to Death Valley (see p.230). The centre has practical and historical information on the whole of eastern California, including the High Sierra, Owens Valley, White Mountains and Death Valley. Most of the region is protected within the massive **Inyo National Forest**, and if you're planning to spend any amount of time in the area, pick up the very helpful **map** ($1), which covers everything between Mount Whitney and Yosemite National Park, including all hiking routes and campsites. Interestingly, this is the only map that makes clear the extent of the City of Los Angeles' holdings in the Owens Valley – basically the entire valley floor.

Many early Westerns, and the epic *Gunga Din*, were filmed in the **Alabama Hills** west of Lone Pine, a rugged expanse of sedimentary rock that's been sculpted into bizarre shapes by 160 million years of erosive winds and rains. Some of the oddest formations are linked by the **Picture Rocks Circle**, a dirt road that loops around from Whitney Portal Road, passing by rocks shaped like bullfrogs, walruses and baboons; the 100-foot rock faces make it a popular place for rock-climbers to hone their skills. There is a free **campsite** at Tuttle Creek, on the south edge of the hills.

Climbing Mount Whitney

Climbing up to the 14,494-foot summit of Mount Whitney is a real challenge; it's a very strenuous, 21-mile round trip, made especially difficult by the lack of oxygen in the rarefied air. None of this discourages the two thousand or so eager mountaineers who climb the peak each summer, mainly in July and August, starting at dawn from the non-reservable **campsite** (reachable on a shuttle bus) at the end of twisting Whitney Portal Road, which climbs steeply west from US-395. The trail gains over a mile in elevation, cutting up past alpine lakes to boulder-strewn Trail Crest Pass – the southern end of the 220-mile John Muir Trail which heads north to Yosemite. From the pass it climbs along the top of vertical cliffs, finally reaching the rounded hump of the summit itself, where a stone cabin serves as an emergency shelter.

From Memorial Day to the end of September, you have to do the whole trip in a day, unless you've booked one of the strictly limited **wilderness permits** which entitles you to spend the night camped out along the route. Reservations must be made, as soon as possible after 1 March (with a $5 fee per person), through the *Eastern Sierra Interpretive Association*, PO Box 8, Lone Pine, CA 93545. This way you can camp overnight just below the timberline at 10,600-foot **Mirror Lake**, four miles along the trail, which will give you a good headstart and help you acclimatise to the altitude. Stash most of your equipment at the campsite and retrieve it after bagging the summit.

Into the Owens Valley

If the Central Valley is hot, dry and largely boring, the **Owens Valley** – stretching from Lone Pine north beyond Bishop – is hotter, drier and numinously thrilling. This desolate desert landscape, bordered by parallel ridges of fourteen-thousand-foot peaks, is almost entirely unpopulated outside of the few towns along the highway, though a few solitary souls live in old sheds and caravans off the many dirt roads and tracks that cross the valley floor. Years ago the area was a prime spot for growing apples and pears, but since 1913 its plentiful natural water supply, fed by the many streams which run down from the Sierra Nevada, has been drained away to fill the swimming pools of Los Angeles.

Manzanar Relocation Camp and Independence

Just west of US-395, eight miles north of Lone Pine, on the site of the most productive of these orchards, stand the concrete foundations of the **Manzanar Relocation Camp**, where more than ten thousand Americans of Japanese descent were corralled during World War II. Considering them a threat to national security, the US government uprooted whole familes and confiscated all their property; they were released – obviously – at the end of the war, though no apology was ever officially offered, and claims for compensation were only settled in 1988, when the government agreed to pay damages amounting to millions of dollars. The camp was once ringed by barbed wire and filled with row upon row of wooden bunkhouses; now only a couple of guardhouses and a small cemetery remain. As the bronze plaque on the guardhouse says: "May the injustices and humiliation suffered here as a result of hysteria, racism and economic exploitation never emerge again".

An evocative and affecting exhibit about Manzanar, detailing the experiences of many of the young children who were held there, is on display inside the **Eastern California Museum** (Thurs–Sun noon–4pm, weekends from 10am; free, donations accepted), at 155 Grant Street, three blocks west of the porticoed County Courthouse in the town of **INDEPENDENCE**, six miles further north. The cinder-block museum also has displays on the natural environment of the Owens Valley, including the Bighorn Sheep that live in the mountains west of town, and exhibits on the region's history, from native Paiute basketry to old mining and farming equipment. There's also a reconstructed pioneer village behind the museum, made up of old buildings from all over the Owens Valley that have been brought together and restored here.

Practicalities

Independence is not as well supplied with tourist services as Lone Pine. For a **motel** try *Ray's Den* at 405 N Edwards Street, a block off US-395 ($40 doubles; ☎619/878-2122), and for food, stop by *Austin's General Store* at 130 S Edwards Street. The town takes its heroic name not from any great libertarian tradition but from a Civil War fort that was founded north of the town on the 4th of July, 1862. Every year on the day the town holds a parade down Main Street followed by a mass barbecue and fireworks show in **Dehy Park**, along tree-shaded Independence Creek .on the north side of town, marked by a large and unexplained old steam locomotive.

There's a small **campsite** half a mile west of town ($4 a night), reached by following Market Street beside the creek.

Onwards from Independence

The minor Onion Valley Road leads beyond Independence's campsite, twisting and turning up the mountains to **Onion Valley**, ten miles west , where there's another **campsite** ($5) and the trailhead for **hiking** across the Sierra Nevada into King's Canyon National Park, sixteen miles over Kearsarge Pass to Cedar Grove (see p.301). This is the easiest and shortest route across the Sierra; to get the required – free – wilderness permit contact the visitors centre in Lone Pine (see above.

The slopes of Mount Williamson, south of Onion Valley, and of Mount Baxter to the north are the protected home of the rarely seen **California Bighorn Sheep**: nimble-footed creatures that roam around the steep, rocky slopes and sport massive, curling horns, which can be as large as a car tyre. The **Paiute Monument**, a giant boulder standing on the flat ridge of the Inyo Mountains, six miles east of Independence and clearly visible from US-395, resembles nothing so much as the monolith from the movie *2001*. Local legends tell of how members of the Paiute tribe would hide behind the smaller boulders at its base and ambush wild game that had been chased up from the hills below. There are lots of abandoned mine shafts and poorly marked tunnels at the foot of the mountains, so watch your step.

Ten miles north of Independence is the actual start of the **LA Aqueduct**, which sucks water out of the valley to irrigate LA. Follow any of the dirt tracks that head east from US-395 and you can't fail to spot the abandoned railway stations built to haul in the material needed to construct the great ditch – which Space Shuttle astronauts have claimed to see while orbiting the globe.

Big Pine and the White Mountains

The town of **BIG PINE**, twenty miles north, is slightly larger than Independence but it has no greater appeal. There are a few petrol stations; *Greyhound* buses stop once a day in each direction; and there are a couple of **motels** along US-395 – the *Big Pine Motel* (☎619/938-2282) and the *Starlight Motel* (☎619/938-2011) both have doubles from $32. There is also a small **campsite** ($4) just east of town at the junction of Hwy-168. Big Pine is, however, the gateway to two of the most unusual natural phenomena in California: the Palisades Glacier in the Sierra Nevada, west of the town, and the ancient Bristlecone Pine Forest in the barren White Mountains to the east.

The southernmost glacier in the northern hemisphere, the **Palisades Glacier** sits at the foot of the impressive Palisade Crest, centre of one of the greatest concentrations of enjoyably climbable (though only for the experienced) peaks in the Eastern Sierra. To the south is Norman Clyde Peak, named after California's most prolific early mountaineer; Thunderbolt Peak and Mount Agassiz are highlights of the Inconsolable Range to the north of the glacier, itself an excellent introduction to snow and ice climbing; while in the centre the immense bulk of

Temple Crag offers a range of routes unparalled outside of Yosemite Valley. The trailhead for all of these climbs, and the many local hikes, is ten miles west of Big Pine, at the end of Glacier Lodge Road, along which there are a number of $6-a-night **campsites**. Before heading off into the wilderness, get a backcountry camping permit from the small ranger station at Upper Sage Camp, a mile down the road from the trailhead. The snow-covered, icy-white glacier is nine miles from the end of the road on a well-marked trail along the north fork of Big Pine Creek, past a number of alpine lakes.

The White Mountains

Big Pine is also the gateway to the intimidating **White Mountains**, a bald, dry, unwelcoming range, made up of some of the oldest, fossil-filled rock in California, which acts as the eastern wall of the Owens Valley. The mountains are accessible only by car (or bike) via Hwy-168. Be sure to fill up on petrol and **drinking water**, both of which are unavailable east of US-395. The highest point in the range, White Mountain, rises to a height of 14,246 feet. Near the summit, a strenuous fifteen-mile hike from the end of a long dusty road, a research station (closed to the public) studies the physiology of high-altitude plant and animal life, which is in many ways similar to that of the arctic regions.

On the lower slopes, often covered in snow until mid-June, stand the gnarled trees that are the prime reason for coming here, in the ancient **Bristlecone Pine Forest**. Some of these trees have been alive for over four thousand years, earning them a place in the *Guinness Book of Records* as the "world's oldest living things". Battered and beaten by the harsh environment into bizarrely beautiful shapes and forms, even when dead they hang on without decaying for upwards of another thousand-odd years, slowly being eroded by wind-driven ice and sand.

Schulman Grove, named after Dr Edmund Schulman, who discovered and dated these trees in the mid-1950s, is the most accessible collection, at the end of the paved road that twists up from Hwy-168. The grove is split up into two self-guided nature trails. One, the mile-long Discovery Trail, passes by a number of photogenic examples, including the first one found to be over four thousand years old; the other, longer trail loops around past the oldest tree, the 4700-year-old Methuselah. **Patriarch Grove**, eleven miles further, along a dusty dirt road that gives spectacular views of the Sierra Nevada to the west and the Great Basin ranges of the deserts to the east, contains the largest Bristlecone Pine – once more, over four thousand years old.

Beyond here a gate prevents unauthorised vehicles from getting to the research station on the summit, though hikers and all-terrain **mountain bikes** are permitted to continue. In fact, the steep canyons running down from the ridge are tailor-made for thrillseekers, who race down the steep washes at incredibly high speed. **Silver Canyon**, descending from just beyond Schulman Grove, is the route taken by the **Plumline Outback** – the ultimate kamikaze race – held each July; cyclists begin in Bishop, race up to the ridge and career back down again.

There is **camping** available, but no water; the only campsite is at Grandview (no charge), two miles south of Schulman Grove. Backpackers can camp wherever they like, without a permit, though it's a good idea to check in with the rangers in Bishop first, if only to find out which of the springs and small creeks (if any) are flowing.

The Bishop Area

BISHOP, to a Californian, means outdoor pursuits. The largest town (population 3500) in the Owens Valley, it's an excellent base from which to explore the mountains that surround it; and if you've ever wanted to try rock-climbing, hang-gliding, cross-country skiing or even fly-fishing, there's no better place to be, with some of the world's best mountaineers offering their services through lessons and guided trips. Not for nothing was Bishop voted one of the hippest places in the US by readers of the adventure travel magazine *Outside*.

The town

The best feature of Bishop is its proximity to the wilderness, but there's also a laid-back ambience to the town which is worth hanging around to enjoy. It's an easy place to get to; besides the *Greyhound* buses, two scheduled airlines serve the city daily from Los Angeles: *Alpha Air* (☎1-800/421-9353) and *Glazov Airlines* (☎1-800/456-4500), both of which cost about $60 a flight. Finding a **place to stay** is no problem either. The **tourist office** at 690 N Main (☎873-8405) on the north side of town has lists of accommodation, most of it within a block of US-395 (Main Street through the town): the *Bishop Elms Motel*, 233 E Elm Street (☎619/873-8118); the *El Rancho Motel*, 274 W Lagoon Street on the south side of town (☎619/872-9251); and the *Thunderbird Motel*, 190 W Pine Street (☎619/873-4215), all have doubles from around $35 a night.

With two 24-hour *Safeway* stores, and a number of good cafés and diners, Bishop is also a good spot to stock up on food and supplies. *Jack's Waffle Shop*, 437 N Main Street, is open 24 fluorescent-lighted hours a day for breakfasts and burgers; a block away at no. 281 is the *Bishop Grill*, open from 6am for solid breakfasts. For lunch and dinner try *Bar-B-Q Bill's* at 187 S Main Street, or at the other end of town, drop into *Perry's Pizza* at 772 N Main Street. For steaks or pasta dishes try *Whiskey Creek*, 524 N Main Street, which also has a lively **bar** that's open till 2am.

For information on **hiking** and **camping** in the area, contact the White Mountain Ranger Station at 798 N Main Street (☎619/873-4207); they have details on hikes in the White Mountains and the High Sierra, for which they issue the obligatory free wilderness permits. Another place worth a stop is *Wheeler and Wilson Sports*, an excellent mountaineering and sporting goods supply shop at 206 N Main Street.

Around Bishop

US-6 heads north and east from Bishop into Nevada, passing by the **Laws Railroad Museum** (daily 10am–4pm; donations), a restoration of the old town of LAWS, five miles off US-395, with some old buildings and a slender, black narrow-gauge railway train, that used to run along the eastern edge of the Owens Valley. It's worth a quick look on your way to see the **Red Rock Canyon Petroglyphs**, four miles west of US-6: the rock carvings have unfortunately been terribly vandalised, but enough remains of the spacey figures to justify a trip there.

There are petroglyphs all over the Owens Valley – about the only sign of the Paiute Indian tribe that once roamed the area, hunting and gathering and living off the land. Their descendants have been gathered in reservations outside each of the valley towns, the largest just west of Bishop, where they've established the **Paiute Shoshone Indian Cultural Center** at 2300 W Line Street (daily 10am–5pm; free, donations accepted). Here they put on displays of basketry and weaving, food gathering and processing, and of traditional ways of building – and also run a good bookshop.

Further west along this road, which runs up into the foothills of the Sierra Nevada, there are a number of **campsites** – some small, undeveloped and free, others with piped water and costing $5 a night. There are also a number of **hiking routes** which set off up into the High Sierra wilderness from the end of the road. The trail from South Lake over Bishop Pass heads into Dusy Basin, where you can see the effects of centuries of glaciation in the bowl-like cirques and giant "erratic" boulders, left by receding glaciers. Another path follows the northern fork of Bishop Creek under the rusty cliffs of the Paiute Crags, before climbing over Paiute Pass into the Desolation Lakes area of the John Muir Wilderness.

Mammoth Mountain and the Devils Postpile National Monument

Much of the money that flows into Bishop comes from the brigades of fishing enthusiasts who spend their summer holidays fishing for rainbow trout placed in the streams and lakes by the state government. The largest assembly of fisher-folk gather every April around Lake Crowley, an artifical reservoir built to hold water diverted from Mono Lake, twenty miles north. During winter, masses of weekend skiers pass through from LA on their way to the slopes of **Mammoth Mountain**, forty miles from Bishop along Hwy-203, above the resort town of **MAMMOTH LAKES** (northbound on Friday nights, and back again on Sunday nights).

Mammoth Lakes revolves around the skiing and fishing seasons – with an increasing number of on- and off-road cycling races – and if you're not into such active pursuits there's not much to do. The **Mammoth Lakes Visitor Center** (daily 8am–5pm; ☎619/934-2505), on the main highway east of the town centre, has exhibits explaining such local geological activity as earthquakes and hot springs; they also handle wilderness permits for backpackers heading into the Minarets Wilderness in the mountains to the west. For a **place to stay**, there are lots of motels side by side along Hwy-203 west of the heavily shopping malled town centre.

The evocatively named **Devil's Postpile National Monument**, ten miles further west beyond the ski resort, is accessible in summer only, via a shuttle bus ($3.75) from Mammoth Lakes. A collection of slender, blue-grey basaltic columns, some as tall as sixty feet, the Postpile was formed as lava from the eruption of Mammoth Mountain (really a volcano) cooled and fractured into multi-sided forms. The highlight of the monument is Rainbow Falls, a two-mile hike along the San Joaquin River, which drops over a hundred feet into a deep pool, its spray reflecting and refracting, especially at midday, to earn its name. There is a $4-a-night **campsite** in the monument, and excellent camping and backpacking in the adjacent **Minarets Wilderness**, named for the spiky volcanic ridge just south of pointed Mount Ritter – one of the Sierra's most enticing high peaks.

**ADVENTURE TRAVEL SPECIALISTS
IN BISHOP, MAMMOTH LAKES, AND AROUND**

Cross-country Ski Lodges A number of backcountry lodges offer accommodation, skiing trips, instruction and rentals. Try *Rock Creek Winter Lodge*, PO Box 5, Mammoth Lakes 93546 (☎619/935-4452) or the *Tioga Pass Winter Resort*, PO Box 330, Lee Vining 93521 (☎209/379-2420). In Yosemite try *Badger Pass Nordic* (☎209/372-1244).

Downhill Skiing *Mammoth Mountain* (☎619/934-2571), one of the largest ski areas in the US, is packed with skiers from November to July; lift tickets cost a whopping $37 a day. Contact PO Box 24, Mammoth Lakes 93546.

Hang-gliding Lessons and tandem flights offered by *Owens Valley Soaring*, PO Box 8918, Mammoth Lakes 93546 (☎619/872-0247).

Mountain Bike Tours and Rental *Mountain Routes*, Route 1, Keough's #18, Bishop 93514 (☎619/873-8034), offer a variety of off-road cycling tours around the Owens Valley, from half-day trips ($15) to multi-day tours ($50 a day). Rentals cost $20 a day.

Mountaineering and Rock-climbing Guides For expert instruction or guided trips in the High Sierra backcountry contact the *Palisade School of Mountaineering*, PO Box 694, Bishop 93514 (☎619/873-5037); or *Alpine Expeditions*, PO Box 1751, Bishop 93514 (☎619/873-5617 or 213/624-7156). For introductory lessons or Big Wall climbing on 4000-foot granite cliffs, try the *Yosemite School of Mountaineering*, Yosemite 95389 (☎209/372-1335).

Pack Mules If you want to enjoy the wilderness without the burden of a heavy backpack, you can hire a mule to carry your load from a number of outfits on both sides of the Sierra. Cost is around $40 per day. For the southern High Sierra try *Cottonwood Pack Trains* (☎619/878-2015) or *Onion Valley Pack Trains* (☎619/873-8877); further north, there's *Pine Creek Pack Trains* (☎619/387-2797); or contact the local visitors bureau.

Just east of US-395, a mile south of the exit for Mammoth Lakes, there are more pleasurable and easily accessible examples of the region's volcanic activity in the many steaming geysers and hot springs that bubble up at **Hot Creek** (daily dawn–dusk; free), a mile east of the highway along a bumpy dirt road. Jets of boiling water mix with the otherwise chilly, snow-melt water to form pools ranging from tepid to scalding; you have to search to find a happy medium, and it's a bit of a challenge since the flows are ever-changing. Paths and wooden steps lead down to the most likely spots, but wear shoes, because idiots have broken bottles under the water.

Mono Lake and Lee Vining

The blue expanse of **Mono Lake** sits in the midst of a volcanic, desert tableland, its sixty square miles reflecting the statuesque, snow-capped mass of the eastern Sierra Nevada. At close on a million years old, it's an ancient lake, one of the oldest in North America, with two large volcanic islands, one bright white, the other shiny black, surrounded by salty, alkaline water. It looks like a science-fiction landscape, with great towers and spires formed by mineral deposits ringing the shores;

hot springs surround the lake, and all around the basin are signs of lava flows and volcanic activity, especially in the cones of the Mono Craters, just to the south.

The lake's most distinctive feature, the strange, sandcastle-like **tufa** formations, have been exposed over the past forty years since the City of Los Angeles began draining away the waters that flow into the lake. The towers of tufa were formed underwater, where calcium-bearing freshwater springs well up through the carbonate-rich lake water; the calcium and carbonate combine and sink to the bottom as limestone, slowly growing into the weird formations you can see today.

One of the best places to look at these mushroom-shaped hulks is at the **South Tufa Reserve**, four miles east of US-395 via Hwy-120, where rangers offer guided hikes throughout the summer at 11am, and occasional cross-country ski tours in winter (☎619/647-6331). Also here is Navy Beach, where you can swim and float in the salty water, three times as buoyant as seawater. Adjacent to the south shore stands the **Panum Crater** a 700-year-old volcano riddled with deep fissures and 50-foot towers of lava.

The **water level** in Mono Lake has dropped over forty feet since 1941, when the City of Los Angeles extended its Owens Valley Aqueduct into the Mono Basin through an eleven-mile tunnel. This itself was something of an engineering marvel, dug through the volcanically active Mono Craters, but it's been overshadowed by the legal battle surrounding the depletion of the lake itself, which is the biggest environmental controversy currently raging in California, not only because of the lake's unique beauty but also because Mono Lake is the primary nesting ground for the state's seagull population – twenty percent of the world total – and a prime stopover point for thousands of migratory geese, ducks and swans.

Mono Lake is now roughly half its natural size, and so far the City of Los Angeles has refused to stabilise the water level of the lake at a healthy height. As the levels drop, the islands in the middle of the lake, where the seagulls lay their eggs, become peninsulas, and the colonies fall prey to coyotes and other mainland predators. Also, as less fresh water reaches the lake, the landlocked water becomes increasingly alkaline, threatening the unique local ecosystem.

For more details about Mono Lake and the fight for its survival, stop by the **Mono Lake Visitors Center** (daily 9am–9pm, ☎619/647-6386), in the centre of the small town of **LEE VINING**, right on US-395 above the lake's western shore. The centre, which doubles as the local Chamber of Commerce, is operated by the non-profit **Mono Lake Committee** and has exhibits on the history and ecology of the lake, plus information on accommodation, camping and hiking in the region. It's also a good place to meet fellow travellers and perhaps hitch a ride over Tioga Pass into Yosemite National Park, ten miles west (see p.303).

Greyhound buses from the south stop daily in Lee Vining at 2am, but it's perhaps better to arrive from the north on the bus from Reno, which comes in at the more reasonable 11am. There are a couple of **motels** along US-395: *El Mono Motel* (☎619/647-6310) and *Murphey's* (☎619/647-6316) both have doubles from $35. **Eat** at *Nicely's Coffee Shop*, a great Fifties vinyl palace that opens at 6am; in summer, *Yosemite Transit* buses leave from the car park at noon and 4pm for the trip into the park, costing $20. There are a number of **campsites** along Lee Vining Creek off the Tioga Pass Road, Hwy-120; stop by the **ranger station** (☎619/647-6525) one mile west of Lee Vining, for details, and to pick up wilderness permits for backcountry camping.

On the north shore of the lake, along the road to the ghost town of Bodie, stands **Black Point**, at the end of a two-mile dirt road off Hwy-167 – the result of a massive eruption of molten lava some thirteen thousand years ago. As the lava cooled and contracted, cracks and fissures formed on the top, some only a few feet wide but as much as fifty feet deep.

Bodie Ghost Town and Bridgeport

In the 1870s the gold-mining town of **BODIE** boasted three breweries, some thirty saloons and dancehalls and a population of ten thousand, with a well-earned reputation as the raunchiest and most lawless mining camp in the west. Contemporary accounts describe a town that started each day with a shootout on Main Street, and churchbells, rung once for every year of a murdered man's life, that seemed never to stop sounding. The town boomed for about twenty years, taking out over $100 million in gold, but has been all but abandoned since the turn of the century.

Much of the town burned to the ground in a series of fires, but over 150 wooden buildings – about ten percent of the original town – survive in a state of arrested decay among the unrestored ruins around the intact town centre, littered with old bottles and bits of machinery and old stagecoaches. It's definitely the best ghost town in the US, and is far enough out of the way for its evocatively derelict structures to be relatively free of other tourists.

The town stands in a remote, high desert valley, seven thousand feet above sea level, surrounded by sagebrush and grassy hills. The eight-mile, unpaved road that leads here from Hwy-167 is blocked by snow for most of the winter, which gives some idea of how difficult the miners' isolated life must have been. The buildings are maintained in their present condition as a **state park** (daily 9am–dusk), and there's a handy walking tour guide and **map** ($1) of the town available next to the parking area. The **Miner's Union Building** on Main Street was the centre of the town's social life: founded in 1877, the union was one of the first in California, organised by workers at the Standard and Midnight mines. The ruins of the mines stand on the hills east of town, unfortunately off-limits to visitors due to their dangerously rundown state.

An alternative route in and out of Bodie, Hwy-270, turns off from US-395 eighteen miles north of Lee Vining, halfway to the mountain hamlet of **BRIDGEPORT** – an isolated village that provided the new start in life for fugitive Robert Mitchum in the *film noir* masterpiece *Out of the Past*. The gas station he owned in the film is long gone, though the place is otherwise little changed, a pretty little community of ranchers and fishermen, worth stopping at for a look at the dainty white 1880 **County Courthouse** and the small local history **museum** (summer daily 9am–5pm; free), next door in a restored old schoolhouse. From Bridgeport US-395 continues north into the state of Nevada, through the capital CARSON CITY and the gambling city of RENO, both described fully in Chapter Seven.

travel details

IN THE CENTRAL VALLEY

Trains

The twice-daily San Joaquin service runs between Bakersfield and Oakland. There are bus connections from Los Angeles (Union Station, LAX, UCLA, Santa Monica, Long Beach and Glendale) that link with the train at Bakersfield.

From Bakersfield Hanford/Fresno/Merced/Stockton/Oakland (1hr 30min/2hr 25min/2hr 51min/3hr 10min/4hr).

Buses

From Los Angeles to Bakersfield (18 daily; 1hr 25min); Visalia (6; 6hr 15min); Kingsburg (1; 4hr 40min); Fresno (16; 6hr 45min); Merced (9; 9hr); Modesto (12; 8hr 25min); Stockton (11; 6hr 45min).

From San Francisco to Modesto (8 daily; 2hr 10min); Merced (8; 3hr 20min); Fresno (9; 4hr 40min); Visalia (2; 5hr); Bakersfield (7; 7hr 20min).

From Visalia to Hanford (2 daily; 1hr 30min); Reedley (1; 40min).

From Fresno to Merced (15 daily; 1hr 10min); Modesto (17; 2hr 10min); Stockton (9; 3hr); Yosemite (5 a week; 3hr).

From Merced to Yosemite (3 daily; 2hr 25min).

From Stockton to Lodi (5 daily; 30min).

IN THE EASTERN SIERRA

Buses

From Los Angeles one a day, leaving at 5pm for Lone Pine (6hr); Bishop (7hr); Lee Vining (9hr) and Reno (13hr). Note that this bus arrives at most places in the middle of the night.

From Reno one a day, in the opposite direction, leaving at 9am for Los Angeles.

From Lee Vining to Yosemite (2 daily; 2hr).

From Yosemite to Lee Vining (2 daily; 2hr).

CHAPTER SIX

SAN FRANCISCO AND THE BAY AREA

The Bay Area is so beautiful, I hesitate to preach about heaven while I'm here.

Billy Graham

America's favourite city sits at the edge of the Western world, a position which lends even greater romantic currency to its legend. Arguably the most beautiful, certainly the most liberal city in the US, and one which has had more platitudes heaped upon it than any other, **SAN FRANCISCO** is in serious danger of being clichéd to death. But despite its position as the cosy favourite of the tourist boards, San Francisco remains remarkably unchanged: a funky, individualistic, surprisingly small city whose people pride themselves on being the cultured counterparts to their cousins in LA – the last bastion of civilisation on the lunatic fringe of America. A steadfast rivalry exists between the two cities. San Franciscans like to think of themselves as less obsessed with money, less riddled with status than those in the south – a rare kind of snobbery that you'll come across almost immediately. But San Francisco has its own element of narcissism, rooted in the sheer physical aspect of the place. Downtown streets lean upwards on impossible gradients to reveal stunning views of the city, the bay and beyond, and blanket fogs roll in unexpectedly to envelop the city in mist, adding a surreal quality to an already unique appearance. It's a compact and approachable place, one of the few US centres in which you can comfortably survive without a car. This is not however the California of monotonous blue skies and slothful warmth – the temperatures rarely exceed the seventies, and even during summer can drop much lower when consistent and heavy fogs muscle in on the city and the area as a whole.

San Francisco proper occupies just 48, hilly square miles at the tip of a slender peninsula, almost perfectly centred along the California Coast. But its metropolitan area sprawls out far beyond these narrow confines, east and north across to the far sides of the bay, and south back down the coastal strip. This is the **Bay Area**, one of the most rapidly growing regions in the US, and one whose population is expected to double by the turn of the century: well under a million people live in the city, but there are six million in the Bay Area as a whole. It's something of a mixed bag. In the **East Bay**, across one of the two great bridges that connect San Francisco with its hinterland, are industrial Oakland and the radical locus of Berkeley – a student town that's calmed since the peak of its notoriety in the Sixties but is still the closest you'll come to protest in smug California. To the

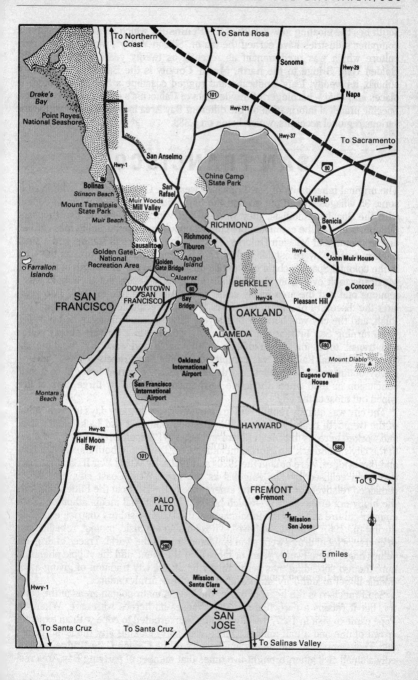

south lies the gloating new wealth of the **Peninsula**, which its multi-billion dollar computer industries have earned the tag of "Silicon Valley", wiping out the agriculture which was predominant as recently as twenty years ago. Across the Golden Gate Bridge to the north, **Marin County** is the Bay Area's wealthiest suburb, its woody, leafy landscape and rugged coastline a bucolic – though in places *very* chic – harbinger of the delights of California's earthy northern coast. Specific practical information on the different Bay Area locales is given within the various regional accounts, which begin on p.383.

SAN FRANCISCO

The original inhabitants of San Francisco were the Ohlone Indians, who lived in some 35 villages spread out around the bay. Within a very few years of contact with the Spanish colonists, they were all but wiped out – some five thousand Ohlone, over half the estimated pre-contact population, are buried in mass graves on the grounds of Mission Dolores. The Mission, which still stands, and a small military *presidio*, were established in 1776 by Juan Bautista de Anza as the sixth in the colonial Spanish chain of Catholic missions that ran the length of the state. Mexicans took over from the Spanish in the early 1820s, but their hold was a tenuous one and the area finally came under American rule in 1846. Two years later the discovery of gold in the Sierra foothills precipitated the riproaring Gold Rush, and the city was born. Within a year fifty thousand pioneers had travelled west, turning San Francisco from a muddy village into a thriving supply centre and transit town for the goldfields to the north and east. By the time the Transcontinental Railroad was completed in 1869 San Francisco was a lawless, rowdy boomtown of bordellos and drinking-holes – a period brought to a swift conclusion in 1906 when a massive earthquake, followed by three days of fire, wiped out most of the city.

The city was quickly rebuilt, and in many ways saw its glory days in the first half of the twentieth century – writers like Dashiell Hammett and Jack London lived and worked here, as did Diego Rivera and other WPA-sponsored artists, and many of the city's landmark structures, including Coit Tower and both the Golden Gate and Bay bridges, were built in the 1920s and 1930s. By World War II San Francisco had been eclipsed by Los Angeles as the main West Coast city, and things remained relatively quiet until the emergence of the Beats in the Fifties, and later the hippy era of the Sixties – which brought international media attention to the counter-culture antics of the inhabitants of the Haight-Ashbury district, especially during the 1967 "Summer of Love", whose fusion of music, protest, rebellion and of course, a lot of drugs were soon emulated around the world. Traces of drop-out values linger some twenty years or more after the event; and the yuppie phenomenon, though spreading, has yet to finally break the city tradition of giving a stiff middle finger to authority, and its libertarian streak firmly endures.

San Francisco is the heart of one of the largest metropolitan areas in the country, but it retains a parochial air, and chooses its heroes with care. When the Pope came to visit in 1987, the city's traffic was rerouted to cope with an expected crowd of one and a half million. Only a very sorry-looking fifty thousand turned out. That same year, the fiftieth anniversary of the Golden Gate Bridge, supposedly a small civil affair, brought five times that number of partying Bay Area residents onto the bridge in celebration of their cherished city – only a Grateful Dead concert could have matched the numbers. Similarly, the earthquake of October 1989 that literally rocked the city, brought the best out of San Francisco – once the casualties had been taken care of and before electricity was restored, a party atmosphere took hold as people barbecued, stuck beers in ice boxes and rounded up neighbours in a show of community spirit and indifference to disaster. They'd be appalled if you suggested they move elsewhere. And in an increasingly conservative America, San Francisco's reputation as a politically liberal oasis continues to grow – the city government was vilified in the US press for offering support to soldiers unwilling to fight in the January 1991 conflict in Kuwait. The entire Bay Area is a firm Democrat stronghold; and as gay capital of the world it is handling a massive AIDS crisis with intelligence and dignity. Indeed as other cities seek to isolate and ignore their gay communities, San Francisco's Mayor openly lends his support on Gay Freedom Day parades. Freedom is the key word, but with responsibility, and for all its failings – the level of homelessness, for example, is among the highest in the US – San Francisco remains one of the least prejudiced and most proudly distinct cities on earth.

Arrival and information

All international and most domestic flights arrive at **San Francisco International Airport** (SFO), about fifteen miles south of the city. There are several ways of getting into town from here, each of which is clearly signposted from the baggage reclaim areas. Cheapest are the half-hourly San Mateo County Transit (*SamTrans*) **buses** ($1.25), which leave from the lower level of the airport – either take the #7F express, which (depending upon traffic) takes around twenty-five minutes to reach the Transbay Terminal downtown; the slower #7B stops everywhere and takes nearly an hour. Bear in mind, though, that you're only allowed as much luggage as you can carry on your lap. The San Francisco **Airporter** bus ($4) picks up from outside each baggage claim area every fifteen minutes and travels to the downtown hotels. If you can spend a little more, the blue **Supershuttle** and the **Yellow Airport Shuttle** minibuses are the best: they pick up every five minutes from the upper level of the airport loop road and will take you and up to five other passengers to any city centre destination for around $12 a head. Be ruthless, though – competition for these is fierce and queues nonexistent.

Taxis from the airport cost $30 to $35 (plus tip) for any downtown location, more for East Bay and Marin County, and are only worth considering if you're in a group. If you're planning to drive, there's the usual clutch of **car hire** agencies at the airport. All of them operate shuttle buses that circle the top level of the airport road, and will take you to their depot free of charge (see "Getting Around" for details).

Several domestic airlines (*America West, Southwest* and *Continental* are three) fly into **Oakland International Airport** (OAK; see p.385 for details), across the bay. This airport is actually closer to downtown San Francisco than SFO, and efficiently connected with the city by the $2 *AirBART* shuttle bus from the Coliseum *BART* station. The third Bay Area airport, **San Jose Municipal** (SJO), also serves domestic arrivals, but is only worth considering if flights into the other two are booked up, or if you're going to be spending time in the Silicon Valley.

Buses, trains and driving

The San Francisco **Greyhound** terminal (☎433-1500) is on Seventh Street just south of Market Street, near the Civic Center. **Green Tortoise** buses (☎285-2441) disembark behind the Transbay Terminal on First and Natoma streets, also south of Market Street, near the Embarcadero *BART* station. **Amtrak** trains stop across the bay in Richmond (where you can transfer easily to *BART)* and continue to Oakland, from where a free shuttle bus will take you across the Bay Bridge to the Transbay Terminal.

The main route **by car** from the east is I-80, which runs via Sacramento all the way from Chicago. The main north–south route through California, I-5, passes by fifty miles east, and is linked to the Bay Area by I-580. US-101 and Hwy-1, the more scenic north–south routes, pass right through downtown San Francisco.

Information

The **San Francisco Visitor Information Center**, in Hallidie Plaza at the end of the cable car line on Market Street (Mon–Sat 9am–5pm, Sun 9am–3pm; ☎974-6900), has free maps of the city and the Bay Area, and can help with accommodation and travel information. San Francisco's major **daily papers** are the *San Francisco Chronicle* in the morning, and in the afternoon, the revamped *San Francisco Examiner,* which is making great efforts to capture the liberal market with in-depth reporting, and, in the case of Hunter S Thompson, controversial columnists. On Sundays the two papers combine into a very large edition, most of which can be discarded apart from the very useful *Calendar* section (also called the "Pink Pages") which gives detailed listings of arts, clubs, films and events. There's an abundance of **free publications**, led by the *San Francisco Bay Guardian* and *SF Weekly,* and in the East Bay by the *East Bay Express,* all of which have lively reporting and invaluable listings.

Getting around the city

Getting around San Francisco is simple. In spite of the literally breathtaking hills, the city centre is small enough to make walking a feasible way to see the sights and get the feel of things. In addition, the excellent public transport system is cheap, efficient and easy to use, both in the city and the more urbanised parts of the surrounding Bay Area. We've detailed public transport options in the relevant Bay Area sections towards the end of this chapter, but to go any further afield you'd do well to hire a car. Cycling, and – outside the city centre – mountain biking, is a good option too, though you'll need stout legs to tackle the many steep hills of San Francisco.

Muni

The city's public transport is run by the **San Francisco Municipal Railway**, or *Muni* (☎673-6864), and made up of a comprehensive network of **buses, trolley buses** and **cable cars**, which run up and over the city's hills, and underground **trains** – which become **streetcars** when they emerge from the downtown metro system to split off and serve the suburbs. On buses and trains there's a flat **fare** of 85¢, \$2 on cable cars; with each ticket you buy, ask for a **free transfer** – good for another two rides on a train or bus, and a fifty percent reduction on the cable car fare if used within ninety minutes. With trains, you must purchase tickets or pay the exact fare at the turnstile before descending to the platforms; on buses and trolleys, correct change is required on boarding.

A **24-hour pass**, costing $6, or a **three-day pass**, costing $10, can be bought from most Market Street *Muni* stations and are good on all *Muni* services. If you're staying more than a week or so and need to rely heavily on public transport, get a **Fast Pass**, which costs $28 and is valid for unlimited travel on the *Muni* system and *BART* stations (see overleaf) within the city limits for a full calendar month. Fast Passes are available from most *Muni* and *BART* stations, supermarkets and newsagents for the first few days of any month.

Muni trains run **throughout the night** on a limited service, except those on the M-Ocean View line, which stop around midnight. Buses, too, run all night – though, again, services are greatly reduced after midnight. For **more information** pick up the handy *Muni* map ($1.50) from the Visitor Information Center or bookshops, though it's unlikely that you'll need to be familiar with more than a few of the major bus routes, the most important of which are listed below. See also the route map overleaf, which details all major bus and *Muni* lines.

SAN FRANCISCO TRANSPORT ROUTES

USEFUL BUS ROUTES

#5 From the Transbay Terminal, west along the north side of Golden Gate Park to the ocean.

#7 From the Ferry Terminal (Market St) along Haight St to the ocean.

#15 From Third St (SoMa) to Pier 39, Fisherman's Wharf, via the Financial District and North Beach.

#20 (Golden Gate Transit) From Civic Center to the Golden Gate Bridge.

#22 From the Mission along Fillmore St north to Pacific Heights.

#24 From Castro St north along Divisadero St to Pacific Heights and Marina.

#37 From Market St to Twin Peaks.

#38 from Geary St via Civic Center, west to the ocean along Geary Blvd.

#30 From the CalTrain depot in SoMa, north to Fisherman's Wharf via North Beach and the Financial District.

MUNI TRAIN LINES

Muni J-CHURCH LINE From downtown to Mission and East Castro.

Muni K-INGLESIDE LINE From downtown to Balboa Park.

Muni L-TARAVAL LINE From downtown west to the zoo and Ocean Beach.

Muni M-OCEAN VIEW From downtown west to Ocean Beach.

Muni N-JUDAH LINE From downtown west to Ocean Beach, via the Haight.

CABLE CAR ROUTES

Powell–Hyde: from Powell St along Hyde through Russian Hill to Fisherman's Wharf.

Powell–Mason: From Powell St along Mason via Chinatown and North Beach to Fisherman's Wharf.

California St: From the foot of California St in the Financial District through Nob Hill to Polk St.

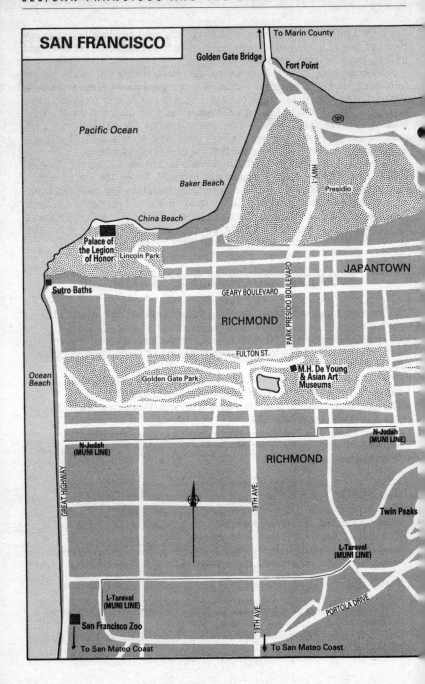

SAN FRANCISCO

To Marin County

Golden Gate Bridge

Fort Point

Pacific Ocean

HWY 101

Presidio

Baker Beach

China Beach

Palace of the Legion of Honor

Lincoln Park

JAPANTOWN

Sutro Baths

GEARY BOULEVARD

PARK PRESIDIO BOULEVARD

RICHMOND

FULTON ST.

M.H. De Young & Asian Art Museums

Ocean Beach

Golden Gate Park

N-Judah (MUNI LINE)

N-Judah (MUNI LINE)

RICHMOND

GREAT HIGHWAY

19TH AVE.

Twin Peaks

L-Taraval (MUNI LINE)

L-Taraval (MUNI LINE)

19TH AVE.

PORTOLA DRIVE

San Francisco Zoo

To San Mateo Coast

To San Mateo Coast

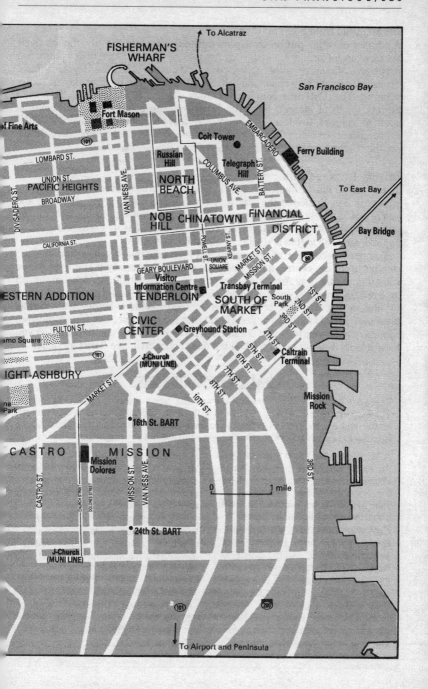

To Alcatraz

FISHERMAN'S WHARF

San Francisco Bay

Fort Mason

of Fine Arts

Coit Tower

Ferry Building

EMBARCADERO

LOMBARD ST.

Russian Hill

Telegraph Hill

COLUMBUS AVE.

VAN NESS AVE.

BATTERY ST.

UNION ST.

PACIFIC HEIGHTS

NORTH BEACH

To East Bay

BROADWAY

DIVISADERO ST.

NOB HILL

CHINATOWN

FINANCIAL DISTRICT

Bay Bridge

CALIFORNIA ST.

POWELL ST.

KEARNY ST.

MARKET ST.

80

UNION SQUARE

MISSION ST.

GEARY BOULEVARD

ESTERN ADDITION

Visitor Information Centre

TENDERLOIN

Transbay Terminal

SOUTH OF MARKET

South Park

1ST ST.

2ND ST.

FULTON ST.

3RD ST.

CIVIC CENTER

Greyhound Station

4TH ST.

amo Square

5TH ST.

Caltrain Terminal

101

J-Church (MUNI LINE)

6TH ST.

IGHT-ASHBURY

MARKET ST.

7TH ST.

na Park

8TH ST.

Mission Rock

10TH ST.

16th St. BART

CASTRO

MISSION

CASTRO ST.

Mission Dolores

MISSION ST.

VAN NESS AVE.

3RD ST.

CHURCH STREET

DOLORES STREET

0   1 mile

24th St. BART

J-Church (MUNI LINE)

101

290

To Airport and Peninsula

Other public transport services

A number of **other public transport networks** run into the city, though these are most useful for the rest of the Bay Area. Along Market Street in downtown San Francisco, *Muni* shares the station concourses with *BART*, the Bay Area Rapid Transit system, linking major points in San Francisco with the East Bay and outer suburbs. The **CalTrain** commuter railway (Depot at Fourth and Townsend Streets, South of Market) links San Francisco with points along the Peninsula south to San Jose. **Golden Gate Ferry** boats leave from the Ferry Building on the Embarcadero, crossing the bay past Alcatraz to Marin County. For more details see the "Getting Around" sections of the various Bay Area accounts.

Driving: taxis and cars

Taxis – as in most American cities, normally coloured yellow – don't crawl the streets in San Francisco the way they do in some cities. If you want one and you're not in a busy part of town or near a big hotel you'll probably have to telephone: try *Veterans* (☎552-1300) or *Yellowcab* (☎626-2345). Fares work out at approximately $3 for the first mile, $1.50 a mile thereafter.

You don't need a **car** to get around San Francisco, but if you're staying some way out from the centre, it can make life easier – especially if you want to see something of the Bay Area while you're here. UK nationals can **drive** in the US on a full UK driving licence, although under-25s will encounter problems if trying to **hire a car** and will probably get lumbered with a higher than normal insurance premium; those under 21 will find it impossible. Car hire companies will also expect you to have a credit card; if you don't have one they may let you leave a hefty **deposit** (at least $200) but don't count on it. See *Basics* for more.

WALKING TOURS

There are some excellent personalised **walking tours** available in San Francisco. The better ones usually have no more than five to a group and can often be an informative and efficient way of getting to know a particular area of town. The Visitor Information Center will be able to give you a full list, but you might like to try:

A.M. Walks, 1433 Clay St (☎928-5965). An early start (7am or 9am), but the cheapest downtown walking tour available. For only $10 San Francisco author John McCarroll will take you on a witty, anecdotal two-and-a-half-hour trek.

Café Walks (☎751-4286). 2–3hr tours of the Haight-Ashbury, Pacific Heights, and, best of all, North Beach and Russian Hill. $18 each, including lunch.

Cruisin' the Castro, 375 Lexington St (☎550-8110). The Supreme Champion of the walking tour circuit in San Francisco, Trevor Hailey, a resident of it's gay community for fifteen years, takes you on a fascinating tour of this area. $25 per person includes breakfast.

Helen's Walk Tour (☎524-4544). Helen Rendon, a four-feet-ten-inch dynamo, leads you around the murals of the Mission. $20, with a stop for coffee and pastries.

San Francisco Art Tours (☎832-2421). Two-hour tours of either the downtown galleries, or (much better) the alternative art spaces South of Market. Traces the history of San Francisco's artistic community and discusses local artists. $15 per person.

San Francisco Discovery Walks, 1200 Taylor St (☎673-2894). Four different tours highlighting major architectural sights. $15–20.

Organised tours

If you've just arrived, you may want to orientate yourself by taking an **organised tour**. *Gray Line Tours* (☎558-9400) will whip you around the city in three fairly tedious hours, stopping at Twin Peaks and Cliff House, for around $25 a head. Skip it unless you're really pushed for time and want to get a general idea of the city's layout with minimal effort.

Excruciatingly expensive but spectacular **aerial tours** of the city and Bay Area in light aircraft are available from several operators, the cheapest of which is *Airship Industries Skycruise* (☎568-4101), who offer one-hour airship cruises for $150. Much cheaper are *Commodore Helicopters* (☎332-4482), who hover over the city for upwards of $70 per hour, with longer tours up and down the coastline available for considerably larger sums. You might prefer one of the more leisurely two-hour **bay cruises** operated by the *Blue & Gold Fleet* (☎781-7877) from piers 39 and 40 – though at $17 a throw these don't come cheap either, and in any case everything may be shrouded in fog.

Accommodation

Visitors count as San Francisco's number-one business, and the city isn't short on places to stay. However, accommodation is a major expense, with prices running at upwards of $10 for the cheapest dormitory bed, $35 a night for the most basic hotel or motel room – $70 for anything fairly decent. The city's stock of bed and breakfast inns, starting at around $50 a night, can often be better value. It's a good idea to make advance reservations in late summer and autumn, but failure to phone ahead rarely results in getting stuck.

If you do have trouble finding a place, call either **Central Reservations of Hotel Group of America** (☎775-4600) on Market Street at Mason, or **Golden Gate Lodging Reservations** at 1030 Franklin Street (☎771-6915), both of which, for a small fee, will find you a room from around $40 for a single, $50 a double. If all else fails and you've got a car, **motels** are legion along the highways and bigger roads throughout the Bay Area, at a fairly standard rate of $35–45 a night. In all cases, bear in mind that all quoted room rates are subject to an **eleven percent room tax**.

Camping isn't really an option in San Francisco itself.

Hostels and YMCAs

At the bottom end of the price scale, there are a number of **hostels** in both the city and the Bay Area in general, some in very beautiful settings. Beds in dormitories go for around $10 on average, and many hostels also offer cut-rate single and double rooms, too.

European Guest House, 763 Minna St (☎861- 6634). Dormitory-style accommodation with communal kitchen. No curfew; safe locker facilities. $11 per night per person.

Globe Hostel, 10 Hallam Place (☎431-0540). Funky, lively hostel with music room, sauna and no curfews. From $15 per person, per night.

International Network Cotel, 1906 Mission St (☎864-3629). Shared dormitory-style accommodation, with some private rooms available, in this upmarket crash-pad with kitchen facilities. $10 per person per night. Private rooms $25–30.

San Francisco International Hostel, Building 240, Fort Mason (☎771-7277). On the waterfront between the Golden Gate Bridge and Fisherman's Wharf. Annoying 11pm curfew, but one of the most comfortable hostels around. $9 per person Nov–April; $9.50 May–Oct.

YMCA Central Branch, 220 Golden Gate Ave, two blocks from the Civic Center (☎885-0460). Well-equipped and centrally located YMCA. Singles $22, doubles $32. Facilities include a gym, swimming pool, squash courts and sauna.

Youth Hostel Central, 116 Turk St (☎346-7835). Bit of a flop house but dorms beds are just $8 per person. Private rooms for $15 (single) and $20 (double).

Hotels, Motels and B&Bs

San Francisco **hotels and motels** have a good reputation for comfort and cleanliness, and there's often little to choose between the two. Hotels in the slightly seedy areas south of Market and the Tenderloin start at around $25 a night or $100 a week, though don't expect a private bath or even toilet for that amount. In the glitzier areas around Union Square and Nob Hill it's hard to find a place for under $100 a night. Few hotels or motels bother to compete with the ubiquitous diners and offer **breakfast**, although there's a trend towards providing free (insipid) coffee (from paper cups) and sticky buns on a self-service basis from the lobby.

Several of the smaller hotels now consider themselves to be **bed and breakfast inns**, which basically means they provide a more personalised service. As well as those we've included in the listings below, you could also contact a specialist agency such as *Bed and Breakfast International* (1181-B Solano Avenue, Albany CA 94706; ☎525-4569)), *Bed and Breakfast San Francisco* (Box 349 San Francisco, CA 94101; ☎931-3083), or, in Britain, *Colby International* (139 Round Hey, Liverpool L28 1RG; ☎051/220 5848).

Downtown

Adelaide Inn, 5 Isadora Duncan Court, between Geary and Post (☎441-2261). Small hotel with shared bathroom facilities. Doubles from $38.

Alexander Inn, 415 O'Farrell St (☎928-6800). B&B in great location, just off Union Square. Doubles $39–49.

Ansonia Hotel, 711 Post St (☎673–2670). A charming B&B inn, three blocks from Union Square and cheap to boot, with breakfast and dinner included in the price. Rooms from $35.

Beresford Arms Hotel, 701 Post St (☎673-2600). Luxury B&B in the heart of town, well worth the few dollars more. Doubles $75.

Beverly Plaza Hotel, 342 Grant Ave (☎781-3566). Clean if uninspiring rooms whose main recommendation is their location in Chinatown. Doubles from $75.

David's, on Theatre Row, Geary St near Taylor (☎771-1600). Not the cheapest place in town, but a great Theater-District location. Rooms $69 for one or two people and all you can eat from the deli downstairs in the morning.

Hotel Mark Twain, 345 Taylor St (☎673-2332). Elegantly decorated colonial-style hotel in the middle of the Theater District. Doubles from $79.

Gates Hotel, 140 Ellis St (☎781-0430). Super-cheap downtown location with double rooms from $35.

Geary Hotel, 610 Geary St (☎673-9221). Affordable, no frills Theater District hotel with rooms from $36 per night.

Grant Plaza Hotel, 465 Grant Ave (☎434-3883). Newly renovated hotel with clean rooms in the middle of Chinatown. Doubles $40.

Lotus Hotel, 580 O'Farrell St (☎885-8008). Sophisticated, European-style hotel with reasonable rates. Rooms from $45 per night.

Pensione International, 875 Post St (☎775-3344). Straightforward B&B accommodation; $30 for a small double, with shared bathroom.

The Northern Waterfront

The Art Center Bed and Breakfast, 1902 Filbert St (☎567-1526). Home away from home, mainly for painters who come to sit in the grounds and attend the classes given by the owners of this quirky little inn. Apartments or suites from $65 to $120.

Bel Aire Travelodge, 3201 Steiner St (☎921-5162). Cheapest of the large motel chains, with rooms available from $50 per night.

Edward II, 3155 Scott St (☎921-9776). Large and comfortable inn-style accommodation with free wine and breakfast. Doubles from $60.

The Mansion, 2220 Sacramento St (☎929-9444). Victorian mansion up on the hill in Pacific Heights. $90 for a double, which considering the luxury you're swaddled in, isn't bad.

Marina Motel, 2576 Lombard St (☎921-9406). Cheapest of the motels around here, with rooms going for under $30 per night.

San Remo Hotel, 2237 Mason St (☎776-8688). Very basic – you'll have to share a bathroom – but for this part of town it's the cheapest you're going to find. Rooms from $30 per night.

The Wharf Inn, 2601 Mason St (☎673-7411). Comfortable, family-style hotel with free parking. Doubles for around $80.

Van Ness Motel, 2850 Van Ness Ave (☎776-3220). Large rooms with TVs within walking distance of Fisherman's Wharf. Doubles $50–60.

Washington Square Inn, 1660 Stockton St (☎981-4220). B&B bang on North Beach's lovely main square with rooms from $65.

Elsewhere in the city

Alamo Square Inn, 719 Scott St (☎922-2055). A beautifully restored B&B, but not cheap; $70–200 for handsome dwellings with fireplaces and a jacuzzi.

Amsterdam Hotel, 749 Taylor St (☎673-3277). Midway between Union Square and City Hall, this is one of the cheaper B&Bs with rooms from $42 per night.

Best Western Kyoto, 1800 Sutter St (☎921-4000). Immaculate hotel in Japantown with steambaths. Doubles around $80.

Dolores Park Inn, 3641 17th St (☎621-0482). Tiny but elegant pension-style hotel in the Mission. Doubles from $35.

Friendship Inn, 860 Eddy St (☎474-4374). Slightly dodgy location, but good rates with rooms starting from $36 per night.

Golden City Inn, 1554 Howard St (☎431-9376). Best of the South of Market hotels, far from a doss-house and smack in the middle of the SoMa nightlife scene. Unbelievably good value with doubles for $23–28.

Grove Inn, 890 Grove St (☎929-0780). Nothing fancy, but good value and a fine location. Rooms from $35 per night.

Hyde Plaza Hotel, 835 Hyde St (☎885-2987). Reasonable, no frills Tenderloin hotel with rooms from $25 per night.

Metro Hotel, 319 Divisadero St (☎861-5364). Homely, clean and cheap. Doubles from $35.

Pensione San Francisco, 1668 Market St (☎864-1271). A good base near the Civic Center, with doubles from $40.

San Francisco Central Travelodge, 1707 Market St (☎621-6775). Dependable chain motel with rooms from around $50 per night.

The Red Victorian Bed and Breakfast, 1665 Haight St (☎864-1978). Bang in the middle of the Haight Ashbury, a lively B&B that's a real relic of the Sixties. Rooms $45–70.

Stanyan Park Hotel, 750 Stanyan St (☎751-1000). Gorgeous small Victorian hotel in a great setting across from Golden Gate Park, with friendly staff and free continental breakfast. Doubles for around $80.

UN Plaza Hotel, Seventh and Market St (☎626-4600). Good location just opposite the Civic Center. Glitzy lobby and large, comfy rooms. Doubles from $55.

Airport hotels

Best Western Grosvenor Hotel, 380 South Airport Blvd (☎873-3200). Large comfortable hotel with pool, health club and free shuttle service to the airport. Rooms from $69 per night.
La Quinta Inn, 20 Airport Blvd (☎583-2223). Overnight laundry service and a pool make this a comfortable stopover. Free shuttle service to the airport. Rooms from $65.
Radisson Inn San Francisco Airport, 275 South Airport Blvd (☎873-3550). Great facilities include pool, jacuzzi, live music and a free airport shuttle. Rooms from $85 per night.
Super 8 Lodge, 111 Mitchell Ave, South San Francisco (☎877-0770). Plain, motel-style accommodations with free laundry service, breakfast and airport shuttle. Rooms from $53.

Luxury hotels

Fairmont Hotel, 950 Mason St (☎772-5000). Most famous of San Francisco's top-notch hotels, the Fairmont is an excessively decorated palace with seven restaurants, ten lounges and fantastic views from the rooms. Rooms go for $145–250 per night.
Huntington Hotel, 1075 California St (☎474-5400). Understated and quietly elegant hotel for the wealthy who don't need to flash it about; the bars opt for simple dark-wood furnishings, a piano player and a very intimate atmosphere. Free limousine service. Rooms cost $160–210.
Mandarin Oriental San Francisco, 222 Sansome Street (☎885-0999). You'll need silly amounts of money if you want to stay in what are reputedly San Francisco's most luxurious hotel rooms. Amenities include valet, concierge and 24hr room service. Rooms cost $230–450 a night.
St Francis, 335 Powell St (☎397-7000). Truly grand hotel with a sumptuous lobby, five restaurants, an elegant bar and disappointingly plain rooms. Its reputation far outstrips the reality of a stay here, but as long as you don't mind the throngs of tourists who pour in to gape at the lobby, you'll be happy. Rooms from $145 to $235.

Gay men's accommodation

There are, of course, a number of places in San Francisco either sympathetic to – or specifically catering for – **gay travellers**. Most are inevitably geared towards men: although it's unlikely that lesbians would be excluded, they may be outnumbered and should refer to "Women's accommodation", below, for more suitable alternatives.

Beck's Motor Lodge, 2222 Market St (☎621-8212). Motel near the Castro. Rooms from $50.
Casa Loma Hotel, 600 Fillmore St (☎552-7100). Mid-sized, friendly hotel with sauna, jacuzzi, sundeck and a lively bar. Singles $30, doubles $38.
Gough Hayes Hotel, 417 Gough St (☎431-9131). Informal favourite in San Francisco, no private toilets but 24hr sauna and sundeck. Singles from $25, doubles from $29.
Inn on Castro, 321 Castro St (☎861-0321). A longstanding favourite with visiting gays, this luxury bed and breakfast doesn't come cheap, but is worth it for the large rooms and good breakfasts. About two minutes' walk from the Castro. Singles $85, doubles $95.
Leland Hotel, 1315 Polk St (☎441-5141). Attractively decorated Russian Hill hotel with singles from $40 and doubles from $68.
Queen Anne Hotel, 1590 Sutter St (☎262-2663). Very much a gay hotel with over-done decor, full valet service and complimentary afternoon tea and sherry. Rooms $95 and up.
24 Henry, 24 Henry St (☎864-5686). Intimate guesthouse in a quiet street just off the heart of the Castro. Singles from $40, doubles $55 and up.
Twin Peaks Hotel, 2160 Market St (☎621-9467). Set in the hills above, this is a quieter and prettier location not far from the Castro, even if the rooms are small and short on luxury. Singles $25, doubles $30.

Women's accommodation

Bock's Bed & Breakfast, 1448 Willard St. A basic, secure and friendly hotel for women. Rooms from $35.

The Langtry, 637 Steiner St (☎863-0538). Each room in this nineteenth-century mansion is dedicated to a famous woman in history. Hot tub, sundeck, views of the city. Fabulous but not cheap with rooms at $75–200 per night.

Women's Hotel, 642 Jones St (☎775-1711). Comfortable, secure building that is sadly situated in the unpleasant Tenderloin district. Weekly rates only: singles $100 per week, doubles $120. A good deal for two women travelling together.

The City

The first and most obvious thing that strikes the visitor is that San Francisco is a city of hills. Becoming familiar with these forty-odd hills is not just a good way to get your bearings; it will also give you a real insight into the city's class distinctions. As a general rule, geographical elevation is a stout indicator of wealth – the higher you live, the better off you are. Commercial square-footage is surprisingly small and mostly confined to the downtown area, and the rest of the city is made up of distinct, primarily residential neighbourhoods, most of which are very easily explored on foot. Armed with a good map you could plough through three a day, but frankly, the best way to get to know San Francisco is to dawdle, unbound by itineraries: the most interesting districts, certainly, merit at least half a day each of just hanging about.

The top right-hand corner of the peninsula, bordered by I-80 to the south, US-101 to the west, and the water, makes up the part of the city known as **downtown**, though really the neighbourhoods themselves make the best orientation points. The core of downtown, mainly north of the city's main artery, **Market Street**, is signalled by the corporate high-rises of the **Financial District**, and just beyond, the department stores and hotels which make up the city's busiest shopping district, around **Union Square**. Above this area, swanky **Nob Hill** with its mansions and grand hotels, sits snootily on its quiet hilltop perch gazing at the action below. A few blocks away, Nob Hill's borders merge with the neon intensity of **Chinatown**, easily the densest part of town and a good bet for cheap food.

At the northernmost tip of the city, **Fisherman's Wharf** and the waterfront is carefully crafted with the visitor in mind – and pulls them in by the tour-load. You'd do better to glimpse the area in passing, though, and make a bee-line for the livelier old Italian enclave of **North Beach**. Though gentrified greatly, it still harbours a vaguely literary Bohemian population that's a hangover from the days of the Beats in the Fifties. Above it, the very desirable neighbourhoods of **Russian Hill** and **Telegraph Hill** flank North Beach on either side affording fabulous views of the shimmering bay. Just west of here, the truly rich enjoy similar vistas from the sumptuous homes of **Pacific Heights.**

Not a million miles from this rampant affluence, the slums of the **Tenderloin** form an at-times alarming quarter that begins a few blocks west of Union Square. The Tenderloin runs south for a six-block stretch of dilapidated urban sleaze before ending abruptly at San Francisco's arterial Market Street – the wide thoroughfare, lined with shops and office buildings that bisects the city centre, and is a main reference point for your wanderings. Crossing over Market Street, **South of Market** (or **SoMa**) was until recently one of the city centre's few industrial enclaves, though in recent years it has gone the way of other comparable inner-city areas and been spruced up by the artistic and nightclubbing crowd. Controversially, even this is likely to be short-lived: SoMa is a prime piece of real estate in the heart of the city, slated for development, and it's only a matter of time before the bulldozers move in and the artists move out. **Civic Center**, a little way west, is San Francisco's municipal – and arts – nucleus and site of some of the city's more grandiose architecture, plonked rather awkwardly between the slowly improving slums that surround it.

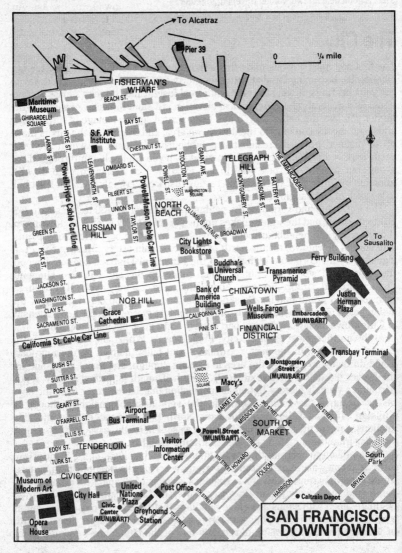

SAN FRANCISCO DOWNTOWN

Walk much further south or west from Civic Center and you're out of downtown and in the more staunchly residential neighbourhoods that enclose the city centre. A lengthy stroll or short bus-ride southwest, the garrulous Hispanic district of **The Mission**, San Francisco's largest neighbourhood, might be a good first choice for a trip further afield, filled with cheap restaurants, bars and clubs, and with a street-life that's about as non-stop as San Francisco gets. **The Castro**, just beyond, has long been the city's primary gay district and makes no bones about it: refurbished for and by gays, and although to some extent tempered by the post-AIDS years, still with an emphasis on vigorous nightlife. West of downtown, the **Haight Ashbury** district was once San Francisco's radical focus and tries hard to hold on to its counter-culture traditions, with a caucus of left-wing bookshops, some taste-fully tatty café-society and a smattering of residents still flying a slightly limp freak flag. At the end of Haight Street, **Golden Gate Park**'s landscaping is the antidote to all this: San Francisco's main city park and a sublime piece of landscape design, stretching west to the Pacific Shore and city beaches.

Downtown: The Financial District

With its plate glass and steel skyscrapers soaring dramatically into the sky to form San Francisco's only real high-rise district, casting long shadows where twenty years ago there were none, the **FINANCIAL DISTRICT** is the city's most dynamic neighbourhood – a Manhattan in miniature that's a symbol of San Francisco's enduring wealth and prosperity. Sharp-suited workers clog the streets in well-mannered rush-hour droves, racing between their offices and the Montgomery *BART/Muni* station on Market Street. Originally, the centre of the city's financial dealings was entirely to the north of Market Street, where the old low-rise banking halls are now flanked by newer, larger structures of corporate power. But to avert the complete demolition of the area for more profitable towers, the city is nowadays directing new development to the south of Market. The area contains a virtually comprehensive library of architectural styles and periods, from Palladian piles to post-modern redoubts. Scattered between the banks and bars are the copy centres and computer boutiques which serve the offices above, with an occasional restaurant of note; the people are as dressed up as they come in this casual town, though they're still largely a testament to comfort before style. There's not a lot here to come for if you're not a high-finance wheeler-dealer, and you'd do well to steer clear altogether during the rush hour. But it has a pleasantly active buzz through weekday lunchtimes, and is worth a stroll through on the way to somewhere else. It's entirely deserted on the weekend, save for gawking tourists.

Once cut off from the rest of San Francisco by the double-decker Embarcadero Freeway – which was damaged in the 1989 Earthquake, and finally torn down in 1991 – the **Ferry Building**, at the foot of Market Street, was modelled on the cathedral tower in Seville, Spain, and before the bridges were built in the Thirties was the main point of arrival for fifty thousand cross-bay commuters daily. A few ferry boats still arive here (see "Getting Around" for details), but the characterless office units inside do little to suggest its former importance. Across the way, the vast **Embarcadero Center**, a modern and rather unimaginative complex of offices, shops and cafés, connected above ground level, stretches for several blocks west from **Justin Herman Plaza** to the grey concrete *Hyatt Regency* hotel, with its twenty-storey lobby atrium and rooftop revolving bar.

From the Embarcadero, it's a few blocks down Market to **Montgomery Street**, main artery of the Financial District, where the grand pillared entrances and banking halls of the post-1906-earthquake building era jostle for attention with the mixed bag of modern towers that is gradually moving in. For a real hands-on grasp of the dynamics of modern finance, the **World of Economics Gallery** in the **Federal Reserve Bank**, 101 Market Street (Mon–Fri 10am–4pm), is unbeatable: computer games allow you to engineer your own stock-market disasters, while gallery exhibits detail recent scandals and triumphs in the financial world. The **Wells Fargo History Room**, 420 Montgomery Street (Mon–Fri 10am–5pm), details the origins of San Francisco's banking and financial boom with exhibits from the days of the Gold Rush. Mining equipment, gold nuggets, photographs and even an old wagon show the far-from-slick roots of San Francisco's big money. There are similar illustrations of the era in the **Museum of American Money from the West** in the **Bank of California**, 400 California Street (Mon–Fri 9am–5pm).

Jackson Square and the Barbary Coast

A century or so ago, the eastern flank of what is now the Financial District was part of the so-called **Barbary Coast**, a rough-and-tumble waterfront district packed with saloons and brothels where hapless young male visitors were given "Mickey Finns" and "Shanghaied" into involuntary servitude on merchant ships. Its wicked reputation made it off-limits for military personnel up until World War II and many of the old dives died an inevitable death. During the 1930s, the Barbary Coast became a low-rent district that attracted writers and artists including Diego Rivera, who had a studio on Gold Street at the height of his fame as the "communist painter sought after by the world's biggest capitalists". Most of these old structures have since been done up and preserved as the **Jackson Square Historic District** – not in fact a square, but a rectangle formed by Jackson, Montgomery, Gold and Sansome streets, making up a dense few blocks of low-rise, mostly brick buildings that now house the offices of advertising agencies and design firms, as well as the requisite cafés and watering holes.

The **Transamerica Pyramid** at the foot of diagonal Columbus Avenue, is San Francisco's most unmistakable (some would say unfortunate) landmark and the city's tallest building, marking the edge of the Financial District and the beginning of North Beach. There was something of a rumpus when this went up, and it earned the name "Pereira's Prick" after its LA-based architect William Pereira. But since then it's become institutionalised as almost a symbol of San Francisco and figures on a great deal of the city's tourist and promotional literature. The original building on this site was the Montgomery Block, the city's first office building of any significance, but known more for the important names which moved in when the businesses moved off to alternative premises. Rudyard Kipling, Bret Harte, Robert Louis Stevenson, Mark Twain and William Randolph Hearst all rented office space in the building and regularly hung around the notorious "Bank Exchange" bar within. Legend also has it that Sun Yat-Sen – whose statue is in Chinatown, three blocks away (see p.341) – wrote the Chinese constitution and devised the successful overthrow of the Manchu Dynasty from his second-floor office here. A little way south, the city's second tallest tower, the **Bank of America** building on Kearny and California, is a plate-glass and marble beast that the bank had to sell off after some over-zealous lending to developing countries. Judging by the prices in its *Carnelian Room* roof-top restaurant, the books are balancing a bit better these days – though you'd do better to skip the food, which is mediocre anyway, and simply take the elevator up for the incredible view.

Union Square

West of Kearny Street, around **Union Square**, the skyscrapers thin out and are replaced by the bright lights and window displays of San Francisco's **shopping district**: a collection of boutiques, speciality shops and department stores which stretches for several blocks in all directions. Limousines are bumper-to-bumper here, as the well-heeled pop in and out of their favourite stores; by contrast, bums and winos sprawl across the green lawns of Union Square, having drifted in from the Tenderloin to do a brisker trade from passing shoppers. The square takes it name from the mass meetings held here on the eve of the Civil War by Northerners demonstrating their loyalty to the Union, but these days it's remembered more for the attempted assassination of President Gerald Ford outside the *St Francis Hotel* in 1975. It was also the location of Francis Ford Coppola's most paranoid (and some would say best) film, *The Conversation*, where eavesdropper Gene Hackman spied on lovers strolling in the square. The hotel played a similar role in many of **Dashiell Hammett's** detective stories, as well as in his own life. In the 1920s Hammett worked there as an operative for the Pinkerton detective agency, investigating the notorious rape and murder case against the silent movie star Fatty Arbuckle. When Hammett later came to write *The Maltese Falcon* and other classic tales, he modelled many of the locations on the *St Francis*.

On Geary Street, on the south side of the square, the optimistically named **Theater District** is a pint-sized Broadway of restaurants, tourist hotels and serious and "adult" theatres – as in New York's Broadway, or London's Soho, the Theater District of San Francisco shares space with less rarefied institutions, namely porn and prostitution. Also part of this district, just north of the Square along Post and Sutter are downtown's least visible landmarks – some fourteen private clubs hidden behind discreet facades. Money isn't the only criteria for membership to these highly esteemed institutions, though being *somebody* usually is. Most notorious is the **Bohemian Club** at Post and Taylor. Better known for its *Bohemian Grove* retreat at the Russian River, where ex-Presidents and corporate giants get together for masonic rituals and schoolboy larks, the San Francisco chapter is housed in a Lewis Hobart Moderne-style building. Organised in the late 1880s by newspaper men and artists, it evolved into a businessmen's club with an arty slant, including Frank Norris, Ambrose Bierce and Jack London among its members.

On the eastern side of the square you'll find still more shops and **Maiden Lane**, a chic little urban walkway that before the 1906 earthquake and fire was one of the city's roughest areas, where prostitutes solicited openly and homicides averaged around ten a month. Nowadays, aside from some prohibitively expensive boutiques, its main feature is San Francisco's only **Frank Lloyd Wright** building, the pricey little **Circle Gallery** that was a try-out for the Guggenheim in New York. Inside, a gently curving ramp rises toward the skylighted ceiling, taking you past some of the city's most expensive artwork.

If you're heading back up to the waterfront, **cable cars** run along Powell Street but are usually too packed to board at their Market Street origin. Move a few blocks up the hill where there are fewer people trying to get on, and climb to palatial Nob Hill before descending once more to the water's edge.

Nob Hill

Nob Hill, the hill of palaces, must certainly be counted the best part of San Francisco. It is there that the millionaires gather together, vying with each other in display. From thence, looking down upon the business wards of the city, we can decry a building with a little belfry, and that is the stock exchange, the heart of San Francisco; a great pump we might call it, continually pumping up the savings of the lower quarter to the pockets of the millionaires on the hill.

Robert Louis Stevenson

If the Financial District is representative of new money in the city, the posh hotels and masonic institutions of **NOB HILL**, just above, exemplify San Francisco's old wealth; it is, as Joan Didion wrote, "the symbolic nexus of all old California money and power". Perhaps San Francisco's most revered address, it's worth the stiff climb (the wise will take the cable car) to view the mansions, hotels and elitist restaurants that serve those who come closest to being San Francisco gentry. There are very few real sights as such, but nosing around is pleasant enough, taking in the aura of luxury that distinguishes the neighbourhood, and enjoying the views over the city and beyond.

Originally called the California Street Hill, the area became known as Nob Hill after robber-baron industrialists like Leland Stanford and Charles Crocker came to the area to construct the Central Pacific Railroad and built their mansions here. Only one of these ostentatious piles survived the 1906 fire – the brownstone mansion of James C. Flood, which cost a cool $1 million in 1886 and is now the *Pacific Union Club*, a private retreat for the ultra-rich. Other, later residences have given way to hotels, the most elaborate of which is the **Fairmont Hotel** on California and Mason Streets, perhaps San Francisco's classiest joint and setting for the television soap opera *Hotel*. One block west on California stands one of the biggest hunks of sham-Gothic architecture in the US, **Grace Cathedral**. Construction began soon after the 1906 earthquake, though most of it was built, of faintly disguised reinforced concrete, in the early Sixties. One part that's worth a look is the entrance, adorned with faithful replicas of the fifteenth-century Ghiberti doors of the Florence Baptistry.

But the invention that made high-society life on the hills possible and practical – the **cable car** (the sort that runs along the ground, not swings precipitously from mountainsides) – is Nob Hill's dominant feature. Since 1873 when Scotsman Andrew Hallidie piloted the first of these little trolleys up the Clay Street hill to Portsmouth Square, they have been an integral part of life in the city. At their peak, just before the earthquake, over six hundred cable cars travelled 110 miles of track throughout the city, though by 1955 their usage had dwindled to such an extent that nostalgic citizens voted to preserve the remaining seventeen miles of track as a moving historic landmark. Today there are three lines, two of which run from Powell Street to Fisherman's Wharf, and the steepest and best which climbs Nob Hill along California Street from the Embarcadero. To climb the hills, they have to fasten on to a moving two-inch cable which runs beneath the streets, gripping on the ascent then releasing at the top and gliding down the other side. These cables are powered by huge motors which you can see in the **Cable Car Barn**, at Washington and Mason streets, recently renovated as a working museum (daily 10am–5pm; free) with exhibits of cars and trolleys. During the summer, trolley cars from all over the world (including an English one from Blackpool) are hauled out of storage and run along otherwise disused routes around the city.

Chinatown

Completely distinct from any other neighbourhood in the city, 24 square blocks of seeming chaos smack in the middle of San Francisco make up **CHINATOWN**. Dense, noisy, smelly, colourful and overcrowded, the second largest Chinese community outside Asia manages to be almost entirely autonomous, with its own schools, banks and newspapers. In among the brightly lit streets of restaurants, foodstores and souvenir shops, however, the occasional dark and gloomy alleyway reminds you that the commercial enterprise has not brought prosperity to all of the city's Chinese population.

CHINESE NEW YEAR

If you're visiting at the end of January or early February, make an effort to catch the celebration of **Chinese New Year**, when the streets almost self-combust with energy and noise. Floats and papier maché monsters crawl past as people hang off balconies, out of windows and shin up lampposts until there isn't an inch of space

---

The first Chinese arrived in Northern California in the late 1840s, many of them fleeing famine and the opium wars at home and seeking the easy fortunes of the Gold Rush. Later, in the 1860s, thousands more were shipped across to build the Transcontinental Railroad. At first the Chinese, or "coolies" as they were called (taken from the words *ku li*, meaning "bitter toil"), were accepted as hard-working labourers, but as the railway neared completion and unemployment rose, many moved to San Francisco, to join what was already a sizeable community. The city didn't extend much of a welcome: jingoistic sentiment turned quickly into a tide of racial hatred, manifest in sometimes vicious attacks that bound the Chinese defensively into a solid, homogenous community. The population stagnated until the Sixties, when the lifting of the anti-Chinese immigration restrictions swelled the area's numbers to close on 160,000. Nowadays it's not just Chinese, but Vietnamese, Koreans, Thais and Laotians: by day the area seethes with activity and congestion; by night the traffic moves a little easier, but the blaze of neon and marauding diners gives you the feeling that it just never lets up. Overcrowding is compounded by a brisk tourist trade, and sadly, Chinatown boasts some of the most egregiously tacky shops and facades in the city. Genuine snatches of ethnicity are sullied by pseudo-Chinese Americana at every turn.

You can approach Chinatown from many directions: as well as Nob and Russian Hills, North Beach blends into its eastern edges and if you're coming from the south, Union Square is just a few blocks away. It is from this direction that you'll encounter the large dragon-clad archway (a gift from the Government of Taiwan, and, judging by the look of it, not one that broke the bank) that crosses the intersection of Bush Street and **Grant Avenue**, a long, narrow street, crowded with gold ornamented portals and brightly painted balconies which sit above the souvenir shops and restaurants. Plastic buddhas, floppy hats and chopsticks assault the eye from every doorway. Parallel to Grant, **Stockton Street** is closer to the real thing – Chinatown's main street, crammed with exotic fish and fruit and veg markets, bakeries and spice shops. Your dollar will go further here than anywhere else in the neighbourhood and your search for the authentic face of Chinatown will be better rewarded. Two blocks down, **St Mary's Square** holds a sculpture of Sun Yat-Sen, founder of the Chinese Republic, its little old ladies and pastoral ambience a far cry from the days when this was the red light district of Chinatown. Similarly, before the days of all-consuming tourism, Grant Avenue was known as Dupont Street, a wicked ensemble of opium dens, bordellos and gambling huts policed and frequently terrorised by Tong hatchet men – gangs who took it upon themselves to police and protect their district in any (usually extremely violent) way they saw fit. Their original purpose was to retaliate against the racial hooliganism, but they developed quickly into Mafia-style family feuding – as bloody as any of the Chicago gang wars. These days there isn't much trace of them on the streets, but the mob continues to operate, battling for a slice of the lucrative West Coast drug trade.

Chinatown's history is well documented in the **Chinese Historical Society of America** at 17 Waverly Place (daily 9am–4pm; donations), which traces the beginnings of the Chinese in the US and has a small but worthy collection of photographs, paintings and artefacts from the pioneering days of the last century. Also in Waverly Place are three opulently decorated but skilfully hidden temples (numbers 109, 125 and 146), their interiors a riot of black, gold and vermillion. They're still in use today and open to visitors, but the variable opening times mean you'll have to take pot luck to get in. More accessible is **Buddha's Universal Church** at 720 Washington Street, where America's largest Zen sect give tours on the second and fourth Sunday of each month. This five-storey building was painstakingly built by the sect-members from an exotic collection of polished woods, adorned everywhere by the mosaic images of Buddha. Not as rich with history, the **Chinese Cultural Center**, 750 Kearny Street (Tues–Sat 10am–4pm), does nonetheless have a regular programme of art shows, mostly contemporary, that go some way to dispelling the popular myth that Chinese art is all pastel colours and oblique images.

The best of Chinatown's very few **bars** is **Li Po's**, at 916 Grant Avenue, a dimly lit retreat from the confusion of the surrounding streets – is named after the Chinese poet, and something of a hangout for the small contingent of Chinese writers in the city. However, you are more likely to have come here to **eat** in one of over one hundred restaurants (see p.366 for recommendations). Some are historical landmarks in themselves, none less so than **Sam Woh's**, at 813 Washington Street, cheap and churlish ex-haunt of the Beats where Gary Snyder taught Jack Kerouac to eat with chopsticks, and had them both thrown out for his loud and passionate interpretation of Zen poetry.

One block further west, **Portsmouth Square** was the original centre of the city, and the place where Sam Brannan announced the discovery of gold, an event which transformed San Francisco from a sleepy Spanish pueblo into a rowdy frontier city. Though not the most attractive of parks these days, built on top of a multi-storey car park, it's nonetheless an oasis in a very cramped part of town. Old men come to play chess while younger ones fly past on skateboards; in the northwest corner there's a monument to Robert Louis Stevenson, who, it's claimed, used to come here and write.

North Beach

Resting in the hollow between Russian and Telegraph Hills, and split down the middle by Columbus Avenue, **NORTH BEACH** likes to think of itself as the happening district of San Francisco. Originally the city's Italian quarter, since the Fifties – when the more prominent figures of the Beat movement gathered here – it has been among the city's most sought-after neighbourhoods for anyone vaguely alternative. There's still an Italian slant to the neighbourhood, somehow resisting the encroaching neon of the strip joints and sex clubs on Broadway, and North Beach is home to some of the most loyally patronised bars and restaurants in the city. Rocketing real estate prices are inevitably bringing about change, and die-hard free-thinkers wrestle to maintain their territory amidst the growing numbers of sharp-suited young professionals slumming it at North Beach's traditionally scruffy cafés. But for the moment it's one of the city's most likeable neighbourhoods, still inhabited by a solid core of people who remember what Bohemia was really like. The anecdotes connected with North Beach are legion – get chatting to any barfly over fifty, they seem to know them all.

San Francisco's most visible landmark, the **Transamerica Pyramid**, on Montgomery Street at Columbus, marks the southern edge of North Beach and the beginning of the more corporate identity of the Financial District. A little way along Columbus, the green flatiron **Columbus Tower** looks somewhat surreal against the corporate backdrop of the downtown skyline. Developers have been trying to knock it down for years, but the efforts of its owner, San Francisco-based film-maker Francis Ford Coppola, have so far ensured its survival. Across Columbus, the now defunct *Purple Onion* nightclub, and the *Hungry i* down Jackson Street hosted some of the biggest names of the Fifties San Francisco scene. Politically conscious comedians like Lenny Bruce (who made himself a name in the area for regular doped-out attempts to throw himself from the upper windows) and Mort Sahl performed here and even though these places have now closed or changed beyond recognition, the district continues to trade on a reputation earned decades ago.

Further along Columbus at Broadway, amidst the flashing neon and sleazy clubs, the **City Lights Bookstore** was the first paperback bookshop in the US. It was established in 1953, and is still owned by poet and novelist Lawrence Ferlinghetti. The vast collection of avant-garde, contemporary and Beat works is kept open for business and browsing until midnight, seven days a week. North Beach has always been something of a literary hangout: it was home to Mark Twain and Jack London for a while, among other boomtown writers. But it was the **Beat Generation** in the late Fifties that really put the place on the map, focusing media attention on the area – and *City Lights* – as literary capital of California. The first Beat writings had emerged a decade earlier in New York's Lower East Side from Jack Kerouac, Allen Ginsberg and William Burroughs, who like many writers of the time were frustrated by the conservative political climate of the time, and whose lifestyle and values emphasised libertarian beliefs that America wasn't perhaps ready for. Nothing really crystallised, however, until a number of the writers moved out West, most of them settling in North Beach and forming an esoteric cluster of writers, poets, musicians and inevitable hangers-on around the *City Lights* bookstore. It wasn't long before the Beats were making news. In 1957 a storm of controversy rose up when police moved in to prevent the sale of Ginsberg's poem *Howl* under charges of obscenity – an episode the press latched onto immediately, inadvertently hyping the Beats to national notoriety, as much for their hedonistic antics as for the literary merits of their work. Within six months, Jack Kerouac's *On the Road*, inspired by his friend Neal Cassady's benzedrine monologues and recorded in a marathon two-week session in New York six years earlier – previously rejected by all the publishers he had taken it to – shot to the top of the bestseller lists.

As well as developing a new, more personal style of fiction and poetry, the Beats eschewed most social conventions of the time, and North Beach soon became almost a symbol across the nation of a wild and subversive lifestyle. The roadtrips and riotous partying, the drug-taking and embrace of eastern religion, were revered and emulated nationwide. Whether the Beat message was an important one is a moot point; in any case, the Beats became more of an industry than a literary movement, and whatever they might have had to say was ultimately trivialised as tourists poured into North Beach for "Beatnik Tours" and the like. The more enterprising fringes of Bohemia responded in kind with "The Squaresville Tour" of the Financial District, dressed in Bermuda shorts and carrying plaques that read "Hi Squares". The legend has yet to die, not least in North Beach itself, where Ferlinghetti recently had his wish granted by City Hall and many of the city's streets have been renamed as a tribute to the famous figures who have graced the neighbourhood; indeed the small alley which runs down the side of the store has been called "Jack Kerouac Lane".

Next to the bookstore, **Vesuvio's** is an old North Beach bar where most of the local writers hung out at some point. The likes of Dylan Thomas and Kerouac regularly got loaded here, and while times have changed considerably since then it remains a haven for the lesser-knowns to get ploughed with impunity and pontificate on the state of the arts. Assuming you leave Vesuvio's with your brain intact, you'll find yourself at the crossroads of **Columbus and Broadway**, where poetry meets porn in a raucous assembly of strip joints, rock venues and drag queens. Most famous, the now-derelict *Condor Club* is where Carol Doda's infamous revealing of her silicone-implanted breasts started the topless waitress phenomenon. Her nipples are now immortalised in neon above the door as a tribute to the years of mammary fascination in the clubs around here – though nowadays business seems a bit slack along the strip as the doormen try to lure you into their darkened doorways.

As you continue north on Columbus Avenue, the bright lights fade and you enter the heart of the old **Italian neighbourhood,** an enclave of restaurants, cafés and delicatessens set against a background of narrow streets and leafy enclosures. A quick diversion along any of the side streets will lead you to the small landmarks like the **Café Trieste**, a literary morning spot since the days of the Beats and still a reminder of more romantic times: the jukebox blasts out opera classics to a heavy-duty art crowd, toying with their capuccinos and browsing a slim volume of poetry. Traces of a minor hippy occupation in the Sixties linger on in places like the **Sixties Poster Shop**, on Columbus, where the visages of icons like Hendrix, Joplin and Morrison are immortalised in psychedelic rainbows.

A couple of hundred yards further along Columbus Avenue, **Washington Square Park** isn't, with five sides, much of a square; nor due to urban overcrowding is it much of a park either. However, it's big and green enough for the elder Italians to rest on the benches and the neighbouring Chinese to do their Tai Chi routines on a Sunday morning. On the north side of the park the lacy spires of the **Church of St Peter and Paul**, where local baseball hero Joe DiMaggio married Marilyn Monroe, dominate the centre of the neighbourhood. Two steep hills dwarf the dainty towers of the church: to the east of Columbus Avenue, **TELEGRAPH HILL** is a neighbourhood of small alleys and houses perched on 45-degree inclines. It was once an extension of the wilder North Beach territory, but is now firmly rich country, its elegant homes dangling precipitously on the steep hills below **Coit Tower** (daily 10am–6pm) – a monument to the firefighters who doused the flames of 1906, decorated with WPA murals depicting musclebound Californians working on the land. Greatest reward for the trudge uphill, though, are the panoramic views out over the waterfront, from the Golden Gate Bridge in the west to the hills of Berkeley across the bay to the east.

To the west of Columbus, **RUSSIAN HILL** was named after the Russian sailors who died on an expedition here in the early 1800s and were buried on its southeastern tip. The neighbourhood today draws a steady stream of visitors, who come to drive down **Lombard Street**: a narrow, tightly curving street with a 5mph speed limit and a tailback of cars waiting to get on to it. Surrounded by palatial dwellings and herbaceous borders, Lombard is featured as often as the Golden Gate Bridge in San Francisco publicity shots, and at night when the tourists leave and the city lights twinkle below, it makes for a thrilling drive. But even if you're without a car the journey up here is worth it for a visit to the **San Francisco Art Institute**, 800 Chestnut Street (Tues–Sat 10am–5pm; free). As the oldest art school in the west, the Institute has been central in the development of the arts in the Bay Area, and has four excellent galleries, three dedicated to painting and one to surrealist photography. The remarkably high standard of work puts some of San Francisco's galleries proper in a very shady second place. But the highlight of the institute is unquestionably the **Diego Rivera Gallery**, which has an outstanding mural done by the painter in 1931 at the height of his fame. A small **cafeteria** at the back of the building offers cheap refreshments and great views of North Beach, Telegraph Hill and the bay.

Fisherman's Wharf, Alcatraz and the Waterfront

San Francisco doesn't go dramatically out of its way to please the tourist on the whole, but with **Fisherman's Wharf**, and the nearby waterfront district, it makes a rare exception. The area's crowded and hideous ensemble of waterfront kitsch and fast-food stands make for a sad and rather misleading introduction to the city. Hard to believe now, but this was originally a serious fishing port, trawling in real crabs and not the frozen sort now masquerading as fresh on the stands; the few fishermen that can afford the exorbitant mooring charges are usually finished by early morning and get out before the tourists arrive. The shops and bars here are among the most over-priced in the city and crowd-weary families do little to add to the ambience: it's pretty enough and has a handful of good seafood restaurants, but the best thing to do at the Wharf is leave.

Almost directly opposite, the **Cannery**, on Leavenworth Street, is a fruit-packing factory which has experienced similar refurbishment. And at the far end of the Wharf, about half a mile away, **Pier 39** is another shopping complex, contrived to look like San Francisco of old but failing rather miserably and charging heavily for the privilege of visiting. In between there's a cluster of exorbitantly priced museums and exhibitions designed to relieve you of more of your money; none is worth expending time on at all, even if you're with kids. Further east, **Ghirardelli Square** at 900 N Point Street, is perhaps a fitting conclusion to this part of the waterfront, a former chocolate factory whose major parts have been refurbished as a Covent-Garden-like complex of pricey shops and restaurants – although some small-scale production does continue.

Two-hour **cruises of the bay** depart from piers 39 & 40 several times a day, and, provided the fogs aren't too heavy, they give good views of the city from the water (see "Getting Around" for details).

ALCATRAZ

The rocky little islet of **Alcatraz**, rising out of San Francisco Bay, was originally home to nothing more than the odd pelican (*alcatraz* in Spanish). In the late nineteenth century, the island became a military fortress, and in 1934 it was converted into America's most dreaded **high-security prison**. Surrounded by freezing, impassable water it was an ideal place for a jail, and safely kept some of America's most wanted criminals behind bars – Al Capone and Machine Gun Kelly were just two of the villains imprisoned here. The conditions were about as inhuman as you'd expect: inmates were kept in solitary confinement, in cells no larger than five by nine feet, most without light; they were not allowed to eat together, read newspapers, have a game of cards or even talk; relatives were allowed to visit for only two hours each month. Escape really was impossible. In all, nine men managed to get off the rock, but there is no evidence that any of them made it to the mainland.

For all its usefulness as a jail, the island turned out to be a fiscal disaster, and after years of generating massive running costs, not to mention whipping up a storm of public protest for its role as a prison for petty criminals, it closed in 1963. The remaining prisoners were distributed among decidedly less horrific detention centres, and the island remained abandoned until 1969, when a group of native Americans staged an occupation as part of a peaceful attempt to claim the island for their people – citing treaties which designated all federal land not in use as automatically reverting to their ownership. Using all the bureaucratic trickery they could muster, the government finally ousted them in 1971, claiming the operative lighthouse qualified it as active.

Nowadays the only people to set foot on the island are the annual 750,000 tourists who participate in the excellent hour-long, self-guided audio tours ($3) of the abandoned rows of cells, which include some sharp anecdotal commentary and the opportunity to spend a minute (it feels like forever) locked in a darkened cell.

Boats across to Alcatraz leave hourly from pier 41, beginning at 8.15am, with the last boat back at around 6pm (cost $7 per person).

West from the Wharf

A little way west of the Wharf, beyond Ghirardelli Square, the **Golden Gate National Recreation Area** was established in 1972 to protect much-needed central park space for the people of the city. It now encompasses almost seventy square miles of waterfront property, from the beach areas of the city to the south right up to the cliffs of Marin County on the other side of the Golden Gate Bridge. Closest to the Wharf, a complex of buildings known as **Aquatic Park** groups around the foot of Hyde Street, at its centre the "bathhouse" – a bold, art deco piece of architecture which is now home to the **National Maritime Museum** (summer daily 10am–6pm, winter Wed–Sun 10am–6pm; free). It's worth dropping by just to see Hilaire Hiler's mural, symbolising the lost continent of Atlantis in 37 individual hallucinogenic panels which dominate the main room. The rest of the complex includes a maritime library, and a fairly forgettable collection of ocean-going memorabilia. **Hyde Street Pier**, one of the few working piers remaining at the Wharf, is adjacent to the museum and has five old wooden ships, open to the public daily for free, anchored and choc-full of seafaring trinkets. One of them, the *Balclutha*, the sole survivor of the great sailing ships that journeyed around Cape Horn in the 1800s, later had bit parts in movies like *Mutiny on the Bounty*.

Fort Mason, half a mile west along the waterfront, sits behind a park at the end of the MUNI bus line #30. Originally used for defence purposes during the Civil War and now turned over to public use, the site includes a **youth hostel** (see p.332), the acclaimed **Magic Theater** (see "Nightlife") and two museums. The **Museo Italo Americano** (Wed–Sun noon–5pm; free) has displays relating to the culture and history of the Italian community in the US; the rather better **Mexican Museum** in Building D (Wed–Sun noon–5pm; $3) houses a small but important collection of pre-Hispanic, colonial and folk art with regular exhibitions by the likes of Diego Rivera and Frida Kahlo.

San Francisco's most theatrical piece of architecture lies at Marina Boulevard and Baker Street. **The Palace of Fine Arts** is not the museum its name suggests, but instead a huge freely interpreted classical ruin originally built of wood and plaster for the Pan Pacific Exhibition in 1915 to celebrate the rebirth of the city after the 1906 fire. Sentimental San Franciscans saved it from immediate demolition after the exhibition, and it crumbled with dignity until a wealthy resident put up the money for its reconstruction in 1958, making it the sole survivor of the Pan Pacific pageant, surrounded by a swan-filled lagoon and other nice touches of urban civility. The rather unsightly, shed-like building next door is the **Exploratorium** (Tues & Thur 1–5pm, Wed 1–9pm, Sat & Sun 10am–5pm; $4, Wed), with over five hundred hands-on exhibits demonstrating scientific principles of electricity, sound, lasers and more. From here the waterfront stretches west through the Presidio Army Base to the Golden Gate Bridge and beach area close to the park (see p.354).

The area around the Palace of Fine Arts is known as the **MARINA** district to the young, image-conscious, money-no-object sort of professionals who live there. One of the city's greenest districts, the Marina enjoys a prime waterfront location, open spaces and lots of trees. Ironically, though it was built specifically to celebrate the rebirth of the city after the massive earthquake of 1906, the Marina was the worst casualty of the earthquake in 1989 – tremors tore through fragile landfill and a good number of homes collapsed into smouldering heap. The neighbourhood's commercial centre runs along **Chestnut Street** between Broderick and Fillmore streets. As a neighbourhood, it has a reputation for being something of a haven for swinging singles; the local watering holes are known as "high intensity breeder-bars" and even the local *Safeway* has been dubbed "The Body Shop" because of the inordinate amount of cruising that goes on in the aisles.

The Tenderloin, Civic Center and South of Market

While much of San Francisco tends to be depicted as some kind of urban utopia – and in some cases, almost lives up to the promise – the adjoining districts of the Tenderloin, Civic Center and South of Market reveal a city of harsh realities. Pretty tree-lined streets, hills and stunning views are conspicuously absent, and for the most part these areas are a gritty blue-collar reminder that not everybody here has it so easy. The homeless and disaffected are very much in evidence – the flipside of Californian prosperity is alive and unwell. Sporadic attempts are made to improve the areas (like the removal of over three hundred homeless people who set up camp outside the offices of the Mayor), but these are at best well-meaning hit and misses or at worst, patently cosmetic gestures that are bound to fail. However, these districts are not uninteresting and neither are they menacing.

The Tenderloin

West of Union Square, on the north side of Market, the **TENDERLOIN** provides bold contrast with the rest of San Francisco– still a predominantly poor neighbourhood sandwiched between Civic Center and the downtown area. A small, uninviting area no more than four blocks by five, it remains the poorest and shabbiest spot in the city. However, it is the cheapest area around for accommodation and you may find yourself staying in one of the numerous budget hotels and lodgings. Most recently it has been home to a wave of Vietnamese and Laotian immigrants, though soup kitchens and flop houses remain the area's major industry. The Tenderloin is at least smack in the middle of town, and you'll be safe as long as you keep your wits about you and don't mind bums asking you for money.

Partly as an attempt to spruce the area up, the city has gone to great lengths to design a "tramp-proof" **park** on Jones and Eddy streets, replete with every imaginable barrier to dissuade the locals from establishing residence. On a good day, and with heavy patrolling by local police, it can claim to be a success. With common sense you shouldn't find the Tenderloin threatening, though areas you might take care to avoid are those along **Taylor** Street and around **Eddy** and **Turk** streets. Gangs have made this their territory and nonchalantly mooching around is not recommended.

Attempts to dignify **Polk Street** to the west have fortunately, been less successful. Even the police find this wild stretch hard to control, with cars kerbcrawling the strip of dodgy-looking bars for rent boys and prostitutes. Refreshingly sleazy after the sometimes tedious charm of San Francisco, Polk Street is a neon haven of gay bars, affordable, small shops, movie theatres and further up towards Russian Hill, some pretty good restaurants.

Civic Center

Born out of a grand, celebratory architectural scheme, **CIVIC CENTER,** squashed between the quasi-slums of the Tenderloin and SoMa, is an impressive layout of majestic federal and municipal buildings, that can't help but look strangely out of synch, both with its immediate neighbours and with San Francisco as a whole. Its grand Beaux Arts structures, flags and fountains are at odds with the quirky wooden architecture that characterises the rest of the city. It's the city's centre for the performing arts, and by night can look quite impressive – beautifully lit, and swarming with dinner-suits heading in and out of the ballet, opera and symphony hall. But by day it's much less appealing, populated either by office-workers from the various local government departments situated here, or by the homeless who loiter on the grass verges of the elegant central quadrangle.

Emerging from the MUNI/BART station, the first thing you see is the **United Nations Plaza**, a memorial to the founding of the UN here in 1949 – though the only sign of life here is on Wednesdays when it's the site of San Francisco's largest and cheapest **fruit and vegetable market**. Most other days it's a rather dismal location for elderly, disabled and poor people to beg for small change around the fountains in front of the **City Hall**, at the northern edge of the quadrangle. Modelled on St Peter's in Rome, this huge, green-domed Baroque building of granite and marble is the city's most grandiose structure and forms the nucleus of Civic Center. It was here in 1978 that conservative councillor Dan White got past security and assassinated Mayor George Moscone and gay Supervisor Harvey Milk; later, when White was found guilty of manslaughter (not murder), it was the scene of violent demonstrations, as gay protesters set fire to police vehicles and stormed the doors of the building. A number of galleries are beginning to group themselves around the district: the **Vorpal Gallery**, 393 Grove Street (daily 11am–6pm) has earned a reputation for consistently high-class contemporary paintings, while the **San Francisco Women's Artists Gallery**, 370 Hayes Street (Tues–Sun 11am–5pm), provides much needed exhibition space for mainly photographic works by women.

Directly behind City Hall are San Francisco's cultural mainstays – the ritzy War Memorial Opera House, the giant aquarium-like Louise M. Davies Symphony Hall and, pending construction of its own home, **The Museum of Modern Art** (Tues–Sun 10am–4pm; $4.50) – occupying the top two floors of the Veteran's Building, which was built in tribute to those who fought in World War I. While not a big-league museum, the permanent collection includes works by some major contemporary artists. Small enough to take in during one visit, it was the first California museum to set up an architecture and design department, and has recently widened its net further by exhibiting video installations – an emerging art form to which the responses of most established museums have, at best, been lukewarm.

The permanent collection is distinguished by some major paintings from the **American Abstract Expressionist school**, most notably Clyfford Still, Jackson Pollock and Philip Guston. The museum shows strength in **German Expressionism** – with the recent arrival of works by Paul Klee – **Fauvism** and **Mexican Painting** by Frida Kahlo and Diego Rivera. There's a smattering of works by Dali, Matisse, Picasso and Kandinsky, but by no means their best, and the museum excels most with its collection of twentieth-century **photography**, which includes work by both European and American photographers – Cartier-Bresson and Brassai, as well as Man Ray and Ansel Adams, all get a look in. By appointment, there's also access to an exhaustive **Fine Arts Library** with over twelve thousand volumes for the committed archivist, though most will be happy with the **bookshop's** extensive stock of posters and art-related literature.

South of Market

Although traditionally among San Francisco's least desirable (and notorious) neighbourhoods, the district South of Market, aka **SOMA**, enjoyed a bit of a renaissance in the 1980s and has entered the 1990s with a slightly altered reputation. It's reminiscent in a way of New York's SoHo, and while by day it can seem a bleak expanse of largely deserted warehouse spaces, by night it can fairly claim to be the epicentre of San Franciscan nightlife. The decline of San Francisco's shipping and rail freight industry in the Fifties and Sixties left much of the area desolate, but since the city planners put a stop to all new development in the Financial District, there's been a boom in new construction here, highlighted by major projects like the **Moscone Convention Center**, named after the Mayor who was assassinated along with Harvey Milk, and the **Yerba Buena Center** – a massive project of offices and condominiums, aimed at restoring the disused docks and railyards. Many of the abandoned warehouses have been converted into studio space and small art galleries, and the neighbourhood is now home to artists, musicians, hep-cat entertainers and a number of trendy restaurants. After years of public wrangling and public protest, the **Mission Bay Project** – a huge and contentious expansion scheme aimed at restoring the disused docks and railyards to lucrative industry – looks set to bring thousands of new residents to town. Of all the planned buildings, the most talked-about has been the new home of the **Museum of Modern Art**, designed by Mario Botta, which will more than double its current exhibition space and – optimists predict – make San Francisco a foremost centre for contemporary art on the West Coast.

Above all, SoMa is the nucleus of **clubland**, the only place any self-respecting San Franciscan night owl will be seen after dark, and it's a chance to see the city's wildlife at its best. Folsom Street was a major gay strip, the centre for much lewder goings-on than the now-respectable Castro, but in recent years the mix has become pretty diverse and you should expect to find anything but the very tame – this is not the home of the mainstream. The kernel of activity is around 11th and Folsom, where the largest grouping of clubs are bars draw crowds who don't mind queuing at weekends. Comparatively little traffic uses this intersection during the day and it comes are a surprise to see the bumper to bumper and double-parked vehicles after midnight. If you find yourself here during the day and want to check out the area, head for the block of Folsom Avenue between Seventh and Ninth streets. *Brainwash* at 1122 Folsom Avenue is the epitome of SoMa, a cafe where you can also do your laundry. There's also a small handful of galleries in the area, most interestingly **Artspace** at Ninth and Folsom – an avant-garde space for the exhibition of unusual works and video installations.

Nestled between Brannan and Bryant, and Second and Third Streets about half a mile away, **South Park** is the sole survivor of what in the 1870s was San Francisco's most upscale district, a small square designed by an English architect to mirror London's fashionable Georgian squares. The building of the Bay Bridge – which has its western foot just a block away – spelled the end of this as a residential neighbourhood; long an industrial district, South Park has recently been rediscovered and increasingly houses the offices of architects and designers, who can be seen lunching at the chic and genuinely French *South Park Café* on the square. Around the corner, where Third Street meets Brannan, a **plaque** marks the birthplace of *Call of the Wild* writer Jack London, though he soon escaped what were then pretty mean streets, enjoying his better days in Oakland and the valleys of Sonoma.

Rising impressively out of the desolation of this changing but still predominately industrial area, the **Old Mint Museum**, Fifth and Mission Streets (Mon–Wed 10am–4pm; free), is an unexpected sight. Classically styled from brick and stone, the building is no longer used as a mint, but a stroll around will still allow you to glimpse an awful lot of money. As well as a million dollars in gold, there's a million-dollar coin collection, and lots more valuables beside. Before you return to the movement of Market, stop at the **Tattoo Museum**, at 30 Seventh Street – actually a working tattoo parlour – and check out Lyle Tuttle's bizarre recordings of the flesh canvases that have fallen under his needle.

With all the new development in progress, it can be hard to imagine what SoMa looked like before, but the real spirit of blue-collar, industrial San Francisco can still be found around the abandoned docks and old shipyards known as **China Basin** and **Mission Rock**. Not much goes on here now, but the site has an isolated, romantic quality suited to desolate walks, stopping off for drinks at the few places that dot the shoreline. The easiest way to reach the area is to follow Third Street south from Market as it curves round to meet the docks at the **Switchyards** where the drawbridge crosses China Basin Channel. It was here that **Jack Kerouac** worked as a brakeman in the Fifties, at the same time writing the material that was later to appear in *Lonesome Traveller*, detailing scenes of SoMa skid row hotels, drunks and whores. A short walk south takes you to the heart of the China Basin, the old water inlet and Mission Rock – the old Pier 50 that juts out into the bay. This was the focus of the old port where freight ships used to dock from Asia. Occasionally the odd ship will sail by, but these days it's more likely to be the military ships from the Oakland Naval Base cruising the bay than the freight liners that used to jam the waterways. A few small boat clubs have sprung up along the waterfront, but most people come to visit the *Mission Rock Resort* or *The Ramp* – two creaky wooden structures that are local landmarks. *The Ramp* in particular is quite the place to be on Sunday when people gather to hear live jazz on the small pier.

The Mission and Castro

Low-rent, hip, colourful, occasionally dangerous and solidly working-class, the **MISSION** is easily San Francisco's funkiest neighbourhood. Positioned way south of downtown, it is also the city's warmest, avoiding the fogs which blanket most of the peninsula during the summer months. Stretching from SoMa at its northern end down to Army Street in the south, the Mission is a large district, although with *BART* stations at each end, getting here isn't a problem.

As a first stop for immigrants to the city, the Mission is something of a microcosm of the history of San Francisco. It was first inhabited by Scandinavians and Germans, later the Irish, then the Italians – and most recently San Francisco's Hispanic population. Perhaps because of this the area also has a marked political edge: there's active Hispanic campaigning and a fair concentration of feminist and lesbian activities, as well as a thriving Latin literary scene – possibly San Francisco's most vibrant since the Beats. For the rest, it's a noisy melange of garages, bookshops, furniture and junk stores, old movie houses and parking lots; food is cheap and there's a fair concentration of lively nightspots, making the Mission a good base if you're staying in the city for any length of time.

The district takes its name from the old **Mission Dolores**, 16th and Dolores (daily 10am–4pm; $1), the most ancient building to survive the 1906 earthquake and fire. Founded in 1776, it was the sixth in a series of missions built as Spain staked its claim to California, trying to "civilise" the native Indians with Christianity while at the same time utilising their (cheap) labour. Cruel treatment and neglect, however, led to disease and many Indians died; their graves, and those of white pioneers, can be seen in the cemetery next door. **Dolores Park** a few blocks along at Dolores and 18th Street, high on a hill at the edge of the neighbourhood, is a pretty, quiet space to rest and take in the good views of the city, plagued though it is with defecating doggies and children on BMX bikes.

Most of the Mission's action goes on between 16th and 24th Streets, between the *BART* stations along Mission, Valencia and Dolores street. The heart of things is the area around 16th and Valencia, where there's a concentration of restaurants, thrift stores, cafés and bookstores – all good for picking up flyers and free magazines to find out what's going on in the area. The one sight here is the **Levi Stauss & Co** factory at 250 Valencia Street (Mon–Fri 10am–5pm; free), where you can see how the world's most famous jeans are made. Tours of the plant include the cutting and sewing operations, and how to "stonewash" a pair of jeans and make your new pair look old. What really sets the Mission apart from other neighbourhoods, however, are its **murals** – though with so many splashed about (there are over 200 in all) it's hard to know what to look at first. If you can't stomach taking yourself on an unexpurgated tour you should at least go and see the brilliant tribute to local hero **Carlos Santana** adorning three buildings where 22nd Street meets South Van Ness. For more controversial subject matter take a walk down **Balmy Alley** between Folsom and Harrison off 24th Street (unquestionably the axis of Latino shopping, with Nicaraguan, Salvadorean, Costa Rican, Mexican and other Latin American stores and restaurants), where every possible surface is covered with murals depicting the political agonies of Central America. It was started in 1973 by a group of artists and community workers and has become the most quietly admired public art in San Francisco. Several organisations conduct walking tours of the Mission – see "Getting Around" for details.

The Latin literary scene means there are some worthy bookshops around, particularly **Old Wives Tales**, 1009 Valencia Street, where *Shameless Hussy* and the *Women's Press Collective* publish a large number of titles, but you should refer to the bookshops section of the listings for further details. The **Valencia Rose Restaurant Cabaret**, 766 Valencia Street, is the hot literary nightspot at the moment and has a full schedule of readings, poetry shouting jousts and the like. **Bars** too are thick on the ground, and people arrive from all over town to visit places like *Caesar's Palace*, *El Rio* and *The Uptown*. (See listings for details of the best places).

The Castro

Arguably San Francisco's most progressive, if no longer most celebratory neighbourhood, **THE CASTRO** is the city's avowed Gay Capital and, as such, the best barometer for the state of the AIDS-devastated gay scene. As a district, the Castro occupies a large area which stretches south from Market Street as far as Noe Valley (see below), but in terms of visible street life the few blocks from Market to 20th Street contain about all there is to see. People say many things about the changing face of the neighbourhood – some insist that it's still the wildest place in town, others reckon it's a shadow of its former self – but all agree that things are not the same. A walk down the Castro ten or even five years ago would have you gaping at the revelry, and while most of the same bars and hangouts still stand, these days they're host to an altogether different, younger and more conservative breed. But while there are no sights as such, a visit to the district (inevitably somewhat voyeuristic) is a must if you're to get any idea of just how progressive San Francisco really is.

Harvey Milk Plaza, by the Castro MUNI station, is as good a place as any to start your wanderings, dedicated to the gay supervisor (or councillor) who before his assassination in 1978 owned a camera shop and was a popular figure in the Castro. Milk and Moscone's assailant, Dan White, was a disgruntled ex-supervisor who resigned when the liberal policies of Moscone and Milk didn't coincide with his conservative views. He later tried to get his post back but was refused by Moscone, and soon after, sauntered into City Hall and shot them both. At the trial, White pleaded temporary insanity caused by harmful additives in his diet of fast food – a plea which came to be known as the "twinkie defence" (twinkies are sweets) – and was sentenced to five years' imprisonment for manslaughter. The gay community reacted angrily to the brevity of White's sentence, and the riots that followed were among the most violent San Francisco has ever witnessed, protesters marching into City Hall turning over and burning police cars as they went. White was released in 1985 and moved to Los Angeles, where he committed suicide shortly after.

Before heading down the hill into the heart of the Castro, take a short walk across Market Street to the headquarters of the **Names Project** at 2362 Market Street (daily 10am–7pm). The organisation was founded in the wake of the AIDS crisis and sponsored the creation of "The Quilt" – a gargantuan blanket composed of panels, each 6ft x 3ft (the size of a gravesite) and bearing the name of a man lost to the disease. Made by their lovers, friends and families, the panels are stitched together and regularly toured around the country; it was spread on the Mall in Washington DC in 1987 and 1988 to dramatise the epidemic to the seemingly indifferent government. Sections of the quilt, too large to be exhibited in any one place in its entirety, continue to tour the world to raise people's awareness of the tragedy and keep the care programmes alive. Inside the showroom, you can see the thousands of panels stored on shelves; some are hung up for display and machinists tackle the endless task of stitching the whole thing together.

Back on Castro Street, one of the first things you see is the **Castro Theater**, self-described as "San Francisco's landmark movie palace". It's undeniably one of San Francisco's better movie houses, as popular for its pseudo-Spanish baroque interior as it is for its billing, which includes revival-fare, twenty-minute performances on a Wurlitzer and some plush velvet surroundings. A little further down the hill, the junction of **Castro and 18th Street,** known as the "gayest four corners of the earth", marks the Castro's centre, cluttered with bookshops, clothing stores, cafés and bars. The side streets offer a slightly more exclusive fare of exotic delicatessens, fine wines and fancy florists, and enticingly leafy residential territory that keeps a neat distance from the bright lights and noise of the main drag.

Before leaving the Castro, make an effort to go to **Twin Peaks**, about a mile and a half along Market from the Harvey Milk Plaza. (Travel west until you hit Twin Peaks Boulevard; the #37 Corbett bus will take you to Parkridge.) The highest point in the city, this gives a 360-degree view of the peninsula. Real estate prices in the city are gauged in part by the quality of the views, so it's no surprise that the curving streets which wind around the slopes of Twin Peaks hold some of the city's most outrageously unaffordable homes. During the day, busloads of tourists arrive to point their Pentaxes and often, during the summer, crowds build up while waiting for the fog to lift. Better to go at night, picking out landmarks from either side of the shimmering artery of Market Street.

HALLOWEEN IN THE CASTRO

The Castro is at its best during **Halloween** – a big deal in San Francisco anyway but here the zenith of the social calendar. Six-foot beauties be-decked in jewels and ballgowns strut noisily between Market Street and the junction of Castro and 20th streets stopping at the most popular watering holes. Those not in their finery strip down and take their beautifully worked-on pectorals out for a stroll. Police block-off roads and turn a blind eye to minor indiscretions. Not to be missed.

You might also consider a quick visit to **NOE VALLEY**, on the far side of the hill, remarkable only for its insignificant status in the pantheon of San Francisco neighbourhoods; in fact, so good is it at failing to capture imaginations that it is fondly tagged "Noewhere Valley" by those who have any notion of where it is and what it's like. Sitting snugly in a sunny valley, the main vein of which runs along 24th Street, crammed with delicatessens, coffee shops, small boutiques and some excellent venues for lunch, it has an air of rugged unfashionableness manifest in clean streets, blue-collar sports bars and a noticeable lack of street crime and vagrancy. Refreshing, after the contrivedness and sleaze of the Mission and SoMa.

Haight Ashbury, Golden Gate Park and the beaches

Two miles west of downtown San Francisco, **HAIGHT ASHBURY** is a neighbour-hood that lent its name to an era, giving it a fame that far outstrips its size. A small area, spanning no more than eight blocks in length, centred around the junction of Haight and Ashbury Street, and bordered by Golden Gate Park at its western edge, "The Haight", as it's known, was a respectable Victorian neighbourhood-turned-slum that emerged in the Sixties as the mecca of the counter-cultural scene. Since then it's become gentrified, but it retains a collection of radical book-stores, laid-back cafés, record shops and secondhand clothing stores that recall its era of international celebrity – when to some it was the scene of one the most significant of Sixties protest movements, to others the best Acid party in history.

The Haight today has few real sights, relying instead on the constant turnover of hip clothing stores, popular cafés and bookstores to sustain its legend. Two blocks east of the Haight-Ashbury junction, **Buena Vista Park** is a mountainous forest of Monterey pines and California redwoods, used by dogwalkers in the daylight hours but come nightfall the locale of much sex-in-the-shrubbery. Walk here accompanied by day and not at all at night. You might also look in on the **Holos Gallery** at 1792 Haight Street, which has the largest collection of holo-grams in California, a darkened gallery that comes across as almost a microcosm of the Sixties – trashy, empty and vacuous, but a good idea at the time. The **"Haight Ashbury Free Clinic"**, at 558 Clayton Street, is a more worthwhile hangover from the Sixties era: an unusual phenomenon, certainly, by American standards, which first began providing free health care when drugs-related illnesses became a big problem in the Haight. It now survives – barely – on contri-butions, continuing to treat local drug casualties and the poor, both disproportion-ately large groups in this area of the city. Otherwise, stroll along the Haight and take advantage of what is still one of the best areas in town to **shop**. It shouldn't take more than a couple of hours to update your record collection, dress yourself up and blow money on good books and cold beers. Things get more lively as you

HIPPIES

The first **hippies** were an offshoot of the Beats, many of whom had moved out of their increasingly expensive North Beach homes to take advantage of the cheap rents and large spaces in the Victorian houses of the Haight. The post-Beat Bohemia that subsequently began to develop here in the early Sixties was a small affair at first, involving the use of drugs and the embrace of Eastern religion and philosophy, together with a marked anti-American political stance and a desire for world peace. Where Beat philosophy had emphasised self-indulgence, the hippies, on the face of it at least, attempted to be more embracing, emphasising self-coined concepts like "universal truth" and "cosmic awareness". Naturally it took a few big names to get the ball rolling, and characters like Ken Kesey and his Merry Pranksters soon set a precedent of wild living, challenging authority and dropping (as they saw it) out of the established norms of society. The use of drugs was particularly important, and was seen as an integral – and positive – part of the movement. LSD, especially, the effects of which were just being discovered and which at the time was not actually illegal, was claimed as an avant-garde art form, pumped out in private laboratories and distributed by Timothy Leary and his network of supporters with a prescription ("Turn on, tune in, drop out") that galvanised a generation into inactivity. An important group in the Haight at the time was The Diggers, who were famed for their parties and antics and also believed LSD could be used to raise the creativity of one and all. Before long life in the Haight began to take on a theatrical quality: Pop Art found mass-appeal, light shows became legion, dress flamboyant, and the Grateful Dead, Jefferson Airplane and Janis Joplin began to make names for themselves. Backed by the business weight of promoter Bill Graham, the psychedelic music scene became a genuine force nationwide, and it wasn't long before kids from all over America started turning up in Haight Ashbury for the free food, free drugs . . . and free love. Money became a dirty word, the hip became "heads", and the rest of the world were "straights".

Other illustrious tenants of the Haight at this time include Kenneth Rexroth, who hosted a popular radio show and wrote for the *San Francisco Examiner*. Hunter S Thompson, too, spent time here researching and writing his book *Hell's Angels*, and was notorious for inviting Angels round to his apartment on Parnassus Street for drinking and drug-taking sessions which were invariably noisy, long and sometimes even dangerous.

Things inevitably turned sour towards the end of the decade, but during the heady days of the massive "be-in" in Golden Gate Park in 1966 and the so-called "Summer of Love" the following year, this busy little intersection became home to no less than 75,000 transitory pilgrims who saw it as the mecca of alternative culture.

move west, the increasing number of street musicians merging eventually into the hard-core hippy guitarists along the **Panhandle**, the finger-slim strip of greenery that eventually leads into Golden Gate Park.

The eastern end of Haight Street, around the crossing with Fillmore Street, is the funkiest corner of the district. Known as the **Lower Haight**, and the centre of black San Francisco for decades, it is now emerging from a period of transition to be the major stomping ground for the sort of fashion-victims usually spotted South of Market. Some of the city's best bars and meeting places are here, as well as a growing mix of ethnic restaurants, and given its proximity to downtown it's a fine place to get a cheap breakfast, browse the bookstores, rake through vintage clothing shops and drink yourself silly.

Ten blocks north of here, up Geary Street, **WESTERN ADDITION** is also firmly black, one of the city's most relentlessly poor neighbourhoods – not at all tourist territory and in parts even dangerous. Its boundaries reach to **JAPANTOWN,** something of a misnomer for what is basically a shopping mall with an eastern flavour – the Japan Center – around which only a small percentage of San Francisco's Japanese Americans actually live. Visit only to check out the **Kabuki Hot Springs,** (1750 Geary Boulevard; ☎922-6000. Mon–Sat 10am–10pm) – community baths with shiatsu massage, steam baths and other luxuriating facilities for around $20 per hour. If you're in the area, jump over a few blocks to where Geary Boulevard meets Gough and look at the monumentally provocative **St Mary's Cathedral**.

Golden Gate Park

Unlike most American cities, San Francisco is not short on green space, but **Golden Gate Park** is its largest, providing a massively bucolic antidote to the centre of town. Despite the throngs of joggers, polo players, roller-skaters, cyclists and strollers it never gets overcrowded and you can always find a spot to be alone. Designed by Frederick Olmsted, the creator of Central Park in New York, in the late nineteenth century, this is one of the most beautiful, and safest, corners of the city, with none of the menace of its New York counterpart. Spreading three miles or so west from the Haight as far as the Pacific shore, it was constructed on what was then an area of wild sand dunes, buffeted by the spray from the nearby ocean, with the help of a dyke to protect the western side from the sea. John McLaren, park superintendent for fifty-odd years, planted around a million trees here, and it's nowadays the most peaceful – and most skilfully crafted – spot to relax in the city, over a thousand acres of gardens, forests, lakes, waterfalls and museums.

The park is huge, no question, and exploration of all its corners could take days of footwork. Among its more mainstream attractions, there's a Japanese Tea Garden, a horticultural museum (modelled on the Palm House at Kew Gardens), a Shakespeare Garden with every flower or plant mentioned in the writer's plays, not to mention the usual contingent of serious joggers, cyclists and roller-skaters. But most people come here to do nothing whatsoever, save the odd stretch. If you're feeling energetic, activities are many and quite cheap: **boat hire** is available on Stow Lake (parallel with 19th Avenue) for around $6 per hour, **horseriding** on offer for around $20 per hour from the *Golden Gate Stables*, on J.F. Kennedy Drive and 34th Avenue.

There's also a number of museums in the park, of which the **M.H. de Young Museum** (Wed–Sun 10am–5pm; $4, first Wed of each month and Sat mornings free) is the largest, with San Francisco's most diverse range of painting and sculpture, ranging from the ancient art of Greece and Rome to an outstanding twentieth-century collection in the American Wing – a hundred or so paintings bequeathed by John D. Rockerfeller III. There are good showings, too, by Rubens, Rembrandt and seventeenth-century European painters. You can get an exhaustive commentary on all with a free "Directors Tour", actually a walkman which you wear for about an hour. Next door, in the West Wing, the **Asian Art Museum** (same times) has a rather less impressive, in fact drearily exhaustive collection of ten thousand paintings, sculptures, ceramics and textiles from all over Asia. Donated by Avery Brundage in 1966, the collection receives much attention for its sheer vastness, but it's only worth seeing if you're an enthusiast.

There are more museums opposite, in the **California Academy of Sciences** (daily 10am–5pm; $4) – the perfect place to amuse restless children. There's a natural history museum with a thirty foot skeleton of a 130 million-year-old dinosaur and life-size replicas of humans throughout the ages. But the show-stealer is the collection of 14,500 specimens of aquatic life in the **Steinhart Aquarium** (daily 10am–5pm; $3), the best of which are the alligators and other reptiles lurking in a simulated swamp. Also, if you catch it at the right time, the **Morrison Planetarium** (schedule varies; ☎387-6300) can be a great experience. Laser shows and rock music draw often acid-crazed crowds for evening performances.

Slightly west of the museums is the usually crowded **Japanese Tea Garden** (daily 8am–6pm; $2 admission charged 9am–5pm). Built in 1894 for the California Midwinter Exposition, the garden was beautifully landscaped by the Japanese Hagiwara family, who were also responsible for the invention of the fortune cookie (despite the prevalent belief that fortune cookies are Chinese). The family looked after the garden until World War II, when, along with other Japanese Americans, they were sent to internment camps. A massive bronze Buddha dominates the garden, and bridges, footpaths, pools filled with shiny over-sized carp, bonsai and cherry trees lend a peaceful feel – but for the busloads of tourists that pour in regularly throughout the day. The best way to enjoy the garden is to get there around 8am when it first opens and have a breakfast of tea and fortune cookies in the tea house.

The best things to do at the park are outdoors and free. On Sundays, in the central space near the museums, **music** can be heard for free at the **Music Pavilion** bandstand; to enjoy the quieter corners of the park head west through the many flower gardens and eucalyptus groves towards the ocean. Perhaps the most unusual thing you'll see in the park is the substantial herd of bison, roaming around the **Buffalo Paddock** off JFK Drive near 38th Avenue; you can get closest to these noble giants at their feeding area, at the far west end. Moving towards the edge of the park at Ocean Beach, passing a tulip garden and large windmill, you'll come to the **Beach Chalet** facing the Great Highway. This two-storey, white-pillared structured designed by Willis Polk is home to some of San Francisco's lesser-known public art. A series of frescoes painted in the 1930s depict the growth of San Francisco as a city and the creation of Golden Gate Park.

The Golden Gate Bridge

The orange towers of the **Golden Gate Bridge** – probably the most beautiful, certainly the most photographed, bridge in the world – are visible from almost every point of elevation in San Francisco. As much an architectural as engineering feat, the bridge took only 52 months to design and build and was opened in 1937. Designed by Joseph Strauss, it was the first really massive suspension bridge, with a span of 4,200 feet, and until 1959 ranked as the world's longest. It connnects the city at its northwesterly point on the peninsula to Marin County and Northern California, rendering the hitherto essential ferry crossing redundant, and was designed to stand winds of up to a hundred miles an hour. Handsome on a clear day, the bridge takes on an eerie quality when the thick white fogs pour in and hide it almost completely.

You can either drive or walk across. The drive is the more thrilling of the two options as you race under the bridge's towers, but the half-hour walk across it really gives you time to take in its enormity and absorb the views of the city behind you and the headlands of Northern California straight ahead. Pause at the midway point and consider the seven or so suicides a month who chose this spot, 260 feet up, as their jumping off spot. Monitors of such events point out that victims always face the city before they leap. Perhaps the best-loved symbol of San Francisco, in 1987 the Golden Gate proved an auspicious place for a sunrise party when crowds gathered to celebrate its fiftieth anniversary. Some quarter of a million people turned up (a third of the city's entire population); the winds were strong and the huge numbers caused the bridge the buckle, but fortunately not to break.

Standing beneath the bridge is almost as memorable as travelling over it. The **Fort Point National Historic Site**, a brick fortress built in the 1850s to guard the Golden Gate, gives a good sense of the place as the westernmost outpost of the nation. Part of the massive **Presidio** army base which occupies a huge area on San Francisco's northwesterly tip, it was originally to have been demolished to make way for the bridge above, but the redesign of the southern approach – note the additional arch which spans it overhead – left it intact. It's a dramatic site, the surf pounding away beneath the great span of the bridge high above – a view made famous by Kim Novak's suicide attempt in Alfred Hitchcock's *Vertigo*. It is alleged by some that the water here makes for one of the best (if most foolhardy) surfing spots in the area. There's a small **museum** (daily 9am–4pm; free) inside the fort, showing some rusty old cannons and firearms, although a far superior military collection can be seen in the **Presidio Army Museum** (Tues–Sun 10am–4pm; free) at Lincoln Boulevard and Funston Avenue in the Presidio proper, with uniforms, photographs and some detailed documentation of San Francisco's military history.

Although much of the Presidio is closed to the public, Hwy-1 cuts through its centre linking it with the Golden Gate Bridge to the north, Golden Gate Park to the south and the suburban **RICHMOND** district in between. Richmond is a staunchly middle-class immigrant neighbourhood, originally home to Russian families, although in recent years Asians have been making their prescence felt as they leave the overcrowded Chinatown and slowly bring their business to this stable, family district. Clement Street especially is home to an inexhaustible supply of South East Asian restaurants. The part of the Presidio you most definitely can explore is the **Golden Gate Promenade**, a 3½-mile-long path spanning the northern waterfront, linking up the bridge with the Marina district and beyond to the downtown water's edge around Fisherman's Wharf.

San Francisco's best waters are to be found by walking in the opposite direction, around the tip of the peninsula towards the city's **beaches**. From the San Francisco side of the bridge, follow Hwy-1 to Lincoln Boulevard and travel west for about three miles until you reach the coastal road and **Baker's Beach**. Partly due to the weather, partly due to the people, beach culture doesn't exist the way it does in Southern California and people here tend to watch the surf rather than ride it. Dangerous riptides and very cold water make it almost impossible to swim with any confidence and more often than not nude sunbathing is as adventurous as things get. To reach the beach by bus takes about three connections from Geary Street and it's probably less trouble to walk through the Presidio Army Base – a thirty-minute hike. A little further along, **China Beach** is emptier than Baker's but again hard to reach. Bus #29 from Geary will take you closest, although it's still a twenty-minute walk from there to the beach.

Above the beaches, paths stretch south around the peninsula to **Lands End**: it takes about half an hour to get round the cliffs, tricky to negotiate but worth it for the brilliant views of the ocean. A small beach in a rocky cove beneath the cliffside walk is a favourite spot for gay sunbathers. Inland lies **Lincoln Park**, primarily a golf course, but as part of the Point Lobos Headlands, it has some striking trails.

The isolated **California Palace of the Legion of Honor** (Wed–Sun 10am–5pm; $4, free the first Wednesday of each month; take the #38 bus from Geary Boulevard and get off at the Lincoln Park Golf Course) is a white-pillared twin of the more famous Legion d'Honneur in Paris. Arguably San Francisco's best museum, it is probably also its most beautifully located – the romantic setting, graceful architecture and colonnaded courtyard combining to lend a truly elegant impression.

Built from a donation from the wealthy San Franciscan Spreckels family, the Legion of Honor was built in 1920 and dedicated on Abraham Lincoln's birthday in 1921. Until a major re-sort a couple of years ago, the collection was mainly French and not particularly strong, but with many new additions it has emerged as the city's best collection of fine art. Divided into 23 galleries across two floors, the collection on display is almost entirely permanent, with only one gallery dedicated to travelling and usually contemporary exhibits. The **Renaissance** is represented with the works of Titian, El Greco and sculpture from Giambologna, hung in high-ceilinged, well-lit, spacious marble halls. Some great canvases by Rembrandt and Hals, as well as Rubens' magnificent *Tribute Money*, are highlights of the seventeenth-century Dutch and Flemish collection. The **impressionist** and **post-impressionist** galleries contain works by Courbet, Manet, Monet, Renoir, Degas and Cezanne, but the section dedicated to the sculpture of **Rodin** steals the show. Bronze, porcelain and stone pieces including *The Athlete, Fugit Amor, The Severed Head of John the Baptist* and a small cast of *The Kiss* are scattered around an enormous hall, said to be one of the world's finest collections of Rodin sculptures. Stanford University's art museum makes a similar claim but the works here certainly take some beating.

A rather bigger stop for the tour-buses is the **Cliff House**, dangerously balanced on the western tip of the peninsula above the head of Ocean Beach. There's a **visitors center** here with information on the surrounding area and an exhibit on the Cliff House itself (Mon, Tues, Thurs, Fri 11am–5pm, weekends 10am–5pm). There's also a **museum** (daily 10.30am–7pm; free) which claims to have the largest collection of fruit machines and one-armed bandits in the world. The Cliff House Restaurant is where most visitors end up, though avoid it unless you want to pay through the nose to sit in a bar with an ocean view (no big deal in a city flanked on three sides by water). But stick your head around the door to take a look at the photos of the original Cliff House, which burned down long ago. Down by the water you'll find more picturesque ruins – of the **Sutro Baths**: a collection of recreational pools built for the city by Adolf Sutro, and very popular until demolished by a vicious storm earlier in this century. From here you can explore the ramparts and tunnels of the fortified coastline. It's a bit frightening here at night, when the surf really starts crashing, but there's a certain romance too, and on a rare warm evening it becomes one of the city's favourite snogging spots.

Finally, you might want to visit San Francisco's small but expertly designed **zoo** (daily 9am–4pm; $4): as zoos go, not a bad one, thoughtfully crafted to resemble the natural habitat as much as possible. It's closer to the beaches than the city though, and unless you've got a car you'll have to go back downtown and board the L Taraval MUNI to get here.

Drinking and eating

To experience San Francisco as the locals do, you're going to have to spend a lot of your time **eating** and **drinking** in the city's many cafés, restaurants and bars. Wining and dining is second nature to most San Franciscans, and, given the reasonable prices and sheer number of bars and restaurants in the city, it should also prove to be the most pleasurable of activities. The city prides itself on its fresh gourmet foods and fine wines, and in some places the taking of nourishment is treated with a reverence – and done with a protocol – normally reserved for affairs of state. That's not to say that simple fare and casual snacks can't be found, just that food and drink receives an uncommon amount of attention.

We've listed **bars** geographically by neighbourhood, followed by a rundown of **cafés** and a section detailing the city's many and varied **gay and lesbian** watering holes. **Restaurants** are listed by cuisine together with a round-up of where to eat around-the-clock.

Drinking: bars and cafés

Since its lawless, boomtown days, San Francisco has been a **drinking** town. Even as the rest of California cleans up its act and guzzles mineral water, San Franciscans continue to indulge with impunity, and the city's huge array of bars, varying from seedy late-night dives to rooftop piano lounges touting glittering views, can be one of its real pleasures. On the whole San Francisco's bars are rough-hewn, informal affairs, although slicker places can be found around the downtown area and in the Financial District. Most open mid-morning (the legal opening time is 6am) and close around 2am, although after-hours drinking is not uncommon in the smaller neighbourhood joints.

San Francisco is also home to a higher proportion of **cafés** than most American cities – informal places, patronised more during the day than at night and with the emphasis more on good coffee than alcohol. Both bars and cafés normally have some kind of food available, even if it's only sandwiches or pretzels, though cafés will often have hot meals, too. Unsurprisingly, the city has many specifically **gay bars**, most plentifully in the Castro – although few bars are at all threatening for either gay men or lesbians, or women on their own.

Downtown bars

The Blue Lamp, 561 Geary St. For daytime slumming within five minutes of Union Square, this is unbeatable.

Dashiell's, *Hotel Union Square*, 114 Powell St. Stylish hotel bar playing up its Hammett connections – he wrote a number of his "Thin Man" stories from one of the upstairs rooms.

Li Po's Bar, 916 Grant Ave. Named after the Chinese poet, *Li Po's* is Chinatown's only bar and something of a literary hang-out amongst the Chinatown regulars. Enter through the false cavern front and you can sit at the very dimly lit bar where Wayne Wang filmed *Chan is Missing*.

1001 California, 1001 California St. A swish Nob Hill hang-out where you can sit and watch the rich get loaded. Worth it for the premium liquor and polished piano playing.

The Redwood Room, *Clift Hotel*, 495 Geary St. Gorgeous redwood-panelled, Art-Deco-style lounge, dulled only slightly by the wealthy geriatric hotel guests who frequent it. Definitely worth a look.

ROOFTOP BARS

The Carnelian Room, 555 California St, in the Bank of America building. Best of the rooftop cocktail lounges, 52 floors up and a truly elegant spot for some refined drinking. Bring lots of cash.

Equinox, *Hyatt Regency,* the Embarcadero. Revolving rooftop cocktail lounge, good for novelty value only. You get 360° views of the city without ever leaving your seat.

The Starlight Roof, top floor of the *Sir Francis Drake Hotel,* 450 Powell St. Very tacky, but an experience. Panoramic views and free Happy-Hour food compensate for the expensive cocktails.

Top of the Mark, *Mark Hopkins Hotel,* California St at Mason. Its reputation surpasses the actual experience of drinking up here, but if you're determined to do all the rooftop cocktail lounges, this should be on your agenda.

Bars in North Beach and the Northern Waterfront

Balboa Cafe, 3199 Fillmore St. A favourite with the young, upmarket singles of the Marina. Very good food, too.

Harry's, 2020 Fillmore St. A bona fide saloon, this elegantly decorated hang-out serves a mixed, unpretentious crowd and makes for a great night's drinking.

Perry's, 1944 Union St. Sophisticated meat-market, featured in Armistead Maupin's *Tales of the City* as the quintessential breeder bar.

The Saloon, 1232 Grant Ave. This bar has stood for over a hundred years and seen use as a whorehouse and prohibition speakeasy. Today the old structure creaks nightly as blues bands and crowds of enthusiastic dancers do their thing.

Savoy Tivoli, 1434 Grant Ave. Definitely North Beach's most attractively decorated and populated bar, and also serving good, reasonably priced food – although the emphasis is definitely on liquid enjoyment.

Spec's, 12 Adler St. Long-standing North Beach bar with a good, jocular drinking crowd enjoying the cocktail shakers full of martini for just $3. Particularly handy for women drinking alone: the barman will hand a card which reads "Sir, the lady is not interested in your company" to anyone that hassles you. A most civilised place to get ploughed.

Tosca's, 242 Columbus Ave. The theme is opera here, in stylish surroundings; mingle with media people and pay through the nose for a drink. Worth the investment if you like to dress up and be seen.

Vesuvio's, 255 Columbus Ave. Legendary North Beach Beat haunt in the Fifties, and still catering to an arty but friendly crowd who prop up the bar into the small hours. Situated next to *City Lights Bookstore,* it's a good place for browsing your new purchases with a drink.

Bars in Civic Center, SoMa and the Mission

The Edinburgh Castle, 950 Geary St. Most of the so-called pubs are embarrassingly twee, but this one pulls it off – and features bagpipes on Fri and Sat. Good fish and chips, too.

Bouncers Bar, 64 Townsend St. Old waterfront hang-out, with free live music and a very earthy crowd.

Brainwash, 1122 Folsom St. Great idea – café/bar and laundromat where you can have breakfast and a beer while you do your washing. Needless to say, it's popular with the young and novelty-conscious.

Cadillac Bar and Grill, 1 Holland Court. Noisy Mexican-style bar with good food available, although most people come just to drink the margaritas.

El Rio, 3158 Mission St. When it isn't staging one of its specials (samba on Sun, comedy on Wed and dancing on Fri), this is a great place for a quiet drink and a game on the best-looking pool table in town.

Mission Rock Resort, 817 China Basin. Scruffy, blue-collar bar down on the old dockyards, great for a cheap beer and views of the bay.

Paradise Lounge, 1501 Folsom St. Mainly a venue for bands, but the upstairs bar has lots of room and pool tables – good for early evening beers and a game.

Rockin Robin's, 133 Beale St. Fifties rock and roll music and lots of boys in leather. Good fun if you can stand to hear that much Elvis in one evening. Mon–Fri only.

The Uptown, 200 Capp St. Best of the Mission's neighbourhood bars, embracing an eclectic crowd who shoot pool, drink like fiends and fall around on the scruffy, leatherette upholstery. A more bizarre collection of characters would be hard to find. Don't miss it.

Bars in the Central Neighbourhoods

Casa Loma Hotel, 600 Fillmore St. Very neighbourly Lower-Haight hang-out for a well-behaved young crowd. A must for the Lower-Haight bar-hopping schedule.

The Deluxe, 1511 Haight St. Formerly a hang-out for older gays, the *Deluxe* is now gaining a well-earned reputation as one of the better pool halls in town.

Jimmy's West Point, 669 Haight St. The joint is jumping most nights at this black neighbourhood bar, where Philadelphia soul and Motown blare out relentlessly from the jukebox. Sleazed to perfection in 1970s vinyl upholstery, this is the perfect place for one last shot before you stagger home.

The Mad Dog in the Fog, 530 Haight St. Aptly named by the two Birmingham lads who own the joint, this is one of the Lower Haight's most loyally patronised bar with darts, English beer, copies of *The Sun* and a typical pub menu that includes bangers and mash, hearty ploughmans and the like.

The Rat and the Raven, 4054 24th St. Friendly, hard-drinking neighbourhood bar with pool, darts, and, if you're into country music, one of the best jukeboxes in town.

Tropical Haight, 582 Haight St. Best decorated bar in the district; the theme is tropical, the crowd most definitely are not. Impromptu performances on Tuesdays provide the biggest laugh you're likely to have.

Cafés

Bohemian Cigar Store, 566 Columbus Ave. Small, informal North Beach hang-out for sipping coffee or slinging beers.

Buena Vista Cafe, 2765 Hyde St, Fisherman's Wharf. If you like your coffee with a kick, this is the place for you. Claims to be the home of the world's first Irish coffee, which is hard to believe – it's certainly the best in town and the crowds who pack the place are testimony to the generously laced coffee. Good, inexpensive food, too.

Cafe la Boheme, 3138 24th St. A staggering range of coffees brings in the Mission's caffeine addicts from morning until late at night.

Cafe Flore, 2298 Market St. Lively, partly gay café near the Castro serving meals until 3pm. A popular cruising spot for the locals – drown in a sea of newspapers and pretty faces.

Cafe Picaro, 3120 16th St. Very popular, no-frills spot where you can get cheap lunches and browse through the hundreds of books that line the walls. Opposite the *Roxie* cinema in the Mission.

Cafe Trieste, 609 Vallejo St. Noisy North Beach Italian café, popular with a serious literary crowd. Opera classics boom from the jukebox. Saturday lunchtimes are a treat – the family who run the place get up and sing. Get there by noon if you want a seat.

Gay and lesbian bars

San Francisco's **gay or lesbian bars** are many and varied, ranging from cosy cocktail bars to full no-holds-barred leather-and-chain hang-outs. It's true to say the scene is no longer as wild as its reputation would have you believe, but at its best it can still be hard to beat. The **Castro** holds the thickest concentration of gay men's bars, though its establishments have matured in recent years and you need to visit **SoMa, Polk Street** – or to a lesser extent the **Mission** – for anything outside the mainstream. Specifically women's bars are fewer than you might expect, and right now are pretty much confined to the Mission. Bear in mind, though, that the increasingly integrated nature of the gay scene means that formerly exclusively male bars now often have a sizeable lesbian contingent. Most, too, are perfectly welcoming places for straight people, especially those in the Castro.

Many of the places listed below as bars may switch on some music later on and transform into a club; we've listed the better ones that do this under "Nightlife".

Amelia's, 647 Valencia St. Trendy hang-out for mostly younger, fashion-conscious women. The lipstick lesbian scene.

The Bear, 440 Castro St. Friendly neighbourhood bar that draws a chatty, non-cruisy crowd – nice patio out back.

Cafe Flore, 2298 Market St. Very much the in spot before dark. Attractive café with leafy outdoor area and no shortage of people sizing each other up.

The Corral, 2140 Market St. Country and western bar with large dance floor and cheerful crowd. Dolly Parton fans alight here.

Castro Station, 456 Castro St. Noisy disco bar that packs 'em in even in the middle of the day. Very much the die-hard scene of the 1970s with a fair number still in leather gear.

Deluxe, 1511 Haight St. Large, comfy bar with pool tables and slightly older gay guys, but getting a reputation as a good pool hall and drawing an increasingly mixed crowd.

Eagle, 12th & Harrison St. Legendary SoMa biker bar. Not for wimps.

El Rio, 3158 Mission St. Mixed crowds gather for cabaret on Wednesdays but most nights of the week this is an exclusively gay bar popular with Hispanics from the local Mission district. Dancing to live samba on Sunday afternoons. Recommended.

Female Trouble, 1821 Haight St. Wednesday dance club with female bands and dancing. A lot of fun.

Francine's, 4149 18th St. Something of a female biker bar in the Castro – a friendly (if butch) joint with pool tables and the sort of women you'd want on your side if a fight started.

La India Bonita, 3089 16th St. Casual neighbourhood bar, mostly Latin but anybody welcome, with occasional drag acts.

Maude's, 937 Cole St. Situated in one of the busier parts of the Haight, this tends to be full most nights with a mixed female crowd.

Midnight Sun, 4067 18th St. Young, white boys dressed to the nines and cruising like maniacs in this noisy Castro video bar.

Moby Dick, 4049 18th St. Beautifully decorated men's neighbourhood bar in the Castro with music and video, but the accent definitely on light-hearted chatting and a few drinks.

The Phoenix, 482 Castro St. The Castro's only dance bar; draws a large, lively crowd.

Powerhouse, 1347 Folsom St. Full-on leather boys. Definitely not for the faint-hearted.

Rawhide, 280 Seventh St. If men in chaps are your scene, go no further than this dimly lit SoMa bar/dance club that plays country and western and bluegrass favourites.

Sofia's, 527 Valencia St. Popular women's meeting place in the Mission.

Eating

With over four thousand restaurants crammed on to the small peninsula, and scores of bars and cafés which are open all day (and many all night), **eating** in San Francisco is never difficult. Perhaps the most cuisine-orientated place in

California, San Franciscans gourmandise expertly around the city and most people will have at least four restaurant recommendations up their sleeves. Eating out doesn't have to be all that expensive – in some cases not much more so than cooking your own food. Options among the **budget places** range from the usual array of pizza and burger joints, to a broad selection of **Chinese** restaurants in Chinatown and the **Mexican** eateries of the Mission – really, these are the two cuisines that San Francisco does best. More expensively, **Italian** restaurants are common, in North Beach and around much of the rest of downtown, **Thai** cuisine is becoming rapidly more popular, and **French** food is a perennial favourite, at least with the power-broking crowd; and although *nouvelle cuisine* is finally beginning to loosen its grip on San Franciscan menus, its obsession with the beautifully presented tiny portion lives on in the city's **California cuisine** eateries. **Japanese** food, notably sushi, is also still massively popular though not always affordable.

Not surprisingly, health-conscious San Francisco also has a wide range of **vegetarian** and **wholefood** restaurants, and it's rare to find anywhere that doesn't have at least one meat-free item on the menu. Remember also that with the vineyards of Napa and Sonoma Valley on the city's doorstep, quality **wines** are a high-profile feature in most San Francisco restaurants.

Restaurants in the East Bay – especially Berkeley – are every bit as good as those in the city itself; you'll find suggestions later in this chapter.

Budget eating: breakfasts and burgers

Bagdad Cafe, 2295 Market St (☎621-4434). Good hearty breakfasts and burgers served 24 hours a day.

Church Street Station, 2100 Market St (☎861-1266). Big American steak-and-salad restaurant. Possibly the largest portions you'll find for the price – around $5 for a burger and fries.

David's Delicatessen, 474 Geary St (☎771-1600). Kosher food in giant portions. Eat until you expire for under $10.

Hamburger Mary's Organic Grill, 1582 Folsom St (☎626-5767). One of the rowdier eateries in town, in which punky waiting staff will slap burgers, sandwiches and several vegetarian options on your table for less than $7. Usually full of ravenous SoMa club-goers.

Holey Bagel, 1206 Masonic St (☎626-9111). Every type of bagel you could think of, stuffed with the filling of your choice and served with coffee for around $1.75.

Hot 'N Hunky, 4039 18th St (☎621-6365). As the name suggests, the burgers are heavy-duty masses of red meat, in what is generally considered San Francisco's best burger joint. Negligible atmosphere, but an average single serving could feed a family of four.

Limbo, 299 Ninth Street (☎255-9945). Super cheap and ultra-trendy, so you can be sure that you won't be alone if you come for dinner here. Wholefood and burgers from under $4.

Mission Rock, 817 China Basin (☎621-5538). Good cheap breakfasts and lunches, served outside on the wharf when the weather's good.

Orphan Andy's, 3991 17th St (☎864-9795). Favourite hang-out in the Castro for filling burgers, omelettes and breakfasts.

Sparky's Diner, 240 Church St (☎621-6001). Inexpensive 24-hour diner cooking up burgers, pastas and pizzas and delicious breakfasts, particularly a marvellous eggs florentine. Beer and wine as well.

Spikes, 139 8th Street (☎255-1392). Newly opened Sixties-style diner that often has coupons for cheap dinners in the local press. Even without a discount card, you can get a big breakfast or cheap lunch.

Spaghetti Western, 576 Haight St (☎864-8461). Best breakfasts in town and a lively Lower-Haight crowd to look at while you chow down.

American and Californian

Bix, 56 Gold St (☎433-6300). Jackson Square restaurant kitted-out like a majestic ocean liner, with torch singer, sax player and pianist. The food is great – straightforward, classic dishes. Not surprisingly, a hot spot you'd be well advised to book. Dinner for two will probably set you back around $50, but if you're into elegant dining experiences you should definitely go.

The Connecticut Yankee, 100 Connecticut St (☎552-4440). Not cheap, but this Potrero Hill restaurant does great weekend brunches served with generous cocktails.

Hard Rock Café, 1699 Van Ness Ave. Standard *Hard Rock* clone. Loud music, rock-and-roll decor and the sort of crowd who don't mind queuing for hours to get in.

John's Grill, 63 Ellis St (☎986-0069). Straight out of the *Maltese Falcon* (Dashiell Hammett was a regular). Burgers, steaks and other all-American fare.

Mayes Original Oyster House, 1233 Polk St (☎474-7674). In business since the 1860s, turning out reasonably priced, well-cooked fish dishes. Oysters by the half-dozen with a beer at the bar for the budget-conscious or less hungry.

Original Joe's, 144 Taylor St (☎775-4877). Inexpensive American/Italian restaurant, good for steaks, ribs, salads, pasta and the like.

Pazzaz, 3296 22nd St (☎824-8080). American food with a Chinese twist. Inexpensive and usually crowded.

Trader Vic's, 20 Cosmo Place (☎776-2232). A San Francisco "Society" institution. Ostensibly Polynesian/Indian, but ethnicity stops at the dinner plate. Dining moneyed-American style.

Washington Square Bar & Grill, 1707 Powell St (☎982-8123). Stylish American grill with an Italian tilt and a media/politico patronage. Food cooked to rich and heavy perfection and sublime martinis. A wander down the cheaper side of the menu (burgers, sandwiches, etc) should get you out unscathed for around $15 per head with a few drinks. If you want to see the upper echelons of San Francisco society power-lunching, this is your scene.

Zuni Cafe, 1658 Market St (☎552-2522). The chic place to be and be seen, with Californian *nouvelle cuisine* portions as minimal as the elegant decor for around $30 a head with wine.

Italian and Pizza

Blondie's, 63 Powell St (☎282-6168). Union Square pizzeria, usually packed out; they do well-topped pizzas for $1.25 a slice.

Calzone's, 430 Columbus Ave (☎397-3600). Busy, noisy bar and restaurant smack in the middle of North Beach, serving lush pizzas and fat calzones, as well as regular Italian fare.

Capp's Corner, 1600 Powell St (☎989-2589). Funky, family-style Italian restaurant in North Beach, with a fashionable clientele who line up for the big portions.

Golden Boy, 542 Grant St (☎982-9738). This North Beach venue is the best place to sample slices of exotic pizza without it costing a bomb.

Gold Spike, 527 Columbus Ave (☎986-9747). More like a museum than a restaurant, with enough photographs, mooseheads and war souvenirs to keep you occupied for what can be a long wait for the excellent value $12 six-course dinner.

Green Valley Restaurant, 510 Green St (☎788-9384). Good, hearty fare in a basic but busy place, full of local North Beach families and birthday celebrants. Eat till you drop for under $10.

Il Pollaio, 555 Columbus Ave (☎362-7727). You'll be hard pushed to spend more than $6 for a blow-out meal in this postage-stamp restaurant, in which sheer value for money more than compensates for the lack of elbowroom.

La Traviata, 2854 Mission St (☎282-0500). Friendly, noisy and cheap Mission Italian restaurant.

Little Joe's, 523 Broadway (☎433-4343). Always a queue for tables, but worth it for the cheap, enormous portions of well-cooked food in this North Beach institution.

Noe Valley Pizza, 3898 24th St (☎647-1664). If you love garlic this is your place – every pizza is loaded up with it.

North Beach Pizza, 1499 Grant Ave (☎433-2444). Good location in one of the best bar-hopping areas in town. Tasty and cheap, it's just the ticket for a drink-induced munchie.

Ristorante Firenze, 1421 Stockton St (☎421-5813). Modern decor, traditional food, quick service – an attractive combination.

Tommaso's, 1042 Kearny St (☎398-9696). Always a wait for tables, but worth it to stuff yourself with these delicious pizzas and admire the scruffy decor and classical murals.

Vicolo Pizzeria, 201 Ivy St (☎863-2382); Ghirardelli Square, Fisherman's Wharf (☎776-1331). The consummate designer pizza parlours, these two turn out some very fancy fare and charge for the privilege. The Civic Center restaurant has a better atmosphere for a sit-down dinner – the Wharf branch is a bit of an eat-and-run joint.

French

Cafe Landais, 489 Third St (☎495-6944). SoMa bistro that's about the cheapest place for French food in town. Popular with connoisseurs on a budget.

Ernie's, 847 Montgomery St (☎397-5969). Certainly not cheap, but a lovely Victorian interior and an *haute cuisine* menu made famous by Hitchcock's *Vertigo* – it figured in some of the crucial scenes.

Le Trou, 1007 Guerrero St (☎550-8169). About as reasonably priced as you'll get, this is French food on a budget.

Zola's, 395 Hayes St (☎864-4824). Very fancy, beautifully prepared and presented French *nouvelle cuisine* in stylised surroundings. Smoke-free and quite expensive.

Chinese, Thai and Indonesian

Bangkok 16, 3214 16th St (☎431-5838). Moderately priced Thai restaurant in the Mission, with a great selection for vegetarians – and for meat-eaters they do a mean lamb saté.

Brandy Ho's Original Hunan, 217 Columbus Ave (☎788-7527). Excellent long-established Hunan cuisine restaurant. Another, new branch at 450 Broadway (☎362-6268).

Celadon, 881 Clay St, Chinatown (☎982-1168). Fancy Cantonese restaurant. Far from bargain-basement food, but worth shelling out for the beautifully presented, fragrant dishes.

China Moon Cafe, 639 Post St (☎775-4789). Standard Cantonese cuisine, but the restaurant is more notable for its excellent, cheap dim sum lunches.

Cloisonne, 601 Van Ness Ave (☎441-2232). First-class Cantonese cooking, moderately priced and served in luxurious surroundings. Quite formal; you won't be refused if you turn up in jeans, but you might feel out of place.

Empress of China, 838 Grant Ave (☎434-1345). The poshest Chinese place in town. An incredible selection of dishes and amazing views over North Beach. You'll be lucky to pay less than $18 for a main course. A good place to be decadent.

Indonesian Restaurant, 678 Post St (☎474-4026). Small, unassuming and affordable.

Jing Wah, 1634 Bush St (☎922-5279). Highly rated Cantonese cuisine served at reasonable prices in very unpretentious surroundings in the middle of Polk Gulch.

Manora's Thai Cuisine, 1600 Folsom St (☎861-6224). Massively popular, and you may have to wait, but it's worth it for light, spicy and fragrant Thai dishes at around $6 each.

New Asia, 772 Pacific Ave (☎391-6666). Amazing place for such a cramped neighbourhood. Some of the most authentic dim sum in town.

Pot Sticker, 150 Waverly Place (☎397-9985). Popular Chinatown favourite; extensive but inexpensive menu of Szechuan and Hunan dishes.

Sam Woh's, 813 Washington St (☎982-0596). Much tamer since the death of hilariously surly waiter Edsel Ford Fong some years ago, this late-night (until 3am), very basic eatery – you have to clamber up dodgy old steps through the kitchen to reach the eating area – still manages to attract the North Beach crowds when the bars turn out.

Thep Phanom Restaurant, 400 Waller St (☎431-2526). Delicate decor and beautifully prepared dishes in the Lower Haight. Just $7 for a main course, but expect to queue.

Yank Sing, 427 Battery St (☎362-1640). Join the Financial District workers at lunchtime and eat dim sum in the fanciest of surroundings.

Yuet Lee, 1300 Stockton St (☎982-6020). Cheap and cheerful Chinese restaurant with a good seafood menu and enthusiastic crowds of diners. No alcohol; take your own beer or wine.

Japanese and Korean

Asuka Brasserie, *Miyako Hotel*, 1625 Post St (☎922-3200). Very flash indeed. Great Japanese food in beautiful surroundings, priced way beyond the means of most.

Benkay, *Hotel Nikko*, 222 Mason St (☎394-1111). Hi-tech, minimal and ultra-modern, *Benkay* is the Jean-Paul Gaultier of the restaurant biz. The theme is *Kaiseki*, a succession of many exquisite courses served by kimono-clad waitresses. Dinner for two could easily be $100.

Mifune, 1737 Post St (☎922-0337). Moderately priced seafood and Japanese fare to take away.

Mitoya, 1855 Post St (☎563-2156). Inexpensive sushi and seafood. The adjoining bar has singers and is an excellent place to warm up before dinner.

Moshi Moshi, 2092 Third St (☎861-8285). Out-of-the-way gem of a restaurant in SoMa. Excellent sushi and seafood, moderately priced.

Mun's, 401 Balboa St (☎668-6007). Western Addition venue serving inexpensive, simple Korean fare.

Sanppo, 1702 Post St (☎346-3486). Small, busy and unpretentious Japantown eatery – the decor might be negligible but the food is cheap and first rate.

Silver Moon, 2301 Clement St (☎386-7852). Seafood and vegetarian Japanese fare. Very light, healthy dishes.

Sushi Bar, 1800 Divisadero St (no phone). Bright, cheap and quick.

Yoshida-Ya, 2909 Webster St (☎346-3431). Genuine sushi bar; kick off your shoes and eat at low tables on futoned floors. Expect to pay around $20 a head, with a few drinks.

Indian, Greek and Middle Eastern

Gaylord, Ghirardelli Square, 900 North Point, Fisherman's Wharf (☎771-8822). One of very few Indian restaurants in San Francisco and probably the best, though you should expect to pay around $15 for a main course. Still, if you're dying for a curry . . .

The Grapeleaf, 4031 Balboa St (☎668-1515). Way out in the western suburbs, this small Lebanese bistro serves unusual and spicy food, but what really makes it are the spirited belly-dancers who gyrate round the restaurant.

India House, 350 Jackson St (☎392-0744). Again, not cheap, but lavish decoration and extraordinarily punctilious service help soften the blow when the bill arrives.

Mamounia, 441 Balboa St (☎752-6566). Eat Moroccan food with your fingers and pay for it through the nose.

The Peacock, 2800 Van Ness Ave (☎928-7001). Indian restaurant near Fort Mason. Hot tandoori dishes and fragrant Indian breads. Very tasty, moderately priced and quite formal.

Steve the Greek, 1431 Polk St (no phone). Authentic Greek (including plastic tablecloths) and ultra cheap.

Mexican and Hispanic

El Cubane, 1432 Valencia St (☎824-6655). Big portions of Cuban food with a Tues–Fri lunch special for $4.

El Tapatio, 475 Francisco St (☎981-3018). Not as cheap as the Mission's Mexican restaurants, but the food in this North Beach eatery is notably better – and the margaritas larger.

El Tazumal, 3522 20th St (☎550-0935). Interesting Salvadorean restaurant where you can try tripe, tongue and spicy rice dishes for around $5 for a lunch and up to $9 for a dinner. Small but lively, and with an interesting crowd.

El Toro, 3071 16th St (☎431-3351). Always a queue outside for the massive burritos.

Ensenada Restaurant, 2976 Mission St (☎826-4160). One of the more cheerful-looking of the Mission's inexpensive Mexican restaurants. Full meals for around $4–5.

Mom's Cooking, 1192 Geneva St (☎586-7000). Small and crowded, on the fringes of the Mission. You may have to queue for the super-cheap fresh Mexican food.

New Central Restaurant, 301 South Van Ness Ave (☎431-8587). Small, family-run restaurant serving moderately priced, hearty dishes to a ravenous crowd.

La Taqueria, 2889 Mission St (☎285-7717). Always busy with locals, which is as good a recommendation as any for its fairly standard Mexican menu.

Vegetarian and wholefood

Amazing Grace, 216 Church St (☎626-6411). Rated highly by local vegetarian buffs, with standard veggie fare for around $4 a dish.

Greens, Building A, Fort Mason Center, Fort Mason (☎771-6222). A converted US Army supply warehouse that's now San Francisco's only Zen Buddhist restaurant, serving unusual and delicious macrobiotic and vegetarian food to an eager clientele. Always busy, so book in advance, and count on spending around $30 a head for a five-course dinner.

Marty's, 508 Natoma St (☎621-0751). Stuck down a little alley, this isn't the sort of place you'd stumble over, but if you're into macrobiotic food, you should definitely make the effort. Thurs–Sun only.

Real Good Karma, 501 Dolores St (☎621-4112). Hearty and nutritious portions of vegetarian and wholefood dishes in informal surroundings.

Nightlife

Compared to many US cities, where you need money and attitude in equal amounts, San Francisco's **nightlife** scene demands little of either. This is no 24-hour city, and the approach to socialising is often surprisingly low-key, with little of the pandering to fads and fashions that goes on in New York or LA. The casualness is contagious, and manifest in a **club scene** that – far as it is from the cutting edge of hip – is encouragingly cheap compared to other cities; $30 can get you a decent night out, including cover charge, a few drinks and maybe even a taxi home. San Franciscans may be relatively out of touch with fashion, but there are decent **live music** venues all over town, many entertaining you for no more than the price of a drink.

The city has a somewhat better reputation for **opera** and **classical music**, its orchestra and opera association among the country's most highly regarded.

Theatre is more accessible and much cheaper, with discount tickets available, but most of the mainstream downtown venues are mediocre, mainly staging Broadway re-runs, and you'd do better to take some time to explore the infinitely more interesting fringe circuit. The city's **cabaret and comedy** scene is more up-tempo: there are some excellent clubs, hosting an increasingly healthy and varied diet of good comedians.

Live music: rock, jazz and folk

San Francisco's **music scene** reflects the character of the city: laid-back, eclectic, and not a little nostalgic. The options for catching **live music** are wide and the scene is definitely on the up and up, with the city spawning some good young bands. However, it has never recaptured its crucial Sixties role, and these days lacks the influence of many other American cities, better as a venue for good R&B, psychedelia, folk and rock standards, and – of late – country and western and Latin American bands. Sadly, not all jazz haunts are commensurate with the amount of talent in the greater Bay Area – if you want to hear some really good stuff, you'll need to head over to the East Bay, where a couple of excellent clubs more than make up for the relative paucity in the city.

Unlike the club scene, which is concentrated in the South of Market area, **live music** tends to be more spread out across the city, though the Haight, North Beach and the Mission tend to have more venues than most. Be sure to check the music press, the best of which is San Francisco's free *BAM (Bay Area Music)* – which has exhaustive listings of events in the city and Bay Area as a whole and is available in most record stores.

The large performance venues

Although San Francisco has a couple of major-league venues, some of the Bay Area's best auditoria are across the bay in Oakland and Berkeley, and this is where the big names tend to play. See the relative listings later in this chapter.

Great American Music Hall, 859 O'Farrell St (☎885-0750). Theater District venue too small for major names, but too large for local yokels. It hosts a range of musical styles from balladeers to thrash bands. Seating for several thousand.

The Warfield, 982 Market St (☎775-7722). Can usually be relied upon to stage major rock crowd-pullers. Chart bands, big-name indie groups and popular old-timers keep it packed.

Rock, folk and country

Bouncers Bar, 64 Townsend St (☎397-2480). Near the SoMa waterfront, this was originally a rowdy sailors' hang-out. These days the sailors are gone, but the rowdiness lives on in this hardcore drinkers' bar staging obscure country, blues and R&B bands. No cover.

Full Moon Saloon, 1725 Haight St (☎775-6190). Pot luck – expect anything from reggae and funk to bluegrass. Consistently lively punters and good fun. No cover.

I-Beam, 1748 Haight St (☎668-6023). Haight-Ashbury's most famous venue, usually host to some fairly big names. It's not the place to see bands on the cheap, although midweek you can generally get in for around $5–10.

JJ's, 2225 Fillmore St (☎563-2219). Trendy Pacific Heights hang-out for the better-dressed live music fan. Good bar and cruisy singles crowd. Usually a cover charge of $6–12.

Lou's, 300 Jefferson St (☎771-0377). Country/rock and blues bar down on Fisherman's Wharf that hosts some good local bands. Weekend lunchtimes are a good time to check out the lesser-knowns in relative peace. Come nightfall it's madness. No cover before 9pm.

Nightbreak, 1821 Haight St (☎221-9008). Slightly shabby, small Haight venue for a lot of new wave and goth bands playing to a matching crowd. Very dark, very loud, very crowded, and charging a small cover only at weekends.

Paradise Lounge, 11th and Folsom St (☎861-6906). Good, cheap SoMa venue to see new wave, rock and occasionally country bands. See the band and dance downstairs, or take a break and a game of pool upstairs. Free Sun–Thurs, $5 cover Fri and Sat.

Paul's Saloon, 3251 Scott St (☎922-2456). Stands alone in San Francisco as the only place to see genuine, foot-tappin' bluegrass bands who twang and fiddle hard nightly from 9pm until 1am. Drinks are remarkably cheap; one of the city's most comfortable old watering holes.

The Saloon, 1232 Grant St (☎397-3751). Always packed to the gills, this is North Beach's best spot for some rowdy R&B. No cover.

Slim's, 33 11th St (☎621-3300). Slick but reliable venue for rock and R&B.

The Stone, 412 Broadway (☎391-8282). Solid San Francisco venue with consistently good billing of rock and new wave bands. Open until 6am Fri and Sat for a very danceable rock disco after the bands finish. Young, fun clubbers, cover around $8.

Tar & Feathers, 2140 Union St (☎563-2612). Young, casual, country and western. The Marina's the place to go for a few beers and a singalong when you can't face the singles bars.

Jazz and Latin American

Bahia Tropical, 1600 Market St (☎861-8657). Expensive, yuppie hang-out and supper club with good Brazilian and samba bands. Cover $7.

Bajone's, 3140 Mission St (☎648-6641). Unusual – and refreshing – age-mix for San Francisco, ranging from 25 to 65. Excellent Latin jazz that plays nightly. Casual, unpretentious and genuine. $5 cover at weekends.

Jack's, 1601 Fillmore St (☎567-3227). Small, intimate bar with jazz and blues seven nights a week. Recommended. No cover.

Pasand Lounge, 1875 Union St (☎922-4498). Unusual club where you can come to eat Indian food and listen to very mellow jazz in the comfortable lounge. Open Wed–Sat. Sometimes a small cover.

The Rite Spot Cafe, 2099 Folsom St (☎552-6066). Informal, café-style club with jazz and R&B bands. Snacks, drinks and coffee until 1am. Mon–Sat, small cover at weekends.

Roland's, 2513 Van Ness Ave (☎567-1063). Classic and Latin jazz for the serious jazz fans who like their music a bit on the esoteric side in a dark, smoky atmosphere. Open Tues–Sun. Small cover at weekends.

Slim's, 333 11th St (☎621-3330). Slick, medium-sized venue staging mainly jazz bands with the occasional big name topping the bill. Friendly, comfortable club. Cover depends on the bill, usually $7–10.

The Tonga Room, basement of the *Fairmont Hotel*, 950 Mason St (☎772-5000). An absolute must for fans of the ludicrous or just the very drunk. Decked out like a Polynesian village with a pond and simulated rain storms. The grass-skirted band play terrible jazz and pop covers on a raft in the middle of the water. Worth every penny of the cover charge and outrageously priced cocktails. Cover $4.

Clubbing

Trading on a reputation earned decades ago, the city's **nightclubs** continue to trail vapidly behind those of other large American cities. That said, the compensations are manifold – no queuing for hours, or high cover charges, ridiculously priced drinks and feverish posing. Instead you'll find a diverse range of small to medium-sized affordable clubs in which leather-clad goths rub shoulders with the bearded and beaded, alongside a number of gay hang-outs still rocking to the sounds of high-energy funk and Motown. The greatest concentration of clubs is in **SoMa**, especially the area around 11th Street and Folsom; indeed SoMa is your best bet for club and bar hopping – most places don't mind you leaving and re-entering provided you've got your regulation hand-stamp.

Several places charge no **cover** at all and only the most chi-chi of clubs will charge a fortune for drinks. The entry age to clubs, as with bars, is 21, and it's a good idea to carry **ID** with you at all times: as a general rule, if you look under thirty you'll definitely need it. Clubs are cracking down in general, and becoming very fussy about **drugs** in particular: a crafty joint is enough to get you thrown out of some places.

Many **gay and lesbian clubs** are bars that host various club nights at least once a week. Pleasingly unpretentious, the city's gay clubs rank among the city's best, and although a number are purely male affairs, with women-only discos few and far between, the majority welcome gay people of both sexes – and even straights. The distinction between gay bars and **gay clubs** is a fine one, and many gay and lesbian bars convert to discos in the evening.

The Clubs

Caesar's Latin Palace, 3140 Mission St (☎826-1179). A big laugh: Latin, jazz and disco rock for those who want to relive late 1970s disco-mania. Naff enough to have achieved cult status.Cheap drinks and late licensing (until 6am at weekends). $6 cover.

Chatterbox, 853 Valencia St (☎821-1891). Good no-nonsense rock'n'roll in a room resembling a pool hall. Mixed, beer-drinking biker crowd. Daily until 2am; cover around $5.

Covered Wagon Saloon, 917 Folsom St (☎974-5906). Definitely one of the better SoMa places, especially on Thursday when they have their "Love Shack" hi-tech psychedelic night, and on Saturday for hip-hop. Cover $4–6.

Crystal Pistol, 842 Valencia St (☎695-7887). One of the newer gay men's clubs, enjoying a very healthy patronage. Good dancing and a young, well-turned-out set .

DNA Lounge, 375 11th St (☎626-1409). Changes its music style nightly, but draws the same young hipsters. Large dance floor downstairs and when the dancing gets too much you can lounge around in comfy sofas on the mezzanine. Cover $7. Open Tues–Sun 9pm–4am.

DV8, 540 Howard St (☎777-1419). Huge, ornate and fashionable, this is the closest San Francisco gets to rivalling the big clubs of New York and Los Angeles, decorated by Keith Haring pop-art and playing high-energy funk and house music. About the only club in town worth dressing up for. Cover $10. Open Wed–Sat.

El Rio, 3158 Mission St (☎282-3325). Latin, jazz and samba are the speciality here, with live bands on Sunday, dancing to modern funk on Friday, and cabaret on Wednesday in a friendly, anything-goes atmosphere. Open seven nights 3pm–2am, until 6am at weekends. No cover. See also "Comedy Clubs".

The Endup, Harrison and 6th St (☎495-9550). A mostly gay crowd, but has recently been discovered by the weekend clubbers. A good place for the hard-core party animal – especially on "Wet jockstrap night". Open continuously from 6am on Sat morning until 2am Mon. Small cover.

Esta Noche, 3079 16th Street (☎861-5757). Gay disco-mania Latin-style. Young men and their pursuers dance to a high-energy disco beat reminiscent of the 1970s.

Firehouse 7, 3160 16th St (☎621-1617). Not to be missed; bar/club with a broad cross-section of music styles and clientele. Reggae night Wed, live music Fri, house music Sat. Relaxed, informal crowd and pool tables for those not into dancing. $3 cover at weekends.

Holy Cow, 1535 Folsom St (☎621-6087). Young club-fiends trying hard to be cool, but a good rave once it warms up. A huge plastic cow hangs outside. Tues–Sun. Usually no cover.

I-Beam, 1748 Haight St (☎668-6006). One of San Francisco's longest-standing rock venues, featuring both familiar names and lesser-knowns for around $5. Tickets for the bigger shows can be pricey, but dancing afterwards keeps the place packed until 2am. Tea dances on Sunday afternoons, popular with the gay community.

Kennel Club, 628 Divisadero St (☎931-9858). Most popular for its "Box" club on Thursday and Saturday for the gay crowd. Friday is "Club Q" for women, and Sunday reggae and worldbeat music. Good fun, mixed crowd. Cover $6.

The New Martini Empire, 1015 Folsom St (☎626-2899). Club with an international bent where you'll be able to hear some of the more unconventional sounds of Brazilian, salsa, Arabic, African and Soca. Open Fri–Sun. Cover $4.

Nightbreak, 1821 Haight St (☎221-9008). Small Haight club where the slogan is "All the funk that's fit to pump" – house, hip-hop and funk most nights, except for Wednesday when it becomes "Female Trouble", lesbian dance night – not much dancing or posing and as such better for drinking and chatting than serious funking. Small cover at weekends.

Oasis, 11th and Folsom St (☎621-8119). One of the few places in town where you have to queue, but usually worth it to dance on the open-air plexi-glass covered swimming pool to new wave, rock and house music. Tues–Sun; $7 cover at weekends.

Rapture, 1484 Market St (no phone). Saturday night dance club for women. Tends to draw the younger, well-dressed lipstick-lesbian crowd.

Rawhide, 280 Seventh St (☎621-1197). Gay country and western dance hall. Hysterical good fun if you're into square dancing and the like.

Rock & Bowl, 1855 Haight St (☎752-2366). Try this one for a change – a bowling alley that turns up the music at weekends so that you can dance while you bowl. Definitely good fun if there's a group of you.

Rockin Robin's, 1840 Haight St (☎221-1960). A real mixture, including rock'n'roll, Motown on Tuesday and Karaoke (get up on the mike and howl to your favourite tunes) on Thursday. No cover.

The Stud, 399 Ninth St (☎863-6623). An oldie but a goodie. A gay scene mainstay for its energetic, uninhibited dancing and good times. No cover charge.

Townsend, 177 Townsend St (☎974-6020). A must for house fans, this place really cranks up the bass and keeps it blaring. Thurs–Sat. Cover $5.

Classical music, opera and dance

Though the San Francisco arts scene has a reputation for provincialism, this is the only city on the West Coast to boast its own professional **symphony**, **ballet** and **opera** companies, each of which has thriving upper-crust social support wining and dining its way through fundraisers and the like. These companies rely entirely on private contributions for their survival and cheap tickets are rare, if not nonexistent.

Look out also in summer for the **free concerts in Stern Grove** (at 19th Avenue and Sloat Blvd) where the symphony, opera and ballet give open-air performances for ten successive Sundays (starting in June).

Louise M. Davies Symphony Hall, 201 Van Ness Ave (☎431-5400). Permanent home of the San Francisco Symphony, which offers a year-round season of classical music and sometimes performances by other, often offbeat musical and touring groups. The least expensive seats going for around $20 – and availability is nowhere near as much of a headache.

War Memorial Opera House, 401 Van Ness Ave (ticket and schedule information: ☎864-3330). The very opulent venue for both the San Francisco Opera Association and the ballet, designed by architect Arthur Brown Jr – creator of City Hall and Coit Tower – means that a night at the opera in San Francisco is no small-time affair. By far the strongest of San Francisco's cultural trio, the company has won critical acclaim for its performances of Beethoven's *Fidelio* and Puccini's *La Boheme* and *Madame Butterfly*. Its main season runs from the end of September for thirteen weeks, and its opening night is said to be one of the principal social events on the West Coast. Sporadically, they have a summer season during June and July and in general these tickets are easier to come by. Performances tend to be booked up way in advance, so unless you plan to spend more than a week or two in the city, your chances of getting tickets may be slim. If you do succeed, expect to pay upwards of $40 – for which you do at least get supertitles with the foreign operas.

The San Francisco Ballet (☎893-2277). The city's ballet company is the oldest and third largest in the US, and puts on an ambitious six-month – January to June – programme of both classical and contemporary dance annually. Since the appointment of Icelandic Helgi Tomasson, "premier danseur" of the New York City Ballet, as artistic director in 1985, the company can seem to do no wrong and some proud San Franciscans are already tagging it "America's premier ballet company". The demand for tickets doesn't quite match the opera, but a decent seat will cost you upwards of $30.

Theatre

The majority of San Francisco's **theatres** congregate downtown around the Theater District. Most aren't especially innovative (although there is a handful of more inventive fringe places in other parts of town, notably SoMa), but tickets are reasonably inexpensive – up to $20 a seat – and there's usually good availability. You can either buy tickets direct from the box offices of the theatres, or more commonly book through one of the ticket agencies (see above) using a credit card. Failing that, try the *STBS* ticket booth on the Stockton Street side of Union Square (Mon–Sat 11am–6pm; ☎433-7717), which regularly has last-minute tickets for as much as thirty percent off the price.

Downtown

American Contemporary Theater, *Geary Theater*, 450 Geary St (☎775-5811). Despite suffering the wholesale destruction of their theatre in the 1989 earthquake, the Bay Area's leading resident theatre group have bounced back and continue to stage impressive plays from temporary bases around the city. Phone for location details of current performances.

Cable Car Theater, 430 Mason St (☎771-6900). Home for the last eight years of *Greater Tuna*, a scathing two-man portrait of small town Texan bigotry that has yet to lose its ability to draw the crowds. Small, comfortable theatre and extremely funny production.

Golden Gate Theater, 1 Taylor St (☎775-8800). Originally built in the 1920s and recently restored to its former splendour, the *Golden Gate* is San Francisco's most elegant theatre, with marble flooring, rococo ceilings and gilt trimmings. A pity the programme doesn't live up to the surroundings – generally a mainstream diet of Broadway musicals.

Lorraine Hansberry Theater, 25 Taylor St (☎474-8842). Radical young group of black performers whose work covers traditional theatre as well as more contemporary political pieces and jazz/blues musical reviews. Impressive.

Stage Door Theater, 420 Mason St (☎433-9500). Attractive, medium-sized turn-of-the-century theatre with a reputation for serious productions.

Theater On The Square, 450 Post St (☎771-6900). Converted Gothic theatre with drama, musicals, comedy and mainstream theatre pieces. San Francisco's main fringe venue.

Elsewhere

Beach Blanket Babylon Series, *Club Fugazi Cabaret*, 678 Green St (☎421-4222). One of the few musts for theatre-goers in the city, its formality smacks of a Royal Command Performance, but the shows themselves are zany and fast-paced cabarets of jazz singers, dance routines and comedy very slickly put together. Currently in its sixteenth year.

Climate Theater, 252 Ninth St (☎626-9196). Small, reputable SoMa theatre, specialising in fringe/alternative productions. Cheaper and probably a lot more stimulating than some of the downtown efforts.

The Lab, 1805 Divisadero (☎346-4063). Mixed media centre with gallery and changing exhibitions downstairs, a small theatre for drama and dance upstairs. Usually something locally based and interesting going on.

The Magic Theater, Fort Mason Center, Building D (☎441-8822). Busiest and largest company after the *ACT* and probably the most exciting, the *Magic Theater* specialises in the works of contemporary American playwrights and emerging new talent: Sam Shepard traditionally premieres his work here. They have been described as the "most adventuresome company in the West".

Theater Artaud, 450 Florida St (☎621-7797). Very modern theatre in a converted warehouse that tackles the obscure and abstract: visiting performers, both dance and theatrical, always something interesting.

Theater Rhinoceros, 2926 16th St (☎861-5079). San Francisco's only uniquely gay theatre group, this company, not surprisingly, tackles productions that confront gay issues, as well as lighter, humorous productions.

Comedy

Comedians have always found a welcoming audience in San Francisco, but in recent years the alternative **comedy and cabaret scene** has experienced a rebirth. Even so, with any cabaret venue you take your chances, and what could be a good club one week might have dodgy acts the next, and vice versa. You should expect to pay roughly the same kind of cover in most of the clubs ($7–10), although be aware that most places impose a two-drink minimum. There are usually two shows per night, the first kicking off around 8pm and a late show starting at around 11pm. For bargains, check the press for no-cover "Open Mike" nights when unknowns and members of the audience get up and have a go.

Cobbs Comedy Club, The Cannery, 2801 Leavenworth (☎563-5157). Popular small venue, where new performers often get the chance of their first live appearance.

El Rio, 3158 Mission St (☎282-3325). Wednesday night comedy shows, with a choice of performers that is often a lot riskier than in the established clubs. Very alternative, and, more often than not, extremely funny.

Finocchio's, 506 Broadway (☎982-9388). A San Francisco institution. The small cast of female impersonators run through "saucy" textbook routines. Once considered outrageous; these days it's more than a little tame, good for cheap laughs and expensive drinks.

509 Cultural Center, 509 Ellis St (☎346-1308). Seedy, but worth visiting on Tuesdays for "Open Mike Night".

Holy City Zoo, 408 Clement St (☎386-4242). Supreme champion of the alternative circuit, *Holy City* plays host to the best of the genre in a small, funky club. Make an effort to go.

The Improv, 401 Mason St (☎441-7787). The chain store of the comedy world, this is the latest of a string of *Improv*s around the country, which get the acts after the other clubs have finished with them. Some good established talent and up-and-coming acts. Monday is the cheapest and best night to go.

Morty's, 1024 Kearny St (☎986-6678). Old North Beach club that evokes the Lenny Bruce era, even if none of the acts are quite as good as he was.

The Punch Line, 444 Battery St (☎397-7553). Frontrunner of the city's "polished" cabaret venues. Intimate, smoky feel; ideal for downing expensive cocktails and laughing your head off. The club usually hosts the bigger names in the world of stand-up, and is always packed.

Film

After eating, watching **films** is the favourite San Francisco pastime. For one thing it's cheap (rarely more than $6, sometimes as little as $2), and secondly there's a staggering assortment of current-release and repertory film houses. There are rarely queues, and the cinemas are often beautiful Spanish-revival and Art-Deco buildings that are in themselves a delight to behold.

The Alhambra, Polk St and Union (☎775-2137). With its gorgeous, plush, Moorish-looking interior, this cinema is one of the city's grandest, showing a selection of current releases and re-runs.

The Castro Theater, 429 Castro St (☎621-6120). Perhaps San Francisco's most beautiful movie house, offering a steady stream of re-runs, Hollywood classics and (best of all) a Wurlitzer organ played between films by a man who rises up from the stage. A fond favourite with the gay community, it hosts the annual Gay and Lesbian Film Festival each June.

The Clay, 2261 Fillmore St (☎346-1123). Small, elegant art house cinema.

Kabuki Cinemas, Post and Fillmore St (☎931-9800). Attractive, modern building in the Japancenter complex, housing eight cinemas showing mainly current-release movies. The centre for the San Francisco Film Festival, in the first couple of weeks in May, which specialises in political and short films you wouldn't normally see.

The Roxie, 317 16th St (☎863-1087). San Francisco's trendiest, independent rep house in the heart of the Mission, showing a steady diet of punk, new wave and political movies.

The Strand, 1127 Market St (☎621-2227). Dark, appropriately scruffy surroundings for cult films and B-movies.

The York, 2789 24th St (☎282-0316). Large, comfortable collective movie house specialising in *film noir* seasons.

Gay and Lesbian San Francisco

San Francisco's reputation as a city for gay celebration is not new – in fact it could even be outdated. This is still the undoubted gay capital of the world, but despite a high profile, the gay scene hasn't had much to celebrate in the last few years and there's been a definite move from the outrageous to the mainstream. It's unlikely that even AIDS will wipe out the increasing number of gay activists in public office, but it has made them more conservative in approach, if not in policy. The exuberant energy that went into the posturing and parading of the 1970s has taken on a much more sober, down-to-business attitude, and these days you'll find more political activists organising conferences than drag queens throwing parties. Things have changed.

It's still America's most liberal city for gay men *and* women, who, it's true to say, can genuinely enjoy their sexualities openly and without fear here. However, the moral backlash caused by AIDS has inevitably awakened prejudice in San Francisco as it has everywhere. The basic principles of tolerance and support endure, though, and have even in some senses been reinforced. (It's interesting to note that on the same day the homophobic "clause 28" bill was being rushed through parliament in Britain, San Francisco's mayor, Art Agnos, rode through the streets of San Francisco in support of the Gay and Lesbian Freedom Day Parade.)

Certainly, post-AIDS, San Francisco's gay scene is a different way of life altogether. The Seventies were notorious for the bar and bathhouse culture and the busy and often anonymous promiscuity which went with it, but this toned down abruptly when AIDS first became a problem in the latter part of the decade. This wasn't a foregone conclusion by any means. Many men saw the closure of the bathhouses as an infringement on their civil liberties, rooted in homophobia – and the rumour that AIDS is germ warfare by the US government has yet to die.

Socially, San Francisco's gay scene has also mellowed, though in what is an increasingly conservative climate in the city generally, gay parties, parades and street fairs still swing better than most. Like any well organised section of society, the gay scene definitely has its social season, and if you're here in June, you'll coincide with the Gay and Lesbian Film Festival, Gay Pride Week, the Gay Freedom Day Parade and any number of conferences. Come October, the street fairs are in full swing and Halloween still sees some of the most outrageous carrying-on.

The 1980s also saw the flowering of a **lesbian** culture to rival the male 1970s upsurge, and while there still isn't anything like the number of women's bars and clubs that exist for men, they are catching up quickly.

You'll find details of gay accommodation, bars and clubs under the relevant headings earlier in this chapter.

Neighbourhoods

Traditionally, the area for gay men has been the **Castro**, together with a few bars and clubs in the **SoMa** area – though gay life these days is much less ghettoised and there are bars and clubs all over town. Rent boys and pimps prowl **Polk Street**, not the safest area at 2am but hardly a danger zone if you use common sense. Lesbian interests are more concentrated in the East Bay than the city, although women's activities thrive in the **Mission**.

Publications

New clubs and groups spring up all the time and you should keep an ear to the ground as well as referring to the many free gay publications available: *The Sentinel, Coming Up, The Bay Area Reporter* and *Gay Times* all give listings of events, services, clubs and bars in the city and Bay Area. Women should also keep an eye out in bookshops for *On Our Backs* and *Bad Attitude*, two magazines that often have useful pointers to lesbian organisations in town. Also useful for both men and women is *The Gay Book*, a telephone-cum-resource book that's available in gay bookshops.

Contacts and Resources

AIDS Hotline (☎863-2437). 24-hour information and counselling.

Bay Area Bi-Sexual Network, 2404 California St (☎654-2226). Referral service for support groups, social connections and counselling.

Dignity, 133 Golden Gate Ave (☎584-1714). Catholic worship and services.

Gay Cocaine Counselling Service (☎1-800/2622463).

Gay Legal Referral Services, Box 1983 SF (☎621-3900). Enquiries regarding legal problems and legal representation.

Lesbian/Gay Switchboard (☎841-6224). 24-hour counselling and advice. Contacts and activities referral service.

Gay Men's Group, 450 Stanyan St (☎750-5661). Support group and advice on places to go, contacts, etc.

Gay Men's Therapy Center (☎673-1160). How to cope with AIDS issues and fears, grief counselling, etc.

Gay Therapy Center, 3393 Market St (☎558-8828). Counselling and help with coming out.

SF AIDS Foundation, 25 Van Ness Ave (☎864-4376). Referral service providing advice, testing, support groups.

Shanti Project, 525 Howard St (☎777-1162). AIDS support group that offers care of victims, advice, testing and counselling.

SOL (Slightly Older Lesbians), Pacific Center, 2712 Telegraph Ave, Berkeley 94705 (☎841-6224). A gathering-place and referral service for women over thirty.

Woman to Woman (☎939-6626). Confidential introductions.

Women's San Francisco

The flip side of San Francisco's gay revolution has in some women's circles led to a separatist culture, and women's resources and services are sometimes lumped together under the lesbian category. While this may be no bad thing, it can be hard to tell which organisations exist irrespective of sexuality. Don't let this stop you from checking out anything that sounds interesting, nobody is going to refuse you either entry or help if you're not a lesbian – support is given to anybody who needs it. Similarly women's health care is very well provided for in San Francisco and there are numerous clinics you can go to for routine gynaecological and contraceptive services: payment is on a sliding scale according to income, but even if you're flat-broke, you won't be refused treatment.

Contacts and Resources

Bay Area Resource Center, 318 Leavenworth St (☎474-2400). Services, info and clothing.

Metropolitan Community Church, 150 Eureka St (☎863-8843). A "women's spirit group" is held here each Wednesday at 7.30pm.

Radical Women, 523A Valencia St (☎864-1278). Socialist feminist organisation dedicated to building women's leadership and achieving full equality. Meetings held on the second and fourth Tuesday of each month.

Rape Crisis Line (☎647-7273). 24-hour switchboard.

Women's Building, 3543 18th St (☎431-1180). Central stop in the Mission for women's art and political events. A very good place to get information also – the women who staff the building are happy to deal with the most obscure of enquiries. Don't be afraid to ask.

Women's Health Center No.1, 3850 17th St (☎558-3908). Free contraception, AIDS testing, pregnancy testing and a well-women's clinic.

Women's Needs Center, 1825 Haight St (☎221-7371). Low-cost health care and referral service.

Women's Yellow Pages, 270 Napoleon St (☎821-1357). Call for a copy of this invaluable directory, with everything from where to stay to where to get your legs waxed.

Shops and galleries

San Francisco does have the large-scale shopping facilities you'd expect in a major city, with the usual international names prominent in its downtown shop windows. However, most places are low-key and unpretentious. Not only does this mean slightly lower prices, but it also makes shopping a more pleasant, stress-free activity all round.

If you want to run the gauntlet of designer labels, or just watch the style brigades in all their consumer fury, **Union Square** is the place to aim for. Heart of the city's shopping territory, it has a good selection of big-name and chic stores – expense account stuff admittedly, but good for browsing, especially in the district's many art galleries.

For things that you can actually afford to buy, you'll have a less disheartening and more interesting time in neighbourhoods like **Haight-Ashbury** and the **Mission**, where the secondhand, quirky and plain bizarre are in abundance, fascinating to pick through if you're at a loose end or on the lookout for some good American kitsch and unique souvenirs; the Mission, especially, has some marvellous secondhand clothing stores. The city in general is home to a small but excellent array of **bookstores**, and its one-off, independent **record shops** are unbeatable for rare birds to add to your collection.

Department stores

Emporium-Capwell, 835 Market St, near Powell St *Muni* (☎764-2222). San Francisco's largest general department store with a very average range of merchandise – everything the suburban home could possibly need.

I. Magnin, Geary and Stockton St (☎362-2100). A stylish, if rather conservative store selling well-made clothes at not terribly outrageous prices. Top designer names.

Macy's, Stockton and O'Farrell St (☎397-3333). Probably the city's best-stocked store, though it's not a patch on its New York counterpart. Nonetheless, brimming with the trinkets of the consumer society, and a dangerous place to go with a wallet full of money.

Nieman Marcus, 150 Stockton St (☎362-3900). The sheer cheek of the pricing department has earned this store the nickname "Needless Mark-up". Undoubtedly Union Square's most beautiful department store, however, with its classic rotunda, and enjoyable for browsing.

Sak's Fifth Avenue, 384 Post St (☎986-4300). Pathetic compared to its New York sister store. A dodgy selection geared towards the middle-aged shopaholic.

Woolworth's, 898 Market St (☎286-2164). Unlike the fast-sprucing-up British Woolies, this is the original "five & dime" store – great for essentials as well as tacky souvenirs.

Shopping malls

Crocker Galeria, Kearny and Post St (☎392-5522). The most recent in the new wave of shopping malls, this has been built to as modern and attractive a design as possible, and features some very pricey showcase boutiques. It's all very nice for a wander, but don't plan on spending money unless your reserves are bottomless.

Embarcadero Center, The Embarcadero, Market St (☎772-0500). Ugly, four-plaza shopping complex with almost 200 shops, distinguished from other anaesthetic shopping malls only by the occasional work of art and a reasonably carefully planned layout. The place where San Franciscans indulge in a spot of consumer therapy.

Japan Center, three blocks bounded by Post, Sutter, Laguna and Fillmore streets, Japantown (☎922-6776). A five-acre complex of shops, cinemas and restaurants run by and for the Japanese community. Interesting, costly shopping.

Drugs, beauty products and toiletry stores

The Body Shop, 2072 Union St (☎922-4076). Since it opened across the bay in Berkeley in the late Sixties, this now national chain has been putting out a full range of aromatic natural bath oils, shampoos and skin creams.

Common Scents, 3920 24th St (☎826-1019). Natural oils, cures, remedies and bath salts.

Fairmont Pharmacy, 801 Powell St (☎362-3000). Huge pharmacy, perfumery and toiletry supply store that also has a good selection of maps and books on San Francisco.

Mandarin Pharmacy, 895 Washington St (☎989-9292). This amiable, well-stocked drug-store is a sanctuary in the bustle of Chinatown.

Thrifty JR, 2030 Market St; 4045 24th St (☎626-7387). General prescription and non-prescription drug and medical needs.

Walgreen Drugs, 135 Powell St (☎391-4433). Central and open long hours. Also 24-hour branches at 498 Castro St and 3201 Divisadero St.

Clothes and accessories

Banana Republic, 224 Grant Ave (☎777-0250). Stylish clothes for the travelling yuppie, in this main branch of the San Francisco-based nationwide chain.

Comme Des Garçons, 70 Geary St (☎3620-6400). Beautiful clothes that only the lucky few can afford to get decked out in. The store is a total design environment – minimal decor and clothing sparsely scattered around the large space. Good fantasy browsing.

Esprit, 16th St at Illinois (☎648-6900). Warehouse-sized store in SoMa that is the flagship of the wildly successful international chain selling sporty "California-style" casual wear in ghastly colours. For basics, t-shirts, etc, it's pretty good.

Groger's Western Wear, 1445 Valencia St (☎674-0700). Mission store selling cowboy boots, Stetson hats, boot tips and traditional brand-name Western clothes. Fun shopping.

Gucci, 253 Post St (☎392-2808). Classic Italian shoes, bags and apparel that you need a trust fund to indulge in. Snoop around the store and be fascinated by the rich ladies that come in and say "I'll have one of those, two of those, one of those", etc.

Hats on Post, 201 Post St (☎392-3737). Interesting, odd designs, very contemporary, but only worth shelling out for if you're *really* into hats.

North Beach Leather, 190 Geary St (☎362-8300). Leather everything, and in some pretty sickly colours, but for basic black jackets and simple pieces, there are some pretty well-made styles. Actually in the Union Square district, despite the name.

Rolo, 535 Castro St (☎431-4545). Tiny shop, crammed with unusual and attractive one-offs by lesser-known designers. Moderately priced and well-made clothing.

Tiffany, 252 Grant Ave (☎781-7000). The staff are extraordinarily courteous and will let you try on luxury trinkets and jewellery even if it's perfectly obvious that you can't afford them.

Wilkes Bashford, 375 Sutter St (☎986-4380). Five floors of fabulous designer finery for men. A fashion victim's fantasy.

Thrift Stores and Secondhand clothes

Aardvarks Odd Ark, 1501 Haight St (☎621-3141). Large secondhand clothing store in Haight-Ashbury: some junk, but also some priceless pieces and an infinite supply of perfectly faded Levis.

Community Thrift, 625 Valencia St (☎861-4910). Gay thrift store in the Mission with clothing, furniture and general junk. All proceeds are ploughed back into gay community groups.

Mascara Club, 1408 Haight St (☎863-2837). Vintage clothing in the heart of Haight-Ashbury, heavy on the psychedelic and more recently Wild Western garments.

Past Tense, 665 Valencia St (☎621-2987). Mission district store selling 1930s to Sixties collectable vintage clothing. One of the smarter secondhand stores.

Purple Heart, 1855 Mission St (☎621-2581). Top quality junk and kitsch.

San Francisco Symphony Thrift Store, 2223 Fillmore St (☎563-3123). Top-rate vintage clothing store in Pacific Heights, with flamboyant and original pieces going for top dollar.

Spellbound Vintage Clothing, 1670 Haight St (☎863-4930). Not cheap, but truly classy rags from yesteryear.

St Vincent de Paul, 1519 Haight St (☎863-3615). Queen of the junk shops, St Vinnies, as it's known, will keep you amused for hours. You could spend money all day and still have change from $50. Also at 4452 Mission St in the Mission.

Thrift Town, 2101 Mission St (☎861-1132). Quite upmarket for a thrift shop, with some of San Francisco's better quality trash as well as some pretty stylish secondhand clothing bargains.

Worn Out West, 1850 Castro St (☎431-6020). Gay secondhand cowboy gear store – a trip for browsing, but if you're serious about getting some Wild West kit, this is about the cheapest place in town to pick out a good pair of boots, stylish western shirts and chaps.

Food and drink

Auntie Pasta, 3101 Fillmore St (☎921-7576). Fresh pasta and sauces for you to heat and eat. Great if you don't want to dine out or cook.

Boudin, 156 Jefferson St, Fisherman's Wharf (☎928-1849). They only make one thing – sourdough bread – but it's the best around.

California Wine Merchant, 3237 Pierce St (☎567-0646). Before you set off for the Wine Country, sample a selection at this Marina wine emporium so you know what to look out for.

Cannery Wine Cellars, The Cannery, Fisherman's Wharf (☎673-0400). Astounding selection of wines and imported beers, as well as Armagnac and Scotch, lines the walls

Canton Market, 1135 Stockton St (☎982-8600). Exotic Chinatown deli; the decor may be a bit stark and crowds unbearable, but the selection (and prices) makes it worth the effort.

David's, 474 Geary Blvd (☎771-1600). The consummate Jewish deli, open until 1am and a downtown haven for the after-theatre crowd and night owls.

Liguria Bakery, 1700 Stockton St, North Beach (☎421-3786). Marvellous old world Italian bakery, with deliciously fresh *focaccia*.

Marasco's, 3821 24th St (☎824-2300). The dipsomaniac's dream – hundreds of wines and exotic spirits taking booze shopping to its zenith.

Rainbow Wholefoods, 1899 Mission (☎863-0620). Progressive politics and organic food in this Mission wholefood store.

Tokyo Fish Market, 1908 Fillmore St (☎931-4561). Every type of fish. Makes for fun looking even if you don't want to buy.

Books

About Music, 375 Grove St (☎647-3343). Tiny, hole-in-the-wall place crammed with books on classical and contemporary music.

Around the World, 1346 Polk St (☎474-5568). Musty, dusty and a bit of a mess, this is a great place for hours of poring over first editions, rare books and records.

Books Etc, 538 Castro St (☎621-8631). Stocks the gamut of gay publishing, from psychology to soft-core porn.

The Booksmith, 1644 Haight St (☎863-8688). Good general Haight-Ashbury bookstore with an excellent stock of political and foreign periodicals.

Bound Together Anarchist Collective Bookstore, 1369 Haight St (☎431-8355). "Radical and progressive" Haight-Ashbury store. They even stock *Class War*.

City Lights Bookstore, 261 Columbus Ave (☎362-8193). America's first paperback bookshop, and still San Francisco's best. The range of titles includes their own publications.

Columbus Avenue Books, 540 Broadway (☎986-3872). North Beach store with a good selection of new and used books, and a large guide and travel books section.

A Different Light, 489 Castro St (☎431-0891). Well-stocked and diverse gay bookstore.

Fanning's Bookstore, Second Floor, Ghirardelli Square, Fisherman's Wharf. Speciality bookshop offering the works of only Northern Californian writers – Hammett, London, Twain and Steinbeck among others.

Field's Bookstore, 1419 Polk St (☎673-2027). Metaphysical and New Age books.

Great Expectations, 1512 Haight St (☎863-5515). Radical liberal bookstore with hundreds of t-shirts bearing political slogans, some funnier than others.

Modern Times, 968 Valencia St (☎282-9246). Largely radical feminist publications, but a hefty stock of Latin American literature and progressive political publications. It also stocks a good selection of gay and lesbian literature, and stages regular readings of authors' works.

Rand McNally, 595 Market St at Second St (☎777-3131). Brand new store selling travel guides, maps and paraphernalia for the person on the move.

Small Press Traffic, 3599 24th St (☎285-8394). Don't be misled by the unprepossessing Mission storefront: this is San Francisco's prime outlet for independent, contemporary fiction and poetry, with an astounding range. It's also the best place, along with *City Lights*, to find out about readings and writing workshops.

Tillman Place Bookstore, 8 Tillman Place, off Grant Ave, near Union Square (☎392-4668). Downtown's premier general bookshop, with a beautifully elegant feel.

William Stout Architectural Books, 804 Montgomery St (☎391-6757). One of San Francisco's world-class booksellers, with an excellent range of books on architecture, building, and urban studies.

Records

Aquarius Music, 3961 24th St (☎647-2272). Small neighbourhood store with friendly, knowledgeable staff. Admirably reluctant to stock CDs. Emphasis on indie rock, jazz and blues.

Discolandia, 2964 24th St (☎826-9446). Join the snake-hipped groovers looking for the latest in salsa and Central American sounds in this Mission outlet.

Discoteca Habana, 24th and Harrison St (no phone). Caribbean and samba recordings.

Embarcadero Discs and Tapes, 2 Embarcadero Center, the Embarcadero (☎956-2204). Not a piece of vinyl in sight – up-to-the-minute CDs and tapes.

Jack's Record Cellar, 254 Scott St (☎431-3047). The city's best source for American roots music – R&B, jazz, country and rock & roll. They'll track down rare discs and offer the chance to listen before you buy.

Magic Flute, 756 Columbus Ave (☎661-2547). Fine classical music store with a smattering of rock, jazz and vocals.

Reckless Records, 1401 Haight St (☎431-3434). If you can't complete your Sixties collection here, you never will.

Record Finder, Noe and Market St (☎431-4443). One of the best independents, with a range as broad as it's absorbing. Take a wad and keep spending.

Record House, 1550 California St (☎474-0259). Nob Hill archive library of over 25,000 Broadway and Hollywood soundtracks. Great record-finding service.

Record Rack, 3987 18th St (☎552-4990). Castro 12" single emporium with a few albums, but the accent is definitely on stuff you can dance to.

Recycled Records, 1377 Haight St (☎626-4075). Good all-round new and used store for records, tapes and CDs, as well as a good selection of music publications. If you can't live without the *NME* and don't mind paying the import price, you'll be all right.

Rooky Ricardo's, 448 Haight St (☎864-7526). Secondhand soul and funk, some albums but mostly 45s. Brilliant.

Rough Trade, 1529 Haight St (☎621-4395). Because of its London connections, this is the first place in town to get imports. Good reggae and indie rock.

Star Records, 551 Hayes St (☎552-3017). Secondhand rap, soul, jazz, gospel and reggae specialist, out in Western Addition. Any track ever cut by a black artist, you'll find here.

Art galleries

American Indian Contemporary Arts, 685 Market St (☎495-7600). The only non-profit gallery in the country run by contemporary native American artists.

Artspace, Ninth and Folsom St (no phone). Adventurous, avant-garde gallery that often exhibits video installations.

Atelier Dore, 771 Bush St (☎391-2423). Salon-style gallery hung floor-to-ceiling with top-quality paintings. Historical genre paintings from California, including WPA works, as well as nineteenth- and twentieth-century black American painters.

Joseph Chowning Art Gallery, 1717 17th St (☎626-7496). Massive forum for humorous and bizarre art.

Contemporary Realists Gallery, 506 Hayes St (☎863-6556). One of the more interesting galleries and the first California gallery dedicated to promoting current realist drawing.

Crown Point Press, 871 Folsom St (☎974-6273). With a showcase that changes monthly, you never know what to expect from one of SoMa's most eclectic galleries, which has a reputation for taking a chance on new talent.

SF MOMA Rental Gallery, Building A, Fort Mason (☎441-4777). Large exhibition space of over 500 artists trying to break into the commercial art world.

Smile, A Gallery With Tongue In Chic, 1750 Union St (☎771-1909). From the whimsical to the very serious, this gallery is one of very few into it just for fun. They'll exhibit anything.

Listings

Airlines *American Airlines*, 433 California St (☎498-4434); *British Airways* Powell St (☎247-9297); *Continental Airlines*, 433 California St (☎397-8818); *Delta Airlines*, 433 California St (☎552-5700); *Pan Am*, 721 Market St (☎221-1111); *TWA*, 605 Market St (☎864-5731); *United Airlines*, 433 California St (☎397-2100).

American Express 237 Post St (☎981-5533). Mon–Fri 9am–5:30pm, Sat 9:30am–4:30pm.

Baby-sitting *Bay Area Babysitting Agency* (☎991-7474).

Children San Francisco is very much a place for adults – more so than, say, LA, where Disneyland and Universal Studios are major attractions – and there aren't many things to occupy young ones. Of the few places that exist, the *Exploratorium* in the Marina District is excellent, as is the *Steinhart Aquarium* in Golden Gate Park; and the *Lawrence Hall of Science* in Berkeley will captivate any young mind. For more organised distractions, try the *Great America* amusement park in San Jose, or the animal-themed *Marine World/Africa USA* in Vallejo, accessible by transbay ferry.

Consulates *United Kingdom*, 1 Sansome St (☎981-3030); *Ireland*, 655 Montgomery (☎392-4212); *Australia* (for *New Zealand* as well) 360 Post St (☎362-6160); *Netherlands*, 601 California St (☎981-6454).

Cycle and Scooter Hire *California Scooter*, 640 Stanyan St (☎751-4100), rent out scooters for around $45 a day; *Park Cyclery*, 1865 Haight St (☎221-3777)have touring bikes for $18 a day, mountain bikes $25 a day, weekly rates from $75.

Dentist *Castro Dental Group*, 375 Castro St (☎392-9018).

Disabled Visitors Steep hills aside, the Bay Area is generally considered to be one of the most barrier-free cities around, and physically challenged travellers are well catered for. Most public buildings have been modified for disabled access, all *BART* stations are wheelchair accessible, and most buses have lowering platforms for wheelchairs – and, usually, understanding drivers. In San Francisco, the *Mayor's Council on Disabilities* puts out an annual guide for disabled visitors; write to them c/o Box 1595, San Francisco CA, or phone (☎554-6141). The *Center for Independent Living,* 2539 Telegraph Avenue in Berkeley (☎841-4776), has long been one of the most effective disabled people's organisations in the world; they have a variety of counselling services and are generally a useful resource.

Drug and Suicide Hotline ☎752-3400.

Ferries *Golden Gate Ferries* to Marin County, The Ferry Building, east end of Market St (☎332-6600); *Red & White Fleet* ferries to Alcatraz from Pier 41, Fisherman's Wharf (☎546-2805).

Gambling Tours Try your luck in Reno with *Lucky Tours*, 1111 Mission St (☎864-1133); $39 buys you transport, accommodation, and $15 worth of food coupons and gambling chips.

Grateful Dead Hotline ☎457-6388. Join the Deadheads and find out about upcoming gigs and other essential Dead facts.

Hospital The *San Francisco General Hospital*, 1001 Protrero Drive (☎821-8111), has a 24-hour emergency walk-in service. *Health Center No. 1*, 3850 18th St (☎558-3905), offers a drop-in medical service with charges on a sliding scale depending on income, and free contraception and pregnancy testing. The *Haight Ashbury Free Clinic*, 558 Clayton St (Mon–Fri noon–9pm; ☎431-1714), provides a general health care service with special services for women and detoxification.

Laundry All but the most basic hotels do laundry but it'll be a lot cheaper (about $1.50) for a wash and tumble dry in a launderette (US *laundromat*) – found all over the place. Take plenty of quarters. *Brainwash*, 1122 Folsom Street in SoMa, is a combo bar-and-launderette, not a bad way to pass the time.

Left Luggage *Greyhound*, 50 Seventh St (☎433-1500); open daily 5:30am–12:30am.

Legal Advice *Lawyer Referral Service* (☎764-1616).

Passport and Visa Office US Dept of Immigration, 525 Market St (☎974-9941).

Poisonings *Poison Control Center* (☎476-6600).

Post Office Main post office with telephone and post restante facilities at Seventh & Mission sts. (Mon–Fri 9am–5:30pm, Sat 9am–1pm).

Public Library Civic Center, between Market St and Van Ness Ave. (☎558-3191). Mon–Sat 9am–6pm, until 9pm Tues and Thurs.

Sierra Club 730 Polk St (☎776-2211) Information and publications on camping and environmental issues; and camping trips.

Sports Super Bowl champions the *San Francisco 49ers* (☎468-2249), play at Candlestick Park in South San Francisco, as do the baseball team, *San Francisco Giants* (☎467-8000). Ticket prices vary from $6 for standing room in the gods to $100 for a field-side box.

Swimming Pools *Hamilton Pool*, Geary and Steiner sts (☎931-2450); *Mission Pool*, 19th and Linda sts (☎282-6950); *North Beach Pool*, Lombard and Mason St (☎421-7466).

Tax In San Francisco and the Bay Area the sales tax is 7.5 percent, plus a 0.5 percent "earthquake" tax. Hotel tax will add 5–11 percent onto your bill.

Telegrams *Western Union*, 697 Howard St (☎495-7301). Open daily 7am–midnight.

Travel Agents *Council Travel*, 312 Sutter St, San Francisco (☎421-3473); 2511 Channing Way, Berkeley (☎848-8604). *STA Travel,* 166 Geary St, Suite 702 , San Francisco (☎391-8407).

Venereal Disease Hotline ☎495-6463.

Whale Watching *The Oceanic Society* (☎441-1106) runs seven-hour boat trips from the Marina to observe the Gray Whales on their migration from Alaska to Baja. Incredible, but even the strongest constitutions will need travel sickness pills to survive the choppy seas in the small boat. Trips cost $35 and should be booked in advance.

THE BAY AREA

Of the six million people who make their home in the San Francisco Bay Area, only a lucky one in every eight lives in the actual city of San Francisco. Everyone else is spread around one of the many smaller cities and suburbs that ring the bay, either down the peninsula or across one of the two impressively engineered bridges that span the chilly waters of the world's most exquisite natural harbour. There's no doubt about the supporting role which these places play in respect to San Francisco – always "The City" – but each has a distinctive character, and contributes to the range of people and landscapes that make the Bay Area one of the most desirable places in the US to live or to visit.

South of the city, the Peninsula holds some of San Francisco's oldest and most upscale suburbs, reaching down along the bay into the computer belt of the Silicon Valley around San Jose – California's fastest-growing city – though apart from some fancy houses there's not a lot to see. The beaches down here are excellent, though – sandy, clean and surprisingly uncrowded – and there's a couple of youth hostels in old lighthouses hard on the edge of the Pacific.

Across the grey steel Bay Bridge, eight miles from downtown San Francisco, the East Bay is more interesting, home to the lively, left-leaning cities of Oakland and Berkeley, which together have some of the best bookshops and restaurants, and most of the live music venues in the greater Bay Area. The weather's generally much sunnier and warmer here too, and it's easy to reach by way of the space-age BART trains which race under the bay. The rest of the East Bay is filled out by Contra Costa County, which includes the short-lived early state capital of California – the near-ghost town of Benicia – as well as the homes of writers John Muir and Eugene O'Neill.

For some of the most beautiful land-and-seascapes in California, cross the Golden Gate Bridge or ride a ferry boat across the bay to Marin County, a mountainous peninsula that's one-half wealthy suburbia and one-half unspoilt hiking country, with redwood forests rising sheer out of the thundering Pacific Ocean. A range of 2500-foot peaks divides the county down the middle, separating the yacht clubs and plush bay-view houses of Sausalito and Tiburon from the nearly untouched wilderness that runs along the Pacific coast, through Muir Woods and the Point Reyes National Seashore. North of Marin County, at the top of the bay, and still within an hour's drive of San Francisco, the Wine Country regions of the Sonoma and Napa Valleys make an excellent day out, tasting fine wines or soaking in natural hot springs; they're detailed in the Northern California chapter, beginning on p.459.

The East Bay

The largest and most-travelled bridge in the US, the **Bay Bridge**, heads east from San Francisco, part graceful suspension bridge and part heavy-duty steel truss. Completed just a year after the more famous (and better-loved) Golden Gate, the Bay Bridge works a whole lot harder for a lot less respect: a hundred million vehicles cross the bridge each year, though you'd have to search hard to find a postcard of it. Indeed its only claim to fame – apart from the fact that its partial collapse during the 1989 earthquake was captured on videotape, and broadcast repeatedly on the TV news – is that **Treasure Island**, where the two halves of the bridge meet, hosted the 1939 World's Fair. During World War II the island became a US Navy base, which it remains, but just inside the gates there's a small **museum** (daily 10am–3pm; free) with pictures of the Fair amidst maritime memorabilia. The island also gives some great views of San Francisco and the Golden Gate.

The Bay Bridge – and the *BART* trains which run under the bay – finishes up at the heart of the East Bay in **Oakland**, a hard-working, blue-collar city that earns its livelihood from shipping and transport services, evidenced by the massive Port of Oakland whose huge cranes dominate the place, lit up at night like futuristic dinosaurs. Oakland spreads north along wooded foothills to **Berkeley** (pronounced as for Busby), an image-conscious college town that looks out across to the Golden Gate and collects a mixed bag of pin-striped Young Republicans, ageing 1960s radicals and Nobel prizewinning nuclear physicists in its many cafés and bookshops. Berkeley and Oakland blend together so much as to be virtually the same city, and the hills above them are topped by a twenty-mile string of forested **regional parks**, providing much-needed fresh air and quick relief from the concrete grids below. The rest of the East Bay is filled out by Contra Costa County, a huge area that contains some intriguing, historically important waterfront towns – well worth a detour if you're passing through on the way to the Wine Country region of the Napa and Sonoma valleys – as well as some of the Bay Area's most insular suburban sprawl.

Curving around the **North Bay** from the heavy-industrial landscape of Richmond, and facing each other across the narrow **Carquinez Straits**, Benicia and Port Costa were both vitally important towns during California's first twenty years of existence, after the 1849 Gold Rush; they're now strikingly sited but little-visited ghost towns. In contrast, standing out from the soulless dormitory communities that fill up the often-baking hot **inland valleys**, are the preserved homes of an unlikely pair of influential writers: the naturalist **John Muir**, who, when not out hiking around Yosemite and the High Sierra, lived most of his life near Martinez; and playwright **Eugene O'Neill**, who wrote many of his angst-ridden works at the foot of **Mount Diablo**, the Bay Area's most impressive peak.

Arrival

You're probably unlikely to visit the East Bay unless you're staying in San Francisco, but it is possible (and may even be cheaper) to fly direct to **Oakland Airport**, particularly if you're coming from elsewhere in the US. It's an easy trip from the airport into town: take the *AirBART Shuttle* van (every 15min; $2) from outside the terminal direct to the Coliseum *BART* station, from where you can reach Oakland, Berkeley, or San Francisco. Several privately operated shuttle buses cost from $10; coming directly from SFO, try *Bayporter* (☎467-1800), which costs $15. Coming **by bus**, Oakland's *Greyhound* station (☎834-3070) is in a dodgy part of town, on the north side of downtown Oakland on San Pablo Avenue at 21st Street. If you come to the Bay Area **by train**, the end of the line is the *Amtrak* station on 16th and Wood streets in the depths of West Oakland, but a better option is to get off at Richmond and change there on to *BART*.

Getting around

BART (from San Francisco ☎788-BART, from the East Bay ☎465-BART), the ultra-modern *Bay Area Rapid Transit* system, links San Francisco with the East Bay, via the underground transbay tube, Monday to Saturday 6am to midnight and 9am to midnight on Sunday. Three lines run from **Daly City** through San Francisco and on to downtown Oakland, before diverging to service East Oakland out to **Fremont**, Berkeley and north to **Richmond**, and east into Contra Costa County as far as **Concord**. Fares range from 80¢ to $3, and the cost of each ride is deducted from the total value of the ticket, purchased from machines on the station concourse. If you're relying on *BART* to get around a lot, you'd do well to buy a **high-value ticket** ($5 or $10) to avoid having to queue up to buy a new ticket each time you ride.

From East Bay *BART* stations, pick up a free transfer saving you 35 cents off the $1 fares of AC Transit (☎839-2882), which provides a good bus service around the entire East Bay area, especially Oakland and Berkeley. *AC Transit* also runs buses on a number of routes to Oakland and Berkeley from the Transbay Terminal in San Francisco. These operate throughout the night, and are the only way of getting across the bay by public transport once *BART* has shut down; they cost $2.25 from SF, but only $1.25 on the way back, when they give a great view of the Financial District from the Bay Bridge. Excellent free **maps** of both *BART* and the bus system are available from any station.

There are also two smaller-scale bus companies you might find useful on occasion. The *Contra Costa County Connection* (☎676-7500) runs buses to most of the inland areas, including the John Muir and Eugene O'Neill historic houses. The *Benicia Bay Connection* (☎707/642-1168) operates buses between the Pleasant Hill *BART* station and downtown Benicia.

One of the best ways to get around is **by bike**; a fine cycle route follows Skyline Boulevard along the wooded crest of the hills between Berkeley and Lake Chabot. If you haven't got one, touring bikes are available for $15 a day (mountain bikes cost $25) from *Carl's Bikes* (☎835-8763), 2416 Telegraph Avenue in Oakland. For those interested in **walking tours**, the city of Oakland sponsors free "discovery tours" (☎273-3234) of various neighbourhoods every Wednesday and Saturday at 10am. Another good option is the ferry route to Jack London Square from San Francisco's Ferry Building and Pier 39, which costs around $3.50 and leaves every ninety minutes.

Information

The **Oakland Convention and Visitors Bureau**, at 1000 Broadway near the 12th Street *BART* station downtown (Mon–Fri 8.30am–5pm; ☎839-9000), offers free maps and information on the whole of the East Bay; the **Berkeley Chamber of Commerce**, 1834 University Avenue (Mon–Fri 9am–4pm; ☎549-7000), is less helpful. If you're spending any time at all in the Berkeley area, pick up a copy of *Berkeley Inside/Out* by Don Pitcher (Heyday Books, $12.95), an indispensable and informative guide that'll tell you everything you ever wanted to know about the town and its inhabitants. For information on hiking or horse-riding in the many parks that top the Oakland and Berkeley hills, contact the **East Bay Regional Parks District**, 11500 Skyline Boulevard (☎531-9300). The widely available (and free) *East Bay Express* – in many ways the best newspaper in the Bay Area – has the most comprehensive listings of **what's on** in the vibrant East Bay music and arts scene. The troubled Oakland daily *Tribune* (25¢) is also worth a look for its coverage of local politics and sporting events.

Accommodation

Surprisingly, it's not a great deal cheaper to stay in the East Bay than in San Francisco, and anyway there's not much to choose from. The only hostel is solely for men, but the **motels** and **hotels**, at around $30 a night, are slightly better value for money than their San Francisco equivalents. **Bed and breakfast** is a more pleasant option, particularly in Berkeley, one of the first places in the US to offer this type of accommodation. There are two fine **campsites** in the East Bay, though both are hard to reach without a car.

Inexpensive

Berkeley YMCA, 2001 Allston Way at Milvia St, a block from Berkeley *BART* (☎848-6800). Ideal bargain accommodation for male travellers; single rooms for $22 a night including use of the excellent gym and pool. Men only, first-come, first-served.

Golden Bear Motel, 1620 San Pablo Ave, West Berkeley (☎525-6770). The most pleasant of the many motels in the "flatlands" of West Berkeley, but a bit out of the way; $37 doubles.

University of California Housing Office, Ida Sproul Hall, 2400 Durant Avenue, Berkeley (☎642-5925). Rents dorm rooms in summer for $34 single, $44 double.

Moderate to expensive

Waterfront Plaza Hotel, 21 Jack London Square, Oakland (☎836-3800). A plush, modern hotel moored on the best stretch of the Oakland waterfront, close to the *AC Transit* bus #51 route. Weekend doubles from $80.

Claremont Hotel, 41 Tunnel Rd at Ashby Ave on the Oakland–Berkeley border (☎843-3000). At the top end of the scale, this grand Victorian palace has panoramic bay view rooms from $190 a night. All-inclusive "weekend breaks" are also available.

Hotel Durant, 2600 Durant Ave, Berkeley (☎845-8981). Fairly plain but well-worn and comfortable, and very handy for the UC Berkeley campus. Doubles $75–85.

London Lodge, 700 Broadway, downtown Oakland (☎451-6316). Spacious rooms, some of which have kitchens, make this a good option for families or groups. Doubles from $48.

Shattuck Hotel, 2086 Allston Way, Berkeley (☎845-7300). Very central and newly refurbished. Doubles from $85.

Bed and breakfast

Bed and Breakfast International, 1181-B Solano Ave, Albany (☎525-4569). Not an inn but a clearing house that books rooms in private homes throughout the East Bay. There's a two-night minimum, but rooms start at a bargain $35 including breakfast, and it's a great way to get to know some local people.

Gramma's, 2740 Telegraph Ave, Berkeley (☎549-2145). Pleasant if slightly dull rooms – with fireplaces – in a mock-Tudor mansion half a mile south of UC Berkeley. Doubles from $85.

East Brother Light Station, East Brother Island, San Pablo Bay (☎233-2385). More of a retreat than a handy base for seeing the sights, this converted lighthouse serves up gourmet meals for its lucky overnight guests. Doubles from $285 a night, all inclusive.

Camping

Chabot Regional Park (☎531-9043), off I-580 in East Oakland. Walk-in, tent-only places, with hot showers and lots of good hiking nearby; in summer, reservations are handled by MISTIX (☎1-800/442-7275).

Mount Diablo State Park (☎837-2525). Twenty miles east of Oakland off I-680 in Contra Costa County. RV and tent places; likewise, book through MISTIX in summer.

Oakland

A quick trip across the Bay Bridge or on *BART*, **OAKLAND** is a solidly working-class balance to upwardly mobile San Francisco: the workhorse of the Bay Area, the largest port on the West Coast, and the western terminus of the railway network. It's not all hard graft, though: the climate is rated the best in the US, often sunny and mild when San Francisco is cold and dreary, and there's great hiking around the redwood- and eucalyptus-covered hills above the city – and views right over the entire Bay Area. However, everywhere you'll see sad reminders of the firestorm which ravaged the city in October 1991.

Oakland is better served by historical and literary associations than important sights, of which it has very few. **Gertrude Stein** and **Jack London** both grew up in the city, at about the same time though in entirely different circumstances – Stein a stockbroker's daughter, London an orphaned delinquent. The macho and adventurous London is far better remembered – most of the waterfront, where he used to steal oysters and lobsters, is now named in his memory – while Stein is all but ignored. Perhaps this is due to her book, *Everybody's Autobiography,* in which she wrote: "what was the use of me having come from Oakland, it was not natural for me to have come from there yes write about it if I like or anything if I like but not there, *there is no there there*" – a quote which has haunted Oakland ever since.

Jack London's mildly socialist leanings set a style for the city, and Oakland has been the breeding ground for some of America's most unabashedly revolutionary **political movements** in the years since. The 1960s saw the city's fifty percent black population find a voice through the militant Black Panther movement, and in the 1970s Oakland was again on the nation's front pages, when the radical Symbionese Liberation Army demanded a ransom for kidnapped heiress Patty Hearst in the form of free food distribution to the city's poor. More recently, when Nelson Mandela visited the US he came to Oakland, not San Francisco, to thank local people for supporting the anti-apartheid campaign.

Oakland is still very much its own city, one whose diversity and dynamism take time to get a feel for. A good place to start, if you're here in the spring, is at the annual Festival at the Lake, celebrated each June on the shores of Lake Merritt. Also, although civic pride has never fully recovered from the defection of the *Oakland Raiders* football team to the bright lights of Los Angeles a few years back, sports fans still rally behind the many times American League and World Series champion *Oakland A's* baseball club.

Downtown Oakland

Coming by *BART* from San Francisco, get off at the 12th Street–Civic Center station and you're in **DOWNTOWN OAKLAND**, a compact district of spruced-up Victorian shopfronts overlooked by modern hotels and office blocks that has been in the midst of an ambitious programme of restoration and redevelopment for the last decade or so. It's a project that's been fraught with allegations of illegal dealings and incompetent planning, and so far it's anything but a success. To make way for the moat-like I-980 freeway – now the main route through Oakland since the collapse of the Cypress Freeway in the 1989 earthquake – entire blocks were cleared of houses, some of which were saved and moved to **Preservation Park** at 12th Street and Martin Luther King Jr Way, where they now sit empty and slowly falling apart. The late nineteenth-century commercial centre along Ninth Street west of Broadway, now tagged **Victorian Row**, underwent a major restoration some years ago, but the buildings have since been boarded up awaiting tenants. Certainly, the centrepiece of the redevelopment – and the one part thus far complete – is the brand-new Oakland Convention Center opposite the *BART* station, hardly an inviting-looking construction, dominated by the space-age international *Hyatt Regency* hotel with its trademark atrium lobby. By way of contrast, stroll a block east of Broadway, between Seventh and Ninth streets, to Oakland's **Chinatown**, whose bakeries and restaurants are as lively and bustling – if not as picturesque – as those of its more famous cousin across the Bay.

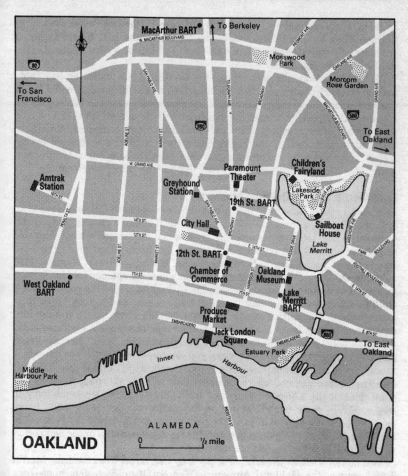

OAKLAND

To Berkeley

MacArthur BART

W. MACARTHUR BOULEVARD

To San Francisco

Mosswood Park

Morcom Rose Garden

To East Oakland

Amtrak Station

Paramount Theater

Greyhound Station

19th St. BART

City Hall

12th St. BART

West Oakland BART

Chamber of Commerce

Produce Market

Jack London Square

Middle Harbour Park

Inner

Harbour

Estuary Park

Children's Fairyland

Lakeside Park

Sailboat House

Lake Merritt

Oakland Museum

Lake Merritt BART

To East Oakland

ALAMEDA

0   ½ mile

Luckily not all of downtown Oakland has the look of a permanent building site. The city experienced its greatest period of growth early in the twentieth century, and many of the grand buildings of this era survive a few blocks north along Broadway, centred on the awkwardly imposing, earthquake-damaged 1914 **City Hall** on 14th Street. Two blocks away, at 13th and Franklin streets, stands Oakland's most unmistakable landmark, the chateau-esque lantern of the **Tribune Tower**, home of the Oakland *Tribune* newspaper.

Further north, around the 19th Street *BART* station, are some of the Bay Area's finest early twentieth-century buildings, highlighted by the outstanding Art-Deco interior of the 1931 **Paramount Theater** at 2025 Broadway (tours Sat at 10am; $5; ☎465-4600). Nearby buildings are equally exuberant in their decoration, ranging from the wafer-thin Gothic "flatiron" office tower of the **Cathedral Building** at Broadway and Telegraph, to the Hindu temple-like facade of the

3500-seat **Fox Oakland** on Telegraph at 19th Street – the largest cinema west of Chicago when built in 1928 – and, across the street, the 1931 **Floral Depot**, a grouping of small Moderne shopfronts faced in black and blue terracotta tiles with shiny silver highlights.

West of Broadway, the area around the *Greyhound* bus station on San Pablo Avenue is a fairly dodgy one. San Pablo used to be the main route in and out of Oakland before the freeways were built, but many of the roadside businesses are now derelict, especially around the industrial districts of **EMERYVILLE**, a mile north. Some of Emeryville's old warehouses have been converted into artists' lofts and studios, though any gentrification there might be is diffused by the scenes on the street, where prostitutes and drug-dealers hang out under the neon signs of the gambling halls and dingy bars that line the murky pavements.

Lake Merritt and the Oakland Museum

Five blocks east of Broadway, the eastern third of downtown Oakland is made up by **Lake Merritt**, a three-mile-circumference tidal lagoon that was bridged and dammed in the 1860s to become the centrepiece of Oakland's most desirable neighbourhood. All that remains of the many fine houses that once circled the lake is the elegant **Camron-Stanford house**, on the southwest shore at 1418 Lakeside Drive, a graceful Italianate mansion whose sumptuous interior is open for visits (Wed 11am–4pm, Sun 1–5pm; free). The lake is also the nation's oldest **wildlife refuge**, and migrating flocks of ducks, geese and herons break their journeys here. The north shore is lined by **Lakeside Park**, where you can hire canoes and rowing boats ($4 an hour) and a range of sailboats and catamarans ($4–10 an hour) from the Sailboat House (daily 10am–5pm in summer, weekends only rest of year; ☎444-3807) – provided you can convince the staff you know how to sail. There's also a miniature Mississippi riverboat ($1) that makes half-hour lake cruises on weekend afternoons, and kids will like the puppet shows and pony rides at the *Children's Fairyland* (daily 10am–5.30pm, weekends only in winter; $1.50), along Grand Avenue on the northwest edge of the park. Every year, on the first weekend in June, the park comes to life during the **Festival at the Lake**, when all of Oakland gets together to enjoy non-stop music and perfor-mances from local bands and entertainers.

Two blocks south of the lake, or a block up Oak Street from the Lake Merritt *BART* station, the **Oakland Museum** (Wed–Sat 10am–5pm, Sun noon–7pm; free, except for special exhibitions) is perhaps a more worthwhile stop, not only for the exhibits but also for the superb modern building in which it's housed, topped by a terraced rooftop sculpture garden that gives great views out over the water and the city. The museum covers many widely differing areas: there are displays on the **ecology** of California, including a simulated walk from the seaside through various natural habitats up to the fourteen-thousand-foot summits of the Sierra Nevada mountains; state **history** – with objects ranging from old mining equipment to the guitar that Berkeley-born Country Joe MacDonald played at the Woodstock festival in 1969; and a broad survey of works by California artists and craftspeople, some highlights of which are pieces of turn-of-the-century **arts and crafts furniture**, and excellent **photography** by Edward Muybridge, Dorothea Lange and Imogen Cunningham. The museum also has a collector's gallery which rents and sells works by California artists.

The Waterfront, Alameda and West Oakland

Half a mile down Broadway from downtown Oakland on *AC Transit* bus #51A, or even better direct from The City by ferry boat, **Jack London Square** is Oakland's sole concession to the tourist trade. Stretching along the waterfront, this aseptic complex of boutiques and eateries was named after the self-taught writer who grew up pirating shellfish around here, but is about as far away from the spirit of the man as it's possible to get. Jack London's best story, *The Call of the Wild*, was written about his adventures in Alaskan Yukon, where he carved his initials in a small **cabin** that has been reconstructed here; another survivor is *Heinhold's First and Last Chance Saloon*, a scruffy bar where London spent much of his wayward youth.

There's not much reason to linger, if you're not a keen fan of London – and if you are, you'd be better off visiting his Sonoma Valley ranch (see p.469). It's more enjoyable to walk a few short blocks inland to the **Produce Market**, along Third and Fourth streets, where there are some very good places to eat and drink among the railroad tracks (see p.406). This bustling warehouse district has fruit and vegetables by the forklift load, and is at its most lively early in the morning, from about 5am.

AC Transit bus #51A continues from Broadway under the inner harbour to **ALAMEDA**, a quiet and conservative island of middle-America dominated by a large naval air station, where massive nuclear-powered aircraft carriers sometimes dock. Alameda was severed from the mainland as part of a harbour improvement programme in 1902, and the fine houses along the original shoreline on Clinton Street were part of the summer resort colony that flocked here to the *contra costa* or "opposite shore" from San Francisco, near the now-demolished **Neptune Beach** amusement park. The island has since been much enlarged by dredging and landfill, and 1960s apartment blocks now line the long, narrow shore of **Robert Crown Memorial Beach**, along the bay.

WEST OAKLAND – an industrial district of warehouses and railway tracks, wartime housing projects and decaying Victorian houses – is the nearest East Bay *BART* stop to San Francisco, but is light years away from that city's prosperity. Except for the few artists and others who have ventured into the area – most noticeably at the *PRO-Arts Gallery* (☎763-4361), an artists' collective at 461 Ninth Street which organises a popular "Open Studios" tour each June – the only time anyone pays any attention to it is when something dramatic happens. Two examples are when Black Panther **Huey Newton** was gunned down here in a drug-related revenge attack, and when the double decker I-880 freeway which divided the neighbourhood from the rest of the city collapsed onto itself in the **1989 earthquake**, killing dozens of commuters.

Local people are resisting government plans to rebuild the old concrete eyesore (its replacement should be completed by 2001), and where the freeway used to run through is now the broad and potentially very attractive Cypress Boulevard, rechristened the Nelson Mandela Parkway. But otherwise West Oakland remains the Bay Area's poorest and most neglected neighbourhood; if you visit, do so during the day, preferably by car, and don't take anything you'd want to lose.

For a long time the area was known as "the place where the trains stopped" – which it still is: take *Amtrak* to San Francisco and you'll arrive at the old **Southern Pacific Depot** at the end of 16th Street (from where buses run across the bay). The station is interesting for the interior alone, cut by huge blue-tinted arched windows and seemingly untouched for the last fifty years. However, since the structure was damaged in the 1989 quake it may soon be demolished; in the meantime you can peer in and watch the colonies of stray cats who've taken over the lobby. Trains still use the platforms, and a temporary waiting room and ticket office has been built next door.

Half a mile south, near the West Oakland *BART* station, Seventh Street was the heart of the Bay Area's most vibrant entertainment district from the end of Prohibition in 1933 until the early 1970s, when many of the bars and nightclubs were torn down in the name of urban renewal. Seventh Street runs west between the docks and storage yards of the Oakland Army Base and the US Naval Supply Depot, ending up at **Portview Park**, one of the best places to watch the huge cargo ships that cruise by. The small park stands on the site of the old transbay ferry landing, used by as many as forty million passengers a year at its peak in the 1930s before the Bay Bridge was completed. Though the park has been closed since the earthquake, nip around the fence and join the people fishing from the small pier, or just enjoy the unmatched view of the San Francisco skyline framed by the Bay and Golden Gate bridges.

East Oakland

The bulk of Oakland spreads along foothills and flatlands to the east of downtown, in neighbourhoods obviously stratified along the main thoroughfares of Foothill and MacArthur boulevards. Gertrude Stein grew up here, though when she returned years later in search of her childhood home it had been torn down and replaced by a dozen **Craftsman-style bungalows** – the simple 1920s wooden houses that cover most of **EAST OAKLAND**, each fronted by a patch of lawn and divided from its neighbour by a narrow concrete driveway.

A quick way out from the gridded streets and pavements of the city is to take *AC Transit* bus #15A east from downtown up into the hills to **Joaquin Miller Park**, the most easily accessible of Oakland's hilltop parks. The park stands on the former grounds of the home of the "Poet of the Sierras", Joaquin Miller, who made his name playing the eccentric frontier American in the literary salons of 1870s London. His poems weren't exactly acclaimed (his greatest poetic achievement was rhyming "teeth" with "Goethe"), although his prose account, *Life Amongst the Modocs*, documenting time spent with the Modoc Indians near Mount Shasta, does stand the test of time. It was more for his outrageous behaviour that he became famous, wearing funny clothes and biting debutantes on the ankle. His house, a small white cabin called **The Abbey**, still survives, as do monuments he built to his friends Robert and Elizabeth Browning, and the thousands of trees he planted.

Perched in the hills at the foot of the park, the pointed towers of the **Mormon Temple** look like missile-launchers designed by the Wizard of Oz – unmissable by day or floodlit night. During the holiday season, speakers hidden in the landscaping make it seem as if the plants are singing Christmas carols. Only confirmed Mormons can go inside, but there are great views out over the entire Bay Area and a small **museum** (daily 9am–9pm; free) that explains the tenets of the faith.

Two miles east along Hwy-13 sits the attractive campus of **Mills College**. Founded in 1852 as a women-only seminary and still decidedly female after a recent much-publicised struggle against plans to make it co-ed, Mills is renowned for its music school, considered one of the best and most innovative in the US, and worth a visit for its **museum** (Sept–June Tues–Sun 10am–4pm; free), which has a fine collection of Chinese, Japanese, and pre-Columbian ceramics. A broad stream meanders through the lushly landscaped grounds, and many of the buildings, notably the central campanile, were designed in solid California Mission style by Julia Morgan, architect of Hearst Castle as well as some five hundred Bay Area structures. Further east, **Oakland Zoo** in Knowland Park is not worth the $2 entry fee, plus $2 to park, but you can hire **horses** (☎569-4428) from the stables at 14600 Skyline Boulevard, and ride around **Lake Chabot** in the forested hills above.

Along the bay south to San Jose stretch some twenty miles of tract house suburbs, and the only vaguely interesting area is around the end of the *BART* line in **FREMONT**, where the short-lived Essanay movie studios were based. Essanay, the first studios on the West Coast, made over seven hundred films in three years, including Charlie Chaplin's *The Tramp* in 1914. Not much remains from these pre-Hollywood days, however, and the only real sight is the **Mission San Jose de Guadalupe** on Mission Boulevard south of the I-680 freeway (daily 10am–5pm; donations), which in the best traditions of Hollywood set design was completely rebuilt in Mission style only a few years ago.

North Oakland and Rockridge

The pretty hillside homes around Broadway in **NORTH OAKLAND** look out across the bay over the flatlands that were the proving grounds of Black Panthers Bobby Seale and Huey Newton, who first studied politics at the old Merritt College campus on Martin Luther King Jr Way. The area has very few things to see but contains some of the best **nightclubs** in the entire Bay Area (see "East Bay Listings").

The **Oakland Rose Garden**, on Oakland Avenue three blocks north of MacArthur Boulevard (daily April–Oct; free), repays a look if you do come during the day; in between runs one of Oakland's most neighbourly streets, **Piedmont Avenue**, lined by a number of small bookshops and cafés. At the north end of Piedmont Avenue, the **Mountain View Cemetery** was laid out in 1863 by Frederick Law Olmsted (designer of New York's Central Park), and holds the elaborate dynastic tombs of San Francisco's most powerful families – the Crockers, the Bechtels and the Ghirardellis. No one minds if you jog or ride a bike around the well-tended grounds.

Pleasant Valley Road leads back to Broadway, from where *AC Transit* bus #76 climbs up Broadway Terrace, through neighbourhoods ravaged by the fire of 1991, to **Lake Temescal**. You can swim here in summer, or continue on up to the forested ridge at the **Robert Sibley Regional Preserve**, which includes the 1761-foot volcanic cone of Round Top Peak and panoramas of the entire Bay Area. Skyline Boulevard runs through the park and is popular with cyclists, who ride the twelve miles south to Lake Chabot or follow Grizzley Peak Boulevard five miles north to Tilden Park through the Berkeley Hills.

Most of the Broadway traffic, including the *AC Transit* #51 bus, cuts off onto **College Avenue** through Oakland's most upscale district, **ROCKRIDGE**, at the foot of wooded hills and with views out over the bay. Spreading for a half-mile on either side of the Rockridge *BART* station, the quirky shops and eateries here, especially the parade of shops on College Avenue just north of Claremont Boulevard, have emerged as the East Bay's gourmet centre. Despite their undeniably yuppie overtones, they're some of the best around, and make for a pleasant afternoon's wander. Both in geography and in atmosphere it's as near as Oakland gets to the café society of neighbouring Berkeley.

Berkeley

This Berkeley was like no somnolent Siwash out of her own past at all, but more akin to those Far Eastern or Latin American universities you read about, those autonomous culture media where the most beloved of folklores may be brought into doubt, cataclysmic of dissents voiced, suicidal of commitments chosen – the sort that bring governments down.

Thomas Pynchon, *The Crying of Lot 49*

More than any other American town, **BERKELEY** conjures up an image of dissent. During the Sixties and early Seventies, when American university campuses were protesting against the Vietnam War, it was the students of the University of California, Berkeley, that led the charge, gaining a name for themselves as the vanguard of what was increasingly seen as a challenge to the very authority of the state. Pitched battles were fought almost daily here for a time, on the campus and on the streets of the surrounding town, and there were times when Berkeley looked almost on the brink of revolution itself. If you've seen the Hendrix film *Jimi Plays Berkeley* you'll have some idea of the violent skirmishes that took place when students (and others) throwing stones and petrol bombs were met with tear-gas volleys and truncheons by National Guard troops under the nominal command of then Governor Ronald Reagan. It was, of course, most inspired by the mood of the time, and post-Gulf War campus politics are decidedly conservative. But – despite an influx of non-rebellious students of the Eighties, a thriving bedrock of exclusive California Cuisine restaurants and the high-tone types they attract – the progressive legacy lingers around the town and campus, noticeable in the many small bookshops and in the agenda of the local city council, which has long been a progressive trend-setter, establishing recycling programmes at home while supporting any number of left-leaning, anti-oppression movements abroad.

The **University of California** completely dominates Berkeley, and, as it's right in the centre of town, it makes a logical starting point for a visit. Its many grand buildings and thirty thousand students give off a definite energy that spills down the raucous stretch of **Telegraph Avenue**, which runs south from campus, holding most of the studenty hang-outs, including a dozen or so lively cafés, as well as several of Berkeley's many fine bookshops. Older students, and a good percentage of the faculty, congregate in the **Northside** area, popping down from their woodsy hillside homes to partake of goodies from the "Gourmet Ghetto", a stretch of Shattuck Avenue that collects many of Berkeley's internationally renowned restaurants, delis and bakeries. Of quite distinct character are the flatlands that spread through **West Berkeley** down to the bay, a poorer but increasingly gentrified district that mixes old Victorian houses with builder's yards and light industrial premises. Along the bay itself is the **Berkeley Marina**, where you can hire windsurfing boards and sailboats or just watch the sun set behind the Golden Gate.

The University of California

Caught up in the frantic crush of students who pack the **University of California** campus during term-time, it's nearly impossible to imagine the bucolic learning environment its high-minded founders intended. When Reverend Henry Durant and other East Coast academics decided to set up shop here in the 1860s, the rolling foothills were still largely given over to dairy herds and wheatfields, the last remnants of the Peralta family's Spanish land-grant *rancho* which once stretched

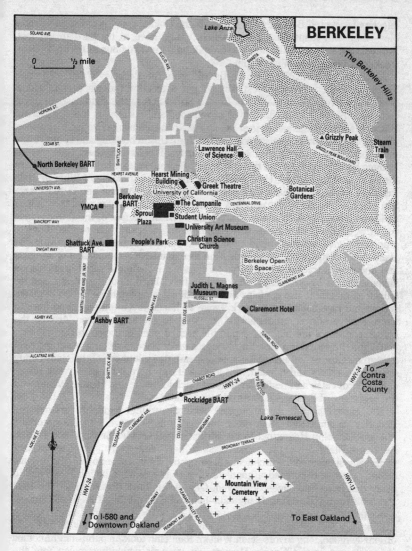

over most of the East Bay. Construction work on the two campus buildings –
imaginatively named North Hall and South Hall – was still going on when the first
two hundred students, including 22 women, moved here from Oakland in 1873.
Since then an increasing number of buildings have been squeezed into the half-
mile-square main campus, and the state-funded university has become one of
America's most highly respected, with so many Nobel laureates on the faculty
that it's said you have to win a Nobel Prize just to get a parking permit.
Overcrowding aside, the beautifully landscaped campus, stepping down from the

eucalyptus-covered Berkeley Hills towards the Golden Gate, is eminently strollable – and with maps posted everywhere, you'd have to try hard to get lost. Enthusiastic students will show you around on a free two-hour **tour** (☎642-5215), weekdays during term-time at 1pm.

A number of footpaths climb up the hill from the Berkeley *BART* station on Shattuck Avenue, but the best way to get a feel for the place is to follow Strawberry Creek from the top of Center Street across the southeast corner of campus, emerging from the groves of redwood and eucalyptus trees at **Sproul Plaza**. It's the newest and largest public space on campus, enlivened by buskers playing for quarters on the steps of the **Student Union** building and conga drummers pounding away in the echoing courtyard below. **Sather Gate**, which bridges Strawberry Creek at the north end of Sproul Plaza, marks the entrance to the older part of campus. Up the hill, past the imposing facade of Wheeler Hall, the 1914 campus landmark **Campanile** is modelled after the one in the Piazza San Marco in Venice; you can take a lift to the top for a great view of the campus and the entire Bay Area (daily 10am–4pm; 25¢). At the foot of the tower stands red-brick **South Hall**, the sole survivor of the original pair of campus buildings.

Inside the plain white building next door, the **Bancroft Library** (Mon–Sat 10am–5pm) displays odds and ends from its exhaustive accumulation of artefacts and documents tracing the history of California, including a faked brass plaque supposedly left by Sir Francis Drake when he claimed all of the West Coast for Queen Elizabeth. It also contains an internationally important collection of manuscripts and rare books, from Mark Twain to James Joyce – though you have to show some academic credentials if you want to see any of these. Around the corner and down the hill, just inside the arched main entrance to Doe Library, you'll find the **Morrison Reading Room**, a great place to sit for a while and read foreign magazines and newspapers, or just ease down into one of the many comfy overstuffed chairs and unwind with a book. From here it's a quick walk to the collection of cafés and restaurants lining Euclid Avenue and Hearst Avenue and the beginning of Berkeley's Northside (see below).

The Hearst family name appears with disturbing regularity around the Berkeley campus, though in most instances this is due not to the notorious William Randolph Hearst but to his altruistic mother, Phoebe Apperson Hearst. Besides inviting the entire senior class to her home every spring for a giant picnic, she sponsored the architectural competition that came up with the original campus plan, and donated a good number of the campus buildings, including many that have since been destroyed. One of the finest that survives, the 1907 **Hearst Mining Building** (daily 8am–5pm) on the northeast edge of campus, conceals a delicate metalwork lobby topped by three glass domes, above ageing exhibits on geology and mining – which is how the Hearst family fortune was originally made, long before scion William Randolph took up publishing. Another Hearst legacy is the **Greek Theatre**, an open-air amphitheatre cut into the Berkeley Hills east of campus, which hosts a summer season of rock concerts.

Higher up in the hills, above the 100,000-seat Memorial Stadium, is the lushly landscaped **Botanical Garden** (daily 9am–5pm; free), good for defeating on-campus claustrophobia with its thirty acres of plants and cacti. Near the crest, with great views out over the bay, a full-size fibreglass sculpture of a sei whale stretches out in front of the space-age **Lawrence Hall of Science** (daily 10am–5pm; $3.50, children free), an excellent museum and learning centre that features earthquake simulations, model dinosaurs and a planetarium, plus a number of

BERKELEY'S BOOKSHOPS

Berkeley's **bookshops** are as exhaustive as they are exhausting – not surprising for a university town. Perfect for browsing and taking your time, you won't be made to feel guilty or obliged to buy a book you've been poring over for ages.

Black Oak Books, 1491 Shattuck Ave, North Berkeley (☎486-0698). Some new books, some secondhand; also regular evening readings by internationally regarded authors.

Cody's Books, 2454 Telegraph Ave (☎845-7852). The flagship of Berkeley booksellers, with an excellent selection of fiction, poetry and criticism.

Comics and Comix, 2461 Telegraph Ave (☎845-4091). Great selection of comic books, both current and classic.

The Holme's Book Company, 274 14th St, downtown Oakland (☎893-6860). Not in Berkeley, but the largest new and secondhand bookstore in the Bay Area. Good local history section.

The Map Center, 2440 Bancroft Way (☎841-6277). Well-stocked map and guide store.

Moe's Books, 2476 Telegraph Ave (☎849-2087). The biggest (and most expensive) of Berkeley's bookshops, selling secondhand books at new book prices; there's an excellent art section on the top floor though.

Serendipity Books, 1201 University Ave, West Berkeley (☎841-7455). Damp and disorganised, but with an incredible selection of first editions and out-of-print books – a must for collectors of twentieth-century American fiction and poetry.

Shakespeare and Company, 2499 Telegraph Ave (☎841-8916). Crammed to the ceiling with quality secondhand and new books at reasonable prices. The best place to linger and scour the shelves for finds.

hands-on exhibits for kids in the Wizard's Lab. Both the gardens and the Lawrence Hall of Science are accessible on weekdays via the free *UC Berkeley Shuttle* bus from the campus or the Berkeley *BART* station.

In the southeast corner of campus, the **Lowie Museum of Anthropology** in Kroeber Hall (Thurs–Tues 10am–4pm; $2, free Thurs) has a variety of changing exhibits and an intriguing display of artefacts made by Ishi, the last surviving Yahi Indian, who was found near Mount Lassen in Northern California in 1911. The anthropologist Alfred Kroeber (the father of novelist Ursula K. Le Guin) brought Ishi to the museum (then located on the UC San Francisco campus), where he lived under the scrutiny of scientists and journalists – in effect, a state of captivity – until his death from tuberculosis a few years later. Also in Kroeber Hall, the Worth Ryder Art Gallery in room 116 shows varying degrees of quality in the work of Berkeley's art students.

The brutally modern, angular concrete of the **University Art Museum** across Bancroft Way (Wed–Sun 11am–5pm; $3) is in stark contrast to the campus's older buildings. Its skylit, open-plan galleries hold works by Picasso, Cezanne, Rubens and other notables, but the star of the show is the collection of Fifties American painter Hans Hofman's energetic and colourful abstract paintings, on the top floor. The best thing about the museum are its cutting-edge, changing exhibitions: the main space hosts a range of major shows – like Robert Mapplethorpe's controversial photographs – while the Matrix Gallery focuses on lesser known, generally local artists. Works on paper are shown downstairs outside the **Pacific Film Archive**, which shares the building, showing new films from around the world that you won't see elsewhere, as well as revivals from its extensive library (see p.408 for details).

Telegraph Avenue and South Berkeley

Downtown Berkeley – basically a few banks, a post office and the City Hall building – lies west of the university campus, around the Berkeley *BART* station on Shattuck Avenue, but the real activity centres on **Telegraph Avenue**, which runs south of the university from Sproul Plaza. This thoroughfare saw some of the worst of the Sixties riots, and is still a frenetic bustle, especially the four short blocks closest to the university, which are packed to the gills with cafés and secondhand bookshops. Sidewalk vendors hawk hand-made jewellery and brilliantly coloured t-shirts, while down-and-outs hustle for spare change and spout psychotic poetry.

People's Park, now a seedy and overgrown plot of land a block up from Telegraph between Haste Street and Dwight Way, was another battleground in the late 1960s, when organised and spirited resistance to the university's plans to develop the site into student dormitories brought out the troops, who shot an onlooker dead by mistake. To many, the fact that the park is still a community-controlled open space (and outdoor dosshouse for Berkeley's homeless legions) symbolises a small victory in the battle against the Establishment, though it's not a pleasant or even very safe place to hang about, especially after dark. A mural along Haste Street remembers some of the reasons why the battles were fought, in the words of student leader Mario Savio: "There's a time when the operation of the machine becomes so odious, makes you so sick at heart, that you can't take part, you can't even tacitly take part. And you've got to put your bodies upon the gears and upon the wheels, upon the levers, upon all the apparatus, and you've got to make it stop" – ideals that can't help but be undermined by the state of the place these days. In late 1991 a misguided effort by the University (which has legal title to the land) to build volleyball courts in the middle of the park resulted in predictably violent demonstrations and rioting on surrounding streets, and as yet no clear plan for the park's future has emerged, with the University threatening to bulldoze the entire block and activists still resisting any change in the status quo.

The results of a more restrained but no less radical effort faces the allotment gardens of People's Park across Bowditch Street. One of the finest buildings in the Bay Area, Bernard Maybeck's **Christian Science Church**, built in 1910, is an eclectic but thoroughly modern structure laid out in a simple Greek cross plan and spanned by a massive redwood truss with carved Gothic tracery and Byzantine painted decoration. The interior is only open on Sundays for worship and for tours afterwards at 11am, but the outside is worth lingering over, its cascade of many gently pitched roofs and porticoes carrying the eye from one hand-crafted detail to another. It's a clever building in many ways: while the overall image is one of tradition and craftsmanship, Maybeck also succeeded in inconspicuously incorporating such unlikely materials as industrial metal windows, concrete walls and asbestos tiles into the structure – thereby cutting down costs.

Though many of the largely residential neighbourhoods elsewhere in South Berkeley ("Southside") – especially the Elmwood and Claremont districts around College Avenue – are worth a wander, there are a couple of specific sights worth searching out. One of these is the **Judah L. Magnes Museum**, a few blocks south of campus at 2911 Russell Street (Sun–Fri 10am–4pm; free). Located in a rambling old mansion, it has California's largest repository of Judaica, and the exhibits detail the history of Jewish life from ancient times to the present day. The other Southside attraction is much harder to miss, towering as it does over the Berkeley–Oakland border. The half-timber castle imagery of the **Claremont Hotel** gives a fairly clear hint as to what's inside – it's now one of the Bay Area's plushest resort hotels, with the three-storey Tower Suite going for a cool $750 a night. Built in 1914, just in time for San Francisco's Panama-Pacific Exposition, the *Claremont* was designed to encourage day-trippers out across the bay in the hope that they'd be so taken with the area they'd want to live here. The ploy worked, and the hotel's owners (who incidentally also owned the streetcar system that brought people here, and all the surrounding land), made a packet.

North Berkeley

NORTH BERKELEY, also called "Northside", is a subdued neighbourhood of professors and postgraduate students, its steep, twisting streets climbing up the lushly overgrown hills north of campus. At the foot of the hills, some of the Bay Area's finest restaurants and delicatessens – most famously *Chez Panisse*, started and run by Alice Waters, the acclaimed inventor of California Cuisine – have sprung up along broad and busy Shattuck Avenue to form the so-called "Gourmet Ghetto" (see p.406 for details), a great place to pick up the makings of a tasty *al fresco* lunch.

Above the Gourmet Ghetto on Euclid Avenue (if you want to avoid the fairly steep walk, take *AC Transit* bus #65 from Hearst Avenue, the northern edge of campus), there's no more pleasant place for a picnic than the **Berkeley Rose Garden**, a terraced amphitheatre filled with some three thousand varieties of roses and looking out across the bay to the Golden Gate and Mt Tamapais. Built as part of a WPA job-creation scheme during the Depression, a wooden pergola rings the top, stepping down to a small spring. Opposite the Rose Garden, through a pedestrian tunnel, is **Codornices Park**, a broad expanse of manicured lawn edged by a baseball diamond, basketball courts and lots of play equipment, best of which is a long concrete helter-skelter that's good fun to hurtle down, and not only for kids. A **footpath** leads up from the park along Codornices Creek, burbling with small waterfalls after a good rain. Though the hills are steep, the homes here – built in an eclectic range of styles, designed to meld seamlessly into the wooded landscape – are some of the finest and most impressively sited in the Bay Area. All repay many times over the effort it takes to see them, if only for their marvellous setting. Complementing the picturesque houses of the Berkeley Hills are a number of enticing **parks**, all with great views over the bay. The largest and highest of these, at the end of the bus route, is **Tilden Regional Park**, where you can swim in Lake Anza, ride the old carousel or take a miniature **steam train** through the redwood trees.

West Berkeley and the Waterfront

From downtown Berkeley and the UC campus, **University Avenue** runs downhill towards the bay, lined by increasingly shabby frontages of motels and massage parlours. The liveliest part of this **WEST BERKELEY** area is around the junction of University and San Pablo avenues – the pre-freeway main highway north – where a community of recent immigrants from India have set up shops and markets, and restaurants that serve some of the best of the Bay Area's rare curries. Otherwise there's not much reason to stop.

The area between San Pablo Avenue and the bay is the oldest part of Berkeley, and a handful of hundred-year-old houses and **churches** – like the two white-spired Gothic Revival ones on Hearst Avenue – survive from the time when this district was a separate city, known as Ocean View. The neighbourhood also holds remnants of Berkeley's industrial past, and many of the old warehouses and factory premises have been converted into living and working spaces for artists and craftspeople. Along similar lines are the cafés, workshops and galleries built in the late 1970s along **Fourth Street** north of University Avenue, which have since become somewhat yuppified but are still good places to wander in search of handicrafts and household gadgets.

One of the few places you can visit here is the **Takara Sake Tasting Room**, just off Fourth Street south of University Avenue at 708 Addison Street (daily noon–6pm; free). Owned and operated by one of Japan's largest producers, this plant is responsible for more than a third of all sake drunk in the US. You can sample any of the five varieties of California strain sake (brewed from California rice), best drunk warm and swallowed sharply. Though no tours are offered, they will show you a slide presentation of the art of sake brewing.

The I-80 freeway, and the still-used railway tracks that run alongside it, manage to cut Berkeley pretty well off from its **waterfront**. The best way to get there is to take *AC Transit* bus #51M, which runs regularly down University Avenue. Once a major hub for the transbay ferry services – to shorten journey times, a three-mile-long pier was constructed, much of which still stands stuck out into the bay – the **Berkeley Marina** is now one of the prime spots on the bay for leisure activities, especially windsurfing. If you're interested in having a go on the water, contact the *Cal Sailing Club* (see "Sports and Outdoor Activities" in *Basics* for details). The surrounding area, all of which is landfill largely owned by the Southern Pacific railway, has long been the subject of heated battles between developers and the environmentalists who want to preserve it as a shoreline park. For the moment, the winds off the bay make it a good place to fly a kite, and there are some short hiking trails.

The North Bay and Inland Valleys

Compared to the urbanised bayfront cities of Oakland and Berkeley, the rest of the East Bay is sparsely populated, and places of interest are few and far between. The **North Bay** area is home to some of the Bay Area's heaviest industry – oil refineries and chemical plants dominate the landscape – but also holds a few, remarkably unchanged waterfront towns that merit a side trip if you're passing by. Away from the bay, in the **inland valleys**, it's a whole other world, of dry rolling hills dominated by the towering peak of Mount Diablo. Dozens of tract house developments have made commuter suburbs out of what had been cattle ranches and farms, but so far the region has been able to absorb the numbers and still feels rural, despite having doubled in population in the past twenty years.

The North Bay

North of Berkeley there's not a whole lot to see or do. In ALBANY *Golden Gate Fields* has horse-racing from October to June, and EL CERRITO's main contribution to world culture was the band Creedence Clearwater Revival, who did most of their "Born on the Bayou" publicity photography in the wilds of Tilden Park in the hills above. **RICHMOND**, at the top of the bay, was once a boomtown, building ships during World War II at the Kaiser Shipyards, which employed 100,000 workers between 1940 and its closure in 1945. Now it's the proud home of the gigantic Standard Oil refinery, the centre of which you'll drive through before crossing the **Richmond–San Rafael Bridge** ($1) to Marin County. About the only reason to stop in Richmond is that the city marks the north end of the *BART* line, and the adjacent *Amtrak* station is a better terminal for journeys to and from San Francisco, than the end of the line in West Oakland.

Though not really worth a trip in itself, if you're heading from the East Bay to Marin County **POINT RICHMOND** repays a look. A cosy little village tucked away at the foot of the bridge between the refinery and the bay, its many Victorian houses are rapidly becoming commuter territory for upwardly mobile professionals from San Francisco. Through the narrow tunnel that cuts under the hill stands the most obvious sign of this potential gentrification: "Brickyard Landing", an East Bay version of London's Docklands, with modern bay-view condos, a private yacht harbour, and a token gesture to the area's industrial past – disused brick kilns, hulking next to the tennis courts on the front lawn. The rest of the waterfront is taken up by the broad and usually deserted strand of Keller Beach, which stretches for half a mile along the sometimes windy shoreline.

The Carquinez Straits

At the top of the bay some 25 miles north of Oakland, the land along the **Carquinez Straits** is a bit off the beaten track, but it's an area of some natural beauty and much historic interest. The still-small towns along the waterfront seem worlds away from the bustle of the rest of the Bay Area, but how long they'll be able to resist the pressure of the expanding commuter belt is anybody's guess. *AC Transit* bus #70 runs every hour from Richmond *BART* north to **CROCKETT** at the west end of the narrow straits – a tiny town cut into the steep hillsides above the water that seems entirely dependent upon the massive C&H Sugar factory at its foot, whose giant neon sign lights up the town and the adjacent Carquinez Bridge.

From Crockett the narrow **Carquinez Straits Scenic Drive**, an excellent cycling route, heads east along the Sacramento river. A turning two miles along drops down to **PORT COSTA**, a small town that was dependent upon ferry traffic across the straits to Benicia until the bridge was built at Crockett, and the town lost its livelihood. It's still a nice enough place to watch the huge ships pass by on their way to and from the inland ports of Sacramento and Stockton. If you haven't got a bike (or a car), you can enjoy the view from the window of the *Amtrak* train, which runs alongside the water twice a day from Oakland and Richmond, not stopping until MARTINEZ, at the eastern end of the straits, two miles north of the John Muir house (see below).

On the north side of the Straits, and hard to get to without a car (see "Getting around", p.385), **BENICIA** is the most substantial of the historic waterfront towns, but one that has definitely seen better days. Founded in 1847, it at first rivalled San Francisco as the major Bay Area port, and was even the state capital for a time; but despite Benicia's better weather and fine deep water harbour, San Francisco eventually became the main transport point for the fortunes of the Gold Rush and the town very nearly faded away altogether. Examples of Benicia's efforts to become a major city stand poignantly around the very compact downtown area, most conspicuously the 1852 Greek Revival building that was used as the **first State Capitol** for just thirteen months. The building has been restored as a **museum** (daily except Tues and Wed 10am–5pm; $1), furnished in the legislative style of the time, with top hats on the tables and shiny spitoons every few feet.

A walking tour map of Benicia's many intact Victorian houses and churches is available from the **tourist office** at 831 First Street (☎707/745-2120), including on its itinerary the steeply pitched roofs and elaborate eaves of the **Frisbie-Walsh house** at 235 East L Street – a prefabricated Gothic Revival building that was shipped in pieces from Boston in 1849 (an identical house was put up by General Vallejo at his house in Sonoma; see p.467). Across the City Hall park, the arched ceiling beams of **St Paul's Episcopal Church** look like an upturned ship's hull; it was built by shipwrights from the Pacific Mail Steamship Company, one of Benicia's many successful nineteenth-century shipyards. Half a dozen former brothels and saloons stand in various stages of decay and restoration along First Street down near the waterfront, from where the world's largest train ferries used to ply the waters between Benicia and Port Costa until 1930.

Vallejo and Marine World/Africa USA

Across the Carquinez Bridge from Crockett, **VALLEJO**, like Benicia, was an early capital of California. Though it now lacks any sign of its historical importance, Vallejo has remained economically vital, in contrast to most of the other Gold Rush-era towns along the Straits. That's largely because of the massive US military presence here at the **Mare Island Naval Shipyard**, a sprawling, relentlessly grey complex that covers an area twice the size of Golden Gate Park. Its less than glamorous history – the yard builds and maintains supply ships and the like, not carriers or battleships – is recounted in a small **museum** in the old city hall building at 734 Mare Street (Tues–Fri 10am–4.30pm; $1), whose highlight is a working periscope that looks out across the bay. Though not a great thrill, it merits a quick stop; it's right on Hwy-29, the main route from the East Bay to the Wine Country, in the centre of town.

The only reason you might conceivably come to Vallejo is for **Marine World/Africa USA** (daily 9.30am–6.30pm; $16.95; ☎707/643-6722), five miles north of Vallejo off I-80 at the Marine World Parkway (Hwy-37) exit. Operated by a non-profit educational group, it offers a standard range of performing sea lions, dolphins and killer whales kept in approximations of their natural habitats, as well as water-ski stunt shows and a large aviary full of cockatoos, macaws and other tropical birds. It can be a fun day out, especially for children, and it's not bad as these things go, but nonetheless you can't deny that the creatures pay a much bigger price to be here than the families of tourists who crowd it on summer weekends. The best way to get here from San Francisco is the *Red and White Fleet* catamaran **ferry boat** (☎546-2896) from Fisherman's Wharf, which takes an hour each way and adds another $12 on to the admission price.

The Inland Valleys

Most of the **inland East Bay** area is made up of rolling hills covered by grasslands, slowly giving way to suburban housing developments and office block complexes, as more and more businesses abandon the pricey real estate of San Francisco. Dominating the region is the great peak of **Mount Diablo**, twice as high as any other Bay Area summit and surrounded by acres of campsites and hiking trails. There are also two historic homes that serve as memorials to their literate and influential ex-residents, **John Muir** and **Eugene O'Neill**.

BART tunnels from Oakland through the Berkeley Hills to the leafy-green stockbroker town of ORINDA, continuing east through the increasingly hot and dry landscape to the end of the line at **CONCORD**, site of chemical plants and oil refineries and a controversial nuclear weapons depot. A few years ago, a peaceful, civilly disobedient blockade here ended in protestor Brian Willson losing his legs under the wheels of a slow-moving munitions train. The event raised public awareness – before it happened few people knew of the depot's existence – but otherwise it's still business as usual.

From Pleasant Hill *BART*, one stop before the end of the line, *Contra Costa County Connection* bus #116 leaves every half-hour for **MARTINEZ**, the seat of county government, passing the preserved home of naturalist **John Muir** (daily 10am–4.30pm; $1), just off Hwy-4, two miles south of Martinez. Muir, an articulate, persuasive Scot whose writings and political activism were of vital importance in the preservation of America's wilderness as National Parks, spent much of his life exploring and writing about the majestic Sierra Nevada mountains, particularly Yosemite. He was also one of the founders of the Sierra Club – a wilderness lobby and education organisation still active today. Anyone who is familiar with the image of this thin, bearded man wandering the mountains with his knapsack, notebook and packet of tea might be surprised to see his very conventional, upper-class Victorian home, now restored to its appearance when Muir died in 1914. The house was built by Muir's father-in-law and so doesn't reflect much about Muir himself, except for the parts he added to it, like the massive, rustic fireplace he had built in the East Parlour so he could have a "real mountain campfire". The bulk of Muir's personal belongings and artefacts are displayed in his **study**, on the upper floor, and in the adjacent room an exhibition documents the history of the Sierra Club and Muir's battles to protect America's wilderness.

At the foot of Mount Diablo, fifteen miles south, near DANVILLE, playwright **Eugene O'Neill** used the money he got for winning the Nobel Prize for Literature in 1936 to build a home and sanctuary for himself, which he named Tao House. It was here, before he was struck down with Parkinson's Disease in 1944, that he wrote many of his best-known plays: *The Iceman Cometh, A Moon for the Misbegotten*, and *Long Day's Journey into Night*. Readings and performances of his works are sometimes given in the house, which is open to visitors, though you must reserve a place on one of the free guided **tours** (twice daily at 10am & 1.30pm; ☎839-0249). To get to the house, take the *Contra Costa County Connection* bus #121 from Walnut Creek *BART* station – it stops close by.

As for **Mount Diablo** itself, it rises up from the rolling ranchlands at its foot to a height of nearly 4000 feet, its summit and flanks preserved within **Mount Diablo State Park** ($3 parking; ☎837-2525). The main road through the park (there's no public transport, though the Sierra Club sometimes organises day trips: see *Basics*) reaches within a hundred metres of the top, so it's a popular place for an outing, and you're unlikely to be alone to enjoy the marvellous view. On a clear day you can see over two hundred miles in every direction, from San Francisco to the High Sierra – it's said to be the most extensive panorama on earth, after Mount Kilimanjaro. The fifteen thousand acres of parkland surrounding the peak offer many miles of hiking and some of the only **camping** in the East Bay.

Livermore and Altamont

Fifteen miles southeast of Mount Diablo, on the main road out of the Bay Area (I-580), the rolling hills around **LIVERMORE** are covered with thousands of shining, spinning, hi-tech **windmills**, placed here by a private power company to take advantage of the nearly constant winds. It's the largest wind-farm in the world – you'll probably have seen it used in a number of TV adverts, as a space-age backdrop to hype flashy new cars or sexy perfumes. The US government provides no funding for this non-polluting, renewable source of energy, but spends billions of dollars every year designing and testing nuclear weapons and other sinister applications of modern technology at the nearby **Lawrence Livermore Laboratories**, where most of the research and development of the US nuclear arsenal and the "Star Wars" Strategic Defense Initiative takes place. Hands-on exhibits show off various scientific phenomena and devices at the small visitors centre (Mon–Fri 9am–4.30pm, Sat & Sun noon–5pm; free), two miles south of I-580 on Greenville Road.

Up and over the hills to the east, where I-580 joins I-5 for the 400-mile route south through the Central Valley to Los Angeles, stand the remains of **Altamont Speedway**, site of a nightmarish Rolling Stones concert in December 1969. The free concert, which was captured in the film *Gimme Shelter*, was intended to be a sort of second Woodstock, staged in order to counter allegations that the Stones had ripped off their fans during a long US tour. In the event it was a complete fiasco: three people died, one of whom was kicked and stabbed to death by the Hell's Angels "security guards" – in full view of the cameras – after pointing a gun at Mick Jagger while he sang "Sympathy for the Devil". Needless to say, no historical plaque marks the site.

East Bay Listings

Life doesn't end the other side of the Bay Bridge, and even if you're staying and spending most of your time in San Francisco, there are many reasons for popping across. One of the best things about visiting the East Bay is the opportunity to enjoy its many **cafés**. Concentrated most densely around the UC Berkeley campus, they're on a par with the best of North Beach for bohemian atmosphere – heady with the smell of coffee, and from dawn to near midnight full of earnest characters wearing their intellects on their sleeves. If you're not after a caffeine fix, you can generally also get a glass of beer, wine or fresh fruit juice, though for serious drinking you'll be better off in one of the many **bars**, particularly in rough-hewn Oakland. Grittier versions of what you'd find in San Francisco, they're mostly blue-collar, convivial, and almost always cheaper. Not surprisingly, Berkeley's bars are brimming with students, academics, and those who don't mind mixing with them.

As befits the birthplace of California Cuisine, the **restaurants** are as varied and no less excellent than those of San Francisco. Berkeley in particular is an upmarket diner's paradise, but it's also a student town where you can eat cheaply and well, especially around the southern end of the university, along and around Telegraph Avenue. The rest of the East Bay is less remarkable, except for when it comes to American food like barbecued ribs, grilled steaks and seafood or deli sandwiches – or especially breakfasts, for which it's unbeatable.

Nightlife is where the East Bay really comes into its own. Even more so than in San Francisco, dancing to canned music and paying high prices for flashy decor is not the done thing, which means that **discos** are virtually nonexistent; however, dance music – from the likes of Oakland's own MC Hammer and Digital Underground – is thriving. Dozens of **live music venues** cover the range of musical tastes and styles – from unpretentious little jazz clubs to buzzing R&B venues. Oakland's hotspots are the hottest of the lot. Though not bad by San Francisco standards, the East Bay **theatre** scene isn't exactly thriving, and shows tend to be politically worthy rather than dramatically innovative. By contrast, the range of films is top-rate, with a dozen **cinemas** showing new releases and Berkeley's *Pacific Film Archive*, one of the world's finest film libraries, filling its screens with obscure but brilliant art flicks.

Check the free *East Bay Express* or the *Berkeley Monthly* for details of who and **what's on** where in the entire East Bay region.

Cafés

Cafe Mediterranean, 2475 Telegraph Ave, Berkeley. Berkeley's oldest café, straight out of the Beat Generation archives: beards and berets optional, books *de rigueur*.

Cafe Milano, 2522 Bancroft Way, near Telegraph Ave, Berkeley. Airy, artsy warehouse-like space just off the UC campus.

Cafe Strada, 2300 College Ave at Bancroft Way, Berkeley. Upmarket open-air café where art and architecture students mix with lawyers and chess wizards.

Coffee Mill, 3363 Grand Ave, Lake Merritt. Spacious room that doubles as an art gallery, and often hosts poetry readings; the coffee's good, too.

Mama Bear's, 6536 Telegraph Ave, North Oakland. Mainly a women's bookshop, it doubles as a café and meeting place, and has regular readings, often for women only, by lesbian and feminist writers. Open daily 10am–7pm, later for readings.

Peet's Coffee, 2124 Vine St, North Berkeley. Mostly for take-home coffee-buyers; regular cups for 50¢, massive ones for 80¢, minus 10¢ if you bring your own cup. Another branch at 2916 Domingo near the *Claremont Hotel*. Also has an excellent range of hot teas at 85¢ a pot.

Bars

Brennan's, Fourth St and University Ave, Berkeley, under the I-80 freeway overpass. Solid blue-collar hang-out for watching a game on TV, jostling noisily at the bar and escaping the droves of students. Cheap drinks and cafeteria food, with lots of room.

Heinhold's First and Last Chance Saloon, Jack London Square, Oakland. Authentic waterfront bar that's hardly changed since the turn of the century, when Jack London himself drank here.

The Kingfish, 5201 Claremont Ave, two blocks from Telegraph Ave in North Oakland. Less a bar than a tumbledown shed, selling cheap cold beer. Popular with UC Berkeley rugby players and other headbangers.

Larry Blake's, 2367 Telegraph Ave, Berkeley. Upstairs there's a small bar, downstairs there's a R&B club and large bar; in between the two there's a good value restaurant.

The Pub, 1492 Solano Ave, North Berkeley. Good range of English beers, quaffable on their tree-shaded outdoor deck.

Rickey's Sports Lounge, 15028 Hesperian Blvd, San Leandro, near Bayfair *BART*. With seven giant-screen TVs, and 35 others spread around the cavernous room, this bar-cum-restaurant is *the* place to watch sporting events, especially *A's* and *Raiders* games.

Starry Plough, 3101 Shattuck Ave, South Berkeley. An Irish bar with Guinness and Anchor Steam on draught, Powers Whiskey on call, happy hours and sporadic collections for the IRA. Near Ashby *BART*, and with live music some nights; see p.408.

The White Horse, 6560 Telegraph Ave at 66th St, North Oakland. Smallish, friendly mixed bar (it was one of the first Bay Area bars openly to welcome gay men and lesbians), with dancing and a pool table.

Budget food: diners and delis

Bette's Ocean View Diner, 1807 Fourth St, West Berkeley (☎548-9494). Named for the neighbourhood and not for the vista. Huevos rancheros and home fries served from 6.30am.

The Brick Hut, 3222 Adeline Street (☎658-5555). Very popular Lesbian-run breakfast cafe, with the best Eggs Benedict in the East Bay, right across from Ashby *BART*.

Flint's Barbeque, 3314 San Pablo Ave, downtown Oakland (☎658-9912). Open until the early hours of the morning for some of the world's best takeaway barbecued chicken and ribs. Also at 6609 Shattuck Ave, North Oakland (☎653-0593), and 6672 E 14th St in East Oakland (☎569-1312).

Lois the Pie Queen, 851 60th St, North Oakland (☎658-5616). Famous for southern-style sweet potato and fresh fruit pies, this cosy diner serves massive down-home breakfasts and Sunday dinners that'll keep you full for a week.

Mabel's Cafe, 635 First St, Benicia (☎707/746-7068). Timeless American diner food in a homely, small front room.

Rockridge Cafe, 5492 College Ave, Rockridge (☎653-1567). Chrome-and-lino breakfast and burger bar with good desserts, opens at 7am every day.

Cafe Intermezzo, 2442 Telegraph Ave, Berkeley (☎849-4592). Huge and healthy sandwiches and platefulls of salad for under $5.

Top Dog, 2534 Durant St, Berkeley (no phone). Not just a hot dog stand, and open late for bockwurst, bratwurst, kielbasas and Louisiana Hot Sausages.

American food

Bay Wolf Cafe, 3853 Piedmont Ave, North Oakland (☎655-6004). A comfortable restaurant serving moderately expensive grilled steaks and seafood on an ever-changing menu.

Chez Panisse, 1517 Shattuck Ave, North Berkeley (☎548-5525). The first and still the best of the California Cuisineries – although at $50 a head *prix-fixe* you may prefer to try the comparatively cheap *Cafe* upstairs, especially if you haven't made the obligatory three-months-in-advance reservation.

Gulf Coast Oyster Bar & Specialty Co., 736 Washington St, downtown Oakland (☎839-6950). Popular and reasonably priced Cajun-flavoured seafood restaurant.

Oakland Grill, in the Produce Market at Franklin and Third St, Oakland (☎835-1176). Good all-American food all day, every day, in an airily remodelled warehouse.

Spenger's, 1919 Fourth St, West Berkeley (☎845-7111). About as far as you can get from the subtle charms of Berkeley's high-style eateries, this is nonetheless very much a local institution: the largest restaurant in the whole Bay Area, serving up tons of seafood to thousands of customers every day. Full meals from $8 to $15.

Pizzas, Mexican and South American food

Alameda Taqueria, 1513 Park St, Alameda (☎865-9380). Small and family run, with some of the freshest and best-tasting burritos in the Bay Area.

Alvita's Restaurant, 3522 Foothill Blvd, East Oakland (☎536-7880). Arguably the best Mexican restaurant in the Bay Area, with great *chiles rellenos*, *carnitas* and a range of seafood dishes.

Blondie's Pizza, 2340 Telegraph Ave, Berkeley (☎548-1129). Takeaway New York-style pizza by the slice ($1.25) or by the pie; open late (2am) and always crowded.

Cafe Oliveto, 5655 College Ave, Rockridge (☎547-5356). Trendy sidewalk tapas bar with good-sized portions costing around $4 a plate.

Juan's Place, 941 Carlton St, West Berkeley (☎845-6904). The original Berkeley Mexican restaurant, with great food (tons of it) and an interesting mix of people.

Mario's La Fiesta, 2444 Telegraph Ave at Haste St, Berkeley (☎540-9123). Usually crowded enough to keep things going at a dull roar, and the food is very good for the little you pay.

Tambo Cafe, 1981 Shattuck Ave near University Ave, Berkeley (☎841-6884). Brilliant, reasonably priced Peruvian food – *papas huacainas* (potatoes in spicy cheese sauce) and *empanadas* (meat or vegetable pies), as well as marvellous *ceviche* – served up fresh and fast.

Zachary's Pizza, 5801 College Ave, Rockridge (☎655-6385). Good salads and arguably the best pizzas in the East Bay. Also at 1853 Solano Ave, Berkeley (☎525-5950).

Asian, African and Indian food

The Blue Nile, 2525 Telegraph Ave, Berkeley (☎540-6777). Go here with a group and share the giant platters of Ethiopian stewed meats and veggies, eaten by hand with pancake-like *injera* bread.

Byul Mi House, 308 14th St, downtown Oakland (☎839-3993). Small, quiet Korean café with excellent *bulgoki, kim chee*, and other delicacies; $5 for a set lunch, $9 for dinner.

Cha-Am, 1543 Shattuck Ave, North Berkeley (☎848-9664). Climb the stairs up to this unlikely, always crowded small restaurant that serves up deliciously spicy Thai food at bargain prices.

Jade Villa, 800 Broadway, downtown Oakland (☎839-1688). For *dim sum* lunches or traditional Cantonese meals, this is one of the best places to go in Oakland's thriving Chinatown.

Maharani, 1025 University Ave, West Berkeley (☎848-7777). One of the best of the handful of eateries that have sprung up here in Little India, and certainly the cheapest, with $6 all-you-can-eat lunchtime buffets during the week.

Sorabol, 372 Grand Ave, Lake Merritt (☎839-2288). Excellent Korean restaurant, featuring addictive barbecued meats for around $8 a dish.

Steve's Barbeque, in the Durant Center, 2525 Durant St, Berkeley (no phone). Excellent cheap Korean food (*kim chee* to kill for).

Ice cream and desserts

Edy's, 2201 Shattuck Ave, Berkeley (☎843-3096). If you can bear the orange vinyl booths, the sundaes, banana splits and milk shakes are great.

Fatapples, 1346 Martin Luther King Way, North Berkeley (☎526-2660). Excellent apple and fruit pies, and a menu full of countless versions of hamburgers.

Fenton's Creamery, 4226 Piedmont Ave, North Oakland (☎658-4949). A brightly lit Fifties ice cream and sandwich shop, open until midnight seven days a week.

Schuyler's, 1854 Euclid Ave, North Berkeley (☎841-6374). Borrow a book from the wall of paperbacks while you down a hot fudge sundae or two.

Speciality shops and markets

Acme Bread, 1601 San Pablo Ave, West Berkeley (☎524-1327). A small bakery that supplies the majority of Berkeley's better restaurants; the house speciality is delicious sourdough baguettes.

Cheese Board, 1504 Shattuck Ave, North Berkeley (☎549-3183). Collectively owned and operated since 1967, this was one of the first outposts in Berkeley's Gourmet Ghetto and is still going strong, offering over 200 varieties of cheese and a range of delicious breads.

La Farine, 6323 College Ave, Rockridge (☎654-0338). Small but highly rated French-style bakery, with excellent *pain chocolat*.

Monterey Foods, 1550 Hopkins St, North Berkeley (☎526-6042). The main supplier of exotic produce to Berkeley's gourmet restaurants, this boisterous market also has the highest quality fresh fruit and vegetables available.

Poulet, 1685 Shattuck Ave, North Berkeley (☎845-5932). Famed for their ready-cooked, free-range chickens, the shop also sells a variety of chicken-based pâtés and salads.

Live music venues

Ashkenaz, 1317 San Pablo Ave, Berkeley (☎525-5054). World music and dance café. Acts range from modern Afrobeat to the best of the Balkans. Kids and under-21s welcome. Admission $5–8.

Caribe Dance Center, 1408 Webster St, downtown Oakland (☎835-4006). For reggae, rockers, calypso, soca, dub, salsa or lambada, this new place is hard to beat. Admission $3–8.

Eli's Mile High Club, 3629 Martin Luther King Jr Way, North Oakland (☎655-6661). The best of the Bay Area blues clubs. Waitresses balance pitchers of beer on their heads to facilitate a safer passage through the rocking crowds. Cover $5–8.

Gilman Street Project, 924 Gilman St, West Berkeley (☎648-3561). On the outer edge of the hardcore punk scene. No booze, all ages, admission $3–6.

Kimball's East, 4800 Shellmound St, Emeryville (☎658-2555). Fairly slick, high-style jazz and dancing venue. Cover $10–20.

Koncepts Cultural Gallery, 480 Third St, downtown Oakland (☎763-0682). Excellent, ground-breaking jazz club, hosting a wide variety of different acts. Admission $8–15.

Yoshi's, 6030 Claremont Ave, North Oakland (☎652-9200). Spacious and comfortable jazz and blues club. Cover $8–20.

Larger performance venues

Berkeley Community Theater, 1930 Allston Way, Berkeley (☎845-2308). Jimi Hendrix played here, and the 3500-seat theatre still hosts major rock concerts and community events.

The Oakland Coliseum Complex, Coliseum *BART*, near the airport (☎639-7700). Mostly stadium shows, inside the 18,000-seat Arena or outdoors in the adjacent 55,000-seat Coliseum.

Paramount Theater, 2025 Broadway, downtown Oakland (☎465-6400). Beautifully restored Art-Deco masterpiece, hosting classical concerts, big-name crooners, ballets and opera. Tickets $6–15.

Zellerbach Hall and the outdoor **Greek Theatre** on the UC Berkeley campus (☎642-9988). Two of the prime spots for catching touring big names in the Bay Area. Tickets cost $15–20.

Cinemas

Coliseum Drive-in, 5401 Coliseum Way, East Oakland (☎536-7491). If you've never been to a drive-in, here's your chance.

Grand Lake Theater, 3200 Grand Ave (☎452-3556). The grand dame of East Bay picture palaces, right on Lake Merritt, showing the best of the current major releases.

Pacific Film Archives, 2621 Durant Ave, Berkeley, in the University Art Museum (☎642-1412). For the serious film fan, this is perhaps the best cinema in all California, with seasons of contemporary works from around the world, plus revivals of otherwise forgotten favourites. Two films a night; $4.25 each, $5.25 for both.

UC Theater, 2036 University Ave, Berkeley, just below Shattuck Ave (☎843-6267). Popular revival house, with a huge auditorium and a daily double feature. $4.

Theatre

Berkeley Repertory Theater, 2025 Addison St, Berkeley (☎845-4700). One of the West Coast's most highly respected theatre companies, presenting updated classics and contemporary plays in an intimate modern theatre. Tickets $6–20.

Black Repertory Theater, 3201 Adeline St, Berkeley near Ashby *BART* (☎652-2120). After many years of struggling, this politically conscious company moved into their own purpose-built home in 1987. Since then they've been encouraging new talent with great success. Tickets $4–12.

California Shakespeare Festival, Siesta Valley, Orinda (☎548-3422). After 15 seasons in a North Berkeley park, this outdoor festival was forced to move to a larger home for the 1991 season. Tickets $8–15.

Julia Morgan Theater, 2640 College Ave (☎548-7234). A variety of touring shows stop off in this cunningly converted old church. $8–15.

Zellerbach Playhouse, UC Berkeley (☎642-9988). Occasionally brilliant visiting productions. Tickets $5–15.

The Peninsula

The city of San Francisco sits at the tip of a five-mile-wide **Peninsula**. Home of old money and new technology, this stretches for fifty miles of relentless suburbia south from San Francisco along the bay past the wealthy enclaves of Hillsborough and Atherton, to wind up in the futuristic roadside landscape of the so-called "Silicon Valley" near **San Jose** – though your only glimpse of the area may be on the trip between San Francisco and the airport. There was a time when the region was covered with orange groves and fig trees, but the concentration of academic interest around Stanford University in **Palo Alto**, and the continuing boom in computers – since the Seventies the region's biggest industry – has laid to rest any chances of it hanging on to its agricultural past.

Surprisingly, most of the land along the **coast** – separated from the bayfront sprawl by a ridge of redwood-covered peaks – remains rural and undeveloped; it also contains some of the best **beaches** in the Bay Area, and a couple of affably down-to-earth farming communities, all of which are well served by public transport.

Getting around and information

BART only travels down the Peninsula as far as DALY CITY, from where you can catch **SamTrans** (☎761-7000) buses south to Palo Alto or along the coast to Half Moon Bay. For longer distances, **Caltrain** (☎557-8661) offers an hourly rail service from its terminal at Fourth and Townsend in downtown San Francisco, stopping at most bayside towns between the city and San Jose, for $1–5; *Greyhound* runs regular buses along US-101 to and from their San Jose terminal at 70 S Almaden (☎408/297-8890) as well. **Santa Clara County Transit** (*SCCT*) (☎408/287-4210) runs buses around metropolitan San Jose. If you're going to be spending most of your time down here, it's possible to **fly** direct into **San Jose International Airport** (SJO), surprisingly close to downtown San Jose on the frequent *SCCT* bus #64.

The **Palo Alto Chamber of Commerce**, 325 Forest Avenue (Mon–Fri 9am–noon & 1–5pm; ☎324-3121), has lists of local eateries and cycle routes; for information on nearby Stanford University, phone ☎723-2560. To find out **what's on** and where, pick up a free copy of the *Palo Alto Weekly*, available at most local shops. At the southern end of the bay, the **San Jose Convention and Visitors' Bureau**, 333 W San Carlos Street (Mon–Sat 9am–5pm; ☎408/295-9600), is the best bet for tourist information; for local news and events pick up a copy of the excellent *San Jose Mercury* newspaper, or the free weekly *Metro*.

Accommodation

There are dozens of $40-a-night **motels** along Hwy-82, "El Camino Real", the old main highway, and, with a bit of advance planning (and a car), you could save money by staying here rather than in the city. Also, if you're arriving late or departing on an early flight from SFO you might want to avail yourself of one of the many **airport hotels**, listed on p.334. Perhaps the best reason to spend the night down on the Peninsula is its many cheap and pleasant **hostels**, two of which are housed in old lighthouses bang on the Pacific coast.

Hostels

Hidden Villa Hostel, 26807 Moody Rd, Los Altos Hills (☎941-6407). Located on an 1800-acre ranch in the foothills above the Silicon Valley; closed June–Sept. $11 a night.

Montara Lighthouse Hostel, on Hwy-1 in Montara, 25 miles south of San Francisco (☎728-7177). Dorm rooms in a converted 1875 lighthouse, accessible from the city via *SamTrans* bus #1A. $11 a night.

Pigeon Point Lighthouse Hostel, on Hwy-1 south of Pescadero, fifty miles south of San Francisco (☎879-0633). Worth planning a couple days around, this beautifully sited hostel is ideal for exploring the redwoods in the hills above or watching the wildlife in nearby Año Nuevo State Reserve. $11 a night.

Motels and hotels

Best Western Inn, 455 S Second St, San Jose (☎408/298-3500). Right in downtown San Jose, with pool and sauna for $55 a double.

Best Western Stanford Park Hotel, 100 El Camino Real, Menlo Park (☎322-1234). Doubles from $65.

San Benito House, 356 Main St, Half Moon Bay (☎726-3425). Twelve restful rooms in a 100-year-old building, just a mile from the beach. Doubles from $80 a night, including breakfast.

Town House Motel, 4164 El Camino Real, Palo Alto (☎493-4492). A mile from anywhere but the rooms are particularly clean and well-kept. $42 for a double.

Valley Inn, 2155 The Alameda, San Jose (☎408/241-8500). Standard motel not far from the Rosicrucian Museum. Doubles $45.

Camping

Butano State Park, Pescadero (☎879-0173). RV and tent spaces in a beautiful redwood forest. Free camping.

Half Moon Bay State Beach, Half Moon Bay (☎726-6238). Sleep out along the beach for free, or in the campsite for $10.

South along the Bay

US-101 runs south from San Francisco along the bay through over fifty miles of unmitigated sprawl to San Jose, lined by light industrial estates and shopping malls. The only place worth stopping at is the **Coyote Point Museum** (Wed–Fri 9am–5pm, Sat & Sun 1–5pm; free), four miles south of the airport off Poplar Avenue in a large bayfront park, where examples of the natural life of the San Francisco Bay – from tidal insects to birds of prey – are exhibited in engaging and informative displays, enhanced by interactive computers and documentary films.

A more pleasant drive is via **I-280**, the newest and most expensive freeway in California, which runs parallel to US-101 but avoids the worst of the bayside mess by cutting through wooded valleys down the centre of the Peninsula. Just beyond the San Francisco city limit the road passes through **COLMA**, a unique place made up entirely of cemeteries (which are prohibited within San Francisco). Beyond Colma the scenery improves quickly as I-280 continues past the **Crystal Springs Reservoir**, an artificial lake which holds the water supply for San Francisco – pumped here all the way from Yosemite. Surrounded by twenty square miles of parkland, hiking trails lead up to the ridge from where San Francisco Bay was first spotted by eighteenth-century Spanish explorers; it now overlooks the airport to the east, but there are good views out over the Pacific Coast, two miles distant.

At the south end of the reservoir, just off I-280 on Canada Road in the well-heeled town of **WOODSIDE**, luscious gardens surround the palatial **Filoli Estate** (tours Tues–Sat 10.30am & 1pm; $6; ☎364-2880). The 45-room mansion, designed in 1915 in neo-Palladian style by architect Willis Polk, may seem familiar – it was used in the TV series *Dynasty* as the Denver home of the Carrington clan. It's the only one of the many huge houses around here that you can actually visit, although it's the gardens that are most worth coming for, especially in the spring when everything's in bloom.

Palo Alto and Stanford University

PALO ALTO, just south and three miles east of Woodside between I-280 and US-101, is a small, leafy community with all the contrived scruffiness you'd expect to find in a student town, but little of the vigour of its northern counterpart, Berkeley. Though a visit doesn't really merit the expense of a night's accommodation, you could spend a lazy day in the bookshops and cafés that line **University Avenue**, the town's main drag. Or, if you're feeling energetic, try cycling round the town's many well-marked bike routes; various sorts of bike are available for $12 to $25 a day from *The Effortless Bike* at 401 High Street (☎328-3180), near the *Caltrain* station a block west of University Avenue.

Stanford University, spreading south from the end of University Avenue, lends Palo Alto what liveliness it has. The private university is one of the best – and most expensive – in the Bay Area, though when it opened in 1891, founded by railroad magnate Leland Stanford in memory of his dead son, it offered free tuition. Ridiculed by East Coast academics, who felt that there was as much need for a second West Coast university (after UC Berkeley) as there was for "an asylum for decayed sea captains in Switzerland", Stanford was defiantly built anyway, in a hybrid of Mission and Romanesque buildings on a huge campus that covers an area larger than the whole of downtown San Francisco.

Stanford, recently under fire for misspending millions of dollars of US government research monies, hasn't always been such a smug and somnolent place, though you wouldn't know it to walk among the preppy future-lawyers-of-America who seem to comprise ninety percent of the student body. **Ken Kesey** came here from Oregon in 1958 on a writing fellowship, working nights as an orderly on the psychiatric ward of one hospital here, and getting paid $75 a day to test experimental drugs (LSD among them) in another. Drawing on both experiences, Kesey wrote *One Flew Over the Cuckoo's Nest* in 1960 and quickly became a counter-culture hero. These days Stanford attracts a more prosaic body of students, preferring to bolster its departments in medicine, science and engineering.

Approaching from the Palo Alto *Caltrain* and *SamTrans* bus station, which acts as a buffer between the town and the university, you enter the campus via a half-mile-long, palm-tree-lined boulevard which deposits you at its heart, the **Quadrangle**, bordered by the phallic **Hoover Tower** and the colourful, gold-leaf mosaics of the **Memorial Church**. Free hour-long walking **tours** of the campus leave from here daily at 11am and 2pm, though it's fairly big and is best seen by car or bike.

San Jose

The fastest-growing city in America's fastest-growing state, **SAN JOSE**, save the odd Burt Bacharach song, is not strong on identity, though in area and population it's close on twice the size of San Francisco. Sitting at the southern end of the Peninsula, with a location that's almost central to the state, an abundance of cheap land brought developers and businessmen into the area in the 1960s, hoping to draw from the concentration of talent in the commerce-orientated caucuses of Stanford University. Fuelled by the success of computer firms like Apple and Hewlett-Packard, in the past 25 years San Jose has emerged as the civic heart of Silicon Valley, surrounded by miles of faceless hi-tech industrial parks where the next generations of computers are designed and crafted.

Ironically enough, San Jose is one of the oldest settlements in California, though the only sign of it is at the late eighteenth-century **Mission Santa Clara de Asis**, on a pedestrianised stretch of San Jose's main drag, the Alameda, and just a short walk from the Santa Clara *Caltrain* station. Next to the mission, the small **De Saisset Museum** (Tues–Fri 10am–5pm, Sat & Sun 1–5pm; $1) has artefacts from the Mission era; but otherwise there's only really one good reason to subject yourself to San Jose's relentlessly boring cityscape – to visit the **Rosicrucian Museum**, 1342 Naglee Avenue (Tues–Fri 9am–4.30pm, Sat–Mon noon–4.30pm; $3), reachable from the *Caltrain* station on *SCCT* bus #36. Languishing in the suburbs, this grand structure contains a brilliant collection of Assyrian and Babylonian artefacts, with displays of mummies, amulets, a replica of a tomb and ancient jewellery.

You could also stop off at the **Winchester Mystery House**, 525 S Winchester Boulevard, just off I-280 near Hwy-17 (daily 9.30am–4.30pm; $9). Sarah Winchester, heir to the Winchester rifle fortune, was convinced by an occultist upon her husband's death that he had been taken by the spirits of men killed with Winchester rifles. She was told that unless a room was built for each of the spirits and the sound of hammers never ceased, the same fate would befall her. Work on the mansion went on 24 hours a day for the next thirty years, with results that need to be seen to be believed – stairs lead nowhere, windows open on to solid brick. It is however a shameless tourist trap, and you have to run a gauntlet of ghastly gift shops and fizzy drink stands to get in or out.

One other Peninsula place might exercise a certain attraction, particularly to those fond of roller coasters, log rides, and all-American family fun: **Great America** (daily 10am–10pm in summer, weekends only in winter; $16.95, $8.95 under-6s) – a huge, 100-acre amusement park on the edge of San Francisco Bay, just off US-101 north of San Jose. It's not in the same league as Disneyland, but neither does it suffer from the same crowds and lengthy queues, and the range of high-speed thrills and chills – from the loop-the-looping "Demon" to "The Edge", where you free-fall in a steel cage for over 100 feet – is well worth the entry fee, especially on weekdays when you may well have the run of the place. The whole park is laid out into American-themed areas like "Hometown Square", "Yankee Harbor" or "County Fair", filled up with all sorts of sideshow attractions and funfair games.

The Coast

The **coastline** of the Peninsula south from San Francisco is more appealing than inland – relatively undeveloped, with very few buildings, let alone towns, along the 75 miles of coves and beaches that extend down to the resort city of Santa Cruz. The bluffs protect the many nudist beaches from prying eyes, and make a popular launching-pad for hang-glider pilots, particularly at Burton Beach and Fort Funston, a mile south of the San Francisco Zoo – also the point where the earthquake-causing San Andreas Fault enters the sea, not surfacing again until Point Reyes. From here Skyline Boulevard follows the coast past the repetitious tracts of identical ticky-tacky houses that make up DALY CITY, where it is joined by Hwy-1 (and *SamTrans* bus #1A) for the rest of the journey.

Some fifteen miles south of Daly City, the suburban sprawl gives way to the clothing-optional sands of **Gray Whale Cove State Beach** (daily dawn–dusk; $2 to park). Despite the name it's not an especially great place to look for migrating gray whales, but there is a stairway from the bus stop down to a fine strand. Two miles south, the red-roofed buildings of the **Montara Lighthouse**, set among the windswept Monterey pine trees at the top of a steep cliff, have been converted into a **youth hostel** (see "Accommodation", above, for details), where you can rent bikes for $10 a day. There are a few good places to stop for a drink or a bite to eat in the village of MOSS BEACH, across Hwy-1.

South of the lighthouse, the **James Fitzgerald Marine Reserve** strings along the shore, a two-mile shelf of flat, slippery rocks that make excellent tidepools. The ranger often gives guided interpretive walks through the reserve at low tide, the best time to explore. At the south end of the reserve, Pillar Point juts out into the Pacific, just east of which, along Hwy-1, fishing boats dock at Pillar Point Harbour. The ramshackle village adjacent to the waterfront, **PRINCETON-BY-THE-SEA**, has a few stands selling fish – sometimes freshly caught – and chips.

Half Moon Bay

HALF MOON BAY, twenty miles south of the city and the only town of any size between San Francisco and Santa Cruz, takes its name from the crescent-shaped bay formed by Pillar Point. Lined by miles of sandy beaches, the town is surprisingly rural considering its proximity to San Francisco and Silicon Valley, and sports a number of ornate Victorian wooden houses around its centre. The oldest of these is at the north end of Main Street: built in 1849, it's just across a little stone bridge over Pillarcitos Creek. The **Chamber of Commerce** (Mon–Fri 9am–5pm; ☎726-5202), housed in an old railway carriage on Hwy-1, half a mile south, has free walking tour maps of the town, and information on the two annual festivals for which the place is well known. These are the **Holy Ghost and Pentecost Festival**, a celebratory parade and barbecue held the sixth Sunday after Easter, and the **Pumpkin Festival**, celebrating the harvest of the area's many pumpkin farms, just in time for Halloween, when the fields around town are full of families searching for the perfect jack-o'-lantern to greet the hordes of trick-or-treaters. There are free, primitive **campsites** all along the coast in Half Moon Bay State Park, a half-mile west of the town.

Half Moon Bay is also the southern end of the *SamTrans* bus #1A route; to continue south, transfer here to route #90C, which runs every three hours to Waddell Creek, twenty miles south. **San Gregorio State Beach**, ten miles south of Half Moon Bay, is best seen in the spring, after the winter storms, when flotsam architects construct a range of driftwood shelters along the wide beach south of the parking area. In summer the beach is packed with well-oiled bodies; things are quieter around the bluffs to the north, and clothing is optional.

The Butano Redwoods and the Año Nuevo State Reserve

If you've got a car and it's not a great day for the beach, head up into the hills above, where the thousands of acres of the **Butano redwood forest** feel at their most ancient and primaeval in the greyest and gloomiest weather. About half the land between San Jose and the coast is protected from development in a variety of state and county **parks**, all of which are virtually deserted despite being within a half-hour's drive of the Silicon Valley sprawl. Any one of a dozen roads will take you through endless stands of untouched forest, and even the briefest of walks can lead seemingly miles from any sign of civilisation. Hwy-84 climbs up from San Gregorio through the **Sam McDonald County Park** to LA HONDA, from where you can continue on to Palo Alto, or, better, loop back to the coast via Pescadero Road. A mile before you reach the quaint village of **PESCADERO** – which has two of the best places to eat, *Duarte's* and *Dinelli's Cafe*, on the Peninsula – Cloverdale Road heads south to **Butano State Park**, where you can hike and camp overlooking the Pacific. If you're here in December or January, continue south another ten miles to the **Año Nuevo State Reserve** for a chance to see one of nature's most unusual happenings – the mating rituals of the northern elephant seal (see p.282). The reserve is also good for bird-watching, and in March you stand a chance of getting a good look at migrating gray whales. From Año Nuevo it's another twenty miles south to the resurgent, earthquake-shattered beach resort of Santa Cruz.

Eating and drinking

Though the culinary establishments of the Peninsula hardly compete with those of San Francisco, if you find yourself down here there are a number of places to **eat** and **drink** that are well worth searching out, if only because the pace is more relaxed and you get more for your dollar. Most of the places listed are centrally located in the downtown areas of the various Peninsula cities, though a few others are worth almost any effort to get to. Also, as most of the restaurants are good spots for a drink and vice versa, we've listed them all together. For late-night partaking, check out the clubs described under "Nightlife", below; all serve drinks until the early hours.

Barrio Fiesta, 909 Antoinette Lane, South San Francisco (☎871-8703). Hard to find amidst the shopping malls of South City, but well worth it for the huge portions of beautifully presented, delicious Filipino dishes, especially seafood. Full meals cost around $15; bring your own wine or beer.

Dinelli's, 1956 Pescadero Rd, Pescadero (☎879-0106). Probably the best roadside café in the known world, with great burgers and a house speciality, fried artichoke hearts, that brings people from all over the Bay Area.

Duarte's, 202 Stage Road, Pescadero (☎879-0464). Platefuls of traditional American food for around $10, plus wonderful fresh fruit pies.

Eulipia, 374 S First St, San Jose (☎408/280-6161). Upscale and stylish spot featuring well-prepared versions of California Cuisine staples like grilled fish and fresh pastas. Full bar; dinner and drinks will set you back $15–25.

Fresco, 3398 El Camino Real, Palo Alto (☎493-3470). Wide range of pastas, pizzas and salads with palpably fresh ingredients in unusual combinations. Opens early.

Krung Thai Cuisine, 1699 W San Carlos St, San Jose (☎408/295-5508). Delicious, unusual seafood dishes – start off with a *po-tak* soup of clams and crab legs in citrus broth – and excellent satays.

Original Joe's, 301 S First St, San Jose (☎408/292-7030). Grab a stool at the counter or settle into one of the comfy booths and enjoy a burger and fries or a plate of pasta at this San Jose institution, where $10 goes a long way.

Pudley's Burger Saloon, 255 University Ave, Palo Alto (☎328-2021). Burgers ($4) and beers ($1.50) in retro-American 1940s setting.

Nightlife

Though many San Franciscans would deny it and think you were crazy even to suggest the possibility, there's a surprisingly good **nightlife** scene on the Peninsula, particularly in San Jose but also in the studenty environs of Palo Alto.

Cactus Club, 417 S First St, San Jose (☎408/280-1435). One of two very good clubs near each other in downtown San Jose, hosting some of the better up-and-coming bands with music ranging from roots reggae to hardcore thrash. Cover $4–8.

The Edge, 260 California Avenue, Palo Alto (☎324-EDGE). Cheap drinks and low (or no) cover charge make this dance club a lively option. Good live bands some nights, when tickets cost $5–7.

FX: The Club, 400 S First St, San Jose (☎408/298-9796). The other San Jose club, more for drinking and dancing; 21 and over only. Closed Mon and Tues, cover $4–6.

Hard Disk Saloon, 1214 Apollo Way, Sunnyvale (☎408/733-2001). Near US-101 at Lawrence Expressway in the heart of the Silicon Valley; live blues most nights, no cover Sun–Wed.

Marin County

Across the Golden Gate from San Francisco, **Marin County** (pronounced Ma-RINN) is an unabashed introduction to Californian self-indulgence: an elitist pleasure-zone of conspicuous luxury and abundant natural beauty, with sunshine, sandy beaches, high mountains and thick redwood forests. Often ranked as the wealthiest county in the US, Marin has drawn a sizeable contingent of northern California's wealthier young professionals to live in its swanky waterside towns, many of whom grew up during the Flower Power years of the 1960s, and lend the place its New Age feel and reputation. Locals get their shiitake-mushroom pizzas delivered in Porsches, and think nothing of spending $1000 to see the Grateful Dead play at the Pyramids. Though many of the cocaine-and-hot-tub devotees who seemed to populate the place in the 1970s have traded in their drug habits for mountain bikes, life in Marin still centres around personal pleasure, and the throngs you see hiking and cycling at weekends, and the hundreds of bizarrely esoteric self-help practitioners – Rolfing, Re-Birthing and soul-travel therapists fill up the classified ads of the local papers – prove that Marinites work hard to maintain their easy air of physical and mental well-being.

Flashy modern ferry boats sail across the bay from San Francisco and give a good initial view of the county: heading past desolate Alcatraz Island, curvaceous **Mount Tamalpais** looms larger until you land at its foot in one of the chic bayside settlements of **Sausalito** or **Tiburon**. **Angel Island**, in the middle of the bay but accessible most easily from Tiburon, provides relief from the excessive style-consciousness of both towns, retaining a wild untouched feeling among the eerie ruins of derelict military fortifications.

Sausalito, Tiburon, and the lifestyles that go with them, are only a small part of Marin. The bulk of the county rests on the slopes of the ridge of peaks which divides the peninsula down the middle, separating the sophisticated harbourside towns in the east from the untramelled wilderness of the Pacific coast to the west. The **Marin Headlands**, just across the Golden Gate Bridge, hold time-warped old battlements and gun emplacements that once protected San Francisco's harbour from would-be invaders, and now overlook surfers and backpackers enjoying the acres of open space. Along the coastline that stretches north, the broad strand of **Stinson Beach** is the Bay Area's finest and widest stretch of sand, beyond which Hwy-1 clings to the coast past the rural hamlet of **Bolinas** to the seascapes of **Point Reyes**, where in 1579 Sir Francis Drake landed and claimed all of California for England.

Inland, the heights of Mount Tamalpais, and specifically **Muir Woods**, are a magnet to sightseers and nature-lovers, who come to wander through one of the few surviving stands of the native coastal redwood trees that once covered most of Marin. The trees were chopped down to build and rebuild the dainty wooden houses of San Francisco, and the long-vanished lumber mills of the rustic town of **Mill Valley**, overlooking the bay from the slopes of Mount Tam, as it's locally known, bear the guilt for much of this destruction; it's the oldest town in Marin County, and now home to an eclectic bunch of art galleries and cafés. Further north, the largest town in Marin, **San Rafael**, is best passed by, though its outskirts contain two of the most unusual places in the county: Frank Lloyd Wright's peculiar Civic Center complex and the preserved remnants of an old Chinese fishing village in China Camp State Park. The northern reaches of Marin County border the bountiful wine-growing regions of the Sonoma and Napa valleys, detailed in the following chapter.

Arrival and getting around

Just getting to Marin County can be a great start to a day out from San Francisco. *Golden Gate Transit* (☎322-6600) ferries leave from the **Ferry Building** on the Embarcadero, crossing the bay past Alcatraz Island **to Sausalito and Larkspur;** they run from 5.30am until 8pm, approximately every half-hour during the rush hour, less often the rest of the day, and every two hours at weekends and holidays. Tickets cost $3.50 single to Sausalito, $2.20 to Larkspur Monday to Friday ($3 weekends) – and there's a full bar on board. The more expensive *Red and White Ferries* ($9 return; ☎546-2805) sail from Pier 431/2 at **Fisherman's Wharf to Sausalito** and from the **Ferry Building to Tiburon** – from where the *Angel Island Ferry* ($3 return, plus $1 per bicycle; ☎435-2131) nips back and forth to Angel Island State Park daily in summer, weekends only in the winter. The only services between Marin County and the East Bay are offered by *Traveler's Transit* (☎457-7080) minibuses, running between the Richmond *BART* station and downtown San Rafael for $2 a trip.

Golden Gate Transit also runs a comprehensive **bus service** around Marin County, and across the Golden Gate Bridge from the **Transbay Terminal** in San Francisco (from Marin County, ☎453-2100), and publishes a helpful and free system **map** and timetable, including all ferry services. Bus **fares** range from $1 to $3, depending on the distance travelled. If you'd rather avoid the hassle of bus connections, *Gray Line* (☎896-5915; $37.50) offer four-hour guided **coach tours** from San Francisco, taking in Sausalito and Muir Woods, daily at 9am, 11am and 1.30pm.

One of the best ways to get around Marin is by **bike**, particularly by mountain bike, cruising along the many trails that crisscross the county. If you want to ride on the road, Sir Francis Drake Highway – from Larkspur to Point Reyes – makes a good route, though it's best to avoid it at weekends, when the roads can get clogged up with cars. All ferry services allow you to bring a cycle from San Francisco, or you can hire one from local outlets like *Ken's Bikes*, 94 Main Street in Tiburon (☎465-1683), or *Point Reyes Bikes*, 11431 Hwy-1 in Point Reyes Station (☎663-1768).

Information

For further **information** regarding Marin County, there are three main on-the-spot sources: the **Marin County Visitors Bureau**, 30 N San Pedro Road, San Rafael (Mon–Fri 9am–5pm; ☎472-7470); the **Sausalito Chamber of Commerce** at 333 Caledonia Street (Mon–Fri 9am–5pm; ☎332-0505); and the **Mill Valley Chamber of Commerce**, 85 Throckmorton Avenue (Mon–Fri 9.30am–4pm; ☎388-9700), in the centre of the town. For information on **hiking and camping** in the wilderness and beach areas, depending on where you're heading, contact the Golden Gate National Recreation Area, Building 201, Fort Mason Center (daily 9am–4pm; ☎556-0560), Mount Tamalpais State Park, 801 Panoramic Highway, Mill Valley (daily 9am–5pm; ☎388-2070), or the Point Reyes National Seashore, Bear Valley, Point Reyes (daily 9am–5pm; ☎663-1092). For information on **what's on** in Marin, there are widely available local freesheets, like the down-to-earth *Coastal Post* or the New-Agey *Pacific Sun*.

Accommodation

You might prefer simply to dip into Marin County using San Francisco as a base, and if you've got a car or manage to time the bus connections right it's certainly possible, at least for the southernmost parts of the county. However, it can be nicer to take a more leisurely look at Marin, staying over for a couple of nights in some well-chosen spots. Sadly there are few **hotels**, and those that there are often charge in excess of $100 a night; **motels** tend to be the same as anywhere, though there are a couple of attractively faded ones along the coast. In any case, the best bet for budget accommodation is a dorm bed in one of the beautifully situated **hostels** along the western beaches.

Hostels

Golden Gate Youth Hostel, Building 941, Fort Barry, Marin Headlands (closed 9.30am–4.30pm; ☎331-2777). Hard to get to unless you're driving – it's near Rodeo Lagoon just off Bunker Road, five miles west of Sausalito – but worth the effort for its setting, in a cosy old army barracks building just across the Golden Gate Bridge.

Point Reyes Hostel, in the Point Reyes National Seashore (closed 9.30am–4.30pm; ☎663-8811). Housed in an old ranchhouse, and surrounded by meadows and forests. Dorm beds $11 a night.

Motels and hotels

Casa Madrona, 801 Bridgeway, Sausalito (☎332-0502). Deluxe hideaway tucked into the hills above the bay; doubles $100.

Motel Alto, 817 Redwood Highway, Mill Valley (☎388-6676). A bit hard to find – take the Seminary Drive exit of US-101, and it's just west of the freeway – but worth it for the low prices. Singles $30, doubles $40.

Ocean Court Motel, 18 Arnold St, Stinson Beach (☎868-0212). Just a block from the beach, west of Hwy-1. Large double rooms with kitchens for $85 a night.

Stinson Beach Motel, 3416 Shoreline Highway, Stinson Beach (☎868-1712). Basic roadside motel right on Hwy-1, ten minutes' walk from the beach. Doubles $45 a night.

Bed and breakfast

The Bed and Breakfast Exchange, 45 Entrata Drive, San Anselmo (☎485-1971). Not an inn but a letting agency, with rooms available in comfortable private homes all over Marin County from $50 a night for two, ranging from courtyard hideaways on the beach in Tiburon to houseboats in Sausalito.

The Blue Heron Inn, 11 Wharf Rd, Bolinas (☎868-1102). Lovely double rooms in an unbeatable locale for $75 a night.

Lindisfarne Guest House, part of the *Green Gulch Zen Center*, Muir Beach (☎383-3036). Restful rooms in a meditation retreat set in a secluded valley above Muir Beach. Doubles $50 a night, and the price includes excellent vegetarian meals.

Camping

China Camp State Park, off North San Pedro Rd north of San Rafael (☎456-0766). Walk-in plots (just 200m from the car park) overlooking a lovely meadow. First-come, first-camped for $8 a night per plot.

Marin Headlands, just across the Golden Gate Bridge (☎331-1540). The best of dozens of plots here are at Kirby Cove, at the northern foot of the Golden Gate Bridge. Free.

Mount Tamalpais State Park, above Mill Valley (☎388-2070). Free plots for backpackers on the slopes of the mountain, and a few rustic cabins ($20 a night) along the coast at Steep Ravine.

Samuel Taylor State Park, on Sir Francis Drake Blvd, fifteen miles west of San Rafael (☎488-9897). Deluxe, car-accessible plots with hot showers, spread along a river for $12 a night. In summer, reserve a place through MISTIX (☎1-800/445-7275).

Across the Golden Gate: Marin Headlands and Sausalito

The headlands across the Golden Gate from San Francisco afford some of the most impressive views of the bridge and the city behind. Take the first turning past the bridge, and follow the road up the hill into the **Marin Headlands** section of the Golden Gate National Recreation Area – largely undeveloped land, except for the concrete remains of old forts and gun emplacements standing guard over the entrance to the bay. The coastline here is much more rugged than it is on the San Francisco side, and though it makes a great place for an aimless, cliff-top scramble, or a walk along the beach, it's impossible not to be at least a little sobered by the presence of so many military relics – even if none was ever fired in a war. The oldest of these artillery batteries date from the Civil War, and the newest were built to protect against a Japanese invasion during World War II, but even though the huge guns have been replaced by picnic tables and brass plaques – one of the concrete bunkers has even been painted to make a *trompe l'oeil* Greek temple – you can't overlook their violent intent. Battery Wallace, the largest and most impressive of the artillery sites, is cut through a hillside above the southwestern tip, and the clean-cut military geometry survives to frame views of the Pacific Ocean and the Golden Gate Bridge. If you're interested in such things, come along on the first Sunday of the month and take a guided tour of an abandoned 1950s ballistic missile launchpad, complete with disarmed nuclear missiles. The one non-military thing to see, the **Point Bonita Lighthouse**, stands at the very end of the Headlands, where it's open for tours at weekends, except during the winter.

Most of what there is to do out here is concentrated half a mile to the north, around the rocky cliffs and islets of the point. Adjacent to the **Marin Headlands Visitor Center** (daily 8.30am–4.30pm; ☎331-1450) – also the end of the *Muni* bus #76 route from San Francisco on Sundays and holidays – there's a wide sandy **beach** in between the chilly ocean and swimmably warm-water **Rodeo Lagoon**. The visitor centre has maps and information, and handles reservations for the Headlands' free campsites (see above), each three miles from the beach and nearest road. Next to the centre, the **Marine Mammal Center** rescues and rehabilitates injured and orphaned sea creatures, whom you can visit while they recover; there's also a series of displays on the marine ecosystem, and a bookshop that sells t-shirts and posters. The largest of the old army officers' quarters in the adjacent Fort Barry, half a mile to the east, has been converted into the spacious and homely **Golden Gate Youth Hostel** (see above for details), an excellent base for more extended explorations of the inland ridges and valleys.

Sausalito

SAUSALITO, along the bay below US-101, is a pretty, smug little town of exclusive restaurants and pricey boutiques along a picturesque waterfront promenade. Very expensive, quirkily designed houses climb the overgrown cliffs above Bridgeway Avenue, the main road and bus route through town. Sausalito used to be a gritty community of fishermen and sea-traders, full of bars and bordellos, and despite its upscale modern face it's still a fun day out from San Francisco by ferry, the boats arriving next to the Sausalito Yacht Club in the town centre. Hang out for a while along the marina and watch the crowds strolling along the esplanade, or climb the stairways across Bridgeway and amble among the many grand houses.

The old working wharves and warehouses that made Sausalito a haven for smugglers and Prohibition-era rum-runners are long gone. Most have been taken over by dull steakhouses like the *Charthouse* – fifty years ago one of the settings for Orson Welles' waterfront murder-mystery, *The Lady from Shanghai*. However, some oceanside stretches have, for the moment at least, survived the tourist onslaught. Half a mile north of the town centre along Bridgeway Avenue, an ad hoc community of exotic barges and **houseboats**, some of which have been moored here since the 1950s, is being threatened with eviction to make way for yet another luxury marina and bay-view office-block development. In the meantime many of the boats – one looks like a South Pacific island, another like the Taj Mahal – can be viewed from the marina behind the large brown shed that houses the Army Corps of Engineers **museum** (summer Tues–Sun 10am–6pm, other times Mon–Sat 9am–4pm; free), which features a massive working model of the San Francisco Bay, simulating changing tides and powerful currents.

The Marin County coast to Bolinas

The Shoreline Highway, Hwy-1, cuts off west from US-101 just north of Sausalito, following the old main highway through the dull outskirts of MARIN CITY. The first turning on the left, Tennessee Valley Road, leads up to the less-visited northern expanses of the Golden Gate National Recreation Area. You can make a beautiful three-mile hike from the car park at the end of the road, heading down along the secluded and lushly green **Tennessee Valley** to a small beach by a rocky cove; or you can take a guided tour on horseback from *Miwok Livery* ($15 per hr; ☎383-8048).

Highway 1 twists up the canyon to a crest, where Panoramic Highway spears off to the right, following the ridge north to Muir Woods and Mount Tamalpais (see below); *Golden Gate Transit* bus #63 to Stinson Beach follows this route every hour on weekends and holidays only. Two miles down from the crest, a small unpaved road cuts off to the left, dropping down to the bottom of the broad canyon to the **Green Gulch Farm and Zen Center** (☎383-3134), an organic farm and Buddhist retreat, with an authentic Japanese tea house and a simple but refined prayer hall (see "Accommodation", above). Beyond the Zen Center, the road down from Muir Woods rejoins Hwy-1 at **Muir Beach**, a surprisingly dark and usually uncrowded strand around a semicircular cove. Three miles north – assuming Hwy-1 has been reopened since the massive mudslide of January 1990 – **Steep Ravine** drops sharply down the cliffs to a small beach, past very rustic $20-a-night cabins and a $6-a-night campsite, bookable through Mount Tamalpais State Park (see above for details). A mile on is the small and lovely **Red Rocks** nudist beach, down a steep trail from a parking area along the highway. **Stinson Beach**, which is bigger, and more popular (it's packed at weekends in summer, when the traffic can be nightmarish) despite the rather cold water, is a mile further. You can hire surfboards and wetsuits for $10 a day from the *Livewater Surf Shop* (☎868-0333) along the highway at the south end of a short parade of shops.

Bolinas

At the tip of the headland, due west from Stinson Beach, is the village of **BOLINAS**, though you may have a hard time finding it – road signs marking the turnoff from Hwy-1 are removed as soon as they're put up by locals hoping to keep their hamlet all to themselves. The campaign may have backfired, though, since press coverage of the "sign war" has done more to publicise the town than any road sign every did; to get there, take the first left beyond the estuary and follow the road to the end. The village itself is a small enclave of artists and writers (the late trout-fishing author Richard Brautigan and basketball diarist Jim Carroll among them), and there's not a lot to see – though you can get a feel for the place (and pick up a tasty sandwich and bags of fresh fruit and veg) at the *Bolinas People's Store* in the block-long village centre.

Beyond Bolinas there's a rocky beach at the end of Wharf Road west of the village; and **Duxbury Reef Nature Reserve**, half a mile west at the end of Elm Road, is well worth a look for its tidepools, full of starfish, crabs and sea anemones. Otherwise, Mesa Road heads north from Bolinas past the **Point Reyes Bird Observatory** (☎868-0655) – best visited in the morning, though open for informal tours all day. The first bird observatory in the US, this is still an important research and study centre: if you time it right you may be able to watch, or even help, the staff as they put coloured bands on the birds to keep track of them.

Beyond here the road is no longer paved, and leads on to the **Palomarin Trailhead**, the southern access into the Point Reyes National Seashore (see p.423). The best of the many beautiful hikes around the area leads past a number of small lakes and meadows for three miles to **Alamere Falls**, which plunge down the cliffs onto tiny **Wildcat Beach**.

Mount Tamalpais and Muir Woods

Mount Tamalpais dominates the skyline of the Marin peninsula, hulking over the cool canyons of the rest of the county in a crisp yet voluptuous silhouette, and dividing the county into two distinct parts: the wild western slopes above the Pacific coast and the increasingly suburban communities along the calmer bay frontage. Panoramic Highway branches off from Hwy-1 along the crest through the centre of **Mount Tamalpais State Park**, which has some thirty miles of hiking trails and many campsites, though most of the redwood trees which once covered its slopes have long since been chopped down to form the posts and beams of San Francisco's Victorian houses. One grove of these towering trees does remain, however, protected as the **Muir Woods National Monument** (daily 8am–sunset; free), a mile down Muir Woods Road from Panoramic Highway. It's a tranquil and majestic spot, with sunlight filtering three hundred feet down from the treetops to the laurel- and fern-covered canyon below. The canyon's steep sides are what saved it from Mill Valley's lumbermen, and today it's one of the only first-growth redwood groves between San Francisco and the fantastic forests of Redwood National Park, up the coast near the Oregon border. Being so close to San Francisco, Muir Woods is a popular target, and the trails nearest the car park have been paved and are often packed with coach-tour hordes. However, if you visit during the week, or outside midsummer, it's easy enough to leave the crowds behind, especially if you're willing to head off up the steep trails that climb the canyon sides.

Mill Valley

From the East Peak of Mount Tamalpais, it's a quick two-mile hike downhill, following the Temelpa Trail through velvety shrubs of chaparral, to the town of **MILL VALLEY**, the oldest and most enticing of the inland towns of Marin County, also accessible every half-hour by *Golden Gate Transit* bus #10 from San Francisco and Sausalito. This was originally a logging centre, from which the destruction of the surrounding redwoods was organised, but for many years the town has made a healthy living out of tourism. The *Mill Valley and Mount Tamalpais Scenic Railway* – "the crookedest railway in the world" the blurb goes – was cut into the slopes above the town in 1896, twisting up through nearly three hundred tight curves in under eight miles, a trip which proved so popular with tourists that the line was extended down into Muir Woods in 1907, though road-building and fire combined to put an end to the railway by 1930. You can, however, follow the old railway from the end of Summit Avenue in Mill Valley, a route that's popular with daredevils on all-terrain **mountain bikes** (which were, incidentally, invented here). There's more sport each June, when runners and assorted masochists come together for the **Dipsea**, a fiercely competitive seven-mile cross-country race over the mountains through Muir Woods to Stinson Beach.

The town centres today around the *Book Depot and Cafe* (daily 7am–10pm), a popular bookshop, café and meeting place on Throckmorton and Miller. The **Chamber of Commerce** (Mon–Sat 9am–5pm; ☎388-9700), next door, has listings and maps that show the many local cafés, restaurants, and hiking trails.

Tiburon and Angel Island

TIBURON, at the tip of a narrow peninsula three miles east of US-101, is, like Sausalito, a ritzy harbourside village to which hundreds of people come each weekend, via direct *Red and White Fleet* ferries from Pier 41 near Fisherman's Wharf in San Francisco, and regular buses from elsewhere in Marin. It's a relaxed place, less touristy than Sausalito, and if you're in the mood to take it easy and watch the boats sail across the bay, it's a good place to sit out on the sunny deck of one of many cafés and bars and key in on the life of the town. There are few specific sights to look out for, but it's quite pleasant just to wander around, popping into the odd gallery or antique shop.

Tiburon, however, is soon exhausted, and you'd do best to take the hourly *Angel Island Ferry* a mile offshore ($3 round trip, plus $1 per bicycle; ☎435-2131) to the largest island in the San Francisco Bay, ten times the size of Alcatraz. **Angel Island** is now officially a state park, but over the years it's served a variety of purposes, everything from a home for Miwok Native Americans to a World War II prisoner-of-war camp. It's full of ghostly **ruins** of old military installations, and, with oak and eucalyptus trees and sagebrush covering the hills above rocky coves and sandy beaches, feels quite apart from the mainland. It's another excellent place to **cycle**: a five-mile road rings the island, and an unpaved track (and a number of hiking trails) leads up to the 800-foot hump of **Mount Hamilton**, which gives a 360-degree panorama of the Bay Area.

The ferry arrives at **Ayala Cove**, where there's a small **snack bar** selling hot dogs and cold drinks – the only sustenance available on the island, so bring a **picnic** if you plan to spend the day here. The nearby **visitors' center** (daily 9am–4pm; ☎435-1915) has displays on the island's history, in an old building that was built as a quarantine facility for soldiers returning from the Philippines after the Spanish–American War.

Sir Francis Drake Boulevard and central Marin County

The quickest route to the wilds of the Point Reyes National Seashore, and the only way to get there on public transport, is by way of **Sir Francis Drake Boulevard**, which cuts across central Marin County from the Larkspur ferry landing through the inland towns of San Anselmo and Fairfax, reaching the coast thirty miles west at a crescent-shaped bay, where. in 1579, Drake landed and claimed all of what he called Nova Albion for England. The route makes an excellent day-long cycling tour, and there are good beaches, a youth hostel and some tasty restaurants at the end of the road.

SAN ANSELMO, set in a broad valley two miles north of Mount Tam, calls itself "the antiques capital of Northern California" and sports a tiny centre of speciality shops, furniture stores and cafés that draws out many San Francisco punters at weekends. The ivy-covered **San Francisco Theological Seminary** dominates the town from the hill above, and the very green and leafy **Creek**

Park along the creek winds through the town centre, but otherwise there's not a lot to do but eat and drink – or browse through fine **bookshops** like *Oliver's Books*, at 645 San Anselmo Avenue.

Center Boulevard follows the tree-lined creek west for a mile to **FAIRFAX**, a town that's much less ostentatiously hedonistic than the harbourside towns, though in many ways it still typifies Marin lifestyles, with an array of wholefood stores and bookshops geared to a thoughtfully mellow crowd. From Fairfax, the narrow **Bolinas Road** twists up and over the mountains to the coast at Stinson Beach, while Sir Francis Drake Boulevard meanders through a pastoral land-scape of ranch-style houses hidden away up oak-covered valleys – an area that was used as the location for Alan Parker's tear-jerking saga of Marin County life, *Shoot the Moon*, in which a slobby Albert Finney starred as a philandering writer.

Ten miles west of Fairfax along Sir Francis Drake Boulevard, **Samuel Taylor State Park** has excellent **camping** (see p.418 for details); five miles more brings you to the coastal Hwy-1 and the village of OLEMA, a mile north of which sits the town of **POINT REYES STATION**, a good place to stop off for a bite to eat or to pick up picnic supplies before heading off to enjoy the wide-open spaces of the Point Reyes National Seashore just beyond. *Point Reyes Bikes*, 11431 Hwy-1 at Main Street (☎663-1768), hires out **mountain bikes** for $20 a day, much the best way to get around.

The Point Reyes National Seashore

From Point Reyes Station, Sir Francis Drake Boulevard heads out to the western-most tip of Marin County at Point Reyes through the **Point Reyes National Seashore**, a near-island of wilderness that's surrounded on three sides by more than fifty miles of isolated coastline – pine forests and sunny meadows bordered by rocky cliffs and sandy, windswept beaches. The wing-shaped landmass is something of an aberration along the generally straight coastline north of San Francisco, and is in fact a rogue piece of the earth's crust that has been drifting slowly and steadily northwards along the San Andreas Fault, having started some six million years ago as a suburb of Los Angeles. When the great earthquake of 1906 shattered San Francisco, the land here at Point Reyes, the epicentre, shifted over sixteen feet in an instant, though damage was confined to a few skewed cattle fences.

The park **Visitors' Center** (daily 9am–5pm; ☎663-1092), two miles southwest of Point Reyes Station near Olema, just off Hwy-1 on Bear Valley Road, has engag-ing displays on the geology and natural history of the region; rangers can suggest good places to hike or cycle to, and have up-to-date information on the **weather**, which can change quickly, and be cold and windy along the coast even when it's hot and sunny here, three miles inland. They also handle permits and reserva-tions for the various **campsites** within the park. Nearby, a replica of a native Miwok village has an authentic religious roundhouse, and a popular hike follows the Bear Valley Trail along Coast Creek four miles to **Arch Rock**, a large tunnel in the seaside cliffs that you can walk through at low tide.

North of the visitors' centre, Limantour Road heads west six miles to the **Point Reyes Youth Hostel** (see above), continuing on another two miles to the coast at **Limantour Beach**, one of the best swimming beaches and a good place to watch the seabirds in the adjacent estuary. Bear Valley Road rejoins Sir Francis

Drake Boulevard just past Limantour Road, leading north along the Tomales Bay through the hamlet of **INVERNESS**, so-named because the landscape reminded an early settler of his home in the Scottish Highlands. Eight miles west of Inverness, a turning leads down past *Johnson's Oyster Farm* – where you can buy bi-valves by the dozen for half the price you'd pay in town – to **Drake's Beach**, the presumed landing spot of Sir Francis in 1579. Appropriately, the coastline here resembles the southern coast of England, often cold, wet and windy, with chalk-white cliffs rising above the wide sandy beach. The main road continues west another four miles to the very tip of Point Reyes, where there's a precariously sited **lighthouse** standing firm against the literally crashing surf. You can't tour the lighthouse, which is reached via a tiring 300 or so steps down the steep cliffs; even if you don't make that trek, the bluffs along here are excellent places to look out for sea lions and, in winter, migrating **gray whales**.

San Rafael and northern Marin County

You may pass through **SAN RAFAEL** on your way north from San Francisco, but there's little worth stopping for. It's the county seat and the only big city in Marin County, and it has none of the woodsy qualities that make the other towns special, though there are a couple of good restaurants and bars along Fourth Street, the town's main drag. The one sight to see in town is an old Franciscan **Mission** (daily 11am–4pm; free), in fact a 1949 replica that was built near the site of the 1817 original, on Fifth Avenue at A Street. The real points of interest are well on the outskirts: the Marin County Civic Center to the north and the little-known China Camp State Park along the bay to the east.

The **Marin County Civic Center** (Mon–Fri 9am–5pm; free; ☎472-3500), spanning the hills just east of US-101 a mile north of central San Rafael, is a strange, otherworldly complex of administrative offices, plus an excellent performance space, that looks like a giant railway viaduct capped by a bright blue-tiled roof. The buildings were architect **Frank Lloyd Wright**'s one and only governmental project, and although the huge circus tents and amusement park at the core of the designer's conception were never built, there are some interesting touches, like the atrium lobbies that open directly to the outdoors.

From the Civic Center, North San Pedro Road loops around the headlands through **China Camp State Park** (☎456-0766), an expansive area of pastures and open spaces that's hard to reach without your own transport. It takes its name from the intact but long-abandoned Chinese shrimp-fishing village at the far eastern tip of the park, the sole survivor of the many small Chinese communities that once dotted the California coast. The ramshackle buildings, small wooden pier, and old boats lying on the sand seem straight out of a John Steinbeck tale, the only recent addition a chain-link fence to protect the site from vandals. At the weekend you can get beers and sandwiches from the old shack at the foot of the pier, but the atmosphere is best during the week, at sunset, when there's often no one around at all. There's a **campsite** at the northern end of the park, about two miles from the end of the *Golden Gate Transit* bus #39 route.

Six miles north of San Rafael, the **Lucas Valley Road** turns off west, twisting across Marin to Point Reyes. *Star Wars* film-maker George Lucas lives and works here – his sprawling *Skywalker Ranch* studios are well concealed from the road – but the name is a coincidence. Hwy-37 cuts off east, eight miles north of San

Rafael, heading around the top of the bay into the Wine Country of the Sonoma and Napa valleys (see p.463).

Eating

For all its healthy and wealthy prosperity, Marin County's **eating** options don't really compare with those in the rest of the Bay Area. However, there are plenty of **restaurants** worth searching out if you're in the area, serving anything from pizzas and Mexican food to vegetarian crêpes and standard soup-and-sandwich combos, as well as some fine places whose settings – on the waterfront or high up in the hills – make them quite special indeed.

Casa Madrona, 805 Bridgeway, Sausalito (☎331-5888). Mediterranean staples meet California Cuisine in this delectable hotel-restaurant, which does excellent fresh seafood. Great view of the harbour, and service is anything but hurried.

Dipsea Cafe, 1 El Paseo, Mill Valley (☎381-0298). Hearty diner food, especially good for breakfast before a day out hiking on Mount Tamalpais.

Greater Gatsby's, 39 Caledonia St, Sausalito (☎332-4500). Handy, inexpensive pizza parlour a block from the waterfront on the north side of town.

Hilda's, 639 San Anselmo Ave, San Anselmo (☎457-9266). Great breakfasts and lunches in this down-home, cosy café.

Jenny Low's Chinese Cuisine, 38 Miller Ave, Mill Valley (☎388-8868). Whether you're after Cantonese, Hunan, Mandarin or Szechuan food you'll find it here. Main dishes cost $4–8.

Milly's, 1613 Fourth St, San Rafael (☎459-1601). Extremely healthy, wide-ranging vegetarian dishes such as Thai vegetable curries and jalapeno ravioli. Evenings only.

New Morning Cafe, 1696 Tiburon Blvd, Tiburon (☎435-4315). Lots of healthy whole-grain sandwiches, plus salads and omelettes.

Pelican Inn, Hwy-1, Muir Beach (☎383-6000). Great fish and chips ($8) or roast beef and Yorkshire pudding ($15) in a coaching-house atmosphere.

Rice Table, 1617 Fourth St, San Rafael (☎456-1808). From the shrimp chips through the crab pancakes and noodles on to the fried plantain desserts, these fragrant and spicy Indonesian dishes are worth planning a day around. Dinners only, with very filling set meals for around $15..

Sam's Anchor Cafe, 27 Main St, Tiburon (☎435-2676). Rough-hewn, amiable waterfront café. Good burgers, soups and sandwiches, plus Sunday brunch.

Station House Cafe, Main St at Third St, Point Reyes Station (☎663-1515). Open for breakfast, lunch and dinner every day but Tuesday, this friendly local favourite attracts people from miles around.

Drinking and nightlife

Almost every Marin town has at least a couple of **cafés**, open long hours for a jolt of caffeine, and, if you're after more relaxing liquid refreshments, any number of saloon-like **bars** where you'll feel at home immediately. While the nightlife is never as charged as it gets in San Francisco, most of the honchos of the Bay Area music scene – from impresario Bill Graham to psychedelic rangers the Grateful Dead – and dozens of lesser-known but no less brilliant sessionmen and songwriters live here, so Marin's **nightclubs** are unsurpassed for catching big names in intimate locales.

Cafés

Book Depot and Cafe, 87 Throckmorton Ave, Mill Valley (☎383-2665). Lively café housed in an old railway station, which it shares with a bookstore and newsstand.

Caffe Nuvo, 556 San Anselmo Ave, San Anselmo (☎454-4530). Great coffees and pastries, with a large balcony overhanging a creek, plus poetry readings and live music most nights

Mill Valley Coffee Roasters, 2 Miller Ave, Mill Valley (☎383-2912). Boisterous, always crowded coffee house right in the centre of town.

Patrick's Bookshop and Cafe, 9 Bolinas Rd, Fairfax (☎454-2428). Coffees and teas, and tasty soups and sandwiches, in this low-key hippie holdout; good selection of books and mags too.

Sweden House, 35 Main St, Tiburon (☎435-9767). Great coffee and marvellous pastries on a jetty overlooking the yacht harbour, all for surprisingly reasonable prices.

Bars

no name bar, 757 Bridgeway, Sausalito (☎332-1392). A thriving ex-haunt of the Beats which still hosts poetry readings and evening jam sessions.

Marin Brewing Company, 1809 Larkspur Landing, Larkspur (☎461-4677). Lively pub opposite the Larkspur ferry terminal, with half a dozen tasty ales – try the malty *Albion Amber* or the creamy *St Brendan's Irish Red* – all brewed on the premises.

Pelican Inn, Hwy-1, Muir Beach (☎383-6000). Good selection of traditional English and modern Californian ales, plus fish and chips (and rooms if you overdo it).

Sam's Anchor Cafe, 27 Main St, Tiburon (☎435-2676). Slightly posey hang-out for yachtsmen and wharf rats right on the water. It's packed on weekend afternoons but better after the sun goes down or during the week. A good range of food.

Sweetwater, 153 Throckmorton Ave, Mill Valley (☎388-3820). Large open room full of beer-drinking locals that after dark evolves into Marin's prime live music venue (see below).

Nightlife

Fourth Street Tavern, 711 Fourth St, San Rafael (☎ 454-4044). Gutsy, no-frills beer bar with free, bluesy music most nights.

New George's, 842 Fourth St, San Rafael (☎457-1515). Large dance floor and wide range of music in a friendly, good-time place that doubles as a charcoal grill restaurant. Performers range from local cover bands to Leon Redbone to Robyn Hitchcock, and cover varies from nothing to $15.

Sweetwater, 153 Throckmorton Ave, Mill Valley (☎388-3820). Small, comfortable saloon that brings in some of the biggest names in music, from jazz and blues all-stars to Jefferson Airplane survivors.

travel details

Buses

Greyhound

From San Francisco to Los Angeles (11 daily; 8hr); San Diego (11; 10hr 30min); Sacramento (4; 2hr); Redding (4; 7hr 30min); Portland (4; 16hr); Seattle (4; 20hr); San Jose (6; 1hr); Reno, Nevada (6; 5hr).

Green Tortoise

From San Francisco to Los Angeles (3 weekly; 11hr; $40); Seattle (2 weekly; 20hr; $70). Tours of Northern California and Yosemite also available, see *Basics*.

Trains

Amtrak shuttle bus from Transbay Terminal to depot in Oakland from where there is a daily service north to Portland and Seattle, east to Sacramento and across the country and south to Los Angeles and San Diego.

CHAPTER SEVEN

THE GOLD COUNTRY AND LAKE TAHOE

T he single most enduring image of California, after surfers and movie stars, is that of the rough and ready 49ers. Not the Joe Montana, football-playing variety, but the argonauts of the Gold Rush of 1849, who came from all over the world to get rich quick in the gold fields of the Sierra Nevada foothills, 150 miles east of San Francisco. The first prospectors on the scene sometimes found large nuggets of solid gold sitting along the river banks. Most however worked long hours in the hot sun, wading through fast-flowing, ice-cold rivers to recover trace amounts of the precious metal that had been eroded out of the hard-rock veins of the **Mother Lode**, the name given by miners to the rich source of gold which underlies the heart of the mining district. Many of the mining camps that sprung up around the Gold Country vanished as quickly as they appeared, but although there's been practically no development in the intervening years, about half the towns survive today. Some are bustling – and appealing – resorts, standing on the banks of white-water rivers in the midst of thick pine forests; others just eerie ghost towns, all but abandoned on the grassy rolling hills.

The **Gold Country** ranges from the foothills near Yosemite National Park to the deep gorge of the Yuba River two hundred miles north. The heart of the Mother Lode, where gold was first discovered in 1848, is Sutter's Mill in Coloma, in the foothills forty miles east of **Sacramento**. The largest city in the Gold Country – now the state capital and much the best jumping-off spot for the area as a whole – Sacramento was a tiny military outpost and farming community which boomed as a supply town for miners setting off in search of gold. The mining areas spread to the north and south of Sacramento and preserve distinct identities. The **northern mines**, around the twin towns of **Grass Valley** and **Nevada City**, were the richest fields, and today retain most of their Gold Rush buildings, in a beautiful, near-alpine setting halfway up the towering peaks of the Sierra Nevada mountains. The hot and dusty **southern mines**, on the other hand, became depopulated fast: they were the rowdiest and wildest of all the mines, and it's not too hard to imagine that many of the abandoned towns sprinkled over the area once supported upwards of fifty saloons and gambling parlours, each with its own cast of card sharks and thieves, as immortalised by writers like Bret Harte and Mark Twain.

Most of the mountainous forest along the Sierra crest is preserved as near-pristine wilderness, with excellent hiking, camping and backpacking. There's great skiing in winter, around the mountainous rim of **Lake Tahoe** on the border

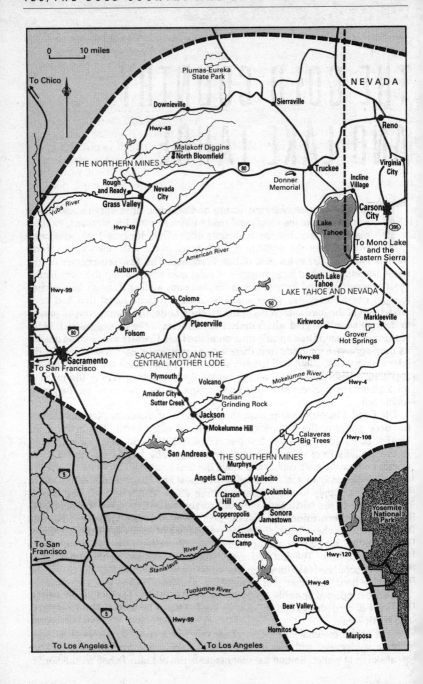

between California and Nevada, aglow under the bright lights of the nightclubs and casinos that line its southeastern shore. East of the mountains, in the dry Nevada desert, sit the highway towns of **Reno**, famed for low-budget weddings and speedy divorces, and **Carson City** – the Nevada state capital and one-time boomtown of the Comstock silver mines.

Hwy-49 runs north to south, linking most of the sights of the Gold Country; two main highways, US-50 and I-80, along with the transcontinental railway, cross the Sierra Nevada through the heart of the region, and there are frequent *Greyhound* bus services to most of the major towns. If you're just passing through, a quick stopover by public transport will be enough to give a palpable taste of the region, though to get a real feel for the Gold Country, and to reach the most evocative ghost towns, you'll need a car. Also, though it's all very pretty, the Gold Country is far too hilly, and the roads too narrow, to be much good for cycling.

The area code for Sacramento and the northern half of the region, including Lake Tahoe, is ☎916; the south is ☎209, and Nevada is ☎702.

RIVER RAFTING IN THE GOLD COUNTRY

Although plenty of people come through the area to see the Gold Rush sights, at least as many come to enjoy the thrills and spills of **white-water rafting** and kayaking on the various forks of the American, Stanislaus, Tuolumne and Merced rivers, which wind down through the region from the Sierra crest towards Sacramento. Whether you just want to float leisurely downstream, or fancy "eskimo rolling", careering through five-foot walls of water, contact one of the many river trip operators, like *Gold Rush River Runners* (☎1-800/344-1013), *Mother Lode River Trips* (☎1-800/367-2387), the *Sierra Kayak School* (☎916/626-8006), or *Zephyr River Expeditions* (☎209/532-6249), who also offer a variety of multi-day tours renowned for their gourmet cook-outs.

SACRAMENTO AND THE CENTRAL MOTHER LODE

Before gold was discovered in 1848, the area around what's now the state capital at Sacramento belonged entirely to one man, John Sutter. He came here from Switzerland in 1839 to farm the flat, marshy lands at the foot of the Sierra Nevada mountains, and the prosperous community he founded became a main stopping-place for the few trappers and travellers who made their way inland or across the range of peaks. But it was upon the discovery of flakes of gold in the foothills forty miles east that things really took off. Although Sutter tried to keep it a secret, word got out and thousands soon flocked here from all over the world, to mine the rich deposits of the Mother Lode.

This area is still very much the centre of the Gold Country, though it's rather richer in history than specific attractions. **Sacramento**, roughly midway between San Francisco and the crest of the Sierra Nevada mountains and well connected by *Greyhound* and *Amtrak* and the arterial I-5 motorway, is likely to be your first stop, a green open city of wide tree-lined streets centring on the grandiose buildings of the state government, and a somewhat sanitised waterfront quarter restored from the days of the Pony Express. From Sacramento two main routes climb east through the gentle foothills of the Mother Lode: US-50 passes through the old supply town of **Placerville** on its way to Lake Tahoe, and I-80 zooms by **Auburn** over the Donner Pass into Nevada. Both towns have retained enough of their Gold Rush past to merit at least a brief look if you're passing through, and Auburn in particular makes a good base for the more picturesque towns of the northern mines.

Sacramento

California's state capital, **SACRAMENTO**, is not at the top of most travellers' itineraries; indeed it had, until recently, the reputation of being decidedly dull, a suburban enclave of politicians and bureaucrats surrounded by miles of marshes and farmland. However, while it still doesn't even come close to San Francisco for action, Sacramento has been undergoing something of a transformation of late. Flashy office towers and hotel complexes, catering to expense-account promoters and lobbyists, have sprung up out of the rather suburban streetscape, enlivening the flat grid of leafy, tree-lined blocks; and multi-million-dollar redevelopment efforts have gone some way toward resurrecting the rowdy, free-for-all spirit of the city's Gold Rush past.

Set at the confluence of the Sacramento and American rivers in the flatlands of the northern Central Valley, Sacramento was founded in 1839 by a Swiss immigrant, **John Sutter**, on fifty thousand acres granted to him by the Mexican government. Sutter was a determined settler, and for ten years worked hard to build the colony into a busy trading centre and cattle ranch, only to be thwarted by the discovery of gold at a nearby sawmill. Instead of making his fortune, the gold left Sutter a broken man. His workers quit their jobs to go prospecting, and many thousands more flocked to the gold fields without any respect for Sutter's claims to the land. The small colony was soon overrun: since the ships of the day could sail upriver from the San Francisco Bay, Sacramento quickly became the main supply-point for miners bound for the isolated camps in the foothills above. The city prospered, and in 1854 Sacramento was chosen to be the fourth and final capital of the young state of California, equidistant to the gold mines, the rich farmlands of the Central Valley and the financial centre of San Francisco. As the Gold Rush faded, Sacramento remained important as a transport centre, first as the western terminus of the Pony Express and later as the western headquarters of the transcontinental railway.

Arriving, getting around and information
Sacramento is the hub of all the long-distance transport networks: being at the intersection of the I-5, I-80, US-50 and Hwy-99 freeways, it's dead easy to reach, and to leave. **Trains** (☎444-9131) from Los Angeles, San Francisco and Chicago stop four times a day at the station at Fourth and I Streets, near Old Sacramento, while an almost continuous stream of *Greyhound* **buses** (☎444-6800) pull into the station at 1107 L Street, a block from the K Street Mall. There's an **airport** twelve miles northwest of downtown that's served by most major domestic airlines: *Sacramento Airport Transit* vans (☎424-9640; $6) will take you from the terminals to downtown.

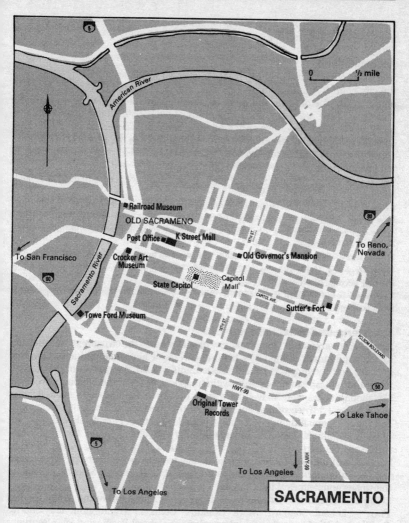

Downtown Sacramento, divided by the I-5 freeway into Old Sacramento along the river, and the modern centre along the K Street Mall, contains almost everything you'd want to see. The entire city is compact, deadly flat and entirely walkable, though many locals get around (especially along the 25-mile riverfront bikepath) by **bike** – hireable from *Sacramento Bike Rentals* at 916 Second Street in Old Sacramento (☎441-3836; $12 a day).

The **tourist office** at 1421 K Street (Mon–Fri 8am– 5pm; ☎442-5542) has maps and listings of accommodation and places to eat and drink, and the **State Office of Tourism** at 121 L Street (Mon–Fri 9am–5pm; ☎322-1396) holds tons of back-ground and practical information on the rest of California. The *Sacramento Arts*

Hotline (☎449-5566) has details of art exhibitions and cultural events, as do local freesheets like *Primal Urge* and *The Good Life*.

Accommodation

Sacramento has plenty of cheap places to stay, all within easy walking distance of the city centre. A number of motels cluster around the old Governor's Mansion on the north side of town, and there are dozens more along the highways on the outskirts. There are a few, somewhat down-at-heel 1930s hotels downtown, and many more flashy new ones springing up every year. There's no good **camping** anywhere within easy reach of Sacramento, but there is the new *AYH Gold Rush Home Hostel*, 1421 Tiverton Avenue (☎421-5954), near I-5. Prices listed below do not include the city's twelve percent hotel tax.

Americana Lodge, 818 15th St (☎444-3980). Central and low-priced (around $35 a night) motel, near the old Governor's Mansion.

Central Motel, 818 16th St (☎446-6006). Another cheap central motel – rooms roughly $35.

The Briggs House, 2209 Capitol Ave (☎441-3214). Attractive 1901 Colonial Revival house set in spacious grounds, just a half-mile from the State Capitol. Doubles with full breakfast cost from $60 a night.

Hotel Berry, 729 L St (☎442-2971). Faded old downtown hotel, near *Greyhound*.

Hyatt Regency, 12th and L Streets (☎443-1234). Brand new and very flashy, perfect for an expense account blowout to impress some high-flying politico.

Vagabond Inn, 909 Third St (☎446-1481). Near the river and Old Sacramento, with a swimming pool and doubles from $55 a night.

The riverfront: Old Sacramento

Sacramento grew up along the riverfront, where the wharves, warehouses, saloons and stores of the city's historic core have been restored and converted into the novelty shops and theme restaurants of **Old Sacramento**, inevitably a major tourist trap but not entirely without appeal. Most of the buildings are original, though some were moved here from nearby in the Sixties to make way for the massive I-5 freeway that cuts between the river and the rest of Sacramento, and the area, small though it is, has a period aspect not completely sanitised out of all recognition. Beyond the unassuming old chambers of the first **State Supreme Court** (daily 9am–5pm; free), upstairs from the *Wells Fargo* office on Second and J Streets, there's not a great deal to actually see. For Wild West fanatics, the **Information Center** across the way at 1031 Second Street has walking tour maps and historical information.

A block north from here is the hardware store, now a **museum**, where the **Big Four** – Leland Stanford, Mark Hopkins, Collis P. Huntington and Charles Crocker – first got together to mastermind the Central Pacific and later Southern Pacific Railroads that monopolised transportation and dominated the economy and politics of California and the western US for many years to come. For an initial investment of $15,000, the four financiers, along with the railway designer and engineer, Theodore Judah, who died before its completion, received federal subsidies of $50,000 per mile of track laid – twice what it actually cost. On top of this, they were granted half the land in a forty-mile strip bordering the railway: as the network expanded, the Southern Pacific became the largest landowner in the state, owning over twenty percent of California. An unregulated monopoly – caricatured in the liberal press as a grasping octopus – the railway had the power to make or break farmers and manufacturers dependent upon it for the transport of goods. In the cities, particularly Oakland and Los Angeles, the railway was able to demand massive concessions from local government as an inducement for rail connections, and by the end of the 1800s the Big Four had extracted and extorted a fortune worth over $200 million each. Strangely, it's their humble beginnings that are stressed in the exhibits on display here, mainly a collection of old wood-working and blacksmith's tools; upstairs there's a low-key idealisation of the men, with a re-creation of their boardroom and an archive of railway history.

There's a much better collection of railway artefacts on the northern edge of the old town, inside the **California State Railroad Museum** (daily 10am–5pm; $3), which brings together a range of lavishly restored 1860s locomotives straight out of a kid's cartoon, with "cow-catcher" front grilles and huge bulbous smoke-stacks. There are also a number of opulently decked-out passenger cars, includ-ing the 1929 St Hyacinthe Pullman sleeper car, which simulates movement with flashing lights and clanging bells and a gentle swaying back and forth. The old passenger station and freight depot a block south have also been restored as part of the museum; in summer a refurbished **steam train** ($3) makes a seven-mile, 45-minute round trip along the river.

There's another museum two blocks south across the I-5 freeway, at Third and O Streets: the **Crocker Art Museum** (Wed–Sun 10am–5pm, Tues 1–9pm; $2), which exhibits European paintings collected by Supreme Court judge Edwin Crocker, brother of railway baron Charles, in an odd complex of Renaissance Revival and modern buildings. More appropriate to its Sacramento setting, however, in the shadow of the massive interchange of the I-5 and I-80 freeways along the river and two blocks south, is the **Towe Ford Museum** (daily 10am–6pm; $1) – the world's most complete collection of antique Ford cars and trucks, from Model Ts and As to classic '57 T-birds and the "woody" station wagons beloved of the Beach Boys.

K Street: the modern centre

Running east from the riverfront and the Old Sacramento development, past the *Greyhound* and *Amtrak* stations, the **K Street Mall** is the commercial heart of Sacramento, with the downtown end of the modern suburban tramway running through the centre of a pedestrianised shopping precinct, amid a growing forest of new office blocks and hotels that tower over art deco movie theatres and neon-signed shopfronts.

Two blocks north of the mall at 16th and H Streets is the old **Governor's Mansion** (daily 10am–4pm; $1), the elaborate Victorian home of California governors up to Ronald Reagan; when this white, 1874 structure was condemned as a firetrap, he abandoned these high ceilings and narrow staircases in favour of a ranch-style house on the outskirts of town.

Isolated from downtown – just as the capital itself is isolated from the rest of the state – the noble dome of the **State Capitol** stands proudly in the middle of a spacious green park two blocks south of the mall, at the geographical centre of Sacramento. Recently restored to its original nineteenth-century elegance, and still very much in use as the seat of state government, the building is luxuriously appointed and brimming over with finely crafted details. Although you're free to walk around, you'll see a lot more if you take one of the free **tours** (daily 9am–5pm) that leave hourly from room B-27 on the lower ground floor, passing through the old legislative chambers decked out in turn-of-the-century furnishings and fixtures.

Sutter's Fort (daily 9am–5pm; $1), on the east side of town at 27th and L streets, is a re-creation of Sacramento's original settlement. An adobe house displays relics from the Gold Rush, and on summer weekends local volunteers dress up and act out lives in the manner of the 1850s. The adjacent **Indian Museum** (daily 10am–5pm; $1) on K Street displays tools, handicrafts and ceremonial objects of the native Americans of the Central Valley and the Sierra Nevada mountains.

Eating and drinking

Dozens of fast-food stands and pricey restaurants line the riverfront in the Old Sacramento district, but they're generally tourist-thronged joints with a vaguely Western theme, and best avoided. You'd do better to search out the city's many good eateries, a few of which are listed below. The watering holes of Old Sacramento, especially when one of the regular summer weekend music festivals is in full swing, are better after dark.

Ambrose Heath, 924 J St (☎448-4526). Healthy, stylish sandwiches in airy downtown café.

Annabelle's, 200 J St (☎448-6239). Bustling Old Sacramento Italian joint with all-you-can-eat lunchtime buffets.

Paraguay's, 1401 28th St (☎457-5737). Giant-size portions of pasta, and tasty brick-oven pizzas, for not much money.

Rubicon Brewing Company, 2004 Capitol Ave. One of Sacramento's more enjoyable haunts, with good Mexican bar food washed down by pints of the flavourful house-brewed *Amber Ale*, and live jazzy music weekend nights.

The Tower Cafe, 1518 Broadway (☎441-0222). Nineties version of a Fifties diner, good for burgers, vege-burgers, and late-night caffeine fixes.

Listings

Airport Sacramento Metro Airport is twelve miles north of the city centre on I-5, and served by a number of domestic airlines including *America West* (☎448-8364), *American* (☎443-3399), *Delta* (☎446-3464) and *USAir* (☎922-8021).

Area Code ☎916.

Car Hire *Thrifty*, 500 12th St (☎447-2847); *Budget*, 830 L St (☎973-8411).

Hospital *Davies Medical Center*, 15 miles west of Sacramento, has a 24-hour casualty ward (☎453-3790).

Post Office 801 I St (☎921-4383). Open Mon–Fri 8.30am–5pm, Sat 8.30am–noon; zip code 95814.

Riverboat tours The Paddlewheel steamboat *Matthew Mckinley*, departs at 2pm daily from the L Street landing in Old Sacramento for 90-minute cruises on the river (☎441-6481; $12.50 per person).

The Central Mother Lode

US-50 and I-80 head east from Sacramento through the heart of the Gold Country, up and over the mountains past Lake Tahoe and into the state of Nevada. The highways closely follow the old stagecoach routes over the Donner Pass, and in the mid-1860s local citizens, seeking to improve dwindling fortunes after the Gold Rush subsided, joined forces with railroad engineer Theodore Judah to finance and build the first railway crossing of the Sierra Nevada over much the same route as that used by *Amtrak* – even along much of the same track – today. However, while the area holds much historic interest, its towns aren't nearly as nice as those elsewhere in the Gold Country. Neither Placerville nor Auburn, where I-80 and US-50 respectively cross Hwy-49, is worth much more than a quick look. Coloma and Folsom, in between the two highways, have slightly more to offer.

Folsom

FOLSOM, halfway between US-50 and I-80 in the low foothills of the Sierra Nevada, has a single main street of restored homes and buildings that date from the days of the Pony Express, though the town is best-known as the site of the stone-faced **Folsom State Prison**, made famous by Johnny Cash. At the main gate, two miles north on Green Valley Road, an arts-and-crafts gallery sells works by prisoners, who get the proceeds when released. Across the road a small **museum** (daily 10am–5pm; $1) is filled with grisly photographs and the medical records of murderers and thieves who were hanged for their crimes. US-50 continues east to Placerville and the central Mother Lode, where gold was first discovered along the American River.

Placerville

PLACERVILLE, forty miles east of Sacramento, takes a perverse delight in having been known originally as *Hangtown* for its habit of lynching alleged criminals in pairs and stringing them up from a tree in the centre of town. Despite this gruesome start, Placerville has always been more of a market than a mining town, and is now a major crossroads, halfway between Sacramento and Lake Tahoe at the junction of US-50 and Hwy-49. For a time it was the third largest city in California, and many of the men who went on to become the most powerful in the state got their start here: railway magnates Mark Hopkins and Collis P. Huntington were local merchants, and car-mogul John Studebaker made wheelbarrows for the miners.

The modern town spreads out along the highways in a string of fast-food restaurants, petrol stations and motels. The old Main Street, running parallel to US-50, retains some of the Gold Rush architecture, with an effigy dangling by the neck in front of the *Hangman's Tree* bar; there also are many fine old houses scattered amongst the pine trees in the steep valleys to the north and south of the centre. Nearby, one of the better of the Gold Country museums is located in the sprawling El Dorado County Fairgrounds, just north of US-50. This, the **El Dorado County Historical Museum** (Wed–Sat 10am–4pm; free), gives a broad historical overview of the county, from the Miwok Indians to the modern day, including logging trains and a mock-up of a general store.

Placerville practicalities

Greyhound buses to Lake Tahoe stop three times a day in **Placerville** at 1750 Broadway (☎622-7200), a long walk east of town, where there are a number of $30-a-night **motels**, like the *Hangtown Motel* (☎622-0637) and the *El Dorado* (☎622-3884). The **Chamber of Commerce** office at 542 Main Street (Mon–Fri 9am–5pm; ☎626-2344) has local information and can help set up **river rafting** trips or find you a room in a local **bed and breakfast inn** for about $50 a night.

For **eating**, try the local concoction known as "Hangtown Fry" (included in the *Penguin Book of American Cookery*), an omelette-like mix-up of bacon, eggs and breaded oysters that you can taste at the *Miners Café* in the centre of town, opposite the Hangman's Tree. Also worth searching out, and not to be passed by if you've got a car, is *Poor Red's Barbeque*, housed in the old *Adams and Co* stagecoach office in El Dorado on Hwy-49 three miles south of Placerville, which serves the Gold Country's best barbecued dinners for under $6, with $1 beers and two-fisted margaritas.

Coloma and the Gold Discovery

Sights along Hwy-49 north of Placerville are few and far between, but it was here that gold fever began, when on 24 January 1848 James Marshall discovered flakes of gold in the tailrace of a mill he was building for John Sutter along the south fork of the American River at **COLOMA**. By the summer of that year thousands had flocked to the area, and by the following year Coloma was a town of ten thousand – though most left quickly following news of richer strikes elsewhere in the region, and the town all but disappeared within a few years. The few surviving buildings, including the cabin where Marshall lived, have been preserved as a **state park** (daily 10am–5pm; $3 parking fee).

A reconstruction of **Sutter's Mill** stands along the river, and working demonstrations are held at weekends at 10am and 1pm. There's a small historical museum across the road, and on a hill overlooking the town a statue marks the spot where Marshall is buried. Marshall never profited from his discovery, in fact it came to haunt him. At first he tried to charge miners for access to what he said was his land along the river (it wasn't), and he spent most of his later years in poverty, claiming supernatural powers had helped him to find gold.

Other supernatural forces are at work in the *Vineyard House Inn* (closed Monday; ☎622-2217), adjacent to the state park on Cold Springs Road, where the ghost of a man tormented by his wife haunts the cellar – now a popular **bar**, with music on weekend nights. If you want to sleep off a night's revelry, **bed and breakfast** is also available from around $65 a night for a spacious double room.

Auburn and Dutch Flat

If you're heading for the northern mines you might stop off at **AUBURN**, eighteen miles north of Coloma at the junction of I-80 and Hwy-49: *Greyhound* **buses** (☎885-9422) from Sacramento to Reno stop at 160 Harrison Avenue, for connections to Grass Valley and Nevada City (though there are also direct buses from Sacramento to these places if Auburn doesn't appeal). The outskirts of the town are sprawling and modern, but the Old Town district just off Hwy-49 has been preserved: a cluster of antique shops and saloons around California's oldest post office and the unmissable red and white tower of the 1891 **Firehouse**. For a free map stop by the **Chamber of Commerce** office at 1101 High Street (☎885-5616). South of the Old Town the **Placer County Historical Museum** (Tues–Sun 10am–4pm; $1) has the standard displays of guns and mining equipment. If you're stuck overnight, try the *Auburn Hotel* (☎885-8132), which has doubles for $35.

The twenty or so miles of Hwy-49 north of Auburn is a dull but fast stretch of freeway to one of the best parts of the Gold Country: the twin cities of Grass

Valley and Nevada City. For an interesting side-trip on the way there, or if you're heading for Lake Tahoe, take I-80 from Auburn 27 miles east to the small town of **DUTCH FLAT**, where old tin-roofed cottages are sprinkled among the pine and aspen-covered slopes. Miners here used the profitable but very destructive method of hydraulic mining (see p.442) to get at the gold buried under the surface, with highly visible consequences.

THE NORTHERN MINES

The northern section of the Gold Country includes some of the most spectacularly beautiful scenery in California. Fast-flowing rivers cascade along the bottom of steeply walled canyons, whose slopes in autumn are covered in the flaming reds and golds of poplars and sugar maples highlighted against an evergreen background of pine and fir trees. Unlike the freelance placer mines of the south, where wandering prospectors picked nuggets of gold out of the streams and rivers, the gold here was (and is) buried deep underground, and had to be pounded out of hardrock ore. In spite of that, the mines here were the most profitable of the Mother Lode – more than half the gold that came out of California came from the mines of **Nevada County**, and most of that from **Grass Valley's** Empire Mine, now preserved as one of the region's many excellent museums. Just north, the pretty Victorian houses of **Nevada City** make it perhaps the most enticing of all the Gold Rush towns.

A few miles away, at the end of a steep and twisting back road, the scarred landforms of the **Malakoff Diggins** stand as an exotic reminder of the destruction wrought by over-zealous miners, who, as gold became harder to find, washed away entire hillsides to get at the precious metal. Hwy-49 winds up further into the mountains from Nevada City, along the Yuba River to the High Sierra hamlet of **Downieville**, at the foot of the towering Sierra Buttes. From here you're within striking distance of the northernmost Gold Rush ghost town of **Johnsville**, which stands in an evocative state of arrested decay in the middle of the forests of **Plumas-Eureka** state park, on the crest of the Sierra Nevada.

There are very good transport links, via *Greyhound*, from Sacramento to Grass Valley and Nevada City, but you'll need a car to get to any of the outlying sights. Hitching is generally a pretty safe bet on the small, backcountry roads. Though there are no youth hostels there are a few inexpensive motels and a handful of bed and breakfasts; **camping** is an option too, often in unspoilt sites in gorgeous mountain scenery.

Grass Valley and Nevada City

Twenty-five miles north of Auburn and I-80, the neighbouring towns of **GRASS VALLEY** and **NEVADA CITY** were the most prosperous and substantial of the gold mining towns, and are today still thriving communities, four miles apart in beautiful surroundings high up in the Sierra Nevada mountains. Together they make one of the better Gold Country destinations, with museums and many balconied, elaborately detailed buildings, climbing irregularly up hills and hanging out over steep gorges.

Gold was the lifeblood of the area as recently as the mid-Fifties, and although both towns look largely unchanged since the Gold Rush days, they're by no means stuck in the past: the engineering expertise that enabled miners to extract millions of dollars' worth of gold from veins deep underground is now being put to work to make electronic equipment for television studios and space-age freeze-dried food for backpackers. Also, since the Sixties a number of artists and crafts-people – recently including songwriter Jonathan Richman – have settled in the old houses in the hills around the towns, lending a vaguely alternative feel that's reflected in the *Community Endeavor* newspaper, the KVMR 89.5FM non-commercial community radio station, and in the friendly throngs that turn out for the annual Bluegrass Festival at the end of August.

There are a number of inexpensive places to stay, a choice of cosy if more pricey bed and breakfast inns, and an indigestible number of places to eat and drink. *Greyhound* stops four times a day at 123 Bank Street in Grass Valley from Sacramento via Auburn (☎272-9091), and getting around is easy; both towns are very compact, and connected every half-hour daily between 8am and 5pm by the *Gold Country Stage* minibus ($1 a trip, $2 for a day pass; ☎265-1411).

Grass Valley and Nevada City accommodation

Places to stay don't come cheap, but if you can afford to splash out on a bed-and-breakfast, Nevada City in particular has some excellent options. Otherwise there are a couple of revamped old Gold Rush hotels, and a scattering of motels, though be warned that these may be booked up weeks in advance.

Motels

Airway Motel, 575 E Broad St, Nevada City (☎265-2233). Quiet, 1940s motel with swimming pool, ten minute's walk from centre of town. Doubles from $35 a night.

Shady Rest Motel, 10845 Rough and Ready Hwy, Grass Valley (☎273-4232). A little way out of town, but a pleasant walk; rooms from $30 per night or $135 per week.

Sierra Motel, 816 W Main St, Grass Valley (☎273-8133). Close to the centre, but a bit run-down, with doubles from $30.

Hotels and B&Bs

Annie Horan's, 415 W Main St, Grass Valley (☎272-2418). Sumptuous small home with antiques galore; rooms for two from $60 a night.

Downey House, 517 W Broad St, Nevada City (☎265-2815). Pretty 1870s Victorian home at the top of Broad Street looking out over the town and surrounding forest. Rooms for two with full breakfast from $60 a night.

Flume's End, 317 South Pine St, Nevada City (☎265-9665). Across the Pine Creek bridge from the centre of town, this small inn overlooks a pretty waterfall and features lovely gardens ranged along year-round Deer Creek. Rooms $85–125 a night.

Holbrooke Hotel, 212 W Main St, Grass Valley (☎273-1353 or ☎1-800/933-7077). Recently renovated and right in the centre of town, this historic hotel, where Mark Twain once stayed, has an opulent bar and double rooms from $65 to $120 a night.

National Hotel, 211 Broad St, Nevada City (☎265-4551). Another 1850s vintage hotel, with saloon and dining room downstairs and doubles from $50 a night.

Swan-Levine House, 328 S Church St, Grass Valley (☎272-1873). Accommodation with the artist in mind; the friendly owners also give instruction in printmaking. Attractively deco-rated, sunny rooms, in old Victorian hospital, from $50 a night.

Grass Valley

Jonathan Richman wasn't the first performer to settle in **GRASS VALLEY**: Lola Montez, an Irish dancer and entertainer who had been the mistress of Ludwig of Bavaria and a friend of Victor Hugo and Franz Liszt, embarked on a highly successful tour of America, playing to packed houses from New York to San Francisco. Her provocative "Spider Dance", in which she wriggled about the stage shaking cork spiders out of her dress, didn't actually impress the miners, but she liked the wild lifestyle of the town, leading her to give up dancing and retire to Grass Valley with her pet grizzly bear, which she kept tied up in the front yard.

A few mementoes of Lola's life are on display in the Grass Valley **tourist office** (Mon–Sat 10am–5pm; ☎273-4667), housed in a replica of her house, on the south side of town at 248 Mill Street. They have reams of historical information and lists of possible accommodation, and give away a walking tour **map** of the town, pointing out the oldest hardware store in California (which, sadly, closed in 1990 and has been converted into a tacky art gallery) among the wooden awnings and shopfronts of the gas-lighted business district.

The North Star Mining Museum

Grass Valley was the richest and most important of all the California mining towns, and today has two intriguing mining museums. The **North Star Mining Museum** (daily, April–Oct 11am–5pm, irregular hours rest of year; donations) at the south end of Mill Street is far and away the best of the Gold Country museums, both for the quality of the exhibits and the knowledge and enthusiasm of the guides. Housed in what used to be the powerstation for the North Star Mine, the featured exhibit is the giant **Pelton wheel**. Resembling nothing so much as a thirty-foot diameter bicycle wheel, this was patented in 1878 and became one of the most important inventions to come out of the Gold Country. A hundred or so small iron buckets, each divided into bowl-like scoops, are fixed to the rim of the wheel; a jet of water shot into the centre of the buckets is turned around to create a secondary jet, spinning the wheel at a speed of over seventy miles per hour. Many Pelton wheels were used to generate electricity, though the one here drove an air compressor to power the drills and hoists of the mine.

A series of dioramas in the museum describe the day-to-day working life of the miners, three-quarters of whom had emigrated here from the depressed tin mines of Cornwall. Besides their expertise at working deep underground, the "Cousin Jacks", as they were called by the non-Cornish miners, introduced the Cornish pump (and the pasty) to the mines. Some of these pumps had rods over a mile long, made of lengths of wood spliced together with iron plates. The surface mechanism and a mock-up of one of these mammoth beasts is also on display.

These great machines are now peacefully at rest, but when they were in action the racket could be heard for miles around. The noisiest offenders were the thundering **stamp mills**, a scaled-down version of which is operated upon request. In a full-size stamp mill, banks of from ten to eighty huge pistons, each weighing upwards of 1500 pounds, mashed and pulverised the gold-bearing quartz ore, freeing up the gold which was then separated from the gravel and dust by a variety of chemical amalgamation processes.

The Empire Mine State Park

The largest and richest gold mine in the state, and also the last to shut down, was the **Empire Mine**, now preserved as a state park a mile east of Grass Valley, just off Hwy-174 at the top of Empire Street. The 800-acre park (daily 9am–5pm; $1) is surrounded by pine forests, and most of the mining equipment and machinery was sold for scrap after the mine closed in 1956; wandering around today it's hard to imagine the din that shook the ground 24 hours a day, or the cages of fifty men descending the now-desolate shaft into the 350 miles of underground tunnels. After more than six million ounces of gold had been recovered, the cost of getting the gold out of the ground exceeded $35 an ounce, the government-controlled price at the time, and production ceased. Most of the mine has been dismantled, but there's a small but very informative **museum** at the entrance, and you can get some sense of the mine's prosperity by visiting the owner's house, the **Empire Cottage** at the north end of the park: a stone and brick, vaguely English manor house with a glowing, redwood-panelled interior overlooking a formal garden.

Nevada City

NEVADA CITY, four miles north, may have less to see than Grass Valley, but it's smaller and prettier, with dozens of elaborate Victorian homes set on the winding, narrow, maple tree-lined streets that rise up from Hwy-49. It's the least changed of all the Gold Country towns, and a gem for aimless wandering, following the many steep streets up into the surrounding forest.

A good first stop is at the **tourist office** (Mon–Sat 9am–3pm; ☎265-2692) at 132 Main Street, a block north of Hwy-49, to pick up a free walking tour **map** of the town. It's hard to pick out specific highlights, as it's really the town as a whole that's worth seeing, but one place to start is the newly restored **Old Firehouse**, the lacey balconied and bell-towered piece of gingerbread next to the tourist office, which houses a small **museum** (daily 11am–4pm; donations), describing the social history of the region. The heart of town is Broad Street, which climbs up from the highway past the 1852 *National Hotel* and a number of antique shops and restaurants, all decked out in Gold Country balconies and wooden awnings. Almost the only exception to the rule of picturesque nostalgia is the surprising Art Deco 1937 **City Hall**, near the top of Broad Street, which with a flashier paint job would fit quite happily in an episode of *Miami Vice*.

The **Miner's Foundry Cultural Center** (daily 9am–5pm; free), perched precariously above the Deer Creek canyon at 325 Spring Street, is an old tool foundry converted into a multi-use cultural centre, art gallery and evening performance space. Above the town at the top of Pine Street a small plaque marks **Indian Medicine Rock**, a granite boulder with sunbeds worn into the hollows of the rock by native Americans who valued the healing power of sunshine. Broad Street intersects Hwy-49 a block further on, and continues on up into the mountains as the North Bloomfield Road, which twists up the hills to the Malakoff Diggins (see p.442).

Eating and drinking

Both Grass Valley and Nevada City have some good places to eat and drink, including a few cafés that are open only for breakfast and lunch, closing in the early afternoon. After dark head to one of the many bars and saloons, where you'll often be treated to free live music. A couple of things to look out for around here are pasties, brought to the Gold Country by Cornish miners, and crisp-tasting Nevada City beer, brewed locally and available at better establishments.

Cafés and restaurants

Cirino's, 309 Broad Street, Nevada City (☎265-2246). Good deli sandwiches for lunch and Italian specialities at dinner, plus a full bar.

Gold Star Cafe, 207 W Main Street, Grass Valley (☎477-1523). Inventive breakfasts, great omelettes and a range of salads and burgers. Open 7am–2pm.

Main Street Cafe, 213 W Main Street, Grass Valley (☎477-6000). The best bet for a really good meal, this casual but refined restaurant has an eclectic range of dishes – from pastas to cajun specialities – as well as good grilled meats and fresh fish.

Marshall's Pasties, 203A Mill Street, Grass Valley (☎272-2844). Mind-boggling array of fresh-filled pasties.

Moore's Cafe, 216 Broad Street, Nevada City (☎265-9440). Plain-looking, all-American diner for breakfast and burgers.

Sierra Mountain Coffee Roasters, 316 Commercial Street, Nevada City (☎265-5282). Scrambled eggs and fresh bagels from daybreak, together with a range of coffees served all day.

Saloons, bars and clubs

Friar Tuck's, 111 N Pine Street, Nevada City (☎265-9093). Somewhat kitsch wine bar, with occasional live folk and jazz music.

Gold Exchange Saloon, 158 Mill Street, Grass Valley (☎272-5509). Lively, unpretentious and unthreatening beer bar and saloon, great for quenching a thirst after a day's hiking, biking or prospecting.

The Live Wire, 11990 Plaza Drive, Grass Valley (☎477-0855). The Gold Country's main live venue, with headbanging metal music most nights and bigger name rockers and cabaret performers sometimes passing through. Cover varies, usually around $5. Located just off Hwy-49, halfway between Grass Valley and Nevada City.

Mad Dogs and Englishmen, 211 Spring Street, Nevada City (☎265-8173). Pub-like bar with darts, good beer and regular live and danceable blues and rock music.

Main Street Cafe, 215 Main Street, Grass Valley (☎477-6000). Wine and cocktail bar next to restaurant, with live music most weekends.

CAMPING IN NEVADA COUNTY

One of the best ways to get a feel for the day-to-day life of the miners is to "rough it" yourself, camping out in one of the many easily accessible **campsites** in the surrounding hills, all of which you can only reach by car. On Hwy-20 east of Nevada City towards I-80, *Scott's Flat Lake* (☎265-5302), is privately operated, has the best facilities and charges $10.50 a night; seven miles on, *White Cloud* costs $6 a night; much further out, 24 miles east of Nevada City, *Fuller Lake Campground* is free. Along Hwy-49 north of Nevada City there are half a dozen more campsites, the most attractive of which, the *Sierra* campsite seven miles beyond Sierra City and *Chapman Creek,* another mile upstream, lie along the Yuba River. For details contact the **ranger station** (☎265-4531) in Nevada City, on Coyote Street near the tourist office.

Nevada County and the Malakoff Diggins

Grass Valley, Nevada City and the foothills of **Nevada County** yielded more than half the gold that came out of California. Before the deep, hardrock mines were established in the late 1860s, there were mining camps spread out all over the northern Gold Country with evocative names like "Red Dog" and "You Bet", that disappeared as soon as the easily recovered surface deposits gave out. **ROUGH AND READY**, five miles west of Grass Valley, survives on the tourist trade alone, its visitors coming to take a look at the only mining town ever to secede from the United States, which Rough and Ready did in 1850. The band of veterans who founded the town, fresh from the Mexican-American War, opted to quit the Union in protest against unfair taxation by the federal government, and though they declared their renewed allegiance in time for that summer's Fourth of July celebrations, the conflict was not officially resolved until 1948. Now there's only a handful of ramshackle buildings, including a petrol station and a general store.

Six miles northwest of Rough and Ready, off the winding Bitney Springs Road, the **Bridgeport covered bridge**, the largest in the US, spans the Yuba River: splintery wood shingles disguise the hefty trussed arch structure that's clearly visible from the inside if you walk the 250 feet across. The swimming area underneath offers some relief from a hot summer's day, but don't jump from the bridge – it's further than it looks.

Malakoff Diggins State Park

The waters of the Yuba River are now crisp and clear, but when the bridge was completed in 1862 they were being choked with mud and residue from the many hydraulic mining or **hydraulicking** operations upstream. Hydraulic mining was used here in the late 1850s, to get at the trace deposits of gold which were not worth recovering by orthodox methods. It was an unsophisticated way of retrieving the precious metal: giant nozzles or monitors sprayed powerful jets of water against the gold-bearing hillsides, washing away tons of gravel, mud and trees to recover a few ounces of gold. It also required an elaborate system of flumes and canals to collect the water, which was sprayed at a rate of over 30,000 gallons a minute. Worst of all, apart from the obvious destruction of the landscape, was the waste it caused, silting up rivers, causing floods, impairing navigation and eventually turning San Francisco Bay a muddy brown colour.

The worst offender, whose excesses caused hydraulic mining to be outlawed in 1884, was the **MALAKOFF DIGGINS**, sixteen miles up steep and winding North Bloomfield Road from Nevada City (or reachable via Tyler Foote Road, which turns off Hwy-49 eleven miles northwest of Nevada City), where a canyon more than a mile long, half a mile wide and over six hundred feet deep was carved out of the red and gold earthen slopes. Natural erosion has softened the scars somewhat, sculpting pinnacles and towers into a miniature Grand Canyon, now preserved as a 3000-acre **state park** (daily 10.30am–4.30pm in summer, weekends only for the rest of the year; $5 per car). Inside the park is the restored town of NORTH BLOOMFIELD, where old buildings from ghost towns around the Gold Country are being moved. A small **museum** shows a twenty-minute film on hydraulicking, and there's a $10 a night **campsite** near the eerie cliffs.

Downieville and the High Sierra towns

From Nevada City, Hwy-49 climbs up along the Yuba River gorge into some of the highest and most marvellous scenery in the Gold Country, where waterfalls tumble over sharp, black rocks bordered by tall pines and maple trees. In the middle of this wilderness, an hour's drive from Nevada City, **DOWNIEVILLE**, the most evocatively sited of the Gold Rush towns, spreads out along both banks of the river, crisscrossed by an assortment of narrow bridges. Hwy-49 runs right through the centre of town, slowing to a near-stop to negotiate tight curves that have not been widened since the stagecoaches passed through. Thick stone buildings, some enhanced with delicate wooden balconies and porches, others with heavy iron doors and shutters, face on to raised wooden sidewalks, their backs dangling precipitously over the steep banks of the river.

For what is now a peaceful and quiet little hamlet of four hundred people, Downieville seems strangely proud of its fairly nasty history. It has the distinction of being the only mining camp ever to have hanged a woman, Juanita, "a fiery Mexican dancehall girl", who stabbed a miner in self-defence. A decrepit green gallows, last used in 1885, still stands next to the County Jail, on the south bank of the river, to mark the ghastly heritage. Across the river and two blocks north, on the other side of town at the end of a row of 1850s shopfronts, the **Sierra County Museum** (April–Oct, daily 10am–5pm, weekends only rest of the year; 50¢) is packed full of odd bits and historical artefacts, including a set of snowshoes for horses and a scaled-down model of a stamp mill, "made by the boys of the shop classes 1947–8". Pick up a walking tour map of the town from the **Tourist Office** kiosk (☎386-3122), next to the firebell tower in the centre of town. They can also help out with accommodation, which is provided by two **motels** alongside the Yuba River: *Holt's Riverside Motel* (☎289-3574) or *Robinson's Motel* (☎289-3573), both on Hwy-49 in the centre of town, with doubles for $35 a night.

The full-size original of the county museum stamp mill is maintained in working order at the **Kentucky Mine Museum** (Wed–Sun 10am–5pm in summer, weekends only rest of the year; $2.50), a mile east of SIERRA CITY further up Hwy-49, where a guided tour looks inside a reconstructed miner's cabin, down a mine shaft and at various other pieces of equipment used for retrieving the gold-bearing ore until the mine was shut down during World War II. The ore was dug out from tunnels under the massive Sierra Buttes, the craggy granite peaks which dominate the surrounding landscape.

Fifteen miles beyond Sierra City, up and over the seven-thousand-foot Yuba Pass, Hwy-49 is joined by Hwy-89 for the next five miles until they diverge at the town of SIERRAVILLE, where the nearby **Campbell Hot Springs** (☎994-8984) are an excellent place to rest your road-weary bones, three-quarters of a mile east of town at the end of Campbell Hot Springs Road. These springs, in a wooded glade at the edge of the broad green meadow of the Sierra Valley, have been popular since the Gold Rush times and currently cost $8 for a day-long soak. They're also the home of the **Consciousness Village** spiritual training centre, a New Age community concentrating on the use of "conscious breathing", inspired by the Hindu-based teachings of Leonard Orr. Seminars and workshops are held erratically (and cost $200 a week), but the setting is superb.

Hwy-49 continues east for another thirty-five miles beyond Sierraville, ending near US-395, while Hwy-89 runs forty miles south along the Sierra crest to Lake Tahoe.

Johnsville

One of the few Gold Country sights not on Hwy-49, and after Bodie (see p.320) the best-preserved and most isolated genuine ghost town in California, **JOHNSVILLE**, just west of Hwy-89, 25 miles north of Sierraville, slumps in photogenic ruin surrounded by over 7000 acres of pine forest and magnificent alpine scenery, at the centre of the **Plumas-Eureka** state park – which has **camping** and miles of hiking trails. The huge stamp mill and mine buildings are being restored, and in the meantime a small **museum** (daily 9am–5pm) describes the difficult task of digging for gold in the High Sierra winters.

THE SOUTHERN MINES

Though never as rich or successful as the diggings further north, the camps of the **southern mines** had a reputation for being the liveliest and most uproarious of all the Gold Rush settlements, and inspired most of the popular images of the era: Wild West towns full of gambling halls, saloons and gunfights in the streets. The mining methods here were quite different from those used in the north. Instead of digging out gold-bearing ore from deep underground, claims here were more often worked by itinerant, roving prospectors searching for bits of gold washed out of rocks by rivers and streams, known as *placer* gold (from the Spanish word meaning both "sandbar", where much of the gold was found, and "pleasure", which the finding presumably incurred). Nuggets were sometimes found sitting on the riverbanks, though most of the gold had to be laboriously separated from mud and gravel using handheld pans or larger sluices. It wasn't a particularly lucrative existence: freelance miners roamed the countryside until they found a likely spot, and if and when they struck it rich quickly spent most of the earnings either in celebration, or buying the expensive supplies needed to carry on digging.

The boomtowns that sprung up around the richest deposits were abandoned as soon as the gold ran out, but a few slowly decaying ghost towns have managed to survive more or less intact to the present day, hidden away among the forests and rolling ranchland. Other sites were buried under the many **reservoirs** – built in the Sixties to provide a stable source of water for the agricultural Central Valley – that cover much of the lower elevations.

During spring the hillsides are covered in fresh green grasses and brightly coloured wildflowers, though by the end of summer the hot sun has baked everything a dusty golden brown. Higher up, the free-flowing rivers rush through steep canyons lined by oak trees and cottonwoods, and the ten-thousand-foot granite peaks in the Sierra Nevada mountains above offer excellent skiing in winter, and hiking and camping in the pine and redwood forests year-round. South from Placerville, Hwy-49 passes through **Jackson**, which makes a good base for exploring the many dainty villages scattered around the wine-growing countryside of **Amador County**, continuing on through the mining towns of **Calaveras County.** The centre of the southern mining district, then as now, and the only place you can get to without a car, is **Sonora**, a small but prosperous town of ornate Victorian houses set on ridges above steep gorges. Once an arch-rival but now a ghost town, neighbouring **Columbia** has a carefully restored Main Street that gives an excellent – if slightly contrived – idea of what Gold Rush life might have been like. The gold-mining district actually extended as far south as **Mariposa**, but the mines here were comparatively worthless and little remains to make it worth the trip, except perhaps as a quick stop on the way to Yosemite National Park.

The area code for the Southern Mines is ☎209.

Amador County

South from Placerville and US-50, the old mining landscape of **Amador County** has been given over to the vineyards of one of California's up-and-coming wine-growing regions, best known for its robust *Zinfandel*, a full-flavoured vintage that thrives in the sun-baked soil. Most of the wineries are located above Hwy-49 in the Shenandoah Valley near PLYMOUTH on the north edge of the county.

Amador City and Sutter Creek

Coming direct from Sacramento, Hwy-16 joins Hwy-49 at **AMADOR CITY**, whose short strip of false-fronted antique shops give it a distinctive, Old West look. The landmark *Imperial Hotel* at the northern edge dominates the town, its four-foot-thick brick walls standing at a sharp bend in Hwy-49. The hotel has just been done up, with sunny double **rooms** (☎267-9172) from $65 a night, and the **restaurant** on the ground floor is one of the more sophisticated in the Mother Lode, but otherwise there isn't much to the place.

The real appeal of **SUTTER CREEK**, a much larger town two miles south of Amador City and an hour's drive east of Sacramento, is at first obscured behind the tidy facades of the cloying touristy restaurants and antique shops that line up along Hwy-49 through town. Though there are a number of surprisingly large Victorian wooden houses – many styled after Puritan New England farmhouses – the town lacks the dishevelled spontaneity that animates many of the other Gold Rush towns, perhaps because its livelihood was based not on independent prospectors panning for *placer* gold but on hired hands working underground in the more organised and capital-intensive hardrock mines. It was a lucrative business for the mine owners: the Eureka Mine, on the south side of town, operated until 1958 and was owned by Hetty Green, at one time the richest woman in the world; while the Lincoln Mine made enough money for owner Leland Stanford to become a railway magnate and Governor of California. One unusual place that's worth a quick look, for closet Luddites and fans of Dickensian technology, is three blocks up Eureka Street from Hwy-49, where the cavernous and dimly lit **Knight's Foundry** uses huge belts and wooden pulleys, driven by a water-powered mill to make the moulds for cast-metal gears and machine parts.

Sutter Creek also holds the bulk of Amador County's accommodation and eating places, with two $75-a-night B&Bs, *The Foxes* (☎267-5882) and the larger *Sutter Creek Inn* (☎267-5606), side by side in the centre of town. The Eureka Street Courtyard, a half-block east of Hwy-49, has a handful of eating places like the *Sutter Creek Wine and Cheese Company*, where you can sample a dozen of the best local vintages and enjoy an *al fresco* picnic.

Jackson

After Sutter Creek, the town of **JACKSON**, four miles south, can seem distinctly blue-collar, mainly because of the huge *Georgia Pacific* lumber mill that serves as its northern gateway. Despite this first impression, Jackson makes a more afford-able base for exploring the surrounding countryside. Its well-preserved centre of photogenic brick facades makes a fine frame for the 1939 Art Deco front of the **County Courthouse**, at the top of the hill, and further along the crest, the **Amador County Museum** at 225 Church Street (Wed–Sun 10am–4pm; $1) has displays of all the usual Gold Rush artefacts, but is most worth a look for its detailed models of the local hardrock mines which were in use up until World War II, with shafts over a mile deep. The headframes and some of the machinery from the mines are still standing a mile north of the museum, on Jackson Gate Road, where two sixty-foot diameter **tailing wheels**, which carried away the waste from the Kennedy Mine, are accessible by way of short trails that lead up from a well-signposted parking area. The headframe of the six-thousand-foot shaft, the deepest in North America, stands out at the top of the grade, along Hwy-49. The other major mine in Jackson, the **Argonaut Mine**, of which nothing remains, was the scene of a tragedy in 1922, when 47 men were killed in an underground fire.

The **Jackson Chamber of Commerce** (☎223-0350) gives away an excellent *Visitors Guide to Amador County*, full of maps and interesting local anecdotes, at its office along Hwy-49 behind Main Street. The best **place to stay** is the *National Hotel* (☎223-0500) at the foot of Main Street, a down-to-earth, friendly hotel with double rooms from $35 a night; if it's full, try the *Amador Motel* (☎223-0970) on Hwy-49, north of town. If you're hungry, *Mel's Diner,* on Hwy-49 near the town centre, is open all day for breakfasts and burgers; for more refined fare, try *The Balcony*, 164 Main Street. For **drinking,** the *Pioneer Rex Pool Hall and Card Room* at 32 Main Street is the modern equivalent of a Wild West saloon, with cheap beers and all-night poker games behind swinging louvre doors.

Indian Grinding Rock and Volcano

Hwy-88 heads east from Jackson up the Sierra Crest through hills which contain one of the most fitting memorials to the native Americans who lived here for thousands of years before the Gold Rush all but wiped them out. Nine miles from Jackson, off Hwy-88, a side-road passes by the restored remains of an old Miwok Indian settlement at **Chaw Se Indian Grinding Rock**, where thousands of small cups were carved into the limestone boulders by Indians for use as mortars for grinding acorns into flour. The state has begun to develop the site into an inter-pretive centre and museum of native American life, and have so far constructed replicas of Miwok dwellings and religious buildings – interesting even if they haven't managed to disguise the nails. Descendants of the Miwok gather here at the end of September to celebrate the survival of their culture, with traditional arts and crafts, and to play a spirited game a bit like soccer.

VOLCANO, a mile north, was named for the crater-like bowl in which it sits, and once boasted over thirty saloons and dancehalls – though the town is now little more than a shadow of its Gold Rush self. The densely forested countryside around, however, makes it well worth a visit, especially during spring, when **Daffodil Hill** north of Volcano is carpeted with flowers. The few bulbs planted a hundred and some years ago have since multiplied to over three hundred thousand. Signs directing you there are only displayed when the daffs are in bloom. A narrow, scenic road follows Sutter Creek twelve miles down a wooded canyon back to the eponymous town.

Hwy-88 heads east beyond the Volcano turnoff over the Sierra Nevada mountains through Carson Pass, closely following the route of many early settlers. This, the **Eldorado National Forest**, is beautiful during autumn, and winter snows turn the mountain and meadows around **Lake Kirkwood**, close to the Nevada border, into one of California's best ski cross-country resorts. **Grover Hot Springs State Park** sits on the Sierra Crest near Markleeville, and has $10-a-night **campsites**, hiking trails and 105°F natural (although sometimes crowded) hot springs.

Calaveras County

Calaveras County lies across the Mokelumne River, eight miles south of Jackson. There are a few good swimming and hiking spots on the north side of the river, along Electra Road; or you can push straight over the bridge, where a barely marked "Historic 49" turnoff loops around through the centre of **MOKELUMNE HILL**, perhaps the most evocative – and least touristed – town in the southern Gold Country, standing on a hilltop just east of the highway. Moke Hill, as it's called, was as action-packed in its time as any of the southern Gold Rush towns, but locals have resisted the onslaught of tourism, and the town today is an intriguing concoction of ruined and half-restored buildings. It also has a couple of good **bars**, one on the south side of town in the lobby of the *Hotel Leger* and another inside the three storey **Odd Fellows Hall** at the north end of Main Street, where the *Adams and Co* saloon – and ad-hoc historical museum – is one of the few places in the region that retains much of the rowdy spirit of the pioneer years. On a more sober note, the range of names and languages on the headstones of the **Protestant Cemetery**, set on a hill a hundred yards west of town, gives a good idea of the mix of people who came from all over the world to the California mines.

After the haunting decay of Moke Hill, **SAN ANDREAS**, eight miles south, seems hardly to warrant a second look: the town is now the Calaveras County seat and about the biggest for miles, but it has sacrificed any historic character it once had in exchange for commercial sprawl. What remains of old San Andreas survives along Main Street, on a steep hill just east of the highway, where the 1893 granite and brick County Courthouse has been restored and now houses one of the more interesting collections of Gold Rush memorabilia in the **Calaveras County Museum** (daily noon–4pm; 50¢). Local nightlife revolves around the *Black Bart Inn* across the street, named for the gentleman stagecoach robber, Black Bart, who was captured and convicted here. Black Bart led a double life. In San Francisco he was a prominent citizen named Charles Bolton, who claimed to be a wealthy mining engineer; in the mining camps he made his name by committing some thirty robberies between 1877 and 1883, always addressing his victims as "Sir" and "Madam" and sometimes reciting bits of poetry before escaping with the loot. He was finally discovered after dropping a handkerchief at the scene of a hold-up; police traced the laundry mark and got their man.

The mining camps of southern Calaveras County were some of the richest in the Gold Country, both for the size of their nuggets and for the imaginations of their residents. The author Bret Harte spent an unhappy few years teaching in and around the mines in the mid-1850s, and based his short story, *The Luck of the Roaring Camp*, on his stay in **ANGELS CAMP**, thirty miles south of Jackson. There isn't much to see here these days, except for the saloon in the *Angels Hotel*, on Main Street, where the 29-year-old **Mark Twain** was told a tale that inspired him to write his first published short story, the *Celebrated Jumping Frog of Calaveras County*. **CARSON HILL**, now a ghost town along Hwy-49, four miles south of Angel's Camp, boasted the largest single nugget ever unearthed in California: 195 pounds of solid gold that was fifteen inches long and six inches thick, worth $43,000 then and well over a million dollars today.

Nine miles east of Angels Camp, up the fairly steep Hwy-4, **MURPHYS'** one and only street is shaded by locust trees and graced by rows of decayingly monumental buildings. One of the Gold Country's few surviving wooden water flumes still stands on Murphys' northern edge, while the oldest structure in town now houses the **Oldtimer's Museum** (daily 10am–5pm), a small collection of documents and a wall-full of rifles. The *Murphys Hotel* (☎728-3454) across the street hosted some of the leading lights of the time and you can stay in the same rustic double rooms for around $50 a night. The **Big Trees of Calaveras**, a state park fifteen miles east, holds six thousand acres of gigantic Sequoia trees and makes for fine ski touring in winter, with hiking and **camping** the rest of the year.

LIMESTONE CAVERNS IN THE GOLD COUNTRY

Limestone caverns abound around the southern Gold Country. Three have been developed for the public, and are open daily from around 9am to 5pm; at $6 a go, it's not likely you'll want to visit more than one, though any of them can provide, at the very least, a cool and constant 55°F relief from the sometimes baking-hot summer days. At Vallecito, just south of Hwy-4, five miles east of Angels Camp on Parrot's Ferry Road, the **Moaning Cavern** is the largest in California, filled with strange rock formations, 150 feet below ground; the human remains on display here greeted gold-seekers who found the cave in 1851. The natural acoustics of the cavern, which caused the low moaning sounds for which it is named, were destroyed by the insertion of the spiral staircase that takes visitors down into its depths. **Mercer Caves**, a mile north of Murphys, focus on an 800-foot-long gallery of sculpted limestone, which takes the shape of angel's wings and giant flowers; the third cave system, California Caverns, are just east of San Andreas.

Sonora, Columbia and Jamestown

The centre of the southern mining district, and the only place you can get to easily without a car, is **SONORA**, fifteen miles southeast of Angels Camp, and a two-hour bus ride from the San Francisco Bay Area. Now a logging town, set on steep ravines, Sonora makes a good base for exploring the southern region, with a thriving commercial centre that manages to avoid the tourist overkill. There's not much to see beyond the false-fronted buildings and Victorian houses on the main **Washington Street** and the Gothic **St. James Episcopal Church** at its far end. But the town is friendly and animated, and well worth ambling through.

Architectural and historical walking-tour **maps** (25¢) are available from the tourist office desk inside the small **Tuolumne County Museum**, 158 W Bradford Avenue in the old County Jail (Mon–Sat 10am–3.30pm, plus Sun in summer; free), which is worth a look for the restored cellblock, if not for the collection of old clothes and photographs.

There's a *Calaveras Transit* (☎209/728-1193) **bus** service to Sonora, once daily at 11am from the Pleasant Hill *BART* station, in the San Francisco Bay Area, and three times daily from the *Greyhound* station in the Central Valley town of Stockton. The *Tuolumne County Visitors Bureau*, 16 W Stockton Road (☎533-4420 or 800/446-1333), a block from Washington Street, is the best source of **information** on the area, but for details on camping, backpacking or outdoor recreation try *Sonora Mountaineering* at 173 S Washington Street (☎532-5621).

For a **place to stay** there's the *Miner's Motel* (☎532-7850) on Hwy-49, or the old adobe *Gunn House* at 286 S Washington Street (☎532-3421); a much nicer place to stay is the *Ryan House*, 153 S Shepherd Street (☎533-3445), a very comfortable and welcoming old home set in lovely rose gardens, two blocks east of the town centre, with B&B accommodation for $70 for two. For breakfast or lunch try *The Whitewater Cafe*, 79 N Washington Street (☎532-3543), or the gourmet health foods at *Good Heavens*, 51 N Washington Street (☎532-3663). After dark you'd do better heading to Jamestown (see overleaf).

Columbia

Perhaps the most striking introduction to the southern Gold Rush towns is **COLUMBIA**, three miles north of Sonora on Parrots Ferry Road. It's now a ghost town but it experienced a brief burst of riches, after a Dr Thaddeus Hildreth and his party picked up thirty pounds of gold in just two days in March 1850. Within a month over five thousand miners were working claims limited by local law to ten feet square, and by 1854 it was California's second largest city, with fifteen thousand inhabitants supporting some forty saloons, eight hotels and one school. The town missed becoming the state capital by two votes – just as well, since by 1870 the gold had run out and the town was abandoned, after over two and a half million ounces of gold (worth a billion dollars at today's prices) had been taken out of the surrounding area.

Columbia is preserved as a state historic park, but there is no main gate or entrance fee: the dusty streets and wooden boardwalks are open all the time. Most of the buildings that survive date from the late 1850s, built of brick after fire destroyed the town for a second time. Roughly half of them house historical exhibits – including a dramatised visit to the frontier dentist's office, complete with 100-proof anaesthetic and tape-recorded screams. The rest, somewhat unfortunately, have been converted into shops and eateries, where you can sip a sarsaparilla or munch on a Gold Rush hot dog. There's even a **stagecoach ride** ($3) along the old mining trails around the town, which leaves from in front of the Wells Fargo Building. Needless to say it's all a bit contrived, and summer weekends can be nightmarishly crowded, especially on Living History Days when volunteers dress up and act out scenes from the old days. But most of the year the tree-lined streets are empty, and the place as a whole makes for a reasonably effective evocation of Gold Rush life. If you want to stay nearby, the *Columbia Gem Motel* (☎532-4508), on Parrott's Ferry Road, has fairly basic accommodations in rustic cabins for $25 to $40.

Jamestown

Three miles south of Sonora on Hwy-49 lies **JAMESTOWN**, a somewhat saccharine-sweet little village that serves as the southern gateway to the Gold Country for drivers coming on Hwy-120 from the San Francisco Bay Area. Much of Jamestown burned down in a fire in 1966, but before that the town was used as location for many movies, most famously for the filming of *High Noon*, the train from which is now the biggest attraction of **Railton 1897 State Park**, a block east of Main Street – a collection of old steam trains that's open summer weekends, and offers half-day trips on restored local railways. Along with its train collection, Jamestown is one of the few Gold Country towns that still has a working mine – the huge open-pit Sonora Mining Corp operation west of town on Hwy-49 – and a number of outfits take visitors on gold-mining expeditions. One, called Gold Prospecting Expeditions ($35; ☎984-4653), gives some brief instruction in the arts of panning, sluicing and sniping, kits you out and gives you two hours to pan what you can from their local stream.

Main Street, lined with old balconied Gold Rush hotels like the *National* (☎984-3446) and the *Royal* (☎984-5271) – both of which have doubles from $50 a night – is the town's main drag, and also holds a few good places to eat. The *Mother Lode Coffee Shop* is popular with locals, and the more touristy *Smoke Cafe* (☎984-3733) has fairly tame Mexican food and huge margaritas. Across the street, *Michaelangelo* is a stylish trattoria, which serves up a range of pastas and pizzas.

Mariposa County and south to Yosemite

Hwy-49 winds south from Sonora through some sixty miles of the sparsely populated, rolling foothills of **Mariposa County**, passing near the remains of the town of **CHINESE CAMP**. It was here that the worst of the Tong Wars between rival factions of Chinese miners took place in 1856, after the Chinese had been excluded from other mining camps in the area by white miners.

Racism was rampant in the southern Gold Rush camps, something which also accounts for its most enduring legend, the story of the so-called Robin Hood of the Mother Lode, **Joaquin Murieta**. Very little is actually known of the truth behind the stories of this figure, yet virtually every southern Gold Rush town has some tale to tell of him. A romantic hero, rather than a real one, Murieta was probably a composite of many characters, mostly dispossessed Mexican miners driven to banditry by violent racist abuse at the hands of newly arrived white Americans. In May of 1853, the State Legislature hired a man named Harry Love to capture any one of five men named "Joaquin" wanted for cattle theft. Love soon returned with the head of a man pickled in a glass jar, and collected the reward. A year later J. R. Ridge wrote a story called *The Life and Times of Joaquin Murieta, the Celebrated California Bandit*, mixing together flights of fancy with a few well-placed facts – including the pickled head – and the legend was born.

Many towns tell tales of Murieta, but the town with the most likely claim to his patronage is **HORNITOS**, twenty miles west of BEAR VALLEY on the southern edge of the Gold Country. Hornitos, which is Spanish for "little ovens", was named for the oven-shaped tombs in the cemetery at the edge of town and was once a quiet little Mexican pueblo, one of the few in the area founded before the

Gold Rush. Now it's a heap of substantial ruins grouped around a central plaza. The population swelled to over fifteen thousand when Mexican miners were exiled from nearby mining camps by white miners who didn't feel like sharing the wealth, and the town became notorious for its saloons, opium dens and gambling halls, a favourite haunt of many an outlaw like Murieta – who, it's claimed, had his own secret escape route out of town via an underground tunnel.

Hwy-49 continues south to **MARIPOSA**, the county seat and the largest town for miles. The **Mariposa Museum and History Center** (daily 10am–4pm, weekends only in winter; donations), behind the *Bank of America* off Hwy-49 at the north end of town, has a little bit of everything to do with the Gold Rush – from miners' letters home to ancient bottles of *E & J Burke's Guinness Stout* – and is well worth a look if you're passing through. From Mariposa Hwy-140 heads east along the Merced River into Yosemite National Park (see p.303); *Yosemite Buses* ($9; 722-0366) do the trip four times daily from the *Frost Shop* on Hwy-49.

LAKE TAHOE, RENO AND CARSON CITY

High above the Gold Country, just east of the Sierra ridge, **Lake Tahoe** sits placidly in a dramatic valley, surrounded by high peaks and miles of thickly wooded forest. The sandy beaches around the shores attract thousands of families throughout the summer, and in winter the snow-covered slopes of the nearby peaks are packed with skiers. The eastern third of the lake lies in the state of Nevada, where flashy casinos cater to well-heeled gamblers, and neon signs shine out for miles around.

Truckee, twenty-five miles north of Lake Tahoe, ranges along the Truckee River, which flows out of Lake Tahoe down into the desert of Nevada's Great Basin. It's a main stop on *Greyhound* and *Amtrak* cross-country routes, but is otherwise little-visited, its life revolving around the lumber mill that dominates its old centre. **Donner Pass**, just west of town, was named in memory of the pioneer Donner family, many of whom lost their lives when trapped here by heavy winter snows.

Across the border in Nevada, **Reno**, at the eastern foot of the Sierra Nevada, is a downmarket version of Las Vegas, popular with slot-machine junkies and elderly gamblers; others come to take advantage of Nevada's lax marriage, divorce and prostitution laws. **Carson City**, thirty miles south, is more interesting: though far smaller than Reno, it's the Nevada state capital and has some engaging museums, many recounting the town's frontier history. Heading deeper into Nevada, in the arid mountains further east, the silver mines of the Comstock Lode, whose wealth paid for the building of much of San Francisco, are buried deep below the tourist-centre of **Virginia City**.

The two main trans-Sierra highways, I-80 and US-50, head east from Sacramento and are kept open year round, regardless of snowfall, passing by Truckee and Lake Tahoe respectively. Both places are well served by *Greyhound*, and there are also frequent services from the Nevada cities to the Tahoe casinos, though there's no public transport between Truckee and the lake.

Lake Tahoe

One of the highest, largest, deepest, cleanest, coldest and most beautiful lakes in the world, **Lake Tahoe** is perched in an alpine bowl of forested granite peaks, just east of the Sierra Nevada crest. Longer than the English Channel is wide, and more than a thousand feet deep, it's so cold at its depths that cowboys who drowned over a century ago have been recovered in perfectly preserved condition, gun holsters and all. Its position straddling the border between California and Nevada lends it a schizophrenic nature, varying from the forested state parks of the California side to the glitzy casinos of the eastern shore.

Getting there, getting around and information

Lake Tahoe is a hundred miles east of Sacramento on US-50, and well served by *Greyhound* and a number of coach tours, mainly catering to weekend gamblers. The ten daily *Greyhound* buses from San Francisco and Sacramento stop at the big Nevada casinos before returning to the **depot** (☎544-2241), on the California side at 1099 Park Avenue in South Lake Tahoe. As for tours, *See Tahoe Tours* (☎702/832-0713; $12) run eight buses a day from Reno to Incline Village on the north shore of Lake Tahoe, and *LTR Stage Lines* (☎702/323-3088; $18) run frequent buses from the well-served Reno airport to South Lake Tahoe; for "gambler's special" coach tours from San Francisco, see p.382.

STAGE buses (☎573-2080) run 24 hours a day all over the South Lake Tahoe area, and will take you anywhere within a ten-mile radius for a flat $1 fare. Around Tahoe City, on the northwest shore, *START* buses (☎581-6365) run hourly from Tahoma to Incline Village from 6am–6pm; a single ride costs $1, an all-day pass $2.50. **Car hire**, at about $30 a day, is available through the South Lake Tahoe outlets of all the national chains: *Avis* (☎541-7800); *Budget* (☎541-5777); *Hertz* (☎544-2327); and *National* (☎541-2277) – as well as slightly cheaper local firms like *Tahoe Rent-a-car* (☎544-4500) and *Aspen* (☎541-1613). Better, though, is to hire a **bicycle** from any of over a dozen lakeside shops, such as *Anderson Bike Rental* (☎541-0500) or the *Clean Machine Bike Shop* (☎544-7160), both in South Lake Tahoe.

Local **information**, maps, and help with finding a place to stay is available through the *South Lake Tahoe Visitors Bureau* at 3066 US-50, just west of El Dorado beach (☎544-5050); the *North Lake Tahoe Chamber of Commerce* in the Lighthouse shopping centre, Tahoe City (☎583-2371); or the *Incline Village Visitors Bureau*, 999 Tahoe Boulevard (☎831-4440). The US Forest Service **ranger station** (☎544-6420) at Emerald Bay has information on the many excellent **hiking** trails.

Lake Tahoe accommodation

Most of the hundred or so motels that circle the lake are collected together along Hwy-50 in South Lake Tahoe – the lake's largest settlement and home to the main Greyhound station – and on the north shore in and around Tahoe City. During the week, except in summer (the peak season), many have bargain rates, from around $30 for a double; however, these rates can easily double at weekends, so be sure to confirm all prices. If you get stuck for a room, the visitors bureau (☎1-800/288-2463) runs a free **reservation service**. Unlike Las Vegas or Reno, the casinos rarley offer good-value accommodation. **Camping** is only an option during summer (Tahoe gets upwards of twenty feet of snow every winter), and is best done at *Emerald Bay State Park* (☎525-7277) or *Nevada Beach* (☎544-6420) on the south shore, or at any number of backcountry sites in the surrounding forest.

Caesar's Tahoe Resort/Casino, 55 US-50, Stateline Nevada (☎702/588-3515 or ☎1-800/648-3353). Deluxe resort and upmarket casino, right on the lake; double rooms start at around $100 a night.

Falcon Motor Lodge, 8258 North Lake Tahoe Blvd (☎546-2583). Just east of Hwy-267 in Tahoe City, with doubles from $35 a night.

Lamplighter Motel, 4143 Cedar Ave, South Lake Tahoe (☎544-2936). Just off US-50, near the casinos and a short walk from the lakeshore. Doubles from $35. Other similar places nearby include the *Green Lantern* (☎544-6336) or the *Seven Seas* (☎544-7031).

Motel 6, 2375 Lake Tahoe Blvd, South Lake Tahoe (☎542-1400). Huge but nonetheless filled throughout the ski season and in summer. The best bet for budget accommodation. Doubles $38.

Around the lake

Though many stretches are breathtakingly beautiful, the 75-mile **drive** around the lake can be a bit of a disappointment if you're looking forward to non-stop scenic vistas. A better way to see the lake is to take one of two **paddlewheel boat** cruises: the *Tahoe Queen*, sets sail from the end of Ski Run Boulevard in South Lake Tahoe (daily 11am, 1.30pm and 4pm; $12.50; ☎541-3364); the *M.S. Dixie*, an authentic, restored Mississippi riverboat, leaves daily at noon from Zephyr Cove, three miles north of Stateline, for a two-and-a-half hour cruise ($11 per person; ☎702/588-3508) to Emerald Bay.

Perhaps most impressive is the view of the lake from above, either skiing in winter or hiking along the many trails that rim the lake basin, particularly the section of the **Pacific Crest Trail** which follows the Sierra ridge west of the lake on its way from Canada to the Mexican border. The lazy way to get up is by way of the **Heavenly Valley Tram** (daily 10am–10pm; $8), a ski-lift to Lake Tahoe's largest ski resort that operates in summer to shift tourists up the 10,000 feet mountain from South Lake Tahoe. Just over the Nevada border from here lies the gambling town of **STATELINE**, a mile north of which **Nevada Beach** is a fine sandy strand.

The prettiest part of the lake by far is along the southwest shore, where **Emerald Bay State Park**, ten miles from South Lake Tahoe (daily dawn–dusk; $3 parking fee), surrounds a narrow, rock-strewn inlet and the lake's one island, Fanette Island. The park has many good shoreline **campsites** and **Vikingsholm**, believe it or not an authentic reproduction of a Viking castle that's open for **tours** (daily 10am–4pm; $1) during the summer, at the end of a mile-long trail from the car park. Other grand old mansions, dating from the days when Lake Tahoe was accessible only to the most well-heeled of travellers, line the lakeshore two miles north in **D.L. Bliss State Park**, where the fifteen-thousand-square-foot **Ehrman Mansion** (daily 11am–4pm; free) is open for guided tours on the hour. The house is decorated in 1930s-era furnishings, and the extensive lakefront grounds were used as a location for the movie *Godfather II*.

Eating and drinking

Lake Tahoe has very few exceptionally good restaurants, but there are dozens of homely burger and steak places, rustic in decor with raging fireplaces standard.

For cheap food it's hard to beat the Nevada casinos: *Harrah's*, for example, has $1.99 breakfasts, $2.99 barbecued beef lunches and a range of full dinners from $4.99. The casinos are also good places to **drink** – roving barmaids bring free cocktails to gamblers – and hold most of the region's entertainment options as well: crooners and comedians mostly, plus small-scale versions of Las Vegas revues.

Bobby's Cafe, Hwy-267 at Hwy-28, King's Beach (☎546-2329). Excellent and inexpensive North Shore diner, with good breakfasts and Tahoe's best barbecued ribs.

Carlos Murphy's, 3678 US-50, South Lake Tahoe (☎542-1741). Pseudo-Mexican cantina, serving up large platefuls of anodyne Mexican-American food; come early in the evening for free Happy Hour nachos, cheap margaritas and $1 shots of Jose Cuervo.

Nephele's, 1169 Ski Run Blvd, South Lake Tahoe (☎544-8130). At the foot of Heavenly Valley ski resort, with good all-American grilled meat, fish and pasta dishes.

Red Hut Waffle Shop, 2723 US-50, South Lake Tahoe (☎541-9024). Always popular coffee shop, crowded early mornings with carbo-loading skiers.

Steamers Bar and Grill, 2236 US-50, South Lake Tahoe (☎541-8818). Fairly cruisey après-ski hangout that gets especially lively when there's a big game on the big-screen TV; bar food is good value.

Truckee and Donner Lake

Just off I-80, along the main transcontinental *Amtrak* train route, **TRUCKEE**, 25 miles north of Lake Tahoe, is a refreshing change from the tourist-dependent towns around the lake. A small town, lined up along the north bank of the Truckee River, it retains a fair degree of its late nineteenth-century wooden architecture along its main street, Commercial Row – some of which appeared in Charlie Chaplin's silent film *The Gold Rush*. It's more of a stopoff than a destination in its own right though, its livelihood dependent on the forestry industry and the railway. The town's rough, lively edge makes it a good base from which to see Lake Tahoe. There's no public transport between the two places, but it's not a bad day's cycling tour.

Truckee practicalities

Greyhound (☎587-3882) buses from San Francisco stop eight times a day, and *Amtrak* trains once a day from both directions, at the station on Commercial Row in the middle of town; there's a small but helpful **tourist office** (daily 10am–5pm; ☎587-2757 or ☎1-800/548-8388) in the lobby, with assorted maps and historical information. To get around, hire a **mountain bike** from *Mountain Bikes Unlimited* (☎587-7711) at the west end of Commercial Row for $20 a day; **cross-country skis** for $10 a day, $15 for telemark gear, from *Alpenglow Sports* (☎587-2025) on Bridge and Jibbom streets; or a **car** from *Rent-a-Dent* (☎587-6711) for $25 a day.

The best and cheapest **place to stay** is the *Star Hotel/AYH Youth Hostel* at 10015 W River Street (☎587-3007), on the south side of the river and the railway tracks, which has dormitory beds for $12 a night and double rooms for $30 to $50. A block away, the *Alta Hotel* at 10101 W River Street (☎587-6668), also has doubles for $35, as does the *Cottage House* (☎587-3108) on the west end of Commercial Row, though this is more shabby. There are a number of free **campsites** along the

Truckee River between the town and Lake Tahoe, off Hwy-89: the closest and largest is at Granite Flat, a mile and a half from Truckee; others are at Goose Meadows and at Silver Creek, four and six miles south respectively.

Truckee has a couple of good **places to eat**, especially *Coffee and*, a diner opposite the railway station, or, more expensively, the *River Street Café*, on River Street at Hwy-267. Though the old *Bucket of Blood* saloons of frontier-lore are long-gone, there are a couple of good places to stop for a **drink**, including the *Bar of America* or *The Passage* at the east end of Commercial Row – both of which have free **live music** most nights.

Donner Lake . . . and the Donner Party

A mile west of Truckee, surrounded by alpine cliffs of silver-grey granite, **Donner Lake** was the site of one of the most gruesome and notorious tragedies of early California, when pioneers trapped by winter snows were forced to cannibalise the bodies of their dead companions. The **Donner Party**, named for two of the families among the group of 89 travellers, had set off for California in April 1846 from Illinois across the Great Plains, following a short cut recommended by the first traveller's guide to the West Coast (the 1845 *Emigrant's Guide to California and Oregon*) that actually took three weeks longer than the established route. By October they had reached what is now Reno, and decided to rest a week to regain their strength for the arduous crossing of the Sierra Nevada mountains – a delay which proved fatal. When at last they set off, early snowfall blocked their route beyond Donner Lake, and the group were forced to stop and build crude shelters, hoping that the snow would melt and allow them to complete their crossing; it didn't, and they were stuck.

Within a month they were running out of provisions, and a party of fifteen set out across the mountains to try and reach Sutter's Fort in Sacramento. They struggled through yet another storm, and a month later, two men and five women stumbled into the fort, having survived by eating the bodies of the men who had died. A rescue party set off from Sutter's Fort immediately, only to find more of the same: thirty or so half-crazed survivors, living off the meat of their fellow-travellers.

The horrific tale of the Donner Party is recounted in some detail in the small **Emigrant Trail Museum** (daily 10am–4pm; $1) – just off Donner Pass Road, three miles west of Truckee in **Donner Memorial State Park** – which shows slides and a dramatised film of the events. The park also includes a memorial pillar, and the remains of some of the party's shelters. Nearby, on the southeast shore of the lake, there's a **campsite**.

Above Donner Lake the Southern Pacific railroad tracks climb west over the **Donner Pass** through tunnels built by Chinese labourers during the nineteenth century – still one of the main rail routes across the Sierra Nevada. For much of the way the tracks are protected from the usually heavy winter snow by a series of wooden sheds, which you can see from across the valley, where Donner Pass Road snakes up the steep cliffs. Rockclimbers from the nearby *Alpine Skills Institute* can often be seen honing their skills on the 200-foot granite faces; the institute offers a variety of climbing and mountaineering courses and trips. At the crest the road passes the *Soda Springs*, *Sugar Bowl* and *Royal Gorge* ski areas before rejoining I-80, which runs east from Donner Pass to Reno, Nevada, and west to Sacramento.

Into Nevada: Reno and around

If you don't make it to Las Vegas, you can get a feel for the non-stop, neon-lit gambler's lifestyle by stopping in **RENO, NEVADA**: "the biggest little city in the world", as it likes to call itself. Reno is a downmarket version of the glitz and glamour of Vegas, with miles of gleaming slot machines and poker tables, surrounded by tacky wedding chapels and quickie divorce courts.

Situated on I-80 at the foot of the Sierra Nevada, thirty miles east of Truckee, Reno is quick and easy to reach, and has plenty of cheap places to stay and eat, making it a good – and unique – stop off if you're doing the long haul by bus or train across the country from the east. The town itself may not be much to look at – apart from the countless neon signs – but its setting is magnificent, with the Truckee River winding through and the snow-capped Sierra peaks as a distant backdrop. It is also cyclist Greg LeMond's hometown.

There are three things to do in Reno: gamble, get married, and get divorced. To learn the ins and outs of the **casinos** before you blow your cash, invest $5 in the two-hour *Learn to Win Gaming Tour* (daily noon and 2pm), which leaves from next to the tourist office and includes lessons in the basics of craps, roulette, and blackjack ("21"), before taking you on a guided tour of the backrooms of a casino – where you can watch the gamblers being watched from behind mirrors and on closed-circuit TV.

GETTING MARRIED (AND DIVORCED) IN RENO

If you've come to Reno to get **married**, you and your intended must be at least eighteen years of age and be able to prove it, swear that you're not already married, and appear before a judge at the **Washoe County Court**, south of the main casino district on the corner of Virginia and Court Street (daily 8am–midnight; ☎702/785-4172), to obtain a **marriage licence**, which costs $27. There is no waiting period or blood test required. Civil services are performed for an additional $25, $30 during peak periods, at the **Commissioner for Civil Marriages** 195 S Sierra Street. If you want something a bit more special, wedding chapels all around the city will help you tie the knot; across the street from the courthouse, the *Starlight Chapel* – "No Waiting, Just Drive In" – does the job for a bargain $30, providing a pink chintz parlour full of plastic flowers and heart-shaped seats. If it doesn't work out, you'll have to stay in Nevada for another six weeks before you can get a **divorce**.

Reno practicalities

Reno's Cannon International **airport** is served by most major domestic carriers – including *American* (☎702/329-9217); *Delta* (☎702/323-1661); *US Air* (☎702/329-9365); and *United* (☎702/329-1020) – and there is an hourly, $2 bus from the terminals to the casinos in Reno's town centre. *Greyhound* (☎702/322-2974) and the *Amtrak* California Zephyr from Chicago both stop in the centre of town, on Second Street. Reno is also another good place from which to see Lake Tahoe, which you can either do independently or by taking an organised tour: *LTR Stage Lines* run a service to South Lake Tahoe (☎702/323-3088; $18), and *See Tahoe Tours* (☎702/832-0713; $12) run eight buses a day to Incline Village on the North Shore. To **hire a car**, try *Alamo* (☎702/329-5115) or *Thrifty* (☎702/329-0096 or 800/367-2277).

A good first stop in Reno is the **Visitor Center** at 135 N Sierra Street (☎827-RENO or ☎800/FOR-RENO), near the main casinos. They can help find you a cheap **place to stay**, and offer discount vouchers worth up to $15 in cash and $30 in credits for use in the casinos. For sleeping you could also try *Circus Circus*, at 500 N Sierra Street (☎1-800/648-5010), or the *Grand Hotel*, at 239 E Plaza Street (☎702/322-2944), both of which have off-peak (i.e. Sun–Thurs) doubles from $25, though prices usually double on holiday weekends. Reno also has some good places to eat, like the tasty Italian *La Trattoria* at 719 S Virginia, and the casino food is as cheap as, and much better than, what you get in Las Vegas.

Carson City

US-395 heads south from Reno along the jagged spires of the High Sierra past Mono Lake, Mount Whitney and Death Valley. Just thirty miles south of Reno, **CARSON CITY**, state capital of Nevada, is small by comparison but has a number of elegant buildings, some excellent historical museums and three world-weary casinos, populated mainly by old ladies armed with buckets of nickels which they pour ceaselessly into the "one-arm bandits".

Greyhound buses stop once a day in each direction between Reno and Los Angeles. There are a couple of cheap **motels** in town: the *Westerner* at 555 N Stewart Street (☎702/883-6565), behind the *Nugget* casino, and the *Trailside Inn* at 1300 N Carson Street (☎702/883-7300). The **Chamber of Commerce**, on the south side of town at 1191 S Carson Street (Mon–Sat 9am–5pm; ☎702/882-1565 or 800/634-8700), can help with practical details and runs architectural walking and driving **tours** of the town, particularly of the many fine 1870s Victorian wooden houses and churches on the west side.

Carson City was named after frontier explorer Kit Carson in 1858 and is still redolent with Wild West history. A good introduction is the **Nevada State Museum** at 600 N Carson Street (daily 8.30am–4.30pm; $1.50), across the road from the impressively restored **State Capitol**. Housed in a sandstone structure built during the Civil War as the Carson Mint, the museum's exhibits deal with the geology and natural history of the Great Basin desert region, from prehistoric days up through the heyday of the 1860s, when the silver mines of the nearby Comstock Lode were at their peak. Amid the many guns and artefacts, the two best features of the museum are the reconstructed **Ghost Town**, from which a tunnel allows entry down into a full-scale model of an **underground mine**, giving some sense of the cramped and constricted conditions in which miners worked.

Virginia City

Much of the wealth on which Carson City – and indeed San Francisco – was built came from the silver mines of the Comstock Lode, a solid seam of pure silver discovered underneath Mount Hamilton, fourteen miles east of Carson City off US-50, in 1859. Raucous **VIRGINIA CITY** grew up on the steep slopes above the mines, and a young writer named Samuel Clemens made his way west with his older brother, who'd been appointed acting Secretary to the Governor of the Nevada Territory, to see what all the fuss was about. His descriptions of the wild life of the mining camp, and of the desperately hard work men put in to get at the valuable ore, were published years later under his adopted pseudonym, **Mark Twain**. Though Twain also spent some time in the Gold Rush towns of California's Mother Lode on the other side of the Sierra – which by then were all but abandoned – his accounts of Virginia City life, collected in *Roughing It*, give a hilarious, eyewitness account of the hard-drinking life of the frontier miners. There's not much to Virginia City nowadays, since all the old storefronts have been taken over by hot-dog vendors and tacky souvenir stands, though the surrounding landscape of arid mountains still feels remote and undisturbed.

travel details

Trains

From Oakland to Sacramento (2 daily at 11.50am and 9pm; 2hr).

From Sacramento 1 daily leaving at 1.45pm to Truckee (3hr 30min); Reno (4hr 30min).

From Reno one daily leaving at 8.30am to Truckee (1hr) and Sacramento (4hr 30min).

Buses

Greyhound

From San Francisco to Sacramento (25 daily, 2hr); Auburn (4, 3hr 30min); Truckee (3; 4hr

30min); Reno (14; 5hr 30min); Placerville (7; 3hr 30min); South Lake Tahoe (11; 6hr).

From Sacramento to Auburn (8 daily; 1hr); Grass Valley (4; 2hr); Truckee (5; 2hr); Reno (18; 3hr); Placerville (6; 1hr 30min); South Lake Tahoe (12; 4hr).

Calaveras Transit (☎209/728-1193) runs one bus a day at 11am **from Pleasant Hill** _BART_ in San Francisco, and three daily **from Stockton** to Sonora (2hr).

LTR Stage Lines (☎702/323-3033) run every two hours **from Reno** to Carson City (1hr) and South Lake Tahoe (2hr).

CHAPTER EIGHT

NORTHERN CALIFORNIA

California's **northern coast and interior** covers around a third of the state, a huge area four hundred miles long and over half as wide of sparsely populated, densely wooded and almost entirely unspoilt terrain. A massive and eerily silent land of volcanic proclivity, this is California at its most deeply rural, and much of the region has more in common with the states of Oregon and Washington further north than with the built-up areas that make up much of the south (which you could say lucked-out in terms of money, but lost out on looks to the north). Commerce is thin on the ground, and most settlements are small towns populated by a mixture of diehard locals, supported by the backbone of the logging, fishing and farming activities, and ex-city dwellers who have spilled over from San Francisco's hippie days, venturing north to work on the marijuana farms of the so-called "Emerald Triangle". For both groups, the uniting factor is the land – and a deep-rooted suspicion of the big cities to the south.

As with elsewhere in California, the first inhabitants of the North were native Americans, whose past has all but been erased, leaving only the odd reservation or crafts museum. Much later, the Russians figured briefly in the region's history, when they had a modest nineteenth-century settlement at Fort Ross on the coast, ostensibly to protect their interests in otter hunting and fur trading though more likely to promote territorial claims. Mexican explorers and maintenance costs that exceeded revenues prevented them extending their hunting activities further south and in the 1840s they sold the fort to the Americans. It was the discovery of gold in 1848 that really put the north on the map, and much of the countryside bears the marks of this time, with abandoned mining towns, deserted since the gold ran out. Not a lot has happened since, although recently New Ageism has triggered a kind of future for the region, and cheap land prices are drawing more and more devotees up here to sample the delights of a landscape they see as rich with the rural symbolism of their movement. More realistically, it will probably be the upsurge in weekend homes for the wealthy that will save the region's bacon.

Immediately north of the Bay Area, the **Wine Country** might be your first – indeed your only – taste of Northern California, though it's by no means typical. The two valleys of Napa and Sonoma unfold in around thirty miles of rolling hills and premium real estate, home to the Californian wine barons and San Francisco weekend refugees wanting to rough it in comfort. The third, though less significant wine growing area **Lake County**, lies to the north of its prosperous counterparts on the other side of Mount St Helena, a mountain that deters most visitors, leaving it blissfully empty and easily affordable. Most people see the Wine Country as a possible day trip from San Francisco, though it is also feasible to take the area in before encountering the grittier territory further north, hooking up to the coast by bus from Santa Rosa.

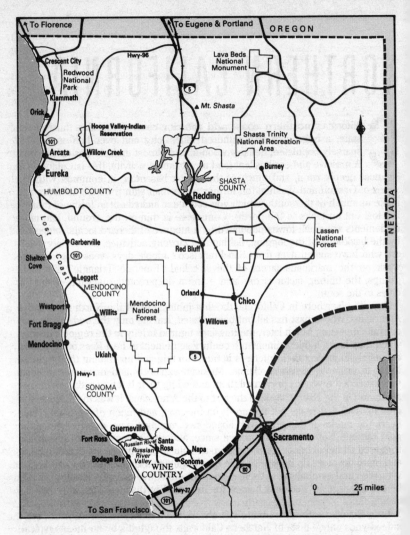

It's the **coast** which provides the most appealing route through the region, beginning just north of Marin County and continuing for four hundred miles of rugged bluffs and forests as far as the Oregon border. The three principal counties you pass through seem to vary little at first, but given time reveal tangible shifts, from the cutesy seaside homes of **Sonoma** to the coastal elegance of **Mendocino** and the big logging country further north in **Humboldt**. Trees are the big attraction up here: some thousands of years old and hundreds of feet high, dominating a landscape swathed in swirling mists and very sparsely populated. In summer, areas like the **Redwood National Park**, stretching into the most northerly **Del Norte** county, teem with campers and hikers, but out of season it can be idyllic. Even if things are rarely exactly swinging, towns like **Eureka** and **Arcata** at the top end of the northern coast make a lively refuge when the great outdoors begins to pall.

The **interior** is more remote still, an enchanting land whose mystery and sheer physical enormity can't help but leave a lasting impression. I-5 neatly divides the region, cutting through the forgettable Sacramento Valley northeast to the **Shasta Cascade**, a mountainous area of isolated towns, massive lakes and a forbidding climate. In winter much of this corner of the state is completely impassable and the region's commercial activities are centred around the lower, warmer climes of the largest town and transportation hub of **Redding** – not an especially inviting place, too big to retain any vestige of small-town cordiality, but too small to have many of the social amenities of a city. It is, however, the only feasible base if you want to explore the outlying regions of the **Whiskeytown-Shasta-Trinity National Recreation Area** and the **Lassen Volcanic National Park** – massive slabs of wilderness set aside for public use. During the summer months you'll find them packed with campervans, windsurfers and hikers, but, again, outside of peak season you're on your own.

Public transport services are not surprisingly sparse all over Northern California, and to enjoy the region you'll need to be independently mobile. *Greyhound* buses run from San Francisco and Sacramento up and down I-5 and Hwy-101, which stretches to the top of Humboldt County on the coast, stopping off at towns along the highway and branching off to Mendocino and Fort Bragg on the coast – though they are infrequent and do not solve the problem of actually getting around once you've arrived. Frankly, your best bet is a driving tour, fixing on a few points. Only the largest of Northern California's towns have any local bus service and for some of the remoter spots you could, perhaps, consider an organised trip, notably *Green Tortoise's* one-week tours – see *Basics* for details.

THE WINE COUNTRY

San Francisco during summer can be a shock – persistent fog and often cool temperatures can dog the city throughout the peak-season months. But you only need travel an hour north to find a warm and sunny climate among the rolling hills of **Napa** and **Sonoma Valley**. These valleys have long been the centre of the American wine industry, particularly Napa, and have attracted growers, many from Europe, for over a century. The vines withered during prohibition, but the growers struggled back, and these days their 29,000 grape-acres manage to turn out premium vintages that satisfy a wine snobbery that is often every bit as rampant as in Europe. It's a wealthy region, and a rather smug one, thriving as much on its role as San Francisco suburbia as on its wine connection – though the wine industry does dominate most aspects of life here. The soap opera *Falcon's Crest* is set in the Napa Valley and unravels the tales of feuding growers and their plonk empires. The Wine Country is also a major tourist attraction, both for foreign visitors and Californians: every year cars jam the entire length of the central Hwy-29 as visitors embark on a day's free drinking, thinly disguised as an avid interest in wine.

By and large **Napa** is home to the bigger concerns: of a combined total of over two hundred wineries in the valleys, 155 are in Napa, and as a region it's responsible for the lion's share of the four hundred million gallons of wine that are consumed every year in the US. With business ever in mind, Napa's prestigious wineries lay on organised tours and tasting, but you often have to pay for them. The smaller backroads wineries of the **Sonoma** valley are more down-to-earth and certainly less crowded than those of the Napa valley. Family-run businesses in the main, they are usually tucked away in obscure locations and harder to find, but the effort is worth it for the *free* tours and the elbowroom in the tasting hall. Lastly, **Lake County** takes a bit more determination to reach and isn't really recommended unless you want to lose the crowds altogether and spend most of your day getting there. What it does have to offer has less to do with wine than it does with its namesake, the magnificent **Clear Lake** – California's largest natural lake, surrounded by small settlements that depend almost totally on the folks with weekend homes around it for their survival. If you get fed up with trailing around wineries in the heat, you can always take a boat out on the lake for the price of a few good bottles.

Just west of the valleys, **Santa Rosa** is the main centre in the region, and holds most of its more affordable accommodation (hard to find in Napa especially); it's also the place to pick up connections on to US-101 and the coast, although beyond that there's little to draw you there. You can see the Wine Country fairly thoroughly by using San Francisco as a base and day-tripping it by *Greyhound* to Napa (around an hour's journey), and returning to the city at night – though this is more difficult if you want to see much of the Sonoma Valley, which isn't directly linked with San Francisco. Bear in mind also that peak tourist days see an estimated fourteen thousand cars and buses on Hwy-29, the main route through the region, and just getting to the valleys can take considerably longer than you might be bargaining for.

Wine tasting

If you're into **wine** you can have a lot of fun touring the various wineries, although you should be aware that vintages mean less in California than they do in Europe, thanks to the state's relatively benign climate. Having said this, Californian wines have been scooping up awards (much to the consternation of the Europeans) all over the place for some time now, and should not be dismissed because of their origin; the days of cheap Californian plonk and little else, certainly, are over. When touring, limit yourself to about three wineries a day: any more and it becomes not only a bore, but your ability to judge a wine tends to be severely impaired. The more you drink, the more coated your mouth is, and subtle differences are harder to detect. Eating salty foods between tastings goes some way to restoring the palate to its virgin state but will not revive one violated by its third bottle in a day.

In tasting, **colour** is a consideration, though not an overriding one: a good white should have a rich yellow or gold tone, anything paler could indicate something either insipid or unmanageably dry. Clarity, too, is important, and anything slightly cloudy should be immediately discarded. For reds, look for a faint purple tinge unless it's a particularly full-bodied claret, in which case you shouldn't be able to see through the glass. **Smell** is less crucial and used mainly as a formality to ensure that the wine hasn't "turned" – a common enough occurrence in restaurants, but unlikely in a winery. All wines will have a slightly vinegary smell due to the acescence (which occurs during fermentation) and you shouldn't be put off unless a wine smells particularly virulent. The **taste** itself is of course entirely personal, but as a general rule Californian whites should be light and somewhat acidic, with the exception of dessert wines, for which a smooth port-like texture is more appropriate. A quality red should be powerful enough to linger on the palate for a good ten seconds after tasting. But above all, be ruthless and don't just nod appreciatively at any old bottle. Winery owners will respect a discerning palate and if you really sound as if you know what you're talking about, they might drag out the good stuff. Hot tips for reds: *Cabernet Sauvignon*, *Pinot Noir* and *Zinfandel* from 1974, 1978 and 1980. Good whites include *Chardonnay*, *Chenin Blanc* and *Reisling* from 1975, 1977 and 1980 respectively. Most wineries will have a good selection, each claiming that theirs is the best; for non-experts, there isn't much between them.

The Napa Valley

A 35-mile strip of gently landscaped corridors and lush hillsides, the **Napa Valley** looks more like rural England than a near-neighbour of the Pacific Ocean. In spring the valley floor is covered in brilliant yellow rape which mellows into mulled-autumnal shades by grape-harvest time. The Indian tribes who lived here named the once-rich river that runs through the valley "Napa", which means "fish". The name stuck, even after Spanish explorers wiped out the tribal settlements and replaced them with a series of ranchos and farming communities. By the 1850s Napa town had grown up at a strategic location at the head of the tidewater, and the Napa river was used for transporting agricultural produce south to San Francisco – though before long this route was usurped by vehicular traffic. The area's superior climate saved it from ending up a simple rural backwater, encouraging a variety of mainly fruit crops, and eventually the grape, which spawned the now super-lucrative wine industry.

Practicalities

Hwy-29 runs the length of the valley from the town of Napa at the southern end to Calistoga, Mount St Helena and, beyond, to Clear Lake in the north. *Greyhound* (1620 Main St, Napa; ☎226-1856) buses connect Napa and St Helena to San Francisco, Sacramento and Santa Rosa, although for touring the valley itself *Napa City Bus*, 1130 First Street, Napa (☎255-7631), is a better bet. To avoid dependency on public transport, hiring a bike is a good, if energetic, way to see the valley: *Napa Valley Cyclery*, 4080 Byway East, Napa (☎255-3377), rent bikes for $20 per day, and if you stick to the prettier **Silverado Trail**, which parallels Hwy-29, your chances of being mowed down by the sports cars and recreational vehicles that pack the road are slimmer. However you work things, you'll need a good map; most wineries give away maps of the valley for free, but for a really detailed one giving addresses and phone numbers of the wineries, try the **Napa Chamber of Commerce**, 1900 Jefferson Street, Napa (☎257-1122; daily 9am–4pm), who'll also give you full lists of lodgings in town. **Accommodation** is extra-pricey, the staple provision being upmarket bed and breakfasts at around $80-plus a night for a double room – if you can find one that isn't fully booked (unlikely without reserving well in advance, apart from in the depths of winter). If you absolutely have to rest up, there's a *Motel 6* at 3380 Solano Avenue (☎226-1811; doubles $43 per night). There are two **campsites** in the area: *Bothe-Napa Valley State Park* (☎942-4575), a few miles north of St Helena on Hwy-29, has sites with showers from $9 per night; further north in Calistoga, the *Calistoga Fairgrounds*, 1435 Oak Street, Calistoga (☎942-5111), has places from $10 per person per night.

Napa town and the wineries

The town of **NAPA** is bland and expensive. But for a small civic block with its proud courthouse, it could be any surburban sprawl of annoying one-way systems and no centre. Picking up a bus and passing through should be your only objective – if you're in a car you can bypass it completely by staying on Hwy-29. You might want to stop off for **food**, but Napa's restaurants are prohibitively pricey (though fast food abounds) and for good smash-and-grab meals you're better off dropping in on the numerous general stores and delis as you head north through the valley on Hwy-29 – best of these is the *Oakville Grocery Co*, 7856 St Helena Hwy, just south of St Helena, that's not a grocery store so much as a top-class deli, with truffles, pâté, caviar and exotic cheeses as well as the more standard sandwiches and salads. If you really need a good sit-down meal, try the *Joseph Mathew Winery*, 1171 Main Street (☎226-3777); skip the winery tour and head straight for the restaurant and oyster bar, where you can have some top-class food with good wine. Slightly cheaper, the *Red Hen Cantina*, 5091 St Helena Highway (☎255-8125), serves pseudo-Mexican cuisine and enormous pound-size burgers wrapped in tortillas.

Winery tours differ greatly according to the size and inclination of the producers. Most are open daily, though you should always call ahead to check – many will only receive guests on an appointment basis. The southern end of the valley tends to be home to the larger operations, which draw big crowds for some pretty rigid free tours of the cellars and tasting rooms. Tours are generally accompanied by a quick (often glorified) historical synopsis of how the institution in question came to be so great, and you'll usually have to shuffle around in a pack for about half an hour, by which time you'll have built up quite a thirst and be ready for the tasting hall. Again, though, at the larger producers this is no great shakes, and you normally have to pay – though this at least is on an ad-lib basis, whereby you buy a glass (for around $3–4) and then fill up on as much as you like from bottle to bottle until it's time to leave.

Of the many southerly wineries, one that is worth checking out is **Domaine Chandon**, California Drive off Hwy-29 (Tues–Sun 11am–9pm; ☎944-8848), a few miles into the valley at YOUNTVILLE. Owned by the French company *Moet & Chandon*, they specialise in champagne here, which is excellent, and boast an (albeit very pricey – $35-plus a head) open-air *nouvelle cuisine* restaurant. Well worth it to dine with the sound of champagne flutes tinkling around you. Just to the west of Napa in Green Valley (take the Green Valley exit off Hwy-80 for two miles) , **Chateau de Leu**, 1635 West Mason Road (☎864-1517), gives tours by appointment only, but it's worth the call ahead to check out its imposing Tudor-style chateau and modern winery pumping out an incredible twenty-five thousand cases per year. In the adjacent village of SUISUN, the **Wooden Valley Winery**, 4756 Suisin Valley Road (Tues–Sun 9am–5pm; ☎864-0730), bottles more than just wine. As well as a list of forty different kinds of wine, it produces sherries, vermouths and champagne, some of which are bottled under the strangely named *Mario Lanza* label.

A little way further up the valley there are less crowded concerns around **ST HELENA** – not much more than a large village really, and much prettier than Napa. The **Silverado Museum**, 1490 Library Lane (Tues–Sún noon–4pm), has a collection of over eight thousand articles relating to Robert Louis Stevenson, who spent just under a year in the surrounding area recovering from an illness (actually near Calistoga – see below). But again it's the wineries that are the major focus of interest. **The Christian Brothers Vineyard**, Spring Mountain Road, off Hwy-29 (by appointment only; ☎967-3112, 10am-4pm), was the world's largest winery when erected in 1889, but was a bit of a white elephant that kept changing hands until its present owners – oddly enough a Catholic education order – bought it in 1950, and it now turns out some of the best sparkling wines and champagnes in the valley. The winery tour is among the more interesting the valley has to offer and the tasting room a model of elegance. At the northern end of St Helena, bang on Hwy-29 are the impressive buildings of **Berringer Brothers Winery** (daily 9.30am–4pm; closed in August; ☎963-7115). Known as the Rhine House, this is the Napa Valley's most famous piece of architecture, gracing the cover of many a wine magazine and modelled on an ancestral Gothic mansion in the brothers' native Germany. Spacious lawns and a grand tasting room, heavy on the dark wood, make for quite a regal experience. A little further north where Hwy-128 crosses the Silverado Trail, the **Conn Creek Winery**, on the Silverado Trail (by appointment only; ☎963-5133), is quite different from these two wineries, a truly modern organisation whose lightweight stone and steel building is worlds away from the cutesy old-stone image that's the norm in the rest of the valley. It's owned by the family responsible for half the Napa valley's annual grape crop; *Cabernet Sauvignon* is their star wine, lashed out generously at tastings.

Calistoga and around

Beyond St Helena, towards the far northern end of the valley, the wineries become prettier and the traffic thinner. At the very tip of the valley, nestling against Mount St Helena, **CALISTOGA** is far and away the best of the valley towns. It enjoys a lot of sunshine and has a good share of wineries but is really better known for its mudbaths, whirlpools and the mineral water that bears its name, which adorns every Californian supermarket shelf: all evidence of a mineral abundance lent by the proximity of the volcanic mountain. It's a homely, health-conscious kind of place, with many spas and mudbaths of the walk-in variety that draw jaded city-dwellers up here for the weekend.

Greyhound buses from Napa serve Calistoga, though you might find **accommodation** prices prohibitive. The extravagant might enjoy checking out *Dr Wilkinson's Hot Springs*, 1507 Lincoln Avenue (rooms and treatment from $70-per night; ☎942-4102) – a legendary health spa and hotel whose heated mineral water and volcanic ash tension-reliever treatments have been featured on the TV show, *Lifestyles of the Rich & Famous*. If you're short on time however, and can't afford the decadence of *Dr Wilkinson's*, head back into town and try **Nance's Hot Springs**, 1614 Lincoln Avenue (☎942-6211), who can offer you a full mineral rubdown, blanket sweat, steam bath and massage for around $35. Reasonable accommodation can be found down the road at 1865 Lincoln Avenue, the *Comfort Inn* (☎942-9400) has rooms from $45 per night. **Eating** can be pricey too, with most of Calistoga's restaurants catering for the town's traditionally well-heeled visitors; best stick to delis and sandwich bars if you're on a budget.

Of Calistoga's wineries, the best is **Chateau Montelena**, 1429 Tubbs Lane (☎942-5105), just north of town. One of the valley's oldest and smallest wineries, the medieval facade of the building makes it look more like feudal Bordeaux than modern California and lends a certain dignity to what, in essence, is a free binge. It's also a good place to sample California's mystery grape, the *Zinfandel* (though it is available in most Napa wineries) – thought to be of Italian origin. Lighter and crisper in texture than most other varieties, and known for its fragrance and gulp-ability, it comes in red, white and rosé.

Wineries apart, Calistoga's appeal lies in its natural phenomena, of which the **Old Faithful Geyser** (daily 9am–5pm; $3), two miles north of town also on Tubbs Lane off Hwy-128, is probably the most spectacular example – a geyser which spurts boiling water sixty feet into the air at fifty-minute intervals. The water source was discovered while drilling for oil here in the 1920s, when search equipment struck a force estimated to be up to a thousand pounds a square foot; the equipment was blown away and despite heroic efforts to control it, the geyser has continued to go off like clockwork ever since. Land owners finally realised that they'd never tame it and turned it into a high-yield tourist magnet. Worth a look too, is Calistoga's **Petrified Forest,** 4100 Petrified Forest Road, (☎707/942-6667; daily 10am-5pm, $2.50) about five miles west of Calistoga on the way to Santa Rosa. These gnarled relics are the result of Mount St Helena blowing her top three million years ago, leaving fossilised remains of ancient redwoods. The trail through the forest is a little over a quarter of a mile long and won't take all your day if you fancy a quick look.

Twelve miles north of Calistoga on Hwy-29 **Robert Louis Stevenson State Park** (daily 8am–sundown; $3) covers a largely abandoned area of over 3,200 acres with a disused silver mine at the top of the winding road. Notorious for highwaymen who came to rob the mine payroll, it was here that in 1880 Stevenson spent his honeymoon in a bunkhouse with Fanny Osborne, recuperating from tuberculosis and exploring the valley. The bunkhouse remains, but there is little else about the park's winding roads and dense shrub-growth to evoke its days of former notoriety, though it's a pretty enough place to take a break from the wineries and have a picnic. Stevenson liked the area and wrote about it copiously. In his novel, *Silverado Squatters*, he describes the highlight of the honeymoon as the day he managed to taste eighteen of local wine baron Jacob Schram's champagnes in just one sitting. Quite an extravagance when you consider that Schramsberg champagne is held in such high esteem that Richard Nixon took a few bottles when he went to visit Chairman Mao.

The Sonoma Valley

On looks alone the crescent-shaped **Sonoma Valley** beats Napa hands down. This altogether more rustic valley curves between oak-covered mountain ranges from the Spanish colonial town of Sonoma a few miles north along Hwy-12 to Glen Ellen. It's also known as the "Valley of the Moon", after the Native American legend popularised by longtime resident Jack London that tells how, as you move through the valley, the moon seems to rise several times from behind the various peaks.

The Sonoma Valley is far smaller than Napa, and most of its wineries are informal, family-run businesses, within a few miles of Sonoma itself, where a charge for tasting is still frowned upon and visitors are few – very much the stress-free alternative to a day out in the Napa Valley. You could even skip the wineries altogether and check out the many farms in the Sonoma Valley area, where production of fruits, jams, honey, flowers and christmas trees (not to mention the rearing of goats, rare pigs and poultry and even llamas) make for a good change of scenery away from tasting halls. Pick up a copy of *Farm Trails* from the chamber of commerce (see below) which details what there is and where you can hope to find it.

Sonoma

Behind a layer of touristy shops and restaurants, the small town of **SONOMA** retains a good deal of its Spanish and Mexican architecture. Set around a spacious plaza, the town has a welcoming feel that's refreshing after brash Napa, although as a popular retirement spot, with a median age of about fifty and a matching pace, it's not exactly bubbling with action. If it weren't for the wineries, it would be a bore. The **tourist office** (daily 9am–4pm; ☎996-1090), in the middle of the leafy central plaza, has walking-tour plans of the town and excellent free maps and guides to the wineries. What there is to see in the town itself will take no more than an hour – Sonoma is a place better known for its history than its sights.

It's hard to believe now that this valley was the site of a key turning point in the eventual American takeover of California – the **Bear Flag Revolt**. American settlers in the region had long lived in uneasy peace under Spanish and, later, Mexican rulers, and in 1846, in response to the expulsion of all non-Mexican immigrants from California, a band of thirty armed settlers descended upon the disused and unguarded *Presidio* at Sonoma, taking the retired and much-respected commander, Colonel Guadalupe Vallejo, as their prisoner. Ironically, Vallejo had long advocated the American annexation of California and supported the aims of his rebel captors, but he was nonetheless bundled off to Sutter's Fort in Sacramento and held there for the next two months while the militant settlers declared California an independent republic. The Bear Flag, which served as the model for the current state flag, was raised on Sonoma Plaza. A month later the US declared war on Mexico, and without firing a single shot took possession of the entire West Coast.

Around the plaza there are some rusty old cannons and a romantic monument to the Bear Flag revolutionaries. A few steps north of here, the restored **Mission San Francisco Solano de Sonoma** (daily 10am–5pm; free) was the last and northernmost of the California missions, and the only one established on the northern coast by the nervous Mexican rulers, who were fearful of expansionist Russian fur-trading activities. Along Spain Street, in the northeastern corner of the plaza, are the spooky-looking old military barracks; half a mile further on is the ornate old home of General Vallejo, dominated by profusely decorated filigreed eaves and slender Gothic arched windows. A chalet-style storehouse next door has been turned into a **museum** (daily 9am–5pm) of artefacts from the General's reign.

The wineries

The best Sonoma wineries are the closest, in a concentrated – and well-signposted – group a mile east from the town plaza down E Napa Street, near the railway lines. Most are within walking distance, but often along quirky back-roads, so take a winery map from the tourist office and follow the signs closely. Oldest and perhaps grandest of the wineries is the **Buena Vista Winery**, 18000 Old Winery Road (daily, 10am-5pm; ☎938-1266), with champagne cellars, tunnels of oak caskets and a high-ceilinged tasting room, although the wine itself has a reputation for being pretty mediocre. They're very generous with the tastings, however, and will courteously explain the relative merits of each type of grape to an uninitiated taster. Close by, the **Hacienda Wine Cellars**, 1000 Vineyard Lane (weekdays by appointment only ☎938-3220), is, like its neighbour, a lavish Spanish colonial building, with some great topiary in the gardens and extensive vineyards. The wines are inexpensive, middle-of-the-range vintages that appeal to the pocket and palate alike; if you're looking to buy a case, this one's a safe bet. The **Gundlach-Bundschu** winery, 2000 Denmark Street, (☎938-5277), set back about a mile away from the main cluster, is more highly regarded for its wine, having stealthily crept up from the lower ranks of the wine league to the position where it now regularly steals awards away from the big names. The rather plain, functional building is deceptive – this is premium stuff and definitely not to be overlooked.

Sonoma Practicalities

Unfortunately **public transport** connecting Sonoma with the outside world is scarce, though *Sonoma County Transit* (☎527-7665) has a weekday bus service linking the town to Napa in the east and Santa Rosa in the north. At weekends you'll have to hitch.

Just as in the Napa Valley, most **accommodation** in Sonoma is priced out of any reasonable budget; if you're on a shoestring you might prefer to see it on a day trip from San Francisco, or maybe drive to Santa Rosa and find a cheap-ish motel. If you do decide to stay overnight, the *Sonoma Hotel*, 110 West Spain Street, Sonoma (☎996-2996) has antique crammed doubles from $65 per night – as well as the town's best bar.

Eating is a relatively uncomplicated process in Sonoma, faring better in sandwich shops and delicatessens than full-blown restaurants. Among the best places are: *The Cheese Factory* on First Street West, on the western side of the main square which has been making its own cheese from the same stone building since the 1930s turning out nutty, dry cheeses like the famous *Monterey Jack*, as well as more unusual raw milk cheddars. Served with homemade salads in the garden at the back, it's a good option for lunch. The best place for bread is the *Sonoma French Bakery*, 468 First Street, where they queue round the block to pick up yeastless sourdough, and carnivores will be happy to order at the *Sonoma Sausage Company*, a few doors down at 453 First Street. For a good sit-down, try the above-mentioned *Sonoma Hotel*, which isn't cheap but you can be sure of some first-rate grub. A bit more downmarket is *La Casa*, 121 Spain Street East, that serves comfortingly large portions of Mexican food; but for something really unusual try *Little Switzerland* just west of town on the corner of Grove Street and Riverside Drive (☎707/938-9990). An old bordello that has evolved into a cabaret with acordion and drums while they serve bratwurst and goulash dinners – a full bar helps it all go down easier, but all the same, it's quite mad.

Up the valley

As the valley tapers north, the sights begin to peter out, and while it makes for a soothing drive there's really very little to see apart from a few small villages and the **Jack London State Park** (daily 8am–dusk; $3 per car) – just ten minutes from Sonoma on the London Ranch Road which curves sharply off Hwy-12 close to tiny GLEN ELLEN village. Jack London lived here with his wife for the last years of his short, unsettled life, on a 140-acre ranch in the hills above what he described as the "most beautiful, primitive land in California". A series of paths and walking trails lead through densely wooded groves to the remains of the **Wolf House**, where they lived until an arson attack reduced most of it to a pile of rubble in 1913, leaving only the huge stone chimney and fireplaces. London died three years later and is buried on a hill above the trail to the Wolf House. After his death London's wife built the more formal **House of Happy Walls**, which today serves as a small **museum** (daily 9am–4pm; free), with many mementoes and information detailing the writer's life.

The *Jack London Lodge*, near Glen Ellen at 13740 Arnold Drive (☎707/938-8510) compares reasonably with the Wine Country B&B's, and has rooms from $65.

Santa Rosa

Twenty miles northwest of Sonoma, **SANTA ROSA** marks the end of the Sonoma Valley, and more or less of the Wine Country too. As one of the fastest growing towns in Northern California, its current population of around one hundred thousand can be expected to swell over the next few years as part of the Bay Area dormitory community. Nevertheless, it remains a mid-sized American town indistinguishable from hundreds of others across the nation. Wineries do exist around here, some even do well, but they'll never have the cachet, or indeed charm, of the valleys to the south.

Santa Rosa describes itself confidently as a "town designed for living", but shopping malls and one-way systems obscure what little appeal it has. You may nonetheless find yourself here either as a base for the Wine Country or to pick up bus connections. *Greyhound*, 503 5th Street (☎542-6400), run services to San Francisco, north along US-101 and out to the coast at Mendocino; *Sonoma County Transit* (☎576-7433) link Santa Rosa to Sonoma, the Russian River area and the Sonoma Coast at Duncans Mills.

Of things to see in town, the **Luther Burbank Home and Gardens** (April to Sept only, Wed–Sun 10am–3.30pm; $1), at the junction of Santa Rosa and Sonoma Avenues, may help you to kill an hour or two. California's best-known turn-of-the-century horticulturalist is remembered here in the house where he lived and the gardens where he bred some of his most unusual hybrids. If you're not into gardening, nip across the street to the **Ripley Museum**, 492 Sonoma Avenue (Wed–Sun 11am–4pm, March to Oct only; $1.50), where you might expend twenty minutes or so in one of the cartoonist Ripley's mediocre "believe it or not" chain of museums – Santa Rosa was Ripley's home town.

Like other Wine Country settlements, Santa Rosa can get quite hot come midday. Rather than drag yourself around museums of limited interest, you might prefer to drop by **Spring Lake**, 5585 Newanga Avenue, where the 75-acre lagoon for swimming and sailing is usually uncrowded – especially mid-week. To reach the lake, head east of Santa Rosa on Hwy-12 to Hoen Avenue, take a left on Summerfield Road then right onto Newanga. The journey takes ten minutes by car.

Practicalities

Santa Rosa's **Chamber of Commerce**, 637 First Street (Mon–Sat 9am–5pm, Sun 10am–4pm; ☎545-1414), is in the most interesting part of town, the old Railroad Square district, and has useful lists of motels and restaurants as well as comprehensive maps and guides to the Wine Country. There are several **motels** on the approach roads to Santa Rosa off US-101 – often cheaper than the small hotels in town. *Motel 6*, 2760 Cleveland Avenue off US-101 (☎546-9563), is about the cheapest, with doubles from $35. Also on the same road, the *Sandman Motel*, 3421 Cleveland Avenue (☎544-8570), has sparse but clean rooms from $37 per night. There's a **campsite** ten miles north of town along Hwy-128 at HEALDSBURG, the *Thunderbird Ranch*, 9455 Hwy-128 (☎433-3729), which has places with showers and a swimming pool for $11 per person, though it's closed during July and August for summer camp.

The town's best **restaurants** are concentrated in the town centre near Mendocino Avenue. Try the very healthy *Good Earth*, 610 Third Street, which serves wholesome salads and organic meals from as little as $4. More exotic is *Le Gare*, at 208 Wilson Street on Railroad Square, who for not much more will feed you with well-prepared French Provençale dishes. For fun, you could try eating at *Studio Kafe*, 418 Mendocino Avenue, from where live broadcasts of "gourmet radio" (FM 96) are transmitted; the food is mostly cajun and pretty good, but your motivation for going should definitely be to get in on the act. For **bars and nightlife**, stick to the First–Fourth Street area and wander around until you spot something to your liking – there are any number of lively haunts. Try *Acapulco* at 505 Mendocino Avenue, good for happy hour cocktails between 4pm and 7pm, or *Joe Frogger's*, a few blocks away at 527 Fourth Avenue, which has regular live music until 1.30am.

Lake County

The frumpy folks of **Lake County**, hidden away behind the bulk of Mount St Helena, are far removed from the often-contrived lifestyles of the Napa valley. In fact, with the biggest drunk driving problem in California, and some pretty worrying unemployment figures, Lake County people have their hands full just getting by.

The area's big attraction, **CLEARLAKE**, California's largest natural lake sitting snug under the shadow of the active volcano Mount Konocti, made it an area that could support some world-class health spas back in the late nineteenth century, but the money moved south in the early part of this century, leaving behind a friendly working-class resort and retirement area. The smart money is starting to buy cheap weekend homes that cling to the steep slopes of Mount Konocti overlooking some pretty spectacular scenery, and it can only be a matter of time before Lake County's fortunes take a turn for the better. About three hours from San Francisco along Hwy-29, a road that curves often perilously over Mount St. Helena, it's a place that most travellers can't be bothered with when busier, far more glamorous resorts lie closer to home. In truth, there's not a terrific amount to see or do and if you make it up here, it'll be to see a few wineries, maybe take a boat out on the lake and generally enjoy the slow pace. As a destination you could probably do better, but as a stopover before heading on to more northerly reaches of the state, it's a good, cheap option.

Practical details

Several small towns dot the edge of the lake, within a few miles of each other. Your first stop should be the **Chamber of Commerce** in **LAKEPORT** at 290 S Main Street (☎707/263-5092), Lake County's largest settlement at the northern edge of the lake. They'll be able to offer you details of accommodation around the lake, plus maps detailing the wineries and watersports available. **Camping** is not a bad option; there's an excellent site at *Clearlake State Park,* 5300 Soda Bay Road, Kelseyville (☎707/279-4293) that has sites for $10. Reasonable **hotels** while not plentiful, do exist: in Lakeport, try the *Anchorage Inn,* 950 N Main Street (☎707/263-5417), a comfortable mid-sized hotel with double rooms from $40. Better sited, bang on the edge of the lake a few miles away in **Kelseyville** is the *Konocti Harbour Inn,* 8727 Soda Bay Road (☎707/279-4281), where motel-style rooms and beach-cabins cost from $55. *Konocti* also has swimming pools, tennis courts, and preferential hire rates for taking boats on the lake.

Eating is not an expensive affair in Lake County – wherever you chose to stay you'll find a reasonable choice. *The Helmsman Restaurant,* 1873 High Street, Lakeport, serves massive breakfasts, bulging sandwiches and hearty dinners in the $6-7 bracket. For good fish try *Captain Bill's Seafood Grotto,* 460 S Main Street, Lakeport. *Anthony's Restaurant,* 2509 Lakeshore Boulevard, Lakeport, has a more varied menu of American and Italian-style dishes.

THE NORTHERN COAST

Rugged in the extreme, often foggy, always dangerous and thunderously dramatic, the **Northern Coast** is leagues away from the gentle, sun-drenched beaches of Southern California. The climate along here, at best moderate, means that sunbathing is out, as is swimming; sudden ground swells and strong under-tow make even surf play risky, and it's worth bearing in mind that there is no life-guard service along any of the beaches. Instead, this is an area to don hiking boots, wrap up warm and experience the enormous forests with their plentiful camping facilities.

The only way to see the coast properly is on the painfully slow but scenically magnificent Hwy-1, which hugs the coast for two hundred miles through the wild counties of **Sonoma** and **Mendocino** before turning sharply inland at Legget to join Hwy-101 and **Humboldt County**. The shore it misses has become known, appropriately, as the **Lost Coast**, the hundred miles of coastline never reached by California's coastal highway. North of here, **redwood forests** clothe the landscape as far as the Oregon border, doubling as raw material for the huge logging industries (the prime source of employment in the area) and the region's prime tourist attraction, most notably in the **Redwood National Park**. **Eureka** and **Arcata** are the main towns here, both easily reached on public transport and the principal centres of nightlife and action for the coast as a whole.

You'll need to be fairly independent to **get around** this region: *Greyhound* buses travel the length of US-101, which parallels the coastal highway, but only link up with the coast south of Humboldt County at Mendocino and Fort Bragg. On balance you need a car, although hitching is generally good: it's not an area known for its danger and the people who live here often hitch to get around. Women hitching alone should of course be extra vigilant (see p.19 for more on hitching).

The Sonoma Coast and Russian River

Proximity to San Francisco means the **Sonoma Coast** and **Russian River Valley** areas have never been short on weekend visitors. But tourist activity is confined to a few narrow corridors at the height of summer, leaving behind a network of north coast villages and backwater wineries which for most of the year are all but asleep. The coast is colder and lonelier than the villages along the valley, and at some point most people head inland for a change of scene and a break from the fog that dogs the coastline. What both areas have in common, however, is a reluctance to change. As wealthy San Franciscans cast their eyes coastwards for potential second-home sites, the California Coastal Commission endeavours to keep the architects at bay, keenly maintaining beach access for all, and most farmers have so far managed to resist the considerable sums offered for their grazing land. For the time being the Sonoma coastal area remains relatively undeveloped, the majority of it state beach, with good access to hiking trails and views.

The Sonoma coast

BODEGA BAY, about fifty miles north of San Francisco, is the first Sonoma village you reach on Hwy-1, actually little more than two restaurants, a much depleted fishing industry and some twee seaside cottages. Originally discovered by the Spanish in 1755, this is where Hitchcock filmed *The Birds* – an unsettling number of them are still squawking down by the harbour. With one small bar to serve the entire community, you'll be hard put to whoop it up in the evening and this is more a place for long moody walks and early nights. Certainly, if you're travelling the whole coast it makes a good first stop: there's a **campsite** two miles north of the village on Hwy-1 at the tip of a windy peninsula known as **Bodega Head**: the *Bodega Dunes Campground* (☎875-3382), is laid out across sand dunes that end in coastal cliffs behind the beach and has places for $10 a night. And there are hiking and horseriding trails around the dunes behind the beach – though in summer these tend to be packed with picnicking families, and for less crowded routes you should head up the coast. Unfortunately, the only other option for sleeping is expensive, if extremely comfortable; the *Bodega Coast Inn*, 521 Coast Hwy (☎1-800/346-6999) has lovely rooms with fireplaces that will set you back a minimum of $85 per night during the week and $120 at weekends.

North of Bodega Bay, along the **Sonoma Coast State Beach** – actually a series of beaches separated by rocky bluffs – the coastline coarsens and the trails become more dramatic. It's a wonderful stretch to hike, although the shale formations are often unstable and you must stick to the trails, which at best are demanding. Of Sonoma's thirteen miles of beaches, the finest are **Salmon Creek Beach**, opposite which you'll find the park headquarters for maps and information, and at the top of the Sonoma coast near the mouth of the Russian River, the busy **Goat Rock Beach**. The Russian River joins the ocean at Goat Rock and a massive sand spit at its mouth provides a breeding ground for harbour seals from March to June. An experienced hiker could cover the full thirteen miles in a day; the less hardy will probably need to stop at **Wrights Beach**, about halfway along the coast, which has primitive camping facilities.

North of the tiny village of JENNER (which marks the turn-off for the Russian River), the population evaporates and Hwy-1 turns into a slalom course of hairpin bends and steep inclines for about eight miles as far as **Fort Ross State Historic Park** (daily 8am–5pm; $2). At the start of the nineteenth century, San Francisco was still the northernmost limit of Spanish occupation in Alta California, and from 1812 to 1841 Russian fur traders quietly settled this part of the coast, building a fort to use as a trading outpost and growing crops for the Russian stations in Alaska. Officially they posed no territorial claims, but by the time the Spanish had gauged the extent of the settlement, the fort was heavily armed and vigilantly manned with a view to continued eastward expansion. They traded here for thirty years until over-hunting and the failure of their shipbuilding efforts led them to pull out of the region altogether. There are **guided tours** of the fort at weekends; during the week, walkie-talkie-like wands given out at the entrance transmit the fort's history. There are a lot of empty bunkers and storage halls but the most interesting buildings are the Russian Orthodox Chapel and the Commandant's house, with its fine library and wine cellar. At the entrance, a potting shed which labours under the delusion that it is a museum provides cursory details on the history of the fort, with a few maps and diagrams.

Fort Ross has a small **beach** and picnicking facilities, but the nearest **campsite** is at **Salt Point**, six miles north of the fort on Hwy-1 (☎884-3723). Also at Salt Point, the **Kruse Rhododendron State Reserve** is a sanctuary for twenty-foot-high rhododendrons: indigenous to this part of the coast and at their best in early summer. The beaches on this last stretch of the Sonoma coastline are usually completely empty save a few abalone fishermen, driftwood and the seal-pups who rest here. Again, good for hiking and beachcombing but stick to the trails.

The Russian River Valley

Hwy-116 begins at JENNER and turns sharply inland, leaving behind the cool fogs of the coast and marking the beginning of a relatively warm and pastoral area known as the **Russian River Valley**. The tree-lined highway follows the river's course through about twenty miles of what appear to be lazy, backwater resorts but in fact are the major stomping-grounds for partying weekenders from San Francisco. The fortunes of the valley have come full circle; back in the Twenties and Thirties it was a recreational resort for well-to-do city folk who abandoned the area as the building of new roads took them elsewhere. Drawn by low rents, back to the landers started arriving in the late Sixties, and the Russian River took on a hippy flavour that lingers today. More recently an injection of affluent property seekers have sustained the region's economy and the funky mix of loggers, sheep farmers and wealthy weekenders gives it an off-beat cachet that has restored its former popularity.

The road that snakes through the valley is dotted with campsites every few miles, most with places for the asking, although during the last week of September, when the region hosts the **Russian River Jazz Festival**, things can get a bit tight. The jazz festival is something of a wild week around here and a good time to come: bands set up in the woods and along the riverbanks for impromptu jamming sessions as well as regular scheduled events.

Sonoma County Transit (☎576-7433) run a fairly good weekday bus service (though patchy at weekends) between the Russian River resorts and Santa Rosa, although ideally you need a car to see much of the valley.

Guerneville

The main town of the Russian River valley, **GUERNEVILLE**, is described by the tourist office as a place where "a mixture of people respect each other's lifestyles". Unofficially, but quite clearly, it's a **gay resort**, and has been for the last ten years or so: a lively retreat that's popular with tired city-dwellers who favour the pace of the town and its surrounding area.

If you don't fancy venturing along the valley, there's plenty to keep you busy without leaving town. On the river in the centre of town there's a place for swimming and hiring boats, but Guerneville's biggest natural asset is the magnificent **Armstrong Redwoods State Reserve**, two miles north at the top of Armstrong Woods Road – 750 acres of massive redwood trees, hiking and riding trails and primitive camping sites. Take food and water and don't stray off the trails: the densely forested central grove is quite forbidding and very easy to get lost in. A natural amphitheatre provides the setting for the **Redwood Forest Theatre** which (when the countless outdoor wedding ceremonies aren't being performed) stages dramatic and musical productions during the summer. If you can't face the very basic camping, there's a **campsite** with full amenities just before the entrance to the reserve; failing that, nip back into Guerneville and find a room.

Weekend visitors flock to Guerneville for the canoeing, swimming and sunbathing that comprise the bulk of local activities. The **tourist office** at 14034 Armstrong Woods Road just off Main Street (daily 10am–5pm; ☎869-9009) can supply you with good free maps of the area, and **accommodation** listings. As with most of the valley, bed and breakfast inns are the staple; *The Willows*, 15905 River Road (☎869-3279), is a homely guesthouse with doubles from $60 per night, while *The Estate*, 13555 Hwy-116 (☎869-9093) is a luxury B&B where doubles cost upwards of $115. A dearth of cheap motels (unless you head east to Hwy-101) may make camping the economical answer. *Austin Creek State Recreation Area*, Armstrong Woods Road (☎865-2391), is guaranteed RV-free and has places for $10 per night, as does *Johnson's Resort* on First Street (☎869-2022), which also has cabins and rooms available from around $40 per night, making them about the cheapest in the area.

Eating is not a problem; Guerneville has a good selection of reasonably priced, reliable restaurants. Places you might try include *Hamburger Molly's* at *Molly Brown's Saloon* (below), and *'Bout Time* on Main Street – both serve large portions of wholesome, fresh food. Really, though, it's the nightlife which makes Guerneville a worthwhile stop: the *Rainbow Cattle Company* on Main Street and *Molly Brown's Saloon* on Old Cazadero Road are good for some dining, dancing and ballyhoo in the company of cowboys. On Saturday afternoons, *Molly Brown's* has a "beer bust", when for $5 you can consume all the beer you can manage.

Monte Rio

The small town of **MONTE RIO**, a few miles south along the river from
Guerneville, is definitely worth a look; a lovely, crumbling old resort town with
big Victorian houses in stages of graceful delapidation. Over recent years it has
earned itself a name as the Haight Ashbury of the Russian River for its non-
conformist air; for much longer it has been the entrance to the 2500-acre
Bohemian Grove, a private park that plays host to the San Francisco-based
Bohemian Club. A grown-up summer camp, its membership includes the very
rich and very powerful male elite – ex-Presidents, financiers, politicians and the
like. Every year they descend for "Bohemian Week" in July – the greatest men's
party on earth, noted for its high-jinks and high-priced hookers, away from prying
cameras in the seclusion of the woods.

If you're touring the area by car, the Cazadero Highway just to the west makes
a nice drive from here. This lonely, narrow road, curves north through the
wooded valley and leads back to Fort Ross on the coast.

Russian River Valley wineries

The Guerneville tourist office (see above) issue an excellent *Sonoma County
Farm Trails* map, which lists all the **wineries** and small farms which spread
along the entire course of the Russian River. Unlike their counterparts in Napa,
the wineries here neither organise guided tours nor charge for wine-tasting. You
can wander around at ease, guzzling as many and as much of the wines as you
please. Some of the wines (the *Cabernet Sauvignons* and *Merlots* in particular) are
of remarkably good quality, if not as well known as their rivals in Napa. **Topolos
at Russian River Vineyards**, 5700 Gravenstein Highway, in Forestville, five
miles from Guerneville along Hwy-116 (Wed–Sun 10.30am–5pm; ☎887-2956) and
the **Field Stone Winery**, 10075 Highway 128, Healdsburg (daily 10am–5pm;
☎433-7266), are two of the most accessible wineries.

Even if you're not "doing" the wineries, you shouldn't miss the *Korbel
Champagne Cellars*, 13250 River Road, Guerneville (☎707/887-2294). The bubbly
itself – America's best-selling premium champagne – isn't anything you couldn't
find in any supermarket, but the wine and brandy are sold only at the cellars and
are of such notable quality, that you'd be mad not to swing by for a snifter. The
estate where they are produced is lovely, surrounded by hillside gardens covered
in blossoming violets, coral bells and hundreds of varieties of roses – perfect for
quiet picnics. By car, you could easily travel up from the Sonoma Coast and check
out a couple of Russian River wineries in a day, although the infectiously slow
pace may well detain you longer.

The Mendocino coast

The coast of Mendocino County, 150 miles north of San Francisco, is a dramatic
extension of the Sonoma Coastline – the headlands a bit sharper, the surf a bit
rougher, but otherwise more of the same. Despite the best efforts of the local
chambers of commerce, this remains a remote area, its small former lumbering
towns served by limited public transport. One *Greyhound* (☎937-4382) bus per
day connects Santa Rosa, some sixty miles south, with the main towns of
Mendocino and **Fort Bragg** to the north and runs services between these two
towns; in addition, *Mendocino Stage and Transit Authority* (☎964-0167) link

Mendocino and Fort Bragg, and run south from Mendocino to the small villages of Navarro and Gualala. Inland there is a small contingent of wineries, but little else. Stick to the coast where there is at least some sign of life, and content yourself with brisk walks and brooding scenery.

Mendocino

Fifty miles along the coast from the Sonoma border at Gualala, **MENDOCINO** is about the first viable stop, a weathered, quaint kind of place that errs on the dangerous side of cute. Its reputation for being something of an artists' colony draws the curious up the coastal highway, and while people here make a big thing out of loathing tourists, there's a fairly extensive network of bed and breakfasts, restaurants and bars. Prices are inevitably hiked up, but provided you stay away from the chintzy hotels on the waterfront, adequate **rooms** can be found for around $40 a night on the streets behind. The *Seagull Inn*, 44594 Albion Street (☎937-5204), is the best of the affordable options, and has nightly jazz in the bar (see below). The *Joshua Grindle Inn*, 4480 Little Lake Road (☎937-4143), is a friendly bed and breakfast with rooms from $48 per night; and there are also several **campsites** within about five miles of town. *Russian Gulch State Park* (☎937-0497), two miles north on Hwy-1, is the nearest, or there's *Van Damme State Park* (☎937-0841) three miles south on Hwy-1. For a more comprehensive list of lodgings and free maps and information about Mendocino, visit the **North Coast Visitor Center**, 991 Main Street (☎937-1913).

Like other small settlements along the coast, Mendocino was originally a lumber port, founded in the late nineteenth century by merchants who thought the proximity to the redwoods and exposed location made it a good site for saw-milling operations. The industry has now vanished, but a large community of artists gives the place a low-key, raffish charm and has spawned craftsy commerce in the form of art galleries, gift-shops and boutique-delicatessens. The **Mendocino Arts Center**, 45200 Little Lake Street (daily 10am–5pm; free), gives classes and has a gallery showing some good works (if a little heavy on the seascapes) of mainly Mendocino-based artists. The **Kelley House Museum** on Main Street (Tues–Sat 10am–5pm) has exhibits detailing the town's role as a centre for shipping redwood lumber to the miners during the Gold Rush, and conducts **walking tours** of the town every Saturday morning at 11am – though you could do it yourself in under an hour, picking up souvenirs from the galleries as you go.

Otherwise there's plenty to occupy you around the town: **hiking** and **cycling** are popular, with bikes available for hire for around $25 a day from *Mendocino Cyclery*, behind the deli on Main Street. If you do hire one, the **Russian Gulch State Park**, two miles north of town, has bike trails, beautiful fern glens and waterfalls. A walk along the **Mendocino Headlands**, a bracing beach area of cliffs and rocks at the end of Main Street, is good for appetite-building, and just south of town hiking and cycling trails weave through the unusual **Van Damme State Park**, on Hwy-1 (☎937-5804; $3), which has a **Pygmy Forest** of ancient trees, stunted to waist-height because of poor draining and soil chemicals.

Practicalities: hot tubs, food and nightlife
The best thing to do in Mendocino is to pamper yourself. **Hot tubs** and **saunas** are a big thing here, and as the main tourist attraction they're pricey. *Sweetwater*

Gardens, 955 Ukiah Street (☎937-4140), offer the usual hot tub, steam and sauna menu for around $10 per hour, though often it can be crowded and the waiting-time irksome. Better to travel five miles north to **CASPAR**, a tiny village of a few houses and an excellent **health spa**, which offers open-air hot tubs for $7 per hour. Caspar also has the best **bar** in the area, the *Caspar Inn*, which has a nightly billing of rock, jazz and rhythm and blues. Of Mendocino's bars, one of the best is *The Seagull*, on the corner of Albion and Lansing, which has a good, reasonable restaurant upstairs and a lively cellar bar with nightly jazz. *The Seagull* plays a major hosting role in the two-week **Mendocino Music Festival** in July, bringing in blues and jazz bands from all over the state, although the emphasis is largely on classical and opera.

For an earthier experience (and cheaper beer), *Dick's Place* on Main Street is Mendocino's oldest bar, with all the robust conviviality you'd expect from a spit-and-sawdust saloon. Of the town's **restaurants**, *Café Beaujolais*, 961 Ukiah Street, serves a solid plate of bangers and mash as well as its standard French options, while the *Wellspring* just along the road at 955 Ukiah Street, is a good if more formal choice, specialising in seafood.

Fort Bragg, Willits and Leggett

FORT BRAGG is very much the blue-collar flipside to its comfortable neighbour. Where Mendocino exists on wholefood and art, Fort Bragg brings you the rib-shack and lumberjack, and sits beneath a perpetual cloud of steam choked out from the lumber-mills of the massive Georgia Pacific Corporation, who monopol-ise California's logging industry and to whom Fort Bragg owes its existence. There was once a fort here, but it was only used for ten years until the 1860s when it was abandoned and the land sold off cheap. The otherwise attractive **Noyo Harbour** (as you enter town on Hwy-1), has been crammed full of commercial fishing craft and the billowing smog does little to add to the charm. But its proximity to the more isolated reaches of the Mendocino Coast, an abundance of cheap accommodation and all-you-can-eat restaurants make it a good alternative to Mendocino.

Greyhound, 140 E Laurel Street (☎964-0877), have only one southbound **bus** daily; if you want to travel north, you'll have to hitch or catch the Skunk Train (see below) forty miles inland to **WILLITS**, where you can pick up *Greyhound*. Most of the **cheap motels** cluster along Hwy-1 in the centre of town, the cheapest and most visible of which is *The Surf Motel*, South Main Street (☎964-5361), with rooms from $28 per night. The *Old Coast Hotel*, 101 N Franklin Street (☎964-6443), is a good family-run hotel offering meals and comfortable rooms from $40 a night; or there's the excellent *Grey Whale*, 615 North Main Street (☎964-9800), with good views from the rooms which cost from $43 per night. **Camping** is another good way to stay in Fort Bragg: the **MacKerricher State Park**, three miles north of town, is set among coastal pines on a secluded stretch of beach with a ranch that offers horse-rides along the coast.

Eating in Fort Bragg may be tricky for vegetarians, as all the restaurants (and there are plenty) serve either massive mill-portions of ribs, steaks and suchlike or specialise in seafood. *The Restaurant* at 418 Main Street, has great cajun and creole fish dishes, for around $6; *David's Deli & Restaurant*, 450 S Franklin Street, does runaway sandwiches at lunchtime. But what Fort Bragg really does best is its meat. Both *Jenny's Giant Burger*, 940 N Main Street, and the *Redwood Cookhouse*, 118 E Redwood Avenue, serve huge tree-felling dinners of steaks, ribs and burgers, and are usually full of men from the mills. For big breakfasts, try *Egghead Omelettes of Oz* at 326 North Main Street (daily 7.30am–3pm).

As for things to do, or even just a convenient way from getting to or from the coast, you can amuse yourself on the **Skunk Train**, operated by the *Californian Western Railroad* (☎964-6371 $18 one-way, $39 return), which runs twice daily forty miles inland to US-101 and the town of **WILLITS**. Officially the county seat thanks only to its location in the centre of Mendocino, Willits differs not at all from other strip-development, mid-sized American towns – stop only to get a drink. The trains take their name from the days when they were powered by gas engines and could be smelt before they were seen, piled up with timber through the redwood forests. The railroad now operates almost exclusively for the benefit of tourists, but it is fun to ride in the open observation car of the steam train as it tunnels through mountains and across the thirty-odd high bridges on its route through the towering redwoods. You can pick up the train at 9am onwards from the railroad depot on Laurel Street, one block down from North Main.

If you've got a car, a short drive south of Fort Bragg will take you to the **Mendocino Coast Botanical Gardens** (daily 9am–5pm; $2), where you can see more or less every wildflower under the sun spread across seventeen acres of prime coastal territory. The coast here is also reputed to be one of California's best areas for **whale-watching**: if you're visiting in November when they pass on their way south to Baja to breed, a few patient hours spent on the beach may be rewarded by the sighting of a grey whale.

Hwy-1 continues north for another twenty miles of slow road and windswept beaches before leaving Mendocino county and the coastline to turn inland and meet Hwy-101 at **LEGGETT**. Redwood country begins in earnest here: in Leggett they've even got a tree you can drive through for $2, though you'd do better to stay on course for the best forests further north.

The Humboldt Coast

Of the coastal counties, **Humboldt** is by far the most beautiful – overwhelmingly peaceful in places, in others plain eerie. The coastal highway doesn't get to its southern reaches, guaranteeing isolation and lending the region the name of the "Lost Coast". Humboldt is perhaps most renowned for its "Emerald Triangle", as it's known, which produces the majority of California's largest cash crop, marijuana. As the fishing and logging industries slide, more and more people have been turning to growing California's primo smoke to make ends meet. The Bush Administration has taken steps to crack down on the business with CAMP (Campaign against Marijuana Planters), and sporadically sends out spotter planes to pinpoint the main growing areas. Aggressive law enforcement and a steady stream of crop-poaching has been met with a defiant, booby-trapped and frequently armed protection of crops, and production goes on – the camouflage netting and irrigation pipes you find on sale in most stores clearly do their job.

Apart from considerable areas of clandestine agriculture, the county is almost entirely forestland, vast areas of which are protected in national parks. The highway rejoins the coast at **Eureka** and **Arcata**, Humboldt's two major towns and spirited jumping-off points for the **redwoods,** which stretch up the coast with a vengeance to the north of here. These prehistoric giants are the real crowd-pullers in this part of the state, at their best in the **Redwood National Park** – three state parks in all, altogether covering some 58,000 acres of skyscraping forest. Again, **getting around** is going to be your biggest problem. Although *Greyhound* buses run the length of the county along US-101, they're hardly a satis-factory way to see the trees, and you'll have to beg, borrow or steal a car to make the trip worthwhile. For information on **what's on** in Humboldt, there are two excellent, free county newspapers, *The Activist* and *North Coast View*, which detail the local scene and people, and where to go and what to do in the area.

Southern Humboldt: Garberville and the "Lost Coast"

The inaccessibility of the Humboldt Coast in the south is ensured by the **Kings Range,** an area of impassable cliffs that shoots up several thousand feet from the ocean, so that even a road as sinuous as Hwy-1 can't negotiate a passage through. To get there you have to travel US-101 through deepest redwood territory as far as **GARBERVILLE,** a one-street town with a few good bars that is the centre of the dope industry and a lively alternative to the wholesome, happy-family nature of much of this part of California. Each week, the local paper runs a "bust-barometer", which charts the week's pot raids; and, as a complement to all the good grass, the town hosts a **Reggae on the River** festival every August, draw-ing big names for its night-long jam session. Tickets cost $20 but are well worth it.

Greyhound (☎923-3259) **buses** pull into town three times daily and have connecting services north to Eureka and south to San Francisco. Sadly, most of the town's **accommodation** is overpriced. Of a couple you might try, the *Benbow Inn,* 445 Lake Benbow Drive (☎923-2124), is a flash place for such a rural location (former guests include Eleanor Roosevelt and Herbert Hoover), and charges $75-plus for a double; the *Johnston Motel,* 839 Redwood Drive (☎923-3327), is more affordable, if a lot scruffier, with rooms from $30 a night. This road, parallel to Hwy-101 has several other motels and it may be worth cruising up and down the strip until you find something you like and can afford.

The closest **campsite** is eight miles away, but if you're independently mobile you can head for the **Richardson Grove State Park,** south of town on US-101 (☎247-3318) which charges $10 per night.

Even if you don't intend to stay, at least stop off to sample some of Garberville's **restaurants** and **bars,** which turn out some of the best live bluegrass you're likely to hear in the state. The town's main street is lined with bars, cafés and restaurants: the *Eel River Café,* 801 Redwood Drive, is a good bet for breakfast; in the evening try the cheap, reliable Italian food at *Sicilio's,* 445 Conger Lane. You're spoilt for choice when it comes to drinking. All the bars tend to whoop it up in the evening; the noisiest of the lot is probably *The Cellar,* at 728 Redwood Drive, with a small cover for its nightly live music.

From Garberville, via the adjoining village of REDWAY, a road winds 23 miles to the **Lost Coast** at **SHELTER COVE,** set in a tiny bay neatly folded between sea cliffs and headlands. First settled in the 1850s when gold was struck inland, its isolated position at the far end of the Kings Range has kept the village small: just two restaurants, a bar and a few retirement homes. There's nowhere to stay, but it's the closest real settlement for **hiking** and **wildlife** explorations of the Kings Range, which remains inhabited only by deer, river otter, mink, black bear, bald eagles and falcons. Hiking trails run for sixteen miles north along the cliffs, dotted with primitive **campsites**, all free with no permit required.

The heart of redwood country begins in earnest a few miles north of Garberville along US-101, when you enter the **Humboldt Redwoods State Park**: over 48,000 acres of virgin timber, protected from lumber companies, make this the largest of the Redwood parks. The serpentine **Avenue of the Giants** weaves for 33 miles through trees which block all but a few strands of sunlight. This is the habitat of *sequoia sempervirens*, a coastal redwood with ancestors dating back to the days of the dinosaur. John Steinbeck described them as "ambassadors from another time" – and indisputably they're big, some over 350 feet tall, evoking a potent sense of solitude that makes a day of stopping off along the highway time well spent. Small stalls selling lumber products and refreshments dot the course of the highway. The three **campsites** within the park fill up quickly in the summer months; you must book (on ☎946-2436).

The avenue follows the south fork of the Eel river, eventually joining US-101 at Pepperwood. Ten miles before this junction, the turn-off to **HONEYDEW** provides a possible respite from the trees. In a region thin on even small settlements, Honeydew is a postage-stamp town popular with marijuana growers who appreciate its remote location – and the two hundred inches of annual rain that sustains the crops.

Eureka

EUREKA, the largest coastal settlement north of San Francisco, is an industrial, gritty and often foggy lumbermill town near the top of the north coast of California between the Arcata and Humboldt Bay. It's not, as its name might suggest, a place that will make you think you've struck paydirt, but at least it's a useful stopover. Downtown Eureka is fairly short on charm, lit by the neon of motels and pizza parlours, and surrounded by rail and shipyards, but an abundance of affordable **motels** around the Broadway area at the northern (and noisy) end of town make the place bearable for a night or two. The *Bayview Motel*, Broadway and Henderson Streets (☎442-1673), has rooms from $33; the *Safari Budget 6 Motel*, 7th and Broadway Streets (☎443-4891), from $26 – if you're lucky you'll get one with a waterbed; the *Sea Breeze Motel*, 2846 Broadway (☎443-9381) is cheapest of all, with rooms from only $22, and a jacuzzi. There are several **campsites** between Eureka and Arcata along US-101, best of which is the *KOA* (☎822-4243), a large site with copious amenities five miles north of town. Transport **links** are good: *Greyhound*, 1603 Fourth Street, (☎442-0370) connect Eureka to San Francisco in the south and Portland in the north three times daily. *Redwood Transit* operate two buses per day from the Greyhound terminal east along the winding and treacherous Hwy-36 through the mountains to REDDING. For getting around town and up the coast as far as TRINIDAD, *Humboldt Transit*, 133 V Street (☎443-0826), have a weekday service.

The so-called **Old Town**, bounded by C, G, First and Third Streets, at the edge of the bay, is in the process of smartening up. For the moment, though, the peeling Victorian buildings and poky bars of the old sailors' district are pretty much rundown though they have a certain seedy appeal, along with a handful of lively, mostly Italian cheap eateries. More conventional sights include the **Carson Mansion** at Second and M Streets, an opulent Gothic pile built in the 1880s by a rich lumberman that now operates as a private gentleman's club behind the gingerbread facade. There's a collection of Native American applied art at the **Clarke Memorial Museum**, Third and E Streets (Tues–Sat 10am–4pm; donations), though this can't hold a candle to the stuff at the **Indian Art Gallery**, 241 F Street (Mon–Sat 10am–4.30pm; free), a rare opportunity for Native American artists to show and market their works in a gallery setting, and a very rare opportunity to get your hands on some incredibly good, inexpensive silver jewellery. If dragging yourself around town for these low-key sights doesn't appeal, **Rudene's Massage & Stress Release Center**, 322 P Street (☎445-2992), has salt-rubs, tranquillity tanks and saunas. Special offers include a thirty-minute massage with hot tub and sauna for $20.

A few minutes by car from town across the Samoa bridge, squashed against the Louisiana-Pacific plywood mill, is the tiny community of **SAMOA**, a company town that is the site of the last remaining cookhouse in the west. **The Samoa Cookhouse** was where the lumbermen would come to eat gargantuan meals after a day of felling redwoods, and although the oilskin tablecloths and burly workers have gone, the lumbercamp style remains, with long tables, the most basic of furnishings, and massive portions of red meat. Other **eating** possibilities include most of the Italian restaurants of the Old Town, notably *Sergio's* on Second and C Streets, and *Mazzotti's* on Third and F Streets, both serving good family-sized portions for less than $5 per head. Great seafood can be had at *The Landing*, at the foot of C Street, with great views of the bay. For food with entertainment, the *Old Town Bar & Grill*, on Second and E Street, serves quality Italian/American dishes to a backdrop of serenades by the Humboldt Blues Society. For the best (or at least the biggest) breakfasts in town, *Deb's*, Fourth & N Street, serve up tasty variations on the theme of bacon and eggs.

Arcata and around

ARCATA, twelve miles across the bay from Eureka, is by far the more appealing of the two centres, a small college town with a large throwback Sixties community whose presence is manifest in some raunchy bars and an earthy, mellow pace. The beaches along the coast north of town are some of the best on the north coast, white-sanded and windswept, and known for their easy hikeability and random parties.

There's a small *Greyhound* bus station on Tenth Street that connects with the Eureka services going north and south, and a weekday *Humboldt Transit* link with Eureka. The small but helpful **Chamber of Commerce**, 1062 G Street (Mon–Sat 10am–5pm summer only; ☎822-3619), has free maps and lists of **accommodation**. Motels just out of town on US-101 are cheaper than the increasingly popular bed and breakfast, if a little less inviting, and can usually be found for under $40 per night. Three blocks from the bus station, the *Arcata Crew House Hostel*, 1390 I Street (May–Sept only; ☎822-9995), is easily the best deal in town with rooms for $8.75 per night. Reasonable accommodation can be had at the *Fairwinds Motel*, 1674 G Street (☎822-4824) from $38 per night. If you've a bit more money, *Hotel Arcata*, 708 9th Street (☎826-0217), on the town's main square, is a very stylish way to get rid of it – $70 for elegant turn-of-the-century rooms with huge brass beds and clawfoot tubs in the bathrooms. Of bed and breakfasts, *The Plough & The Stars*, 1800 27th Street (☎822-8236), have adequate rooms from $40 per night. There are several **campsites** north of Arcata along the coast, but none within easy reach of town unless you've got a car. *Big Lagoon County Park*, (☎445-7650) fifteen miles north of town on Hwy-1, has spaces for $4, as does the nearby *Clam Beach County Park* (☎445-7650), four miles north of town on US-101.

The town is centred around a main square of shops and bars, with everything you're likely to want to see and do within easy walking distance. In the middle of the square the statue of President McKinley was intended for nearby McKinleyville but after falling off the train stayed put in Arcata. Dotted around the plaza and tangential streets, it's Arcata's **bars** that set the town apart. *The Jambalaya* at 915 H Street is the best of the bunch, drawing a longhaired crowd for its nightly diet of R&B, jazz and rock bands. There's also the *Finnish County Sauna and Tubs* on the corner of 5th and J Streets, a busy, friendly café with hot tubs in the garden behind for $5 per hour. *The Humboldt Brewery*, 856 10th Street, is a working beer factory with its own bar and cheap restaurant, where you can sample the preferred stronger, darker brews of Northern California.

Around Arcata: up the coast and the Hoopa Valley Reservation

If Arcata's nightlife doesn't appeal, there's not much else to the town apart from a **bird sanctuary**, about a mile from the main square at the end of South Street. Developed from an old landfill, the sanctuary is a peaceful and remote area, good for cycling and lazing around on the wooden boardwalks. Those with a car might do better to explore the coastline just north of Arcata along Hwy-101. **Moonstone Beach**, about ten miles north of town, is a vast, sandy strip that, save the odd beachcomber, remains empty during the day, and by night hots up with guitar-strumming student parties which rage for as long as the bracing climate allows. **Trinidad Harbor**, a few miles further on, is a good stop for a drink, to nose around the small shops or just sit down by the sea wall and watch the fishing boats being tossed about beyond the harbour.

A more adventurous (some would say insane) destination is the **Hoopa Valley Indian Reservation** sixty miles inland. In recent years the site of often violent confrontation between Native Americans and whites over fishing territory, Hoopa is now seen by some as the badlands of Humboldt and few take the time to check out the valley. To get there, take Hwy-299 west for forty miles until you hit Hwy-96 at **WILLOW CREEK** – self-proclaimed gateway to "Bigfoot Country". Reports of giant 350 to 800-pound humanoids wandering the forests of northwestern California have circulated since the late nineteenth century, fuelled by long-established Indian legends, though they weren't taken seriously until 1958, when a road maintenance crew found giant footprints in a remote area nearby. Photos were taken and the Bigfoot story went worldwide, since when over forty separate sightings of Bigfoot prints have kept the story alive. At the crossroads in Willow Creek stands a huge wooden replica of the prehistoric looking man-ape, with its slanted forehead, flared nostrils and short ears, an identikit of the creature who in recent years has added kidnapping to his list of alleged activites. Beside the statue is a small **Chamber of Commerce** that has details of Bigfoots escapades as well as information on the Hoopa Valley Reservation and other local sights.

Hwy-96 out of Willow Creek leads for twelve miles to Tish Tang Road, marking the edge of the Hoopa Indian Reservation, set in a pretty valley of hills and streams. There's a **campsite** here, well signposted inside the reservation, a bingo hall (a *must* if you're here on a Friday night) bar, general store and the **Hoopa Tribal Museum** (Mon–Sat 10am–4pm; $1.50) – full of crafts, baskets and jewellery of the Hupa and Yurok tribes. Otherwise the reservation has a dead, lawless feel, the locals hanging around listlessly outside their caravans or roaring up and down the dirt tracks on their Harley-Davidsons. The nervous will want to move on quickly, but if you're here in the last week in July you should make an effort to catch the All Indian Rodeo which is held southwest of the village.

The Redwood National Park

Some thirty miles north of Arcata, the small town of **ORICK** marks the southernmost end of the **REDWOOD NATIONAL PARK**, a massive area that stretches up into Del Norte County at the very top end of California, ending at the unattractive town of CRESCENT CITY. Three state parks make up the Redwood park, which contains the world's first, third and sixth highest trees – the pride of California's forestland, especially between June and September when every school in the state seems to have organised its summer camp here. Increasingly, it's also becoming a controversial area, and despite its designation as a World Heritage Site by UNESCO, campers awake to the sound of chainsaws and huge lumber trucks ploughing up and down the highway. Despite this, locals are still dissatisfied and claim that they've lost much of the prime timber they relied on before the days of the park to make their living.

You can drive through the park, and this is as ever the best way; pausing where you want to and taking in the incredible vistas. *Greyhound* buses, if asked, will stop (and if you're lucky can be flagged down) along part of the highway that cuts through the forests, but – unless you want to single out a specific area and stay there (not the way to see the best of the park) – a dire lack of any other public transport in the area makes it almost impossible to get through unless you've got a car or are of a very determined breed of hitchhiker.

The park

The 58,000 acres of the park divide into distinct areas: the southern entrance and **Orick Area**; the **Prairie Creek State Park**, past the riverside town of **KLAMATH**; and the area in the far north around the **Del Norte** and **Jedediah Smith State Parks** in the environs of CRESCENT CITY in Del Norte County. The park headquarters are in Crescent City at 1111 Second Street (☎464-6101), but the **visitors centers** and **ranger stations** throughout the park are perfectly adequate (even better) for maps and information. There are **campsites** in each of the areas of the park, many are primitive and free, but the three that have showers and water cost around $8 a night; they are, *Prairie Creek* on US 101, five miles north of Orick; *Mill Creek*, eight miles south of Crescent City and *Jedediah Smith*, five miles north of Crescent City on Smith River. If you must come in summer (and it does get very crowded), make reservations (☎619/452-1950) or try the **Redwood Hostel** (☎482-8265) halfway between Eureka and Crescent City on

US-101 at **KLAMATH**, which has rooms at around $17 per night. If you're really desperate, get onto US-101 and look for **motels** around Crescent City.

One word of warning: while there is no imminent danger, you should be aware of the presence of **bears;** as friendly as they appear, they are *wild* animals. Most fundamentally, they will be after your food, so it's essential to store it in airtight containers when camping and be careful where you leave your garbage; never attempt to feed them (frequently they'll beg, but once fed will become aggressive in their demands for more), and never get between a mother and her young. Young animals are cute, irate mothers are not.

Orick Area

As the southernmost, and therefore most-used, entrance to the Redwood National Park, the Orick area is always busy. Its major attraction is **Tall Trees Grove**, home of the world's tallest tree – a mightily impressive specimen that stands at some 367 feet. Many hike the 8.5 mile trail from the **ranger station** (daily 8am–5pm; ☎488-3461) at the park's entrance to the grove, but if you're unsure of your footing amongst all this lush undergrowth, there's a **shuttle bus** ($3) service five times daily. Less demanding is a hike along the Redwood Creek Trail to the imaginatively named Tall Trees Grove. North of Orick take a right onto Bald Hills Road, then, 0.3 miles along you fork off to the picnic area, where the trail starts. The bridge, 1.5 miles away, is passable in summer only – heavy rainfall in winter makes it impossible. If you can make it from here, a bit further east, another trail turns off Bald Hills Road and winds for half a mile to Lady Bird Grove – a collection of trees dedicated to the former U.S. President's wife, Lady Bird Johnson, a big lover apparently, of flora and fauna.

In Orick itself (actually two miles north of the park entrance and ranger station), *Lane's Pack Station* (☎488-5225), offer **horseback trips** through the forests and along the coast. Trips vary from two-hour rides along coastal trails, to full weekends in the forest where they provide the camping equipment, cook and guide. There are several stores and cafés north along US-101, where you can pick up supplies, buy a lot of burl and have a sit-down meal. Of several places, the *Elkhorn Saloon*, halfway between Orick and Prairie Creek, is your best bet for avoiding the crowds.

Prairie Creek State Park

Of the three state parks within the Redwood National Park, Prairie Creek is the most varied and popular, and while bear and elk roam across all three, it's only here that you can be taken around by the rangers for a hand-held **tour** of the wild and damp profusion of a solidly populated redwood forest. Whether you take a map and do it independently or opt for an organised tour, main features include the meadows of **Elk Prairie** in front of the **ranger station** on US-101 (daily 8am–5pm winter, 8am-6pm summer, ☎488-2171),where herds of Roosevelt Elk, massive beasts weighing up to four hundred pounds, roam freely, protected from poachers. A mile north of the ranger station, a magnificent redwood tree, more than one hundred metres tall, overlooks the road – which given its accessibility is usually jam-packed with passing traffic stopping for a peek. Ferns, lichen and mosses are everywhere, especially at **Fern Canyon** with its slippery fifteen-metre walls.

Prairie Creek also has the park's main concentration of **restaurants** on the southern apporach on US-101. All do a good line in wild boar roasts, elk steaks and the like, as well as a more traditional fare of burgers and breakfasts: *Ima's Burger Bar* and *Rolf's Park Restaurant*, just before the park entrance, are two you might try.

Klamath Area

Though technically not part of the Redwood park, Klamath has spectacular coastal views from trails where the Klamath River meets the ocean, a reliable hostel (see above), and, for a bit of fun, **Trees of Mystery** (daily 8am–6pm; free), on US-101, where you'll notice two huge sixty-foot wooden sculptures, one of Paul Bunyan and one of Babe (who was apparently his blue ox). You can drive through, jump over, lumber under the trees, with the exception of the most impressive specimen of all – the **Cathedral Tree**, where nine trees have grown from one root structure to form a spooky circle. Never slow to cash in, enterprising Californians hold wedding services here throughout the year. The most spectacular scenery in Klamath is to be had, not by the trees, but by the ocean: take Requa Road about three quarters of a mile down to the estuary, a point known as the **Klamath Overlook**, from where there is an awe-inspiring view of the sea and coast. From here, a coastal trail begins and leads for ten miles along some of California's most remote beach, ending at Endert's Beach in Crescent City.

Crescent City, and Del Norte and Jedediah Smith State Parks

The northernmost outpost of the national park, the Del Norte and Jedediah Smith state parks sit either side of **CRESCENT CITY**, a woebegone place with little to recommend it apart from its proximity to the parks. However, if you've come this far, and are tired of camping and inadequate food supplies, it could save you from despair. There are several good motels on US-101: *Curly Redwood Lodge*, 701 US-101 South (☎464-2137), has doubles from $35, and, even cheaper, the *Townhouse Motel*, 444 US-101 South (☎464-4176), has rooms from $28. **Del Norte Park**, seven miles south of Crescent City, is worth visiting less for its redwood forests (you've probably had enough by now anyway), than its fantastic beach area and hiking trails. Pick up maps from the ranger station at the park entrance; they also conduct guided tours, although most of the hiking trails are an easy two miles or so along the coastal ridge where the redwoods meet the sea, and can be done just as well independently. From May to July, wild rhododendron and azalea shoot up everywhere, creating a floral blanket across the park's floor. **Jedediah Smith Park**, nine miles east of Crescent City, is named after the European explorer who was the first white man to trek overland from the Mississippi to the Pacific in 1828, before being killed by Comanche tribes in 1831. Not surprisingly his name is everywhere and no less than eighteen separate redwood groves are dedicated to his memory. Sitting squatly on the south fork of the Smith River, the park attracts many people to canoe downstream or, more quietly, sit on the riverbank and fish. Of the hiking trails, the **Stout Grove Trail** is the most popular, leading down to a most imposing goliath – a twenty-foot diameter redwood.

If you're heading further east and can't face more highway (101 and US 99), opt for the painfully slow, but scenic route that follows Howland Hill Road from Crescent City through the forest to the Hiouchi ranger station about five miles away. Branching off this are several trails that are blissfully short and easy (average 800m) where you're unlikely to meet the hordes of hikers that plague the major parts of the park. At the end of the Howland Hill Road are picnicking facilities.

THE NORTHERN INTERIOR

As big as Ohio, yet with a population of only 250,000, the **Northern Interior** of California is about as remote as the state gets. Cut off from the coast by the **Shasta Cascade** range, it's a region dominated by forests, lakes, some fair-sized mountains – and two thirds of the state's precipitation. It's largely uninhabited too, and infrequently visited. This is, of course, the greater part of its appeal, and while it doesn't have the biggest waterfalls, the bluest lakes or the highest mountains, it lacks the congestion that marks many of California's better-known areas. Those who do visit stick to a few easily accessible locations, leaving vast miles of the state for the more adventurous (or crowd-weary) to explore.

I-5 leads through the very middle of this near wilderness, forging straight up the **Sacramento Valley** through acres of unspectacular farmland up to **Redding**: neatly placed for the best of the northern interior's natural phenomena. Redding isn't much of a place in itself, but it's a good idea to use the town as a base, venturing out on loop trips a day or so at a time. Most accessible, immediately west and north of Redding, the **Whiskeytown-Shasta-Trinity National Recreation area** is a series of three lakes and forests set aside for what can be heavily subscribed public use, especially in summer when it's hard to move for campervans, windsurfers and packs of happy holidaymakers. The drought of recent years has meant that the water in certain lakes has dropped to dangerously low levels, and as a result the resorts that rely on watersports for their existence are finding it harder and harder to survive. East of here the **Lassen National Volcanic Park** enjoys its biggest crowds in the winter months when the volcanic summits and slopes make for some increasingly fashionable skiing territory, but come the summer thaw it returns to a much emptier panorama. The **Plumas National Forest**, which spreads southeast from here as far as the borders of Nevada and the Gold Country, will hold no surprises: another mountainous cloak of forestland with almost repetitive appeal. If you have to hit the boonies, save your petrol for the very northeastern tip of the state and the loneliest of all California's verdant landscapes, the **Modoc National Forest**. The volcanic **Lava Beds National Monument** here is for most of the year inaccessible, and even when the roads do open, very few people visit.

It's the usual story with **public transport**: buses connect San Francisco and Sacramento to Portland via I-5, stopping off at the Sacramento Valley towns and Redding on the way; and, weather permitting, Redding is also connected by bus to the coast at Eureka. But neither route provides anything like comprehensive access to the area, and if you're going to come here at all it should be in a car. Anything worth seeing lies at least five miles from the nearest bus stop. The area is too big and the towns too far apart to make public transport even faintly enjoyable. Hitching, too, unlike on the coast, can be a cold and frustrating way of getting around due to unreliable weather and at times very patchy traffic flow.

The Sacramento Valley

The **Sacramento Valley** lays fair claim to being California's most uninteresting region, a flat, largely agricultural corridor of small, sleepy towns and endless vistas of dull arable land. Luckily, I-5 makes it easy to pass straight through, whether you're driving or not, and this is much the best thing you could do. The half-empty, speedy freeway cuts an almost two-hundred mile-long swathe through the region, and you could forge straight through to the more enticing far north quite painlessly in half a day.

Chico

CHICO, about halfway between Sacramento and Redding, and some thirty miles east of I-5, might be a good stop-off if you don't want to attempt to cover the whole valley from top to bottom in one day. It's a typical small American university town in every way, its charm lying in its homely suburban appeal rather than anything you can see or do once you get here. Having said that, it could be the best of the bunch if you're here to visit Lassen Volcanic Park and need somewhere to stay.

The town is on the Seattle–Sacramento train-line and *Greyhound* stop here five times a day on their north–south routes. The **Chamber of Commerce**, 500 Main Street (☎891-5556; Mon-Fri 9am-4pm) can supply you with maps and a street-plan as well as comprehensive lists of accommodation and eating options in the area.

Short on sights as Chico is, you might try the three-storey **Bidwell Mansion**, 525 Esplanade (tours daily 10am-4pm $2 ☎895-6144). Built in 1868 by the man who is considered to be the town's founder, General Bidwell, it's an attractive enough Victorian building filled with the leftovers from a wealthy but otherwise insignificant family. It is however unequivocally rather boring, and you might prefer to opt for a picnic in the adjoining **Bidwell Park**, which extends from the centre of the town for ten miles to the north. This is again unremarkable, though perhaps a little spiced up by the knowledge that the first Robin Hood film, starring Errol Flynn, was made here in the old Oak forest.

More interestingly, the **Sierra Nevada Brewing Company**, 1075 E 20th Street (☎893-3520), give free tours of the brewery from Tuesday to Friday at 12.30pm, and on Saturday at 2pm showing how one of California's best beers is made and, more usefully, giving the chance to get some cheap samples before you leave.

Accommodation

Fortunately Chico has much more in the way of **accommodation** than it does in sights. Motels are everywhere in town, particularly in the Main Street and Broadway area.

Chico Motor Lodge, 725 Broadway (☎895-1877). The cheapest and most central motel in town, if somewhat run down. Rooms from $28 per night.

The Matador, 1937 The Esplanade (☎342-7543). A pretty Spanish Revival building, set out around a courtyard, with rooms from $38.

O'Flaherty House Bed and Breakfast, 1462 Arcadian Ave (☎893-5494). Sumptuous bedrooms cost $60 per night and upwards.

Thunderbird Lodge, 715 Main St(☎343-7911). Not a bad motel at all, with rooms for around $32 – and the largest neon sign in town.

Eating

Chico also does itself proud when it comes to **food**. Being a university town there are many cheap, excellent places aimed at the younger (and poorer) customer, as well as a handful of lively pubs and bars to while away your evenings.

La Comida, 954 Mangrove Ave. Cheap Mexican food daily until 9pm.

The Gashouse, 2359 Esplanade. Pizzas, salads and the like.

The Graduate, 344 W Eighth St. Massive hall with long tables at which students enjoy hamburgers, steaks and salads. Good value if you can put up with the video screens that glare at you from every available patch of wall space.

Jack's Family Restaurant, 540 Main Street. 24-hr diner, a bit on the greasy side, but good for late-night filling up.

Madison Beer Garden, 316 W Second St. As the name suggests, a place for swigging beer with students from the campus nearby.

Oy Vey's, 146 W Second Street. Large Jewish delicatessen that bakes the only bagels available in Chico and serves thumping great breakfasts for around $5. Bargain food, beautifully prepared.

The Rededengray Pub, 912 W First St. Large, pub-like place with draught beers from around the world with live music at weekends.

Trader Mou's, 2201 Pillsbury Road off Cohasset Road. Chinese food for around $5 per person. At 9pm the place turns into a dance emporium playing everything from country to Motown.

Red Bluff

RED BLUFF, around thirty miles north from Chico up I-5 is not a particularly exciting place – and has long since outgrown the small-town friendliness exuded by Chico. You may well see no more of the place than its *Greyhound* station, but if you're weary and want to stay over there's a reasonable selection of $30-a-night motels along Main Street: the *Crystal Motel*, 333 S Main Street (☎527-1021), has rooms from $23 per night and there are a handful of diners and burger-joints to fill up in town.

Red Bluff is on the other hand the one point at which you can pick up **public transport** to Lassen National Volcanic Park (see p.492). *Mount Lassen Motor Transit* (☎529-2722) operate a daily service – apart from Sundays and public holidays – via mail truck from Red Bluff's *Greyhound* station to the park entrance at Mineral.

Redding and around

After the high-flown descriptions of Northern California's isolated beauty and charm, **REDDING**'s sprawl of franchise motels and fast-food chains comes as something of a shock to most visitors, and the town doesn't improve with longer acquaintance. But Redding's position close to both the Whiskeytown-Shasta-Trinity National Recreation Area to the west and the Lassen Volcanic National Park to the east make it a premium transit point and the major source of accommodation for those wanting to sample the best of this part of the state. It's a railway centre basically, a characterless assembly of cheap lodgings and little else whose streets only really brighten during midsummer when the tourists hit town.

If conditions don't suit hiking, there's not a lot to do in Redding, though the **Redding Museum Art Center**, 1911 Rio Drive (Tues–Sun 10am–5pm; free), might amuse for half an hour or so with its collections of Native American artefacts and contemporary art by local artists.

Redding practicalities

Public transport is woefully inadequate; *Greyhound* (☎241-2643) have a station on Pine and Placer Streets with regular connections north and south, and a local bus system, *Municipal Bus* (☎241-2877) operates weekdays around Redding. But to get out of town and into the parks, the car-less will have to employ their thumbs. Those with cars will have to check ahead for weather conditions and if necessary, make extra provisions (anti-freeze, tyre chains, etc) in case of snow-storms. Though fiercely hot in summer, the temperature drops forbiddingly in some of the surrounding areas in winter, and what looks like a mild day in Redding could turn out to be blizzard conditions a few miles up the road (and several thousand feet up a mountainside).

The cheaper **motels** are concentrated along Redding's main strip, Market Street (Hwy-273), and Pine Street, four blocks from the *Greyhound* station. *Budget Lodge*, 1055 Market Street (☎243-4231), has rooms from around $35. Down the road a little, the *Redding Lodge*, 1135 Market Street (☎243-5141), offers slightly more luxurious rooms from $40. **Restaurants** are as ubiquitous as motels, many of them 24-hour, most of them unappealing: *Denny's*, 735 Cypress Avenue, is an all-night diner serving cheap burgers and breakfasts, and *Gibsons Pub & Grill*, 610 N Market Street, serves beer, and meat and two veg dishes, well into the night. You can also get Chinese food for less than $5 at the *Temple Chinese Restaurant*, 1400 Pine Street. You can get excellent sandwiches at the *Italian Sandwich Shop* in Cypress Square Village Plaza.

The **Redding Convention and Visitors Bureau**, 777 Auditorium Drive (Mon–Fri 9.30am–4.30pm; ☎225-4100), has advice on accommodation in Redding and some information on camping in the outlying areas and hiring camping equipment. For information more specifically on the surrounding area the **Shasta Cascade Wonderland Association**, on Pine Street and Parkview Avenue (opening times vary, call ahead; ☎243-2643), is manned by outdoor experts and has a more detailed collection of maps and information. They'll give you the best tips on hiking and weather conditions, geological features, the best campsites and suchlike. As a general rule, Lassen National Volcanic Park is for the hardier and more experienced hikers, and novices are pointed in the direction of the Whiskeytown-Shasta Trinity National Recreation Area, where there are warmer climes and easier trails.

Shasta

SHASTA, some fifteen miles west of Redding on Hwy-299, is altogether more appealing as a destination. It was a booming gold-mining town when Redding was an insignificant dot on the map, but the two towns' fortunes changed when the railroad tracks were laid to Redding and Shasta was abandoned. It remains today a row of half-ruined brick buildings that were once part of a runaway prosperity, and literally the end of the road for prospectors. All roads from San Francisco, Sacramento and other southerly points terminated at Shasta; beyond, rough and poorly marked trails made it almost impossible to find gold diggings along the Trinity, Salmon and Upper Sacramento Rivers, and diggers contented themselves with the rich pickings in the surrounding area, pushing out the local Native Americans in a brutal territorial quest for good mining land. The **Courthouse**, on the east side of Main Street, has been turned into a museum (daily 10am–3pm; $2), full of mining paraphernalia and paintings of past heroes, though best are the gallows at the back and the prison cells below – a grim reminder of the daily executions that went on here. The miners were largely an unprincipled lot, and in the main room of the Courthouse a charter lays down some basic rules of conduct:

IV Thou shalt neither remember what thy friends do at home on the sabbath day, lest the remembrance may not compare favourably with what thou doest here.

VII Thou shalt not kill the body by working in the rain, even though thou shall make enough money to buy psychic attendance. Neither shalt thou destroy thyself by "tight" nor "slewed" nor "high" nor "corned" nor "three sheets to the wind", by drinking smoothly down brandy slings, gin cocktails, whiskey punches, rum toddies and egg nogs.

From the Miners Ten Commandments

The **Shasta State Historic Park** (daily 9am–5pm; free), also on Main Street, is less grand than it sounds, not much bigger than a beer garden really, with old painted wagons and a good picnic area under the trees to have your lunch from the burger-shack next door

Whiskeytown-Shasta-Trinity National Recreation Area

Travelling on from Shasta, Hwy-299 is a deserted, often precipitous but enjoyable road that leads into the western portion of the **Whiskeytown-Shasta-Trinity National Recreation Area**, ten miles out from Redding. Assuming the road's open – it's often blocked off due to bad weather – this huge chunk of land is open for public use daily, year-round. Its series of three impounded lakes – Clair Eagle, Whiskeytown and Shasta – have artificial beaches, forests and camping facilities designed to meet the needs of anyone who has ever fancied themselves as a water-skier, sailor or wilderness hiker. Sadly, during summer it's completely congested as windsurfers, motorboats and recreational vehicles block the narrow routes which serve the lakes. To compound the problem, severe drought in the last few years has led to receding water levels, evidenced by the red band of hitherto unexposed rock just above the surface of the water. But in the winter, when the tourists have all gone, it can be supremely untouched, at least on the surface. In fact there's an extensive system of tunnels, dams and aqueducts directing the plentiful waters of the Sacramento River to California's Central Valley to irrigate cash crops for the huge agribusinesses. The lakes are pretty enough, but residents complain they're not a patch on the wild waters that used to flow from the mountains before the Central Valley Project came along in the 1960s.

Of the three lakes, **Whiskeytown**, just beyond Shasta, is the smallest, easiest to get to, and inevitably the most popular. Ideal for watersports, it hums with the sound of jet-skis and powerboats ripping across the still waters. Those that don't spend their holiday in a wet-suit can usually be found four-wheel driving and pulling action-man stunts on the primitive roads all around. The best place for **camping** and **hiking** is in the **Brandy Creek** area – a hairy five-mile drive along the narrow Kennedy Memorial Drive from the main entrance and **Visitor Information Center** on Hwy-299. There's a small store at the water's edge in Brandy Creek and three campsites about a mile behind in the woods.

Northeast on Hwy-3 (off Hwy-299 forty miles west of Whiskeytown) **Clair Eagle Lake** is much quieter, rarely used in summer and in winter primarily a picturesque stopoff for skiers on their way to the **Salmon-Trinity Alps** area beyond, part of the extensive **Salmon Mountains** range. Cold temperatures year-round keep it empty, and most people who make it this far west are coming only to see **WEAVERVILLE** and its **Joss House**, a small Chinese temple built during the Gold Rush years that is still in use today. Should you get stuck in the area, there's a motel in **Douglas City**, just south of Weaverville; *Indian Creek Lodge,* 1.5 miles east of town (☎916/623-6294) has rooms for around $30. In Douglas City itself there are a couple of grub-stops (you could hardly call them restaurants) where you can grab a burger.

But this is a diversion only for the desperate, and what time you have should be used to move north of Redding along US-151 to visit **Shasta Lake**, biggest of the three lakes, but not the most popular due to the unsightly and enormous (180-metre high and 1-km long) **Shasta Dam** bang in the middle. Built between 1938 and 1945 as part of the enormous Central Valley irrigation project, the dam backs up the Sacramento, McCloud and Pit rivers to form the lake, the northern outpost of the Central Valley Project. In terms of size it is eclipsed only by two other dams in the world, and it sits imposingly in the otherwise concrete-free landscape. The best views are from marked vista points on the approach road (US-151), but a more vivid way to experience the 465-foot-high structure is to drive across the narrow precipice itself, think of how much water is gushing about beneath you and note the silence. There's a **Visitor Center** on the approach to the dam that has slide shows and information about the dam for fans of engineering.

On the north side of the lake the **Shasta Caverns** (daily 10am–3pm; $4; ☎916/238-2341) just off I-5 about twenty minutes north of Redding on the Shasta Caverns Road, are of slightly more interest, their massive limestone formations – the largest in California – jutting above ground, visible from the freeway. The interior, however, is something of a letdown: a fairly standard series of caves and tunnels in which stalactite and stalagmite formations are studded with crystals, flowstone deposits and miniature waterfalls. The steep, rugged granite rocks of the CASTLE CRAGS STATE PARK are located west of Hwy 5, just beyond Castella. Turn off down Castle Creek Country Road and after about 750 metres, on the right-hand side, you'll come to the park headquarters, where you can obtain a map and information. A steep, incredibly winding road leads up past several small campsites to a vantage point. From here on, you can hike along the tough, 2.7-mile long Crags Trail and Indian Springs Trail to the granite Castle Dome.

Mount Shasta

The lone peak of **Mount Shasta**, at 14,162 feet one of the highest volcanoes in the country, dominates the landscape for a hundred miles all around. Although it experienced its last volcanic eruption over two hundred years ago, it's still considered active. A scenic road branches off I-5 at the small town of DUNSMUIR, to close-by, pushing on eight thousand feet up the slopes to the tiny town that describes itself as "the best kept secret in California"; **MOUNT SHASTA**, hard under the enormous bulk of the mountain. It's a rewarding journey, and easily done by *Greyhound* (305 N Mt Shasta Blvd; ☎926-3797) which connects the town with Redding in the south and Oregon in the north.

The main purpose of a visit is of course to climb the mountain, although it should be noted that every year there are several deaths and numerous injuries sustained through inexperience and over-ambition. Also there are the packs of hunters who roam the slopes of the mountain looking for deer, bear and antelope to contend with. The wise will stick to the clearly marked trails laid out in the excellent maps given out by the **Mount Shasta Ranger District Office**, 204 W Alma (☎926-3781). More exciting is the llama trekking organised by *Shasta Mountain Guides*, 1938 Hill Road (☎926-3117) who can also arrange for you to see the mountain from a jeep. And if you're into some real thrills, you can arrange **white-water rafting trips** through *Turtle River Rafting* (☎926-3223). Because of the rough weather, even clearly marked trails will be difficult to follow unless you visit in the "weather-safe" June to August period. If you come outside of these months then it will probably be just to rest up for the night and get some food en route to warmer climes.

For information on places to stay, check out the the *Mount Shasta Chamber of Commerce*, 300 Pine Street (☎926-2620) who can also furnish you with a town plan and answer miscellaneous enquiries. Despite its size and general lack of things to do, **accommodation** in Mount Shasta does not come as cheap as you'd imagine and you should expect to pay upwards of $35 for a room for the night. Amongst those you might try are: *Mountain View Lodge,* 305 McCloud Road (☎926-4704) and the *Das Alpenhaus Motel,* 504 Mount Shasta Boulevard (☎926-4617) both have rooms for around $30 or $40 and are about the cheapest around. Really nice places like the *McCloud Guest House,* 606 W Colombero Drive (☎964-3160) set in the former headquarters of the old logging company, will set you back about $65, as will a stay at the stylish *Mount Shasta Ranch,* 1008 W Barr Road (☎926-4029).

There are campsites all over the surrounding area, but few with full amenities (hot showers are vital when the mercury drops). One that has it all, and unfortunately a few recreational vehicles besides, is *KOA*, 900 N Mt Shasta Boulevard (☎926-4029), two blocks from the centre of town, which charges $12 per site. The most picturesque campsite in the area is the *Lake Siskiyou Campground* (☎926-2618) which lies four miles west of the town, in a wood on a lake with the same name. It has picnic areas and bathing and you can hire boats.

For **eating**, try the *Mt Eddy Bagel Bakery*, a moderately priced soup and sandwich place a block from the ranger station on E Alma Street. *Bellissimo's*, at 204 E Lake Street, serves delicious well-priced meals; *Marilyn's* on 1136 Mt Shasta Boulevard, has standard American fare; *Lalo's*, a stone's throw from the *KOA* campsite, is a reliable Mexican. An excellent Italian restaurant, *Mike and Tony's,* 501 Mount Shasta Boulevard, is a bit more expensive, but you can wash down your food with some good wines.

Lassen National Volcanic Park

Around forty miles directly east from Redding, the 106,000 acres that make up the pine forests, crystal-green lakes and boiling thermal pools of the **Lassen National Volcanic Park** are one of the most unearthly parts of California. A forbidding climate, which brings up to fifty feet of snowfall each year, keeps the area pretty much uninhabited with the roads all blocked by snow and apart from a brief June to October season completely deserted. Dominating the park at over 10,000 feet is Mount Lassen itself. Quiet in recent years, Lassen erupted in 1914 beginning a cycle of outbursts which climaxed in 1915 when the peak blew an enormous mushroom cloud some seven miles skyward, tearing the summit into chunks that landed as far away as Reno. Although seventy years of geothermal inactivity have since made the mountain a safe and fascinating place, scientists predict that of all the West Coast volcanoes, Lassen is the likeliest to blow again.

The northern entrance to the park is at the junction of Hwy-44 and Hwy-89 at Manzanita Lake where Lassen is beautifully reflected in the water. You can walk around this using simple trails which stay on level ground.

Hwy-89 leads through Lassen to the southwestern corner park entrance at Mineral, reachable from Red Bluff on an 8am *Mount Lassen Motor Transit* (☎529-2722) mail truck/bus; round-trip tickets cost $22 and return buses leave at 10.30am and 3.50pm. The **Visitor Centers** at Manzanita and Mineral (daily 8.30am–4.30pm; ☎335-4266) have free maps and information on the park: in particular, you should pick up a copy of *Lassen Trails*, which describes the most popular hikes and the free *Lassen Park Guide*.

You should also speak to rangers who'll point you toward the routes best suited to your ability – the park's generally high elevations will leave you short of breath unless you're an experienced hiker, and you should stick to the shorter trails at least until you're acclimatised. The only **campsite** with hot showers and toilets is at Lake Manzanita near the visitor centre and is open only from the end of June until the end of September, but there are free primitive **campsites** at South Summit, North Summit and Sulphur Works, operating on a first-come first-served basis There are few times of the year when conditions are ideal for camping and hiking; even in August night temperatures hover around freezing, and many opt instead for a leisurely drive through.

For **food**, you don't have an awful lot to choose from. There's nothing actually in the park itself, and you'll have to content yourself with stocking up beforehand at the cafeteria/grocery stores in Mineral and Manzanita Lake.

The Park

Starting at the northern entrance, a thorough tour of the park by car along Hwy-89 should take no more than a few hours. The park road is thirty miles long and although its first few miles are unremarkable, it's worth persevering a few miles south until you reach the **Devastated Area**, where 65 years ago molten lava from Lassen poured down the valley, denuding the landscape as it went, ripping out every tree and patch of grass. Slowly the earth is recovering its green mantle, but the most vivid impression is one of complete destruction. Marking the halfway point, **Summit Lake** is a busy camping area set around a beautiful icy lake, close to which are the park's most manageable hiking trails. There's a hikers' trail from the lake's eastern shore to ECHO LAKE (seven miles, about four hours) and LOWER TWIN LAKE (eight miles, about five hours). At this point you meet the Pacific Crest Trail again, which bisects the park from north to south.

If you head further south along Hwy 89, you reach the parking area (eight thousand feet up) where the steep five-mile ascent to LASSEN PEAK begins. Experienced hikers can reach the peak in four hours. Take sufficient water, warm clothing and a map, and watch out for the first signs of mountain (ie altitude) sickness. Wilderness seekers will have a better time pushing east to the **Juniper**

Lake area, where steep trails weave for about four miles round to a primitive campsite on the east side

Continuing south along Hwy-89, Lassen's indisputable show-stealers are **Bumpass Hell** and **Emerald Lake**, the former (named after a man who lost a leg trying to cross it) a steaming valley of active pools and vents which bubble away at a low rumble all around. It looks dangerous, but the trails are sturdy and easy to manage. Be warned, though, that the crusts over the thermal features are often brittle, and breaking through them could literally plunge you into very hot water – *never* venture off the trails. The paths around Emerald Lake are spectacular in a much quieter fashion: the lake looks like a sheet of icy-green glass, perfectly still and clear but for the snow-covered rock-mound which rises from its centre. Only during summer does the lake approach swimmable temperatures, and if you're visiting outside of July or August you'll have to content yourself with gazing at its mirror-like surface.

Before leaving the park at Mineral, make an effort to stop at **Sulphur Works**, a boiling cauldron of steam vents, whose acrid smell reminds you that Lassen is in fact a volcano. A magnificent but gruelling trail leads for a mile around the site to the avalanche-prone summit at **Diamond Peak**, and great views over the entire park and forestland beyond.

Lava Beds National Monument

After seeing Mount Shasta you may well want to push on to the **Lava Beds National Monument** (open May–Sept only) in the far northeastern corner of the state, especially if you've plans to continue on into Oregon. Be warned, however, that even from Mount Shasta the journey takes about four hours by car; only if you're bitterly determined to see the Lava Beds should you even attempt this journey.

This is the most remote and forgotten of California's parks: part of the huge **Modoc National Forest**, it's actually a series of volcanic caves and huge black lava flows with a history as violent as the natural forces that created it. Until the 1850s Gold Rush it was home to the Modoc tribe of Indians, but repeated and bloody confrontations between the indigenous people and the miners led the government to order the Indians into a reservation shared with another, traditionally enemy, tribe. After only a few months the Modocs drifted back to their homeland in the lava beds, and in 1872 the army was sent in to return them by force to the reservation. They were driven off by 52 Modoc warriors under the leadership of a tribesman known as Captain Jack, who held back an army twenty times the size of his for five months, from a stronghold at the northern tip of the park

Eventually Captain Jack was captured and hanged and what was left of the tribe sent off to a reservation in Oklahoma where most of them died of malaria. Today the lava beds are inhabited only by the wild deer and three million migrating ducks who attract the trickle of tourists that make it up here.

The most accessible and useful of the two entrances to the park – neither of which can be reached without a car – is in the southeastern corner along Hwy-139, 160 miles from Redding and twenty-five miles south of **TULELAKE**. This latter town is your last chance to buy supplies if you're going to camp – there's nothing in the park itself. It also has the area's only accommodation options –

several roadside budget **motels** – and a few cheap restaurants. *Park Motel* (☎667-2913) just south of town on Hwy-139, and the *Ellis Motel* (☎667-5242) on the same road a mile north, have rooms starting from $28 per night. Elevation throughout the park ranges from 4000 to 5700 feet and at any time of the year cold weather is possible, snowfall occurring throughout most months; in summer, daytime temperatures can reach the seventies, but freezing nights can make **camping** uncomfortable. There is one **campsite** in the park, at Indian Wells near the entrance and **visitor center** (daily 8.30am–5.30pm; ☎667-2283), and all off-road camping throughout the forest is free.

The area around the visitor centre also holds the largest concentration of caves (around two hundred) and if you've managed to hitch into the park you won't need a car to get around. **The Mushpot Caves**, as they're known, were formed from lava flows which left cylindrical tubes that you can now scamper through. Some are so small that you have to crawl along on all fours, while others are an enormous 75 feet in diameter. Some of the caves contain Native American petroglyphs, not to be confused with the names painted on the cave walls by J.D. Howard, one of the first white men to explore and name the caves. Ranger-led tours from the visitor centre will explain the history of the more important caves, like **Labyrinth** and **Golden Dome**, distinguishable both for their geological features and one-time Native American inhabitants.

A car is vital, however (as is the visitor centre map), if you're to tackle the northern reaches of the park around **Captain Jack's Stronghold**, which was where he and his tribe holed up for five months in a natural fortress of caves.

When you get there you'll see how they managed to hide through the passage-ways of the hill, which on the outside looks like nothing special, and a self-guided trail will take you through the fort, pointing out significant spots along the way. While you're allowed to explore the caves alone, it takes considerable nerve to enter the darkness and most opt for the ranger-led tours which leave the visitor centre daily at 2pm. If you insist on going it alone, you must report to the ranger and collect flashlights from the visitor centre before heading off.

travel details

Buses

From San Francisco to Redding (3 daily; 5hr); Santa Rosa (5; 1hr 30min).

From Eureka to Redding (2 daily; 4hr).

From Portland to Redding (2 daily; 12hr).

From Santa Rosa to Mendocino (1 daily; 2hr 30min); Fort Bragg (1; 2hr 45min); Eureka (1;4hr 30min).

From Sacramento to Redding (4 daily; 3hr 30min).

Trains

From San Francisco, 1 daily to Sacramento (2hr 45min); Chico (4hr 30min); Redding (5hr 44min)/ Klamath Falls (8hr 51min); Eugene (14hr 4min); Portland (17hr 55min); Seattle (21hr 55min).

PART THREE

WASHINGTON AND OREGON

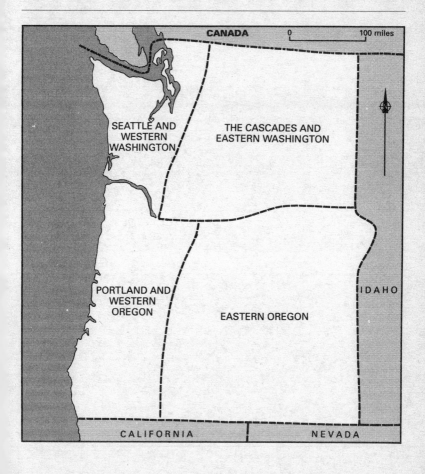

CANADA 0 100 miles

SEATTLE AND
WESTERN
WASHINGTON

THE CASCADES AND
EASTERN WASHINGTON

PORTLAND AND
WESTERN
OREGON

EASTERN OREGON

IDAHO

CALIFORNIA NEVADA

CHAPTER NINE

SEATTLE AND WESTERN WASHINGTON

Every part of this soil is sacred, in the estimation of my people

Chief Seattle, 1854

Does it ever stop raining?

Californian hitch-hiker, 1989

D espite the sunny-side-up statistics of the tourist board, **Western Washington** is for most of the year very wet: only the summers (late June to September) are usually warm and blue-skied. But even seen through a haze of fine, grey drizzle, the region is incredibly beautiful. Vast forests shelter all kinds of wildlife, remote islands scatter the sea, driftwood-strewn beaches are unchanged since the native Americans used them to launch whaling canoes; and, edging the region to the east, the Cascade mountains provide a snow-capped backdrop. There's a kind of challenge in all this, and to get the most out of coming here, you have to be prepared to tackle at least a few hiking trails (well laid-out, easy to follow and available in manageably short versions); otherwise Washington's great, green outdoors with its everlasting expanses of trees can just make you feel very small indeed.

Of course, Western Washington does have its cities. But even **Seattle**, commercial and cultural capital of the Northwest, is only really a prelude to the surrounding scenery. Perched on the edge of the Puget Sound, it's the hub of a ferry system offering glorious rides to rural islands and peninsulas.

At the southern end of the Puget Sound, heavy industry at blue-collar **Tacoma** has caused a worrying amount of pollution – a matter which, among other things, is debated in the stately government buildings of **Olympia**, Washington's capital, thirty miles or so beyond. Further south, I-5 races past the volcanic remains of Mount St Helens on toward the Oregon border. **North from Seattle** mountains, forests and lakes surround the spreading communities and at weekends Puget Sounders escape from the cities to the rural parts of **Whidbey Island**, further north to the beautiful **San Juan Islands**, or inland to the steep mountains of Mount Baker and north to Canada.

Cross an island or two from Seattle to the west, and you come to the **Olympic Peninsula**, fringed with logging communities and circled by the US-101 highway. The rugged mountains at its core are home to rare Roosevelt elk, lush vegetation that merges into rain forest in its western valleys, with miles of wilderness beaches on its Pacific edge: amazing stuff, but again you'll need to use your feet to see the best of it. Washington's **lower coast,** to the south, is more accessible but not as appealing, splodged with industrial towns and holiday resorts.

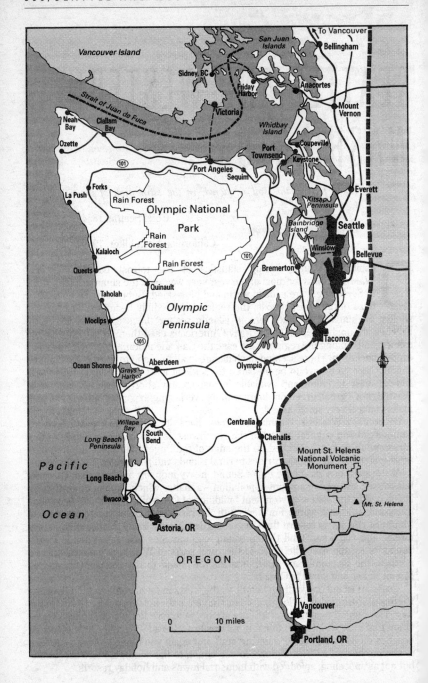

The drawback to this remoteness is that you'll have to hire a car (or bike, if you've got strong legs) to get to many of the most enticing parts: the ferries will carry you around the waterways and *Greyhound* provides useful services between the main towns (*Amtrak* only serves the larger cities). Limited local bus services extend the network.

SEATTLE AND AROUND

Curved around the shore of Elliott Bay, with Lake Washington behind and the snowy peak of Mount Ranier hovering faintly in the distance, **Seattle** is beautifully set, its insistently modern skyline of shiny glass skyscrapers gleaming across the bay, emblem of two decades of vigorous urban renewal. And Seattle in many ways feels like a new city, still groping for a balance between its smart highrises and a downbeat streetlife that reflects its tough port past. Its old central working-class areas, narrowly saved from the jaws of the bulldozer by popular outcry, have been restored as colourful historic districts – now, like so much of the city, home to a new core of urban sophistication that is mushrooming up in clusters of chic and pricey restaurants and wine bars.

Broad and deep like an inland sea, the Puget Sound stretches its clutter of tiny islands and ragged peninsulas surrounded by enough saltwater to make boats and bridges an essential part of life **around Seattle**. Bays and inlets house every kind of watercraft: yachts are moored in picturesque marinas, ocean-going ships unload containerised consumer goods at ports, and fishing trawlers pull in with catches from Alaska.

Seattle

Considering its pre-eminent standing in the economic and cultural life of the Pacific Northwest, Seattle's **beginnings** were inauspiciously muddy. Flooded out of its first location on Alki Beach, in the 1850s the small logging community here built its houses on stilts over the soggy ground of what's now the Pioneer Square historic district. As the surrounding forest was gradually felled and the wood sawed and shipped abroad, Seattle grew slowly as a timber town and a port until the Klondike Gold Rush of 1897 put it firmly on the national map and boosted Seattle's shipbuilding trade. The city was soon a large industrial centre, one that to this day holds a significant place in US labour history. Trades unions grew strong and the *Industrial Workers of the World* or "Wobblies" made Seattle their base, coordinating the country's first general strike in 1919, during the time of high unemployment which followed the end of World War I.

World War II brought a new impetus to growth, and the decades since have seen Seattle thrive as the economic centre of the booming Pacific Northwest. Today Seattle is among the most prosperous cities in the US, seemingly immune to the downturn in the economy everywhere else. Still, there's a sharp contrast between the obvious wealth and power of Seattle's many high-tech companies – such as *Boeing*, the world's biggest manufacturer of airplanes, or *Microsoft*, the largest US producer of computer software – with the very high levels of homelessness, and even more pointedly, Seattle's surprisingly large and visible community of teenage runaways, all very tangible reminders that not everyone shares in the city's good fortune. That said, for the short-term visitor Seattle offers all the fringe benefits of urban life – cafés, good bookshops and numerous cultural and counter-cultural events – amidst an idyllic, waterfront setting.

Arrival, information and getting around

International flights land at Seattle/Tacoma's **Sea-Tac Airport**, fourteen miles south of downtown; after customs, your luggage is taken away again and you follow in an underground train to the main terminal, where there's a small **visitor's information kiosk** (daily 9.30am–7.30pm) in front of the baggage carousel. Outside, the *Gray Line Airport Express* **bus** ($5) leaves every half-hour for the thirty-minute journey downtown, dropping off at major hotels, though further along, the local *Metro* bus makes regular runs along much the same route for 85¢ and takes only ten minutes more. Major **car hire** firms have airport branches, and operate shuttles to their pick-up points: once you're behind the wheel, Hwy-99, the Pacific Highway, leads into town. You can also pick up a car downtown – see "Listings" for details.

Arriving **by car**, you'll probably come in on **I-5**, the main north–south highway between California and the Canadian border; for downtown, take the Stewart Street or Union Street exit. The **Amtrak** station at Third Avenue and Jackson Street (☎1-800/872-7245 or 464-1930), south of downtown near the International District, and the **Greyhound** station, at Eighth Avenue and Stewart Street (☎624-3456) east of downtown, are both a bus-ride from downtown accommodation. *Green Tortoise*, with twice-weekly runs to and from Portland and San Francisco, drops off and picks up at Ninth Avenue and Stewart Street (☎324-RIDE).

For **information**, the **Seattle-King County Visitor's Bureau**, 666 Stewart Street in the Convention Center (Mon–Fri 8.30am–5pm, summer also Sat 10am–4pm; ☎461-5840), has racks of brochures on Seattle and Washington State, as well as handy free maps. The **AIA Resource Center**, 1911 First Ave near Pike Place Market, has the best range of walking tour maps and guides to Seattle's rich architectural heritage.

> The area code for Seattle is ☎206.

Getting around

Getting around Seattle is best done on foot and by **bus** downtown, where the buses (some of which run underground along Third Avenue) are free. Cross out of the free zone – to the University District for example – and you pay the driver as you get off; come back in and you pay as you enter. Single fares are between 55c and $1, depending on the zone and time of day; tickets are valid for an hour. **Day passes** are a good deal at $2.50, even better at weekends when they only cost $1; buy them from the driver or from the **Metro Customer Assistance Office** at 821 Second Ave, which also has information and timetables (☎447-4800 for bus information). Weekday passes also include a free return trip on the **monorail** (otherwise 60¢ each-way) which runs overhead on thin concrete stilts from a downtown stop at Fifth Avenue and Stewart Street to the Seattle Center. Bus passes and valid bus tickets can also be used on the **streetcar** (60¢) which runs up and down the waterfront.

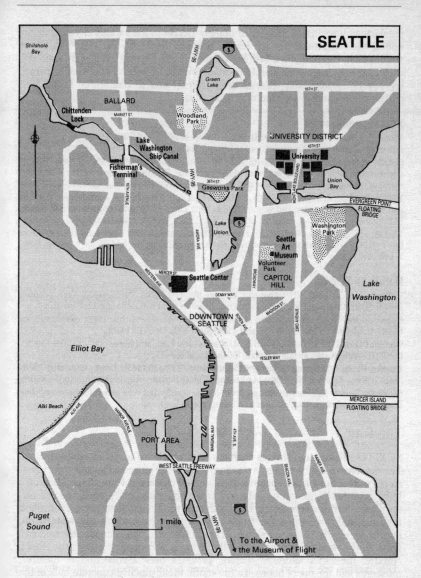

Finding a place to stay

While there's no shortage of hotel space in Seattle, it can be difficult to find the middle ground between smart, expense-account-type places and the seedy dives of the destitute. Budget travellers are in for a treat at the newly opened Seattle International **Hostel** on the waterfront, but otherwise reasonable accommodation is hard to come by. There are all the usual **motels** along the highways on the outskirts of town, and a number of homely **B&Bs** in the various city neighbour-hoods; the reservation agency *Pacific Bed and Breakfast*, 701 NW 60th Street (☎784-0539), can find you a bed, but requires a $25 deposit (credit cards will do) with your booking, which should be made well in advance. If you want to **camp**, try *Fay Bainbridge State Park* at the northeast end of Bainbridge Island (see p.519), where there are a handful of basic sites.

Hostels and motels

Motel 6, 18900 S 47th Avenue (☎241-1648). Cheapest of the nationally known motels, but it's miles out of town near the airport; exit 152 from I-5. Doubles from $35.

Seattle International Youth Hostel, 84 Union St, behind Pike Place Market (☎622-5443). Comfortable and well-equipped, with dorm beds for $10 (*AYH* members) or $13 (non-members) a night. Midnight curfew, and you'll need a sheet sleeping bag. Closed 10am–5pm.

YMCA, 909 Fourth Ave (☎382-5000). By far the best option if you want your own room, clean and safe and open to men and women. Dorm beds cost $17, private rooms from $38 single, $44 double – a few dollars more for private TV and bath. Weekly rates from $160.

YWCA, 1118 Fifth Ave (☎461-4888). For women only, and slightly older (and cheaper) than the *YMCA*. Large clean rooms cost from $24 single, $35 double; add $5 for a private bath. Weekly rates from $150.

Hotels and B&Bs

College Inn, at 4000 NE University Way in the U District (☎633-4441). Very popular, friendly B&B that's well worth the extra cost. Doubles from $40 including a full breakfast.

Commodore Hotel, 2013 Second Avenue (☎448-8868). Cheap but cheerless downtown hotel – doubles with bath from $35, and a few dorm beds for $11 a night.

Gaslight Inn, 1727 15th Ave (☎325-3654). Capitol Hill landmark home converted into attrac-tive B&B, with its own swimming pool. Doubles cost $55–75.

Pacific Plaza, 400 Spring Street (☎623-3900 or ☎1-800/426-1165). Newly renovated 1920s hotel, halfway between Pike Place Market and Pioneer Square, with doubles from $63 a night.

St Regis Hotel, 116 Stewart Street (☎448-6366). Scruffy but well located, cheap and safe downtown hotel, with doubles from $32, $5 more with bath.

The City

SEATTLE divides into several districts, all of which are easily accessible by bus. The **downtown** core would be a standard affair of tall office blocks and department stores were it not for two enclaves of colour and character: **Pike Place Market**, a busy, crowded collection of stalls and cafés, and **Pioneer Square**, a small old-town area of restored redbrick, lined with taverns. The fabulous views over Elliott Bay, too, help to lighten the feel – best perused from along **the waterfront**, despite its clutter of tourist shops. From downtown, you can ride the monorail north to the **Seattle Center**, where the flying-saucer-tipped tower of the **Space Needle**, the city's futuristic symbol, presides over a collection of theatres, museums and the opera house. To the south, the distinctive concrete bulk of the **Kingdome** sports arena/concert hall maroons the small Southeast Asian-dominated **International District** behind its stretch of car parks, and further south still, the huge **Museum of Flight** charts the development of air-travel from Icarus on. A couple of the city centre's outlying districts are often livelier than downtown: **Capitol Hill**'s cafés and bars form the heart of the city's gay scene (and holds some of the best city parks); and the **University District** is, as you'd expect, a studenty district of cheap cafés with some uptempo nightlife.

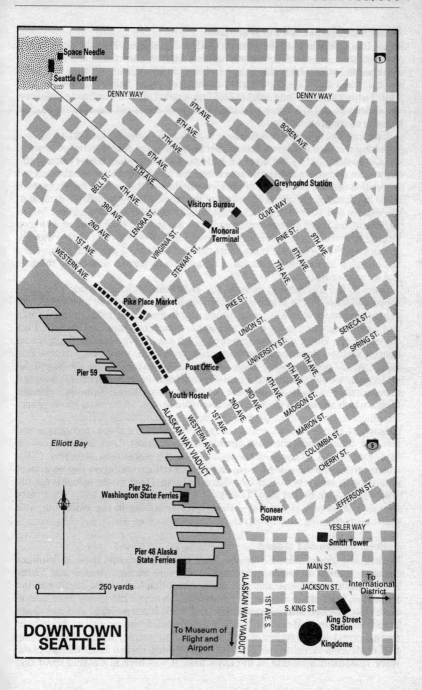

Space Needle

Seattle Center

DENNY WAY
DENNY WAY

9TH AVE.
8TH AVE.
7TH AVE.
6TH AVE.
5TH AVE.
BELL ST.
4TH AVE.
3RD AVE.
LENORA ST.
2ND AVE.
VIRGINIA ST.
1ST AVE.
WESTERN AVE.

BOREN AVE.

Greyhound Station

Visitors Bureau

OLIVE WAY

Monorail
Terminal

PINE ST.

9TH AVE.
8TH AVE.
7TH AVE.

STEWART ST.

Pike Place Market

PIKE ST.

UNION ST.

SENECA ST.
SPRING ST.

UNIVERSITY ST.

Post Office

6TH AVE.
5TH AVE.
4TH AVE.
3RD AVE.

Youth Hostel

Pier 59

MADISON ST.

2ND AVE.
1ST AVE.

MARION ST.

ALASKAN WAY VIADUCT

WESTERN AVE.

COLUMBIA ST.

CHERRY ST.

5

Elliott Bay

JEFFERSON ST.

Pier 52:
Washington State Ferries

Pioneer
Square

YESLER WAY

Smith Tower

Pier 48 Alaska
State Ferries

MAIN ST.

To
International
District

0   250 yards

JACKSON ST.

1ST AVE. S.

S. KING ST.

ALASKAN WAY VIADUCT

King Street
Station

Kingdome

**DOWNTOWN
SEATTLE**

To Museum of
Flight and
Airport

Pike Place Market and the Waterfront

Pike Place Market, at the bottom of Pike Street (conveniently close to the youth hostel), is one of downtown Seattle's biggest attractions, and rightly so. Buskers and street entertainers play to busy crowds, smells of coffee drift from the cafés and stalls are piled high with lobsters, crabs, salmon, vegetables and fruit. Further into the long market building, craft stalls sell handmade jewellery, woodcarvings and silk sceen printing, while over the street small shops stock a massive range of ethnic foods.

Farmers first brought their produce here in 1907, lowering food prices by selling straight from the barrow. The market boomed in the poverty-stricken years of the Depression, but by the Sixties it had become shabby and neglected, and the authorities decided to flatten the area altogether. Architect Victor Steinbrueck led a horrified protest: he wanted to preserve the turn-of-the-century buildings, and, more importantly, the whole character of the market as the affordable domain of the elderly and poor. There was a sharp fight between the two lobbies, but in 1971 Seattlites voted overwhelmingly to keep the market. Now restored with low-income facilities, it goes some way to preserving its working-class roots – though, perhaps inevitably, upscale restaurants catering to tourists and local yuppies are fast creeping in, despite the surrounding area being packed with porno theatres and teenage prostitutes.

Stairs in the market lead down to the **Hillclimb**, which descends past more shops and cafés to the **Waterfront**. No longer deep enough for modern ocean-going ships, much of this has been turned over to the tourist trade while the port's real business goes on to the north and south. Almost opposite the Hillclimb, **Pier 59** is one of a line of old wooden jetties which once served the tall ships; it now houses Seattle's **Aquarium** (summer daily 10am–7pm, winter daily 10am–5pm; $4.50), which provides some lively information on marine life in the Sound, an underwater viewing dome and a pool of playful sea otters and seals. A combined ticket admits you also to **Omnidome** next door (daily 10am–8.30pm; $4.95 for two films), which shows 3-D films on a large curved screen, some using clever graphics, others featuring natural dramas like the eruption of Mount St Helens.

South of Pier 59, the waterfront is lined with souvenir shops, restaurants and fish and chips stands, the most famous of which, *Ivar's Acres of Clams*, has its own special stop (*"Clam Central Station"*) on the **waterfront streetcar** (60¢), which carries tourists along the bay in restored vintage carriages. The waterfront gets back to business at Pier 52, where **Colman Dock** is the terminal for the *Washington State Ferries* (see "Listings" for ferry information), and a good place to watch them pull in and out – though it's swarming in the rush hour with commuters crossing from suburban homes over the bay.

Pioneer Square and around

Walk a few blocks inland from the ferry terminal and you come to **Pioneer Square** (actually an area of a few blocks focusing on First Avenue and Yesler Way) – Seattle's oldest section and another spot that had a close brush with the demolition balls of the Sixties. The restoration work is more glossy here than at Pike Place Market, and the square's old red brick, black wrought iron and shady trees bear the unmistakable hallmark of a well-tended historic district, bookshops and galleries adding a veneer of sophistication. Rock music resounds from a group of lively taverns at night (see "Nightlife"): but by day, there's little evidence of the more rumbustious aspects of the city's past. It was here in the mid-1800s that

Henry Yesler erected the Puget Sound's first steam-powered sawmill, felling trees at the top of a nearby hill and rolling the logs down what's now Yesler Way, and was then known as the "skid road". Drunks and down-and-outs gathered here in the later years of the Depression and the term "skid row" passed into its present usage – or that's Seattle's version of it. The whole district was razed in 1889 when a pot of boiling glue turned over in a cabinet maker's shop and set the wooden buildings and streets ablaze. Rebuilding, the city resolved an unsavoury problem with the sewage system (which had a nasty habit of flowing in reverse when the tide was high in the bay) by regrading the level of the land; but this left the entrances to the surviving brick buildings at first-floor level and the ground floors below the earth, connected by underground passages – a literal underworld that soon became a prime location for illicit activities (like drinking during Prohibition). These passages were rediscovered in the Sixties, and can be explored on the **Underground Tours** which leave more or less once an hour from *Doc Maynard's* tavern, 610 First Avenue (☎682-4646 for times and a reservation; $4) – by far the most amusing way to find out about Seattle's seamy past, with witty guides taking an offbeat look at the city's history before leading you underground.

A couple of blocks from Doc Maynard's, at 117 South Main Street, the **Klondike Gold Rush National Park** (daily 9am–5pm; free) is not a park at all, but a small museum where a free film and a few artefacts portray the 1897 rush which followed the discovery of gold in the Klondike region of Alaska. As soon as the first ship docked in the city carrying Klondike gold, Seattle's sharp-eyed capitalists espied massive trading potential in selling groceries, clothing, sledges and even ships to the inevitable rush of gold-seekers, and launched a formidable publicity campaign, bombarding inland cities with propaganda billing Seattle above all other ports as the gateway to Alaskan gold. It worked: prospectors streamed in, merchants (and con-men) scented easy profit, the population escalated and traders made a fortune. The dog population fared less well, as many a hapless mutt was harnessed to a sledge while gold-seekers practised "mushing" up and down Seattle's streets before facing Alaskan snow. Jack London's novel *The Call of the Wild* puts the canine point of view, and gold fever is gloriously sent up in the Charlie Chaplin film *The Gold Rush* – shown free at the museum on weekend afternoons.

Almost opposite the museum the large cobblestoned square of **Occidental Park** holds four recently erected totem poles carved with the grotesque, almost cruel, features of creatures from Northwest native American legends, a sign of the city's growing awareness of its indigenous roots.

The business district

At the corner of Yesler Way and Second Avenue, Seattle's first skyscraper, the white **Smith Tower**, edges the city's financial district. Built in 1914 by the New York typewriter mogul, L.C. Smith, it was for years, as locals love to tell you, the tallest building west of the Mississippi. Today it mostly holds private offices, but if you're passing it's worth looking in on the elegant lobby, decked out with marble and carved Indian heads; restored brass-lined elevators take you to an observation deck at the top – though this is often closed. To the north, the prestigious new glassy office blocks of the business district loom over the Smith Tower – not on the whole an inviting sight, although the **Ranier Tower**, balanced on a narrow pedestal, and the dark, 76-storey **Columbia Center**, the tallest of the towers (and aptly nicknamed the "Darth Vader building" or "the box the Space Needle came in"), are city landmarks with a passing interest as engineering feats.

South to Chinatown/International District

A few blocks south of Pioneer Square, your way is blocked by the huge concrete **Kingdome**, Seattle's main sports and concerts arena, and the home of its *Seahawks* football team and baseball team, the *Mariners*. The Kingdome's spread of car parks seems to signal an end to the downtown area, but pushing on east up S Jackson Street, past the redbrick clocktower of the old railway station, the concrete spaces soon give way to the build-up of restaurants and ethnic grocers of Seattle's **CHINATOWN** – officially (and blandly) labelled the **INTERNATIONAL DISTRICT** due to the presence of other far-eastern groups. Aside from some good restaurants, for a city with a strong history of South East Asian immigration it's a rundown and rather scrappy neighbourhood, its tawdry blocks dotted with street-people and few actual sights.

Seattle's Chinatown hasn't always been desolate. In the nineteenth century this was an overcrowded and unruly district, its boarding houses crammed with young Chinese men who'd come over to earn money in the city's mills and canneries. Suspicion of the area's gambling halls and opium dens overflowed into racial hatred during a depression in the 1880s: laws were passed nationally debarring the Chinese from full citizenship and in the Northwest, Chinese workers were attacked and threatened, their homes burned. Seattle did eventually rake up an armed guard which made a belated and botched attempt to prevent mobs expelling the entire community (as happened in Tacoma), but most Chinese left anyway, leaving behind a depleted and scarred community. Later influxes of Japanese, Filipino, Korean and Thai immigrants, and more recently Vietnamese, Laotian and Cambodian newcomers, went some way to restoring a trace of the district's nineteenth-century vigour, but Chinatown has been regarded locally with some trepidation since gang activity exploded into a small massacre here in 1983. In reality the area is more shabby than unsafe, though it is best to take care after dark. The focus of the district, insofar as it has one, is **Hing Hay Park** at Maynard and South Main Street, where an ornate oriental gateway stands beneath a large and rather faded dragon mural. But there's not really anything else to see beyond the absorbing little **Wing Luke Asian Museum** on Eighth and Jackson Street (Tues–Fri 11am–4.30pm, weekends noon–4pm, closed Mon; $1.50, free Thurs), which goes some way to explaining the area's history.

The Museum of Flight

The best and biggest of Seattle's museums, the **Museum of Flight**, 9404 E Marginal Way (daily 10am–5pm, until 9pm Thurs and Fri; $4), more than makes up for the twenty-minute bus ride (#123) south from downtown, through the port's dreary industrial hinterland. As the birthplace of the Boeing company, Seattle has its own stake in aviation history, and has invested heavily in this huge new museum, partly housed in the 1909 "Red Barn" that was Boeing's original manufacturing plant. The displays, accompanied by detailed information plaques and three separate filmshows, take in everything from the dreams of the ancients, through the work of the Wright brothers, with a working model of the wind-tunnel they used, to the growth of Boeing itself, with part of the Red Barn laid out as an early designer's workshop. The best bit of the museum is the huge glass-

and-steel Great Gallery, big as an (American) football field and hung with twenty full-sized aircraft – tiny, fragile-looking mail planes and a red sportscar that could apparently be given wings in minutes. There's also a replica of the Mercury space capsule that took John Glenn into space in 1962. Behind the gallery, museum staff hand out eggboxes and plasticine for the construction of paper planes – one way to learn about aerodynamics.

Alki Beach

West of downtown, on the other side of Elliott Bay (and reachable by bus #37 from downtown), the flat little peninsula of **Alki Point** is where Seattle's founders first tried to settle when they weighed anchor in the Puget Sound, optimistically christening their community "New York Alki" – New York "by and by". Defeated by floods and the lack of space, the town soon shifted over to what's now Pioneer Square, changing its name to Seattle after a local native American chief. The peninsula's now a residential district, interesting only if you want to join the promenaders and cyclists along the narrow strip of **Alki Beach**, which offers nice views of Elliott Bay with the city skyline behind and the Olympic Mountains to the west. You can swim here too, but the water's pretty cold.

The Seattle Center

To the north, downtown peters out around Virginia Street, beyond which lies a district once occupied by Denny Hill and now flattened into the **Denny Regrade**. Considering the momentuous effort that went into knocking the hill down, it's a shame that nothing interesting has been built here – though the area around Bell Street, known as **Belltown**, has some character, its tough taverns now rubbing shoulders with upmarket cafés with French names. This apart, the regrade is probably best viewed from the window of the **monorail**, which runs from Fifth Avenue and Stewart Street downtown (60¢ one-way), crossing the area on thin, concrete stilts, and finishing inside the **SEATTLE CENTER**.

The Seattle Center is an inheritance from the 1962 World's Fair, whose theme was "Century 21" (hence the idea of the spindley Space Needle tower, the fair's – and now Seattle's – adopted symbol). Since then the fair's site has become a sort of culture-park, collecting the city's symphony, ballet and opera, a couple of theatres and a museum alongside the Space Needle and a small amusement park.

The monorail drops you close to the **Space Needle** (observation deck summer daily 7.30am–1am, Sept Sun & Thurs 9am–midnight, Fri–Sat 9am–1am, winter Sun & Thurs 10am–midnight, Fri–Sat 10am–1am; $4.25). Though reminiscent of the *Star Trek* era of space-fascination, this still exudes a fair amount of glamour, especially at night, when it's lit up and Seattle's well-to-do come to eat at its revolving restaurant. The view from the observation deck, where there's a (pricey) bar, is unmatched, and this is much the best place to get an overall orientation of the city and its surroundings.

Back on the ground, the Center's emphasis on the arts is balanced by the excellent **Pacific Science Center** (summer daily 10am–6pm, otherwise Mon–Fri 10am–5pm, weekends 10am–6pm; $4.00), easily recognisable by its distinctive white arches. This is much livelier than it sounds, full of bright, innovative and often noisy exhibits on a huge range of science-based topics, sometimes linked to cultural issues; the permanent *Sea Monster House* exhibit, for example, re-creates a turn-of-the-century native American home.

Capitol Hill

Of all Seattle's neighbourhoods, **CAPITOL HILL**, a fifteen-minute bus-ride east of downtown, has probably raised the most eyebrows over the years. Since young gays, hippies and assorted radicals moved in over the Sixties and Seventies, this has been the city's closest thing to an alternative centre, fulcrum of the arts scene and the city's chancier night-time activities. In fact, the shops and cafés around **Broadway**, the main street, are now pretty mainstream and, despite ubiquitous black leather jackets slung over teenage shoulders, the neighbourhood's days at the cutting edge of Seattle Bohemia are probably over. Still, the concentration of easy-going restaurants, coffee houses and bars provide good day-time café-sitting and night-time drinking (see "Eating" and "Nightlife"), and if you're gay this is still very much the place to be – though homophobic violence can happen here as disturbingly often as it does anywhere in the US.

The northern end of the Capitol Hill district is, by contrast, quietly wealthy, mansions built on Gold Rush fortunes and trimmed with immaculate lawns sitting sedately around **Volunteer Park**, among whose shrubs and trees lies the **Seattle Art Museum** (Tues–Sat 10am–5pm, Thurs 10am–9pm, Sun noon–5pm; $2, free Thurs), which is currently strongest on its Asian art collection, the tiny jade carvings and intricate, many-armed figures oddly juxtaposed with a handful of sombre European paintings. Nearby, the lovely 1912 glass **Conservatory** (summer daily 10am–7pm, winter daily 10am–4pm; free) packs a more immediate aesthetic punch: divided into galleries with different climates (jungle, desert, rain-forest, etc), it has a sweltering mix of perfect flowers and shrubs, and a huge collection of orchids. Also in the park, the old **Water Tower** can be climbed for a grand (and free) panorama across Seattle, albeit through wire mesh.

Ten blocks east of Volunteer Park, **Washington Park** stretches away to the north, encompassing the **University of Washington Arboretum**, whose assortment of trees shade foot and cycle paths – a huge, leafy invitation for summer walks and picnics, and especially beautiful in autumn when the trees turn brilliant shades of red and brown. At the south end of the park, the immaculately-designed **Japanese Gardens** (March–Nov daily 10am to around dusk depending on the season; $1.50) flash banks of pink flowers beside neat little pools.

The University District

Across Union Bay from the park, the **University District** (aka the "U" district) is livelier than Capitol Hill: a busy hotchpotch of coffee houses, cinemas, clothes, book and record shops, all catering to the tastes and budgets of the University of Washington's 35,000 students. The area centres on University Way, known as **"The Ave"** and lined with cheap ethnic restaurants and the cavernous *University Bookstore* – an excellent place to seek out a cheap meal (see "Eating") or the lowdown on the student scene.

The **campus** itself is more serene, its sedate nineteenth-century buildings and landscaped grounds overlooking Union Bay. There are a couple of museums here: the pale brick **Henry Art Gallery**, at NE 15th Avenue and NE 41st Street (Tues, Wed & Fri 10am–5pm, Thurs 10am–7pm, weekends 11am–5pm; $2), houses American and European paintings from the last two centuries, and mounts small, innovative shows, often drawing on local work. The **Thomas Burke Memorial Museum**, on the campus' northwest corner at Seventeenth Avenue and NE 45th Street (Mon–Fri 10am–5.30pm, weekends 9am–4.30pm; free except for special exhibitions), has carved totem poles, painted wooden masks from the Northwest coast, plaited fibre fans from Polynesia and sorcery charms from New Guinea. There's another museum across Montlake Bridge on the other side of Lake Union, the **Museum of History and Industry** (Mon–Sat 10am–5pm, Sun noon–5pm; $3, free Tues), which has a gallery reconstructing Seattle in the 1880s, with homes, storefronts and a free film, though this is rather out on a limb (bus #25 from downtown drops you fairly near) – enthusiasts only.

Lake Washington Canal, Ballard and other northern parts of town

The U district and Seattle's other northern neighbourhoods are sliced off from the rest of town by water. Lake Union, in the middle, is connected to the larger Lake Washington to the east, and the sea to the west by the **Lake Washington Ship Canal**. Built at the turn of the century to carry ships to safe harbours on the inland lakes, the canal was used during World War I to safeguard battleships from exposure to attack in the more open Elliott Bay. If you have an hour to spare, the procession of boats passing from salt water to fresh through a set of canal locks called the **Hiram M. Chittenden Locks**, near the mouth of the canal, makes pleasant viewing (bus #17 from downtown), and migrating salmon bypass the locks via the **fish ladder**, a sort of piscine staircase laid out with viewing windows. In peak migrating season (late summer for salmon, autumn and early winter for trout) the water behind the locks is full of huge, jumping fish.

Behind the locks is Salmon Bay, on the south side of which **Fisherman's Terminal** is crowded with the boats of Seattle's fishing fleet; you can buy freshly caught fish here – assuming you're staying somewhere where you can cook it. On the northern side of Salmon Bay, **BALLARD** (reachable by several buses from downtown) was settled by Scandinavian fishermen. The **Nordic Heritage Museum**, 3014 NW 67th Street (Tues–Sat 10am–4pm, Sun noon–4pm; $2.50), outlines their history from poverty in rural Scandinavia, through immigration problems at Ellis Island and New York tenements to arrival in the West, in a series of rather musty tableaux in the basement of an old school. Bar a couple of nightspots, there's little else to see here, though if you do find yourself passing further east, along the northern shore of Lake Union, look out for **Gasworks Park**, where the rusting black towers of an old gasworks have been left as "urban sculpture", the slag heaps grassed over to become kite-flying mounds. It's worth seeing on summer evenings when skateboarders bring ghetto blasters, and their music echoes round the old industrial site.

Further east at **GREENLAKE**, the **Woodland Park Zoo** (April–Sept daily 8.30am–6pm, Oct & March 8.30am–5pm, Nov–Feb 8.30am–4pm; $3; bus #5 from 3rd and Pine downtown) is an open zoo with natural-ish habitats for the animals.

Eating

You won't have to spend a fortune in Seattle's elegant new French-name restaurants to **eat** well: among the coffee shops of Capitol Hill, the bargain-rate ethnic restaurants of the University district, and above all Pike Place Market there are some excellent pickings. **Seafood** is Seattle's speciality, and even if the budget won't stretch to the plentiful salmon or crab, you'll be able to afford fish and chips, or a steaming bowl of thick clam chowder.

Pike Place Market

During the day, there's no better place to find food than **Pike Place Market**, either in picnic-form from the stalls and ethnic groceries or served up in the cafés and restaurants. If you're staying in the youth hostel, join the stallholders for an early breakfast at *Lowells* café in the main market building, where tables overlook Elliott Bay; next door and sharing the view, the more crowded *Athenian Inn* has been here since 1909, its lengthy menu matched by the beer list. Across the street, tucked inside the market buildings, the tiny *Three Girls Bakery* serves freshly baked goods either to take away or eat at its diminutive counter. There are plenty more good cafés here, but, like the stalls, they mostly close around 6pm (and many don't open Sunday), and in the evening the market's a less tempting prospect. Of the few restaurants that open, try *El Puerco Lloron* on the Hillclimb, a cheap, authentic Mexican restaurant and, above the market on Post Alley, the Italian *Pink Door*, a slightly more expensive trattoria – there's no sign, just look for the pink door.

Pioneer Square and the International District

Though an excellent place to come drinking (see below), **Pioneer Square** isn't the best place to find cheap food: the taverns all serve food because they have to by law, but it's basic sandwich and burger stuff. The *Elliott Bay Book Company*, at First Avenue and S Main Street, serves wholefood in its cosy book-lined basement until 11pm (6pm on Sunday), and light meals are available from *The Bakery*, 214 First Avenue. Among the more pricey restaurants, the *New Orleans Restaurant* in the main part of the square charges moderately for its cajun fare and has live New Orleans jazz. For a cheaper meal, head over to the wealth of bargain ethnic restaurants in the **International District**: the massive *House of Hong* at Eighth and Jackson serves about the best Chinese food, while *Viet My*, 129 Prefontaine Place, has authentic Vietnamese cooking. *Mikado*, 514 S Jackson Street, while not cheap, is a classy Japanese restaurant with a good sushi bar. If you prefer your seafood cooked, pick up fish and chips at *Ivar's Fish Bar* on the waterfront (the adjacent restaurant is overpriced).

Capitol Hill

Options at **Capitol Hill** include chic little coffee and dessert houses like the *B & O Espresso*, 204 E Belmont Street, or the *Dilettante*, 416 Broadway E Street, specialising in chocolate concoctions. There are also ethnic restaurants ranging from the pleasant Greek *Byzantion*, 806 E Roy Street, to *Kokeb*, 926 Twelfth Avenue at the south end of the district, serving low-priced and spicey Ethiopian food; *Piecora's Pizza*, 1401 E Madison Street, is the area's favourite pizza parlour. The laid-back *Deluxe Bar and Grill*, 625 Broadway East, serves nachos, salads and pasta alongside the bargain-rate burgers and beer and has outdoor tables; on the eastern side of the district at Mercer Street and E 15th Avenue, the cheerful *Cause Celebre* café serves first-class wholefood to a mix of gay and straight customers, including excellent Sunday brunch; two other good brunch places are Matzoh Momma's, 509 E 15th Avenue, and Jack's Bistro, 405 E 15th Avenue.

The University District

An obvious target for cheap eating and action, the **University District** is also strong on ethnic restuarants: Chinese, Greek, Italian, Mexican, Vietnamese, Thai

– even British at the *Unicorn*, 4550 University Way, which serves cornish pasties and steak and kidney pies along with British beer (and 50¢ glasses of water). Otherwise finding somewhere good is simply a question of walking up and down University Way until you find what you want; the *Chile Pepper*, 5000 University Way, has good cheap Mexican food, and *Curry House*, 4142 Brooklyn Avenue is a welcome sight in a land where Indian food is still rare. At the far end you'll find *Ave!*, 4743 University Way, and two good cheap Greek places (the *Continental* and *Costa's*); the *College Inn Café*, 4002 University Way, is a pleasant diner open around the clock. The classic student hangout is *Last Exit on Brooklyn*, 3930 Brooklyn Avenue at NE 40th Street, a warm, busy coffee house where would-be intellectuals eye the lively group at the next table over their paperbacks – open until late, often with live music. Bookish types are similarly thick on the ground at the quieter *Grand Illusion Espresso and Pastry* on NE 50th Street at University Way, a cosy adjunct to the *Grand Illusion* arts cinema, and a good spot to sit with the Sunday papers (which they provide).

Nightlife

Though it doesn't have the cultural variety of Los Angeles or San Francisco, taken on its own laid-back terms, Seattle's **nightlife** isn't as bad as you might think, particularly if all you're after is a convivial atmosphere and a beer or two. As far as drinking goes, there's an enormous range of potential watering holes, varying from **taverns** (which in Washington sell beer and wine but not spirits) to **bars**, which sell everything but must be attached to a restaurant. Taverns also often lay on **live music**, usually for a small cover: nothing too revolutionary, predominantly rock & roll or rhythm & blues, with a good dash of jazz, but always enthusiastically delivered and accompanied by **dancing** where there's room. All-round it's a warmly down-to-earth and unpretentious scene. Similarly with **clubs**, where a good proportion of the audience show up in jeans and there's little scope for posing. There are, of course, the dress-up video-dance places you'd find in any US city, but the heart is missing, and they're less uniquely local and certainly less fun.

On the **arts** front things are relatively – and deceptively – sophisticated, particularly in the realm of **theatre**. A dozen or so bright and innovative theatre groups re-work the classics and provide up-to-the-minute and cosmopolitan plays, and the city's a magnet for hopeful young actors, many of whom are marking time behind the craft stalls in Pike Place Market. There's also a fair demand for art and re-run **films**, shown in the city's wonderful collection of tiny, atmospheric cinemas.

For **listings** of what's on where, *The Weekly*, 75¢ from boxes on the streets, is good for reviews and theatre, cinema and arts listings, and the what's on sections of the Friday editions of *The Seattle Times* or *Seattle Post Intelligencer* supply live music details. Some of the most interesting shows are put on by *Rakumi Arts* (☎548-0700), who do a year-round series of jazz and African concerts at various venues around Seattle.

Drinking, live music and dancing

Downtown, there's no better introduction to the tavern scene than **Pioneer Square**, where a concentration of bars – *Doc Maynards, Old Timer's Café*, the

Central Tavern and more – often host bands. Walk around outside until you hear something you like, and look out for "joint cover nights" about every month, when you can get into five or six venues for as many dollars. Near Pike Place Market, the *Virginia Inn*, First and Virginia, is another laid-back place to drink, young professionals mixing with old timers.

Capitol Hill's drinking-places span the range, from chic yuppie bars like *Baffert's*, 314 E Broadway, to the smoky pool-tables of the counter-cultural *Comet Tavern*, 922 E Pike Street, and the mounted moose head and huge neon juke box of *Ernie Steele's* on Broadway, a no-nonsense working men's bar. This district's also a focus for the gay scene – see "Gay Seattle" below.

The **University District** obviously offers a lively student scene. The *University Bistro*, 4315 University Way, has live music nightly and a small cover; the *Scarlet Tree*, 6521 Roosevelt Way, is a busy, sweaty, rhythm & blues venue. West of the U District towards Wallingford, *Murphy's Pub*, 2110 N 45th Street, has a massive beer list and live folk, often Irish, for no cover. Further west in more grown-up but folksy **Ballard**, the *Backstage* club, 2208 NW Market Street, stages quality jazz, rock, reggae or folk acts and serves spirits. The *New Melody Tavern*, 5213 NW Ballard Avenue, loses in atmosphere because of its barn-like size, but puts on classy jazz, bluegrass and folk, with square dancing on Monday nights.

If you're after **dance music**, the easiest venue to get to is the *Borderline* on Pioneer Square. For more sophistication get out to **Shilshole Bay**, northwest of downtown where the Lake Washington Ship Canal joins the sea. The clubs are rather better here: hi-tech *Spinnaker's*, 6413 NW Seaview, has the best view, the nearby *Windjammer*, 7001 NW Seaview, often has live bands. Both charge a small cover ($5) at weekends.

Dance, classical music, opera and the theatre

The **Seattle Center** is the base for the city's cultural institutions: the *Pacific Northwest Ballet* (☎628-0888), the *Seattle Symphony Orchestra* (☎443-4747) and the *Opera Association* (☎443-4711), take it in turns to use the Opera House there. Tickets go for anything between $10 and $55, and, particularly for the Opera Association, tend to sell out in advance; you can sometimes get returns – occasionally at reduced prices – just before performances start.

But it's **theatre** that's Seattle's strongest suit. Numerous small groups serve up serious drama alongside the visiting Broadway shows. Oldest and most established of Seattle's companies is the *Seattle Repertory Company* (☎447-2222) at the Seattle Center's Bagley Wright Theater, performing popular contemporary stuff with a good dash of the classics. By the time the Rep closes down in June for the summer, *A Contemporary Theater (ACT)*, 100 W Roy Street, north of the Seattle Center near Queen Anne Hill(☎285-5110), has started its season (May–Oct) – again mostly mainstream modern stuff. Glamorous musicals come to the *Fifth Avenue Theater*, 1308 Fifth Avenue (☎625-1900) – anything less gets lost in the restored movie palace's flamboyant proportions. For a more offbeat approach, try the *Empty Space* in Pioneer Square at First and Jackson (☎467-6000), which stages adventurous cosmopolitan fare and sparse versions of the classics. For Seattle's most politically right-on stuff, *The Group*, based in the U District's Ethnic Cultural Theater, 3940 Brooklyn NE (☎543-4327), next to the *Last Exit* café, regularly plunges into tough social and political issues.

Film

Seattle has the usual on-release venues, prime among which are the *Varsity*, 4329 University Way (☎632-3131), and the big *Metro Cinemas* complex, 45th and Roosevelt (☎633-0055) – both in the U District and offering several screens. But the city also has number of small, independent cinemas, many concentrated in the U and Capitol Hill districts in rickety old buildings, showing a selection of left-of-field and foreign films, particularly in May when the annual *Seattle International Film Festival* takes place (check local papers for listings). Venues include the cosy little *Harvard Exit*, 807 E Roy Street (☎323-8986), and, housed in an old Masonic Temple, the art deco *Egyptian*, 801 E Pine Street (☎323-4978) – HQ of the annual film festival. The *Seven Gables Theater*, 911 NE 50th Street at Roosevelt Way (☎632-8820), and the tiny *Grand Illusion* at NE 50th Street (☎523-3935), are two more. The *Neptune*, at the corner of 45th and Brooklyn Street (☎633-5545), has a lobby decked out to match its name, and works its way through classic double features. The *Market Theater*, on Lower Post Alley near Pike Place Market (☎382-1171), is downtown's only independent cinema, and a secondary venue for the international film festival.

Gay Seattle

Focusing on the Capitol Hill district, Seattle's **Gay Scene** is lively and well organised. Your best source of local information is the weekly *Seattle Gay News*, a high-quality paper with plenty of local resource information and listings of all that's current; pick up a copy at a decent downtown bookshop, or the exclusively gay bookshop mentioned below.

Gay and lesbian resources

Bookshop *Beyond the Closet Bookstore*, 1501 Belmont Avenue at E Pike St (☎322-4609). A wide range of gay and lesbian books, poetry, magazines and videos, plus occasional readings.

Counselling The primly-named *Seattle Counselling Service for Sexual Minorities* (☎329-8707) can provide counselling, as can the *Gay Men's Health/Support Group* (☎322-7043).

Lesbian Resource Center Women can contact the *Lesbian Resource Center*, 1208 E Pine St (☎322-6697), for information or news of the several groups and goings-on based there.

Students The *Gay/Lesbian Student Organization* is based at Seattle Central Community College in Capitol Hill (☎587-3815 ext 39).

Nightlife

As far as **nightlife** goes, **Capitol Hill** is again the place to head for, though the **downtown** area has a couple of well-established places.

DJ's Nightlife, 1501 E Olive Way. A tavern/dance club mostly for gay men.

Madison Pub, 1315 E Madison St. Again caters for gay men.

The Double Header, 407 Second Ave. The oldest gay bar around, with pool tables and live bands nightly.

Thumpers, 1500 E Madison St. A gay and lesbian venue.

Tug's Belltown Tavern, 2207 First A, Belltown. Another well-established bar, with a women-only lesbian night on Thursday.

Wildrose Tavern, 1021 E Pike St. A popular venue for gay women, with decent food and often live music or entertainment.

Listings

Airlines *British Airways* 1315 4th Ave (☎1-800/247-9297); *Delta* 410 University St (☎241-2300); *Northwest Airlines* 402 University Ave (☎433-3500); *TWA* 1001 4th Ave (☎447-9400).

Airport *Sea-Tac International Airport*, 18612 S Pacific Hwy (general information ☎433-5217).

American Express 600 Stewart St (☎441-8622).

Area Code ☎206.

Banks Major branches include *Bank of California*, 910 Fourth Ave (☎587-6100), *First Interstate*, 999 Third Ave (☎292-3111), *People's National Bank*, 723 First Ave (☎344-2300).

Bookshops The *University Bookstore*, 4326 University Way in the U District, is the city's biggest general bookshop; the *Elliott Bay Book Company*, 101 S Main St in Pioneer Square is convenient and cosy.

Bike Rental None downtown: try *Gregg's*, 7007 Woodlawn Ave in Greenlake (☎523-1822), or *Alki Bikes*, 2722 Alki Ave near Alki Beach (☎938-3322).

British Consulate On the 8th floor of the First Interstate Center at Third and Madison (☎622-9253): surprisingly friendly, though they may well refer you to the dragons in LA.

Car hire *Five and Ten*, 14120 Pacific Hwy S (☎246-4492) only has an airport branch but is the cheapest in town and will take a cash deposit instead of a credit card.

Chemist *LD Bracken Prescription Pharmacy* 1303 Fourth Ave (☎622-2110).

City Tours *Gray Line* (☎626-5208) runs guided half-day tours by coach (covering all major sights with copious commentary) and by boat (more fun but necessarily less comprehensive), both pricey at $16 each but not a bad way to see the city if you've got more cash than time. Pick-up and drop-off is at major downtown hotels.

Dentist 24-hr emergency answering service ☎624-4912; also, *Yesler Terrace Medical Dental Clinic*, 102 Broadway; ☎625-9260.

Doctor 24-hr emergency answering service; ☎622-6900.

Emergencies ☎911.

Ferries *Washington State Ferries*, tickets from Pier 52, Colman Dock (☎464-6400), run to Winslow and Bremerton. You can also buy tickets for these ferries at a reduced rate from the Seattle AYH, at 84 Union St, behind Pike Place Market (☎622-5443). *BC Steamship Company*, tickets from Pier 69 (☎441-5560), to Victoria; *Alaska Marine Highway*, tickets from Pier 48 (☎623-1149), to Alaska.

Hospital *Northwest Hospital*, 1550 N 115th St (☎364-0500). For minor injuries, try the *Country Doctor Community Clinic*, 500 E 19th Ave (☎461-4503); women can use the *Arcadia Women's Health Center*, 112 E Boylston St (☎323-9388).

Launderette The youth hostel and the *YMCA* both have much nicer facilities than the sleazy ones on the streets, such as the 24-hr laundromat beneath the *St Regis Hotel*, 116 Stewart St. In the U district, there's a *Wash'n'Shop* behind the *Pay'n'Save* shop at 45th St and Brooklyn Ave.

Library *Seattle Public Library*, 1000 Fourth Ave (Sept–May Mon–Thurs 9am–9pm, Fri–Sat 9am–6pm, Sun 1–5pm, June–Aug closed Sun; ☎386-4636).

Post Office/post restante The main post office is at Union St and Third Ave downtown (Mon–Fri 8am–5.30pm; ☎442-6255); zip code 98101.

Rape Crisis Line 24 hours; ☎632-7273.

Resource Center for the Handicapped 20150 NE 45th Ave (☎362-2273).

Taxis *Yellow Cab*; ☎622-6500.

Traveler's Aid On the sixth floor of the *YMCA*, Fourth Ave between Madison and Marion St (Mon–Fri 8.30am–9pm, Sat–Sun 1–5pm; ☎447-3888).

Around Seattle

With island-cluttered Puget Sound to the west and the huge expanse of Lake Washington to the east, Seattle has only been able to spread by means of boats (there's one boat for every six Seattlites) and bridges. Most commuters pass over one stretch of water or another on their way into work. Off the water, however, the countryside immediately around Seattle can't compete with the dramatic panoramas you'd get if you put in a few extra miles – to the **Snoqualmie Falls**, for example. But if you find yourself with a spare day (or even, for **Bainbridge Island**, couple of hours) and want to head – or cycle – just a short distance out of the city, there are a number of places worth dipping into.

Though the fares will push up your budget (particularly with a car) the Puget Sound's **ferries** are a glorious way to **get around** and take in the scenery: *Washington State Ferries* link the mainland with the Kitsap Peninsula, Whidbey Island and the San Juans. The major cities are well connected by *Greyhound* and, to a lesser extent, *Amtrak*, but frankly these are not where you'll want to spend your time; to enjoy yourself, you'll really need to budget for renting some kind of wheels – if only a bike.

East of Seattle: Lake Washington and Snoqualmie Falls

Until it was bridged, Lake Washington isolated the city from the countryside and small farms to the east. Ferries laden with farm produce made slow progress across the water, and the lake became a sort of tradesmen's entrance to the city while the centre of Seattle faced the big commercial ships docking in Elliott Bay. All this changed when two long, floating bridges, one built in the Forties, the second in the Sixties, opened up commuting possibilities: business people poured across, tripling the population of one-time rural towns **BELLEVUE** and **REDMOND** – world headqaurters of software giants *Microsoft* – and turning them into affluent city suburbs. Now outgrowing its suburban status to become the state's fourth largest city, Bellevue has its own smart business district and shopping area, the showpiece of which is the elite **Bellevue Square Mall**, elegantly laid-out and expensively stocked, and with a reputation that's the area's most upmarket. Malls aside, the towns have little to recommend them, and the countryside is much more appealing.

I-90, the main eastbound highway, heads off towards the Cascade Mountains and **Snoqualmie Pass**, the lowest and most traversible of the Cascade passes and the regular mountain route for early trappers and traders (it now offers good **skiing** from November to April). Before I-90 reaches the Cascades, there's a turning for Hwy-202 and the rural **Snoqualmie River Valley**, where attractions include the **Puget Sound and Snoqualmie Valley Railroad** (April–June Sun only, June–Oct weekends; $6 round-trip), whose renovated steam and diesel trains chug up the valley from the small town of NORTH BEND to SNOQUALMIE.

Further on from Snoqualmie, **Snoqualmie Falls** – the falls seen at the beginning of the cult TV show *Twin Peaks* – crash into a rocky gorge, sending up a cloud of white spray. Managed, prosaically enough, by the electricity company *Puget Power* (who can switch the falls off if they want), the falls are best viewed

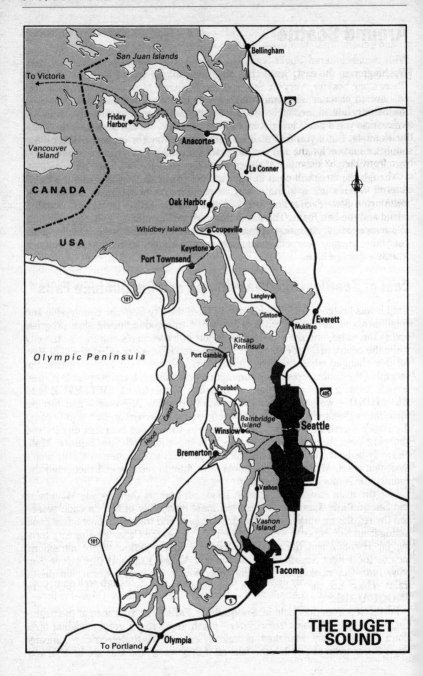

THE PUGET
SOUND

from the bottom of the trail which leads past the shiny metal pipes of an underground generating station to the thunderous foot of the waterfall.

Bainbridge Island and the Kitsap Peninsula

It's hard to think of any commuters blessed with as pleasant a trip as the **Bainbridge Island** set, who wake up to a serene half-hour on the ferry, the city skyline drawing slowly closer across Elliott Bay. This is such a nice journey that the island itself (green and rural, but mostly private land) is for most of its visitors simply an excuse for the ferry ride. *Washington State Ferries* leave about every hour from Pier 52 downtown (return tickets around $4 foot passenger, $7 car; avoid rush hours), landing in **WINSLOW** – a town so small that once you've admired the harbour and had lunch, you'll doubtless be ready to head back to Seattle. However, if you're looking for somewhere to pitch a tent, there's **camping** at the other end of the island in *Fay Bainbridge State Park*.

The main reason to come to Winslow is that the ferry here is the handiest route from Seattle to the national parks and seaside towns of the Olympic Peninsula (see p.533 for more). To get there however, you must first head from Bainbridge Island across the **Kitsap Peninsula.** Sprawling messily into the middle of the Puget Sound, this jagged spit of land bristles with a concentration of defence projects: the naval submarine base at Bangor housing Trident submarines, the Undersea Warfare Engineering Station at Keyport testing torpedoes, and Indian Island ammunition depot just off the peninsula's northwest shore – all of which together add up to a fair dollop of military might.

Bainbridge Island is joined to Kitsap at its northern end by Agate Pass Bridge, on the Kitsap side of which is Port Madison Indian Reservation and the fascinating **Suquamish Museum** (daily in summer 10am–5pm, in winter Wed–Sun 11am–4pm; $2; call ☎597-3311 to check), off Hwy-305 on Sandy Hook Road, southwest of the bridge. The Suquamish tribe, who occupied all of the peninsula and parts of Seattle and Bainbridge Island until white settlers arrived, received, like other tribes, an appallingly bad deal from the carve-up of their land. But the museum's tone is moderate, interspersing exhibits of native canoes and a well-displayed collection of old photographs with quotations from tribal elders, whose recorded voices also overlay a slideshow that portrays the schizophrenic lifestyle of the generation caught between traditional values and white cultural imperialism.

The Suquamish leader when the first settlers arrived here was Chief Sealth, or Seattle, after whom the city was named, and he's buried not far from the museum in the town of **SUQUAMISH**. Two large dugout canoes mark his grave against the incongruous background of a white wooden church, and a plaque proclaims him "The firm friend of the whites" – something of a dubious accolade, considering how things turned out. Continuing across Kitsap, **POULSBO** was founded by Norwegians and is heavily coated in "little Norway" kitsch, though well equipped with cafés if you need a break. In the **Marine Science Center** (Mon–Fri 9am–5pm; donation), 17771 Fjord Drive, you can observe marine fauna from close up. Across the bay, halfway between the Suquamish Museum and Poulsbo, lies **KEYPORT**, "Torpedo Town" of the USA", where all the US torpedos get tested and where the brand-new **Undersea Naval Museum** shows off a collection of submarines and, not surprisingly, torpedos.

Port Gamble

Further north, the small lumber town of **PORT GAMBLE**, though less twee, also has an imported identity, this time from East Machias, Maine. The town's entre-preneurial founders Pope and Talbot made a killing on the Puget Sound timber trade, but satisfied a sentimental attachment to their New England roots by shipping out East Coast elm trees to overhang quaint, New England-style clap-board houses. Behind the restored streets, the Pope and Talbot lumber mill continues to churns out thousands of planks. At the former Port Gamble General Store, where you can still get a cup of coffee for 5¢, the **Port Gamble Historical Museum** (daily 10am–4pm) has local history exhibits on the ground floor, and, upstairs, a well-graded collection of mussels and clam.

The town is close to the **Hood Canal Bridge**, which leads to the Olympic Peninsula. More than a mile in length, the bridge used to be billed as an engi-neering miracle – until a chunk of it floated out to sea during a violent storm in 1979. It was over three years before the bridge was reopened, with assurances that it had been duly strengthened.

Bremerton

The ferry ride from Seattle to **BREMERTON,** at the southern end of the Kitsap Peninsula, is beautiful; the town is anything but. Dominated by the large naval shipyard, Bremerton's town centre has fallen on hard times, its hard-as-nails bars and tattoo parlours offering scant entertainment to bored sailors awaiting the repair of their ship. Bremerton has a **tourist office** (Mon–Fri 9am–5pm; ☎479-3588) at 120 Washington Ave, where you can get hold of a town map with a "historical route" marked in, the main site on which is the **Bremerton Naval Museum** (Tues–Sat 10am–5pm, Sun 1–5pm; free), 130 Washington Ave, basi-cally a collection of ship models.

If you find yourself regretting having got off the Bremerton ferry, while you wait for the next one you might want to ride the passenger ferry that shuttles every ten minutes between Bremerton and **PORT ORCHARD,** where the Log Cabin Museum (Sun & Mon 9am–1pm; free), 416 Sidney St, has a variety of exhibits discussing the more domestic aspects of local pioneer history.

Vashon Island

From Seattle, it's a fifteen-minute ferry ride to **Vashon Island**, a pleasant, cycle-ble island where there's little to do but explore the country roads. The **Vashon Island AYH Hostel** here makes a pleasant change from city accommodation. You'll find it at 168th – Cove Road – and 121st Avenue, housed partly in a hand-built log cabin and partly in tepees (*IYHA* members $7 a night, non-members $10; ☎463-2592). Thy also rent out bikes for $5 a day Once you've worked up an appe-tite with a pleasant cycle or amble around, head for the *Sound Food Restaurant* on Island Highway at 204th SW Street (closed Tues), whose upmarket wholefood brings Seattlites over for weekend brunch – and there's live music on Saturday night.

If you'd rather not return straight to Seattle, you can cross Vashon Island to TAHLEQUAH its southern tip, from where *Washington State Ferries* sail every hour or so to Point Defiance at Tacoma's northern tip (see below); you only have to pay to get to the island – leaving is free.

Switch on the radio in Seattle, and you'll soon hear an advertisement for trips to **VICTORIA** on Vancouver Island in Canada, just a four or five hour ferry ride from Seattle. From May to October, *BC Steamship Company* (☎441-5560) runs the *Princess Marguerite* and the slower *Vancouver Island Princess* daily from Seattle's Pier 69 to Victoria ($22 single, $32 return for passengers, $40 each-way for a car plus driver). You can get there quicker with the *Victoria Clipper* catamaran, also from Pier 69 (☎448-5000) which only takes two and a half hours but costs twice as much ($60 return, no cars).

More alluring (and much more expensive) is the **Alaska Marine Highway**, a two day ferry ride that winds between islands and a fjord-lined coast from Seattle to **SKAGWAY**, Alaska, with stops along the way at Ketchikan, Wrangell, Petersburg, Juneau and Haines. Ferries leave Seattle's Pier 48 (☎623-1149) every Friday at 8pm, May to October, earlier in winter, and arrive in Skagway the following Monday at 12.30pm in summer, later in winter. Summer passages from Seattle to Skagway cost around $260 one-way per passenger, around $30 less in other seasons, excluding food or berths; a berth in a shared room will cost an extra $100 or so – bring a sleeping bag and crash out in the lounge to save money. Cars up to 10 feet in length cost around $275 in addition to the driver's fare, from May to October (at other times drivers travel free), and space for these in the summer should be reserved well (i.e. months) in advance. Contact c/o *Alaska Marine Highway*, PO Box R, Juneau, Alaska 99811 (☎907/465-3941 or ☎1-800/642-0066) and pay in full 45 days before you sail; turn up three hours before departure. You can generally get a walk-on passage at short notice by signing up on the standby list that opens in Seattle every Monday for departure the next Friday; technically, standbys can be off-loaded at any port *en route* if the ferry gets too full, but in practice you're unlikely to get turfed off.

TACOMA, OLYMPIA AND SOUTH

Tacoma, the Puget Sound's southernmost and Washington's second-largest city, is the state's most heavily industrialised corner, with old steel mills and chemical plants rusting away along the otherwise beautiful shoreline. Apart from the gorgeous Point Defiance Park at its northern tip, it's all quite run-down and eminently missable. When Tacoma (and Seattle) boomed in the early 1900s, **Olympia**, the state capital, was left out, its sole money-spinner (apart from politics) the *Olympia Brewing Company*, which set itself up just south of town in 1896 – and is rumoured to attract more visitors than the government buildings. Beyond Olympia, **I-5** skirts the western foothills of the Cascades, passing Mount Rainier and Mount St Helens, and in the far south, near the Columbia River and the Oregon border, tiny **Vancouver**, site of the Hudson's Bay Company fur-trapping colony, the first European settlement in the Pacific Northwest.

Tacoma

TACOMA has a massive credibility problem. The city council claims it's simply unfortunate that "aroma" rhymes with Tacoma, but the smelly label has stuck, making industrial Tacoma the butt of Northwest jokes. There's some truth behind it too: Tacoma's deep Commencement Bay (thought by nineteenth-century explorers to be far superior to anything Seattle had to offer) was recently listed by the Environment Protection Agency as one of the USA's most dangerously polluted areas, and the *Asarco* copper refinery has just closed after years of releasing large quantites of arsenic into the environment. Along with industry, the military are also close at hand, in the shape of the enormous Fort Lewis Army base and McChord Air Force Base. But despite its industrial profile, the city has its moments: Point Defiance Park is beaten only by New York's Central Park as the USA's largest city open space; and there are a couple of fair museums, some impressive old buildings and a redevelopment project that is trying – with some success – to turn around the tawdry downtown area.

It's the shabby side of the city that strikes you first, though: whether you come in by car or bus, you'll pass along sleazy Pacific Avenue with its pawn-shops, boarded-up buildings and prostitutes lingering in the doorways. Pacific is a major artery, dividing the sloping town centre from the industrial area below around the port. On the way in you'll pass the enormous blue-grey roof of the **Tacoma Dome**, an ugly sports and concerts venue of which the city (adopting it as a symbol) is inordinately proud. Things improve slightly in the main downtown area, to the left of Pacific, where the new **Broadway Plaza** pedestrian area is part of a recent scheme to inject new life into the ailing city centre. Its centrepiece is the elegant white **Pantages Center**, a 1918 Vaudeville theatre reopened in 1983 as Tacoma's Performing Arts Center and now staging ballet, plays and concerts. A short walk from here at 12th and Pacific, the **Tacoma Art Museum** (Mon–Sat 10am–4pm, Sun noon–5pm, closed holidays; free) has a few Renoirs, a Pissarro and a Degas among American paintings and Chinese jade and robes. North of downtown, the **Washingon State Historical Society Museum**, 315 N Stadium Way (Tues–Fri 10am–4pm, Sat & Sun noon–4pm; $2, free Tues), runs thoroughly through Washington's history and sets up temporary exhibitions related to the state – photos of Makah tribespeople, paintings from the logging era, quilts made by pioneer women.

Point Defiance Park

Heading away from downtown to the north, Ruston Way follows the curve of Commencement Bay past restaurants touting their scenic views and the now-abandoned tall chimney of the poisonous *Asarco* copper plant (free *BayLiner* buses run hourly from Tenth and Commerce Streets downtown on weekends and Wednesdays; otherwise *Pierce Transit* buses – ☎581-8000 – follow an inland route). At the tip of this jutting piece of land, the vast **Point Defiance Park** – one of the finest city parks in the US – has beaches, gardens, and roads and trails through acres of shady virgin forest as green and lush as the highly-touted "rain forests" of the western Washington coast, as well as a number of more specific attractions. These include a **Zoo and Aquarium** (summer daily 10am–7pm; winter daily 10am–4pm; $3.50); **Camp Six** (Memorial Day to Labor Day only Mon–Fri 11am–5pm, Sat & Sun 11am–6pm; free), a reconstructed logging camp with bunk houses, old logging equipment and a restored and functioning steam engine; and **Fort Nisqually** (museum building summer daily noon–6pm, winter daily 1–4pm, grounds open longer; free) – a reconstruction of the trading post set up by the Hudson's Bay Company in 1833, in the pre-settlement days of the fur traders, when American entrepreneurs were beginning to threaten the monopoly of the British company. Fort Nisqually was seen as a key British foothold in what later became Washington state – an area which the British originally intended to keep.

Tacoma practicalities

Set squarely on the main north–south route between Seattle and Portland, Tacoma is hard to avoid, though you won't necessarily have to see any more of the city than its transport terminals. The *Greyhound* station is in the heart of town at 1319 Pacific Avenue (☎383-4621); the beautifully restored *Amtrak* station at 1001 Puyallup Avenue (☎627-8141) is a bit less central; **local buses** run by *Pierce Transit* (☎581-8000 or ☎1-800/562-8109) serve the Tacoma area. *Pierce Transit* also connect with Seattle's local *Metro* buses, offering a bargain-rate route between the two cities. By **car**, I-5 loops towards the downtown area; come off at exit 133. Bus and city maps are available at the **Chamber of Commerce**, 950 Pacific Avenue (Mon–Fri 8.30am–5pm; ☎383-2459).

With Seattle just up the highway and a very pleasant youth hostel on nearby **Vashon Island** (see above), it's not likely that **accommodation** in Tacoma will be a priority. Hotels downtown are either pricily smart for the business community or grim in the extreme: if you've got a car, keep going to *Motel 6* at 5201 20th Street in Fife (☎922-1270), a few miles east of town (exit 137 off I-5), where clean rooms cost $26 a double. There's **camping** at **Dash Point State Park**, 5700 SW Dash Point Road, Federal Way, five miles northeast of Tacoma with wide beaches and hiking trails.

For **food and entertainment**, again the best places are out of downtown, though it's worth checking what's on at the Pantages Center (☎591-5894 – see opposite). The *Antique Sandwich Shop*, 5102 N Pearl Street, near Point Defiance Park, is an offbeat café which has huge pots of tea and often has live folk or classical music in the evenings. Also a short distance from downtown, *Engine House No. 9*, at 611 N Pine Street, is a lively tavern/café bedecked with firemen's helmets and crowded with locals, who consume excellent pizza, carrot cake and the like with their beer until the early hours.

Olympia and around

Thirty miles south of Tacoma, dominated by the white dome of the state government headquarters, **OLYMPIA** is an odd sort of place for a state capital. No more than a muddy little logging community when it was picked as Washington's territorial capital in 1853 (settlers had only reached the Puget Sound the decade before), Olympia hasn't grown into the metropolis its founders hoped, and after the bustle and industry of Seattle and Tacoma, the town seems rather sleepy and quiet. The Washington State Capitol buildings here, grouped on a "campus" to the south of downtown, make Olympia worth a visit, if only to wonder at the sheer energy of the pioneers, who plotted something along the lines of St Paul's Cathedral in what was then a backwoods beset by native American uprisings. Only completed in 1928, the **Legislative Building** (Mon–Fri 8am–5pm; free) is the one to see, an imposing Romanesque structure topped with a high stone dome, and hung with a massive brass Tiffany chandelier. Epic murals were originally planned for the inside, and the *Twelve Labors of Hercules* by Michael Spafford is indeed up on the walls of one of the government chambers – though Washington's pious legislators were apparently so shocked by the "pornographic" images of the painting that their immediate reaction was to spend $15,000 covering it up with hardboard and curtains – since removed.

Eight blocks south of the Capitol Campus, the small **Washington State Capital Museum**, 211 W 21st Avenue (Tues–Fri 10am–4pm, Sat & Sun noon–4pm, closed Mon and holidays; donation), set in the Mediterranean-looking 1920s mansion of the wealthy Lord family, juxtaposes a restored well-to-do dining room with displays of native American basketwork and natural history exhibits, inadvertently underlining the gap between two vastly different cultural norms. In the other direction, north from the Capitol, the **town centre** offers a few streets of shops and restaurants, presided over by the chateau-like **Old Capitol** at Seventh Avenue between Washington and Franklin Streets, its turreted roofs and arched windows facing a green town square.

Tumwater

A short drive or bus ride (#12 or #13 from Capitol Way and 15th Street) south of Olympia, tiny **TUMWATER** was Washington's first pioneer community, settled in 1845 in part by black immigrants – including a man named George Bush – banned from racist Oregon. The town's name comes from the tumbling water of the Deschutes River, which now goes into the making of Olympia beer at the **Pabst (Olympia) Brewing Company**, by the Tumwater turning (exit 103) off I-5 (tours and tastings daily 8am–4.30pm; free). Smelling strongly of hops, the brewery overlooks **Tumwater Falls**, now enclosed in a park but once a rich salmon fishing site for the Nisqually tribe. Among the pioneers were **Bing Crosby's grandparents**, who lived in the small white **house** at Deschutes Way and Grant Street between I-5 and the river.

Olympia and Tumwater practicalities

Olympia is on I-5 and easily accessible by car or bus; *Greyhound* (☎357-5541) are at Capitol Way and Seventh Avenue, about five blocks north of the Capitol Campus. The *Amtrak* station (☎1-800/872-7245), at Rich Road and 83rd Street, is about eight miles southeast of town and not on the bus route. Elsewhere, *Intercity Transit* provides a **local bus** service around Olympia and Tumwater (☎786-1881 for route and timetable information).

There's a **visitor information centre** across from the Olympia Brewery at 316 Schmidt Place (Mon–Fri 9am–5pm; ☎357-3370). In-town **accommodation** tends, not surprisingly, to cater for business visitors; in Tumwater, *Motel 6*, 400 W Lee Street (☎754-7320), has doubles for $28; take exit 102 off I-5, east on to Trosper Road, right on to Capitol Boulevard and right again on to W Lee. The best place to stay is the *Harbinger Inn*, 1136 E Bay Drive (☎754-0389), a turn-of-the-century balconied B&B with views out over the Puget Sound and doubles from $50 a night. There's **camping** at forested **Millersylvania State Park**, 12245 Tilley Road south of Olympia, two miles east of I-5 (exit 99) and fifteen miles west of Olympia.

If you've come here to **eat**, try the *Urban Onion*, 117 E Legion Way (closed Sun), diagonally across the square from the Old Capitol, which serves its own herb and onion bread. Failing that, *The Spar*, a few blocks away at 114 E Fourth Avenue is a genuine Thirties diner with a long, curved counter.

South along I-5

There isn't actually all that much to see along the sixty-odd miles of I-5 south to Oregon, but a short detour off can bring you to a number of more rewarding places. One of the most worthwhile turnings, just six miles south of Olympia, leads east to the town of TENINO, where the **Wolf Haven** reserve provides a safe breeding ground for the threatened North American timberwolf. Established in 1982 as a sanctuary and open-air hospital for wolves shot or poisoned by live-stock ranchers, Wolf Haven has grown into a 65-acre facility that's now home to over 40 of these surprisingly affectionate, sociable creatures. Close-up, educational **tours** ($2) are given throughout the day, but the best time to come is for the Friday and Saturday night "Howl-Ins" (7pm; $6; ☎264-4695 or ☎1-800/448-9653), when storytellers evoke various wolf-related myths and legends, especially those of the native American peoples; when darkness falls, a sort of call-and-response kicks off between the audience and the nearby wolves, baying their heads off at the rising moon.

Further south I-5 gives access to the Mount St Helens National Volcanic Park (see p.555 for more). Just before reaching the Columbia River, the state border, a turning east at Mill Plain Blvd in the otherwise boring town of VANCOUVER drops you at a fairly credible reconstruction of the Pacific Northwest's first substantial European settlement, the stockaded warehouses of the British-owned *Hudson's Bay Company* in **Fort Vancouver National Historic Site** (daily 9am–5pm; $1). Originally built in the 1830s, for more than twenty years the fortress served as the sole outpost in the region, but as American migrants moved in to the Willamette Valley British claims to the land receded, and when the 49th parallel was determined as the dividing line between the US and Canada, Fort Vancouver was left stranded on US territory. By 1860 the Hudson's Bay Company moved out, and the fort and outbuildings disappeared, only to be mapped and rebuilt by archaeologists in the 1940s. Rangers give interpretive tours through out the day, and the site – basically a dozen one- and two-storey log structures protected within a rectangular palisade – certainly merits at least a quick look, even though it's cut off from the river by the four-lane US-14 highway.

NORTH OF SEATTLE

While the areas south of Seattle aren't among the state's more attractive corners, heading north of the city brings you to some of the most beautiful land and seascapes in Washington. Besides the rural peace and quiet of **Whidbey Island** – whose flat glacial moraine makes it ideal for a cycling tour – there's the unfor-gettable scenery of the San Juan Islands. Washingtonians's most popular holiday destination, and one of the few not-to-be-missed places in the state. Inland stand the snow-capped peaks of **Mount Baker** and sundry other Cascades, while I-5 races north past **Bellingham** to the Canadian border.

Whidbey Island

With sheer cliffs and craggy outcrops, rocky beaches and prairie countryside, **WHIDBEY ISLAND** is a favourite retreat for the Puget Sound's city-dwellers, who take a tent and head for one of the state parks, or spend pampered weekends in one of Whidbey's luxurious bed and breakfasts. Once considered a key stronghold in the defence of the Sound, the island carries military relics from various eras: nineteenth-century blockhouses built against native American attack, concrete bunkers from World War II – and, in the north, a large naval base housing the sophisticated warfare squadrons of modern air and naval defence whose low-flying jets are an occasional but considerable annoyance. But on the whole the island is peaceful enough, the narrow country roads winding through farmland and small villages. If you're heading north to the San Juan Islands (see p.528), or crossing to Port Townsend and the Olympic Peninsula (see p.533), it's much more pleasant to meander through Whidbey than dash up I-5 or loop around US-101.

The Mukilteo ferry lands on the island at the small town of CLINTON. There's not much to see here, and further around the east coast **LANGLEY** makes a better first stop, its short high street of old-west wooden storefronts just about the right side of bogus and set on a bluff overlooking the waterfront. There's a **Chamber of Commerce** (☎321-6765), tucked away upstairs in the small arcade on Langley's high street, with information on the island.

The middle part of Whidbey Island is a National Historic Reserve called **Ebey's Landing**, specifically the spot where Isaac Ebey lived, the son of a pioneer farmer, who rose to prominence as a civil and military leader before coming to a nasty end at the hands of a party of vengeful Canadian Indians. Also inside the reserve is **COUPEVILLE**, a showcase town of immaculately maintained Victorian mansions built by wealthy sea captains, who were drawn from their native New England by the fine, deep harbour of Penn Cove and the abundance of oak and pine trees, which made good money in the lucrative Californian timber trade. Fearing the native Skagit tribe might object to the white annexation of their land, the settlers built **Alexander's blockhouse**, a small, wooden, windowless building intended to protect them from attack, although relations remained remarkably blood-free and the **dugout war canoe** next to the blockhouse was used only in festivals; both the blockhouse and the canoe are cared for by the **Island County Historical Museum**, across Main Street.

Ebey's Reserve also includes two old, windblown forts, now state parks. Three miles southwest of Coupeville, near the Keystone ferry port, **Fort Casey** was built at the end of nineteenth-century as part of a triangle of fortifications across the entrance of the Puget Sound, and a formidable barrage of WWII gun emplacementsnow face starkly out to sea. It is possible to hike the five or so miles north along the the beach from here to **Fort Ebey** (also accessible along the island's winding roads), constructed in 1942 after America's entry into World War II. There are no guns here now, but the fortifications still stand, giving good views out across the water to the Olympic Mountains.

Military matters of a modern and more mundane kind dominate the economy of **OAK HARBOR**, Whidbey's largest – and most unappealing – town. The nearby Naval Air Station, built in 1941, is home to the Navy's tactical electronic warfare squadrons, whose jets and helicopters loudly crowd the skies. The town's ugly suburban sprawl is best passed straight through and unless you're stuck for a motel room (see below) you'd do much better to continue north to **Deception Pass State Park** where a steel bridge arches gracefully over the narrow gorge between Whidbey and Fidalgo Island, connecting-point for the San Juans beyond. Seals sometimes bask on the rocks below, though mist can make the pass obscure.

Getting to and around Whidbey Island

Coming **from Seattle**, the quickest route on to the island is to head north to Mukilteo (near Everett) and catch the ferry from there to Whidbey's southern tip; boats run about every half-hour, and single fares are around $2.50 per person, $4.50 with a car. There's also a bus from Seattle's *Greyhound* depot to Anacortes across the island, making stops along the way (Mon, Wed & Fri; call ☎626-6090 for an up-to-date schedule). Another ferry, from Whidbey to the Olympic Peninsula, leaves Keystone, in the middle of the island, every ninety minutes or so and dropping at Port Townsend; single fares are around $3.50 per person, $7 with a car. To the north Whidbey is connected by bridge across Deception Pass to Fidalgo Island from where you can take ferries to the San Juan islands. A new local bus system, *Island Transit* (☎321-6688), has just started up on Whidbey – though, as with Puget Sound's other islands, you'd be well advised to bring your own car or bike, or come prepared to hitch at least some of the time.

Practicalities

Most of the island's **motels** are around Oak Harbour. *Auld Holland Inn*, at 5861 Hwy-20 (☎675-0724), does indeed have a Dutch owner but isn't exactly cheap with doubles from $58; the *Crossroads*, nearby on Hwy-20 is cheaper(☎675-3145). On the edge of Coupeville, the *Tyee Motel* 403 S Main Street by Hwy-20 (☎678-6616), has doubles from around $35. With a little more cash, you could try **bed and breakfast**, though you'll need to book in advance: contact *Whidbey Island Bed and Breakfasts*, PO Box 259, Langley, WA 98260 (☎321-6272).

The most popular place to stay on the island is the *Capt Whidbey Inn*, two miles west of Coupeville overlooking Penn Cove. This comfortably rustic B&B, built out of local madrone logs, has been run by the same family for over thirty years, and double rooms cost from $75 a night. The *Chart Room* in the inn serves up some of the state's best seafood.

Otherwise, if you want to **eat** on Whidbey, Coupeville has the best range of places: the *Kneed and Feed* is a bakery offering good sit-down lunches and *Toby's Tavern* is a friendly local bar; both are on Front Street near the jetty. In Langley, six miles from the Clinton ferry, the *Dog House Tavern* is a convivial gathering place, with a restaurant round the back.

The best **camping** on Whidbey Island is in Deception Pass State Park, where there are a number of fine, $10-a-night sites on the forested slopes above Cranberry Lake.

Near Whidbey: La Conner

Hwy-20 rejoins the mainland at the top of Whidbey Island about four miles north of **LA CONNER**, a quiet fishing village and artists' retreat that doubles, on weekend at least, as a tacky tourist trap: the painters who settled here in the late Sixties are still around, but heavily outnumbered by visitors. It's pretty enough, though – the bright red **Rainbow Bridge** making a splash of colour along a picture-postcard waterfront, facing across to the Swinomish Indian Reservation, where craftsmen carve (and sell) huge wooden totem poles and smaller fetish sculptures. In town, the restored Victorian Gaches Mansion up the hill on Second Street houses the **Valley Museum of Northwest Art** on its second floor (Fri, Sat, Sun 1–5pm; $1). Further up the hill on Fourth Street, the **Skagit County Historical Museum** (Wed–Sun 1–5pm; $1) has exhibits on the early days of Skagit County, from a small native American section to a 1942 doll of Scarlett O'Hara. At the bottom of the hill on First Street, the *Calico Cupboard* restaurant is absurdly quaint, but serves excellent lunches and afternoon teas; the *La Conner Tavern* on the waterfront has good cheap fish-and-chips and a range of Washington's best beers.

The San Juan Islands

North of Whidbey Island, midway between the Washington coast and Canada, the beautiful **San Juan Islands** scatter across the northern reaches of the Puget Sound, and entirely upstage the rest of the inlet. Perfect retreats for walking, cycling and generally unwinding (bar the weather, which can be wet), this maze of green islands is the breeding-ground of rare birds and sea creatures: white-headed bald eagles circle over tree tops, and families of Orca ("killer") whales pass close to the shores. Farming and fishing communities now share the islands with escapees from the cities, including artists and craftspeople, all in search of tranquillity and solitude – a quest in which they're joined every summer by more visitors than the islands can really accommodate, especially on San Juan and Orcas, the largest of the islands. You'll absolutely need to **book somewhere to stay in advance**: during summer weekend dozens of disappointed travellers end up spending the night at the ferry terminal, something all the tourist authorities work hard to avoid. That said, even in July and August, peaceful corners can be readily found.

Getting to the San Juan Islands

Washington State Ferries run about eight boats a day, more in summer, to the San Juan islands. The ferries only stop at four of the 172 islands, but the slow cruise through the archipelago is a real highlight. Less serene are the long queues of cars that develop at ferry ports in the summer when latecomers inevitably end up waiting for the next boat – it pays to be early; pedestrians and cyclists have less hassle. Summer fares are around $20 return for a car and driver, $5 for foot-passengers and cyclists to San Juan Island, slightly less out of season; make a note of when the last ferry leaves the island for the mainland, as it can sometimes be surprisingly early, especially out of season. One ferry a day (more in summer) continues on from the islands to SIDNEY in British Columbia.

All the ferries depart from **ANACORTES**. This as-yet unreconstructed fishing town, at the end of Hwy-20 and reachable on *Evergreen Trailways* buses from Seattle, is home to the largest working fleet in Washington, as well as many of the larger canneries. Though there's little reason to linger, the waterfront still has a rough-hewn charm, and there are a couple of chandlers and hardware stores along the main Commercial Avenue that make for an hour's diversion. If you want to catch an early ferry (the first one leaves before 6am) you may well decide

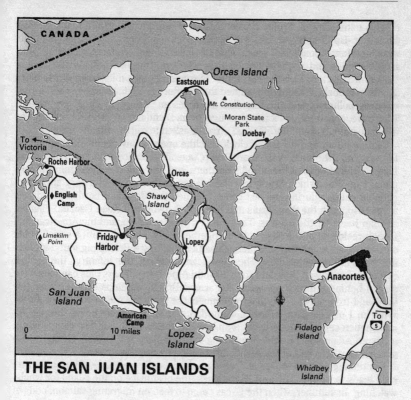

THE SAN JUAN ISLANDS

to spend the night, either at one of the $35-a-night roadside motels like the *Holiday Motel*, 2903 Commercial Avenue (☎293-6511) or the more spacious *Islands Motel*, 3401 Commercial Avenue (☎293-4644). The best place to stay is *The Majestic*, 419 Commercial Avenue (☎293-3355 or ☎1-800/950-3323), a recently renovated grand old hotel with plush doubles from $75; it also has the best restaurant (and bar) in Anacortes. Incidentally, **petrol** on the islands is considerably more expensive than on the mainland, and you'll save by filling up in Anacortes before you leave.

San Juan Island

The ferry's last stop but many people's first is **SAN JUAN ISLAND**, the most accessible of the islands, and the only one where the ferry actually drops you in a town. **FRIDAY HARBOR** may be small, but it's the largest town in the archipelago and the best place to hire transport – which you'll need to see any of the islands properly. **Bikes** can be hired from *Island Bicycle* at 380 Argyle, a few blocks up from the ferry. Ask for advice on cycling routes at the helpful **information center** (winter, daily 8am–4.30pm; longer in summer) at First and Spring Streets, a short walk up from the ferry landing. They also have maps – useful since it's easy to get lost on the islands' twisting and badly marked roads.

This taken care of, Friday Harbor's cafés, shops and waterfront make pleasant browsing. Up First Street, the **Whale Museum** (summer daily 10am–5pm, other seasons 11am–4pm; $2.50) has a mass of whale-related artefacts, including paintings, carvings and a whale stained-glass window. The local whales are Orca or "killer" whales – though the tag "killer" is something of a misnomer, Orcas being gentle mammals. Washington banned their capture in 1976, but they're still threatened by pollution, and the museum promotes an "Adopt an Orca" programme (there are, apparently, 84 left in the Puget Sound) and monitors whale activities on a "whale hotline" (☎1-800/562-8832). You're asked to call in with any sightings.

Setting off around the island clockwise, the open, windy peninsula that tails off to the south is home to **American Camp**, one of two national parks on the island. Like **British Camp** at the island's northern end, the name derives from the infamous **Pig War**, which briefly put the islands at the centre of a very silly international conflict during the last century. When the Canadian border was drawn up in 1846, both the Americans and the British (who still ruled Canada) claimed the San Juans for themselves. This wasn't a great problem, and the American and British residents of the islands lived together fairly amicably until a series of tax squabbles climaxed with an American settler shooting a British pig found munching his garden vegetables. The Americans sent in the infantry; the British responded with warships, and soon 460-odd American soldiers plus cannons were dug in behind a trench opposing five armed British warships carrying over two thousand troops. After a lengthy stalemate, the question was resolved by Kaiser Wilhelm I of Germany in favour of the US, the only casualty being the pig. An information centre at American Camp explains the "war" in full. The camp itself is a barren affair, full of ankle-wrenching rabbit holes, and British Camp, at the greener northern end of the island, makes for a more pleasant walk.

Continuing past the coves and bays on the island's west side, a bumpy gravel road leads to **Limekiln Point State Park**, the best place on the island for whale-watching. In summer, when the Orcas come to feed on migrating salmon, odds of seeing one are about four to one. The lime kilns that give the park its name are just outside, relics of an era when lime quarrying was big business on the island. Further north, **ROCHE HARBOR** (accessible from Friday Harbor by *Primo Taxi*; ☎378-3350), belongs to the same era – originally a company town, its gracious white **Hotel de Haro** was built to accommodate visiting lime-buyers in 1887. The tiny place is now a private resort, but the attractive wharf is worth a peek, and the hotel can provide leaflets and directions to the weird **mausoleum** of its founder, a haunting structure set in the woods, incorporating Masonic symbols.

Sleeping and eating

Camping is the obvious way to stay on San Juan Island, but unfortunately neither of the national parks has sites. There's a very pleasant cyclists-only camp, the *Pedal Inn* at 1300 False Bay Drive, or there's *Lakedale Campground*, almost five miles from the ferry on Roche Harbor Road and reachable on the *San Juan Tour and Transit Co* bus. In Friday Harbor, the *Elite Hotel* (☎378-5555), two blocks from the ferry on First Street, is the island's best budget deal (though you should book ahead, especially in August), with dorm beds from $10 and shared rooms from $30; no kitchen and no curfew. A mile out of town on Guard Street, the friendly and easy-going *Island Lodge* (☎378-2000) has doubles from around $60, less out of season.

There are plenty of places to **eat** in Friday Harbor: *Cannery House* (lunch only) at the top of First Street has a wonderful view from its outdoor terrace; the *Electric Company*, 175 First Street, is a local tavern which also does food and has live music at weekends; and, if you're setting off early, the *San Juan Donut Shop*, 209 Spring Street, serves hefty breakfasts from 5am.

Orcas Island

Horseshoe-shaped **ORCAS ISLAND** is quieter than San Juan, its several holiday resorts so well tucked into distant coves that they hardly touch the island's peace. The tiny community of **ORCAS**, where the ferry lands, is no exception to this, with little beyond the *Orcas Hotel* (☎376-4300) – a grand Victorian building overlooking the ferry landing, its rooms few and pricey, but a good place for a leisurely breakfast . You can hire **mopeds** from *Key Moped Rentals* (☎376-2474) at *The Shoals*, a café in a garage above the ferry dock, after which you'll probably want to follow most of the other people off the ferry north through the island's farmlands – the former heart of the state's apple orchards, until Eastern Washington was irrigated.

The road winds along towards Orcas' main town, **EASTSOUND**, about ten miles from the ferry landing, where the **visitor information** kiosk on North Beach Road, just past Eastsound Square, has maps and information on the island's many sights. Eastsound has a handful of small shops and restaurants – such as *Doty's Cafe*, a homely diner a block inland from the waterfront, and the more upscale *Outlook Inn*, west of the centre – and the small but enjoyable Orcas Island Historical Museum (summer only, daily 9am–5pm; donations), all together within the four-block town centre. About two miles west of Eastsound, at the end of W Beach Road, the *Beach Haven Resort* (☎376-2288) is the best place to stay on the Orcas, its fifty-year-old beachfront log cabins lined up along a densely wooded, sunset-facing cove; in summer the cabins are only available by the week, though out of season they go from $60 a night.

Rising high above the eastern half of Orcas, **Moran State Park** is the island's main attraction, with miles of hiking trails winding through dense forest and open fields around freshwater lakes. **Mount Constitution**, at the heart of the park, is the highest peak on the islands, the summit of which is a steep four-mile hike (or a short drive up a paved road), where the views are as good as you'd expect, looking out as far as Vancouver Island, and back towards snow-capped Mounts Baker and Rainier.

There are four **campsites** in the park, though they all fill up early in the summer. You can also camp at **Doe Bay Village Resort (AYH)**, Star Route 86 (☎376-2291 or 376-2190), tucked round on the east side of the island about as far from the ferry as you can get. It's a lovely place, built on a secluded bay, with echoes of its previous incarnation as a "human potential center" still hanging meditatively around its cabins, cottages and hostel dorms. Cabins go from around $28, cottages $45–70, dorm beds $9.50 with *IYHA* membership, $12.50 without – and there are excellent communal facilities, including an open-air **hot tub**, which can also be used by day visitors ($5).

There's one last little hamlet on Orcas, halfway between Moran State Park and Doe Bay. **OLGA** – basically a general store, a petrol station, a post office and a good **café** – also has some of the San Juan's best and most accessible **tidepools**, stretching northeast along the rocky shore from the village jetty.

Lopez and Shaw

Of the two other islands to be served by the ferry, **SHAW** is the least accessible – mostly in private hands though its ferry dock is, bizarrely enough, operated by Franciscan nuns. The other, **LOPEZ**, isn't exactly on the beaten track either: farming is the main concern, and despite the secluded little coves and a flat landscape well suited to cycling, tourism has a comparatively low profile. **LOPEZ VILLAGE** is quite a way from the ferry terminal – Angie's Cab Courier (☎468-2227) is the only available transport – and there's not much there when you reach it. *Holly B's Bakery* and the wholefood-ethnic *New Bay Café* opposite the post office, both serve good food. South of the village on Fisherman Bay Road, *Lopez Bicycle Works* (☎468-2847) rents out bikes during the summer and by advance arrangement out of season. The best **camping** is at **Odlin County Park** and **Spencer Spit State Park**, both on the north side of the island not too far from the ferry.

North to Canada

While the Puget Sound's islands provide lingering detours to the west, the I-5 speeds north along the mainland towards the Canadian border, cutting past forests, lakes and, eventually, the distant peak of Mount Baker. Of the towns along the way, there's little to tempt you into industrial **EVERETT**, except possibly the free tours of the huge **Boeing Plant**, west off Hwy-526 (tours must be booked in advance; call ☎342-4801), where the wide-bodied 767 and 747 jets are made. As big, the guides claim, as 57 football pitches, the plant houses the great, lumbering shells of Boeings at various stages of construction.

North of Everett stretch the flat, tulip-growing farmlands of the Skagit Valley. If you're in a car, you could come off the interstate here at Burlington and follow the more attractive **Chuckanut Drive** (Hwy-11), which winds a scenic route around the coastline as far as **BELLINGHAM**..

Bellingham

Part-industrial, with a dash of Victoriana and a lively university scene, Bellingham is a sprawling town, created from five smaller communities whose separate street patterns make up a disjointed whole, tricky to navigate.

There's nothing particularly inspiring to look at **downtown**, where industry stretches to the north around Bellingham Bay. The old City Hall, now the **Whatcomb Museum of History and Art** 121 Prospect Street (Tues–Sun noon–5pm; free) overlooks the bay from a bluff, a grandiose 1892 redbrick building, towered and spired, holding artefacts of limited local interest. A more original setting for contemporary artwork is the campus of **Western Washington University**, on a hill to the south of downtown. Billing itself as an "Outdoor Museum", the campus has some offbeat pieces of modern sculpture, including a kinetic "steam sculpture" which blows a white cloud of mist over the grass.

Practicalities

For all its faults, Bellingham makes an obvious base for exploring the surrounding country, and is a major stop on the Seattle to Vancouver *Greyhound* route. If you're coming straight in from I-5, turn off at exit 253, which leads to Potter Street and the helpful **visitor's center** (daily 9am–6pm), who'll give you information on the town, and skiing and hiking details for the surrounding area. The *Greyhound* station (☎733-5251) is downtown at 1329 N State Street, and the **local bus** terminal (*Whatcom County Transit*) is almost next door at Railroad Avenue and Magnolia Street. There are several **motels** at exit 252 off I-5, around Samish Way: *Mac's Motel*, at Samish and Maple Street (☎734-7570), and *Motel 6* (☎671-4494) at 3701 Byron Avenue, which crosses Samish Way both have rooms for around $29 double. Women can stay at the *YWCA*, 1026 N Forest Street (☎734-4820), not far from the *Greyhound* station.

Bellingham's most appealing section is the restored railway community of **Fairhaven Village**, a pleasant drive or bus-ride around the bay from downtown, and the best place to find **food and drink.** *Tony's* at 1101 Harris Avenue is a lovely coffee shop, sometimes hosting live music, while across the road, the beer list at *Bullie's* includes hundreds by the bottle and a good selection on tap.

Mount Baker

Natural sights are what lure most people to northern Washington. **Parks** surrounding Bellingham are laid out with hiking trails, and beyond them to the east are the foothills of **MOUNT BAKER**, 56 miles along Hwy-542. The mountain features in Lummi tribal mythology as a sort of Ararat, the one peak that survived the legendary Great Flood to provide sanctuary for a native American Noah in his giant canoe, though it's better known today for its **skiing**, with a seven-month season (from early November until May) and the best early snow in the Northwest; ☎734-6771 for ski information. There's plenty of good **camping** in the area: near Bellingham, try **Larrabee State Park**, seven miles south of the city on Hwy-11; or on the way to Mount Baker, **Silver Lake Park**, up Silver Lake Road north of Maple Falls.

THE OLYMPIC PENINSULA

The broad mass of the **Olympic Peninsula** projects across the Puget Sound, sheltering Seattle from the open sea. Small towns are sprinkled around the peninsula's edges, but at its core the Olympic Mountains thrust upwards, shredding clouds as they drift in from the Pacific and drenching the coastal area with rain. Conditions are wet enough for the dense vegetation of the peninsula's forests to thicken into rain forest in the western river valleys, and both the forests and the lonely Pacific beaches provide cover for a huge variety of wildlife and seabirds.

It was partly to ensure the survival of a rare breed of elk that Franklin D Roosevelt created a national park here in 1939, and the **Olympic National Park** now has the largest remaining herd of Roosevelt elk in the US. The heart of the peninsula is now protected land, but the large areas of forest surrounding the national park are heavily logged; how much timber should· be cut, and where cutting should be allowed, is contentious. Issues of economy versus ecology are debated with particular intensity. It was the timber trade that brought settlers here in the first place; almost every town has a sawmill, and logging remains crucial for local jobs. Ecologists are now reluctantly favouring tourism as the lesser of environmental evils, and the number of visitors is increasing – an odd marriage with the tough world of the timber trade.

Victorian **Port Townsend** is the most logical and attractive first stop on the peninsula, accessible by ferry via Whidbey Island or by an hour's drive from Seattle, and restored as a "historic" centre, with a lively arts scene. The real economic engine of the peninsula is the more industrial **Port Angeles**, linked by *Greyhound* to Seattle and by ferry to Victoria in Canada. West of here, settlements are smaller and fewer. **Neah Bay,** at the northwest corner of the peninsula, is the headquarters of the Makah Indian Reservation; below it, the small logging community of **Forks** is the only community of any size on the Pacific side of the mountains.

The peninsula's main artery is **Hwy-101**, which loops around the coast. No roads run across the peninsula's mountainous core, though a couple do reach up a fair way into the Olympic National Park. You can get from town to town quite well using a combination of *Greyhound* and local buses, but if you want to do any walking, you'll have problems reaching trailheads without your own transport. A **car** is by far the best way to explore – on a bike beware of narrow roads, sharp corners and hurtling logging trucks – though hitch-hiking isn't an impossibile task.

Port Townsend

With its brightly painted Victorian mansions, convivial cafés and vigorous cultural (and counter-cultural) scene, **PORT TOWNSEND** has always had aspirations beyond its small-time logging roots. A wannabe San Francisco since the midnineteenth century, it was poised for Puget Sound supremacy in the 1890s, when confident predictions of a railway terminus lured in the rich, and Gothic mansions sprung up above the flourishing port. Unfortunately for the investors, the railway petered out before Port Townsend, the hoped-for boom never happened, and the town was left with a glut of stylish residences and a very small business district.

This combination has in recent times turned out to be Port Townsend's trump card, and since the old mansions were bought up and restored in the Sixties, the town has mellowed into an artsy community with hippy undertones and a fair amount of charm. Tourists in search of Victoriana fill plush bed and breakfasts, while jazz fans flock to the annual music festivals, and nearby, two nineteenth-century forts provide ample camping and youth hostel facilities.

Arrival and information

If you've got your own transport, Port Townsend – more than likely your first stop on the Olympic Peninsula – is easy to reach, either by **ferry** from Keystone on Whidbey Island, or by **road** over the Hood Canal Bridge from the Kitsap Peninsula. By **bus**, things get more complicated – *Greyhound*'s first major stop on the Peninsula is Port Angeles, further west. Two *Greyhound* buses a day connect with Port Townsend's local *Jefferson Transit* buses ($1; ☎385-4777) in the town of Port Ludlow, just over the Hood Canal Bridge; *Jefferson Transit* also connect Port Townsend with Winslow (see p.519), where ferries from Seattle dock.

Once in Port Townsend, pick up a map and information at the very helpful **Chamber of Commerce**, 2437 Sims Way (☎385-2722), a half-mile west of the town centre on Hwy-20; to get around, **hire a bike** from the *PT Cyclery,* 215 Taylor Street (☎385-6470).

The town

Port Townsend's physical split – half on a bluff, half at sea-level – reflects Victorian-era social divisions, when wealthy merchants built their houses uptown, well away from the noise and brawl around the port below. The downtown area is at the base of the hill, its shops and pleasant cafés centring on **Water Street** – lined with hefty 1890s brick and stonework of which the town is very proud (timber is the obvious building material in these parts and a big brick building was quite a coup for a pioneer town). The Jefferson County Court House, for example, at the far end of Water Street from the ferry landing, is a heavy red-brick Gothic assertion of civic dignity now housing the **Jefferson County Historical Museum** (Mon–Sat 11am–4pm, Sun 1–4pm; free) – the old court-room and jail essentially, plus three upper floors crammed with antique furniture and photographs. Across Water Street, a delightful dockside promenade and park stretches along the waterfront.

Doubling back from the museum, a block over on Washington Street steps lead towards residential uptown's wooden mansions – some private houses, others converted into upmarket bed and breakfast inns. The **Rothschild House** at Franklin and Taylor Street (summer daily 11am–4pm, winter weekends 11am–4pm; $1) has been restored with period furnishings, although the **Starret House** at Adams and Clay Street (now a bed and breakfast) easily out-Gothics the rest, swarmed with gables and an octagonal tower, and an impressively ornate eliptical staircase that has to be seen to be believed.

Practicalities

The peninsula's best place for **eating and drinking**, Port Townsend has a sociable atmosphere that makes for good café-sitting: try the *Salal Café*, 634 Water Street (though it closes after lunch), or *Bread and Roses* at 230 Quincey Street. For more substantial meals, the *Fountain Café*, 920 Washington Street, serves classy seafood and pasta. Water Street also holds two good fish-and-chip places, the *Lighthouse Cafe* at Tyler Street and the *Day Star*, two blocks north at Quincy; there's also a little stand set up along the dockside promenade. In the evenings, *Russell's Back Alley Tavern*, down an alley off the corner of Water and Tyler Streets, has live music Wednesday to Sunday.

Apart from the youth hostel at Fort Worden (see below) finding a place to stay in Port Townsend can be expensive: this is Washington's B&B capital, with over a dozen places, like the *Lincoln Inn*, 538 Lincoln St (☎385-6677) and the *James House*, 1238 Washington St (☎385-1238), sprinkled around the uptown area. Downtown, the *Water Street Hotel*, 635 Water Street (☎385-5467) has doubles from $40 to $100 a night, and the *Port Townsend Motel*, 2020 Washington Street (☎385-2211), costs around $50 for a double.

Forts and festivals

Fort Worden, two miles north of downtown Port Townsend, was once part of a triangle of forts built to protect the Puget Sound from invasion by a new breed of steam-powered battleships. It's the best preserved of the three, though the old army buildings make rather bleak viewing (they were the set for the film *An Officer and a Gentleman*). Still, the officers' quarters now house the *Centrum Arts Foundation* (☎385-3102), which stages lively **festivals**, particularly over the summer: it's especially worth watching out for *Jazz Port Townsend* towards the end of July, the newer *Hot Jazz* festival in February and *American Fiddler Tunes* in early July – book accommodation well ahead for any of these. Most of the shows are held in the new McCurdy Pavillion, a modern auditorium inserted into an old dirigible hangar.

Also housed in military buildings, the **Fort Worden AYH youth hostel** (☎385-0655) offers Port Townsend's cheapest beds; there's a **campsite** too. Another **youth hostel** (May–Sept only; ☎385-1288) and **campsite** (☎385-1288) can be found twenty miles east of Port Townsend at **Fort Flagler**, the second fort of the triangle (the third's Fort Casey on Whidbey Island). Set on the tip of rural Marrowstone Island, this is usually pretty empty, probably because of the lack of public transport, but cyclists might bear it in mind.

West via Sequim and Dungeness

Local buses from Port Townsend (*Jefferson Transit*) and Port Angeles (*Clallam Transit*) connect at **SEQUIM**, (pronounced "Skwim"), the only town on the rain-soaked peninsula to hold an annual irrigation festival. While drenching everywhere else, the Olympic Mountains cast a "dry shadow" over this area, and the sunshine attracts senior citizens to retire here in scores, as evinced by advertisements for lessons in the foxtrot and two-step in downtown windows and the teashops with olde-worlde spellings strung along the high street. The ultra-quaint *Oak Table Café* towards the end of town at Third and Bell Street serves excellent breakfasts and lunches.

The **visitor bureau** (☎683-6197), 1192 E Washington Rd at US-101, has information on the two main attractions, namely the **Sequim-Dungeness Museum** (Wed–Sun noon–4 pm: free), 175 W Cedar St, which exhibits locally found historical and archaeological objects, including some the oldest traces of humanity in the northwest of the United States, uncovered at nearby Happy Valley. The **Olympic Game Farm** (summer daily from 9am–4pm, winter daily from 10am; $6 per car), six miles north of Sequim, produced the animal stars of Disney classics like *The Incredible Journey* and *Grizzly Adams*, and though it's fascinating to see the peninsula's native bears and cougars close up, the sight of a huge buffalo trailing forlornly after your car in hope of a stale hamburger bun (you buy bagfuls at the entrance) makes for depressing – and far from essential – viewing.

Dungeness National Wildlife Refuge

There are no such indignities for the wildlife on the **Dungeness Spit**, a long sand-spit projecting into the sea six miles northwest of Sequim, beyond the Game Farm. Strewn with rocks and weirdly shaped driftwood, this is a bird refuge and the native home of Dungeness crabs, widely thought by shellfish gourmets to provide the ultimate in crabmeat. You can hike to the lighthouse, which has been in use for 125 years, in a day, but be sure to take provisions and enough drinking water.

As part of the Dungeness National Wildlife Refuge, the tidal zone and parts of the coastal forest have been placed under protection and are the home of numerous waterfowl. Wild geese also come here in winter and spring from the Far North. From US-101, take Kitchen Road through the Dungeness Recreation Area to the protected zone. An 800-metre footpath leads from the parking lot through a forest, and there's a viewpoint here from which you can see Canada. You can also hike further onto the promontory.

Port Angeles

Founded by the Spanish in 1791, and named "Puerto de Nuestra Senora de los Angeles" until confused postal clerks insisted one Los Angeles on the West Coast was enough, **PORT ANGELES** is the peninsula's main town and the most popular point of entry into the Olympic National Park. Though its setting is lovely, it's very much a working town, the main strip of motels and restaurants making few concessions to quaintness; and although the surrounding scenery and ferry connections to and from Victoria BC bring in the tourists, it's timber that's Port Angeles' real business. Heavy logging trucks roll in bearing tree-trunks, while pulp and paper mills – one at each end of six-mile waterfront – send a pennant of steam over the town 24 hours a day. That said, sheltered by the long arm of the Ediz Hook sand-spit, the harbour has its own harsh beauty: industrial chimneys are backdropped by mountains, and out in the bay, cormorants fly over the fishing boats.

As far as sightseeing goes, it's not going to take long to look around: the main sight downtown is **Clallam County Museum**, at Fourth and Lincoln Street (summer daily 9am–4pm, less in winter; free), housed in the old clock-towered Courthouse (Port Angeles' one showpiece of nineteenth-century architecture) and with some good exhibits on the local history. But the town's real attraction is its closeness to the Olympic National Park (see below).

Arrival and information

Port Angeles has the peninsula's best **transport connections**: *Greyhound*, at 215 N Laurel Street (☎452-7611), run a daily service to Seattle, while local *Clallam Transit* buses (☎452-4511 or ☎1-800/858-3747 outside Port Angeles) go part of the way to Port Townsend (change on to a *Jefferson Transit* bus at Sequim), and into the National Park and west around the Peninsula to NEAH BAY and FORKS. *Black Ball Transport* (☎457-4491) and the Victoria Express (☎452-8088 or ☎1-800/633-1589) run **ferries** to Victoria in Canada for a bargain $5 walk-on fare one-way, $22 with car. In Port Angeles itself, the **North Olympic Peninsula Visitors Center** at 121 East Railroad Street, near the ferry terminal (summer daily 7am–10pm, winter daily 10am–4pm; ☎452-2363), can provide a mass of information about the town. Port Angeles also houses the **Olympic National Park Visitor Center** (summer 8am–8pm, winter 8am–4pm; ☎452-4501), at the top of Race Street as you head out of town towards the park , an excellent source of the maps and information you'll need if you're planning any hiking.

Sleeping and eating in Port Angeles

If you're staying, you shouldn't have any problems finding a **motel** – the two parallel one-way main drags, First Street and Front Street, are cluttered with them (though book ahead on summer weekends, when they can all fill up). The rooms at *Aggies*, 602 E Front Street (☎457-0471), for around $45 a double are palatially large, though the *Dan Dee Motel*, 132 E Laurisden Boulevard (☎457-5404), is cheaper at around $30 a double. The nicest place in town is the *Red Lion Inn*, 221 N Lincoln St (☎452-9215), on the waterfront a block from the ferry landing, but rooms cost upwards of $70 per night.

The *House of Health*, 511 E First St (☎452-7494), has **hostel beds** for $10 and discounts on their steam baths and saunas – great for relaxing after a day on the trails. There's plenty of excellent **camping** in the Olympic National Park: six miles south of Port Angeles along Hurricane Ridge Road, the *Heart o' the Hills* campsite is one of the best, though you'll need your own transport to get to this, or any of the park campsites.

The tiny *First Street Haven* café, 107 E First Street, is good for breakfast or lunch; for dinner, the innovative vegetarian *Coffee House Restaurant and Gallery*, practically opposite at 118 E First Street, has low prices and a pleasant atmosphere.

Olympic National Park

With ample opportunity for some spectacular camping, hiking and wildlife-watching, the **Olympic National Park** is the peninsula's greatest highlight. No roads actually cross the park from one side to the other, but many run into it from various points along the coast, so you'll probably end up making several forays into different sections as you work your way around (for information on the beaches and rain forests, see below). Port Angeles is the park's most obvious and accessible point of entry, and the only place where you can get in on public transport.

Get hold of a copy of the free and very useful *Northern Olympic Peninsula's Visitor's Guide* (also available at other tourist information centres on the peninsula), which details camping facilities, ranger stations and hiking trails throughout the park, and will help to plan your route. The usual backcountry rules about not drinking the water and hiding food from bears apply here, and the weather can be particularly dodgy so carry raingear; it's worth noting too that there's a fair amount of snow until as late as June, and snowfields and glaciers survive year-round at the higher elevations. Much of the Olympic National Park is accessible from the western side, especially the **rain forests** of the Hoh, Queets and Quinault river valleys (see below for more)

While you're in the visitor centre, it's worth taking a peek at the **Pioneer Memorial Museum**, with exhibits on the park including a huge slice of a tree whose inner rings date back six hundred years.

Hurricane Ridge and Sol Duc Hot Springs

The closest point of access to the park from Port Angeles is **Hurricane Ridge**, seventeen miles above the town. *Clallam Transit* run buses up here, but only in the winter when there's cross-country skiing; in summer *Gray Line* (☎457-4140) run $9 excursions. The road up to the ridge wraps itself around precipices until the Olympic Mountains are spread magnificently in front of you – the wind blows and cameras click. A **lodge** on the ridge contains tourist facilities and a large relief map of the area, useful for getting your bearings, and **trails** lead off – through masses of wild flowers in the summer – to more isolated spots.

In summer, *Clallam Transit* also operate buses from Port Angeles to **Sol Duc Hot Springs**, twelve miles off Hwy-101 west of Port Angeles (currently open summer only; $3 to use the springs for a day), where mineral water bubbles hot out of the earth, and is channelled into the pools of a 1910 resort set in dense forest. The resort (☎327-3583; call for current prices) rents out cabins and motel units and also has **camping** facilities, and a couple of very attractive trails lead off into the national park. If you prefer bathing *au natural*, the **Olympic Hot**

Springs, at the end of a three-mile hike into the forest, still bubble up through the quickly vanishing remains of another turn-of-the-century health spa.

From the end of the road you can continue hiking along the river to **Soleduck Falls**, and a steep path turns off south, heading along Canyon Creek up into the mountains to the **Seven Lakes Basin**. More ambitious souls can hike across the Bogachiel Peak, past the Hoh Lake and down into the Hoh River valley where there's one of Western Washington's famous rain forests (see p.541). If you want to stay in the mountains overnight, get a **Backcountry Permit** from the ranger station in Port Angeles.

Neah Bay and the Makah Indians

West from Port Angeles, provided the road has been rebuilt since the storms of December 1990, Hwy-119 clings precariously to the coastline as it approaches **NEAH BAY**, the small and rundown last village of the **Makah Indian Tribe**, connected to Port Angeles by *Clallam Transit* buses. The Makah's history is a bitter one but typical of the area: a sea-going tribe, they once lived by fishing and hunting whales and seals, moving around from village to village across the western part of the peninsula. Since then, the tribe have been hit by various restrictions – of which a good example is the turn-of-the-century government decree designed to preserve the few native seals that hadn't been destroyed by white overfishing and forbidding Indians to hunt in anything but traditional canoes – which, thanks to previous pressures to modernise, a new generation had not been taught how to use. Besides such economic Catch 22s, Makah (like other Indian) children were forced to speak English at white-run schools, and missionaries set about changing the tribe's religion.

The Makah's tenuous grip on their tribal past received an unexpected boost in 1970, when a mudslide at Lake Ozette, several miles south of their present reservation, revealed part of an ancient Makah settlement – buried, Pompeii-like, by a previous mudslide some five hundred years before and perfectly preserved. The first people to arrive here encountered bizarre scenes of instantaneous ageing – green alder leaves, lying on the floor where they fell centuries ago, shrivelled almost as soon as they were exposed. But eleven years of careful excavation revealed thousands of artefacts: harpoons for whale hunts, intricately carved seal clubs, watertight boxes made without the use of metal, strangely designed bowls, toys – all belonging to a period before trade began with Europeans. Rather than being carted off to the depths of the Smithsonian, these artefacts have remained in Makah hands, and are now displayed at the purpose-built **Makah Cultural and Research Center** (summer daily 10am–5pm, closed Mon & Tues the rest of the year; $2), along with a full-size replica house and some beautiful turn-of-the-century photographs of Makah people.

If you want to stay, there are a couple of **motels** in the village: the *Thunderbird* (☎645-2450) with doubles from around $40, and the slightly cheaper *Tyee Motel* (☎645-2223). But these are neither cheap nor particularly clean, and if you've got your own transport, *Hilden's Motel* (☎645-2306), east of Neah Bay at Bullman Beach, is a better bet at around $35 a double. The village's two cafés have friendly atmospheres, but the food isn't great: try the *Breakwater Inn* on Hwy-112 near Seiku – or bring a picnic.

The Peninsula's ocean beaches

The wild, lonely Pacific **beaches** that start near Neah Bay and stretch down the Olympic Peninsula's west side still look exactly as they did before the pioneers got here: black rocks point out of a grey sea along a coastline inhabited mostly by loons, grebes, puffins and cormorants and preserved as a wildlife reserve. With strong currents, cold water and hidden rocks, these beaches aren't really suitable for swimming, but the hiking can be magnificent. You do hear the odd horror story about hikers cut off by the tide – carry a tide-table (usually in local newspapers), or copy down times at a ranger station or visitor's centre. You'll need **your own transport** and sturdy legs to get here in the first place – roads tend to be rough, and many end in a parking lot, where a trail leads on to your destination.

From Neah Bay, **Cape Flattery**, at the northern corner of the Makah Reservation is comparatively accessible, at least once you've bumped your way down the unpaved road from Neah Bay. A short hike leads to the cape which once "flattered" Captain Cook with the hope of finding a harbour and is the USA's northwesternmost point (excluding Alaska). Below the cape, the centuries-long crashing of the waves has worn caves in the sheer rock of the cliff-face, while opposite on **Tatoosh Island**, coastguards staff a remote lighthouse. You can drive to **Hobuck beach**, to the south of the cape; south again it's a three-mile hike from the road to crescent-shaped **Shi-Shi Beach**, (pronounced *shy-shy*) which ends to the south in **Point of the Arches**, an array of rocks tunnelled by waves.

Sixteen miles south of Neah Bay, a road leads to the northern tip of **Lake Ozette**, where there's a **campsite**, and trails give the only access to another stretch of wild coastline, including one to **Cape Alava**, where the Makah village was buried – though the archaeological dig closed in 1981. It's possible to hike the eighteen otherwise inaccessible miles from Cape Alava south to **Rialto Beach**, though you'd have to arrange transport at both ends of the trail, and take good care not to get cut off by the tide. At Rialto Beach itself, a broad, sandy stretch, the coast becomes accessible by road again – there's a turning off US-101 about a mile north of FORKS. About six miles from the sea, this road splits into two branches, the northern one heading to Rialto beach via **MORA** – where there's an attractive **campsite** and a couple of **motels** – the southern branch leading to **LA PUSH**, an eight hundred-year-old fishing village on the Quileute Indian Reservation. This is now sad and shabby but has a beautiful sandy beach and trails to more secluded beaches further south.

Forks

Along the densely forested west side of the peninsula, buses from Port Angeles reach no further than **FORKS**, a small logging community set just east of where the Bogachiel river "forks" into two branches. Despite half-hearted attempts to catch the peninsula's growing tourist trade, Forks is still very much a timber town, hit hard by the gradual decline of the industry – though the Mount St Helens explosion in 1980 created a temporary surge of work, as local loggers headed south to clear some of the acres of blasted trees. Today business is slower, though heavy trucks still pull through the town, unloading logs at local sawmills – where they're fed through rotating circular blades to emerge in thin slices known as "shakes" and "shingles" – and hauling sawn lumber away to be shipped out of Port Angeles or Grays Harbor.

When you're surrounded by trees, the history of logging becomes more interesting than you'd otherwise think, and it's worth calling in on the newly expanded **Forks Timber Museum** on US-101 at the south end of town (daily 10am–4pm; free), whose broad range of exhibits depicts life in the logging camps of the Twenties and Thirties, where men were based out in the forest, sleeping in bunkhouses and hitting the towns for only a couple of days every month. Cheaper road-building ended the days of the logging camp after World War II, and various mechanical devices (some on display) made logging less dangerous. The timber trade still inspires innovations – apparently, a few years back, a Japanese company tried logging around here by balloon. There's a very good **visitors bureau** (☎374-2531), with lots of information on hiking in the region, right next door.

Practicalities

Clallam Transit run **buses** between Forks and Port Angeles, with connections to Neah Bay. For **accommodation**, try the *Miller Tree Inn* (☎374-6806 after 4.30pm or at weekends), five hundred yards east of the (only) set of traffic lights in Forks: a relaxed bed and breakfast that charges $40–$45 for a double in high season (less in winter). *Olympic Suites* (☎374-5400 or ☎1-800/262-3433), on the north side of town, also has doubles from $40. Twenty miles south of Forks, the small but very friendly *Rain Forest AYH Hostel* (☎374-2270), off US-101 four miles before RUBY BEACH, puts mattresses in the barn when its twelve **hostel beds** are full.

The Rain Forests

Incredible though it seems in cool Washington, the river valleys of the west side of the peninsula produce an environment akin to a jungle, as the much-joked-about Olympic rain combines with river-water running down from the mountains to exert the overwhelming growing-power you'd associate with a much warmer climate. Temperate rain forests are rare – the only others are in Patagonia and New Zealand – but the peninsula's mild climate has combined with 140 inches of annual rainfall to produce giant trees, some centuries old. Thick mosses and lichens cling to the bark, and hang in pendants from the branches which arch overhead, so sunlight is filtered – lending the forest a somewhat ghostly, fairy-tale air. On the ground, some three hundred species of plants fight for growing space, crowding the ground with ferns, mushrooms, wood sorrel oozing out of the dense, moist soil.

Just a few miles inland from the coast the climate becomes increasingly dry and cool with lengthy periods of frost and snowfalls as the elevation climbs. The forest looks different here, reflecting the harsher conditions. It is sparser and lower and there are fewer species of tree. The rain forests, therefore, are only to be found at lower altitudes, especially in the valleys of the Hoh, Queets and Quinault rivers.

The only way to get through the forests is on the specially cleared, and in places paved, **trails**, which tend to get slippery as moss grows back again – your footwear should grip well. You'll need **your own transport** to get to any of the trailheads, but there is good **camping** at all three areas.

The Hoh River Rain Forest

The **Hoh River Rain Forest**, southeast of Forks, is probably the most popular of the rain forest areas, in part because it has the only large **visitors center** (daily 9am–5pm), nineteen miles along Upper Hoh River Road, which leaves US-101 twelve miles south of Forks. After picking up pamphlets and looking in on the various displays in the visitors centre, you can explore the rain forest along two short trails, the three-quarter mile Hall of Mosses Trail or the slightly longer Spruce Trail, which reaches the Hoh River on a circuit through the forest. More energetic hikers can follow the 36-mile Hoh River Trail right up to the base of 8000-foot Mt Olympus; climbing the ice-covered peak is a major undertaking, but even if you just want to camp out along the route, be sure to check in with the rangers and get a free **Backcountry Permit**. Cougars and other beasts are still very much present in the park.

Beyond the turn-off for the rain forest, US-101 runs parallel to the Hoh River, passing the **Rain Forest Hostel** (see p.541) before hitting the coast at the tiny **Hoh Indian Reservation** beside the rugged mouth of the river. You can wander from here along a driftwood-covered beach.

Kalaloch and the Queets River Rain Forest

US-101 runs right along the coast beyond the Hoh River, passing by a continous strand of windswept beaches, all belonging to the Olympic National Park. At one of the prettiest spots, **KALALOCH**, there's a couple of campsites and the very pleasant *Kalaloch Lodge* (☎962-2271), which has a coffee shop, a good restaurant and large, ocean-view rooms from $55 a night. There's also a **ranger station** on the south edge of the short built-up strip, which has lots of information and suggestions for hiking trips.

South of Kalaloch US-101 cuts inland around the Quinault Indian Reservation (see p.544 for more), while the Queets River, and a 25-mile-long dirt road, heads inland to the **Queets River Rain Forest**, the least visited of the three main rain forest areas. On a marked path around the forest you are given information about the luxuriant flora and fauna, including the **world's tallest Douglas Fir** tree – 220 feet tall and 45 feet in circumference.

Lake Quinault and the Quinault Rain Forest

The most easily accessible and perhaps most beautiful of all the rain forests, though, is the **Quinault Rain Forest,** around the shores of Lake Quinault. The lake itself was already a popular resort area when Teddy Roosevelt visited in the 1900s and decided to proclaim it part of an expanded Olympic National Park. While in places it feels a bit over-developed – with motels, cafés and lodges like the rustic *Quinault Lodge* (where Roosevelt stayed, and where you can too for $85 a night; ☎288-2571 or ☎1-800/562-6672) lining the southern shore – if you take the time to wander the many thick groves that fan off from the road, you'll see why Roosevelt was impressed.

One of the best short hikes starts from the ranger station just north of the lodge, climbing up and along a small stream through some textbook rain forest vegetation. A huge expanse of dense overgrowth covers the eastern shore of the lake, around which winds a narrow but definitely passable road, perfect for a mountain bike tour. The best **camping** is on the northeast shore, at the **July Creek Campground**.

WASHINGTON'S LOWER COAST

As you leave the west side of the Olympic Peninsula for the **southern part of Washington's coast**, the roads improve but the scenery gradually grows tamer. Wilderness beaches give way to holiday resorts, dense virgin forest to privately owned timber land, thinned by the processes of logging and replanting, and punctuated by bald patches of "clear-cutting", where everything has been flattened. The coastline cuts deeply into the mainland at two points: the bay of **Grays Harbor**, at the centre of which lies the industrial town of **Aberdeen**; and at muddy **Willapa Bay**, ringed by oyster beds and wildlife sanctuaries. Just below here, the churning mouth of the Columbia Rover has formed the narrow sandspit of the **Long Beach Peninsula**, lined with old resorts, a last thrust of the Washington coast before the state of Oregon.

The area is covered by two **local bus** services: *Grays Harbor Transit*, based in Hoquiam (☎532-2770/1 or ☎1-800/562-9730), runs north to Lake Quinault, west along the ocean beaches up to Taholah, and as far inland as Olympia to the east. It connects with *Pacific Transit* (☎642-4475) at Aberdeen, which then runs south as far as Astoria in Oregon, covering the Long Beach Peninsula.

South to Grays Harbor

South of the rain forest areas, US-101 loops awkwardly inland around the Quinault Indian Reservation. There have been numerous plans to build a coast road here, but the Quinault tribe has so far vetoed them to preserve its beaches from mass invasion. Routes therefore become somewhat contorted, the main highway travelling inland as far as Aberdeen, where Hwy-109 sneaks back up the coast, ending abruptly at Taholah, the main town. There's inevitably some doubling back in what follows – you could avoid it by cutting across to the coast on tiny back roads.

Grays Harbor and Aberdeen

South of the Quinault Reservation, the bay of **Grays Harbor** takes a big bite out of the coastline. The loggers who settled here in the mid-nineteenth century originally meant to stay only until the dense forest within easy reach of the waterfront had been cut down and the area was "logged out". But railways soon made it possible to transport logs from deeper in the forest, and a combination of this and the plentiful fishing – fish canning factories gradually joined the sawmills along the waterfront – led to the development of the industrial town of **ABERDEEN**, named after the settlement's biggest salmon cannery. Now hit by recession in both fishing and forestry, Aberdeen, and the neighbouring city of HOQUIAM which merges into it, are not the obvious places for a visit; but Aberdeen is making a brave attempt to exploit its key location (on the way to the ocean beaches) to catch passing tourists. At its heart is the **Grays Harbor Historical Seaport** project (east on Heron Street on the north side of the Chehalis River Bridge). Set on the battered, industrial waterfront, the Seaport project has painstakingly reconstructed the *Lady Washington* and *Columbia*, the two eighteenth-century sailing ships of Captain Robert Gray, the American trader who discovered Grays Harbor (and also the Columbia River, which is named after his ship).

Built to conform both with original designs and modern Coast Guard safety regulations, the ships are now floating museums, the cornerstone of a larger scheme to convert the old mills and packing plants of the waterfront into tourist-attracting shops and cafés.

If you want to **stay** in Aberdeen, there are inexpensive **motels** along Wishkah Street, and Grays Harbor Chamber of Commerce operates a useful **information center** at 2704 Sumner Avenue (Mon–Fri 9am–noon & 1–5pm; ☎532-1924), which can also help you with local **bus** times. *Grays Harbor Transit* is based at 3000 Bay Street in Hoquiam (☎532-2770).

The Coast between Aberdeen and the Quinault Indian Reservation

From Aberdeen, Hwy-109 leads around the northern edge of the harbour towards the wide, sandy beaches of the coast; *Grays Harbor Transit* provides a bus service. Coastal weather around here is not usually of a sort to make you reach for the suntan oil, and **clamming** is the main attraction (see p.595 for how to go about it). The right tide can bring out scores of clam-diggers armed with special shovels to dig up the local razor clams, and the Department of Fisheries sometimes have to impose no-clamming seasons to give the clams a fighting chance (check locally). Clams aside, there's little to draw you to **OCEAN SHORES**, a purpose-built Sixties bid for the convention dollar, which aimed to line its wide streets with Atlantic City-style glitter. Until, that is, the money ran out, leaving the town with neither sleaze nor soul, a tidy holiday and retirement centre.

To the north, the wide beach stretches for miles of fine, grey sand to **MOCLIPS**, where more resorts overlook the sea. The road ends north of here at **TAHOLAH**, at the centre of the **Quinault Indian Reservation**, which stretches north and east to Lake Quinault. The Quinault nation, made up of the descendants of several Salish-speaking tribes decimated when early Spanish explorers brought the first of several smallpox epidemics, dates, like most of Washington's reservations, from the treaty-making period in the 1850s, after Washington was made a territory and the demand by settlers for land increased. In 1969, the tribe restricted access to its lovely wilderness beaches to protect them from a growing incursion of litter and graffiti, but you can hike through the beaches and forests in groups led by native American guides; contact the Tribal Office (☎276-8211) in Taholah for details.

South to Willapa Bay

Hwy-105 leads south out of Aberdeen around the lower side of Grays Harbor to **WESTPORT**, which rescued itself from the declining commercial fishing industry by promoting itself to holiday-making amateurs as a "salmon capital" (the Northwest has several), and now makes a living from tourists (particularly fishermen) in the summer. Further south, the area around **GRAYLAND** is cranberry country: the local peat bogs were converted to cranberry fields earlier this century, by Finnish settlers who shipped vast quantities of vines over from the east and worked in the mills at Aberdeen until the project took off. It's all a bit on the dreary side, though, and you'll probably want to head on south to where the coastline dips into **Willapa Bay**.

Too shallow to succeed as a commercial port (despite the zealous promotions of unscrupulous nineteenth-century property developers), Willapa Bay is much less developed than Grays Harbor: its muddy depths support a profitable underworld of oysters, and much of the bay is now lined with private oyster beds. Conditions here are also good for wildlife, and sections of the **Willapa Wildlife Refuge** are scattered around the bay, including **Long Island** at the lower end, which is home to otters, racoons, an ancient cedar grove and some two hundred species of birds. The catch is, you can only get to it by private boat, but there's an **information center** at the south end of the bay on US-101, twelve miles north of ILWACO. More accessible is **Leadbetter Point**, at the tip of the Long Beach Peninsula, whose combination of forest, dunes, mudflats and marsh attracts sandpipers, turnstones, migrating black brandt sea geese and the tiny – and rare – snowy plovers, who nest in a section of the dunes specially closed off from April to August. You'll still need your own transport to get here, though, as the bus route ends at Oysterville, a few miles short of the reserve.

The Long Beach Peninsula

At the southern end of Willapa Bay, the **Long Beach Peninsula** projects a spindly arm between the mainland and the ocean (*Pacific Transit* run buses up and down it). Lined by 28 miles of uninterrupted beach, and less prone to fog than other parts of Washington's coast, the peninsula's been a holiday target since steamboats carried vacationing Portlanders down the Columbia River in the 1890s, and seaside towns like **LONG BEACH** have a nostalgia which is missing from the modern resorts further north. Large wooden figures of sea creatures and the explorers Lewis and Clark loom over you as you enter the town, and the mix of seaside gimcrackery and history feels almost surreal in **Marsh's Free Museum** (open as a shop) where, behind the giftshop paraphernalia of buckets, spades and sea-shells, ancient nickelodeons still turn out whimsical tunes for five cents, and antique peep shows line up behind them. If you're staying in the area – and the town's a nice base for the Leadbetter point wildlife estuary at the top of the peninsula (see above) – the *Sands Lo Motel* on Pacific Highway (☎642-2600) is about the cheapest in town with doubles from around $28. The **food's** nothing special here, though *My Mom's Pie Kitchen*, Pacific Highway and 12th Street, produces some tasty crab quiche alongside its range of gooey pies.

Further up the peninsula, **OYSTERVILLE** made a killing in the late 1800s by shipping oysters to San Francisco, and flogging them to the decadent spirits of the Gold Rush at up to $40 a plate. A few buildings from the 1860s and '70s have been preserved in a small historic district. Overfishing eventually wiped out the local oysters, and a new breed had to be imported from Japan, but the industry is now back on course – there are canneries further up the peninsula at NAHCOTTA.

The Columbia River Mouth

Though there's not much evidence of it now, the area around the Columbia River (served by *Pacific Transit* buses as far as Astoria in Oregon) was once inhabited by the **Chinook tribe**, who evolved "Chinook jargon", an esperanto-style mix of Indian, French and English that was widely used for trading, and later, for treaty-making – much to the confusion of other tribes who didn't speak it. Its baffling effects were put to better use during World War II, when it was employed as a radio code. The Chinooks caught nineteenth-century imaginations with their strangely flattened skulls, the result of pressing a piece of bark firmly to a baby's (padded) forehead every time it went to bed for about a year, and seen as a sign of aristocratic distinction; the explorers Lewis and Clark brought back careful sketches to a curious East. Today, the area's native-American past is signposted mostly by place names and displays in a couple of museums. The town of **ILWACO** was named after Elowahka Jim, the son-in-law of a Chinook chief. Now a rather rundown fishing town, it had a rough reputation at the turn of the century when competition between fishermen with nets and with traps broke into a series of street battles, the *gillnet wars*, fought with knives and rifles, and ending only when fishtraps were banned on the Columbia in 1935 – a blow to the local economy. A large portion of the salmon are now caught by sports-fishing tourists. The **Ilwaco Heritage Foundation Museum**, on Lake Street (summer Mon–Sat 9am–5pm, Sun noon–5pm, winter closed Mon & Tues; free), has displays on Chinook culture and the history of the cranberry along with the usual pioneer artefacts.

South of Ilwaco, **Cape Disappointment** hooks into the mouth of the wide Columbia River, the boundary with Oregon. Disappointed fur trader John Meares named the cape when he couldn't get his ship over the dangerous sandbar at the river's entrance: in fact, Meares was lucky – over two hundred ships were later wrecked on the sandbar, despite the two nineteenth-century **lighthouses** that were built to cut the death toll. Dredges and jetties have now made the bar much safer, but the **Coast Guard Station and Surf School** still trains coastguards off the cape, and you can sometimes see their small boats facing massively high waves. At the tip of the cape, **Fort Canby** is one of a chain of military installations whose bunkers and batteries guarded the Pacific coast (and here, of course, the river mouth) from the late nineteenth century through both world wars. Now a state park with plenty of **camping**, Fort Canby contains the **Lewis and Clark Interpretive Center** (summer daily 9am–5pm, closed Oct, winter weekends 10am–3pm), which follows the trail of Lewis and Clark through miles of then-unknown territory to their arrival at the Pacific.

US-101 runs east along the Columbia from here, eventually crossing a toll bridge into Oregon at Astoria (see p.596) Before the bridge, and just past the tiny town of CHINOOK, you come to turn-of-the-century **Fort Columbia** (grounds open: summer daily 8am-dusk, winter closed Mon & Tues), now renovated to include another **Interpretive Center**, this one portraying early military life from kitchens to mess halls to squad rooms where the troops slept; there are also displays on Chinook Indian history. The fort's old hospital now houses **Fort Columbia AYH Youth Hostel** (summer only; ☎777-8755) – the cheapest place in the area to stay.

travel details

Trains
From Seattle to Tacoma (3 daily; 1hr); East Olympia (3; 1hr 45min); Kelso-Longview (3; 3hr); Portland (3; 4hr); Wenatchee (1; 4hr); Spokane (1; 7hr); Vancouver, British Columbia (2; 3hr).

Buses
South from Seattle to Sea-Tac airport (4 daily; 25min); Tacoma (9; 45min); Olympia (8; 2hr); Castle Rock (1; 3hr 25min); Longview (5; 3–4hr 30min); Portland (10; 2 express buses 3hr 15min,

others up to 5hr). *Green Tortoise* also runs twice-weekly to Portland (4hr 15min).

North from Seattle to Everett (6 daily; 40min); Mt Vernon (6; 1hr 30min); Bellingham (6; 2hr 10min); Vancouver, British Columbia (7; 3hr 20min–5hr); Winslow (2; 1hr); Poulsbo (2; 1hr 15min); Port Ludlow (2; 2hr); Sequim (2; 2hr 30min); Port Angeles (2; 3hr); Anacortes (2; 2hr, except Mon, Wed and Fri, when a third bus runs via Whidbey Island).

Ferries

(All *Washington State Ferries* unless otherwise stated.)

To Alaska from Seattle (1 weekly; leaves Friday evening, arrives Skagway Monday afternoon).

To Bremerton from Seattle (15 daily; 1hr).

To Port Townsend from Keystone, Whidbey Island (Mon–Thurs 7 daily, twice as many Fri–Sun; 30min).

To the San Juan Islands from Anacortes (8; to Orcas 1hr 30min, to Friday Harbour 2hr).

To Vashon Island: from Point Defiance to Tahlequah (18 daily; 15min); from Fauntleroy, W Seattle, to Vashon (around every half-hour from 5.25am–1.40am; 15min)

To Victoria from Seattle (*BC Steamship Company* May–Oct 2 daily; 4-5hr, also a catamaran 2hr 30min); from Port Angeles (*Black Ball Transport* summer 5, spring and autumn 2; 1hr 45min).

To Whidbey Island: from Mukilteo to Clinton (from 6am to 1am every half-hour; 20min); from Port Townsend to Keystone, see above.

To Winslow from Seattle (at least hourly from 6.20am–2.40am; 35min).

CHAPTER TEN

THE CASCADES AND EASTERN WASHINGTON

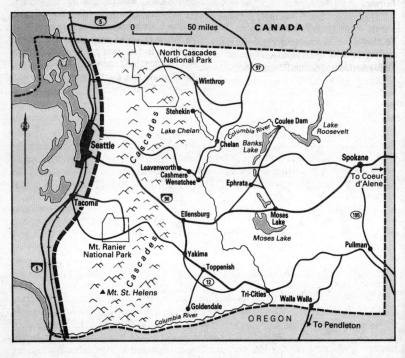

Native American legends say that the thirsty people of **Eastern Washington** once went to the ocean to ask for water. Ocean sent his children Cloud and Rain to water the land, but the people refused to let the spirits return home: Ocean, furious, rescued his offspring and built the **Cascade Mountains** as a great punitive barricade between the people and the sea. Whether or not the gods had a hand in it, the great spine of the Cascades is still a crucial divide, separating the wet, forested, sea-facing regions of the west from the parched prairies and canyonlands of Eastern Washington. Snow-capped and pine-covered, the mountains have a pristine beauty that's almost impossible to take in without putting your hiking boots on and setting off along one of the many winding trails. **Mount Rainier**, set in its own national park and accessible from Tacoma or Seattle, has some of the loveliest. Further afield, the **North Cascades** demand more time; but Hwy-20, the high mountain road that crosses them, is by far the most spectacular route to the east, dipping into the eastern foothills where small villages like **Winthrop, Chelan** and **Leavenworth** bristle with gift shops. And alongside the immaculate peaks to the south, the ashen waste land that was once **Mount St Helens** exudes its own grim fascination.

The **East** is a very different proposition: the huge, sagebrush covered spaces set with big, flat-topped rocks conjure up exciting, cowboy-movie images of the Wild West, especially in the area around the **Grand Coulee Dam**. But the population is thinly spread, and of the towns only **Spokane**, the largest city east of the Cascades, has much sophistication; others – **Ellensburg, Yakima, Walla Walla** – are plain agricultural communities whose residents clearly wonder why on earth you should want to visit. This, in a way, is the point: the great, empty region can be fascinating because of its lack of window-dressing – the rural America of country music, grain silos, Fifties diners, and battered pick-up trucks, of which there's seemingly one for every resident. It's an interesting enough place to pass through, but you need to be a real die-hard traveller to want to spend much time here.

Public transport in the area is less scanty than you might expect. The larger towns of southeast Washington and Spokane are easy enough to get to on *Greyhound* or *Amtrak*; and *Empire Lines* usefully connect Spokane with smaller towns like Chelan and Grand Coulee, close to the dam, as well as running to more major towns already linked by *Greyhound*. If you want to explore the North Cascades or see Mount St Helens, though, you'll have to think seriously about renting a car.

The area code for the Cascades and Eastern Washington is ☎509.

THE CASCADE MOUNTAINS

The first bumps of the Cascades surfaced from the sea 35 million years ago, later splitting apart to give the present mountain range a fiery birth in massive volcanic explosions. Though the snowy peaks that back up almost every Washington view now look the image of serenity, they still conceal a vast and dangerous volcanic power – as **Mount St Helens** proved when it exploded in 1980, causing human death, annihilating wildlife and deluging the Northwest with ash. Aside from the grey (and fascinating) scar left by the blast, the Cascades (now largely protected by a series of national parks) offer mile upon mile of forested wilderness, sheltering all kinds of wildlife and traversed by a skein of beautiful trails – though for all but a few summer months, you'll need snowshoes to follow them. **Mount Rainier National Park** is the most popular access-point, a possible day trip from Seattle and with plenty of visitors' facilities. Further north, the remoter **North Cascades** can be reached along Hwy-20, or dipped into from the sunny eastern foothills, where small resort towns eagerly await summer tourist-traffic and apple orchards fill sheltered valleys.

The North Cascades and the Cascade Loop

When Hwy-20 opened up the rugged **North Cascades** to an admiring public in 1972, the towns of the eastern foothills got together and came up with the **Cascade Loop**, a route which channels tourist traffic from Hwy-20 through several of their number before sending it west again over US-2. This does make a sensible route for taking in plenty of mountain scenery over a few days, but the towns themselves, despite gargantuan efforts – one, **Winthrop**, has dressed itself up in wild west regalia; another, **Leavenworth**, has turned Bavarian – have little lasting appeal, and are best taken simply as bases between trips into the gorgeous scenery. There's immense scope for camping and hiking in the North Cascades, with the remote hiking village of **Stehekin**, at the tip of Lake Chelan, making a particularly good base. Information on trails and campsites in the North Cascades is available from the **National Park Headquarters**, 800 State Street (Mon–Fri 8am–4.30pm) in **Sedro Woolley**.

The loop is only feasible during the summer, as snow closes the mountain passes for much of the year, and completely covers the hiking trails. You'll also need your own transport: unfortunately, there's no bus service over Hwy-20, though *Greyhound* runs along US-2 to Leavenworth – where you can hire bikes – and beyond to urban **Wenatchee**, the area's largest town. *Empire Lines* buses continue to the lakeside resort of **Chelan**.

Over the mountains on Hwy-20

Hwy-20 leaves I-5 about 65 miles north of Seattle at BURLINGTON, running east through the flat, tulip-growing farmlands of the Skaggit Valley and past tumble-down barns and farm buildings, before pine forests and mountain walls finally close in around the road past SEDRO WOOLLEY, where you'll find the National Park Headquarters. What few towns there are after this look well past their prime: cement storage towers, relics from more prosperous days, mark the approach to **CONCRETE**, where at the turn of the century cement factories were drawn by massive local limestone quarries. Production stopped in 1968, and the town's now very quiet. Just east, in **Rockport State Park**, there are lots of hiking trails, through a forest of fine old Douglas firs, which give a good view of the mountains and westwards to the sea; there's also **camping** (☎853-8461).

In the **Skagit River bald eagle Natural Area** you'll see bald eagles, the United States' national bird and adopted symbol, identifiable by their white heads and broad wingspan. They nest year-round along the river between Concrete and Marblemount – though winter is really the time to see them, when the birds gather to feed on the river's salmon, easy pickings as they die after spawning. In order not to disturb the birds, you should stick to the marked paths.

Minuscule MARBLEMOUNT is the last chance for ninety miles to fill up on petrol – and the last good place to eat, too, in the roadside *Mountain Song Restaurant*. Just beyond, you come to a chain of three dams set in the forest, built across the Skaggit River. **NEWHALEM**, near the first, consists of no more than a shop, a restored steam engine, and **information centre** (☎856-5700) for the North Cascades National Park. A few miles up the road, the second dam, **Diablo Dam**, is built at a tricky turn in the river called "Devil's Corner", its name trans-lated into Spanish to cause less offence to early twentieth-century citizens. The road offers a view across the dam and its steep **incline railroad**, built in 1927 to lift men and materials up a near vertical mountainside and now offering free rides to tourists. A little further east, **Ross Dam**, the largest of the three, created **Ross Lake**, which stretches north for pine-rimmed miles past the Canadian border, surrounded by hiking trails and campsites. Stopping-points all along the highway give access to spectacular views, but it's particularly worth looking out for **Washington Pass**, fifteen miles west of Mazama, where a short trail from a roadside carpark leads to a wonderful mountain panorama featuring the jagged, rocky peak of **Liberty Bell Mountain**, to the south. From here, the road winds down into the tamer landscape of the Methow Valley.

Winthrop

Leaving the mountains, Hwy-20 runs straight into **WINTHROP**, landing you among the wooden false fronts, boardwalks, swinging saloon doors and other western paraphernalia that bedecks its high street. Winthrop was actually founded by an East Coast entrepreneur, Guy Waring, who turned up in 1891 with a wagon-load of merchandise and diplomatically named the settlement he founded after John Winthrop, the Governor of his native Massachusetts – the state that had provided his backing. Waring was visited by an old Harvard classmate, Owen Wister, and when Wister later wrote *The Virginian*, widely acclaimed as the first Western novel, the book was clearly (in the town's opinion) based on Winthrop. Waring's large log-cabin home, set on a hill behind the high street, is now the **Shafer Museum** (Mon–Fri 10am–5pm; free), its long porch cluttered with old bicycles and rusty farming equipment.

There are some good places to **eat** in Winthrop, the food ranging from Mexican/American meals at the *Duck Brand Cantina* to late-night pizza at *Three Fingered Jacks*, both on the high street. **Accommodation**, though, is pricey (you'll pay around $50 for a double) and you'll be better off in one of the **campsites** along Hwy-20 west of town. If you do decide to stay, or want to go horseriding, fishing or white water river-rafting, the **Visitor Information Center** (summer only daily 9am–5pm; ☎966-2125) is well stocked with information.

Rooms are cheaper down the road in Winthrop's impoverished neighbour, **TWISP**, eleven miles further south on Hwy-20, though you may not fancy staying here. A quick look round Twisp's battered buildings in fact goes a good way towards explaining Winthrop's shameless bidding for the tourist trade: whatever you make of the wild west motif, Winthrop at least looks like a going concern. Shabby Twisp just looks forlorn.

Chelan and Stehekin

South of Twisp, Hwy-153 follows the Methow River three miles east to Lake Pateros, which edges the road to **CHELAN**, at first sight a dull little resort town where watersports are the only attraction: the *Ship and Shore Drive Inn*, off US-97 south of town rents out canoes, rowing boats and windsurfing boards fairly cheaply. The town also has bus connections to WENATCHEE, Eastern Washington and the Grand Coulee Dam; call the **Chamber of Commerce**, 208 E. Johnson (☎682-2022), for information on *Empire Line* buses, which drop off outside the building.

Chelan's real advantage, however, is that it lies at the eastern tip of **Lake Chelan** – unimpressive from this end, surrounded by low bare hills, but in reality carved long, thin and deep by an Ice-Age glacier, and stretching back over fifty miles to the northwest, through sloping forests of fir trees into the heart of the Cascades. A **ferry**, the *Lady of the Lake* (☎682-2224), sails slowly up the lake, leaving Lake Chelan Boat Dock, a mile south of Chelan, daily in summer at 8.30am and returning early evening ($19). It's a pleasant cruise for tourists, and an important transport link for the people who live in HOLDEN, a Lutheran retreat in a remote valley west of the lake.

At the lake's mountainous western tip, the boat stops briefly in **STEHEKIN**, an isolated village otherwise accessible only by hiking trail or air-taxi ($35 each way from Chelan; ☎682-5555). Stehekin is an ideal base for hiking in the North Cascades, and you can rent bikes and canoes from the *North Cascades Lodge* (☎682-4711), which also runs a shuttle-bus deeper into the mountains. Rooms at the *Lodge* start at $55 for a double and can be hard to get, so it's a good idea to come armed with a tent. For camping and hiking information (and, for some of the trails, a wilderness permit), visit the **ranger station** in Stehekin. Or in advance look in on the helpful **Chelan ranger station**, 428 W Woodin Avenue, at the south end of town by the lake (Mon–Sat 8am–4.30pm).

Wenatchee and the Apple Trade

South of Chelan, **WENATCHEE** is Washington's apple capital, the centre of an industry that fills the valleys of the eastern foothills with orchards, scattering blossom in the spring. Apple-stalls appear beside the roads in the autumn, piled mostly with sweet, outsized *Red Delicious*, the USA's most popular kind – Washington grows nearly half the country's supply. You'll find other varieties too: enormous *Golden Delicious*, tarter red *Winesaps* and giant *Granny Smiths*. The warm climate's ideal for apple growing, although farmers defend their fruit from early frosts with metal heaters, their tall fans easily visible from the road, which often cuts close to the trees.

As apples, rather than tourists, are Wenatchee's main business (you'll pass packing plants on the way in), the town has for the most part a plain, commercial face, its only gesture towards quaintness a short strip of gaudy Victorian buildings whose cafés and shops are dying a quiet death at the south end of Mission Street, quite a walk from the town centre. The friendly staff at the **North Central Washington Museum**, 127 S Mission Street (Mon–Fri 10am–4pm, Sat & Sun 1–4pm; free), will happily switch on an antique apple-sorting machine, hurling fruit across the room with alarming vigour: but most people end up here simply because the town's on the *Greyhound* route. The station's on the corner of First and Chelan Streets (☎662-2183) and is shared by *Empire Lines* who run to Chelan and the Methow Valley and some of eastern Washington. There's also a strip of cheap **motel** rooms along N Wenatchee Avenue.

If you're around in May it's well worth looking in on the **Apple Blossom Festival**, a massively American affair involving carnival floats, interminable marching bands and a semi-official "cruise" where teenagers from miles around cram into cars and pick-up trucks and circle a two-street block from afternoon to night. At any time, shady **Ohme Gardens** (April–Oct daily 9am to dusk; $3), set on a rocky bluff overlooking the town three miles north, provide some pleasant relief from the arid scenery around with alpine plants, trees and fern-lined pools. If you have not yet seen enough dams to last a lifetime, **Rocky Reach Dam**, a couple of miles further on, has a huge and thorough exhibit on electricity, as well as art exhibitions and windows to watch fish climbing the fish-ladder.

Cashmere and Leavenworth

Just before Rocky Reach Dam, US-2 splits and branches west into the mountains, towards two more themed villages. The first of these, **CASHMERE**, can muster up a reasonably tasteful late nineteenth-century main street and a small **Pioneer Village** of restored buildings, tucked in a field behind the **Chelan County Museum** on US-2 – which features displays of stuffed local wildlife and artefacts. The village is also famous, at least locally, for its sweet speciality *aplets* and *cotlets* (as in apricot) – not unlike turkish delight and available in free samples from the **Aplets and Cotlets factory**, 117 Mission Street.

Brace yourself as you head west towards **LEAVENWORTH**. Twenty years ago a small timber and railway town, Leavenworth has warded off economic death by going Bavarian: local motels and stores have been replaced with steeply roofed half-timbered "alpine chalets", complete with wooden balconies and window-boxes; wienerschnitzel, sauerkraut and strudels now feature heavily in local menus; and gift shops sell musical boxes, all to the strains of "alpine" folk music – even the supermarket bids you "Wilkommen zu Safeway".

This can (just about) be fun if you're in the right mood, and even if you aren't the surrounding mountain scenery is gorgeous. In any case it's a stop for *Greyhound* (on US-2 at the *Country Kitchen Drive-In*; ☎548-7015), and the town is an obvious base for hiking in the Cascades if you don't have a car. You can rent **bikes** from *Icicle Bicycle* on US-2 at the far end of town (☎548-7864). The cheapest way to **stay** is to pitch tent at one of the **campsites** ten miles down Icicle Creek Road (last on the left at the far end of town) such as the Icicle River Ranch (☎548-5420); for hotel accommodation try the *Edelweiss* on Front Street (☎548-7015), which has one double room at $20, and more at around $33. There are some wonderful hiking trails near Leavenworth, especially the *Enchantment Lake* trail, although the popularity of this has led to a permit system restricting access: the **ranger station** just off US-2 can advise and provide you with trail guides and other hiking information.

A fifty-mile long round trip via Hwy 209 and Hwy 207 takes you through the Wenatchee National Forest to **LAKE WENATCHEE**, a large mountain lake. If you're fit you can cycle the journey, and in summer you can hire boats at the lake or ride horses through the forest. This is also a popular winter-sports area, with some good cross-country skiing.

From Leavenworth, US-2 runs west through the Cascades over Steven's Pass, emerging to the north of Seattle. Alternatively, US-97 branches off south through the Swauk Mining Districts where prospectors dug for gold in the late nineteenth century. Just off the highway, tiny, ramshackle **LIBERTY** is a curious, though rather gimmicky ghost town, with a year-round population of around seven, still promoting gold panning from its grocery store – about the only solid-looking building there. South of here, the east–west interstate, I-90, cuts over Snoqualmie Pass to the west side of the mountains; it also continues east to Spokane (see p.563).

Mount Rainier National Park

Set in its own National Park, **MOUNT RAINIER** is the tallest and most accessible of the state's Cascade peaks, and a major Washington landmark. People in Seattle look to see if "the mountain's out", the sign of a clear day, and Indian tribes living long ago in the shadow of the mountain evolved their own myths around it. Rainier appears as a jealous wife magically metamorphosed, a giant mountain mysteriously tamed, its high peak seen as spirit country, inscrutable to human eyes (the summit is wreathed in clouds much of the time). There's a lively movement to re-christen Rainier with a native American name like *Tahoma* ("the great mountain, which gives thunder and lightning, having great unseen powers") – something that would at least avoid the current jokes about the mountain's name actually being a description of its weather: often very wet, with heavy snow falls during the long winter season. It's not until late June or July that the snow-line creeps up the slopes, unblocking roads and revealing a web of hiking trails. But in summer, when deer and mountain goats appear at the forest edges, small furry marmots emerge among the rocks and newly uncovered meadows sprout alpine flowers, the mountain makes for some perfect – and, if you pick the right trail, not unduly tough – hiking.

There are four entrances to the national park, all leading to distinct sections, though in summer it's possible to drive between the main **Nisqually entrance** in the park's southwest corner, and the smaller entrance to the southeast. The Nisqually section is the only one kept open year-round (for cross-country skiing; the others open when the snow melts around June) and the only part you can see on any kind of public transport – confined to pricey day trips with *Gray Line* from Seattle (☎626-5208; $29; May–Oct only). Admission to the National Park is $5 per car, $2 hiker or cyclist. It's possible to **stay** in the park at one of the two national park lodges in LONGMIRE and PARADISE (see below), and there's plenty of **camping**, and of course **hiking**, all over

The Nisqually entrance: to Longmire and Paradise

The **Nisqually entrance** to the park, around sixty miles southeast of Tacoma on Hwy-7, then Hwy-706, brings you into the park just short of **LONGMIRE**, a small group of buildings that includes a tiny **wildlife museum** (daily 9am–6pm; free), whose front desk serves as a very useful **hiker information center** with plenty of information on the over thirty trails. In winter you can hire skis in Longmire, and year-round the *National Park Inn* offers accommodation (doubles from $40 without bath; ☎569-2275 for reservations here and at *Paradise Inn*, below).

The **TRAIL OF SHADOWS** is a highly popular, half-hour walk around the hillside meadows which takes you past the ruins of the first hotel built in the area. From the **Cougar Rock Campground** you can also hike along the two-mile **CARTER FALLS WALK** on the Paradise river.

Trails around here are free from snow earlier than those higher up. In midsummer you'll probably want to drive further up the mountain – where the snow is still many feet deep well into June – past waterfalls of glacial snowmelt, towards **PARADISE** – where a larger **visitors center** has films and exhibits on natural history and a round, windowed room for contemplating the mountain. Several routes begin from Paradise, and, a short walk from the visitors centre, bedraggled hikers can dry out by the two large fireplaces of *Paradise Inn*: pricier but more cosy than its counterpart at Longmire (doubles from $45 without bath; ☎569-2275). It's only open May to October; watch out for the special deals at the end of each season.

Paradise is also the starting-point for **climbing Mount Rainier** – a serious undertaking involving ice axes, crampons and some degree of danger. It usually takes two days to get to the summit and back (the first to reach the base camp at Camp Muir, then the strenuous final assult and back down to Paradise) and by all accounts, the climb, and the summit, with its two craters rimmed with ice-caves, are pretty special. Unless you're very experienced (and even then, you have to register with rangers) the way to do it is with the guide service, *Rainier Mountaineering Inc* in Paradise (☎569-2227), who offer three-day courses – one day's practice, then the two-day climb – and rent out equipment for around $230.

If you don't want to exert yourself quite that much, you can take the 1.2-mile **Nisqually Vista Trail** up the mountain and enjoy the fine view of the Mount Rainier glacier. Throughout the summer months park rangers also organise **theme tours**, such as a geology tour along the Nisqually Vista Trail, a tour of the flowers in the Paradise Hill meadows, or a strenuous half-day tour devoted to the ecology of the mountains. The Visitor Center at Paradise (see above) has information.

Other entrances

During summer it's possible to drive from Paradise along rugged **Stephen's Canyon Road** to the park's southeastern corner, otherwise accessible only from the eastern side of the Cascades, off Hwy-12, west of Yakima. Here, the **Ohanapecosh visitors center** (summer only, Sun–Thurs 9am–6pm; Fri & Sat 9am–7pm) is set in deep forest, near the trout-packed Ohanapecosh River. A hiking trail leads along the Grove of the Patriarchs – where some of the trees are over one thousand years old – and another leads off to hot springs enjoyed by the first settlers.

Two further entrances are accessible from Seattle and the west. The **White River entrance** on Hwy-410 in the park's northeastern corner leads to the **Sunrise** visitors centre and wonderful views of Emmons Glacier and the mountain's crest; the **Carbon River entrance** on Hwy-165 in the northwest corner is the least-used, and has no visitors centre and only a few dirt roads. There are **campsites** near each entrance; for overnight backpacking you'll need a wilderness permit (free from any ranger or visitors centre).

Mount St Helens

The Klickitat Indians who called **MOUNT ST HELENS** *Tahonelatclah* ("Fire Mountain") knew what they were talking about. For centuries a perfect snow-capped peak, popular with scout camps and climbing expeditions, Mount St Helens suddenly exploded in May 1980, blasting off its peak and leaving a charred area of almost total destruction. The scene today is grey, crumbly and very quiet, except for the noise of construction work as roads and trails are built through what is now the Mount St Helens National Volcanic Monument.

From its first rumblings in March, the volcano became a big tourist attraction. Residents and loggers working on the mountain's forested slopes were evacuated and roads were closed, but by April the entrances to the restricted zone around the steaming peak were jammed with reporters and sightseers – one crew even ducked restrictions to film a beer commercial at the edge of the crater. People in Portland wore t-shirts saying "St Helens is hot" and "Do it, Loowit" (another Indian name for the mountain). But the mountain didn't seem to be doing anything much, and impatient residents demanded to be let back to their homes. Even the official line became blurred when Harry Truman, the elderly manager of the Lodge at Spirit Lake, refused to move out, became a national celebrity and was, incredibly, congratulated on his "common sense" by Washington's governor.

It was finally decided on 17 May that home-owners could be allowed in to the restricted zone to collect their possessions, and a convoy was actually waiting at the road-barriers when the mountain finally exploded on May 18 – not upwards, but sideways in a massive lateral blast that ripped a great chunk out of the mountainside. An avalanche of debris slid down the mountain into Spirit Lake, raising it by two hundred feet and turning it into a steaming cauldron of muddy liquid. Heavy clouds of ash and rock suffocated loggers on a nearby slope, and, drifting east, caused a small plane spraying crops to crash before raining several feet of ash on the town of Yakima.

Fifty-seven people died in the eruption. A few were there officially, taking a calculated risk to survey or record the mountain, but most, like Harry Truman, had ignored warnings or evaded the restrictions. The wildlife population was harder hit: about a million and a half wild animals – whole herds of deer and elk, mountain goats, cougar and bear – were killed, and thousands of fish were trapped in sediment-filled rivers whose temperatures rose to boiling point. There were dire economic effects, too, as falling ash spoiled crops and killed livestock across the state, and millions of feet of timber were lost when forests were flattened. The long-term effects are less easy to quantify: some have even suggested that the eruption was responsible for climatic changes as far away as Europe.

Seeing the mountain

Visiting the devastation is fascinating, chilling and slow. You'll need **your own transport**, and the roads are narrow and twisting; most are closed by snow for a good part of the year, and some are currently shut for reconstruction (call ☎274-4038 for an update). There's no obvious choice of a good base to make the trip from – it's possible to do it in a day from Portland, but this is heavy on driving-time, and you're probably better off finding a **motel** in one of the small towns close by the mountain or in the otherwise uninteresting larger towns of LONGVIEW and KELSO. There's a *Motel 6* at 106 Minor Road, Kelso – exit 39 off I-5 (doubles $30; ☎425-3229), and plenty of **camping** in the National Forest which surrounds the blast area; *Iron Creek Campsite* on National Forest route 25 is closest.

The main **visitors center** (summer daily 9am–6pm, winter daily 9am–5pm; ☎247-5473), just west of TOUTLE off I-5, is worth dropping into, for exhibits, interpretive programmes and a free film, as well as lots of useful information. You can't see anything of the actual blast area from here, but by the time Hwy-504 is reopened beyond the visitors centre you'll be able to drive well up into the devastated area. At the end of the road, two more visitors centres, one at **Coldwater Ridge** and another at **Johnson Ridge**, above Spirit Lake, are under construction and due to open in the 1992 and 1994 respectively. In the meantime there are **two other routes** up the mountain, but both involve backtracking to I-5 from the visitors centre and at least a further three-hour drive.

Windy Ridge

The easiest route onto the mountain is from the **north**: take I-5 to exit 68, where US-12 leads east to RANDLE, then turn right down Forest Service Road 25 to the tiny **Iron Creek Information Station**, where the journey into the blast area proper begins. Closed by snow in winter, and clogged by cars in summer, the road winds round hairpin bends through dark green forest, until bald, spikey trees signal a sudden change of scene: thousands of grey tree-skeletons lie in combed-looking horizontal rows, knocked flat in different directions as the blast waves bounced off the hillsides. The sheer wastage is staggering: logging companies wanted to salvage what they could, but the decaying wood produces vital nutrients to regenerate the soil, and provides the only available cover to surviving small animals and insects, so the trees have been left to rot naturally. Even though there are signs of renewal – the odd patch of grass or young tree – it's a stark scene. Beside the road, the wrecked car of a couple who ducked the entry restrictions has been left where it was blown by the blast, the rusty roof crushed in. This road ends by a viewpoint across a lake part-jammed with fallen trees; another, narrow route 99, leads on to **Windy Ridge**, an outcrop which overlooks the crater itself – apparently the best view of all, but only accessible once the road has been reconstructed.

The Lava Caves

You can also drive around the mountain from the blast area to its **south** side, where the rushing molten lava from another explosion, centuries ago, channelled long, tube-like **lava caves** under the earth. Rent a light (or bring a torch) and descend to **Ape Cave**, a mile long, and much colder than outside – bring extra clothing. Though it's more atmospheric on your own, the ranger-led tours in the early afternoon point out all kinds of geological oddities you'd otherwise miss. The cave is close to **Pine Creek Information Center**, a good place to pick up maps and information if you're approaching the mountain from the south – exit 21 off I-5, at WOODLAND, then keep going east past COUGAR on Hwy-503.

EASTERN WASHINGTON

Big, dry and empty, Eastern Washington has more in common with neighbouring Idaho than with the green western side of the state. Faded, olive-coloured sagebrush covers mile upon mile of dusty land and huge, reddish flat-topped rocks loom over the prairies. It's the powerful landscape of a thousand western movies, and it's impossible not to be stirred by the sheer scale of the scenery. The towns, though, are no-nonsense agricultural and commercial centres, and only **Spokane** has any degree of cultural life. There are several routes you could follow through the region, ranging from a *Greyhound*-borne sprint across I-90, via **Ellensburg** and Spokane, to pottering among the rocks and coulees around the **Grand Coulee Dam**, one of the biggest concrete structures ever built. *Greyhound* run a second route from Ellensburg, dipping into the fertile Yakima Valley to stop at the railway town of **Yakima**, and running southeast to **Richland**, the World War II site of an "atomic city" where plutonium was secretly produced. **Walla Walla**, a little way east, was once the home of Marcus Whitman, the pioneer missionary who led the first wagon-train over the Oregon Trail and was later massacred by Cayuse Indians. A useful supplement to *Greyhound* is provided by *Empire Lines*, who connect Spokane with Grand Coulee, close to the dam, and run south to Chelan, Wenatchee, Ellensburg and Yakima, and north up US-97 to the Canadian border. *Amtrak* also run to Ellensburg, Yakima, Richland and Spokane from Seattle.

East to Ellensburg

If you're travelling east by *Greyhound* along I-90 your first major stop beyond the mountains will be **ELLENSBURG**, a dusty little town with a late nineteenth-century redbrick core. Like many frontier towns, Ellensburg was razed by fire in its early wooden-buildings days, then rebuilt itself more solidly in brick – the reason so many of the downtown buildings flourish the same "1889" date. One of these post-fire buildings houses the **Kittas County Museum**, on Third Avenue at Pine Street (Mon–Fri afternoons only; free), which features rocks, gems and local agates along with native American and pioneer exhibits. Other than that, there's nothing to detain you unless you're around on Labor Day weekend (early September), when the annual **Ellensburg Rodeo** fills the town with stetsoned cowboys (and cowgirls), who rope steers, ride bulls and sit on bucking broncos, accompanied by much pageantry and unfurling of star-spangled banners. For tickets, call the Rodeo Ticket Office (☎1-800/637-2444 or 925-5381): prices start at around $7, and include admission to the **Kittitas County Fair**, an odd combination of penned livestock and bright carnival rides that takes place at the same time. Needless to say, you should book accommodation ahead for this.

Greyhound and *Empire Lines* stop at Oakanogan Street and Eighth Avenue (☎925-1177), and if you fancy a break between buses, the **Chamber of Commerce**, a short walk away at 436 N Sprague Street (Mon–Fri 8am–5pm; ☎925-3137), can provide a downtown map and advice on **accommodation**. The *Rega Lodge*, in Motel Square, at Sixth and Water streets (☎925-3116), is close to downtown and has doubles from around $30. As for **eating**, the art deco *Valley Café*, 105 W Third Street, is by far the nicest place in town.

The Yakima Valley

While some *Greyhound* buses speed east out of Ellensburg, disappearing in a cloud of dust along I-90 towards Spokane, others take a slower, more varied route, skirting a large military reservation towards the towns of the southeast and the fertile Yakima Valley. If you've got your own transport, Hwy-821, the Yakima Canyon Road, is nicer, following the Yakima River along a route lined in summer with wild roses.

To the east and west of its namesake town , the Yakima Valley turns into fruit-and wine-growing country, where apples, cherries, pears and grapes grow prolifically in what was once sagebrush desert. Though the Yakima Valley's volcanic soil is naturally rich, irrigation is what has made it fertile, and intricate systems of reservoirs, canals and ditches divert water from the Yakima River around the orchards and vineyards. Water rights are a crucial issue for local farmers: priority is given to those who've held the land longest, and in dry years farmers with only junior water rights can find themselves in trouble. The river's fish can be left high and dry, too – irrigation channels can drain the river itself to a shallow trickle, not deep enough to support migrating salmon.

Yakima

Sprawling **YAKIMA** is the valley's urban hub, and although its glossy new convention centre promotes an upmarket image – "Visit Yakima, the Palm Springs of Washington" – the town isn't about to win any beauty contests. Freight trains still run close to the town's centre, and you get the feeling that the railway yard might still be the town's real centre of gravity. It certainly was in the nineteenth century, when the town actually shuffled several miles from its original site in pursuit of a vital railway terminal, meanly located away from the original township by a miffed railway company (the old Yakima is now the smaller neighbouring community of UNION GAP). The town's attractions are few, but it's a potential base for exploring the Cascades to the west (see Mount Rainier, p.554), or the wineries of the Yakima Valley to the east, and *Greyhound* stop at 602 E Yakima Avenue (☎457-5131), sharing the depot with *Empire Lines* (same number) so you might end up here. Pick up a map at the **Visitors and Convention Bureau** at 10 N Eighth Street (Mon–Fri 8.30am–5pm; ☎575-1300), a short walk from the Greyhound station. If you want to stay, there are plenty of motels along N First Street, and the **YWCA**, centrally located at 15 N Naches Avenue (☎248-7796), has beds for women only from $10 a night.

The railway heritage is invoked at one of a couple of new projects aimed at cheering up the part of downtown that hasn't been scooped into the town's main mall. Where Yakima Avenue, the main street, crosses Front Street, **Track 29** is a group of brightly painted 1930s and earlier train carriages housing a small collection of shops, mostly food stalls, the vendors leaning sweaty-faced out of cramped kitchens. Opposite, **Yesterday's Village and Farmer's Market** is turning the old Fruit Exchange building into a nostalgic antiques-and-crafts mall – the kind of thing that has worked better in richer, more touristy areas. Across the tracks, located inside the old Union Pacific Railroad station and, the *Brewery Pub*, 32 N Front Street, serves a half-dozen of *Grants* top-rated ales, lagers and stouts, fresh from the brewery next door; be sure to try the hoppy *Scottish Ale* (and the crisp-tasting local cider), and some of the pub-type **food** in the friendly front room.

While good beer fans will have a field day, there's not really much else to see in Yakima, though you could catch a bus (*Yakima Transit* run a service around the city, but not in the evenings or on Sunday ☎575-6175) into the southwestern suburb where the **Yakima Valley Museum**, 2105 Tieton Drive (Wed–Fri 10am–5pm, Sat & Sun noon–5pm; $1), houses a collection of nineteenth-century buggies, stage coaches and big covered Conestoga wagons.

South through the wine country

Two main roads run parallel out of Yakima toward the southeast. I-82, lined with vineyards, follows the northeast edge of the **Yakima Indian Reservation**, which covers a huge chunk of land to the south. US-97 runs down to TOPPENISH, where it's worth taking time before seeing the wineries to visit the **Yakima Indian Nation Cultural Center** (open very approximately daily 9am–5pm, closed Jan & Feb; free Mon, otherwise $2; call ☎865-2800 to check hours).

Housed in what looks like a stone-built, slate-roofed wigwam, the museum outlines Yakima traditions in a series of big tableaux, featuring models of mountains, marshes and Indian children, and wall displays including a *time-ball* – a sort of macramé diary kept by women after marriage, each major event commemorated by a knot or beads. Women start to form the chain when they marry, so that in old age one's entire life can be recalled by unravelling it. Self-consciously evocative of Indian rituals in its presentation (information plaques are written in simple, fairy-tale language), the museum is sub-titled *the Challenge of Spilyay* – Spilyay being the Yakima version of the god-like coyote figure who crops up in many Indian myths.

Once out of the museum, you can either head south to the Columbia Gorge via US-97 – if you do, set aside at least an hour for a stop at the Maryhill Museum – or continue along I-82 through the wine country – **wineries** are thickly scattered throughout the valley, and they all have tasting-rooms. Much of the labour in this hop- and fruit-growing area is Mexican, and in the tiny town of ZILLAH there's an excellent and cheap Mexican café, *El Ranchito*, 1319 E First Avenue.

Goldendale and the Maryhill Museum

From I-82 at TOPPENISH, US-97 cuts southwest across the Yakima Indian Reservation toward the Columbia River. Thirty miles on, just before the Oregon border, is one unexpected place you won't want to miss: the eccentric **Maryhill Museum** (daily, mid-March to mid-Nov, 9am–5pm; $3), an elaborate house stuffed with the art treasures collected by Sam Hill, an oddball landowner who once planned a Quaker colony here. The Quakers he brought over from Belgium took one look at the parched slopes of the Columbia Gorge and opted out, and he concentrated on the house instead, determined to ensconce his wife Mary in palatial magnificence. The result is an eclectic collection ranging from Russian icons to Indian wickerwork, not to mention one of the country's best collections of Rodin sculptures. On a nearby hill, overlooking the Columbia River, Sam Hill built a miniature copy of **Stonehenge,** in honour of those who died in World War I.

Richland

As I-82 curves southeast towards the Columbia River, it approaches a cluster of three towns known as the TRI-CITIES. Of these, only **RICHLAND** is worth visiting, and then only for its previous incarnation as **Hanford**, when it housed a top-secret plant to produce plutonium during the World War II race for nuclear weapons. The government chose the town for its closeness to the Columbia River – providing both cold water for cooling reactors and hydro-electricity from its new dams – and its remote location in sagebrush-covered wilderness. The sudden arrival of over fifty thousand construction workers from across the US, and the growth of a huge, sprawling makeshift city around what was in 1943 a tiny village of four hundred, must surely have made people suspect something was afoot. But apparently very few, perhaps a dozen top scientists and politicos, knew much about what was happening here.

During the Sixties and Seventies, work at Hanford shifted from military projects towards civic uses of nuclear (and other) forms of energy. But the Reagan years brought defence back to the fore, and now about sixty percent of investment here is in military projects. The saga of the town's atomic past is set out at the **Hanford Science Center**, 825 Jadwin Avenue in the Federal Building next to the post office in downtown Richland (Mon–Fri 8am–5pm, Sat 9am–5pm, Sun noon–5pm; free), where computerised exhibits and a film put the case for nuclear power. It's unlikely that you'll want to hang around Richland for long; but if you do, the **Chamber of Commerce** (☎735-8486) can give you more information.

Walla Walla: the Whitman Mission

US-12 follows the Columbia south from the Tri-cities, then cuts east through the wheat and onion fields that surround the college and agricultural town of **WALLA WALLA**. Once the bare, wild scene of Washingon's most disasterous mission outpost, the town is now known for its onions, *Walla Walla Sweets*, which are allegedly mild enough to be eaten raw like apples. Though there's not much to see here now, the town has a crucial historical significance: it was here in 1836 that **Dr Marcus Whitman**, a key figure in the settling of the Northwest, arrived from the East Coast as a missionary, hoping to convert the local Cayuse Indians from their nomadic ways into church-going, crop-growing Christian citizens.

Whitman and his wife Narcissa made little headway with the Indians, and like other western missionaries turned their attention instead to white settlers. In 1843, Whitman guided the first wagon-train across the Oregon Trail, effectively opening up the Northwest for settlement: his mission became a refuge along the trail, taking in sick and orphaned travellers (including the real-life Sagar children of the story book *Children of the Oregon Trail*). The Cayuse Indians eyed the increasing numbers of emigrants very warily, and when a measles epidemic brought by settlers spread among the tribe, suspicions grew that they were being poisoned to make way for the whites, particularly as Dr Whitman could help (some) whites but few of the Indians – who had no natural immunity to the epidemic. Half the tribe died. Whitman sensed the growing tension, and he must have known the tribal tradition that medicine-men were directly liable for the deaths of their patients, but he continued to take on even hopeless cases. In November 1847 a band of Cayuse Indians arrived at the mission and murdered Whitman, Narcissa and several others. Fifty more at the mission, mostly children, were taken captive, and although they were later released, angry settlers raised volunteer bands against the Cayuse. When the story hit the newspapers back east, it generated such a tide of fear about Indian uprisings that the government finally declared the Oregon land (then including Washington) an official US territory, which meant the army could be sent in to protect the settlers – with drastic implications for the Indians.

The site of the **Whitman Mission** (summer daily 8am–8pm, rest of the year 8am–4.30pm; free), seven miles west of Walla Walla off US-12, is bare but effective. The mission itself was burnt down by the Cayuse after the massacre, and simple marks on the ground plus interpretive plaques show its one-time layout, the place where the Whitman's young daughter drowned in the stream, and the sites of Marcus's and Narcissa's murder. A visitor's centre by the site shows a film on Whitman's work and the massacre, and is well stocked with books on the subject, including Narcissa Whitman's diary.

When the army arrived, they were stationed at **Fort Walla Walla** (June–Sept Tues–Sun 1–5pm, May & Oct Sat & Sun 1–5pm; $2), at the southwest corner of town, off Myra Road. The fort's five enormous shed-like concrete buildings are now home to a collection of relics from the horse-drawn era of agriculture: old ploughs and farm machinery, sturdy wagons and more elegant lightweight buggies, built for nineteenth-century cruising. Below these buildings, a reconstructed log-cabin pioneer village includes a schoolroom, railway station, store and smithy.

Once you've seen these two sights (and of the two, the mission's the more interesting), there's not much point in hanging around, though *Greyhound* stops at 315 Second Street (☎525-9313), and if you fancy a break the **Chamber of Commerce**, Sumach and Colville Streets (Mon–Fri 9am–5pm), is a couple of blocks away, with maps and listing of lodgings. Of the handful of **motels**, the *Whitman Annex*, 204 N Spokane Street (☎529-3400), has reasonably priced rooms a few blocks from the Chamber of Commerce; and for women, the centrally located *YWCA* at First and Birch Streets (☎525-2570) has single rooms from $15 a night.

Pullman and the Palouse Region

From Walla Walla, you can either head south over the Oregon border towards PENDLETON, LA GRANDE and the lovely Wallowa Mountains (see Chapter Twelve), or travel northeast towards Spokane, useful as a launching-point for the Grand Coulee Dam if nothing else. The latter option will take you through the agricultural **Palouse** region, where the land undulates into rows of low hills, covered with wave after wave of wheatfields. **PULLMAN** is the main town in the area – a college town that dies completely when Washington State University's sixteen thousand students take off for the summer. At other times, the studenty atmosphere is convivial, though you can probably see what there is of the town in less than an hour. *Greyhound* stop at NE 115 Olsen Street (☎334-1412), and the **Chamber of Commerce**, N 415 Grand Avenue (Mon–Fri 9am–5pm), can supply information – the 24-hour Visitor Information Center **window** on the university campus filling in when it's closed.

The best views come from the top of one of the cone-shaped hills which scatter the area. Between Pullman and Spokane off US-195, **Steptoe Butte**, named for Colonel Steptoe, whose troops once spent an uneasy night creeping down the hill and through encircling bands of Indians during the struggles of the 1850s, offers a widespread panorama across the rippling land. On a clear day, you can just about make out the Rockies to the east.

Spokane

The wide open spaces and plain little towns of Eastern Washington don't really prepare you for **SPOKANE**. Just a few miles from the Idaho border, it's the region's only real city, and its scattering of grandiose late nineteenth-century buildings – built on the spoils of the Coeur d'Alene silver mines, just across the state divide – sport some unexpectedly elegant, almost colonial touches. But Spokane lost its looks badly when its turn-of-the-century heyday gave way to industrial shabbiness, and despite the extensive revamping that went on before the 1974 World's Fair was held here, shades of the down-at-heel freight town still haunt the modern city. It's not the sort of place you're likely to linger very long, but some pleasant parks, the oddness of the architecture and a couple of museums can easily fill a day or so. Spokane is also a potential base for visiting the Grand Coulee Dam, eighty miles or so to the west, to which *Empire Line* buses provide a convenient connection.

Arriving, getting around and accommodation

Greyhound (☎624-5251) buses use the bus depot at 1125 Sprague Avenue, which they share with *Empire Lines* (☎624-4116). *Amtrak* trains pull in at W First and Bernard Street (☎747-1069). **Local buses** run by *Spokane Transit Authority (STA)* (☎328-7433) cover the city and its outskirts. **Information**, including maps and books of discount coupons (some quite useful), are available at the ornate **Chamber of Commerce** at Riverside Avenue and Jefferson Street (Mon–Fri 8.30am–5pm), a few blocks from Greyhound, or the **Visitors and Convention Bureau**, W 301 Main Avenue (Mon–Sat 8.30am–5pm, Sun 10am–3pm), a block south of Riverfront Park.

The cheapest place to **stay** is the *Brown Squirrel AYH Hostel*, W 1807 Pacific Avenue (☎838-5968), a large, verandahed Victorian house in a residential area a half-hour walk or ten-minute bus ride west of downtown. *Motel 6* at 1508 S Rustle Street (☎459-6120), near the airport in the west – exit 277 off I-90, then north – starts at $32, while the more central *Shilo Inn* at E 923 Third Avenue (☎535-9000) charges $52 and upwards. There's **camping** in *Riverside State Park* (☎456-3964), six miles northwest of Spokane off Hwy-291.

The city

The place to make for **downtown** is **Riverfront Park** – in summer at least the town's focal point. Set beside the Spokane River, the park was originally planned by Frederick Olmsted of Central Park fame, when he was hired by Spokane's wealthy to landscape the city. Though some of Olmsted's suggestions were followed, the big landowners drew the line at sacrificing their own river access, and for almost a century the banks of the Spokane River were covered by an ugly tangle of railway lines and buildings – the price, perhaps, for the city's early railway-based commercial success. But the park was finally laid out in the massive clean-up before the 1974 World's Fair, and is now Spokane's main venue for strolling, picnicking, and general hanging out. Inside are the usual park attractions, but of most interest is probably the **Eastern Washington University Science**

Center (summer Wed–Mon 11am–6pm, Tues 11am–10pm; $2.50), which has bright, modern kiddie-orientated science exhibits – and a snack bar nearby.

At the back of the park, the river tumbles down a series of rocky shelves known as **Spokane Falls**, once a fishing site for the Spokanee Indians and later the site of the first pioneer settlement. Early settlers harnessed the churning water to power their mills, and across the river the **Flour Mill** was an economic cornerstone when it opened in 1896, though it's now been converted to house cutesy shops. Cablecars, known as the **Gondola Skyride** (summer daily 11am–9pm; $2.50), run across the river from the west end of the park, offering panoramic views.

The relics of Spokane's early grandeur are sprinkled all over the town, from the monumental downtown *Davenport Hotel* at Sprague and Post Streets, whose heavy English oak interior is being carefully restored, to the *County Court House*, built like a French Chateau across the river from Riverside Park. But the main concentration is several blocks southwest of the park on W Riverside Avenue, where heavy neo-Classical facades cluster around Jefferson street. Further west, the restored **Grace Campbell House** W 2316 First Avenue (Tues–Sat 10am–5pm, Sun 2–5pm; free), is furnished in a truly tasteless combination of pointedly expensive styles. Next door, and keeping the same hours, the excellent and absorbing **Cheney Cowles Museum**, interspersing thorough and well-presented displays on Spokane's and Eastern Washington's history with lively contemporary quotes from early residents. There's also a large gallery of contemporary Northwest artwork.

There are more interesting pickings in the northern part of town, at the **Museum of Native American Cultures**, 200 E Cataldo Street (Mon–Sat 9am–6pm Sun noon–6pm; $2; bus #6). The fine collection takes in prehistoric artwork from Central and South America – weavings, images, odd little dolls – as well as more local stuff, including a number of small model tableaux showing excruciating-looking native American initiation ceremonies, where the candidates are suspended from hooks embedded in their chests as a test of manhood. Less than a mile from the museum, **Bing Crosby** pops up again at Gonzaga University, which is inordinately proud of its most famous ex-student (recently deposed by Utah Jazz basketball star John Stockton). Bing's family used to live in *Alumni House*, one of the university buildings, and the singer endowed the college with the **Crosby Library**, which sports a shrine to the great man in return. A key from the desk will admit you to a conference room lined with cases of Bing memorabilia – gold discs, sporting awards and suchlike – while a bronze statue of him with golf bag stands outside.

Food, drink and nightlife

For **eating and drinking**, *Morelands*, at the top of a restored nineteenth-century building called the Bennett Block, 216 Howard Street, has good cafeteria lunches with ranges of cheeses, breads and wines; cheerful *Cyrus O'Leary's*, W 516 Main Street, at the bottom of the Bennett Block, serves a long and reasonably priced American menu to rowdy crowds of teenagers; while over at 313 Riverside Avenue, *Auntie's Bookstore and Cafe* offers home-made soups, salads, deserts and a quieter atmosphere. Nearby, the *Onion Bar and Grill*, W 302 Riverside, serves beer, wine and fruit daiquiris over an elegant, polished wooden bar; the food (dressed-up burgers, salads) is quite good, too. At W 230 Riverside, *Henry's Pub* is packed for live rock, Wednesday to Saturday nights. If you're visiting the Native American museum, it's worth saving breakfast or lunch for *Knights Diner*, N 2442 Division Street, a beautifully converted old train carriage in whose narrow confines an astoundingly dexterous chef feeds large platefuls to Gonzaga University students. Big-name rock groups often appear at the **Spokane Coliseum**, N 1101 Howard Street (☎456-3204), also the main venue for big sporting events (including the odd **rodeo**).

The Grand Coulee Dam and around

Eastern Washington's at its most dramatic in the open, swaggering, big country around the **Grand Coulee Dam**, itself a huge-scale work, around eighty miles west of Spokane. *Empire Lines* run a daily service from Spokane to GRAND COULEE, dropping off at the *Coulee Express Mini-Mart*, less than half a block from the dam. Coming from the west, the dam's fifty miles or so east of the Methow Valley along Hwy-173 and 174: *Empire Lines* provide connections.

The dam lies at the heart of what's known as the Columbia Basin, an Ice Age disaster-area scoured and sculpted by ancient floods until it was riven with deep channels called *coulees*. The dam is built in the biggest of these, and **Banks Lake,** one of its reservoirs, now fills the canyon carved long ago when an ice-dam temporarily diverted the Columbia this way. Behind the dam, the backed-up water has broadened the river into another reservoir: long, spindly **Lake Roosevelt**, which stretches all the way to the Canadian border, surrounded by campsites and, further north, by the Colville National Forest and some nice hiking trails. The lake itself offers fishing, sailing and water-skiing and has considerably boosted the area's recreational attractions – though the scattered smaller lakes that lurk less temptingly in coulee-bottoms to the south still attract mammoth campervans to their dry summer resorts.

The Dam

Kingpin of the Columbia dams, Grand Coulee, begun in 1933, was for a while as much a political icon as an engineering feat. Probably the most ambitious of Roosevelt's New Deal schemes to lift America out of the Depression, it symbolised hope for the Northwest and provided jobs for hundreds of workers from all over the country, notably the dustbowl regions further east, whose unemployed agricultural labourers were migrating west in their hundreds. As folk singer Woody Guthrie had it:

> *Columbia's waters taste like sparklin' wine*
> *Dustbowl waters taste like picklin' brine*

Guthrie worked on the Bonneville Dam lower down the river and was commissioned to write some twenty songs about the Columbia project – one of which, *Roll on, Columbia*, you'll hear *ad nauseam* in the Visitors Arrival Center (below). These were originally played at local rallies, held to raise investment money, and to combat propaganda from the private power companies whose interests lay in keeping power production in their own hands. Glowing with optimism, the songs underline the promise the dam held for impoverished working people:

I'm a farmer's boy, my land's all roots and stumps!
It's gonna take a big 'lectric saw to make 'em jump!

The dam is now the world's biggest single producer of hydro-electricity, and has certainly controlled flooding lower down the Columbia. But the power-guzzling demands of the new war industries that were attracted to the Northwest during World War II, and the atomic plant at Richland, switched attention and resources from irrigation, and Guthrie's other vision of "green pastures of plenty from dry desert ground" has been much slower to get underway – even now, only half the area originally planned has been irrigated. There's been ecological criticism of the Columbia project too: salmon migration along the river was reduced to a fraction by the dams, though schemes have since been set up to increase stocks of fish.

The background to the dam's construction is laid out in some detail in the **Visitors Arrival Center**, Hwy-155 on the west side of the dam (summer daily 8am–10pm, rest of the year daily 8.30am–5pm) with photographs, information and a free film detailing everything from the dangerous working conditions of the Thirties to how the turbines operate. As for the **dam itself**, it's initially something of an anti-climax. Though the world's largest concrete structure, it just doesn't look that big, a trick of the huge-scale scenery that surrounds it – best to focus on a car or person on the top for a more impressive perspective. Guided, and self-guided, tours of the dam and its generating plants are available from the visitors centre: views of the churning water are quite exciting, but you'll need a fair amount of enthusiasm for things mechanical to get right into the intricacies of power-generation.

A place to stay: Coulee Dam and Grand Coulee

Set against the surrounding scrubland, the leafy streets and shady lawns of well-sprinkled **COULEE DAM**, across the dam from the visitors centre, are a green advertisement for the difference the Grand Coulee's irrigation schemes actually make. Otherwise Coulee Dam is a stunningly boring little town, not much more than a dormitory centre for the dam's workers, who must get very tired of the bowling alley that makes up the sum of local nightlife it and its less-watered neighbour **GRAND COULEE** can muster. Options for **food** in either place are dire too, though if you need to stay, there are **motels** in both towns (Grand Coulee's are cheaper). More appealingly, there's a choice of more than thirty **campsites** scattered around Lake Roosevelt, becoming more woody and secluded as you get further north; pick up a map from the dam's visitors centre.

South along Banks Lake to Dry Falls

South of the Grand Coulee dam, Hwy-155 follows the shore of Banks Lake through more of the Columbia Basin's big country: endless plains sparsely coated with scrubby vegetation and broken by enormous flat-topped rocks, like **Steamboat Rock**, set in its own state park at a turning off Hwy-155, where a few trails loop half-heartedly over the dry land. It's worth getting out of the car, though: butterflies flit over the sagebrush, brightly coloured insects crawl across the path and the odd snake rattles as you walk by.

Banks Lake ends at Dry Falls Dam, named for **Dry Falls**, a few miles further on, which had their moment of glory during the Ice Age when the Columbia, temporarily diverted this way, poured a tremendous torrent over a drop twice as high and almost four times as wide as Niagra. It must have been quite a sight, but a waterfall without water is not that impressive, and all you can see today is a wide, bare, canyon-walled hole, the remnants of a lake lurking apologetically in its flat-bottomed depths. A little before Dry Falls, at Dry Falls Dam, US-2 will take you west towards WENATCHEE (see p.552); or Hwy-17, then Hwy-282, leads south to I-90.

travel details

Trains
From Spokane one daily to Ephrata (2hr); Wenatchee (3hr 15min); Everett (6hr 25min); Seattle (8hr). Another to Pasco (2hr 40min); Portland (7hr 15min).

Buses
Greyhound
From Seattle to Leavenworth (3 daily; 3hr); Cashmere (3; 3hr 15min); Wenatchee (3; 3hr 30min); (5; 2hr); Ellensburg (7; 2hr); Yakima (4; 3hr); Toppenish (2; 4hr 25min); Richland (3; 5hr 30min); Pasco (3; 6hr 20min); Walla Walla (2; 7hr); Spokane (7; 5hr 15min/8hr).
From Yakima to Goldendale (1 daily; 1hr 30min); Biggs, Oregon (1; 2hr); Portland (1; 8hr).
From Spokane to Portland (1 daily; 9hr, change in Biggs).

Empire Lines
From Spokane to Grand Coulee (1 daily; 2hr 30min), with connections to Chelan, Brewster, Okanogan, Oroville, Wenatchee, Ellensburg and Yakima.

CHAPTER ELEVEN

PORTLAND AND WESTERN OREGON

For nineteenth-century pioneers, driving in covered wagons over the mountains and deserts of the Oregon Trail, the green **Willamette Valley** was the promised land. Rich and fertile, it became the home of Oregon's first settlement and towns, and the valley is still the heart of the state's social, political and cultural existence. Most of Oregon's population is concentrated here, either in the cities strung along the river valley or in the hinterland of rural villages, linked by weaving country roads. The pace remains firmly provincial and there's a dreamy, alternative/hippy culture that survives intact from the Sixties. Even **Portland**, Oregon's largest city and commercial and cultural centre, can feel very much like an overgrown village, with an urbanised centre that quickly gives way to rolling countryside. Just east of Portland, beyond the point where the Willamette empties into the Columbia River, waterfalls cascade down mossy cliffs along the **Columbia River Gorge**, and south of here the twisting path of an old pioneer road leads through more gorgeous scenery around **Mount Hood**.

South from Portland, the main I-5 highway races through the Willamette Valley, passing by a number of medium-sized towns like **Salem**, the state capital, and student-orientated **Eugene**, both of which lie along the river with forested mountains seemingly right on their doorstep. Further south, **Crater Lake National Park**, a pristine alpine lake held within the shell of a burnt-out volcano, sits on the crest of the Cascade Mountains, only an hour's drive east of I-5, while near the California border, tiny **Ashland**'s summer-long Shakespeare Festival acts as a magnet for arts-orientated travellers.

Several highways link the Willamette Valley to the rugged Oregon **coast**, where wide expanses of sand are broken by jagged, black monoliths: white lighthouses look out from stark headlands and rough cliffs conceal small, sheltered coves. Dramatically varied, the coast takes in acres of sand-dunes and dense forests – not as warm as its Californian counterpart but every bit as appealing. As for towns, there are a couple of working ports – **Astoria** and **Coos Bay** – but most, like **Seaside**, **Newport** and **Bandon**, are small resorts, busy in summer, half-deserted out of season, when only storm-watchers come to see the wind lash stupendous waves against the rocks.

With *Greyhound* and, to a lesser extent, *Amtrak* linking major towns, and local bus services extending the network, **getting around** on public transport is less of a problem here than in other parts of the Northwest, but there are large areas that you just can't cover without your own transport. The coast especially is ideal for cycling; and obviously, a car will make things much easier – particularly as hitching is, strictly speaking, illegal in Oregon.

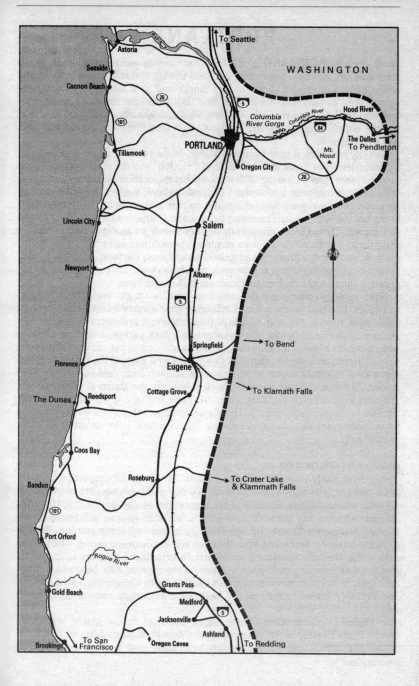

PORTLAND

Small, friendly **PORTLAND** is not the most obvious tourist destination. It has museums, art galleries, a colourful weekend market and any number of cheerful coffee houses, bars and plenty of jazz music; and as a base for exploring the surrounding countryside, it's hard to beat. But somehow the city doesn't quite have the thrill of San Francisco, or even Seattle: it lacks any really major sights, and the nightlife can be patchy. Portland's fans (and there are plenty) say that's part of the appeal.

The city was named after Portland, Maine, as the result of a coin toss between its two ardent East Coast founders in 1843 ("Boston" was the other option). It was then no more than a clearing in the woods, but its location on a deep part of the Willamette River, near a hinterland of fertile valleys, made it a perfect trading port, and the town grew fast, expanding quickly and replacing its humble clapboard houses with ornate Florentine facades and Gothic bursts of twirling towers and gables. Through the nineteenth century it was a raunchy, bawdy shipping and railway town, notorious for its gambling, prostitution and opium dens. When the new ports in the Puget Sound gained ascendancy, Portland declined, leaving behind huge swaths of derelict riverside warehouses and rail yards, linked by the dozens of heavy-duty bridges that span the Willamette River.

Now ecology-conscious, arts-conscious and – more recently – citizen-conscious, Portland is scrupulously salvaging what's left of its nineteenth-century past, while risking the odd splash of post-modernist architectural colour. City planners in the Seventies faced a downtown in tatters, part-gentrified, part low-life waterfront, its historic buildings decayed or sacrificed to car parks and expressways. There's been much assiduous gap-filling since, even to the extent of grassing over a riverside highway to convert it to parkland. Pockets of seediness remain, but much of the downtown area now bears the stamp of these renewal projects, with redbrick replacing concrete, cycle routes and an extensive public transport system replacing cars. There's a way to go yet perhaps but, overlooked by extensive parkland on the green west hills, Portland is an attractive and very liveable city.

Arrival and information

You're most likely to arrive by **bus or train**. Terminals for *Greyhound*, 550 NW Sixth Avenue (☎243-2340), and *Amtrak*, 800 NW Sixth Avenue, are conveniently situated within walking distance of the centre. *Green Tortoise* (☎225-0310) drop off and pick up a way out from downtown at NW 23rd Avenue and Savier Street, near *McMenamin's Tavern*. By **car**, the I-5 highway will bring you into the city from the north or south, I-84 from the east: aim for Burnside Street, which channels traffic through downtown. **Portland International Airport** is in the far northeast of the city: get into town either on the express *RAZ* bus, which drops off regularly at major downtown hotels ($5), or more cheaply on a local *Tri-Met* bus #12(85¢), coded "purple rain" – both leave from right outside the airport's doors.

The **Visitors Information Center**, along the river in the glassy Willamette World Trade Center, 26 SW Salmon Street (Mon–Fri 8.30am–5pm; ☎222-2223 or ☎1-800/345-3214), can provide good free maps and lots of other useful information.

Orientation and getting around

The Willamette River divides Portland in half; the downtown area, where you'll probably spend most time, is on the west bank, while the east is mostly residential. The city is further divided north to south by Burnside Street: street numbers get bigger in both directions from Burnside – make sure you're in the right quadrant, as 1800 SW Fifth Avenue is a *long* way from 1800 NW Fifth Avenue. **Downtown Portland,** focusing on Pioneer Courthouse Square, is a compact mix of gleaming new offices and crumbly old plasterwork, punctuated by grassy strips of small parks and liberally sprinkled with statues. It's here you'll find the malls, the department stores, theatres, the main museums. Just north along the riverfront are the restored nineteenth-century buildings of **Old Town,** where smart new restaurants and shops face groups of streetpeople crowded around the Salvation Army mission. Restaurants and coffee houses also cluster in the quaint **Nob Hill** district, a mile northwest of the town centre, and further out **Washington Park** offers leafy trails, formal gardens, a couple of museums and the best city views.

Portland's a compact city and you can see much of it on foot, but, if only to get to where you're staying, you may have to avail yourself of the excellent public transport. The *Tri-Met* **bus system** is based at the downtown "transit malls": two bus-shelter-lined stretches along Fifth Avenue (southbound) and Sixth Avenue (northbound). Each shelter is labelled with a small environmentally orientated symbol – brown beaver, blue snowflake, purple rain – which serves as a code for the route; video displays and telephones inside the shelters give more information. Though designed for simplicity, the system can still be pretty confusing: contact the **Tri-Met Customer Assistance Office,** close by on Pioneer Square, (Mon–Fri 8am–6pm; ☎233-3511) to get sorted out. Buses (and trams, see below) are free in the downtown zone, edged by the Willamette to the north and east, and the Stadium Freeway to the south and west. Outside here, fares are between 85¢ and $1.35 – pay the driver exact change.

There's also **Max,** Portland's new light railway, which shunts tourists around downtown and the old town area, then carries commuters over the river through the northwest neighbourhoods as far as suburban GRESHAM – you'll see its tracks along the streets. And vintage **streetcars** have returned to run the downtown streets, just as they did at the start of the century – though this lot are imported from Portugal.

Accommodation

There are plenty of very cheap old hotels scattered around the downtown area, but most are fairly shabby, inside and out. A better bargain is a room at one of the two hostels or, for women, the downtown YWCA. Dozens of motels can be found off the Interstates and along Sandy Boulevard, northeast of the centre, and there are also some plusher riverside hotels and a scattering of cosy B&Bs.

Hostels and motels

Portland International AYH Hostel, 3031 SE Hawthorne Blvd (☎236-3380). Across the river in a lively neighbourhood of cafés and pubs. Dorm beds, in a surprisingly cheery old Victorian house, cost $9 for AYH members, $12 non-members.

Youth Hostel Portland International, 1024 SW Third St (☎241-2513). Privately run, with a funkier feel, and open 24 hours. Dorm beds $10, private rooms $15–20.

YWCA, 1111 SW Tenth St (☎223-6281). Clean and central – right next to the downtown arts centre – but its very few rooms are often booked solid months in advance. Doubles $20, for women only.

Travelodge, 949 E Burnside St (☎234-8411). Standard, no-frills motel, just half a mile east of Pioneer Square; doubles from $35.

Unicorn Inn Motel, 3040 SE 82nd St (☎774-1176). Far from the thick of things (off I-205 at exit 19) but cheap, clean and comfortable. Doubles with cable TV and pool, from $25.

Hotels and B&Bs

Clinkerbrick House, 2311 NE Schuyler (☎281-2533). Peaceful and quiet, but a way out from the centre, this nicely decorated, 1908 red-brick Dutch Colonial bed and breakfast inn has a lovely garden and comfortable rooms from $60 a night.

Execulodge Convention Center, 1021 N Grand Ave (☎235-8433). Just east of the river, a block from the Metrorail with good views and modern doubles from $70.

General Hooker's House, 125 SW Hooker St (☎222-4435). Small and relaxed bed-and-breakfast inn. Evening cocktails on the roofdeck, and doubles cost $50–75.

Heathman Hotel, 1009 SW Broadway (☎241-4100 or ☎1-800/551-0011). Portland's top hotel, this restored downtown landmark would be a standout anywhere, with its elegant, teak-panelled interior and generous amounts of marble and brass, especially in the high-style lobby bar. Somewhat pricey by Northwest standards – rooms start at over $110 – though you'd pay twice the price for a lot less were it in a ritzier locale.

Mallory Hotel, 729 SW 15th Ave at Yamhill (☎223-6311 or ☎1-800/228-8657). Old and well-worn, with comfortable if slightly spartan doubles from $45, just a few blocks from Pioneer Square.

Riverside Inn, 50 SW Morrison (☎221-0711). For a river view at a reasonable price, this is the best bet. Overlooking the riverfront promenade, and near the Old Town district, with fairly plain rooms starting at $75 a night.

Downtown Portland

When the sun shines, **Pioneer Courthouse Square** is Portland's focal point, cluttered with music and people; in colder weather, only teenagers hang around the corner near Broadway, furtively smoking dope. Red-bricked, and lined with curving shelves of steps, the square is the modern centrepiece of downtown's new look (it used to be a nasty asphalt car park), and brightly upstages the solid nineteenth-century **Pioneer Courthouse** behind. North from here, along Fifth and Sixth Avenues, the redbrick and smoked-glass **transit malls** are another keystone of the city's renovations. Stretches of street are lined with hi-tech bus shelters, a study in user-friendliness, designed to lure car-addicted Americans away from their city-cluttering vehicles.

A block up from Pioneer Square, **Broadway**, more than any other street, pulls together Portland's mix of decayed grandeur and new wealth. Great, white crumbling movie palaces (relics from the Roaring Twenties) share the street with pricey hotels like the modern *Hilton*, towering on an ugly, bunker-like pedestal. One of the old cinemas, the grand *Portland*, has been restored as the **Arlene Schnitzer Concert Hall**, part of the new **Portland Performing Arts Center** complex and home to Oregon's symphony orchestra, opera and ballet. The main arts centre building is next door, an opulent construction of brick and dark glass, topped with a spectral light dome. Look up as you walk round the foyer – the blue dashes in the dome change colour.

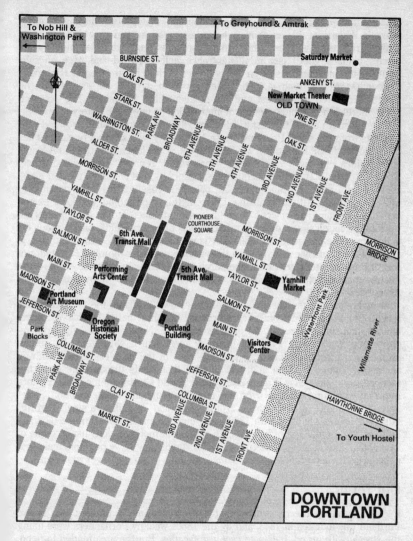

To Nob Hill &
Washington Park

To Greyhound & Amtrak

BURNSIDE ST.

Saturday Market

OAK ST.

ANKENY ST.

STARK ST.

New Market Theater
OLD TOWN

WASHINGTON ST.

PINE ST.

PARK AVE.

BROADWAY

6TH AVENUE

5TH AVENUE

4TH AVENUE

OAK ST.

ALDER ST.

3RD AVENUE

2ND AVENUE

MORRISON ST.

1ST AVENUE

FRONT AVE.

YAMHILL ST.

TAYLOR ST.

PIONEER
COURTHOUSE
SQUARE

SALMON ST.

MORRISON ST.

MORRISON
BRIDGE

6th Ave.
Transit Mall

YAMHILL ST.

MAIN ST.

Performing
Arts Center

5th Ave.
Transit Mall

TAYLOR ST.

Yamhill
Market

MADISON ST.

Waterfront Park

Portland
Art Museum

SALMON ST.

JEFFERSON ST.

Oregon
Historical
Society

Portland
Building

MAIN ST.

Willamette River

Park
Blocks

COLUMBIA ST.

Visitors
Center

PARK AVE.

BROADWAY

MADISON ST.

JEFFERSON ST.

CLAY ST.

3RD AVENUE

COLUMBIA ST.

HAWTHORNE BRIDGE

MARKET ST.

2ND AVENUE

1ST AVENUE

FRONT AVE.

To Youth Hostel

**DOWNTOWN
PORTLAND**

A paved arcade between the concert hall and arts centre leads to a sedate
group of buildings around a long strip of elm-lined grass, dotted with bronze statues of Theodore Roosevelt and other luminaries and called the **Park Blocks**.
Across the park, next to the grandiose columned front of the **Masonic Temple**,
is the long, low, understated facade of 1930s architect Pietro Belluschi's
Portland Art Museum, (Tues, Wed & Fri 11am–7pm; Thurs 11am–9.30pm; Sat
& Sun noon–5pm; $3, free Thurs 5–9.30pm). Founded in 1892, the museum's
collection is wide-ranging and well laid-out, spacious galleries displaying haunting
Northwest Indian masks, squat Mexican statues, ancient Chinese figures,

ornately framed portraits of European aristocrats – and, proudly displayed, one of Monet's *Waterlilies*. It's an above-average art museum, and very popular, especially during the "Museum After Hours" sessions on Wednesday night, when there's (usually good) jazz in the entrance hall and food and wine on sale. Opposite the museum, beside an old, ivy-covered church, the **Oregon Historical Center** (Mon–Sun 10am–4.45pm; free) is worth a peep for its displays on Oregon's covered-wagon past and its excellent little bookshop. The research library here is the definitive source of information on Oregon's history.

Turning south out of the historical centre, the leafy park is often crowded with students from the small **Portland State University**, whose modern campus lies three blocks down. Back down Madison Street, at the junction with Fifth Avenue, is Portland's one sight of national, if not world, renown – architect Michael Graves' **Portland Building**, a squarely-sat concoction of concrete, tile and glass, adorned with pink and blue tiling and pale blue rosettes. It's quite possible to walk straight past without realising this is anything special, but on closer examination it's certainly an eclectic structure, an uninhibited (some say flippant) reworking of classical and other motifs that was one of the most talked-about US buildings of the post-modern 1980s. Portland positively relished the controversy, and, in a burst of civic zeal, hoisted the enormous copper figure of *Portlandia* (a sort of Portlandian *Liberty*) on to the porch above the main entrance – where she kneels, one hand clutching a trident, the other stretched down towards the Fifth Avenue transit mall.

Stretching along the eastern edge of Downtown Portland, the **riverfront** has recently been rescued from over a century of burial beneath wharves, warehouses, and, more recently, an express highway. Now the mile-long strip, rechristened **Waterfront Park**, is lined by trees which will eventually screen promenaders from the less-than-inspiring view of the ugly east bank. Midway along the popular walking and cycling path that winds through the park, the modern, grey and glassy **Willamette World Trade Center** (home of the Visitors Information Center) looms over the gushing fountains of the Salmon Street Springs. A couple of blocks over, around First and Yamhill, the small **Yamhill Historic District** is lined with 1890s buildings. **Yamhill Marketplace** (actually built in 1982, on the site of a nineteenth-century farmer's market) has a couple of fruit and vegetable stalls, though most of its stands now serve hot food, making it popular for rushed professional lunches (and not a bad place to get your own).

Old Town

Old Town, along the river between the Morrison and W bridges, was where Portland was founded in 1843, and by the 1860s wealthy Portlanders were lining the streets with grand, Italianate cast-iron facades. But the area tended to flood, and when the railway came in 1883 the town centre shifted away from the river; the big, ornate buildings became warehouses and the area plummeted down the social scale. 1950s "improvement" schemes almost finished the district off, and gaps lined with peeling plaster still show where buildings were pulled down to make way for car parks. Recent attempts at rejuvenation have been more tactful, and the area is now an odd mixture of restoration work, housing a glut of bistros and boutiques, and old-style dereliction. Along W around the large Salvation Army mission, the well-heeled and the down-and-out eye each other dubiously – in a division that's uncomfortably sharp.

The best time to come here is at weekends, when the **Saturday Market** (March–Christmas Sat 10am–5pm, Sun 11am–4.30pm) packs the area under the W Bridge with arts and crafts stalls, street musicians, spicey foods and lively crowds. In the middle of this, the **Skidmore Fountain** at First Avenue and Ankeny Street is Old Town's focal point, a bronze basin raised by caryatids above a granite pool, designed to provide European elegance for the citizens – and water for hard-worked nineteenth-century horses. Across an angular plaza, an ornamental colonnade salvaged from the cast-iron pediments, arches, columns and other remnants of demolished local buildings stretches from the side of the **New Market Theater**: a Covent-Garden-like combination of theatre and vegetable market that has been restored and is now full of cafés. Not far from here, the **American Advertising Museum**, 9 NW Second Avenue (Wed–Fri 11am–5pm, Sat & Sun noon–5pm; $1.50), gives a fascinating account of the rise of US advertising, beginning with the printed posters that apparently engendered all kinds of social phenomena, from the rise of the cornflake to the rush of volunteers to World War II, moving on to tapes of old radio adverts and videos of classic TV ads. The museum also hosts some lively and intelligent temporary exhibits.

Chinatown and Nob Hill

Away from the river, up W, an ornate oriental gate at Fourth Avenue marks the entrance to what's left of Portland's **CHINATOWN**. By the late nineteenth century, expanding Portland had the second-largest Chinese community in the US, but white unemployment in the 1880s led, as in other places, to racist attacks. Chinese workers were threatened, their homes dynamited or burned, and most were forced to leave; there's little to see here today. The further north and west you go, towards the *Greyhound* and *Amtrak* stations, the sleazier the district becomes, the streets increasingly haunted by drug dealers, addicts, and prostitutes.

Despite the general grimness of things, there are a couple of places worth searching out, especially **Powell's Books** at Burnside Street and Tenth Avenue (Mon–Sat 9am–11pm, Sun 9am–9pm), one of the largest secondhand bookshops on the West Coast – five full floors of new and secondhand books so overwhelming that floorplans are given out at the entrance. Across the street from *Powell's* is another local institution, the **Blitz-Weinhard Brewery** at 1133 W Burnside Street, which fills up most of the surrounding blocks in order to brew the Northwest's most popular lagers and ales, *Henry Weinhard's Private Reserve*; free tours and tastings are given weekday afternoons at 1pm (☎222-4351). Many of the other old warehouses and industrial premises have been converted by artists and craftspeople into studios and loft spaces, a change evident in the many good galleries emerging here, like the *Jamison/Thomas Gallery* at 1313 NW Glisan Street.

A bus ride away, the **NOB HILL** district (often simply called the "Northwest Section") stretches from Burnside Street along a dozen blocks of NW 23rd Avenue and NW 21st Avenue. The name was borrowed from San Francisco, imported by a grocer who hoped the area would become as fashionable as the Nob Hill back home. It did, almost, and a few multicoloured wooden mansions add a San Franciscan tinge – though the main interest up here are the dozens of cafés and restaurants, which are among the city's best.

The West Hills and Washington Park

Directly behind Nob Hill, the wooded bluffs of the **WEST HILLS** hold the elegant houses of Portland's wealthy, some of which are visible from the window of the brightly painted "zoo bus" (#63 from the downtown transit mall) as it winds along its special route towards **Washington Park**. Set aside for public use in 1871, much of the park is green, leafy and twined with trails; it's also home to Portland's **zoo** (summer daily 9.30am–7pm, gates close earlier in other seasons; $3), whose star-turn is its elephants. When baby "Packy" was born here in 1962, he became the first Asian elephant to be born in the western hemisphere, and the zoo now has a sizeable herd. An **Elephant Museum** details the sad effects of the ivory trade, while the new, ambitious Africa exhibition attempts to give a comprehensive view of the continent, including giraffes, rhinos and birds as part of an African environment. Come here on a Wednesday night in summer, and you'll catch the weekly **Zoo Jazz** concert (free with admission to the zoo), followed on Thursdays by a **Zoo Grass** (bluegrass) session.

Across a large car park from the zoo is the **Oregon Museum of Science and Industry (OMSI)** (summer Tues–Sat 9am–9pm, Sun & Mon 9am–6pm, winter Sat–Thurs 9am–5pm, Fri 9am–8pm; $4.50): a modern set-up, much less boring than it sounds, which uses "hands-on" techniques – kids thump, jump and shout at the more robust exhibits, and play astronauts to discover the mysteries of gravity.* Nearby, the **World Forestry Center** (daily 10am–5pm: $1.50) goes in for similar tactics, not least in the seventy-foot "talking" tree which introduces the museum. Beyond it, amongst other things, is a collection of chunks from most of North America's native trees, and a dramatic push-button reconstruction of the "Tillamook Burn", a fire that ravaged one of Oregon's coastal forests in the 1930s.

A miniature train ($2) connects the zoo with two formal gardens further into the park. The **International Rose Test Gardens** are at their best between May and September, when eight thousand rose bushes cover layered terraces with a gaudy range of blooms. Home of America's oldest and largest rose-growing society, the city at one point in its early days had more rose bushes than people, and Portland now calls itself the "City of Roses". During the crowded and colourful **Rose Festival** each June, everyone flocks to Burnside Bridge to watch a big parade, and that claim seems fair enough. On the hill above, the **Japanese Gardens** (summer daily 10am–6pm, winter daily 10am–4pm: $3.50) are more subtle, with cool, green shrubs reflected in pools, and an abstract sand and stone garden making minimal use of colour.

If you've got a car, you might consider driving the few miles northwest from the park to the opulent **Pittock Mansion** (daily 1–5pm, closed early Jan; $2.50), set in its own park the other side of W Burnside Street – there's a bus from downtown, but it drops you half a mile from the entrance. Henry Pittock came to Portland in 1853 as a sixteen-year-old printer's devil; eight years later he became editor of *The Oregonian*, still Oregon's most influential newspaper, and in 1909 started to build this enormously flashy chateauesque home, furnishing rooms in styles alternately Jacobean, Victorian and French Renaissance. All in all, a convincing declaration of wealth and success.

---

*An expanded version of OMSI is under construction along the Willamette just east of downtown, and is due to open late in 1992.

East of the river

While the west side of the Willamette river provided a deep port, the **east side** was too shallow for shipping and the area remained undeveloped for the first fifty years of Portland's life. The Morrison Street Bridge crept across the river at the end of the last century, since when most of Portland's population has lived here, in various neighbourhoods that are almost entirely residential. Restaurants, bars, nightclubs and the youth hostel are the features most likely to draw you over, but of a few things to see, the **Crystal Springs Rhododendron Garden** (daily during daylight hours; free), opposite ivy-covered **Reed College** in the southeast section, provides colourful strolling in April and May. And in the far northeast, **The Grotto**, NE 85th and Sandy Boulevard (daily 8am–dusk; free), contains a marble replica of Michelangelo's *Pieta*, surrounded by candles and set in a cave in a cliff face – the centrepiece of a bizarre outdoor church and monastic complex.

Eating

Friendly and unpretentious are the two words that come to mind most often to describe Portland's eating options, the bulk of which are concentrated in the downtown area, with quite a few in the Nob Hill area to the northwest and a handful on the less-touristed east side of the river, on and around Hawthorne Boulevard. There's a surprisingly good range of top-notch restaurants, with fresh fish dishes, especially salmon, the local speciality, and many more down-to-earth, bistro-style neighbourhood joints, as good for quaffing local brews and vintages as they are for tasty meals. For flavourful fast food at low prices, pop into either of two popular local chains, *Hot Lips Pizza* (based at 1909 SW Sixth Ave) or the anarchic *Macheesmo Mouse* (723 SW Salmon St), both of which have branches all over town.

Inexpensive

B Moloch's Bakery and Pub, 901 SW Salmon St (☎227-5700). Great pizzas – topped with all manner of designer ingredients – plus salads and daily specials, and some of the Northwest best micro-brewed beers, around twenty on tap. Huge and very popular, but worth waiting for.

Besaw's Cafe, 2301 NW Savier St at 23rd Ave (☎228-3764). Old-fashioned, NY-style bar and grill. Lots of dark wood panelling, good-sized burgers, steaks and sandwiches, plus onion rings to kill for.

Cisco and Pancho's, 107 NW Fifth Ave (☎223-5048). Lively, inexpensive Tex-Mex restaurant with free live jazz or blues most evenings.

Hamburger Mary's, 840 SW Park St (☎223-0900). Relaxed and occasionally bizarre burger and salad bar with a decidedly non-conformist clientele.

Metro on Broadway, 911 SW Broadway St (☎295-1200). A dozen distinct low-priced stands offer food from around the world, under one roof; live jazz piano most evenings.

Old Wives' Tales, 1300 E Broadway St (☎238-0470). Feminist café with great breakfasts, sandwiches and innovative vegetarian fare; it's also the place to come to find out about local women's issues.

Rose's, 315 NW 23rd Ave (☎227-5181). Long-established family-run place, as near to a Jewish New York City deli as you get in the Northwest. Bagels, blintzes, and a killer *kreplach* soup.

Rusty's, 1212 NW Glisan St (☎221-0205). Old workingman's cafe out amongst the derelict rail-yards and warehouses of the Loft District, now catering to gallery-hopping young trendies.

Vat and Tonsure, 822 SW Park Ave (☎227-1845). You don't need to don a beret or grow a beard to get served in this unreconstructed Beat Generation hangout, but it wouldn't hurt. The animated conversations are kept energised by good-sized portions of bistro-style food, copious amounts of wine, and reasonable prices.

Moderate to expensive

Brasserie Montmartre, 626 SW Park Ave (☎224-5552). Pseudo-Left Bank, Paris-in-the-1930s bistro, with free live jazz and very good food – it's the only place in Portland where you can get fresh pasta with pesto and scallops at 2am.

Bread and Ink Café, 3610 SE Hawthorne Blvd (☎239-4756). Bustling morning to night, this spacious café puts together an anarchically varied menu of bagels, burritos, and Mediterranean food; come on Sunday for the special Jewish brunch or one of Portland's best breakfasts.

Jake's Famous Crawfish, 401 SW 12th Ave (☎226-1419). For nearly 100 years this polished wood oyster bar has been Portland's prime spot for fresh seafood, though at weekends it's packed and veers toward singles bar territory. The food, especially the daily fish specials, is excellent and not exorbitantly priced, but be sure to save room for dessert.

L'Auberge, 2601 NW Vaughn St (☎223-3302). One of the classiest restaurants on the West Coast, serving up exquisitely prepared traditional French dishes with a nouvelle emphasis on fresh local ingredients; prix fixe meals start at a reasonable $35, plus wine. The upstairs bar is surprisingly cosy and unpretentious – on Sunday night they show old movies on the walls – and has a good value menu of burgers, grilled fish and salads.

McCormick and Schmick's, 235 SW First Ave (☎224-7522). Another of Portland's many excellent fish restaurants, with a variety of ultra-fresh nightly specials; there's also a lively oyster bar, where besides bivalves you can get a range of burgers and pasta dishes.

Drinking and nightlife

Though sometimes clogged with cars and clubbers on summer weekends, Portland's streets can seem pretty quiet at night, yet generally there's a lot more going on here than you might at first think. **Coffee houses** – including some of the best in the US – and dozens of **bars** form the fulcrum of a lively scene, and the city is a beer-drinker's heaven, with dozens of local micro-breweries proof of the resurgence of the Northwest's proud brewing traditions.

Music is another thing Portland does well, with a handful of decent folk and rock clubs and some good jazz and blues – downtown, on and off-Broadway, is the place to head. *The Downtowner* and *Willamette Week*, available free on most street corners, have up-to-the-minute listings of what's on and where; the younger and livelier *PDXS*, also free, has the rundown on more alternative happenings.

Coffee houses

Anne Hughes Coffee Room, inside *Powell's Books*, 1005 W Burnside St (☎228-4651). Not too big on atmosphere, but brought to life by the many earnest characters leafing through their books and partaking of caffeine.

Cafe Omega, 711 SW Ankeny St (☎226-2508). Hyper-trendy, post-industrial, 24-hour Old Town espresso bar just off Burnside St, next to the *Elvis is King* sound and light automated freak show.

Coffee People Immediate Care Center, 817 NW 23rd Ave (☎226-3064). "Good coffee – no backtalk" is the motto, and they deliver, at least on the first count. Excellent espresso, straight up or smothered in whipped cream. For a real eye-opener, try the *Depth Charge*: filter coffee supercharged with a shot of espresso.

Papa Hayden's, 701 NW 23rd Ave (☎228-7317). Chic, upscale ice-cream café that brews up some good coffees to wash down their sugar-shock-inducing desserts, including a world-class chocolate mousse.

Rimsky Korsakoffee House, 707 SE 12th Ave (☎232-2640). Looks like someone's house from the outside, but inside live chamber music enlivens a very pleasant if slightly cliquish café.

Bars and pubs

B Moloch's, 901 SW Salmon St (☎221-5700). Always crowded downtown brew-pub pouring some Oregon's finest pints – from Widmer's weisen lagers to Deschutes's Black Butte Porters, and every shade in between.

Bridgeport Brewpub, 1313 NW Marshall St (☎241-7179). Huge old warehouse that's now one of the city's largest and liveliest beer bars, pouring pints of homebrewed Bridgeport Ale. There's food too, including a top-rated, malt-flavoured pizza.

Dublin Pub, 3104 SE Belmont St at 31st Ave (☎230-8817). As if you couldn't have guessed from the name, this is one of Portland's many traditional Irish pubs, with regular live folk music, including bagpipes, and well-kept pints of Guinness. A short walk from the youth hostel.

East Bank Saloon, 727 SE Grand Ave (☎231-1659). Rowdy sports bar with an occasionally obnoxious, very male clientele; the best place, other than courtside, to watch a Rip City Portland Trailblazers basketball game.

The Hospital Pub, 2845 SE Stark St. Laid back, mixed gay and straight East Portland pub, popular with pool-players and off-duty nurses.

Produce Row Café, 204 SE Oak St (☎232-8355). Just across the river amongst the still-working fruit-and-vegetable warehouses, with about a million different beers and gigantic sandwiches to help soak it up. Pool tables and a varied crowd keep things interesting.

Virginia Café, 725 SW Park Ave (☎227-0033). Step back into the 1940s for $1 drinks and plush wooden booths in this popular downtown bar; open all day (the food's cheap), but the later it gets the more interesting the crowd.

Rock venues

Eli's Hard Rock Café, 424 SW Fourth Ave (☎223-4241). What you'd expect.

Melody Ballroom, 615 SW Alder (☎232-2759). Cavernous old dancehall that's become one of Portland's prime venues for up-and-coming pop bands and touring indie stars – keep an eye out for the Dharma Bums and other local faves.

The Roseland Theater, 8 NW Sixth Ave (☎227-0071). Portland's prime mid-sized venue; tickets usually around $15.

Satyricon, 125 NW Sixth Ave (☎243-2380). Somewhat foreboding post-punk club that mixes live bands, peformance art and various oddball acts. In a seedy neighbourhood, but cheap (cover free–$5) and with good bar food inside.

X-Ray Café, 214 W Burnside St (☎721-0115). Anarchic hardcore punk club in Old Town storefront ; all ages, no alcohol, low (or no) cover.

Blues and folk venues

Dakota Café, 239 SW Broadway (☎241-4151). Relaxed downtown club that has live bands most nights.

Dandelion Pub, 31 NW 23rd Place (☎223-0099). Bluesy, pub-rock venue way out in the warehouse wilderness of the Northwest waterfront.

East Avenue Tavern, 727 E Burnside St (☎236-6900). Located about half a mile east of the river, with nightly Irish, folk or bluegrass music.

Key Largo, 31 NW First Ave (☎223-9919). Tropical decor, steamy dance floor, and the hottest blues bands. Cover at weekends only.

Jazz venues

Brasserie Montmartre, 626 SW Park Ave (☎224-5552). Nightly live jazz for the price of a dinner or a drink (see "Eating" above for more).

The Hobbit, 4420 SE 39th Ave (☎771-0742). A long way out from downtown, but worth the ride for the city's best late-night live jazz, from traditional Dixieland through bebop and beyond. Cover varies; free–$12.

Parchman Farm, 1204 SE Clay St (☎235-7831). Intimate club with good pizzas and great jazz most nights. No cover.

Remo's, 1425 NW Glisan (☎221-1150). This always lively restaurant – the bar food's outstanding and good value – is housed in a converted fire station, but the real attraction is the nightly live jazz. No cover.

Nightclubs and discos

The City, 13 NW 13th Ave (☎224-2489). Portland's largest and livest gay nightclub, with huge dance floors and occasional live acts. Thurs–Sun only, till 4am Fri and Sat; cover $2–6.

Portland Underground, 333 SW Park Ave (☎775-7232). All sorts of bands, rappers and DJs mixing up a range of house and reggae and generally arty, alternative sounds; cover under $5.

Quest, 126 SW Second Ave (☎479-9113). Portland's biggest disco, mostly under-18 and all under-21: no alcohol allowed. Cover under $5.

Red Sea, 318 SW Third Ave (☎241-5450). Small dance floor hidden away in the back of an Ethiopian restaurant, grooving most nights to DJ'ed reggae and rockers tunes. No cover, strong drinks.

Shanghai Lounge, 309 SW Montgomery St in River Place (☎220-1865). Portland's main pick-up joint, a yuppie meat market made almost pleasant by the great views out over the Wilamette River. Mostly Top 40 with some live bands. Cover around $4.

Classical music, theatre and cinema

The opening of the new *Performing Arts Center* on Broadway, coupled with the opulent restoration of the *Arlene Schnitzer Concert Hall* next door, has given Portland's **arts scene** a new lease of life. For up-to-date what's on and ticket information, call the **events hot line** on ☎233-3333; the *Willamette Week* (see above) carries listings and reviews. The **Oregon Symphony Orchestra** perform at the Concert Hall (☎243-7350) from September to April; tickets range from $15–$40 for evening performances, but you can catch a Sunday afternoon concert for as little as $7. At other times, the Concert Hall is used for visiting acts – classical, jazz, country and rock. Keep an eye open for **free concerts**, especially in Pioneer Square or at the zoo in the summer, and year-round at the *Old Church*, Eleventh Avenue and Clay Street downtown, every Wednesday at noon.

The *Performing Arts Center* (☎248-4496) is the focus of Portland's **theatre** scene. One of its two small auditoria, the cherry-wood panelled *Intermediate Theater*, is also the main venue for the local chamber orchestra and ballet companies; the other, the hi-tech *Winningstad Theater*, is used by the *Storefront Theater*, performing tough, original plays; and *New Rose Theater*, who tend to keep more to the classics. A few blocks away at SW Third Avenue and Clay Street, the *Civic Auditorium* (☎248-4496) is a venue for big musical extravaganzas, operas and anything else that needs a large stage.

You'll find **cinema** listings in *Willamette Week*, but for stuff out of the mainstream try the *Northwest Film and Video Center*, 1219 SW Park Avenue in the Art Museum (☎221-1156), or *Movie House*, 1220 SW Taylor Street, both showing foreign and art films.

Listings

Airlines *American Airlines*, 802 SW Sixth Ave (☎241-9145); *Delta*, 1210 SW Sixth Ave (☎228-2128); *Northwest Airlines*, 910 SW Second Ave (☎225-2525).

American Express 7000 SW Hampton (☎639-7807), Travel Service with **poste restante**, Standard Plaza Bldg, 1100 SW 6th St (☎588-0834). There are automatic cash dispensers at the airport.

Area code ☎503.

Banks Central branches include *First Interstate Bank*, 400 SW Fifth Ave and *US Bank of Oregon*, 321 SW Sixth Ave.

Bike Rental None downtown. Try *The Complete Cyclist*, 2610 SE Clinton St (☎230-0317), out in the southeast district.

Books *Powell's Bookstore*, 1005 W Burnside St, is a huge book-lined labyrinth of new and secondhand books. There's a branch directly on Pioneer Square where you can buy travel guides and maps.

Car Hire *Budget*, 2033 SW Fourth Ave (☎649-6500); *Hertz*, 1009 SW Sixth Ave (☎249-5727); *Rent-a-Dent*, 8400 SE 82nd Ave (☎777-4702); *Rent-a-Wreck*, 283 NE Sandy Blvd (☎231-1640); *Thrifty*, 632 SW Pine St (☎227-6587).

Consulate The British Consulate (☎227-5669) seems to exist only as an answerphone, redirecting you to Seattle or Los Angeles.

Gay Hotline (☎228-6785), nightly 7–11pm. The *Phoenix Rising Foundation*, at 333 SW Fifth Ave (☎223-8299). Gay and lesbian counselling and health centre.

Hospital The Good Samaritan Hospital and Medical Center, 1015 NW 22nd Ave (information ☎229-7711, emergency dept ☎229-7260).

Launderette *Springtime Laundry*, 2942 SE Hawthorne Blvd, not far from the youth hostel.

Police 1111 SW Second Ave (796-3097); 222 Second Ave at Main St (☎294-2300).

Post Office 715 NW Hoyt St (☎294-2424), zip code 97208. Open Mon–Fri 8.30am–8pm, Sat 8.30am–5pm.

Taxi *Broadway Cabs* (☎227-1234) or *Portland Taxi Co* (☎256-5400).

Women's politics *National Organization of Women*, Portland chapter, 408 SW Second Avenue (☎223-6722).

Women's Crisis and Rape Lines Crisis line (☎235-5333). Rape line (☎232-4176). There's also an office at 3020 E Burnside St (Mon–Fri 9am–4pm; ☎232-9751) offering counselling to women who've been raped.

THE COLUMBIA RIVER GORGE AND MOUNT HOOD

Carved by the Columbia River as it powered through volcanic layers to the sea, the **Columbia River Gorge**, twenty or so miles northeast of Portland, was scoured deep and narrow by huge glaciers and rocks during the Ice Age. Now it's covered with green fir and maple trees, which turn fabulous shades of gold and red in the autumn. Narrow, white waterfalls cascade down its sides over mossy, fern-covered rocks. To its south, the forested slopes of **Mount Hood** become increasingly lonely as you follow the path of the old pioneer Barlow Road back towards Portland. The best way to see the gorge is by **car**: *Greyhound* buses run along the gorge stopping at **Cascade Locks**, but they take the freeway and you really want to be on the smaller, more scenic route. *Gray Line* run day **tours** from

Portland during the summer for around $23 (☎226-6755), but many of the water-falls deserve a closer look, and it's frustrating not to have time to follow the trails.

For this reason, too, it's much better not to attempt the gorge and Mount Hood in one day, whatever the tourist leaflets say. A nice **Mount Hood Loop** takes you round both areas (turn south from the gorge onto Hwy-35 at HOOD RIVER, then west on Hwy-26), but if you want to do any walking, you'll need two days for this. No matter when you come, be sure to get out of the car (or off your bike)and walk the many trails, otherwise the gorge can be somewhat disappointing: it's not breathtakingly sheer-walled or deep, as you might expect from the name, but it does have dozens of waterfalls and countless other cascades and streams, all flow-ing through the lushly forested ravine.

The Columbia River Gorge

A tired Lewis and Clark were the first whites to pass through the **Columbia River Gorge**, floating down it on the last stage of their 1804 trek across the conti-nent. Just forty years later it had become the perilous final leg of the Oregon Trail, negotiated by pioneer families on precarious rafts. Soon after that, when gold was discovered in eastern Oregon, the Columbia turned into a lifeline for pioneering miners and farmers and a prime target for a lucrative transport monopoly, when a Portland-based company put steamboats on the river, and was soon raking in profits from the dependent (and bitter) residents of the arid east. By the 1880s, the steamboats were already carrying tourists, too.

The beginning of car-born tourism prompted the construction of the **Columbia River Scenic Highway** in 1915 – and this is still the road you should take through the gorge. The old road, now bypassed by I-84 (and *Amtrak* trains), is by far the most popular day out from Portland and so can be quite crowded; if you can come during the week, and manage to ignore the freeway and the nearly constant rumble of freight trains, the road certainly rates among the more scenic stretches of blacktop going. Most people come via I-84, getting off at the Troutdale exit and following the signs along the Sandy River; there's another access point at the east end of the Scenic Highway, and a third in the middle near Multnomah Falls.

The tallest and most famous of the many falls along the highway, two-tier **Multnomah Falls** plummets 542 feet down a mossy rockface, collects in a pool, then falls another 70 feet to the ground. Apparently, when a sickness once threat-ened the Multnomah tribe, the chief's daughter threw herself over the Falls to appease the Great Spirit, and you're supposed to be able to see her face in the mist. The stone *Multnomah Falls Lodge* (actually a gift shop and restaurant) has been catering for legend-enamoured tourists since 1925.

While Multnomah Falls can feel quite crowded, if you head just a short way east or west you'll come to a half-dozen equally impressive but much less visited cascades. **Wahkeena Falls** at the western end of the gorge is the start-point for a number of hiking trails into the backcountry of the Mount Hood National Forest, while at the east end the powerful torrent of **Horsetail Falls,** right along the road, is balanced by the quieter and prettier Pony Tail Falls, at the end of an easy mile-long trail. Perhaps the best of the many short hikes within the gorge heads up **Oneonta Gorge,** half a mile west of Horsetail Falls, following a shallow stream along the bottom of the sheerest of the Columbia Gorge's many side-canyons.

Back on I-84, five miles further east of the gorge, **BONNEVILLE** is the site of a massive dam, a WPA project that's the first of the chain of dams which made the Columbia River the biggest producer of hydro-electric power in the world (for more on the Columbia dams, and Woody Guthrie, who wrote a series of songs about them, see p.565). There's a **visitors center** and **fish ladder** here (open daily 10am–5pm; free). Four miles on, at **CASCADE LOCKS**, you can look back along the river to the **Bridge of the Gods** – or at least the twentieth-century version. The story goes that a natural stone bridge once crossed the water here, but it was misused by sparring gods and the Great Spirit broke it down again; a small **museum** on a hill above the south end of the bridge fills in the details.

Hood River and The Dalles

The next bridge across the Columbia River is at the town of **HOOD RIVER**, depending upon the time of year one of the most popular windsurfing, mountain biking and cross-country skiing centres in the Pacific Northwest. Though the town itself isn't exactly pretty, the outdoor recreation opportunities more than make up for it: hire a windsurfer for around $40/day from the *Rhonda Smith Windsurfing Center* (☎386-WIND), which also gives lessons and has a café right on the river near the main launching spot, under the bridge. *Windsor Bikes*, 1788 Eighth Street (☎386-4172) rents out mountain bikes and can suggest which of the many nearby trails might be most to your taste. If you just want to see the scenery, ride the Mount Hood Railroad ($15; ☎386-3556) halfway up the mountain.

After dark, join the sailors and bikers for a pint of *Full Sail Ale* in the *Hood River Brewing Company*, 506 Columbia Street (☎386-2247) or sample the barbecue ribs at the *Mesquitery*, 1219 12th Street (☎386-2002). For a place to stay, there's the clean and good value *Vagabond Inn*, 4070 Westcliff Drive (☎386-2992), as well as a handful of pricier B&Bs; contact the **tourist office** (☎386-2000) in Marina Park for more information.

From Hood River, Hwy-35 turns southwards towards Mount Hood (see below), Hwy-141 heads north to the Maryhill Museum , across the border in Washington (see p.560), and I-84 continues upriver from here toward **THE DALLES**, an old military outpost and later gold mining town that's now the closest settlement to the controversial **Dalles Dam**, just beyond. Until the dam was built, the water tumbled over a series of rocky shelves called **Celilo Falls**, used by Native Americans as fishing grounds since prehistory, and the source of much of the area's wealth of Indian lore ("the great fishing place of the Columbia", Washington Irving, drawing on the experience of early fur-traders, called it). Celilo Falls were flooded when the Dalles Dam opened, to the anguish of local native Americans; the compensation money went to build the *Kah Nee Tah* resort east of the Cascades (see p.609). Close to where the falls were, on the Washington side of the river, the village of **WISHRAM** was a great Indian trading centre: ancient petroglyphs are relics of its one-time cultural role, though there's little else here today.

Mount Hood

The most spectacular part of the gorge is, however, well west of Hood River and The Dalles; and there's a good case for turning instead south towards **Mount Hood**, the tallest of the Oregon Cascades. Hwy-35 runs through the Hood River Valley (fruit-growing country, whose speciality is red *Anjou* pears), climbing out of the valley and up the mountain, with lovely views, until it comes to the highest point on the loop road, **Barlow Pass**, named after Samuel Barlow, a wagon train leader who pioneered a new finish to the Oregon Trail. The Columbia River Gorge was impassable by wagon, and pioneers had previously been forced to carry all their goods around Celilo Falls, then float down the river on rafts – or to pay extortionate rates to the two boats operating on the river. In 1845, Barlow led his party off to blaze a new trail around the south side of Mount Hood. They were trapped by snow while chopping their way through thick forests, and had to leave their wagons behind in the struggle to reach the Willamette Valley before they starved or froze. But Barlow returned a year later to build the **Barlow Road** (much of which is still followed by Hwy-26), and many emigrants chose to brave its steep ridges, where wagons frequently skidded out of control and plummeted down hill, rather than face the Columbia. You can still see deep gashes on some of the trees where ropes were fastened to check the wagon's descent.

Shortly after Hwy-35 leads into Hwy-26, there's a turning up the mountain towards **Timberline Lodge** (☎272-3311), solidly built in stone and furnished with craftwork in wood, textiles, wrought iron and mosaic – like Bonneville Dam, a New-Deal job-creation scheme. During winter Timberline is the headquarters of a busy ski-resort, and in summer there's plenty of hiking; you can rent ski-equipment here, and rooms go from around $55 double. Out of season, though, the deserted roads around here can feel downright eerie, especially once the real-isation begins to dawn that Timberline was the set for the horror film *The Shining*.

THE WILLAMETTE VALLEY AND SOUTH

South of Portland, the I-5 highway cuts through a series of inland valleys towards the Californian border, stringing through the region's main towns – though it bypasses historic **Oregon City** on the outskirts of Portland, once the end of the Oregon Trail and the first state capital. **Salem**, a quiet nineteenth century mill-town, is the modern capital, while at the southern end of the Willamette valley, **Eugene** is Oregon's second largest city, a lively university town with a strong reputation for sport.

Further south, the Umpqua and Rogue river valleys are fertile basins in a mountainous region, scattered with logging and agricultural towns like outdoors-orientated **Grants Pass,** a popular base for white-water river rafting along the turbulent Rogue River, **Jacksonville**, a restored relic of Gold Rush times, and **Ashland**, which hosts the *Oregon Shakespeare Festival*, a spring and summer-long dose of Shakespeare and more contemporary drama. East of the valleys, **Crater Lake National Park** is the region's one real tourist magnet, a deep blue lake cradled in an old volcano.

Transport in this area shouldn't be too much of a problem: *Greyhound* run regularly along the I-5, stopping at most places, and *Green Tortoise*'s twice-weekly bus down I-5 provides a cheaper alternative. *Amtrak* links up Oregon City, Salem and Eugene before swinging east across the Cascades. Local buses provide useful services between Grants Pass and Ashland, and around Eugene.

Oregon City

Set by the falls of the Willamette River, about thirteen miles south of Portland (and connected by the city's *Tri-Met* bus service), **OREGON CITY** is, in a sense, where the state began. This was the end of the Oregon Trail and the first capital of the Oregon Territory – though ironically enough it was actually founded by the British-owned *Hudson's Bay Company* during the early nineteenth-century anglo-American scramble to settle the Northwest. Today, the split-level town consists of a short, turn-of-the-century high street, connected by steps, steep streets and a cliff-face elevator to an uptown area of old wooden houses set on a bluff.

It's on this upper level that you'll find the town's two main sights. The small **Oregon Trail Interpretive Center** at the corner of Fifth and Washington streets (Tues–Sat 10am–4pm, Sun noon–4pm, closed Jan; $2), commemorates the often dangerous route followed by the pioneer wagon-trains of the 1840s with exhibits and a short film, eagerly presented by the volunteer staff. Nearby, among a number of nineteenth-century wooden mansions, the restored **McLoughlin House** on Center Street (Tues–Sat 10am–5pm, closing at 4pm in winter, Sun 1–4pm; $2) was the home of Dr John McLoughlin, head of the *Hudson's Bay Company*, the town's founder, and something of a local hero. Ignoring political antagonisms, he provided the Americans who survived the Oregon Trail with food, seed, and periodic rescue from hostile Indians. He's now regarded as one of Oregon's founding fathers, and although his main base was north of here in the town of Vancouver, Washington, he retired to Oregon City in 1846. The house has been refurnished in period style, with a good scattering of McLoughlin's own possessions; he and his wife are buried in the grounds.

Salem: the State Capital

The build-up of motels and fast-food chains that ushers you into **SALEM** doesn't really prepare you for the city's humble size. In fact Salem is a small and rather staid little town, content dutifully to point visitors around its quota of attractions – the Capitol building, Mission Mill Village and Willamette University – but not particularly expecting them to linger. It was founded by the Methodist missionary Jason Lee, who set up Oregon's first US mission a few miles north of Salem in 1834. Lee originally intended to convert the Indians, but his sermons went down better with the white fur-traders who had retired to farm in the area, and Lee, deciding white settlement was the best way to further the cause, requested more recruits. The Methodist Missionary Board sent a shipful of pioneers, and, usefully, the machinery for a grist mill and a sawmill, which Lee set up by a dam in Salem, building himself a house nearby and thus laying the cornerstone for the present town. His ideal of a self-sufficient Willamette farming community was advanced further when an enterprising pioneer managed to herd a flock of high-grade sheep over the Oregon trail in 1848 – no mean feat in itself. The woollen mills that resulted, worked mostly by local women, sprang the rural valley into the industrial age – and Salem, like Oregon City, became established as a mill town.

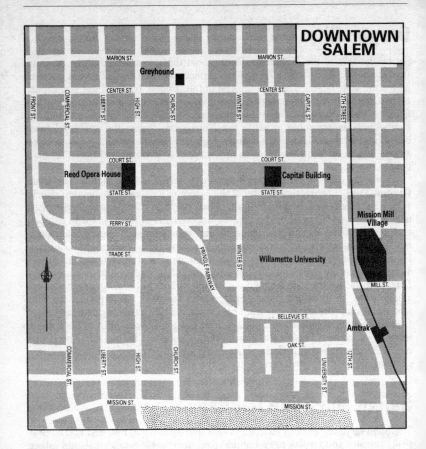

The town

Downtown Salem has a compact collection of nineteenth-century redbrick, the showpiece of which is the 1869 **Reed Opera House**, once the centre of local cultural and political activity and now a classy mall, full of antique shops. But a short walk from the downtown shopping area the tall, white, Vermont marble **Capitol Building** is the town's real centrepiece, finished in 1938 and topped with a gold-leaf pioneer, axe in hand, eyes towards the west. There's a marble carving of explorers Lewis and Clark processing regally towards (presumably) the Willamette Valley at the entrance to the building, its caption "Westward the Star of Empire Takes its Way" – an odd sort of motto, considering the amount of blood and effort spent throwing out British imperialism only a few years before Lewis and Clark set off. Inside are murals celebrating the state's beginnings, and on the floor there's a large bronze version of the state seal, in which wheat, a covered wagon and trading ships symbolise the new Oregon state of 1859, under the wings of a bald eagle. There are periodic tours to the top of the tower – the **information desk** inside the rotunda has the times – and outside, manicured gardens surround the building, with statues of Jason Lee and Dr McLoughlin on the east side.

Next to the Capitol, tree-lined **Willamette University** is the oldest university in the West, originally a mission school set up by Jason Lee. But to get a more vivid (albeit prettified) glimpse of Salem's early history, head further out of downtown towards **Mission Mill Village**, 1313 Mill Street, which groups a nineteenth-century woollen mill, a small museum and the old frame houses of two early pioneers with a café and several small shops. There's a **visitors bureau** here too (summer Mon–Fri 9am–5pm, Sat 10.30am–4pm, Sun 1–4.30pm; winter Mon–Fri 9am–5pm). Around the back, the small **Marion Museum of History** (Tues–Sat 1.30–4.30pm; $1) has an exhibit on the Kalapuyan Indians, who lived in the Willamette Valley until a combination of white settlers, the Klickitat tribe and disease drove them out. As much as ninety percent of the native population were killed by a nineteenth-century malaria epidemic.

Practicalities

Only an hour from Portland, and easy to reach along the main I-5 corridor, Salem can be visited on a day trip from Portland or, better, on the way south towards Eugene and Ashland. The *Greyhound* (☎362-2428) station is at 450 Church Street NE, *Green Tortoise* drops off at the Bingo truck stop, exit 263 from I-5 and the *Amtrak* station is at 13th and Oak Streets (☎588-1551); *Cherriots* buses (☎588-2877) provide a local bus service. For **a place to stay**, the best option for women is probably the *YWCA*, 768 State Street (☎581-9922), next to the university, for around $13 a day – though much of its space goes to longer-term residents. Space is even tighter at the *YMCA*, 685 Court Street (☎581-9622), two blocks away, though it's always worth a try. There are plenty of motels around: *Motel 6*, 2250 Mission Street SE (☎588-7191), has doubles for $29, though it's quite a way out from the centre of town. More central is the *City Center Motel*, 510 Liberty St, south of Trade St, (☎364-0121).

The area around the university does not turn up the busy **food** scene you might expect, though the *Ram Border Cafe*, 515 12th Street SE, is a pleasant bar/restaurant, open until 2am. Downtown, the *Euphoria Café* on Court Street – almost opposite the Reed Opera House – sells good homemade food during the day.

Camping options are limited to a commercial campsite run by *KOA*, 1596 Lancaster Drive SE (☎581-6736), on the outskirts of town; 26 miles east of Salem, **Silver Falls State Park**, 20024 Silver Falls Highway (☎873-8681), has a much more attractive location.

Covered Bridges of the Willamette Valley

The I-5 highway cuts straight through the heart of the Willamette Valley from Salem to Eugene, while the old Hwy-99 potters through smaller towns at a more leisurely pace.

The visitors centre at 435 W First Avenue in **ALBANY** can provide a plan of the area's **covered bridges**. Pioneers here put roofs over their bridges to protect the wooden trusses from the Oregon rain, lengthening the bridge's life-span from ten years to thirty or more – a tradition which continued until fairly recently. Most of the area's covered bridges, centring around **SCIO**, were built in the 1930s, and there's a society dedicated to preserving them. Albany itself, despite an industrial profile, has a concentration of nineteenth-century wooden mansions and churches, its residential districts narrowly saved from the bulldozers when I-5 was constructed.

Eugene

EUGENE dominates the lower end of the Willamette Valley – a lively social mix of students and professionals, loggers and hippies. Named after Eugene Skinner, the first person to build a homestead in the area around 1846, the town is Oregon's second largest centre, and has been a prime cultural focus since travelling theatre groups began to stop here on their way between Portland and San Francisco in the late nineteenth century. Now, beyond the standard downtown shopping malls, Eugene's markets make colourful wandering, and ethnic eateries are out in force. The **University of Oregon** campus in the city's southeast corner (you can walk or catch a local bus from downtown) lends a youthful – and cost-conscious – feel and has a very decent **Museum of Art** (Wed–Sun noon–5pm; free), whose highlight is a strong Asian collection, plus contemporary Northwest and American paintings.

Eugene is also something of a **sports** capital – the city and university have hosted the US Olympic Track and Field Trials, the *Nike* sports shoes company was started here; locals even claim to have started the jogging revolution which swept the US – and Europe – in the 1970s. Trails and paths abound for runners and cyclists, both in the city centre and along leafy river banks. In fact, if you intend to spend some time here, a bike's a good way to get around: you can hire one for $2.50 an hour from *Pedal Power,* 535 High Street (☎687-1775) though you'll need a credit card or $100 cash deposit for rentals over 24 hours. **University sports facilities** are open to the public from mid-June to mid-August for $2 a day – contact the recreation office, 103 Gerlinger Hall (☎686-4113); the **Obsidian Hiking Club** organises weekend trips from the *YMCA* (Patterson and 20th); and the *EMU Waterworks Co*, 1395 Franklin Boulevard (☎686-4386), rents out **canoes and kayaks** in the summer.

Though short on sights as such, Eugene puts on a highly watchable display of its social diversities at its two big markets, especially the weekly **Saturday Market** (Eighth and Oak between April and Christmas), which began in 1970 as a local craftsmarket but has since expanded into something of a carnival, with live music and street performers. Tie-dye and wholefoods set the tone, but rastas, skateboarders, punks and students join the hippies, and make a cheerful throng. **Fifth Street Public Market** (to the north at Fifth and High), though more touristy, is another lively affair, its three levels of shops around a brick inner courtyard (actually a clever conversion of an old chicken processing plant) selling arts, crafts, and clothes, as well as a huge variety of ethnic food, from Chinese to Mexican to fish and chips. **Skinners Butte Park**, north of the *Amtrak* station along High Street, is leafy and green and worth alook for the Shelton Murphy House, an 1888 Queen Anne Victorian with a sharply pointed spire and all manner of ornate flourishes.

Arrival, information and sleeping

Getting to Eugene is easy: the *Greyhound* terminal is at Tenth Avenue and Pearl Street (☎344-6265); *Amtrak* pull in at Fourth Avenue and Willamette (☎485-1092); while *Green Tortoise* stop three times a week at 15th Avenue and Kincaid Street (by the University) on their way to and from Seattle (☎937-3603 or ☎1-800/227-4766). The local bus service, *Lane Transit District (LTD)* (☎687-5555), have a central boarding-point and information centre at Tenth Avenue and Willamette

Street – or pick up a route map from *7-11* stores. There's a **visitors information office** at 307 W Seventh Avenue (Mon–Fri 8.30am–5pm; ☎484-5307 or ☎1-800/ 547-5445), between Lincoln and Lawrence Streets – it's signposted from the highway. There are lots of cheap **motels**, concentrated along W Sixth Avenue – though it's worth noting that at least one (*Notel Motel*), features "adult" films and hourly rates over weekends. No such goings-on at the *Executive House*, 1040 W Sixth Ave (☎683-4000) or the *Budget Host*, 1190 W Sixth Ave (☎342-7273); *Motel 6*, 3690 Glenwood Drive (☎687-2395), where doubles cost $26, is a mile from the university, two from downtown. **Campsites** are much further out: *Fern Ridge Lake* is the closest, twelve miles west on US 126, and there are three lakeside campsites twenty miles southeast of town on Hwy-58.

Eating and nightlife

With over fifteen thousand students to feed, Eugene is well supplied with **eateries and entertainment**. both around the campus and **downtown**, where there's more choice. *Café Zenon*, 898 Pearl Street, is an upbeat bistro with marble-topped tables, tile floors and an eclectic though pricey menu ranging from (tasty) pasta to (bland) curry; *Keystone Café*, 395 W Fifth Street, is cheaper and less glamorous but serves high quality American and Mexican food. Right **opposite the university**, *Taylor's Bayou Kitchen*, 394 E 13th Street, has good, well-priced Cajun cooking and nightly live music, and *Guido's*, 801 E 13th Street (☎343-0681), offers decently priced Italian fare, plus chart music on Wednesday, Friday and Saturday nights.

For **evening entertainment** lots of bars have live music but the city's new showpiece is the *Hult Performing Arts Center*, Sixth and Willamette Street (☎687- 5000), which features everything from Bach to blues, its annual *Bach Festival* in late June drawing musicians from all over the world; call the 24-hour *Concert Line*; ☎342-5746, for an update. The older **WOW Hall**, 291 W 8th Street (☎687- 2746), once a meeting hall for the *Industrial Workers of the World* (or "Wobblies"), is more informal, featuring up-and-coming bands across the musical spectrum, with some vigorous Saturday night dancing.

Around Eugene: countryside and country fairs

Eugene's biggest event of the year is the **Oregon Country Fair** ($6 a day), held twenty minutes west on US-26 in **VENETA** over three days on the second weekend in June – a big, crowded hippy-flavoured festival of music, arts, food and dancing that's well worth making the effort to get to. Traffic for the fair is heavy, and even with a car you might be better taking Eugene's local *LTD* buses (see above), which run to Veneta every half-hour during the fair for 25¢. At other times (when buses run less frequently) a bus ride to Veneta sets you up for the sixty-mile hitch from Eugene to the coast.

Across the river from Eugene, neighbouring **SPRINGFIELD** is only likely to be of interest as the gateway to the **McKenzie River Valley**: Hwy-126 follows the path of the McKenzie river into the depths of the Willamette National Forest and eventually the valley, passing lakes, waterfalls and trails before heading up to the high lava fields around McKenzie pass. On the way to the pass, you come to **Cougar Hot Springs**, fifty miles east of Eugene: turn right at Cougar Dam, then drive three miles to a small lake with a waterfall on its south shore – a trail on the north shore leads to the springs, where clothing is optional.

There's plenty of hiking and camping in the forest, and you can loop back again on Hwy-20. Pick up information at the **Eugene Parks and Recreation Dept**, 858 Pearl Street, in the City Hall (Mon–Fri 7.45am–5pm; ☎687-5333), or from the **Willamette National Forest Service**, 211 E Seventh Avenue (☎687-6521).

Twenty miles south of Eugene on I-5, **COTTAGE GROVE** once had gold-fever. The **Chamber of Commerce**, 710 Row River Rd (☎942-2411), have maps of old local mines and mining towns, while *The Goose*, a 1914 vintage steam-train, takes passengers on a two-hour run through mining territory and into the Cascades (departs summer weekends 10am and 2am from the Oregon Pacific and Eastern Railroad Depot; ☎942-3368; $7.50). There's a summer festival here, too, **Bohemia Mining Days**, on the third week of July, recalling the nineteenth-century gold-strike of one James Bohemia Johnson.

Oakland

The historical little town of **OAKLAND**, thirty miles south of Cottage Grove and a mile east of I-5, dates from the end of the last century and has been restored in the traditional style. Besides antique shops and iron mongers, you'll also find a **local history museum** (Mon–Sat 1.30–4.30pm; Sun 1–5pm) housed in the former grocery store and post office at 126 Locust Street, the main street through town. The City Hall around the corner has town plans and tips for walks around Oakland, pointing out what happened where and when among the various rebrick buildings.

Roseburg

Seventy miles south of Eugene along I-5, fifteen miles south of Oakland, the timber town of **ROSEBURG** is the urban centre of the fertile Umpqua valley. There's really not much to see in the town, but the Douglas County Museum (Tues–Sat 10am–4pm; free) along I-5 on the south side of town portrays the lives of the loggers with great effect, and has a library on the ground floor where you can pore over old photos and books. Apart from a very much lived-in **historical district**, along Mill and Pine street along the railway and the river, and a dozen more **covered bridges** sprinkled round the region, there's not a lot to see; the tourist office, 410 SE Spruce Street along the river (☎672-9731), has the low-down on everything in and around the town. Eat and drink at the friendly *Little Brother's Pub*, 428 SE Main St, or stay the night at the *Garden Villa Motel*, 760 Garden Valley Blvd (☎672-1601), off I-5 on the north side of town.

Crater Lake

The Northwest's best-looking volcanic crater is just 75 scenic miles east of I-5 and the Umpqua valley towns, high up in the Cascade Range, where the shell of Mount Mazama holds **Crater Lake**; blue, deep and resoundingly beautiful. For half a million years Mount Mazama sent out periodic sprays of ash, cinder and pumice, later watched apprehensively by Klamath Indian tribes, who saw in them signs of a war between two gods, Llao and Skell, and kept well clear. The mountain finally burst, blowing its one-time peak over eight states and three Canadian provinces in an explosion many times greater than the more recent Mount St Helens blast. Two cone-like mini-volcanoes began to grow again within the hollowed mountain-top, but when the mountain cooled the basin was filled by springs and melted snow, and the growths, now dormant, became islands in a new, blue lake. In its snow-covered isolation, the lake is awe-inspiring, especially in summer, when wildflowers bloom, wildlife (deer, squirrels, chipmunks, elks, even bears) emerge from hibernation, and boats run out to **Wizard Island**, the larger of the two volcanic cones.

Though it's a stop well worth making, Crater Lake, set high in the mountains and protected in a national park, is not easy to reach: you'll need a car, and of the two approach-roads, the northern entrance (off Hwy-138 from Roseburg) is closed by snow from mid-October to July, as is the 33-mile **"Rim Drive"** road around the crater's edge. The southern access road (off Hwy-62, which leads off US-97), is kept open year-round, though of course the hiking trails at the top are also snow-covered for much of the year, and except at midsummer are used mainly by cross-country skiers.

At the north end of the lake, the steep, mile-long **Cleetwood Trail** leads to the shore, the only way down from the Rim Drive. The southern approach road brings you to the lake and tiny **Rim Village**, where there's not much beyond a **visitors center** (open daily in summer), a café, and a **Lodge** (☎594-2511) where rooms cost around $35. There are two **campsites**, the large *Mazama*, near the park's southern entrance, and the more remote *Lost Creek*, three miles down a branch road off Rim Drive's eastern portion, where there are a dozen basic plots. Alternatively, you'll find cheap motels either in, or on the way to, the Umpqua Valley towns or, to the east, the logging town of KLAMATH FALLS.

Klamath Falls

Sixty-odd miles southeast of Crater Lake, and over twice that from BEND (see p.618), isolated **KLAMATH FALLS** is a logging and agricultural town often used either as a budget base for visiting the national park or as a pit-stop for long-distance truck drivers, whose mighty vehicles fill the motel car parks along the town's northern approach. It's something of a nexus for public transport too, and if you're on your way to California there's a fair chance you'll wind up here. *Greyhound* arrive from Portland and Eugene at 1200 Klamath Avenue (☎882-4616); and *Amtrak* pull in at 1600 Oak Street (☎884-2822). While the town has few actual sights, you can at least be sure of a cheap **room** and **meal**: prices, aimed at working-class locals rather than tourists, are low. The **visitors bureau**, 125 N Eighth Street (Mon–Fri 8.30am–5pm; ☎884-5193), four blocks west and a block north of the bus depot, has maps and listings of motels like the *Pony Pass Motel*, 75 Main Street (☎884-7735), which has doubles at around $26 and the *Maverick Motel*, 1220 Main St (☎882-6688). A nicer option is *Thompson's B&B*, 1420 Wild Plum Court (☎882-7938), which overlooks Klamath Lake and is probably the only inn with a resident pair of bald eagles; doubles cost from $45. There's nothing too fancy by way of **food**: walk along Main Street and check out the menus.

Set at the southern tip of enormous Upper Klamath Lake, Klamath Falls sits on a geothermally active area, and much of the small town centre is heated by naturally hot water; including the **Klamath County Museum**, 1451 Main Street (Tues–Sat 9am–5pm; free), which details the underground quirks and runs through the sparse pioneer history of the area, with an account of the *Modoc War*

– a bitter nineteenth century struggle which turned into the US Army's most expensive Indian campaign, fought mostly in the maze-like Lava Beds just over the Californian border. At the other end of Main Street, just over the bridge, the **Favell Museum**, 125 W Main Street (Mon–Sat 9.30am–5.30pm: S3), is an idiosyncratic, cluttery private collection of vast quantities of Indian arrowheads, variously mounted, mixed with renderings of the Old West by local artists, more of which are on sale upstairs. South of Klamath Falls along US-97, most of the marshy Klamath Basin has now been drained and turned to potato and onion farmland, but the remaining wetlands have been saved as the **Klamath Basin National Wildlife Refuges**, six separate but similar areas devoted mostly to waterfowl – pelicans, cormorants, herons, ducks, geese and, in the winter, bald eagles. Most of the reserve is actually just over the California border. Because it's generally flat and little travelled, the roads here make excellent cycling country.

South to the California border

Back on the western side of the Cascades on I-5, **GRANTS PASS** lies on the Rogue River, which tumbles vigorously from the Cascade mountains to the sea. Like GOLD BEACH, at the river's mouth, Grants Pass seems to earn its living by strapping its visitors into bright orange life-jackets, and packing them in to rafts to bounce over the river's white-water rapids. A half-day's rafting or kayak tour will cost around $35, a full day $45 – the **Visitor and Convention Bureau**, 1501 NE Sixth Street (☎476-7717 or ☎1-800/547-5927) can provide brochures from the more than two dozen *licensed* (and therefore safer) river guides operating from the town; you can rent paddle-boats and canoes, too. With such exciting surroundings the town is rather on the dull side, mostly modern, neon-lit shops with a few old brick buildings and churches dating from the turn of the century. Hwy-99, the old main route through the valley, cuts along Seventh Street (northbound) and Sixth Street (southbound), holding the bulk of the town's budget accommodation, like the *Flamingo Inn* at 728 NW Sixth Street (☎476-6601) and the *Travelodge*, 748 SE Seventh Street, (☎476-7793).

Thrilling though rafting undoubtedly is, it's easier to concentrate on the scenery around the Rogue River Canyon on foot: the forty-mile *Rogue River Trail* begins (or ends, if you're coming from the coast – see p.606) at GRAVE CREEK, 27 miles to the northwest of Grants Pass. It's a sweaty walk in summer, and muddy to the point of impassibility in winter, but in spring or autumn it's an excellent trek for serious walkers. There's more easily accessible **camping** sixteen miles east of town in the **Valley of the Rogue State Park**.

The Oregon Caves

Hwy-199 leaves I-5 at Grants Pass, and wanders down the Illinois River Valley towards the Northern Californian coast. At the small town of **CAVE JUNCTION** there's a turning for the **Oregon Caves**, tucked in a wooded canyon at the end of a narrow, twisting road (*Greyhound* run to Cave Junction, but you have to make your own way to the caves, twenty miles away). The caves were discovered in 1874, when a deerhunter's dog chased a bear into a hole in the mountainside, but they only became famous when the poet Joaquin Miller described his 1909 visit in such ringing phrases that "the marble halls of Oregon" were preserved as Oregon's only National Monument.

Inside, the caves – actually, one enormous cave with smaller passages leading off it totalling three miles in length – are the stuff of geology lessons. The marble walls were created by the centuries-long compression of mucky lime, mud and lava, then carved out over the eons by subterranean water. Limestone dissolved into the remaining water, and long years of steady dripping have created elaborate formations from the lime deposits: clinging stalactites hang from the ceiling, some met by stalagmites to form columns, while rippled flows of rock run from the walls. The caves are open year-round, and are always cool, so you'll need extra clothes: hours vary according to season – call the nearby *Caves Chateau* hotel on ☎592-3400 for an update. You have to go in with the 75-minute tour ($5.25): while you're waiting (tours leave regularly but can get full in the summer, when it's wise to turn up early in the day), two nature trails ramble up the mountain above the caves and look out magnificently over the surrounding Siskiyou mountains.

Eight miles from Cave Junction, twelve miles from the cave, the **Fordson Home Hostel**, 250 Robinson Road (☎592-3203), offers a cheap bed ($3–6, but you need to book in advance), **camping** and $2 discount off entry to the caves for non-Americans with the hostel's stamp on their *IYHA* cards. There's plenty of other camping around, either at the two US Forest Service campsites near the caves or at *Woodland Echoes Motel and Campground*, 7901 Caves Highway (☎592-3406: motel rooms around $20 a night).

Medford and Jacksonville

Heading south inland on I-5 rather than toward the coast on Hwy-199, it's a short journey from Grants Pass to **MEDFORD**, the Rogue River Valley's urban centre – an industrial goliath squatting amongst huge paper mills and piles of sawdust. Best passed through as quickly as possible, there's a turning here for smaller and prettier **JACKSONVILLE**, a short drive west. The largest of Oregon's 1850s Gold Rush towns, Jacksonville saw its fortunes take a nose-dive when the gold boom ended: it crumbled, quietly, until it was old enough to attract tourists, and now the whole town has been restored and is listed as a national historic landmark. The **Jacksonville Museum**, on Fifth Street in the County Courthouse, sometimes stages performances of pioneer scenes in nineteenth-century costume, and, like the **Children's Museum** next door, has exhibits on the town's chief celebrity, Pinto Colvig – who provided the voices of Goofy and Pluto in the Disney films. If you're around in July and August, look out for the **Britt Music Festival** (☎773-6077 or ☎1-800/882-7488 for further info), which fills the town with musicians and dancers (and visitors). Jazz, classical, bluegrass and folk music plays everywhere, and accommodation – always pricey here – becomes impossible (you'll find cheaper beds in ASHLAND). You'll find a small **tourist office** (☎889-8118) inside the old railway depot, at Oregon and C streets, where you can pick up a free walking tour map of the town, and if you want to stay the night, the plush *Jacksonville Inn*, 175 E California St (☎889-1900) is right in the centre of town; there are also lots of quaint $75-a-night B&Bs in restored old homes.

Ashland and the Shakespeare Festival

Throughout Oregon, the small town of **ASHLAND** is identified with the works of Shakespeare, a bizarre cultural anomaly among the timber and dairy-farming towns of the state's rural, folksy south. The idea of an **Oregon Shakespeare**

Festival came to a local teacher, Angus Bowmer, fifty years ago, and now through-out the summer Shakespeare t-shirts and mugs fill the shops, and actors in Elizabethan costume pack audiences into a half-timbered replica of sixteenth-century London's open-air *Fortune Theatre* – here the **Elizabethan Theater** – while Shakespearian (and other) plays are staged in other, indoor venues from February to October.

Despite the obvious phoniness of it all, Ashland is nowhere near as tacky as Shakepeare's birthplace in England, and in some ways has the distinct edge. Performance standards are high, and there's some excellent contemporary fringe theatre around – not to mention pleasant cafés and a young, friendly atmosphere when the nearby Southern Oregon State College is in session. Ashland's setting, between the Cascade and the Siskiyou mountains, is magnificent, enabling good skiing in the winter and river rafting in summer,

Lithia Park is appealing too: stretching around the Elizabethan theatre close to Ashland's two main streets of shops and cafés, it was designed by John McLaren (of Golden Gate fame) with shrubs, trails and a brook, its spreading trees sheltering both family picnics and meditating hippies. The park was created during Ashland's pre-festival incarnation as a spa-town, a project of New York advertising mogul, Jesse Winburne. He overestimated the appeal of the nasty-tasting local Lithia Spring water, and the spa idea failed, but it did lodge the germ of Ashland's potential as a tourist town.

Seeing the plays

The **festival** runs from February to October. Shakespeare is performed at the *Elizabethan* and the modern *Angus Bowmer* theatres, both in Lithia Park, while the smaller *Black Swan*, opposite the park off Pioneer Street, tends to stage contemporary plays. Ticket information for all three is available from the *Oregon Shakespeare Festival* (☎482-2111) – expect to pay anywhere from $8 to $20. Lots of performances sell out in advance, but you can sometimes pick up half-price tickets on the day, and the Elizabethan sells standing-only tickets for $5. Contemporary drama comes cheaper ($5–10): try the *Actors' Workshop Theatre*, 295 E Main Street (☎482-9659: tickets from the *Blue Dragon* bookshop), the *Oregon Cabaret Theatre*, in a renovated pink church at First and Hagerdine Street (☎488-1926), or the *New Playwright's Theatre*, 31 Water Street (☎482-9286).

Practicalities

Greyhound (☎482-2516) stops in the centre of Ashland at 91 Oak Street; *Rogue Valley Transport* (☎799-BUSS) runs local buses between Ashland, Jacksonville and Medford. The **Chamber of Commerce**, 110 E Main Street (☎482-3486), has bus schedules and other information about the area. For **accommodation**, the Ashland *AYH Youth Hostel*, 150 Main Street (☎482-9217 – book ahead), or one of the **motels** along Main Street, should suffice. There are also some motels along the main street, such as the inexpensive *Manor Motel*, 476 N Main Street, ☎482-2246. Otherwise accommodation in the town is relatively expensive, especially the numerous B&Bs which charge up to $150 for a double room.

There are also quite a few good places to eat and drink, ranging from soup-and-sandwich spots like the *Ashland Bakery Cafe,* 28 E Main Street, to more upscale haunts like *Alex's Plaza Restaurant,* 35 N Main Street; the best place to drink is the *Rogue River Brewery,* 31-B Water Street just off N Main Street, which has a dozen of Oregon's best micro-brewed beers as well as pizzas and nightly live music.

THE OREGON COAST

Although the **Oregon Coast** is as beautiful as any the West has to offer, the California trump card of more sun (summer temperatures on the Oregon coast stay in the sixties and seventies) draws off the tan-seeking masses, leaving Oregonians to hike and dig clams along their own four hundred miles. And while holiday homes and extensive logging operations detract somewhat from the natural beauty, the entire coast is public land: when private ownership threatened to turn Oregon's beaches into havens for the monied elite during the Sixties, the state passed a bill preserving the lot for "free and uninterrupted" public use. State park after state park lines the shore, scattering campsites thickly; there are two strategically-separated hostels, and extensive and often isolated beaches offer a multitude of free activites, from beach-combing for Polynesian glass floats and sea-carved driftwood, to shell-fishing, whale-watching, or, in winter, storm-watching. This isn't to say that Oregon has escaped commercialism: small fishing towns, hard-hit by decline, are jumping on to the tourism bandwagon, and it's a lucky traveller who finds a cheap room without booking ahead in July and August.

The coast is almost perfect for cycling (pick up the *Oregon Coast Bike Route* map from the tourist board which also shows inclines, wind directions and other

---

FOOD FORAGING ALONG THE COAST

With patience, the beaches can yield a hearty free meal – though there are often limits on the numbers of shellfish and crabs you're allowed to catch, so you'll need to check for local restrictions. You need, also, to know what you're looking for. There are several sorts of **clams**: *razor* clams are the hardest to catch, moving through the sand remarkably quickly; others are easier game. *Gapers*, found at a depth of 14 to 16 inches, and *softshells*, found 8 to 14 inches deep in firmer mud flats, both have meaty and rather phallic-looking "necks"; *cockles* don't have these (a decided advantage if you're at all squeamish) and are also the easiest to dig, lying just below the surface. Arm yourself with bucket and spade and find a beach where other people are already digging – obviously a likely spot.

Cleaning and cooking gapers and softshells is not for the faint-hearted. You immerse them in fresh warm water until the neck lengthens and the outer skin will slip off easily, then prize the entire clam out of its shell with a sharp knife, peel off the outer skin from the neck, and slit lengthwise. Split open the stomach, remove all the cark material and gelatinous rod and cook as preferred – steamed, fried, battered or in a chunky chowder soup. Cockle clams are much less messy; you just steam them in fresh or salt water until their shells open – some people prefer them almost raw.

For **crabbing**, you'll need to get hold of a crab ring (often rentable) and scrounge a piece of fish for bait. You lower the ring to the bottom of the bay from a boat, pier or dock – and wait. The best time to crab is an hour before or an hour after low and high tides; and you're not allowed to keep babies (less than 5.75 inches across), females (identified by a broad round flap on the underside – the male flap is narrow) or softshells (ones that have recently shed their skins): when you're putting these back in the water, pick them up in the middle from behind to avoid getting pinched by their claws. To cook a crab, boil it in water for twenty minutes, then crack it, holding its base in one hand, putting your thumb under the shell at midpoint, and pulling off its back. Turn the crab over to remove the leaf-like gills and "butter" from its centre – then pick the meat from its limbs.

handy information for cyclists), and a car is the ultimate blessing for less ener-getic souls. US-101 follows the coast closely right down to the Californian border, sometimes offering spectacular panoramas, and with your own wheels you can escape onto the many, smaller "scenic loop" roads that cling to the clifftops or wind through the inland forests.

You can get to most places by bus: *Greyhound* run up the coast as far as **Lincoln City**, then cut inland to Portland, from where *Raz Buses* branch out on a coastal loop to **Seaside** and north to **Astoria**. But this leaves a sizeable gap in the northern third of the coast, some of which is covered by a local bus service but the rest of which – between Lincoln City and **Tillamook** – is completely inaccess-ible by public transport.

Astoria

Set at the mouth of the Columbia River, **ASTORIA** was the first American attempt at colonising the West Coast. It was founded as a private commercial venture by the millionaire John Jacob Astor, who wanted to set up a massive Pacific business empire, based on the lucrative Northwest fur trade. Established in 1811, "Fort Astoria" struggled on for a painful year and a half, beset by natural disasters, internal feuding and supply-line difficulties before selling out to the British: Washington Irving made the best of the saga in his chunky novel *Astoria*. There's a small replica of the old fort at the junction of 15th and Exchange Streets, but nowadays Astoria is really a working port, with enough on the histori-cal side to attract a few tourists, but little of the candy-floss razzmataz of the communities further south.

The road into Astoria runs parallel with the waterfront – a rough place during the nineteenth century, crammed with saloons and brothels, many of which had built-in trap-doors for shanghaiing drunken customers, who might wake up half-way across the Pacific, sold into an inadvertent naval career. Shanghaiing got so out of hand at one point that workers on quayside canneries had to carry guns to get themselves safely to the nightshift. It's all much tamer now, though the odd drunk sailor still rolls out of the downtown bars. Exhibits from Astoria's sea-faring past are on display at the huge, sail-shaped **Columbia River Maritime Museum**, at 17th and Marine Drive (daily 9.30am–5pm, closed Mon in winter; $3), including the red-hulled *Lightship Columbia* that was used to guide ships over the treacherous bar at the mouth of the Columbia River.

From Marine Drive, numbered streets climb towards the uptown area, where wealthy nineteenth-century merchants sea captains and politicians built their elegant mansions, well away from the noise of the port. Several still stand along Franklin and Grand Avenues, and **Flavel Mansion**, Duane Avenue and Eighth Street, (summer daily 10am–5pm, winter daily 11am–4pm; $2) has been restored and refurnished in the style of its turn-of-the-century owner, Captain George Flavel, who made his fortune piloting ships across the Columbia river bar. The admission charge here also covers the **Heritage Center**, 1618 Exchange Avenue in the old City Hall (same hours), which houses exhibits on the region's history. Further up still, on the top of Coxcomb Hill (take Coxcomb Hill Road), the **Astoria Column** is coated with a faded mural depicting the town's early history: inside, a spiral staircase leads up to a view across the town and the river, as far north as Mount St Helens. Near the column is an **Indian Burial Canoe**, a memorial to Chief Comcomly of the Chinook tribe. He was on fairly amicable terms with the first settlers, one of whom even married his daughter, until he caught his son-in-law hoeing potatoes (woman's work in the chief's opinion). Another of Comcomly's relatives turns up in the saga of **Jane Barnes**, a barmaid from Portsmouth who arrived on an English ship in 1814 to become, Astorians claim, the first white woman in the Northwest. Proposed to by Comcomly's son, among others, Jane turned him down, wreaking havoc with local race-relations. None the less, local taverns still nominate honorary barmaid Janes to take part in **Jane Barnes Day**, held in the second week of May.

Practical details

The *Raz/Greyhound* station is at 364 9th Street (☎325-5641), connected daily with Portland and south to Seaside. Of the **local bus** services, *Pacific Transit* (☎642-4475 ext.450) up the Washington coast, and *TBR Transit* (☎325-3521) serves Astoria itself. The **Visitors Center** (daily 8am–8pm in summer, till 6pm in winter; ☎325-6311), at 111 W Marine Drive, near the base of the US-1010 bridge over the Columbia River, is well signposted and well stocked. Unless you're **camping**, (in which case see *Fort Stevens State Park*, below), you'll probably end up staying in a **motel**: the *Lamplighter Motel*, 131 W Marine Drive (☎325-4051), the *Rivershore Motel*, 59 W Marine Drive (☎325-2921), and the *City Center Motel*, 495 Marine Drive (☎325-4211), are much of a muchness. Or there's **bed and breakfast** at *Franklin Street Station*, 1140 Franklin Street (☎325-4314), for around $50 a double. There's a **youth hostel** on the other side of the Columbia River in *Fort Columbia State Park* (see p.546).

For **food** try the *Pacific Rim Restaurant*, 229 W Marine Drive, somewhat shabby-looking but near the tourist office and with excellent pasta and pizza. More centrally, the tiny *Columbian Café*, 1114 Marine Drive, has tasty vegetarian food, though the opening hours are as erratic as the menu. *Café Uniontown*, 215 W Marine Drive, is quite pricey for dinner, but has a friendly piano bar.

Near Astoria: Fort Clatsop and Fort Stevens

Having finally arrived at the mouth of the Columbia River in November 1805, the explorers Lewis and Clark needed a winter base before the long trudge back east. They built **Fort Clatsop** (summer daily 8am–6pm, winter daily 8am–5pm; free), six miles southwest of Astoria and had a thoroughly miserable time there. It rained on all but twelve of their 106 days, and most of the party caught fleas. Lewis and Clark's log stockade has been reconstructed and the Fort Visitors Center has a good film show on the expedition. In the summer, staff don furs and britches and act out a "living history" programme.

Ten miles west of Astoria off US-101, **Fort Stevens State Park** is a massive recreational area with trails, a lake, camping and miles of beaches, on one of which lies the **wreck of the Peter Iredale**, a British schooner that got caught out by high winds in 1906. Fortifications were first put up at Fort Stevens to guard againt Confederate raiders entering the Columbia River during the Civil War, though **Battery Russell** was part of World War II defences. It did, in fact, get shelled one night by a passing Japanese submarine, which makes it, incredibly, the only military installation on the mainland US to have been fired on by a foreign power since 1812.

South to Seaside and Cannon Beach

Seventeen miles down the coast from Astoria, **SEASIDE** is a small-town American resort, full of amusement arcades, hot dogs, cotton candy and all the other things its name suggests. The local authorities have recently tried to spruce the place up, tidying the main street, Broadway, and promoting Seaside as a conference centre. Fortunately they haven't entirely suceeded, and it's really the enduring holiday tackiness that lends the town its character.

Not surprisingly, it's the long sandy **beach** which provides the main focus in town and it won't take long to exhaust Seaside's other few features. Walk a short way along the two-mile boardwalk (actually concrete) and you come to the **Salt Cairn,** where two members of the Lewis and Clark expedition once spent a tedious few weeks boiling down gallons of seawater to make salt – vital to preserve meat for the journey back. The small **Historical Museum**, at 570 Necanicum Drive (summer daily 1–4pm, closed Mon–Tues in winter) north of the **Convention Center** details other aspects of the town's history.

Seaside details

Seaside's on the *Raz* route between Portland and Astoria, stopping at 325 S Holladay Drive (☎738-5121); *North Coast Transit* (☎738-7083) runs from there up to Astoria, In the summer, too, there's a free double-decker bus between here and Cannon Beach; details, and general information, from the helpful **Chamber of Commerce**, 7 N Roosevelt, opposite the end of Broadway (summer Mon–Fri 8am–6pm, Sat 10am–4pm, Sun noon–4pm; shorter hours in winter; ☎738-6391 or ☎1-800/444-6740).

There are plenty of **motels**, but also lots of tourists in the summer; as with elsewhere along the coast, book ahead. The *Riverside Inn*, 430 S Holladay Drive (☎738-8254), officially a bed and breakfast, is a good cut above the average motel: the *Mariner-Holladay Motel*, 429 S Holladay Drive (☎738-3690) next door, is cheaper. *Saddle Mountain State Park,* fourteen miles east of Seaside on US-26, has camping; there's nothing too remarkable by way of **food**, though there are plenty of low-priced restaurants and cafés along Broadway.

Cannon Beach

Nine miles south of Seaside, **CANNON BEACH** is a more upmarket resort. The town, which takes its name from several cannon that washed on to the beach from the wreck of the **Sloop-of-War Shark** in 1846, now sees itself as an artists' colony, and has building regulations to match – there are no neon signs, and even the supermarket is tastefully draped with Fifties advertisements for coffee and cigarettes. On the tiny main street, painters sell their work from weathered cedar galleries, while tourists and visiting Portlanders wander from bookshop to bistro. The artistic element really comes in to its own during the great annual **Sandcastle Competition**, held every May: what Cannes is to film, Cannon Beach is to sandcastle-building, and past subjects have included dinosaurs, sphinxes, even the Crucifixion. Photographs of past masterpieces are on display at the **Chamber of Commerce**, at the corner of Spruce and E Second Streets (Mon–Fri 11am–5pm, Sun 11am–4pm; ☎436-2623), which also has a very good range of practical information.

The wide, seven-mile-long sandy beach is dominated by the great, black mono-lith of **Haystack Rock**, crowned with nesting seagulls and puffins while starfish, mussels and other shellfish shelter at its base. But increasing numbers of tourists among the sea-creatures has caused ecological consternation, and now, during the summer, volunteers are strategically placed with information and binoculars.

Cannon Beach practicalities

Get to Cannon Beach in the summer on *Raz* from Seaside or Portland; or catch the summer double-decker between here and Seaside. **Accommodation** is always tight over the summer, and booked solid during the sandcastle competi-tion. The *Mcbee Motel*, 888 S Hemlock Street (☎436-2569), is close to the beach and has doubles from around $35. *Hidden Villa*, 188 E Van Buren Street (☎436-2237), just up the road, costs about the same. The *Blue Gull Inn,* 632 S Hemlock Street, (☎436-2714), is somewhat more expensive, but does have a sauna.

For **food**, the outlook is good: *Lazy Susan Café*, 126 N Hemlock Street, next to the Coaster Theater, does excellent health-food brunches and lunches; *Osburn's Deli*, just down the road at 240 N Hemlock Street, has a good deli selection and sidewalk seats; the *Bistro*, 263 N Hemlock Street (☎436-2661), has a tasty range of fresh seafood and the town's best bar.

South to Tillamook

During the summer, *Raz* runs down the coast as far as Tillamook, stopping at many small towns on its way. Windsurfers crisscross the bay at **MANZANITA** and holidaymakers search for shrimp and mussels in the shallow waters and fly kites on the beach, while behind the town, **Neahkahnie Mountain** has been linked with legends of buried treasure since a Spanish galleon was wrecked here in the 1700s; there's a steep two-mile trail to the summit. At **ROCKAWAY BEACH** the beach stretches for five desolate miles of white sand and wind-swept dunes while the small and tacky-looking fishing town of **GARIBALDI** sells excel-lent fresh fish.

A few miles inland from here, fifteen miles south of Cannon Beach, the **Tillamook State Forest** stretches vast and green, although in 1933 it was devas-tated by a forest fire, which devoured five hundred square miles of timber-land in a week-long blaze – economically disasterous for the nearby logging communi-ties. The scorched area, known as the *Tillamook Burn* and made worse by later fires, prompted Oregon to begin state-managed forestry, and a massive scheme was launched to replant the trees, completed in 1973.

TILLAMOOK itself is a plain dairy town whose two cheese-making factories are trying hard to turn themselves into tourist attractions. Two miles north of the town on US-101, a quick glimpse of workers in wellington boots bent over large vats of orange-coloured Tillamook cheddar is all you get in the **Tillamook County Creamery Association** before the factory's cavernous gift shop/restaurant takes over. Further along US-101, the **Blue Heron French Cheese Factory** is slightly less gimmicky and has wine tasting – but in either factory you have to be fiendishly skilful with a cocktail stick to spear a sizeable free cheese sample (and the cheese is pretty bland anyway). The **Chamber of Commerce,**

3705 Hwy 101, across the car park from the Tillamook Creamery (summer Mon–Fri 9am–5pm, Sat & Sun 2–5pm; shorter hours in winter), provides information and sticks accommodation information on the door when it's closed. Downtown, the **Tillamook County Pioneer Museum**, at Second and Pacific streets (summer Mon–Sat 8.30am–5pm, Sun noon–5pm, winter closed Mon; $1), in the old county courthouse, has displays on wildlife and pioneer life, including a portrayal of logging developments from the beginning of the century, with a full-size fire-watch station.

Most of the **motels** are on Hwy 101 in the north of town, such as the inexpensive *Green Acres Motel,* 3615 Hwy 101, (☎842-2731), and the newer *Shilo Inn*, 2515 Main Street, (☎842-7971).

Scenic loop roads to Lincoln City

Without your own transport, you're stuck for the next 44 miles down the coast to Lincoln City – remember hitching, while far from impossible, is technically illegal in Oregon, and calls for discretion. With a car or bike, however, the clifftop detour around the **Three Capes Scenic Loop** is much more exciting than the main route down US-101. Leading west out of Tillamook, the loop begins by climbing **Cape Meares**, on the southern arm of broad **Tillamook Bay** (once called "Murderer's Harbor" after Indians killed a sailor from Gray's expedition here in 1788). The restored Lighthouse (Wed–Sun 11am–6pm), built at the end of the last century, has a small photo exhibition inside, and outside you have a truly magnificent view of the rocky coast.

Further south, in **Cape Lookout State Park,** there's a shallow bay surrounded by dunes and with a picturesque, small rocky island, beyond which the road then twists around 35 miles of rocky ocean scenery, bringing you out at the foot of **Cape Kiwanda**, near the tiny town of **PACIFIC CITY**. It's worth scanning the beach below Cape Kiwanda for signs of the **dory fleet** – special fishing boats based at Pacific City which can be launched through the surf straight into the oncoming breakers. Overhead, hang-gliders often launch themselves off the cape, landing (they hope) on the wide sandy beach. Further along US-101 at NESKOWIN, there's a turning for another detour, the **Cascade Head Scenic Loop**, this one taking you inland through forest and farmland coming out at the one-shop town of OTIS (where cheap, tasty food makes the *Otis Café* worth a visit).

Lincoln City

After this, there's no avoiding **LINCOLN CITY** – probably the ugliest town on the coast – without swinging miles inland. Actually the merged version of five small beach towns, run together in 1965, Lincoln City sprawls along the highway for seven and a half congested, motel-lined miles. **Greyhound** buses, 316 SE US-101 (☎994-8418), reappear here, running to Portland and south down the coast, so you might even end up staying – especially since Lincoln City will have rooms long after other beach towns are full up. The **visitors center,** 3939 N US-101 (Mon–Fri 9am–5pm, Sat 10am–5pm, Sun 10am–4pm; ☎994-8378 or ☎1-800/452-2151 has lists of motels like the clean and fairly cheap *City Center Motel*, 1014 NE US-101 (☎994-2612); the *Nidden Hof*, 136 NE US-101 (☎1-800/98COAST), is slightly more expensive. The **food** is as you might expect: *Li'l Sambo's*, 3262 NE US-101, is at least exuberantly kitschy, with vinyl tigerskin cushions, plastic palm trees and the like, although the food is better at *Kyllo's Seafood Grill*, 2733 NW US-101.

One faint ray of interest in Lincoln City is the **World's Longest Kite Festival**, which runs between May and September. Conditions for kite-flying along the long, windswept beach, can be excellent. The *Catch the Wind Kite Shop* coastal chain have their headquarters here at 266 SE US-101; they have kites in all shapes and colours and for all the different types of wind conditions. **Lacey's Doll and Antique Museum**, 3400 N US-101 (summer daily 8am–5pm, rest of the year 9am–4pm $1.50), has Dolly Parton and Shirley Temple dolls among its bizarre exhibits.

The actual centre of town lies around **Devils Lake,** right off US-101. On the northern shore of the lake you can hire paddle boats and curve in and out of the windsurfers. From behind the bridge over the "D" river, you can walk to the beach with its myriad colourful kites and windsocks fluttering in the sky.

The coast to Newport

Greyhound cover the coast south of Lincoln City, but with your own transport, it's worth turning off the highway two miles south of the small harbour town of DEPOE BAY to reach the **Otter Crest Loop**, a four-mile section of the old Coast Highway, which edges its way precariously around the sheer rock walls of **Cape Foulweather**. The cape was discovered and named by a jaded Captain Cook, whose historic expedition up the Pacific Coast had nearly been dispatched to a watery grave by a sudden Northwest storm – the wind up here can reach 100mph. Further on a turning leads to the **Devil's Punchbowl,** a sandstone cave whose roof has fallen in, the sea foaming up cauldron-like at high tide and receding to reveal pools of sea-creatures. Back on the highway, just before Newport there's a turning to **Yaquina Bay Lighthouse** (summer daily noon–5pm; 50c). This gives an unsurpassed view of the coast, overlooking **Agate Beach**, where winter storms toss up agates from gravelly beds under the sea. If you walk along the beach towards the sun on an outgoing tide, the agates (after a winter storm, at least) sparkle up at you: *moonstone* agates are clear, *carnelians* are bright red and transparent, and *ribbon* agates have coloured layers. Local shops provide both information and more accessible agates.

Newport

NEWPORT, like so many other coastal fishing towns, is slowly turning into a resort. Although a pleasant enough place to pass a couple of days it's currently a strange hybrid. It's not the presence of the tourist industry so much as the chicness of the packaging that seems surprising. Turn off US-101 towards the bayfront and you'll find, opposite the dented, corrugated metal walls of the old fish canneries, the smart grey wood, dark glass and sophisticated neon logos of the *Mariner Square* tourist development; seagulls, perching on old packing cases, are weirdly juxtaposed with new neon parrots. There's an artsy undertone to the place, manifest in a new Performing Arts Center and two small art museums on the beach at **Nye Beach**, a short distance north of town from the main bayfront (narrow

Newport, built around an inlet, faces the sea on two sides). The centre of town is on the northern side, and you can watch fishermen unloading their catch at the town port, at the end of Hurburt Street off US-101. Nye Beach is worth walking to anyway for its long and less crowded stretch of sand. It's naturally the ocean that continues to provide Newport's main appeal, and the bayfront proper nowadays pulls the crowds with its over-priced tourist attractions (waxworks and the like).

The **Mark O. Hatfield Marine Science Center** (summer daily 9.30am–6pm, winter daily 10am–4pm; free) on Marine Science Drive on the other side of arching Yaquima Bay bridge, is the base of Oregon State University's coastal research, and various curious sea-creatures swim around in display tanks; by the end of 1992, the brand-new, state-of-the-art **Oregon Coast Aquarium** next door should have opened its more entertaining and educational displays.

Practicalities

Newport's certainly a nice place to stay over: there's a pleasant, relaxed feel to the town, some appealing cafés and restaurants, and a couple of good budget **accommodation** options, the highlight of which is the *Sylvia Beach Hotel*, 267 NW Cliff (☎265-5428). Named after the owner of the *Shakespeare and Co.* bookshop in Paris during the Twenties and Thirties, the hotel aims to encourage modern would-be writers – there's a cosy attic library, and dorm beds go for $20 a night, including breakfasts. Other rooms are decorated in the styles of various writers (the Poe room has a guillotine over the bed), but they're small and pricey: $50–110 for a double. As far as **motels** go it's the usual story – less of the roar of the sea, and more of the roar of US-101. The best of them is probably the *Penny Saver*, 710 N Coast Highway (☎265-6631); doubles from around $32. The *Puerto Nuevo Inn*, 544 SW Coast Highway (☎254-5767 or ☎1-800/999-3068), is new and has good rooms with a view of the sea. There are **campsites** in Beverly Beach State Park (☎265-9278), north of town and in the South Beach State Park (☎867-4715), two miles south of the bridge.

Maps with complete motel and campsite listings are available from the **Chamber of Commerce**, 555 SW Coast Highway (summer Mon–Fri 8.30am–5pm, Sat & Sun 10am–4pm, winter Mon–Fri 8.30am–5pm; ☎1-800/262-7844). *Greyhound* pulls in at 956 SW 10th Street (☎265-2253). For **food**, the *Whale's Tale* on Bay Boulevard has a good, if varied menu (German, Greek, Cajun, vegetarian), live music at weekends – and a large piece of whale's vertebrae suspended from the ceiling. At lunchtime the *Broadwalk Cafe* on Bay Boulevard serves good soups, sandwiches and desserts. Nearby, the *Canyon Way Restaurant and Bookstore*, 1216 SW Canyon Way, is another pleasant eatery; at Nye Beach, the *Chowder Bowl* is good value, as is the Italian *Don Petrie's*, across the road.

Cape Perpetua and the Sea Lion Caves

South of Newport, the huge **Siuslaw National Forest** closes in around the highway, threaded by shady forest roads, and scattered with campsites and state park beaches. Cape Perpetua, twenty-five miles out from Newport, is the centre of one of the most spectacular stretches of the Oregon coast. The drive (or ride) along US-101 is incredibly scenic, with dense forests climbing above the anything-but-Pacific surf crashing against the rocks below. Numerous hiking trails loop around from the well-marked **Cape Perpetua Visitors Center** (daily 10am–4pm; ☎547-

3289), just off US-101, and there's more hiking, and camping, at **Washburne State Park**, eight miles south.

Just beyond Washburne State Park, a small turning leads down to a very pretty beach at the foot of a graceful old highway bridge; just north along the rocky shore stands the Heceta Head Lighthouse, an 1893 Queen Anne-style structure, looking far too petite to withstand the endless onslaught of the sea. The views along US-101 get less incredible as you continue south, the natural splendour having all but vanished (only for a while, though) by the time you reach the **Sea Lion Caves** (daily 8am–6pm; $5) the year-round home of hundreds of sea lions, who sprawl over the rocks during the summer breeding season but in the winter hide away in a massive cave, whose rock walls echo the combined roar of sea and beast.

Florence and the Dunes

FLORENCE, on the mouth of the Siuslaw river, twelve miles south of the Sea Lion Caves, was once a Siuslaw settlement; nowadays, the town doesn't look like much from the highway, but azaleas and rhododendrons grow wild along the roadside (there's an annual **Rhododendron Festival** in the third week of May, when they're all in bloom), and the **Old Town**, along the harbour front, has been pleasantly revamped.

Practicalities

Greyhound buses drop off at 2107 US-101 (☎997-8782), just north of the town centre, and there's a **Chamber of Commerce**, at 270 US-101 (☎997-3128), just north of the river bridge. **Accommodation** is on the pricey side, though the *Money Saver Motel*, 170 US-101 (☎997-7131) near Old Town, has doubles from around $35, as does the *Silver Sands Motel*, 1449 US-101 (☎997-3459); *Driftwood Shores*, north of town at Heceta Beach, is Florence's only beachfront resort, with fairly standard, sea-view doubles for $65.

For **food**, head down to the Old Town waterfront, just north of the US-101 bridge, where the *Harbour House Cafe*, 1368 Bay Street, and the more upmarket *Bridgewater Restaurant* across the street do a top-notch range of fresh seafood.

The Dunes

It's **the Dunes**, just south of Florence, that dominate this area: 41 miles of shifting sandhills, higher in places than the Sahara, and punctuated with pockets of forests and lakes. It's thought they were formed by the crumbling of the sandstone mountains behind the area. Sediment was washed down from the mountains in the rivers, dried out on the beach, then picked up by the wind. Hiking trails wind through the windy dune country, and the giant hills are also haunted by manic buggy riders. The **Oregon Dunes National Recreation Area Information Center**, 855 US-101 (summer Mon–Fri 8am–4.30pm, Sat & Sun 10am–5.30pm, winter Mon–Fri 8am–4.30pm; ☎271-3611), is further south in REEDSPORT, and has masses of information on hiking, camping and wildlife in the dunes. Real dune fanatics can rent ATVs ("all-terrain vehicles") in Florence from *Sandland Adventures*, on US-101 at 10th Street, behind the Shell Station in Florence ($25 for the first hour, $50 deposit; ☎997-8087), or *Gary's Rentals*, 586 US-101 (☎997-6755; similar prices, but also with mopeds at $6 an hour).

Around Coos Bay

The dunes end as the coastline curves into **Coos Bay**, which groups around its large, deep natural harbour the merged industrial towns of North Bend and Coos Bay, and the smaller fishing town of Charleston. Forestry and shipping are the economic mainstays here. You'll pass the huge plant of **Weyerhauser**, the biggest name in the Northwest timber industry, on US-101 in North Bend: it offers tours of its sawmill if you're interested. Heavy freighters pull in to pick up shiploads of timber further on in **COOS BAY**, the largest and most industrial town along the Oregon coast. If you want to stop off here, there are tours of the **House of Myrtlewood**, just off US-101 at First Street, where rare myrtlewood, indigenous to southwest Oregon, is carved by craftspeople.

The **tourist office** (☎269-0215 or ☎1-800/762-6278), at the south foot of the McCullough Bridge, shares space with a small local history museum; there's also a small but oddly intriguing Coos Bay Art Musuem (Tues–Sun 10am–4pm), at 235 Anderson off US-101 in the down-at-heel town centre. *Greyhound* stops at 275 N Broadway (☎267-6517), and a short walk away there's the summer-only *Sea Gull Youth Hostel* , 438 Elrod St (☎267-6114). Lots of **motels are** scattered along US-101. One bright spot in this none-too-cheering town is the homemade food and long list of imported beers at the *Hurry Back Café* on US-101 at Commercial Street.

Further out on the south arm of the bay, the small and rather tatty sports-fishing town of **CHARLESTON** is surrounded by a trio of parks, connected by a three-mile hiking trail. Enclosed by sandstone cliffs, **Sunset Bay** three miles west of Charleston, is shallow, protected and ideal for swimming, while next to it, **Shore Acres State Park** was once the estate of a shipping tycoon – his lavish mansion burnt down, but the formal gardens survived and are laid out with exotic plants and open to the public. South of Shore Acres, **Cape Arago** offers whale-watching, and a view of the seals and sea lions who breed on nearby reefs: tidal pools around the cape's coves house anemones, purple sea urchins, starfish and crabs. More wildlife can be seen at the **South Slough National Estuary Sanctuary**, also near Charleston. These 26 miles of forest and tideflats preserve numerous plants, animals and birds, and are thought to be the inspiration for a local Native American legend about "Baldiyasa" – the place where life began.

Bandon and around

Twenty-four miles south of Coos Bay, easy-going **BANDON**'s combination of old town restoration work and New Age style make it a rather more enticing place to pass a few days. Certainly, if you're in Oregon to seek out the state's alternative circles, this is a good place to come: since former habitués of Haight Ashbury and Venice Beach in California moved up here in the late Sixties, the town has grown into something of an arts and crafts centre, and "far-out" theories abound. Equipped with one of the state's largest metaphysical bookshops, *Winter River*, Bandon stands, according to a local New Age chiropractor, directly on a ley-line going from the Bering Sea to the Bahamas, making it one of the earth's "acupuncture points".

Located rather more obviously at the mouth of the Coquille River, Bandon was originally an native American settlement, but the town really only developed in the mid-nineteenth century with the onset of the Gold Rush. This century began rather ominously, when townsfolk dynamited Tupper Rock, a sacred tribal site, to build the sea wall, and the town was cursed to burn down three times: it's happened twice so far, in 1914 and 1936, and the superstitious are still waiting; in 1990, the rock was deeded back to the Indians, in order to ward off any more bad vibes.

Bandon's main attraction today is its rugged **beach**, whose unusual rock formations have given rise to Native American legends. Magnificent in stormy weather, the beach's prolific quantities of shellfish make this a prime venue for **crabbing and clamming** (see p.595). In the town, Bandon's history is on display at the **Coquille River Museum**, in the Coast Guard building overlooking the river mouth (summer Tues–Sun 1–4pm, rest of the year Thurs–Sat noon–4pm), and the **Rose** paddle steamer runs daily cruises along the river ($8 for two hours). Further out, there's **swimming** at Bradley Lake, a fresh water lagoon sheltered by trees and sand dunes two miles south along Beach Loop Road (there's no signpost – look for a layby on the bend just before Blue Jay Campground). Cranberries are big business in Bandon – you'll see them growing in bogs – and the annual extravaganza here is the **Cranberry Festival** in mid-September, featuring a parade, square dancing and a food fair with numerous recipes for the rampant red berry.

Practicalities

Unquestionably the best place to **stay** in Bandon is the *Sea Star Hostel*, in the centre of town at 375 Second Street (☎347-9632) – it's the only *AYH* hostel in the state that doesn't have a curfew. Behind the hostel, overlooking the harbour, the *Sea Star Guest House* is run by the same management and offers a little more luxury: doubles from $45–80 in the summer, less out of season. For a motel try the *Sunset Motel*, 1755 Beach Loop Road (☎347-2543 or ☎1-800/842-2407). There's **camping** just north of town at **Bullards Beach State Park** (☎347-2209), where a refurbished 1896 lighthouse stands guard over miles of windswept wilderness. You can eat out at *Andrea's Old Town Cafe,* a block from the hostel on Baltimore, while the small *Sea Star bistro* in the hostel itself does a good range of salads and sandwiches. The **visitors information center** (daily 9am–5pm; ☎347-9616)) is right off US-101 in the town centre. Their daily *Coffee Break* free news-sheet lists local news and activities, and they also have a handy walking tour map of the town.

The coast to California

Towns become fewer and further between as you travel south along US-101, which passes dozens of secluded **beaches**. *Greyhound* stops at the *Port Orford Motel,* 1034 Oregon Street (☎332-1685), but there's actually not much to tiny **PORT ORFORD** beyond its rugged setting. Because the small harbour is relatively unprotected from the fierce storms, the fishing boats that moor here are lifted out of the water with a huge crane.

Just south of the town, the rocky outcrop of **Battle Rock** was the site of an early struggle between white settlers and local Native Americans, and an

information booth opens in the summer at the park here. The town itself has dusted off some of its nineteenth-century buildings, and has several places to eat. There's **camping** nine miles north of town at windblown **Cape Blanco State Park**, or six miles south at **Humbug Mountain State Park**, where you can also hike to the top of the mountain (the tallest along the coast) for spectacular views.

Gold Beach and the Rogue River

South of Port Orford, grass-covered mountains sweep smoothly to the shoreline. The wild and scenic **Rogue River** reaches the sea at **GOLD BEACH**, a small town largely devoted to packing visitors off on rafts and jet-boats, up canyons and through roaring rapids into the depths of the **Siskiyou National Forest**. During the summer, *Mail Boat Hydro-Jets* (☎247-7033), *Jerry's Rogue Jets* (☎247-4571 or ☎1-800/451-3645) charge roughly the same for either a six-hour trip as far as the town of AGNESS, and back ($25), or a longer eight-hour trip, which bounces you over stretches of white water ($50); times include two-hour lunch breaks at a mountain resort, but food isn't included in the price.

If you don't fancy a boat-trip, but want to see something of the mountains, head to the **Shrader Old Growth Forest**, nine miles east of town via Jerry's Flat Road, which winds along the south bank of the river. It's one of the few coastal groves that's never been logged, so the dense stands of cedars, firs and tanoaks here are a haven for a variety of wildlife, notably the threatened Spotted Owl. A mile-long trail winds through the forest, and there's a pamphlet which describes the various features of this rare undisturbed environment – which seems all the more special after you've passed through the clear-cut hillsides on the way here. If you're a good hiker, you might also consider the forty-mile **Rogue River Trail**, which follows the north bank of the river twelve miles inland, eventually linking up with other routes to reach all the way to Grave Creek, 27 miles northwest of GRANTS PASS.

Details on this and other hikes, and information on **camping** in the area, is available from the Gold Beach **Ranger District Office** (Mon–Fri 7.30am–5pm; ☎247-6651), 1225 S Ellensburg St on the south side of town. Less adventurously, the **Curry County Museum** (summer Wed–Sun 1–5pm, rest of the year Fri–Sat noon–4pm; free) at 920 S Ellensburg Street has old pictures of the town.

Practicalities

Greyhound have a terminal at 310 Colvin Street (☎247-7246), and the **Chamber of Commerce**, 510 S Ellensburg Street (Mon–Fri 9am–5pm, Sat & Sun 10am–4pm; ☎452-2334), can provide you with all manner of practical and historical information. For **food**, the *Crow's Nest* on the north edge of town at 565 N Ellensburg Street does pizzas and burgers, while *Rogue Landing* is a good place to stock up on breakfast/brunch before an energetic day, though it's a mile-long trek up Jerry's Flat Road. Further out, 32 miles east in the mountain village of AGNESS, *Lucas Pioneer Lodge* (☎247-7443) welcomes weary hikers with all-you-can-eat chicken and home-grown corn-on-the-cob dinners for $7.95. They also have **cabins** from $30 a night; otherwise the nicest of Gold Beach's dozen motels is the *River Bridge Inn* (☎247-4533 or ☎1-800/759-4533), just off US-101 at the south end of the Rogue River Bridge, with clean and quiet doubles from $40.

Brookings

Down towards the California border is Oregon's "banana belt" – of which **BROOKINGS**, 29 miles south of Gold Beach, is the capital. Warmed by drifting thermal troughs from the Californian coast, this area is unusually sunny (often over 70°F in January) making it popular with retirees, and the local industry is, appropriately enough, the genteel art of flower growing – most of North America's Easter lilies are grown here, and some of the local azaleas are over twenty feet high and three hundred years old, inspiring the annual **Azalea Festival** on Memorial Day weekend at the end of May. *Greyhound* (☎469-3326) stops at Cottage and Pacific, and there's a **Chamber of Commerce** (Mon–Fri 9am–5pm; ☎469-3181) on the left hand side of US-101, opposite the shopping mall. But a quick look at the harbour is all Brookings really merits, and there's little here to keep you from the **beaches and state parks** that stretch out on both sides of the town.

The coastline immediately north of Brookings, especially along the ten-mile stretch of **Samuel Boardman State Park**, is magnificently rugged, the roadway dangling above rocky coves and giving sweeping views out over the Pacific. There isn't much between Brookings and California, but just over the border are the Jedediah Smith Redwoods (see p.483), which you'll have to pass in order to make the loop to the Oregon Caves and Grants Pass on Hwy-199, the only way over the mountains.

travel details

Trains
From Portland to Salem (1 daily; 1hr 25min); Eugene (1; 2hr 30min); Klamath Falls (1; 6hr 30min); San Francisco (1; 18hr); Los Angeles (1; 29hr); The Dalles (1; 1hr 40min); Pendleton (1; 4hr), La Grande (1; 6hr 15min); Baker (1; 7hr 15min); Boise, Idaho (1; 10hr); Tacoma (3; 3hr); Seattle (3; 4hr); Vancouver, Canada (2; 8hr).

Buses
Greyhound/Raz runs **from Portland** to Oregon City (1 daily; 1hr 30min); Salem (9; 1–1hr 30min); Eugene (10; 2hr 30min–3hr 30min); Grants Pass (5; 7hr); Medford (7; 6–8hr); Ashland (5; 7–9hr); Klamath Falls (3; 7–8 hr); San Francisco (4; 16–30hr); Seattle (11; 3–5hr); Bend (2; 45min); Boise (1; 13hr).

Green Tortoise runs twice a week **from Portland** to Salem (1hr 45min), Eugene (3hr 15min), Ashland (10hr), San Francisco (20hr) and Seattle (5hr).

CHAPTER TWELVE

EASTERN OREGON

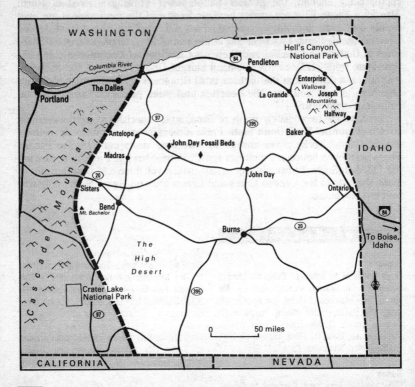

E ast of the Cascades, Oregon, like Washington, grows wilder and more dramatic. The temperature rises, the drizzle stops, and green valleys give way to scrubby sageland, bare hills and stark rock formations fringed with pines and ragged juniper. Though nowhere near as popular a destination as the lush coastal areas, it still has its attractions, particularly in the north. At the **John Day Fossil Beds**, prehistoric skeletons of plants and animals lie embedded in crumbly red and green rock. Further northeast are small-town farming and ranching communities such as **Pendleton**, **La Grange** and **Baker**, and the snow-capped peaks of the Wallowa Mountains overlook the long deep slash of **Hells Canyon**. In the south, around the small but pleasant town of **Bend**, ancient volcanoes have produced the oddly scarred landscape of the **Lava Lands** – though it comes as a surprise to most first-time visitors that the rest of southeastern Oregon is barren desert and virtually uninhabited.

None of this terrain looked very promising to early immigrants, who hurried on along the Oregon Trail, and returned east only when the prime western land was taken. In doing so, they displaced the native Americans who had been roaming the land since prehistory. Early pioneer homesteading was a precarious, stockaded affair, at one point forbidden by officials who feared for the safety of the white settlers, and saw the Cascades as "a valuable separation of the races". But the lure of land-ownership – and gold – was irresistible. White versus Indian skirmishes escalated into a series of bitter mini-wars, only to come to an end when the native inhabitants were confined to reservations. Violence was also rife between pioneer cattle-ranchers and sheep-farmers. Cattlemen formed themselves into terrorist squads, and "Sheepshooters" associations committed dire atrocities on the woolly usurpers during Eastern Oregon's "range wars". Sheep and cows now safely graze side-by-side, and some small towns still celebrate their cowboy roots with annual rodeos – most famously the Pendleton Round-Up, one of the largest in the US.

Probably because of the small population, **public transport** isn't too good: *Greyhound* run east from Portland along the Columbia River, serving Pendleton, La Grande and Baker in the northeast corner on the way to Boise, Idaho. A second route from Portland to Boise dips through Bend and cuts east further south, through **Burns**, a remote town in the southeast. *Amtrak* parallels *Greyhound* to Pendleton, La Grande and Baker, and crosses the Cascades below Eugene to run south to California via Klamath Falls. At a local level, public transport is practically negligible, and hitching, as with the rest of Oregon, is illegal – if you want to explore, you'll really need a car.

NORTHEASTERN OREGON

The remoteness and isolation of northeast Oregon can be romantic, but just getting around can be tough: even along US-26, the main east–west highway, tiny battered hamlets boasting two rusting petrol pumps and (maybe) a café punctuate long stretches along which you can drive for miles without seeing so much as a coke machine. And drive you'll have to: the quiet little backwaters of Pendleton, La Grande and Baker are served by *Greyhound* and *Amtrak*, but are worth a look only as bases from which to explore the badlands of the John Day Fossil Beds, the lovely Wallowa Mountains, or wild Hells Canyon.

East from Portland: US-26

US-26 from Portland leaves the path of the old Barlow road halfway around the base of Mount Hood (see p.583), to dip southeast through miles of forest into the **Warm Springs Indian Reservation**, within which the scenery changes from mountain forest to the hot, dry landscape of the east. Near the reservation's southeast edge, you pass a turning for the very popular **Kah–Nee–Ta** resort, the "Gift of the Gods" – a catchy, but ironic, piece of hyperbole for what is in fact a canny commercial project set up by the Confederated Tribes of Warm Springs and financed by federal compensation for the flooding of their ancestral fishing grounds at Celilo Falls along the Columbia River. Native culture here is packaged

into a jolly tourist product (accommodation in tepees, Indians dancing in feathered head-dresses while the audience munches vast quantities of traditionally
baked salmon), and the venture is widely hailed as a commercial success.

ANTELOPE AND THE BHAGWAN

These days, there's nothing much to see at **ANTELOPE**, fifty or so miles east of
the Warm Springs Reservation on Hwy-218. However, the town's story is probably
the most bizarre and well known in Oregon's recent history, and you'll no doubt
hear mutterings about it at some time during your stay wherever you're travelling
in the state. In 1981, followers of the Indian guru, Bhagwan Shree Rajneesh, bought
the old **Big Muddy Ranch**, twenty miles east of Antelope, converting it to an agricultural commune. Dressed exclusively in shades of red – and thus sometimes
known as "the orange people" – Bhagwan's followers were a middle-class lot,
mostly graduates in their thirties who came from all over the world. The
commune's mish-mash of eastern philosphy and western Growth Movement thera-
pies raised great (and initially sympathetic) interest across Oregon – and eyebrows
in conservative Antelope. Despite the commune's agricultural success in what still
is a relatively depressed region, relations disintegrated fast, especially when
Rajneeshis took over the town council; and the appearance of Rajneeshi "peace
patrols" clutching semi-automatic weapons did little to restore confidence in the
guru's good intentions.

The Rajneeshis' hold on the community was, however, fairly short-lived. Just
before the local county elections, the Rajneeshis began a "Share a Home" project
that involved bussing in street-people from across the US and registering them to
vote here. Many vagrants later turned up in neighbouring towns (without the promised bus ticket home), saying they'd been conned, drugged or both, and creating big
problems for the local authorities. Worse, an outbreak of salmonella-poisoning in the
nearby town of The Dalles turned out to have been part of a Rajneeshi strategy to lay
their voting opponents low. When the law eventually moved in on the commune – by
now an armed fortress – they discovered medical terrorism (more poisoning, the
misdiagnosis of AIDS) had been used on Rajneeshi members themselves in an internal power-struggle. The culprits were jailed and commune members dispersed. The
Bhagwan, after a bungled attempt to flee the country, was deported to India and his
notorious fleet of Rolls Royces sold off, along with the ranch, to pay debts. By 1986,
the embattled Antelope was quiet again. A plaque on a new memorial flagpole in the
town centre, dedicated to the triumph of the Antelope community over the
"Rajneesh invasion", is the only sign that anything ever happened.

Madras, Redmond and Sisters

The wealth of buried fossils and agates around **MADRAS,** on US-26 ten miles
beyond the Warm Springs Reservation, makes it popular with so-called "rock-
hounds" or amateur excavators: the **Chamber of Commerce** at 366 Fifth Street
(☎475-2350) has details if you want to go digging; and you'll see signs advertising
agates for sale all along the road. US-97 runs south from Madras along the eastern foot of the Cascades for 27 miles before reaching the small, plain town of
REDMOND, where Hwy-126 cuts off west towards **SISTERS.** A tourist town with
a pseudo-Western high street, but beautifully set, Sisters is genuinely exciting
during the annual **rodeo**, held on the second weekend in June, which draws big
crowds to watch the cowboys hang grimly on to tough, mean-looking bulls;

contact the Chamber of Commerce, 340 SW Cascade (☎549-0251). The white-capped triple peaks of "Faith", "Hope" and "Charity", the **Three Sisters Mountains**, behind the town, provide a perfect backdrop. Two roads lead into the mountains from Sisters, both eventually climbing over high Cascade passes to the west side of the mountains, the **Mackenzie Pass Highway** (Hwy-126, open summers only) to the south, and US-20 over **Santiam Pass** to the north – both beautiful drives through dense mountain forests, with hiking trails and campsites en route.

The John Day Fossil Beds

East from Madras or Redmond, US-26 begins its dry trek across the state, emerging from a brief, green passage through the **Ochoco National Forest** into a bare, sun-scorched landscape of ochres and beige that extends for hundreds of miles. Many features of the area are named after John Day – a fur-trapper from the Astoria colony in the west of Oregon, who fell victim to the elements and local Indians and was later discovered wandering lost and naked by another party of trappers – including a river, a town and most importantly the **John Day Fossil Beds**, a little way north of US-26. Made up of three separate sites, this carefully excavated area of strange-coloured rock-forms holds some of the most revealing fossil formations in the US. Trails wind through barren hills over crumbly textured earth and information plaques point out the various geological and palae-ontological oddities. The fossils date from the period just subsequent to the extinction of the dinosaurs: before the Cascade mountains raised their rain-blocking peaks to the west, a sub-tropical rainforest covered this land in a dense jungle of palms, ferns and tropical fruits, inhabited by weird creatures that predate the evolution of current species – *Hpertragulus*, a tiny, mouse-sized deer, *Diceratherium*, a cow-sized rhinoceros, and *Miohippus*, a small, three-toed horse. As the Cascades sputtered into being, volcanic ash poured down on the forest, mixing with the rain to make a thick, muddy poultice, which fossilised bits of the leaves and fruit. Other layers trapped the bones and teeth of the animals. Palaeontologists first visited the area in the 1860s, and have since been able to put together a massive epic of evolution and extinction.

The three sites of the fossil beds are spread far apart, and vary greatly in accessibility. You'd have to be a real fossil fanatic to push up to the rocky **Clarno** unit, seventy miles off US-26 on Hwy-218. However, the **Painted Hills** unit, down a (marked) side road six miles west of the one-horse town of MITCHELL, is more accessible, though the interest here lies as much in the hills themselves as the relics embedded in them: striped in shades of rust and brown, they look like sandcastle mounds, the smooth surface quilted with rivulets worn by draining water. Close up, the hills are frail, their clay surface cracked by dryness; the colours become brighter when it rains and the pores in the earth close up.

Further east, the final section of the fossil beds, **Sheep Rock,** takes its name from the volcanic capstone which looms like the Matterhorn over the John Day River valley. The staff at **Cant Ranch Visitor Center**, housed in the ranch-house of an old sheep farm at the foot of the rock, can tell you more than you ever wanted to know about prehistory, and there are plenty of fossils on display. Two miles north of the visitors centre there's a turning for an area known as **Blue Basin**, where the rock is more of a pale, greeny colour, mixed in with more of the soft, crumbly dark red of the painted hills. The *Island in Time* trail takes you into the "blue basin" itself – a rock-surrounded natural amphitheatre – past perspex-covered fossil exhibits, including a tortoise that hurtled to its death millions of years ago and a sabre-toothed cat.

John Day town

Centered around a bright, white-painted wooden nineteenth-century church, small, dry **JOHN DAY** is, despite its size (2100 inhabitants) the largest town you'll come across along US-26. If you're going to spend a night anywhere between Bend and Baker, this is probably the place – try the inexpensive *Little Mac's Motel*, 250 E Main Street, (☎575-1751) or the more luxurious *John Day Inn*, 315 W Main St, (☎575-1700). **Information** and maps are obtainable at the Chamber of Commerce, 281 W Main Street, (☎575-0547).

Like many of the towns around here, John Day was originally a Gold Rush settlement, founded when gold was discovered at nearby Canyon Creek in 1862. Along with the rush of hopeful white miners came Chinese immigrants, often to work sites abandoned as unprofitable by the wealthier whites. Despite high-pitched racial tensions across the Northwest, a Chinese herbalist, "Doc" Ing Hay made quite a name for himself treating patients of both races, and his two-storey house (which was also the local shop, temple and opium and gambling den) is now open as the **Kam Wah Chung & Co. Museum**, (summer only Mon–Thurs 9am–noon & 1–5pm, Sat & Sun 1–5pm; $1.50) next to the City Park on the north-west side of town.

Baker City

Continuing east on US-26, passing turnings that lead to sagging gold-boom ghost towns like SUMPTER, where old dredging equipment still looks poised for action, the road leads eventually to **BAKER CITY**. Eighty miles east of John Day and with a more substantial feel to it, the downtown here is a solid affair of brick and stone. I-84 from Portland passes through, and public transport reappears – *Greyhound*, 1932 Main Street (☎523-5011) and *Amtrak*, 2803 Broadway, both run to Portland, though there's no local transport to take you anywhere interesting once you're here. Still, Baker City (usually called simply *Baker*), makes a good stopover, and is well equipped with motels. The *New Image Motor Inn*, 134 Bridge Street (☎523-6571), is about the best value in town with doubles from around $25, and the surrounding area is sprinkled with campsites. Baker's **Chamber of Commerce**, 490 Campbell Street (☎523-5855), has more informa-tion. You'll find **restaurants** around Main Street – the *Blue and White Café*, 1825 Main Street (closed Sun), is full of old regulars, lingering over their 10¢ coffees.

Unlike its ghost-town neighbours, Baker outlived its gold-boom days – now remembered by a collection of gold nuggets in a cabinet in the **US National Bank** on Main Street – and branched out into agriculture and cattle-rearing. Large herds would assemble here, headed for the dinner-plates of the East, and farming's still the area's main business. The Oregon Trail once dipped through the town, but the **Oregon Trail Regional Museum** at Campbell and Grove Streets (summer daily 10am–4pm; free), while assembling a jumble-sale's worth of pioneer clothes, really concentrates on its enormous collection of rocks. Precious stones, agates, minerals, petrified woods, fossils and shells crowd the shelves, and, in a dark room, fluorescent crystals glow weirdly under ultra-violet light. Opposite the museum is the large green city **park**, in a corner of which rusty metal spikes driven into the earth for nineteenth-century horseshoe-throwing games still stick up alongside the old pioneer trail.

La Grande and around

From Baker, I-84 runs north through cattle-grazing rangeland and into the distinctly shaped **Grande Ronde Valley** – large, round, flat and rimmed by mountains. Now mostly drained to become farmland, the valley was once a marsh – a breeding place for birds, but fatally boggy to the wheels of pioneer wagons, forcing the Oregon Trail to keep to the higher but tougher ground around the hills as it headed northwest towards the tortuous Blue Mountains.

The centre of the valley is **LA GRANDE**, a simple lumber-and-railway town, linked with Portland by public transport. *Greyhound* stop at *A-Z Travel*, 2108 Cove Avenue (☎963-5165), *Amtrak* at Depot and Jefferson streets. La Grande is also the gateway to ENTERPRISE and JOSEPH in the Wallowa mountains (see p.614), to which *Wallowa Valley Stage Line* (☎569-2284), who use the *Greyhound* pick-up point, provide daily transport. The **Visitor Information Center** at 1502 N Pine Street, near the railway station (Mon–Fri 8.30am–5pm; ☎963-8588) can supply maps and information about the area. **Motels** gather along Adams Avenue (US-30) and prices aren't bad. Doubles at the *Broken Arrow Lodge* at no. 2215 (☎963-7116), or *Stardust Lodge* at no. 402 (☎963-4166) are around $29, while bed and breakfast at the luxurious *Stange Manor*, 1612 Walnut Street (☎963-2400) costs around $54 for two. There's **camping** at Morgan Lake, two miles west of town down B Avenue. **Restaurants** also line Adams Avenue; *Mamacita's* at 110 Depot Street is the best place for Mexican food.

If you've got time to spare in La Grande (and it won't take you long to look around the town), **Hot Lake Mineral Springs** on Hwy-203, eight miles from La Grande (Wed–Sun 1–9pm; $6, bring a bathing costume) offer relaxing sessions in naturally heated mineral baths or saunas, at a resort on the shore of a hot lake – the steam hanging in clouds over the water. The lake was once a summer gathering place for several Northeast Indian tribes, who used it as a medicinal spa. Later, pioneers took a break from the Oregon Trail here, and in 1864 a hotel was built, which later became a hospital, and then turned into the present spa – still equipped with the long, turn-of-the-century hall of cast-iron bath tubs in which you sit and soak.

Pendleton

From La Grande I-84 runs northwest, climbing out of the Grand Ronde valley and into the Blue Mountains, following the route of the Oregon Trail. Pioneer wagon trains rested at what is now **Emigrant Springs State Park** before making the steep, dangerous descent into the flat land below. Out of the mountains, the pine trees give way to a vast patchwork of wheat fields and farmland, and cattle-ranches reappear. Connected by *Greyhound*, 320 SW Court Avenue (☎276-1551), and *Amtrak*, S Main and Frazer Street, to Portland, **PENDLETON** cultivates its cowboy-country reputation, and there's a great build-up to its immensely popular annual bash, the **Pendleton Round-Up**. Traditional rodeo stuff – bareback riding, steer roping and of course the bucking bronco – is mixed with extravagant pageantry, parades and a few dubious cultural hybrids ("the American Indian Beauty Contest") for four days in mid-September: tickets from the *Round-Up Association*, PO Box 609, Pendleton, OR 97801 (☎276-2553 or ☎1-800/824-1603 inside Oregon; $5-12 per rodeo session). At other times, you can see the evidence – including a one-time star horse, now stuffed – at the **Round-Up Hall of Fame**, SW Court Avenue on the Round-Up grounds.

As well as the Round-Up, Pendleton is known for its woollen goods: sheep-farming gained a hold on the local economy after the ugly days of the nineteenth-century range wars. However, the turn-of-the-century **Pendleton Woolen Mills**, 1307 SE Court Place (Mon–Fri 8am–4.45pm, Sat 8am–noon; guided tours on week-days; ☎276-6911) does nothing more exciting than initiate you into the mysteries of mechanised carding, spinning, warp dressing and weaving. The Round-Up's much more fun, but it's the mill that really put Pendleton on the map. The other attraction in town is the **Pendleton Underground**, 370 SW First Street (Mon–Sat 8am–5pm; $5), basically a tour of the town's extensive network of subterranenan passageways, which were used up through Prohibition as saloons, card-rooms and brothels, and as housing for the area's much-abused Chinese population.

If you're staying over in Pendleton, the **Chamber of Commerce** at 25 SE Dorion Avenue (Mon–Fri 9am–5pm; ☎276-7411), a short walk from the *Greyhound* station, has maps, leaflets and other information, and **motels** are usually quite cheap (except during the Round-Up, when you should book as far in advance as possible). The *Longhorn Motel*, 411 SW Dorion Avenue (☎276-7531), is close to *Greyhound*, with doubles from around $24. Perched on a hill southeast of the town is the plush *Red Lion Motor Inn* 304 SE Nye Avenue (☎276-6111), and further out, *Motel 6*, 325 SE Nye Avenue (☎276-3160) southeast of town near exit 210 off I-84, has doubles for $27. **Restaurants** tend to be plain, all-American affairs featuring burgers, steaks, baked potatoes and huge breakfasts; you should find something along Main Street.

The Wallowa Mountains

If it's not Round-Up time in Pendleton (and you've got a car), it's much more tempt-ing to leave I-84 at La Grande and head east instead on Hwy-82 towards the **Wallowa Mountains**, one of Eastern Oregon's loveliest and least discovered areas. The road takes you through tiny, backwater towns like **ELGIN** where the only solid-looking building doubles as police-station and one-time **Opera House**, its ornately embossed tin ceiling and plush seats a curious dash of old-time opulence; and descends into the Wallowa Valley until the High Wallowa moun-tains come spectacularly into sight. **ENTERPRISE**, in a region of small farming towns, hints at underlying sophistication – perhaps it's the cosy, well-stocked bookshop. There's a **visitor information** office here, housed in a kiosk at the Court House in the town's small mall, and a nice restaurant, *A Country Place on Pete's Pond* on Montclair Street, tucked around the back of town. In Enterprise, the weekend after Labor Day in early September is given over to celebration of **Hells Canyon Mule Days**, with highly amusing mule parades, mule rodeos and other competitions.

Joseph

Set at the northern tip of glacially carved Wallowa Lake, the mountains rearing behind, the tiny town of **JOSEPH** is a perfect spot to spend the night and a good base for exploring the surrounding scenery or continuing on to Hells Canyon. The **WALLOWA COUNTY MUSEUM on** Main St (daily 10am–5pm; free) is in an old, stone corner building dating from the year 1888. It used to house Wallowa County's first bank, the office of the daily newspaper and a private school. On the ground floor the history of the Nez Perce Indians, and Chief Jospeh, for whom the town is named, is dealt with in detail. Exhibits include a wigwam and Indian clothing. The upper storey is devoted to the pioneers, with the womenfolk and children receiving the appropriate quota of attention.

Wallowa Valley Stage (☎432-3531) run a daily van service from La Grande, stopping in Joseph at the Chevron station. There are a handful of **motels** here, but with just a little more money (doubles from $45), the friendly *Bed, Bread and*

CHIEF JOSEPH AND THE NEZ PEARCE INDIANS

The original inhabitants of the land on which modern Joseph now stands were the **Nez Perce** Indians, so called by French-Canadian trappers for their shell-pierced noses. The Nez Perce came into conflict with the US government soon after settlers started to move into the Wallowa Valley in the early 1870s. The discovery of gold, and white pressure for more space, led to a proposed treaty under which ninety percent of tribal land would be taken away. Chief Joseph refused to sign, pointing out that this was sacred land, where the tribe's ancestors were buried (you can still visit the grave of Old Chief Joseph, the chief's father, by Wallowa Lake). After much bureaucratic fuddling, the government decided to go ahead with their plans anyway, and gave the Indians thirty days to get out of the valley before the army moved in. Chief Joseph asked for more time, to round up stock and avoid crossing the Snake River at a high and dangerous time, but the general in charge, fearing delay (and knowing abandoned stock would fall to white ranchers), refused: the Indians had to leave cattle and horses behind, and more livestock drowned on the perilous river-crossing.

In the angry aftermath, a handful of white settlers were murdered, and the sad march to a reservation became a dramatic combination of flight and guerilla warfare, the Nez Perce group (the bulk of whom were women, children and old people) out-manoeuvring army columns over twice their strength in a series of hair-breadth escapes, almost as far as the relative safety of the Canadian border. The flight had its bizarre moments – a group of tourists in search of the Wild West wandered into the Nez Perce warpath in Yellowstone National Park. But only thirty miles from the border, the Indians were cornered: and Chief Joseph (reportedly) made his much-quoted speech of surrender:

> *Hear me my chiefs! I am tired. My heart is sick and sad. From where the sun now stands I will fight no more forever.*

The Indians had been told they would be put on a reservation in Idaho; instead, they were taken to Kansas, where marshy land caused a fatal malaria epidemic. The survivers were brought back to the Idaho reservation, though Chief Joseph and a few others were taken to the Colville reservation in Washington, where the Chief eventually died in 1904, having campaigned consistently to return with what was left of the tribe to the Wallowa Valley.

Trail Inn **bed and breakfast inn**, 700 S Main Street (☎432-9765) includes a big morning feed; for **camping**, see below. The Wallowa area, like Washington's San Juan Islands, attracts artists by sheer force of beauty, and a few years ago a bronze foundry was set up in Joseph to cast sculptors' work in metal. The foundry's been very successful, drawing craftspeople to the area and encouraging the development of local talent. Some of the finished works are on display at the **Eagle Mountain Gallery**, 107 SW 1st Street, and they have information on tours of the foundry, where you watch delicate metal artwork emerging from clumsy-looking casts.

Around Joseph

A mile or so south of Joseph, mountain-rimmed **Wallowa Lake** is supposedly inhabited by an Oregonian version of the Loch Ness monster. At its far end, **Wallowa Lake State Park** has **camping**, and houses the bottom terminal of the **Wallowa Lake Tramway** (operates summer daily 10am–4pm; $8) – a cable-car system that hoists you up into the mountains where short trails lead to magnificent overlooks. Much of the mountain scenery south of the lake belongs to the **Eagle Cap Wilderness** area, whose lakes, streams and peaks are accessible only along trails (no roads). Backcountry hiking and camping here really is remote – contact the **Forest Service station**, 612 SW Second Street (☎426-3104) by Hwy-82 in Enterprise for details.

During the summer months, various **Pack Stations** at Wallowa Lake, Joseph, Enterprise, Elgin and elsewhere in the northeast offer one- and several-day mule tours into the wilderness. You can also arrange to be transported to a remote mountain lake or some such spot, and picked up again a few days later. The cheapest half-day trips are $30; an organised tour – including food and most of the necessary gear – costs perhaps $100 per person per day.

Hells Canyon

East of Joseph, along the Idaho border, the Snake River has carved the deepest canyon on the continent. Though **Hells Canyon** is a thousand feet deeper than the Grand Canyon, it lacks something of the overwhelming impact because it's what's known as a low-relief canyon, edged by a series of gradually ascending false peaks rather than sheer cliffs. But it's impressive enough, with Idaho's Seven Devils mountain range rising behind and the river glimmering in its depths. Since prehistoric times, the canyon's sheltered depths have provided a winter sanctuary for wildlife and local Indians, and stone tools and rock-carvings have been found at old Nez Perce village sites.

Though the Nez Perce are long gone, the canyon area is now preserved for wildlife and backpackers as the **Hell's Canyon National Recreation Area**: deer, otters, mink, black bears, mountain lions and whole herds of elk live here, along with less attractive, even poisonous, beasties – rattlesnakes and black widow spiders. Part of the Canyon area is designated wilderness land, where mechanical vehicles are banned above water-level (boats along the Snake are allowed); so the only way to explore is on foot or on horseback. There are roads through the rest of the recreation area, but they tend to be rough and slippery, and many are closed by snow for much of the year: it's best to check with either the **Hells Canyon National Recreation Area Headquarters**, above the post office at the junction of Hwy-82 and Hwy-3 in Enterprise (☎426-3151), or the **Wallowa Whitman National Forest Headquarters** in Baker (☎523-6391), before you set out. They (and some tourist information offices in surrounding towns) will be able to supply you with maps and a complete list of **camping** facilities.

Reaching the canyon from Joseph

There are two ways of getting to the canyon from the Oregon side: either via Enterprise and Joseph, west of La Grande, or, at the canyon's southern end, via Halfway, west of Baker. Coming from Joseph gives the ultimate view over the canyon, from **Hat Point**, 54 miles northeast of Joseph along Hwy-350: drive to the hamlet of IMNAHA then a further 24 miles along a rough, slow, unpaved road which ends in a lookout high over the canyon's riverbed. Another National Forest Road, 4260, forks off from Imnaha down towards **Dug Bar** and the river itself, bringing you to the beginning of the three-mile **Nee-Me-Poo trail**, which follows the path of Chief Joseph and the Nez Perce Indians as they left their Wallowa Valley home.

Halfway, and the canyon by boat

The reconstruction of the **Wallowa Mountain Loop Road** (National Forest Road 39) makes it possible to drive south from Joseph through the Wallowa mountains to **HALFWAY**, near the Canyon's southern end (you can also get here by taking Hwy-86 west out of Baker). Tiny and tin-roofed, Halfway, 40 miles south of the Oxbow Dam, makes a good base for exploring the southern end of the canyon: rooms at *Granites Motel* (☎742-5868), or at the *Winter Creek Inn* (☎742-5722) go for around $30 a double; if you can afford it *Clear Creek Farm* (☎742-2233/2238; call for directions from the town – it's complicated), is a lovely, rural **bed and breakfast**, well worth the extra money: doubles go from around $45.

Hwy-86 winds towards the canyon from Halfway, meeting the Snake River at Oxbow Dam, where a rough Forest Service road leads on to Hells Canyon Dam, the launching-point for **jet boat** and **raft** trips through the canyon. *Hells Canyon Adventures Inc* (☎785-3352) and *Hells Canyon Challenge* (☎569-2445) have daily motorboat tours in summer for $40–70, or two-day tours for $150. The boats take you skimming over white-water rapids between the deceptively low, bare hills, past rocks faintly coloured with ancient Indian rock carvings, to an old homestead where pioneers once tried to eke a living out of the dry, lonely canyonland. The companies also operate a "drop-off" service, taking you to hiking trails along the canyon and picking you up either later in the day or the week (fee from $20 per person).

A narrow road follows the eastern shore of the Snake River from the Oxbow Dam to **Hells Canyon Spilway**, a dam at the southern end of the Snake River Wilderness. During the summer, at the parking area at the end of the road two miles beyond the dam, there's a mobile Information Centre; otherwise there are notices about the geology and history of the valley and the hiking paths in the area.

BEND AND THE SOUTHEAST

You can't go far along the Cascades' eastern slopes without encountering some manifestation of the mountains' massive volcanic power. Nowhere is quite as impressive as Washington's Mount St Helens, but the green, alpine scenery is everywhere counterpointed by stark cones and lava flows, especially in the Lava Lands area that surrounds **Bend**, the southeast's one sizeable town. Bend itself is a young and lively place, full of ski bums in winter and mountain bikers all summer long, with a number of good cafés, bars and restaurants as well as Eastern Oregon's best brewery.

Fortunately, you needn't venture far into the vast Great Basin desert of **Southeastern Oregon,** just to get a taste of it: the High Desert Museum, one of the best natural history museums in the US, is right outside the town. If you've got a car, or a bike and strong legs, you may well want to explore the empty spaces, which spread east from Bend all the way into Nevada and Idaho; Bend itself is about the only place you can get to on public transport.

Bend

A convenient mid-point between the Cascade mountains and the wilder landscapes to the east, **BEND** is really your best base in Eastern Oregon, giving access both to Cascade grandeur and the eerie landscape of Oregon's untouched desert reaches. These surroundings, rather than the town itself, are the main attraction, though Bend (easily reached by *Greyhound* from Portland) is a pleasant enough little place, set on a bend in the Deschutes River: early hunting trails struck away from the river-path here, and hunters came to know the place as "farewell bend" – a name which stuck until an impatient post office abbreviated it.

Once a ramshackle scattering of half-deserted ranches and small houses, Bend was turned into a town by a turn-of-the-century East Coast entrepreneur, and followed the rickety, uneven development of the Western frontier (cars came here before gaslights or electricity). The recent explosion of interest in leisure pursuits, especially following the development of the ski resort on Mount Bachelor, shot Bend to its current in-status with the more sophisticated western part of the state, and now outdoorsy Oregonians pour into Bend from the Willamette Valley, roof-racks laden with skis, mountain bikes or fishing tackle.

Practicalities

As is the case almost everywhere in Eastern Oregon, getting around without a car is far from ideal. *Greyhound* will get you here (at midnight) from Portland, and their station is a long way east of town at 2045 E Hwy-20 (☎382-2151); there's no *Amtrak* service. The **Central Oregon Welcome Center** (Mon–Sat 9am–5pm; ☎382-3221 or ☎1-800/547-6858) along US-97 on the north side of town has maps, accommodation listings, and piles of pamphlets on outdoor recreation opportunities in the surrounding area. Rent a mountain bike and get information on the many local trails from Mt Bachelor Bike and Sport, 1244 NW Galveston Street (☎382-4000) west of the river.

The many **motels** along Third Street (US-97) are pretty cheap, but they tend to fill up by the end of the day, especially at weekends. The *Royal Gateway*, 475 SE Third Street (☎382-5631), and the *Edelweiss Motor Inn*, 2346 Division Street (close to where it leads off US-97 at the north end of town; ☎382-6222), both have doubles for around $30; more central and quieter, however, is the *Motel West*, 228 NE Irving Street (☎389-5577), behind the *Sizzler* restaurant. The *Mill Inn*, 642 NW Colorado Street (☎389-9198) is a very pleasant and reasonably priced B&B, with rooms from $40. There's **camping** during the summer in *Tumalo State Park* (☎388-6055), five miles along US-20 northwest of town, and at numerous sites in the Deschutes National Forest.

As far as **eating** goes, Bend has several pricey little bistros like the *Old Bend Blacksmith Shop and Broiler*, 211 Greenwood Avenue – which serves classy American homecooking – and the *Pine Tavern Restaurant*, 962 NW Brooks Street, (☎382-5581). *D&D Bar and Grill* at 927 NW Bond Street and *Arvard's Lounge and Café*, opposite at no. 928, serve up big portions of diner food at low prices. Lots of places along Bond Street are good for a drink, but no beer drinker will want to miss the chance to sample some of the Northwest's best microbrewed ales and stouts at the *Deschutes Brewery*, 1044 NW Bond Street(☎382-9242), which also does a good range of pastas, pizzas and salads.

Mount Batchelor and the Cascades Lake Highway

Bend owes a good slice of its new-found popularity to the development of the Northwest's largest ski-resort at **Mount Batchelor**, 22 miles southwest of town. The season runs from around mid-November to as late as July, snowfall permitting, and you can rent cross-country and downhill skis (☎382-8334 for details).

The main ski lift runs in summer so from the end of May on (Memorial Day) non-skiers can also reach the top without exerting themselves excessively. On a clear day, the view of the Cascades is stupendous.

Mount Batchelor is also the first stop on the **Cascade Lakes Highway**, also called "Century Drive" – a hundred-mile mountain loop road which winds around the Cascade lakes, giving access to trailheads into the **Three Sisters** (see p.611), or further south, the **Diamond Peak** wilderness areas, and a sprinkling of campsites. Check with the **Deschutes National Forest Office**, 1645 East Hwy-20 (☎388-2715), or the Lava Lands Visitors Center (see overleaf) just outside Bend for details.

The High Desert Museum

Whether or not you intend to travel through Oregon's sandy southeast, it's well worth spending half a day in the fascinating **High Desert Museum**, three miles south of town off Hwy-97 (daily 9am–5pm; $5). Unfortunately, however, no bus runs here. As much a zoo as a museum, this account of natural life in Oregon's arid interior sets out its best exhibits around an outdoor path, where pens and pools of creatures – otters, birds of prey, comically ambling porcupines – are interspersed with displays of trees and shrubs, and historical exhibits: a pioneer log cabin and a sheep-herder's wagon, with relics of a lonely nineteenth-century life spent guarding the animals against natural perils and sheep-shooting cowboys during the "range wars". Try to time your visit for one of the daily talks or (more fun) the otter feedings: call the museum (☎382-4754) for details.

The exhibits on the region's geography and history are displayed very effectively in several rooms, with the **Spirit of the West Gallery** being particularly noteworthy. Historical scenes of life as it once was are reproduced in faithful detail, even down to the taped birdsong and chirping crickets. The first scene is of a Paiute Indian settlement beside a swamp; you then see the fur traders on the Snake River Plateau and at the fortified trading station, followed by the arrival of the first settlers in northeastern Nevada. Then come the land surveyors of Central Oregon and the gold miners: you wander through the narrow mining shafts into one of the former towns. Through doorways and dusty windows you see a Chinese grocery store, the bank, a photographic studio and other shops in Silver City, Idaho. The last room is devoted to the **buckaroos**, the cowboys who roamed the open range well into this century.

The Lava Lands

Characterised by weird formations of solidified lava, the **Lava Lands** cover a huge area of central Oregon, stretching roughly from Madras way down to Fort Rock in the south. But the concentration of geological oddities in the Bend area makes this the Lava Lands' focal point. The volcanic forms – neat conical buttes, caves and solidified trees – date back seven thousand years to the eruptions of Mounts Newberry and Mazama (today's Crater Lake; see p.590), which dumped enormous quantites of ash and pumice across the region. The process is depicted in a series of dioramas, complete with dramatic narrative and collapsing plastic peaks, at the **Lava Lands Visitors Center** (daily in summer 9am–5pm; ☎593-2421), eleven miles south of Bend on Hwy-97. Histrionic history aside, the visitors centre is an excellent source of maps and practical information on the many hiking trails that wind through the lava country. Also, right on its doorstep is the large, dark cinder cone of **Lava Butte**, breached by a gush of molten lava which spilled over the surrounding land. A trail from the visitors centre leads through the cracked moonscape of the lava flow, and a road spirals to the top of the butte, giving an overview of dark green pine forest interrupted by chocolate-coloured lava. The butte is cratered at the top, the basin-like hole tinged red where steam once oxidized the iron in the rock; an **interpretive center** nearby explains the mini-volcano's geological impact. Drive up **Pilot Butte**, just east of the city at the junction of Highways 97 and 20, and you'll get a panorama over Bend to the white-topped Cascades, and across the dry bumps of the lava lands.

A mile south of the Lava Lands visitors centre, just east of US-97, the **Lava River Cave** (summer daily 8.30am–6pm; $1, plus 50¢ for a lamp), takes you down a long, subterranean passage into the volcanic underworld. The cave was created by a rush of molten lava during the turbulent Ice Age: most of the lava eventually cooled and hardened around the hottest, still-molten centre of the flow; and when this drained away, it left an empty lava-tube, over a mile long, discovered only when a part of the roof fell in. There are supposedly all kinds of formations along the cave, but even with a lantern it's hard to see much beyond the next few steps; still, the long cave has a magicky atmosphere – though it's cold even in summer and you'll need extra clothes and stout shoes.

South of the cave (and a bumpy twelve miles down an unpaved forest road), the **Lava Cast Forest** contains the casts formed when, centuries ago, lava poured into a forest of Ponderosa pines, leaving empty moulds when the trees disintegrated. This batch of lava came from what was once the towering Mount Newberry, but is now the sagging **Newberry Crater** (there's a small road leading to the crater east off US-97, about twenty miles south of Bend). When the mountain finally collapsed, worn out by long years of deluging its surroundings in lava, two lakes were formed, **Paulina** and **East Lake**. Trails lead through the crater, including the **Trail of Glass**, which travels around a mass of glassy, volcanic rock – obsidian – used by ancient Indian tribes to form tools.

Southeastern Oregon

Very few people travel through Oregon's big, arid southeast: the one *Greyhound* bus a day runs along Hwy-20 from Bend, stopping at BURNS, VALE and ONTARIO, on the Idaho border, before continuing to Boise. It's mostly barren land, part-coated with dry sagebrush and punctuated with great flat-topped, cowboy-movie rocks and canyons. Early exploration of the area was mostly accidental: the best-known tale of desert wanderings is that of the **Blue Bucket Mine Party** of 1845, who left the Oregon Trail in search of a short cut and got lost in the parched land with neither food nor water. Most of them were eventually rescued, and caused great excitement with an account of a big nugget of gold, discovered in the bottom of a blue bucket of water brought by children from a creek: members of the party even went back to look for the lost gold mine, but it was never found.

The land beyond Bend was actually settled at the turn of the century, its homesteaders conned by unscrupulous promoters, who painted rich pictures of the land's farming potential. In fact, the desert homesteaders faced bleak, lonely country where water was scarce, dust blew in clouds and gardens turned green in the spring only to wilt under the summer sun – a grim life, which few could stick for long. When World War I broke out, most homesteaders left to take jobs in the new war industries, and today the area seems empty, its scattered towns seldom-visited, and very small when you do get to them.

Still, it was in the southeast that the earliest signs of human life in Oregon have been found: excavations at **FORT ROCK** (seventy-odd miles south of Bend off Hwy-31) have uncovered ancient sandals, woven from sagebrush nine thousand years ago. To the east, 130 miles from Bend on Hwy-20, **BURNS** comes as a welcome watering hole, and is on the *Greyhound* route from Bend (☎573-2736 in Burns). There's not much to the town, but 37 miles south along Hwy-205 the **Malheur National Wildlife Refuge**, around ominously named Lake Malheur, is a major bird refuge: cranes, herons, hawks, swans, ducks and geese stop off in its soggy marshland during their spring and autumn migrations.

The 30-mile stretch of Hwy-205 passes through the refuge before ending at the end-of-the-world hamlet of FRENCHGLEN, the starting point for a loop-road up **Steens Mountain**. The road follows a gradual slope up this massive fault-block, giving way at the top to abrupt views into craggy gorges, and over the hard sands of the **Alvord Desert**, which stretches to the east. Just north of where this road rejoins Hwy-205, another route cuts off west through the even more desolate expanse of the Hart Mountain Antelope Refuge, where you should keep an eye peeled for spritely Pronghorn Antelope.

travel details

Trains

From Klamath Falls to Eugene (1 daily; 4hr 10min); Albany (1; 4hr 50min); Portland (1; 7hr 30min).

Buses

From Portland to Bend (2 daily; 4hr); Pendleton (2; 4hr); La Grande (2; 5hr 30min); Baker (2; 6hr 15min).

From Bend to Burns (1 daily; 3hr 30min); Ontario (1; 7hr 15min).

PART FOUR
THE
CONTEXTS

THE HISTORICAL FRAMEWORK

To many, the West Coast of the United States seems one of the least historic places on the planet. Unburdened by the past, it's a land where anything seems possible, whose inhabitants live carefree lives, wholly in and for the present moment. The very name California, appropriately for all its idealised images, is itself a work of fiction, free from any historical significance. The word first appeared as the name of an island, located "very near to the terrestrial paradise" and inhabited entirely by Amazons "without any men among them", in a popular Spanish picaresque novel of the early 1500s, *Las Sergas de Esplandián* by Garcí de Montalvo.

NATIVE PEOPLES

For thousands of years prior to the arrival of Europeans, the aboriginal peoples of the West Coast flourished in the naturally abundant land, living fairly peacefully in tribes along the coast and in the deserts and the forested mountains. Anthropologists estimate that over half a million people – almost half the native population then living within the boundaries of the present-day US – lived spread throughout what's now the three West Coast states, in small, tribal villages of a few hundred people,

each with a clearly defined territory and often its own distinct language. Since there was no political or social organisation beyond the immediate level of the tribe, it was not difficult for the colonising Spaniards to divide and conquer, effectively wiping them out – though admittedly more through epidemics of disease than outright genocide.

Very little remains to mark the existence of the West Coast Native Americans: they had no form of written language, relatively undeveloped craft skills, and built next to nothing that would last beyond the change of seasons. About the only surviving signs of the coastal Indian tribes are the piles of sea shells and discarded arrowheads that have been found, from which anthropologists have deduced a bit about their cultures. Also, a few examples of **rock art** survive, as at the Chumash Painted Cave, near Santa Barbara on California's Central Coast. Similar sorts of petroglyph figures were drawn by the Paiute Indians, who lived in the deserts near Death Valley, the Miwok Indians from the Sierra Nevada foothills, the Nez Perce in Oregon's Hell's Canyon and other tribes across the West Coast.

DISCOVERY AND EARLY EXPLORATION

The first Europeans to set foot on the West Coast were Spanish explorers, intent on extending their colony of New Spain, which under the 1494 Treaty of Tordesillas included all the New World lands west of Brazil and all of North America west of the Rocky Mountains. In 1535, **Hernán Cortéz**, fresh from decimating the Aztecs, headed westward in search of a short cut to Asia, which he believed to be adjacent to Mexico. Though he never reached what's now California, he set up a small colony at the southern tip of the Baja (lower) California peninsula. He thought it was an island, and named it Santa Cruz, writing in his journals that he soon expected to find the imagined island of Amazons.

The first explorer to use the name California, and to reach what's now the US state, was **Juan Cabrillo**, who sighted San Diego harbour in 1542, and continued north along the coast to the Channel Islands off Santa Barbara. He died there six months later, persistent headwinds having made it impossible to sail any further north. His crew later made it as far north as Oregon, but were unable to find any safe anchorage and returned home starved and half-dead from scurvy. It was fifty years before another Spaniard braved the difficult journey: **Juan de Fuca**'s 1592 voyage caused great excitement when he claimed to have discovered the Northwest Passage, a potentially lucrative trade route across North America. It has long since turned out that there is no such thing as the Northwest Passage (de Fuca may have discovered the Puget Sound), but Europeans continued to search for it for the next two hundred years.

The British explorer **Sir Francis Drake** arrived in the *Golden Hinde* in 1579, taking a break from his piracy of Spanish vessels in order to make repairs. His landing spot, now called Drake's Bay, near Point Reyes north of San Francisco, had "white bancks and cliffes" that reminded him of Dover. Upon landing, he was met by a band of native Miwok Indians, who feted him with food and drink and placed a feathered crown upon his head; in return, he claimed all of their lands – which he called Nova Albion (New England) – for Queen Elizabeth, supposedly leaving behind a brass plaque that's now on display in the Bancroft Library at the University of California.

Setting sail from Acapulco in 1602, **Sebastián Vizcaíno**, a Portuguese explorer under contract to Spain, made a more lasting impact than his predecessors, undertaking the most extensive exploration of the coast, and bestowing most of the place-names that survive. In order to impress his superiors he exaggerated the value of his discoveries, describing a perfect, sheltered harbour, which he named **Monterey** in honour of his patron back in Mexico. Subsequent colonisers based their efforts, 150 years later, upon these fraudulent claims (the windy bay did not live up to Vizcaíno's estimation), and the headquarters of the missions and military and administrative centre of the Spanish government remained at Monterey, 100 miles south of San Francisco, for the next 75 years.

COLONISATION: THE SPANISH AND THE BRITISH

The Spanish occupation of the West Coast, which they called *Alta* (upper) *California*, began in earnest in 1769 in a combination of military expediency (to prevent other powers from gain-

ing a foothold) and Catholic missionary zeal (to convert the heathen Indians). Father **Junipero Serra** and a company of three hundred soldiers and clergy set off from Mexico for Monterey, half of them by ship, the other half overland. After establishing a small mission and *presidio* (fort) at San Diego, in June 1770 the expedition arrived at Monterey, where another mission and small *presidio* were constructed.

The Spanish continued to build missions all along the California coast, ostensibly to Catholicise the Native Americans, which they did with Inquisitional obsession. The mission complexes were broadly similar, with a church and cloistered residence structure surrounded by irrigated fields, vineyards, and more extensive ranchlands. The labour of the Indian converts was co-opted: they were put to work making soap and candles, were often beaten and never educated. Objective accounts of the missionaries' treatment of the Indians are rare, though mission registries record twice as many deaths as they do births, and their cemeteries are packed with Indian dead. Not all of the Indians gave up without a fight: many missions suffered from raids, and the now ubiquitous red-tiled roofs were originally a replacement for the earlier thatch to better resist arson attacks.

Most of the mission structures that survive today were built to the designs of Serra's successor, Father **Férmin de Lasuén**, who was in charge of the missions during the period of their greatest growth. By the time of his death in 1804, a chain of 21 missions, each a long day's walk from its neighbours and linked by the dirt path of *El Camino Real* (The Royal Road), ran from San Diego to San Francisco.

During this time the first towns, called **pueblos**, were established in order to attract settlers to what was still a distant and undesirable territory. The first was laid out in 1777 at San Jose, south of the new mission at San Francisco. Los Angeles, the second *pueblo*, was established in 1781, though neither had more than a hundred inhabitants until well into the 1800s.

One reason for Spain's military presence on the West Coast – which all told consisted of four *presidios*, with twelve cannons and only two hundred soldiers – was to prevent the expansion of the small **Russian** colony based in Alaska, mostly trappers collecting beaver and otter pelts in the Northwest. The two countries were at peace and relations friendly, and in any case the Spanish *presidios* were in no position to enforce their territorial claims. In fact, they were so short of supplies and ammunition that they had to borrow the gunpowder to fire welcoming salutes whenever the two forces came into contact. Well aware of the Spanish weakness, in 1812 the Russians established an outpost, called **Fort Ross**, sixty miles north of San Francisco. This further undermined Spanish sovereignty over the region, though the Russians abandoned the fort in 1841, selling it to John Sutter (who features prominently in later California history).

In fact, the biggest threat to Spain's West Coast supremacy came from the British. In 1776 **Captain James Cook** scoured the coast in search of the Northwest Passage; naturally he didn't find it, nor did he notice the useful Columbia River, later discovered by the American Robert Gray, and he was murdered in Hawaii on the way home. He did, however, open up the **Northwest fur trade**, having established valuable trading links with the Chinese. George Vancouver's 1792 explorations en route to the island that now bears his name strengthened British claims, and the British-based *Hudson's Bay Company* was soon operating a cosy monopoly on the lucrative commerce in sea-otter and beaver pelts (beaver-skin top hats were then the vogue in Europe).

The overland route to the Northwest was blazed by the explorers **Lewis and Clark**, sent by US President Thomas Jefferson in 1804 to map the still-mysterious Northwest Territory, collect notes on the plant and animal life, and make friends with the Indians (with an eye to inland trade). After Lewis and Clark negotiated their incredible trip across the continent (and back), American settlers began to make their way west with varying degrees of success. **Astoria**, a fur-trading outpost set up by New York millionaire John Astor, was a financial flop, and the enterprise was sold at a knock-down price to the invading British during the brief **War of 1812**, a last-ditch effort to win back their American colonies. Small groups of rough-living American trappers, the much-mythologised mountain men, fared rather better, and the British decided to defend their monopoly through the cynical practice of "trap-ping out" the land; the fur trade equivalent of a "scorched earth" policy, which very nearly succeeded in making the region's beavers and sea otters extinct.

THE MEXICAN ERA

While Spain, France and England were engaged in the bitter struggles of the Napoleonic Wars, the colonies of New Spain rebelled against imperial neglect, with Mexico finally gaining independence in 1821. The Mexican Republic, or the United States of Mexico as the new country called itself, governed California as a territory, though none of the fifteen distinct administrations it set up – lacking the money to pay for improvements and the soldiers needed to enforce the laws – was ever able to exercise any degree of authority.

The most important effect of the Mexican era was the final **secularisation** in 1834, after years of gradual diminution, of the Franciscan missions. As most of the missionaries were Spanish, under Mexican rule they had seen their position steadily eroded by the increasingly wealthy, close-knit families of the *Californios* – Mexican immigrants who'd been granted vast tracts of ranch land. The government's intention was that half of the missions' extensive lands should go to the Indian converts; however, this was never carried out, and the few powerful families divided most of it up among themselves.

In many ways this was the most lawless and wantonly wasteful period of California's history, an era described by **Richard Henry Dana** – scion of a distinguished Boston family, who dropped out of Harvard to sail to California – in his 1840 book *Two Years Before the Mast*. Most of the agriculture and cottage industries that had developed under the missionaries disappeared, and it was a point of pride amongst the *Californios* not to do any work that couldn't be done from horseback. Dana's Puritan values led him to heap scorn upon the "idle and thriftless people" who made nothing for themselves. For example, the large herds of cattle that lived on the mission lands were slaughtered for their hides and sold to Yankee traders, who turned the hides into leather which they sold back to the *Californios* at a tidy profit. "In the hands of an enterprising people", he wrote, "what a country this might be."

NATIVE PEOPLES

Throughout the Mexican and Spanish eras, foreigners were legally banned from settling, and the few who showed up, mostly sick or injured sailors dropped off to regain their health, were often jailed until they proved themselves useful, either as craftsmen or as traders able to supply needed goods. In the late 1820s the first **Americans**, males without exception, began to make their way to California. They tended to fit in with the existing Mexican culture, often marrying into established families and converting to the Catholic faith. The American presence grew slowly but surely as more and more people emigrated, still mostly by way of a three-month sea voyage around Cape Horn. Among these was **Thomas Larkin**, a New England merchant who, in 1832, set up shop in Monterey, and later was instrumental in pointing the disgruntled *Californios* towards the more accommodating US; Larkin's wife Rachel was the first American woman on the West Coast.

It was another eleven years before the first overland routes to the West Coast were established. The missionary Marcus Whitman (later murdered in a gruesome Indian massacre) helped to open up the **Oregon Trail**, previously used only by fur-trapping mountain men. When the first wagon train attempted the trail in 1843, Whitman alone was convinced that the wagons could be driven right through the Oregon Territory's Blue Mountains: after some sweaty forest-felling and road-building along the way, he was proved right, and the successful crossing inspired scores more in the "big" migrations that continued throughout the 1840s. The emigrants came west for a variety of reasons: some, like Whitman and fellow missionary Jason Lee, were religious zealots motivated by the desire to convert the Indians and spread Christianity, but most came simply for the chance of some cheap acreage and a fresh start in a new land.

The first people to make the four-month journey to California overland – in a covered wagon like in so many Hollywood Westerns – arrived in 1844, having forged a trail over the Sierra Nevada mountains via Truckee Pass, just north of Lake Tahoe. The next year over two hundred people followed in their tracks, though in 1846 forty migrants, collectively known as the **Donner Party**, died when they were trapped in the mountains by early winter snowfall. The immense difficulties involved in reaching California and the West Coast, over land and by sea, kept population levels at a minimum, and by 1846 just ten thousand people, not counting Native Americans but including all the Spanish and Mexicans, lived in the entire region.

THE MEXICAN–AMERICAN WAR

From the 1830s on – inspired by **Manifest Destiny**, the popular, almost religious belief that the United States was meant to cover the continent from coast to coast – US government policy regarding California was to buy all of Mexico's land north of the Rio Grande, the river that now divides the US and Mexico. President Andrew Jackson was highly suspicious of British designs on the West Coast – he himself had been held as a (14-year-old) prisoner of war during the Revolutionary War of 1776 – and various diplomatic overtures were made to the Mexican Republic, all of which backfired. In April 1846 Jackson's protege, President James Polk, offered 40 million dollars for all of New Mexico and the California territory, but his simultaneous annexation of the newly independent Republic of Texas – which Mexico still claimed – resulted in the outbreak of war.

Almost all the fighting of the **Mexican-American War** took place in Texas; only one real battle was ever fought on California soil, at San Pasqual, northeast of San Diego, where a roving US batallion was surprised by a band of pro-Mexican *Californios*, who killed 22 soldiers and wounded another 15 before withdrawing south into Mexico. Monterey, still the territorial capital, was captured by the US Navy without a shot being fired, and in January 1847, when the rebel *Californios* surrendered to the US forces at Cahuenga, near Los Angeles, the Americans controlled the entire West Coast.

Just before the war began California had made a brief foray into self-government: the short-lived **Bear Flag Republic**, whose only lasting effect was to create what's still the state flag, a prowling grizzly bear with the words "California Republic" written below. In June 1846, American settlers in the Sonoma Valley took over the local *presidio* – long abandoned by the Mexicans – and declared California independent, which lasted for all of three weeks until the US forces took command.

THE GOLD RUSH

As part of the Treaty of Guadalupe Hidalgo, which fomally ended the war in 1848, Mexico ceded all of the *Alta California* territory to the US. Nine days before the signing of the accord, in the distant foothills of the Sierra Nevada mountains, flakes of **gold** were discovered by workmen building a sawmill along the American River at Coloma, though it was months before this momentous conjunction of events became known.

At the time, California had a total non-Indian population of just seven thousand people, mostly concentrated in the few small towns along the coastal strip. Early rumours of gold attracted a trickle of prospectors, and, following news of their subsequent success, by the middle of 1849 – eighteen months after the initial find – men were flooding in to California from all over, in the most madcap migration in world history. **Sutter's Fort**, a small agricultural community, trading post and stage stop which had been established six years earlier by John Sutter on the banks of the American River, was overrun by miners, who headed up into the nearby foothills to make their fortune. Some did, most didn't; but in any case, within fifteen years most of the gold had been picked clean. The miners moved on or went home and their camps vanished, prompting Mark Twain to write that "in no other land, in modern times, have towns so absolutely died and disappeared as in the old mining regions of California".

At first it looked as though the California Gold Rush would drain Oregon of settlers, but canny Oregonians soon discovered a more steady market in "mining the miners"; charging them exorbitant prices for Northwest-grown food and building materials. The Northwest's own Gold Rushes were less dramatic than California's, but played a large part in opening up the area east of the Cascades – and displacing the Indians who had previously been assured they'd be allowed to remain there. Vital to Seattle's ascendancy as a major West Coast port, however, was the 1898 **Klondike Gold Rush** to Alaska (written about by Jack London in *The Call of the Wild*), when Seattle became the jumping-off point for Alaska-bound miners, and grew big enough to rival San Francisco.

STATEHOOD

Following the US takeover after the defeat of Mexico, a **Constitutional Convention** was held at Monterey in the autumn of 1849. The men who attended were not the miners – most of whom were more interested in searching for gold – but those who had been in California for some time (about three years on average). At the time, the Territory of California extended all the way east to Utah, so the main topic of discussion was where to draw the eastern boundary of the intended state. The drawing-up of a state constitution was also important, since it was the basis on which California applied for admission to the US. In it were a couple of noteworthy inclusions. To protect the dignity of the manually labouring miners, **slavery** was prohibited; and to attract well-heeled **women** from the East Coast, California was the first state to recognise in legal terms the separate property of a married woman. In 1850, California was admitted to the US as the 31st State.

Statehood for the Northwest, now more manageably divided along the Columbia River to create the Washington Territory, was delayed over the pernicious question of slavery. Oregon was finally admitted as a free state in 1859, though with a notoriously invidious State Constitution which also forbade *free* black people from living there, effectively banning any black population at all; this later became unconstitutional when federal law was changed after the Civil War. Sparsely populated Washington only managed to muster enough residents to qualify for statehood in 1889.

THE INDIAN WARS

Though the US Civil War had little effect on the West Coast, many bloody battles were fought throughout the 1850s and 1860s by white settlers and US troops against the various Native American tribes whose lands the immigrants wanted. At first the government tried to move willing tribes to fairly large reservations, but as more settlers moved in the tribes were pushed onto smaller and smaller tracts. The most powerful resistance to the well-armed invaders came in the mountainous northeast of California, where a band of **Modoc Indians** fought a long-running guerrilla war, using their superior knowledge of the terrain to evade the US troops.

In the Northwest, the massacre of Marcus Whitman and others at his Walla Walla mission by Cayuse Indians in 1847 persuaded the government to declare Oregon an official US territory: later wars in the region were small, desperate affairs fought almost entirely east of the Cascades, the most famous episode being the dramatic flight of **Chief Joseph** and his small band of Nez Perce Indians (see p.615) from the Wallowa valley in 1877.

Due to a combination of disease and lack of food, as well as deliberate acts of violence, the Native American population was drastically reduced, and by 1870 almost ninety percent had been wiped out. The survivors were concentrated onto small, relatively valueless reservations all over the West Coast, where their descendants still live. In California, the Cahuila near Palm Springs, the Paiute/Shoshone in the Owens Valley, and the Hupa on the northwest coast continue to live near their ancestral homelands, and are quite naturally defensive of their privacy. Others, like the Makah tribe in northwest Washington, are more accessible, with an excellent museum (see p.539); in eastern Oregon, the Warm Springs Indian Reservation operates a successful commercial resort.

THE BOOM YEARS: 1870–1900

After the Gold Rush, **San Francisco** boomed into a boisterous frontier town, exploding in population from 500 to 50,000 within five years. Though far removed from the mines themselves, the city was the main landing spot for ship-borne argonauts, and the main supply town. Moreover, it was the place where successful miners went to blow their hard-earned cash, on the whisky and women of the **Barbary Coast**, then the raunchiest waterfront in the world, full of brothels, saloons and opium dens. Ten years later, San Francisco enjoyed an even bigger boom as a result of the silver mines of the Comstock Lode, in Nevada but owned in the main by San Franciscans, who displayed their wealth by building grand palaces and mansions on Nob Hill – still the city's most exclusive address.

The completion of the **transcontinental railroad**, built using imported Chinese labourers, in 1869, was a major turning-point in the settlement of California and the West Coast.

Whereas the trip across the country by stage-coach took at least a month, and was subject to scorching hot weather and attacks by hostile Indians, the crossing could now be completed in just five days.

In 1875, when the Santa Fe railroad reached Los Angeles (the railroad company having extracted huge bribes from local officials to ensure the budding city wasn't bypassed) there were just ten thousand people living in the whole of **Southern California**, divided equally between San Diego and Los Angeles. A rate war developed between the two rival railroads, and ticket costs dropped to as little as $1 for a one-way ticket from New York. Land speculators placed advertisements in East Coast and European papers, offering cheap land for homesteaders in towns and suburbs all over the West Coast that as often as not existed only on paper. By the end of the nineteenth century, thousands of people, ranging from Midwestern farmers to the East Coast elite, had moved to California to take advantage of the fertile land and mild climate.

Railway development in the **Northwest** came slightly later, though accompanied by a similarly sordid saga of bribery and fraud: Portland had its transcontinental line by 1883, a step ahead of its rival ports in the Puget Sound, who didn't get their transcontinental link until 1887.

MODERN TIMES

The greatest boost to West Coast fortunes was, of course, the **film industry**, which moved here from the East Coast in 1911, attracted by the temperate climate that enabled films to be shot outdoors year-round, and by the incredibly cheap land that allowed large indoor studios to be built at comparatively little cost. Within three years movies, like D.W. Griffith's *Birth of a Nation* – most of which was filmed along the dry banks of the Los Angeles River – were being cranked out by the hundred.

Hollywood, a suburb of Los Angeles that was the site of many of the early studios – and ever since the buzzword for the entire entertainment industry – has done more to promote the mystique of California as a pleasure garden landscape than any other medium, disseminating images of its glamorous lifestyles around the globe. Los Angeles is still the centre of the world's film industry, making two out of three films screened, most American TV programmes, and, increasingly, is an international centre for the music business as well.

This widespread, idealised image had a magnetic effect during the **Great Depression** of the 1930s, when thousands of people from all over the country descended upon California, which was perceived to be – and for the most part was – immune from the economic downturn which crippled the rest of the US. From the Dust Bowl Midwest, entire families, who came to be known as **Okies**, packed up everything they owned and set off for the farms of the Central Valley, an epic journey captured by John Steinbeck's bestselling novel *The Grapes of Wrath*, in the photographs of Dorthea Lange, and in the baleful tunes of folk singer Woody Guthrie. Some Californians who feared losing their jobs to the incoming Okies formed vigilante groups and, with the complicity of local and state police, set up roadblocks along the main highways to prevent unemployed outsiders from entering the state.

One Depression-era initiative to alleviate the poverty, and to get the economy moving again, were the US government sponsored **Works Progress Administration (WPA)** construction projects, such as the Grand Coulee Dam in Eastern Washington. Many smaller works were carried out all over the West Coast, ranging from restoring the California missions to building trails and park facilities, and commissioning art works like the marvellous Social Realist murals in San Francisco's Coit Tower.

Things turned around when **World War II** brought heavy industry to the West Coast, as shipyards and aeroplane factories sprang up across the three states, providing well-paid employment in wartime factories. After the war, most stayed on, and the aviation industry that grew out of the war effort remains one of the West Coast's biggest employers. In Seattle, the troubled Boeing Aircraft Company builds the 727s and 747s that make up most of the world's passenger fleets, while California companies — McDonnell Douglas, Lockheed, Rockwell and General Dynamics, for example – make up the roll call of suppliers to the US military and space programmes. More recently, the "Silicon Valley" area south of San Francisco has been at the forefront of hi-tech developments in the computer industry.

After the war many of the soldiers who'd passed through on their way to the battlegrounds of the South Pacific came back to the West Coast and decided to stay on. There was plenty of well-paid work, the US government subsidised house purchases for war veterans and, most importantly, constructed the **freeways** and Interstate Highways that enabled land speculators to build new commuter suburbs on land that up until then had been used for farms and citrus orchards.

The **1950s** brought prosperity to the bulk of middle-class America (typified by President Eisenhower's goal of "two cars in every garage and a chicken in every pot"), and the West Coast, and San Francisco in particular, became a nexus for alternative artists and writers, spurring an immigration of intellectuals that by the end of the decade had become manifest as the **Beat Generation**, pegged "Beatniks", in honour of Sputnik, the Soviet space satellite, by San Francisco columnist Herb Caen (see p.343 for more).

California remained at the forefront of youth and social upheavals into and throughout the **1960s**. In a series of drug tests carried out at Stanford University – paid for by the CIA, who were interested in developing a "truth drug" for interrogation purposes – unwitting students were dosed with LSD. One of the guinea pigs was the writer Ken Kesey, who had just published the highly acclaimed novel *One Flew Over the Cuckoo's Nest*; Kesey quite liked the experience and soon secured a personal supply of the drug (which was as yet still legal) and toured the West Coast to spread the word of "**Acid**". In and around San Francisco Kesey and his mates, the Merry Pranksters, turned on huge crowds at Electric Kool-Aid Acid Tests – in which LSD was diluted into bowls of the soft drink Kool-Aid – complete with psychedelic light shows and music by the Grateful Dead. The Acid craze reached its height during the **Summer of Love**, 1967, when the entire Haight Ashbury district of San Francisco seemed populated by barefoot and drugged Flower Children.

Within a year the superficial peace of Flower Power was shattered, as protests mounted against US involvement in the **Vietnam War**; Martin Luther King and Bobby Kennedy, heroes of left-leaning youth, were both gunned down – Kennedy in Los Angeles after winning the California Primary of the 1968 Presidential election. By the end of the 1960s the "system", on the West Coast especially, seemed to be at breaking point. The militant **Black Panthers**, a violent group of black radicals based in Oakland, terrorised a white population that had earlier been enthusiastic supporters of the Civil Rights Movement, and the atrocities committed by **Charles Manson** and his Family proved what the rest of the US had known all along: that California was full of madmen and murderers.

The antiwar protests, concentrated at the University of California campus in Berkeley, continued through the early **1970s**. Emerging from the milieu of revolutionary and radical groups, the Symbionese Liberation Army, a small, well-armed and stridently revolutionary group, set about the overthrow of the US, attracting media (and FBI) attention by murdering civil servants, robbing banks and, most famously, kidnapping 19-year-old heiress **Patty Hearst**. Amid much media attention Hearst converted to the SLA's cause, changing her name to Tanya and for the next two years – until her capture in 1977 – went underground, provoking national debate about her motives and beliefs.

After the unrest of the previous decade, the **late 1970s** were decidedly dull. The one interesting phenomenon was the rise of **cults**, among them LA's Scientology Church, megalomaniac L. Ron Hubbard's personality-testing sect; the Moonies, pestering people at airports and public places all over the coast; and San Francisco's People's Temple, of which over a thousand members died when their leader, Jim Jones, dosed them with cyanide in a religious service held at their commune in Guyana. The most public and visible of the lot were the followers of the **Bhagwan Shree Rajshneesh**, clothed entirely in shades of red. Their town-sized commune in Eastern Oregon (see p.610) folded in 1986, among (proven) accusations of some nasty poisonings, and the Bhagwan, who fled in disgrace, has since died.

West Coast **politics**, after Watergate and the end of American involvement in Vietnam, seemed to lose whatever idealistic fervour they might once have had, and popular culture withdrew into self-satisfaction, typified by the smug harmonies of musicians like the Eagles and Jackson Browne. While the Sixties upheavals were overseen by California Governor Ronald Reagan, who was ready and willing to fight the long-haired hippies, the 1970s saw the reign of "Governor Moonbeam" Jerry Brown, under whose leadership California enacted some of the most stringent **anti-pollution** measures in the world – one of which pays environmental activists to expose corporate polluters, offering a 25 percent commission on the multi-million-dollar fines imposed by the courts. The state also actively encouraged the development of renewable forms of energy such as solar and wind power, and protected the entire coastline from despoilation and development. Oregon and California also decriminalised the possession of under an ounce of marijuana (though it remains an offence to grow or sell it), and the harvesting of **marijuana** in both states continues to account for over $1 billion each year, making it the number-one cash crop in the number-one agricultural region in the US.

The easy-money **Eighties** crash-landed in a tangled mess, with LA junk-bond king Michael Milkin convicted of multi-billion-dollar fraud and the S&L banking scandals enmeshing such high-ranking politicos as California Senator Alan Cranston. While the Pacific Northwest has so far been comparatively immune to the downturn in the economy, for California the **Nineties** kicked off with a stagnant property market, rising unemployment and no sign of hope on the horizon. In the cities the picture is especially bleak. In Los Angeles, **gang violence** continues to take dozens of lives every month, and a videotape of police beating a handcuffed black man has inflamed longstanding racial tensions. San Francisco has been hardest hit: on top of **AIDS**-related illnesses stretching health services to the breaking point (more than one in every hundred residents has already died from it), the area has been hit by a series of natural disasters of almost Biblical proportions. An **earthquake** in October 1989 devastated much of the San Francisco Bay Area, followed two years later by a massive **fire** in the Oakland Hills which burned over two thousand homes and killed two dozen people – the third worst fire in US history.

Despite all this, California still retains its aura as something of a promised land, and, barring its complete destruction by the **Big**

One – the earthquake that's destined one day to drop half of California into the Pacific and wipe out the rest under massive tidal waves – the West Coast seems set to continue much as it is: source (and home) of so much of the nation's wealth, yet displaying the starkest examples of some of its most pressing social problems.

WEST COAST WILDLIFE

For sheer range of landscape, California and the West Coast is hard to beat. Though popularly imagined as little more than palm trees and golden sand beaches, the West Coast contains just about every kind of geography there is: glaciated alpine peaks and meadows, desolate desert sand dunes, flat, fertile agricultural plains, even fecund rain forests; and it's no wonder Hollywood film-makers have so often and successfully used West Coast sites to simulate so many distant and exotic locales. The diverse landscapes of the West Coast also support an immense variety of plant and animal life, most of which – due to the protection offered by the various state and national parks, forests and wilderness areas – is both easily accessible and unspoiled by encroaching civilisation.

BACKGROUND: LANDSCAPES GEOLOGY & EARTHQUAKES

This mixed bag of landscapes has been formed over millions of years through the interaction of all the main geological processes: Ice Age glaciation, erosion, earthquakes and volcanic eruptions. The most impressive bits of geology are collected in **Yosemite National Park**, east of San Francisco, where solid walls of granite twice the size of the Rock of Gibraltar have been sliced and shaped into unforgettable cliffs and chasms. In contrast, the sand dunes of **Death Valley** are being constantly shaped and reshaped by the dry desert winds, surrounded by foothills tinted by oxidised mineral deposits into every colour of the spectrum.

Earthquakes – which earned Los Angeles the truckdriver's nickname "Shakeytown" – are the most powerful expression of the volatile unrest underlying the placid surface. The West Coast sits on the "Ring of Fire", at the junction of two tectonic plates slowly drifting deep within the earth. Besides the occasional earthquake – like the 1906 quake which flattened San Francisco, or the 1971 tremor which collapsed many of LA's freeways – this instability is also the cause of the many **volcanoes** which dot the West Coast. Distinguished by their symmetrical, conical shape, almost all of them are now dormant, though Mount Lassen, in Northern California, erupted in 1914, destroying much of the surrounding forest, and Mount St Helens, in Washington, blew her top – on national TV – in 1980. Along with the steaming geysers that accompany even the dormant volcanoes, the most attractive features of volcanic regions are the bubbling **hot springs** – pools of water that flow up from deep underground, heated to a sybaritically soothing 100°F plus. Hot springs occur naturally all over the western US, and though some have been developed into luxurious health spas, most remain in their natural state, and you can soak your bones *au naturel* surrounded by mountain meadows or wide-open deserts. The best of these are listed throughout the *Guide*.

Of the **wildlife**, though some of the most fantastic creatures, like the grizzly bear – ten-foot-tall, two-ton giants that still adorn the state flag of California – and the California condor – the world's largest bird, with a wingspan of over eight feet – are now extinct in their natural habitats, plenty more are still alive and thriving, like the otters, elephant seal and grey whales seen all along the coast, and the chubby marmots; shy mammals often seen sunning themselves on rocks in higher reaches of the mountains. Plant life is equally varied, from the brilliant but short-lived desert wildflowers to the timeless Bristlecone pine trees, which live for thousands of years on the arid peaks of Great Basin desert.

Below you will find details of the major **ecosystems** of California, Oregon and Washington. They are inevitably brief: the area encompasses almost 320,000 square miles, stretching from moist Cascadian forests to Death Valley, 276 feet below sea level with an annual rainfall of two inches, and is inhabited by multitudes of species. Native to California alone are 54 species of cactus, 123 species of amphibians and reptiles, 260 species of birds, and 27–28,000 species of insects. See the books listings section for recommendations of more specific habitat guides. Bear in mind, also, that there are a number of museums all over the West Coast region that examine and exhibit in depth, notably Monterey's superb Aquarium, the diorama-filled Oakland Museum and the innovative High Desert Museum in Bend, Oregon – see the *Guide* for details.

THE OCEAN

The Pacific Ocean largely determines West Coast climate, keeping the coastal temperatures moderate all year round. In spring and summer, cold nutrient-rich waters rise or upwell to produce cooling banks of fog and abundant crops of phytoplankton (microscopic algae). The algae nourishes creatures such as krill (small shrimps) which provide baby food for juvenile fish. This food chain fodders millions of nesting seabirds, as well as harbour and elephant seals, California sea lions and whales. **Grey whales**, the most common species spotted from land, were once almost hunted to the point of extinction, but have returned to the coast in large numbers. During their southward migration to their breeding grounds off Mexico, from December to January, it is easy to spot them from prominent headlands all along the coast, and most harbours have charter services offering whale-watching tours. On their way back to the Arctic Sea, in February and March, the new-born whale pups can sometimes be seen playfully leaping out of the water, or "breaching". Look for the whale's white-plumed spout – once at the surface, they usually blow several times in succession.

TIDEPOOLS

West Coast shorelines are composed of three primary ecosystems: tidepools, sandy beach and estuary. To explore the **tidepools**, first consult a local newspaper when the low tides (two daily) will occur. Be careful of waves, don't be out too far from shore when the tide returns, and also watch your step – there are many small lives underfoot. There are miles of West Coast beaches with tidepools, some of the best at Pacific Grove near Monterey. Here you will find sea anemones (they look like green zinnias), hermit crabs, purple and green shore crabs, red sponges, purple sea urchins, starfish ranging from the size of a dime to the size of a hub cap, mussels, abalone and chinese-hat limpets – to name a few. Black oystercatchers, noisily heard over the surf, may be seen foraging for an unwary, lips-agape mussel. Gulls and black turnstones are also common and during summer brown pelicans dive for fish just offshore.

The life of the tidepool party is the **hermit crab**. It protects its soft and vulnerable hind-quarters with scavenged shells, usually those of the aptly named black turban snail. Hermit crabs scurry busily around in search of a detri-tus snack, or scuffle with other hermit crabs over the proprietorship of vacant snail shells.

Pacific Grove is also home to large populations of **sea otters**. Unlike most marine mammals, sea otters keep themselves warm with a thick soft coat rather than blubber. The trade in sea otter pelts brought entrepreneurial Russian and British fur-hunters to the West Coast, and by the mid-nineteenth century, the otters were virtually extinct. In 1938, a small population was discovered near Big Sur, California, and with careful protection otters have re-established themselves in the southern part of their range.

Sea otters are charming creatures with big rubbery noses and Groucho Marx moustaches. With binoculars, it's easy to spot them amongst the bobbing kelp, where they lie on their backs opening sea urchins with a rock, or sleep entwined within a seat belt of kelp which keeps them from floating away. The bulk of the population resides between Monterey Bay and the Channel Islands, but – aside from Pacific Grove – the best places to see them are Point Lobos State Park, the 17-Mile Drive and the Monterey Wharf, where, along with sea lions, they often come to beg for fish.

Many of the **seaweeds** you see growing from the rocks are edible. As one would expect from a Pacific beachfront, there are also **palms**

– sea palms, with 10cm-long rubbery stems and flagella-like fronds. Their thick root-like holdfasts provide shelter for small crabs. You will also find giant **kelp** washed up on shore – harvested commercially for use in thickening ice cream.

SANDY BEACHES

hThe long, golden sandy **beaches**, for which California is so famous, may look sterile from a distance. However, observe the margin of sand exposed as a gentle wave recedes, and you will see jetstreams of small bubbles emerge from numerous clams and mole crabs. Small shorebirds called sanderlings race amongst the waves in search of these morsels, and sand dollars are often easy to find along the high tide line.

The most unusual sandy shore bathing beauties are the **northern elephant seals**, which will tolerate rocky beaches but favour soft sand mattresses for their rotund torsos. The males, or bulls, can reach lengths of over six metres and weigh upwards of four tons; the females, or cows, are petite by comparison – four metres long, and averaging a mere 2000 pounds in weight. They have large eyes, adapted for catching fish in deep or murky waters; indeed, elephant seals are the deepest diving mammals, capable of staying underwater for twenty minutes at a time, reaching depths of over 4000 feet, where the pressure is ninety times that at the surface. They have to dive so deeply in order to avoid the attentions of the great white sharks who lurk offshore, for whom they are a favourite meal.

Like otters, elephant seals were decimated by commercial whalers in the mid-nineteenth century for their blubber and hides. By the turn of the century less than a hundred remained, but careful protection has partially restored the California population, which is concentrated on the Channel and Farallon Islands and at Ano Nuevo State Park.

The only times elephant seals emerge from the ocean are when they are breeding or moulting; their name comes from the male's long trunk-like proboscis, through which they produce a resonant pinging sound that biologists call "trumpeting", which is how they attract a mate. The Ano Nuevo beach is the best place to observe this ritual. In December

and January, the bulls haul themselves out of the water and battle for dominance. The predominant, or alpha, male will do most of the mating, siring as many as fifty young pups, one per mating, in a season. Other males fight it out at the fringes, each managing one or two couplings with the hapless, defenceless females. During this time, the beach is a seething mass of ton upon ton of blubbery seals – flopping sand over their back to keep cool, squabbling with their neighbours while making rude snoring and belching sounds. The adults depart in March but the weaned pups hang around until May.

Different age groups of elephant seals continue to use the beach at different times throughout the summer for moulting. Elephant seals are completely unafraid of people, but are huge enough to hurt or even kill you if you get in their way, though you're allowed to get close, except during mating season, when entry into the park is restricted to ranger-guided tours. See the *Guide* for more details.

ESTUARIES

Throughout the West Coast, many **estuarine or rivermouth habitats** have been filled, diked, drained, "improved" with marinas or contaminated by pollutants. Those that survive intact consist of a mixture of mudflats, exposed only at low tide, and salt marsh, together forming a critical wildlife area that provides nurseries for many kinds of invertebrates and fish, and nesting and wintering grounds for many birds. Cordgrass, a dominant wetlands plant, produces five to ten times as much oxygen and nutrients per acre as does wheat.

Many interesting creatures live in the thick organic ooze, including the fat Innkeeper, a revolting-looking pink hot dog of a worm that sociably shares its burrow with a small crab and a fish, polychaete worms, clams and other goodies. Most prominent of estuary birds are the great blue herons and great egrets. Estuaries are the best place to see wintering shorebirds such as dunlin, dowitchers, least and western sandpipers and yellowlegs. Peregrine falcons and osprey are also found here.

Important West Coast estuaries include Elkhorn Slough, near Monterey, San Francisco Bay, Bolinas Lagoon, and Willapa Bay.

COASTAL BLUFFS

Along the shore, coastal meadows are bright with pink and yellow sand verbena, lupines, sea rocket, sea fig and the bright orange California poppy – the state flower – which is also found in Washington and Oregon. Slightly inland, hills are covered with coastal scrub, which consists largely of coyote brush. Coastal canyons contain broadleaf trees such as California laurel (called myrtlewood in Oregon), alder, buckeye and oaks – and a tangle of sword ferns, horsetail and cow parsnip.

Common rainy season canyon inhabitants include four-inch-long banana slugs and rough-skinned newts. In winter, orange and black Monarch butterflies inhabit large roosts in a few discreet California locales, such as Bolinas, Monterey and Pacific Grove. Coastal thickets also provide homes to weasels, bobcats, grey fox, racoons, black-tailed deer, California quail, and garter snakes. Tule elk, a once common member of the deer family, have also been reintroduced to the wild: a good place to view them is on Tomales Point at the Point Reyes National Seashore.

RIVER VALLEYS

Like most fertile **river valleys**, the Sacramento, Central (San Joaquin) and Williamette valleys have all been greatly affected by agriculture. Riparian (streamside) vegetation has been logged, wetlands drained and streams contaminated by agricultural runoff. Despite this, the riparian habitat that does remain is a prime wildlife habitat. Wood ducks, kingfishers, swallows and warblers are common, as are grey fox, racoon and striped skunks. The Gray Lodge and Sacramento National Wildlife Refuges have the world's largest concentration of snow geese during winter months. Other common winter migrants include Canada geese, green-winged and cinnamon teals, pintail, shovelers and wigeon. These refuges are well worth visiting, but don't be alarmed by large numbers of duck-hunters – the term "refuge" is a misnomer. However, most have tour routes where hunting is prohibited.

Vernal pools are a valley community unique to California. Here, hardpan soils prevent the infiltration of winter rains, creating seasonal ponds. As these ponds slowly evaporate in April and May, sharply defined concentric floral rings come into bloom. The white is meadow-foam, the blue is the violet-like downingia, and the yellow is goldfields. Swallows, meadow-larks, yellowlegs and stilts can also be found. Jepson Prairie Nature Conservancy Reserve is the easiest to visit, south of Sacramento near the small town of Rio Vista.

FORESTS

Perhaps the most notable indigenous features of West Coast forests are the wide expanses of **redwood and sequoia trees**. It is easy to confuse the coastal species, *Sequoia sempervirons*, or redwood, with the *Sequoiadendron giganteum* or giant sequoia (pronounced suk-oy-ah). Redwoods are the world's tallest trees; sequoias have the greatest base circumference and are the largest organism on earth. Both can live for over 2000 years. Their longevity is partially due to their bark, which is specially adapted to resist fire; the seeds also need fire to germinate and establish themselves. The wood of these great trees is much sought after not only for its beauty – near any forest you'll see signs advertising redwood burl furniture – but also for its resistance to decay.

As you might expect, most of the old-growth redwood forests are gone, and a tremendous battle between environmentalists and loggers is being waged over the remaining acres. These virgin forests provide homes to unique creatures such as the spotted owl and marbled murrelet. The floor of the redwood forest is a hushed place with little sunlight, the air suffused with a rufous-red glow from the bark, which gives the trees its name.

Redwoods are a relict species, which means that they flourished in a moister climate during the Arcto-Tertiary (just after the golden age of the dinosaurs), and now occupy a much-reduced range. As the weather patterns changed, redwoods slowly retreated to their current near-coastal haunts. Today, they are found from just north of the Oregon border to just south of Monterey.

One of the commonest ground covers in the redwood forest is the redwood sorrel, or oxalis. It has shamrock leaves and tubular pink flowers. Ferns are also numerous. Birds are usually high in the canopy and hard to see, but you might hear the double whistled song of the varied thrush or the "chickadee" call from the bird of that name. Roosevelt elk, larger than the tule elk, also inhabit the humid northwest forests. Prairie Greek Redwoods State Park, near the Oregon border of California, has a large herd, as does the Olympic National Park in Washington.

Sequoias are found on the western slopes of the Sierra Nevada, most notably in Yosemite and Kings Canyon National Parks. About 75 groves remain. The sequoia forest tends to be slightly more open than the redwood forest. Sequoias are also highly adapted to fire.

MOUNTAINS AND BASINS

THE CASCADES

The **Cascades**, glaciated volcanoes, have thick conifer-rich forests and wild alpine meadows. Depending on the elevation, you can find Engelmann spruce, larch, Douglas fir, lodgepole pine and mountain hemlock. One of the most unexpected high-country plants is a microscopic algae, a miniature plant that lives only where there is late-lying snow. It appears to stain the snow pink and is also known as "watermelon snow" because of its distinctive watermelon-like smell. Beware, however, of sampling this unusual delicacy – it can cause diarrhoea.

The slopes of Mount Rainier, the tallest of the Cascades, have some of the best wild-flower displays. It is also a good place to view mountain goats – white shaggy critters with beards – though probably all you'll see is a white dot high in the crags. During autumn, elk court and mate, making a thin nasal sound that is called "bugling". Respect their privacy, since rutting elk have uncertain temperaments.

Grey jays are one of the common Cascadian birds. They're easy to spot begging by camp-grounds and roadside rests. Ptarmigan are plump partridge-like birds that are as tame as any barnyard chicken. They moult into white plumage in the winter to provide camouflage in the snow.

THE SIERRA NEVADA

In the late nineteenth century, the environmental movement was founded when John Muir fell in love with the **Sierra Nevada** mountains, which he called the Range of Light. Muir fought a losing battle to save Hetch Hetchy, a valley said to be more beautiful than Yosemite, but in the process the Sierra Club was born and the move to save America's remaining wilderness began.

The Sierra mountains, which run down California, have a sharper, craggier, more freshly glaciated look than the Cascades. Many of the same conifers can be found as in the forests further west, but ponderosa and lodge-pole pines are two of the dominants, and the forests tend to be drier and more open. Lower elevation forests contain incense cedar, sugar pine (which has the biggest pinecones – over a foot long – in the world) and black oak. The oaks, along with dogwood and willows, produce spectacular autumnal colour. The east side is drier and has large groves of aspen, a beautiful white-barked tree with small round leaves that tremble in the wind. **Wildflowers** flourish for a few short months – shooting star, elephant's head and wild onions in early spring; asters and yarrow later in the season.

The dominant campsite scoundrels are two sorts of noisy, squawking bird: Steller's jays and Clark's nutcrackers. If you're lucky, a black bear may make a raid on your campsite. They pose more danger to iceboxes than humans, but nonetheless treat them with caution. The friendly twenty-pound pot-bellied rodents that lounge around at the fringes of your encampment are **marmots**. Marmots probably do more damage than bears; some specialise in chewing on radiator hoses of parked cars.

Other common birds include mountain chick-adees, yellow-rumped warblers, white-crowned sparrows and juncos. Deer, golden-mantled ground squirrels and chipmunks are also plentiful.

GREAT BASIN

The little-known **Great Basin** borders the eastern side of Washington south almost to Death Valley, encompassing all of Nevada and parts of all bordering states. It's a land of many shrubs and few streams, and what streams do exist drain into saline lakes rather than the ocean.

Mono Lake, reflecting the 13,000-foot peaks of Yosemite National Park, is a spectacular example. Its salty waters support no fish but lots of algae, brine shrimp and brine flies, the latter two providing a smorgasbord for nesting gulls (the term "seagull" isn't strictly correct – many gulls nest inland) and migrating phalaropes and grebes. Like many Great Basin lakes, Mono Lake faces destruction through diversion of its freshwater feeder streams, which provide water to the city of Los Angeles.

Great Basin plants tolerate hot summers, cold winters and little rain. The dominant Great Basin plant is sagebrush. Its dusky green leaves are very aromatic, especially after a summer thunder storm. Other common plants include bitterbrush, desert peach, junipers and pinyon pines. Pinyon cones contain tasty nuts that were a mainstay of the Paiute Indians' diet.

The **sage grouse** is one of the most distinctive Great Basin birds. These turkey-like birds feed on sage during the winter and depend on it for nesting and courtship habitat. In March and April, males gather at dancing grounds called leks, where they puff out small pink balloons on their necks, make soft drumbanging calls, and in general succeed in looking and sounding rather silly. The hens coyly scout out the talent by feigning greater interest in imaginary seeds.

Pronghorns are beautiful Africanesque tawny-gold antelope. Although they can be seen in many places in the Great Basin, the Hart Mountain Antelope Range in southeastern Oregon is a good place to search for them. Watch for their twinkling white rumps as you drive.

Other Great Basin denizens include golden eagles, pinyon jays, black-billed magpies, coyotes, feral horses and burros, black-tailed jackrabbits and western rattlesnakes. Large concentrations of waterfowl gather at Malheur in eastern Oregon and Tule Lake in northeastern California. The latter is famous for hundreds of wintering bald eagles, which are most numerous in November before the cold really sets in.

DESERT: THE MOJAVE

The **Mojave Desert** lies in the southeast corner of California, near Death Valley. Like the Great Basin, the vegetation consists primarily of drought-adapted shrubs. Creosote, with its olive-green leaves and puffy yellow flowers, is one of the commonest shrubs. Death Valley is renowned for its early spring wildflower shows. The alluvial fans are covered with desert trumpet, gravel ghost and pebble pincushion. Quantity and timing of rainfall determines when the floral display peaks but it's usually some time between mid-February and mid-April in the lower elevations, late April to early June higher up.

Besides shrubs, the Mojave has many interesting kinds of cactus. These include barrel, cottontop, cholla and beavertail cactus. The yucca family also has many representatives. Yuccas have stiff, lance-like leaves with sharp tips. A conspicuous representative is the **Joshua Tree**, which has twisting arm-like branches covered with shaggy upward-pointing leaf fronds, which can reach to thirty feet high.

Many Mojave desert animals conserve body moisture by foraging at night, including the kit fox, wood rat and various kinds of mice. The **kangaroo rat**, an appealing animal that hops rather than runs, has specially adapted kidneys that enable it to survive without drinking water. Other desert animals include mammals such as the Mojave ground squirrel, bighorn and coyote; birds like the roadrunner, ash-throated flycatcher, ladder-backed woodpecker, verdin and Lucy's warbler; and reptiles like the Mojave rattlesnake, sidewinder and chuckwalla.

THE WEST COAST ON FILM

The West Coast, and California in particular, is probably the nearest America has come to providing itself with the proverbial land of milk and honey. It's also the home of the world's film industry: filmmakers shifted to Hollywood as far back as the 1910s, drawn here by the climate and cheapness of the land and the rich array of natural landscapes, and as such the region has figured regularly in countless movies, either as itself or masquerading as somewhere else in the world.

Where appropriate we've mentioned a number of films in the *Guide*. What follows is a selection of (inevitably) mainly California-based films, which runs a gamut from the obvious to what are hopefully a few surprises. It's a wide and disparate list, but if there is a factor which links the movies it's perhaps the West Coast's obsession with itself – and just how much mileage an almost auto-erotic navel-gazing, starry-eyed and often thick-headed Hollywood has got out of zealously rooting about in its own backyard and pulling skeletons from its own luxurious closet.

Alex in Wonderland (Paul Mazursky 1970). Hollywood satire given a Fellini slant, as first-time director Donald Sutherland frets and fantasises over his next picture. Plenty of late-1960s Hollywood ambience.

All Night Long (Jean-Claude Tramont 1981). Charming underrated comic romance about LA businessman Gene Hackman relinquishing his obligations after he meets a toned-down, blonde, Barbara Streisand.

American Gigolo (Paul Schrader 1980). Arty, muted, pulp thriller about hunky male prostitute Richard Gere framed for political murder. High-sheen view of LA life and mores.

American Graffiti (George Lucas 1973). Remarkable cast in enormously popular, influential small-town teen rites of passage movie, based on Lucas's hometown of Modesto.

The Bad and the Beautiful (Vincente Minnelli 1952). Overwrought Hollywood self-analysis at its best, with Kirk Douglas as a ruthless movie producer trying to reclaim those he launched and subsequently lost.

Bad Day at Black Rock (John Sturges 1954). Creepy cinemascope exposé of the racial tension that arises in a small Mojave Desert town over the covered-up murder of a Japanese farmer. Spencer Tracy stars as the one-armed stranger out to set things right.

Bagdad Café (Percy Adlon 1988). Lovable, inspiring fable about a bunch of ill-matched drifters thrown together in the Mojave Desert, the US debut of German director Adlon.

Barfly (Barbet Schroeder 1987). Entertaining self-indulgence, penned by low-life specialist Charles Bukowski and featuring an admirably scatty, brave performance from Mickey Rourke as a drunken writer.

Beverly Hills Cop (Martin Brest 1984). Street-smart Detroit cop Eddie Murphy let loose in LA's ritziest environs in this phenomenally successful crime comedy.

The Big Sleep (Howard Hawks 1946). Over-plotted detective classic, starring Humphrey Bogart as Chandler's moral shamus Philip Marlowe and ripe with the corrupt atmosphere of nocturnal, studio-bound LA.

Big Wednesday (John Milius 1978). Highly admired in some quarters, this is a California surfing movie of epic intentions, following the lives of three beach buddies during the 1960s.

A Bigger Splash (Jack Hazan 1974). Meandering, semi-documentary cult film about the California influence on David Hockney's paintings.

Bird Man of Alcatraz (John Frankenheimer 1962). Earnest but overlong study of real-life convicted killer Robert Stroud (Burt Lancaster) who becomes an authority on birds while in prison.

The Birds (Alfred Hitchcock 1963). Some brilliant set-pieces in this allegory about our hostile feathered friends, set on the Northern California coast.

Bob and Carol and Ted and Alice (Paul Mazursky 1969). Still funny hit film about Southern California attitudes and values, contrasting the sexual hang-ups and experimentations of two married couples.

Bullitt (Peter Yates 1968). Steve McQueen gives an assured central performance in this overpraised but entertaining cop thriller, which contains the definitive San Francisco car chase.

California (John Farrow 1946). Mia's dad directed Barbara Stanwyck and Ray Milland in an elaborate Western about the founding of the state.

California Suite (Herbert Ross 1978). Maggie Smith and Jane Fonda shine in two episodes of gagmeister Neil Simon's four-part omnibus script, set in the *Beverly Hills Hotel*. The tone ranges from low-grade slapstick to bittersweet sentimentality.

Car Wash (Michael Schultz 1976). Crude, cool microcosmic black American comedy recording a day in the life of an LA carwash. A big hit.

Chan Is Missing (Wayne Wang 1982). Low-budget sleeper hangs a thoroughly impressive, unpredictable study of San Francisco's Chinatown and the Chinese-American experience on a mystery-suspense peg. Often satirical, it shows a Chinatown tourists don't usually see.

Chinatown (Roman Polanski 1974). Superlative detective thriller, with Jack Nicholson sleuthing in a 1930s LA crawling with corruption. Faye Dunaway and John Huston co-star in Robert Towne's intricately structured, Oscar-winning script.

Choose Me (Alan Rudolph 1984). Excellent erotic comedy set in the world of LA's neon-lit bars and morning-after pick-ups, with Keith Carradine and Genevieve Bujold as the agony aunt of the airwaves.

Citizen Kane (Orson Welles 1941). Some call it the greatest film ever made, and it's relevant to the West Coast for its depiction of Xanadu, which was more than loosely based on William Randolph Hearst's San Simeon – where the ageing tycoon Kane (Welles) holes up in massively empty luxury with his no-talent mistress (Dorothy Comingore).

Coming Home (Hal Ashby 1978). Overrated, award-winning drama, as politically naive volunteer nurse Jane Fonda falls in love with paraplegic Jon Voight while her husband Bruce Dern is off fighting the Vietnam War. It reeks of soft-centred, California liberal attitudes circa 1968.

Colors (Dennis Hopper 1988). Gritty location shooting enhances this violent, controversial LA gang warfare drama, with Robert Duvall and Sean Penn turning in resourceful performances as a veteran cop and his young firebrand sidekick.

The Conversation (Francis Ford Coppola 1974). This chilling character study of San Francisco surveillance expert Harry Caul (Gene Hackman at his finest) is one of the best films of the Watergate era. The key, titular sequence is set in Union Square, San Francisco.

Cutter's Way (Ivan Passer 1981). Cult film teaming beachbum Jeff Bridges with crippled Vietnam vet John Heard in investigating upper echelon homicide in soured California paradise. Santa Barbara is the main setting.

The Day of the Locust (John Schlesinger 1975). Overdone treatment of Nathanael West's famous novel that brings the apocalypse to Hollywood.

Dead Again (Kenneth Branagh 1991). Film noir meets the New Age in this clever tale of murder and mischief. Ken and Emma flash back to previous lives as darlings of Thirties LA society, but Robin Williams steals the show as a wise-cracking defrocked shrink.

Deadly Pursuit (Roger Spottiswoode 1987). Stunning Northwest mountain locations highlight this teaming of Sidney Poitier and trail guide Tom Berenger as they seek a killer.

Dim Sum (Wayne Wang 1985). Appealing little film about a more-or-less westernised Chinese family in San Francisco. A treat.

Dirty Harry (Don Siegel 1971). Sleek and exciting sequel-spawning thriller casts Clint Eastwood in epitomal role as neo-fascist San Francisco cop. Morally debatable, technically dynamic.

D.O.A. (Rudolph Mate 1949). Surprisingly involving suspense in which Edmond O'Brien tries to discover who poisoned him before he dies. Excellent use of LA and SF locales.

Double Indemnity (Billy Wilder 1944). Sensational film noir has femme fatale Barbara Stanwyck duping LA insurance salesman Fred MacMurray into murdering her husband.

Down and Out in Beverly Hills (Paul Mazursky 1986). Upwardly mobile hobo Nick Nolte works wonders on the neurotic family of Richard Dreyfuss and Bette Midler, in this satire of filthily nouveau riche Californians.

Earthquake (Mark Robson 1974). Top-notch special effects saddled with stock B-movie characterisations, as LA topples to the ground. Starring square-jawed Charlton Heston.

Escape From Alcatraz (Don Siegel 1979). Tense, well-crafted picture, based on a true story about an escape from the famous prison.

Family Plot (Alfred Hitchcock 1976). The master's last film is a lark about stolen jewels, kidnapping and psychic sleuthing in and around San Francisco.

Faster, Pussycat! Kill! Kill! (Russ Meyer 1965). Meyer's wonderfully lurid action flick unleashes a trio of depraved go-go girls upon an unsuspecting California desert. One of a kind.

Fat City (John Huston 1972). Superb cast in a beautifully directed portrait of barflies, has-beens and no-hopes on Stockton's small-time boxing circuit.

52 Pick-up (John Frankenheimer 1986). Blackmailed businessman Roy Schneider is up against three of the slimiest LA extortionists imaginable in this well-crafted adaptation of Elmore Leonard's novel.

Forty Pounds of Trouble (Norman Jewison 1962). This Tony Curtis comedy about an orphan who enters the life of a casino manager has some neat character acting and a climactic visit to Disneyland.

Foxes (Adrian Lyne 1980). Underrated if sometimes slick study of four troubled teenage girls in the San Fernando Valley.

Gates of Heaven (Errol Morris 1978). Cult documentary about California pet cemeteries (particularly the Bubbling Well Pet Memorial Park in Napa) that's oddly humorous and touching in its revelations about the human condition.

The Goddess (John Cromwell 1958). Paddy Chayefsky is responsible for this overwritten, intensely acted saga of a Monroe-like film star (Kim Stanley).

The Grapes of Wrath (John Ford 1940). California as a dubious Promised Land in tremendous adaptation of Steinbeck's novel about uprooted Depression-era sharecroppers.

The Graduate (Mike Nichols 1967). Dustin Hoffman in his breakthrough role as the college grad whose attentions shift from mother Anne Bancroft to daughter Katharine Ross. Dated, but understandably a huge hit. UCLA doubles for Berkeley campus.

Greed (Erich von Stroheim 1924). Legendary, lengthy silent masterpiece about the squalid, ultimately tragic marriage of a blunt ex-miner with a dental practice on San Francisco's Polk Street, and a simple girl from nearby Oakland. Dated but unforgettable, including the classic finale in Death Valley.

Hardcore (Paul Schrader 1980). Bible Belt bimbo takes a bus to Disneyland and ends up in a mire of debauchery and pornography, pursued by her distraught father, excellently played by George C. Scott. Good shots of LA, San Diego and San Francisco.

Harper (Jack Smight 1966). High-powered cast, led by gumshoe Paul Newman, in flat-footed but popular attempt to recreate the spirit of the old Bogart private eye films set in typically overripe Southern California.

Hicky and Boggs (Robert Culp 1972). Down-at-heel detectives Culp and Bill Cosby trail stolen money and a black power group through an LA of deserted public areas: parks, beaches and the Coliseum.

House of Games (David Mamet 1987). Playwright-turned-film-maker Mamet's debut feature is a cunning Seattle-set drama about shame and stings, as psychiatrist Lindsay Crouse gets seduced by the shady world of con-man Joe Mantegna.

Hollywood Cowboy (Howard Zieff 1975). Engaging low-key comedy set in 1930s Hollywood, as naive pulp Western writer Jeff Bridges trades life in Iowa for a stint as an extra in low-budget westerns.

Hollywood Hotel (Busby Berkeley 1937). The title says it all – an amiable flick full of guests and music. Songs include "Hooray for Hollywood".

Hollywood Shuffle (Robert Townsend 1987). Townsend wrote, directed and stars in this sharp send-up of racial stereotyping in the movie industry. Very entertaining, once you overlook the minuscule budget and shaky narrative.

Hollywood on Trial (David Helpern Jnr 1976). Valuable documentary about the Hollywood Ten, a group of screenwriters and producers persecuted for their possible Communist leanings. Includes footage of the HUAC hearings, plus contemporary interviews.

In a Lonely Place (Nicholas Ray 1950). Curiously hollow yet still compelling psychological melodrama about the ill-fated romance between Gloria Grahame (Ray's soon-to-be ex-wife) and dangerously temperamental screenwiter Humphrey Bogart. Hollywood atmosphere well-evoked.

Inside Daisy Clover (Robert Mulligan 1965). Natalie Wood as a brassy young Hollywood discovery who refuses to be eaten up by the movie industry.

Into the Night (John Landis 1985). Yuppie insomniac Jeff Goldblum gets mixed up with on-the-run Michelle Pfeiffer in this badly directed action-comedy that nevertheless scores valid points against LA's rampant freeway/junk/celebrity culture.

Invasion of the Body Snatchers (Don Siegel 1956). Low-budget sci-fi horror classics don't come much better than this taut, allegorical tale about the takeover of Santa Mira, California by emotionless pod people.

The Killer Elite (Sam Peckinpah 1975). Familiar themes of betrayal and trust in this mostly straightforward action flick, built around the internal politics of an underground San Francisco company and a wounded agent (James Caan) who seeks revenge. Excellent set-pieces include a Chinatown shoot-out and dockland siege.

The Last Tycoon (Elia Kazan 1976). Harold Pinter's version of F Scott Fitzgerald's unfinished Hollywood novel is all prestige and pedigree, with a star-filled cast and little energy or invention.

The Laughing Policeman (Stuart Rosenberg 1973). Walter Matthau and Bruce Dern pair up in another brutal San Francisco cop thriller, triggered off by a busload of people being gunned down in the Mission District. Queasy use of gay characters.

The Long Goodbye (Robert Altman 1973). Raymond Chandler's private eye Philip Marlowe confronts 1970s me-generation LA in terrific update starring Elliot Gould. Funny and serious, the film superbly evokes the city's sick, sun-drenched, shadowy soul.

The Loved One (Tony Richardson 1965). Perverse fun in this three-ring circus adaptation of Evelyn Waugh's satirical novella, inspired by Forest Lawn Memorial Park. Robert Morse and Rod Steiger head an amazingly diverse cast.

The Maltese Falcon (John Huston 1941). Humphrey Bogart is San Franciscan Sam Spade in this candidate for best detective movie ever made. Diamond-hard and near perfection.

McCabe and Mrs Miller (Robert Altman 1971). Set in the wintry Northwest, there's not another western like it. Gambler Warren Beatty and madame Julie Christie become business partners in a frontier town.

Monterey Pop (D.A. Pennebaker 1969). The first major rock concert movie includes turns by Jimi Hendrix, Otis Redding, Janis Joplin, the Who, Simon and Garfunkel, and many others.

Murder, my Sweet (Edward Dymytryk 1944). Former crooner Dick Powell changed his lightweight image to play LA detective Philip Marlowe in the character's first screen appearance. The picture exudes a splendidly seedy atmosphere.

My Own Private Idaho (Gus van Sant 1991). Quirky, highly stylised tale of a narcoleptic Portland hustler searching for his mother and his Idaho past.

Never Give an Inch (Paul Newman 1971). Disappointing adaptation of Ken Kesey's novel *Sometimes a Great Notion*, despite the presence of Newman, Henry Fonda and Lee Remick. About a hard-headed Oregon logging family and shot on location in Newport.

The Onion Field (Harold Becker 1979). Grim crime thriller based on Joseph Wambaugh's best-selling account of a real-life 1963 cop killing near Bakersfield.

The Outside Man (Jacques Deray 1972). Undeservedly little-known crime picture; French hit-man-on-the-run Jean-Louis Trintigent meets up with LA cocktail waitress Ann-Margret and much violence. Good location shooting.

The Parallax View (Alan J. Pakula 1974). Intriguing police action-thriller stars Warren Beatty as a reporter whose investigations begin after an American presidential candidate is assassinated in Seattle's Space Needle.

Petulia (Richard Lester 1968). San Francisco surgeon George C. Scott takes up with unhappily married kook Julie Christie in richly detailed, deliberately fragmentary comedy-drama set in a messy, decadent society.

Play it as it Lays (Frank Perry 1972). Tuesday Weld wanders around in numb anguish in this movie version of Joan Didion's novel that presents Hollywood as a stylised hell.

Play It Again, Sam (Herbert Ross 1972). Woody Allen as a (what else?) neurotic San Francisco film critic who has an affair with his best friend's wife, Diane Keaton.

Play Misty for Me (Clint Eastwood 1971). Eastwood made his directorial debut with this precursor of "Fatal Attraction", about the consequences of a DJ's affair with a psychotic fan (the top-notch Jessica Walter). Scary, and much of it shot on big Clint's own 200 acres of Monterey coastland.

Point Blank (John Boorman 1967). Virtuoso brutality around LA and at Alcatraz, as vengeance-seeking hood (the genuinely scary Lee Marvin) goes after some underworld bosses. One of Hollywoods's definitive 1960s "art" films.

Rebel Without a Cause (Nicholas Ray 1955). The iconographic James Dean in seminal youth flick set in Hollywood High School.

Remember My Name (Alan Rudolph 1978). Geraldine Chaplin as the spidery habitual criminal who comes back to avenge herself on remarried ex-husband Anthony Perkins in laid-back Southern California.

Repo Man (Alex Cox 1984). Clever cult comedy, set in a wonderfully sleazy LA, about a young punk (Emilio Estevez) who accidentally lands a job repossessing cars.

San Francisco (W.S. Van Dyke 1936). Elaborate, entertaining hokum about a Barbary Coast love triangle circa 1906. The script is upstaged by the climactic earthquake sequence.

The Sandpiper (Vincente Minnelli 1965). A camp classic of of awfulness, as clergyman Richard Burton has an affair with bounteous beatnik Elizabeth Taylor on the beaches of Big Sur.

Seconds (John Frankenheimer 1966). Superb sci-fi thriller in which a bored, middle-aged businessman pays a secret organisation to give him a new body and identity in bohemian, beachside California.

Shadow of a Doubt (Alfred Hitchcock 1943). A sterling comedy-drama from Thornton Wilder's script, set in well-scrubbed Santa Rosa.

Shampoo (Hal Ashby 1975). Great cast in a spot-on adult comedy sees LA as a big bed on the eve of the 1968 American Presidential Election. Co-writer Warren Beatty has one of his best roles as an inarticulate, confused, priapic Beverly Hills hairdresser.

Singin' in the Rain (Stanley Donen/Gene Kelly 1952). Everybody's favourite movie musical is a lovingly made satire of the transition from silents to talkies. A pinnacle of pure pleasure.

S.O.B. (Blake Edwards 1981). Cynical comedy about a cynical business, as movie producer mopes in his Malibu home because his latest picture is a disaster. Neither as funny nor as scathing as it likes to think.

Stand and Deliver (Ramon Menendez 1988). Fine ensemble playing lifts this inspirational low-budget drama, based on a true story about a middle-aged computer programmer who quits his high-paying job to teach remedial maths at East LA's notoriously tough Garfield High School.

A Star is Born (William Wellman 1937). Janet Gaynor and Fredric March in the first version of inside-Hollywood weepie about a couple: her career goes up while his plunges down. The Judy Garland/James Mason (1954) remake is much better – though the later Streisand version definitely isn't.

The State of Things (Wim Wenders 1982). Avant-garde European film-maker runs out of money and winds up doing deals in his Hollywood mobile home. Excellent soundtrack, with songs by the band X.

Streetwise (Martin Bell 1984). A Life magazine article prompted blistering cinema-verité study of teenage squalor in the environs of Seattle's Pike Street.

Sunset Boulevard (Billy Wilder 1950). Screenwriter William Holden in the clutches of half-mad ex-silent film star Gloria Swanson in this bitter satirical drama. A classic.

Tequila Sunrise (Robert Towne 1988). Casual romantic comedy-thriller set in San Pedro and other LA beach communities and given star voltage by Mel Gibson and Michelle Pfeiffer.

The Terminator (James Cameron 1984). Terrifically paced action flick stars Arnold Schwarzenegger as roving robot from a gladiatorial LA of the future.

Terminator 2 (James Cameron 1984). Arnie's on the side of the good guys in this effects-filled replay, getting lessons in Valley-speak and racing around the LA freeways.

Three Women (Robert Altman 1977). Fascinating, hard-to-categorise film about identity exchange set in and around a geriatric centre in Desert Springs, California. Brilliant, until it gets stuck in its own mysticism. With Shelley Duvall and Sissy Spacek.

The Times of Harvey Milk (Robert Epstein 1984). Exemplary feature-length documentary about America's first "out" gay politician chronicles his career in San Francisco and the aftermath of his 1978 assassination.

To Live and Die in LA (William Friedkin 1986). Successful flick that's as cynical and brutal about LA crime as "French Connection" was about New York.

True Confessions (Ulu Grosbard 1981). 1940s LA corruption vividly depicted in this nonetheless muffed and emotionally muffled crime drama linking brothers Robert de Niro (a monsignor) and Robert Duvall (a cop).

Vertigo (Alfred Hitchcock 1958). A tragedy of obsession, stunningly set in San Francisco, in which detective James Stewart tracks down two Kim Novaks.

Whatever Happened to Baby Jane (Robert Aldrich 1962). No-holds-barred performance from Bette Davis, co-starring with real-life rival Joan Crawford, as ageing sisters, former child stars, living horrifically in a rotting Malibu house.

What Price Hollywood (George Cukor 1932). Aspiring actress Constance Bennett, a waitress at the Brown Derby restaurant, is befriended by alcoholic director Lowell Sherman. His career hits the skids as her star rises.

What's Up Doc? (Peter Bogdanovich 1972). Some people went bananas over this screwball comedy pastiche, set in San Francisco and starring Barbara Streisand and Ryan O'Neal as a cook and a naive professor.

Who Framed Roger Rabbit (Robert Zemeckis/Richard Williams 1988). Dazzling, groundbreaking, wildly popular fusion of live-action and animation, as private eye Bob Hoskins investigates dirty doings in Toontown, Hollywood's cartoon ghetto, circa 1947.

The Wild Angels (Roger Corman 1966). Members of the Venice branch of the Hell's Angels motorcycle gang appear in this crude exploitation flick starring Peter Fonda.

The Wild One (Laslo Benedek 1954). Marlon Brando is the magnetic antihero of this prototypical motorcycle film, based on events in 1947 when 4000 leather-clad bikers terrorised the town of Hollister, California. Not as good as legend would have it, but Brando is ace.

The Wild Party (James Ivory 1975). James Coco and Raquel Welch in drama based on the 1920s sex scandal involving silent screen clown Fatty Arbuckle.

Zabriskie Point (Michelangelo Antonioni 1970). Visually gorgeous though thematically pretentious outsider's view of disaffected youth and the American system, shot in LA and Death Valley.

BOOKS

While the West Coast may be mythologised as the ultimate stimulant for the imagination, it's inspired comparatively few travel books, and virtually no books of any kind on the region as a whole. In contrast, floods of fiction have poured out of California, in particular Los Angeles, regularly over the last few decades, not only shaping perceptions of the area in general, but often redefining the whole course of contemporary American writing.

TRAVEL AND IMPRESSIONS

Tim Cahill *Jaguars Ripped my Flesh* (Penguin). Adventure travel through California and the world, including skin-diving with hungry sharks off LA and getting lost and found in Death Valley. Thoughtful and sensitive yet still a thrill-a-minute.

Richard Gilbert *City of the Angels* (Secker & Warburg o/p). Readable mid-Sixties impressions from a goatee-bearded English postgraduate in a year-long teaching post at UCLA.

Mark Twain *Roughing It* (Penguin). Vivid tales of frontier California, particularly evocative of life in the silver mines of the 1860s Comstock Lode, where Twain got his start as a journalist and storyteller.

John Waters *Crackpot* (Fourth Estate). Odds and ends from the Pope of Trash, the mind behind cult film *Pink Flamingos*, including a personalised tour of LA.

Edmund White *States of Desire* (Picador). Part of a cross-country sojourn that includes a rather superficial account of the gay scene in 1970s LA.

Tom Wolfe *The Electric Kool-Aid Acid Test* (Black Swan). Take a trip with the Grateful Dead and the Hell's Angels on the magic bus of Ken Kesey and the Merry Pranksters as they travel through the early days of the psychedelic 1960s, turning on California youth to LSD. Wolfe at his most grippingly readable.

HISTORY

Walton Bean *California: An Interpretive History* (McGraw-Hill). Blow-by-blow account of the history of California, including all the shady deals and back-room politicking, presented in accessible, anecdotal form.

David Boorstin *The National Experience* (Cardinal). Heavy-going because of the glut of detail but otherwise an energetic appraisal of the social forces which shaped the modern US, with several chapters on the settlement of the West.

Matthew H. Case *Northwest Frontier* (BCS Educational Aids Inc). By far the most concise and readable history of pioneer Washington and Oregon in print.

Washington Irving *Astoria* (KPI). An account of Oregon's first American fur-trading colony, orginally published in 1839, that offers fascinating, if lengthy, insights into contemporary attitudes to the then still unsettled Northwest.

Merriweather Lewis and William Clark *The Original Journals of the Lewis and Clark Expedition, 1804–1806* (Dodd, Mead and Co., New York, o/p). Eight volumes of meticulous jottings by the Northwest's first inland explorers, scrupulously following President Jefferson's orders to record every detail of flora, fauna and native inhabitant. Interesting to dip into, though booklets of extracts sold at historic sites in the Northwest are more use to the casual reader.

POLITICAL, SOCIAL AND ETHNIC

Jean Baudrillard *America* (Verso). Scattered thoughts of the trendy French philosopher, whose (very) occasionally brilliant but often overreaching exegesis of American Pop Culture, especially in LA, is undermined by typos and factual inaccuracies.

Ella C. Clark *Indian Legends of the Pacific Northwest* (UC Press). Good selection of tales from several tribes, organised by theme and linked by useful critical passages.

Mike Davis *City of Quartz: Excavating the Future in Los Angeles* (Verso). The best modern history of LA bar none, with a wealth of factual and anecdotal info painting a clear picture of a city on the edge of apocalypse.

Joan Didion *Slouching towards Bethlehem* (Penguin). Selected essays from one of California's best journalists, taking a critical look at the West Coast of the Sixties, from the acid-culture of San Francisco to a profile of American hero John Wayne. In a similar style, *The White Album* (Penguin £3.95) traces the West Coast characters and events that shaped the Sixties and Seventies, including The Doors, Charlie Manson and the Black Panthers.

Frances Fitzgerald *Cities on a Hill* (Picador). Intelligent and sympathetic exploration of four of the odder corners of American culture, including San Francisco's gay Castro district and the bizarre Rajneeshi community that recently folded in eastern Oregon.

Russel Miller *Barefaced Messiah* (Sphere). An eye-opening study of the rise and rise of L. Ron Hubbard and his Scientology cult, who have their world HQ in LA and their devotees lurking everywhere.

Jay Stevens *Storming Heaven: LSD and the American Dream* (Heinemann). Aside from being an engaging account of psychedelic drugs and their relationship with American society through the Sixties, the epilogue brings things up-to-date with "designer drugs" – Venus, Ecstasy, Vitamin K – and the inner space they help some modern Californians chart.

Danny Sugarman *Wonderland Avenue* (Sidgwick & Jackson). Publicist for The Doors and other seminal US rock bands from the late Sixties on, Sugarman delivers a pacey autobiographical account of sex, drugs and LA rock'n'roll.

ARCHITECTURE

Reyner Banham *Los Angeles: The Architectecture of Four Ecologies* (Pelican). The most lucid account of how LA's history has shaped its present form – and the author's enthusiasms are infectious.

Sam Hall Kaplan *LA Lost and Found: An Architectural History of Los Angeles* (Viking). The text is informative but dull, but the outstanding photos vividly portray the city's growth and the trends in its design.

Charles Moore *The City Observed: Los Angeles* (Vintage). The best book to guide you around the diffuse buildings and settings of LA, loaded with maps and illustrations and combining historical anecdotes with perceptive explanations.

HOLLYWOOD/THE MOVIES

Kenneth Anger *Hollywood Babylon* (Arrow). A vicious yet high-spirited romp through Tinseltown's greatest scandals, although the facts are bent rather too often. A seldom-seen second volume covers more recent times, but was hurriedly put together and shoddily researched.

Paul F. Boller Jnr & Ronald L. Davis *Hollywood Anecdotes* (Macmillan). As the title suggests, this contains some of the better anecdotes from the golden years. Very entertaining.

David Bordwell, Janet Staiger and Kirstin Thompson *The Classical Hollywood Cinema* (Routledge). Aimed at the serious student but still a generally interesting account of the techniques used in the best-known Hollywood movies up to 1960.

Bruce Crowther *Film Noir: Reflections in a Dark Mirror* (Columbus). A welcome down-to-earth description of the background and realisation of the American *film noir* genre.

David King Dunaway *Huxley in Hollywood* (Bloomsbury). How famed English author Aldous Huxley became a failed scriptwriter, searching for money and enlightenment in the Hollywood of the Forties. Very evocative of the period – and the man.

Joel W. Finler *The Hollywood Story* (Octopus). A remarkably comprehensive and informative account of the inner workings of the movie industry, packed with illuminating features, facts and statistics.

Clayton R. Koppes & Gregory D. Black *Hollywood Goes To War* (I.B. Tauris). Masterly examination of the influence of World War II on the film industry – and vice versa.

Ed: Doug McClelland *Star Speak: Hollywood on Everything* (Faber). An intriguing gathering of quotes from big screen names on all aspects of everything: Life, Sex, Money, Death ... and Marilyn Monroe.

Barry Norman *Talking Pictures: The Story of Hollywood* (BBC/Hodder & Stoughton). The most accessible mainstream outline of the growth of movies in Hollywood, informative and pleasantly irreverent in tone. And why not?

Julia Phillips *You'll Never Eat Lunch in This Town Again* (Heinemann). From the woman who became a Hollywood somebody by co-producing *The Sting*; a diary of drug abuse, spouse abuse and film-business bitching.

Ken Schessler *This is Hollywood* (Ken Schessler Publishing). A near-overwhelming by-numbers account of scenes of gore and scandal all around LA but predominantly in Hollywood.

David Strick *Our Hollywood* (Arrow). Grainy black and white photos that explore behind the movie-fostered myths and find the real Hollywood; often not a pretty – but always a compelling – sight.

SPECIFIC GUIDES

California Coastal Commission *California Coastal Access Guide* (UC Press). The most useful and comprehensive wildlife guide to the entire Californian coast, packed with maps and background information.

Tom Kirkendall and Vicky Spring *Bicycling the Pacific Coast* (Mountaineers). Detailed guide to the cycle routes all the way along the coast from Mexico up to Canada. See also Mountaineers' other backcountry bicycling books – to the Puget Sound and other parts of Washington and Oregon – and their extensive list of hiking, climbing and wildlife guides to the whole of the Northwest region (see below). Contact The Mountaineers, 306 2nd Avenue W, Seattle, WA 98119.

John McKinney *California Coastal Trails* (Capra Press). Comprehensive guide to the best of the state's coastal hikes.

National Geographic Society *A Field Guide to the Birds of North America* (National Geographic). Self-explanatory – and thoroughly useful.

Peterson Series Field Guides (Houghton Mifflin): *A Field Guide to Western Reptiles and Amphibians; A Field Guide to the Insects of America North of Mexico; A Field Guide to Pacific State Wildflowers*. Excellent general field guides to the flora and fauna of the three West Coast states.

Schaffer *The Pacific Crest Trail (California)* (Cordee). A guide to the southern section of the trail that leads all the way from Mexico to Canada through the Sierra Nevada mountains.

Schaffer *The Pacific Crest Trail (Washington & Oregon)* (Cordee). Guide to the second half of the Pacific Crest Trail, from California to the Canadian border.

David and Kay Scott *Travelling & Camping in the National Park Areas: the Western States* (Bradt). How to get around and camp in the West's national parks, including Yosemite, Kings Canyon, etc.

William L. Sullivan *Exploring Oregon's Wild Areas* (Mountaineers). A detailed guide to backpacking, climbing, rafting and other outdoor activities across the state.

THE WEST COAST IN FICTION

James Robert Baker *Boy Wonder* (Futura). Overlong, but often spikily accurate black comedy, built around the recollections of the family, friends and lovers of a lived-fast, died-young movie iconoclast.

Ray Bradbury *The Martian Chronicles* (Grafton). Brilliant, lyrical study of colonisation, new worlds and new lands – and it's very easy to read the Martian setting as a Californian one. Bradbury's first, and still best, book.

Charles Bukowski *Post Office; Women* (Allison & Busby). Three-hundred-hangovers a year Henry Chinaski (the author, thinly veiled) drinks and screws his way around downbeat LA, firstly as a misfit mailman, then as a moderately successful writer with his own tab at the local liquor store and an apparently endless supply of willing female fans. Savage and funny, and quite unique. See also *Factotum* (Allison & Busby), which recounts Chinaski's early days.

James M. Cain *The Five Great Novels of James M. Cain* (Picador). Haunting stories of smouldering passion told with clipped prose and terse dialogue and including his best-known works, *Double Indemnity* and *The Postman Always Rings Twice*.

Raymond Carver *The Stories of Raymond Carver* (Picador). Set mostly in the Northwest and Northern California, Carver's deceptively simple eye-level pictures of plain-dealing Americans, concise and sharply observed, are difficult to put down.

Raymond Chandler *The Chandler Collection. Vols 1, 2 & 3* (Picador). The first two especially are essential reading, some of the toughest and greatest LA crime fiction of the Thirties and Forties – including *The Big Sleep, The Little Sister, The Lady in the Lake* and *The Long Goodbye*, to name only the best.

Susan Compo *Life After Death and Other Stories* (Faber). Strange and zany romp through the clubs, clothes and characters of LA's goth scene; completely original in style and scope yet very believable.

Philip K. Dick *A Scanner Darkly* (Grafton). Of all Dick's erratic but frequently brilliant books, this is the best evocation of California. Set in the mid-1990s, when society is divided between the Straights, the Dopers and the Narks, it's a dizzying study of individual identity, authority and drugs. Among the pick of the rest of Dick's enormous legacy are *Blade Runner/Do Androids Dream of Electric Sheep?* (Grafton), set (unlike the movie) in San Francisco and the radiation wasteland of Oregon, and *Flow My Tears The Policeman Said* (Grafton), in which a chat-show host loses his bearings in a future LA after a new drug alters not only the user's perceptions of reality, but reality itself.

Joan Didion *Run, River* (Penguin). Focuses on the Sacramento Valley of the author's childhood and follows its change from agriculture into a highly-charged consumer society. In contrast, but just as successfully done, *Play it as it Lays* (Penguin) is an electrifying dash through the pills, booze and self-destruction linked with the LA film world.

Bret Easton Ellis *Less Than Zero* (Picador). A numbing but highly readable account of wealthy LA teen-life. A classic brat pack tome, with an influence and fame far in excess of its worth.

James Ellroy *The Black Dahlia* (Mysterious Press). A classic of the Forties hard-boiled style, in which two LAPD detectives compete in their obsessive quest to solve the gory murder of a film star – with no bloody detail spared.

Robert Ferringo *The Horse Latitudes* (Sphere). Drug-dealer turned lecturer on Mayan civilisation returns to his Newport Beach house after a midnight swim to find his wife has run off – leaving behind a corpse.

David Freeman *A Hollywood Education* (Michael Joseph). Cumulatively powerful collection of short stories concerning a writer's lot in Hollywood.

Ursula le Guin *Always Coming Home* (Grafton). Impressive "archaeology of the future", describing the lifestyles and culture of a mysterious race living in Northern California many years from now.

Dashiell Hammet *The Four Great Novels* (Picador). Seminal detective stories including *The Maltese Falcon* and starring Sam Spade, the private investigator working out of San Francisco. See also the absorbing biography of Hammet: Diane Johnson's *The Life of Dashiell Hammet* (Picador).

Joseph Hansen *Death Claims; Gravedigger; Skinflick; Troublemaker* (Grafton). Entertaining tales of Dave Brandsetter, a gay insurance claims investigator, set against a vivid Southern California backdrop.

Aldous Huxley *After Many a Summer; Ape & Essence* (Grafton). Huxley spent his last twenty years earning a crust as a Hollywood screenwriter, and both these novels are products of that time: one, based on William Randolph Hearst, concerns a rich, pampered figure who surrounds himself with art treasures and dwells on the meaning of life; the other chronicles moral degeneracy and Satanic rituals in post-apocalypse Southern California.

Richard Kadrey *Metrophage* (Gollancz). Sci-fi adventure set in an almost-believeable LA of the future, where society has gone to the wall and the street gangs are all powerful.

Karen Karbo *Trespassers Welcome Here* (Serpent's Tail). Wildly funny and acutely observed vignettes of Soviet emigre life in Los Angeles, and the attendant conflicts of language, culture and expectations.

Jack Kerouac *Desolation Angels; The Dharma Bums* (Grafton). The most influential of the Beat writers on the rampage in California and contemplating the stars and Great Truths on a Washington mountain. If you haven't already read it, see also *On The Road* (Penguin), which has a little of San Francisco and a lot of the rest of the US.

Ken Kesey *Sometimes a Great Notion* (Methuen). A sweaty and rain-drenched evocation of Oregon's declining timber industry provides the background for a tale of psychological quirkiness from the author of *One Flew Over The Cuckoo's Nest*.

David Lodge *Changing Places* (Penguin). Thinly disguised autobiographical tale of an English academic who spends a year teaching at UC Berkeley and finds himself bang in the middle of the late 1960s student upheaval.

Jack London *The Call of the Wild and Other Stories* (Penguin). *The Call of the Wild*, a short story about a tame dog discovering the ways of the wilderness while forced to labour pulling sleds across the snow and ice of Alaska's Klondike, made London into the world's best-selling author almost overnight. Afterwards, frustrated by the emptiness of his easy fame and success, the young, self-taught author wrote the semi-autobiographical *Martin Eden* (Penguin), in which he rails against the cultured veil of polite society. Besides his prolific fiction, London also wrote a number of somewhat sophomoric political essays and socialist tracts, the most effective being *The Iron Heel* (Everyman Press), presaging the rise of Fascism.

Alison Lurie *The Nowhere City* (Abacus). A nice New England couple spend six months in LA and the city forces a complete reassessment of their relationship and their own personalities. Clever, uncontrived stuff.

Ross MacDonald *The Barbarous Coast; Black Money; The Blue Hammer; The Far Side of the Dollar; The Moving Target* (W.H. Allen). Following in the footsteps of Sam Spade and Philip Marlowe, private detective Lew Archer looks behind the glitzy masks of Southern California life to reveal the underlying nastiness of creepy sexuality and manipulation. All captivating reads.

Armistead Maupin *Tales of the City; Further Tales of the City; More Tales of the City* (Black Swan). Lively and witty soap operas detailing the sexual antics of a select group of archetypal San Francisco characters of the late 1970s/early 1980s. See also *Babycakes* (Black Swan), which continues ths story, though in more depth, and *Significant Others* (Black Swan) – set several years on.

Brian Moore *The Great Victorian Collection* (Paladin). A professor dreams up a car park full of Victoriana, which becomes the biggest tourist attraction in the town of Carmel, California.

Walter Mosely *Devil in a Blue Dress* (Serpent's Tail). The sleazy side of LA circa 1948 seen through the eyes of a war veteran embroiled in an ultra-noir murder plot.

Ken Nunn *Tapping the Source* (Delacorte). Amusing murder mystery set among the surfers and bikers of Huntington Beach.

Thomas Pynchon *The Crying of Lot 49* (Picador). Follows the hilarious adventures of techno-freaks and pot-heads of 1960s California, and shows off the sexy side of stamp collecting.

Richard Rayner *Los Angeles Without a Map* (Paladin). An English non-driving journalist goes to LA on a romantic whim and lives out movie fantasies made even more fantastic by the city itself.

Danny Santiago *Famous All Over Town* (Simon & Schuster). Coming-of-age novel set among the street gangs of East LA, giving a vivid depiction of life in the Hispanic community.

Vikram Seth *The Golden Gate* (Faber). A novel in verse which traces the complex social lives of a group of San Francisco yuppies.

Mona Simpson *Anywhere But Here* (Abacus). Bizarre and unforgettable saga of a young girl and her ambitious mother as they pursue LA stardom for the daughter.

Gustav Sobin *Venus Blue* (Bloomsbury). Gripping and lucidly written story of one man's obsession with a Hollywood starlet of the Thirties.

John Steinbeck *The Grapes of Wrath* (Pan). The classic account of a migrant family forsaking the Midwest for the Promised Land. For more localised fare, read the lighthearted but crisply observed novella *Cannery Row* (Pan), capturing daily life on the pre-war Monterey waterfront, or the epic *East of Eden* (Pan), which updates and re-sets the Bible in the Salinas Valley and details three generations of familial feuding.

Michael Tolkin *The Player* (Faber). Convincing, multilayered story of a movie executive using his power and contacts to skirt justice after committing murder.

A. Rutgers Van der Loeff *Children of the Oregon Trail* (Puffin). Children's adventure story based on the true struggle of the orphaned Sager children to cross the Oregon Trail and reach safety at the Whitman Mission – reasonably enough, the story ends before the massacre which wiped out half the brood.

Nathanael West *Complete Works* (Picador). Includes *The Day of the Locust*, an insightful and caustic tale that is *the* classic satire of early Hollywood.

INDEX

HELP US UPDATE

We've gone to a lot of effort to ensure that this second edition of the *Rough Guide: California and West Coast USA* is completely up-to-date and accurate. However, from the moment of publication things will, of course, begin to change. Prices will rise, opening hours will alter, restaurants and hotels will close, and new ones will appear.

A crucial element in keeping this book up to date is the response we get from readers. Please write and let us know if you spot anything that is no longer true, or if you feel we have omitted anything that deserves inclusion. We will credit all contributions, and send a copy of any *Rough Guide* to the writers of the best letters. We would also welcome correspondence from the owners of any establishments reviewed in this book, with news of updated prices or facilities, and will send researchers to those who are not mentioned and feel that they should be.

Please write to Rough Guides (California & West Coast USA), 1 Mercer Street, London WC2H 9QJ.

You are
A STUDENT

You travel
THE WORLD

You want
TO SAVE MONEY

Here's how

The International
Student Identity Card

Available at Student Travel Offices Worldwide.

Entitles you to discounts and special services worldwide.

BEFORE YOU TRAVEL THE WORLD, TALK TO AN EXPERIENCED STAMP COLLECTOR.

At STA Travel we're all seasoned travellers so we should know a thing or two about where you're headed. We can offer you the best deals on fares with the flexibility to change your mind as you go – without having to pay over the top for the privilege. We operate from 120 offices worldwide. So call in soon.

74 and 86 Old Brompton Road, SW7, 117 Euston Road, NW1. London.
Manchester. Leeds. Oxford. Cambridge. Bristol.
North America **071-937 9971**. Europe **071-937 9921**. Rest of World **071-937 9962**
(incl. Sundays 10am-2pm). **OR 061-834 0668 (Manchester)**
Africa Desk 071-465 0486.

WHEREVER YOU'RE BOUND, WE'RE BOUND TO HAVE BEEN. STA

 Retail Agents for ATOL Holders

STA TRAVEL